Encyclopedia of
American War Films

Garland Reference Library of the Humanities
(Vol. 873)

Encyclopedia of
American War Films

Larry Langman and Ed Borg

Garland Publishing, Inc.
New York & London   1989

Library of Congress Cataloging-in-Publication Data

Langman, Larry.
Encyclopedia of American war films / by Larry Langman and Ed Borg.
p.   cm. — (Garland reference library of the humanities ; vol. 873)
Bibliography: p.
ISBN 0-8240-7540-4 (alk. paper)
1. War films—United States—Dictionaries.   I. Borg, Ed.
II. Title.   III. Series.
PN1995.9.W3L36   1989
791.43′58′03—dc20   89-1491

Printed on acid-free, 250-year-life paper

MANUFACTURED IN THE UNITED STATES OF AMERICA

"There's something rotten about a world
that's got to be wet down every thirty years
with the blood of boys. . ."

What Price Glory? (1926)

Contents

Preface

Before beginning work on this encyclopedia, the authors—one an avid film buff, author of several film books and former English instructor; the other a free-lance writer, former history instructor and war buff—examined numerous books, both in and out of print, dealing with American war movies. Although many of these volumes were entertaining and informative, we found that each had at least one deficiency. None completely covered the whole genre of American war films. Few attempted to present historically related material which formed the bases for many of these films. Some of these books were devoted solely to one conflict, usually either of the two World Wars. Others concentrated only on the most popular war movies or those that emanated from a few major studios.

We have tried in this volume to remedy these shortcomings. We have included in our reviews virtually every war-related feature and most of the documentaries, short subjects, serials and cartoons. These works came from both the major and lesser known American film studios, some long defunct. In addition to reviewing some 2,000 films, we analyzed the accuracy of selected movies in terms of how they portrayed the period, people and historical events. In short, we wanted to make this the most complete and accurate one-volume book on American war films.

The term "war" generally has narrow definitions in most dictionaries; e.g., "hostilities," "conflict," "struggle," "aggression," and so on. When applied to film, however, the expression "war" takes on a much broader meaning. Films about revolution, the home front, spies, refugees and even comedies and musicals made during wartime may tell us more about a conflict and its period than straight combat dramas. We have adopted this wider view and included these movie categories as well.

To make this work comprehensive and yet keep it within the confines of one volume, we set certain arbitrary criteria. Each combat-based drama and comedy has its own entry. Films about revolution, insurrection and civil strife also received individual entries. Dramas about the home front closely associated with a particular war received similar treatment. Peripheral films about war are cross-referenced and discussed under broad topic entries such as Cold War, Spy Films, War Humor and Musicals, to mention a few.

How the Book Is Arranged

All films, historical figures, events and war-related subjects are arranged alphabetically. Films with the same title appear chronologically. Remakes are noted as such. If the plot of a remake is very similar to the original, the remake is given less space. If a biographical or historical entry has the same title as a film ("Juarez," *Juarez*), the former takes precedence and appears first. The director, screenwriter and major cast credits follow the date of release. In some rare cases we were unable to find the name of a particular director or screenwriter. On occasion, a person's name is spelled differently from one film to another (Sig Ruman, Sig Rumann; Josef Swickard, Joseph Swickard). We have kept the original spellings as they appeared in the screen credits.

The lengths of individual film entries do not necessarily reflect upon the work's artistic quality. Sometimes a particular aspect of a low-budget, routine drama may have a special interest that lends itself to greater analysis and discussion. At other times the circumstances under which a film was made or how it was accepted upon its release may be of particular concern. We have included these tidbits to satisfy both the serious researcher and the browsing reader.

Pertinent historical information often accompanies an individual film entry. When several films refer to the same war, battle, incident or person, the historical background appears as a separate and often more comprehensive entry to avoid repeating the informa-tion in each film entry. Most films about fictitious wars and nations have been omitted. For purposes of clarity or illustration, some repetition has unavoidably crept into the book, and the authors hereby plead guilty to pursuing too eagerly the Goddess of Completeness.

War documentaries—from one- or two-reelers to full-length films—are generally treated as full entries, as are dramatic or comedy war-related shorts. The titles of shorter works are identified by quotation marks; longer films are italicized. All serials, regardless of length and subject, appear under "Serials." They are difficult to summarize because of their obligatory length. Besides, they are concerned with pure action and escapism and have only the most tenuous connection to plot and real events. We handled animated films, or cartoons, in similar fashion and placed them under "Cartoons."

Acknowledgments

The authors wish to thank several people who have helped in the compilation of this encyclopedia: film researcher Paul Gold for his fresh insights and war reference materials; film collector Joseph A. Molinari who generously opened his vast assortment of films to us; film collector Billy Shelley for his unique knowledge of film history; Harry Friedman for his clerical help; and Ron Harvey for assisting in the selection of stills. We would also like to extend our appreciation to Jerry Ohlinger's Movie Material Store and Movie Star News, both located in New York City, for the materials they made available. Finally, Phyllis Korper, senior editor at Garland Publishing, deserves a special thanks for her practical editorial suggestions, steady encouragement and extreme patience.

Introduction

One day in 1898 a brash but resourceful young man lugged some primitive movie equipment to the roof of a New York City building and photographed a uniformed figure lowering the Spanish colors from a pole. J. Stuart Blackton, who made those few feet of film, titled his little work "Tearing Down the Spanish Flag," and released it as an authentic scene from the Spanish-American War. He had made film history by turning out the first American war movie.

Blackton's short film had an important impact on the young and developing movie industry. His drama, with its overtones of patriotism and propaganda, only hinted at the potential of this new medium. Within a few years a stream of war films rushed forth to merge with other popular genres. Blackton, and other resourceful pioneers who soon followed him, proved that historical events could be recreated satisfactorily and their depiction accepted by the public.

The genre offered more than entertainment and historical re-enactment; the films echoed many of society's attitudes and values. Although war movies released between 1900 and 1920 stressed glory, honor and heroism as noble goals, some began to examine war's futility, waste and destruction. The silent war film as a propaganda tool reached its peak during World War I. By 1915 American studios were producing pacifist films blatantly describing the evils of war. Simultaneously, preparedness films appeared, showing the devastating consequences of military complacency.

During the 1920s the flow of war films slowed to a trickle. Americans, it seemed, wanted to put the conflict behind them and forget about its costs in human lives or destruction. By the second half of the decade,

the war film reappeared as a viable and popular genre with such major productions as *The Big Parade* (1925), *What Price Glory?* (1926) and *Wings* (1927).

The advent of sound brought a new approach to war films. Stories of World War I now placed less emphasis on heroism, honor and glory, and focused instead on war's destructive effects, particularly upon the individual. This gave rise to a series of powerful antiwar dramas such as *All Quiet on the Western Front*, *Journey's End* and *The Dawn Patrol*, all released in 1930. They were to set a pattern that would continue until 1939 with *Nurse Edith Cavell*. Hitler's aggressive policies and the eruption of World War II once again compelled Hollywood to change its course.

After that conflict ended, America turned its attention to the Cold War. The House Un-American Activities Committee (H.U.A.C.), investigating Communist influence in the film industry, led to the blacklisting of suspected performers, directors and writers. The studios, perhaps as a sign of patriotism, turned out a flood of anti-Communist films such as *My Son John* (1952). Some combat films reverted to World War II but changed the face of the enemy. The real culprits, they suggested, were not the Nazis or Japanese, but the ineffectual military officers (*Attack!*, *The Bridge at Remagen*), politicians on both sides (*Command Decision*) or the nature of war itself (*The Longest Day*).

Hollywood had a much more difficult time dramatizing the Korean and Vietnam Wars. After a brief flurry of Korean War films in the 1950s, interest faded. Korea became the "forgotten war." The major studios stayed away for many years from the controversial Vietnam War which, in its later stages in the

1960s, provoked riots in the U.S. War films made during this period concentrated on World War II, the "good" war with its easily identifiable heroes, villains and causes.

Not until the latter half of the 1980s did Hollywood begin to scrutinize the Vietnamese conflict in big-budgeted films with major performers. Some of these—the strictly action dramas—tended to bend history by making their American heroes into super warriors and the enemy into blundering incompetents. A few, such as *Apocalypse Now* (1979) and *Platoon* (1986), portrayed the conflict in tones of surrealistic violence.

However, Hollywood has failed to convey America's military confrontations in the 1980s. Few films dealt with the rising threat of international terrorism. Movies ignored the Lebanese Civil War that resulted in the deaths of 241 U.S. Marines in Beirut in 1983. Also missing were films exploring the U.S. bombing of Libya, the invasion of Grenada and the undeclared naval war in the Persian Gulf.

Recent war films continue to move in two directions. Some, like *Platoon*, heighten our abhorrence to the cruelty, death and destruction that accompany war. Others, like the Rambo series, cater to our desires for vicarious thrills. Past and present war films evoke many questions. To what extent were the directors and writers affected by the events which surrounded them? How accurate are the historical backgrounds of these films? To what extent have films influenced society's attitudes about historical events, famous personalities or the nature of war itself? The authors of this book had several purposes in mind: to extract historical and topical trends and interpretations from the familiar and popular war movies, as well as a host of the more obscure ones; to stress relevant political, economic and social events suggested by the films; and, just as importantly, to explain the times in which those movies were first released. We equated others with their remakes, compared some films with those of similar plots and themes, and searched for other meanings within subgenres. War movies can tell us about our society and ourselves and how we view other societies and peoples. Although some films may not present as flattering a portrait as we would like, they are always worth thinking about.

One of the chief aims of this book is to point out how war films both inform and misinform. A significant portion of the movie-going public tends to get its understanding of history from films. Some dramas, such as *The Longest Day* (1962), are starkly accurate historical accounts. Many movie-goers, however, could just as easily gain a false view of history. One might believe, for example, that famed Indian war chief Geronimo was gunned down as depicted in *I Killed Geronimo* (1950). In truth, the Apache leader lived to a ripe age and became a celebrity before passing away early in this century.

Some war films reflect or reinforce social and political attitudes, even to the extent of pandering to popular stereotypes and prejudices. The anti-German dramas released before America's entry into World War I and the numerous westerns portraying the American Indian as a bloodthirsty savage provide ample proof. In other instances, a film may play a decisive role in changing its audience's beliefs and understandings. *Home of the Brave* (1949), for example, gave a sympathetic portrait of a black soldier confronted with racism in his own unit. This book describes these shifts and relates them to the climate of the time in which these films appear.

Whether a particular movie was meant solely to entertain or to shed light on a problem, its nuances nevertheless affect the viewer. Meanwhile, each viewer brings to every film his or her own personal values. The cumulative effect of this blend upon society is difficult to evaluate. The making of these dramas has undergone extensive technological advances since Blackton's first elemental work in 1898. But the basic emotional appeal upon which war dramas feed remains constant.

Abbreviations

AA	Allied Artists
AE	Associated Exhibitors
AI	American International
APD	Allied Producers and Distributors Corporation
APR	Associated Producers
AR	American Releasing Company
Avco	Avco Embassy
BFB	Brody-Freed-Brandchild
BV	Buena Vista
Cin.	Cinerama Releasing Corporation
Col.	Columbia
CU	Commonwealth United
FBO	Film Booking Offices
FN	First National
GN	Grand National
MGM	Metro Goldwyn Mayer
Mon.	Monogram
NC	Nation Cinema Pictures
NG	National General Pictures
Par.	Paramount
PDC	Producers Distributing Corporation
PRC	Producers Releasing Corporation
Rep.	Republic
RKO	RKO Radio Pictures
TCF	Twentieth Century-Fox
U	Universal
UA	United Artists
UI	Universal-International
WB	Warner Brothers
WW	Sono Art-Worldwide

Sources

Atlas of United States History. Maplewood, NJ: Hammond, 1971.

Bailey, Thomas A. *The American Pageant.* 2nd ed. Boston: D.C. Heath, 1961.

Barbour, Alan G. *Saturday Afternoon at the Movies.* New York: Bonanza Books, 1986.

Beebe, Lucius, and Charles Clegg. *The American West.* New York: E. P. Dutton, 1955.

Bridgwater, William, and Seymour Kurtz, eds. *Columbia Encyclopedia.* 3rd ed. New York: Columbia University Press, 1968.

Brownlow, Kevin. *The War, the West, and the Wilderness.* New York: Alfred A. Knopf, 1979.

Bullock, Alan. *Hitler: A Study in Tyranny.* New York: Harper and Row, 1962.

Catton, Bruce. *This Hallowed Ground.* New York: Doubleday, 1956.

Churchill, Winston S. *The Second World War.* Boston: Houghton Mifflin, 1953.

Clubb, Edmund O. *20th Century China.* New York: Columbia University Press, 1964.

Cowie, Peter. *Seventy Years of Cinema.* New York: Castle Books, 1969.

Dolan, Jr., Edward F. *Hollywood Goes to War.* New York: Gallery Books, 1985.

Dooley, Roger. *From Scarface to Scarlett: American Films in the 1930s.* New York: Harcourt, Brace, Jovanovich, 1979.

Dunan, Marcel, ed. *Larousse Encyclopedia of Modern History.* New York: Crescent Books, 1987.

Dunn, Jr., J. P. *Massacres of the Mountains: A History of the Indian Wars of the Far West 1815–1875.* New York: Archer House, 1965.

Dupuy, R. Ernest, and Trevor N. Dupuy, eds. *Encyclopedia of Military History.* New York: Harper and Row, 1986.

Eames, John Douglas. *The MGM Story.* New York: Crown Publishers, 1979.

——————. *The Paramount Story.* New York: Crown Publishers, 1985.

Film Daily Year Book of Motion Pictures (annually). New York: Distributed by Arno Press, 1970.

Freidel, Frank. *Over There: The Story of America's First Great Overseas Crusade.* New York: Bramhall House, 1964.

Griffith, Richard, and Arthur Mayer. *The Movies.* New York: Simon and Schuster, 1957.

Grun, Bernard, and Werner Stein. *The Timetables of History.* New York: Simon and Schuster, 1979.

Halliwell, Leslie. *The Filmgoer's Companion.* New York: Hill and Wang, 1977.

Hart, John Mason. *Revolutionary Mexico.* Berkeley: University of California Press, 1988.

Henderson, Robert M. *D. W. Griffith: His Life and Work.* New York: Oxford University Press, 1972.

——————. *D. W. Griffith: The Years at Biograph.* New York: Farrar, Straus and Giroux, 1970.

Hirschhorn, Clive. *The Universal Story.* New York: Crown Publishers, 1983.

——————. *The Warner Bros. Story.* New York: Crown Publishers, 1979.

Hoffman, Mark S., ed. *World Almanac and Book of Facts.* New York: Pharos Books, 1988.

Hoyt, Edwin P. *The Bloody Road to Panmunjom.* New York: Stein and Day, 1985.

Hyams, Jay. *War Movies.* New York: Gallery Books, 1984.

Insdorf, Annette. *Indelible Shadows: Films and the Holocaust.* New York: Vintage Books, 1983.

Isenberg, Michael T. *War on Film: The American Cinema and World War I, 1914–1941.* East Brunswick, NJ: Associated University Presses, 1981.

Jewell, Richard B., and Vernon Harbin. *The RKO Story.* New York: Crown Publishers, 1982.

Jones, Emrys, ed. *Webster's Color Atlas of the World.* London: Octopus Books, 1978.

Josephy Jr., Alvin M. *The Patriot Chiefs.* New York: Viking Press, 1962.

Karnow, Stanley. *Vietnam: A History.* New York: Viking Press, 1983.

Knight, Arthur. *The Liveliest Art: A Panoramic History of the Movies.* New York: Macmillan, 1957.

Kohn, George C. *Dictionary of Wars.* Garden City, NY: Anchor Books, 1987.

Lahue, Kalton C. *World of Laughter: The Motion Picture Comedy Short, 1910–1930.* Norman, OK: University of Oklahoma Press, 1966.

Langer, William L., ed. *Encyclopedia of World History.* Leicester, Eng.: Harrap/Galley Press, 1987.

Langguth, A. J. *Patriots: The Men Who Started The Revolution.* New York: Simon and Schuster, 1988.

Langman, Larry. *A Guide to American Film Directors: The Sound Era, 1929–1979.* Metuchen, NJ: Scarecrow Press, 1981.

————. *A Guide to American Screenwriters: The Sound Era, 1929–1982.* New York: Garland Publishing, 1984.

Levey, Judith S., and Agnes Greenhall, eds. *Concise Columbia Encyclopedia.* New York: Columbia University Press, 1983.

Maltin, Leonard. *The Great Movie Shorts.* New York: Bonanza Books, 1972.

Manvell, Roger. *Films and the Second World War.* New York: Dell, 1976.

Mayer, S. L., Alan Wykes and Ian Hogg. *Great American Generals of World War II.* Greenwich, CT: Bison Books, 1984.

McCracken, Harold, ed. *Frederic Remington's Own West.* New York: Dial Press, 1960.

Miller, Don. *B Movies.* New York: Ballantine Books, 1987.

Morris, Richard B., ed. *Encyclopedia of American History.* New York: Harper and Row, 1982.

New York Times Film Reviews (1913–1980). New York: Quadrangle Books, Inc.

Palmer, R.R. *A History of the Modern World,* 2nd Ed. New York: Alfred A. Knopf, 1963.

Parrish, Thomas, ed. *Encyclopedia of World War II.* New York: Simon and Schuster, 1978.

Pratt, Julius W. *A History of United States Foreign Policy.* New York: Prentice-Hall, 1955.

Quigley, Martin, Jr., and Richard Gertner. *Films in America, 1929–1969.* New York: Golden Press, 1970.

Schlesinger, Arthur M., ed. *Almanac of American History.* New York: Bramhall House, 1986.

Shindler, Colin. *Hollywood Goes to War.* Boston: Routledge & Kegan Paul, 1979.

Shirer, William L. *The Rise and Fall of the Third Reich.* New York, Simon and Schuster, 1960.

Siepman, Kate, ed. *Benet's Reader's Encyclopedia.* 3rd ed. New York: Harper and Row, 1987.

Smith, Graham. *When Jim Crow Met John Bull: Black American Soldiers in World War II Britain.* New York: St. Martin's Press, 1988.

Spears, Jack. *Hollywood: The Golden Era.* New York: Castle Books, 1971.

Todd, Lewis Paul, and Merli Curti. *Rise of the American Nation.* New York: Harcourt, Brace and World, 1969.

Truman, Harry S. *Memoirs.* New York: Doubleday, 1955.

Tuchman, Barbara W. *The Guns of August.* New York. Macmillan, 1962.

Utley, Robert M. *The Indian Frontier of the American West; 1864–1890.* Albuquerque: University of New Mexico Press, 1984.

Variety Film Reviews 1907–1984. New York: Garland Publishing, 1986.

Waldman, Carl. *Atlas of the North American Indian.* New York: Facts on File Publications, 1985.

Ward, Christopher. *The War of the Revolution.* New York: Macmillan, 1952.

Wellman, Paul I. *The Indian Wars of the West.* New York: Doubleday and Co., 1954.

White, David Manning, and Richard Averson. *The Celluloid Weapon: Social Comment in the American Film.* Boston: Beacon Press, 1972.

Young, Desmond. *The Desert Fox.* New York: Harper and Row, 1950.

The
Encyclopedia

A

Abbott and Costello in the Foreign Legion (1950). See Service Comedy. ▪

Abenaki (Abnaki) Wars. See *Northwest Passage* (1940). ▪

About Face (1942). See Service Comedy. ▪

Above and Beyond (1952), MGM. *Dir.* Melvin Frank, Norman Panama; *Sc.* Melvin Frank, Norman Panama; *Cast includes:* Robert Taylor, Eleanor Parker, James Whitmore, Larry Keating.

This World War II drama deals with the pilot who flew over Hiroshima with the first atomic bomb and how it affected him. Robert Taylor portrays Colonel Paul Tibbets, a flier recalled from Europe to the U.S. during the war and assigned the task of assembling an anonymous group of bombers and crews as well as testing a special long-range bomber. All is kept secret until the actual mission is carried out by the crew of the *Enola Gay.* Eleanor Parker plays Taylor's wife in this story that places its characters under stress until the bomb is dropped.

Tibbets, born in 1915, flew antisubmarine patrols over the Atlantic coast of the U.S., flew 25 bomber missions in Europe and participated in the North African campaign before being reassigned to the U.S. He piloted the *Enola Gay,* a B-29 bomber, over Hiroshima and, on August 6, 1945, dropped the first atomic bomb in history.

One of several post-World War II dramas to focus on actual events and use the names of real participants, *Above and Beyond* in this respect differs from such combat films as *Wake Island* and *Bataan* released during the war. These earlier works, which are based on real events, employ fictional characters. ▪

Above Suspicion (1943). See Spy Films: the Talkies. ▪

Abraham Lincoln (1924). See American Civil War. ▪

Abraham Lincoln (1930). See American Civil War. ▪

Abroad With Two Yanks (1944). See Service Comedy. ▪

According to the Code (1916), Essanay. *Dir.* Charles Michelson; *Sc.* Charles Michelson; *Cast includes:* Lewis Stone, Marguerite Clayton, Florence Oberle.

A complex domestic drama with a Civil War setting, the film is told through several flashbacks. A Southerner meets and marries a northern girl and they settle in the South. When war breaks out, the husband, now also a father, becomes a captain in the Confederate army. During an engagement, he finds a wounded Union captain and brings him home to recuperate. The husband returns to battle and is reported killed in action. The Union officer, fully recovered, falls in love with the wife and marries her. He takes her and the child to his home in the North. Later, the first husband returns. The film has at least two worthy qualities—its effective Civil War battle sequences and a strong climactic courtroom scene. ▪

Ace of Aces (1933), RKO. *Dir.* J. Walter Ruben; *Sc.* John Monk Saunders, H. W. Hanemann; *Cast includes:* Richard Dix, Elizabeth Allan, Ralph Bellamy, William Cagney.

A World War I airplane drama, the film stars Richard Dix as a sensitive sculptor who is transformed into a bloodthirsty killer when

1

Richard Dix (c.) and fellow World War I airmen enjoy a short respite from battle as images of death and war wait in the background. *Ace of Aces* (1933).

he enters the war as an aviator. His romantic relationship with Elizabeth Allan, who encouraged him to enlist, disintegrates as he grows more obsessed with shooting down enemy aircraft. He soon begins to evaluate the cost in human lives with the medals he has won. Ultimately, he is killed in action. The film provides several lively action sequences, some of which were borrowed from *Hell's Angels*, the 1930 airplane epic directed by Howard Hughes.

This was one of the earliest war stories to follow the trend set by *All Quiet on the Western Front* and several other films released in 1930 which seriously tried to blend the element of adventure with a strong antiwar theme. ■

Across the Atlantic (1928). See Veterans. ■

Across the Pacific (1926), WB. *Dir.* Roy Del Ruth; *Sc.* Darryl Zanuck; *Cast includes:* Monte Blue, Myrna Loy, Jane Winton, Walter McGrail, Charles Stevens.

The drama is set in the Philippines following the Spanish- American War. Rebel islanders are on the verge of overthrowing the democratic regime when Monte Blue, portraying an American spy, is sent to uncover the leader. He makes love to one of the natives, a half-caste islander (Myrna Loy), so that he can learn the whereabouts of the rebel leader. The film concludes with an action-filled battle between the dissidents and American troops. Edgar Kennedy supplies the comic relief. Warner Brothers used the title again in

the 1940s but for an entirely different story starring Humphrey Bogart and Mary Astor. ■

Across the Pacific (1942), WB. *Dir.* John Huston; *Sc.* Richard Macauley; *Cast includes:* Humphrey Bogart, Mary Astor, Sydney Greenstreet, Charles Halton, Sen Yung.

The strategic Panama Canal is the subject of this World War II spy drama starring the three leads of director John Huston's previous hit, *The Maltese Falcon* (1941). Humphrey Bogart plays an American agent posing as a court-martialed army officer who is on the trail of Sydney Greenstreet, suspected of collaborating with the Japanese. Mary Astor provides the romantic interest and lure for Bogart as he temporarily joins forces with the espionage network. He eventually foils a plot to bomb the canal in this suspenseful film of intrigue and action.

Huston left the film before its conclusion when he was called for active service. Vincent Sherman completed the direction in the taut Huston style which included a rather implausible escape by Bogart, who was being held captive by the spies. ■

Act of Violence (1948). See Veterans. ■

Action in Arabia (1944). See Women and War. ■

Action in the North Atlantic (1943), WB. *Dir.* Lloyd Bacon; *Sc.* John Howard Lawson; *Cast includes:* Humphrey Bogart, Raymond Massey, Julie Bishop, Ruth Gordon, Sam Levene, Dane Clark, Alan Hale.

A tribute to the U.S. Merchant Marine and the navy gun crews of World War II, the film reveals the story of the liberty ships and their crews that fought their way through the U-boat-infested waters of the Atlantic during the Murmansk run. Humphrey Bogart portrays a first mate aboard an oil tanker whose captain is Raymond Massey. Their ship is torpedoed by a Nazi submarine. Massey, Bogart and a handful of the survivors climb aboard a raft which is purposely smashed by the surfaced German submarine. The men luckily swim to a nearby raft as the crew of the U-boat mock them. "Go on, laugh, you apes!" Massey cries out to the U-Boat as it disappears into the night. "You had your blood and fire to make you laugh! But I swear to God our time is comin'. We'll pay you back! We'll hunt you down and slice you like a piece of cheese!" "They can't hear you," Bogart says quietly. "No," Massey replies, "but God can." Bogart gets his turn to utter his share of patriotic remarks when a young seaman from Kansas is buried at sea. "A lot more people are going to die before this is over," he says, "and it's up to the ones who make it through to make sure they didn't die for nothing." They are rescued and returned to the States where they rejoin their families until their next assignment.

Alan Hale provides the comic relief. In one scene during a storm that tosses the tanker about as if it were a toy, Hale says to a fellow sailor: "This is the kind of day I'd like to be home with a blonde and a book." "Since when can you read?" his pal reminds him. "Who said I could read?" Hale fires back.

Typical of the war movies released during the 1940s, the film contains a fair amount of propaganda. When a merchant seaman (Dane Clark) complains back in port that he prefers to stay at home rather than return to sea, a fellow seaman (Sam Levene) blasts him. "So you want a safe job?" Levene says. "Go ask the Czechs and the Poles and the Greeks. They wanted safe jobs. They're lined up in front of guns digging each other's graves. The trouble with you is you think America is just a place to eat and sleep." Clark signs on again. When their second ship finally reaches Murmansk after being stranded from the convoy, torpedoed by a U-Boat and bombed and strafed by German planes, a naval officer of the convoy, watching the listing tanker sail into port, remarks, "It's a miracle." "It's no miracle," says another, "it's American seamanship." The finale includes a voice-over by President Roosevelt: "We shall build a bridge of ships to our allies over which we shall roll the implements of war. The goods will be delivered where they are needed and when they are needed. Nothing on land, in the air, on the sea or under the sea shall prevent our final victory." ∎

Address Unknown (1944), Col. *Dir.* William Cameron Menzies; *Sc.* Herbert Dalmas; *Cast includes:* Paul Lukas, Carl Esmond, Peter Van Eyck, Mady Christians, Morris Carnovsky, K.T. Stevens.

This pre-World War II drama, which takes place in the late 1930s, underscores how the callousness and brutality of the Nazi regime affect the individual who succumbs to its influence. Paul Lukas and Morris Carnovsky, as two German-American business partners, have a flourishing concern in the United States. Lukas returns to Germany to handle affairs there while Carnovsky, who is Jewish, asks his partner to look after his daughter (K.T. Stevens), a German actress and the fiancee of Lukas' son who has remained in America. Lukas soon becomes a loyal follower of the Nazi party and distances himself from the young Jewess. She is harassed by the Nazis and finally taken away to a concentration camp.

The film then introduces the theme of parricide. Lukas' son, in an act of revenge, purposely sends coded letters from the U.S. to his father. The Nazis, of course, censor the mail and accuse Lukas of treason. The last letter is returned and stamped "Address Unknown." This idea appears also in *The Purple Heart*, released the same year, in which a young Chinese kills his father, a local official who is collaborating with the Japanese. Even traditional family ties are no defense against the exigencies of war.

The plot follows Lukas' slow degeneration from a caring and humane figure to one who places Nazi ideology and self-interest above human life. The story, written by Kressmann Taylor, switches back and forth between the two countries and is told through a series of letters. ∎

Adele (1919), U. *Dir.* Wallace Worsely; *Sc.* Jack Cunningham; *Cast includes:* Kitty Gordon, Mahlon Hamilton, Wedgewood Nowell, Joseph Dowling.

In this World War I romantic drama a nurse and her sweetheart both go to France, she to help with the wounded and he to fight for his country. He is wounded and placed in her hospital, but the Germans attack and capture the wounded and the nurses. The invaders promise to save the boy's life if she will go to England and spy for them. She agrees, but once in England she goes to the authorities who give her useless information to transport back to the Germans. A British counterattack retakes the town and the hospital. ∎

Advance to the Rear (1964), MGM. *Dir.* George Marshall; *Sc.* Samuel A. Peeples, William Bowers; *Cast includes:* Glenn Ford, Stella Stevens, Melvyn Douglas, Jim Backus, Joan Blondell.

A wrong-headed Union colonel causes a multitude of problems for his troops in this

Civil War comedy. Melvyn Douglas, as the commander of a troop of misfits, insists on making all the military decisions. But they usually turn out to be disasters. Glenn Ford portrays a sensible-minded captain who is frustrated by his eccentric colonel. Stella Stevens, as a Confederate spy, provides the romance. Joan Blondell plays a madam whose group of prostitutes provide the customary diversions for the men. Veteran character player Alan Hale portrays a sergeant. One of the highlights of the farce is a comical battle between the Yankees and the Confederates. ■

Adventure in Sahara (1938), Col. *Dir.* D. Ross Lederman; *Sc.* Maxwell Shane; *Cast includes:* Paul Kelly, C. Henry Gordon, Lorna Gray, Robert Fiske, Marc Lawrence.

An action drama of the Foreign Legion, this low-budget film centers on a tyrannical captain who is eventually overthrown by the men serving under him and tossed into the desert to fend for himself. He swears to return to the fort and punish the mutineers. When he does, hostile Arabs decide to attack, and the men who have secured the fort allow their former captain and his troops to enter. After Arab hordes are repelled, the men are rewarded for their bravery. But the captain insists on carrying out the courts-martial of his men until an outspoken lieutenant explains the intolerable circumstances to the proper officials. The accused are then exonerated in this cliché-ridden plot that often resembles *Mutiny on the Bounty* (1935). ■

Adventures of a Rookie, The (1943). See Service Comedy. ■

Adventures of Buffalo Bill, The (1914), Essanay. *Dir.* Theodore Wharton; *Sc.* General Charles King; *Cast includes:* William "Buffalo Bill" Cody, Chief Running Hawk, General Nelson Miles.

William "Buffalo Bill" Cody portrays himself in this early epic that deals with the Indian wars. The drama covers several historical battles, including those at Warbonnet Creek, Summit Springs and Wounded Knee, the last being the climactic highlight. Cody, who acted as producer, was determined to give an accurate account of the events while making a permanent record of the resistance of the Sioux. General Miles, a Civil War veteran who later captured Geronimo and sub-

dued several tribes, acted as technical adviser. The U.S. government supported the project and lent cavalry troops to Cody.

The final production caused some controversy. Indian spokesmen attacked the depiction of the battle at Wounded Knee as inaccurate. They claimed the cavalry killed innocent women and children while their men were away. The film shows the braves present and ready to turn in their arms to the soldiers when a shot is fired accidentally. Suddenly, the soldiers, fearing an uprising, begin shooting wildly. As a result, many braves, women and children lay dead. Criticism also came from historians who disputed the accuracy of different events. Unfortunately, much of the film has been lost. The drama was exhibited under a variety of titles, including, among others, *Buffalo Bill's Indian Wars* and *The Indian Wars Refought*. ■

Adventures of Casanova (1948), Eagle Lion. *Dir.* Roberto Gavaldon; *Sc.* Crane Wilbur, Walter Bullock, Karen DeWolf; *Cast includes:* Arturo De Cordova, Lucille Bremer, Turhan Bey, John Sutton.

The legendary lover, Casanova, temporarily puts aside his vigorous amorous pursuits as he fights to liberate Sicily from Austrian oppression in this historical action drama. Arturo De Cordova portrays the adventurer who is loved by every Sicilian woman and envied by every Sicilian man. Even when told by one of his conquests that "love is a constant search for something you never find," he is already thinking of other matters. He leads the peasants in a revolt against the Austrian establishment, ambushing their patrols and feeding the local natives. Lucille Bremer, whom Casanova finds time to woo, portrays the daughter of the governor. John Sutton plays the corrupt emissary of the Austrian regime. George Tobias contributes to the comic relief, especially in the sequence in which he portrays a spy masquerading as a clergyman. Despite the historical background, the film has the familiar trappings of a conventional western.

The plot is fundamentally inaccurate. Although Sicily had at one time been under Austrian domination, the island came under rule of the Bourbon kings of Naples in 1738. That rakish Italian adventurer and author, Casanova (1725–1798), would have been 13 years old, according to the film, in his resistance against Austria. There is no evidence

Arturo De Cordova (l.c.), representing the oppressed peasants, challenges the seat and luxury of Austrian power. *Adventures of Casanova* (1948).

that Casanova, who was expelled from the priesthood for immoral conduct, served in the Venetian army and acted as a spy for the Venetian Inquisition, had ever been entangled in political events in Sicily. ■

Adventures of Robin Hood, The (1938),

WB. *Dir.* Michael Curtiz, William Keighley; *Sc.* Norman Reilly Raine, Seton I. Miller; *Cast includes:* Errol Flynn, Olivia De Havilland, Basil Rathbone, Claude Rains, Patric Knowles, Eugene Pallette, Alan Hale.

Filled with spectacle, action, romance and adventure, the film brings to life the famous folk legend of the bandit of Sherwood Forest. Warner Brothers allotted a big budget for the large cast, the lavish sets and the use of Technicolor to help the production along. Errol Flynn plays Robin Hood, defender of the poor and downtrodden Saxons against the Normans, led by Prince John, usurper to the throne, whose brother, King Richard, is away fighting in the Crusades. Flynn finds time to woo Maid Marion, played by Olivia De Havilland, while evading John's troops and ambushing his rich caravans to raise the ransom money needed for Richard's release. Later,

when the rightful king returns disguised as an abbot, he meets Robin in Sherwood Forest and tests his loyalty. "You condemn the Holy Crusades?" inquires Richard. "I condemn anything that prevents Richard from defending the country from outlaws like me," Flynn replies. Historically, Richard spent very little time in England during his reign.

The film, a remake of the 1922 silent version with Douglas Fairbanks as the hero, provides plenty of action, including attacks on the Prince's caravans; a hand-to-hand battle within Prince John's castle; and a rousing sword fight between Flynn and Basil Rathbone, who plays the treacherous Sir Guy. Claude Rains portrays a sinister Prince John. Most of Robin Hood's legendary friends appear—Little John (Alan Hale), portly Friar Tuck (Eugene Pallette) and Will Scarlet (Patric Knowles). The film was one of the major box-office successes of the year and became Errol Flynn's most popular film. Warner Brothers originally planned to star William Cagney in the title role in the mid-1930s but set aside the project for a few years.

Researchers in the region where the famed outlaw was supposed to have dwelled have uncovered a Robin Hood-like figure who had been born about 1220 during the reign of Henry III (1216–1272). Old documents list Robert de Kyne, part nobleman of Saxon descent, as having helped to lead a revolt against corrupt Norman officials and clergy who were imposing excessively heavy taxes on the poor. Some historians question the outlaw's social magnanimity, stating that very few references in existing ballads mention his sharing of his thefts with the poor. They suggest that Robin Hood may have been a simple common thief. In the early 1950s, during the Cold War, stories of the outlaw's exploits were banned from several school districts in the U.S. He had been labeled a harmful "Communist role model" who "smeared law and order." ■

Aerial Gunner (1943), Par. *Dir.* William H. Pine; *Sc.* Maxwell Shane; *Cast includes:* Chester Morris, Richard Arlen, Lila Ward, Jimmy Lydon, Dick Purcell.

Two enemies in civilian life find themselves at the same gunnery school in this World War II action drama. Chester Morris portrays a sergeant and instructor at the base while Richard Arlen plays his long-time foe. The entire unit upon completion of its training is sent into combat in the Pacific. Morris and Arlen, attacked by a swarm of Japanese fighters, are forced to land their bomber on a Japanese-occupied island. The former sacrifices his life so that the other can escape with the plane. Besides the limited battle scenes in the sky, the film contains several early sequences of the different training exercises of the gunners. Lila Ward provides the love interest of the two rivals in this routine tale. ■

Afghanistan War (1979–). See *Rambo III* (1988). ■

Affair of Three Nations, An (1915). See Russo-Japanese War. ■

Afraid to Fight (1922). See Veterans. ■

African Queen, The (1951), UA. *Dir.* John Huston; *Sc.* James Agee, John Huston; *Cast includes:* Humphrey Bogart, Katharine Hepburn, Robert Morley, Peter Bull, Theodore Bikel.

This adventure comedy, set in Africa during World War I and based on C. S. Forester's novel, depends more on characterization for its humor than on incident or plot. And it is precisely the two characters, Charlie Allnut and Rose Sayer, as portrayed by Bogart and Hepburn, respectively, that make this such a winning film. Rose, the spinster sister of Reverend Sayer, an English missionary, has been in Africa ten years playing the organ during services for the natives. Charlie is the gin-guzzling skipper of the beat-up *African Queen*, a 30-foot launch that chugs along the rivers of German East Africa. The film opens in 1914. World War I has broken out in Europe, and the German soldiers are burning villages along the river and rounding up the male natives as recruits.

When Rose's brother dies after being brutalized by the Germans, Charlie takes her aboard his boat to safety. But she has other plans. She is determined to use Charlie's boat to destroy the *Louisa*, a German gunboat guarding a great lake that the English must use to transport their troops. At first Charlie resists, but her stubbornness induces him to give in half-heartedly. That night he gets drunk and refuses to go on, calling her a "crazy, psalm-singing old maid." While he is asleep, she dumps his case of gin overboard and refuses to speak to him until he continues the journey as he originally promised. He finally agrees, and they navigate their little boat past a German fort and through treacherous rapids toward their final destination. Exhilarated with their success in surmounting these dangers, they embrace and kiss, then pause and draw back in surprise, realizing that they have fallen in love. They continue down the river, acting like two young lovers who have discovered love for the first time.

After a series of new hardships, they encounter the *Louisa* and, through a set of unexpected circumstances, succeed in sinking it. Rose, who had repressed her emotions for most of her life, first begins to discover a change while riding down the dangerous rapids. "I never dreamed that any mere physical experience could be so stimulating," she confesses to Charlie. "I've only known such excitement a few times before . . . in my brother's sermons when the spirit was upon him." Later, when they are picked up by the German captain of the gunboat, she is the quintessence of English determinism and pride. She admits the purpose of their journey and tells how they traversed the allegedly unnavigable river. The captain, in disbelief, exclaims, "It's impossible." Rose smiles and replies with self-satisfaction: "Nevertheless." Charlie, a shy bachelor who has spent most of his life avoiding people and getting drunk, changes under Rose's strong influence. Bogart won an Academy Award for his role.

Although it is basically a comedy adventure, the film may also be viewed on an allegorical level. Rose Sayer represents the high-minded spirit of the English people who refuse to succumb to temporary defeat. She responds with a strong determination to retaliate against those who have chosen to make her their enemy. Her steadfastness of purpose eventually arouses the cynical Charlie Allnut, a symbol of American apolitical isolationism who, once convinced that her cause is just, uses his ingenuity and strength to help her destroy the German gunboat.

Byron Farwell, in his book *The Great War in Africa, 1914–1918,* suggests that the sequences in the film involving the *Louisa* and Charlie's launch may have been inspired by an actual World War I incident. A small British expedition transported two launches overland to Lake Tanganyika in the Belgian Congo. The two boats then proceeded to attack a larger German gunboat, forcing it to surrender. ∎

After Mein Kampf (1961), Joseph Brenner. *Dir.* Ralph Porter; *Sc.* Ralph Porter.

A documentary depicting the horrors loosed upon the world by the Nazis during World War II, the film depends almost entirely upon newsreel footage of the period, most of which has been seen before. Hitler's rantings and ravings at German rallies, Nazi soldiers marching to martial songs and shocking scenes of the death camp victims dominate the work. Other scenes, borrowed from feature films and other sources, include the rape of a Norwegian woman by a German soldier and the forced attempt by prostitutes to revive a moribund figure. The film, especially with its focus on specific atrocities, is reminiscent of those documentaries and propaganda dramas that appeared during World War I. They, too, emphasized rape and showed the Huns in the worst possible light. ∎

After the War (1918), U. *Dir.* Joseph De Grasse; *Sc.* Harvey Gates; *Cast includes:* Grace Cunard, Herbert Prior, Edward Cecil, Dora Rogers.

Part fantasy and part melodrama, this World War I film takes place in postwar Berlin where German military leaders are being executed for war crimes following their trials. Although it was released at war's end, the drama continued the anti-German sentiment that prevailed during the conflict. The plot concerns a French soldier, a former prisoner of war, who shows his gratitude to a Prussian officer for sparing his life. He then discovers that his fiancee was forced to marry the Prussian in exchange for her lover's life. The obvious message—that the Germans were not to be trusted—was not lost on American audiences. ∎

After Tonight (1933). See Spy Films: the Talkies. ∎

Air Force (1943), WB. *Dir.* Howard Hawks; *Sc.* Dudley Nichols; *Cast includes:* John Garfield, Gig Young, Harry Carey, George Tobias, Arthur Kennedy.

This World War II drama extols the virtues of camaraderie and teamwork as the crew members of a B-17 Flying Fortress, affectionately named *Mary-Ann,* work and fight together through several tough obstacles. A pursuit plane flier, played by James Brown, is transported from Hawaii to Manila aboard the *Mary-Ann* and soon learns why the crew takes particular pride in its bomber. John Garfield portrays a sulky aerial gunner who failed as a flying officer. He is just biding his time to resign—until the sneak attack on Pearl Harbor changes his attitude. Harry Carey plays a World War I veteran and crew chief, proud of his son who has won his wings. He later learns that the boy was killed at Wake Island by Japanese pilots. Tension mounts as the B-17 is shuttled from island to island to escape the invading Japanese. As they leave Wake Island and the small force of 400 marines, one of the officers of the bomber asks: "Anything we might do for you in Manila?" "You might send us more Japs," a marine officer says jokingly. Finally, a marine commandant orders the damaged plane destroyed, but the crew repairs it in time. On the way to Australia, the men spot a Japanese invasion fleet and signal nearby bases for help. American bombers and fighter planes join the *Mary-Ann* in destroying the enemy ships. The last sequence of the film shows a squadron of bombers taking off to bomb Tokyo. President Roosevelt's voice is heard announcing the strategy of the U.S. "We shall carry the attack against the enemy. We shall hit him and hit him again wherever and whenever we can reach him. For we intend to bring the battle to him on his own home ground." The flagwaving that occurs at times does not take away from the strong human elements of the story. The film cleverly integrates actual footage from the Battle of the Coral Sea, which heightens the overall realism. ∎

Air Raid Wardens (1943). See Spy Comedies. ∎

Aircraft in war. Although the work of the Wright brothers is given major credit for ushering in the air age, the first recorded use of aircraft in war predated the Wrights' accomplishments. The French used hot-air balloons, the first examples of military air power, for observation in the Battle of Fleurus (1794). Napoleon even toyed with the tactic of using balloons to invade England during the Napoleonic Wars. Austria in 1849 carried out history's first aerial bombing attack when it sent unmanned bomb-carrying balloons against Venice. Lighter-than-air machines first received extensive military application during the American Civil War. Union forces in 1862 used balloons to report on the disposition and movement of Confederate ground troops. Unfortunately, Hollywood has overlooked this historical background and its entertainment potential.

Lighter-than-air craft continued to intrigue military thinking into World War I. Count Ferdinand von Zeppelin pioneered in 1902 a rigid-framed, hydrogen-celled airship powered by engines. Germany used his designs, known as zeppelins or dirigibles, in World War I raids over London. *Hell's Angels* (1930) featured a battle over London between a zeppelin and British fighter planes. *The Zeppelin's Last Raid*, a 1917 pacifist drama in which a German zeppelin commander, influenced by his nonviolent sweetheart, refuses to bomb an enemy city, was one of the earliest war films to use this aircraft.

Airplanes, however, soon overshadowed zeppelins for several reasons. Early dirigibles used highly flammable hydrogen. In addition, their slow speed and bulk made them easy targets for ground fire and airplane attacks. As a result, by 1916, the emphasis had shifted overwhelmingly to airplanes. But the zeppelin continued to appear on screen in an occasional drama.

Airplanes were introduced into war films to add a bit of freshness to conventional stories dealing with romance, heroism and action. Eventually the airplane and its pilot began to interest audiences more than the trite plots and routine characters in the same way that alien creatures or exotic settings have come to dominate science fiction stories. Airplanes appeared in early American films about real and imaginary wars. One of the earliest in this genre, "Warfare in the Skies," released in 1914, concerned an insurrection in a fictitious country with both sides using airplanes for bombing and dogfights. *A Romance of the Air* (1918) recounted the true experiences of Lt. Bert Hall, a flier with the Lafayette Escadrille. The film included a romantic plot that was not part of his book.

As World War I progressed, airplanes performed functions other than simply gathering information, and soon there were bombers, fighters, seaplanes, and attack planes. The idea of attacking enemy targets away from the battlefield quickly took hold. The British bombed sites in Germany in 1914. Germany in 1915 undertook a series of air raids on London and other British cities.

The invention of an interrupter mechanism in 1915 enabled a pilot to fire his forward machine guns more accurately through a turning propeller. By 1917 aerial dogfights involving 100 or more planes were not uncommon. Planes darted about the sky in a wild melee of high, individual drama with the hunter often becoming the hunted. This deadly individual combat created such World War I air aces as Baron Manfred von Richthofen (The Red Baron) and Max Immelman of Germany; Georges Guynemer and Rene Fonck of France; Edward Mannock and Albert Ball of Great Britain; Roy Brown—who downed von Richthofen—of Canada; and Edward Rickenbacker of the U.S. *Von Richthofen and Brown* (1971) recounted the exploits of the famous "Red Baron" and the Canadian flier who ultimately downs the German ace.

The film that actually launched the air war genre was William Wellman's *Wings* (1927), starring Buddy Rogers and Richard Arlen as two American pilots. Despite a bland romantic plot, scenes of spectacular dogfights, crashes and bombings helped to make it a popular success and established the format for future films. *Legion of the Condemned* (1928), also directed by Wellman, soon followed, starring Gary Cooper as an American airman in the Lafayette Escadrille who volunteers for several perilous assignments because of unrequited love.

Two major films in the air cycle appeared in 1930. *Hell's Angels*, directed by Howard Hughes, an eccentric millionaire, consumed millions of dollars and took years to complete before it got off the ground. A spectacular production, it featured exciting air fights and a zeppelin attack on London. The weak romantic plot also catapulted Jean Harlow to fame as a sex symbol of the 1930s as a result of her sensual role. *The Dawn Patrol*, directed by Howard Hawks and released the same year, suggested a pacifist theme amidst the trappings of heroism and duty. It focused on British fliers and their reactions to the constant threat of death they faced, rather than on sensational battle sequences. The film was remade in 1938 starring Errol Flynn, David Niven and Basil Rathbone.

Air power achieved recognition as a commanding weapon in World War II, both on land and at sea. Germany's use of its powerful air force showed an astonished world the devastating manner in which aircraft could be used to weaken and demoralize the enemy's ground units and civilian populations. Screaming dive bombers spread both panic and destruction among victims of the Nazi Blitzkrieg.

The development of heavy, long-range bombers in World War II made aircraft the chief instrument for carrying the attack deep into the enemy's heartland. Massive bombing raids not only disrupted production of war supplies but aimed at terrorizing the population to weaken its resolve to continue in the war. Hitler first employed this tactic, though unsuccessfully, in the Battle of Britain (1940–1941). The Allies refined and enlarged this form of warfare in the latter stages of the conflict as they developed high altitude, nighttime and saturation bombing, sometimes using massive incendiary raids that created a fire storm in selected Axis cities. Such films as *Bomber's Moon* (1943) and *The Thousand Plane Raid* (1969) exemplified this phase of the air war.

The importance of carrier planes and carrier task forces grew during the war. The aircraft carrier task force, especially in the Pacific, became the main long-range weapon against enemy naval and ground forces. The Battles of the Coral Sea and Midway in 1942 and Leyte Gulf in 1944, engagements that shaped the outcome of the war in the Pacific, were primarily air-sea duels with little or no direct contact between opposing surface ships. *Wing and a Prayer* (1944), *Task Force* (1949) and *Midway* (1976) were only some of the dramas about the Pacific War.

Jet aircraft, introduced by Germany in limited fashion near the end of World War II, developed into the main form of air power in subsequent limited conflicts such as the Korean and Vietnam Wars. U.N. (principally American) jets in Korea helped neutralize the effect of numerically superior Communist ground troops by pounding the enemy with searing napalm and rocket assaults. The Korean War films *Sabre Jet* (1953), *The Bridges at Toko-Ri* (1954) and *The Hunters* (1958) highlighted the jet plane.

Helicopters made their appearance in the Korean War where they were used extensively to ferry the wounded straight from the battlefield to military hospitals. *Battle Taxi* (1955) demonstrated this function. They became hovering gunships in the Vietnam War, directing their fire against Communist guerrillas and regulars in the jungles. Several Vietnam War films, including *Apocalypse Now* (1979) and *Platoon* (1986), showed the devastating fire power of the helicopter.

In less than a century, the airplane has progressed from a simple, wooden, one-man machine used as an auxiliary instrument to a major, independent and potent weapon. At the same time, air dramas went through their own phases of development. During the late 1920s and 1930s they stressed two major themes—the former war ace as a tragic figure and the emotional damage of war on pilots. Veteran fliers of World War I, usually unable to find employment, endanger their lives when they join air shows as in *The Flying Fool* (1929) starring William Boyd. Sometimes a strong antiwar theme accompanied the romance and drama as in *Ace of Aces* (1933). Richard Dix portrays a sensitive and talented sculptor in peacetime, who, after enlisting as a flier, is changed by war into a cold-hearted killer obsessively pursuing enemy planes. Several decades later American studios returned to World War I as the background for air dramas. *The Blue Max* (1966), for example, highlighted spectacular aerial shots and action sequences of dogfights, bombings and strafings.

World War II air dramas chiefly followed the pattern of earlier films. They were filled with conventional heroes who adhered to, or learned by bitter experience to accept, the codes of honor, courage and self-sacrifice of war in the air. Patriotic themes were usually woven into the story. Robert Taylor, as a recently graduated pilot assigned to a navy fighter squadron in *Flight Command* (1940), has to prove himself to his fellow airmen. A carefree American flier (Tyrone Power) joins the British in *A Yank in the R.A.F.*, released the same year. More dedicated to romancing Betty Grable than to stopping the Nazis, he changes his attitude when he witnesses the death of his friend.

In some films the focus shifted from fighter aircraft to bombers, allowing the writers to emphasize camaraderie and teamwork among the crew. The B-29 Superfortress was featured in several postwar films, including *The Wild Blue Yonder* (1951), starring Forrest Tucker, Wendell Corey and Vera Ralston, and *Above and Beyond* (1952), with Robert Taylor and Eleanor Parker. The latter focused on the *Enola Gay*, the plane that dropped the atom bomb on Hiroshima.

Some of the best airplane dramas about World War II appeared after the conflict. Delving more deeply into character, they attempted to explore the various types of stress that fliers and the top brass are subjected to. In *Command Decision* (1948) Clark Gable, as an American brigadier general, has to answer to visiting politicians and justify the heavy casualties his crews suffer over Nazi-occupied territory. Gregory Peck in *12 O'Clock High* (1949) has to rebuild the shattered morale of his English-based American bomber squadron plagued with heavy losses.

Hollywood, in its eagerness to satisfy the public's interest in the airplane, has often paid tribute to those who fly the nation's planes in peace and war. Perhaps Fredric March, as the commander of an aircraft carrier in the Korean War drama *The Bridges at Toko-Ri*, best sums up this spirit of admiration when he ponders the dedication of one such flier (William Holden) killed in action: "Where do we get such men?" ∎

Alamein, Battles of El (July 1942 and October 23, 1942–November 4, 1942).

Both Adolf Hitler and Winston Churchill showed by their statements they understood the significance of the fighting at El Alamein in North Africa in World War II. When Africa Corps commander Erwin Rommel petitioned Hitler

to be allowed to withdraw in orderly fashion in the face of impending defeat at the second Battle of El Alamein, the Nazi dictator answered: ". . . stand fast, yield not a yard of ground and throw every man into the battle . . . As to your troops, you can show them no other road than to victory or death." Hitler needed a victory at Alamein to keep alive his dream of capturing the Suez Canal and severing the Allied supply line through the Mediterranean. Churchill's succinct comment, delivered after the same battle, was: "Up to Alamein we survived. After Alamein we conquered."

A desert town on Egypt's Mediterranean coast, El Alamein straddles the main highway and rail line between Egypt and Libya. Its strategic location made it the focus of two major battles in 1942 between Britain's Eighth Army, defending Egypt, and invading Axis forces from the west from Italy's colony, Libya.

The first engagement took place in July between Rommel's Africa Corps and British forces under General Sir Claude Auchinleck. The British stopped an Axis invasion that had penetrated 250 miles into western Egypt to reach within 50 miles of Alexandria and 150 miles of the Suez Canal. Although the battle was a stalemate it bought time for the British to rebuild for an offensive against the Africa Corps, tired after a five-week desert campaign, supply lines badly extended and facing growing shortages of material.

The second battle, starting October 23, 1942, resulted in Rommel's first crushing defeat and marked the beginning of the Axis collapse in North Africa. During the interval between the first and second engagements, Auchinleck had been replaced by Generals Sir Harold Alexander and Bernard Montgomery who built up the troops and material under their command in preparation for a drive to repel the enemy. In the ensuing battle Montgomery, as field commander, dictated the location and nature of the fight due to his superiority in arms and men.

The opposing sides clashed on a 40-mile front in which Rommel's maneuverability was restricted by the Qattara Depression to the south—a rough, impassable extended area of salt flats— and the Mediterranean Sea to the north. British infantry cleared a corridor for its armor through extensive German minefields, and the final Allied breakthrough took place on November 4.

Rommel, on sick leave in Germany at the time the clash began, hurried back to his troops and determined that only an orderly retreat would save his corps from defeat and possible annihilation. Hitler's refusal to allow such a plan contributed to his problems. The Axis suffered large losses at Alamein, including 50,000 troops of which 30,000 were taken prisoner, and an extensive number of tanks and supplies. Hitler's handling of the North African campaign so destroyed Rommel's faith in the Nazi leader that the Panzer commander ultimately joined in a generals' plot on Hitler's life two years later. The Allied victory at Alamein, coupled with an invasion of western North Africa (Operation Torch) later that same month, caught Axis forces in a pincer movement that led to their defeat and expulsion from North Africa by early 1943.

How did Hollywood handle an event that some military historians consider a turning point in World War II in the west? It came up with *El Alamein* (1953) that concerned itself with a small Allied unit fighting the Nazis over a supply dump. Totally missing from the cast of characters was the architect of that important desert victory, who became known as Montgomery of El Alamein. The Axis calamity at Alamein was touched upon in *At The Front In North Africa* (1943), a documentary that was shown commercially during World War II, and in *The Desert Fox* (1951), starring James Mason in a superb and sympathetic portrayal of Rommel. It was also mentioned in the last sequence of *Sahara* (1943), starring Humphrey Bogart as an American tank sergeant. He and his handful of exhausted soldiers who had been holding off a German column, hear the welcome news from a member of a British relief force, "We held them at El Alamein." ∎

Alamo, The (1960), UA. *Dir.* John Wayne; *Sc.* James Edward Grant; *Cast includes:* John Wayne, Richard Widmark, Laurence Harvey, Frankie Avalon, Patrick Wayne, Linda Cristal.

A large-scale production of the historical battle at the Alamo in 1836, the film recounts the events that led up to the defense of the old mission that was converted into a small fort. The film concentrates on three of the principal heroes—Colonels Crockett, James Bowie and William Travis. Richard Widmark, as Bowie, abandons his Mexican wife

to fight at the sides of the Texans and later learns that his wife has died. Laurence Harvey portrays a strong-willed Travis. John Wayne portrays Davy Crockett, who epitomizes what the 187 defenders will ultimately lay down their lives for when he unabashedly muses: "Republic . . . I like the sound of the word." Richard Boone has a small role as Sam Houston. Linda Cristal provides the romantic interest for Wayne.

The second half of the film contains the more interesting sequences, including a late-night foray by some Texans against General Santa Anna's Mexican soldiers and the climactic battle between the defenders of the converted mission and the thousands of attacking troops. Some critics suggested that Wayne instilled his own philosophy into the film, employing the 1836 massacre as a metaphor for his personal anti-Communist pronouncement. Regardless of the political and ideological theories it may conjure up, the film is a bright and fitting tribute to the Americans and Texicans who resisted Santa Anna's 7,000 troops. Moreover, it is quite accurate in its recreation of many events. For example, the conflict between Travis and Bowie about who is better qualified to assume command of the small force defending the Alamo is based on fact. The battle sequences are handled expertly, as are small details such as costumes and uniforms. Wayne took a gamble in turning out this type of action feature more in tune with the 1930s and 1940s than with the 1960s when this genre was falling out of favor with American audiences. Wayne's long-time director, John Ford, supposedly helped during the action sequences. ∎

Alamo, Battle of the (Feb. 23–Mar. 6, 1836). Skirmishes between American colonists in Texas seeking independence and opposing Mexican forces had already broken out on several occasions prior to the Battle of the Alamo. Mexican dictator-general Antonio Lopez de Santa Anna had determined to crush the budding revolution by leading 3,000 troops into Texas to attack the Alamo, a former Spanish Roman Catholic mission in San Antonio that Texans had fortified and held with 188 men. The defenders were jointly led by Colonels William Travis, a young lawyer, and James Bowie, a well-known frontiersman. They were soon aided by newcomer David Crockett. They turned down offers to surrender and held out in a siege beginning February 23 until March 6 when Santa Anna's forces overwhelmed the survivors, all of whom were killed in the final assault. Although the battle was a victory for Mexican forces, the defeat served to inspire the fighters for Texas independence, who, joined by increasing numbers of American volunteers, took up the battle cry "Remember the Alamo" in future engagements. Now a historic site, the Alamo has been labeled "the cradle of Texas Liberty" because of its role in the fight for Texan independence.

Hollywood made several dramas of this historic event. *Heroes of the Alamo* (1938), one of the earliest sound versions of the battle, was a low-budget entry that focused more on action than on characters. In *The Last Command* (1955), along with the final battle scenes, an earnest attempt was made to show the unsuccessful meetings that took place between leaders of the American colonists and Mexican officials. These talks illustrated the gulf between the two sides. The battle and its aftermath were covered in *The First Texan* (1956), a film biography of Sam Houston starring Richard Dix. *The Alamo* (1960), directed by and starring John Wayne, focused on the roles of the three most prominent persons in the Alamo—Travis, Bowie and Crockett. The drama presented a stirring version of the final battle in which all the defenders were killed. The films overwhelmingly favored the heroic defenders. ■

Alexander the Great (1956), UA. Dir. Robert Rossen; Sc. Robert Rossen; Cast includes: Richard Burton, Fredric March, Claire Bloom, Dannielle Darrieux, Harry Andrews.

This large-scale biographical drama of the Greek conqueror pictures Alexander, played by Richard Burton, as a larger-than-life figure. He saw himself as a god ("I am not Philip's son," he exclaims. "I am the son of God.") and believed he was destined to unify the world of his time. The film covers his boyhood, his principal battles and his incursions into Persia and India. Fredric March portrays Philip of Macedonia, Alexander's father and famous in his own right. Dannielle Darrieux, as the conqueror's mother, plots to help him realize his providence. Claire Bloom plays the woman he loves. The film contains several lavish battle sequences although the production often bogs down in court scenes and intrigues.

The dialogue is more literate than usual for this type of epic. Barry Jones, as Aristotle, describes the enigmatic young warrior to Philip: "Alexander is many things. He is logic and he's dreams; he's warrior and he's poet; he's man and he's spirit; he's your son but he's also hers; and he believes himself to be a god." Darius, the King of Persia, who dismisses Alexander as an "impudent and shameless boy" and a "thief," sends him a message: "I send you a whip, a ball and a bag of gold. The whip to train you, the ball so that you may play with boys your own age and not meddle in the affairs of men and a bag of gold for your expenses." Alexander, poised for a bold attack upon the Persian army, replies with equal wit: "If I slay you, which I intend to do, it will be said that this great king and warrior died by the hand of a little Greek boy."

Alexander the Great (356–323 B.C.), or Alexander III, King of Macedonia in northern Greece, was one of the most powerful and important figures of the ancient western world. His empire, the result of his conquests of the Persian empire and Egypt, spanned parts of three continents and helped the spread of civilization and trade in the Eastern Mediterranean and the Middle East. He single-handedly created a Hellenistic world in which Greek culture spread and fused with the native civilizations of Egypt and Persia. The film, a creditable biographical spectacle that covers extended aspects of his life, touches upon his youth and has extensive detail on his successful invasions of Persia and Western India.

He was tutored as a youngster by the Greek philosopher Aristotle, a situation covered in the film. Alexander became King of Macedonia in 336 B.C., following the assassination of his father, King Philip. Alexander believed he had a divine destiny to rule the world, a point the film emphasizes. Towards the end of his glorious but short career, Alexander began to take on the attitude of a living God and encouraged worship of himself.

He initiated his conquest of the Persians, under Darius, when he crossed the Dardanelles in 334 B.C. into Asia Minor at the head of a combined Greek army of some 35,000 troops. Following his victory in Asia Minor, he conquered Syria, then northern Egypt, and within four years, by 330 B.C., had completed his conquest of the Persians, at that time the largest and most powerful empire in the Middle East. His chief opponent, Darius, was killed by a Persian usurper, an event shown in the film. By 326 B.C., Alexander had crossed the Indus and was involved in the conquest of western India.

The film presents large battle scenes as it chronicles Alexander's triumphs. He founded several cities bearing his name, the most notable being the Egyptian port of Alexandria. Alexander sought to unify his empire by enouraging intermarriage between his troops and the Persians. He, for example, took one of Darius' daughters as his wife, an event noted in the film. By removing trade barriers and facilitating communication within his empire through the adoption of Greek as the official language, he helped spread trade and knowledge through the region. He died on June 13, 323 B.C., after a ten-day illness following a banquet in which he drank heavily. The empire quickly fell into separate military kingdoms because he had not officially appointed an heir. ▪

Algerian-French Wars (1830–1847). France gradually extended its control over the North African state of Algeria in the 19th century, starting with a fortified trading post around 1827 and through a series of wars during the early to mid-1800s. The area had been nominally under Turkish control but in reality ruled as a semi-autonomous region by a local Dey (military governor). A dispute between the Dey and the French consul in 1827 led to a French invasion in 1830 that resulted in the defeat of the Dey's forces.

However, Abd el-Kader, an Algerian Muslim leader and Emir of Mascara, attempted to stop increasing French encroachment by initiating three wars between 1832–1847 against the intruders. El-Kader successfully led his rifle-wielding native cavalry in the first two wars (1832–1834 and 1835–1837), and, by defeating French forces he restricted French presence in Algeria.

When France continued its efforts to increase the area under its control, el-Kader launched a holy war in 1839 that sought to unify Algeria into a Muslim state. *The Song of Love* (1924) describes a tribal leader—not unlike el-Kader—who initiates a holy war designed to drive the French from Algeria. France responded in 1840 with a full invasion to conquer the whole area and drive el-Kader from power. French General Thomas R. Bugeaud sent raiding columns through the

desert to destroy el-Kader's arsenals and weaken his opponent's economic base by seizing cattle, crops and groves of olive and fruit trees. Bugeaud decisively defeated the Muslim leader's 45,000-man army at the Battle of Isley River on August 14, 1844. El-Kader continued fighting a diminishing guerrilla war from bases in Morocco until 1847 when he surrendered. This marked the end of large-scale, organized native resistance to French rule though local challenges continued for many years.

A representative but fictitious uprising was dramatized in *The Dishonored Medal* (1914), a romantic drama in which the abandoned son of a French officer and an Algerian woman unknowingly kills his own father during a native revolt. Other films to touch upon these desert conflicts include *The Bugler of Algiers* (1916) and its 1924 remake, *Love and Glory*. ▪

Algerian War (1954–1962). See *Lost Command* (1966). ▪

Alias Mike Moran (1919), Par. *Dir.* James Cruze; *Sc.* Will M. Ritchey; *Cast includes:* Wallace Reid, Ann Little, Emory Johnson, Charles Ogle.

Wallace Reid, as a fortune-hunting slacker in this World War I drama, is called to serve in the army. He exchanges places with an ex-convict, Mike Moran (Emory Johnson), who is eager to fight but is rejected because of his past. When Moran dies a hero's death in France, Reid, now posing as Moran and working at a shipyard, has a change of attitude. He enlists in the Canadian army and is sent overseas where he, too, becomes a hero. Ann Little, who provides the romantic interest, finds him when he returns home and professes her love for the belated hero. Although released after the war, this patriotic tale reflected the national resentment toward slackers during the conflict. Reid took a chance with his career by agreeing to portray such an unsympathetic character for the first half of this three-reel film. ▪

Alien Enemy, An (1918), Panalta. *Dir.* Wallace Worsley; *Sc.* Monte M. Katterjohn; *Cast includes:* Louise Glaum, Thurston Hall, Mary Jane Irving, Albert Allardt.

A World War I drama, the film concerns a young woman of German heritage who marries an important American involved in military matters. A German agent threatens the couple unless they turn over to him secret documents. The film contains patriotic scenes of American troops liberating French villages as well as sequences of a prisoner-of-war camp where Germans attempt to escape. Louise Glaum, the star of the film, plays a dual role, that of a mother and her daughter. ■

All My Sons (1948), UI. *Dir.* Irving Reis; *Sc.* Charles Erskine; *Cast includes:* Edward G. Robinson, Burt Lancaster, Mady Christians, Howard Duff, Louise Horton.

Based on Arthur Miller's play about war profiteering, the film stars Edward G. Robinson as Joe Keller, a business partner who, during World War II, sold defective airplane cylinders to the government, an act which ultimately leads to the death of several American fliers. Larry, one of his sons who is serving in the air force, commits suicide out of shame. Robininson let the blame fall on his partner, who is arrested and in prison when the film opens. Attempting to rationalize what he knows to have been a criminal act, Robinson claims family responsibility. "It's a crime only when you get caught," he says later. "The main thing is to survive." But he fails to convince Chris, his other son.

Burt Lancaster portrays the idealistic Chris who is outraged when he learns of his father's actions. At one point, he tries to kill him. The bewildered industrialist cannot comprehend his son's anger until Lancaster drills home the idea of social responsibility. "There's a universe outside and you're responsible to it," he reminds his father. "Don't you think of other people? Don't you live in the world?" Mady Christians, as Robinson's wife, refuses to believe that her aviator son is dead. She maintains his room and cares for his clothes as though he were coming home any day. "Sometimes it's better to let things stay as they are," she suggests to her dead son's fiancee, "not disturb them, no matter what."

The static but grim film version, which brings out several universal truths, including the father's ultimate realization of the enormity of his actions ("They were all my sons," he admits before taking his own life), skirts one of the major points of the original play. Miller suggested that the flawed capitalistic system with its emphasis on greed should be condemned for producing such men who value profit above human life. ■

Lew Ayres tries to shut out the horrors of World War I by muffling the cries of mortally wounded Raymond Griffith, an enemy soldier. *All Quiet on the Western Front* (1930).

All Quiet on the Western Front (1930), U. *Dir.* Lewis Milestone; *Sc.* George Abbott; *Cast includes:* Lew Ayres, Louis Wolheim, John Wray, Raymond Griffith, Slim Summerville, Russell Gleason.

Based on Erich Maria Remarque's 1928 novel of German youth in World War I, the film depicts the war experiences of Paul Baumer, an idealistic adolescent played by Lew Ayres, and his classmates. Scenes include their enthusiastic enlistment in the army, their harsh training under a martinet corporal (John Wray), their first frightening days and nights under bombardment, their eventual disillusionment with the war and their final days of desolation as one by one they fall victim to the endless killing. As the war grinds on, the Western Front becomes a virtual slaughterhouse. Most of Paul's companions are either dead or wounded. He stops a piece of shrapnel and is temporarily removed from the front lines.

On leave, he finds many changes in his home town. Visiting his former teacher, he is pointed to with pride. To impress the present class of prospective recruits, he is asked to relate some of his glorious experiences while fighting for the Fatherland. Paul instead paints a bleak picture of the filthy, rat-infested trenches and the pitiable men who inhabit them. "When it comes to dying for your country," he pleads, "it is better not to die at all." The teacher and the students cry him down with jeers and abuse. Disgusted with the illusions held by those at home, he returns to the front where "there are no lies."

Back in the trenches, he loses his best friend, Kat (Louis Wolheim), a cynical, humane corporal. Then one overcast day, while reaching out of his trench toward a lonely butterfly, Paul is killed by a single bullet.

The film contains numerous compelling and unforgettable moments. Battle sequences show rows of men falling under the deadly accuracy of machine guns. One scene displays a charge which results in a soldier being blown to bits, with only his hands clinging to barbed wire. In another scene Paul seeks shelter in a shell-hole. When an enemy soldier jumps in after him, Paul stabs him with his bayonet. As the man lay dying, Paul is stricken with remorse. "Forgive me, comrade," he cries. "Oh, God, why do they do this to us? We only wanted to live, you and I."

The film remains quite faithful to the novel, except for the ending. The book reports Paul's death matter-of-factly on an otherwise uneventful day on the Western Front. Director Milestone decided to add the poignant bit about the butterfly with all its ramifications. This may be one of the few times that a film improved upon the ending of an original work.

Aside from winning numerous awards, the film has had a long history of controversy. Some factions in America condemned it as propaganda designed to cripple the military. It was not permitted to be shown at several army posts in the United States. In Germany, Nazi propaganda leader Goebbels attacked its pacifist theme and claimed it harmed his country's reputation. Whatever the criticism, the film remains a damning condemnation of the futility and stupidity of war. ∎

All the Young Men (1960), Col. *Dir.* Hall Bartlett; *Sc.* Hall Bartlett; *Cast includes:* Alan Ladd, Sidney Poitier, James Darren, Glenn Corbett, Mort Sahl.

Several U.S. Marines, assigned to defend an abandoned farmhouse, face the problem of racism as well as the enemy in this implausible action drama set near the 38th parallel during the Korean War. Alan Ladd, as a bigoted marine, resents taking orders from a black sergeant (Sidney Poitier) who assumes command when their lieutenant is killed. The problem is resolved when Ladd requires a blood transfusion and the only fellow marine with his blood type is Poitier. The offbeat cast includes stand-up comic Mort Sahl, who delivers several monologues, and former

Space used as symbol of bigoted marine Alan Ladd's alienation in the Korean War. *All the Young Men* (1960).

boxing champion Ingemar Johansson. The film contains lively action sequences that are interspersed between those of racial conflict within the farmhouse. *Battle of Blood Island*, released the same year, was another weak attempt to deal with prejudice (anti-Semitism) on the battlefield. ∎

All This and World War II (1976), TCF. *Dir.* Susie Winslow.

A documentary about World War II with an updated musical soundtrack, the film attempts to present a fresh approach to the horrors of the conflict. Some of the songs are meant to provide ironic commentary to the compilation of newsreel footage, but most of the effort seems to fall short of its target. The film is aimed at those who were too young to remember or who were not yet born during the war years. Some of the groups and vocalists heard in the background include The Bee Gees, The Four Seasons, Elton John, Frankie Laine, Tina Turner and Frankie Valli. ∎

All Through the Night (1941). See Spy Comedies. ∎

Allegheny Uprising (1939), RKO. *Dir.* William A. Seiter; *Sc.* P. J. Wolfson; *Cast includes:* Claire Trevor, John Wayne, George Sanders, Brian Donlevy, Robert Barrat.

A weak action drama of colonial America in the mid-1700s, the film stars John Wayne as a colonist who rebels against the tyrannical rule of a local English officer (George

Union troops fight off a Confederate attack. *Alvarez Kelly* (1966).

Sanders). Wayne organizes the local farmers to resist the oppressive yoke that Sanders has forced upon the settlers of the Pennsylvania valley. Meanwhile, he and his followers must battle hostile Indians who have bought guns and whiskey from greedy white men. Claire Trevor plays Wayne's sweetheart who is madly in love with him. The events in the film provide the impetus for the eventual rebellion of the colonies against England. The chemistry between Wayne and Trevor that was so telling in *Stagecoach*, released only months before this film, was lacking in this bland tale based on the novel *The First Rebel* by Neil H. Swanson.

The parallels between England's treatment of the colonists and Nazi Germany's attitudes toward its neighbors that audiences drew from the film angered many British who had just gone to war against Hitler. American critics joined their cousins across the Atlantic in attacking the film as ill-conceived. Studio heads discreetly ordered some cuts to make the drama more palatable to British audiences. ■

Allotment Wives (1945). See Home Front. ■

Alvarez Kelly (1966), Col. Dir. Edward Dmytryk; Sc. Franklin Coen, Elliott Arnold; *Cast includes:* William Holden, Richard Widmark, Janice Rule, Patrick O'Neal.

Confederate troops steal much-needed cattle destined for the Union army and divert the herd for the starving South in this Civil War action drama. William Holden, as an Irish-Mexican cattleman who believes only in "money, whiskey and women," is forced to assist in driving the cattle to the South. Richard Widmark, as a Confederate colonel, directs the cattle raid against the Union. Patrick O'Neal plays a Union major. Janice Rule provides the romantic interest as Widmark's sweetheart who leaves him for a sea captain. The film, which lacks the traditional western or war hero, treats both the Union and Confederate troops as equally ruthless. The story is based on an actual, little-known incident that occurred during the conflict between the North and the South. ■

Ambush (1949), MGM. Dir. Sam Wood; Sc. Marguerite Roberts; *Cast includes:* Robert Taylor, John Hodiak, Arlene Dahl, Don Taylor, Jean Hagen.

The Apaches are on the warpath again in this action drama set in the late 1800s. Robert Taylor, as an Indian scout, falls in love with the fiancee (Arlene Dahl) of a cavalry captain (John Hodiak). When Dahl's sister is captured by the hostiles, the cavalry rides into action. The film contains two good battle sequences. The first concerns the soldiers' victory over the Apaches and the second in which the surviving Indians ambush the cavalry just before Taylor arrives with reinforcements to finish off the enemy. Director Sam Wood died soon after the film was completed. ■

Mickey Rooney, wounded in battle and about to be captured, sits on live grenades as he lures Japanese soldiers into his trap. *Ambush Bay* (1966).

Ambush Bay (1966), UA. *Dir.* Ron Winston; *Sc.* Marve Feinberg, Ib Melchior; *Cast includes:* Hugh O'Brian, Mickey Rooney, James Mitchum.

A patrol of nine marines is sent on a secret mission in the Philippines in this action drama that takes place during World War II. Their goal is to contact a Japanese who has vital information concerning General MacArthur's proposed invasion. The leathernecks meet stiff resistance as they traverse the jungle and lose several of their buddies as well as their native guide before they locate their contact. To their surprise, the person is a young Japanese woman from California. She informs the patrol that the enemy has mined the location of the landing. With their radio destroyed and their number reduced to two, the pair are forced to destroy the mines before the American ships reach the mine field.

The film contains an abundance of heroics. Hugh O'Brian, as a tough, determined ser-

geant, takes command of the patrol when its officer is killed the first day. O'Brian dies manning a machine gun while giving his fellow marine time to detonate the mine field. Mickey Rooney portrays an experienced combat marine who voluntarily goes to his death blowing up several Japanese soldiers while cracking a joke. Wounded in a previous gun battle, he waits for the enemy to approach, holds out two grenades and quips: "Guess what I got for you. Baked potatoes. You can eat these with the jackets on them." As the Japanese discharge their rifles into him, he tosses the grenades into their midst. Tisa Chang, the Japanese-American spy, aids the remnants of the patrol. She offers herself to the leader of the pursuing Japanese, giving the marines a chance to escape. When the Japanese officer discovers her ploy, he kills her. James Mitchum, as a green private, narrates the tale and is the only survivor in this routine drama.

The film ends with a voice-over of General MacArthur's "I shall return" speech to the Filipinos as the camera focuses on Mitchum waiting on the shore for a submarine to pick him up. Although MacArthur's words were (and still are) very poignant, they have little to do with the actual film, which relies more on heroics and bravado than on realism or historical perspective. ■

America (1924), UA. *Dir.* D.W. Griffith; *Sc.* Robert W. Chambers; *Cast includes:* Neil Hamilton, Carol Dempster, Erville Alderson, Lionel Barrymore.

D.W. Griffith's large-scale production unfolds the birth of America through the experiences of two young lovers, a Boston patriot (Neil Hamilton) and the daughter (Carol Dempster) of an aristocratic family divided by the rebellion. The film brings to life numerous historical figures, including Paul Revere, George Washington, Samuel Adams, John Hancock, Thomas Jefferson, Patrick Henry and William Pitt.

The Hamilton-Dempster love story is woven through the lengthy film, with Lionel Barrymore portraying a villainous royalist who ruthlessly creates obstacles for the lovers. Sidney Deane plays Dempster's royalist father who is unaware that his son (Charles Emmett Mack) has been killed at Bunker Hill fighting on the side of the patriots. But it is the actual events and people taken from the pages of the nation's history that dominate the spectacle.

One such important character is William Pitt (1708–1778), the Earl of Chatham, a well-known English statesman who opposed King George's policies for the American colonies. His speeches to the House of Lords consistently urged a more conciliatory tone in dealing with the growing American colonial revolt, short of independence. Pitt has remained a neglected figure on the American screen except for his portrayal by Charles Bennett in *America* (1924), a film in which Pitt has a featured role in the director's depiction of the American Revolution.

Several historical incidents have been faithfully recreated in this paean to democracy. There is a climactic attack by the Mohawk Indians on the early colonists. Harry O'Neill re-enacts Paul Revere's ride with some difficulty (his horse threw him, but director Griffith decided to leave the shot in). Washington's inauguration stands out as a memorable sequence, as does the Battle of Bunker Hill.

This was the last of Griffith's memorable silent epics. The director had difficulties recovering the initial cost of the production. The idea for the film was suggested by the Daughters of the American Revolution, who realized the potential of the relatively young medium as an effective educational conduit. The film gained a degree of popularity in an area that even its director was unable to predict. The historical incidents were dramatized with such accuracy that excerpts were used for many years in classrooms around the country to supplement the teaching of American history. ■

"America at War" (1942). See "The March of Time." ■

"America Prepares" (1941). See "The March of Time." ■

America Preparing (1916). *Dir.* Lawrence Kemble.

This early documentary shows the training of American soldiers, sailors and marines. It also points out that, in 1916, the United States was at its peak of preparedness. A screen title proudly exclaims: "Quality we possess—we must have quantity." The film contains scenes of various military bases ranging from New York State to Texas as well

as West Point and Annapolis; a long column of battleships poised for battle; a seaplane flying gracefully above Pensacola. Other sequences depict the leisurely life of the servicemen when they are off duty.

The film, released shortly after the appearance of several fictional works that showed invaders occupying American shores and U.S. cities being bombed (*The Fall of a Nation* (1916), etc.), was in part an answer to those often hysterical depictions of an America poorly prepared. ■

America Under Fire (1937). *Dir.* R. H. Igleston.

A World War I documentary, the film is narrated by Corporal R. H. Igleston, who shot all the scenes during the conflict. The corporal concentrates chiefly on military units from the Midwest, the area he has targeted for the distribution of the film. Various scenes show the men at home and at the front during the fighting. The footage was resurrected from U.S. government vaults. ■

American Civil War (1861–1865). Also known as The War Between The States; War of Secession. Tension had been building steadily after Lincoln's election (1860) to the presidency. Seven Southern states, beginning with South Carolina on December 20, 1860, had dissolved their ties with the Union and formed a new Confederate government headed by President Jefferson Davis. By early April 1861 several Southern states had seized federal forts and property within their borders. Though peace, however tenuous, still existed, both sides were sitting on a powder keg with feelings running high. *Santa Fe Trail* (1940), with Errol Flynn as Jeb Stuart and Ronald Reagan as George Custer, conveys some of the tension of this period.

But at Fort Sumter, which guarded the approach to Charleston harbor, a crisis developed when U.S. Army Major Robert Anderson refused to turn the fort over to a delegation of Confederate officers. The Confederate government, fearing the Union might try to strengthen the garrison, ordered Southern batteries ringing Charleston harbor to subdue the bastion by force.

Soldiers at Sumter, in the early morning darkness of April 12, saw flashes of light from the shore. A few seconds later shells began to pound against the masonry. The bombardment continued for 34 hours before the outgunned and outnumbered defenders ceased their weak, return fire and accepted surrender at 2:30 P.M. on April 13. The American Civil War had begun.

Before it was over almost exactly four years later, the country would undergo the bloodiest domestic convulsion in its history. Nearly 600,000 Americans were killed and at least another 375,000 wounded. In proportion to the nation's population at that time, the Civil War stands as the costliest in our experience. The animosity and bitterness created by the conflict would last for generations.

The causes of the dispute were complex, rooted in the economic, social and geographic differences between North and South. These differences all came together in the emotional issue of slavery. Should it be allowed to expand beyond the deep South, and should it be ended everywhere in the nation? The South interpreted Abraham Lincoln's election on the Republican Party ticket as a signal that the right to own slaves would be destroyed, hence Southern secession.

Both sides went into the war in a holiday spirit with recruits flocking in unexpected numbers to join their respective forces. There was, however, a deeper personal sadness embedded in the political split, for oftentimes members of the same family and neighbors found themselves fighting on opposite sides. For example, Kentucky Senator Crittendon saw one son become a Confederate general while the other held a similar rank in the Union. President Lincoln's wife, Mary, had members of her family in Confederate uniforms. The armed forces suffered on the highest level from this division as well. Virginia-born Robert E. Lee turned down Lincoln's offer to become field commander of the Union Army in order to accept a similar post in his native Virginia. At the same time, fellow Virginian Winfield Scott continued as General-in-Chief with the Union.

Though the Civil War formally began with the shelling of Sumter, blood had already been spilled. The incident occurred during a sectional dispute in a miniature civil war in Kansas ("Bleeding Kansas") as early as 1856 when each side tried to control the area's position on slavery. Two films, both about the radical abolitionist John Brown, graphically dramatize this dispute—Santa Fe Trail (1940) and Seven Angry Men (1955).

The South at first was successful in the east under Robert E. Lee in holding off superior Northern forces. However, Union forces in the west, under Grant, split the Confederacy in 1862 by gaining control of the Mississippi River. The Union navy gradually tightened its blockade of Southern ports, and from mid-1862 virtually isolated the South. Lincoln made Grant supreme field commander in 1864, and Grant wore down Lee's forces in Virginia in a war of attrition during the last year of the conflict.

Over 2,400 skirmishes and battles took place in the four years of fighting; some stood out in importance. In the two Battles of Bull Run (Manassas Junction) (July 21, 1861 and August 29–30, 1862), the Confederates stopped Northern drives into Virginia. However, General McClellan halted Lee's attempt to invade Maryland at Antietam Creek (September 17, 1862), in the bloodiest engagement of the war. An early silent film, The Battle of Bull Run (1913), captures some of the spirited fighting.

The first battle of ironclad warships (March 9, 1862), between the Monitor and the Merrimac, occurred off Hampton Roads, Virginia. The battle ended in a draw. Hearts in Bondage (1936) recreates this famous sea clash. In the west, Grant's victories at Shiloh (April 6–7, 1862) and Vicksburg (July 4, 1863), coupled with Admiral Farragut's capture of New Orleans (April 25, 1862), gave the Union control of the Mississippi. They effectively split the Confederacy into eastern and western parts. Several silent and sound dramas have highlighted these battles, including The Battle of Shiloh (1913); D.W. Griffith's The Crisis (1915), about Vicksburg; and The Southerners (1914), with its re-enactment of the Battle of Mobile Bay.

The Battle of Gettysburg (July 1–3, 1863), at which Union forces under General Meade turned back Lee's second attempted invasion of the North, is considered the turning point of the war in the east. From then on, Lee was gradually forced deeper into Virginia and faced increasing problems of supply and reinforcements. Only a few films covered this important engagement, including "General Meade's Fighting Days" (1909), The Battle of Gettysburg (1913, 1936) and Between Two Fires (1914).

General Sherman on May 4, 1864, began his drive from Chattanooga through Georgia to the Atlantic coast and split off the deep South from the upper South in the east. Along the way, Sherman took Atlanta (September 2, 1864), an important transportation junction and industrial center, and Savannah (December 22, 1864) to close one of the few remaining Southern ports on the Atlantic coast. Sherman's troops intentionally laid waste to the cities and countryside through which they passed to weaken the South's industrial and emotional capability to continue the war. Sherman's march occurs in Griffith's masterpiece, *The Birth of a Nation* (1915), and *When Sherman Marched to the Sea*, also 1915. It also plays a role in *Gone With the Wind* (1939), along with the burning of Atlanta, a dramatic highlight in the film.

Grant's capture of Petersburg, an important transportation junction, followed by the conquest of the Confederate capital of Richmond (April 2, 1865), gave Lee no choice. He surrendered on April 9, 1862 at Appomattox Court House, effectively ending the war. Several films recreated the historic surrender, including *The Slacker* (1917) and *Only the Brave* (1930).

The clash left deep resentments between the sections that were further exacerbated by the assassination of Lincoln (April 14, 1865). The former Confederate states, for almost 100 years after the war, raised racial barriers. Local and state "Black Codes" and Ku Klux Klan activities effectively restricted the political, economic, and social rights of former slaves and their descendants. Lincoln's assassination, the abuses of Reconstruction and the rise of the Klan are all vividly portrayed in *The Birth of a Nation*.

Hollywood produced well over 100 Civil War-related films. They chiefly echo the major historians' views—Lincoln was well liked in the North; the Confederates generally were gallant and fought bravely for an ill-fated cause; and slavery was one of the main issues of the conflict. Some films covered specific aspects of the war. *Friendly Persuasion* (1956) recounted the Quakers' lack of participation on religious grounds. *The Raid* (1954) and *The Horse Soldiers* (1959) told about two of several behind-the-lines assaults. *Tap Roots* (1948) was based on an actual Southern insurrection. *Rebel City* (1953) dealt with the controversial Copperheads. Finally, the war inspired at least one classic comedy, Buster Keaton's *The General* (1927), which was based on a true incident.

Generally, Hollywood points no accusing finger at either side. Both protagonists were usually given sympathetic treatment as noble opponents in an honorable cause. Not uncommonly, though it raises a question about reality, slaves are shown as loyal to their masters. Some films show the harshness of Union troops as they cut a destructive path through the South. Other dramas show the abuses of Southern rebels. If there are villains, they are usually irregulars and renegades bent on looting and raping. Southern officers appear to be more gallant than their Northern counterparts. Southern women retain their sectional loyalties even when they fall under control of Union invaders. Officers and troops on both sides exhibit bravery in battle. This evenhanded approach may well be attributed more to the studios' interest in box-office receipts than to any higher purpose.

A curious blend of cavalry-vs.-Indian and Civil War action film emerged in the 1950s. These action dramas show Confederate and Union troops putting aside their differences to help each other in fighting the Indians. In *Two Flags West* (1950), for example, Confederate prisoners who volunteer to man an outpost drop their plan to escape and, instead, return to help their Union brothers when the Indians attack. In *Rocky Mountain* (1950) a band of Confederate soldiers, led by their stalwart officer (Errol Flynn), lay down their lives to protect a small unit of Union soldiers being attacked by Indians. *Revolt at Fort Laramie* (1957), which takes place at the beginning of the Civil War, reverses the roles of rescuer and the rescued. A Southern major in charge of Fort Laramie departs with those troops loyal to the Confederacy. When hostiles attack the major and his unit, the Northern captain leads his troops to the rescue of their fellow soldiers. *The Last Outpost* (1951) carries brotherly concern beyond politics by showing two brothers, who are on opposing sides during the Civil War, temporarily joining forces to fight the Apache. These films barely stop short of sending a racist message, that whites must stand together against enemies of another color.

Films about the Civil War usually skirt the more profound issues, particularly in the silent era which focused on romance, action and heroism. Hollywood's image as a factory devoted chiefly to entertainment held true for Civil War films. Certain exceptions did appear, as with Griffith's *The Birth of a Nation*. The advent of sound brought forth films which continued the same themes. It was not until after World War II, when social comment became acceptable through such American films as *Gentleman's Agreement* (anti-Semitism) and *Pinky* (racism), that Civil War dramas offered more frank themes. Although action, romance and sometimes spectacle seemed to play dominant roles, such topics as the abolition of slavery in *Tap Roots* (1948), pacifism in *No Drums, No Bugles* (1971) and the horror of war in *The Horse Soldiers* (1959) began to seep in. ∎

American Consul, The (1917), Par. *Dir.* Harvey Thew; *Sc.* Harvey Thew, Thomas Geraghty; *Cast includes:* Theodore Roberts, Maude Fealy, Dorothy Drake, Jack Mulhall.

An Indiana lawyer goes to Washington to see a senator that he once helped for a political appointment. The senator gives the lawyer a position as consul in a Central American country. The new consul takes his role seriously and when threatened by revolutionaries, he refuses to go against his own country's interests. U.S. Marines come to his rescue. The drama contains a romantic subplot involving the consul's daughter and an American engineer.

The plot of the film may have referred to several topical incidents. To protect American nationals, the U.S. intervened in Haiti in January, February and October, 1914, when that small country was going through a period of unrest, and again in 1915 when insurrection threatened. The U.S. interceded as well in the affairs of the Dominican Republic, also faced with an insurrection, in May 1916. ∎

American Guerrilla in the Philippines (1950), TCF. *Dir.* Fritz Lang; *Sc.* Lamar Trotti; *Cast includes:* Tyrone Power, Micheline Presle, Tom Ewell.

A small group of American and native forces battle the invading Japanese from 1942 until General MacArthur's return to the Philippines in this World War II action drama. Tyrone Power, as a U.S. ensign, and a fellow sailor, played by Tom Ewell, take refuge in the jungle after their PT boat is destroyed. They soon join forces with Filipino guerrillas against the Japanese. Micheline Presle, as the wife of a French plantation owner who is killed, provides the romantic interest for Power. The film contains several rousing action scenes involving suspenseful encounters between the guerrillas and the enemy troops. ∎

American Revolution (1775–1783). It was the shot heard 'round the world. An unplanned confrontation at a small New England village started the American Revolution and the ultimate separation of Britain's 13 North American colonies to form a new nation. A simmering revolt flared into armed hostilities on that crisp, New England afternoon of April 19, 1775, when a small band of Massachusetts militiamen (Minute Men), drawn up on the Lexington village green, attempted to stop a considerably larger column of British troops. The soldiers, paradoxically, were on a mission to neighboring Concord to seize colonial military supplies and, hopefully, prevent the outbreak of armed rebellion. The brief exchange of gunfire and the actions of the Minutemen are portrayed in detail in *The Heart of a Hero* (1916), a biographical drama of Nathan Hale, and *Cardigan* (1922), an historical romance set before and during the revolution. The Battle of Lexington and Concord was refought in at least one other historical drama *Johnny Tremain* (1957).

The Battle of Lexington and Concord was not the first example of colonial violence towards the British crown. There had been other incidents generally directed against individuals such as British-appointed customs agents and commissioners charged with upholding the law. Lexington, however, marked the first formal armed confrontation between rival troops, and from that moment on, each side was wedded to a policy of using military coercion to enforce its view.

The causes of the American Revolution are beyond the scope of this book. It is sufficient for general understanding, however, to point out that the seeds of rebellion were planted in English colonial policy beginning at least a decade prior to the skirmish at Lexington. American colonists were antagonized by several laws such as the Proclamation of 1763 that closed lands west of the Appalachians to settlement so as to prevent, from Britain's view, future conflict with the Indians; the Declaratory Act of 1766 that upheld Parliament's right to make all laws for the colonies; and the various tax measures such as the Stamp Act and Tea Act for raising revenue or controlling commerce.

Hollywood's view of the American Revolution steered away from the political complexities and generally involved some highly selective focusing on a few events and people.

To rely on movies for an understanding of the revolution—the military successes and defeats, the political and economic problems, the important roles of some of the chief participants—will produce a spotty and disjointed view of one of the most important events in our nation's history. Two early silents, both titled "The Spirit of '76," one released by Biograph in 1905, the other by Selig in 1908, were chiefly short patriotic tracts.

In dealing with the background of events that brought on the revolution, Hollywood focused on at least two incidents which were important to an understanding of the period. They were the Boston Tea Party (1773), when colonists dressed as Indians threw a shipload of English tea into Boston Harbor rather than pay a tea tax, and Paul Revere's ride (April 19, 1775) warning of the coming of British troops. Edison presented a one-reel depiction of the tea-dumping as early as 1908 titled "The Boston Tea Party." *Janice Meredith* (1924) and *The Howards of Virginia* (1940) are examples of more elaborate re-enactments of this incident. Paul Revere's famous ride was depicted in more than half a dozen films. One of the earliest was "The Midnight Ride of Paul Revere," a short Edison production directed by film pioneer Edwin S. Porter. *Washington at Valley Forge* (1914), *Cardigan* (1922), *Janice Meredith*, *America* (1924) and *Johnny Tremain* (1957) are other films which include Revere's historical ride.

However, the Boston Massacre (1770), when British troops harassed by colonials responded by firing into the crowd, goes virtually unmentioned in filmdom, despite the importance of the event in inflaming colonial sentiment against British military presence. The Battle of Lexington and Concord, that started the fighting, seems to be the only major military engagement that merited full-length film treatment.

Several major figures appear in historical and biographical dramas in roles of varying importance. *America*, D.W. Griffith's epic production, features Paul Revere, Patrick Henry, John Hancock, Thomas Jefferson and William Pitt. The young French sympathizer, Lafayette, is portrayed in *Janice Meredith* and *Johnny Tremain*. Betsy Ross is rewarded with her own biography in 1917, aptly titled *Betsy Ross*, while the traitorous Benedict Arnold is the major character in *The Scarlet Coat* (1955). The musical *1776* (1972), based on the Broadway play, presents a host of notable figures of the period, including Thomas Jefferson, Benjamin Franklin and John Adams.

Surprisingly, considering Hollywood's love affair with war movies, most of the outstanding battles and military events in the revolution get either very skimpy treatment or none at all. Missing from Hollywood's version of American history is the Battle of Bunker Hill (1775), the first formal, large-scale fight between the two sides. There is mention, though, of Valley Forge in the winter of 1777–1778, a low point for the American side. *Washington at Valley Forge* (1914) is a chiefly fictional account of the general's exploits. *The Howards of Virginia* (1940), on the other hand, gives a more accurate account of the hardships these early patriots suffered.

But there is either no detailed account or only limited coverage of such important engagements as the Battle of Trenton (1777), Washington's first major victory after a string of losses—only mentioned in *Janice Meredith*, or of the Battle of Saratoga (1777), when British General Burgoyne surrendered his whole British army of 6,000, thereby ending the plan to split the colonies.

Hollywood does some justice to the successful guerrilla war conducted in the Carolinas by Col. Francis Marion in such early silents as "General Marion, The Swamp Fox" (1911) and "Francis Marion, the Swamp Fox" (1914). However, it neglects the efforts of Generals Nathaniel Greene and Daniel Morgan, whose harassing actions in the south forced Cornwallis to retreat to Yorktown where Britain suffered its final defeat (1781), shown in *Janice Meredith* and *The Howards of Virginia*.

Films missed out on the opportunity to explore the lives and problems of a number of other colorful and important figures. Some were in the enemy camp, such as Cornwallis, Burgoyne and the two Howes. Others were within the ranks of the patriots such as General Horatio Gates—a brief rival to Washington for supreme commander, and "Mad" Anthony Wayne, whose New England Green Mountain Boys played such a critical role in denying the British control of the Champlain valley, the invasion route south from Canada.

One film on the Revolution, the controversial *The Spirit of '76* (1917), was to hound its writer-producer Robert Goldstein for years. It presented a blistering anti-British picture of the Wyoming Valley Massacre of Americans by redcoats. Many thought the film was ill-timed in coming out when the U.S. had entered World War I on Britain's side and might create problems for Allied unity.

Considering the importance of the American Revolution to our nation's history, the struggle has suffered both in the quantity and quality of films turned out by American moviemakers. In addition, many were made in the days of silent movies. What conclusions, if any, can we draw from this? It appears that Hollywood may believe that the farther back in time an event occurred, the less value it has as potential for screen entertainment. Either that, or modern filmmakers may feel less comfortable with using earlier American wars as a basis for screen productions. ■

Americanization of Emily, The (1964), MGM. *Dir.* Arthur Hiller; *Sc.* Paddy Chayefsky; *Cast includes:* James Garner, Julie Andrews, Melvyn Douglas, James Coburn.

A satirical black comedy set in England during World War II, the film concerns an overly proud American admiral who prefers that the first fighting man to be killed during the upcoming Normandy invasion be a navy man. James Garner, as a resourceful aide to the admiral and a confirmed coward, is selected for the heroic job. He survives the invasion, much to the dismay of navy public relations who have already released stories of his glorious death. Julie Andrews, as an English chauffeur who has been widowed by the war, provides the romantic interest for Garner. When James Coburn, as a navy officer who spends most of his time bedding "nameless broads," proudly informs Andrews that Garner was the first man to be killed on Omaha Beach, she fires back: "Was there a contest?" Melvyn Douglas, as an eccentric admiral, refuses to let the army ride roughshod over his sailors and attain all the glory. The film, from Paddy Chayefsky's cynical screenplay, was one of the earliest antiwar films of the 1960s. ■

America's Answer (1918), Bureau of Public Information. *Sc.* Kenneth C. Beaton.

Another documentary in the series released by the Division of Films of the Committee on Public Information, the film shows scenes of U.S. Army and Navy personnel as they go about their business of fighting in France and defending the nation's shores. Some highlights of the propaganda film include aircraft guns firing at enemy planes, a daylight raid, U.S. airplanes in France and scenes of the trenches. The film emphasizes the importance of those at home who manufacture the armaments and other war materiel and those at the front who care for the wounded.

A sequel to *Pershing's Crusaders*, the film was the second U.S. government documentary designed to stir the war spirit of the American public. ■

"America's New Army" (1942). See "The March of Time." ■

Andersonville Prison. See Prisoners of War. ■

Andrews' Raid (also known as the Great Locomotive Chase). This bold raid behind Confederate lines on April 22, 1862, by a small force of Northern soldiers, began the tradition of awarding the Congressional Medal of Honor, the nation's highest military award, for unusual bravery.

A squad of 22 Union soldiers under James J. Andrews volunteered to penetrate Confederate lines and cut rail communication between Marietta, Georgia, and Chattanooga, Tennessee. The troop seized a train pulled by a locomotive named *The General* and headed west to destroy bridges and other communication links on the line. Confederate forces discovered the plan and chased the Northerners in another locomotive named *Texas* for a distance of about 90 miles and captured the hijack squad after *The General* had used all its fuel. Andrews and seven of his troop were executed as spies. The remainder, after surviving internment in prisoner-of-war camps, were the first ones to be awarded the Congressional Medal of Honor.

The historic raid inspired two silent films and a Walt Disney feature. "Railroad Raiders of '62" (1911), a short drama by the Kalem studio, presented a generally accurate account of the incident. Buster Keaton, in his highly acclaimed comedy classic *The General* (1927), retained the framework of the original raid but added many inventive gags. Walt Disney Studios produced *The Great Locomotive Chase* (1956), a fictionalized but colorful version of the incident. ■

Anglo-Saxon Rebellions (1066–1174). From the time of the Norman conquest of England in 1066 by William I, until late in the

1100s, several uprisings took place that pitted primarily native Anglo-Saxon lords against the ruling Norman aristocracy. William faced rebellions from 1066 to 1070 and fought a serious insurrection in 1075. Resentment against Norman rule continued to surface for nearly one hundred years.

One of the biggest rebellions occurred in 1173–1174 during the reign of Henry II, one of William's descendants. Henry's four sons and his ambitious wife, Eleanor of Aquitane, made use of latent anti-Norman resentment to mount a rebellion against the king. Though granted kingdoms ranging from the Pyrenees to Scotland, Henry's sons had no real power, and, together with their mother and the King of France, they began a revolt in 1173 in Normandy against their father. The rebels were soon joined by some disgruntled Anglo-Saxon barons in England and Scotland's King William the Lion. The beleaguered Henry II fought battles both in Normandy and in England. His tactical genius resulted in the defeat of all his enemies. The Scottish king, after being taken prisoner, was forced to grant his lands as a fief to the English king.

Henry eventually pardoned his sons but did not grant them any more powers while he still ruled. Following Henry's death, his youngest son succeeded to the throne as King John I (1199–1216). John's arbitrary rule resulted in a baronial revolt that brought forth the Magna Carta (1215). By the time of the baronial revolt, however, the dispute with the king was no longer divided simply along ethnic lines. It represented an attempt by many of his lords, from both ethnic backgrounds, to check John's abuse of power. The few Hollywood dramas that take place during these stormy times avoid the court intrigues and political ramifications of the internal conflict. Instead, they emphasize the pageantry and romanticism of the period. *The Adventures of Robin Hood* (1938), starring Errol Flynn in the title role, has the bandit of Sherwood Forest defending the poor and downtrodden Saxons against the Normans, led by Prince John, usurper to the throne, whose brother, King Richard, is away fighting in the Crusades. In the costume drama *The Black Rose* (1950) the illegitimate son of a Saxon (Tyrone Power) is forced into exile when officials learn that he has led a revolt to free Saxon prisoners from jail, an act considered treasonous against the Norman King. In the lavishly produced *Ivanhoe* (1952), made in England, Robert Taylor portrays Sir Walter Scott's brave Saxon leader who battles to free King Richard from Austrian imprisonment and to restore him to the throne of England. ∎

Anglo-Spanish Wars (1587–1729). England and Spain fought three major wars during this period, (1587–1604), (1655–1659), and (1727–1729) as well as being in conflict before and after these times, either in undeclared naval war or sometimes as part of a broader war. Their rivalry involved religious differences, control of the sea and fighting for New World treasures. Such films as *The Sea Hawk* (1940) reflect this turbulent period. Errol Flynn, as an English pirate, brings to England some of the riches of the New World that he has plundered from the Spanish, and earns the plaudits of Queen Elizabeth I (Flora Robson) for filling her coffers.

Sir Francis Drake's raids on Spanish shipping (1577–1595), the destruction of the Spanish Armada (1588) and other intermittent attacks by English corsairs—actually royally encouraged pirates—on Spain's treasure ships and Caribbean colonies, provide fertile ground for swashbuckling sea dramas. *Seven Seas to Calais* (1963), with Rod Taylor as Sir Francis Drake, dramatizes his raids on Spanish wealth in the New World and the defeat of the Spanish Armada. ∎

Angry Hills, The (1959), MGM. *Dir.* Robert Aldrich; *Sc.* A. I. Bezzerides; *Cast includes:* Robert Mitchum, Elisabeth Mueller, Stanley Baker, Gia Scala, Theodore Bikel.

An American war correspondent, carrying vital information about members of the Greek underground, attempts to escape from Greece while he is pursued by the Gestapo in this World War II spy drama. Robert Mitchum, as the reporter who agrees to help the Greek resistance, becomes the target of the Nazis who want the list of names while anti-Nazi forces try to assist him in his escape. Elisabeth Mueller provides the romantic interest. Stanley Baker, as the head of the Gestapo in Greece, is treated too sympathetically for a Nazi in this routine espionage tale. ∎

Animation. See Cartoons. ∎

Annapolis Story, An (1955), AA. *Dir.* Don Siegel; *Sc.* Dan Ullman, Geoffrey Homes; *Cast includes:* John Derek, Diana Lynn, Kevin McCarthy, Alvy Moore, Pat Conway.

The U.S. Naval Academy and the Korean War provide the backgrounds for this drama of a group of midshipmen who undergo rigorous training before joining their comrades in battle. John Derek and Kevin McCarthy portray brothers who compete for the affections of Diana Lynn. They carry their dispute through graduation and to Korea where they are assigned as navy pilots. When McCarthy, the older of the brothers, is shot down, Derek rescues him from the ocean in this routine service tale. ■

Annihilators, The (1985), New World. *Dir.* Charles E. Sellier, Jr.; *Sc.* Brian Russell; *Cast includes:* Gerrit Graham, Lawrence Hilton-Jacobs, Paul Koslo, Christopher Stone.

A group of Vietnam War veterans, former members of an elite fighting force, reunite in the 1980s to battle a vicious street gang in this action drama. The story opens in Vietnam with Christopher Stone leading his elite group of fighters on a special mission. Overwhelmed by a large force of North Vietnamese troops, the American soldiers are saved by one of their buddies (Dennis Redfield) who is severely wounded in the battle. As a result of his sacrifice, Redfield is permanently confined to a wheelchair.

The drama then shifts to a Georgia town in the 1980s where Redfield helps his father in a local grocery story. The community is being terrorized by a gang of hoodlums headed by their crazed leader (Paul Koslo). When Redfield tries to organize his neighbors against the thugs, he is brutally beaten to death. His former army buddies (Stone, Lawrence Hilton-Jacobs, Gerrit Graham, Andy Wood) arrive in town, train the local citizens in self-defense and help them to defeat the predators. The second half of the film, which is dominated by street action, makes little reference to the war. ■

Another Dawn (1937), WB. *Dir.* William Dieterle; *Sc.* Laird Doyle; *Cast includes:* Kay Francis, Errol Flynn, Ian Hunter, Frieda Inescort.

A weak romantic melodrama of three souls isolated at a remote British outpost in North Africa, the film stars Kay Francis as the wife of the post commander (Ian Hunter) who is in love with Captain Roark (Errol Flynn). She marries Hunter in England with the understanding that she respects and admires him but does not love him. Deeply in love with

her, Hunter agrees to her terms. They return to his command where she falls for Flynn, who reminds her of her former lover who has died in an airplane crash. Meanwhile a native chieftain is stirring up trouble. Flynn takes out a patrol that is nearly wiped out. He returns wounded. The chief then dams a river supplying water to 500 families. Hunter, who overhears his wife and Flynn profess their love for each other and their determination not to betray Hunter, takes off in an airplane on a suicidal mission to bomb the dam. The next morning at dawn the two lovers receive news of his death. The film presents only one desert battle between a patrol of British soldiers led by Flynn and a horde of natives. One moving scene involves Herbert Mundin, as the commander's orderly. Taunted by his fellow soldiers and branded a coward because of his actions in a previous battle, he redeems himself in the desert skirmish when he sacrifices his life to retrieve a container of ammunition. ■

Antiwar films. The American antiwar film has been a viable force since the early days of the movie industry. Ironically, more films denigrating war appeared during World War I (although only a handful) than during the second world conflict. In fact, between 1940 and 1948 virtually no feature film containing a key antiwar statement appeared from either the major or independent studios. Obviously as the result of the political climate, the bulk of antiwar movies show up either before or after a conflict.

The term "antiwar" was seldom used during the first few decades of this century. The film studios, historians and critics tended to label films with antiwar themes as pacifist dramas. Current film historians generally reserve the term "pacifist" for those films released before and during World War I and "antiwar" for those of the postwar period—although both terms are often used interchangeably.

Progressive America, with its religious, humanitarian and pacifist roots, embraced the view that all war was hateful and particularly condemned World War I. The war provided the fuel to the controversy, and a few outspoken producers and directors supplied the fuse. The young American film industry had hardly crawled from its cradle when it became entangled in the pacifist controversy.

Films with antiwar themes released before

America's entry into World War I were generally set in fictitious countries or mythical kingdoms. The bellicose leaders, however, resembled the Kaiser. The uniforms and headgear of the military were suspiciously similar to those of Germany. One of the earliest antiwar films, *War o' Dreams*, appeared in 1915. An inventor who has developed a powerful new explosive has a dream in which he witnesses the pain and agony on the faces of parents whose sons have been killed as a result of the modern inventions of war. The next day he decides not to sell his secret to the military. Thomas Ince's *The Despoiler* (1915) describes another dream that turns into a nightmare. A colonel during an unnamed war threatens to loose his troops upon the women of an occupied town if he is not paid a large sum of money. Later, when the colonel learns that his chief officer has been killed, he orders the murderer shot, realizing too late that it is his own daughter.

Ince's now classic *Civilization* (1916) tells the story of another fictitious country ruled by a militaristic king (a thinly disguised Kaiser). When he plans to start a war, the spirit of Christ appears and shows the warlike ruler images of death and destruction that follow in the wake of war. The king, stirred by these scenes, ends hostilities. *War Brides* (1916) was one of the most popular films of the period. Also set in a mythical kingdom, its populace is governed by a ruler who decrees that women have more babies for the purpose of producing future soldiers. A defiant citizen (the international actress Nazimova) shoots herself in protest against the command. Other women rise up and vow not to have any more births until war is outlawed in their land.

As the U.S. became more entangled in the European war, films echoing the call of preparedness began to replace those with antiwar motifs. *The Zeppelin's Last Raid* (1917), also directed by Ince, was one of the last pacifist dramas of the period. The German commander of one of these lighter-than-air vehicles, who is influenced by his pacifist fiancee, refuses to bomb an enemy city. Mortally wounded in a gun battle with his crew, he blows up the airship rather than rain destruction on the defenseless people below. Charlie Chaplin's satirical comedy, *Shoulder Arms* (1918), suggests antiwar elements in his attacks on authoritarian figures, life in the trenches, tallies of enemy dead and the general absurdity of the war.

Not only did antiwar films disappear from the screen during World War I, but pacifists in dramas and comedies were treated derisively. They were shown as empty-headed, naive idealists or, worse, as traitors. An example of the former was *Perkins' Peace Party* (1916), in which a dim-witted pacifist-professor and his companions journey to New York so that they can sail to Europe to stop the war. Following a succession of blunders, they eventually drop the idea. In the short comedy "Tell That to the Marines" (1918) the main character, a bumbling pacifist, becomes the butt of most of the humor. *In-Again, Out-Again* (1917), starring Douglas Fairbanks, is an example of the latter. The acrobatic star persuades his sweetheart, a member of a pacifist group, that the others are surreptitiously selling war materiel to the enemy.

Following the Armistice, a stream of war movies poured out of Hollywood and continued into the 1930s. A brief respite occurred in the early 1920s when audiences tired of the romances and heroics that invariably blended leave in wartime Paris with life in the trenches. The popularity of the *The Big Parade* (1925) rejuvenated the genre. The themes varied from romance, heroism and glory to disillusionment and hatred of war. One of the earliest postwar films to condemn the conflict was the bitter drama *Uncle Sam From Freedom Ridge* (1920). A patriotic Virginia mountain man has accepted the loss of his son in France until he learns that there are those who are trying to stop President Wilson's goal of abolishing all wars through the League of Nations. The embittered father wraps himself in his beloved stars and stripes and shoots himself in protest. Director D.W. Griffith, who turned out virulent anti-German films during the war such as *The Great Love* (1918), also made *Isn't Life Wonderful* in 1924 in which he treats his central German characters sympathetically. An impoverished family struggles to survive in the midst of the economic and political instability of postwar Germany. A similar theme appears in Fred Niblo's *The Enemy* (1928), in which a recently married Austrian couple (Ralph Forbes and Lillian Gish) pay the price of their nation's war. While Forbes suffers at the front, Gish, desperate for money to feed her newborn baby, enters a brothel. By the time her husband returns, the baby has died.

During the next decade, antiwar themes

dominated the military dramas. *All Quiet on the Western Front* (1930), the most important and highly acclaimed of the group, set the tone and standard for others to follow. The drama offers no heroes, no acts of glory, no talk of national honor. It tells the tragic tale of a group of idealistic German students who discover that war offers only endless hardships, a daily struggle to survive and senseless death. Two other films released the same year, *Journey's End* and *The Dawn Patrol*, reflect some of the antiwar qualities of the former work, but they retain strong elements of national pride and honor. *Beyond Victory* (1931), with William Boyd, plays down the glory and heroics on the battlefield and suggests the dangers of national prejudice as one of the major causes of war. *Ace of Aces* (1933) tells about a sensitive sculptor (Richard Dix) who is transformed into a callous killer once he becomes a flier. Films about war's destructive influence on the individual would surface in the aftermath of World War II, Korea and Vietnam as their backgrounds.

Not all antiwar movies of the 1930s dealt with life in the trenches. Phillips Holmes, as a French veteran in *The Man I Killed* (1932), visits the parents of a German soldier he has killed in the war. But he cannot bring himself to reveal his identity when he sees the family still grieving for their boy. Meanwhile the villagers, renewing their old hatreds for the French, threaten the boy until the father (Lionel Barrymore) reminds them that it was these same national prejudices that caused the war and resulted in so many deaths. *The Road Back* (1937), based on Erich Maria Remarque's intended sequel to *All Quiet on the Western Front*, examines the experiences of those returning German soldiers who were fortunate to survive the horrors of battle. They encounter food riots and threats of revolution. The pessimistic ending hints at the rise of militarism once again.

The results of World War I disillusioned many. The U.S. was the only Allied nation not to claim any territory; war debts went unpaid or were temporarily suspended. Isolationism was on the rise; popular figures called for America's disengagement from all political ties with Europe. Nazism in Germany and Fascism in Italy loomed like a dark cloud over Europe. In addition to dramas, antiwar documentaries occasionally found their way to the screen. They often were comprised of newsreel footage gathered from various sources, including the Allied and Central powers, and reflected the growing pacifist mood in the country. *The Unknown Soldier Speaks* (1934) uses World War I footage to introduce its thesis that the ideals of the war have been forgotten or betrayed. The film proceeds to show the rise of Hitler and Mussolini. The munitions makers are the targets of *Dealers in Death* (1934), a documentary examining the secret deals between French and German arms dealers and the two nations during the war. The film points out the agreements that prevented the bombings of munitions factories in both countries, the destruction of which would have shortened the war. *The Dead March* (1937) traces various world conflicts, employing various newsreel footage, including that of World War I, Japan's invasion of China and Mussolini's conquest of Ethiopia, to underscore the dangers of plunging the world into another war. *The Fight for Peace* (1938) covers much the same ground and uses similar footage in its attack on Fascism and Nazism, two militant ideologies bent on threatening the already fragile peace. *Why This War?*, released in 1939, attacks the imperialists, munitions makers and militarists for initiating World War I and bringing the world to the brink of another global conflict. The film ends with a gold-star mother condemning war. The documentary came too late to have any effect. The armies of Europe were once again on the march down the familiar road of destruction and death.

Following World War II and its almost endless stream of propaganda dramas and documentaries, antiwar films once again began to appear. *The Boy With Green Hair* (1948), an almost forgotten and underrated film, as well as one of the earliest antiwar dramas, pleads for world peace through tolerance for others by employing images of war orphans. Young Dean Stockwell becomes their voice. Stanley Kubrick's scathing *Paths of Glory* (1957), which returns to the trenches of World War I, is more of an attack on machiavellian military leaders than on war in general. Dalton Trumbo's *Johnny Got His Gun* (1971), also set during World War I, gives an uncompromisingly grisly picture of war. Timothy Bottoms, as a youth bursting with life and vitality, goes willingly to the trenches only to return as a quadriplegic, an anomaly that exposes all the lies about honor, duty and country. The embarrassed militarists and politicians decide to shut him away in a dark, locked room.

Such anti-Vietnam War films as *Coming Home* (1978), *Platoon* (1986) and *Full Metal Jacket* (1987) show the horrors of that conflict. *Hearts and Minds* (1974), one of several antiwar documentaries of the Vietnam conflict, traces the different stages in which the U.S. became involved in the war. Much of the footage concerns the Vietnamese people. The realistic dramas of the war that began to appear with regularity in the late 1980s deal more with the ordeals of that particular conflict and its effects on the common soldier than with the horrors of war in general. These horrors, however, are strongly suggested in the above dramas as well as many straight combat action films, intentionally or otherwise. ▪

Antony, Mark (c. 82–30 B.C.). Antony, a leading Roman general, tribune and supporter of Caesar, delivered an emotional eulogy after Caesar's assassination (44 B.C.) that turned the Roman mob against the killers, Brutus and Cassius. He then joined with Octavian (later Augustus) and Lepidus to form a triumvirate as rulers of Rome. In the civil war that followed, the triumvirate battled the Republican forces of the Senate, headed by Brutus and Cassius, and defeated them at the Battle of Philippi (42 B.C.). The killers of Caesar committed suicide rather than face capture.

The triumvirate divided the empire, and Antony was granted rule over the eastern portion. After 40 B.C. he lived in Alexandria, Egypt, where he became the lover of Egyptian Queen Cleopatra, formerly Caesar's mistress. Another civil war soon broke out, this time between Rome under Octavian and Egypt under Antony and Cleopatra. The dispute was possibly caused by political jealousy between Octavian and Antony, as well as Antony's decision to divorce his wife, Octavia, sister of Octavian, and marry Cleopatra, who bore him three children. Roman forces defeated Antony and Cleopatra at Actium (31 B.C.). Upon receiving false information that Cleopatra had killed herself, Antony committed suicide. Cleopatra soon followed Antony's example when she heard she would be treated as a prisoner in Rome.

Antony has been portrayed in several ways by dramatists and writers. He has appeared both as a strong individual who was, nevertheless, driven to destruction by a more cunning and seductive Cleopatra, and also as a weakling whose ambitions were greater than his abilities. The routine film *Serpent of the Nile* (1953) portrays a rather simplistic Mark Antony who falls for the charms of the treacherous Egyptian queen. Shakespeare's *Julius Caesar* paints Antony as Caesar's staunch supporter who delivers a famous speech attacking the assassins. He then proceeds to defeat Brutus and Cassius in battle. Director-screenwriter Joseph A. Mankiewicz in his 1953 film version of the play adheres to this image of Antony (Marlon Brando), showing him defeating the assassins at Philippi.

In another drama, *Antony and Cleopatra*, Shakespeare characterizes Antony as a declining hero who is torn between ambition and his desire for Cleopatra. *Cleopatra* (1963), also directed by Mankiewicz, generally reflects this latter portrait of Antony (Richard Burton). This is an Antony in his middle years—a warrior, politician and lover. Still envious of the abilities of a dead Caesar and powerless against Cleopatra's seduction, he is aware that he has neglected his public duty for private pleasure. The epic Battle of Actium is a closing highlight of the film. See also Cleopatra, Roman Civil Wars. ▪

Anybody's War (1930), Par. *Dir.* Richard Wallace; *Sc.* Lloyd Corrigan; *Cast includes:* George Moran, Charles Mack, Bert Swor, Joan Peers, Neil Hamilton, Walter Weems.

A World War I comedy starring the comedy team of Moran and Mack, the film is disappointing in its humor except for one or two routines. Moran and Mack, who appear in blackface as they did on stage as the "Two Black Crows," are dogcatchers at the beginning of the film. They go into the army and are soon sent over to France. The highlight of the film is their dice game with other soldiers. When their sergeant breaks up the event, Moran swallows the dice to hide the evidence. Mack wants his payoff since Moran did not make his number. To settle the dispute, they use a fluoroscope to see the numbers inside Moran's body. ▪

Anzio. The Allied invasion fleet edged forward in the dark to anchor in the shallows off the Italian coast. It carried a combined American-British force ready to begin an operation that might shorten the Allied campaign in Italy. There was no sign of a waiting enemy as troops splashed up onto the wide beaches of Anzio and nearby Nettuno, about

Earl Holliman (c.) and his fellow G.I.s meet stubborn Nazi resistance amid the rubble of war in Italy. *Anzio* (1968).

30 miles south of Rome, at 2 A. M. on January 22, 1944.

The Anzio landing, potentially one of the most important invasions of World War II, caught the Germans and Italians completely by surprise. There was no resistance, except for very light, sporadic small arms fire, along most of the 10-mile beachhead. "Maybe the war is over and we don't know it," said Lt. Col. Edgar Coleman, an officer in the invading force.

The Allies had several objectives in mounting a leapfrog action up the Italian coast: cut the Axis supply lines that ran out of Rome to the main battlefronts in the mountains further south and enable the Allies to end the bloody stalemate into which the Italian campaign had fallen; secondly, capture the capital of Fascist Italy, important to the enemy as a transportation junction and for political and morale reasons too; and, additionally, entrap and capture a large body of enemy troops whose escape routes would be cut off.

Within two days, the invading force had pushed 10 miles inland and appeared well on the way to gaining its objectives. But it took close to four-and-a-half months to cover the last 20 miles and capture Rome. What had started out so well turned into a bitter struggle to keep from being driven back into the sea. Major General John Lucas, commanding the invasion force, failed to exploit the effects of a surprise landing and decided to consolidate his supplies and reserves on the beachhead before moving ahead. Axis troops, meanwhile, poured into the area to, in Hitler's words, "eliminate the abscess," and actually drove back the invaders in some areas.

The main Allied forces in the south eventually fought their way up to the Anzio perimeter by May 25, slightly more than four months after the landing. During the interval, Lucas was replaced as commander of the Anzio operation by Major General Lucien Truscott, Jr. Following the linkup, Allied armies under General Mark Clark entered Rome on June 4, but enemy troops had withdrawn safely from the planned trap. Almost as disappointing as the turn of events is the main film on this battle, *Anzio* (1968). Its slow pace and lack of direction fail to present the drama of what happened at Anzio. One reviewer labeled the movie "less than memorable." The film did hint at the foul-up by higher brass for not moving quickly to seize important objectives. A film character, General Leslie, played by Edgar Kennedy, bears more than a thin resemblance to the real-life General Lucas, both in his cautious attitude and even to having a last name with the same initials and number of syllables.

The blockbuster *The Big Red One* (1980), which chronicles the adventures of the First Division throughout the war, includes action scenes of the Anzio operation in which the division participated. *To Hell And Back* (1955), a biography of much-decorated war hero Audie Murphy, in which he plays himself, also has segments pertaining to the Battle of Anzio in which he took part.

Unfortunately for that portion of the movie-going public that gets its understanding of history through films, Hollywood's treatment of this battle in *Anzio* is a prime example of its failure to do justice to what happened in real life. The Battle of Anzio had all the ingredients for an engrossing action drama replete with opportunity for solid characterization. Hollywood could have made a better film by staying closer to history. ∎

Anzio (1968), Col. *Dir.* Edward Dmytryk; *Sc.* Harry A. L. Craig; *Cast includes:* Robert Mitchum, Peter Falk, Earl Holliman, Robert Ryan, Reni Santoni.

One of the more important European campaigns of World War II is trivialized in this weak drama. Robert Mitchum stars as a cynical newspaper correspondent who belittles the top military brass who progress from one blunder to the next. Robert Ryan portrays an American general more interested in making the front pages than in fighting the war efficiently. Arthur Kennedy, as another general, is overcautious, losing strategic opportunities against the enemy. Action sequences include the Anzio invasion, but the rest of the film is rather slow. ∎

Apache (1954), UA. *Dir.* Robert Aldrich; *Sc.* James R. Webb; *Cast includes:* Burt Lancaster, Jean Peters, John McIntire, Charles Buchinsky.

A defiant Apache, who learns from the U.S. Cavalry that might makes right, wages a lone war against the U.S. in this implausible outdoor drama. Burt Lancaster, as Massai, the defiant, sympathetic main character, fights for his tribe's honor against the encroaching army. Susan Peters plays his wife. John McIntire, as the army's chief scout, is determined to kill the elusive Indian. Lancaster, using knives, arrows and a rifle, takes a heavy toll against his pursuers. The army finally acknowledges his one-man battle as a war and offers him amnesty if he will make peace. Resolved to fight a warrior's battle to the death, he finally accepts the offer after he hears the cries of his new-born child. He then becomes a legend among his people. Charles Buchinsky, who will later change his name to Bronson, has a small role in this story based on historical incidents. ∎

Apache Drums (1951), U. *Dir.* Hugo Fregonese; *Sc.* David Chandler; *Cast includes:* Stephen McNally, Coleen Gray, Willard Parker, Arthur Shields.

A conventional action western, *Apache Drums* unfolds the story of a group of settlers in Spanish Boot, a small town in the Southwest that comes under attack by a band of hostile Apaches. Stephen McNally, a gambler and drifter, falls in love with Coleen Gray, who in turn attracts the attention of Willard Parker, the local blacksmith and mayor. The two rivals vie for her affections as they fight off the hostiles led by Victorio, their chief. In the rousing climax the surviving defenders barricade themselves in the town church and fight off the braves until the cavalry comes to their rescue.

Chief of the Ojo Caliente tribe of the Apache, Victorio was a master of guerrilla warfare. His small band of warriors kept the Mexican-American border in a state of turmoil with his attacks during the late 1870s in part of the period collectively known as the Apache Wars. When the American government did away with his tribal reservation located in ancestral territory and attempted to move his people to the arid San Carlos reservation, along with several other Apache bands, Victorio and his group fled to the Mexican border. He terrorized the border country with repeated raids and massacres. It took a combined force from the Mexican army, the Texas Rangers and about 2,000 U.S. troops to finally subdue Victorio's group of less than 200 warriors.

Chief Victorio, who died in 1880 (there is no record of his date of birth), raided and murdered numerous Mexican sheepherders and small ranchers during the Apache wars, but there is no evidence of the events depicted in the film, especially the incident of his being wounded. He ranked below Cochise and Geronimo as an eminent warrior. See also Apache Wars. ∎

Apache Rifles (1964), TCF. *Dir.* William Witney; *Sc.* Charles B. Smith; *Cast includes:* Audie Murphy, Michael Dante, Linda Lawson, L. Q. Jones.

An Indian-hating cavalry commander in the Southwest learns a lesson in tolerance in this routine action drama. Audie Murphy, as an army officer, falls in love with a missionary (Linda Lawson) with Indian blood. His sympathies begin to change for the Apaches, who have to contend with greedy miners seeking the gold on the tribe's land. The whites manage to have Murphy replaced with an officer more sympathetic to their needs until the finale when a battle rages and Murphy is proven correct. John Archer plays the officer who replaces Murphy. ∎

Apache Uprising (1966), Par. *Dir.* R. G. Springsteen; *Sc.* Harry Sanford, Max Lamb; *Cast includes:* Rory Calhoun, Corinne Calvert, John Russell, Lon Chaney, Gene Evans.

A minor action drama blending a gold theft scheme with warring Apaches, the overly talkative film centers on a group of stagecoach passengers who stop at a way station. Rory Calhoun stars as the hero. Corinne Calvert, as a passenger with a questionable past, provides the romantic interest. John Russell portrays the head of a gang of outlaws. Veteran screen performers include Lon Chaney as a happy-go-lucky stagecoach driver, Johnny Mack Brown as a sheriff who becomes interested in Calvert and Richard Arlen as a U.S. Cavalry officer. The title has little to do with the plot and general action of this routine drama. ∎

Apache Warrior (1957), TCF. *Dir.* Elmo Williams; *Sc.* Carroll Young, Kurt Neumann, Eric Norden; *Cast includes:* Keith Larsen, Jim Davis, Rudolfo Acosta, John Miljan.

The clash of cultures causes problems for an Apache scout in this weak drama. Keith Larsen, as the Apache Kid, a scout working with the U.S. Cavalry to stamp out minor pockets of Apache resistance following the defeat of Geronimo, avenges the murder of his brother at the hands of a fellow Indian.

Although Larsen has acted according to his tribal customs, the army major considers him a criminal and imprisons him. Larsen and a band of Indians led by Rudolfo Acosta break out and in the fracas a white scout (Jim Davis), a close friend of Larsen, is wounded by Acosta. Davis pursues the prisoners, thinking it was Larsen who has shot him. ∎

Apache Wars (1871–1886). Apache chief Geronimo's surrender to General Nelson Miles in late 1886 brought an end to one of the longest and bitterest conflicts between the U.S. and a native tribe. To white settlers and government forces in the Southwest in the late 19th century, the Apaches were feared as agents of death and destruction. Here's how an army trooper talking to Frederic Remington, a noted western writer and artist in the late 1800's, described his feelings toward the Apaches: "It is hardly possible to convey in words . . . the panic and terror spread throughout the country by Apaches on the warpath . . . Their (Apache) murder strokes came like thunderbolts from a clear sky . . . bang! bang! bang! all capable of resistance would be shot dead in their places. . . ."

Composed of several linguistically related bands located in the southwestern part of the U.S., the Apache resisted and terrorized invaders from three nations into their homeland— Spain, Mexico and the U.S. Prolonged and vicious conflict between the U.S. and the Apache occurred after the U.S. acquired the Southwest as a result of the Mexican War (1846–1848). Numerous Americans crossed through Apache territory as land-hungry settlers streamed westward during the 19th century. The discovery of gold in Apache country soon after the Mexican War attracted additional hordes of miners. The tribe, led by such outstanding fighting chiefs as Mangas Colorado, Geronimo, Cochise and Victorio, became one of the most difficult to subdue in the history of Indian wars.

Conflict between the U.S. and the Apache first erupted in 1851 when Mangas Colorado, chief of the Mimbrenos Apaches in southwest New Mexico, tried to resist encroaching gold miners upon his tribe's territory. Caught and publicly flogged in humiliating fashion by some miners, he retaliated with brutal raids against settlers and transients until he was killed by Union soldiers in 1863. *Apache Rifles* (1964) brings up the role of greedy gold miners in the start of hostilities.

Conflict spread to another band in 1861 when Cochise, chief of the Chiricahua Apache, went to war because of the army's execution of five of his relatives for a crime he claimed they never committed. Cochise and his group conducted intermittent raids against the whites until 1871, when war erupted on a larger scale over the massacre of more than 100 Apaches at Camp Grant, Arizona. The incident, covered in *Fort Bowie* (1958), is considered the start of the Apache Wars. A campaign mounted against just one band of about 200 warriors led by Victorio, chief of the Oro Caliente Apache, provides an example of how formidable the Apaches were as fighters. It required the combined forces of a portion of the Mexican army, the Texas Rangers and nearly 2,000 American troops to subdue the braves.

Another group, the Chiricahua Apache under Geronimo, joined the revolt in 1876 after the Chiricahua reservation was abolished and its inhabitants forcibly transferred to an arid site on the San Carlos reservation in New Mexico. Geronimo's band fled to Mexico and hid in the Sierra Madre Mountains between raids into Arizona. Geronimo and his group were captured in 1881 and 1885, but he managed to escape each time and continue a guerrilla war against both Mexicans and Americans.

The American film industry seized upon the American-Apache conflict for a series of action dramas which depicted Indians as hostile semi-savages while under-emphasizing the role of whites as invaders. Victorio, the Apache chief, appeared in *Apache Drums* (1951) besieging settlers barricaded in a church before being driven off by the cavalry. Even future President Ronald Reagan got into the action in *The Last Outpost* (1951), his first film as a western star, as he led the cavalry to rescue a threatened post. *Geronimo* (1939), with Preston Foster, shows a highly fictionalized version of the capture of the great Indian warrior. Corrupt traders who provoked the Apaches and sold guns and ammunition to them is covered in the films *Geronimo* (1939) and *Valley of the Sun* (1942), delineating the white man as a partial cause of hostilities.

Films about the Apache overwhelmingly played up the animosity between Indians and whites and served primarily as vehicles for showing bloody action in rugged western settings. Few films mention that the Apache originally welcomed Americans as friends because they both fought the Mexicans. It was a fragile friendship, however, that ended once American settlers and gold miners replaced Mexicans in encroaching upon Apache territory.

The word "Apache" became a code word for hostile Indians. Only a few films have digressed from the stereotyped image of the Apache as bloodthirsty savages. *Broken Arrow* (1950), starring Jeff Chandler as Cochise, was the first movie to present an Apache chief as a reasonable man willing to live in peace under the American government. *Apache* (1954), in which Burt Lancaster, as an Indian, fights for his people's honor until he is granted amnesty, portrayed the Apache favorably. Audie Murphy in *Apache Rifles* (1964) appears as a cavalry officer who is convinced that the Apache, repeatedly wronged by greedy gold miners, will eventually rise up. His beliefs are vindicated in a resulting battle.

These movies effectively demonstrated the mutual animosity of many Indian and white leaders. Collective retribution was a feature of Indian society that was handily reciprocated by white military forces. When either side attacked the other, there was no question of the individual victim's innocence or guilt. It was all-out war between one "tribe" and another. Any person or group from the other side was considered a target in a mutual war of retribution.

Hollywood's treatment of the Apache lacks balance. Little earnest attempt was made to show how the Apache suffered at the hands of whites. True, the Apaches fully earned their reputation as merciless raiders and wily warriors. But their history in dealing with Americans from 1850 until the tribe's final pacification in 1886 is replete with incidents involving official and unofficial white encroachment upon their lands. They were the victims of many broken pledges. They too suffered massacres as vicious as those they in turn inflicted upon the whites. In aiming at box office appeal, Hollywood generally portrayed a one-sided view of the conflict. In time, perhaps, screenwriters may use the power of commercial films to reveal the full, true story behind the Apache-white conflict. See also Geronimo, Cochise. ∎

Apocalypse Now (1979), UA. Dir. Francis Ford Coppola; *Sc.* John Milius, Francis Ford Coppola; *Cast includes:* Marlon Brando, Martin Sheen, Robert Duvall, Fred Forrest, Sam Bottoms.

Director Francis Coppola's epic about the Vietnam conflict and its effects on its participants consciously draws upon Joseph Conrad's 1911 novella *Heart of Darkness*. Both works concentrate chiefly on a river journey that ultimately leads into darkness, terror and death in which the pivotal character of each exclaims: "The horror! The horror!"

Martin Sheen portrays an Intelligence officer sent into Cambodia by his superiors to "terminate" the command of Kurtz (Marlon Brando), a megalomaniac American officer whose military tactics are disapproved of by the top brass. "There's a conflict within every human heart between the rational and the irrational," a superior officer explains to Sheen, "but the good does not always triumph." During his trip on the river Sheen encounters an enigmatic colonel (Robert Duvall) who commands a squadron of helicopters. Duvall, a surfing enthusiast, orders a helicopter raid on a Viet Cong village while his loudspeakers blast out Wagner's *Die Walkure*. Before he engages in surfing, he orders one last napalm attack on some nearby enemy mortar positions. "I love the smell of napalm in the morning," Duvall admits.

When Sheen finally arrives at Brando's camp, he witnesses corpses dangling from trees, scattered skulls and crucified bodies. Sheen meets privately with the renegade leader who leads a private army of tribesmen. Brando, seen mostly in shadows, engages in some arcane commentary and concludes that "we must make friends with moral terror," that "it is judgment that defeats us." Using a knife, Sheen carries out his assignment. This final sequence has been attacked by audiences and critics alike as muddled and incomprehensible.

Throughout most of the film, however, Coppola transcends the realistic world of warfare to evoke a surrealistic environment of mist and darkness symbolizing conspiracy and evil. When he uses lights, as in a night sequence at a USO station along the river, they represent a carnival world of fantasy for the soldiers as well as the crew of Sheen's patrol boat. "Beautiful," says one of the sailors, "it's just beautiful." The film is less a depiction of the Vietnam War than it is of a nightmarish and ironic vision of horror and death. ■

Appointment in Berlin (1943). See Spy Films: the Talkies. ■

Appointment in Tokyo (1945), WB. *Dir.* Major Jack Hively; *Sc.* Capt. Jack Handley, Capt. Jesse Lasky, Jr.

A World War II documentary produced by the War Department, the film covers the Pacific campaign from the fall of Bataan to Japan's surrender. Using footage from the U.S. Army as well as that captured from the enemy, the compilation depicts jungle warfare, street battles, the burning of Manila by the Japanese, the invasion of the Philippines by the U.S. Marines and the beachhead at Leyte. The film not only captures the larger scope of war, such as American planes bombing and strafing enemy targets, but the human side as well by showing the faces of marines as they are about to land on various islands and during battle. ■

Arch of Triumph (1948), UA. *Dir.* Lewis Milestone; *Sc.* Lewis Milestone, Harry Brown; *Cast includes:* Ingrid Bergman, Charles Boyer, Charles Laughton, Louis Calhern.

Ingrid Bergman and Charles Boyer portray tragic lovers in this atmospheric romantic drama set in France on the eve of World War II. Boyer, as a refugee doctor who has escaped to France in his flight from the Nazis, saves the life of fallen woman Ingrid Bergman as she is about to commit suicide. The strangers soon fall in love. Meanwhile, the war erupts and the Nazis march into Paris. But the conflict remains in the background as the film concentrates on the two lovers. Bergman is fatally wounded by an envious suitor. Boyer is placed in a concentration camp. The film is based on a novel by Erich Maria Remarque. ■

Are We Civilized? (1934), Raspin. *Dir.* Edwin Carewe; *Sc.* Harold Sherman; *Cast includes:* William Farnum, Anita Louise, Frank McGlyrna, Leroy Mason, Oscar Apfel.

A pretentious antiwar drama, the film invokes historical precedents (through the use of excerpts from old features and newsreels) to show the folly of war. William Farnum portrays the chief of an international news syndicate, a pacifist whose writings are burned in a thinly disguised, nameless state that resembles Germany. Farnum shows the leader the fallacy of choosing the road to war as a means to his end through flashbacks in history, including such figures as Christ, Moses, George Washington, Napoleon and Abraham Lincoln. The film was released during Hitler's rise to power in Nazi Germany and Mussolini's popularity in Fascist Italy, both of whom were causes for concern to their immediate neighbors. ■

"Argentine Question, The" (1942). See "The March of Time." ■

Arise, My Love (1940), Par. *Dir.* Mitchell Leisen; *Sc.* Charles Brackett, Billy Wilder; *Cast includes:* Claudette Colbert, Ray Milland, Dennis O'Keefe, Walter Abel, Dick Purcell.

A romantic drama with strife-torn Europe as the background, the film stars Claudette Colbert as an ambitious American reporter and Ray Milland as a young idealistic flier willing to fight for any underdog against oppression. Sent to France to report on the latest women's fashions, Colbert is quickly bored with this assignment. She decides to journey to Spain to seek more newsworthy headlines. Finding a fellow American (Milland) about to be executed, she poses as his wife and effects his release. But the couple are pursued by soldiers once the commandant who released Milland finds the American's "Last Will and Testament" which states that he is a bachelor. They steal an airplane and narrowly escape their pursuers across the border to France. As a reward for this front-page story, her editor sends her to Berlin. Following a slight holiday with Milland, they decide to sail for home. But the ship they are on is torpedoed by a Nazi submarine. The disaster brings the couple to the realization that their romantic bliss must be postponed while the world is in flames. Colbert sends in the story to alert the world of the ruthless sinking while Milland enlists in the Royal Air Force. The film title comes from "The Song of Solomon"— "Arise, my love, my fair one, come away"—which Milland is fond of quoting and which Colbert paraphrases in the last scene as a call to all Americans to defend themselves against the encroaching tyrannical forces.

Director Mitchell Leisen manages to take a romantic, and often humorous, story and combine it with serious world events. One of Milland's two buddies, who fought with him in Spain against the Fascists, reminds him why they are so far from home: "Because you said a lot of big guys were kicking the tar out of some little guys, and you said it wasn't fair, and you said it was up to us to come over to even things out." ■

Arizona Bushwhackers (1968), Par. *Dir.* Lesley Selander; *Sc.* Steve Fisher; *Cast includes:* Howard Keel, Yvonne De Carlo, John Ireland, Marilyn Maxwell, Scott Brady.

More a western than a Civil War drama, the film deals with the efforts of a Confederate prisoner of war to re-establish law and order in a crooked frontier town. With the Union busy fighting the war and prison camps overcrowded with captured Southerners, President Lincoln permits several Confederates who take an oath to the Union to leave the wretched conditions of incarceration and work as lawmen in the West. Howard Keel portrays a Southerner who accepts the terms but privately welcomes the opportunity to spy for the Confederacy. He is assigned to end the corruption in a town controlled by a dishonest sheriff (Barton MacLane) and a villainous saloon owner (Scott Brady). Yvonne De Carlo, as a milliner, helps Keel in his spying and provides the romantic interest. John Ireland plays Keel's rebel-hating deputy. ■

Arizona Raiders (1965), Col. *Dir.* William Witney; *Sc.* Alex Gottlieb, Mary and Willard Willingham; *Cast includes:* Audie Murphy, Michael Dante, Ben Cooper, Buster Crabbe.

Two former Confederate soldiers serving a 20-year prison sentence volunteer to help capture the notorious Quantrill and his band of raiders in this routine action drama loosely based on historical events. Audie Murphy and Ben Cooper portray the buddies who are captured by a Union officer (Buster Crabbe) and sentenced to prison for riding with Quantrill, played by Fred Graham. When the rebel leader turns from guerrilla activities to a general reign of terror for pure profit, Murphy and Cooper decide to help bring him in. Their prison break is arranged and they join up with the outlaws. Quantrill is brought to justice by Murphy with the help of friendly Yaqui Indians but not before Cooper is killed by one of the gang. Gloria Talbott, as the Indian chieftain's daughter, provides the romantic interest. This film is just one of several concerning the legendary Confederate leader. ■

Armada. See Spanish Armada. ■

Armenian massacres. The Armenian people, a subjugated Christian minority in Moslem Turkey, suffered through three massacres during revolutions around the turn of the 20th century. The mass killings directed by the Turkish government may have been the first recorded case of attempted genocide in modern times. Few American films focused attention on this period. *Auction of Souls* (1919), a dramatic recreation of Turkey's barbarous acts, scathingly attacked that country for her atrocities. The adventure drama *The Last Outpost* (1935) depicted the Turkish-inspired Kurdish attacks upon defenseless civilians only in a superficial way.

The most devastating of the three massacres occurred in 1915, during World War I, when an estimated 600,000 Armenian civilians lost their lives. Armenian revolutionaries, seeking to gain independence while Turkey was at war, revolted in eastern Turkey and received assistance from invading Russian Czarist troops. The Turkish government considered all Armenians a threat and ordered their death or deportation. Over one million fled. Many died from exhaustion, starvation, disease and execution on a forced march through present-day Syria and Iraq. The Turks often killed those who collapsed from weakness. *Auction of Souls* included graphic sequences of the Turks slaughtering children and old people.

Earlier Turkish massacres occurred during Armenian revolutions in 1894–97, when an estimated 250,000 were killed, and in 1909. The western world, horrified by Turkish inhumanity, intervened to stop the slaughter in 1909. Many Armenians eventually settled in southern Russia, in the present-day Armenian Soviet Republic. ■

Armored Command (1961), AA. *Dir.* Byron Haskin; *Sc.* Ron W. Alcorn; *Cast includes:* Howard Keel, Tina Louise, Warner Anderson, Earl Holliman, Burt Reynolds.

A female Nazi spy employs her sexual charms in an attempt to gather information concerning a strategic Allied position in this routine World War II action drama. She ensnares an innocent American sergeant (Earl Holliman) and a private (Burt Reynolds) who brawl for her affections. But her scheme is thwarted in the nick of time by a battle-hardened colonel (Howard Keel). During the ensuing battle, the spy vindictively shoots Reynolds and in turn is killed by Holliman. The film provides an exciting climactic battle sequence. ■

Arms and the Girl (1917), Paramount. *Dir.* Joseph Kaufman; *Sc.* Charles Whittaker; *Cast includes:* Billie Burke, Thomas Meighan.

In this comedy drama, Billie Burke portrays a young American woman on vacation in Belgium as World War I erupts. She misses her train and becomes entangled in military matters as Germans enter the town where she is staying. At first accused of spying, she is freed, but another American, an engineer, is suspected and sentenced to death by a firing squad. Posing as the condemned man's fiancee, she comes to his rescue. The sentimental German general orders them married while her real fiance arrives. This was one of the earliest films to treat World War I lightly. A comedy film in the midst of the Great War was a risky business as casualty reports, newspaper accounts and newsreels were revealing in graphic terms that the war, now in its third year, had turned into a "bloody slaughterhouse." Burke, a Broadway comedy star, made her second screen appearance in this film which received mixed reviews. ■

Army Girl (1938). See Tank Warfare. ■

Army Surgeon (1942), RKO. *Dir.* A. Edward Sutherland; *Sc.* Barry Trivers, Emmett Lavery; *Cast includes:* James Ellison, Jane Wyatt, Kent Taylor, Walter Drake.

A romantic drama of World War I, the film is a flashback of a love triangle between a doctor and the woman he loves, who has come overseas to be near her lover, and her former boyfriend. Her ex-flame shows up as a wounded airman and tries to rekindle the relationship. Jane Wyatt portrays the sought-after nurse while James Ellison, as an army doctor, and Kent Taylor, as the flier, portray the rivals. There are bits of battle scenes in this otherwise low-budget, routine film that ended up losing money in a year that almost all other war dramas did well at the box office. One sequence has the trio buried alive at a field hospital with the rivals competing bravely to save their love. ■

Army Wives (1944). See Home Front. ■

Arnold, Benedict. See *The Scarlet Coat* (1955). ■

Arrowhead (1953), Par. *Dir.* Charles Marquis Warren; *Sc.* Charles Marquis Warren; *Cast includes:* Charlton Heston, Jack Palance, Katy Jurado, Brian Keith, Mary Sinclair.

The Apache once again threaten the peace of the southwest in this routine outdoor action drama. Charlton Heston, as an army scout who has been raised among the Indians, continually warns his cavalry officers not to trust the treacherous Apaches. Jack Palance, as the son of an Apache chief, arouses the young braves to go on the proverbial warpath. Katy Jurado, as a Mexican-Indian, spies on Heston but also is attracted to him. Brian Keith plays a naive post commander who takes over after the previous commander and his troop are killed by the Apaches. Mary Sinclair, as a widow at the outpost, competes with Jurado for the affections of Heston.

Having lived with the Apaches has not stirred any sympathy in Heston for the Indians. To the contrary, he has developed a deep hatred. Although he warns the first commander not to trust the Apaches, the officer rides into an ambush and is killed. He later warns the commander's replacement, who also ignores him. Dismissed by the army for his strong anti-Apache attitude, Charlton eventually restores peace to the territory after being permitted to lead the army troops against the hostiles and engaging Palance in hand-to-hand combat. As with most films of this genre, the characters and incidents are almost entirely fictitious. However, one bit of accuracy is allowed to seep through. Brian tries to convince the Indians to move to a Florida reservation. Historically, the Apache tribe was resettled in Florida. ■

As in a Looking Glass (1916). See Washington, D.C. ■

Assignment in Brittany (1943), MGM. *Dir.* Jack Conway; *Sc.* Anthony Veiller, William H. Wright, Howard Emmett Rogers; *Cast includes:* Jean Pierre Aumont, Susan Peters, Richard Whorf.

Pierre Aumont, who later changed his name to Jean-Pierre, plays a dual role in this World War II drama based on the novel by Helen MacInnes. He portrays a British agent who impersonates his look-alike, a pro-Nazi Frenchman, for the purpose of locating a secret Nazi submarine base. Working with the French underground, he finds the camouflaged base and relays the information to the British Commandos who raid the site on the coast of Brittany and destroy it. Susan Peters provides the romantic interest in this overly familiar plot.

The film gets caught up in its own earnest

attempts at presenting a patriotic message, most notably the final singing of the "Marseillaise," already done more effectively in *Casablanca* (1942). The plot contrivances of the masquerading hero almost being exposed by those who know the real French collaborator whom he is impersonating and his romance with a true daughter of the cause have been seen on the screen too many times before. ■

Assignment—Paris. See Cold War. ■

At the Front in North Africa (1943), WB.

A World War II documentary of the African front produced by the U.S. Army Signal Corps, the film provides several strong battle scenes, including those between Allied airplanes and enemy bombers as well as a short sequence of a tank battle. For further propaganda purposes, several shots are shown of a damaged church and hospital train, the latter clearly marked as such. The action sequences concern the battles in Algeria and Tunisia. The film depicts the lives of those G.I.s who manned the tanks in the artillery duels with their German counterparts. Twentieth Century-Fox's former executive, Darryl F. Zanuck, a colonel in the Signal Corps during the war, supervised the making of the documentary. ■

"At Old Fort Dearborn" (1912), Bison. *Dir.* Frank Montgomery; *Cast includes:* Mona Darkfeather, Charles Bartlett.

An early silent drama of the Indian-U.S. Cavalry conflicts, the film features Mona Darkfeather, a popular performer of the period who made several films playing sympathetic Indians. She portrays Singing Bird, a sensitive young Indian woman who falls in love with a white trooper who is captured by her tribe. She helps the soldier to escape, but in so doing she forfeits her own life. ■

At War With the Army (1951). See Service Comedy. ■

Atlantic Convoy (1942), Col. *Dir.* Lew Landers; *Sc.* Robert Lee Johnson; *Cast includes:* Bruce Bennett, Virginia Field, John Beal, Larry Parks, Lloyd Bridges.

Iceland is the location of this World War II spy drama. John Beal plays a weather man who is suspected of supplying Nazi submarines with information about American shipping. Although he rescues an injured American pilot and several children in a daring airplane landing, he is unable to cast off suspicions of collaborating with the enemy. He eventually absolves himself when he leads the U.S. air patrol to the location of a German submarine. Virginia Field provides the romantic interest in this low-budget but well-paced film. ∎

Atrocities in film. Some war dramas portrayed heinous crimes inflicted upon the helpless by troops or officials. Originally, atrocities in films served as a form of propaganda that evoked even deeper personal feelings of revulsion and hostility toward an enemy.

Films with atrocity scenes first appeared during World War I and were usually blatantly propagandistic. American studios generally portrayed Germany as the perpetrator of cruelties, and her victim was often Belgium. In *A Maid of Belgium* (1917), for instance, a young Belgian wife loses her memory as a result of the German atrocities she witnesses during the war. In *To Hell With the Kaiser* (1918), a fanciful drama, Belgian civilians seeking sanctuary in their local church from German invaders see the mother superior shot dead when she objects to the Germans' attempt to enter the church.

Some World War I films underscored German brutality toward children. In *Till I Come Back to You* (1918), for example, Belgian youngsters transported to Germany are used for slave labor in munitions factories where they are beaten and deprived of food. *The Heart of Humanity* (1919) presented the dual horror of a potential rape and infanticide. A Red Cross nurse (Dorothy Phillips) fights off the lustful desires of a sinister Prussian officer (Erich von Stroheim), who, as a particularly brutal Hun, tosses a crying infant out a window. Belgium, on and off screen, emerged as a nation that was martyred by the Allies for its struggle against the enemy.

Belgians were not the only screen victims of German brutality during World War I. *Bullets and Brown Eyes* (1916) told of a fictitious war between Germany and Poland, with the latter suffering atrocious horrors at the hands of the former. *For France* (1917) portrayed the Huns as bestial figures who take advantage of defenseless French women. In one scene, a peasant mother is attacked by a Prussian officer and his aide. Why did Hollywood, even before America's entry into World War I in 1917, depict Germany in such an unsavory role? An anti-German mood had already developed in America early in the conflict. The public initially became appalled by the Kaiser's callous invasion of tiny, neutral Belgium in the opening days of the war as a means of getting around France's formidable defenses on the German border. As the fighting continued, America lost lives and ships because of Germany's unrestricted submarine warfare aimed at cutting supply lines to Britain and France. The sinking of the British liner *Lusitania* in 1915, with the loss of 128 Americans, was perhaps the most dramatic event to fuel public dislike towards Germany. Some German atrocities in prisoner-of-war camps were publicized in alleged newsreels included in *My Four Years in Germany* (1918), based on former American Ambassador James W. Gerard's book. British propaganda often exaggerated Germany's inhumanity with great effect on the American people. Hollywood, by making anti-German atrocity films, not only reflected the general public's mood but sought to insure a good box office response for its product.

Other silent films dealt with atrocities in different times and places. *Auction of Souls* (1919), for example, recreated the Turkish slaughter of 600,000 Armenians in 1915. The atrocities so incensed *Variety's* critic that he concluded his review with the following: "If (the film) may be given credit for the removal of Turkey from the map of the world, it will have helped in part to avenge Armenia. . . ."

Films also attributed atrocities to American Indians in colonial America. One such example occurs in the 1920 silent version of *The Last of the Mohicans*, featuring Wallace Beery, and in the 1936 sound version with Randolph Scott, both set during the French and Indian War. Although the French promise safe passage from Fort Henry to the defeated American and English defenders of the garrison, an Indian war party, allied to the French, brutally massacres the retreating troops who surrendered in good faith.

War films depicting graphic inhuman acts subsided during the 1920s and early 1930s until the coming of World War II. That global bloodbath witnessed the greatest outpouring of atrocities in fact and in film. Many dramas and documentaries showed Japan and Germany inflicting torture and death upon civilians and war prisoners.

In *China* (1943), for example, Japanese

troops brutally ravish a young Chinese student, a gruesome reminder of the wholesale rape suffered by the people of Nanking following its capture by the Japanese in December 1937. Japanese soldiers torture American prisoners of war in *The Purple Heart* (1944) before sentencing them to death. The film was based on stories that filtered out of Japanese-held territories of atrocities practiced upon prisoners. *Back to Bataan* (1945) re-enacted the infamous Death March forced upon captured American and Filipino troops by the Japanese. Some Japanese military leaders were tried and executed after World War II for directing or condoning atrocities against captured civilians and members of the armed forces.

American films gave even greater exposure to Nazi atrocities. The documentary *Hitler's Reign of Terror* (1934), a harbinger of the ordeal that would engulf Europe during the next decade, included footage of Jews being tortured. Atrocities were usually ascribed to the dreaded Gestapo. *Beasts of Berlin* (1939), the first Hollywood feature to openly attack Nazi atrocities, described the Gestapo's brutal methods and the inhuman treatment of prisoners in Hitler's concentration camps. Such films as *Edge of Darkness* (1943) and *The Moon Is Down* (1943) revealed the suffering that Norwegians had to endure under German occupation. *The North Star* (1943) told of Nazi atrocities in Russia, including the use of Russian children's blood for wounded German soldiers. *Hangmen Also Die* (1943) and *Hitler's Hangman*, released the same year, depicted the cruelty of the hated Reinhardt Heydrich, known as the Hangman, who plied his trade in Czechoslovakia before he was assassinated. James Cagney in *13 Rue Madeleine* (1946) perhaps best exemplified the merciless torture to which captured American agents were subjected by the Gestapo.

Post-World War II films of the holocaust focused more sharply on the horrors perpetrated by Hitler's Germany upon the innocent. *The Diary of Anne Frank* (1959), taken from the published diary of a young death camp victim, concerns the lives of a family of Dutch Jews living in hiding and includes actual footage taken at the infamous death camps. *Judgment at Nuremberg* (1961), directed by socially conscious Stanley Kramer, questioned individual responsibility for war crimes ordered by the state as victims of ster-

ilization and other medical experiments testify before the tribunal. *The Pawnbroker* (1965), a disturbing film directed by Sidney Lumet, blended the present life of an embittered Holocaust survivor (Rod Steiger) living in New York with flashbacks of his experiences during the war. One of many disturbing scenes shows a crowded trainload of Jews journeying to the inevitable gas chambers; in another, Steiger is forced to watch the rape of his wife by a Nazi official. Alan J. Pakula's *Sophie's Choice* (1982) offered a sensitive study of a Polish-Catholic survivor of the Nazi death camp at Auschwitz who is forced to choose which of her children will survive. Several World War II combat dramas made after the conflict included atrocity sequences. In Edward Dmytryk's *The Young Lions* (1958), based on Irwin Shaw's novel, Marlon Brando, as a disillusioned German officer, stumbles upon a concentration camp and is revolted by what he discovers. The film hints at the possibility that not all Germans knew of or condoned the barbaric practices of the Nazis. Writer-director Samuel Fuller related some of his own World War II experiences in *The Big Red One* (1980). Mark Hamill, as a foot soldier, is reluctant to kill the enemy until he witnesses a Nazi concentration camp and its pitiful survivors hastily abandoned by the retreating Germans. He finds a German hiding in one of the ovens and empties his weapon into the soldier. *The Executioners* (1961), one of several documentaries about Nazi atrocities, traced the careers of the principal defendants in the Nuremberg Trials.

Only a few films about the Korean War dramatized the brutal treatment American prisoners suffered under the yoke of their Communist captors. About half the Americans captured by the Communists perished in captivity. In *Prisoner of War* (1954), featuring Ronald Reagan, captives are subjected to beatings and torture and, on occasion, are killed. The film was based on actual interviews of former prisoners and documented evidence of Communist North Korean atrocities. In *The Manchurian Candidate* (1962) Communist Chinese officials brainwash American prisoners of war to become assassins. In one particularly shocking scene, a hypnotized prisoner, following orders, kills a fellow captive.

Vietnam War films such as the Rambo series, starring Sylvester Stallone, and some of the action dramas of Chuck Norris, concentrated on the horrors inflicted upon American servicemen captured by the Viet Cong. In *The Deer Hunter* (1978) one scene shows three American soldiers, boyhood friends, who are captured by the Communists and forced to engage in the deadly game of Russian Roulette while their captors bet on the outcome. Although this exact incident may not have occurred during the conflict, it served as a metaphor for the depravations of captivity and the insanity of war.

However, by 1970, a major shift began to take place in the portraying of film atrocities. The barbarous acts no longer deal only with a foreign enemy. Combat dramas began to examine the actions of American troops. For example, *Soldier Blue* (1970), based on the infamous Sand Creek Massacre of 1864, focused on the carnage U.S. soldiers inflicted upon the American Indian. The U.S. Cavalry wantonly attacks a Cheyenne village in spite of the Indian chief's attempt to surrender by holding out a white flag of truce and the Stars and Stripes. After killing the Braves, the soldiers engage in rape, mutilation and scalping, and end by annihilating the women and children.

American atrocities have been further explored in Vietnam War films. *Apocalypse Now* (1979) includes an American helicopter raid on a suspected enemy village that results in the machine-gunning and bombing of civilians, many of them children. In *Platoon* (1986) a squad of American grunts, after suffering through an attack by an elusive enemy, brutalize the inhabitants of a Vietnamese village that the soldiers believe is harboring and aiding enemy guerrillas. The film incident echoes the 1968 My Lai massacre.

War films with atrocities are no longer conventional propaganda films that seek to arouse hatred toward a foreign enemy. They have emerged as a more frank and realistic mirror of events. By dramatizing atrocities committed by Americans, these films have contributed to self-criticism and a re-examination of a nation's values. They try to point out that war is the true enemy because it dehumanizes all those involved. War creates an atmosphere that is conducive to atrocities by unleashing the capacity to commit these dark acts that is within us all. ■

Attack! (1944), Office of War Information.

A documentary depicting the American assault and capture of the Japanese-held island of New Britain in the South Pacific, the hour-long film provides realistic details of every phase of the operation. Members of the U.S. Army Signal Corps show close-ups of the G.I.s, their equipment and their weapons. The camera follows the men from their intricate training, to their landing and to their battles with the Japanese deep in the jungle. The island assault, the film points out, was a combined effort of the navy, air force and infantry. ■

Attack! (1956), UA. *Dir.* Robert Aldrich; *Sc.* James Poe; *Cast includes:* Jack Palance, Eddie Albert, Lee Marvin, Robert Strauss, Richard Jaeckel, Buddy Ebsen.

A stinging World War II drama about corruption and cowardice among officers, the film is relentless in its presentation of its theme and realistic portrayals. A cowardly captain who fails to support his lieutenants during the Battle of the Bulge is murdered by his own men in this gritty tale. Eddie Albert portrays a spineless officer who freezes with fear when he is called upon to back up his men; they are needlessly killed in battle because of his actions. Jack Palance, as the next lieutenant about to embark on a similar assignment, tries to get Albert relieved of his command. But the colonel in charge (Lee Marvin), who is from Albert's home town, sees a possible political and financial advantage for himself after the war in protecting the captain. Instead of acting upon Palance's advice, he reassigns the unit to a safer zone. But the enemy attacks that position, and Palance is forced to lead his men in defense. He threatens to personally kill Albert if the captain doesn't help him. "I'll shove this grenade down your throat and pull the pin," he warns the cowardly officer. When Albert again acts true to form, Palance returns mortally wounded but collapses before he can keep his promise. Another lieutenant then kills the weak captain.

The production has several shortcomings. At times, it seems overly melodramatic. It also betrays its stage origins (from a play by Norman Brooks) with its limited sets. However, the few action sequences are graphically presented. The film has gained a reputation as a singularly gutsy war drama released during the generally passive Eisenhower years. ■

Attack on the Iron Coast (1968), UA. *Dir.* Paul Wendkos; *Sc.* Herman Hoffman; *Cast includes:* Lloyd Bridges, Andrew Keir, Sue Lloyd, Maurice Denham.

A Canadian officer leads a perilous raid on a German naval base on the French coast in this World War II action drama. Lloyd Bridges stars as a major in charge of training a squad of Commandos for the above special mission given the name Operation Mad Dog. Lloyd comes under pressure when he learns that a previous raid failed, resulting in the deaths of many Commandos. The team starts out as scheduled, but Lloyd and his men don't get the promised air cover as they cross the channel. The film, a conventional war story, has enough suspense and action sequences to sustain it in spite of its slower portions. ■

Attila the Hun. See *Sign of the Pagan* (1954). ■

Auction of Souls (1919), Selig. *Dir.* Oscar Apfel; *Sc.* Nora Wain, Frederic Chapin; *Cast includes:* Irving Cummings, Aurora Mardiganian, Anna Q. Nilsson, Howard Davies, Hector Dion.

A terrifying dramatization of the 1915 Armenian massacre, the film shows in many graphic sequences the brutal atrocities carried out by Turkish troops upon the Armenian civilian population, chiefly the elderly and children. The drama employs a conventional plot to tell the story of the horrors. Irving Cummings portrays the hero who performs a series of courageous deeds. The film, originally titled *Ravished Armenia*, is based on the life of Aurora Mardiganian, the sole survivor of a family of seven. She plays the role of heroine. Henry Morganthau appears as himself.

The savagery depicted on the part of the Turks so stirred the film critic of *Variety* that he concluded his review with these words: "If (the film) may be given credit for the removal of Turkey from the map of the world, it will have have helped in part to avenge Armenia. . . ." ■

Austin, Stephen (1793–1836). By bringing American settlers into Mexico's northern state of Texas, he started a chain of events that led first to a successful revolt for Texan independence, followed shortly by the region's annexation by the U. S. A boundary dispute involving the newly admitted area brought on the Mexican-American War which resulted in the United States gaining much of our southwest and California.

A native of Virginia, Stephen Austin grew up in Missouri where he served in the territorial legislature from 1814–1820. His father Moses Austin secured permission in 1821 from Spanish authorities, then in control of Mexico, to populate a land grant in Texas with American settlers, but the older man died before carrying out the proposal. Stephen continued the plan and organized the first settlement of Americans between the Colorado and Brazos Rivers in 1822. He reconfirmed the conditions of the grant in 1823 with the authorities of newly independent Mexico.

American colonization expanded rapidly during the remaining 1820s, but friction soon developed between the settlers and Mexican authorities. Austin, at first, opposed the idea of independence and even went to Mexico City in 1833 to try to secure more home rule for American settlers. The authorities jailed him on grounds of treason. Upon his release in 1835, he became one of the leaders of the drive for independence and an opponent of Mexican leader General Santa Anna, whose policy was to crush the growing revolt in Texas.

During the revolution, Austin served as one of the Texas commissioners sent to Washington to procure aid from the United States government. He lost his bid for the presidency of independent Texas in 1836 to Sam Houston and served briefly, until his death later that year, under Houston as Secretary of State.

Surprisingly, although he played such an important role in the founding of Texas, there is no film with Austin as the central character. He appeared only incidentally in action dramas concerning the Texas revolt, as in *Heroes of the Alamo* (1938) and *The First Texan* (1965), basically a biography of Sam Houston. In fact, Hollywood, for some unexplained reason, rewrote history by taking Austin's part as a peace-seeking representative to the Mexican government before the outbreak of war and attributing it to James Bowie in *The Last Command* (1955). ■

"Australia at War" (1941). See "The March of Time." ■

Australian convict revolts. See *Captain Fury* (1939). ■

Austrian Succession, War of the. See *A Celebrated Case* (1914). ■

A kamikaze pilot is about to strike a U.S. Navy attack transport. *Away All Boats* (1956).

Austro-Italian Wars. See *The Lady In Ermine* (1927). ▪

Away All Boats (1956), U. *Dir.* Joseph Pevney; *Sc.* Ted Sherdeman; *Cast includes:* Jeff Chandler, George Nader, Julie Adams, Lex Barker, Keith Andes.

A U.S. Navy attack transport provides the subject of this World War II drama. Jeff Chandler, as its heroic captain, takes command of the *Belinda* as it leaves the shipyard. Burdened with an inexperienced crew and officers, Chandler quickly begins a series of strict training exercises to prepare those under his command for battle. "Failing to remember the past," an officer recalls, quoting Santayana, "we seem doomed to repeat it." George Nader portrays a former captain in the U.S. Merchant Marines who gives up commanding his own vessel to become a lieutenant in the regular navy. Lex Barker, as a lax officer who in the beginning shirks his duties, proves himself under fire. The film traces the exploits of the ship and its crew through several battles and invasions, including Makin and Okinawa, and a harrowing kamikaze attack. Chandler is mortally wounded during the battle and dies aboard the vessel. "All of us are better than we thought we could be because of what he gave us," an officer eulogizes. "And we'll go home again because of him." ▪

AWOL (1972). See Vietnam War. ▪

B

Back at the Front (1952). See *Up Front* (1951). ■

"Back Door to Tokyo" (1944). See "The March of Time." ■

"Back From the Front" (1943). See War Humor. ■

Back to Bataan (1945), RKO. *Dir.* Edward Dmytryk; *Sc.* Ben Barzman, Richard Landau; *Cast includes:* John Wayne, Anthony Quinn, Beulah Bondi, Fely Franquelli, Richard Loo.

A World War II action drama of American and Filipino guerrillas battling the ruthless Japanese after U.S. forces are compelled to leave, the film stars John Wayne as an American colonel who stays behind to help organize native resistance against the invaders. The heroic fighters have more in common with the Americans than with the Japanese, who try to persuade the Filipinos that the U.S. is their enemy. The guerrillas are shown contributing substantially to the defeat of the Japanese when American troops land at Leyte. Anthony Quinn, as a passionate Filipino patriot, sees his sweetheart turn collaborator in this routine war yarn. Vladimir Sokoloff, as a local native schoolteacher, dies at the hands of the Japanese when he refuses to lower the American flag outside his school house. The film contains several effective sequences, including the infamous Death March forced upon captured American and Filipino troops by the Japanese. It is during this tragic march that resulted in the deaths of numerous prisoners that Wayne rescues Quinn from the prisoners.

The film is an interesting blend of fact and fiction. It re-enacts several actual incidents besides the Death March, one of which includes the liberation of the Cabanatuan prison camp where, among others, American soldiers, sailors and marines were held as prisoners of war. Some of these men were later used in the production of the drama. ■

Back to Life (1925). See Veterans. ■

Background to Danger (1943). See Spy Films: the Talkies. ■

Balaklava, Battle of. See *Charge of the Light Brigade* (1936); Crimean War. ■

Balkan Wars (1912–1913). See *The Captive* (1915). ■

Bamboo Blonde, The (1946), RKO. *Dir.* Anthony Mann; *Sc.* Olive Cooper, Lawrence Kimble; *Cast includes:* Frances Langford, Ralph Edwards, Russell Wade, Iris Adrian.

A New York nightclub singer becomes the inspiration for an American B-29 bomber crew in this bland World War II musical comedy drama. When army pilot Russell Wade is seen by his crew with singer Frances Langford, the men decide to paint her picture on their plane. They ship out that night for overseas duty in the Pacific where, in a short time, they gain a reputation for destroying the most Japanese planes and ships. The national publicity of the heroic crew of the bomber, "The Bamboo Blonde," propels Langford into stardom. The story is told in flashback by Ralph Edwards, who plays the nightclub owner where Langford got her start. He is now involved in a lucrative business selling "Bamboo Blonde" products. ■

Bamboo Prison, The (1954), Col. *Dir.* Lewis Seiler; *Sc.* Edwin Blum, Jack DeWitt; *Cast includes:* Robert Francis, Dianne Foster, Brian Keith.

This Korean War film suggests that some American prisoners of war held by the Communists and who turned collaborator were actually agents working for the U.S. Government. The story takes place during the peace negotiations at Panmunjon. Robert Francis portrays one such U.S. intelligence agent at a prison camp who is despised by his fellow inmates for cooperating with the enemy. Brian Keith plays another prisoner and fellow spy. E.G. Marshall portrays a Communist who masquerades as a priest in the camp to spy on the prisoners. One of the earliest Korean War films to explore the fate of American prisoners of war, the drama suggests one of the major differences between this conflict and World War II. Americans were confronted with torture and brainwashing by the North Koreans; dissension arose among the prisoners as some suspected others of going over to the enemy. After the war, some were accused of collaborating with the Communists. ■

Bandido (1956), UA. *Dir.* Richard Fleischer; *Sc.* Earl Felton; *Cast includes:* Robert Mitchum, Ursula Thiess, Gilbert Roland, Zachary Scott, Henry Brandon.

Strife-torn Mexico circa 1916 serves as the setting for this action drama of gun runners, rebels and Mexican troops. Robert Mitchum, as a mercenary gun runner, promises to deliver an arms shipment to rebel leader Gilbert Roland. Mitchum intends to steal the guns from a rival arms merchant played by Zachary Scott. He also manages to take Scott's dissatisfied wife (Ursula Thiess) away from his competitor. The revolutionaries finally obtain their guns after a violent battle in this leisurely paced tale that deals superficially with the ideologies and politics of the Mexican Revolution. ■

"Barbara Frietchie" (1908), Vitagraph. *Dir.* J. Stuart Blackton; *Sc.* Liebler; *Cast includes:* Julia Arthur, Edith Storey, Earle Williams.

John Greenleaf Whittier's famous poem about the game old gal who defended the Stars and Stripes appeared on the movie screen in no less than four different versions. This one was the first and starred Julia Arthur, a popular stage actress of the period. J. Stuart Blackton, an experimental producer-director, had given the fledgling film industry its first war film in 1898, a work entitled "Tearing Down the Spanish Flag," which concerned the Spanish-American War and ran for less than one minute. A second adaptation of the Whittier poem was released in 1911 by Champion. Little is known about this film. ■

Barbara Frietchie (1915), Metro. *Dir.* Clarence J. Harris; *Sc.* Clarence J. Harris; *Cast includes:* Mary Miles Minter, Mrs. Thomas W. Whiffen, Guy Coombs.

This adaptation of Clyde Fitch's stage version of John Greenleaf Whittier's popular poem starred the young actress, Mary Miles Minter, as the granddaughter of the strongheaded and brave old woman who shook the American flag in the face of Stonewall Jackson and his troops as they marched through her town. Veteran stage actress Mrs. Thomas Whiffen plays the title role in this screen version. There were two earlier silent screen adaptations of the poem. Vitagraph produced one in 1908 and Champion released its version in 1911. ■

Barbara Frietchie (1924), PDC. *Dir.* Lambert Hillyer; *Sc.* Agnes Christine Johnson; *Cast includes:* Edmund Lowe, Florence Vidor, Emmett King, Joe Bennett, Charles Delaney.

With John Greenleaf Whittier's poem and Clyde Fitch's stage play as its inspiration, this fourth film version tells the immortal story of the courageous woman who grasps her country's flag to her bosom and, from her window, defends it against the bullets of Stonewall Jackson's invading army. In this romantic drama Trumbull pledges his love to Barbara who lives in Frederick, Maryland. But when the Civil War erupts, he joins the Union army. Later, as a captain, he returns with his troops and saves the life of Barbara's brother. The Confederates then attack and drive the Union soldiers out. Barbara, thinking the captain killed, mounts the American flag at half mast in front of her house just as General Stonewall Jackson comes riding by. She utters her immortal words. Then suddenly a soldier fires and wounds her in the shoulder. When the war ends, she marries the captain. The scene then switches to 1917 with the grandson of the couple marching off to fight in the trenches of France.

It is interesting to note the obvious embellishments to the original poem. Fitch was forced to add the love story and other events so that he had a full-length play, while the writers of the film version decided to update the story to the twentieth century with the introduction of World War I. None of the four interpretations could diminish the strength and courage of Whittier's title character. ■

Barbarous Mexico (1913) State Rights. *Sc.* H. Hood.

A documentary covering the early stages of the Mexican Revolution (1910–1921), the film includes Francisco Madero's abortive revolt against dictator Porfirio Diaz, his flight to the U.S. and his eventual triumphant return and military victory. Other scenes show a hand grenade assault, Madero's capture of the city of Juarez and his inauguration as president. One sequence depicts American troops on guard in Texas. ■

Barbary Pirate (1949), Col. *Dir.* Lew Landers; *Sc.* Robert Libbot, Frank Burt; *Cast includes:* Donald Woods, Trudy Marshall, Lenore Aubert, Stefan Schnabel.

An army officer is sent to Tripoli to help stop Barbary pirates from attacking American shipping in this drama set in the days following the American Revolution. Donald Woods portrays the gallant hero who allows himself to get caught, cultivates a friendship with Yusof, the Bey of Tripoli (Stefan Schnabel), and uncovers the traitor in Washington who has been supplying the pirates with information concerning the cargo of American ships. Trudy Marshall, whom Woods rescues, provides the romantic interest. The low-budget film contains a fair amount of action as Woods battles his way to freedom.

Although characters and incidents are completely fictitious, the plot is based on historical events. Barbary pirates did indeed prey upon American as well as European shipping. The U.S. paid annual tributes to several North African Muslim states for safe passage, but the piracy continued, resulting in the Tripolitan War of the early 1800s. See Tripolitan War. ■

Barbary pirates. See Tripolitan War, Stephen Decatur. ■

Barbed Wire (1927), Par. *Dir.* Rowland V. Lee, Erich Pommer; *Sc.* Jules Furthman; *Cast includes:* Pola Negri, Clive Brook, Elinar Hanson, Claude Gillingwater.

A French farm girl falls in love with a German prisoner of war, causing anger among her neighbors, in this World War I romantic drama. Pola Negri portrays the young heroine who has lost a brother in the war. Her once-happy community now becomes the site of a prisoner-of-war camp where she meets and falls for one of the inmates (Clive Brook). When they decide to marry, the other villagers are shocked and enraged at her decision. After the war, her brother, who was thought to have been killed, returns home sightless. "I came home to my own people to find peace," he says. "Instead I find bitter hatred in your hearts—a hatred strong enough to start another war." His pleas to accept the German touch the community. Claude Gillingwater portrays Negri's father.

The film was one of several made after the armistice that attempted to soften the image of the German from a bestial figure bent on rape and pillage to a sympathetic soul misled by power-hungry leaders. Brook, as the German prisoner, describes to the heroine how his people suffered almost as much as the French. The original novel, published in 1923, was written by Hall Caine, who considered himself a pacifist although he upheld the Allied cause. The original story is set on the Isle of Man. The couple, unable to cope with the hatred aimed at them by others in the community, commit suicide. Loyal civilians of German heritage are forced to leave their homes and sent to Germany. Also changed in the film is anything that would appear anti-British. ■

Barricade (1939), TCF. *Dir.* Gregory Ratoff; *Sc.* Granville Walker; *Cast includes:* Alice Faye, Warner Baxter, Charles Winninger, Arthur Treacher, Keye Luke, Willie Fong.

Chinese bandits threaten the lives of Americans in this action drama set in the East. Bewildered American citizens seek safety in a consulate compound when native outlaws rise up in strife-torn China. The besieged group consists of a dance-hall girl (Alice Faye) who is on the run from the law, a foreign correspondent (Warner Baxter) and character actor Charles Winninger as the consul. They are ultimately rescued by the Chinese army after Baxter and Faye elude the attackers and telegraph for help in this minor film. See also Chinese civil wars. ∎

Bastogne, Battle of. See Battle of the Bulge. ∎

Bat 21 (1988), Tri-Star. *Dir.* Peter Markle; *Sc.* William C. Anderson, George Gordon; *Cast includes:* Gene Hackman, Danny Glover, Jerry Reed, David Marshall Grant.

Gene Hackman portrays an American intelligence officer whose plane is shot down somewhere over Vietnam in this war drama. As Lt. Col. Iceal Hambleton, whose only knowledge of the Vietnam War has come from behind a desk or at 30,000 feet above the conflict, Hackman soon experiences some of the truths about the war. Landing in the hostile jungle, he must learn to avoid enemy patrols. He witnesses the terrible effects of napalm upon its victims. He is forced to shoot an incensed villager who attacks him with a machete. For the first time in his long career in the military he witnesses the deaths of fellow Americans. His two-way radio allows him to remain in contact with his eventual rescuer (Danny Glover). The title refers to the downed officer's code name. Based on a book by William C. Anderson, the film recounts the actual experiences of Hambleton who had to survive for several days before being rescued by a black air force captain who honed in on the colonel's radio signal. ∎

Bataan. A peninsula west of Manila Bay, Bataan became the scene of fierce fighting early in World War II when U.S. and Filipino troops unsuccessfully attempted to repel the invading Japanese. The defenders, under the command of General MacArthur, withdrew south on December 24, 1941, where they hoped to stop the enemy. The Japanese pressed their advance on January 9, despite heavy losses. MacArthur was ordered to leave in March. General Wainwright, the new commander, faced with a critical lack of supplies and renewed attacks, was compelled to surrender in April. The emaciated prisoners were then mercilessly forced to march 60 miles to a prison camp, many dying along the way. The incident became known as the Bataan death march. The sacrifice of the de-

fenders prevented Japan from using Manila Bay for several months.

Embattled Bataan has been the subject of several dramas. The most notable film, MGM's glossy production of *Bataan* (1943), is discussed below. *Cry Havoc* (1943), about a group of volunteer nurses on Bataan before its fall, points out the brutality of the Japanese who repeatedly bomb a hospital. In *So Proudly We Hail!* (1943) another group of heroic nurses suffer through the siege of Bataan. In *Back to Bataan* (1945) American and Filipino guerrillas battle the ruthless Japanese after U.S. forces are driven out. John Wayne, as an American colonel, stays behind to help organize native resistance against the invaders. The infamous death march is recreated in one sequence. In *I Was an American Spy* (1951) Ann Dvorak plays the title role based on the true experiences of Claire Phillips during World War II. The film opens with the fall of Manila to the Japanese. When Mrs. Phillips' husband is killed during the Bataan death march, she joins a band of guerrillas. ∎

Bataan (1943), MGM. *Dir.* Tay Garnett; *Sc.* Robert D. Andrews; *Cast includes:* Robert Taylor, George Murphy, Thomas Mitchell, Lloyd Nolan, Lee Bowman, Robert Walker, Desi Arnaz.

Thirteen American soldiers are selected to delay the advance of Japanese troops in this World War II drama about the fall of Bataan. The conventional Hollywood platoon, composed of various ethnic types from different backgrounds, battles bravely although heavily outnumbered. As each soldier dies, he is buried by the others until only one remains, a sergeant, played by Robert Taylor. After digging his own grave, he mans a machine gun and fires away at the hordes of attacking Japanese as the film fades out. The drama transcends others of the same genre in certain respects. This was one of the earliest war entries in which a black soldier, played by Kenneth Spencer, appears on equal footing with other fighting men. Also, the characters are fully developed, thereby adding to the dramatic impact of seeing each soldier fall in battle. Young Robert Walker makes his film debut as a sailor who stays behind to help the doomed men fight the Japanese. It is his words in a letter to his mother that gave impetus to the sacrifice of the troops on Bataan for millions of Americans back home: "It don't matter where a man dies so long as

Lee Bowman, Robert Taylor, George Murphy (standing, l. to r.) and a handful of other Americans prepare to slow down a Japanese advance. *Bataan* (1943).

he dies for freedom." Lloyd Nolan plays the part of a rugged private with a shady background while Thomas Mitchell portrays a Jewish corporal. Desi Arnaz, who was later to gain fame as Lucille Ball's husband, is a young, happy-go-lucky Hispanic-American from California.

Critics acclaimed the film's realism when it was first released. Subsequent viewings reveal flaws in this assessment. Aside from the obvious back-lot studio set, some of the battle sequences are poorly staged. In one Japanese attack upon the small handful of defenders, for example, wave after wave of the enemy is annihilated. Suddenly, for no reason, the five or six Americans rise from their cover and advance into the dense jungle to engage the overwhelming force of Japanese in hand-to-hand combat. When they return, only two Americans have fallen. This sequence probably rated high as propaganda when the film was released, but it strains plausibility. ∎

"Battle, The" (1911), Biograph. *Dir.* D. W. Griffith; *Sc.* D. W. Griffith; *Cast includes:* Blanche Sweet, Robert Harron, Charles West, Donald Crisp.

Another in director D. W. Griffith's early series of short Civil War dramas, the film concerns a young coward who is inspired by his sweetheart to perform acts of heroism. As a battle rages near the home of the young woman (Blanche Sweet), the young soldier (Robert Harron) recoils in fear and darts into her quarters seeking shelter. Her mocking laughter at his spineless behavior gives him the necessary impetus not only to rejoin his unit but volunteer to go for much-needed supplies. Although the journey is perilous, he manages to accomplish his mission. Griffith directed dozens of one- and two-reel films during his stay with Biograph, eleven of which had Civil War backgrounds. Made between 1908 and 1912, the films were shot chiefly in New Jersey. Several of them contained characters and incidents that were to reappear in his 1915 epic masterpiece, *The Birth of a Nation*. ∎

Battle and Fall of Przemysl, The (1915), American Correspondent Film Co.

A documentary film, the scenes depict the German and Austrian-Hungarian advance in North Galicia and upon the city. Shots of the big guns smashing the defenses of the Czar's troops, hand grenades being tossed and men dying from a barrage of bullets bring the reality of the battle and the war in general to the spectator. This was one of the earliest American documentaries to deal with the Great War. Other similar works came to these shores from France and England.

The Austrian army tried desperately to rescue the fortress city of Przemysl, which was under siege by the Russians. After 194 days its garrison of 110,000 troops surrendered on March 22, 1915, to the Russians who then organized a counteroffensive. By early May the Austro-German armies not only halted the Russian assault but but broke through the enemy defenses. The fortress was retaken on June 3. It was this second phase of the battle that the documentary depicted in part. ∎

Battle at Apache Pass, The (1952), UI. *Dir.* George Sherman; *Sc.* Gerald Drayson Adams; *Cast includes:* John Lund, Jeff Chandler, Beverly Tyler, Bruce Cowling, Susan Cabot.

Conflict erupts between the U.S. Army and the Apaches in New Mexico territory at the time of the Civil War when a corrupt Indian Affairs adviser stirs up Geronimo. The belligerent Indian chief is the leader of the Mogollons, one segment of the Apaches. John Lund, as a burdened major, tries to keep the uneasy peace. Jeff Chandler, as Cochise, is the leader of the Chiricahuas, the more passive faction of the Apaches. He ends up in a hand-to-hand combat with Geronimo, driving the bellicose leader into exile. Susan Cabot plays the home-loving wife of Cochise.

Following the trend-setting *Broken Arrow* (1949) which presented a fair and sympathetic picture of the plight of the Indians, director George Sherman and screenwriter Gerald Adams attempted a similar in-depth study of the abuses suffered by the Apaches at the hands of unscrupulous whites. However, the routine plot weakened the overall effect. ∎

Battle at Bloody Beach (1961), TCF. *Dir.* Herbert Coleman; *Sc.* Richard Maibaum, Willard Willingham; *Cast includes:* Audie Murphy, Gary Crosby, Dolores Michaels, Alejandro Rey.

Filipino guerrillas battle the Japanese troops who have occupied their islands in this World War II action drama. Audie Murphy, as a free-lance adventurer, sells arms to the resisters. Murphy manages to rescue a handful of Americans from the Japanese. Meanwhile, a romantic triangle develops when his wife (Dolores Michaels) becomes involved with a guerrilla leader, played by Alejandro Rey. Gary Crosby, as Murphy's partner, is killed during the course of events in this routine story. Producer and co-screenwriter Richard Maibaum went on to write several of the early James Bond films. ∎

Battle Circus (1953), MGM. *Dir.* Richard Brooks; *Sc.* Richard Brooks; *Cast includes:* Humphrey Bogart, June Allyson, Keenan Wynn, Robert Keith.

Humphrey Bogart portrays an experienced army surgeon in the Mobile Army Surgical Corps during the Korean War in this routine drama. Between sequences in which he is patching up the wounded, he has a romance with an idealistic, self-sacrificing nurse, played by June Allyson. She arrives with a new team of nurses and immediately catches Bogart's eye. Keenan Wynn, as a former circus employee, is in charge of striking and setting up the mobile hospital. The film contains several realistic action sequences, especially those showing the wounded being picked up by helicopter crews who work under fire at the front line. The Mobile Army unit, as screen material, was used more effectively as the background for the black comedy, M*A*S*H, two decades later. ∎

Battle Cry (1955), WB. *Dir.* Raoul Walsh; *Sc.* Leon Uris; *Cast includes:* Van Heflin, Aldo Ray, Mona Freeman, Nancy Olsen, James Whitmore.

This World War II drama of a group of U.S. Marines focuses more on the private, sexual lives of the men and their women than on the battles they fought in the Pacific. Van Heflin,

Audie Murphy leads Filipino guerrillas against Japanese troops during World War II. *Battle at Bloody Beach* (1961).

as a tough, battle-hardened major, molds his troops, including the principal characters, into an effective fighting unit. James Whitmore plays a no-nonsense master sergeant in the outfit. Aldo Ray, as a ladies' man and former logger, and Nancy Olsen, as a New Zealand widow, find love in the midst of war. Tab Hunter, as another marine, ends up with the girl he left behind (Mona Freeman) although he has an affair with a married woman (Dorothy Malone) in San Diego. The film, based on the novel by Leon Uris, provides several realistic battle sequences among its many clichés. ■

Battle Cry of Peace, The (1915), Vitagraph. *Dir.* Wilfred North, *Sc.* J. Stuart Blackton; *Cast includes:* Charles Richman, Norma Talmadge, L. Roger Lytton, James Morrison, Mary Maurke, Louise Beaudet.

Based on the book *Defenseless America* by Hudson Maxim, this propaganda film extolling the values of preparedness resulted in a sensation at the box office, numerous public debates and a lawsuit between producer J.

Stuart Blackton and industrialist Henry Ford. The drama consists of five parts: "The Warning," "The Invasion," "In the Hands of the Enemy," "The Price" and "The Remedy." The inflammatory story begins with Mr. Vandergriff, a peace advocate, and John Harrison, who fancies Vandergriff's daughter. He tries to explain to the father that disarmament is wrong, but the older man disregards the warning. Later, while the father officiates at a pacifist meeting, foreign vessels appear off shore and shell New York City, which falls to the invaders. Troops swarm through the city, their uniforms not unlike those of German soldiers. Civilians who resist are slaughtered, and young women are rounded up and locked away for the pleasures of the soldiers. The film relies heavily on spectacular aerial shots of New York, scenes of the enemy fleet, the bombardment of the city, brutal acts by the invaders and the use of allegorical sequences for its overall effect. Blackton, for the final part, was able to enlist the appearances of actual political and military leaders. The personal story adds a human element and contributes to the horror of the invasion, especially the scene in which a mother realizes the impending fate of her two daughters. She shoots them and then goes mad.

Part of the controversy that stalked this preparedness film involved Maxim, the author of the book, who was related to the family that manufactured the Maxim machine gun. Charges quickly rose that the movie was designed to promote munitions sales. Blackton, an advocate of America's entry into the Great War, helped to stifle the voices for peace. Henry Ford, a peace activist, paid for full-page advertisements in several newspapers condemning the film for promoting war hysteria. Conversely, the film was endorsed by the Red Cross, the Army and Navy Leagues, the National Security League and the American Legion. In his unpublished autobiography Blackton states that Theodore Roosevelt, a strong advocate of preparedness, used his influence to help in the production of the work. Roosevelt persuaded Major General Wood, an army commander, to "lend" Blackton 2,500 marines. ■

Battle Flame (1959), AA. *Dir.* R. G. Springsteen; *Sc.* Elwood Ullman; *Cast includes:* Scott Brady, Elaine Edwards, Robert Blake, Wayne Heffley.

The Korean War provides the background for this action drama concerning a rescue mission behind enemy lines. When a group of American nurses is captured by North Korean soldiers, Scott Brady, as a marine lieutenant, leads his men into action and manages to rescue the young women. Elaine Edwards, as one of the captives, also provides the romantic interest who has to choose between the heroic Brady and a navy surgeon to whom she is engaged. This routine film intermixes several stock action sequences with other specific battle shots related to the plot. ■

"Battle for the Marianas, The" (1944), U.S. Marine Corps.

A two-reel documentary produced by the Marine Corps, the film depicts the various stages of battle which resulted in the capture of the Marianas by U.S. forces. There are scenes of marine landings, dive bombers hitting enemy installations and flame throwers clearing out the more stubborn enemy from caves and crevices. Included are combat sequences on Saipan, Tinian and Guam. The film was shot by combat photographers—six of whom died during the battle. ■

Battle Hymn (1956), U. *Dir.* Douglas Sirk; *Sc.* Charles Grayson, Vincent B. Evans; *Cast includes:* Rock Hudson, Martha Hyer, Dan Durea, Don DeFore, Anna Kashfi.

Based on the actual events in the life of Colonel Dean Hess, a fighter pilot and clergyman, this Korean War drama stars Rock Hudson as Hess. The pilot has never shaken the nightmare of his accidental bombing of a German orphanage during World War II. Hess volunteers during the Korean War to train pilots. Later, he airlifts 1,000 Korean orphans to safety. The film interjects suspenseful and exciting action sequences with human interest scenes. Martha Hyer portrays his understanding wife. Anna Kashfi, as a Korean heroine, is killed while helping Hess to save the children. ■

Battle of Blood Island (1960), Filmgroup. *Dir.* Joel Rapp; *Sc.* Joel Rapp; *Cast includes:* Richard Devon, Ron Kennedy.

Two American soldiers, the sole survivors of a failed invasion of a Japanese-held Pacific island, learn a lesson in tolerance in this weak drama set during World War II. Forced to take cover after their unit is annihilated, the two G.I.s (Richard Devon and Ron Kennedy) hide out in a cave. Later, they witness a mass suicide by the Japanese who learn that they have lost the war. The Americans then begin to turn on each other. Kennedy, in frustration, calls Devon a "lousy Jew." Instantly regretting his outburst, he shoots himself in his arm. They are then rescued by an American ship. The incident of anti-Semitism seems to come about too suddenly for the film to be an effective character study of a bigot, unless the author intended to suggest that bigotry remains dormant in the heart of each of us. ■

Battle of Britain (1943), U.S. Army. *Sc.* Col. Frank Capra.

Another documentary in the U.S. government's series titled "Why We Fight," and produced and supervised by Frank Capra, the film describes the life-and-death struggle of Great Britain in its air war against Germany's Luftwaffe. As Hitler flew superior numbers of planes against England's embattled R.A.F., the stalwart Britons displayed their bulldog courage and tenacity as they held out to eventually break the back of the German Air Force. British airmen, heavily outnumbered, flew their Spitfires against German fighter planes and bombers, inflicting heavy losses upon the enemy. Failing to knock out the R.A.F. or destroy England's air bases, Germany decided to weaken the country's will to fight by bombing London. Again Germany suffered heavy air losses. Hitler's next move was to send his bombers over by night. Although London and other cities were severely damaged, the English were determined to carry on. The film provides previously unseen footage as well as captured Nazi films while Walter Huston and others furnish the narration. The documentary ends with Winston Churchill's famous tribute to the gallant British fliers: "Never in the field of human conflict was so much owed by so many to so few."

The Battle of Britain was a crucial one not only for the nation, but for the Allies as well. England's holding out and tying up of Germany's air force was one of the factors that led to Italy's capitulation to the Allies. The six-week air war cost Britain 40,000 deaths and 50,000 wounded. The R.A.F., outnumbered 10 to 1, fought hard, and together with anti-aircraft batteries, destroyed more than 3,000 Axis planes. Hitler's plan for the destruction of England met the same fate as his once-glorious air force. ■

Battle of Bull Run, The (1913). See American Civil War. ■

Battle of China, The (1943), U.S. Army. *Dir.* Frank Capra, Anatole Litvak; *Sc.* Anthony Veiller.

An almost epic World War II documentary of China's struggle against Japan, the film traces the history of one of the oldest civilizations from its beginnings to the mid-1940s. The film details most of the important events in China's battle against Japan, including the latter's occupation of Manchuria in 1931 and invasion in 1937 north and south of Shanghai. Japan then proceeded to bomb the city, killing thousands of civilians. "The Japanese," the narrator announces, "introduced the world to a new kind of war—a war of deliberate terrorization, deliberate mass murder . . ."

Hampered by a lack of unity, obsolete weapons and a poorly trained army, China was forced to retreat westward across the Yellow River while its better-equipped enemy overran cities and provinces. The film shows the fall of the strategic city of Nanking, where 40,000 men, women and children were murdered. Captured Japanese newsreels show some of the atrocities committed by the invading forces. But the rape of Nanking united China. The nation mobilized; it exchanged land for time. Scenes show the mass migration of its people as 30 million Chinese moved west, taking with them their culture and their machinery.

Other highlights point out the contributions of General Chennault and his Flying Tigers—Americans flying in defense of war-scarred China; the building of the Burma Road by the Chinese people; the Japanese bombing of Pearl Harbor; and, finally, a major Chinese victory at Changsha where the Japanese suffered a terrible blow.

The film mentions Japan's attack upon and sinking of a U.S. gunboat, the *Tanay*, in the late 1930s, for which it later apologized. Also mentioned several times is the infamous Tanaka Memorial, a secret Japanese document formulated in the 1920s which outlines Japan's plan for the conquest of China and the Pacific. "In order to conquer the world," it stated, "we must first conquer China." The film ends with Madame Chiang Kai-shek's address to the U.S. Congress. "We in China, like you," she explains, "want a better world—not for ourselves alone, but for all mankind, and we must have it."

The documentary has been criticized by some for presenting a less than complete picture of the Chinese political situation during the Sino-Japanese War. It omitted, for example, all references to Chinese Communist forces who also fought the enemy. However, it remains an outstanding testament to the will and spirit of the Chinese people who stood alone for so many years against such overwhelming odds. ■

Battle of Gettysburg, The (1914), Mutual. *Dir.* Thomas Ince; *Sc.* C. Gardner Sullivan; *Cast includes:* Willard Mack, Charles French, Enid Bennett, Herschal Mayall.

In the longest film of the Civil War released up to this date, the one-hour drama focuses almost entirely on the famous three-day battle. A romantic subplot is introduced early in this silent film, but it is subordinated to the main theme of the grim reality of war and death. The incidents may not be entirely accurate, but the overall effect, with its scenes of slain soldiers and animals and the movements of troops, brings a sense of horror as it suggests what the conflict must have been like to its participants. ■

"Battle of Gettysburg, The" (1936). See Gettysburg, Battle of. ■

"Battle of Midway, The" (1942), U.S. Navy.

A documentary depicting the bloody air, sea and land battles that resulted in victory for U.S. forces over those of Japan, the film was produced for the U.S. Navy under the supervision of director John Ford, who was commissioned as lieutenant commander by the service. The grim war scenes show a Red Cross hospital being hit by Japanese planes, wounded pilots and G.I.s hurried to dressing stations, enemy ships hit or sunk and scores of Japanese planes shot down. The battle for Midway resulted in the loss of four Japanese aircraft carriers, the damage of 28 other warships and the destruction of 300 enemy planes. ■

Battle of Paris, The (1929). See Musicals. ■

Battle of Russia (1943), U.S. Army. Col. Sc. Frank Capra.

Another entry in the U.S. Government's "Why We Fight" series of documentaries supervised by Hollywood director Frank Capra, the film depicts the history of Russia from the time of Alexander Nevsky until the heroic defense of Stalingrad. Using footage from the U.S. Signal Corps, captured newsreels, Russian sources and historical dramas, the film underscores the united effort of the Soviet people and the reasons for their sacrifice. Excerpts from Sergei Eisenstein's 1939 Russian film *Alexander Nevsky* underscore that country's determination to resist all invaders. The theme of the drama—"He who comes with the sword shall perish by the sword"— spoken by the charismatic Nevsky, develops into the theme of *Battle of Russia*. Sweden in the 1700s, France under Napoleon in the 1800s and Hitler's Germany all tried to conquer the vast Russian lands, and all were defeated, suffering heavy losses.

The film covers Hitler's attack on Russia on June 22, 1941, the defenders' scorched earth policy, guerrilla warfare and the battles for Moscow, Leningrad and Stalingrad. The heroic defense of these cities is emphasized. Graphic scenes show the hardships the defenders endure. Eventually the Red Army is seen counterattacking and driving the Germans back. They inflict heavy losses on the enemy and capture thousands of prisoners, including several generals. An obvious work of propaganda indicative of the documentaries of the period, the film makes no mention of the Hitler-Stalin nonagression pact of August 1939. Dimitri Tiomkin prepared the musical score that was played by the Army Air Force band. See also "Why We Fight." ■

"Battle of San Pietro, The" (1945), U.S. Signal Corps. *Dir.* John Huston.

A half-hour World War II documentary made by director John Huston while he served as a major with the U.S. Signal Corps, the film brings home to American audiences the realism and brutality of the conflict. The film deals with the Fifth Army's assault on San Pietro, a small Italian town, in December of 1943. After a narrator explains the strategic importance of the town, the cameras join the U.S. infantrymen as they move in for the attack. Huston concentrates on the faces of the G.I.s during combat. Following the actual battle scenes, the cameras show the stunned faces of the inhabitants who greet the weary American soldiers. Many critics single out the film as the best documentary to come out of World War II. ■

Battle of Shiloh, The (1913). See Shiloh, Battle of. ■

Battle of the Bulge (1965), WB. *Dir.* Ken Annakin; *Sc.* Philip Yordan, Milton Sperling, John Nelson; *Cast includes:* Henry Fonda, Robert Shaw, Robert Ryan, Dana Andrews, Pier Angeli.

A highly fictionalized drama of the pivotal battle that helped to end World War II, the film is a series of sprawling action sequences including tank engagements, bombardments and skirmishes as well as personal human dramas. Henry Fonda stars as an American colonel who tries to convince his superiors of an impending German offensive. Dana Andrews, as an arrogant general, and Robert Ryan portray the top brass who question Fonda's judgment until the German counterattack breaks through American defenses in the Ardennes sector and throws the U.S. forces into disarray.

A banner spells out one of the ironies of war as U.S. troops, caught unaware, face a German offensive. *Battle of the Bulge* (1965).

Robert Shaw, as Colonel Hessler, commander of the German offensive, portrays the consummate warrior—cool under pressure, resourceful, calculating, fascinated by tactics and strategy and disdainful of his superiors who attempt to manipulate him from behind their desks. He delights in trying to outmaneuver his adversaries. The film depicts him as a proud, natural leader hampered by incompetence from above. In the end, the Germans are forced to retreat. The tank battles dominate the action sequences as the superior German Tiger tanks subdue their American counterparts. Other highlights include those in which English-speaking Germans masquerade as G.I.s. They switch signposts, salvage bridges from destruction for the German tanks to cross and create general mayhem for the retreating Americans. ∎

Battle of the Bulge—The Brave Rifles, The (1966), Mascott. *Dir.* Lawrence E. Mascott; *Sc.* Lawrence E. Mascott.

A documentary of the historic World War II battle in which Nazi Germany desperately at-

tempted to halt the Allied advance, the film uses actual footage gathered from both sides of the conflict. Fighting in the areas of the Belgian Ardennes, Eisenborn, St. Vith and Bastogne is highlighted. Lawrence Mascott, who took part in the battle, focuses on some of the Americans who performed heroically as the narrator relates each individual's story. But this is not a romantic treatment of war; the grimness and fury of the battle dominate almost every sequence as the Americans struggle to contain the German breakthrough. ∎

Battle of the Coral Sea, The (1959), Col. *Dir.* Paul Wendkos; *Sc.* Daniel Ullman, Stephen Kandel; *Cast includes:* Cliff Robertson, Gia Scala, Teru Shimada, Patricia Cutts.

Members of an American submarine crew, on a reconnaissance mission in the Pacific, are captured by the Japanese in this World War II action drama that takes place on the eve of the important sea battle in the title. The seamen gather photographic evidence of enemy warships, but before they can return

A tense moment aboard a U.S. aircraft carrier during a Japanese air attack. *Battle Stations* (1956).

to their base they are caught and forced to surrender. While held on the island, three of the officers manage to escape in a Japanese torpedo boat. Cliff Robertson portrays the submarine captain. Gia Scala provides the romantic interest. Teru Shimada, as the enemy commandant, displays sympathy for his captors but does not allow his feelings to interfere with his duty and loyalty in this low-budget film. ■

Battle Stations (1956), Col. *Dir.* Lewis Seiler; *Sc.* Crane Wilbur; *Cast includes:* John Lund, William Bendix, Keefe Brasselle, Richard Boone.

Life aboard an aircraft carrier during World War II forms the basis for this routine drama that offers little in the way of action. Richard Boone, as the demanding captain, is dedicated to repeated drills of the men under him. John Lund portrays the vessel's chaplain. William Bendix plays the robust chief bos'un. Battle sequences in the Pacific against the Japanese come chiefly from old newsreels and documentaries. ■

Battle Taxi (1955), UA. *Dir.* Herbert L. Strock; *Sc.* Malvin Wald; *Cast includes:* Sterling Hayden, Arthur Franz, Marshall Thompson, Leo Needham.

United Artists salutes the U.S. Air Rescue Service in this Korean War drama. Sterling Hayden portrays the commander of an air rescue squadron of helicopters. Aside from impressing upon his crews that their major job is to save the lives of downed pilots, he has to contend with a few members who resent their non-combatant role, preferring instead to battle the enemy. Arthur Franz, as an ex-jet pilot who has been assigned to Hayden, must discover the hard way that his commander is right. The film, devoid of any female players and made with the cooperation of the Department of the Defense, relies too heavily on newsreel and documentary footage for its action sequences. ■

Battle Zone (1952), AA. *Dir.* Lesley Selander; *Sc.* Steve Fisher; *Cast includes:* John Hodiak, Linda Christian, Stephen McNally, Martin Milner.

A tribute to the combat photographers of the U.S. Marines during the Korean War, the film stars John Hodiak as a member of this group of cameramen who has re-enlisted. He and his buddy, played by Stephen McNally, are assigned to photograph enemy installations behind North Korean lines. Romantic interest is supplied by Linda Christian, as the former sweetheart of Hodiak and the recent interest of McNally. Hodiak, when not engaged in military duties, attempts to rekindle their old flame. Battle sequences include newsreel footage as well as those created in the studio. ■

"Battlefields of the Pacific" (1942). See "The March of Time." ■

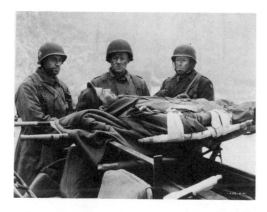

John Hodiak, Van Johnson and George Murphy grimly watch as a wounded comrade is driven away during the Battle of the Bulge. *Battleground* (1949).

Battleground (1949), MGM. *Dir.* William A. Wellman; *Sc.* Robert Pirosh; *Cast includes:* Van Johnson, John Hodiak, Ricardo Montalban, George Murphy, Marshall Thompson.

This World War II drama pays tribute to the men who stopped the Nazis at Bastogne in the famous Battle of the Bulge. Known affectionately as the "battling bastards of Bastogne," these stalwart G.I.s figured the war would be over by Christmas of 1944. Instead, they found themselves surrounded by the enemy. But they held their ground against overwhelming odds and stopped the German advance.

As in most war films of this type, the fictional part of the battle focuses on a group of weary infantrymen from all walks of life who gripe, chase the French girls and talk about their postwar dreams. Van Johnson, as an easygoing, likable soldier, takes time out to woo Denise Darcel. George Murphy, as an old-timer who is discharged, finds himself a civilian in the midst of the German counterattack. John Hodiak, as a cynical newspaperman, enlisted after reading and believing his own columns. James Whitmore's portrayal of a seasoned sergeant won him critical acclaim. The film focuses in on a paratroop company whose division (the 101st Airborne) is trapped during the Germans' daring attack. Some of the more striking sequences include the enemy's dressing up in American uniforms to confuse and infiltrate Allied positions and the brutal killing of American troops who surrendered to the Germans. Some veterans of the actual battle were quick to point out that the marching song highlighted in the film was never sung in that sector or during the period of the battle. It was during this encounter that General McAuliffe's famous reply, "Nuts," was given to the German commander who requested the surrender of the American troops. The drama, shot entirely within a studio, has been singled out for introducing a "new realism" in war films and as partially responsible for reviving the popularity of the war drama. Robert Pirosh won an Oscar for his screenplay.

Gen. Anthony C. McAuliffe (1898–1975), acting division commander (General Maxwell Taylor was absent on leave), received wide praise for his defense of Bastogne. Encircled by German troops, he was presented by enemy messengers on December 22 with an ultimatum to surrender or suffer "annihilation." He at first responded orally, then put his answer on a note which read: "To the German Commander: Nuts! —The American Commander." The German officer who sought the American surrender and received instead the now famous reply was General Heinrich von Luttwitz. ■

Battles of a Nation, The (1915), American Correspondents Film Co. *Dir.* Albert K. Dawson; *Sc.* Tom Bret.

A World War I documentary showing the advance of German and Austrian-Hungarian troops in North Galicia, the film depicts the fall of Lemberg and Warsaw. Highlights consist of the big guns blazing at the fortressed cities, aerial reconnaissance planes in action and the miles of provisions stored and waiting to be devoured by the German war machine. This was one of the earliest American documentaries concerning the war. The European nations involved in the conflict, acutely aware of the power of motion pictures, were already turning out official propaganda newsreels and documentaries as early as 1914. ∎

Battles of Chief Pontiac (1952), Realart. Dir. Felix Feist; Sc. Jack De Witt; Cast includes: Lex Barker, Helen Wescott, Lon Chaney, Berry Kroeger, Roy Roberts.

An inept action drama set during the French and Indian War, the plot concerns skullduggery on the part of a harsh Hessian mercenary. While the British are attempting to negotiate a peace treaty with Chief Pontiac (Lon Chaney), the Hessian officer (Berry Kroeger) wants to kill off the Indians by introducing smallpox to the tribe. His plan backfires, and he suffers the fate he plotted for the native Americans. Lex Barker, as a Ranger lieutenant, is assigned the task of making peace with Pontiac.

Although the film is chiefly fictitious, the incident in which whites deliberately sent blankets infested with smallpox germs to some Indian tribes is historically accurate. Contrary to the film, Pontiac was a staunch ally of the French and hoped by aligning his warriors with them, he could drive the British and colonists off his lands.

Pontiac, who died in 1769, was chief of several tribes, including the Chippewa and Ottawa. He fought against the British in the French and Indian War (1754–1763) and after, until 1766, when peace was negotiated. This three-year postwar conflict, known as Pontiac's Rebellion, was an attempt on the chief's part to regain lost territory from the British lost by the French. The Ottawas, under Pontiac's command, captured nearly all the British forts from Pennsylvania to Lake Superior. Pontiac and his braves were eventually defeated in 1766. ∎

Bavu (1923), U. Dir. Stuart Paton; Sc. R. L. Shrock, A. G. Kenyon; Cast includes: Wallace Beery, Estelle Taylor, Forrest Stanley, Sylvia Breamer, Joseph Swickard.

A drama of the early days of the Russian Revolution, the film centers on Bavu (Wallace Beery), an illiterate and brutish peasant who rises to the rank of treasurer of the revolutionary forces. He incites the mob to loot a city so that he can line his own pockets. Meanwhile, Mischa (Forrest Stanley), a more noble soul who is also appointed as an official of the Revolution, saves the life of Princess Annia (Estelle Taylor) from the violent masses. Before the Revolution, he had worked for her family. Mischa loves her and helps her to escape across the border while Bavu, who follows them and wants the princess for his own purposes, perishes in his lustful pursuit. ∎

Fear grips three U.S. marines after they land on a Japanese-held Pacific island. *Beach Red* (1967).

Beach Red (1967), UA. Dir. Cornel Wilde; Sc. Clint Johnston, Donald A. Peters, Jefferson Pascal; Cast includes: Cornel Wilde, Rip Torn, Patrick Wolfe, Jean Wallace.

A war-hating captain leads his men in battle on a Japanese-held island in this grim action drama set during World War II. Cornel Wilde stars as the officer, a lawyer in civilian life who reluctantly has left his wife. After a series of skirmishes with the enemy in which his unit loses several men, he muses: "I'll have a lot of letters to write."

Rip Torn, as a sadistic sergeant and foil to the captain, enjoys the war, especially the killing. When Wilde learns that Torn has broken both arms of a prisoner, he is outraged. "Was it necessary to break both arms?" the captain asks. "I'm a marine," the sergeant replies. "I'm gonna kill those bastards, I'm gonna shoot them, I'm gonna bayonet them, I'm gonna break their arms . . . That's what we're here for—to kill. The rest is just crap." Wilde's only reply is that he doesn't want the young men in his command to become professional killers.

Wilde, who also directed the work in a

war-is-hell style, inserts several stark scenes that show severed limbs and men dying in agony. There are plenty of battle sequences, including a beachhead landing by the marines and the strafing and bombing of a Japanese platoon caught in the open by American planes. The film switches back and forth from the marines to the Japanese soldiers who, through flashbacks, are depicted as having the same thoughts of home and their families as those of the American troops. ■

Beachhead (1954), UA. *Dir.* Stuart Heisler; *Sc.* Richard Alan Simmons; *Cast includes:* Tony Curtis, Frank Lovejoy, Mary Murphy, Eduard Franz, Skip Homeier.

In this routine action film set on a Pacific island near Bougainville during World War II, four marines are assigned to contact a French planter (Eduard Franz) who has a detailed map of Japanese minefields near the above island that the Americans plan to invade. The information will save thousands of lives. Frank Lovejoy, as a sergeant who has lost a platoon at Guadalcanal and is constantly reminded of the incident by a handful of survivors, leads Tony Curtis and two other leathernecks through terrain swarming with Japanese troops. After several exciting and suspenseful skirmishes with the enemy in which two marines are killed, Lovejoy and Curtis find the planter and his young daughter (Mary Murphy) who soon becomes the object of the two soldiers' rivalry.

The action scenes are generally satisfactory, but the implausible romantic triangle detracts from the basic plot. The dialogue is often trite, especially when it was designed to be tough. "It's a long war," Curtis utters for no particular reason. "Everybody dies." The planter's daughter, who has lived on the island most of her life, confides to Curtis: "I always dreamed that someday a boy would come by and take me away."

Bougainville, the largest of the Solomon Islands, was invaded by the Japanese in World War II. The United States, deciding that the island was strategically important as a potential base in which to carry out its air war against Japan, sent in the Third Marine Division on November 1, 1943. Three bomber and two fighter fields were eventually built. The island was finally secured by Australian troops in 1945. ■

"Beachhead to Berlin" (1944), WB.

A two-reel World War II documentary, the film depicts the U.S. Coast Guard in action during the invasion of Normandy. Scenes show how the Coast Guard participated in transporting troops and supplies across the channel to the assault beaches. Other scenes show the removal of the wounded and dead. The film, produced and released by Warner Brothers, was shot by combat photographers of the Coast Guard. ■

Bear Flag Republic Revolt (1846). About a thousand American settlers, attracted by the fertile soil of California—then part of northern Mexico, had taken up residence there by 1845. U. S. President Polk, in that year, even offered to pay $25 million for the territory, an offer the Mexican government refused. Polk and many Americans, however, continued to covet the area as part of America's 19th century dream of "Manifest Destiny," a philosophy of expansion to the Pacific coast.

During the Mexican War (1846–48), a small band of Americans in California under explorer Captain John Fremont revolted against Mexican control and briefly set up an independent nation called the Bear Flag Republic on June 14, 1846, at Sonoma. The following month an American naval force, under Commodore John Sloat, captured California's capital, Monterey, from the Mexicans and claimed the whole territory for the U.S. Mexico formally ceded California in 1848 as part of the peace settlement ending the war. The film *Kit Carson* (1940) with Jon Hall as the title character and Dana Andrews as Fremont, gives a highly fictional account of the revolt. *The Californian* (1937), features Ricardo Cortez as a Robin Hood type hero who protects the rightful landowners from eastern land-grabbing villains after the state is annexed to the Union. ■

Beast of Budapest, The (1958), AA. *Dir.* Harmon C. Jones; *Sc.* John McGreevey; *Cast includes:* Gerald Milton, John Hoyt, Greta Thyssen.

The unsuccessful Hungarian revolt of 1956 provides the background for this drama of resistance. The film attempts to trace the developments that led to the uprising, depicting those who fought against the oppressive regime and others who helped crush the revolt. Gerald Milton portrays the title role, head of the dreaded secret police. His job is to collaborate with the Russians and maintain an iron fist on the Hungarian populace. Violet Rensing, as an ardent Communist who likes the son of a liberal professor, allows her politics to interfere with their relationship. The film uses newsreel footage of the Russian tanks quelling the revolt. ■

Beasts of Berlin (1939), PDC. *Dir.* Sherman Scott; *Sc.* Shepard Traube; *Cast includes:* Roland Drew, Steffi Duna, Greta Granstedt, Alan Ladd, Lucien Prival, Vernon Dent.

A strong anti-Nazi drama, one of the earliest to be released during the early days of World War II, the film tells of a group of German underground resisters who struggle against the Nazi party in their land. There are scenes showing the brutal methods that the Gestapo employs to gather information, break men's spirits and terrorize in general. Other sequences describe the inhuman treatment of prisoners in Hitler's concentration camps. The plot of the film itself does not equal the importance of its message—that of a national policy of brutality that at first jars and then angers the conscience of decent and compassionate people.

The film was originally titled *Goose Step*—the title of Shepard Traube's novel from which it was adapted, then *Hitler—Beast of Berlin*, before it assumed its present title. Producers Distributing Corporation, a new kid on the block, scheduled this drama as its first release. To avoid controversy, the studio softened the title to the final one. This, however, was only the beginning of its problems. Fearing an outcry from the numerous German Bund branches in the nearby states, the New York board of censors decided to ban the film. The company was forced to delete some material before the ban was lifted. When the drama finally premiered in New York, the critics, surprised at its candor, praised its outspokenness and avoided pointing out its weak plot elements and other deficiencies such as its inept German locales. Despite its faults, it was the first Hollywood feature to openly attack the Nazi techniques and atrocities that later were to become a familiar mainstay of World War II propaganda films. ■

Beau Geste (1926), Par. *Dir.* Herbert Brenon; *Sc.* John Russell, Paul Schofield; *Cast includes:* Ronald Colman, Neil Hamilton, Ralph Forbes, Alice Joyce, Mary Brian, Noah Beery, William Powell.

Percival Wren's popular novel has been faithfully translated to an absorbing adventure drama in this first of several adaptations. Ronald Colman, as Beau Geste, one of three brothers, protects the family honor by stealing a counterfeit diamond. He then joins the French Foreign Legion, which is currently facing a Tuareg uprising in North Africa. His brothers soon follow in his tracks. Complications develop when Boldini, a villainous fellow Legionnaire, overhears the three discuss the diamond. The sergeant of the regiment learns of the precious stone and plots to steal it for himself. Meanwhile, hordes of Arabs attack the fort, and in the battle that ensues Beau is killed. Later another brother sacrifices his life so that the third member of the family can return to the English estate safely. Amid the complicated plot, the film provides plenty of action of desert warfare while the story has become a minor adventure classic. See also Empire Films. ■

Beau Geste (1939), Par. *Dir.* William A. Wellman; *Sc.* Robert Carson; *Cast includes:* Gary Cooper, Ray Milland, Robert Preston, Brian Donlevy, Susan Hayward, J. Carrol Naish, Albert Dekker.

This remake closely follows the plot of the 1926 silent version of Wren's story. Gary Cooper plays the stalwart and tight-lipped Beau Geste while Ray Milland and Robert Preston portray his brothers who follow him into the ranks of the Foreign Legion. Brian Donlevy, who received an Academy Award nomination for his role as a particularly nasty sergeant, props up the bodies of slain Legionnaires into fighting position to mislead the attacking Arabs. The film retains the same grim opening of a deserted fort manned only by corpses before the flashback begins. Other adaptations followed through the years, but this version is considered by many as the best. See also Empire Films. ■

Beau Geste (1966), U. *Dir.* Douglas Heyes; *Sc.* Douglas Heyes; *Cast includes:* Guy Stockwell, Doug McClure, Leslie Nielsen, Telly Savalas.

Guy Stockwell portrays the title role in this third and weakest version of the Percival Wren story about brotherly love. Stockwell, accepting the blame for a crime of which he is innocent, enlists in the Foreign Legion. His brother, John (Doug McClure), follows him into the service. They both fall under the control of a deranged sergeant (Telly Savalas) whose sadistic nature is shown by his inhuman treatment of the soldiers in his company. The remainder of the film follows the familiar plot, including desert battles with the warring Tuareg tribe and the slaughter of all the defenders of Fort Zinderneuf. Several changes in the original story have been made. Digby, the third brother, has been omitted, and the nationality of the Gestes has been altered from English to American. See also Empire Films. ∎

Beau Ideal (1931), RKO. *Dir.* Herbert Brenon; *Sc.* Paul Schofield; *Cast includes:* Ralph Forbes, Loretta Young, Lester Vail, Frank McCormack, Don Alvarado, Irene Rich.

A sequel to *Beau Geste* and based on Percival Wren's characters and story, the film centers on John Geste, once again played by Ralph Forbes, whom we meet as a prisoner incarcerated in a desert dungeon for fallen Legionnaires. Lester Vail portrays Otis Madison, an American who was a childhood friend of the Geste boys. Madison has joined the Foreign Legion to find John Geste to tell him that Isobel Brandon loves him and not Madison. The film contains several desert battles before Geste is freed and the two friends sail for England.

Herbert Brenon, the director who also turned out the original silent version of *Beau Geste* in 1927, tried to establish himself as a director of sound features with the above entry. But the film showed a loss at the box office and was judged the studio's worst production of the year. ∎

Beau Sabreur (1928), Par. *Dir.* John Waters; *Sc.* Tom Geraghty; *Cast includes:* Gary Cooper, Evelyn Brent, Noah Beery, William Powell, Mitchell Lewis.

Gary Cooper stars in this quasi-sequel to *Beau Geste.* (Cooper would appear in his own version of *Beau Geste* in 1939.) Again based on the writings of Percival Wren, the film takes place in the Algerian desert where Cooper, a major in the French Foreign Legion, is assigned the task of implementing a treaty to prevent an impending native insurrection. William Powell, as a former Legionnaire, is inciting the natives while Evelyn Brent, as an American writer, is seeking local color for her novels. The film has limited action sequences. ∎

Bedford Incident, The (1965). See Cold War. ∎

Bedknobs and Broomsticks (1971). See Musicals. ∎

Beggar of Cawnpore, The (1916), Triangle. *Dir.* Charles Swickard; *Sc.* C. Gardner Sullivan; *Cast includes:* H.B. Warner, Lola May, Wyndham Standing, H.E. Entwhistle.

With the Indian Mutiny of 1857–1858 as background, the drama presents a series of intrigues as well as colorful battles between the rebellious sepoys (Indian soldiers) and British troops. H.B. Warner portrays a physician in the employ of the British East India Service. During a cholera epidemic at a remote outpost, he takes morphine when he comes down with fever. He later discovers that he is addicted to the drug. Cashiered from the service, he becomes one of the numerous beggars of Cawnpore. When the sepoy rebellion erupts, he rescues his former sweetheart (Lola May) and conquers his addiction. ∎

Behind the Door (1919), Par. *Dir.* Irvin Willat; *Sc.* Luther Reed; *Cast includes:* Hobart Bosworth, Jane Novak, Wallace Beery, James Gordon.

Hobart Bosworth stars in this World War I tale of revenge. He marries Jane Novak against her father's wishes. When war is declared, he enlists and is made a captain in the U.S. Merchant Marine. He takes his wife, disguised as a nurse, aboard his vessel. A German submarine torpedoes his boat, and he and his wife find refuge on a small raft. The commander of the U-boat takes the wife aboard, leaving the husband to the elements. Bosworth swears revenge upon the commander. Days later he is rescued and eventually gets command of another vessel which he uses to hunt down the submarine. By luck, he is able to find the U-boat and sink it. He pulls the commander out of the water and takes him to his cabin where the man is tricked into telling how he ravished the young wife who died soon after. He then threw the body into the sea. The husband reveals himself and exacts his revenge upon the commander.

The story is told by the use of a flashback. The husband, a broken old man, runs a dilapidated shop. At the end of the narrative he sees an apparition of his beautiful bride. His own spirit rises from his body and joins her in an embrace. The film is considered the first realistic description of submarine warfare. ∎

Behind the Enemy Lines (1945), Globe.

A World War II documentary, the film is a compilation of captured German and Japanese footage. Scenes from German cameramen include the invasions of Poland and Russia while those taken by Japanese photographers depict the attack on Pearl Harbor, the fall of Corregidor and various scenes of the bombing and destruction of Chinese villages. The hour-long film also shows the bombing of Tokyo by American airmen and the burning of Berlin. ∎

Behind the Front (1926), Par. Dir. Edward Sutherland; Sc. Ethel Doherty; Cast includes: Wallace Beery, Raymond Hatton, Mary Brian, Richard Arlen, Chester Conklin.

In this World War I comedy Wallace Beery and Raymond Hatton portray a pair of army recruits and friendly enemies who have been duped into joining up. A girl who wants to help her brother meet his quota of volunteers gives her photograph to a score of men and promises to be each one's sweetheart if they sign up. Beery, a not-too-bright cop, and Hatton, a small-time pickpocket, decide to put aside their rivalry and become buddies while in the army. This sloppy-looking pair of doughboys arrive in France and immediately begin chasing the local women. Eventually they are shipped to the trenches where they continue their misadventures, all the time suffering at the hands of their cruel sergeant. In one particular sequence Beery confronts his former butcher, now a German soldier. He pays the man the few dollars he owes him and then witnesses the butcher's death. The war finally ends and they return home. This gives them the opportunity to get revenge on their sergeant in a funny sequence. When Beery discovers that Hatton has stolen his pocket watch, he begins to chase his former army buddy as the picture draws to a close.

Not truly a film comedy team in the fashion of Abbott and Costello or Laurel and Hardy (Beery and Hatton had separate careers before and after this feature and made only a few films together), they did to some degree anticipate the teams to come and did make one of the earliest war comedies featuring a comedy team. The film was so successful that they were called upon to appear in two sequels, We're in the Navy Now, released the same year, and Now We're in the Air, released one year later. In the latter, a runaway circus balloon takes the pair into enemy territory. When they return to their own lines, they are picked up as spies and barely escape execution. ∎

Behind the Lines (1916), Bluebird. Dir. Henry McRae; Sc. Walter Woods; Cast includes: Harry Carey, Edith Johnson, Ruth Clifford.

Harry Carey, more familiar to his contemporary audiences as a western hero, portrays a doctor in this silent drama. The background concerns the United States-Mexican border disputes that made headlines at the time of the film's release. Although the American physician is dedicated to his profession, he soon finds himself entangled in the border fighting. Edith Johnson provides the romantic interest. The film combines battle sequences and diplomatic manipulations into a suspenseful tale.

Tensions between the U.S. and Mexico began in 1913 when, between September 5–7, several marines landed at Ciaris Estero to help evacuate Americans and other foreigners during Mexico's civil strife. The situation escalated into open hostilities by 1914 and continued until 1917, with Pancho Villa's raids across the border in 1916 and Pershing's punitive expedition into Mexico that same year. ∎

Behind the Rising Sun (1943), RKO. Dir. Edward Dmytryk; Sc. Emmett Lavery; Cast includes: Margo, Tom Neal, J. Carrol Naish, Robert Ryan, Gloria Holden.

This World War II drama, set chiefly in Japan, focuses on a Japanese family before and after the attack on Pearl Harbor. J. Carrol Naish portrays a newspaper publisher with important ties to government officials who rises to minister of propaganda. He believes in his country's aspirations of world conquest. His U.S.-educated son (Tom Neal), on the other hand, has many American friends and defends the American way of life. But in time he is indoctrinated with Japan's imperialistic ideas. He returns from the war against China as a strong supporter of his country while his father suspects Japan will be defeated by the U.S. Neal, reassigned as a pilot, goes to his death defending Japan against American planes during a raid over Tokyo. His father, disillusioned with Japan's political and military aims, takes his own life. Of his son's death, he writes: "To have died without reason is to have lived without reason." Of his own misguided life, he concludes: "One cannot build honor upon dishonor."

The film describes a host of Japanese atrocities. Chinese civilians are brutalized, and their children forced into slave labor. Captured American civilians and pilots receive similar treatment. Many of the incidents depicted on the screen were based on a factual book written by James R. Young, a foreign correspondent for the International News Service and stationed in prewar Tokyo. One of the more interesting aspects of this wartime drama is its depiction of some Japanese, represented by Neal's father and Neal's ex-fiancee (Margo), who are opposed to their country's goals of conquest. ■

Behold a Pale Horse (1964), Col. *Dir.* Fred Zinnemann; *Sc.* J. P. Miller; *Cast includes:* Gregory Peck, Anthony Quinn, Omar Sharif, Raymond Pellegrin.

Gregory Peck portrays a former guerrilla fighter in the Spanish Civil War of the late 1930s. Although it is twenty years later, he continues to fight the war with forays into Spain from France. A disheveled, tired old warrior, Peck is lured into a trap when a disdainful police captain, played by Anthony Quinn, sends out word that Peck's mother is dying. Although the woman's priest, during a journey to France, warns Peck about the police captain's trap, the old soldier decides to visit his mother. Peck realizes his struggle is in vain, but he carries on with a nobility envied by his adversary who ponders why Peck ever returned. Omar Sharif portrays the youthful priest who must choose between his own morality and the law. The film contains some actual footage of the war to help establish the background. ■

Belgian, The (1917), Olcott Players. *Dir.* Sidney Olcott; *Sc.* Frederic Arnold Kummer; *Cast includes:* Walker Whiteside, Valentine Grant, Arda La Croix, Sally Crute.

A romantic drama set prior to the German invasion of Belgium, the film tells the story of two Belgian innocents—a fisherman and his sweetheart—who fall prey to enemy agents. Walker Whiteside portrays the young fisherman whose talent for sculpture takes him to Paris where he falls for the charms of a countess who is a German spy. Meanwhile, back in his village, Valentine Grant, as his girlfriend, becomes involved with the local postmaster, who is also a German agent. When World War I erupts and the Germans invade Belgium, the sculptor enlists in the Belgian army to defend his country and is wounded. Hospitalized and on the verge of losing his eyesight, he pines for the countess, unaware that the nurse caring for him is his sweetheart. When he regains his sight, he realizes the true meaning of love.

The film is more significant for its brutal battle sequences and scenes of German atrocities committed against the Belgian people than for its romantic story. This was only one of many propaganda features to appear during the war that depicted the ruthlessness of the German soldier toward Belgium, a nation that was martyred by the Allies for its struggle against the enemy. ■

Bell for Adano, A (1945), TCF. *Dir.* Henry King; *Sc.* Lamar Trotti, Norman Reilly Raine; *Cast includes:* John Hodiak, William Bendix, Gene Tierney, Roman Bohnen, Montague Banks.

A poignant World War II drama of the American occupation of Adano, a small Italian town, the film depicts the struggle of a sensitive major (John Hodiak) to win the hearts and minds of the natives. The townspeople, after years of Fascist indoctrination, are distrustful of the Yanks. However, Hodiak manages to introduce them to the rudiments of democracy when he obtains what they want most—a bell. This is no easy matter, since he has to clash with the top brass. Gene Tierney plays a young Italian woman whom Hodiak falls in love with while William Bendix and Henry Morgan provide the comic relief. Richard Conte has an interesting role as a cynical, realistic American G.I. who has witnessed the death of another soldier. When the girl who knew the dead man asks if his last thoughts were of her, Conte replies that the soldier simply cried out for his mother. The simple story is a tribute to human decency. The film, based on a popular novel by John Hersey, contains several changes from the original work, most of them minor. But wartime propaganda still prevailed when this film was made, so that any derogatory references to members of the American forces were quickly censored. Therefore, one major alteration occurs in reference to a brutal American general who appears in the novel. In the film, the general terms "brass" or "higher-ups" substitute for the character. ■

Beloved Enemy (1936), UA. *Dir.* Henry C. Potter; *Sc.* John Balderston, Rose Franken, David Hart, William B. Meloney; *Cast includes:* Merle Oberon, Brian Aherne, Karen Morley, Jerome Cowan, Henry Stephenson, David Niven.

A romantic drama set during the Irish Rebellion of the 1920s, the film stars Merle Oberon as the titled daughter of a British dignitary and Brian Aherne as a noble leader of the Irish rebels. An idyllic but implausible love affair of the two principals, the "beloved enemies" of the title, develops until British troops follow the unsuspecting Oberon and surround Aherne's quarters. The rebel chief leads the soldiers in a lively chase across rooftops as he makes his getaway. More implausibility occurs when the heroine influences the British to make peace with the rebel forces. This is accomplished, but when Aherne returns to his people he is mortally wounded by one of his own men (Jerome Cowan) who is convinced that the leader has sold out the revolution. Aherne dies in his lover's arms in a Dublin drugstore.

The film was supposedly based on the events surrounding the Irish leader Michael Collins. His negotiations with English representatives resulted in the creation of the Irish Free State. But his compromise, which left four northern counties under the control of the British, resulted in the belief of some of his men that he betrayed them. ■

Ben Hur (1926, 1959). See Sea Battles. ■

Bengal Brigade (1954), U. *Dir.* Laslo Benedek; *Sc.* Seton I. Miller; *Cast includes:* Rock Hudson, Arlene Dahl, Torin Thatcher, Arnold Moss, Daniel O'Herlihy.

This action film takes place in 1856 in India. Rock Hudson, as a captain in the British army, is in charge of a unit of sepoys, or Indian soldiers. During a battle against rebel forces, his own men fall into a trap. He leads a charge to free them, deliberately disobeying orders to retreat. Following a court martial in which he is reprimanded, he resigns his commission in disgust. Later, during an uprising of the Indian soldiers against the British, Hudson, now a civilian, rescues his former colonel (Torin Thatcher) and the colonel's daughter (Arlene Dahl). He also foils a general rebellion.

One disconcerting flaw in the structure of the film is that the major battle occurs in the opening scenes. All other action sequences, therefore, seem anticlimactic. A routine action feature with stock characters, the film takes itself too seriously.

In reality, the Indian Mutiny of 1857–58 was not brought under control until the British employed a large army against the sepoys and fiercely punished those they considered rebels. One of the causes of the revolt was the Indian soldiers' objections to biting open the British cartridges that were greased with animal fats. This was brought out in the film by the colonel who confides to Hudson: "The first cartridges that were made for the new rifles were greased with a concoction of beef and pork fat. As the Hindus considered themselves damned if they eat beef and the Moslems are no better off if they eat pork, with one master stroke of stupidity we very nearly succeeded in alienating the entire Indian army." Other causes, such as the abuses of the East India Company, are not discussed in the film. See also Empire Films, Indian Mutiny of 1857–58. ■

Berlin airlift. See Cold War. ■

Berlin Correspondent (1942). See Spy Films: the Talkies. ■

Berlin Express (1948). See Cold War. ■

Berlin via America (1918), Fordart. *Dir.* Francis Ford; *Sc.* Elsie Van Name; *Cast includes:* Francis Ford, Edna Emerson, Jack Newton, George Henry.

Director Francis Ford, brother of John Ford, also portrays an American flier employed by the Secret Service in this World War I spy drama. Posing as a traitor to his country, he gains the confidence of Prussian spies and is transported to Germany where he joins Baron von Richthofen's Flying Circus. He soon emerges as one of their leading aces while secretly dropping messages to the Allies concerning imminent enemy advances. Eventually, he escapes to America where he exposes a German spy. The patriotic fervor of the period permitted a character who used stealth and deception for the Allied cause to be considered a hero. However, when a foe used similar tactics to aid his country's cause, he was branded as vile and treacherous. To emphasize the morality of the actions even more strongly, film studios used their most popular leading men in the former while utilizing their traditional "heavies" in the latter features. ■

Berlin wall. See Cold War. ■

Best Years of Our Lives, The (1946), RKO. *Dir.* William Wyler; *Sc.* Robert E. Sherwood; *Cast includes:* Myrna Loy, Fredric March, Dana Andrews, Teresa Wright, Virginia Mayo, Harold Russell.

The most highly acclaimed film of 1946—the winner of six Academy Awards—this post-World War II drama tells the story of three returning servicemen to civilian life and the problems they face. Fredric March, as an infantry sergeant, has difficulties adjusting to his former bank job. "Last year it was 'Kill Japs.' This year it's 'Make money,'" he reflects. His wife (Myrna Loy) and his two teen-age children at times seem like strangers to him. He begins to drink heavily as a temporary escape from his disorientation.

Dana Andrews, as a decorated air force captain, returns to his unfaithful wife and his lowly job as a drug store soda jerk. He visits a junkyard of discarded bombers that he had seen previously from the air on his return home. "What we would have given for those in '43," he mused at the time. Now he is reminded that, like the heaps of rusting metal, his moments of past glories are gone forever. He meets March's daughter and begins to fall in love with her, finding in her a sensitivity lacking in his mercenary wife.

Harold Russell, a newcomer to acting, portrays Homer, a sailor who has lost both hands

which have been replaced with prosthetic devices. His main fear as he arrives in his home town is meeting his sweetheart (Cathy O'Donnell). When she urges that their marriage still take place as scheduled, he demonstrates what she will have to witness each night as he goes through the ritual of removing the artificial devices. Another exceptional moment concerning Homer occurs when his mother first becomes aware of his artificial hands and her eyes begin to tear. Russell had actually lost both hands as the result of a hand grenade accident.

Hollywood studios produced several films during this period depicting the problems of veterans and their readjustment, but seldom has a film captured the pain and emotion of the men and their loved ones or affected the public so strongly as did this drama. The film won Oscars for Best Picture, Best Director, Best Actor (March), Best Supporting Actor (Russell), Best Screenplay and Best Musical Score.

As a result of his appearance in the film, Russell won a second award "for bringing hope and courage to his fellow veterans." He was appointed chairman of the President's Council on Hiring the Handicapped in 1964 and appeared in Richard Donner's *Inside Moves* (1980). ■

Betrayal From the East (1945). See Panama Canal. ■

Betrayed (1954). See Resistance. ■

Betsy Ross (1917), World. *Dir.* Travers Yale, George Cowl; *Sc.* H. A. duSouchet; *Cast includes:* Alice Brady, John Bowers, Lillian Cook, Victor Kennard.

A biographical drama that blends events in the life of Betsy Ross with those of the American Revolution, the film takes certain liberties with both aspects. Betsy (Alice Brady) and her sister are Quakers living in Philadelphia with their father. Betsy is forced by her father to marry John Ross, who is killed in the Revolutionary struggle. She sets up an upholstery business which attracts General Washington, who is looking for someone to make a flag he has designed. Meanwhile some spying is going on around her store, but all ends well for Betsy, Washington and the fledgling nation.

The legend that Betsy Ross (1752–1836) designed and sewed the first official Ameri-

U.S. Marines face the anonymity of war on a Pacific island. *Between Heaven and Hell* (1956).

can flag to show the stars and stripes is just that—a legend for which there is no accurate historical record. The story is based on a historical paper written in the late 1800s by William J. Canby, grandson of Betsy Ross, who related a family tale passed on by his aunt, a daughter of Betsy by her third husband.

Betsy Ross was a flagmaker in Philadelphia and did make American flags during the Revolution. Francis Hopkinson, an artist-designer and signer of the Declaration of Independence, more likely originated the flag that Congress accepted on June 14, 1777, as the national emblem. Bills exist showing that Congress paid him to create the design for the first Stars and Stripes. However, the Betsy Ross story continues to be part of our national myth. ∎

Better 'Ole, The (1926), WB. *Dir.* Charles Reisner; *Sc.* Darryl F. Zanuck, Charles Reisner; *Cast includes:* Syd Chaplin, Doris Hill, Harold Goodwyn, Jack Ackroyd, Edgar Kennedy, Charles Gerrard, Tom McGuire.

A World War I comedy based on the En-glish cartoon characters of Captain Bruce Bairnsfather, the film stars Charlie Chaplin's half-brother, Syd Chaplin, as a happy-go-lucky English soldier. He and his army cronies, played by Harold Goodwyn and Jack Ackroyd, go through a series of misadventures while in the front lines. By the time this farce ends—and following a string of funny gags—the Germans are routed. Chaplin's major, who is actually a German spy, is caught and Syd wins sergeant's stripes. An English film version of the cartoonist's characters, bearing the same title, appeared in 1919. ∎

Between Heaven and Hell (1956), TCF. *Dir.* Richard Fleischer; *Sc.* Harry Brown; *Cast includes:* Robert Wagner, Terry Moore, Broderick Crawford, Buddy Ebsen, Robert Keith.

American military officers come under criticism in this World War II drama set chiefly in the Pacific. One colonel is portrayed as deranged while another is depicted as a coward. Robert Wagner, the hero of the film, plays an arrogant soldier who undergoes a change for the better by the end of the film. His outfit consists mainly of poor

Southerners whom he looks down upon. Wagner's family belongs to the Southern aristocracy. He is demoted to private after he strikes an officer who is responsible for the deaths of several G.I.s. Broderick Crawford plays the disturbed colonel. Most of the battle sequences in the film have a hard edge of realism about them.

Made more than a decade after the war, this film, as well as a handful of others, began to take a more critical look at the men and officers who fought in the conflict. *Attack!*, another film set during World War II and released the same year as the above work, centers on a cowardly major who is responsible for the deaths of several of his officers and men. One of his lieutenants murders him. ■

Between Two Fires (1914). See Battle of Gettysburg. ■

Beware! (1919), WB. *Dir.* William Nigh; *Cast includes:* Maurine Powers, Frank Norcross, Julia Huxley.

A World War I cautionary drama, the film tries to alert its audience of Prussian treachery. After the war, it suggests, Germany should fall under the supervision of its civilized neighbors and never again be allowed to rise to military or political power. The anti-German feeling expressed is so strong that in one sequence the Kaiser is shown facing a war-crimes trial. The film is a sequel to *My Four Years in Germany*, released one year earlier.

Historically, President Woodrow Wilson called for Wilhelm's abdication as a requirement of peace negotiations. Under pressure at home, the Kaiser fled to Holland in 1918 and eventually abdicated. ■

Beyond Victory (1931), RKO. *Dir.* John Robertson; *Sc.* Horace Jackson, James Gleason; *Cast includes:* William Boyd, ZaSu Pitts, Lew Cody, Marion Shilling, Lissi Arna, James Gleason, Russell Gleason.

A World War I pacifist drama about four American buddies in the same outfit, the film tells of each one's romance through flashbacks. Their job is to slow down the advancing enemy while American forces withdraw. Eventually two of the friends are killed. One, a farmboy, has left behind an aging mother. The remaining two, played by William Boyd and James Gleason, make it through until the

armistice. Boyd falls in love with a German girl. Gleason, who provides the comedy, has a wife back home who is a knife thrower, and says he enlisted to escape being her target. Boyd's romance underscores one of the themes of the film— that of the evils of national prejudice—a rather bold suggestion for the time and especially for an American film. The story also implies that perhaps it was wrong for many who enlisted to leave their families and their homes. The film ends gloomily, lacking much of the glory of battle displayed in earlier war adventures, and plays down the heroics American audiences were accustomed to. "We're fighting over something that don't exist!" one of the doughboys cries out. These antiwar elements were part of a new wave of realistic war movies begun by its superior predecessor, the highly acclaimed *All Quiet on the Western Front*, released the previous year. But unlike the earlier film, *Beyond Victory* failed to arouse the critics or score at the box office. The title comes from the phrase "Beyond victory lies the dream of man's desire." ■

Big Drive, The (1933), First Division.

A World War I documentary compiled by J. C. Rule, the film depicts the events of the Great War chronologically. Many of the sequences are from newsreel footage previously used in other documentaries. Scenes show the battle for Belgium, the Argonne offensive, the *Lusitania*, the Yanks at Chateau Thierry, the Marne and Verdun. The film, which has a narrator, has been assembled from footage from the military archives of England, France, Germany, Italy, the U.S. and Austria. ■

"Big Horn Massacre, The" (1913). See George Custer. ■

Big Jim McLain (1952). See Cold War. ■

Big Lift, The (1950). See Cold War. ■

Big Noise, The (1944). See Spy Comedies. ■

Big Parade, The (1925), MGM. *Dir.* King Vidor; *Sc.* Harry Behn; *Cast includes:* John Gilbert, Renée Adorée, Hobart Bosworth, Claire Adams, Karl Dane, Tom O'Brien.

One of the major war films of the 1920s, *The Big Parade* brought back the genre to movie houses across the country. Prior to its

In a lighter moment during World War I, American doughboy John Gilbert offers chewing gum to Renée Adorée, who promptly swallows it. *The Big Parade* (1925).

release, Hollywood producers were hesitant about turning out films whose subject matter was devoted so thoroughly to gritty details of World War I. They and the critics believed that the public was tired of all the war movies released at the time of the conflict and did not want to be reminded of the struggle in the years immediately following the war. But this film and *What Price Glory*, released the following year, proved them wrong. *The Big Parade* tells the story of three young men who meet as recruits and stay together through most of the war. John Gilbert, as the son of a wealthy mill owner, enlists not out of any particular ideological commitment, but because he is caught up with the spirit of war. Karl Dane, as a former ironworker, contributes much of the comic relief, including the uncanny ability to put out a candle flame with a well-directed mouthful of tobacco juice. Tom O'Brien, as a bartender in civilian life, makes up the third member of the trio.

Once in France, Gilbert falls in love with a French peasant, played by Renée Adorée, but they are soon separated in a touching scene when Gilbert and his unit are ordered to the front lines. In the harrowing battles that follow, Gilbert's two close buddies are killed. He returns home after the armistice. He has lost a leg, but he is alive. He grows restless and impatient with those around him because they do not understand him or what he has been through. He returns to France and the girl with whom he had fallen in love.

Vidor, the director, personalized the film.

Each soldier he focused upon reacted according to his own character. He utilized the images of men moving in unison, whether it was the "big parade" of the Yanks filled with fighting spirit at the beginning of the film as they embarked for France, the soldiers marching to the front, or the men moving silently and cautiously through the enemy-infested Argonne forest during battle. The rhythm is pervasive. Vidor utilized the rhythm of a metronome to emphasize the slow, measured advance of the doughboys through the woods. This contrasted with the hectic pace in the sequence depicting the caissons, motorcycles and trucks moving toward the front lines. The numerous battle scenes are realistic, especially the American advance through the woods, the hand-to-hand combat and the deadly accuracy of the machine guns.

The soldiers who fought in World War I were the first American combat troops in the history of the United States to see films of themselves and their buddies in battle through the endless footage shot by the army signal corps and foreign cameramen. This feature was the closest piece of fiction film that attempted to tell with any realism their personal story of their war experiences. The film was a commercial and artistic success although the British were critical. They objected to its depicting the Americans as the predominant force in winning the war. ∎

Big Red One, The (1980), UA. *Dir.* Samuel Fuller; *Sc.* Samuel Fuller; *Cast includes:* Lee Marvin, Mark Hamill, Robert Carradine, Bobby Di Cicco, Kelly Ward.

Based on his own experiences as an infantryman in World War II, director Samuel Fuller traces the exploits of the First Infantry Division—the Big Red One of the title—in North Africa and Europe. He accomplishes this chiefly through the experiences of five G.I.s to whom the war has only one meaning—to survive. In fact, one of the squad echoes this in the final line of the film: "Survival is the only glory in war." The battle sequences cover North Africa, Sicily, Omaha Beach, Belgium, Germany and Czechoslovakia. Fuller provides plenty of action, much of it raw and realistic, as he captures the brutality of war. Brave men give up their lives trying to destroy a barbed wire barricade; formidable tanks overrunning American positions and scattering the troops underscore the fragility of life at the front.

Lee Marvin portrays a battle-hardened sergeant who had fought in World War I (a role planned for John Wayne decades earlier, but production was aborted). The film opens during World War I showing Marvin after a battle. When an enemy soldier comes running towards him shouting in German that the war is over, Marvin, who doesn't comprehend what the man is saying, stabs him in the gut. At the end of the film, in a note of ironic horror, the incident is repeated, and again Marvin stabs a Nazi soldier. But when he learns that the war has ended, he tries to save the man's life. Earlier in the film he briefs one of his soldiers: "We don't murder, we kill."

Mark Hamill, as a foot soldier, is reluctant to kill the enemy until he witnesses a Nazi concentration camp and its pitiful survivors hastily abandoned by the retreating guards. He finds a German hiding in one of the ovens and empties his weapon into the soldier. Robert Carradine, Kelly Ward and Bobby Di Cicco portray other members of the squad. ■

Biloxi Blues (1988). See Service Comedy. ■

Robert Harron prepares to lead a courageous but doomed Confederate charge against Union troops. The *Birth of a Nation* (1915).

Birth of a Nation, The (1915), Mutual. *Dir.* D. W. Griffith; *Sc.* D. W. Griffith, Frank Woods; *Cast includes:* Lillian Gish, Mae Marsh, Henry Walthall, Miriam Cooper, Mary Alden, Ralph Lewis, George Siegmann, Walter Long.

Griffith's epic production of the Civil War has been the continuous subject of film schol-

ars and historians. Chiefly as a result of this film, Griffith has been called the father of the cinema as well as a racist. It has been the cause of controversy from its inception. Based on Thomas Dixon's novel and play *The Clansman*, the film covers the prewar period, the war itself and the years immediately following the conflict. The story revolves around the friendship of two families, the Stonemans from Pennsylvania and the Camerons from South Carolina. Two Stoneman brothers are invited to spend their vacation with the Camerons in the town of Piedmont. Phil Stoneman is attracted to Margaret Cameron, the older of two daughters. He shows his Southern friend, Ben Cameron, a picture of his sister, Elsie. He forgets to take the picture back and Ben puts it in his pocket. Meanwhile the head of the Stoneman household is shown to be a powerful political figure. War breaks out and both families see their sons march off to war. A Northern guerrilla force raids Piedmont but is defeated by a company of Confederate troops. On the battlefield the two friends meet, the younger Cameron and Stoneman boys. Before they have a chance to renew their friendship, they are killed. Ben, now a colonel, is wounded and captured by Union troops and hospitalized. He recognizes Stoneman's sister, Elsie, a volunteer nurse, from her picture.

The battle sequences have been shot from many different positions. There are long shots of the entrenchments of both armies as cannon and flares burst overhead. Medium shots depict the Southerners as they try to break through Union lines. Close-ups show Ben Cameron's elation as he thrusts the staff of the Confederate flag down the muzzle of a Northern cannon. Griffith also employs masks in showing shots of Generals Lee and Grant as they each observe the battle. The second half of the film, entitled "Reconstruction," depicts the racial tensions in the South. Stoneman assigns his protege, Silas Lynch, a mulatto, to oversee the town of Piedmont. His abuses of the white citizens gives rise to the Ku Klux Klan who ride in their white costumes to avenge the injustices heaped upon them. Lynch also has plans for Elsie to become his wife. In the dramatic climax in which he holds Elsie a prisoner, Ben Cameron assembles the entire Klan to relieve a cabin under siege, rescue Elsie and overthrow Lynch's forces in Piedmont.

Griffith's innovative camera and visual

techniques—his use of masks, close-ups, panoramic shots of battle scenes, tracking shots, and his first sustained use of crosscutting in a feature—help to enhance the spectacle. His tableaus, "historical facsimiles," including Lincoln's signing the proclamation for the first call for 75,000 volunteers, and the re-enactment of historical incidents such as General Sherman's march to the sea and Booth's assassination of the President at Ford's Theater, add dramatic power and authenticity to the work.

Griffith's attempts to show his hatred of war, human suffering and the tragedy of a nation torn by prejudice and geographical differences were undermined by his depiction of blacks and the glorifying of the Klan. Both he and the film have been attacked on these grounds. Film critic Richard Schickel calls the film a "flawed masterpiece." Black leaders and other critics have labeled it blatantly racist. After President Wilson viewed the film he described it as "history written in lightning." He was later forced to retract his statement under pressure of opposing groups. When the feature was originally released, blacks in several cities rioted. In this sense, the film contributed to the rise of the fledgling organization, the National Association for the Advancement of Colored People. Griffith continued to resist charges of prejudice and, possibly as an act of redemption, made *Intolerance*, another large production, the following year. ∎

Birth of a Race, The (1919). *Dir.* John W. Noble; *Sc.* Rudolph de Cordoba, John W. Noble; *Cast includes:* John Reinhardt, Jane Grey, George Le Guerre, Ben Hendricks, Mary Carr.

A dramatic, large-scale spectacle, the film covers a variety of historical events to develop its multiple themes. There are highlights from the arrival of Adam and Eve, the story of Noah, the latter part of Christ's life, the signing of the Declaration of Independence, Lincoln's Gettysburg Address and the beginning of World War I. The modern story concerns two sons of a German-American family, one who goes to Germany to fight for the Kaiser and the other who enlists in the American army. They later meet at a hospital where the American brother is recovering from his battle wounds. Meanwhile the father has fired patriotic Americans from his munitions factory and replaced them with those loyal to Germany, causing a riot to break out.

The film suggests that the power of love is stronger than that of hate; that all wars should be abolished; and that America, in order to survive, must be united in its struggles against those forces that would seek to destroy it. Released in the wake of World War I, the film also attempts to address some of the international causes that led to the conflict by showing the destructive forces of excessive nationalism. ∎

Bitter Tea of General Yen, The (1933). See Chinese Civil Wars. ∎

Black Book, The. See *Reign of Terror* (1949). ∎

Black Dakotas, The (1954), Col. *Dir.* Ray Nazarro; *Sc.* Ray Buffum, DeVallon Scott; *Cast includes:* Gary Merrill, Wanda Hendrix, John Bromfield, Noah Beery, Jr.

During the Civil War, a Confederate agent, sent by the South, attempts to stir up Indian troubles in the West to divert Union troops from the battlefield in this routine drama. Southerner Gary Merrill disrupts President Lincoln's plan to make peace with the Sioux so that Union troops can be redeployed to fight against the South. Merrill, however, turns crooked and decides to keep the gold earmarked for the Indians. Wanda Hendrix, as the daughter of a Rebel spy, provides the romantic interest. The hero of this routine film is played by John Bromfield, a stage line owner. The plot allows for several battles between the Indians and the cavalry. ∎

Black Dragons (1942). See Spy Films: the Talkies. ∎

Black Fox, The (1963), Capri. *Dir.* Louis C. Stoumen; *Sc.* Louis C. Stoumen.

Another documentary on the infamous career of Adolf Hitler, the film covers his rise, his support by the German people in the belief that he would bring economic recovery to the nation and the eventual war with all its horrors. Various scenes depict several of Hitler's assistants in action as well as images of the death camps. Aside from using the usual newsreel footage from World War II, Louis Stoumen applies the analogy of Goethe's allegorical *Reynard the Fox.* ∎

Black Parachute, The (1944), Col. *Dir.* Lew Landers; *Sc.* Clarence Upson Young; *Cast includes:* John Carradine, Osa Massen, Larry Parks, Jeanne Bates, Jonathan Hale.

Espionage and guerrilla warfare are the ingredients of this World War II spy drama set in an unnamed Nazi-occupied country whose citizens take up arms against the invaders. Larry Parks portrays an American agent sent into the country by parachute to rescue its king who is held hostage by the Nazis. He joins forces with the local underground in their struggle against the Nazis. Parks finally succeeds in his mission so that the king can broadcast against the ruthless occupiers. Osa Massen portrays a German spy while John Carradine plays a ruthless Nazi general responsible for the king's downfall in this implausible tale in which all the Germans are stereotyped. ■

Black Rose, The (1950), TCF. *Dir.* Henry Hathaway; *Sc.* Talbot Jennings; *Cast includes:* Tyrone Power, Orson Welles, Cecile Aubry, Jack Hawkins.

This medieval costume drama about Saxon rebellion against Norman rule in England during the 13th century stars Tyrone Power as the illegitimate son of a Saxon. He is forced into exile when officials learn that he has led a revolt to free Saxon prisoners from jail, an act considered treasonous against the Norman King Edward, played by Michael Rennie. Power journeys to the East with a well-known bowman (Jack Hawkins) where they meet a Mongol leader, played by Orson Welles, who allows them to accompany his caravan to the court of Kublai Khan. Power falls in love with Cecile Aubry, the Black Rose, and witnesses war and conquest before he returns to England where he is pardoned. The film, shot chiefly in England and North Africa, suggests many battles but shows none, except the results of conflict. ■

Black Watch, The (1929), Fox. *Dir.* John Ford; *Sc.* John Stone; *Cast includes:* Victor McLaglen, Myrna Loy, David Rollins, Lamsdon Hare.

Victor McLaglen portrays Captain Donald King, a Scottish officer, in this early talking film that takes place during World War I. He is sent to India to stop an uprising. Meanwhile his regiment is leaving for the trenches in France. When he arrives in India, he is immediately embroiled in an incident staged by others so that a group of extremists plotting a revolt against British rule can make their escape. Several battles occur between the rebel forces and McLaglen and his handful of troops.

Director John Ford manages to stage the action sequences effectively, adding elements which will later become part of his unique style. His use of bagpipes contributes authenticity to the military aspect of the film. In almost all his works to follow he will utilize music and songs of the particular period, whether the setting is the American West, Scotland or Ireland. The film also has its sentimental touches, broad humor and silhouetted long shots of soldiers, other familiar Ford characteristics. ■

Blackburn, Donald D. See *Surrender—Hell!* (1959). ■

Black Hawk War. See "The Fall of Black Hawk" (1912). ■

Blaze o' Glory (1930), WW. *Dir.* Renaud Hoffman, George J. Crone; *Sc.* Renaud Hoffman; *Cast includes:* Eddie Dowling, Betty Compson, Frankie Darro, Henry B. Walthall, William Davidson.

One of the earliest war musicals, the film stars Eddie Dowling singing and acting his way through a murder trial in this story with a World War I background. Eddie is on trial for murder as his wife sits watching the proceedings while his former commanding officer whom Eddie disobeyed is the prosecuting district attorney. Through a series of flashbacks we learn that Eddie sacrificed one of his lungs during an enemy gas attack to save a fellow doughboy (he continually coughs through the trial scenes). The unfolding drama is interspersed with four songs: "Welcome Home," "The Doughboy's Lullaby," "Put a Little Salt on the Bluebird's Tail," and "Wrapped in a Red, Red Rose," all sung by Eddie with occasional help from others. Several battle sequences occur between the sentimental scenes and the musical numbers in this unique war movie. The film was eventually re-edited, eliminating much of Eddie's coughing and singing as well as shortening other scenes. ■

"Blitz on the Fritz" (1943). See War Humor. ■

Blockade (1938), UA. *Dir.* William Dieterle; *Sc.* John Howard Lawson; *Cast includes:* Madeleine Carroll, Henry Fonda, Leo Carrillo, John Halliday, Vladimir Sokoloff, Reginald Denny.

Producer Walter Wanger's superficial drama of the Spanish Civil War attempts to depict the devastation thrust upon cities and the suffering of civilian populations as a result of modern warfare. Airplanes rain down disaster on military targets and civilians with equal destruction. Submarines impose a tight blockade while spies inform the U-boats of the position of supply ships.

Amid the chaos emerges a romantic plot involving Madeleine Carroll, whose father is an international spy, and Henry Fonda, who portrays a peasant-soldier fighting for his country. Once Carroll witnesses the misery she has helped to bring about, she reveals the location of the spies to Fonda. Meanwhile, high-ranking military officers are in collusion with enemy agents. Fonda pleads for peace in this antiwar film that manages to remain neutral. "Where is the conscience of the world that it allows the killing and maiming of civilians to go on?" he asks.

Although the film was cautious not to side with either the Loyalists or Franco's forces, it met with much controversy. The Hays Office, Hollywood's self-governing censorship committee, suggested numerous changes in the script to avoid antagonizing foreign nations. At its release it received the support of American Communists while the Catholic press and the Knights of Columbus condemned it. In New York City demonstrators gathered in front of Radio City Music Hall, protesting the showing of the film. *Blockade*, with all its ambiguity and artificiality, was the first significant film to deal with the war in Spain. *The Last Train From Madrid*, released the previous year, was even more nebulous about the conflict, simply using the war only as background for a weak drama. One decade later, *Blockade* was used against screenwriter John Howard Lawson when he was brought before the House Un-American Activities Committee investigating Communist influence in Hollywood. Excerpts from the film were used in *The Good Fight*, a 1984 documentary about the Spanish Civil War. ■

Block-Heads (1938), MGM. *Dir.* John G. Blystone; *Sc.* Felix Adler, A. Belgard, Harry Langdon, James Parrott, Charles Rogers; *Cast includes:* Stan Laurel, Oliver Hardy, Billy Gilbert, Patricia Ellis, Minna Gombel, James Finlayson.

Laurel and Hardy made one of their better feature-length comedies when they starred in this film with a World War I background. Stan and Ollie are doughboys on the front line in France when the film begins. Their commanding officer, about to lead his regiment "over the top," orders Stan to guard the trench until he is relieved. The war ends, and the screen reveals the passage of years. It is now 1938 and the scene shows Stan still guarding the trench which now has indentations from his marching back and forth during the last 20 years and a huge pile of empty cans of beans. No one has informed him that the war had ended! Ultimately, he is found and sent back to a soldiers' home in the United States.

When Ollie arrives to take his pal home, he finds Stan seated in a chair designed for an amputee and assumes the worst. He is overly gentle with Stan and begins to carry him, not noticing that he has both legs. After struggling with his friend, he finally realizes the situation and in exasperation demands to know why Stan didn't tell him he had the use of both legs. "Well," Stan replies, "you didn't ask me." He then adds softly, "I've always had them." The remainder of the film deals with a series of funny situations in Hardy's apartment and with a mix-up involving a neighbor's wife. ■

Blood and Steel (1959), TCF. *Dir.* Bernard L. Kowalski; *Sc.* Joseph C. Gillette; *Cast includes:* John Lupton, James Edwards, Brett Halsey, John Brinkley.

Four American sailors, members of the U.S. Navy's Construction Battalion (Seabees), are assigned to explore a Japanese-held island in the Pacific for use as a future airbase in this low-budget action drama set during World War II. The remainder of the film consists of Japanese troops, led by their captain (Allen Jung), pursuing the Americans. John Lupton portrays the leader of the Seabees. James Edwards, as one of the sailors, is wounded in a skirmish with the enemy. Ziva Rodann, as a native, attempts to assist Edwards and is accidentally killed for her efforts in this routine tale. A better tribute to this special force is *The Fighting Seabees* (1944) with John Wayne. ■

English riflemen make a futile attempt to stop a German plane from strafing their comrades in World War I. *The Blue Max* (1966).

Blood on the Sun (1945). See Tanaka Memorial. ∎

"Blue and the Grey or the Days of '61, The" (1908).

This short silent drama takes place during the Civil War. A Union soldier who hides his Confederate counterpart, a former West Point classmate and friend, is sentenced to be shot for aiding the enemy. The compassionate youth's sister, in love with the Southerner, comes to the rescue of her brother with a pardon from President Lincoln. The film contains battle scenes and portrayals of historical figures, including Lincoln and Generals Grant and Lee. Several Civil War films, including Griffith's *The Birth of a Nation* (1915), have used similar incidents to emphasize Lincoln's compassion for the common soldier. ∎

Blue Eagle, The (1926), Fox. *Dir.* John Ford; *Sc.* L. G. Rigby; *Cast includes*: George O'Brien, Janet Gaynor, William Russell, Robert Edeson.

Two rival gang leaders take their feud with them aboard a U.S. battleship where they serve as stokers in this raucous World War I drama. George O'Brien and William Russell portray the two adversaries who are about to battle it out in a formal boxing match when their vessel suddenly comes under attack from an enemy submarine. Their feud then continues into the postwar period. Finally, they combine forces to put some narcotics smugglers out of business. Director John Ford's use of burly characters engaged in rowdy scenes was to continue into the sound era in other films with military backgrounds such as *She Wore a Yellow Ribbon* (1949) as well as non-military features (*The Quiet Man*, released in 1952). ∎

Blue Max, The (1966), TCF. *Dir.* John Guillermin; *Sc.* David Pursall, Jack Seddon, Gerald Hanley; *Cast includes*: George Peppard, James Mason, Ursula Andress, Jeremy Kemp.

World War I provides the background for this drama about German air aces and their exploits both in the skies and on the ground.

George Peppard, as an ambitious airman from the lower classes, rises to distinction by his many successes in the air war against the enemy. Coveting Germany's highest award, a blue cross known informally as "the Blue Max" and named after Max Immelmann, a famous air ace, Peppard is ruthless in his dogfights. James Mason, as an unscrupulous nobleman in charge of the squadron, exploits Peppard as a national symbol of heroism to boost the flagging morale of the German people. Ursula Andress, as Mason's husband, has a steamy affair with the young pilot who is eventually sent to his death when Mason no longer has need of him.

The best segments of the film are the realistic action sequences involving the World War I planes. The new breed of knights engage in deadly dogfights, strafe the defenseless troops below and often go to their deaths consumed in smoke and flame. A particularly effective sequence concerns an air duel in which Peppard challenges a fellow ace, played by Jeremy Kemp, to a series of stunts that lead to the latter's death. ■

Bob Hampton of Placer (1921), FN. *Dir.* Marshall Neilan; *Sc.* Marion Fairfax; *Cast includes:* James Kirkwood, Wesley Barry, Marjorie Daw, Pat O'Malley, Noah Beery, Frank Leigh.

This outdoor western drama, based on a novel by Randall Parrish, concerns an army captain who is accused of killing a major during a fight involving the captain's wife. The officer goes to prison and when he is released changes his name to Hampton. He turns to gambling as a career, has two wards to raise and soon becomes entangled in the Indian uprisings and Custer's last stand. The film depicts the famous battle at Little Big Horn on a large scale but with little factual accuracy. Custer is portrayed realistically by Dwight Crittendon. ■

Body and Soul (1931), Fox. *Dir.* Al Santell; *Sc.* Jules Furthman; *Cast includes:* Charles Farrell, Elissa Landi, Humphrey Bogart, Myrna Loy, Donald Dillaway.

A weak World War I romantic drama, the film concerns three friends in the Royal Flying Corps. Humphrey Bogart portrays one of the fliers who marries before being shipped to France where he soon becomes involved in another romance. He dies during an attack on an observation balloon. Charles Farrell,

aboard the plane, is forced to land. Back in England, he meets Bogart's widow (Elissa Landi). She is under suspicion as an enemy agent who is responsible for the deaths of several fliers. However, the real spy (Myrna Loy) is ultimately revealed. The film has several aerial combat sequences. ■

Boer War. See South African War. ■

Boer War, The (1914), General Film Co. *Dir.* George Melford; *Cast includes:* Larry Peyton, Marin Sais, William Brunton, Edward Clisbee, Jane Wolfe.

The Boer War serves as background for this drama of self-sacrifice. Larry Peyton, as a captain, assumes the blame for a theft to protect the brother of the woman (Marin Sais) he loves. Forced out of the service, Peyton re-enlists under a pseudonym and wins fame for his actions in battle. The brother, a lieutenant in Peyton's unit, writes a note home confessing his own guilt, but Peyton destroys it. He then saves the brother's life in another battle but loses his sight. When both return home, the brother tells all and Sais promises to care for the misjudged hero who is rewarded for his acts of heroism. ■

Bold and the Brave, The (1956), RKO. *Dir.* Lewis R. Foster; *Sc.* Robert Lewin; *Cast includes:* Wendell Corey, Mickey Rooney, Don Taylor, Nicole Maurey.

A World War II drama that focuses on the lives of three very different G.I.s during the Italian campaign of 1944, the film depicts how each comes to terms with the war. Wendell Corey portrays an idealist with pacifist sympathies who has difficulties with killing the enemy. Mickey Rooney, as a soldier obsessed with winning enough money in a crap game to open his restaurant after the war, finally manages to parlay his winnings to $30,000. Later in the film he is killed while on patrol as he tries to protect his winnings. Don Taylor, as a religious fanatic, becomes involved with a local prostitute (Nicole Maurey), but his narrow views of real life strangle his emotions to the point that he is afraid to act out of fear of committing a sin. The film concentrates more on character development than on the actual conflict. ■

Bold Caballero, The (1935). See Bear Flag Republic Revolt. ■

Bombardier (1943), RKO. *Dir.* Richard Wallace; *Sc.* John Twist; *Cast includes:* Pat O'Brien, Randolph Scott, Anne Shirley, Eddie Albert, Robert Ryan.

A routine World War II drama with sufficient action sequences to satisfy its audiences, the film concerns the rivalry between Pat O'Brien, portraying a major, and Randolph Scott, as a captain, over who is more important to a bomber's mission, the pilot or the bombardier. They also squabble over Anne Shirley, who provides the romantic interest. By the end of the film Scott sacrifices his life so that a bombing mission over Japan proceeds as scheduled. Between plot clichés, the film enlightens its audiences about high-level precision bombing as practiced by the U.S. Army. For melodramatic effect and as effective propaganda, the plot includes a downed American bomber crew who are captured and tortured by the Japanese. A conglomeration of plot clichés, the film nevertheless scored with audiences and proved lucrative for the studio. ∎

Bomber's Moon (1943), TCF. *Dir.* Charles Fuhr; *Sc.* Kenneth Gamet, Aubrey Wisberg; *Cast includes:* George Montgomery, Annabella, Kent Taylor, Walter Kingsford, Martin Kosleck.

George Montgomery portrays an American pilot who is shot down behind German lines in this World War II drama. Captured and tossed into prison with a female Russian lieutenant (Annabella) in the medical corps, the two prisoners escape and make their way to freedom. Annabella goes to Holland, and Montgomery, after stealing a German plane, heads for England. On route to his destination, he manages to shoot down a German pilot who earlier had machine-gunned his brother while parachuting from his burning plane. Kent Taylor portrays a Nazi posing as a fellow Allied prisoner. The film contains more romance than action. ∎

Bombs Over Burma (1942). See Burma Road Campaign. ∎

"Bond, The" (1918), Liberty Loan Committee. *Dir.* Charlie Chaplin; *Sc.* Charlie Chaplin; *Cast includes:* Charlie Chaplin, Sydney Chaplin, Henry Bergman.

A one-reel propaganda short, based on a political cartoon and released during World War I, the film stars Chaplin as a patriotic citizen who turns over a bag of money to Uncle Sam. The money passes to Industry who in turn hands a soldier a rifle. Charlie then proceeds to pummel the Kaiser with an oversized mallet. He then places one foot on the flattened Kaiser and addresses the audience to buy Liberty Bonds.

Chaplin was criticized by some during the war for not enlisting in the armed forces. Those at home thought that Chaplin, a native and citizen of Britain, should have set an example for his fellow Englishmen by joining up. However, he made a short propaganda film for Britain and toured the U.S. for several months with other famous screen stars selling Liberty Bonds. His supporters felt that he did more for Allied propaganda by making comedies that cheered up both those at the front and those at home. ∎

Bonnie Annie Laurie (1918), Fox. *Dir.* H. Millarde; *Sc.* L. Liebrand; *Cast includes:* Peggy Hyland, Henry Hallam, Dan Mason, Marion Singer.

World War I provides the dramatic background for this romantic triangle. Peggy Hyland portrays a Scottish lass whose beau marches off to the war. She meets an American officer who is suffering from loss of memory. While nursing him back to health, she falls in love with him. He regains his memory and returns to the front lines where he meets the Scottish boy friend who loses his sight in battle. Hyland appears as a nurse to help him regain his sight and simultaneously rekindles her love for the American. When the Scottish lad's sight is restored, she returns to Scotland with him. ∎

Bonnie Scotland (1935), MGM. *Dir.* James W. Horne; *Sc.* Frank Butler, Jeff Moffitt; *Cast includes:* Stan Laurel, Oliver Hardy, June Lang, William Janney, James Finlayson.

Disappointing to critics but welcomed by their fans, the film has Laurel and Hardy performing their particular style of comedy as Scottish soldiers in colonial India during native unrest. After being disenchanted as heirs to an inheritance that adds up to one bagpipe and one snuff box, Stan and Ollie inadvertently end up in the British army and are sent to India. A chain of mishaps culminates in a climactic battle in which the pair engage the warring natives by tossing beehives at them. Their perennial nemesis, James Finlayson, appears as their sergeant. The film is hampered in part by a romantic subplot with June Lang as heroine and William Janney as soldier-hero and the local hostilities which are often unrelated to problems of the two comics. ∎

Boone, Daniel (1734–1820). A hunter, trapper, wartime fighter, explorer and sometime politician, Boone became a legend in his own lifetime. Unfortunately for the moviegoing public, the few dramas that touch upon his life are pale shadows of the real adventures and accomplishments of this famous early American frontiersman.

Boone, a native of Pennsylvania, worked as a trapper and hunter while still a youth. He had his first brush with an important event in American history at the age of 21. He served as a teamster and blacksmith under British General Edward Braddock in the ill-fated expedition of 1755 against the French in the Ohio Valley at the start of the French and Indian War. After Braddock was killed by ambush, survivors of his force, including Boone, were led back to safety in Virginia by young Colonel George Washington of the Virginia militia. No films touch upon this early dramatic incident in Boone's life.

Boone made several trips into the Kentucky wilderness from 1767–1771, and though others either preceded him or accompanied him, his early association with Kentucky gave rise to the false legend crediting him with its discovery. His first attempt to lead a group of settlers into Kentucky was turned back by a Cherokee Indian attack in 1773 that resulted in a personal tragedy. His son James was captured, tortured and killed.

Boone succeeded in his next venture when he led a band in 1775 that made the first permanent settlement in Kentucky, establishing a fort at the site of future Boonesboro. *Daniel Boone* (1936), and *Daniel Boone, Trail Blazer* (1957) both deal extensively with the problems of creating that first settlement. *Young Daniel Boone* (1950) presents a true incident detailing his rescue of two white girls who had been kidnaped by Indians.

During the American Revolution, Boone was captured by Shawnees in 1778 and adopted by one of their chiefs. He escaped and managed to get back to Boonesboro to warn the community of an impending attack by British and Indian forces which the settlers repulsed. A similar incident appears in *Daniel Boone*. After the war he held several local public offices. Though respected for his qualities of leadership, Boone never became prosperous. In fact, he lost extensive landholdings for failing to register his claims properly. He moved to what is today West Virginia, living there from 1788–1798, then left to resettle on a land grant in Spanish territory in Missouri. ∎

Border River (1954), U. *Dir.* George Sherman; *Sc.* William Sackheim, Louis Stevens; *Cast includes:* Joel McCrea, Yvonne De Carlo, Pedro Armendariz.

Joel McCrea portrays a Confederate major trying to purchase much-needed arms in Mexico for the Southern cause in this Civil War action drama. After seizing $2 million in gold from a Union mint, McCrea and his small band travel into Mexico to buy weapons crucially needed back home to continue the struggle. Others, however, have their own plans to relieve the major of the gold, including bandits and swindlers. Yvonne De Carlo, as a cafe owner, is in league with a renegade Mexican general (Pedro Amendariz), both of whom try to swindle McCrea. ∎

Border Wireless, The (1918). See Spy Films: the Silents. ∎

Born Reckless (1930). See Crime and War. ∎

Born to Love (1931), RKO. *Dir.* Paul L. Stein; *Sc.* Ernest Pascal; *Cast includes:* Constance Bennett, Joel McCrea, Paul Cavanagh, Frederick Kerr, Anthony Bushell.

Constance Bennett portrays an American nurse stationed in England during World War I in this familiar romantic drama. She falls in love with an American flier (Joel McCrea) who is soon shot down over Germany. Bennett, who gives birth to his child, thinks he has been killed in action. When a sympathetic English officer (Paul Cavanagh), who also loves Bennett, hears her story, he marries her. Two years after the Armistice McCrea returns. The couple are finally reunited, but not until several tearjerking situations unfold, including the death of their child. ∎

Boston Tea Party (December 16, 1773). It was not the pleasant social occasion that the name implied. The Boston Tea Party was a well-planned, organized act of vandalism enlisted in the cause of protecting the political and commercial rights of American colonists.

Duties and regulations on imported English tea became an issue that poisoned relationships between England and its American colonies during the early 1770s. Colonists showed their hostility to Parliament's arbitrary tax on imported goods by refusing for a number of years to pay the tax on English tea. Meanwhile, they bought tea smuggled in by American merchants and shippers. Though England took steps to lower the price of "legal" tea to the point where it was cheaper than the smuggled product, many Americans refused to sacrifice their principles for the price of cheaper tea. Attempts to land "legal" tea in Philadelphia, New York, Boston and Charleston resulted in mass meetings, and in some cases, tea ships were driven out of port. In Boston, the dispute took an even more dramatic turn.

Sam Adams and the Sons of Liberty organized a mass protest over the tea issue that attracted 8,000 people. When the British governor refused to allow the tea ships to leave without paying port customs, Adams led a band of colonists dressed as Mohawk Indians to the wharves at night where they boarded the tea ships and threw all 342 tea chests overboard. No other cargo was molested.

Parliament responded early the following spring by passing a series of laws that effectively closed Boston harbor to all shipping until compensation had been paid for the destroyed tea. The closing of Boston's port brought on mass unemployment which further inflamed relations between the mother country and the Americans.

The Boston Tea Party has been depicted in a handful of films, the earliest being a 1908 Edison one-reeler titled "The Boston Tea Party." A two-reel remake followed in 1915. The silent historical romance *Janice Meredith* (1924) includes the incident as one of a series of historical events that occurred around the American Revolution. In Frank Lloyd's *The Howards of Virginia* (1940) the event serves as background to this drama of colonial America. In the historical drama *Johnny Tremain* (1957), the title character, a young boy, becomes an eyewitness to some of the major historical events of early America, including the Boston Tea Party. In all three films the incident is realistically portrayed—considering they are American productions. ∎

Bowery Blitzkrieg (1941). See Spy Films: the Talkies. ∎

Bowie, James (1796–1836). James Bowie, born in Kentucky, was already a famous frontiersman in Louisiana before moving to Texas in 1828 where he became a leading figure in the resistance against Mexico. He had joined other Americans settling in Texas under the leadership of Stephen Austin who had gained approval from Mexico for a plan to bring in American colonists to help populate the country's sparsely settled northern region.

Bowie married the daughter of the Mexican Vice-Governor of Texas. His Mexican marriage and the problems it engendered are covered in John Wayne's *The Alamo* (1960), a large-scale production featuring Richard Widmark as Bowie, one of the principal characters in the film. *The Last Command* (1955), a film in which Bowie, played by Sterling Hayden, is the main character, takes liberties with his role in Texas politics. It portrays him as a personal friend of the Mexican dictator-general, Santa Anna, and one who sought to negotiate a peaceful settlement in the growing dispute between the American colonists and the Mexican government, contrary to historical record.

Bowie accepted a colonel's commission in the army of Texas when war broke out, and together with William B. Travis, organized the defense of the Alamo, a fortified former mission building in San Antonio. Bowie was killed, along with all the other defenders, in Santa Anna's attack on the Alamo. He was reportedly shot while he lay sick on his cot. (This is depicted in *The Last Command*). His reputed invention of the Bowie knife—often the center of action in several of his film biographies—is an unverified legend. ∎

Boxer Rebellion (1900). A long-smoldering resentment against foreigners in China exploded into an anti-foreign rebellion that resulted in the killing of hundreds of foreigners and Chinese Christians and caused much property damage before it was suppressed by foreign military forces. The revolt, encouraged by the Dowager Empress who wished to rid her country of foreign influence and exploitation, was carried out by a secret militant organization known as the Righteous Harmonious Fists, commonly called "Boxers" in English.

The conflict had its roots in the Opium War (1839–1842) which Britain provoked over trading privileges. Britain's easy victory exposed China's military weakness, and soon a parade of imperialist nations moved in to carve up China into colonies and economic spheres of influence. By 1900, the nations of England, Russia, France, Germany and Japan had taken territory and extracted commercial trading rights from China. The principle of extraterritoriality that the foreign powers had wrung from China particularly galled the Chinese. Under this rule, a foreign national was literally beyond Chinese law, for he had the right to refuse to be tried in a Chinese court for breaking a civil or criminal law. Instead, the foreigner could request a trial in his own national court.

The Boxers at their peak numbered 140,000 troops. They were active in several regions including Shantung, Shansi, and Manchuria. In Shansi province alone, they killed at least 231 civilians, chiefly missionaries. Chinese Christians were also attacked for adhering to western religions. After killing Germany's minister, Baron von Ketteler, the Boxers besieged the foreign legations in Peking for eight weeks. The siege was broken by a combined force of British, Russian, French, German, American and Japanese troops.

Only a handful of American films deal with the Rebellion. *The Marked Woman* (1914), one of the earliest, concerns a young Russian woman and her American lover caught up in the turmoil. Action sequences show fighting between the Boxers and American troops. The film is based on a play by Owen Davis. Two later dramas, *Foreign Devils* (1928) and *55 Days at Peking* (1963), include battle scenes relating to the siege of the legations and the heroic actions of the besieged but fail to detail any of the background leading to the event.

After the revolt was quelled, China was required to pay an indemnity of nearly $740 million. Later, in 1908, the United States refunded some of its award as excessive and used the money to finance scholarships for Chinese students in the United States. China emerged from the rebellion under great debt and, in essence, a subjugated nation. ∎

Boy With Green Hair, The (1948). See Refugees. ∎

Boys in Company C, The (1978), Col. *Dir.* Sidney J. Furie; *Sc.* Rick Natkin, Sidney J. Furie; *Cast includes:* Stan Shaw, Andrew Stevens, James Canning, Michael Lembeck.

A handful of green recruits experience the futility of the Vietnam War and the incompetence of the military brass in this action drama. Stan Shaw, as a drug pusher, turns the young marines into a fighting unit. Andrew Stevens portrays a grunt who becomes hooked on drugs. James Canning, as an ambitious author, acts as chronicler of the war. Craig Wasson, as a hippie, adjusts to the marine corps and the war but retains his pacifist disposition. Lee Ermy, who appears as a tough boot camp drill instructor, repeated the role with even greater distinction almost a decade later in Stanley Kubrick's striking Vietnam War drama *Full Metal Jacket* (1987).

As in several World War II films made during the 1960s which reflect a general anti-military tone, this drama attacks the competency and corruption of several officers. Several soldiers are killed transporting supplies to an army post. The crates contain liquor, cigarettes and furniture for a general. Other officers with their petty rules and insensitivity place the lives of the men under them in constant danger. "You are the enemy," exclaims Shaw to an officer.

The film showcases the talents of several actors who are the offsprings of earlier Hollywood performers. Andrew Stevens is the son of Stella Stevens. Michael Lembeck is the son of Harvey Lembeck, who was featured in several war films and service comedies. James Whitmore, Jr. is, of course, the son of Whitmore Senior, who was featured in *Battleground* (1949), a major war movie about World War II, and other films. ∎

Brady's Escape (1984), Satori. *Dir.* Pal Gabor; *Sc.* William W. Lewis; *Cast includes:* John Savage, Kelly Reno, Ildiko Bansagi.

John Savage portrays an American airman who is shot down over Nazi-occupied Hungary in this World War II action drama. The story begins with a flashback in which Savage, at his Wyoming ranch, shoots an old, ailing mare. The sound of the rifle recalls for him his exploits during the Second World War. Forced to bail out of their bomber after it is hit by anti-aircraft fire, Savage and a wounded buddy fall into the hands of *csikos*, Hungarian-style cowboys, who hide the Americans from the Germans. A local doctor's daughter, played by Ildiko Bansagi, prepares Brady for his eventual escape by teaching him Hungarian and provides some romantic interest. A young orphan boy (Kelly

Reno) befriends Savage. Meanwhile, a company of German troopers as well as an SS officer hunt for the downed airmen. Savage's buddy dies of his wounds. The lone American wins the respect of the community when he proves he can ride with the best of the local cowboys. He finally makes his escape with Reno as his guide as his German pursuers enter the village and brutally torture its inhabitants. ■

Brand of Cowardice, The (1916), Metro. *Dir.* John Noble; *Sc.* Charles Maigne; *Cast includes:* Lionel Barrymore, Grace Valentine, Robert Cummings, Kate Blancke, Louis Wolheim.

With the Unites States-Mexican border as the background for this silent drama, the film concerns a spoiled young man who resigns his commission in the state militia when his unit is called to active service. The call to duty interferes with his social life. But his resignation leads to charges of cowardice and rejection by his betrothed who returns his ring. To prove himself worthy of her, he enlists as a private in another regiment and ends up on the Mexican border where he has an opportunity to rescue his loved one. Several battles with Mexican bandits occur.

The film is based on actual border incidents of that period. Beginning in 1914, the U.S. and Mexico became embroiled in a series of undeclared hostilities. Pancho Villa, a rival of Mexico's President Carranza, resented the U.S. shipment of arms to Carranza. Villa and his followers reciprocated by killing 18 American citizens in Mexico in January 1916 and raided a town in New Mexico, leaving another 17 Americans dead. General John J. Pershing was ordered to cross the Mexican border and pursue the Villistas. Pershing and his troops failed to overtake the raiders and returned in 1917. ■

Brass Target (1978), UA. *Dir.* John Hough; *Sc.* Alvin Boretz; *Cast includes:* Sophia Loren, John Cassavetes, George Kennedy, Robert Vaughn, Patrick McGoohan.

This weak drama depicts a fictionalized version of General Patton's death at the hands of assassins and a contrived plot about the theft of Nazi Germany's gold. Robert Vaughn portrays an American colonel who, along with two other officers in occupied Germany, schemes to seize the gold that the Third Reich plundered during the war. They are abetted by Patrick McGoohan, as the head of the Office of Strategic Services. George Kennedy, as General Patton, is forced to investigate the theft and is killed when he gets too close to the truth. John Cassavetes, as a veteran of the O.S.S., helps in the investigation. Sophia Loren portrays the lover of Max Von Sydow, the general's assassin. In reality, Patton was killed in an automobile accident. The film is based on a novel by Frederick Nolan in which the character who is murdered is fictional. ■

Brave Warrior (1952), Col. *Dir.* Spencer G. Bennet; *Sc.* Robert F. Kent; *Cast includes:* Jon Hall, Christine Larson, Jay Silverheels, Michael Ansara.

An American agent is assigned to uncover traitors who are inciting the Indians in this action drama set on the eve of the War of 1812. Jon Hall portrays the government representative who tries to prevent the hostiles from joining the British cause. Jay Silverheels, as Tecumseh, chief of the Shawnees, helps Hall. Christine Larson provides the romantic interest in this low-budget film. In attempting to depict the conflict between American and British sympathizers of the period, the film stretches historical facts. Actually, the Shawnee sided with the British against the Americans during the War of 1812. Also, Chief Tecumseh was firmly antagonistic toward the fledgling nation.

Tecumseh proved to be a Shawnee war chief with a grand dream. He strove to unite all eastern Indian tribes in one great confederacy with sufficient power to stop the piecemeal loss of individual tribal lands to expanding white pressure. Each tribe in the confederacy would preserve its unique and traditional way of life under its own leaders. His idea, through his courage, leadership and energy, almost succeeded.

Settlers in the old Northwest of the Ohio Valley during the early 1800s feared him for the terror and destruction he unleashed against them. However, within a few years after his death in battle, some of his chief foes praised Tecumseh as a leader who belonged among the ranks of the great figures in history. General William Henry Harrison, who commanded American forces against Tecumseh, called the native leader "one of those uncommon geniuses, which spring up occasionally. . . . If it were not for the vicinity of the United States, he would perhaps be the founder of an empire that would rival in glory that of Mexico or Peru."

American historian Henry Trumbull labeled him as "the most extraordinary Indian that has appeared in history." Tecumseh was a brave patriot and a distinguished speaker, quite different from the stereotyped monosyllabic, Hollywood-grunting Indian presented to movie audiences. He was an individual noted for his integrity and humaneness even by his opponents. His 20th-century biographer, Glenn Tucker, considers him the greatest native leader in the long, tragedy-wracked history of Indian resistance to white rule.

Although he had good reasons to hate whites who had broken an earlier treaty with the Shawnee and murdered his father, he retained his humanity. A settler recounted how Tecumseh berated a band of Indians who burned a captured settler at the stake. Other settlers related further incidents of Tecumseh's sense of morality and chivalry.

Tecumseh claimed that Indian land was held in common by all tribes and that no chiefs had the right to sell any part of their heritage. He was supported in this appeal by his brother, "The Prophet." His brother, a mystic, gathered adherents by preaching that Indians could become stronger by abstaining from alcohol, renouncing white ways, stopping intertribal warfare and practicing a code of humanity. The Prophet's defeat at the Battle of Tippecanoe (1811) by General Harrison and his subsequent flight to Canada weakened Tecumseh. He was portrayed in *Brave Warrior*.

During the War of 1812 Tecumseh joined the British, who made him a brigadier general. He was killed at the Battle of the Thames River, just over the Canadian border in Ontario, by General Harrison's forces. The idea of a united Indian nation died with Tecumseh. ■

"Brave Women of '76" (1909), Lubin.

This short silent film of the American Revolution depicts how a group of civilians, especially the women whose men are away fighting for the colonies, defend themselves against alleged enemy troops approaching the small community. Armed with a variety of makeshift weapons ranging from pitchforks to shotguns, the women descend upon the invaders only to discover their own husbands and sweethearts. ■

Breakthrough (1950), WB. *Dir.* Lewis Seiler; *Sc.* Bernard Girard, Ted Sherdeman; *Cast includes:* David Brian, John Agar, Frank Lovejoy, Bill Campbell.

This World War II drama depicts the story of an infantry company during the battle of Normandy. David Brian portrays an experienced and hard-bitten captain of the foot soldiers. John Agar, as an inexperienced lieutenant, gains savvy after each encounter with the enemy. He is aided by an understanding and sympathetic sergeant, portrayed by Frank Lovejoy. The film includes several inserts of actual war footage. In their attempts to focus on the effects of battle on the individual soldier, the misdirected scriptwriters tried to show the positive as well as negative sides to the war. ■

Breath of the Gods, The (1920). See Russo-Japanese War. ■

Bridge at Remagen, The (1969), UA. *Dir.* John Guillermin; *Sc.* Richard Yates, William Roberts; *Cast includes:* George Segal, Robert Vaughn, Ben Gazzara, Bradford Dillman.

Both American and German troops wage a desperate battle for control of the last remaining bridge over the Rhine in 1945 in this action drama that re-enacts an actual World War II battle. George Segal, as a tough American platoon leader, fights to save the Ludendorff Bridge for future Allied crossings. He despises his gung-ho and personally ambitious major (Bradford Dillman) who constantly volunteers his platoon for the most perilous assignments. Ben Gazzara, as a sergeant in Segal's outfit, spends much of his time removing rings and watches from Nazi corpses. "Everybody makes a profit out of war," he rationalizes to Segal, "why shouldn't I?" The Nazi high command orders the bridge destroyed to prevent the Allied advance. But a German major (Robert Vaughn) protests, pointing out that more than 50,000 German troops will be stranded and at the mercy of the enemy. Disobeying orders and eventually paying the price with his life, he delays its destruction so that the abandoned German troops can get safely across. Meanwhile, the killing continues until it is too late for the bridge to be blown up. The Americans are triumphant in gaining control of the coveted bridge although most of Segal's unit is killed.

Besides containing plenty of action, the

film underscores the lack of concern by the military commanders on both sides for the lives of their troops. E. G. Marshall, as an American general who knows the bridge is about to be blown, gambles that Segal's platoon can capture it and detach the explosives in time. On the German side, the general staff is quick to abandon its stranded forces as long as the Americans don't cross the bridge. The drama was one of several released during the 1960s which altered the conventional themes of World War II stories. Attacks on totalitarianism and antiwar statements were replaced by antimilitary themes; corrupt, incompetent or cowardly commanding officers were the new villains. As the German major is about to be executed for disobeying orders, he asks about some airplanes in the distance. "Ours or theirs?" "Enemy planes," a soldier replies. "But who is the enemy?" the condemned man muses.

The film is based on the 1945 attack by American troops as they pushed across the Rhine River into Germany. On March 7, the Ludendorff Bridge at Remagen became the coveted goal of the U.S. 9th Armored Division. German engineers set charges to destroy the bridge, but it remained standing for ten days after the explosion, enough time for Allied tanks and troops to pour across. It became the first Allied bridgehead across the Rhine.

Politics and art clashed during the making of the film, which was shot in Czechoslovakia in the final days of that country's attempt at democratization under Alexander Dubcek. Soviet tanks roared into Czechoslovakia to suppress the uprising and forced the film production to come to a halt. Communist newspapers and politicians alleged that the film was a C.I.A. project. The production had to be completed in Italy. ■

Bridge to the Sun (1961), MGM. Dir. Etienne Perier; Sc. Charles Kaufman; Cast includes: Carroll Baker, James Shigeta, James Yagi, Sean Garrison.

Based on the experiences of Gwen Terasaki, this biographical drama recreates the story of an American who marries a Japanese diplomat. Carroll Baker, as the courageous wife of James Shigeta, accompanies her husband to Japan and remains there throughout World War II. They prevail through a series of crises precipitated by her origin and his views. Shigeta, as the husband, opposes

the war between his country and the U.S. In one poignant scene Baker, aboard a train, looks out the window and into the forlorn eyes of an American P.O.W. The film is based on Gwendolyn Terasaki's autobiography. ■

American jets face heavy ground fire as they try to knock out strategic targets during the Korean War. *The Bridges at Toko-Ri* (1954).

Bridges at Toko-Ri, The (1954), Par. Dir. Mark Robson; Sc. Valentine Davies; Cast includes: William Holden, Grace Kelly, Fredric March, Mickey Rooney, Robert Strauss.

This Korean War drama tells the story of one U.S. Navy pilot and his part in the bombing of the heavily defended five bridges at Toko-Ri, a strategic pass in Korea. William Holden portrays a reserve pilot who is reluctant to leave his wife and child when he is recalled to active duty in the navy. Fredric March, as a conscience-stricken admiral of a task force off Korea, concerns himself about sending pilots to their death. He takes a liking to Holden, who reminds him of his own two sons who were killed in action. During the fateful mission, Holden is unable to return in his plane and is forced to land in enemy territory. Mickey Rooney, as a helicopter rescue pilot, comes to his aid, but both are killed in a gun battle with the Koreans. The final scene in this realistic drama shows March at his post on the aircraft carrier after hearing of the loss. "Where do we get such men?" he ponders. The film is based on James A. Michener's novel. ■

Bright Shawl, The (1923), FN. Dir. John S. Robertson; Sc. Edmund Goulding; Cast includes: Richard Barthelmess, Dorothy Gish, Luis Alberni, Mary Astor.

The drama is set in Cuba during the 1870s when it was ruled by Spain. Richard Barthelmess portrays a wealthy American who, out of sympathy for the oppressed Cuban masses, accompanies his friend, a Cuban patriot (Endre Beranger), to the strife-torn country. Barthelmess aids a group of revolutionaries plotting against the tyrannical colonial rulers. He passes information that he receives from a dancer (Dorothy Gish), who has fallen in love with him, to the rebel leader. However, the American is actually in love with his friend's sister (Mary Astor). Meanwhile, a Spanish spy, upon learning how the information is being leaked, endangers Beranger's entire family. But Barthelmess and those under suspicion are able to escape to the U.S.

Cuba's Ten Years' War (1868–1878), one of several revolutions, was declared by Carlos Manuel del Castillo, a rich planter and lawyer. The civil war ended badly for the rebels who were promised sweeping reforms and other concessions, none of which were fulfilled by Spain. Once again dissent from the colonists was met with a firm despotic fist. The United States, weakened by its own civil strife, did not intervene in Cuba until decades later. ■

Bright Victory (1951). See Veterans. ■

"Britain's R.A.F." (1940). See "The March of Time." ■

British Agent (1934), WB. *Dir.* Michael Curtiz; *Sc.* Laird Doyle; *Cast includes:* Leslie Howard, Kay Francis, William Gargan, Phillip Reed, Irving Pichel, Walter Byron.

A spy drama set in the early stages of the Russian Revolution, the film stars Leslie Howard as the British consul-general in strife-torn Russia. He is determined to keep Russia in World War I although the country is seeking to make peace with Germany while attending to the revolt at home. England at first unofficially assigns Howard this task so that military pressure may continue on Germany during World War I. Howard promises officials of the Communist regime that England will provide money and munitions. However, his superiors never respond, and Howard is betrayed by his own government. Although his life is in danger, Howard continues his own crusade against the Communists.

Early in the film Howard saves the life of Lenin's secretary (Kay Francis), and the two fall in love. But their political differences threaten their relationship. "There'd be no more wars if nations would mind their own business," Francis remarks in reference to England's interference in Russia's plan to withdraw from the conflict. "And abandon their friends?" Howard questions. "If England had starved in the trenches," she explains, "as Russia had, and fought with shells filled with sawdust, I'd like to know what she'd do." "Shall I tell you?" Howard replies. "She'd go on fighting—for humanity."

Howard is captured and placed in a structure to be blown up. Francis joins him, but at the last moment news reaches the soldiers that Stalin is recovering from a gunshot wound and they go off to celebrate. The lovers are spared. Several historical figures portrayed on screen include Lenin, Trotsky and Lloyd George.

The film exemplifies early Hollywood's anti-Communist approach. Revolutionary forces are pictured as ill-bred rabble who murder the innocent. In the autobiography by R. H. Bruce Lockhart, the wartime British diplomat on whose experiences the story is based, there is no such dedication or obsession on the part of the author, whom Howard portrays, to continue the campaign against Bolshevism. Howard's betrayal by his own country anticipates the cynical plots of several Cold War films, including *The Spy Who Came in From the Cold*, starring Richard Burton. ■

British Intelligence (1940), WB. *Dir.* Terry Morse; *Sc.* Lee Katz; *Cast includes:* Boris Karloff, Margaret Lindsay, Holmes Herbert, Bruce Lester.

Based on Anthony Paul Kelly's successful 1918 play about intrigue and German spies operating in England during World War I, the film stars Boris Karloff as a master spy who cleverly installs himself as an employee in the home of a high-ranking British war official. Margaret Lindsay, as a double agent, poses as a Germany spy to learn the identity of the leader of the enemy agents. The film features a climactic air raid of zeppelins over London intent on destroying British military headquarters. This is the third screen version of Kelly's play, the other two released in 1926 and 1930 under the original title, *Three Faces East*. The 1930 adaptation features Erich von Stroheim as the head of the German spy network. He received top billing over Constance Bennett and garnered the best reviews from the critics.

Not unlike other major studios, Warners remade many of its old silent and early sound properties, embellishing them with updated material, slick production values and fresh faces. One slight addition that someone at the studio thought would be clever gave this third version an ironic touch. A fumbling German corporal wore a Chaplinesque mustache and had some of his dark hair fall over one eye. ∎

Britton of the Seventh (1916), Blue Ribbon. *Dir.* Lionel Belmore; *Sc.* Cyrus Townsend Brady; *Cast includes:* Darwin Karr, Charles Kent, Bobby Connelly.

The film recounts the massacre of General George Armstrong Custer and the famous 7th Cavalry at the hands of the Sioux. The story begins in the 20th century with a 70-year-old veteran regaling his grandson with tales of the West. The drama then flashes back to when the man was only 30 and a lieutenant in the U.S. Cavalry. Although one of the early silent screen versions of Custer's last stand, it was not the first. "On the Little Big Horn," a one-reeler, was released in 1909, and Thomas Ince's more elaborate "Custer's Last Raid" appeared in 1912. ∎

Broken Arrow (1950), TCF. *Dir.* Delmer Daves; *Sc.* Delmer Daves; *Cast includes:* James Stewart, Jeff Chandler, Debra Paget, Will Geer.

A landmark film in its sympathetic treatment of the American Indian, this sentimental drama stars James Stewart as Tom Jeffords, a frontiersman who strives to bring peace between the Apache and the whites. Fed up with the slaughter on both sides, he boldly rides into the camp of Cochise, played by Jeff Chandler, chief of the Apaches. He convinces the feared warrior to end the hostilities between their people, promising that the whites will do the same. Cochise and Jeffords strive to maintain the fragile peace. Meanwhile, the frontiersman falls in love with a young Indian woman (Debra Paget) whom he soon marries. The uneasy accord is broken by several unscrupulous whites and treacherous Apaches until the cavalry is forced to intervene. In the wake of the ensuing clashes, Paget is killed in a savage ambush. Peace between the warring factions again descends

upon the territory, but Stewart finds little consolation in it as he rides off into the distance.

The film sparked a string of similar dramas starring some of Hollywood's major personalities, including, among others, Charlton Heston in *The Savage* (1952), Burt Lancaster in *Apache* (1954) and Rock Hudson in *Seminole* (1953). Jeff Chandler repeated his role as Cochise in *Battle at Apache Pass* (1952). ∎

Broken Lullaby. See *The Man I Killed* (1932). ∎

Brought to Action (1945), Office of Strategic Services.

A World War II documentary shot chiefly by U.S. Navy cameramen, the film covers the October 1944 second sea battle of the Philippines off Leyte. Graphic sequences show the heavy air and sea fighting while the narration explains the naval strategy. Some of the footage of enemy ships and planes comes from captured Japanese newsreels. ∎

Brown, John (1800–1859). Martyr, murderer or madman? To his contemporaries, he was any one of these. He was hanged for leading a raid on October 16, 1859, on the federal arsenal at Harpers Ferry, Virginia, to gain arms for a rebellion of slaves and militant abolitionists. Brown's act and subsequent execution contributed to the growing tension between pro- and anti-slavery forces that would shortly engulf the United States in civil war.

He first rose to prominence during the 1850s as an ardent abolitionist. He was active in Missouri and Pennsylvania in the "underground railroad," a secret network devised to aid escaping slaves. Two incidents in Kansas may have led to his belief that slavery could only be eradicated through violence. He had moved to Kansas with a portion of his large family in 1855 to take part in the forthcoming territorial election to decide whether the area should be free or slave territory. The results of the election, which many historians contend was fraudulent, angered him. Outside supporters of slavery swarmed into the region and helped elect a pro-slavery legislature. Subsequently, a pro-slavery band sacked the "free-soil" town of Lawrence. Brown, in retaliation, led a group in 1856 in the massacre of five alleged pro-slavers at Pottawatami Creek.

Seven Angry Men (1955), with Raymond

Massey as Brown, emphasized Brown's attitude in Kansas. He was portrayed as a single-minded, religious zealot who considered himself a God-driven avenger charged with the mission of wiping out the wrongs of slavery at any price, including the murder of innocent people.

Brown decided in the late 1850s to initiate a slave rebellion. Settled on a farm outside Harpers Ferry, he made plans to attack the nearby federal arsenal and distribute the seized arms and ammunition to slaves and militant abolitionists. The rebel group, according to his plans, would then establish a Negro free state in the Southern mountains.

On Sunday night, October 16, 1859, Brown led a successful raid against the arsenal, killing seven people in the process. *Santa Fe Trail* (1940) and *Seven Angry Men* re-enacted the incident. However, Brown's anticipated slave rebellion never materialized. Army forces under then Col. Robert E. Lee captured him and his band.

Brown's deportment at his trial and execution raised him to the level of a martyr in the eyes of a growing number of people. He was always calm, articulate and respectful—the very antithesis of the wild-eyed murderous radical described by his detractors. His final statement to a reporter from the *New York Herald* after the trial has become a classic that won adherents to his role of martyr. "I pity the poor in bondage; that is why I am here," he said. "You may dispose of me easily, but this question is still to be settled—the Negro question—the end of that is not yet. . . . Now if it is deemed necessary that I should forfeit my life for the furtherance of the ends of justice and mingle my blood further with . . . the blood of millions in this slave country whose rights are disregarded by wicked, cruel and unjust enactments, I say, 'Let it be done.'" The final dramatic speech attributed to Brown in *Santa Fe Trail*, although passionate, lacks the depth and serenity of his actual declaration.

The film *Santa Fe Trail* lacks focus, despite Massey's creditable performance. It begins as a cavalry western drama that wanders into the story of Brown's career and then intertwines with a fictional love rivalry involving Jeb Stuart and George Armstrong Custer. *Seven Angry Men* is a better-than-average historical drama that adheres closer to history and permits Raymond Massey to enlarge upon his role as Brown in *Santa Fe Trail*. ■

Buccaneer, The (1938), Par. *Dir.* Cecil B. DeMille; *Sc.* Edwin Justus Mayer, Harold Lamb, C. Gardner Sullivan; *Cast includes:* Fredric March, Franciska Gaal, Akim Tamiroff, Margot Grahame, Walter Brennan, Ian Keith.

Fredric March portrays the title character, Jean Lafitte, in this swashbuckler set during the War of 1812. The British offer him a large sum of money and a full pardon for him and his men. Lafitte, who prefers to help the U.S., then informs the American governor who does not believe him and sends an American army and naval force against the colony. Although Lafitte suffers some losses of men and equipment, he later joins forces with General Andrew Jackson against the British. Lafitte meanwhile has his own romantic problems. He must choose between a pretty Dutch girl who has fallen in love with him and a beautiful young woman from New Orleans whom he loves. Jackson and his backwoodsmen are a poor match for the well-trained, well-armed British soldiers until Lafitte's men join the fray.

Director DeMille provides sufficient action on land and sea in this large production. The film opens with the burning of Washington by the British and concludes with the Battle of New Orleans. Hungarian actress Franciska Gaal was imported especially for the role of a little Dutch beauty whom Lafitte saves when the ship she is traveling on is sunk. Hugh Sothern, as General Jackson, is a good lookalike. The film was remade in 1958.

The famous Battle of New Orleans depicted in the film, in which so many British soldiers were killed, was fought one week after the peace treaty had been signed in London. Unfortunately, it took time for the news to travel to the United States. ■

Buccaneer, The (1958), Par. *Dir.* Anthony Quinn; *Sc.* Jesse L. Lasky, Jr., Bernice Mosk; *Cast includes:* Yul Brynner, Charlton Heston, Claire Bloom, Charles Boyer, Inger Stevens.

The exploits of the famous pirate Jean Lafitte in America during the War of 1812 serve as background for this large-scale remake. Early in the film Lafitte accepts responsibility for the sinking of an American ship at the hands of a renegade pirate and is exiled from the United States. Yul Brynner, as the well-dressed, urbane pirate, later redeems himself when he and his men come to the aid of Andrew Jackson and his troops in their battle with the British. Charlton Heston portrays a tough-minded Jackson whose shrewd sense of expediency leads him to accept Lafitte's help. Claire Bloom, as an emotionally charged young woman, falls in love with the pirate. Most of the action sequences are on land in this routine remake of Cecil B. DeMille's 1938 film. ■

Buck Privates (1928). See Service Comedy. ■

Buck Privates (1941). See Service Comedy. ■

"Bud's Recruit" (1918). See Propaganda. ■

Buffalo Bill. See William Frederick Cody. ■

Buffalo Bill's Indian Wars. See *The Adventures of Buffalo Bill* (1914). ■

Bugle Call, The (1916), Triangle. *Dir.* E. A. Martin; *Sc.* William A. Corey; *Cast includes:* William Collier, Jr., Wyndham Standing, Anna Lehr.

This adventure yarn takes place at a remote American cavalry army post. Billy is the 12-year old son of the captain of the post. One day, hearing about an Indian uprising, the captain rides out with a large force to crush the insurrection. But the Indians, using the incident as a ploy, attack the outpost. Little Billy, hiding in the nearby hills, blows his bugle, and the Indians think the cavalry is nearby. Eventually, the captain returns to save those under siege. ■

Bugle Call, The (1927), MGM. *Dir.* Edward Sedgwick; *Sc.* C. Gardner Sullivan, Josephine Lovett; *Cast includes:* Jackie Coogan, Herbert Rawlinson, Claire Windsor, Tom O'Brien.

A remake of the 1916 drama of the same name, this version features the popular child star of the period, Jackie Coogan, as an ingratiating but mischievous 12-year-old bugle boy living with his stepmother (Claire Windsor) at a western frontier fort. Herbert Rawlinson portrays a cavalry officer whose heroism is established in his battles with local hostile Indians. Young Coogan, following a stream of sentimental scenes including those in which he displays grief for his departed mother, gets the chance to rescue the garrison with his trusty bugle. The routine cavalry-versus-Indians drama has several good battles with the hostiles and provides the screen debut of Johnny Mack Brown, former football star. ■

Bugle Sounds, The (1941). See Tank Warfare. ■

Bugler of Algiers, The (1916), Bluebird. *Dir.* Rupert Julian; *Sc.* Elliot J. Clawson; *Cast includes:* Kingsley Benedict, Rupert Julian, Eida Hall.

Gabrielle, a French peasant girl, has to part with her young brother and her lover when, in 1871, the two young men are called upon to serve their country in Algiers. The brother distinguishes himself in battle, and the two friends return to their village. But Gabrielle is gone and the village has been ransacked by raiders. Fifty years pass and the French government finally gets around to offering the brother a medal. The two elderly men who have remained together through the years decide to walk to Paris. On the way the brother dies and his friend takes his place. Officials meanwhile learn the whereabouts of the hero's missing sister. She recognizes her lost lover as the man being decorated but does not reveal his identity. Later, they both return to where the brother's body rests and place the medal on him. The lovers, separated for half a century, embrace.

Based on the story *We Are French* by Perley Poore Sheehan and Robert H. Davis, the film was remade in 1924 as *Love and Glory* starring Charles De Roche, Wallace MacDonald and Madge Bellamy. Rupert Julian, who acted in the above version, directed the remake. ■

Bugles in the Afternoon (1952), WB. *Dir.* Roy Rowland; *Sc.* Geoffrey Homes, Harry Brown; *Cast includes:* Ray Milland, Helena Carter, Hugh Marlowe, Forrest Tucker.

Ray Milland, as a former army officer who has been branded a coward during the Civil War, re-enlists as a cavalryman to regain his reputation. He not only battles his old enemy (Richard Carlson), now his superior officer at a U.S. Cavalry outpost in the west, but the warring Sioux as well. Carlson, a captain at the fort, continually assigns Milland to perilous duties. Meanwhile they both vie for the affections of Helena Carter. Lively skirmishes occur between the troopers and the hostile braves, including the famous battle at Little

Big Horn with the slaughter of General Custer (Sheb Wooley) and the 7th Cavalry. ∎

Bulge, Battle of the (December 16, 1944–January 16, 1945). Although German armies in mid-1944 were retreating toward Germany after their defeat in France, Hitler proposed a counteroffensive that would send the Allies reeling, cut off major portions of British and American forces and perhaps permit him to negotiate a separate peace with the West. Success depended upon three factors: the initial breakthrough, control of Allied fuel supplies and key communications areas including Bastogne and expansion of the original break in the Allied lines.

The counteroffensive came on December 16–19, 1944, by way of the Ardennes forest region in Belgium. The Germans threw 24 divisions, including 10 armored, against 600,000 surprised American troops. By December 19, General Eisenhower committed reserve troops to the battle, and the Germans were halted at Bastogne. General Patton, advancing in the south, was ordered to turn north and attack the Germans' southern flank. Although a German armored force pushed through at St. Vith, Hitler's bold plan was doomed as a result of the delay. German armor failed to seize Allied fuel dumps. A small force of 18,000 American troops held out tenaciously at Bastogne from December 26, 1944 to January 2, 1945. Hitler's demands that the town be taken were futile. The Germans finally withdrew under an Allied counteroffensive, and the "bulge" in the Allied lines was corrected. The battle resulted in a six-week delay in Allied plans and the commitment of vital German reserves, including 120,000 men killed, wounded or missing; 600 tanks destroyed; 1,600 planes lost; and 6,000 vehicles gone. Among American losses were more than 80 prisoners brutally machine-gunned by the 1st Panzer Division.

The two films that dramatize the battle at some length are earnest attempts to capture the significance and intensity of the breakthrough. The Academy Award-winning *Battleground* (1949) pays tribute to the men who stopped the Nazis at Bastogne. It also recounts the murders of American prisoners. *Battle of the Bulge* (1965), a highly fictionalized drama of the pivotal battle and the breakthrough at Ardennes, features Henry Fonda as an American colonel who tries to convince his superiors of an impending German offensive and Dana Andrews as an arrogant general.

Two documentaries present graphic accounts of events. *The True Glory* (1945) covers, among other topics, the Battle of the Bulge and the gallant American stand at Bastogne. *The Battle of the Bulge—The Brave Rifles* (1966) includes the fighting in the areas of the Ardennes, Eisenborn, St. Vith and Bastogne. ∎

Bull Run, Battles of. See American Civil War. ∎

Bullets and Brown Eyes (1916) Triangle. *Dir.* Scott Sidney; *Sc.* J. G. Hawks; *Cast includes:* William Desmond, Bessie Barriscale, Wyndham Standing, J. J. Dowling.

William Desmond portrays a prince in this romantic drama set during a fictitious war between Germany and Poland in the early part of the twentieth century. Bessie Barriscale, as a countess who falls in love with Desmond, is ordered by her powerful brother to betray the prince. Sentenced to face a firing squad, Desmond is finally rescued by the countess. He then rejoins his regiment in their battle against their invading neighbors. Several large-scale battle sequences as well as individual combat scenes occur frequently. Desmond gets to ride off with his pretty rescuer by the end of this tale.

The film, released prior to America's entry into World War I, depicts Germany as an aggressor nation, and, along with dozens of other features, contributed to the negative propaganda that plagued Germany immediately before, during and after the war. Filmmakers, no doubt, were only reflecting the anti-German sentiments of their audiences. At least one earlier film, *The Fall of a Nation* (1916), that expressed such views was attacked by both screen critics and Washington politicians. But this did not prevent the flow of dramas that projected the German as villain. ∎

Burma Convoy (1941), U. *Dir.* Noel Smith; *Sc.* Stanley Rubin, Roy Chanslor; *Cast includes:* Charles Bickford, Evelyn Ankers, Frank Albertson, Cecil Kellaway.

A minor drama set during the Sino-Japanese War about a group of brave truck drivers who transport munitions to Chinese troops from Rangoon to Chungking over the Burma Road, the film stars Charles Bickford who is in charge of the operation. He is plagued with hijackings and ambushes as he tries to unravel how the guerrillas know the schedules in advance. It seems a Eurasian spy ring is at the bottom of all his problems. His younger brother, played by Frank Albertson, had been mixed up with the agents and was found murdered. Bickford avenges his brother's death in this low-budget film. ■

Burma Road campaign. (December 1943–March 1945). With Japan in control of China's main ports by late 1941 in world War II, the Burma Road, the "back door to China," took on a critical role as a major supply route for Chinese forces. The Japanese, realizing the road's importance, launched an invasion into Burma from Thailand and severed this last ground link between China and the outside world by April 1942. Supplies had to be air ferried over the Himalayan "hump" from India to China for the next two years, a method that was risky and incapable of providing the quantity of materiel necessary to bolster a Chinese offensive against the Japanese.

A combined British, American and Chinese force launched a series of drives in the winter of 1943–1944 to recapture and reopen the road. The Allies were under the overall command of Vice Admiral Lord Louis Mountbatten. General William Slim headed British and empire ground units, and American General Joseph Stilwell directed American and Chinese troops. Allied ground units slogged through monsoon-drenched jungles while airborne and glider troops leapfrogged mountains to enable the Allies, in a year-long campaign, to overcome strong Japanese resistance and reach the Burma Road on January 27, 1945. The first truck convoy traversed the Allied-held northern portion of the road between Namkham in Burma, and Kunming in China between January 28, 1945-February 4, 1945. It took another three months of fighting to clear the Japanese from the southern portion of the Burma Road.

Hollywood was quick to capitalize on contemporary headlines by releasing a series of dramas relating to this remote but vital region. In the spy drama *Burma Convoy* (1941) Charles Bickford is hampered by hijackings and ambushes as he attempts to send supply trucks over the road. *Bombs Over Burma* (1942), a weak low-budget drama featuring Anna May Wong as a Chinese secret agent,

concerns spies, operating along the Burma Road, who are trying to halt the shipment of essential supplies for the war effort. In *Half Way to Shanghai* (1942) Nazi agents attempt to get maps of Chinese defenses and ammunition depots in this low-budget World War II spy drama set in Burma in 1942. *A Yank on the Burma Road* (1942) concerns American hero Barry Nelson who is hired by the Chinese to lead a convoy of trucks carrying medical supplies to Chungking. "Back Door to Tokyo" (1944), a "March of Time" documentary, emphasizes the importance of keeping the Burma Road open as a supply route to China. ■

Burning Sands (1922), Par. *Dir.* George Melford; *Sc.* Olga Printzlau, Waldemar Young; *Cast includes:* Milton Sills, Wanda Hawley, Louise Dresser, Jacqueline Logan, Robert Cain.

The romantic drama is set in Egypt during the Sanusi Anti-British Revolt where a desert tribe is about to rise up against British rule. The British governor, whose headquarters are in Cairo, assigns Milton Sills to look into rumors of impending trouble among some of the tribes. The governor's daughter (Wanda Hawley) falls in love with Sills, who has ignored her at a ball given in her honor. Sills, warned of a possible uprising among a particular tribe, journeys into the desert to prevent the revolt. Several battles occur as Sills overpowers a traitor and British troops crush the revolution. ■

Burr, Aaron (1756–1836). He was an American Revolutionary war officer who later became more famous for his political actions. Burr served under Benedict Arnold in the ill-fated invasion of Canada (1775–1776). Later, he was on the staff of General Washington and then that of General Putnam in the Battle of Kips Bay (1776), part of Washington's unsuccessful fight to retain control of New York City. In that engagement, Burr saved Putnam and his army from certain capture by British troops when he guided the general along a lesser known road away from advancing enemy forces. Promoted to lieutenant colonel in 1777, he then retired from active service because of poor health.

After the revolution Burr had an active political career that often kept him in the public's eye. While serving as vice president (1800–1804) under Jefferson he killed Alexander Hamilton in a duel (1804) over political differences. Burr was linked to a conspiracy in 1806, although never proven in court, over a plot to either seize a portion of Mexico for the United States or engineer the secession of some western states.

Hollywood generally treated Burr as a minor figure. For instance, in *My Own United States* (1918), a panorama of American historical highlights, Burr was one of several figures. In the 1925 adaptation of Edward Everett Hale's historical drama *The Man Without a Country*, Lieutenant Nolan, the main character, becomes entangled in the Burr conspiracy. His largest role is in the fictitious biographical drama *Magnificent Doll* (1946), in which Burr (David Niven) is influenced to abandon his claims for the presidency by Dolly Madison, whom he admires. ■

Busses Roar (1942). See Spy Films: the Silents. ■

C

C.P.I. (Committee on Public Information). See Documentary. ■

Caesar, Julius (102?–44 B.C.). A complex individual in both his private and public life, Caesar has remained a fascinating historical figure for both scholars and the general public. Born of an old-line Roman aristocratic family, he championed the cause of the people. As a leading general he expanded Rome's control in western Europe. He exhibited great physical endurance but wrote and spoke with sensitive eloquence. He combined attitudes of magnanimity and generosity toward his supporters and those he defeated in Rome with severe brutality toward non-Romans. He used these qualities of character to advance his career in the military and in politics.

One incident in Caesar's life illustrates his determination. Forced to leave Rome about 75 B.C., because of his unpopularity with the Senate aristocracy whom he attacked regularly, he was captured by a band of Mediterranean pirates. He raised the ransom for his release, then outfitted a naval party that sought and captured the pirates and had them publicly crucified.

From about 80 B.C., when Caesar first entered public life, he began to acquire fame and a following as a politician, military leader, writer and administrator. Among his non-military accomplishments, the creation of the Julian calendar stands out. He recorded victories in Spain, Britain and Gaul. He became so popular with his troops and the common people that a jealous and fearful Roman Senate, in 50 B.C., ordered him to disband his forces, give up his command and return to Rome. He refused to do so and, instead, marched on Rome in 49 B.C., picking up more supporters along the way. His entrance into Rome was actually a triumphal march, that resulted in his Senate enemies fleeing to Greece to regroup their forces.

Caesar's actions set off a civil war (49 B.C.–44 B.C.) in which he defeated his leading rivals, including Pompey who was killed in Egypt. In pursuit of Pompey, Caesar went to Egypt and, finding Cleopatra and her husband-brother in conflict over the throne there, Caesar placed Cleopatra in control. He fell in love with the Egyptian queen while in Egypt, and though she was married, she accompanied him back to Rome as his mistress (46 B.C.–44 B.C.) Caesar apparently fathered a child with her, Caesarean (Ptolemy XIV).

Upon returning to Rome, Caesar set about improving housing conditions, passed laws to help farmers and reformed the corrupt and inefficient Roman bureaucracy. He became dictator in 44 B.C. His actions led to a Senatorial conspiracy to assassinate him, both for the monarchal way in which he conducted government as well as the damage he caused to the personal interests of some senators. Two men who Caesar favored, Cassius and Brutus, were among the conspirators. The killing of Caesar on March 15, (the Ides of March) 44 B.C., set off another decade of civil war between his supporters and forces representing most of the Senate.

Caesar holds an important place in Roman history. He ended a period of corruption, decline and anarchy. He unified the empire, which resulted in improved trade and the spread of culture, and created a more efficient government. His imperious methods, however, marked the end of the Roman republic and the beginning of one man military rule—a trend that would ultimately weaken

Rome. The greatness associated with Caesar eventually made his name a synonym for royal authority. Later Roman emperors called themselves Caesar, and variations of his name as a title, such as Kaiser in German and Tsar or Czar in Russian, existed into the 20th century.

Hollywood has never attempted a complete biography of Caesar but has made several movies about specific portions of his life, usually within that short period from 49 to 44 B.C., when he held power. Although Caesar is characterized in only a handful of American films, he is often portrayed as a strong and perceptive ruler who is vulnerable to a woman's charms. He is shown as a heroic figure whom others envy. For example, Louis Calhern as *Julius Caesar* (1953) is frequently photographed from below, making him appear high in stature, almost arrogant. In *Cleopatra* (1963) he (Rex Harrison) is more earthy as he falls for the Egyptian queen's charms all the while knowing her motives. Even after Caesar's assassination Antony is haunted by the dead man's powerful image as a masterful general and Roman leader. Cecil B. DeMille's stagy film *Cleopatra* (1934) presents a similar Caesar (Warren William)—one who is amused by the Egyptian but also seduced by her. See also Cleopatra, Roman Civil Wars. ∎

Caine Mutiny, The (1954), Col. *Dir.* Edward Dmytryk; *Sc.* Stanley Roberts; *Cast includes:* Humphrey Bogart, Jose Ferrer, Van Johnson, Fred MacMurray, Robert Francis, May Wynn.

The questions of responsibility of military command and devout loyalty of subordinates come under scrutiny in this World War II drama based on the novel by Herman Wouk. The film traces the ruin of the emotionally unstable Captain Queeg (Humphrey Bogart), who inwardly suffers from an inferiority complex and outwardly rolls two steel balls between his fingers. A career navy man who goes by the book, he dispenses punishments for petty or imagined infractions. Lieutenant Keefer (Fred MacMurray), a free-lance writer who observes Queeg's gradual disintegration, maliciously undercuts the captain and breeds suspicions in Captain Maryk (Van Johnson), the executive officer. "He's a Freudian delight," Keefer announces. "He crawls with clues—his fixation on the little rolling balls, his chattering of second-hand phrases, his in-

ability to look you in the eye . . ." Slowly becoming convinced that Queeg is mentally unfit, Maryk relieves him of command during a typhoon.

A court martial ensues in which Maryk's attorney, Lieutenant Greenwald (Jose Ferrer), demolishes Queeg's defense. The two defendants, Maryk and Keefer, are exonerated and later join their fellow officers in a celebration. Greenwald, now quite drunk, enters and extols Queeg. "While I was studying law and Keefer was writing his stories and you (Keith) were tearing up the playing fields of dear old Princeton, who was standing guard of this big, fat, dumb country of ours, eh? Not us . . . We knew you couldn't make money in the service. So who did the dirty work for us? Queeg did." He accuses Keefer of instigating the entire mutiny. He then tosses his drink into Keefer's face and reminds the group that their rejection of Queeg when he called upon them for their cooperation was unconscionable. "You don't work with a captain because you like the way he parts his hair," he explains. "You work with him because he's got the job. Or you're no good."

When the film was about to go into production, there was a question about gaining the navy's assistance. The service at first was hesitant about the story, priding itself on its record of never experiencing a mutiny. However, as can be seen in the film, the U.S. Navy finally lent its manpower and ships, giving full cooperation to the studio. ∎

Cairo (1942). See Spy Comedies. ∎

California (1927), MGM. *Dir.* W. S. Van Dyke; *Sc.* Frank Davis; *Cast includes:* Tim McCoy, Dorothy Sebastian, Marc MacDermott, Frank Currier, Fred Warren.

This action drama is set in old California in the days when Mexico governed the territory. Tim McCoy, as a U.S. Cavalry officer, falls in love with a Spanish girl who at first rejects him because he is a Yankee. Several battles occur in the film between the Mexicans (although they are never named as such) and the Americans, with McCoy thwarting all evil attempts against the American inhabitants. Historical figure Kit Carson (Fred Warren) has a small role in the plot, probably included to add a touch of authenticity to the film. ∎

California Conquest (1952), Col. Dir. Lew Landers; *Sc.* Robert E. Kent; *Cast includes:* Cornel Wilde, Teresa Wright, Alfonso Bedoya, Lisa Ferraday.

Set in early California when the territory was under Mexican rule and coveted by other nations, this action drama concerns a Russian plot to seize the land. Cornel Wilde portrays the leader of a group of Spanish-Californians who favor joining the U.S. A rich landowner (John Dehner) plots to turn California over to the Russians, who promise him an important political role. Alfonso Bedoya, as an outlaw chief, is hired to lead a rebellion. Wilde foils the revolt by locating the bandit's cache of arms. Teresa Wright plays the daughter of a gunsmith who is killed by the outlaws. ■

California Revolt (1846). See Bear Flag Republic Revolt. ■

California Romance, A (1923), Fox. Dir. Jerome Storm; *Sc.* Charles Banks; *Cast includes:* John Gilbert, Estelle Taylor, George Seigmann, Jack McDonald.

A satirical comedy about the early days of California, the film stars John Gilbert as a Spaniard who is rejected by his sweetheart. It seems he does not want to take up arms against the Americans who are invading the Spanish territory. A smooth-talking stranger arrives and convinces the natives to join him in the battle against the Americans. Meanwhile he is planning after the battle to scoop up the land grants, kill the rich owners and capture their women. The U.S. Cavalry rides to the rescue and saves the people from this self-appointed leader and his band of outlaws. ■

Californian, The (1937). See Bear Flag Republic Revolt. ■

Call of the Blood (1913). See Indian Wars. ■

Call Out the Marines (1942). See Spy Comedies. ■

Campbells Are Coming, The (1915), U. Dir. Francis Ford; *Sc.* Grace Cunard; *Cast includes:* Francis Ford, Grace Cunard, Duke Worne, Harry Schumm, Lew Short.

The Indian Mutiny of 1857–1858 is the subject of this action-filled silent drama directed by and starring Francis Ford, John Ford's older brother. Several battles between British troops and the rebellious natives suggest the actual violence of the uprising that led to atrocities by both sides. Ford portrays the chief villain who instigates the rebellion and lusts for a pretty Scotch lass (Grace Cunard). The film attributes Britain's ultimate victory over the sepoys to a Scotch regiment that is seen arriving in time to save a besieged garrison. ■

"Canada at War" (1940). See "The March of Time." ■

Captain Blood (1924), Vitagraph. Dir. David Smith; *Sc.* Jay Pilcher; *Cast includes:* J. Warren Kerrigan, Jean Paige, Charlotte Merriam, Allen Forrest, Otis Harlan.

Based on Rafael Sabatini's popular sea story, the silent version stars J. Warren Kerrigan as the title character who is unjustly sent to the penal colony on Barbados. As a physician, Peter Blood maneuvers into the good graces of the governor. When the Spanish attack the island, Blood and his fellow prisoners escape by taking over the Spaniards' ship while its crew members are carousing on shore. Blood and his crew become pirates since they cannot return to England. James II, who had sentenced Blood to the penal colony, is overthrown and William III takes the throne. Meanwhile Captain Blood saves the governor's life and is offered the position of running the island if he will abandon his career as pirate. He accepts. ■

Captain Blood (1935), WB. Dir. Michael Curtiz; *Sc.* Casey Robinson; *Cast includes:* Errol Flynn, Olivia De Havilland, Lionel Atwill, Basil Rathbone, Ross Alexander, Guy Kibbee, Henry Stephenson.

A remake of the 1924 film based on Rafael Sabatini's popular novel, the sound version benefits from Erich von Korngold's music score as well as from the dialogue. The film opens in 1685 during the rule of King James II. Errol Flynn, in his first swashbuckling role, portrays Peter Blood, a physician who has tired of his life as a soldier and adventurer. "I'm a healer, not a slayer," he replies to his acquaintances who chide him for not joining the rebellion against the tyrannical king. One night a friend gallops to his quarters and informs Blood that another is wounded. Dr. Blood goes to the injured man to aid him. The king's soldiers barge in and arrest everyone, including Blood, denouncing them as traitors.

Following a brief and unjust trial, the accused are sent to Port Royal, a British colony in the New World, to be sold into slavery. Two years pass. One day Spanish pirates attack Port Royal. That night Blood and a group of fellow slaves escape from the plantation and capture the pirates' ship while the invaders celebrate their victory on shore. The next morning the former slaves turn the cannon on the returning pirates and blast their long boats out of the water. They then set sail for the open sea with Blood as their captain. "We are men without a country," he reminds the crew, "outlaws in our own land and outcasts in any other." Exhilarated by their newly won freedom, the men unanimously decide on a life of piracy while Blood formalizes their oath of allegiance: "We pledge ourselves to be bound together as brothers in a life-and-death friendship."

During the following year the name of Captain Blood emerges as a symbol of fear and dread among other captains and crews traveling the unprotected, pirate-infested seas. England, meanwhile, dispatches an official emissary of the king to rid the shipping lanes of Captain Blood, who has temporarily joined forces with another pirate, a French cutthroat played by Basil Rathbone. The two captains meet on an island and duel over the possession of Olivia De Havilland. (Flynn and Rathbone were to meet again in another, more elaborate sword fight three years later in *The Adventures of Robin Hood*.) Blood kills the pirate and returns to his ship where he learns that James has been driven out of England and replaced by William of Orange. Blood and his crew have been pardoned. They celebrate by lifting the siege of Port Royal by the French, who are now at war with England. As a reward, Blood is appointed governor of Port Royal.

The film includes several effective sea battles and sword fights although many of the sequences aboard ship are studio shots with painted backdrops and the battles of the galleons reveal the work of models. However, the close-ups and the excitement of the fighting are well staged. Several screen titles, a holdover from the days of silent films, help to explain the political events and move the plot along. The film has been colorized for television and is one of the few examples in which this relatively new process has enhanced the original work.

Historically, the film is quite accurate in its references to the king and his exile. When James occupied the throne after the death of Charles II, the old specter of religious war reappeared. In 1688 the English reacted by expelling James to France in their Glorious Revolution. Parliament welcomed the Protestant William of the Netherlands and his wife, Mary, James' daughter, as the new sovereigns. They ruled England from 1689 to 1702. Another area in which the film is correct is the allusion to the pledge of brotherhood among the pirates. Frank Sherry, in his book *Raiders and Rebels: The Golden Age of Piracy*, suggests that the buccaneers of the late 17th and 18th centuries formed a sort of democratic and international brotherhood that instilled in men from the lower classes of Europe a rare taste of freedom and power. ∎

Captain Carey, U.S.A. (1950). See Office of Strategic Services. ∎

Captain Caution (1940), UA. *Dir.* Richard Wallace; *Sc.* Grover Jones; *Cast includes:* Victor Mature, Louise Platt, Leo Carrillo, Bruce Cabot, Robert Barrat.

The War of 1812 serves as background for this sea adventure concerning an American bark that is captured by a British man-of-war. Victor Mature portrays the title character, a prudent seaman who takes over the American ship when its captain dies. The men mistake his cautious nature for cowardice until he swings into action in a rousing battle against the British and exposes a traitor (Bruce Cabot). To give an air of authenticity to the plot, based on a novel by Kenneth Roberts, the historical figure of Captain Stephen Decatur (Ted Osborne) is interjected into the events. Louise Platt provides some romantic interest. Weak comedy relief is left in the hands of Leo Carrillo, El Brendel and Vivienne Osborne. ∎

Captain Eddie (1945), TCF. *Dir.* Lloyd Bacon; *Sc.* John Tucker Battle; *Cast includes:* Fred MacMurray, Lynn Bari, Charles Bickford, Thomas Mitchell, Lloyd Nolan.

This biographical drama covers chiefly the early years in the life of Captain Eddie Rickenbacker, the famous World War I ace. The film opens during World War II with the passengers of a downed army plane getting into a

Lobby card with Brian Aherne (c.) about to be hanged for resisting tyranny in Australia. *Captain Fury* (1939).

raft. One is Rickenbacker, played by Fred MacMurray. The remainder of the film is composed of a series of flashbacks telling of the aviator's life as a child interested in machines, a young automobile salesman and a pilot during World War I. His war career is treated briefly. Lynn Bari provides the romantic interest in this routine film that fails to capture the larger aspects of the famous flier's life.

Edward Rickenbacker (1890–1973) downed 26 German planes during World War I. A member of the illustrious "Hat-in-the-Ring" air squadron, he received the Congressional Medal of Honor for his air exploits. During World War II he was assigned to inspect bases in the South Pacific. On one such inspection in 1942 his plane was shot down. He survived 23 days in a raft. ∎

Captain Fury (1939), UA. Dir. Hal Roach; Sc. Grover Jones, Jack Jevne, William De-Mille; *Cast includes:* Brian Aherne, Victor McLaglen, Paul Lukas, June Lang, John Carradine, George Zucco.

An action drama with early Australia as the background, the film stars Brian Aherne as an Irish patriot sentenced to serve a prison term in Australia. Forced to labor under a tyrannical land baron (George Zucco), the defiant Aherne escapes, taking with him several other prisoners including Victor McLaglen. They form a band of outlaws that harass Zucco while aiding the oppressed ranchers. Eventually the despot meets his fate, and the gallant freedom fighters are pardoned. June Lang provides the romantic interest in this well-paced but conventional tale.

Considering that Australia was first settled by convicts and political exiles from Britain, beginning with the first penal colony in 1788 on the approximate site of present day Sydney, it should come as no surprise that the island continent experienced several revolts in the first century of its history as a settlement.

Britain, during the early 1800s, followed a policy of exiling captured Irish revolutionaries to Australia. At least two Australian rebellions were composed wholly or in part of

Irish prisoners. The first one occurred in 1804 when prisoners, sent there after the suppression of an Irish rebellion in 1798, rose up and were put down ruthlessly. German and Irish revolutionaries, in 1854, tried to set up a local republic of Victoria, but the colonial government easily quashed the movement.

Captain Fury took this background of rebellion by Irish prisoners as a base for a fictitious story in which Brian Aherne, as an exiled Irish patriot, leads several of his group, together with oppressed settlers, in an uprising against a local land baron. The movie does not appear to be about any specific rebellion. ∎

Captain Horatio Hornblower (1951), WB. *Dir.* Raoul Walsh; *Sc.* Ivan Goff, Ben Roberts, Aeneas Mackenzie; *Cast includes:* Gregory Peck, Virginia Mayo, Robert Beatty.

Warner Brothers went to England to film the adventures of a 19th century British naval captain during the Napoleonic Wars. Gregory Peck portrays the dispassionate but always stalwart title character whose sea battles against the Spanish and French were made famous in the novels of C. S. Forester. Several rousing action sequences, including a major sea fight between the British and Napoleon's fleets, keep the plot moving. As a result of Hornblower's deeds during a battle at La Teste harbor where he manages to bottle up the French fleet, he is transformed into a national hero. Virginia Mayo, as the sister of the Duke of Wellington, falls in love with the intrepid Hornblower. But the captain, who is already married, rejects her love. ∎

Captain Lightfoot (1955), U. *Dir.* Douglas Sirk; *Sc.* W. R. Burnett, Oscar Brodney; *Cast includes:* Rock Hudson, Barbara Rush, Jeff Morrow, Kathleen Ryan.

A costume drama about Ireland's rebellion against England, the film stars Rock Hudson as a young, quick-tempered Irishman who joins the rebels. Jeff Morrow portrays the leader of the insurrectionists. Barbara Rush, as his sister, provides the romantic interest for Hudson, who continues the skirmishes against the oppressors while Morrow recovers from his wounds after his escape from an English prison. The routine film was photographed in Ireland. ∎

Captain Newman, M.D. (1963). See Doctors in War. ∎

Captain of the Guard (1930), U. *Dir.* John S. Robertson; *Sc.* George M. Watters, Arthur Ripley; *Cast includes:* John Boles, Laura La Plante, Sam De Grasse, Stuart Holmes, Evelyn Hall, Lionel Belmore.

A romantic drama with the French Revolution as background, the film stars John Boles as Rouget de Lisle, the composer of "La Marseillaise." He is a Royalist, a captain of the guard and a music teacher who falls in love with one of his students, an innkeeper's daughter (Laura La Plante). Their love suffers when the existent social and political tensions compel her to side with the revolutionists. The film contains the usual sequences of the masses storming through the streets of Paris as the Revolution reaches its peak. Such historical figures as Marie Antoinette, Danton and Robespierre occasionally appear to add some authenticity to a chiefly inaccurate historical account. This is acknowledged in an opening credit. Boles sings several semi-operatic songs, the first musical about the French Revolution. The studio originally planned to title the film *La Marseillaise* with Paul Fejos as the director. ∎

Captain Swagger (1928), Pathe. *Dir.* Edward H. Griffith; *Sc.* Leonard Praskins; *Cast includes:* Rod La Rocque, Sue Carroll, Richard Tucker, Victor Potel.

In this implausible melodrama that opens during World War I, Rod La Rocque portrays an American air ace serving in France with the Lafayette Escadrille. He is assigned to bring down a German pilot who has been the cause of high casualties among the other fliers. La Rocque, having just returned from carousing in Paris and still quite drunk, takes on the German terror and shoots him down over enemy territory. He lands his own plane to pull the enemy flier from his burning wreck when a German patrol arrives. The grateful downed flier helps La Rocque escape to safety, giving the American his own gun as a souvenir. The film switches to New York eleven years later. La Rocque, down on his luck, considers using the gun for a stickup. He meets a young woman, a potential victim, and falls in love with her instead. He later comes across the German ace who is now a gang leader. The man buys back his gun from La Rocque through an intermediary for $200, thereby once again helping his old enemy. ∎

Captains of the Clouds (1942), WB. *Dir.* Michael Curtiz; *Sc.* Arthur T. Horman, Richard Macauley, Norman Reilly Raine; *Cast includes:* James Cagney, Dennis Morgan, Brenda Marshall, Alan Hale, George Tobias, Reginald Gardiner.

A tribute to the Canadian bush pilots of the northwest, the film tells the story of four of these brave and reckless airmen who enlist in the Royal Canadian Air Force to train young recruits. Their decision is motivated by a radio broadcast of Sir Winston Churchill's speech following the battle of Dunkirk. James Cagney, as a brash flier, refuses to settle down to a career as a training officer. Held responsible for injuries to a young recruit and the loss of a training plane, he is dismissed from the Royal Canadian Air Force. Later, he volunteers as a civilian to fly bombers to England. When a German fighter plane downs one of the bombers and threatens the other unarmed planes, Cagney crashes his bomber into the enemy craft, thereby saving the other men and bombers.

To add a note of authenticity and some patriotic spirit to the drama, the film utilizes two eminent figures of the period. World War I air ace William Bishop is seen addressing recently graduated fliers at an air base where he presents them with their hard-earned wings. As with several patriotic dramas released during the war, the film ends with a stirring speech. This time the voice of Winston Churchill is heard on the soundtrack. "We shall go on to the end," he affirms. "We shall fight on the seas and oceans. We shall fight with growing confidence and growing strength in the air. We shall fight in the fields and in the streets. We shall never surrender." ■

Captive, The (1915), Lasky. *Dir.* Cecil B. DeMille; *Sc.* Jeanie Macpherson, Cecil B. DeMille; *Cast includes:* Blanche Sweet, House Peters, Gerald Ward, Sage Peters.

With the Balkan Wars as background, this silent drama concerns a Turkish soldier who is captured by Montenegrins. He and other prisoners are sent to work on local farms, replacing the men who are fighting. The young Turk is assigned to a farm run by Blanche Sweet, who guards him with a revolver. Following a battle, the town is retaken by Turkish troops, and their officer, in a drunken stupor, attempts to attack the farm girl. The young captive saves her. The town again

changes hands, and the Montenegrins are back in control. When the war ends, the captive, who has returned home, has his property confiscated and is sent into exile because of his actions toward the Turkish officer. On the road he meets the farm girl.

The Balkan Wars (1912–1913) consisted of two successive conflicts. In the first, Serbia joined Bulgaria, Greece and Montenegro to form the Balkan League which was responsible for driving Turkish forces, who had been unduly brutal to Christians, out of the region. In 1913 the second war erupted when members of the League fought among themselves over the newly won territories. Serbia came out victorious by doubling the size of her land. However, the above film deals only with the first Balkan War. ■

Captive God, The (1916), Triangle. *Dir.* Charles Swickard; *Sc.* Monte J. Katterjohn; *Cast includes:* William S. Hart, Enid Markey, P.D. Tablor, Dorothy Dalton.

This unusual romantic drama is set in the 16th century, a period when only Aztecs and Indians inhabited Mexico and Arizona. The plot concerns a Spanish boy, the sole survivor of a shipwreck, who is adopted by a tribe of peaceful Indian cliff dwellers. Years later the lad, now a man, has become a leader of his people. The Aztecs attack his tribe and capture many women and children, but the young Spaniard and some of his warriors escape. He persuades several other tribes to join him in a war against the Aztecs. Silent western screen star William S. Hart temporarily hung up his cowboy outfit to play the young hero in this offbeat film which received very good reviews.

The film is based on several historical facts. The Aztec civilization, a theocratic state during this period, practiced human sacrifice among its rituals. Local Indian tribes, more peaceful in nature, feared and disliked the Aztecs. The Indians, courted by Hernan Cortes, helped the Spanish conquistador defeat the Aztecs in 1521. ■

Captive Women (1952). See Future Wars. ■

Captured! (1933), WB. *Dir.* Roy Del Ruth; *Sc.* Edward Chodorov; *Cast includes:* Leslie Howard, Douglas Fairbanks, Jr., Paul Lukas, Margaret Lindsay, Arthur Hohl, Robert Barrat, J. Carrol Naish.

A romantic triangle develops in the midst of a German prisoner-of-war camp during World War I. Leslie Howard portrays a captured English captain, recently married, who tries to bring a semblance of order among his fellow prisoners. Douglas Fairbanks, Jr., as Howard's friend, is later captured and sent to the same camp. He and Howard's wife have fallen in love while Howard has been interned. Unable to tell his friend the truth, Fairbanks effects a desperate escape.

Meanwhile, another prisoner has raped and murdered a young German woman on the same night as the escape, and Fairbanks is blamed for the crime. When the Germans request that Fairbanks be returned to stand trial, the British agree, especially since Howard has signed the request. Fairbanks is returned to the German camp, put on trial and found guilty. He accuses Howard, who has learned of the secret love affair, of wanting Fairbanks out of the way. The real murderer-prisoner leaves a confession note and commits suicide. After a slight hesitation, Howard presents the note which saves Fairbanks' life. Howard then initiates a large-scale prison break, sacrificing his life so that 250 Allied prisoners can escape.

The most absorbing aspect of this otherwise routine and implausible drama is the mutual sense of honor concerning the return of the escaped British prisoner. The English officer who agrees to the German request rationalizes his decision by stating that the English would have expected the same cooperation of the Germans if the situation were reversed. Another point of interest is the character of the new German commandant (Paul Lukas) who takes control of the prison camp. More tolerant and humane than his predecessor, he agrees to Howard's requests for reforms and enjoys sharing reminiscences with the English captain about their years at Oxford. ■

Cardigan (1922), AR. *Dir.* John W. Noble; *Sc.* Robert W. Chambers; *Cast includes:* William Collier, Jr., Betty Carpenter, William Pike, Charles E. Graham.

A romantic drama based on the novel by Robert W. Chambers, the film is set in the Colonial period just before the American Revolution. The conflict concerns which side the Indian tribes would ally themselves with—the Tories or the Colonists. William Collier, Jr. portrays the title character, a young patriot who is in love with Betty Carpenter, another Colonial rebel. Collier emerges as a key figure in the historical incidents leading to the Revolution. The events he witnesses transform him from a reluctant servant of King George III to a loyal patriot.

The plot allows for several historical figures and events to be introduced. Young Collier gains admittance to a secret meeting of the Minute Men where he is greeted by Paul Revere, Patrick Henry and John Hancock. Historical events include the Battle of Lexington and Concord and the famous ride of Paul Revere. Action sequences involving Indians, British troops and Colonials all serve as background for the young hero who rescues Carpenter from an unsavory captain and pledges to return to her when the war is over. ■

Cardinal, The (1963). See Religion and War. ■

Careful, Soft Shoulders (1942). See Washington, D.C. ■

Carlson's Raiders. See *Gung Ho!* (1943). ■

Carson, Kit (1809–1868). Though without formal education and illiterate until later in life, Christopher Carson matured into a man of many accomplishments—frontiersman, guide, sheep rancher and soldier. But it was as an Indian fighter that he achieved his greatest prominence. As colonel of the New Mexico Volunteer Cavalry, which he organized and commanded in response to Indian attacks on white settlements in New Mexico during the Civil War, Carson played a major role in the subjugation of the Mescalero Apache and Navajo tribes in his area. The western satire *Do and Dare* (1922), starring Tom Mix as Carson, romanticizes several of the hero's battles with the Indians. An entirely fictitious film, *Kit Carson* (1928), with cowboy star Fred Thomson in the title role, had the famed Indian scout trying to settle a dispute between the Blackfeet tribe and white settlers.

Carson, a native of Kentucky, moved several times before settling in 1826 in Taos, New Mexico, then Mexican territory, where he earned a living for the next 14 years as a guide, cook, teamster and hunter for western explorers. He earned a reputation as a reliable guide for Fremont's expeditions into

California in the early 1840s. This part of his career became the basis for a film biography *Kit Carson* (1940), with Jon Hall in the title role and Dana Andrews as Fremont.

Carson's work as a guide got him involved with military activity in California's Bear Flag Revolt where he served under Fremont in the capture of Los Angeles in 1846. (The above film gave a highly fictionalized account of his heroic efforts to defeat the Mexican troops in a battle sequence reminiscent of the Alamo.) Later in the Mexican War, while Carson served under General Kearny in the latter's westward invasion of California, Carson and several companions slipped through enemy forces that had trapped Kearny's troops and reached San Diego to procure aid.

After the Mexican War, Carson attempted to settle down as a sheep rancher near Taos, but Indian attacks caused him to become a leader in local volunteer forces trying to repel the hostiles. During the Civil War, Indian action increased as a result of the departure of federal troops to fight elsewhere. Carson organized and assumed command of the New Mexico Volunteer Cavalry. He fought the Apache, Comanche and Navajos. His volunteers forced the surrender of the Mescalero Apaches in 1863.

Carson's most famous actions pitted him against the Navajo in 1863–1864. The tribe in April 1863 had been ordered to move to the Bosque Redondo reservation in a barren area in eastern New Mexico. Their refusal brought Carson and his soldiers driving deep on a mission of destruction into their homeland around the Canyon de Chelly that summer. Carson's raid set off attacks against the Navajos by other unfriendly tribes and whites seeking to gain plunder. By that summer, the Navajo had suffered 78 killed, 40 wounded and the loss of 5,000 domesticated animals.

Carson, in the following year, led his troop through the length of the Canyon de Chelly, considered the citadel of Navajo power. Though Indians on the canyon rims let loose a shower of arrows and rocks on the soldiers wending their way along the canyon bottom, the troop methodically tore up orchards and seized the hostiles' sheep. Sixty Indians immediately surrendered. Two months later, eight thousand natives gathered to begin the long, forced trek to an arid reservation in a journey that paralleled, to a lesser extent, the Trail of Tears experienced by the eastern

Cherokee earlier in the century. His successful campaign against the Navajos brought Carson an appointment shortly after the Civil War as a brigadier general in the regular army. He was posted to Fort Garland, Colorado, where he died, as an Indian agent, in 1868.

Except for the above-mentioned biography and several one- or two-reel dramas, including "Kit Carson" (1903) and "Kit Carson" (1910), the famous frontiersman was illtreated by Hollywood. Many films exploiting his name were based on pure fiction; e.g., "Kit Carson's Wooing" (1911), "The Covered Wagon" (1911) and three subsequent serials. A weak remake of the 1940 biography appeared in 1961 titled *Frontier Uprising*, but Carson's name was changed. Carson suffered a similar fate in *Custer's Last Stand*, a 1936 serial in which his name was altered to Kit Cardigan. ■

Cartoons. American cartoons dealing with war themes came into prominence during the country's entry into World War II. Of the nearly 1,000 cartoons produced by the major studios during the war years, almost one-third were war-related. The bulk of these appeared in 1942 and 1943—dark years for the U.S., which was facing setbacks in its struggle against the enemy, especially in the Pacific.

These seven- or eight-minute additions to the movie theater schedule reflected the topical issues of the period. Their subject matter ranged from life on the home front to escapades on a variety of battlefields. The plots concerning civilians covered such topics as the draft, home defense, rationing and the black market while those of the military included the conflict between the Allies and the Axis Powers, life on various fighting fronts and the activities of spies. Like the feature films they accompanied, many contained extensive propaganda. They also poked fun at numerous institutions and world leaders, including rationing, draftees, military life and, most of all, the enemy. Some were quite clever and sophisticated, particularly the war allegories and those offering caricatures of contemporary figures. Many were specifically aimed at an adult audience. Those from Warner Brothers, for example, offered more mature material while the cartoons from Walt Disney were particularly designed for younger audiences.

The home front was a popular subject. In "Scrap Happy Daffy" (1943) Daffy Duck, in a patriotic mood, collects scrap metal for the war effort but is hindered by a German goat who eats the stock pile. "The Fifth Column Mouse," also released in 1943, tells of an oppressive cat who controls the destinies of local mice by enlisting the help of a Quisling mouse. "Meatless Flyday" (1944) concerns a spider who finally catches his prey but is prevented from devouring his victim because the government has decreed that day as a meatless one.

Cartoons parodied the draft and military. In "Meet John Doughboy" (1941), starring Porky Pig, U.S. draft policy comes under attack. "The Rookie Revue," also released in 1941, satirizes military life. Daffy Duck in "Draftee Daffy" (1945) tries in vain to escape a ubiquitous draft board representative who keeps popping up wherever our hero hides.

Spy dramas were the target of several cartoons. "Confusions of a Nutsy Spy" (1942), an obvious takeoff on the 1939 film *Confessions of a Nazi Spy*, has Porky Pig involved with railroad saboteurs. In "Plane Daffy" hero Daffy Duck, on special assignment, matches wits with the notorious Axis spy Hata Mari.

The world of the cartoon expanded to far-flung battlefields where the heroes, often outnumbered, decimate enemy troops. In "Daffy Commando" (1943) Daffy Duck parachutes into Germany and creates havoc among the foe. In "Bugs Bunny Nips the Nips" (1944) our stalwart, wisecracking rabbit ends up on a Japanese-held island where he conquers the enemy with little trouble. He returned the following year in "Herr Meets Hare" where he travels to Germany to take on Goering and Hitler.

Two exceptional cartoons of the war years that retain their humor today are "The Ducktators" (1942) and "Tokyo Jokio" (1943). The former traces the rise of dictatorship while reducing Hitler, Mussolini and Hirohito to absurdity. The latter, a parody of propaganda newsreels and documentaries, concerns a captured Japanese newsreel that focuses on that country's incompetence. ■

Casablanca (1942), WB. *Dir.* Michael Curtiz; *Sc.* Julius and Philip Epstein, Howard Koch; *Cast includes:* Humphrey Bogart, Ingrid Bergman, Paul Henreid, Claude Rains, Conrad Veidt, Sydney Greenstreet, Peter Lorre, S. Z. Sakall.

This drama of love and redemption takes place during World War II, prior to Pearl Harbor, in a city where international intrigue and a flourishing black market dominate the lives of many of its inhabitants. Rick (Humphrey Bogart), a cynical, disillusioned American in self-exile, runs a cafe. One day Ilsa (Ingrid Bergman), Rick's former sweetheart, enters his cafe with her husband, Victor Laszlo (Paul Henreid), a leader of anti-Nazi resistance. That night, while sitting alone and drinking heavily, Rick ponders: "Of all the gin joints in all the towns in all the world—she walks into mine." Ilsa, in desperation, turns to Rick to help her husband who is being sought by the Gestapo. At first he refuses, but when she promises to stay with him, he reluctantly decides to help them both. Rick outwardly professes a lack of interest in her that reassures Victor of his wife's devotion. Providing the couple with special letters of transit, Rick arranges for their flight out of Casablanca. He then walks down that familiar tarmac with his friend, Renault (Claude Rains), a witty and charmingly corrupt police captain. Their lost ideals rekindled, the two men join the Allies in their fight against totalitarianism as Rick announces: "Louie, I think this is the beginning of a beautiful friendship."

The film has rightfully earned its reputation as a classic. It tells a highly romanticized story that captivates its audiences. Rarely has a cast been so well chosen to play the rich assortment of characters. The anti-Nazi propaganda that permeates the work is not only unobtrusive, it is essential to the characters and the plot. For example, when someone warns Laszlo that he and other leaders like him will be caught, he replies defiantly: "Thousands will rise in their places." And when Laszlo says to Rick, "Welcome back to the fight. This time I know our side will win," the audience empathizes with both men. In one inspiring scene in the cafe, which has become a microcosm of the embattled nations of Europe, several Nazi officers break into a chorus of "Die Wacht am Rhein" but are drowned out when Laszlo leads the French patrons in a stirring rendition of the "Marseillaise."

The film opened only weeks after Allied forces landed in French North Africa (November 8, 1942). This was followed by the

Casablanca conference between Roosevelt and Churchill on January 23, 1943—two fortuitous events that no doubt heightened interest in the film. The historical conference contributed to the allegorical speculations about the role of Rick, the neutral American who remains uninvolved until the appropriate moment and then enters the fight. "I stick my neck out for nobody," he announces early in the film. When he allows a young refugee couple, desperate for exit visas, to win at one of his gambling tables, the wife cries: "He is an American. You see, America must be a wonderful place." When the arrogant Col. Strasser (Conrad Veidt), recently arrived from Berlin, dismisses Rick as "just another blundering American," Renault is quick to correct this assessment. "We mustn't underestimate American blundering," he adds. "I was with them when they blundered into Berlin in 1918." American isolationism is suggested in Rick's casual musings: "I bet they're asleep in New York. I bet they're asleep all over America." The film is so affecting that no one cares that historically there never were any "letters of transit." Romantic drama at its best, *Casablanca* was what America needed in the gloomy days of 1942. ∎

Casanova. See *Adventures of Casanova* (1948). ∎

Case of Sergeant Grischa, The (1930), RKO. *Dir.* Herbert Brenon; *Sc.* Elizabeth Meehan; *Cast includes:* Chester Morris, Betty Compson, Alec B. Francis, Jean Hersholt.

A depressing World War I drama about an illiterate Russian soldier, the film stars Chester Morris in the role of the title character. While the war rages on, Grischa, who yearns only to see his mother once more, escapes from a German prison camp and hides out in a forest. Here he meets a German girl (Betty Compson) and seduces her. The authorities search relentlessly for him as he makes his way back to his own lines. When he is finally caught, he gives his captors another soldier's name. Ironically, it is the name of a Russian spy, and he is sentenced to be shot. The German military bureaucracy displays its callousness and depravity when it disregards evidence of the soldier's innocence and has him executed.

Evidently intended as an antiwar film in the spirit, if not the style, of *All Quiet on the Western Front*, released the same year, the film chastises the German high command for its blatant misuse of its powers in the unnecessary execution of the Russian. Some critics found the theme about the fate of one soldier inane since thousands were dying in battle during the entire incident. Others, however, felt that the Russian youth crystallized the plight of the common soldier caught up in the dehumanizing bureaucracy and machinery of war. Herbert Brenon, the director, had made an earlier antiwar film in 1916 titled *War Brides*. ∎

Case of the Legless Veteran: James Kutcher, The (1981), Mass Production. *Dir.* Howard Petrick.

A documentary about a World War II veteran who, as a victim of the Cold War, lost his job and his pension. James Kutcher lost both legs during the battle of San Pietro. After the war he obtained a job as clerk with the Veterans Administration. When government officials learned that Kutcher had been a member of the Socialist Workers Party since 1938, they labeled him as a subversive and had him fired. Within a short time he was threatened with the loss of his pension. Not an otherwise extraordinary man, Kutcher nevertheless decided to fight to get his job back and have his pension restored; there followed a ten-year struggle with government forces as Kutcher relentlessly pursued his rights. Organized labor, which at first took up his cause, buckled under the panic of the Cold War period. To help capture the mood of the times, the film uses newsreel footage ranging from the Spanish Civil War to the 1950s. ∎

Cassino to Korea (1950), Par. *Dir.* Edward Genock; *Sc.* Max Klein.

A documentary composed chiefly of World War II footage, the film attempts to compare certain aspects of the battle for Cassino with that of Korea. Scenes show troops landing on beachheads under heavy fire, forced marches and the final capture of Cassino. These views are then blended with those depicting the tough assignment undertaken by United Nations troops in Korea. Quentin Reynolds, a noted journalist and writer of the period, provides the necessary commentary. ∎

Cast a Giant Shadow (1966), UA. *Dir.* Melville Shavelson; *Sc.* Melville Shavelson; *Cast includes:* Kirk Douglas, Senta Berger, Angie Dickinson, Frank Sinatra, John Wayne.

Kirk Douglas stars as Colonel David (Mickey) Marcus, an American Jew who fought in Israel's war of independence, in this biographical drama. A West Point graduate, a New York lawyer and police officer, a soldier in the U.S. Army during World War II, Marcus at first has difficulties identifying with the Jews in Palestine who are on the verge of establishing their own state. His innate restlessness and proclivity for adventure initially draw him into the conflict where he is invited to train the Jews in Palestine. Eventually, he is won over to the Jewish dream of a homeland.

Angie Dickinson portrays his sympathetic wife who understands his need to journey to the Middle East. John Wayne, as Marcus' superior officer in the World War II flashbacks, cautions him not to take part in the Middle East struggle. Senta Berger, as an Israeli soldier, becomes entangled romantically with Marcus. Yul Brynner plays a leader in the Jewish underground while Frank Sinatra, as an American pilot, provides some humor. The second half of the film contains plenty of action as the Jews battle the Arabs in a life-and-death battle. ∎

One of the horrors of battle on the European front during World War II. *Castle Keep* (1969).

Castle Keep (1969), Col. *Dir.* Sydney Pollack; *Sc.* Daniel Taradash, David Rayfiel; *Cast includes:* Burt Lancaster, Patrick O'Neal, Jean Pierre Aumont, Peter Falk, Astrid Heeren.

Burt Lancaster portrays an American major who, with a handful of G.I.s, decides to make a stand against the advancing Germans in this satirical World War II action drama. A pragmatic officer, Lancaster and his eight battle-weary soldiers stop at a Belgian castle owned by a middle-aged count (Jean Pierre Aumont). They soon begin to enjoy the facilities offered to them, including some of the female occupants. This idyllic respite from the horrors of war comes to an end when the Germans begin to approach. The inhabitants are torn between making a stand and endangering the art treasures of the castle or withdrawing and allowing the Germans to occupy the estate. The count and Lancaster decide to defend the castle against overwhelming odds. The enemy eventually wipes out the small group of defenders, with both sides paying a high price.

The action sequences in the latter half are exciting and plentiful although the film seems pointless and, at times, anachronistic. "Someday," Lancaster remarks upon seeing a Volkswagen on the castle grounds, "the world is going to be peopled by Volkswagens." Patrick O'Neal, as a captain, is concerned with protecting the priceless art collection of the castle. Peter Falk, as a happy-go-lucky soldier and former baker, woos the baker's wife. Astrid Heeren, as the count's wife, provides the romantic interest for Lancaster. The count, who is impotent but would like to have a son, encourages the sexual liaison. ∎

Castro, Fidel. See Cuban Revolution (1956–1959). ∎

Catch-22 (1970), Par. *Dir.* Mike Nichols; *Sc.* Buck Henry; *Cast includes:* Alan Arkin, Martin Balsam, Richard Benjamin, Arthur Garfunkel, Jack Gilford, Buck Henry.

Based on Joseph Heller's best selling novel, this black comedy set in Italy during World War II captures some of the satire and dark humor of the original work. Alan Arkin portrays Captain Yossarian, a peace-loving, battle-weary American flier who simply wants to serve his required number of bombing missions. But this turns out to be a losing battle against the military establishment that applies convoluted reasoning (Catch-22) to keep him in the air. First, his commander keeps raising the number of missions. Second, if Yossarian claims that he is unfit to fly because of mental illness, then his own acknowledgment of his problem proves he is rational and capable of further missions. In the end, it is the high command that symbolizes the insanity of war with its terrible execution and inhuman policies.

The men at the air base engage in selling, trading and plundering, all representing the greed and exploitation that follow in the wake of war. Many are incompetent. Martin Balsam, as an ambitious officer, keeps upping the number of missions needed for completion of duty and does not believe in giving the men leave. Jon Voight, as the ultimate trader in black market goods and organizer of a chain of local brothels, advances to a corporate-military position and ends up dealing with the enemy. He steals the pilots' parachutes and trades them for their silk content. "We're going to come out of this war rich," he boasts to Arkin. "You're going to come out rich," Arkin says. "We're going to come out dead." Orson Welles, as a pompous general, leads a retinue that includes a moronic son-in-law as his aide and a voluptuous mistress. Buck Henry plays Balsam's weak-kneed faithful aide. Anthony Perkins appears as an ineffectual and bewildered chaplain. Bob Newhart, as a confused officer in charge of laundry, is advanced in rank because his last name is Major. The film, episodic in its treatment of the novel and offering little in the way of compassion, manages to reflect some of the surrealistic insanity of the original work. ∎

Caught in the Draft (1941). See Service Comedy. ∎

Cavalcade (1933), Fox. *Dir.* Frank Lloyd; *Sc.* Reginald Berkeley; *Cast includes:* Diana Wynyard, Clive Brook, Herbert Mundin, Una O'Connor, Beryl Mercer.

Based on Noel Coward's stage hit, the film unfolds the story of an English family and how it endures various crises including wars, economic depression and scandal. The story opens with the advent of the Boer War, touches upon such events as the death of Queen Victoria and the sinking of the *Lusitania* and moves on to World War I and the Jazz Age. The Marryot family survives with dignity although, like many other families, tragedy strikes from time to time. One son is lost aboard the doomed *Lusitania* while another falls in battle during the Great War. Noel Coward's songs are kept intact, contributing to the tone of the drama. Perhaps the final speech by the principal couple exemplifies the heart of the film and the fortitude of the

English: "Let's drink to the spirit of gallantry and courage . . . let's drink to the hope that one day this country of ours, which we love so much, will find dignity and greatness and peace again."

One of the numerous films made during and after World War I which depicted the British as the central subject, the drama was indicative of the heroism and determination of a people faced with adversity. Hollywood's favorable image of the British people continued well into the World War II years with such films as *Mrs. Miniver* (1942), a war drama that genuinely stirred American audiences and gained sympathy for a nation under fire. ∎

Cavalry Command (1963), Parade. *Dir.* Eddie Romero; *Sc.* Eddie Romero; *Cast includes:* John Agar, Richard Arlen, Myron Healey, Alicia Vergel, Pancho Magalona.

American occupation forces in the Philippines have problems with local guerrillas in this action drama set during the Philippine Insurrection following the Spanish-American War. U.S. Cavalry troops under the command of Lieutenant Worth (Myron Healey) manage to capture Captain Magno, a fanatic who continues to resist occupation. Worth decides to imprison the captain rather than have him executed, thereby not turning him into a martyr. Later upon his release, Magno thinks the Americans want to kill him. He retaliates by burning down a schoolhouse the troops recently had helped to construct. But his attitude changes when he realizes the Americans have been helping the Filipinos by bringing in food and medical supplies. The film was made in the Philippines. ∎

Cavalry films. Few scenes can match the visual excitement of a rousing cavalry charge thundering across the screen. Cavalry charges played a prominent role in warfare before the 20th century, and Hollywood has occasionally turned to this adventure genre with some striking success. From the time the Hittites first used horses in battle, at the latest by 1200 B.C., until the 19th century, the cavalry was an important if not dominant part of military organization in several parts of the world. Several early famous conquerors from Alexander the Great to Genghis Khan raised the use of cavalry to a highly disciplined force.

The Egyptian cavalry was one of the earliest to be depicted on screen. Cecil B. DeMille's *The Ten Commandments* (1923) has the Pharaoh's cavalry charging headlong after Moses and his people who have fled from the tyrannical ruler. The Mongols under Genghis Khan also were among the earliest mounted warriors to be featured in a film. Genghis Khan and his hordes swept out of Asia in the early 13th century to conquer the greatest land mass of any group in history. Within a generation, the Mongols ruled large sections of Asia and a small part of eastern Europe. The flat, open terrain was well suited to the tactics of Mongol horsemen. Several films dramatized the Mongols in action. The 1951 costume drama, *The Golden Horde*, was a highly fictionalized account of the Mongolian chief's siege of Samarkand in 1220. *The Conqueror* (1956), a large-scale action drama and possibly one of the worst films ever made, recounted the Mongol-Tartar conflicts, with John Wayne portraying the Mongol leader.

During the European Middle Ages and the Crusades, the mounted, heavily armored knight became the core of military strength. Such films as *The Crusades* (1935) and *The Black Arrow* (1948) reflect this. Mounted knights, however, faced a serious drawback: once dismounted, they were practically immobile. Massed foot soldiers using bows and swords did most of the fighting.

The Cossacks, raised from early youth in the skills of horse-borne warfare, became the terrors of the Russian plains, and later the Russian imperial army, beginning in the 15th century. In *Taras Bulba* (1962), starring Tony Curtis and Yul Brynner, hundreds of horsemen thunder across the landscape of 15th-century eastern Europe as Cossacks and Polish troops clash in battle. The plot may be inept, but the thrill of all those horsemen sweeping across the screen more than makes up for the film's inadequacies.

Napoleon relied more on his infantry, rather than cavalry tactics, for his successes. This may have been because of the nature of his army, largely a peasant force with little experience on horseback. Although cavalry action played a significant role in Napoleon's final defeat at Waterloo, such films as *Conquest* (1937), featuring Charles Boyer as Napoleon, and *Desiree* (1954), with Marlon Brando as Bonaparte, failed to detail this aspect.

The film that epitomizes the romanticism of a cavalry charge in all its glory is *The Charge of the Light Brigade* (1936). The movie involves an event in the Battle of Balaklava in the Crimean War between Russia and Britain. The climactic battle, with stalwart Errol Flynn leading the Light Brigade against formidable Russian artillery positions, is recognized as one of the best action sequences ever filmed.

Wars in which thousands of cavalry troops charged with lances and sabers against breech-loading guns, rifles and cannon were all but obsolete by the time of the Crimean War, and the British cavalry suffered a heavy toll in that engagement. However, those who watched the gallant 600 ride into the "jaws of death" did not object to the film's romanticized view of history. Meanwhile, other films recreated the cavalry in action during the 19th century. *The Soldier and the Lady* (1937), the third version of Jules Verne's novel *Michael Strogoff*, concerned the 1870 Tartar revolt against Russia's Czar Alexander II. The drama presented several stirring Tartar and Russian cavalry charges.

The American Civil War and the Indian Wars of the mid-to-late 1800s presented the most effective use of light cavalry in modern times. General Lee at first struck successfully against the Union with his cavalry, especially under Jeb Stuart. The North, slow to develop its own cavalry units, eventually formed an effective striking force, best exemplified by Phil Sheridan. The battles for control of the strategic Shenandoah Valley were largely a series of cavalry actions and tactics. Several early silent films dramatized these battles, including "Sheridan's Ride" and "In the Shenandoah Valley," both released in 1908, and *Shenandoah* (1913).

Cavalry charges began to diminish by 1863. In their place rose mounted riflemen who used their animals mainly for transport and were trained to fight on foot and on horseback. *They Died With Their Boots On* (1941), also starring Errol Flynn—this time as George A. Custer—recounted some of the cavalry action of the Civil War. Flynn's dashing portrayal of Custer leading several rousing cavalry charges against Lee's forces, however erroneous, almost exonerates the film from its digressions from the facts. Other Civil War films, such as John Ford's *The Horse Soldiers* (1959), starring John Wayne as a battle-hardened Union colonel, conveyed the concept of the mounted rifleman in several battle sequences.

The U.S. Cavalry was very important in combating the Indians on the western plains and in the southwest. Horse soldiers were the only means to quickly traverse the large areas between forts. In addition, cavalry was the only way to counter the threat of several tribes such as the Sioux, Apache and Comanche, who had become highly expert mounted fighters—rated among the best light cavalry in history by some military analysts. Unfortunately, few films have stressed this native talent, opting instead to dramatize the glory of the U.S. Cavalry. *Stagecoach* (1939), John Ford's western masterpiece, illustrates the expertise of the Apache mounted warriors during their attack upon a lone stagecoach across the vast salt flats.

John Ford did more to illustrate the life and times of the cavalry on the Southwest frontier than any other director. His trilogy, *She Wore a Yellow Ribbon* (1949), *Rio Grande* (1950) and *Fort Apache* (1951), set in the post-Civil War period, remains the definitive film depiction of the U.S. Cavalry. Ford draped his cavalry troops in myth and glory as they rode across the rugged Southwest frontier protecting settlers from marauding Indians. His screen images of cavalryman and Indian closely resemble the western paintings of Frederic Remington.

The British, during the early stages of the Boer War (1899–1902), relied mostly on infantry. Their few small cavalry units were equipped only with sword or lance. The Boers, lacking the numbers and equipment of their adversaries, used mounted riflemen fluidly to wreak havoc upon the British, who eventually reorganized their forces and defeated the Boers. Early American films of this conflict, such as "The Highlander's Defiance" (1910) and "The Second In Command" (1915), which viewed the war from the British point of view, failed to convey Britain's tactical error in the conduct of the war.

Cavalry units and charges were employed in limited fashion on both the Eastern and Western fronts during World War I. *The Gay Diplomat* (1931) and *Storm at Daybreak* (1933), two World War I dramas, emphasize the use of cavalry by the Russians and Hungarians respectively. The development of machine guns and other automatic weapons, and the stagnant, heavily fortified trench warfare that emerged in the west, soon made cavalry forces virtually useless. Such films as *The Big Parade* (1925) and *Wings* (1927)

merely hinted at the use of cavalry during the conflict. Meanwhile, the cavalry played a more prominent role in the Middle Eastern theater where British and Arab forces defeated the Turks. *The Last Outpost* (1935) starring Cary Grant covered this aspect of the war.

The last major use of the cavalry as a fighting force occurred early in World War II. Poland, in September 1939, sent its gallant but outdated horse-borne troops against the highly mobilized German army with the expected results. In *The North Star* (1943), Lewis Milestone's controversial tribute to embattled Soviet Russia, a local Russian home guard of outnumbered and poorly armed mounted troops bravely attacks the Nazi occupiers of a Russian village.

Once mechanized cavalry (the tank) was introduced, the horse cavalry faded into history, taking with it the romantic tales of poets and storytellers. Filmmakers, by recreating these stories and historical events, have kept alive the tradition and glory of the cavalry. ■

Cease Fire (1953), Par. *Dir.* Owen Crump; *Sc.* Walter Doniger.

A Korean War documentary based on frontline activities during the cease-fire negotiations at Panmunjom, the film focuses on a patrol of G.I.s going about their daily routines. The men are assigned to investigate enemy activity on a nearby mountain. Individual scenes capture the constant dangers the G.I.s face as they perform their routine assignments while awaiting the completion of the negotiations. The film was originally shot in 3-D, a popular fad in movie theaters during the early 1950s. ■

Cease Fire (1985). See Veterans. ■

Celebrated Case, A (1914), Kalem. *Dir.* George Melford; *Sc.* Gene Gaunthier; *Cast includes:* Alice Joyce, Alice Hollister, Marguerite Courtot, James B. Ross.

The silent film is a domestic drama that takes place during the War of the Austrian Succession, particularly at the time of the Battle of Fontenoy in Belgium. A French soldier, wrongly accused of murdering his wife and convicted on the incorrect testimony of his own little daughter, is sentenced to the galleys. The scenes of the famous battle are realistically enacted.

The War of the Austrian Succession (1740–

1748) was fought over the right of Maria Theresa to succeed her father, Holy Roman Emperor Charles VI, to the throne of the Austrian Hapsburg empire. Some European powers wanted to divide up the empire. A general struggle ensued among most of the nations of Europe with Britain emerging as Maria Theresa's principal ally. The Battle of Fontenoy (May 11, 1745) was one of the largest of many big engagements in the war. The French routed a combined army of Austrian-English-Dutch-Hanoverian troops at Fontenoy. Maria Theresa's claim to the crown was eventually upheld after much bloodshed, but Austria did give up some territory. ∎

Chaco War (1932–1935). The discovery of oil in a disputed border area brought on conflict between Paraguay and Bolivia. The contested region in the northern part of the Gran Chaco had been considered part of Bolivia when Spain controlled most of South America, but it had been largely ignored since 1810 although claimed by both countries.

Paraguayan settlers moved into the district in increasing numbers and Paraguayan soldiers gradually pushed out the wild Indian tribes. With the discovery of oil, Bolivia sought to re-establish its claim, but the Paraguayans refused to leave. Border clashes started in 1928, leading to full-scale war in 1932. Over 100,000 people were killed before a peace treaty was signed in 1935 after arbitration by six nations, including the U.S. By the terms of the treaty, Paraguay received about three-quarters of the land while Bolivia received access to the Paraguay River and the right to construct port facilities there as a trade outlet to the sea.

Only one American film deals with this event—*Storm Over The Andes* (1935), a fictional love-adventure tale with little relevance to the actual conflict. However, excerpted newsreels from the Chaco War were used several years later in portions of an antiwar documentary entitled *The Dead March* (1937). The film used footage from several conflicts to show the stupidity and destruction of modern war. ∎

Chances (1931), FN. *Dir.* Allan Dwan; *Sc.* Waldemar Young; *Cast includes:* Douglas Fairbanks, Jr., Rose Hobart, Anthony Bushell, Mary Forbes, Holmes Herbert.

Two brothers fall in love with the same girl in this World War I romantic drama. Douglas Fairbanks, Jr. portrays the older brother while Anthony Bushell plays the younger. They meet Rose Hobart in London while on a three-day pass and quickly lose their hearts over her. Both are assigned to the field artillery in France where Bushell stays at his post after the outfit is ordered to retreat in the face of the advancing Germans. He resigns himself to his death thinking that his brother and the girl have deceived him. The film contains several rousing battle sequences. ∎

Charge at Feather River, The (1953), WB. *Dir.* Gordon Douglas; *Sc.* James R. Webb; *Cast includes:* Guy Madison, Frank Lovejoy, Helen Westcott, Vera Miles.

The U.S. Cavalry enlists the aid of an Indian fighter to rescue two white women held captive for several years by warring hostiles in this action drama. Guy Madison portrays the hero who leads a detachment of soldiers—volunteers from the guardhouse— on the perilous mission. Although he succeeds in rescuing the two captives, Madison is faced with other problems. One of the girls, Helen Westcott, is ashamed to face her peers. The other, Vera Miles, has embraced Indian life and has fallen for the chief. When they return to the outpost, they discover it has been destroyed. As they try to reach another fort, they are stalked by Indians. The small force makes its stand at Feather River, with Madison pitting his skills against the Indians. Because the film was originally released in 3-D, many scenes depict various objects, including lances and arrows, being hurled at the screen. ∎

Charge of the Lancers (1954), Col. *Dir.* William Castle; *Sc.* Robert E. Kent; *Cast includes:* Paulette Goddard, Jean Pierre Aumont, Richard Stapley, Karin Booth.

Romance blooms between a gypsy and a French captain during the Crimean War in this routine drama. Paulette Goddard portrays the passionate gypsy while Jean Pierre Aumont portrays the captain. The lovers are caught by the Russians, but they manage to spy upon the enemy and rescue a British officer (Richard Stapley). Karin Booth, as a Russian agent, masquerades as an English nurse. Goddard and Aumont return with their vital information which helps the British to capture the Russian naval base at Sebastopol. Historical records report that the introduction of a new type of cannon played the principal role in the battle. See also Empire Films. ■

Lobby card for *The Charge of the Light Brigade* (1936).

Charge of the Light Brigade, The (1936), WB. *Dir.* Michael Curtiz; *Sc.* Michel Jacoby, Rowland Leigh; *Cast includes:* Errol Flynn, Olivia de Havilland, Patric Knowles, Henry Stephenson, Nigel Bruce, Donald Crisp, David Niven.

Based on Tennyson's famous poem, this historical drama captures the sweep of the period and the glory of the British cavalry during the Crimean War. The film romanticizes the historical events and people with little regard for accuracy. However, it provides realistic details in such matters as uniforms which are exact replicas of those worn by the 27th Dragoons. Errol Flynn, as Major Geoffrey Vickers, a British officer, witnesses a massacre of women and children in India by the brutal Surat Khan (C. Henry Gordon), and from that moment he pledges to avenge the slaughter. Khan, a shrewd, literate leader of numerous tribesmen, feels cheated when the British cut off a hefty stipend paid to his father at the elder's death. He earlier voices his discontent at a ball given by the British, who suspect he has been flirting with Russia. "I sometimes think that a great government resembles a beautiful woman," he says to the English ambassador to India, "who, intoxicated with the power of her own beauty, is apt to withdraw from her sincere suitor the favors she always granted—and when she finds the suitor consoles himself with another beauty, regrets her coldness."

Flynn and his troops, many the widowers and fathers of the slain, get their chance to avenge the massacre on the plains of Balaklava in the Crimean War when they learn that Khan has joined the Russians. This becomes the motivation for the climactic immortal charge. Flynn changes an official order so that the light brigade can attack the Khan's position, a ride that means almost certain death. "Our chance has come," he announces to the mounted 600. "Show no mercy. Let no power on earth stop you. Prove to the world that no man can kill women and children and boast of it. Men of the 27th—our objective is Surat Khan. Forward!" Romance is introduced by Flynn and his brother (Patric Knowles), both of whom love the colonel's daughter, played by Olivia de Havilland.

Michael Curtiz was singled out by critics for his expert direction of the film although the climactic battle, recognized as one of the best action sequences ever filmed, was directed by B. Reeves Eason, a second unit director. The film was not without its controversy. Animal lovers and organizations criticized the mistreatment and unnecessary deaths of the horses. To dramatize the action and the fighting sequences, the special effects department attached long wires to the hoofs of the creatures so that they would stop short and their riders would spill over in front of the animals. The result made for good visual effects, but it broke the legs of many of the horses.

The Battle of Balaklava (October 25, 1854) was initiated by Russia, who wanted to recapture this port city from occupying British, French and Turkish forces. Both sides indulged in furious cavalry assaults. One of the British cavalry charges, by the 670 men of the Light Brigade under Lord Cardigan, was immortalized in Tennyson's poem. The Russians failed to dislodge the invaders in this engagement. See also Crimean War; Empire Films. ■

Charley One-Eye (1973), Par. *Dir.* Don Chaffey; *Sc.* Keith Leonard; *Cast includes:* Richard Roundtree, Roy Thinnes, Nigel Davenport, Jill Pearson.

Richard Roundtree plays a black Union Army deserter who seeks refuge in Mexico in this allegorical drama about violence. Roundtree had murdered his commanding officer before escaping across the border where he meets an Indian (Roy Thinnes) who has been ostracized by his tribe because he is crippled and a half-caste. The two homeless figures soon develop an odd relationship with Roundtree treating the Indian cruelly while Thinnes responds unemotionally. The deserter's penchant for violence leads to his killing of two Mexicans and, ultimately, to his own death. Nigel Davenport plays a brutal bounty hunter in this unusual Civil War tale. ∎

Charlie Chan in Panama (1940). See Detectives at War. ∎

Charlotte Corday (1914), Kennedy Features.

A silent drama of the French Revolution, the film depicts the events that led up to the death of Marat at the hands of Charlotte Corday. The story begins before the revolution when he meets Charlotte and her lover Barbaroux, whom he convinces to join the uprising. A year later, with the Revolution at its height and Marat's power the cause of numerous executions, Charlotte goes to his rooms. He threatens to sentence Barbaroux to death unless she concedes to become his mistress. Feigning agreement to his demands, she takes out a concealed dagger and fatally stabs him. Barbaroux is freed while she goes to the guillotine. ∎

Charmer, The (1917). See Home Front. ∎

Che! (1969), TCF. *Dir.* Richard Fleischer; *Sc.* Michael Wilson, Sy Bartlett; *Cast includes:* Omar Sharif, Jack Palance, Robert Loggia, Woody Strode, Barbara Luna.

A biographical drama of Dr. Ernesto Che Guevara, the film concentrates on his role in the Cuban revolution and his strong influence on Fidel Castro. The script depicts Guevara, played by Omar Sharif, as a malevolent, ingenious figure who delighted in violence and attempted to divert the revolution and Castro toward evil ends. This almost complete exoneration of Fidel Castro of the events that followed the upheaval may not be accepted by many viewers. The charismatic Guevara is credited as the architect of the revolutionary strategy that toppled the previous regime of Batista and as the major writer of Castro's radio speeches from his mountain hide-out. Jack Palance portrays Castro in this low-budget film that has been photographed in a semi-documentary style. It contains limited action sequences, chiefly concerning guerrilla warfare.

The original script called for a more sympathetic, idealistic figure of little substance who died for his convictions. "What I'm trying to do," Director Richard Fleischer explained in an interview with Newsweek magazine, "is an objective character study of a very complex man . . . But I'm not so sure that five years from now anyone will remember him . . ." Guevara (1928–1967), considered Castro's chief lieutenant, was a dedicated Marxist revolutionary for much of his adult life. Born in Argentina and educated as a physician, he adopted Marxism and took part in riots against Argentine dictator Juan Peron in 1952. Within the next year, he was active with revolutionary groups in Bolivia, where he also worked in a leper colony, and in Guatemala, where he became associated with the pro-Communist government of Jacobo Arbenz-Guzman. Guevara fled from Guatemala to Mexico in 1954, following the overthrow of Arbenz-Guzman.

While in Mexico, he joined Fidel Castro and accompanied him in the 1956 Cuban invasion and subsequent guerrilla war that resulted in the overthrow of Cuban dictator Fulgencio Batista in 1959. Guevara held several posts in Castro's government, including president of the national bank and minister of industry. He was credited with being a major influence in shifting Cuba's economic ties from the U.S. to the Communist bloc. Guevara resigned from the government in 1961 but continued to be a powerful figure in leftist revolutionary circles. His book *Guerrilla Warfare* became a manual for Marxist insurgents.

Guevara, ever the revolutionary, surfaced in Bolivia in 1967, where he took part in an allegedly Cuban-directed guerrilla war against the government. Bolivian peasants gave very limited support to the insurgency.

Guevara was killed in 1967 in a skirmish with government troops. His diary was said to have been sold to Castro by a member of Bolivia's ruling clique. ∎

Chennault, Claire Lee (1890–1958). One of the regular army's early proponents of air power and a pioneer in air pursuit tactics as a pilot in World War I, Chennault became prominent for his accomplishments in Asia prior to and during World War II. He retired from the Army Air Force in 1937 to become an adviser to General Chiang Kai-shek, leader of Nationalist China, in that nation's conflict with the Japanese invaders. Chennault helped organize China's air defenses.

He achieved even greater recognition with the American public beginning in early 1941 when he created and trained the American Volunteer Group, an air unit that became more popularly known as the Flying Tigers. The unit, composed of volunteer American fliers, successfully fought superior Japanese air forces in the period immediately before and briefly after America's entry into World War II.

In his activities in China, Chennault had the unofficial encouragement and assistance of the U.S. government. Though technically neutral in the Asian war between China and Japan before the attack on Pearl Harbor, the U.S. sympathized with China and its efforts to counter Japanese aggression starting in 1937. The U. S., besides sending war supplies to Chiang, allowed American air personnel to temporarily withdraw from the air force to fight in the Flying Tigers. The unit was disbanded shortly after the U.S. entered the war, and many of its personnel returned to the Army Air Force.

Chennault resumed active duty in the A.A.F., gaining promotion as a brigadier general in 1942, and served as U.S. Air Force Commander in China for the remainder of the war. He was promoted to Major General in 1943. Chennault, who emphasized a greater role in tactical air power in the war against Japan, repeatedly clashed with his American superior officer, General Joseph Stilwell. Chennault retired in 1945 as a major general.

Hollywood's handling of Chennault's career and contributions to the conduct of World War II in Asia is yet another example of how American war films often trivialize or even ignore what is important. That part of his career in which he was involved with the

Flying Tigers is only touched upon, and in the briefest fashion, in *God Is My Co-Pilot* (1945), in which Raymond Massey plays a supporting role as Chennault in the semi-biographical story of Colonel Robert Scott, one of his fliers. *Flying Tigers* (1942), purportedly a story of the highly glamorized unit made at a time when its exploits were still fresh in the public's mind, completely ignores the career of the man who organized, trained and inspired the group. The drama, starring John Wayne, is just another stock air action piece about a fictional hero. The documentary *The Battle of China* (1944), part of Frank Capra's "Why We Fight" series made for the government during the war, shows Chennault and his Flying Tigers in action in several scenes. None of the films delve into the political ramifications of Chennault's group in China before U. S. entry into the war, or his clashes with superiors over the role of air power in a modern war. ∎

Chetniks (1943), TCF. *Dir.* Louis King; *Sc.* Jack Andrews, E. E. Paramore; *Cast includes:* Philip Dorn, Anna Sten, John Sheppard, Virginia Gilmore.

This World War II film pays tribute to Yugoslavia's heroic General Draja Mihalovitch and his brave guerrillas who fought against their Nazi occupiers. In this straightforward drama the general, played by Philip Dorn, and his band are shown outwitting the invaders at almost every turn. They ambush an Italian supply column and eventually capture an entire town held by the enemy after the general's wife (Anna Sten) and child are caught and held as hostage.

The film was based on contemporary news reports filtering out of Nazi-occupied Europe as well as biographical information supplied by officials of the Yugoslavian Embassy in the United States. The Chetniks, highly regarded in the West early in the war and who represented Serbian nationalism, soon found themselves out of favor with the Allies, who instead recognized Mashall Tito and his partisans. ∎

Cheyenne Autumn (1964), WB. *Dir.* John Ford; *Sc.* James R. Webb; *Cast includes:* Richard Widmark, Carroll Baker, James Stewart, Edgar G. Robinson, Karl Malden, Sal Mineo.

The plight of the Cheyenne Indians after their surrender to the U.S. Army in 1877 is the subject of this sprawling drama. The tribe of more than 900 men, women and children who are forced to leave their Yellowstone River country and relocate on a barren Oklahoma reservation has been reduced by lack of medication and starvation to 286. Disgusted with government decrees, the Cheyenne decide to escape and return home to Wyoming with its more fertile land. They manage to circumvent their pursuers, the U.S. Cavalry, during most of their journey. Richard Widmark, as a sympathetic army captain, pleads the Indian cause to Washington officials. Ricardo Montalban plays Red Shirt, a Cheyenne chief, while Gilbert Roland portrays Dull Knife, another Cheyenne leader. Carroll Baker, as a Quaker schoolteacher, accompanies the tribe on its journey while caring for the children.

The film is based on the book by Mari Sandoz which in turn was taken from an actual historical incident. In 1878 a band of Cheyenne, interned in Oklahoma's Indian Territory where they were subjected to malnutrition and disease, chose to return to their own home in Wyoming. Numbering almost 300, they journeyed the 1,500 miles by foot, all the while threatened by local settlers whose property they were forced to cross and hounded by the cavalry. Only a handful survived. ■

Cheyenne Wars (1864–1878). Until gold was discovered in 1858 in Colorado on Cheyenne territory, the tribe was generally peaceful toward whites. One noted Cheyenne chief, Yellow Wolf, impressed by the military strength of union forces in his area, counseled his people to live in peace with whites, and, in fact, seek to learn the white man's ways. When occasional conflict arose between swarming gold-seekers and Indians, the Southern Cheyenne agreed in an 1861 peace treaty to reside on a reservation in southeastern Colorado. However, they could not survive in the arid area that comprised most of the reservation. Adjacent settlers claimed that Indian raiding parties took cattle. Supported by federal troops, settlers attacked the Indians, who, while defending themselves, killed several soldiers. Incidents such as these resulted in the first of two major wars between the U.S. and the Cheyenne.

The first conflict, the Cheyenne and Arapaho War of 1864–1868, erupted despite an attempt by several chiefs of the Southern Cheyenne to settle the escalating dispute in Colorado peacefully when settlers and the army continued to harass the Indians. Cheyenne war parties retaliated by attacking stage coaches and wagon trains passing through the area as well as way stations, farms and army outposts.

In the fall of 1864, a band that had originally been given permission to settle peacefully near Fort Lyon was driven away by a newly appointed commander. The Cheyenne, along with some Arapaho, settled into a winter camp at Sand Creek in southeastern Colorado. They were shortly to become victims to one of the worst blood baths, the Sand Creek Massacre, perpetrated by an army unit in the long history of vicious Indian-army warfare.

The incident provoked a general uprising of the Cheyenne and other southwestern tribes. The army sent several columns against the Indians over the next four years. One, under Col. George Custer, destroyed Black Kettle's camp on the Washita River in 1868. Fighting between the army and the Southern Cheyenne all but ceased after that incident, except for occasional raids.

The Northern Cheyenne, a few years later, allied themselves with the Sioux in the Sioux War of 1876–1877, in resisting attempts to send them to a reservation that was not part of their historic hunting grounds. Elements of the Northern Cheyenne took part with the Sioux in the massacre of Custer and his unit in the Battle of Little Bighorn River (June 25, 1876). Several films dealing with Custer's last stand refer to the fact that the Cheyenne joined forces with the Sioux, including a 1936 serial titled *Custer's Last Stand*. Following the eventual defeat of the two tribes, the Northern Cheyenne were forced to move south to join the Southern Cheyenne on a reservation in Oklahoma. The film *White Feather* (1955) gives a poignant but fictional account of some of the more dissident warriors, led by Jeffrey Hunter, who resist the U.S. Cavalry in its attempt to relocate the Cheyenne.

Many among the Northern Cheyenne were dissatisfied with life in Oklahoma. A band of 300, under Chiefs Dull Knife and Little Wolf, broke out in September 1878 and became embroiled in another conflict, the Cheyenne War of 1878. John Ford's *Cheyenne Autumn* (1964) presents an embellished but fairly accurate account of the incident, with Gilbert Roland portraying Dull Knife. The Indians held off four separate army attacks. One

Victor Mature (c.), as the title character in *Chief Crazy Horse* (1955), is betrayed by his own fellow Sioux.

group, under Dull Knife, blundered into a pursuing camp of cavalry during a snowstorm, were captured and interned at Camp Robinson. Faced with an ultimatum to return to the reservation from which they had escaped, the band broke out of camp. The army pursued them relentlessly. In one engagement a group of 30 Indians who were trapped in a canyon were completely annihilated by pursuing troopers.

As news of the treatment of the Indians spread across the country, a ground swell of protest forced the government to undertake a more understanding and humane treatment of the remaining members of the tribe. As a result, the Tongue River Reservation, in Montana, was set up for that segment of the Northern Cheyenne that had not gone south.

The Yellow Tomahawk (1954), an otherwise routine cavalry-vs.-Indians action drama, manages within the confines of fiction to incorporate many of the actual abuses the Cheyenne suffered at the hands of the military. Warner Anderson, a symbol of ruthless officers, breaks peace treaties with the Cheyenne, antagonizes the tribe by building a

military outpost on their land and, finally, slaughters their women and children. This last incident, reminiscent of the Sand Creek Massacre, results in an uprising in the film which again parallels historical events. See also Sand Creek Massacre. ■

Chief Crazy Horse (1955), U. Dir. George Sherman; *Sc.* Franklin Coen, Gerald Drayson Adams; *Cast includes:* Victor Mature, Suzan Ball, John Lund, Ray Danton.

Victor Mature portrays the title character, a brave, idealistic Lakota-Sioux chief, in this action drama. He lives out the dream of a dying Sioux chief who predicts that a mighty warrior will emerge and lead the Sioux in triumph over the encroaching white man. The film presents several realistic battle sequences between the Sioux and the cavalry, including Crazy Horse's victory over General Custer. After the Indian chief makes peace with the U.S. Army, a renegade Sioux, played by Ray Danton, murders Crazy Horse. This was part of the vision the dying chief presaged. Suzan Ball plays the bride of Crazy Horse.

Continuing the trend set by *Broken Arrow*

(1950), with James Stewart as an ex-soldier trying to make peace between the Apaches and the whites, *Crazy Horse* is generally sympathetic to the Indian, providing justification for his taking to the warpath against the invaders. But the characterization of the chief as a half-crazed eccentric who is obsessed with visions, strange voices and ancestors' ghosts has been criticized by Indians and historians as an inaccurate portrait of one of the greatest Indian military leaders and major forces in the defeat of Custer. ■

Children in war. Periodically, American film companies exploited the role of children during war, manipulating them to serve a variety of purposes. Most often the young functioned as a convenient metaphor for all that was malevolent in war—loss of parents and home, physical abuse by the foe, degeneration of the human spirit, corruption by an indifferent society and innocent victims in a world gone mad.

The child as a victim of war appeared on screen in different conflicts. One of the earliest was the American Revolution. In *The Spirit of '76* (1917) an English soldier is seen bayoneting a Colonist's child during the bloody Wyoming Valley Massacre. D. W. Griffith, in his early western and Civil War cycles, often included children trapped with their parents in a cabin while enemy troops or warring Indians surround them. Director John Ford presented a visually dramatic and ironic sequence of a children's army on the march in his Civil War drama *The Horse Soldiers* (1959). A behind-the-lines Union raid on a Confederate rail link provokes an elderly headmaster of a military academy to lead his eager young boys in a march against the Yankee cavalry. John Wayne, as the officer in charge of the raid, wants no part of this phase of the battle and orders a retreat. Ford directed the scene for laughs although its effect is closer to cruel humor or black comedy.

Several World War I films depicted children as victims. *Till I Come Back to You* (1918) and *The Heart of Humanity* (1919) are representative. In the former, Belgian children are transported to Germany where they are beaten and starved and forced into slave labor in munitions factories. In the latter, a Prussian officer (Erich von Stroheim), about to rape an American nurse, is annoyed by a crying baby. He picks up the infant and drops it out of a window.

Children also served on the home front in war dramas and comedies, chiefly as little patriots who harassed local slackers or detectors of spies bent on harming the war effort. In *A Little Patriot* (1917) Baby Marie, anxious to help her country, forces her unemployed father to join the army; she also provokes her pals to spit on those whose fathers are slackers. Wallis Brennan, as a young boy in "Bud's Recruit" (1918), embarrasses his older brother into enlisting by impersonating him at a recruiting office. Jane and Katherine Lee, popular twins of this period, portray French orphans who journey to their uncle in America where they help to uncover a nest of spies plotting to blow up a munitions factory.

World War II films with children as their subject generally leaned more towards drama. Unfortunately, many of them were overly sentimental. *The Man I Married* (1940) and *Hitler's Children* (1942), both set in Nazi Germany, explore the effects of Nazi ideology on children. The former concentrates on regimentation, and the latter focuses on genetic experimentation designed to produce a superior race. In *The Pied Piper* (1942) an irascible old codger (Monty Woolley) reluctantly ends up transporting a group of European refugee children to safety. On vacation in France when the Nazis invade that country, he volunteers to escort an English couple's two children to England. Other orphans begin to find their way to him. Margaret O'Brien, a popular child star during World War II and a proficient crier, portrays an English war orphan in *Journey for Margaret* (1942). She is adopted by an American war correspondent (Robert Young) and his wife (Laraine Day). The film contains several compelling scenes of the effects of German air strikes. In one particular scene a dazed mother stares with disbelief at her dead child. *China* (1943), starring Alan Ladd and Loretta Young, exemplifies the war dramas which vividly depict the vulnerability of young females who fall into the hands of lecherous soldiers. A young Chinese student is brutally raped by Japanese troops. *Tomorrow the World* (1944), one of the most powerful dramas of the period, concerns a 12-year-old German boy who has been indoctrinated with Nazi ideology. Now an orphan, he arrives in America to live with a close friend of his anti-Nazi father who has died in a concentration camp. The boy, influenced by the Hitler *Jugend*, hates the weaknesses he discovers in a democratic America and has a negative influence on adults and other children. Patience, kindness and affection of those close to him have their effect, and he finally breaks out into tears.

Post-World War II films continued to depict the horrors laid upon the young as a result of the conflict. *The Search* (1948), featuring Montgomery Clift as an American soldier stationed in occupied Germany, explores the shattered and tragic lives of those children left homeless and abandoned by the war. The plot centers on a mother' search for her lost nine-year-old son among the ruins and in various children's agencies. Clift finds the child and cares for him until he is reunited with his mother. *Hornet's Nest* (1970), an unconvincing action drama, has Rock Hudson as an American paratrooper who uses a group of Italian war orphans to help him destroy an important dam.

The Korean War brought forth *Battle Hymn* (1956), also starring Rock Hudson and based on the true experiences of Colonel Dean Hess. After accidentally bombing a German orphanage during World War II, the conscience-stricken Hess volunteers to train pilots in the Korean War. He later manages to airlift 1,000 Korean orphans to safety.

Dennis Christopher, as an irresponsible medic in *Don't Cry, It's Only Thunder* (1982), a Vietnam War drama, is regenerated by a mortally wounded buddy and the efforts of an army doctor (Susan Saint James). He devotes his time to helping a group of war orphans. The film, a culmination of many earlier dramas with a similar theme, depicts the young as helpless victims of war. American films have often captured the sharp, ironic contrast between the innocence and honesty of children and the cruelty and senselessness of war. ■

China (1943), Par. *Dir.* John Farrow; *Sc.* Frank Butler; *Cast includes*: Alan Ladd, Loretta Young, William Bendix, Philip Ahn.

Alan Ladd portrays an American salesman in China in this drama of the Sino-Japanese War. At first he works for the Japanese, disinterested in the politics of the war. When a Chinese village is bombed and strafed by Japanese warplanes, he quickly exits with his truck. He is stopped along the road and persuaded to transport a group of female students and their American teacher (Loretta

Young) to safety. When his truck is strafed by the Japanese, he decides to choose sides with the Chinese and fights with them against the Japanese. There is a brutal scene in which three Japanese soldiers rape a Chinese girl. Ladd, in an act of rage, kills the soldiers. William Bendix portrays his buddy in this action drama.

Ladd's easy conversion from profit-motivated salesman to patriotic guerrilla fighter and his uncanny ability to annihilate hordes of Japanese soldiers may seem implausible, but the film satisfied his many fans and the wartime audiences hungry for action dramas of the conflict. By the time the film was released, Ladd was in uniform serving his country. His exaggerated heroics and the deaths of so many enemy troops somewhat anticipate the "Rambo" and "Missing in Action" films of the post-Vietnam War period starring Sylvester Stallone and Chuck Norris respectively. ■

China Bound (1929), MGM. *Dir.* Charles F. Reisner; *Sc.* Sylvia Thalberg, Frank Butler; *Cast includes*: Karl Dane, George K. Arthur, Josephine Dunn, Polly Moran.

The film comedy team of Karl Dane and George K. Arthur starred in their last feature together in this comedy about a Chinese revolution. The boys get mixed up in the foreign rebellion as they perform their familiar antics. Josephine Dunn and Polly Moran, portraying their sweethearts, give ample support to this slight film. Karl Dane, who spoke with a heavy accent, had difficulties adjusting to sound films. He had been a popular feature player in numerous silents, some of which were major productions and highly successful (*The Big Parade*). He continued to work as a carpenter on the back lot at MGM until 1934, when he committed suicide. Arthur switched to the production end of filmmaking when he sensed his screen career was fading. ■

China Doll (1958), UA. *Dir.* Frank Borzage; *Sc.* Kitty Buhler; *Cast includes*: Victor Mature, Li Li Hua, Ward Bond, Bob Mathias, Johnny Desmond, Stuart Whitman.

This tragic wartime romance, set in strife-torn China in 1943, concerns an American pilot and his female Chinese housekeeper. Victor Mature portrays a heavy-drinking, hard-living pilot. Having unwittingly purchased the young woman (Li Li Hua) while he was drunk, Mature gradually falls in love with her. They marry and have a child. Tragedy strikes when Mature's wife is killed during a Japanese air raid. He hides his child and goes on a mission against the enemy from which he never returns. Years later the daughter of the ill-fated couple, raised in orphanages, is taken to America by Mature's former service buddies to live with friends of Hua's parents. The action sequences are chiefly those derived from wartime newsreel footage. ■

"China Fights Back" (1941). See "The March of Time." ■

China Gate (1957), TCF. *Dir.* Samuel Fuller; *Sc.* Samuel Fuller; *Cast includes:* Gene Barry, Angie Dickinson, Nat King Cole, Paul DuBow, Lee Van Cleef.

The French Indo-China War provides the background for this action drama about a patrol of French Legionnaires assigned to blow up a secret Communist ammunition dump. The soldiers are led through enemy territory by Angie Dickinson, who portrays a Eurasian posing as a Red sympathizer. Gene Barry, as a Legionnaire, had been married to her in the past but left when their baby was born with Chinese features. Their romance is rekindled during the mission. Although the mission is accomplished, Dickinson is killed in the explosion. Director-writer Samuel Fuller, who had been the first upon the screen with a Korean war film (*The Steel Helmet*), again scooped Hollywood with this drama of the French Indo-China War. ■

China Girl (1942), TCF. *Dir.* Henry Hathaway; *Sc.* Ben Hecht; *Cast includes:* Gene Tierney, George Montgomery, Lynn Bari, Victor McLaglen, Alan Baxter.

This World War II drama is set in Mandalay and China during the Sino-Japanese War, prior to Japan's attack on Pearl Harbor. George Montgomery, as an American newsreel cameraman, falls in love with Gene Tierney, who portrays a young Chinese woman educated in the U.S. Meanwhile, Japanese agents plot against China and Japanese planes bomb China's cities. When Tierney is killed during one of the raids, Montgomery wreaks revenge upon the Japanese planes with a machine gun. Lynn Bari and Victor McLaglen play spies, with Bari falling for

Montgomery. The film has several exciting war scenes in an otherwise routine tale. ■

China Seas (1935), MGM. *Dir.* Tay Garnett; *Sc.* Jules Furthman, James K. McGuinness; *Cast includes:* Clark Gable, Jean Harlow, Wallace Beery, Lewis Stone, Rosalind Russell, Dudley Diggs, C. Aubrey Smith, Robert Benchley.

This action drama involving pirates and romance aboard a passenger ship traveling from Shanghai to Singapore stars three of Hollywood's major screen personalities of the period. Clark Gable, as the courageous captain, is tortured by the pirates. Jean Harlow, as a tart, ultimately falls for Gable. Wallace Beery as a ruthless pirate chief, travels incognito aboard Gable's vessel. Lewis Stone portrays a discredited former skipper who eventually redeems himself when he sacrifices his life to save the others.

When Gable rejects Harlow, she turns over the keys to the ship's arsenal to Beery. The pirates board and torture Gable for the whereabouts of a hidden gold shipment. He manages to get the upper hand and fights off the pirates in several action-filled scenes. Robert Benchley provides the comic relief in this above-average, well-paced drama. The film proved to be one of the studio's biggest moneymakers of the year. ■

China Sky (1945), RKO. *Dir.* Ray Enright; *Sc.* Brenda Weisberg, Joseph Hoffman; *Cast includes:* Randolph Scott, Ruth Warrick, Ellen Drew, Anthony Quinn.

The Sino-Japanese War provides the background for this routine romantic drama. Randolph Scott and Ruth Warrick portray courageous American doctors who work in a small Chinese village that is also a base for a guerrilla leader, played by Anthony Quinn. The relationship between the two physicians is platonic. When Scott leaves temporarily to raise funds, he meets and marries Ellen Drew. Upon the couple's return to the village, Drew, who plays a spoiled, rich young woman, grows jealous of Warrick. Meanwhile, Quinn leads his gallant fighters against a Japanese invasion of the village. The film, based on the novel by Pearl S. Buck, somehow loses the author's theme of Chinese-American cooperation. Although the critics attacked the cliché-ridden drama, audiences responded enthusiastically. ■

China Venture (1953), Col. *Dir.* Don Siegel; *Sc.* George Worthing Yates, Richard Collins; *Cast includes:* Edmond O'Brien, Barry Sullivan, Jocelyn Brando, Leo Gordon.

A small group of U.S. Marines and navy men is assigned by Navy Intelligence the task of bringing in a downed Japanese admiral on the China coast for questioning. The Americans successfully reach the admiral (Philip Ahn) who was hurt in a plane crash. Their journey back, however, is fraught with a variety of problems, including battles with Japanese and Chinese guerrillas. An internal conflict arises when a battle-hardened marine captain (Edmond O'Brien) clashes with his inexperienced superior navy officer (Barry Sullivan). Ultimately, the latter proves himself by his sacrifice to stay behind to hold off the advancing Japanese. ■

China's Little Devils (1945), Mon. *Dir.* Monta Bell; *Sc.* Sam Ornitz; *Cast includes:* Harry Carey, Paul Kelly, Ducky Louie, Gloria Ann Chew.

Chinese orphans disrupt the activities of their Japanese occupiers and help to rescue downed American fliers in this low-budget but well-produced World War II drama. Harry Carey portrays a missionary whose children have organized themselves into a quasi-Commando group. Paul Kelly, as a pilot in the Flying Tigers, adopt Ducky Louie, a teen-age orphan. The boy leads the children on raids against the Japanese who are depicted as unusually brutal and inhuman in their treatment toward the Chinese population. ■

Chinese civil wars (1911–1937, 1945–1949). China was torn by almost constant civil strife for most of the first half of the 20th century. The first major upheaval, in 1911, saw republican forces under Sun Yat-Sen overthrow the corrupt and hide-bound imperial Manchu dynasty. The new government faced a resumption of internal unrest beginning in 1913, first from factions within the government, and later with regional warlords and bandits, some with sizable military forces, fighting each other and the central government for local control.

Many Hollywood films during the late silent and early sound periods exploited the military, political and social upheavals that plagued China during the 1920s as background for simple action dramas. *Moran of the Marines*, starring Richard Dix, and *Streets of Shanghai*, both released in 1928, portrayed tough American servicemen rescuing their fellow countrymen from marauding Chinese bandits. Dix returned to the strife-torn land as a riverboat captain in *Roar of the Dragon* (1932) who rescues his passengers from the clutches of a local bandit.

Sometimes Hollywood injected steaming romance into the turmoil. In *Shanghai Express* (1932), starring Marlene Dietrich as Shanghai Lily and Clive Brook as her former lover, the two are threatened by local warlord Warner Oland. *The Bitter Tea of General Yen* (1933) concerned a romance between a white woman (Barbara Stanwyck) and a Chinese warlord (Nils Asther). *The General Died at Dawn* (1936) had idealistic gun runner Gary Cooper and Madeleine Carroll at the mercy of bandit warlord Akim Tamiroff. Arguably the best film about this period, *The Sand Pebbles* (1966), starring Steve McQueen, concerns the adventures of a U.S. gunboat, the *San Pablo*, and its crew amidst the upheavals of 1920s China. Its captain (Richard Crenna) must walk a thin line to avoid having his ship and crew become enmeshed and destroyed by the escalating political and international tensions.

The power of local warlords diminished greatly by 1927 as a result of military pressure from a stronger central government, where Chiang Kai-shek's conservatives began to exercise more authority. But, at that time, a new division surfaced in the national government between supporters of Chiang Kai-shek's nationalists, the Kou Min Tang party, and the Communists under Mao Dze-Dung. The nationalists steadily attacked Communist strongholds in southern China from 1927–1934, and finally forced the Communists to withdraw in the Long March (1934–1935) to the northwest. Without referring to political parties, the low-budget action film *War Correspondent* (1932) dealt with this period. Ralph Graves, as an American reporter, broadcasts the daily events to his radio audience while arguing with a mercenary flier (Jack Holt) in the employ of the government. After two more years of strife (1935–1937), the two sides agreed to a cessation of hostilities to present a common front against invading Japanese forces.

The collapse of Japan (1945) and the end of World War II in Asia resulted in renewed civil war between the nationalists and Communists. Despite massive U.S. financial assistance to Chiang Kai-shek, the Communists eventually triumphed on the mainland and drove the nationalists to the island of Taiwan by 1949.

Although Hollywood did not take political sides in adventure and romantic films based on this period, the dramas were particularly unsympathetic to fictional ruthless leaders who attacked the defenseless. In John Ford's *Seven Women* (1965), bandits in 1935 are depicted assaulting an American mission inhabited chiefly by women. What these films did offer their audiences was a graphic and personal account of the upheaval and violence that the Chinese people had to endure. ■

Cipher Bureau (1938). See Spy Films: the Talkies. ■

Civil War. See individual countries. ■

Civilian Clothes (1920), Par. *Dir.* Hugh Ford; *Sc.* Clara Beranger; *Cast includes:* Thomas Meighan, Martha Mansfield, Marie Shotwell, Alfred Hickman.

Thomas Meighan portrays an American captain fighting in the trenches during World War I who meets and marries a Salvation Army volunteer. At one point in the drama he is reported as having been killed in action, but when he returns in "civilian clothes" his wife, who turns out to be a conceited aristocrat, rejects him. He accepts a position as butler in her family estate to teach her a lesson in humility. One of the earliest postwar films to treat the problems of the returning doughboy, it barely scratches the surface. Other dramas, such as Frank Borzage's *Humoresque* (1920), Louis Gasnier's *The Hero* (1923) and Herbert Brenon's *The Side Show of Life* (1924) tackled the subject with more depth and compassion. ■

Civilization (1916), Triangle. *Dir.* Thomas H. Ince and others; *Sc.* C. Gardner Sullivan; *Cast includes:* Herschel Mayall, Lola May, Howard Hickman, Enid Markey.

Producer Thomas Ince's silent film makes a strong plea for pacifism. A peaceful nation is suddenly thrown into war by a self-interested king greedy for conquest. He orders one of his counts to blow up an enemy ship carrying civilians. When the count refuses, his men mutiny. The count sinks his own ship and sacrifices his life rather than take the lives of innocent people. The king has the body brought to a laboratory where scientists try to restore the count's life so that the king can learn the dead man's secret about a new type of submarine. Life returns to the count in the spirit of Christ who preaches peace and love to the warlike king. Christ shows the ruler images of death and destruction, all caused by war. The king, moved by what he has seen, ends the hostilities. Several other directors helped Ince, including Raymond West and Reginald Barker. At the time of its release, the film presented one of the strongest protests against the horrors of war. One title states: "After nineteen centuries of Christian spirit, its mockery is laid bare in the sight of men thirsty for blood." But the relatively few films with a pacifist theme were overshadowed by the large number that advocated preparedness. Ince persuaded President Wilson to appear in a special prologue to *Civilization*. The film allegedly assisted him during the 1916 presidential campaign.

Besides its strong antiwar theme, the film was one of the earliest to portray the Germans as villains, thereby contributing to an already strong anti-German sentiment prevalent in the U.S. The Kaiser and his nation were not mentioned in the film, but allusions to both were obvious, such as the king's spiked helmet and the bellicose policies of the mythical kingdom. Perhaps the strongest reference of all was a message sent to a submarine captain: "Sink the liner *Propatria* with full cargo of contraband of war. Passengers used as blind. Disregard sentiment." American audiences were quick to conjure up images of the sinking of the *Lusitania*. ■

Claws of the Hun, The (1918). See Spy Films: the Silents. ■

Clay Pigeon, The (1949). See Veterans. ■

Cleopatra (69–30 B.C.) The life of this famous ancient Egyptian queen is, without doubt, one of the great romantic tragedies of history. As the last Macedonian princess to rule Egypt, Cleopatra was a major character in the intrigues that disrupted the Roman empire during two civil wars, first under Julius Caesar (49–44 B.C.), and later during the ruling triumvirate of Octavian, Lepidus and Mark Antony (43–31 B.C.).

Upon the death of her father, Ptolemy XI, she became the joint ruler of Egypt with her husband-brother, as was the custom in Egypt. Her co-ruler, Ptolemy XII, drove Cleopatra from the throne. She then decided to use her considerable charm and political cunning to ingratiate herself with Caesar when he visited Egypt while he was still fighting his enemies for leadership of Rome. Caesar's support enabled Cleopatra to regain the throne of Egypt as sole ruler, though as a vassal to Rome. Following her husband's death, she remarried to a younger brother, Ptolemy XIII. Nevertheless, she accompanied Caesar back to Rome where she lived as his mistress from 46 to 44 B.C. There she had a son, Caesarian (Ptolemy XIV), believed to be Caesar's. She returned to Egypt after Caesar's assassination.

A few years later, she developed a liaison with Mark Antony, one of the triumvirate who succeeded Caesar as rulers of the empire. She probably had designs of using him to become Queen of Rome. After divorcing his Roman wife, Antony married Cleopatra, who bore him three children. During a falling out among the members of the Roman triumvirate, Antony made her and the children his sole heirs, an act that helped bring on war between Rome, led by Octavian, and Egypt.

The forces of Antony and Cleopatra suffered defeat at the Battle of Actium (31 B.C.). Antony committed suicide and Cleopatra, hearing that she would be paraded through the streets of Rome as a captured prisoner by the victorious Octavian, committed suicide by holding an asp, a poisonous snake, to her breast.

Her eventful life has been the source of several major stage and screen dramas, beginning with William Shakespeare. Cecil B. DeMille's outlandish *Cleopatra* (1934), starring thinly clad Claudette Colbert in the title role, is filled with sensual images and a climactic barge sequence that virtually defines the term "high camp." In *Serpent of the Nile* (1953) Cleopatra (Rhonda Fleming) is portrayed as a treacherous queen who schemes to have Antony killed so that she can assume power in Rome. *Cleopatra*, Joseph Mankiewicz's 1963 spectacular but flawed production, starring Elizabeth Taylor as a slightly plump queen, accurately recounts the major highlights in her colorful life. See also Mark Antony, Roman Civil Wars. ∎

Cleopatra (1963), TCF. *Dir.* Joseph L. Mankiewicz; *Sc.* Joseph L. Mankiewicz, Sidney Buchman, Ranald MacDougall; *Cast includes:* Elizabeth Taylor, Richard Burton, Rex Harrison, Pamela Brown, Hume Cronyn, Roddy McDowall.

This four-hour historical romance, the most costly in Hollywood history up to the time of its release, covers part of the stormy period of the Roman Civil Wars. Opening in 48 B.C., the drama encompasses the personal story of the queen of the Nile's first encounter with Julius Caesar until her death following the defeat of Mark Antony at Actium.

Cleopatra (Elizabeth Taylor), forced to step down from the throne she shares with her brother Ptolemy, allies herself with Caesar, the Consul of Rome. She bears him a son, and he assists her in regaining control of Egypt. At first the simple child-queen of Egypt, she soon matures into a politically astute queen. However, even in her youth she displays an uncanny perception of the affairs of great men and their desires to be linked to the gods. "You Roman generals," she says to Caesar, "become divine so quickly."

Caesar (Rex Harrison) is portrayed as a complex figure who is ambitious and tyrannical and at the same time wise and astute. Having just beaten Pompey at Pharsalia, he journeys to Egypt where he meets Cleopatra. Although enamored of her early in the drama, he is shrewd enough to quickly scrutinize her character. "You have a way of mixing politics and passion," he remarks. He takes her for his lover and later sends for her in Rome. Cleopatra's bliss comes to an abrupt end when he is assassinated.

Mark Antony (Richard Burton), although a successful general in his own right, remains jealous of Caesar's attributes. He becomes Cleopatra's lover but is so consumed in self-pity that he is unable to fulfill her quest for a great political and military leader. He returns with her to Rome, but for political expediency he is compelled to marry Octavia (Jean Marsh), Octavian's sister. Antony, however, returns to Cleopatra's arms, an act that so infuriates Octavian that he attacks Antony's troops at Actium. Antony, defeated in battle, is misinformed that Cleopatra is dead. Utterly despondent, he takes his own life, as does Cleopatra.

The film was plagued with economic waste (final cost of the film: $30 million), a personal scandal involving the three principals, loud altercations on the set between some of the actors and technicians, changes in personnel at the highest level and a string of lawsuits. In addition, Taylor's illnesses led to several delays and mounting costs. Critics disagreed about the merits of the script and the performances. The public rushed to theaters to see what all the publicity was about and exited with general disapproval. The film in many respects is better than some of the harsh criticism it generated. Lavish sequences enhance this sometimes talky film, including the spectacle of Cleopatra's entry into Rome and the large-scale Battle of Actium. Much of the dialogue is literate and witty, with many of the best lines given to Caesar. ■

Clive of India (1935), UA. *Dir.* Richard Boleslawsky; *Sc.* W. P. Lipscomb, R. J. Minney; *Cast includes:* Ronald Colman, Loretta Young, Colin Clive, Francis Lister, C. Aubrey Smith, Caesar Romero.

Ronald Colman portrays Robert Clive, the "heaven-born general" and statesman, in this romanticized biography. The film covers the highlights in Clive's celebrated career, including his humble beginnings as a clerk with the East India Company, his successful relief of the besieged Trichonopoly, his perceptive political dealings with the local native rulers (symbolized by Caesar Romero), his personal marital problems (Loretta Young plays his wife) and his conflicts with Parliament. The story is filled with sweep and color, especially the action sequences involving battle elephants equipped with barbed armor.

Robert Clive (1725–1774), an 18th century soldier and colonial administrator, needs little fictionalization. His accomplishments for the East India Company and ultimately for the benefit of Britain were substantial. In 1746 he was taken prisoner when the Bengalese recaptured Madras. But he managed to escape. He later employed guerrilla warfare to capture Arcot. He retook Calcutta in 1757, defeating the Bengalese. While serving as governor of Bengal, he was accused of embezzling state funds and was forced to return to England. However, Parliament acquitted him in 1772. ■

Cloak and Dagger (1946). See Spy Films: the Talkies. ■

Clock, The (1945), MGM. *Dir.* Vincente Minnelli; *Sc.* Robert Nathan, Joseph Schrank; *Cast includes:* Judy Garland, Robert Walker,

James Gleason, Keenan Wynn, Lucile Gleason, Marshall Thompson.

This wartime romance concerns a corporal's 48-hour leave in New York City and his developing relationship with a young woman he meets at Grand Central Station. Robert Walker and Judy Garland, here in her first dramatic role, portray the principals. Minnelli, the director, had turned out the winning *Meet Me in St. Louis* (1944) starring Judy Garland whom he married the following year. He makes this modest little story believable by cleverly weaving together seemingly insignificant incidents involving the young couple. They walk through Central Park, visit the zoo and a museum, ride the upper deck of a Fifth Avenue bus and befriend a milkman and his wife. Slowly but inevitably, each becomes entangled in the other's life until they both decide to marry before he ships out.

The scenes of Manhattan are even more interesting today because of their nostalgic value. The director and editor blended actual footage with studio shots. The film captures the pulse of wartime New York and gives the appearance of having been shot on location. The war is never mentioned, but it looms over the lives of the two innocents who are caught up in its events. ■

Closed Gates (1927). See Veterans. ■

Clum, John Philip. See *Walk the Proud Land* (1956). ■

Cochise (1815–1874). As chief of the Chiricahua band of the Apache, Cochise was one of the few Indian leaders of major stature in the Southwest who initially believed that his people and white Americans could find a way to live in peace. But his feelings for friendship turned to bitterness in 1861 when five of his relatives were executed by the army for a crime they claimed they never committed. He began a war of revenge against both settlers and military forces in Arizona that lasted close to eleven years and kept the territory in a state of near anarchy. The army, in retaliation, instituted a war of attrition against Cochise's band, even using field artillery in battles against the hostiles.

Cochise and his followers were among the few Apache bands who hadn't accepted pacification and the principle of reservation life by 1865. Finally, in 1871, a friend of Cochise, Thomas Jeffords, accompanied General O. O.

Howard, the Indian Commissioner, to a meeting with Cochise at the chief's mountain base. The talks resulted in peace when the government granted a reservation to the Chiricahua that included much of their native territory. Cochise lived on the reservation for a few short years before his death.

However, two years after Cochise's death, the U.S. government reneged on its promise and moved the Chiricahua to a less desirable location, the arid San Carlos agency. This was one of the factors for the revolt by Geronimo, another Chiricahua chief, and the subsequent Apache Wars that raged through Arizona and New Mexico from 1871 to 1886.

Cochise has appeared as a subject of screen interest several times. One of the earliest films in which he is portrayed is *Valley of the Sun* (1942). Antonio Moreno, a popular actor during the 1930s, portrayed him in this drama concerning an unsavory Indian agent who exploits those under his jurisdiction and forces the braves to take to the warpath. Jeff Chandler, the star of numerous action and adventure films of the 1940s and 1950s, practically made a secondary career of playing the Indian chief. He portrayed Cochise three times—in *Broken Arrow* (1950), *The Battle at Apache Pass* (1952), and *Taza, Son of Cochise* (1954). *Broken Arrow*, a landmark film in its realistic and sympathetic treatment of the Indian, depicts the efforts of Tom Jeffords (James Stewart), mentioned above, to bring peace between Cochise and the whites. *Taza, Son of Cochise* was a loose sequel to *Broken Arrow*. Other portrayals of the noted chief, such as John Hodiak in *Conquest of Cochise* (1953), were almost purely fictional westerns without historical relevance. ■

The Cockeyed World (1929). See Service Comedy. ■

Cody, William Frederick (1846–1917). More commonly known as "Buffalo Bill," Cody estimated he shot over 4,200 buffalo in an 18-month period (1867–1868) while working for a company that supplied food to railroad construction workers on the Kansas-Pacific line. His fame spread through stories about his buffalo hunting and other exploits and from his popular traveling show, "Buffalo Bill's Wild West Show," that he organized in 1883.

Growing up in the West of the late 19th century, Cody was, at different stages in his life, a wagon freight hauler, prospector, hunter, army scout, Indian fighter and showman. The last pursuit brought him national and international prominence. His "Wild West Show," a combined circus and live western museum that featured Sioux Chief Sitting Bull and markswoman Annie Oakley among its performers, toured the U.S. and Europe. It attracted large audiences by presenting an exciting and imaginative picture of the west with whooping Indians, hard-riding cowboys and sharpshooters. Cody's importance to American history, however, is based on more than his success as a showman. He, and others like him, profoundly affected the development of the American West. Collectively they caused changes to the western environment and to the traditional life of semi-nomadic prairie Indians. Even Cody's popular name, "Buffalo Bill," conjures up an image of a West that no longer exists because he helped destroy it.

During the Civil War, he was an army scout in Kansas, Missouri and Tennessee, often in conflicts with the Indians. While serving as a scout for Col. George Custer in the campaign against the Sioux and Cheyenne in 1876, he killed and scalped Cheyenne Chief Yellow Hand. "I scientifically scalped him in about five seconds," Cody stated. (The incident was depicted in William Wellman's large-scale film biography *Buffalo Bill* (1944), starring Joel McCrea as Cody. The film also traced Cody's other exploits, including his years in show business.) Many of these experiences became the basis for a popular series of Buffalo Bill adventure novels of that time. The stories added to Cody's acclaim as a western hero.

Cody, along with other hunters and "sportsmen" who shot at the beasts from moving trains, contributed to the slaughter of the buffalo. This had important repercussions. The buffalo— slow, stupid, lumbering creatures that moved in large herds—were cut down in such vast numbers for meat, hides and sport that their total population went from an estimated 15 million at the end of the Civil War in 1865 to a few thousand head 20 years later. The buffalo's destruction served as one of the chief contributions to the weakening of once powerful prairie Indian tribes such as the Sioux who relied heavily on the animals for food, hides and fur.

Experienced scouts such as Cody, who knew the central plains well, helped the army to crush Indian resistance. By the close of the 19th century the western plains Indians had lost most of their land. In addition, they were forced to exchange their traditional, semi-nomadic hunting culture for re-settlement on reservations. Several battles, including those of War Bonnet Creek, Summit Springs and Wounded Knee, appeared in *The Adventures of Buffalo Bill* (1914). Cody, who played himself, claimed that the film was historically accurate. However, Indian spokesmen and several representatives of historical societies at the time disputed his statement.

After retiring from show business, Cody settled on a ranch in territory granted to him by Wyoming. The area eventually became the town of Cody. He is buried in Denver, Colorado. His exploits, both factual and imaginative, have appeared in a handful of serials and feature films. Cody was portrayed in a minor role in *Custer's Last Stand*, a 1936 serial later converted into a feature. In Cecil B. DeMille's epic western *The Plainsman*, also released in 1936, James Ellison portrayed him as a supporting character to Wild Bill Hickok (Gary Cooper). A weak remake appeared in 1966. Director Robert Altman in *Buffalo Bill and the Indians* (1976) reduced the legendary hero (Paul Newman) to a flamboyant fraud. ■

Cold War (1946–1980s). Shortly after World War II ended, tensions mounted between the western Allies and the Soviet Union and its satellite nations. The term "Cold War" signified this feeling of animosity between the west and the Communist bloc. The West had become increasingly alarmed at the expansion of Soviet controlled territory and power during the war and shortly thereafter. Early in World War II, the U.S.S.R. seized the three Baltic nations of Latvia, Estonia and Lithuania. Sections of Poland, Rumania and Czechoslovakia were later also incorporated into the Soviet Union. Helped by the presence of Soviet troops, Communist governments seized power in East Europe and in parts of Germany and Korea.

Contact between the people in Soviet-dominated areas and the West quickly diminished, leading Winston Churchill, in his 1946 speech at Fulton, Missouri, to say that an "iron curtain" had descended across Eastern Europe. His speech is considered the beginning of open acknowledgment of the split be-

tween the victorious wartime allies. The spread of Communism in post-war Asia, particularly when China became part of the Communist bloc, heightened western fears. The Cold War reached a peak in the 1950s and 1960s and gradually diminished by the 1980s.

The Cold War was fought in several ways— by an extensive military build-up; diplomatically through military alliances such as N.A.T.O. and the Warsaw Pact; by supporting opposing sides in domestic strife as occurred in China; economically through aid and trade programs such as the Marshall plan; and spying. The generally heightened tension sometimes erupted in shooting wars that involved at least one of the great powers such as the Greek Civil War, the Korean War, the Vietnam War and the Afghanistan guerrilla war.

As films about World War II diminished in number, dramas involving the new conflict began to appear on the screen. These films dealt with real and imaginary incidents, intrigue, torture, treachery, defection and escape. Many of the plots were merely reworkings of old material within a Cold War framework. A few were so didactic that they became ludicrous. Others bordered on panic and paranoia as they tried to warn Americans of the dangers of Communist subversion and the threatened downfall of democracy and freedom.

Actual incidents often served as the basis of several Cold War films. One of the earliest and most dramatic post-World War II confrontations between Russia and the West was Russia's attempt to starve the Allied powers—the U.S., Great Britain and France—out of Berlin by a ground blockade. The Allies responded with the Berlin Airlift (June 24, 1948–Sept. 30, 1949) that supplied the city for over a year. *The Big Lift* (1950), featuring Montgomery Clift and Paul Douglas, deals with the problems that air crews encountered during the crisis as well as East-West tensions on the ground.

The Berlin crisis had its roots in the conclusion of World War II in Europe when the four main victorious powers agreed to a joint occupation of Berlin, with each power supervising one section of the city, until a peace treaty was signed with Germany. However, Allied presence in Berlin created problems for the Soviet Union. The occupied city not only served as a pocket of western military strength deep inside Russian-occupied territory, it also became an "escape hatch" for East Germans seeking to flee Communism. The airlift conducted 277,264 flights to carry supplies to keep the city functioning. Seeing that the blockade had failed to achieve its purpose, the Soviet Union lifted travel restrictions to the city on May 12, 1949.

Other incidents, similarly, were turned into dramas. *Guilty of Treason* (1950) was based on the 1949 case of Hungary's Josef Cardinal Midszenty. The cardinal (Charles Bickford) resists Hungarian Communist authorities and is incarcerated. The trial, with its attempts to discredit the Primate of Hungary, inflamed western public opinion. *I Was a Communist for the F.B.I.* (1951), was based on the true story of double agent Matt Cvetic, who posed as a Communist for nine years. Frank Lovejoy, as the double agent, exposes various Communist plots before the House Un-American Activities Committee. The film was made at the height of anti-Red hysteria in the United States.

Berlin became the focus of a new crisis with the construction of the Berlin Wall in 1961 by the East German Communist government. Soviet Premier Nikita Khrushchev supported the action of the East German government which suddenly sealed off the western-controlled portion of the city from the Communist zone with a concrete and barbed-wire wall that effectively closed an escape route to the West for refugees from Communism. The wall, furthermore, prevented those in Communist areas from continuing to witness the contrast in living standards between the democratic and Communist worlds. *Escape From East Berlin* (1962) re-enacts the true experiences of a handful of East Germans who in 1962 tunneled their way under the Berlin Wall, only months before the film was released. The Communist-fomented Greek Civil War (1944–1949) served as the background for *Guerrilla Girl* (1953). The story features Helmut Dantine as a former Greek officer during World War II who returns to his homeland and discovers that Communist revolutionaries are plotting to take over the country.

The closest the world came to a nuclear holocaust in the Cold War occurred in the Cuban Missile Crisis during the fall of 1962. The strained relationships between the U.S. and the Communist states of Cuba and the U.S.S.R. served as background to *Rebellion In Cuba* (1961), a fictionalized view of the aborted American-backed Bay of Pigs invasion.

Some of these Cold War dramas concerned defection or escape from the Communist world. An actual case in 1946 was the basis for *The Iron Curtain* (1948), one of the earliest Cold War films produced in the U.S. Seeking a better life for their child, a Russian embassy clerk (Dana Andrews) working in Canada and his wife (Gene Tierney) turn themselves in to Canadian authorities to whom they reveal the inner apparatus of a Soviet spy network functioning in Canada. The idea of escaping from Communism was used fictitiously in *Man on a Tightrope* (1953) and *Night People* (1954). *The Red Danube* (1949), though fiction, did deal with a real problem, that of reluctant repatriates in postwar Vienna. The Soviets demand that they be sent to the Eastern bloc. Some of the refugees, including Janet Leigh as a ballerina, prefer suicide to a life under Communism. The Rosenberg spy case that dominated the headlines in 1953 created alarm in the United States over attempts by Communists to gain scientific and atomic secrets through spying. That fear was used in a fictional setting in films such as *Walk A Crooked Mile* (1948), *Project X* (1949), *Walk East On Beacon* (1952) and *Security Risk* (1954), all concerned with American efforts to counter Soviet spying in matters of science. In *Five Steps To Danger* (1956), Sterling Hayden seeks to prevent Soviet spies from stealing information on the American ballistic missile program. The bulk of these Cold War films resembled routine spy dramas with the usual traitors, foreign agents and military secrets at stake. The background might well have been the Civil War or any other conflict.

Many Cold War features take place in foreign cities whose exotic structures and suspicious-looking inhabitants add to the tangled webs of intrigue. Some examples are *Diplomatic Courier* (1952), Salzburg; *Assignment—Paris* (1952), Paris and Budapest; *The Steel Fist* (1952), behind the Iron Curtain; *Never Let Me Go* (1953), the Soviet Union; *The Kremlin Letter* (1970), Mexico, Rome, New York and Russia; *Target Hong Kong* (1952), Asia; and *Tangier Incident* (1953), Africa.

One film rises above the pack in attempting to get across a serious message on the conduct of the Cold War. It is *The Ugly American* (1963), loosely based on the episodic novel by William J. Lederer and Eugene Burdrick, and starring Marlon Brando as American ambassador to a fictitious southeast Asian country. The film underscores the general ignorance of American politicians and an indifferent public concerning relations with underdeveloped countries. "We can't hope to win the Cold War," Brando warns, "unless we remember what we are for as well as what we are against." Films sometimes used fictitious military incidents to capture the tension and danger for both adversaries as the world stood at the brink of disaster. In *The Bedford Incident* (1962) American submarines on surveillance in the North Atlantic engage in deadly cat-and-mouse games with their Soviet counterparts that almost develops into open war. American and British agents clash with Russian forces at the North Pole in *Ice Station Zebra* (1968), starring Rock Hudson. The Soviets want the strategic film that is inside an American space capsule that has landed in the frozen wastes and are willing to fight for it. *Red Dawn* (1984), about a Communist invasion of the U.S., is a grotesque of the genre. It tends toward violence for its own sake and is almost completely devoid of plausibility.

The stress on families of U.S. airmen and the fliers themselves who pilot the giant military aircraft that defend the west from a Communist attack is the subject of *Strategic Air Command* (1955), starring James Stewart and June Allyson. Marital stress is again the subject of *A Gathering of Eagles* (1963), starring Rock Hudson as a dedicated wing commander in the Strategic Air Command.

Cautionary documentaries warned of the perils of Communism and nuclear war. *Death of a Dream* (1950), forcefully written and narrated by Quentin Reynolds, was one of the earliest to depict Communism as an immediate threat to "peace, democracy and security." *If Moscow Strikes* (1952), suggested by Vannevar Bush's book *Modern Arms and Free Men*, advocates national preparedness. It shows through animation the results of an enemy nuclear invasion and its obligatory retaliation. The author, appearing on screen, warns that the planet may not survive a nuclear war. *This Is Your Army* (1954), a documentary produced by the U.S. Army, describes how the military is maintaining peace around the world through 50 foreign bases. Using a strongly provocative title, *We'll Bury You* (1962) traces, through the use of news-

reel excerpts, the rise of Communism in Russia and its bordering states. The film reminds the West of its obligation to meet the threat of Communism. Similar documentaries appeared as late as the 1980s; e.g., *America: From Hitler to M-X* and *Seeing Red*, both released in 1983.

Some dramas presented Americans as dupes or victims of the Communist conspiracy. In *I Married a Communist* (1949), Robert Ryan, as an ex-Communist, is warned by his former party bosses that no one "quits" the party. They want him to foment labor trouble. A shoot-out resolves the plot. *The Red Menace* (1950), another drama, shows how a variety of naive Americans are duped by Communists. The victims, all believing that Communism can change a country's social ills, include a disillusioned veteran, a young black student, an impoverished girl and a refugee.

My Son John (1952), one of the most controversial films of the period, concerns a young American (Robert Walker) from a good home who gets mixed up with Communists. He is suspected by the F.B.I. of associating with Communist spies. His parents (Helen Hayes and Dean Jagger), whose two other sons who are about to embark for Korea, cannot believe that their boy John is a traitor. The drama ends, following his murder, with John's recorded confession that he is a Communist. Several critics and viewers attacked the film as bordering on paranoia in its anti-Communist zeal, particularly in raising the specter of guilt by association.

The flood of Cold War films that followed World War II turned into a trickle by the 1980s as relations improved between the Communist and non-Communist nations. Nevertheless, the frequency and tone of Cold War films in the four preceding decades both reflected and contributed to the tension of the times. ∎

Column South (1953), U. Dir. Frederick de Cordova; *Sc.* William Sackheim; *Cast includes:* Audie Murphy, Joan Evans, Robert Sterling, Ray Collins.

A U.S. Cavalry lieutenant is beleaguered by a potential Navajo uprising and a plot to divert troops for the Southern cause in this drama set on the eve of the Civil War. Audie Murphy portrays the officer who is desperately trying to maintain peace at the New Mexico army outpost between the cavalry and the Navajo. An incompetent Southern captain (Robert Sterling), who keeps blundering into encounters with the Indians, has to be rescued by the more experienced lieutenant. Meanwhile, Ray Collins, as a territorial general who is a Southern sympathizer, plans to have the troops join the South once war erupts between the states. Joan Evans, as Sterling's sister, provides some romantic interludes for the young hero. Murphy, of course, foils the plan in this routine tale.

One of the few Hollywood dramas to pit the Navajo against the U.S. Cavalry, the film in part is loosely based on actual events. The Navajo did offer resistance during this period to government orders in 1863 that they move to a reservation. Colonel Kit Carson was called in to settle the problem. With a force of some 400 troopers, he eventually defeated the tribe early in 1864 and drove them to the Bosque Redondo, an arid reservation in Eastern New Mexico. See Kit Carson. ▪

Comanche (1956), UA. *Dir.* George Sherman; *Sc.* Carl Krueger; *Cast includes:* Dana Andrews, Kent Smith, Linda Cristal, Lowell Gilmore.

Efforts to bring peace between the warring Comanches and the white settlers serve as the basis for this action drama. Dana Andrews, as a stalwart Indian scout, helps to effect a fragile peace treaty with Quanah Parker, the Comanche chief (Kent Smith), but he is hampered on both sides by troublemaking whites and embittered and vindictive Indians. John Litel portrays a bigoted soldier who prefers slaughtering the Indians. Nestor Paiva, as Andrews' sidekick, provides some comic relief while Linda Cristal adds a romantic touch as a beautiful Mexican woman who catches Andrews' eye. Rousing battle sequences between the hostiles, led by a rebellious Comanche (Henry Brandon), and the whites liven things up.

The film is loosely based on historical incidents. Quanah Parker was an actual Comanche chief whose fame resulted in the town of Quanah, Texas, being named after him. He was the son of Peta Nokoni, a Comanche who led an attack on Parker's Fort in northern Texas, sacked it and captured a 13-year-old girl, Cynthia Ann Parker, the granddaughter of John Parker, after whom the fort was named. Nokoni eventually married the captive who, before her rescue by a party of whites, gave him three children. Quanah Parker was their oldest son. ▪

Comanche Territory (1950), U. *Dir.* George Sherman; *Sc.* Oscar Brodney, Lewis Meltzer; *Cast includes:* Macdonald Carey, Maureen O'Hara, Will Geer, Charles Drake.

Macdonald Carey portrays Jim Bowie, the famed adventurer and inventor of the bowie knife in this routine outdoor drama. He is assigned to make a treaty with the Indians, allowing the U.S. government to mine silver in their territory. Meanwhile, some unscrupulous entrepreneurs, led by pretty Maureen O'Hara, intend to steal the valuable metal for themselves. Carey and O'Hara fall in love, and she helps the Indians, who are under siege, by delivering a shipment of rifles to them. Will Geer, as a government official, is robbed of documents which state that settlers are prohibited from occupying Comanche land. ▪

Comanche Wars (1858–1875). With their acquisition of horses, probably from the Spanish, the Comanche became skilled riders and inveterate raiders through western Texas and into northern Mexico. Though the tribe wasn't as large as that of other plains Indians, they were credited with causing more death and destruction, relative to their size, among Spaniards, Mexicans and Texans, than any other plains tribe.

The Comanche often allied themselves with the Kiowa in raids on whites. The army conducted sporadic campaigns against both the Kiowa and Comanche from 1858–1860. In 1864 the two tribes so endangered the Sante Fe Trail that the federal government had difficulty getting supplies through to its forces in New Mexico. The army sent Kit Carson and his New Mexico volunteers against the Indians at Adobe Walls, Texas, but the battle ended with mixed results. The army experienced great difficulty in subduing the Comanche because the Indians cleverly avoided direct, large-scale battles. Their custom of living in remote areas further handicapped the army's efforts to locate them.

At one time, the federal government attempted to keep the Comanche away from more heavily populated white settlements in eastern Texas by constructing a chain of forts as a shield running North and South through mid-Texas. But the military did not have sufficient strength to adequately patrol the vast territory. Comanche raids impeded the settlement of western Texas for some years after the Mexican War (1846–1848). One film that suggested the difficulties of containing the hostile Comanche was *Conquest of Cochise* (1953), with John Hodiak in the title role. According to the plot, Cochise, who had made peace with the whites, joined the U.S. Cavalry against the Comanche in an effort to bring stability to the border region. Historically, the army often made use of Indian scouts from one tribe to help fight another.

The only major defeats suffered by the Comanche came in the Red River War (1874–1875), a concentrated army campaign against several raiding tribes that had fled their reservations and roamed Oklahoma and Texas. In one engagement, the army seized a Comanche village and held 124 women and children as hostages to restrain the raiders. The troopers succeeded in wearing down the resistance of the Comanches by a constant policy of search and harassment that prevented the Indians from resting, making repairs to their tents, hunting and putting up food. By 1875, the Comanche, along with most Plains Indians, had drifted back to their reservation in Oklahoma.

Most Hollywood films portraying the tribe's exploits, such as *Comanche Territory* (1950), are purely fictitious. In fact, one entry, *Last of the Comanches* (1952), relied heavily on a plot borrowed from *Sahara*, a 1943 World War II action drama starring Humphrey Bogart. The western substituted hostile Comanches for a column of German soldiers and a handful of besieged cavalry for Allied soldiers in control of the only water available for miles. ∎

Combat Shock (1986). See Vietnam War. ∎

Combat Squad (1953), Col. *Dir.* Cy Roth; *Sc.* Wyatt Ordung; *Cast includes:* John Ireland, Lon McCallister, Hal March, George E. Stone, Myron Healey.

This Korean War drama follows the exploits of a platoon of American soldiers during the conflict. John Ireland, as a hard-bitten sergeant, guides his charges through a variety of skirmishes with the enemy. Lon McCallister portrays a scared, inexperienced G.I. Ireland takes him under his wing until the youth overcomes his fear. Veteran character actor George E. Stone plays a medic; this is his third war. The battle scenes are lively and realistic in this otherwise routine story. ∎

Come On In (1918), Par. *Dir.* John Emerson; *Sc.* John Emerson, Anita Loos; *Cast includes:* Ernest Truex, Shirley Mason.

A World War I comedy starring Ernest Truex, the film tells of a patriotic young man's abortive attempts to enlist in the army. It seems that he is a half-inch too short. Strolling in a park, he becomes involved in a fight with a German who smashes a bottle on his head. Ernest feels his head and dashes to the nearest draft board. He passes the height requirement because of the bump on his head. Once in the service he continually moves up in rank due to a series of humorous misadventures in which he is able to display his peculiar style of bravery. ∎

Coming Home (1978), UA. *Dir.* Hal Ashby; *Sc.* Waldo Salt, Robert C. Jones; *Cast includes:* Jane Fonda, Jon Voight, Bruce Dern, Robert Ginty, Penelope Milford.

A strong and realistic drama of how the Vietnam War affects the lives of three Americans, the film features Jane Fonda as the conservative wife of a dedicated marine captain who goes off to fight in Vietnam, Jon Voight as a disillusioned soldier crippled as a result of the war and Bruce Dern as Fonda's gung-ho husband. When Dern is sent overseas, Fonda volunteers to help in a veterans' hospital. One of the patients she meets is paraplegic Jon Voight, a former high-school classmate, with whom she eventually falls in love. Her new-found love transforms her into a liberated woman, manifested in her new hair style and zest for life with Voight.

Later, when Dern returns from the war a psychologically disturbed and disillusioned officer, she must choose between the two men. Poignant scenes include Dern's disintegration and ultimate suicide as he walks naked into the ocean and Voight's chaining himself and his wheelchair to a fence as a protest against the war. The film won several Academy Awards, including Best Actor (Voight), Best Actress (Fonda), Best Screenplay and Best Story (Nancy Dowd). ∎

Command Decision (1948), MGM. *Dir.* Sam Wood; *Sc.* William Laidlaw, George Froeschel; *Cast includes:* Clark Gable, Walter Pidgeon, Van Johnson, Brian Donlevy.

Set on an American air base in England

during the bombing of Nazi Germany, this World War II drama shows the human side of the top brass that directed these operations. Clark Gable, in one of his best "mature" roles, stars as a brigadier general who has to live with the fact that each time he orders a raid, a number of young American airmen will not return. He clashes with his superiors and politicians over his daylight bombing strategy.

His superior, played by Walter Pidgeon, has to placate politicians whose constituents criticize the heavy losses. At the same time, he must convince them that he needs more planes and men to complete the job that the air force is committed to. The film, based on a stage play by William Wister Haines, is an intelligent and dramatic depiction of the human tensions that result from these military decisions and political interactions. ∎

Commandos. The British concept of an elite group of highly trained and skilled fighters was shaped by Major Holland in 1938. The men were to be trained in guerrilla tactics and prepared for close combat. The Commandos, named for the Boer farmers who resisted a British force many times their number during the Boer War, were officially established on June 8, 1940. Stationed at various fronts during World War II, they initiated raids on enemy fuel dumps, submarine bases, gun emplacements and other strategic targets on the European continent, in North Africa, in the Mediterranean and in Burma. The Commandos also aided partisans in occupied countries.

This elite military force has been the subject of several British dramas. Occasionally, an American film dramatized its exploits. If the stories are chiefly fictitious, they at least convey the types of missions the men performed and the perils they faced. Many of their actual raids occurred in Nazi-occupied Norway. In They Raid by Night (1942), a low-budget feature, three Commandos drop by parachute into Nazi-occupied Norway to rescue a Norwegian military leader from a Nazi concentration camp. First Comes Courage (1943) highlights a Commando strike force coming to the rescue of a fellow Commando (Brian Aherne) and a Norwegian agent (Merle Oberon) working for the British in Nazi-occupied Norway. In The Commandos Strike at Dawn (1942) Paul Muni, as a humble Norwegian fisherman whose village has come under Nazi occupation, organizes an under-

ground movement against the oppressors and eventually leads a British Commando raid against the Nazis.

Hollywood emulated Commando strikes in other areas as well. Eagle Squadron (1942) features Robert Stack as an American airman flying with the British. He accompanies a Commando raid on the French coast and returns with a captured enemy aircraft of advanced design. The film was also meant to help solidify Anglo-American relations early in the war. In Assignment in Brittany (1943) Commandos, with the help of the French underground, raid a German submarine base on the coast of Brittany and destroy it.

A few post-World War II films include the activities of the Commandos. One of the unit's most daring raids is re-enacted in The Desert Fox (1951). Its suspenseful and unique opening sequence, which appears on screen before the title and credits, shows an unsuccessful British Commando assault designed to kill Field Marshal Rommel. In Operation Cross Eagles (1959) Richard Conte, as a lieutenant on a special mission in Yugoslavia to rescue a captured American officer, enlists the aid of three Commandos, led by Rory Calhoun, who have just completed their own mission and are waiting for their contact to take them back to their base. Operation Crossbow (1965) concerns a special Commando unit assigned the perilous mission of seeking out and helping to destroy a Nazi secret missile base in Holland. In the offbeat Tobruk (1966), with Rock Hudson and George Peppard, a special British force made up of Commandos and German-born Jews are on a special mission to destroy General Rommel's fuel supply and hold a key position at Tobruk until the British navy arrives. ∎

Commandos Strike at Dawn, The (1942), Col. Dir. John Farrow; Sc. Irwin Shaw; Cast includes: Paul Muni, Anna Lee, Lillian Gish, Sir Cedric Hardwicke, Robert Coote.

This World War II drama is set chiefly in a Norwegian village. Its inhabitants, a peaceful people, are soon subjugated under the harsh and brutal rule of the Nazis. Paul Muni, one of the villagers and a humble fisherman by trade, organizes an underground movement against the oppressors. By the end of the film he leads a British Commando raid against the occupiers. The film depicts how a gentle people, when faced with oppression and injustice, can rise up against their oppressors—a story that was repeated many times in different countries during World War II. ∎

Committee on Public Information (C.P.I.)
See Documentary. ∎

Comrades (1928), First Division. *Dir.* Cliff Wheeler; *Sc.* Ruth Todd, Joan Plannette; *Cast includes:* Helene Costello, Gareth Hughes, Donald Keith, Joseph Swickard.

Two good friends at a military academy make an unusual pact in this World War I melodrama. One of the friends is a coward, but agrees to enlist within one year if his friend will switch places with him. The brave one agrees and goes off to fight in the trenches in France. The other joins him but remains cowardly during the war. When news reaches home of particular brave and cowardly acts, of course the wrong boys are cheered and condemned. When the two return from the war, an outraged father who has lost his own son in battle raises a pistol to kill the friend he believes to be a coward. The real coward runs in front of his friend and receives the bullet. As he lies dying, he confesses all. ∎

Concentration camps. A phenomenon chiefly of World War II and one of Nazi Germany's more infamous legacies, the modern concept of the concentration camp was first introduced by the British during the Boer War. It gained a reputation during and after World War II as a place of brutality, torture and death. Perhaps because these camps evoke images too grim for the average moviegoer, American films dealing with this topic are few in number. The majority, released during the war, are either cautionary tales warning of Hitler's New Order or propaganda dramas designed to reinforce the West's determination to defeat the Axis powers.

The earliest hints of the dreaded camps appeared on screen in the late 1930s. *Beasts of Berlin* (1939), one of the earliest films to emphasize Nazi Germany's national policy of brutality, shows the inhuman treatment of prisoners in the camps. Robert Taylor, as an American citizen in *Escape* (1940), plots to free his German-born mother from a concentration camp where she is awaiting execution. The opening scenes paint the camp as a dismal place without hope for its victims. *Underground* (1941), a drama about German resistance within the Nazi state, includes a

compelling concentration camp sequence as well as several vivid descriptions by one of its victims. The full extent of the horrors perpetrated in these camps may not have been known at this time. But the films of the period suggest that enough details had filtered out of Germany to make national leaders and the general public aware of some of the brutalities the Nazis practiced in these places.

With America's entry into the war, films alluding to the camps became more frequent. Philip Dorn portrays a French soldier who has recently returned from a concentration camp in *Paris After Dark* (1943). His spirit for resistance remains broken until late in the film when he decides to join the French underground. In *Address Unknown* (1944), a drama which shifts back and forth between America and prewar Germany, a popular German actress of Jewish heritage is harassed by the Nazis and finally taken away to a concentration camp. Another drama set in prewar Germany, *None Shall Escape* (1944) describes the rise of Nazism through the experiences of a disgruntled World War I veteran (Alexander Knox). The film shows Jews, including a rabbi, being rounded up for deportation to a concentration camp. Germany is once again the setting for the somber film, *The Seventh Cross*, also released in 1944. Spencer Tracy portrays one of seven escapees from a Nazi camp whom the commandant vows to capture. He constructs seven crosses in the camp courtyard, but the last one, designed for the elusive Tracy, a symbol of defiance against Nazi tyranny, remains empty.

After World War II, several films returned to the camps either as a peripheral reference or key sequence. *Arch of Triumph*, a murky drama set in France before and during the war, falls into the former category. Ingrid Bergman and Charles Boyer star as tragic lovers. After Bergman is fatally wounded by a former lover, Boyer is placed in a concentration camp by the Nazis. *A Time to Love and a Time to Die* (1958) explores life inside Germany under the Nazi regime. One sequence includes an officer of a concentration camp who delights in regaling others about his latest methods of torture. *The Young Lions* (1958), starring Marlon Brando, Montgomery Clift and Dean Martin, is one of the few dramas to vividly re-create the scenes of the death camps as witnessed by American troops advancing on Berlin. The wretched condition of the victims disgust and angers the G.I.s who order the local German townspeople to bury the dead. In *The Big Red One* (1980), about the various battles in which America's 1st Infantry Division participated, G.I.s again stumble upon a concentration camp hastily abandoned by the retreating Germans. Mark Hamill, as a young soldier, is reluctant to kill the enemy until he witnesses the pitiful survivors of the camp.

Several documentaries appeared after World War II showing in graphic detail the emaciated corpses, the pathetic survivors who were barely alive and neatly stacked mountains of eyeglasses and other property of the inhabitants of the camps. *Will It Happen Again?* (1948), one such compilation, covers Hitler's rise and fall and includes several newsreel shots of the camps and their victims, a grim reminder of a world gone mad. See also Holocaust. ∎

Concord, Battle of. See Battle of Lexington and Concord. ∎

Confessions of a Nazi Spy (1939), WB. *Dir.* Anatole Litvak; *Sc.* Milton Krims, John Wesley; *Cast includes:* Edward G. Robinson, Francis Lederer, George Sanders, Paul Lukas, Henry O'Neill.

A strong, didactic anti-Nazi propaganda drama, the film opens in 1938 in the United States while in Germany Hitler's war machine gears up to smash its way across Europe. Through German-American organizations such as the Bund, Nazi spies organize a network of agents and collaborators in defense plants, the military services and other occupations who gather classified information that is relayed back to Germany. Edward G. Robinson, as an F.B.I. agent, uncovers the key members of the nest of spies who are quickly brought to trial and found guilty. But before the trial ends, the audience is treated to the Nazi agents' attacks on the U.S. Constitution, the ideals of democracy and those who believe in free speech. Americans of German descent who disagree with the New Order are either beaten up by thugs or sent back to German concentration camps.

Although the message was bold for its time, the film is heavy-handed in its presentation. The one-dimensional spies lack plausibility at times; the strong-arm men in their employ are stereotypes; and the preachy voice-overs during lengthy newsreel shots of Nazi troops on the march and invading other countries

are unnecessary and redundant. Even the prosecutor (Henry O'Neill) at the climactic trial faces the camera as he recites his cautionary summary: "There are those who will say we have nothing to fear—that we are immune—that we are protected by vast oceans from the bacteria of aggressive dictatorships and totalitarian states. But we know and have seen the mirror of history in Europe this last year—the invasions of Poland, Norway and Denmark by Nazi Germany and Russia." He concludes: "America is not simply one of the remaining democracies. America is democracy!"

While the film lauds the American democratic ideals over the German Fascist state, it remains a product of its time. There are no blacks or other racial minorities in the New York street scenes, stores, offices or plants. No characters of other religious groups appear. Only two types dominate the American landscape of this film: white Anglo-Saxon Protestants—the good guys, and the Nazis—the bad guys. The film is based on the writings of Leon Turrou, a former F.B.I. agent who used material from the spy trials of 1937 in which four people were convicted. The trial established that a link existed between Germany and the German-American Bunds, rallies and youth camps that were popular in the United States in the 1930s. Probably the most forceful propaganda film of the period, it was careful to point out that most Americans of German ancestry were loyal, lawabiding citizens. ∎

Confidential Agent (1945). See Spanish Civil War. ∎

Confirm or Deny (1941), TCF. *Dir.* Archie Mayo; *Sc.* Jo Swerling; *Cast includes:* Don Ameche, Joan Bennett, Roddy McDowall, John Loder, Raymond Walburn.

World War II London during the blitz is the setting of this newspaper yarn. Don Ameche, as an aggressive foreign correspondent, meets an English teletype operator (Joan Bennett) during a blackout. The major conflict facing Ameche, who has received highly secret information about Hitler's invasion plans, is whether to publicly announce his scoop and bring down the wrath of the British upon him or suppress the information. Aside from these melodramatics in this weak drama, the film depicts realistically the devastation of parts of London caused by Nazi air raids.

Several American films released during the war years were burdened with an inherent structural dichotomy as exemplified in this film—an implausible story carried by highly romanticized characters placed in realistic surroundings. ■

Conqueror, The (1917), Fox. Dir. Raoul Walsh; Sc. Henry Warnack; Cast includes: William Farnum, Jewel Carmen, Charles Clary, J. A. Marcus.

The film is chiefly a fictionalized life of Sam Houston, the most extraordinary figure in the history of Texas. The drama begins with his early years as a crude youth living with the Cherokee in Tennessee. It goes on to cover his years as a U.S. Senator and Governor of Tennessee and his move to Texas. Using these few facts, the film then adds a love plot and some villainy to heighten the drama. It mentions his failed marriage while he was Tennessee's governor but distorts the facts by showing Houston abandoning his wife to return to his Indian friends when, in reality, she left him. ■

Conqueror, The (1956), RKO. Dir. Dick Powell; Sc. Oscar Millard; Cast includes: John Wayne, Susan Hayward, Pedro Armendariz, Agnes Moorehead, Thomas Gomez.

The 12th-century Mongol-Tartar conflicts provide the background for this large-scale action drama starring John Wayne as Genghis Khan and Susan Hayward as a Tartar princess. Wayne abducts Hayward from her father, the ruthless Tartar leader, played by Ted de Corsia. Spectacular action sequences include the clash of mounted armies of the Mongols and Tartars. Pedro Armendariz portrays the Mongol leader's blood-brother while William Conrad plays Khan's real brother. Despite the epic sweep of the action sequences and the big budget allotted to the film ($6 million), it is considered by many film critics and historians as one of the worst films ever made.

The production has come under continual ridicule, particularly concerning the incongruous casting, the inane story and the strained dialogue. "Yer beautiful in yer wrath," Wayne says to Hayward after she has hurled sundry objects at him in a fit of rejection. But Wayne is confident of winning her love. "I shall keep you in response to my passion," he explains. "Your hatred will kindle into love." Controversy has also surrounded the film which was shot on location in Utah near a radioactive site. Some have attributed the deaths of many of those involved in the film to the locale. It has been alleged that Wayne, Hayward, director Dick Powell and others died from similar cancerous causes. ■

Conquest (1937), MGM. Dir. Clarence Brown; Sc. Samuel Hoffenstein, Salka Viertel, S. N. Behrman; Cast includes: Greta Garbo, Charles Boyer, Reginald Owen, Alan Marshall, Henry Stephenson.

Greta Garbo as the Polish countess Marie Walewska and Charles Boyer as Napoleon Bonaparte are lovers in this historical romance. The romantic and ephemeral tone of the film is set early when the couple first meet. "Are you real, or born of a snowdrift?" Napoleon asks the beautiful countess who was to become his mistress. The doomed love affair covers the last seven years of Napoleon's extraordinary career, including the French retreat from Moscow, his return from Elba, the preparations for Waterloo and his capture and departure for St. Helena. MGM has embellished the production with spectacular battle scenes and lavish settings and costumes.

The real-life romance was perhaps even more interesting than that depicted in the film. The countess was 18 years old when she first met Napoleon, who sent her impassioned notes. During the rare moments in his career when he was not fighting or involved in politics, they managed to spend time together—in Vienna, in Paris, during his exile at Elba. Their son, Alexandre, born in 1810, became a highly successful diplomat, minister of state, envoy and president of the Chamber. ■

Conquest of Cochise (1953), Col. Dir. William Castle; Sc. Arthur Lewis, DeVallon Scott; Cast includes: John Hodiak, Robert Stack, Joy Page.

Indian tribes are forced to curtail their raids upon Mexicans when the U.S. Cavalry begins to patrol the border following the Gadsden Purchase. John Hodiak, as Cochise, chief of the Apaches, decides to end the attacks. The Comanches, however, are bent on continuing their hostilities. Cochise takes a Spanish aristocrat (Joy Page) hostage and then falls in love with her. Robert Stack, as a cavalry major, straightens out differences between the army and Cochise and then joins forces with him to battle the belligerent raiders in this tale set in the 1850s.

References in the film to the Gadsden Purchase were fairly accurate. Following the Mexican-American War (1846–1848) in which the United States gained territory that advanced its southwestern boundary to the Pacific Ocean, railway promoters urged construction of a transcontinental railroad to link the two coasts. The most favorable terrain for constructing a rail line lay just south of the Mexican border. The American minister to Mexico, James Gadsden, found Mexican dictator Santa Anna, whose government was having financial difficulty, receptive to an American bid to purchase the border area. Gadsden negotiated a treaty in 1853 in which Mexico received $10 million for a tract of arid, cactus-dotted land that stretched from the western tip of Texas, near El Paso, across the southern edge of present-day New Mexico and Arizona to the California border.

The American purchase included territory held by the Apache, a fierce southwestern tribe that would soon wage unrelenting war against incursions into their tribal areas by future American settlers and federal troops. Following the pacification of the Indians in the next decade, the Southern Pacific Railroad eventually built a line through the Gadsden Purchase. The area represented the last piece of territory added to the contiguous boundary of the 48 states. ■

Conspiracy (1939), RKO. Dir. Lew Landers; Sc. Jerome Chodorov; Cast includes: Alan Lane, Linda Hayes, Robert Barrat, Charles Foy, J. Farrell MacDonald.

A mythical Central American country is the background for intrigue and revolution in this action drama. Allan Lane portrays an American radio operator forced to flee from his ship when a passenger is murdered and his life is threatened. On shore he meets a revolutionary, played by Linda Hayes. Lane hides out in a local cafe run by a fellow American and experiences several close calls as he is chased by secret police and a speedboat. Ultimately, the intricate and sometimes confusing plot is resolved when the dictator who controls the small nation is toppled from office and democracy and order are restored to the country. This low-budget film is not related to a 1930 release bearing the same title.

With the forces of totalitarianism on the march in Europe in the late 1930s, Hollywood studios by 1939 began to tackle more openly such political issues as Fascism and Nazism while singing the praises of democracy. RKO, besides releasing the above drama, also turned out They Made Her a Spy the same year while Warners produced Confessions of a Nazi Spy. ■

Conspirators, The (1944). See Spy Films: the Talkies. ■

Constitution, U.S.S. The description Old Ironsides is the affectionate and more familiar name given to the oldest and probably most famous warship in the history of the U.S. Navy. Built in Boston, beginning in 1794, the Constitution was one of the first three frigates of the young U.S. Navy. She was originally funded to fight against Algerian, and later French, privateers that preyed upon U.S. ships in the mid-1790's.

The Constitution first saw action in an undeclared and limited naval warfare between France and the U.S. that took place in the Caribbean between 1798–1800. In 1801, the frigate served as the flagship of Commodore Edward Preble's Mediterranean squadron that fought in the Tripolitan War (1800–1805) between the U.S. and the Tripolitan Barbary pirates. The Constitution became famous during the War of 1812, when, under the command of Captain Isaac Hull, she defeated the British man-of-war Guerriere on August 19, 1812, off the coast of Nova Scotia. This engagement served as the basis of the legend that an American seaman, seeing enemy cannonballs bouncing of her sides, affectionately called the ship Old Ironsides, a title that has stayed with her ever since.

Some of the exploits of the warship were re-enacted in the silent film The Man Without a Country (1925). Hollywood paid its greatest tribute to the gallant ship in James Cruze's Old Ironsides (1926), a large-scale production which dramatized her role in the Tripolitan War. Today the ship is a floating memorial museum anchored in Boston and remains on the rolls as the navy's oldest existing vessel. ■

Convoy (1927), FN. Dir. Joseph C. Boyle; Sc. Willis Goldbeck; Cast includes: Lowell Sherman, Dorothy Mackaill, Lawrence Gray, William Collier.

A World War I sea drama, the film revolves around a young woman, portrayed by Dorothy Mackaill, who is called upon by the U.S. Secret Service to uncover a spy. It seems that someone is leaking transport departures to the enemy. The young heroine is told to stay with the suspected agent day and night. During the course of the story her brother is killed in battle and his body is returned home. The film provides several sea battles although most of the story is dominated by the melodramatic spy element. ■

Copperhead, The (1920), Par. *Dir.* Charles Maigne; *Sc.* Charles Maigne; *Cast includes:* Lionel Barrymore, William Carlton, Frank Joyner, Richard Carlyle, Ann Cornwall.

Based on Harold Frederic's 1893 novel which was adapted for the stage in 1918 by Augustus Thomas, the Civil War drama stars Lionel Barrymore in the role of Milt Shanks, a die-hard Southern sympathizer. Residing in a small Illinois town, he enrages the other citizens with his outspoken views and his stance as a conscientious objector during the Civil War. The film version carries the story into the next century and the year 1904, introducing Theodore Roosevelt. It is at that time that Shanks confides to his granddaughter that President Lincoln had secretly assigned him to infiltrate the Copperheads, Northerners who advocated the cause of the South. Barrymore had played the role on stage in 1918 and received high acclaim for his performance. He revived the work in 1926, after which he signed with MGM where he remained for the next 28 years. ■

Copperheads. The term, now used as political insult, was first applied during the American Civil War (1861–65) to Northern and Western peace-democrats and others who favored making peace with the Confederacy for philosophical or commercial reasons. The expression, based on the actions of a copperhead snake that strikes from secrecy, originally denoted one who tries to hurt a cause through secret action. In some cases, Copperhead groups functioned as semi-secret societies whose members assisted deserters and committed occasional acts of terrorism. Others openly adopted the title and even wore badges, made from a copper penny, to identify themselves as part of a political movement.

In modern American politics, the term is

sometimes used pejoratively to describe one who secretly or openly favors an enemy cause. The term was used as late as 1941 by President Roosevelt, in referring to the isolationist views of Charles Lindbergh, who the president claimed was hindering America's attempts to help the beleaguered western allies fighting the forces of fascism.

The controversial Copperheads are rarely mentioned in Civil War-related films. However, they played a major role in at least two dramas, *The Copperhead* (1920) and *Rebel City* (1953), the latter a low-budget drama about Southern sympathizers who stir up trouble in Kansas. ■

"Coquette, The" (1910), Edison.

This silent romantic drama, much of which is implausible, concerns a young woman who vows her love to two soldiers in different regiments. The men meet accidentally during a battle in the Spanish-American War. One of the lovers, mortally wounded, recognizes his ring on the hand of the other soldier. The surviving lover returns to the girl, relating the experience on the battlefield. ■

Coral Sea, Battle of the (May 7–8, 1942). This was the first sea battle in history in which two opposing fleets fought without coming within sight of each other. After a string of successes in the Pacific during World War II, Japan in early 1942 aimed her sights at other targets in the South Pacific, including Australia. U.S. Pacific commander Admiral Nimitz learned of the Japanese plan by way of radio interception and prepared his warships. After a few minor skirmishes, the main carrier duel began on May 8, 1942. American planes sank one Japanese carrier and damaged another. The U.S. lost the carrier *Lexington*. Although the battle was a tactical victory for the Japanese since they knocked out one of the few carriers of the U.S. fleet, they suffered a strategic setback. They were prevented from moving into the South Pacific and threatening Australia.

Only a few films refer to this important engagement. *The Battle of the Coral Sea* (1959) takes place on the eve of the battle. American seamen on a reconnaissance mission gather photographic evidence of enemy warships, but before they can return to their base they are caught. The film shows little of the battle. The first half of *Midway* (1976), a large, pretentious production, covers the Battle of the

Coral Sea and provides much more action. *Air Force* (1943), a drama about a B-17 Flying Fortress and its crew, uses actual footage from the Battle of the Coral Sea. ■

Corporal Kate (1926), PDC. *Dir.* Paul Sloane; *Sc.* Zelda Sears, Marion Orth; *Cast includes:* Vera Reynolds, Julia Faye, Kenneth Thomson.

This weak World War I comedy drama concerns two young American manicurists, Kate and Becky, who put on khaki to entertain the troops in France. In one scene they are shown to their quarters by an indifferent corporal. "Do we have to sleep in a stable?" Kate (Vera Reynolds) inquires. "Not unless you're sleepy," the doughboy growls. They both end up falling in love with the same soldier (Kenneth Thomson). There are scarcely any battle scenes but plenty of bombing by the Germans in this low-budget film. ■

Corregidor. Since Corregidor was a natural fortress that protected Manila Bay, the U.S. converted it into a military base following the Spanish-American War. After the fall of Bataan in 1942, the island was the last symbol of organized resistance against the Japanese invaders in the area. Lieutenant General Jonathan Wainwright led the American troops in fighting off the enemy for 27 days. Under heavy bombardment from Japanese planes and artillery, Wainwright finally surrendered on May 6, 1942. American troops recaptured Corregidor in 1945.

Corregidor (1943), the film that should have told the gallant story of the island's epic defense, concentrates instead on a routine romance. *The Eve of St. Mark* (1944), based on Maxwell Anderson's play, dramatizes a young soldier's experiences during the battle of Corregidor. *They Were Expendable* (1945) deals in part with the nurses and American troops who could not be taken off the "rock" in time. The documentary *Behind the Enemy Lines* (1945) depicts the fall of Corregidor as well as other World war II events. ■

Corregidor (1943), PRC. *Dir.* William Nigh; *Sc.* Doris Malloy, Edgar Ulmer; *Cast includes:* Otto Kruger, Elissa Landi, Donald Woods, Frank Jenks, Ian Keith.

The heroic stand at Corregidor is the subject of this weak World War II drama. The film attempts to depict how the embattled and outnumbered American forces held out for so long against such overwhelming odds as the Japanese tightened their grip on the island. The film gets bogged down in a trite love triangle between Otto Kruger and Donald Woods who compete for the affections of Elissa Landi, all of whom portray doctors. ■

Corvette K-225 (1943), U. *Dir.* Richard Rosson; *Sc.* John Rhodes Sturdy; *Cast includes:* Randolph Scott, James Brown, Ella Raines, Barry Fitzgerald, Andy Devine.

This World War II film tells the story of a corvette, a British-Canadian escort warship used chiefly to support convoys against enemy submarines and aircraft. Randolph Scott portrays a tough Canadian lieutenant commander who, after losing his vessel to German submarines, is anxious to ship out again. He leads his crew and a corvette from Halifax to England while sustaining a torpedo attack and bombardment by German planes. Ella Raines provides the romantic interest as the sister of one officer killed in a previous battle. He had served under Scott's command. She now has another brother currently serving under Scott. Fuzzy Knight and Andy Devine supply the comic relief in this generally realistic drama of life aboard a fighting ship during the war. The film ends with the following tribute to the corvette: "She will carry on, and those who come after her, for her name is legion; and the legend of her and those who fight in her is an inspiration for all men who believe in courage and hope."

The design of the antisubmarine warships was based on the ocean-going whaling ships that could withstand the rough North Atlantic weather. Their weapons included one four-inch gun, anti-aircraft fire power and depth charges. Originally equipped with sonar, the ships later used the more advanced radar. ■

Cossacks, The (1928), MGM. *Dir.* George Hill; *Sc.* Frances Marion; *Cast includes:* John Gilbert, Renée Adorée, Ernest Torrence, Dale Fuller.

John Gilbert, as a Cossack leader's son, at first shuns the fighting tradition of his people in this romantic drama set during the Cossack-Turkish conflicts. Branded by his fellow tribesmen as a coward, Gilbert ultimately proves himself in battle when the Cossacks ride out to meet the Turks in combat. An exciting battle ensues which results in triumph for Gilbert and the Cossacks although they were originally outnumbered by their foes. Ernest Torrence portrays Gilbert's father.

The film has a romantic subplot with Renée Adorée as Gilbert's village sweetheart who earlier, thinking him a coward, had rejected his advances. When he returns, he finds that a visiting prince has proposed to her. After a lover's quarrel, she accepts the prince's marriage proposal. Gilbert springs into action and manages to steal her away from the prospective bridegroom who is then killed by raiding Turks. ∎

Counter-Attack (1945), Col. *Dir.* Zoltan Korda; *Sc.* John Howard Lawson; *Cast includes:* Paul Muni, Marguerite Chapman, Larry Parks, George Macready.

Paul Muni portrays a Russian soldier who holds a handful of German soldiers prisoner in this World War II drama. Both the Russian and the Nazis are trapped in an underground room following an explosion. Meanwhile, Muni tries to wrest from the enemy strategic military information. In a clever battle of wits Muni first discovers which of his prisoners is the officer and then proceeds to work on the German's arrogance until he learns what he wants to know in this tense but stagy tale. Several short battle scenes are interspersed throughout the film to relieve the otherwise claustrophobic effect of the major setting. Marguerite Chapman portrays a Russian soldier who helps Muni guard the prisoners. ∎

Counter-Espionage (1942). See Detectives at War. ∎

Counterfeit Traitor, The (1962). See Spy Films: the Talkies. ∎

Counterpoint (1967), U. *Dir.* Ralph Nelson; *Sc.* James Lee, Joel Oliansky; *Cast includes:* Charlton Heston, Maximilian Schell, Kathryn Hays, Leslie Nielsen.

Members of an American symphony orchestra on tour in Belgium are captured by the Germans in this World War II drama. Charlton Heston portrays a conductor who, along with his performers, is taken prisoner during the Battle of the Bulge. Maximilian Schell, as a music-loving German officer who is ordered to kill all prisoners, is an admirer of the conductor and commands the troupe to play for him. Heston demands that his players be released since they are civilians, but the German officer is unresponsive. In a bat-

tle of wits, Heston stalls in giving the concert, believing they will all be killed when it is over. However, they are saved in the nick of time when local partisans spring a surprise attack on the German troops. Several critics ignored the generally undistinguished plot and lauded the music which included, among other selections, Schubert's "Unfinished" Symphony, Tchaikovsky's "Swan Lake" Ballet and the first movement of Beethoven's "Fifth Symphony." ∎

Court Martial (1928), Col. *Dir.* George B. Seitz; *Sc.* Elmer Harris; *Cast includes:* Jack Holt, Betty Compson, Doris Hill, Pat Harmon.

A Civil War drama about a group of Southern guerrillas, the film stars Jack Holt as the Union officer appointed by President Lincoln to bring in the leader of the marauders who happens to be a female. Holt gains the confidence of the gang members, falls for the leader (Betty Compson) and saves her life during a cavalry battle. In turn, she rescues Holt when the other members discover his secret mission. When he returns to his post, he is court-martialed for aiding the leader instead of capturing her. As he is about to face the firing squad, she appears, mortally wounded by a member of her own gang, determined to save Holt. ∎

Court-martial films. Military trials have been portrayed on screen in various conflicts ranging from the Civil War to Korea. The officers who sit in judgment of the accused tend to be elderly warriors, symbols of the establishment. They have run the gamut from harsh authoritarians to sympathetic humanitarians, depending on the writer's or director's attitude toward the military. Sometimes the trial occurs at the beginning of the drama followed by a long flashback. More often the court martial takes place near the end. As in other genres, a last-minute rescue often saves the hero or heroine.

One of the most frequently used devices in court-martial dramas concerns the trying of an innocent person. In *The Leatherneck* (1929), for example, a marine (William Boyd) is charged with desertion and murder. The court, finding his story incredible, finds him guilty. His wife suddenly appears to prove the events true, and the court reopens his case. Carlos Thompson as a former soldier of the Foreign Legion in *Fort Algiers* (1953) tries to prove that he has been wrongly court-martialed. That same year Rock Hudson faced a similar problem in another part of the globe. As a West Point graduate in *Seminole*, he is wrongly court-martialed for the murder of an Indian chief. He is saved from the firing squad none too soon when an Indian confesses to the killing. In *Under Fire* (1957), a World War II drama, four G.I.s are on trial for desertion until their lawyer (Rex Reason) proves that they were lost, not deserting.

The topic of desertion took a curious turn in *Out of the Ruins* (1928), a World War I drama. Richard Barthelmess, as a French lieutenant, leaves his command to travel to Paris where the woman he loves is about to marry another. While he lingers there, many of his men are killed in battle. Upon his return, he is court-martialed for desertion. His comrades, who make up the firing squad, deliberately miss their mark and he once again heads for Paris and his fiancee.

Cowardice is only occasionally the cause of a court martial in film. It is not too popular a theme since audiences tend to detach themselves from the principal character under indictment. Also, major actors prefer not to play cowards. One of the most popular war dramas with this theme is *The Fighting 69th* (1940). James Cagney plays the thankless role of a coward, supported by Pat O'Brien as the unit's affable chaplain. Cagney portrays a swaggering braggart who falls apart at the first sign of combat. After his cowardice leads to the deaths of several of his comrades, he is court-martialed and sentenced to face a firing squad. Freed from his lock-up by an enemy shell, he redeems himself in battle. He sacrifices his life to save some of his buddies by throwing himself on a live hand grenade.

Mutiny has always been a popular film subject, but seldom used in war dramas. Three years after the huge success of MGM's *Mutiny on the Bounty* (1935), Columbia released *Adventure in Sahara*, starring Paul Kelly and C. Henry Gordon. The latter drama involved a tyrannical Foreign Legion captain who is evicted from a fort by his men. Abandoned in the desert, he vows to return and punish the mutineers. Later, after his men act bravely in driving off an Arab attack, the captain insists on court-martialing the troops. A lieutenant explains the entire circumstances, and the men are exonerated. One of the most popular war movies about mutiny—and one of the most dramatically sustained—is *The Caine Mutiny* (1954), based on Herman

Wouk's best seller. Humphrey Bogart portrays the emotionally unstable Captain Queeg who is eventually relieved of command by his executive officer, Lieutenant Maryk (Van Johnson). Later, at Maryk's court martial, his attorney (Jose Ferrer) demolishes Queeg's testimony and character, thereby acquitting Maryk. After the trial the lawyer accuses Maryk of lack of loyalty to his captain.

Several war dramas present fresh themes within the framework of a court martial. The Korean War introduced a new subject to movie audiences—collaboration with the enemy. Paul Newman, as a former war hero, is charged with collaborating with the Communists in *The Rack* (1956). A court martial finds him guilty after a lengthy trial in which a fellow prisoner of war (Lee Marvin) testifies against the accused. In Stanley Kubrick's highly acclaimed *Paths of Glory* (1957), a drama set during World War I, three French soldiers are chosen at random for a court martial after their unit is accused of cowardice under fire. Used as examples for the rest of the troops, the court finds them guilty and sentences them to death by a firing squad.

The court martial has been used as a ploy in several films to get the hero on good terms with the enemy. In *Across the Pacific* (1942), a World War II spy drama with Humphrey Bogart, Mary Astor and Sydney Greenstreet, Bogart, as an American agent, poses as a court-martialed army officer. He temporarily joins a spy network led by Greenstreet, a Japanese sympathizer. He foils the spies in their attempt to blow up the Panama Canal. Other films dealing with military courts have turned to actual events and historical figures. In *Juarez* (1939) Maximilian (Brian Aherne), the tragic pawn in French politics, is appointed Emperor of Mexico in 1864 and then abandoned by Napoleon III. He resigns himself to his court martial and the ultimate sentence of death. Abraham Lincoln (Frank McGlynn) commutes a young soldier's court martial in the patriotic short, "Lincoln in the White House" (1939). In *The Court Martial of Billy Mitchell* (1954), a military drama rather than a war film, the World War I flier and army general (Gary Cooper) dares to take on the military establishment. His attacks in the 1920s on the military's neglect to recognize the importance of air power led to his court martial for insubordination. He was suspended from the service for five years. In 1926 he resigned from the army. ∎

Coward, The (1915), Triangle. *Dir.* Reginald Barker; *Sc.* Thomas Ince, C. Gardner Sullivan; *Cast includes:* Charles Ray, Frank Keenan, Gertrude Claire, Margaret Gibson.

When the Civil War breaks out, the cowardly son of a proud Virginia colonel refuses to enlist. His father has to physically force him to join the Confederate army at the point of a gun. The boy deserts on his first night of picket duty, and his father substitutes for him. Back at his home, the son overhears Union plans for an attack and captures the plans. He rides furiously to his own lines with the information but is shot down by his own father who mistakes him for the enemy. Although seriously wounded, the boy succeeds in delivering the important papers. ∎

Cradle of Courage (1920). See Crime and War. ∎

Crew members of a U.S. submarine undertake a special mission on shore during World War II. *Crash Dive* (1943).

Crash Dive (1943), TCF. *Dir.* Archie Mayo; *Sc.* Jo Swerling; *Cast includes:* Tyrone Power, Anne Baxter, Dana Andrews, James Gleason, Dame May Whitty.

A tribute to the men of the U.S. Navy who make up the submarine service, this World War II drama follows the exploits of one such undersea vessel through maneuvers and actual sea battles. Tyrone Power portrays a lieutenant assigned to a sub commanded by Dana Andrews. A conflict between the two arises when Power learns that his love interest (Anne Baxter) is the fiancee of his captain. Once the vessel sails into action, however, the trite romantic triangle is submerged along with the vessel as the officers and crew nar-rowly escape enemy depth charges and maneuver through submarine nets. They are assigned to destroy a German mine-laying base, which they handle with dispatch, and sink a German Q-boat, an armed vessel disguised as a merchant ship. One of the earliest war films to employ Technicolor, the film is highly effective in matters of suspense and battle sequences. ∎

Crashing Through to Berlin (1918), U. *Sc.* S. H. Mackean.

A documentary on the history of World War I, the film depicts the war from its beginning to the entrance of the United States. Since the film emanates from an American studio, the point of view is that of the U.S., tracing its preparations for the conflict, the transportation of troops to Europe and its participation in some of the major battles. Titles are used extensively to help describe the visuals. Composed chiefly of official war footage, the film uses several sequences seen previously in other documentaries. ∎

Crazy Horse (184?–1877). A streak of lightning painted on his face, his body covered with hailstone dots, Chief Crazy Horse of the Oglala Sioux presented an imposing figure astride his yellow pinto pony. Calling out to the warriors gathering around him, "Come Lakotas, it's a good day to die!" he and his large band surged out of their tepee encampment on the Little Bighorn River on June 25, 1876 to meet an attacking force of American soldiers under the hated "Long Hair," Col. George Custer.

The resulting clash, the Battle of the Little Bighorn River, also became known as "Custer's Last Stand." The American unit of 267 troopers was totally wiped out in one of the greatest disasters to befall the U.S. Army in its history of Indian warfare. Crazy Horse's victory reinforced his stature as the paramount fighting leader of the Sioux nation.

Born in the 1840s near the present site of Rapid City, South Dakota, in Black Hills country that was the sacred medicine grounds of the Sioux, Crazy Horse spent a good deal of his adult life resisting the encroachments of the white man into the Black Hills. Before the attack on Custer in the Sioux War of 1876–1877, Crazy Horse had participated in several well-known engagements including the Fetterman Massacre (Dec. 21, 1866) and the Wagon Box Raid (Aug. 2, 1867).

Crazy Horse was among those Sioux leaders who resisted forced settlement on a reservation, one of the causes of the Sioux War of 1876–77. Early in the war General George Crook mounted a surprise attack on the camp of Crazy Horse and drove away the hostiles' horses. But Crazy Horse managed to recover the animals and defeat Crook on the Rosebud River in June 1876.

The slaughter of Custer at the Little Bighorn River, though an Indian victory, led to the eventual defeat of the Sioux and the capture of Crazy Horse the following year as a result of increased efforts by the United States government to subdue the tribe and end fighting in the northern Great Plains. Crazy Horse surrendered, turning in his weapons to General Crook, on May 5, 1877, at Fort Robinson.

Seized later that year over fears that he was preparing to lead a new revolt, Crazy Horse got into a struggle with his captors and Indians friendly to the whites. He was bayoneted, ostensibly while trying to escape, by a soldier. His reported last words were, "I am badly hurt. Tell the people it is no use to depend on me any more now." The memory of Crazy Horse is revered today by his tribe.

Only a handful of films touched upon the Indian chief's exploits. Both Indians and whites enacted the role. High Eagle portrayed Crazy Horse as a stereotyped hostile in an inept and highly fictionalized serial titled *Custer's Last Stand* (1936). Anthony Quinn, in a minor role, portrayed him sympathetically in *They Died With Their Boots On* (1941), but he was overshadowed by Errol Flynn as General Custer. Crazy Horse appeared again as a minor but sympathetic character in *Sitting Bull* (1954), this time impersonated by Iron Eyes Cody. The weak plot was filled with historical inaccuracies. Cody repeated his impersonation in *The Great Sioux Massacre* (1965), another retelling of Custer's last stand. Crazy Horse received his best treatment in his own film biography, *Chief Crazy Horse*, in 1955. Portrayed with compassion by Victor Mature, a popular actor of the period, the warrior chief was depicted as a brave and idealistic leader who was fully justified for taking up arms against the encroaching and avaricious whites. ■

Crime and war. As if war doesn't provide enough melodrama and violence, Hollywood, on occasion, has come up with scripts blending crime with the conflict at hand. This has resulted in two broad categories of films. On the one hand, there is the predictable plot of the miscreant who enlists in the military and returns home a changed person. He may even be a small-time hoodlum who becomes involved with enemy agents on the home front. The experience suddenly awakens him to his wasted life. Or he may have been forced into uniform by either the law closing in on him or rival gang members wanting to rub him out. In all these cases, he is usually converted into a better citizen.

On the other hand, a veteran, often a hero in battle, may return from the front to learn that his job has been taken by a slacker or that no work is available. He is then forced to turn to crime. One of the earliest to fit this mold is *The Jolt* (1921). A World War I veteran and former criminal returns with his French wife to New York City where he soon comes upon hard times. Hounded by bill collectors and unable to find work, he reverts to his past life. Fortunately, he is saved by a former army buddy at the last moment. These films, especially those made during the early 1930s, are often more thematic, frequently in a didactic way. They indict society for sending the hero to war where he is trained to kill and where he lives with constant violence. It is no wonder, the films exclaim, that the ex-soldier, with his values twisted, has turned to crime as a way of life.

Several World War I dramas deal with protagonists who had criminal backgrounds but are transformed by their experiences at the front or by the conflict in general. In *Luck and Pluck* (1919), a World War I drama, George Walsh, as a burglar, captures a German spy ring and gives up his life of crime. William S. Hart, as a small-time thief before the war in *Cradle of Courage* (1920), returns from the Great War a hero and joins the police force on the advice of a war buddy. When he tells his mother, who has a strong dislike for the law, that he plans to go straight, she evicts him from her home. Betty Compson, in league with a gang of French pickpockets in *The Green Temptation* (1922), barely escapes the law. When World War I breaks out, she enlists as a nurse. But her past catches up with her when she journeys to America after the war. Alice Calhoun undergoes a similar conversion in *Little Wildcat* (1922). In perpetual trouble with the law, she serves as a Red Cross nurse and spy for the Allies when war erupts. *Into No Man's Land* (1928) relates the story of a big-time gang leader (Tom Santschi) who enlists in the army during World War I to protect his daughter. She is about to marry the district attorney who is ready to arrest her father. Santschi realizes the safest place for him is overseas.

The sound era brought several changes in plot and theme to these crime-and-war dramas although an occasional film with its theme of regeneration lingered on. Such is the case with *The Mighty* (1930), about a prewar criminal (George Bancroft) whose combat experience turns him into a stalwart police chief after the war. Another example is *Born Reckless* (1930), with Edmund Lowe as a suave gangster who is caught for a crime. When he is given a choice of marching off to prison or serving his country, he selects the latter. He distinguishes himself in battle during World War I, falls in love with a socialite when he returns and rescues her kidnaped child from an old rival.

War films as a genre were going through a transition during the early sound era. Dramas such as *All Quiet on the Western Front* and *Journey's End*, both released in 1930, began to treat World War I more realistically, stripping the films of much of their images of heroism, glory and national honor. Cynicism and disillusionment seeped into the next cycle of war films. *The Last Parade* (1931) reflects some of these changes. Two friends who enlist in the war and see action together end up on opposite sides of the law after the Armistice. Jack Holt, as a former reporter, saves his buddy's life in France but loses an eye during the incident. After they return home, his friend (Tom Moore), a former policeman, rises to the rank of detective while Holt, unable to find work, turns to crime. By the end of the film, Holt is on his way to the death chamber, the "last parade." In *They Gave Him a Gun* (1937) a meek clerk (Franchot Tone) is transformed into a gang leader and killer as a result of his experiences in the trenches. Spencer Tracy, as his army buddy, sacrifices his love for Gladys George until Tone is inevitably gunned down by the police. Another drama that graphically links World War I with crime is *The Roaring 20s* (1939). The opening sequences show three buddies (James Cagney, Humphrey Bogart and Jeffrey Lynn) fighting in the trenches in France during World War I. Later, Cagney and Bogart join the lucrative bootlegging

racket during Prohibition while Lynn becomes a lawyer.

During World War II an occasional film reached the screen in which shady characters embraced their country's call to some degree. In *Two Yanks in Trinidad* (1942), another comedy drama, a pair of rival American racketeers (Pat O'Brien and Brian Donlevy) end up in the army where they join forces in capturing a Nazi agent. Alan Ladd, as a gang leader in *Lucky Jordan* (1942), rebels against authority when he is drafted. After escaping from his army camp, he learns that his former mob has thrown in with Nazi agents. Ladd suddenly reforms and saves certain military plans from falling into enemy hands. Dean Jagger, as a counterfeiter in *I Escaped From the Gestapo* (1943), breaks out of prison with the help of Nazi agents. When he learns of their plans to create havoc in financial markets, he helps to effect their capture. In *The Racket Man* (1944), a low-budget drama, former hoodlum Tom Neal goes through a moral patriotic regeneration after he is drafted into Uncle Sam's army. He is sent on a special mission to stop his old gang from dealing in black market merchandise.

The trend continued in postwar films of the conflict. In *When Hell Broke Loose* (1958), for instance, Charles Bronson, as a racketeer serving in the U.S. Army during the war, learns of a Nazi plot to assassinate General Eisenhower. His quick thinking and action saves the commander-in-chief. Some postwar films such as *The Secret Invasion* (1964) and *The Dirty Dozen* (1967) use the ploy of giving convicted criminals and murderers a chance for a pardon if they volunteer for a suicide mission.

The Vietnam War provided the impetus for a series of films in which some returning veterans, either unable to adjust to civilian life or callously mistreated by society, vent their rage in an outburst of violence. In *Welcome Home, Soldier Boys* (1972) four Vietnam veterans, former members of the Green Berets, leave the service and journey through the South. Tired of waiting at a gas station for the attendant and generally frustrated by an uncaring, hostile society, they decide to break the lock on a pump. When the angry station owner fires at them from his window, the vets retaliate with their own firearms. After shooting most of the townspeople, they don their old uniforms, wait for the National Guard and perish senselessly in a hail of bullets. In *First Blood* (1982), an implausible action drama, a former Green Beret (Sylvester Stallone) is hassled by a local sheriff and his deputies. Placed in the slammer and roughed up, he bursts into a rage, crashes out and practically destroys the town. These films often point an anemic finger at society for initiating such a violent war, turning decent young men like Stallone into killing machines and then abandoning them. ■

"Crime Does Not Pay" series. MGM produced a high-quality series of two-reel dramatized documentaries from 1935 to 1947 called "Crime Does Not Pay." Although the majority of the entries were concerned with exposing various illegal activities, several released during World War II dealt with the threat of spies. "While America Sleeps" (1939), for instance, explains how enemy agents operate. "For the Common Defense" (1942) tells of a South American spy network's link to American gangsters. In "Keep 'em Sailing" (1942) an F.B.I. agent exposes sabotage attempts directed at U.S. cargo ships. ■

Crimean War (1854–1856). This conflict could easily have slipped into the shadows of history as just another of many Balkan wars caused by great power rivalries except for the prominence it gained from a poem and the untiring, selfless efforts of a woman in helping the wounded. The poem was Alfred Lord Tennyson's *Charge Of The Light Brigade*. The woman, "the Lady with the Lamp," was Florence Nightingale, founder of modern nursing. Two films highlight these situations— *Charge Of The Light Brigade* (1936), starring Errol Flynn in one of Hollywood's all-time top cavalry spectacles, and *The White Angel* (1936) with Kay Francis in the role of Florence Nightingale.

France's attempt to challenge Russia's role as protector of holy Christian sites in Turkish-controlled Palestine set the stage for this conflict. When the Turks granted France some guardianship privileges and rejected Russian counter-demands in 1853, Russia retaliated by seizing Turkey's vassal Balkan states of Moldavia and Walachia, bringing on a Turkish declaration of war the same year. France and England joined Turkey in the war in 1854 to prevent Russia from penetrating deeper into the Balkans and be in a position to threaten their Mediterranean trade routes.

The allied invasion of the Crimea produced several battles with great losses and notable heroics on both sides. Examples included the battles of Balaklava, that served as the source for Tennyson's poem, and the siege of Sebastopol. Florence Nightingale, an English nurse who founded hospitals to tend the wounded in the Crimea, greatly affected the principles of hospital administration and nursing techniques by her innovations. The famous cavalry charge of the Light Brigade under Lord Cardigan, the result of confused orders, played only a minimal role in preventing the Russians from recapturing Balaklava. The brigade's actions have come to stand for unquestioned heroic obedience to duty as a result of Tennyson's poem.

Charge Of the Light Brigade, loosely based on Tennyson's work, does take some liberties with history. Errol Flynn, as head of the Brigade, is shown leading the charge against the forces of Surat Khan, a fictitious Indian Moslem tribal chief allied with the Russians. Flynn falsifies orders in order to attack Khan and avenge an earlier (fictitious) massacre by the Khan in India. Why Hollywood created this convoluted version of the event is a mystery because both the poem and the actual incident certainly had sufficient basis for filming dramatic heroism and stirring cavalry action. One other movie, *Charge Of The Lancers* (1954), a weak attempt to capitalize on the previous film's success, does show the capture of the Russian fortress city of Sebastopol.

The war brought forth a few innovations. The electric telegraph was introduced to flash battle orders thousands of miles away. Floating mines were employed against enemy ships. This was also the first war to be widely covered by photographs. Russia lost the Crimean War and had to give up the land it had seized. However, Russia continued to harbor designs of expansion into the Balkans. This interest created an explosive situation in the Balkans that ultimately brought on World War I. ■

Crimson Romance (1934), Mascot. *Dir.* David Howard; *Sc.* Milton Krims; *Cast includes:* Ben Lyon, Sari Maritza, Erich von Stroheim, Hardie Albright, James Bush, William Bakewell.

Ben Lyon and James Bush, as two young Americans, join up with the German air force in the early years of World War I in this minor drama. When the Americans enter the conflict, Lyon switches allegiances and fights for the Allies. Bush, born a German-American and fed up with anti-German sentiment back home in the States, continues to fly for the Germans and is eventually killed in battle. When the war ends Lyon returns to the U.S. with his German bride whom he met while flying for her country. They visit the mother of this dead friend. The film ends with her pacifist remarks.

The film is an oddity in its premise that two Americans would have flown for the Germans in the early stages of the war, considering that antipathy for that nation was so prevalent in the U.S. Furthermore, Lyon could have joined the Allied cause by way of Canada. ▪

Crisis (1939), Arthur Mayer. *Dir.* Herbert Kline; *Sc.* Vincent Shean.

An anti-Nazi documentary, the film reveals the methods employed by Nazis in their takeover and control of Czechoslovakia. Scenes of a former tranquil domestic life contrast with troop movements and Nazi storm troopers in the act of terrorizing workers, underscoring the transition of a once peaceful country into an oppressed political state. The narration by screen actor Leif Erickson is more picturesque and informative than the scenes that accompany it. ▪

Crisis, The (1915), Selig. *Dir.* Colin Campbell; *Cast includes:* George W. Fawcett, Bessie Eyton, Matt Snyder, Eugenia Besserer.

An early silent drama set during the Civil War and based on the novel by Winston Churchill, the film was overshadowed by Griffith's Civil War epic, *The Birth of a Nation*, released the same year. One of the historical drama's highlights is the re-enactment of the siege of Vicksburg. Several historical figures are portrayed on screen, including Abraham Lincoln and General Sherman. The government cooperated with the studio by providing original documents and items from the period. Selig, as well as a few other movie studios such as Biograph, had been making historical dramas for several years. Those released from about 1908 through 1913, however, were chiefly one- or two-reelers, especially Griffith's Civil War cycle that he turned out during this period for Biograph. ▪

"Crisis in the Atlantic" (1941). See "The March of Time." ▪

"Crisis in the Pacific" (1940). See "The March of Time." ▪

Crockett, David (1786–1836). When David Crockett died at the Battle of The Alamo after voluntarily joining Americans fighting for their independence from Mexico, he left behind a record as a popular western politician and hero. Born in Tennessee, he served in General Andrew Jackson's army of frontiersmen and militia that fought the British and their Indian allies during the War of 1812. In that conflict Crockett took part in the campaign against the Creek Indians in 1813 and 1814.

Entering politics in his native state, he first won election to the state legislature (1821–1826) and then served three terms as a Tennessee representative (1827–1831, 1833–1835) in the House. While in Congress, Crockett became popular as a conservative who effected a homespun and penetrating wit that he used in comments on contemporary issues. When he failed to gain re-election, he moved to Texas where he quickly aligned himself with the forces battling for independence from Mexico. Crockett joined Colonels William Travis and James Bowie with a force of less than 200 Texans at the Alamo. Following the final successful Mexican assault on the Alamo in which all of the remaining defenders died, Crockett's body was found riddled with bullets.

Films about Crockett usually concentrate on his role at the Alamo, as in *Davy Crockett at the Fall of the Alamo* (1926), starring Cullen Landis. An earlier silent, *Davy Crockett* (1916), starring Dustin Farnum, has him involved with rescuing a heroine from an unscrupulous gambler. He is the main character in *Heroes of the Alamo* (1938) and *The Alamo* (1960) and one of the principal figures in *The Last Command* (1955). John Wayne directed and starred as Crockett in *The Alamo*, a highly fictionalized portrayal of the frontiersman's place in Texas history. *The Last Command* faithfully depicts Crockett's facility as a raconteur. He plays a minor role in *The First Texan* (1956), a biographical drama about Sam Houston. ▪

Cross Bearer, The (1918), World. *Dir.* George Archainbaud; *Sc.* Anne Maxwell; *Cast includes:* Montagu Love, Jeanne Engels, Anthony Merlo, George Morgan.

The drama, set during World War I following Germany's invasion of Belgium, concerns a Belgian lieutenant who is in love with a cardinal's ward. While he is at the front, the German governor-general forces his attentions upon the young woman. The cardinal, deeply angered at the invaders of his land, battles wits with the German while attempting to protect his ward. Eventually he helps to smuggle the lieutenant and the girl into France. Several incidents depict the atrocities brought upon the Belgian people by the Germans although there are no large battle sequences. Montagu Love portrays the cardinal, a symbolic figure of peace, morality and kindness. His strong spiritual faith is more than a match for the brutish, superstitious governor-general who represents the dark forces of human nature. ■

Cross of Lorraine, The (1943), MGM. Dir. Tay Garnett; Sc. Michael Kanin, Ring Lardner, Jr., Alexander Esway, Robert D. Andrews; Cast includes: Gene Kelly, Sir Cedric Hardwicke, Richard Whorf, Joseph Calleia, Peter Lorre, Hume Cronyn.

The barbaric treatment of French prisoners of war in Nazi camps is the subject of this grim World War II drama. Gene Kelly, as a French soldier, resists collaborating with his Nazi captors. He is tortured by a German sergeant (Peter Lorre) who eventually breaks the spirit of the prisoner. Jean Pierre Aumont, portraying another prisoner, plans and executes an escape with his fellow inmates and heads for the border to join the Free French in their struggle against the Germans. Kelly, regaining his fighting spirit while hiding out in a village, arouses that same spark in the local inhabitants who then avenge themselves upon the enemy.

Historically, Germany pledged fair and humane treatment to those French soldiers who surrendered and accepted the terms of the German armistice. What the vanquished did not expect was betrayal of the agreement and the ensuing ruthless treatment, including torture, starvation and brainwashing. The incidents portrayed in the film were based on numerous factual accounts. ■

Crowded Hour, The (1925), Par. Dir. E. Mason Hopper; Sc. Channing Pollack, Edgar Selwyn; Cast includes: Bebe Daniels, Kenneth Harlan, T. Roy Barnes, Frank Morgan.

A romantic drama with World War I as the background, the film stars Bebe Daniels as Peggy, an entertainer, who falls in love with a married producer, Billy Laidlaw (Kenneth Harlan). Billy soon makes stars of Peggy and Matt, her partner in the act. When Billy is sent to France to fight, Peggy and Matt follow. An occasion arises in which Peggy and Matt make an attempt to help Billy, but they are wounded. Billy's wife, who has become a nurse, attends to Peggy in the hospital. They soon reach an understanding and, when Billy, whom both women thought dead, returns, Peggy sends him back to his wife. Numerous battle scenes of trench warfare, attacks and shellings add some realism to the film. ■

Crusades (1095–1291). As the 11th century was coming to an end, Pope Urban II became increasingly disturbed by the situation in the Holy Land. Reports mounted of Christian pilgrims, visiting sacred sites in Palestine, being harassed and persecuted by Moslem Seljuk Turks who controlled the area. It was bad enough in the view of many Christians that non-believers ruled the region where the western church had its roots. The added mistreatment of religious pilgrims impelled the Pope to make an impassioned plea in 1095 to the Church Council of Clermont for an international Christian military force to wrest control of Jerusalem and surrounding Palestine from the Moslems. His call produced an extensive period of religious warfare between Western Christian Europe and the Moslem Middle East that became known as the Crusades from the crosses distributed at the Council. Most of the fighting took place in present-day Israel and Lebanon.

A plea for aid by the Byzantine Christian emperor in Constantinople, whose empire was threatened by Turkish expansion, was probably another factor in determining the time for launching the First Crusade (1095–1099). There were nine Crusades in a span of close to 200 years. Though they achieved only temporary success in dislodging the Moslems from Jerusalem and nearby Palestine, the Crusades, nevertheless, stand as one of history's epochal events that forever altered the nature of society in the western world.

The First Crusade, under Godfrey of Bouillon, captured Jerusalem in 1097 and established the first of several Christian kingdoms in Palestine. Moslem forces under Saladin, however, reconquered the city in 1187 and the

Moslems repulsed all future efforts by Crusaders to regain permanent control. Succeeding Crusades were primarily concerned with giving assistance to the defense of precariously held Christian enclaves in Palestine.

The Third Crusade (1189–1192), led by Frederick Barbarosa of Germany, Philip Augustus of France and England's Richard I (Richard the Lion-Hearted), was called to recover Jerusalem which had been recently retaken by Saladin. Although the Crusade did not retake Jerusalem, Richard's victory at Acre resulted in an agreement with Saladin to grant safe passage to future Christian pilgrims visiting Jerusalem's holy sites. This Crusade became the focus of several films based on the adventures of King Richard.

Richard the Lion-Hearted (1923) is overly concerned with a fictitious love story that pits Richard (Wallace Beery) and Saladin (Charles Gerrard) as romantic and military rivals. *The Crusades* (1935) is a Cecil B. DeMille epic whose title is deceptive in that it deals exclusively with Richard's military and romantic involvements while on the Third Crusade. In *King Richard and the Crusaders* (1954) Richard (George Sanders) struggles against the crafty Saladin (Rex Harrison) as well as with the selfish aspirations of several members of his entourage. DeMille's film presents the greatest spectacle. The climactic battle sequence shows the storming and capture of the fortified city of Acre by Christian forces. It depicts in vivid fashion the techniques and weapons used in medieval warfare. It has scenes of mass sword fights, the use of catapults against the fortifications and retaliation by the defenders who pour burning oil down upon the attackers.

In some cases, European and Byzantine cities on the route of the Crusades were attacked and pillaged by passing Christian forces. European Jews, as non-Christians, were on occasion attacked by those involved in the Crusades. Hollywood, in its customary casual and selective manner of portraying history, has overlooked mining much of this potentially rich lode of drama, action and tragedy.

Though largely a military failure from the point of view of Christian Western Europe, the Crusades are important because they marked the beginning of the end of Western Europe's insularity, ignorance and cultural stagnation that were the legacy of the collapse of ancient Rome and Greece. Indeed, few events have had such a profound effect on the development of modern western culture as the Crusades. European contact with the more advanced Moslem world led to the decline of European feudalism and the rise of trade and a renaissance in learning and the arts. ∎

Crusades, The (1935), Par. *Dir.* Cecil B. DeMille; *Sc.* Harold Lamb, Dudley Nichols, Waldemar Young; *Cast includes:* Loretta Young, Henry Wilcoxon, Ian Keith, Katherine DeMille, C. Aubrey Smith, Alan Hale.

Cecil B. DeMille's pageant of King Richard the Lion-Hearted's adventures and loves during the Third Crusade provides a spectacular final battle scene but a generally spiritless story. Henry Wilcoxon portrays the outspoken and courageous Richard. Loretta Young plays Berangia of Navarre, the romantic interest of Richard. Katherine DeMille, as the sister of King Philip of France, is betrothed to Richard, who joins the Crusade to avoid the promised marriage. Saladin, the leader of the Saracens, played by Ian Keith, is treated intelligently in his dealings with the Christian Crusaders.

The climax of the film, the Battle of Acre, is the most fascinating aspect of the production. Director DeMille, a recognized master at controlling huge crowds and armies, choreographs his thousands of extras in one spectacular scene after another. Hordes of Christian soldiers attack the walls with fire bombs, catapults and swords while the defenders pour burning oil on the invaders. The Christians ultimately win but pay a very high price.

The film plays loosely with history in its depiction of the Third Crusade in which English, French, German, Russian and Hungarian armies unite to reclaim Jerusalem from the non-Christians. An elderly holy man called The Hermit (C. Aubrey Smith) incites King Philip of France (C. Henry Gordon) to lead the Third Crusade against Saladin and cajoles King Richard to join them. Historically, the figure of the zealot was responsible for inspiring the First Crusade in 1095. The Third Crusade did not begin until 1190. DeMille constantly defended his "telescoping" of historical facts by claiming that his audiences did not want historical dates but entertainment. ∎

Cry Havoc (1943), MGM. *Dir.* Richard Thorpe; *Sc.* Paul Osborn; *Cast includes:* Margaret Sullavan, Ann Sothern, Joan Blondell,

Fay Bainter, Marsha Hunt, Ella Raines, Heather Angel.

A stagy World War II drama of a group of volunteer nurses in a bomb shelter on Bataan, the film records their reactions to the war and the dying as the battle grows more intense. Margaret Sullavan, in charge of the nine young women, suffers from malignant malaria but struggles on in her duties. She has volunteered for duty on Bataan to be near her husband, a lieutenant whom she has secretly married. Ann Sothern, as a former waitress, gives Sullavan a tough time. Another volunteer, played by Joan Blondell, was formerly a burlesque entertainer. As the American position becomes more tenuous, Sullavan offers the nurses a chance to leave. They all vote to stay. When her superior, Fay Bainter, expresses surprise at their decision, Sullavan explains: "They're Americans. They believe in happy endings." When the island falls to the Japanese, the nurses march out of the shelter to surrender to the enemy. The film is based on a Broadway play titled *Proof Thro' the Night*.

Typical of the war movies of the period, the film is drenched in propaganda. "In this war," one of the nurses announces, "we're all fighting for the same thing—our lives." She then goes on to elaborate how the enemy intends to make slaves of its captives. The brutality of the Japanese is established by their repeated bombing of the hospital although it is pointed out in the film that in their broadcasts they promised not to do so in future attacks. In another scene a Japanese plane machine-guns one of the nurses who is gently bathing in a stream. The others, outraged at the cowardly act, cry out against the enemy. "We'll get him," one swears, "we'll get every mother's son of them!" ■

Cry of Battle (1963), AA. *Dir.* Irving Lerner; *Sc.* Bernard Gordon; *Cast includes:* Van Heflin, Rita Moreno, James MacArthur.

A low-budget drama set in the Philippines during the early days of World War II, the film concerns a green youth's introduction to love and war. James MacArthur portrays a young American who arrives in the Philippines one day after the bombing of Pearl Harbor. Confused by rapidly developing events, including the Japanese invasion of the island, he joins a guerrilla group. Van Heflin, as a disagreeable eccentric, shares his simple philosophy with the lad. "You fight when you have to, you get a dame when you can, that's about it." Rita Moreno provides the romantic interest in this slow-paced film. ■

Cuban Revolts of 1930–1933. Gerardo Machado, Cuba's first military dictator, served as president from 1925 to 1933. At first sincerely interested in social reforms, he gradually turned his regime into an oppressive one, which culminated in acts of terror and bloodshed carried out by his secret police. Rebel organizations formed and retaliated with their own acts of terrorism and sabotage against Machado's regime. The U.S. eventually interceded, acting as mediator between warring factions. After further incidents of violence, military forces turned against Machado. He fled Cuba in 1933 and died a few years later in Florida. Several American films deal with events during his reign. The documentary *World in Revolt* (1934) covers several rebellions and insurrections, including the anti-Machado revolt in Cuba. In *We Were Strangers* (1949) revolutionaries plot to assassinate the top government leaders of his regime. John Garfield portrays one of the anti-Machado rebels. *The Gun Runners* (1958) stars Audie Murphy as a down-on-his-luck captain who hires out his cabin cruiser to smuggle guns to Cuban rebels. Based on Hemingway's novel *To Have and Have Not*, the film avoids any political references to Machado. ■

Cuban Revolution of 1956–1959. As a result of this uprising, Fidel Castro overthrew dictator Fulgencio Batista y Salvador, who had been in power for over 20 years. Castro headed an organization known as the 26th of July Movement that advocated democratic and economic reforms. He had been imprisoned for earlier anti-government activities, and after being freed by Batista in 1955, he went to Mexico with his small band to reorganize for a new attack on a Cuban government known for corruption and police oppression. Castro returned with 81 followers and a small boatload of arms and ammunition the following year to become entrenched in the rugged Sierra Maestra range in Oriente province.

Castro's group, which now included Che Guevara, a leading Latin-American revolutionary, attracted considerable popular support in guerrilla raids against Batista's troops between 1956–1958. The revolutionists left their mountain refuge and launched a full scale offensive in the fall of 1958 that resulted in the capture of Santa Clara, a provincial capital. Batista, realizing he no longer had the support of even his own troops, fled Cuba on January 1, 1959, to seek asylum in the Dominican Republic.

Castro and his followers entered Havana, Cuba's capital, two days later to be greeted by large crowds who eagerly looked forward to a more efficient and democratic government. Shortly after taking power, Castro, with broad support among the lower class, imposed a Communist economic system and police state on the nation. The U.S. broke relations with Cuba over the problem of nationalized foreign property. Castro then turned to and received massive support from the Soviet Union. The U.S. supported the Bay of Pigs invasion by right wing and democratic elements in 1961 that failed to dislodge Castro.

Che! (1969), one of the few American-produced films about the revolt, is a biographical drama of Dr. Ernesto Che Guevara. It depicts Guevara as a malevolent and ingenious planner of the revolution that toppled the Batista regime. He is shown trying to divert the revolution and Castro toward evil ends. In *Rebellion in Cuba* (1961), a weak and undistinguished piece of fiction, several Americans, disturbed over Cuba's Communist government in such a strategic location, decide to support a revolt against Castro. The film was released shortly after the abortive Bay of Pigs invasion and mirrored many of its details. ■

Cuban War of Independence (1895–1898). Spain's failure to effect promised political reforms after an earlier Cuban revolution led to new demands for independence by the Cuban Revolutionary Party, based in New York. Several prominent Cuban revolutionaries and expatriate fighters returned to the island by the mid-1890s and established a guerrilla republic in eastern Cuba by 1895. Some of the rebel leaders included writer Jose Julian Marti, Antonio Maceo and Maximo Gomez y Baez.

The guerrillas, who avoided direct and large-scale clashes with Spanish troops under General Valeriano Weyler y Nicolau, made gains into western Cuba and by 1896 approached Havana, the island's capital. Weyler's controversial policy of separating the guerrillas from the population by interning civilians in concentration camps caused an outcry in the U.S. press for intervention to free Cuba. The uproar was due to reports that the prisoners suffered and died in increasing numbers from insufficient food, disease and generally bad living conditions.

Some American newspapers created imaginary horrors of the Spanish occupation to whip up sympathy for the Cubans and develop a mood for war within the U.S. The American press, however, generally failed to report that Spain, in 1897, reversed its earlier handling of the revolution by recalling Weyler, disbanding the camps and offering a new promise of home rule. The sinking of the U.S.S. *Maine* in Havana harbor (1898), sent to protect American people and business in Cuba, was the spark that fused the Cuban revolution into the Spanish-American War (1898) and ultimate independence for Cuba. American film studios preferred to exploit the events and personalities of the Spanish-American War, a conflict that directly involved American troops, than focus on Cuba's revolt against Spain. Therefore, very few films used the revolution as background. One of the earliest, "The Dawn of Freedom" (1910), deals with Cuba's struggle for freedom, dramatizing the insurrection as well as several battles. In *Santiago* (1956) Alan Ladd portrays a gun-running mercenary who eventually turns idealistic and involves himself in Cuba's struggle for independence against Spain. ■

Cuba's Ten Years' War. See *The Bright Shawl* (1923). ■

Cushman, Pauline (1835–1893). One of the Union's successful spies in the Civil War, the actress Pauline Cushman came close to losing her life when her ruse was discovered. In 1863, as part of her disguise, she was banished from the North as a supposedly Confederate sympathizer. She did important undercover work for the Union in Kentucky and Tennessee before she was apprehended in possession of valuable Southern papers. After being court-martialed and sentenced to hang, she was saved when the Confederates, in a hasty retreat from Shelbyville, Tennessee (June 1863), inadvertently left her behind. Cushman made a postwar career of lecturing about her spy experiences but ended a troubled life by suicide.

Two Civil War films portray her exploits.

Selig released *Pauline Cushman, the Federal Spy* in 1913. MGM's 1934 Civil War drama *Operator 13* starred Marion Davies as a Union spy who works alongside Pauline Cushman, portrayed by Katherine Alexander. ∎

Custer, George Armstrong (1839–1876). To Lt. Colonel George A. Custer the situation facing him must have seemed ideal for creating another glorious chapter to his already distinguished and highly publicized war record. In pursuit of a large group of Sioux and Cheyenne Indians, he led a frontal assault with 266 troopers from his 7th Cavalry Regiment against an Indian encampment at the Little Bighorn River in present-day Montana on the morning of June 25, 1876.

Custer achieved his goal of gaining more glory and, with it, a permanent niche in American history. But it was at the expense of his life and the lives of all the soldiers in his unit in a battle against an estimated 2,500 Indians that came to be known as "Custer's last stand."

Custer's action was entirely in keeping with his character. He had a reputation for bold and impetuous action. He also had a streak of viciousness that showed itself in his dealings with his soldiers and Indian opponents alike. Following the battle, the Indians celebrated the death of "Long Hair," for they knew him to be a cruel enemy, particularly in his treatment of the Cheyenne. They called him "squaw killer" for his brutal massacre of a portion of their tribe at Washita River a few years earlier.

Graduating last in the West Point class of 1861, Custer more than made up for his poor showing as a student by cutting a dashing figure during the Civil War. With his long, flowing blonde hair and bushy mustache he soon developed into a daring and brilliant cavalry officer and received several quick promotions, culminating in the temporary wartime rank of Brigadier General. He participated in the Battle of Bull Run and distinguished himself at the Battle of Gettysburg. After the war, Lt. Colonel Custer and the 7th Cavalry were assigned to control the Indians in the West. He developed a reputation for harsh, direct action in the unrelenting guerrilla war between natives and white settlers that raged constantly on the western plains during much of the late 1800s. Both Indians and soldiers in his command were victims of

his tempestuous character. He shot troopers, without a trial, who went A.W.O.L. His instability showed when he too went A.W.O.L. He was court-martialed but regained his command.

In 1876, while serving under General A. H. Terry, who was charged with the responsibility for crushing the biggest Sioux uprising in history, Custer went out with an advance probing force of three companies of cavalry to find the enemy camp. He discovered the main camp of allied Sioux and Cheyenne at Little Bighorn River. Custer had been instructed, should he locate the hostiles in sizable numbers, to wait for reinforcements before attacking.

He either ignored reports of the size of the Indian band or didn't realize how large was the enemy force. He decided to attack quickly before the Indians could leave the area. After ordering two of the companies upriver to swing around the concentration of Indians and attack from another direction, Custer mounted a direct charge into the heart of the enemy camp.

Custer's assault failed to penetrate the enemy community. His unit was forced to retreat to a hilltop where they formed a defensive perimeter. The hostiles, in the meantime, attacked the other two separated companies and prevented them from coming to his assistance. Custer's company was wiped out in several hours of fighting by an overwhelming mass of encircling Sioux warriors under Chief Crazy Horse. The Indian victory brought renewed pressure from Generals Terry and Crook, who finally crushed the uprising by the following summer.

Hollywood made more films about Custer than any other officer. Movies about Custer focus heavily on the situation surrounding his final confrontation. Films have portrayed Custer both sympathetically and unfavorably. Virtually all the silent and early sound features and serials paint him heroically. One of the earliest films to depict his historic battle against the Sioux is "Custer's Last Raid" (1912), a short work starring Francis Ford as the title character. The entry is long on action but short on insight, as is "The Big Horn Massacre," released the following year and containing a subplot of a treacherous Indian who leads Custer into the fateful trap. In *Britton of the Seventh* (1916), the massacre is told in flashback by a 70-year-old ex-cavalry officer. Dwight Crittondon portrays the colonel in the historically inaccurate *Bob Hampton of Placer* (1921).

Aided by several Colorado historical societies, *The Scarlet West* (1925) presents Custer's last stand fairly accurately but views the Indians as villains. This was corrected the following year in *The Flaming Frontier*, which blames the Indian uprising on unscrupulous businessmen trying to steal land from the tribes. Inept staging of the battle sequences handicap the film. *Little Big Horn* (1927), another silent, features satisfactory battle sequences.

The sound era continued the Custer myth, picturing him in heroic scale. In *Santa Fe Trail* (1940) Custer (Ronald Reagan) appears as a thoughtful and discerning young West Point graduate who assists Jeb Stuart to track down the fiery abolitionist John Brown on the eve of the Civil War. Errol Flynn portrays Custer in *They Died With Their Boots On* (1941), which justifies the massacre at Little Big Horn by having Custer sacrifice himself and his troops to protect General Crook. Although the film is filled with historical inaccuracies, it does emphasize Custer's boldness and impetuosity.

Occasionally Custer dramas became concerned with attempts to warn Custer of an ambush. In *Little Big Horn* (1951) a small troop of cavalry is sent to inform the general of possible danger, but the men are killed by hostiles before they can accomplish their mission. In *Warpath*, released the same year, Dean Jagger, as a crooked storekeeper attempting to redeem himself, tries unsuccessfully to warn Custer of a potential ambush.

By 1954 Custer's screen image underwent a sharp reversal as feelings toward the Indian became more sympathetic. *Sitting Bull*, released that year, views him as brash and hostile to Indians and treacherous. While a cavalry major tries to negotiate a treaty with the Sioux, Custer, without authorization, attacks the Indians. The movie distorts history by making Custer's action the cause of renewed hostilities. In reality the army was heavily engaged, both before and after that engagement, in an all-out attempt to crush the Sioux uprising. *Chief Crazy Horse* (1955) dramatizes Custer's defeat at Little Big Horn while justifying the Sioux for taking to the warpath. *The Great Sioux Massacre* (1965) attempts to give a more realistic portrayal of Custer as a figure more concerned with his own advancement than with the welfare of Indians. Philip

Carey, as Custer, is a flamboyant figure who takes a hard stand against the Sioux after Washington politicians promise to make him a national hero.

Later films continued to add nuances to his character while retaining his glory-seeking image. *Custer of the West* (1967) presents him as a tragic hero. Sympathetic to the Indian early in his military career, he ultimately becomes a pawn of short-sighted Washington politicians who remain unsympathetic to the Indians' grievances and inept at solving the Indian-white conflict. Unable to cope with political corruption and a changing frontier, he realizes that he is an anachronism. This version attempts to imbue more complexity to Custer's character than any of the earlier films.

Little Big Man (1970) more accurately shows an arrogant and pompous Custer (Richard Mulligan) whose plans for an Indian massacre ironically lead to his own defeat. Released during the Vietnam War, the film led many viewers to equate the brutal actions of Custer with those of present-day military leaders. See also Crazy Horse, Sioux Wars, Sitting Bull. ∎

Custer of the West (1968), Cin. Dir. Robert Siodmak; Sc. Bernard Gordon, Julian Halevy; *Cast includes:* Robert Shaw, Mary Ure, Jeffrey Hunter, Ty Hardin.

Robert Shaw portrays George Custer as a glory-seeking figure who is sympathetic toward the Indian and a victim of failed government policies in this biographical drama. The film, which approaches the real Custer more than other screen portrayals, begins at the close of the Civil War. Custer is ordered to quell the Cheyenne who are protesting the whites' encroaching on Indian land. When Custer, who has struggled to remain apolitical, openly criticizes the corrupt government officials of profiting at the expense of the Cheyenne, he is relieved of his command. He later returns to the territory where he meets defeat in the battle of Little Big Horn by overwhelming odds. Jeff Hunter, as a lieutenant, is conscience-stricken by the abuses thrust upon the Indians. Ty Hardin portrays a loyal major under the command of Custer. Mary Ure plays the general's wife. Lawrence Tierney impersonates a peppery Gen. Phil Sheridan.

The script at times captures some of Custer's vanity and cruelty that historians

Robert Shaw, as the title character in *Custer of the West* (1968), brings to life the legend of Custer's last stand.

have often written about. "You're paying the price for being backward," he announces arrogantly to an Indian. At other moments in the film Custer is transformed into a tragic figure who is endowed with a sense of the inexorable. "Trains, steel, guns that kill by the thousands," he muses. "Our kind of fighting is all over." This vision of the Indian fighter differs sharply from the more popular one epitomized by the dashing Errol Flynn in *They Died With Their Boots On* (1941) which showed Custer as a less pensive and more impulsive, exuberant soldier. ∎

"Custer's Last Fight" (1912), *Dir.* Thomas Ince; *Sc.* Richard V. Spencer; *Cast includes:* Francis Ford, Anna Little, Grace Cunard, William Eagleshirt, Charles K. French.

One of the earliest versions of Col. Custer's battle at Little Big Horn against the Sioux, this silent three-reel film features John Ford's brother, Francis Ford, as a heavily whiskered colonel. The drama has been noted for its realism and visual style. Ince, better known as a producer, vigorously directed the film

while borrowing ideas from such early movie pioneers as William S. Porter and D. W. Griffith, especially in the action scenes. After gaining permission from the government, he used more than a hundred reservation Sioux in this small but costly production. However, this proved to be a serious mistake, for he soon found them difficult to work with. They refused to follow his directions and lacked enthusiasm in the battle sequences. ∎

Custer's Last Stand (1936), Stage & Screen Productions. *Dir.* Elmer Clifton; *Sc.* George Arthur Durlam, Eddy Graneman, Bob Lively; *Cast includes:* Rex Lease, Lona Andre, William Farnum, Ruth Mix, Jack Mulhall.

A feature adaptation of the serial bearing the same title, this western action drama presents a highly fictionalized—as well as incredible—version of the events that led up to General Custer's defeat at the Little Big Horn. Some mention is made of greedy whites encroaching upon Indian territory following the discovery of gold in the Black Hills and of the Cheyennes joining Sitting Bull's Sioux to defend their land. Except for these few historical references, the remainder of the film plunges headlong into fiction. Several historical figures, such as Buffalo Bill and Wild Bill Hickok, have cameo roles in the serial, but they have been cut from this feature version. The climactic re-enactment of Custer's last stand, showing only about twenty troopers battling a similar number of sluggish warriors, is so pathetically staged that it evokes laughter.

The only interesting element of the film is the unusually large number of former silent screen stars who appear in supporting roles. Ex-cowboy star William Farnum plays an Indian agent; Franklyn Farnum (no relation), rugged star of silent films, plays Major Reno; Ruth Mix, former heroine of numerous westerns and the daughter of Tom Mix, portrays Custer's wife; Jack Mulhall has the role of Lieutenant Cook; Helen Gibson, another silent-screen performer, is credited with the role of Calamity Jane; William Desmond has a bit part as a wagon master; and Josef Swickard, who appeared in numerous silents, portrays Major Trent. Frank McGlynn, as General Custer, also portrayed Abraham Lincoln in several historical films. Rex Lease, who stars as Kit Cardigan, the two-fisted hero who is determined to avenge his father's murder, had played leads in many silent dramas and comedies before specializing in westerns during the early sound era. Two years after this serial he was relegated to a minor role, that of William A. Travis, in another historical drama, *Heroes of the Alamo.* ∎

Cvetic, Matt. See Cold War. ∎

D

D-Day. See Normandy Invasion. ◼

D-Day, the Sixth of June (1956), TCF. *Dir.* Henry Koster; *Sc.* Ivan Moffat, Harry Brown; *Cast includes:* Robert Taylor, Richard Todd, Dana Wynter, Edmond O'Brien.

The Normandy invasion of 1944 by Allied forces provides the background for this wartime romantic drama. The film opens on the eve of the invasion aboard an allied transport carrying a special fighting force across the channel for a dangerous mission. The volunteer unit is made up of British, Canadian and U.S. troops who are being sent in before the general assault to knock out particular German artillery and machine-gun emplacements that threaten the overall operation. The plot then lapses into flashbacks to develop the romantic stories of the principal characters.

Robert Taylor, as an American officer aboard the transport, is married. He falls in love with a young Englishwoman, the fiancee of a British officer (Richard Todd), who also is part of the mission and is later killed in action. Dana Wynter, as the woman both men love, falls for Taylor while Todd is fighting in North Africa. When he returns wounded, she decides to devote her life to him although she loves Taylor. Meanwhile, he is reassigned at the last minute to participate in the special mission along with Taylor. When Wynter learns that he has been killed at Normandy, she doesn't tell Taylor, who returns on a stretcher. He speaks highly of Todd, as if the British officer were still alive. Wynter then leaves her lover, knowing that he will return to his wife in the States.

Following these routine romantic entanglements, the film returns to the special mission at hand. There ensues a bloody battle as the

British officer Richard Todd joins American Robert Taylor, both of whom are about to take part in the invasion of Normandy. *D-Day, the Sixth of June* (1956).

small group struggles to wipe out the gun emplacements. They succeed but pay a heavy price. Todd is killed when he steps on a land mine, and Taylor is wounded in the shoulder. The latter part of the film makes good use of actual newsreel footage which is integrated into the battle sequences showing the allied invasion advancing from the beaches. ◼

Dakota Indian Wars. See Sioux Wars. ◼

Dan (1914), Par. *Sc.* Hal Reid; *Cast includes:* Lew Dockstader, Lois Meredith, Gale Kane, Beatrice Clevener.

A Civil War drama, the film tells the story of Dan, a black slave who sacrifices his own life to save that of his master's son. The young man, a Confederate officer, is captured by Union troops and sentenced to death as a spy. Dan gains access to the tent where the prisoner is being held and persuades him to blacken his face to facilitate his escape. In the morning the black servant is executed in place of his white master. Lew Dockstader, the famous minstrel entertainer, was especially selected for the title role, and he blends the appropriate mixture of drama and comedy into his role.

Although the subject matter concerning the servant and his overzealous loyalty to his master is offensive and disagreeable, the film, released in the early days of World War I, was timely for its war background and battle scenes. ▪

Danger in the Pacific (1942). See Spy Films: the Talkies. ▪

Dangerous Business (1920), FN. *Dir.* John Emerson; *Sc.* Anita Loos; *Cast includes:* Constance Talmadge, George Fawcett, Matilda Brundage, Kenneth Harlan.

Constance Talmadge portrays the spoiled daughter of a wealthy family in this romantic comedy set before and during World War I. Always selecting the wrong mate, Talmadge cannot seem to settle down with a proper beau. George Fawcett, as her father's secretary, is in love with her, but she dismisses his advances. When war erupts, the timid Fawcett enlists, goes to France and becomes a hero during battle. When he returns, he displays a new boldness and abducts the woman he loves. He takes her to his mother's home where she spends the night in another room. After further complications, she agrees to marry him only if he consents that they have a child. The last scene shows them bathing their newborn baby.

The concept that military service can change a man for the better was a prevalent one in early silent films, especially those made during World War I when patriotism and propaganda were major forces on the screen. The theme spilled over into the 1920s and showed up in comedies, dramas and westerns in which some of the most popular male stars portrayed cowards, weaklings or slackers until they donned their nation's uniforms. ▪

Dangerous Days (1920). See Spy Films: the Silents. ▪

Dangerous Maid (1923), FN. *Dir.* Victor Heerman; *Sc.* C. Gardner Sullivan; *Cast includes:* Constance Talmadge, Conway Tearle, Morgan Wallace, Marjorie Daw, Tully Marshall.

In this historical drama laid in England on the eve of the Glorious Revolution, Constance Talmadge portrays Barbara Winslow, who, along with her family, favors the Duke of Monmouth as a replacement for the current ruler. A captain in the king's army is sympathetic to the young heroine and is sentenced to face a firing squad for his rebellious actions. Intrigues, battles and love affairs follow, chiefly centering around Barbara. The rebellious forces finally triumph over the tyrannical regime. ▪

Dangerous Partners (1945). See Spy Films: the Talkies. ▪

Dangerously They Live (1941). See Spy Films: the Talkies. ▪

Daniel Boone (1936), RKO. *Dir.* David Howard; *Sc.* Daniel Jarrett; *Cast includes:* George O'Brien, Heather Angel, John Carradine, Ralph Forbes, Clarence Muse.

A biographical drama loosely based on the legendary frontiersman, the film stresses action rather than character development. Daniel Boone, played by George O'Brien, leads his people to Kentucky where they build their settlement. A white renegade (John Carradine) incites the local Indian tribes to unite against the rag-tag group of settlers. The hostiles attack the stockade, but the whites hold out until it rains, supplying them with much-needed water and discouraging the attackers who scatter.

The film is undependable as a factual account except for one sequence in which Boone is taken prisoner by the hostiles. Historically, he had once been captured by Indians. The script provides for an abundance of action, especially that segment concerning the siege. Heather Angel supplies the slight romantic interest. ▪

Daniel Boone, Trail Blazer (1957), Rep. *Dir.* Albert C. Gannaway, Ismael Rodriguez; *Sc.* Tom Hubbard, Jack Patrick; *Cast includes:* Bruce Bennett, Lon Chaney, Faron Young, Kem Dibbs.

This low-budget outdoor drama depicts the trek of Daniel Boone and his group of settlers

Colonel William Darby's specially trained unit undertakes another surprise raid during World War II. *Darby's Rangers* (1958).

from North Carolina to Boonesborough, Kentucky. The journey, which takes place in 1775, is made more unpleasant when British soldiers and a French renegade stir up the Shawnees. Bruce Bennett, as Boone, finally convinces the Indian chief, played by Lon Chaney, that his people want to live in peace with the Shawnees. The film, which was shot in Mexico, has some historical merit and contains sufficient action for those not interested in accuracy. ∎

Darby's Rangers (1958), WB. *Dir.* William A. Wellman; *Sc.* Guy Trosper; *Cast includes:* James Garner, Etchika Choureau, Jack Warden, Edward Byrnes.

This action drama depicts the training and exploits of a special fighting unit created by Colonel William Darby in World War II. James Garner portrays Darby, a dedicated officer who leads his specially trained men on a series of successful missions in North Africa, Sicily and northern Italy. Action highlights include the Rangers' surprise raids, attacks behind enemy lines and wresting coastal defenses at Anzio from the enemy.

Jack Warden plays Darby's aide. Several romances occur, including one between Stuart Whitman and Joan Elan and another involving Edward Byrnes, as a young, inexperienced lieutenant, and Etchika Choureau, an Italian woman carrying the child of a partisan killed by the Germans. The film is based on the book by Major James Altieri.

The actual Rangers unit came into existence in June 1942, after General Lucien K. Truscott suggested that an American unit similar to that of the British Commandos should be formed. General Eisenhower assigned Colonel Darby (1911–1945) to select officers for the special force. Darby was killed in action in Italy. Only 500 men were originally selected from 2,000 volunteers stationed in Northern Ireland. Their name derived from Major Robert Rogers who organized a group of American colonists, whom he called Rangers, to fight in the style of woodsmen and Indians during the wars of 1755–1763. Several different Ranger battalions were formed during World War II. They saw action on different fronts, including Sicily, Italy, France and the South Pacific. See Rogers' Rangers. ∎

Dark Angel, The (1925), FN. *Dir.* George Fitzmaurice; *Sc.* Frances Marion; *Cast includes*: Ronald Colman, Vilma Banky, Wyndham Standing, Frank Elliot.

A World War I drama about two English lovers whose lives are deeply affected by the war, the film stars Ronald Colman and Vilma Banky in the principal roles. The young couple dash off to Dover to marry on the eve of war but arrive too late to obtain a marriage license. They spend the night at an inn without benefit of clergy, and the next day Colman leaves for France. He is blinded in battle while Banky thinks he has been killed. Determined not to be a burden on anyone, especially the woman he loves, he returns to a life of seclusion and spends his time writing novels under a nom-de-plume. Banky discovers he is alive and visits him. Meanwhile Colman, not wanting her sympathy, memorizes where all the objects of his room are located so that he can walk around as though he still had his sight. At first he convinces her that he is self-sufficient and doesn't believe in marriage. But when she leaves his cottage and observes him alone through the window, she learns the truth and returns. She re-enters and the long-parted couple embrace. The film, based on an unsuccessful stage play, was a box-office hit around the country, especially with women, when it was originally released. A remake under the same title appeared ten years later during the sound era. ∎

Dark Angel, The (1935), UA. *Dir.* Sidney Franklin; *Sc.* Lillian Hellman, Mordaunt Shairp; *Cast includes*: Fredric March, Merle Oberon, Herbert Marshall, Janet Beecher, John Halliday.

A remake of the successful 1925 silent original, this sound version of the World War I romantic drama follows essentially the same plot about an English couple who are separated by the war. Fredric March plays the role that Ronald Colman had in the original—that of the soldier who is blinded in battle and chooses a cloistered life as a writer rather than returning home to his family and fiancee, Kitty, portrayed by Merle Oberon. Herbert Marshall, as March's brother, also loves Kitty. Before they sail for France, Marshall believes his brother was unfaithful to Kitty during his last night of leave. When March, after participating in several battles, asks for special leave to marry Kitty, Marshall, as his senior officer, refuses the request. That night

the brothers lead a patrol into enemy territory in which Marshall receives a leg wound and March is assumed killed in an explosion.

The remainder of the film follows the earlier version, including the affecting scene in which the blind veteran, hoping to fool his wife, pretends that he can see. Another poignant scene takes place in a rehabilitation center where all the soldiers who have lost their sight are gathered to hear a minister address them. "I know, my friends," the man of the cloth begins solemnly, "for the things of the eye you must substitute the things of the spirit . . . what are these compared to the inner beauties . . . Your country will be behind you—" Suddenly, one blind youth rises and cries out: "You have to stand there and tell us what we are missing? The things of the spirit! Curse the things of the spirit! Curse them! It's the other things we want to see, and your fine words don't make it any easier!" ∎

Dark Command, The (1940), Rep. *Dir.* Raoul Walsh; *Sc.* Grover Jones, Lionel Houser, F. Hugh Herbert; *Cast includes*: Claire Trevor, John Wayne, Walter Pidgeon, Roy Rogers, George "Gabby" Hayes.

An action drama set before and during the Civil War, the film stars John Wayne as a stalwart Texan who assumes the role of marshal in strife-torn Kansas. Tension mounts among the citizens who are split in their sympathies toward the North and the South. But when guerrillas mercilessly raid the state, Wayne is able to organize the decent folk against their common enemy. Abundant action keeps the film moving in this better-than-average western. Walter Pidgeon plays the Quantrill-like leader of the marauders while Claire Trevor provides the romantic interest.

The film is accurate in at least one area— the historical assault on and burning of Lawrence, Kansas, by the marauders. Quantrill and his raiders have been the subject of several films. See William Clarke Quantrill. ∎

Dark Road, The (1917). See Spy Films: the Silents. ∎

Dark Star, The (1919). See Women and War. ∎

Darling Lili (1970). See Musicals. ∎

Daughter Angele (1918). See Women and War. ∎

Daughter of Destiny (1918). See Women and War. ∎

Daughter of France, A (1918), Fox. *Dir.* Edmund Lawrence; *Sc.* Betta Breuil, Adrian Johnson; *Cast includes:* Virginia Pearson, Hugh Thompson, Herbert Evans, George Moss.

A World War I romantic drama, the film tells the story of a young French maid who has a love-hate relationship with a German officer. Virginia Pearson portrays the heroine while Hugh Thompson plays the Hun. The film is unusual in its tempered treatment of the enemy during the conflict. Virtually every war movie of the period depicted the German as a bestial creature devoid of any human qualities, interested only in destruction, pillage and lust. To portray the German soldier as a lover was a bold move for the studio and in direct contrast to the image American audiences were subjected to at the time. ∎

Davis, Jefferson (1808–1889). Although he had cultivated a reputation for compromise for most of his political career, Jefferson Davis issued the direct order that resulted in the start of the American Civil War. With the election of Lincoln as President of the Union, Davis' position changed and he became one of the leaders urging secession for the South as the only way to retain its tradition of slavery.

"Will you consent to be robbed of your property . . . ?" Davis said to fellow Southerners. "The time for compromise is now past," he remarked in his speech accepting the presidency of the Confederacy on February 16, 1861. He feared the Union might attempt to supply the cut-off garrison at Fort Sumter that blockaded Charleston harbor. On April 9, 1861, he instructed General Beauregard to bombard and subdue the Union-held bastion in South Carolina. The shelling commenced on April 12, precipitating the start of hostilities.

He resigned from the Senate in 1861 after Mississippi seceded. Following the collapse of the Confederacy, Davis was captured in 1865 and confined to a federal prison (1865–67) under conditions that impaired his health. He never requested amnesty and failed to regain his citizenship. The first and

only president of the short-lived Confederacy, Davis is revered in many parts of the South today as a great leader in a lost cause.

He has been portrayed in only minor roles in a handful of films—*The Soul of the South* (1915), *The Heart of Maryland* (1915) and its 1927 remake. ∎

Davy Crockett (1916). See David Crockett. ∎

Davy Crockett at the Fall of the Alamo (1926). See David Crockett. ∎

Dawn Express, The (1942). See Spy Films: the Talkies. ∎

"Dawn of Freedom, The" (1910), Selig.

A weak silent film about Cuba's fight to be free, the drama takes place during the Spanish-American War and depicts an insurrection and several battles. Selig's film studio, along with others like Kalem and Biograph, provided several one- and two-reel historical dramas during these early years, including stories about the Civil War. The majority of studios, however, concentrated either on contemporary dramas or comedies. ∎

Dawn Patrol, The (1930), FN. *Dir.* Howard Hawks; *Sc.* Dan Totheroh; *Cast includes:* Richard Barthelmess, Douglas Fairbanks, Jr., Neil Hamilton, Gardner James.

John Monk Saunders wrote this prize-winning story of a British air squadron during World War I. Neil Hamilton, as a beleaguered commander, must send his gallant fliers into battle against German planes. As new officers continue to arrive to replace their fallen comrades, he observes that they are getting younger each time. This provides him with one more reason to increase his drinking. Richard Barthelmess and Douglas Fairbanks, Jr. portray two of his better pilots whom he has grown particularly fond of. Barthelmess, however, criticizes Hamilton for sending so many men to their death. When they disobey orders and cross enemy lines to shoot up an airfield and destroy a number of enemy planes, Hamilton lashes into them. He then receives orders which reassign him to headquarters. The vacancy moves Barthelmess up as the new commander. Hamilton relishes in this. Now the impulsive and critical Barthelmess will feel what it's like to send young men to almost certain death.

The film has several exciting action sequences although one or two strain credibility. In the final scenes Barthelmess replaces his younger friend, Fairbanks, on a dangerous mission by getting him drunk. He flies over Germany and manages to destroy an arsenal as well as a strategic railhead before he is killed.

Although the film brings out war's brutality, it is not altogether convincing as an antiwar drama. Hamilton, as the commander, makes the one strong antiwar speech in the film: "It's a slaughterhouse, that's what it is, and I'm the executioner." But the power of the words is diminished by the suggested heroics when he adds: "You send men up in rotten ships to die . . . they don't argue or revolt . . . they just say 'right-o' and go out and do it." The dangers the young airmen face, the heroism that several engage in and the sacrifice on the part of Barthelmess only serve to underscore the romanticism and adventure of war. One bit of dialogue even compares the prospect of dying to a school sport. "If you should lose," Barthelmess counsels a green replacement, "be a good loser, just like you would in school." Duty and honor take precedence over the absurdity of war. This is hardly the stuff of pacifism. ■

Dawn Patrol, The (1938), WB. *Dir.* Edmund Goulding; *Sc.* Seton I. Miller, Dan Totheroh; *Cast includes:* Errol Flynn, David Niven, Basil Rathbone, Donald Crisp, Melville Cooper.

A remake of Howard Hawks' 1930 film about the Royal Air Corps in World War I, this version features Basil Rathbone as the resolute officer who must send young recruits into the skies to fight, often to their death. A steady stream of green pilots reports to the British air base in France to replace those who have fallen. Errol Flynn and David Niven portray experienced, war-weary fliers, buddies who have managed to survive the terrible ordeal. When Rathbone, who takes each death personally, is assigned to headquarters, Flynn gets his former commander's dirty job of ordering the new pilots to their death. Niven volunteers to carry out a particularly dangerous mission, but Flynn, who fears for his friend's life, deliberately gets him drunk and flies the mission himself, which leads to his death. One of the best films in the genre, it contains effective battle sequences, crisp dialogue and outstanding performances.

Some critics labeled the film an antiwar drama, but like the 1930 version, it focuses too strongly on the romanticism of danger, duty and sacrifice. The last lines of the film, spoken by Donald Crisp, may have contributed to these critics' conclusions. "A gallant gentleman died this afternoon," Crisp muses upon receiving news of Flynn's sacrifice. "And for what? What have all these deaths accomplished? So many fine chaps who have died and are going to die in this war and in future wars." This is a surprising speech for Warner Brothers to permit as a conclusion, considering the then-current world tensions in general and the rise of Nazism and Fascism in particular. ■

"Day of Battle" (1943), Office of War Information.

A World War II documentary, one of several produced during the conflict for the Office of War Information, this short film depicts the last fight of an American aircraft carrier. The story of the vessel is told from its construction until its final engagement with the enemy and its demise. The footage consists of newsreel shots taken by combat cameramen. ■

Days of Glory (1944), RKO. *Dir.* Jacques Tourneur; *Sc.* Casey Robinson; *Cast includes:* Tamara Toumanova, Gregory Peck, Alan Reed, Maria Palmer, Hugo Haas.

A group of Russian citizens from all walks of life take up arms against the Nazi invaders to become an effective guerrilla force in this low-key, realistically staged World War II tribute to Soviet resistance. Using actors and actresses who have never before appeared on screen, producer Casey Robinson, better known for his successful screenplays, cast Gregory Peck (in his first film) as a guerrilla leader operating inside German lines near Moscow. Tama Toumanova, a ballet dancer in real life, plays a dancer who joins Peck's little band of patriots and eventually falls in love with him. Both go to their deaths when the Russians spring their great counterattack against the Nazis. The film has several effective battle scenes although it was made on a tight budget. Its box-office failure has been attributed to several reasons, including the lack of name players and its depressing ending.

Because of its pro-Russian sympathies, the film joined the ranks of other controversial features released during the 1940s and was later cited by the House Un-American Activities Committee as an example of Communist propaganda being disseminated by Hollywood personnel. During the war years the U.S. government encouraged such films to help cement relations with its Russian allies. Warner Brothers heeded the request with *Mission to Moscow*, as did MGM with *Song of Russia*, both released in 1943. The RKO film as well as the others appear periodically on television in severely cut versions. ■

Dead March, The (1937), Imperial. *Sc.* Samuel Taylor Moore.

An antiwar documentary, the film uses stock newsreel footage from a variety of world conflicts to make its point. There are sequences from World War I, many of which were borrowed from the British War Museum; Japan's incursion into China; the military troubles between Bolivia and Paraguay, also known as the Chaco War; and Mussolini's invasion and conquest of Ethiopia. Also included are scenes of the Spanish Civil War. Boake Carter provides the hard-hitting narration. ■

Deadly Game, The (1941). See Spy Films: the Talkies. ■

Dealers in Death (1934), Topical. *Dir.* Monroe Shaff; *Sc.* Burnet Hershey.

An antiwar documentary attacking munitions manufacturers, the film utilizes newsreel footage and official archive shots of World War I to drive home its point. Facts and figures are used to explore the cost of World War I in terms of losses to the nations involved in the conflict and the huge profits reaped by arms companies. The narrator mentions specific firms and delves into recent exposés that reveal secret deals made between large munitions dealers in France and Germany and the two nations during World War I that prevented the bombing of arms factories in both countries, the destruction of which would have shortened the war. The documentary, which also covers the Sino-Japanese conflict and includes several grisly sequences, was considered by contemporary critics to have been one of the most compelling revelations about the war and a strong indictment of those who make the weapons of destruction. ■

Dear America: Letters Home From Vietnam (1988), Corsair Pictures. *Dir.* Bill Couturie; *Sc.* Richard Dewhurst, Bill Couturie.

A poignant documentary about the Vietnam War, the film traces the conflict from America's early involvement until the nation's withdrawal in 1973. The unique aspect of the work is that the tragic story is told through the letters of the men and women who participated in the events. Some of the readers include Robert De Niro, Michael J. Fox, Kathleen Turner, Ellen Burstyn, Robin Williams and Howard Rollins, Jr. Most of the fighting men are in their late teens or early twenties. Their simple, forthright thoughts, which reveal much about their fears and dreams, pack as much punch as *Platoon* (1986), the highly acclaimed drama of the war. Some believe that their fighting in Vietnam is preventing the war from spreading to the shores of the U.S. Others write home of the horrors they have witnessed. "I was carrying that damned thing (a fellow soldier's leg) all the way back," writes an anguished youth. The voice-over letters are accompanied by actual footage of the war. Casualty figures and other statistics appear periodically. The film was first shown on Home Box Office cable television. ■

Death of a Dream (1950). See Cold War. ■

"Death of Nathan Hale, The" (1911). See Nathan Hale. ■

Decatur, Stephen (1779–1820). Midshipman Stephen Decatur, then 25, probably welcomed the exceptional darkness on the night of February 16, 1804, as he and a small body of men rowed quietly into Tripoli harbor. Their target was the frigate *Philadelphia*, a stranded U.S. Navy warship that the Barbary Moslem pirates had recently captured during the Tripolitan War (1800–1805) with the U.S. The pirates were in the process of outfitting the vessel for their use, and Decatur was charged with the dangerous mission of destroying the ship. He was part of a naval force dispatched to the western Mediterranean by President Thomas Jefferson to put an end to attacks on Christian shipping by the Barbary pirates and the practice of paying tribute to allow safe passage for American vessels.

The Americans stealthily climbed aboard the *Philadelphia*, and in a brief battle, the boarding party overpowered the surprised crew and set the vessel ablaze. The action, in which only one of his men was wounded, earned Decatur an immediate commission as captain and presentation of a ceremonial sword from a grateful American Congress. Britain's Lord Nelson called the assault "the most daring act of the age." Decatur's exploits during this engagement were re-enacted in *The Man Without a Country* (1925), a silent drama based on Edward Everett Hale's popular story, and *Old Ironsides* (1926), a large-scale silent drama that paid tribute to the U.S.S. *Constitution.*

After his daring raid, Decatur took part in subsequent bombardments and assaults against Tripoli's fortifications. During the War of 1812 with Britain, Decatur, as captain of the *United States* and the *President*, captured several enemy vessels. He was wounded during one engagement. After the war with Britain ended, Decatur was transferred to the Mediterranean where he succeeded in subduing the remaining Barbary pirate states of Tripoli, Algiers, Morocco and Tunis that had reinstituted raids against American shipping during the War of 1812. His actions ended all tribute payments by the U.S. to the Barbary pirates and halted future attacks on American vessels as well as secured compensation from the Moslem states for past damages.

Upon returning to the U.S., Decatur responded at a dinner in his honor with a toast that has gone down in history. "Our country! In her intercourse with foreign nations may she always be in the right; but our country, right or wrong." He died in a duel with Commodore James Barron on March 22, 1820. He was also portrayed in the patriotic World War I drama *My Own United States* (1918) and *Captain Caution* (1940) with Victor Mature. ∎

December 7th (1942), War and Navy Departments. *Dir.* John Ford.

The first documentary to cover Japan's sneak attack on Pearl Harbor, the film was commissioned by President Roosevelt "to present accurately the story of the attack." Newsreel footage shows Pearl Harbor before and after the assault. The heavy losses in men and ships are reported unerringly—2,243 Americans were killed and 86 ships were sunk or damaged. However, representative of other such works released during World War II, the film often resorts to propaganda in its coverage of related events. An unidentified narrator quickly skims over the fact that the U.S. Navy was caught off guard, describing instead how American anti-aircraft guns blasted the enemy planes and announcing that the destruction could have been worse if it were not for "Washington's far-sighted programs." "The treachery of an empire was on the wing," the narrator continues, describing Japanese planes as "messengers of death." The film is a curious blend of actual footage and re-enactments, including actors portraying servicemen and civilians and other studio shots of miniature ships being blown up. ∎

Decision Before Dawn (1951), TCF. *Dir.* Anatole Litvak; *Sc.* Peter Viertel; *Cast includes:* Richard Basehart, Gary Merrill, Oskar Werner, Hildergarde Neff.

Allied Intelligence uses prisoners of war as spies during the last days of World War II to speed the end of the conflict. Oskar Werner, as a captured Luftwaffe medic disillusioned with Hitler, acts as a secret agent for the Americans. Although he loves his country, the idealistic German officer abhors the government that has led Germany down the road to destruction. He volunteers to return to Germany as a spy in the belief that by ending the war sooner he will be saving lives. His movements behind the lines provide plenty of suspense as he gathers the necessary information. Although he completes his mission, he is killed while saving an Allied officer's life. Richard Basehart, as the officer, manages to get the information back to headquarters. Gary Merrill portrays the chief of Allied Intelligence. The scenes inside Germany near the end of the war show a country in ruins and a defeated people stunned by the devastation which surrounds them.

This was one of the earliest postwar films to hint that there were some anti-Nazi Germans who voluntarily endangered their lives to help overthrow Hitler's Third Reich. As such, it was unique in exploring the ambivalent feelings in its main character who sees himself both as a defender of his country and traitor—a tragic figure who is torn between causing immediate harm to his fellow countrymen and helping to bring peace by shortening the war. ∎

Deep Six, The (1958), WB. *Dir.* Rudolph Mate; *Sc.* John Twist, Martin Rackin, Harry Brown; *Cast includes:* Alan Ladd, Dianne Foster, William Bendix, Keenan Wynn.

A U.S. Navy gunnery officer during World War II is torn between his pacifist Quaker upbringing and his wartime duty in this routine drama. Alan Ladd portrays the officer who has to come to terms with his religious training. The first important incident while under fire occurs when he hesitates to order his crew to fire upon an approaching aircraft. Fortunately, the plane was a friendly one and Ladd is considered a hero. But when his mates learn of his Quaker views, they shun him. He is removed from gunnery duty and assigned to damage control where he again proves his worth by ridding the ship of an unexploded Japanese bomb.

During a rescue mission on an enemy-occupied island, Ladd, manning a machine gun, hesitates as a Japanese patrol moves forward and mortally wounds his buddy (William Bendix). He then fires upon the enemy as his dying friend utters: "I knew you had it in you all along." Unfortunately, familiar characters, plotting and heroics dominate the film. With Ladd playing a Quaker, Bendix a Jew and Keenan Wynn a bigoted officer, a possible theme of racial prejudice surfaces for a moment but is never developed. ∎

Deer Hunter, The (1978), U. *Dir.* Michael Cimino; *Sc.* Michael Cimino, D. Washburn; *Cast includes:* Robert De Niro, John Cazale, John Savage, Christopher Walken, Meryl Streep.

Michael Cimino's drama of three Pennsylvania steelworkers whose lives are shattered by their Vietnam experience received the New York Film Critics Circle award and won the Academy Award as best picture of 1978. Michael, Nick and Steve, played by Robert De Niro, Christopher Walken and John Savage respectively, are about to enter the service to fight in Vietnam following Steve's wedding. Michael, the reticent member of the trio, likes hunting and seems awkward around women. Nick, the liveliest and the most sensitive of the three, confides to Michael that when they hunt he goes along only because he likes the trees. Steve is the youngest and most pliable. The first part of the film explores the comradeship of this tightly knit group during the wedding. A banner in the wedding hall reads: "Serving God and Country Proudly." Follow-

ing the wedding Michael and Nick are alone in an empty street where the conversation turns to Vietnam. "Whatever happens," Nick says prophetically to his friend, "don't leave me there. You gotta promise." The next day Michael and Nick are joined by several other friends on a short hunting trip during which Michael stalks and kills a deer.

In Vietnam the three friends are captured and forced to engage in Russian Roulette while their captors bet on the outcome. Michael initiates a plan of escape by turning the pistol on the enemy soldiers. They make it back to Saigon where both Nick and Steve are hospitalized. The torture has shattered Nick, who goes A.W.O.L. Meanwhile, Steve loses both legs. Michael is discharged but returns to search for Nick. He finds his friend playing Russian roulette for money and drugs. As Nick places the revolver to his head, Michael pleads with him to return home. But it is too late; Nick's luck has run out. Michael watches as the gun fires into Nick's temple. Back again in Pennsylvania, Michael attends Nick's funeral along with Nick's other close friends. Later, in the back room of the local bar where the small group are assembled for a snack, all are at a loss for words. They slowly break out in a chorus of "God Bless America."

From its earliest showings the film was stalked by controversy. Some critics attacked the stereotyped depiction of the enemy as a throwback to Hollywood's World War II films which pictured all the Japanese as vile and sadistic. Others objected to the distortion of history, claiming that the film was "a criminal violation of the truth," singling out its images of all non-Americans as corrupt, sweaty and depraved. Still other critics attacked the principal metaphor for the insanity of war, the game of Russian roulette, as entirely fictitious. However, the film had as many supporters who found the work powerful and emotionally moving. ∎

Deerslayer, The (1957), TCF. *Dir.* Kurt Neumann; *Sc.* Carroll Young, Kurt Neumann; *Cast includes:* Lex Barker, Rita Moreno, Forrest Tucker, Cathy O'Donnell, Jay C. Flippen.

Lex Barker portrays the title character, a white man raised by the Mohicans in this drama. He and his Chingachgook, his blood brother, come to the rescue of an eccentric hunter (Jay C. Flippen) who lives on a river barge with his two daughters. The fierce Hurons want him dead for killing their braves who in turn have murdered his wife. Rita Moreno and Cathy O'Donnell, as the daughters of the half-crazed old man, provide the romantic interest in this film based on James Fenimore Cooper's novel. ∎

Defense or Tribute? (1916), Radio Film Co. *Sc.* Oscar L. Lamberger.

A documentary advocating preparedness, the film is composed of war and battle scenes borrowed from other documentaries, newsreels and features produced in the United States and abroad. The structure of the film consists of an opening scene of a board meeting in which a member speaks for preparedness. He evokes images of past wars through the centuries while scenes appear on the screen ranging from ancient Roman times, to the Crimean War with its charge of the Light Brigade and, finally, to the Great War. The compilation invokes such historical figures as Abraham Lincoln and General Grant. At the end, a motion is made and passed favoring preparedness. ∎

Denial, The (1925), MGM. *Dir.* Hobart Henley; *Sc.* Agnes Christine Johnston; *Cast includes:* Claire Windsor, Bert Roach, William Haines, Lucille Rickson, Robert Agnew.

Claire Windsor portrays a stern mother whose objection to her daughter's marriage leads her to reflect upon her own failed romance as a young woman during the Spanish-American War. The body of the film is told in flashback. Windsor's austere mother (Emily Fitzroy) refuses to allow her daughter to marry her beau (William Haines), preferring instead a millionaire she has selected for a son-in-law. Haines enlists in the Rough Riders and writes constantly to his love, but the mother intercepts all the letters. Haines is killed in action, and Windsor enters into a bland marriage. After ruminating upon her own shattered romance, she permits her daughter (Lucille Rickson) to marry the young officer (Robert Agnew) whom she loves. ∎

Desert Fox, The (1951), TCF. *Dir.* Henry Hathaway; *Sc.* Nunnally Johnson; *Cast includes:* James Mason, Cedric Hardwicke, Jessica Tandy, Luther Adler, Everett Sloane.

A biographical drama of Field Marshal Erwin Rommel, the film covers his North African defeats, his disillusionment at home with the Nazi general staff and Hitler and his forced suicide. The suspenseful and unique opening sequence, which appears on screen before the title and credits, shows an unsuccessful British Commando raid designed to kill Rommel, played by James Mason. In the next scene, a British officer reads a directive from a general to a group of field commanders concerning their adversary, Field Marshal Rommel: "I wish you to dispel by all possible means the idea that Rommel represents something more than an ordinary German general . . . From a psychological point of view, it is a matter of highest importance."

The remainder of the film deals with Rommel's desert defeat by Montgomery and his reassignment to the defense of Europe. In Germany an old friend tries to warn him of personal danger as well as of Hitler's incompetence. But Rommel, who had angered Hitler by disobeying his leader's orders when he retreated in Africa to save his men and equipment instead of foolishly fighting to the death, remains loyal to his commander-in-chief. A fellow general constantly refers to the dictator as "that Bohemian corporal." He, too, warns Rommel of impending danger. "Victory has a hundred fathers," he says, "defeat is an orphan." Eventually, Rommel gets caught up in an assassination attempt on Hitler's life.

The screenplay, which paints Rommel as a sympathetic character who suffers from ill health, helps to make clear why the general was loved and admired by his troops and respected by his enemies. On the other hand, the film sometimes distorts historical facts by depicting several members of the Nazi military high command (many of whom were considered war criminals) as superior strategists who were defeated only by Hitler's amateurish interference. Allied military strategy and efficacy, borne out by World War II records and battle results, dispute this.

The action sequences are effective, especially the abortive Commando raid on Rommel's headquarters and the stock footage of the Normandy invasion. Jessica Tandy portrays his patient and sympathetic wife. Luther Adler, as an emotional and ranting Hitler, is guided in his military decisions by astrology. The film ends with a voice-over of Winston Churchill's tribute to Rommel: "He deserves our respect because, although a loyal German soldier, he came to hate Hitler and all his works and took part in the conspiracy to rescue Germany by displacing the maniac and tyrant. For this he paid the forfeit of his life.'' ■

Desert Hell (1958), TCF. *Dir.* Charles Marquis Warren; *Sc.* Andre Bohem; *Cast includes:* Brian Keith, Barbara Rush, Richard Denning, Johnny Desmond.

The French Foreign Legion provides the background for this routine action film with a love-triangle plot. Brian Keith, as a captain in the Legionnaires, discovers his wife (Barbara Rush) is having an affair with a lieutenant (Johnny Desmond) in his command. Meanwhile the Legion is plagued by threats of warring Arabs on the move. Keith and Desmond are assigned to a perilous mission. Although they argue over how to execute their assignment, they succeed in accomplishing their mission. However, both are killed. The low-budget film has limited battle sequences. ■

Desert Legion (1953), U. *Dir.* Joseph Pevney; *Sc.* Irving Wallace, Lewis Meltzer; *Cast includes:* Alan Ladd, Richard Conte, Arlene Dahl, Akim Tamiroff.

Alan Ladd, as a captain in the French Foreign Legion, is the only survivor of an ambush in this fanciful drama. He is restored to health by Arlene Dahl, an inhabitant and daughter of the leader of an idyllic community unknown to the outside world. The leader, who has learned of Ladd's reputation as a man who has devoted his life fighting for peace, asks him to join their little "utopia" as their next leader. Ladd, suspicious of the offer and believing they are harboring the rebel leader who has been ambushing Legion patrols, decides to return to his post. When Ladd tells his story to his superiors, they do not believe him. He returns with his sidekick (Akim Tamiroff) to aid Dahl and her father who have been betrayed by a usurper (Richard Conte). A climactic battle between Conte's forces and the Legion resolves the conflict.

The concept of an ideal community hidden from the evils of the outside world, its secret entrance through the mountains, and the characterizations of the elderly leader who selects a peace-loving outsider as his logical successor was executed with more imagination and style in *Lost Horizon* (1937). ■

Desert Rats, The (1953), TCF. *Dir.* Robert Wise; *Sc.* Richard Murphy; *Cast includes:* Richard Burton, Robert Newton, Robert Douglas, Torin Thatcher.

The defense of Tobruk by tenacious British forces serves as the background for this World War II drama. Richard Burton portrays a hard-bitten British captain in command of Australian troops fated to defend the fortress city against overwhelming German forces. At first the Aussies under his command suspect him of not caring for their welfare, but by the end of the film they volunteer to hold a perilous position until a relief column arrives. Burton leads several raids against the enemy in an attempt to disrupt them. General Rommel (James Mason) directs the attack upon Tobruk. The screenwriters contrive a fictitious meeting between Rommel and the British captain, who has been captured during one of his night forays. Rommel confides his general strategy to the English prisoner, suggesting that his taking of Tobruk is unimportant. Burton snaps back that without Tobruk the German general dare not advance on Cairo, and without Cairo Rommel should start planning for the next war.

Robert Newton, as a drunken and cowardly British soldier and Burton's former instructor, arouses Burton's sympathies; otherwise, the captain is overly strict with his men. When the siege of Tobruk is finally lifted by the British relief column at the end of the film, a narrator pays tribute to the gallant defenders. "So, after 242 days," the voice-over announces, "ended the siege of Tobruk—not the biggest action of the war and far from the last—but one in which a sweaty, dirty, hopelessly outnumbered garrison by stubborn courage won for itself an unforgettable place in the world's history of battles." ■

Desert Sands (1955), UA. *Dir.* Lesley Selander; *Sc.* George W. George, George F. Slavin, Danny Arnold; *Cast includes:* Ralph Meeker, Marla English, J. Carrol Naish, John Carradine.

The French Foreign Legion faces yet another Arab uprising in this familiar action drama set somewhere in the Sahara. Ralph Meeker, as a battle-hardened Legionnaire captain, is assigned to take command of a desert fort. He soon learns that a relief column has been wiped out in an Arab attack. He is forced to abandon the fort to the enemy but ultimately recaptures it. Keith Larsen portrays the Arab chieftain while his scheming adviser is played by John Carradine. Marla English, as an Arab princess and sister of chieftain Larsen, falls for Meeker and at one point saves his life. She ultimately is responsible for the defeat of her brother. Character actor J. Carrol Naish plays the typical Legionnaire sergeant, and Ron Randell, as an alcoholic Englishman, demonstrates the right stuff once the climactic battle begins. The otherwise routine film provides plenty of action sequences between the warring tribesmen and the troops. ■

Desert Song, The (1929), WB. *Dir.* Roy Del Ruth; *Sc.* Harvey Gates; *Cast includes:* John Boles, Carlotta King, Louise Fazenda, Johnny Arthur, John Miljan, Myrna Loy.

The first sound operetta to come to the screen, the film stars John Boles as the Red Shadow, a masked figure who bravely leads the Riffs against the French. Without his costume he is Pierre Birbeau, the son of a French general. He finds time to woo a young Frenchwoman (Carlotta King). Johnny Arthur and Louise Fazenda provide the comedy relief. Enough action sequences occur whenever the daring Riffs ride across the desert sands or whenever they confront the French soldiers to keep the plot moving between musical numbers based on Sigmund Romberg's original score, including, among others, "The Riff Song," "The Desert Song," "French Military Marching Song" and "Romance." Some of the scenes were shot in Technicolor. ■

Desert Song, The (1943), WB. *Dir.* Robert Florey; *Sc.* Robert Buckner; *Cast includes:* Dennis Morgan, Irene Manning, Bruce Cabot, Victor Francen, Lynne Overman.

In this updated version of the well-known operetta, Nazi spies scheme to build a railroad in French Morocco in 1939, using Riffs as slave laborers. Dennis Morgan, as an American expatriate who had fought against Franco's Fascists in Spain, works as a piano player in Morocco. Disguised as the Red Rider, he organizes the natives in an uprising against their oppressors. Following a series of desert battles and the unmasking of a German agent, he finally succeeds in gaining freedom for the Riffs. Irene Manning provides the love interest and contributes to some of the sing-

ing. The original songs are retained in this screen version that includes four new numbers. ■

Desert Song, The (1953), WB. *Dir.* Bruce Humberstone; *Sc.* Roland Kibbee; *Cast includes:* Kathryn Grayson, Gordon MacRae, Steve Cochran, Raymond Massey.

Gordon MacRae portrays the mysterious leader of the Riffs and stalwart fighter for justice and freedom in this third version of Sigmund Romberg's popular operetta. MacRae, known to all as a naive anthropology student, assumes his disguise as El Khobar whenever he battles the forces of a ruthless sheik. Kathryn Grayson portrays a general's daughter who is chased by a captain in the Foreign Legion (Steve Cochran) but who has fallen in love with MacRae. Raymond Massey, as the unscrupulous and ambitious sheik, oppresses the Riffs while scheming to overthrow the French. ■

Deserter, The (1971), Par. *Dir.* Burt Kennedy; *Sc.* Clair Huffaker; *Cast includes:* Bekim Fehmiu, Richard Crenna, Chuck Connors, Ricardo Montalban, Brandon De Wilde, Slim Pickens.

The U.S. Cavalry battles the Apache along the Mexican border once again in this weak action drama starring Yugoslavian actor Bekim Fehmiu. The personal story concerns Fehmiu, as a cavalry officer who fights the Indians by traditional means until he finds his wife tortured and mutilated. He deserts and, seeking out the Apaches, goes on a rampage of killing in an attempt to avenge his wife. Richard Crenna portrays his superior officer. John Huston, as a general, assigns Fehmiu to train a special force to deal with the marauding hostiles. The film is long on violence and short on characterization. ■

Design for Death (1947), RKO. *Sc.* Theodor Geisel, Helen Geisel.

A documentary about the rise of the Japanese empire and how power fell into the hands of only a few, the film traces 700 years of that nation's history. Narrators Kent Smith and Hans Conried explain how a handful of greedy "barons" held political and military sway over the land. They exploited the bushido code and Shintoism, employed thought police and even controlled the Emperor while filling their own coffers. The film, which won an Oscar as the best full-length documentary of 1947, suggests that future global conflicts can be prevented only through the democratization of Japan, where an informed and free people can keep power-hungry madmen out of office. The documentary uses much captured Japanese footage. ■

Desire Me (1947). See Veterans. ■

Desiree (1954), TCF. *Dir.* Henry Koster; *Sc.* Phoebe and Henry Ephron; *Cast includes:* Marlon Brando, Jean Simmons, Merle Oberon, Michael Rennie, Cameron Mitchell.

Jean Simmons portrays the title character, a rich Marseilles merchant's daughter, who rejects a down-and-out Napoleon Bonaparte, portrayed by Marlon Brando, in this lavishly produced romantic costume drama. Although Napoleon tries to convince her that someday he will gain fame and fortune, Desiree turns down his marriage offer a second time. He soon rises from artillery officer to his country's leading hero. Desiree travels to Paris to see him and learns that he is about to marry Josephine (Merle Oberon). Despondent, she decides to commit suicide but is saved by a nobleman (Michael Rennie). Desiree then visits relatives in Italy where she records in her diary Napoleon's long list of military successes. She later marries Rennie, who, disillusioned with Napoleon's authoritarian attitude, allies himself with the Russians. His troops badly beaten, Napoleon is eventually forced into exile on Elba. Following his escape, he raises a new army and marches on Paris. Desiree goes to him and dissuades him from continuing his dreams of conquest. He surrenders and accepts permanent exile on St. Helena. Brando, who was reluctant to play the role and undertook the assignment only to fulfill his obligations to the studio, presented a confused Napoleon. Although the basic highlights of his career adhered to historical events, much of the romantic plot is pure fancy. His final surrender at the request of Desiree does a disservice to such a significant historical figure. ■

"Despatch Bearer, The" (1907).

This primitive film is a two-reel silent drama that takes place during an unnamed war. A soldier, carrying a message through enemy lines, is wounded and assisted by a young girl who hides him from his pursuers and volunteers to complete his mission. ■

Desperados, The (1969), Col. *Dir.* Henry Levin; *Sc.* Walter Brough; *Cast includes:* Vince Edwards, Jack Palance, George Maharis, Neville Brand, Sylvia Syms.

Another Quantrill-like figure ravages the land under the guise of acting for the Confederacy. Jack Palance portrays the guerrilla leader who, seeking revenge for his wife's death, leaves a path of death and destruction in the wake of his raids. When one of his sons, played by Vince Edwards, realizes that his father and his followers are nothing more than lawbreakers, he leaves for Texas with his wife (Sylvia Syms). Several years after the Civil War, Edwards, who has made a respectable life for himself, is forced to confront the raiders who have invaded his peaceful community. The climactic battle claims the lives of his entire family. ■

Desperate Journey (1942), WB. *Dir.* Raoul Walsh; *Sc.* Arthur T. Horman; *Cast includes:* Errol Flynn, Ronald Reagan, Raymond Massey, Arthur Kennedy, Nancy Coleman, Alan Hale.

Errol Flynn and Ronald Reagan star in this fast-paced World War II drama about the crew of an English bomber shot down in German territory after completing its mission. Flynn, as a reckless flight lieutenant, takes the plane below the clouds for a better crack at the target after his captain is wounded. The bomber is hit and Flynn is forced to crash-land. From this point on it is one narrow escape after another as the Germans attempt to capture the surviving crew members. When they learn the location of a secret German fighter-plane factory, they are determined to get back to their base. But Flynn convinces the crew to set fire to a factory first, where they lose another crew member. Continuously on the run, they manage to locate a hidden airfield, subdue the German guards and pilots and take off for England. Flynn gets the last word—and the now famous line: "Now for Australia and a crack at those Japs."

Although the story is incredible, the action and suspense are so fast-paced that the viewer is seldom aware of the implausibilities. Warner Brothers did not miss the chance for a little patriotism and propaganda between chases and shootings. Arthur Kennedy, the most cautious member of the downed crew, reminds Flynn that they should try to get back to England without bombing any factories. When Flynn laughingly says that Kennedy won't let the boys have a little fun, Kennedy replies: "I didn't get into this war for fun or adventure or because it was expected of me. I got into it because it was a hard, dirty job that has to be done . . . It's no bright game to me. It's just a job." When they are about to leave Germany, Flynn pleads with a young German woman who has helped them to leave with them. "I must stay here," she explains. "No one's share is done until the war is over. It's our job, the job of the underground." Later, she gives Flynn and the others a message to take home with them: "Tell the people in England that there are people like us left in Germany still living, still hoping, still fighting . . ." ∎

Despoiler, The (1915). See Antiwar Films. ∎

Destination Gobi (1953), TCF. *Dir.* Robert Wise; *Sc.* Everett Freeman; *Cast includes:* Richard Widmark, Don Taylor, Casey Adams, Murvyn Vye, Darryl Hickman.

Members of a U.S. Navy team dispatched to the Gobi Desert to study weather conditions join the Mongols to fight against Japanese forces in this World War II drama. After the Japanese destroy the meteorological station, the American survivors are forced to traverse hundreds of miles of desert before they reach the coast. Richard Widmark portrays a hard-bitten chief petty officer who takes over the command of the sailors when their commanding officer is killed. At one point the Americans befriend the otherwise suspicious native Mongols who rescue Widmark and his men when they are captured by the Japanese. Several skirmishes with the Japanese liven up this offbeat film, reportedly based on actual events. ∎

Destination Tokyo (1943), WB. *Dir.* Delmer Daves; *Sc.* Delmer Daves, Albert Maltz; *Cast includes:* Cary Grant, John Garfield, Alan Hale, John Ridgely, Dane Clark, Warner Anderson.

A U.S. submarine, on a secret mission, penetrates Japan's undersea coastal defenses in this World War II drama. The mission is of such vital importance that the captain and his crew are ordered to sail on Christmas Eve. Their purpose is to gather information for a subsequent air attack from the aircraft carrier Hornet, the first bombing of Japan. To help in this suspenseful and dangerous journey, Warner Brothers assembled an able crew with Cary Grant as commander of the submarine, John Garfield as an unflinching seaman, Dane Clark as a Nazi-hating Greek-American and a host of other competent performers.

The events and places recall those that made the headlines during the war years. After leaving San Francisco harbor, the submarine meets a navy plane off Kiska to take on board a meteorologist. From there it proceeds under sealed orders for Tokyo. Suspenseful moments occur when the sub glides through an underwater mine field and mesh gate into Tokyo's harbor, an appendicitis operation is performed aboard the sub and a crew member attempts to defuse a detonator cap of a bomb. The script follows several conventions of the war genre. The sailors, many of them green youths, come from different parts of the States and reflect various ethnic backgrounds. There is much talk about their sweethearts back home, with Garfield leading the conversation with his numerous affairs, real and imaginary. The typical patriotic and heroic elements are omnipresent.

Although most of the war films of the 1940s contained an abundance of propaganda and heroics, this film—perhaps because much of it takes place within the confined quarters of the sub—seems overly saturated with these elements. Comradeship and harmony dominate life aboard the sub as the jovial crew are quick to volunteer for hazardous assignments. Grant, a sympathetic captain, is close to all his men. Sentimentality runs rampant. The first night out of port finds a handful of crew members strolling through the sub singing Christmas carols. Alan Hale as Cookie, the chef, masquerades as Santa Claus and distributes Christmas presents. An old-timer (Tom Tully) regularly goes off alone to listen to a home recording of his wife's voice. One youth (Jim Hutton) asks the captain for permission to grow a beard. Background music and songs include "Home on the Range" as well as popular tunes. The enemy is depicted in the most derogatory and inhuman terms. When a sailor tries to rescue a downed Japanese pilot from the freezing waters of the Aleutians, the pilot savagely stabs him several times. In another scene Grant discusses the enemy and their culture. "The Japs don't understand the love we have for our women," he comments.

The actual events of the story are difficult to assess, except for General Doolittle's B-25 raid over Tokyo in 1942. However, the film remains fairly representative of the war stories Hollywood turned out at the time and which paid tribute to the bravery of the men of the silent service. See also Submarine Warfare. ■

Destroyer (1943), Col. *Dir.* William A. Seiter; *Sc.* Frank Wead, Louis Meltzer, Borden Chase; *Cast includes:* Edward G. Robinson, Glenn Ford, Marguerite Chapman, Edgar Buchanan.

Edward G. Robinson stars as a World War I navy veteran who desperately wants to serve his country in this World War II drama. As a shipyard worker, he manipulates his way back into the service and is made chief bosun mate on a new destroyer. When things go awry on the ship's first cruise, the captain removes Robinson and gives his job to Glenn Ford. Later, when the vessel is relegated to a mail ship and is damaged by Japanese planes, Robinson heroically repairs it, and the destroyer proceeds to ram an enemy submarine. The old sea dog's reputation is restored. Marguerite Chapman provides the romantic interest in this routine sea tale. ■

Detectives at war. Hollywood sleuths on occasion turned their attentions from battling conventional criminals to tackling enemy agents. Louis Joseph Vance's fictional hero, "The Lone Wolf," for example, had a long screen history, beginning in the silents. In *The False Faces* (1919), set during World War I and starring Henry B. Walthall as the detective, he learns that German spies intend to increase their activities in the United States. Jack Holt portrayed a Robin Hood-type sleuth in *The Lone Wolf* (1924), which concerns some coveted secret papers that contain military plans of the U.S. Columbia studios again pressed their in-house sleuth, the Lone Wolf, into service against enemy agents during World War II. He came out of retirement for *The Lone Wolf Spy Hunt* (1939), in which Warren William as the title character foils a Washington spy network from stealing secret anti-aircraft plans. In *Counter-Espionage* (1942) William, again playing the "Wolf," hunts down a Nazi spy network in World War II London and protects secret military plans. In *Passport to Suez* (1943) William, as a double agent, joins a Nazi spy ring in Egypt as a ploy to retrieve stolen plans of the Suez Canal.

Jack Boyle's popular fictional character Boston Blackie, a former criminal who works on the side of the law, also had a long screen life. In the World War I drama *The Silk-Lined Burglar* (1919) Sam De Grasse, as the regenerated miscreant, plies his safe-cracking talents. He assists a young woman in obtaining evidence against a suspected German spy. Lionel Barrymore, as Boston Blackie in *A Face in the Fog* (1922), becomes entangled in an international plot to restore the monarchy in Bolshevik Russia. During the sound era Chester Morris took over the role. He becomes implicated in a murder in *Meet Boston Blackie* (1941), and to prove his innocence he exposes an entire spy ring.

Basil Rathbone and Nigel Bruce became the most popular team to portray A. Conan Doyle's Sherlock Holmes and Dr. Watson. *The Voice of Terror* (1942) concerned a Nazi radio broadcast that was terrorizing the English citizenry. In *Sherlock Holmes and the Secret Weapon* (1942) Holmes employs a series of disguises to elude the enemy while Dr. Watson remains baffled by his friend's methods. Dr. Moriarty, Holmes' arch-enemy, is again on the loose in this updated version of Doyle's story titled "The Dancing Men." Holmes and Watson then travel to the U.S. to take on an international spy ring in *Sherlock Holmes in Washington* (1943). *Pursuit to Algiers* (1945), another of the updated Sherlock Holmes entries of the 1940s, involves a threat against a young king's life by an unnamed enemy although there are hints that totalitarian forces are behind the plot.

MGM purchased the rights to all the Nick Carter stories, updated the material from its pre-World War I background to the World War II period and featured dapper Walter Pidgeon as the master sleuth in the low-budget series. The undistinguished first entry, *Nick Carter, Master Detective* (1939), directed by Jacques Tourneur, deals with spies trying to steal secret plans from an airplane factory. Comic character actor Donald Meek portrays the detective's assistant. Rita Johnson, as an airline stewardess, serves as romantic interest. The detective series differed from others in that Carter busied himself in tracking down enemy agents and saboteurs rather than run-of-the-mill criminals and murderers. For example, in *Phantom Raiders* (1940), the second entry, saboteurs are busy attacking ships in the Panama Canal region before Carter puts a stop to their activities. The third and final entry, *Sky Murder*, also released in 1940, again concerned foreign spies.

Other detectives also took on an array of enemy agents. In *Charlie Chan in Panama* (1940), the Hawaiian sleuth, working in league with U.S. Intelligence, foils a plot to blow up a portion of the Panama Canal and trap a U.S. fleet passing through during maneuvers. The film, in part, was a remake of *Marie Galante* (1934), which, ironically, had a secret agent of Japan joining forces with those of the U.S. and England to prevent the destruction of the Panama Canal. In *Enemy Agents Meet Ellery Queen* (1942) William Gargan, portraying the master sleuth, exposes a spy ring interested in industrial diamonds for precision instruments, the coveted goal of both Nazi and Free Dutch agents. These diversions by popular screen sleuths into the shadowy world of espionage added a little spark to each series and no doubt contributed to the patriotism of the period. ■

Devil Dogs (1928). See War Humor. ■

Devil Dogs of the Air (1935). See Preparedness. ■

Devil Makes Three, The (1952). See Spy Films: the Talkies. ■

Devil Pays Off, The (1941). See Spy Films: the Talkies. ■

Devil With Hitler, The (1942), UA. *Dir.* Gordon Douglas; *Sc.* Cortland Fitzsimmons; *Cast includes:* Alan Mowbray, Bobby Watson, George E. Stone, Joe Devlin.

Bobby Watson virtually made a career out of impersonating Hitler during the war years. In this World War II comedy he again plays the Nazi leader. The plot concerns the Devil (Alan Mowbray) who is in trouble with the board of directors of Hell. They want to replace him with Hitler. The Devil is given a chance to see whether he can get Adolf to do a good deed. The film pokes plenty of fun at all three Axis leaders. Some of the one-liners are quite funny. Hitler, mourning the loss of Rudolf Hess, who parachuted to England, cries: "I lost my Hess." ■

Devil's Brigade, The (1968), UA. *Dir.* Andrew V. McLaglen; *Sc.* William Roberts; *Cast includes:* William Holden, Cliff Robertson,

Vince Edwards, Andrew Prine, Claude Akins, Richard Jaeckel.

William Holden portrays an American colonel in this World War II action drama about a special forces unit composed of a crack Canadian unit and a slovenly group of American soldiers, most of whom are slackers and misfits. The men undergo intensive training at an abandoned army camp in the United States under Holden and Cliff Robertson, who plays Holden's Canadian counterpart. Holden exploits the competitive spirit between the two units, hoping the Americans will be self-motivated to improve as soldiers. When friction develops between the two diverse groups, Robertson attempts to enlighten Holden, the senior officer of the newly formed brigade, on the virtues of his Canadians. "Many of the Canadian unit fought at Dunkirk," he explains, "so it might be possible that you may want to learn a lesson from their combat experience." "Yes, I might," Holden replies, "if you had won at Dunkirk. You lost. I'm training this outfit to win. Good night, Major."

When the training is completed, the brigade journeys overseas for action in Italy and distinguishes itself during its first assignment by capturing a German-held town and a host of prisoners. Its next mission, however, is much more difficult. The men must take a mountain top by climbing a steep rock wall. They succeed in capturing the mountain in hand-to-hand combat but at a terrible cost in casualties. Robertson is shot by a Nazi officer who has falsely surrendered under a white flag. As the Devil's Brigade descends from the mountain, a voice-over narrated by Holden summarizes the emotions of his men: "It was not much of a mountain, really. But I never knew a mountain could be so tall or plain rock cost so much." At the end of the film he says, again as a voice-over: "The American misfits and the proud Canadians lay dead in a hundred fields and crossroads. Together, they had built a myth. Too many died to keep it true."

The film is based on actual events. The unit, the 1st Special Service Force, organized on July 9, 1942, was made up of American and Canadian volunteers. It was highly successful in several raids and the capture of Monte La Difensa, a strategic target during the battle for Cassino. Winston Churchill singled out the group for its acts of heroism, most notably for its activities in France. ■

Devil's Doorway (1950). See Shoshone Indians. ∎

Diary of Anne Frank, The (1959), TCF. *Dir.* George Stevens; *Sc.* Frances Goodrich, Albert Hackett; *Cast includes:* Millie Perkins, Joseph Schildkraut, Shelley Winters.

A young girl's bounding optimism and joy of life brighten the dark world of those who are forced to share with her a hiding place from the Nazis during World War II. Anne Frank, her parents and a handful of other Dutch Jews hide out in a secret room in Nazi-occupied Amsterdam. Within these restricted confines they maintain their family and religious traditions, live in daily fear of being caught and attempt to keep their dignity as human beings. Anne, 13 years old, never gives up hope. "In spite of everything," she writes in her diary, "I still believe that people are really good at heart."

Joseph Schildkraut, as Otto Frank, Anne's wise and sad father and the sole survivor, provides the appropriate strength for his small family. Gusti Huber portrays Anne's mother, a simple woman who has problems dealing with her maturing daughter. Shelley Winters, as Mrs. Van Daan, Lou Jacobi as Mr. Van Daan, her husband and their son Peter, played by Richard Beymer, share the cramped quarters. Ed Wynn plays Dussel, a local dentist, who joins the fugitives until the fateful moment when the Gestapo appear at the door to their secret room.

The film is based on the popular published diary and the successful Broadway play by Frances Goodrich and Albert Hackett. Controversy arose from some Jewish quarters that condemned the "Anne Frank" syndrome—European Jews who accepted their fate and unrealistically tried to live out their lives as though they were unaffected by external events. These dissenters held that the Jews should have risen up and fought against their assassins instead of merely marching off to their own slaughter. ∎

Dictator, The (1922), Par. *Dir.* James Cruze; *Sc.* Wally Woods; *Cast includes:* Wallace Reid, Lila Lee, Theodore Kosloff, Walter Long, Alan Hale.

A satirical comedy based on the stage play by Richard Harding Davis, the film pokes fun at politics and revolution in a fictitious South American banana republic. Wallace Reid portrays an innocent American hero who stumbles his way into San Manana, a tropical land plagued by revolutions and incompetent politicians. Walter Long, as a tough New York cabdriver, relentlessly follows Reid, trying to collect his cab fare, and becomes embroiled in a firing squad and other threatening escapades.

Several Latin-American countries were plagued with unrest or possible insurrections at the time the film was released, including, among others, Panama (1918–1920), Honduras (1919) and Guatemala (1920), each of which could have been the inspiration for the script. In all three cases, the U.S. intervened either to protect American interests or its legation, to maintain order. ∎

Diplomatic Courier (1952). See Cold War. ∎

Dirty Dozen, The (1967), MGM. *Dir.* Robert Aldrich; *Sc.* Nunnally Johnson, Lukas Heller; *Cast includes:* Lee Marvin, Ernest Borgnine, Charles Bronson, Jim Brown, John Cassavetes.

Twelve criminal soldiers, including rapists and murderers, are given a chance to earn their freedom in this implausible but exciting World War II drama. High-ranking U.S. Army officials conceive of a near-suicide mission in which a handful of specially trained soldiers are dropped by parachute behind the lines to kill as many Nazi officers as possible who periodically assemble at a highly guarded chateau. The purpose is to disorganize the enemy prior to D-Day by ridding them of their key officers. The planners, knowing the odds against surviving such a mission, conjure up the idea of using convicted criminals who have little to lose.

The story opens in England where an unorthodox and troublesome major, played by Lee Marvin, is selected to train and lead the special unit of misfits. He is presented with the plan by a local general (Ernest Borgnine) and his key staff who at first abusively assail the major's previous shaky record. "What do you say, Major?" Borgnine asks, referring to the plan. "I'd say it confirms a suspicion I've had for some time now," Marvin replies. "One of the men we're working for happens to be a raving lunatic." But the major is forced to "volunteer."

He assembles his motley crew and soon whips them into shape for the perilous assignment after he gets the general to promise

Lee Marvin and his unorthodox group of heroes romanticize war as they attack a Nazi stronghold. *The Dirty Dozen* (1967).

amnesty for those who perform their duty. Along with his loyal sergeant (Richard Jaeckel), the men are dropped behind enemy lines and proceed to indulge in a blood bath of killing that includes the Nazi officers and their female companions.

The film was a huge box-office success although several critics attacked the glorification of the convicts and the reckless violence as well as the unbelievable premise that the army would entrust such a critical mission to a group of irresponsible psychopaths and murderers. ■

Dishonored (1931). See Spy Films: the Talkies. ■

Dishonored Medal, The (1914), Mutual. *Dir.* Christy Cabanne; *Sc.* Christy Cabanne; *Cast includes:* George Gebhart, Miriam Cooper, Raoul Walsh, Frank Bennett.

A silent drama set in the French territory of Algiers, the film depicts the story of a French officer who abandons his Algerian sweetheart to return to his native land. She gives

birth to his son and dies, leaving a medal behind that was given to her by her lover. The child is reared by an Algerian who raises the boy and his own son as two brothers. Years later the officer returns and, observing an attractive young native woman that the two young men are in love with, orders her to be brought to his quarters. The young men stir up a revolt and a battle ensues. In the conflict the son mortally wounds the French officer who notices the medal his young slayer is wearing. The son is then informed that he has killed his own father. Bidding farewell to his half-brother and the woman he loves, he remains behind with his slain father to face the consequences. Raoul Walsh, who was to become a major film director of the 1930s and 1940s specializing in action and war movies, portrays the son.

Although the film allegedly takes place during the Algerian-French Wars of the mid-1800s, there is little to suggest any attempt at specific historical accuracy. The suddenness of the revolt initiated by the young men may have some basis in truth as a result of the

Western mythology continues as a troop of U.S. Cavalry rides to glory against hostile Chiricahuas. *A Distant Trumpet* (1964).

earlier military successes of Abd el-Kader, an Algerian Muslim leader who fought a holy war against the French. There was a continual desire on the part of the natives to rid Algeria of the French. ■

Distant Drums (1951), WB. *Dir.* Raoul Walsh; *Sc.* Niven Busch, Martin Rackin; *Cast includes:* Gary Cooper, Mari Aldon, Richard Webb, Ray Teal, Arthur Hunnicutt.

The Seminole War provides the background for this adventure drama set in Florida in 1840. Gary Cooper portrays an army captain who has made the Florida swamps his home where he lives in peace with his young son. A U.S. Navy captain (Richard Webb) is sent to join Cooper on a special mission. They are to destroy the Seminoles' ammunition supply, thereby shortening the war. Several skirmishes occur between the small raiding party and the Indians as well as a rousing battle between army troops, who have come to the rescue of the survivors, and the Seminoles. Cooper also engages in hand-to-hand combat with the Indian chief. Mari Aldon provides the romantic interest. ■

Distant Trumpet, A (1964), WB. *Dir.* Raoul Walsh; *Sc.* John Twist; *Cast includes:* Troy Donahue, Suzanne Pleshette, Diane McBain, James Gregory.

The Chiricahuas take to the warpath in this action drama set in the Southwest after the Civil War. Troy Donahue, as a second lieutenant and recent West Point graduate, is assigned to the outpost responsible for curbing the warring tribe led by War Eagle. Several skirmishes occur between the cavalry and the hostiles, including a rousing climax. James Gregory portrays the general in charge of operations. Both Suzanne Pleshette and Diane McBain provide the romantic interest for Donahue in this otherwise routine story. ■

Dive Bomber (1941), WB. *Dir.* Michael Curtiz; *Sc.* Frank Wead, Robert Buckner; *Cast includes:* Errol Flynn, Fred MacMurray, Ralph Bellamy, Alexis Smith, Regis Toomey, Robert Armstrong.

Released only a few months before Japan's attack on Pearl Harbor, *Dive Bomber* concentrates on the experiments of flight surgeons, especially in regard to their research in high altitude flying and maximum efficiency. It was one of the earliest service dramas to be filmed in color. Errol Flynn and Ralph Bellamy portray navy doctors whose medical research and experiments provide the suspense in this pre-war drama. Fred MacMurray, as a cynical and irascible flight commander, at first rejects the efforts of the medics but later joins them as a test pilot.

Using Ralph Bellamy symbolically, the film stresses the numerous and important contributions of flight surgeons. "He wrecked his heart using himself as a guinea pig on high altitude flights," an officer confides to Flynn. "Now he can't fly anymore . . . He's also the man who doped out Vitamin A for night blindness, optically correct goggles and the shoulder safety belt to stop crash injuries."

The film at its original release no doubt served several purposes. It satisfied the public's curiosity about America's preparedness at a time when Germany's air force was wreaking havoc in Europe. It also contributed to the patriotic fervor by showing dramatic flight formations, the heroism of the pilots and the dedication of the flight surgeons. "A flight surgeon has sometimes been described as a combination Dutch uncle and father confessor because he's more than a pilot's physician," Bellamy explains to a class of navy doctors. Finally, the film certainly must have encouraged many young men to enlist in the army or navy air force. MacMurray, addressing a group of new recruits, extols the glories of naval aviation: "Thirty years ago the navy had one airplane and two pilots. Only 20 years ago a naval aviator was the first man to fly the Atlantic. In those few years the men who've learned to fly here have really built naval aviation. Now you're here to learn to fly and fight and become part of that heritage." ■

Divide and Conquer (1943). See "Why We Fight." ■

Divine Lady, The (1929), WB. *Dir.* Frank Lloyd; *Sc.* Forrest Halsey, Agnes C. Johnston; *Cast includes:* Corinne Griffith, Victor Varconi, H. B. Warner, Ian Keith.

Loosely based on the romance between Lord Nelson and Lady Hamilton, the drama, which takes place during the Napoleonic Wars, stars Corinne Griffith as the attractive Emma Hamilton, Victor Varconi as England's

great naval hero whose illicit affair with Emma creates a London scandal and H. B. Warner as the wronged Lord Hamilton.

The script allows for several naval battles to be introduced, including those of the Nile and Trafalgar. Although they rely heavily on the use of miniatures, the battle sequences are realistically reproduced on screen with careful adherence to early 19th-century naval strategy. The film is chiefly silent except for sound effects and one theme song chanted by the female lead. ■

Do and Dare (1922), Fox. *Dir.* Edward Sedgwick; *Sc.* Edward Sedgwick; *Cast includes:* Tom Mix, Dulcie Cooper, Claire Adams, Claude Peyton.

A western satire on heroes and last-minute rescues, the film stars Tom Mix as the legendary Indian fighter Kit Carson. The story is told in flashback with Mix portraying a descendant of Carson. He is not faring too well in a western town where an old-timer regales the local inhabitants with tales of the old West. He tells how Carson rescued a girl from the clutches of hostile Indians, saved a stockade that was under siege and fought against great odds. The story returns to the present where Tom meets a young woman from South America who wants him to deliver a message to a revolutionary leader in her country. He journeys by airplane to Oliceana and ends up saving its president and his daughter by single-handedly crushing the revolution. Mix's farcical adventures in the fictitious country are quite humorous as he tries to duplicate the heroism of his famous ancestor.

The film may well have been influenced by the headlines of the period, which included stories of unrest and possible revolutions in several countries south of the border. The situation was serious enough for the U.S. to send troops to protect American interests and its legations in Panama (1918–1920), Honduras (1919) and Guatemala (1920). ■

Doctor Zhivago (1965), MGM. *Dir.* David Lean; *Sc.* Robert Bolt; *Cast includes:* Omar Sharif, Julie Christie, Geraldine Chaplin, Tom Courtenay, Ralph Richardson, Alec Guinness, Rod Steiger.

The Russian Revolution provides the background for this epic drama based on Boris Pasternak's Nobel Prize-winning novel. A tribute to the individuality of the human spirit, the story is told through the experiences of the title character, a sensitive poet-physician, played by Omar Sharif, who is an eye-witness to events before, during and after the Revolution. Julie Christie portrays his lover following her disastrous affairs with a lecherous politico (Rod Steiger) and compassionless husband (Tom Courtenay) obsessed with the Communist movement. Ralph Richardson, as a symbol of the past, longs for the genteel world that the revolution has trampled into the ground.

The large-scale production, shot in Spain and Finland and composed chiefly of a British cast, contains several realistic action sequences, including re-enactments of the Revolution and a street massacre. A visually attractive but episodic work, the film was MGM's second largest commercial success (Gone With the Wind being its biggest moneymaker) up to that time. Academy Awards went to screenwriter Robert Bolt, cinematographer Freddie Young, composer Maurice Jarre and costume designer Phyllis Dalton. ∎

Doctors in war. The medical profession has not only been well represented in war films throughout the years but has, on the whole, retained its dignity and integrity on screen. This is not an easy accomplishment when one takes into consideration the fertile imagination and creativity of screenwriters and directors who are constantly on the prowl for drama and conflict. Other professions, such as the law and the military, often portrayed as tainted, corrupt or insensitive, have not fared so well.

Doctors in wartime situations first appeared in early silent movies. One of the earliest is a short 1910 drama, "The Sepoy's Wife." Set in India in the 1850s during the Indian Mutiny, the film concerns an English regimental physician who saves the life of a sepoy's child. Later, the child's mother returns the act of kindness by saving the doctor's wife and child as well as the defenders of a besieged fort. This crude and simple story contains the essential elements of this genre and helps to set the pattern for future films. The medical officer, assigned to duty close to where the fighting takes place, transcends borders, nationalities and politics in helping the sick and wounded.

Surprisingly, very few doctors appear as main or featured characters in the numerous war films released during World War I. In

1916 Behind the Lines thrust a doctor (Harry Carey) into the midst of the border disputes between Mexico and the U.S. It wasn't until after the war that stories integrating doctors and the conflict began to appear. In the romantic drama For Better, for Worse (1919) a doctor is judged a coward by the woman he loves when he chooses to stay at home to help sick children rather than accept a military commission. She marries another who goes off to France. The reverse occurs in Wasted Lives (1923). An idealistic doctor who has set up a children's clinic decides to enlist when World War I breaks out. Leaving his work and wife behind, he goes to France. News arrives that he has been killed in action. His mother threatens to withdraw funds from the clinic while a former lover pursues the wife. But he returns in time to salvage his life and work. Yet another variation of this plot may be seen in The Man From Yesterday (1932). A doctor (Charles Boyer) wants to marry the widow (Claudette Colbert) of a man listed as killed at the front. When the husband, released from a German prison camp, returns, Boyer withdraws his offer. But the husband realizes that his wife loves the doctor and decides to bow out of their lives.

One of the few negative images of the medical profession pertaining to World War I occurs in Johnny Got His Gun (1971), directed by screenwriter Dalton Trumbo and based on Trumbo's novel. The callous doctors, led by their chief medical officer, decide that Timothy Bottoms, a quadriplegic, is incapable of thought or emotions. When he asks to be released from the hospital, they instead lock him up in a dark room out of view of the public.

Doctors have appeared on screen in other wars. William Holden, as a humane army surgeon in the Civil War drama The Horse Soldiers (1959), accompanies a troop of Union soldiers led by John Wayne on a raid behind Confederate lines. When the men depart after carrying out their mission, the doctor volunteers to remain behind to care for the wounded, knowing that he will be taken prisoner and sent to the infamous Andersonville prison. Earlier in the film, following a bloody battle, he spends as much time patching up Southern wounded as he does helping those of the Union. In The Great Sioux Uprising (1953) Jeff Chandler, as a former army medic, helps bring peace between the U.S. Cavalry and the Sioux. Omar Sharif, as the sensitive poet-physician and title character in *Doctor Zhivago* (1965), is an acute observer of events before, during and after the Russian Revolution.

World War II presented the largest number of films about doctors. Errol Flynn and Ralph Bellamy portray dedicated flight surgeons doing research in high altitude flying for the navy in *Dive Bomber* (1940), a patriotic drama released before America's entry into the war. Fred MacMurray, as a cynical flight commander, gives the pair a difficult time before he realizes their invaluable contributions. *Corregidor* (1943) offers one of the earliest war dramas featuring a woman doctor. Elissa Landi, Otto Kruger and Donald Woods portray physicians who form a romantic triangle while they attend the wounded and heroic defenders of the island for 27 days against the Japanese invaders. Cecil B. DeMille's biographical drama *The Story of Dr. Wassell* (1944) recounts the major events in the life of the navy doctor, played by Gary Cooper, who refused to abandon the wounded during the evacuation of Java. Instead, he managed to transport twelve American soldiers to Australia, for which he received the Navy Cross. Clark Gable, as an army doctor in *Homecoming* (1948), falls in love with his nurse (Lana Turner). The affair continues from North Africa to Europe and the Battle of the Bulge. When she dies from war wounds, Gable returns home to his wife.

Not all doctors served at the front or were American in the films about the war. Philip Dorn in *Escape* (1940) portrays a German doctor who works in a concentration camp. Idealistic about his own profession, he is naive about Nazi ideology. "Our children will thank us for the world we are making for them," he announces to Robert Taylor, who has come to visit his sick mother, a prisoner in the camp. In *36 Hours* (1964) a sympathetic German doctor (Rod Taylor) helps an American flier escape from the Gestapo. Charles Boyer, as a refugee doctor who has escaped to Paris in *Arch of Triumph* (1948), saves the life of Ingrid Bergman, who has tried to commit suicide. But tragic events doom the pair who have become lovers.

Doctors were called upon to treat servicemen who suffered from psychological problems. James Edwards, a black soldier in *Home of the Brave* (1949), cracks up when a close buddy is killed. His doctor learns that the G.I. has undergone a long period of racial

abuse which has led to his present condition. Gregory Peck, as a dedicated psychiatrist at an army hospital neuro-psychiatric ward in *Captain Newman, M.D.* (1963), is more concerned about his patients' long-term health than in getting them back to the front lines— as suggested by his superiors. He is assisted by a conniving, good-natured orderly (Tony Curtis).

The Korean War provided two films based on the work of the Mobile Army Surgical Hospital Corps, better known to American movie and television audiences as M.A.S.H. In *Battle Circus* (1953), a bland romantic drama, Humphrey Bogart, as an army surgeon, and June Allyson, as an idealistic nurse, fall in love. They find time for their romance between action sequences which show helicopters picking up the wounded and delivering them to the army base. The black comedy *M*A*S*H* (1970) relegated the former film into obscurity. Donald Sutherland and Elliott Gould portray two highly skilled surgeons who accept the absurdity of the war on their own terms and learn how to survive. Director Robert Altman's irreverent and witty comedy became the basis for the long-running television series.

Two dramas of the Vietnam War feature doctors in major roles. In *Don't Cry, It's Only Thunder* (1982) Susan Saint James, as an army doctor, helps Dennis Christopher, an aimless and irresponsible medic, find himself. He becomes involved in helping a group of war orphans. *Purple Hearts* (1984), a routine romantic drama, has little to do with the Vietnam War. Ken Wahl, as a doctor at a mobile army hospital, falls in love with Cheryl Ladd, a nurse assigned to a hospital in Da Nang. Each of the lovers is reported killed in action, but they both survive and are reunited.

The civil war in El Salvador provides the background for the short documentary "Witness to War" (1984). The film relates the experiences of Charlie Clements, an American volunteer doctor, once a pilot in Vietnam, who patched up soldiers hurt in battle as well as civilians wounded as the result of bombings. ∎

Documentary. Films of actual events with real locales and local people dominated the first few years of the infant movie industry at the turn of the century. Audiences, fascinated with this new and inexpensive form of entertainment, witnessed workers exiting from a factory, a train pulling into a depot or a prize fight. Battles were re-enacted and some wars were filmed. The Biograph studio in 1900 released scenes of the Boer War and the Philippine Insurrection of 1899. But by the second decade the narrative had already replaced the newsreel, travel film and documentary as the major genre. The American war documentary first came into prominence during World War I although there were several previous attempts at this form. As early as 1910 "Troop B, 16th Cavalry, in Maneuvers" appeared. But these short, crudely produced films were more in the realm of newsreels than true documentaries, the latter term implying conscious editing and compiling with a specific point of view, such as the propaganda film. One of the earliest American documentaries about World War I, *The Battle and Fall of Przemysl* (1915), covers the Austrian-Hungarian advance in North Galicia replete with the big guns smashing the Czar's defenses. The same film company produced *The Battles of a Nation*, also released in 1915. This time the action depicts the fall of Lemberg and Warsaw to the Central powers and includes sequences of aerial reconnaissance and the massive number of provisions required to carry out such battles.

As the war in Europe raged on, the mood in the U.S. shifted from pacifism to preparedness. The documentaries followed suit, and for the remainder of the conflict they served an important role as part of the propaganda campaign. *Defense or Tribute?* (1916), for example, advocates an America ready to defend itself by conjuring up past wars through the centuries. The film shows a board meeting of dignitaries finally voting unanimously for preparedness. Meanwhile other documentaries, including *How Uncle Sam Prepares*, *Our Fighting Forces* and *Over Here*, all released in 1917, were informing audiences on the state of the country's military readiness.

Once the U.S. entered the conflict, a flood of propaganda documentaries appeared. Some focused on specific branches of the military ("Flying With the Marines," "Our Invincible Navy"); others concentrated on America's fighting forces in battle ("Crashing Through to Berlin," "Pershing's Crusaders"); and still others emphasized the friendship and unity shared by the Allied nations ("Following the Flag to France," "Under Four Flags").

Most of the war documentaries emanated from the U.S. government's Committee on Public Information and its Division of Films branch. Supervised by George Creel, an industrious journalist, the C.P.I. at first distributed these films, varying in length from one to several reels, to different groups and organizations. To reach larger audiences, the films began to appear in commercial movie theaters. Although documentaries emerged from such private studios as Pathe and Universal, these releases had to conform to the policies of the C.P.I. and obtain its approval. After the Armistice, the Committee was disbanded.

Documentaries about the war continued to be made throughout the next two decades. The U.S. Signal Corps, assigned the task of filming the war, had a backlog of material stored in Europe as well as in the States. Together with the film archives of other European countries, there was a vast storehouse of war film available for resourceful compilers. The Pictorial Sales Bureau, for instance, turned out three films in 1924, *Iowa Under Fire*, *Nebraska Under Fire* and *Wisconsin Under Fire*, each following the training and battle experiences of a particular state's fighting troops. Some documentaries focused on particular battles and added German footage to show both sides of the fighting. *Gold Chevrons* (1927) covers Chateau-Thierry and the Argonne. Others, such as *Men of Purpose* (1926), *Heroes All* (1931), *The Big Drive* (1933) and *War's End* (1934), try to put the events of the war into historical perspective. These compilations, also using footage from the Central Powers, trace the war from its origins to the Armistice and cover some of the lesser known battles, such as those fought by the Russians and Italians.

By the mid-1930s, the war documentary began to look at the conflict critically, as did such war dramas of the period as *All Quiet on the Western Front* and *Journey's End*, both released in 1930. *Forgotten Men* (1933) takes on a note of pacifism as it traces various events of the conflict. *Dealers in Death* (1934) attacks the munitions makers, emphasizing the huge profits their companies reaped as a result of the slaughter. Playwright Laurence Stallings, who had written several works about World War I, wrote and edited *The First World War* (1934), underscoring the senseless horror the soldiers had to live through. Other films included sequences from the conflict to warn against the rebirth of militarism in the world, singling out Germany and Italy as examples. *Why This War?* (1939), one of the last documentaries to rely extensively on World War I footage, attempts to tie in events of that war with the rise of Nazism. But these attempts to stop a future war came too late. The flames were already being stoked.

Documentaries of World War II covered the same subjects as did those of the Great War. They benefited, however, from sound, better and lighter cameras which allowed cameramen more mobility and the expertise of several studio directors who served in the Signal Corps. Occasionally, the film was shot in color. Documentaries like those from "The March of Time" series (*Inside Nazi Germany*, *The Ramparts We Watch* and *America Speaks Her Mind*) set the tone for many to follow. Director Frank Capra produced the highly acclaimed "Why We Fight" series for the Department of War. John Ford turned out the Oscar-winning "The Battle of Midway" (1942) for the U.S. Navy and included scenes of a Red Cross hospital being hit by Japanese aircraft. John Huston's "The Battle of San Pietro" (1945) was another film that received critical praise for its realistic portrait of the foot soldier in combat. William Wyler made *Memphis Belle* (1944), the story of a bomber and its crew that flew 25 missions over German-occupied territory. Louis de Rochemont's Oscar-winning *The Fighting Lady* (1944) focused on the story of an aircraft carrier on duty in the Pacific.

Scores of other documentaries eulogized the different military branches in such films as "We Are the Marines" (1942); highlighted specific battles as in *Battle for Russia* (1943), *Battle of Britain* (1943) and "The Battle for the Mariannas" (1944); or showed how the home front was contributing to the war effort in films like "War Town" (1943). In "The Battle of the Beaches" (1943) the camera accompanied American fighting men from one Pacific island invasion to another. Post-World War II documentaries depicted the tragic results of the conflict in such films as "The Pale Horseman" (1946), which pleaded for American support for the sick and hungry in Europe and Asia. Others traced the military and political history of our former enemies. *Design for Death* (1947), for example, covers the rise of the Japanese empire and concludes that only the democratization of that country

can prevent another world war. But the majority of the postwar films concerned the Cold War, with its threat of Communism and the Korean conflict. *Death of a Dream* (1950), written by foreign correspondent Quentin Reynolds, was one of the earliest to appear and traces the roots of the Korean War. The titles of others reveal their content—*This Is Korea!* (1951), *Why Korea?* (1951) and *If Moscow Strikes* (1952).

By the late 1960s documentaries of the controversial Vietnam War began to reach movie theaters. *Inside North Vietnam* (1967), which opposed America's involvement in the war, places much of the blame for the death and destruction in that nation on U.S. bombers. *A Face of War* (1968) follows a company of U.S. Marines as they battle the hostile terrain and the elusive enemy. *In the Year of the Pig* (1967), another film critical of America's role in Vietnam, uses interviews, speeches and newsreel footage to make its point. *The War at Home* (1979) shows some of the confrontations between those opposed to the war and others who supported government policy.

Documentaries of the 1980s ranged from the role of women in World War II and its effects on contemporary society (*The Life and Times of Rosie the Riveter*) to films about strife in Central America (*El Salvador: Another Vietnam*, *Witness to War*). Sandwiched between these were films of the holocaust during World War II, including *Who Shall Live and Who Shall Die?* (1981) and *Genocide* (1982).

The history of the American documentary resembles a chronicle of the country and is often a barometer of the feelings of its citizens. In prewar years the films provide both antiwar and preparedness views. During wartime, they contribute to the propaganda campaigns. In the aftermath of conflict, they try with more objectivity to explain the causes of the war, pay tribute to the fallen and advocate an end to future wars. ∎

Dog of the Regiment (1927), WB. *Dir.* Ross Lederman; *Sc.* Charles Condon; *Cast includes:* Rin-Tin-Tin, Tom Gallery, Dorothy Gulliver, John Peters.

A World War I drama starring the famous canine Rin-Tin-Tin, the film tells of the dog's heroism during the conflict. A young American lawyer called to Germany before the war to settle an estate falls in love with a young woman. When the conflict begins, he returns to the United States and enlists as a flier. Back in Europe on duty, he is shot down and captured by the Germans. He meets his sweetheart who is working as a Red Cross nurse. Her dog, Rin-Tin-Tin, helps him to escape. The trio head for the border while the dog effects their rescue several times. The story is supposed to be based on true incidents. ∎

Dogs in war. The dog may be man's best friend, but the creature was sorely neglected in the 2,000 war films made in the U.S. during the last 90 years. Dogs appeared on the front line in only a handful of films. In *Find Your Man* (1924), one of the earliest examples of the genre and only a partial war drama, Rin-Tin-Tin goes through his paces as a faithful auxiliary of the Red Cross during World War I before he returns to the States to help his master out of further difficulties. Thunder, another brave canine in World War I, saves the life of George Hackathorne, the wounded hero of *His Master's Voice* (1925). An otherwise forgettable drama, the film is unique in that its story is told from the point of view of the dog to one of his pups. Rin-Tin-Tin returned to active duty in 1927 to rescue a downed American airman who has been captured by the Germans in *Dog of the Regiment*. He then helps his mistress, a Red Cross nurse, and the flier to escape across the border to friendly territory. A dog is featured in several sequences in *Under the Black Eagle* (1928), a World War I drama about a young German pacifist (Ralph Forbes) who finally decides to enter the conflict.

During World War II dogs were recruited for service on the battlefield and the home front. Under the auspices of Dogs for Defense, Inc. and the Quartermaster General of the U.S. Army, 50,000 dogs were recruited and trained for defense and war duties. *Pride of the Army* (1942) describes one of the jobs these canines performed at home. A little boy (Billy Lee) donates his dog for training as a guard at a defense plant. Eventually, the pet uncovers a plot by saboteurs to destroy the factory. The K-9 Corps was another branch in which dogs gave noble service. In *Sergeant Mike* (1945) the title character is a trained dog adept at sniffing out Japanese machine-gun nests and carrying dispatches during the heat of battle. Larry Parks, as a G.I. who is unhappy about being assigned to the canine unit, ultimately comes around to appreciate

the creatures' special talents. Lassie, the most famous screen dog since Rin-Tin-Tin, starred in a popular series that boasted high production values and included talented casts. *Son of Lassie* (1945) traces the exploits of Laddie and his master (Peter Lawford), a pilot in the Royal Air Force. When Lawford's plane is hit during one of his missions, he and his dog bail out over Nazi-occupied Norway. Laddie is subjected to bombings, a sniper's bullets and other hazards in his search for his master. The cast also includes Donald Crisp, Nigel Bruce and June Lockhart. Lassie appeared the following year in *Courage of Lassie*, starring Elizabeth Taylor and Frank Morgan. After being employed by the army as a killer dog and recovering from shell shock, she eventually manages to return home.

Other creatures occasionally were featured in war films. *Keep 'Em Rolling* (1934), for example, focused on Rodney, a horse that saved Walter Huston's life during World War I. Francis, the talking mule, became the subject of a popular film series in the early 1950s. ∎

Dogs of War, The (1981), UA. *Dir.* John Irwin; *Sc.* Gary DeVore, George Malko; *Cast includes:* Christopher Walken, Tom Berenger, Colin Blakely, Hugh Millais, Maggie Scott.

A mercenary force is sent into a fictitious West African country to get rid of a corrupt president in this routine action drama. Christopher Walken is hired by a competitive mining company to organize the coup. He hires a group of professionals who are experts in their particular fields. He then proceeds to visit the country first, posing as a photographer for a national magazine. This gives him the opportunity to study the layout of the president's quarters as well as the strengths and weaknesses of the military force.

Unfortunately, the last part of the film comprises the typical bloodbath of killings, bombings and display of assorted sophisticated weapons that audiences have experienced in dozens of similar plots. One mildly unexpected turn of events occurs at the end. Street-smart Walken, aware that those who have hired him are just as corrupt as the present regime, kills their puppet candidate and helps install the "people's choice," a humane leader he met in prison on his earlier journey. Maggie Scott plays an attractive black woman whom Walken meets on his first trip to the African country. Colin Blakely portrays an alcoholic B.B.C. television journalist working on a documentary in the land targeted for the coup. ∎

Doing Their Bit (1918). See Spy Comedies. ∎

Donovan, William J. See Office of Strategic Services. ∎

Don't Cry, It's Only Thunder (1982), Sanrio Communications. *Dir.* Peter Werner; *Sc.* Paul Hensler; *Cast includes:* Dennis Christopher, Susan Saint James, Lisa Lu, James Whitmore, Jr.

A no-account medic is redeemed through the help of an army doctor in this Vietnam War drama. Dennis Christopher portrays the medic who would rather deal in drugs than become involved in the effects of the war on the civilian population. When his army buddy, who has been helping two Vietnamese nuns and a group of war orphans, is mortally wounded, Christopher promises to carry on in his place temporarily. But obtaining food and other supplies becomes too much of a burden for him and he considers abandoning the project.

Susan Saint James, as the army doctor who at first assists him, persuades Christopher, who by this time has given up trading in drugs and other black market goods, to continue to aid the orphans. Harassed by his superiors and an enemy attack, he perseveres. He grows fond of a 12-year-old mute girl whom he plans to adopt and take back to the States, but she is killed by a terrorist bomb.

Although the film does not deal with the political conflict in this war-torn country, the U.S., in a peripheral sense, appears to be partly responsible for the devastation and suffering. Regardless of who is to blame, the children, the film suggests, are always the victims of war. ∎

Don't Go Near the Water (1957). See War Humor. ∎

Don't Write Letters (1922), Metro. *Dir.* George D. Baker; *Sc.* George D. Baker; *Cast includes:* Gareth Hughes, Bartine Burkett, Herbert Hayes.

In this World War I comedy a store clerk (Gareth Hughes) gets called for military service. Slight of figure, he dreams of becoming a hero during the war. Once in France he is assigned the job of cook. As if this were not degrading enough, the quartermaster supplies him with clothing several sizes too large, making him look even more ridiculous. When one of the shirts contains a letter from a sewing machine operator inviting the wearer to write back, he does so but assumes the role of a much larger figure. After the war he returns to the States, finds the girl and says he is the friend of the letter writer—a heroic soldier who died bravely in battle. Eventually he confesses all, and the girl takes a liking to him. The film was remade as *A Letter for Evie* for World War II audiences in 1945 and featured John Carroll and Marsha Hunt. ∎

Doolittle, James H. (1896–). The aircraft carrier U.S.S. *Hornet*, carrying a force of specially equipped B-25s, steamed toward Japan early in the morning of April 18, 1942. Lt. Col. James H. Doolittle, then 46, commanded the air group. His mission, operating under the cover name of First Special Aviation Project, was to lead a daring carrier-borne air strike against the Japanese homeland and bring the destructive effects of World War II, for the first time, directly to the Japanese people. Doolittle and his group succeeded in carrying out the imaginatively conceived raid. The force struck military targets in Tokyo, Yokohama, Nagoya, Kobe and Yokosuka. He later received the Medal of Honor and immediate promotion to brigadier general in the Army Air Force.

Destination Tokyo (1943), starring Cary Grant, concerned an American submarine assigned to Tokyo Bay where a meteorologist was sent ashore to gather weather information for the upcoming bombing. The preparations for the raid and the attack itself was recounted in much greater detail in *30 Seconds Over Tokyo* (1944), with Spencer Tracy portraying a humane and resolute Doolittle. The raid played a minor role in *Behind the Rising Sun* (1943), a drama about a Japanese family torn apart by the war. Doolittle's raid was one of the boldest strokes of World War II. Coming at a time when Japan seemed to be unstoppable in Asia and the Pacific, the raid, besides boosting American morale, caused a profound shock to the Japanese who had come to believe that their island kingdom was beyond harm. It caused greater destruction than anticipated, partly because of the unprepared state of Japan's air defenses.

Of the 16 planes, one made it to Vladivostok in the U.S.S.R., where its crew members were temporarily interred. Several crash-landed, one was ditched in the sea, and the others were abandoned by their crews, many of whom, including Doolittle, parachuted to safety in China. The Japanese captured eight fliers. Three were executed, one died in confinement and four survived forty months of solitary imprisonment before being freed at the war's end. *The Purple Heart* (1944), a blatant wartime propaganda film, presented stereotyped brutal Japanese military leaders who served as foils to a handful of supremely heroic captured American pilots who undergo a fictionalized account of the trial that results in their ultimate execution. After the raid, Doolittle commanded the 15th Air Force as a lieutenant general and later headed the Eighth Air Force in Europe.

Now in his nineties, Doolittle was able to hear President Reagan's farewell address which included praise for those Americans whose bold initiative and daring exploits contributed to the country's greatness. ■

Doolittle Raid. See James H. Doolittle. ■

Doomed Battalion, The (1932), U. *Dir.* Cyril Gardner; *Sc.* Luis Trenker, Carl Hartl; *Cast includes:* Tala Birell, Luis Trenker, Victor Varconi, Albert Conti, Henry Gordon, Henry Armetta.

A World War I drama shot on location in the Austrian Tryrol, the plot concerns an Austrian battalion holding a vital mountaintop stronghold that is being undermined by an attacking Italian army. The doomed defenders are ordered to hold their position at all costs. Victor Varconi, as the commander of the Italian soldiers, stations himself at the home of his old friend, currently a scout (Luis Trenker) fighting with the besieged troops. Trenker skis down the mountain and penetrates the enemy lines to learn the exact time the Italians plan to set off the explosions. He is the last hope for the soldiers guarding the stronghold.

The film had been made previously in Germany with Trenker as its author and in the same role. Perhaps this explains why Austrians are portrayed as heroic figures in the film—an unusual role for them in a Hollywood production. It was remade again in 1940 as *Ski Patrol*. The incident involving the undermining was based on an actual event that occurred during the war, except that the real victims were Italians. The soldiers who quietly waited while the Germans dug a tunnel were blown up. A similar situation appeared in the 1936 World War I drama *The Road to Glory*, directed by Howard Hawks. ■

Dough Boys (1930), MGM. *Dir.* Edward Sedgwick; *Sc.* Al Boasberg, Sidney Lazarus; *Cast includes:* Buster Keaton, Sally Eilers, Cliff Edwards, Edward Brophy, Victor Potel.

Silent screen comedian Buster Keaton portrays a wealthy bon vivant who blunders his way into the army in this World War I comedy. While seeking to employ a chauffeur, Keaton enters a recruiting office and is quickly inducted into the service. Following some farcical military training he and his outfit are sent to France. Several humorous, although implausible, bits occur in the war sequences, including Keaton's accidental capture of the enemy's war maps. Edward Brophy portrays the tough, shouting sergeant while Cliff "Ukelele Ike" Edwards sings a few ditties. The film ends with Keaton appointing all his war buddies to his board of directors with their former sergeant as a porter. ■

Doughboys in Ireland (1943), Col. *Dir.* Lew Landers; *Sc.* Howard J. Green; *Cast includes:* Kenny Baker, Jeff Donnell, Lynn Merrick, Guy Bonham.

An odd mixture of music, comedy and drama, this minor World War II film stars singer Kenny Baker as bandleader-singer turned soldier who is shipped to Ireland. He pines for his girl (Lynn Merrick) back in the States who has fallen for a producer. Meanwhile, he meets and falls in love with an Irish lass, played by Jeff Donnell. Baker, as part of a Ranger unit, is wounded during a raid on an undesignated coast. When he is discharged from the hospital, he returns to the arms of his Irish sweetheart. ■

Doughgirls, The (1944). See Washington, D.C. ■

Down in San Diego (1941). See Spy Films: the Talkies. ■

Draft 258 (1918). See Propaganda Films: World War I. ■

Dragon Seed (1944), MGM. *Dir.* Jack Conway, Harold Bucquet; *Sc.* Marguerite Roberts, Jane Murfin; *Cast includes:* Katharine Hepburn, Walter Huston, Aline MacMahon, Turhan Bey, Akim Tamiroff, Hurd Hatfield.

Inhabitants of a once-peaceful and docile Chinese village fall under the oppressive yoke of the Japanese, following their invasion in 1937. The farmers slowly begin to resist their oppressors. Katharine Hepburn and Turhan Bey, as a young married couple, put aside their private dreams to fight against the enemy occupiers. Walter Huston and Aline MacMahon portray Bey's hard-working parents who do not understand the violence that the Japanese have brought to the peaceful community. Hurd Hatfield, as Huston's youngest son, changes from a sensitive youth to a vicious killer who enjoys slaying the enemy. Hepburn and Bey, who had left when the Japanese entered the village, return home the following season with their new-born son. They see their child as a symbol of the new China—defiant and proud. Together with Huston's two other sons, the couple organize the villagers into a guerrilla band. Huston at first follows his philosophy of passiveness. "All men are brothers," he affirms, "and they should not kill each other." When he sees that his principles have not worked, he joins the guerrillas on their raids.

Bey and Hepburn encourage the local farmers to burn their crops, thereby depriving the enemy troops of food. Again, Huston at first resists. He then realizes that this is the only way to drive the enemy from his country. "There are others like me with faces I have never seen," he says. "Elsewhere there are men who love peace and long for good and will fight to get these things. A stranger is no longer a stranger to me but a man like me." Huston, his wife and other members of his family leave for the hills as they watch their home and fields ablaze. They see other fires set by their neighbors. Soon the entire valley and village are on fire. Lionel Barrymore provides the off-screen narration. Based on the novel by Pearl S. Buck and made at a time when Hollywood used Caucasians for major Oriental roles, the film pays tribute to the stubborn spirit of the Chinese people in the face of adversity.

Dragonfly Squadron (1954), AA. *Dir.* Lesley Selander; *Sc.* John Champion; *Cast includes:* John Hodiak, Barbara Britton, Bruce Bennett, Jess Barker.

This Korean War drama concerns the building of a South Korean air force prior to the North's invasion. John Hodiak, as a battle-hardened air force major, drives those in his charge almost to the breaking point. When the inevitable attack from the North comes, the men are ready. The Communist tanks push south ready to create havoc, but U.S. planes take to the skies and blast the enemy to smithereens in this routine tale. A romantic triangle occurs when Hodiak renews an old love affair with Barbara Britton, now married to a doctor (Bruce Bennett). ■

Drake, Sir Francis. See *Seven Seas to Calais* (1962). ■

Drum Beat (1954), WB. *Dir.* Delmer Daves; *Sc.* Delmer Daves; *Cast includes:* Alan Ladd, Audrey Dalton, Marisa Pavan, Robert Keith, Charles Bronson, Warner Anderson.

Alan Ladd portrays a frontier Indian fighter assigned by President Grant to negotiate a peace treaty with the Modocs in this action drama set during the Modoc Indian uprising in 1869. The story takes place on the California-Oregon border where Ladd works out a fragile peace with the Indian chief, Captain Jack (Charles Bronson). But a series of killings and retaliations hamper the peace goals. Audrey Dalton provides the romantic interest in this routine tale. Marisa Pavan, as a young Modoc woman, falls for Ladd and sacrifices her life to save him. Robert Keith, as a stage driver, is responsible for a massacre. Several action sequences, including skirmishes and a full-fledged battle between the Modocs and the cavalry, add some excitement to the film.

Historically, the Modocs, in trying to reclaim their native lands, did something no other Indian tribe had ever accomplished in the long history of Indian wars with the U.S. government. They killed a regular army general. Other officers with the rank of general died during the Indian wars, but they did not have regular army commissions at the time.

A portion of this tribe, numbering about 60 families under Chief Kintpuash, commonly called Captain Jack by whites (played by Charles Bronson in the above film), left the Klamath Indian Reservation in southern Oregon in 1872 to reclaim and resettle ancestral lands in northern California. The Modocs rebuffed peaceful attempts to return them to the reservation. When the cavalry responded forcefully and attacked the Modoc village, the band returned the fire and retreated to a wilderness of lava beds with many caves and ravines around Tule Lake.

Kintpuash, with some 60 warriors, held off for four months an army force that at one point reached a thousand soldiers. The government again tried diplomacy, but at a peace meeting on April 11, 1873, Captain Jack shot dead the head of the commission, General Edward Canby. Historical sources indicate that Kintpuash had been taunted by an aggressive faction to prove his bravery and gain a reservation on ancestral lands in one dramatic stroke. The reaction of the government and the nation was totally opposite to what the Modocs had hoped for. Citing the incident as proof that Indians could not be trusted, the army renewed its attacks on the band and gradually hunted them down. Kintpuash and three of his followers were hanged on October 3, 1873. Their heads were cut off and shipped to the Army Medical Museum in Washington. Remaining members of the rebellious band, numbering 155, were resettled in Oklahoma, 1,500 miles to the east. Others remained on a reservation in Oregon. ∎

Drums Along the Mohawk (1939), TCF.

Dir. John Ford; *Sc.* Lamar Trotti, Sonya Levien; *Cast includes:* Claudette Colbert, Henry Fonda, Edna May Oliver, John Carradine.

The hardships faced by settlers of the Mohawk Valley during the American Revolution provide the subject of this historical drama. The film centers on a young farmer and his wife whose lives are affected by the political and military forces of the period. Henry Fonda and Claudette Colbert play a newly married couple who settle in the valley. When the Indians rise up, Fonda must leave, along with other members of the militia, to hunt down the raiding party. A renegade white (John Carradine) stirs up the local tribes to slaughter the peaceful settlers.

John Ford, the director, imbued the work, based on the novel by Walter Edmonds, with local color, action and several moments of comic relief chiefly provided by Edna May Oliver. One particularly poignant sequence concerns the return of the rag-tag remnants of the militia. As the tired and wounded men pass slowly through the village, anxious wives and children search desperately for their loved ones. The film provides lively battle sequences between the settlers and the hostiles but does not depict any major historical event concerning the American Revolution. It does, however, have the distinction of being one of the earliest outdoor historical dramas to be photographed in Technicolor. ∎

Drums in the Deep South (1951), RKO.

Dir. William Cameron Menzies; *Sc.* Philip Yordan, Sidney Harmon; *Cast includes:* James Craig, Barbara Payton, Guy Madison, Barton MacLane.

The plot of this Civil War drama concerns the efforts of a handful of Confederate soldiers to delay General Sherman's march on Atlanta. James Craig portrays a Southern major in charge of a group of 20 Confederate volunteers who are entrenched atop a mountain precipice, a natural fortress, from which they shell the Union general's supply train and repel attempts to dislodge them. A Yankee officer (Guy Madison), a former friend of Craig, is faced with a personal dilemma when he is ordered to blow up the mountain. Barbara Payton, as the wife of a Southern officer, renews her relationship with Craig, her former lover, and spies for him. When Madison mines the entire mountain, she goes to Craig to convince him to surrender, but she is mortally wounded accidentally. Craig orders his men to leave, but he remains, holding Payton in his arms, as the mountain is blown to bits.

The film opens in Georgia in 1861 on the eve of the war. The passage of time is shown in brief battle vignettes until 1864, when the chief plot unfolds. Aside from the slight incident of the two officer-friends from opposing sides, the film offers little insight concerning the war. One of two final screen statements, almost as an afterthought, reads: "Out of the chaos of brother against brother, came a new realization of our common destiny." ∎

Drums of the Desert (1940), Mon.

Dir. George Waggner; *Sc.* Dorothy Reid, Joseph West; *Cast includes:* Ralph Byrd, Lorna Gray, Peter George Lynn, William Castello, Mantan Moreland.

A routine adventure drama of the Foreign Legion, the film stars Ralph Byrd as a lieutenant in the famed Legion. He competes with another officer, Peter George Lynn, for the affections of Lorna Gray until Lynn makes the final sacrifice for both the service and the lovers. The film introduces modern war techniques into the Legion by way of parachute troops, led by comic character actor Mantan Moreland, who probably was on vacation from one of Charlie Chan's detective cases. The film provides some skirmishes with desert tribes in this low-budget tale. ■

Druse Revolt of 1925–1927. See *Sirocco* (1951). ■

Duck Soup (1933). See War Humor. ■

Duel at Diablo (1966), UA. *Dir.* Ralph Nelson; *Sc.* Marvin Albert, Michel Grilikhes; *Cast includes:* James Garner, Sidney Poitier, Bibi Anderson, Dennis Weaver.

Warring Apaches attack a U.S. Cavalry column in this action drama. James Garner portrays an army scout whose Comanche wife was killed by the Apache. Sidney Poitier, as an ex-soldier, sells horses to the cavalry. At first he remains detached in the wars between the hostiles and the whites but eventually takes sides with the soldiers. Bill Travers, as a cavalry lieutenant, has the thankless job of leading the green troops who are attacked by the Apaches. Bibi Anderson plays the wife of a freight driver (Dennis Weaver). Captured by the Apaches and then rescued, she prefers to return to the tribe rather than stay with Weaver. The film provides plenty of action as the two sides battle it out. ■

Dugan of the Dugouts (1928). See Service Comedy. ■

Dunkirk. This port city in northern France became the scene of an almost miraculous evacuation of more than 330,000 British, French and other Allied troops following a German breakthrough early in World War II. Trapped by the Germans and with their backs to the English Channel, these forces faced certain annihilation or surrender. Between May 26 and June 4, 1940, 220 navy ships and 660 other vessels such as sloops, yachts and assorted private craft joined in Operation Dynamo, a bold and desperate plan to rescue the trapped men. The British suffered heavy losses at sea, including six destroyers sunk and eleven damaged; all equipment had to be abandoned at Dunkirk. But the troops who were brought safely to the shores of England would later serve effectively in defeating the Germans.

Dunkirk became a topic in several Hollywood films, often as a rallying cry. An American flier (Tyrone Power) joins the British in *A Yank in the R.A.F* (1941) and takes part in the Dunkirk evacuation. In *Mrs. Miniver* (1942) civilian Walter Pidgeon is called upon to help in the evacuation of Allied troops stranded at Dunkirk. He and scores of other Englishmen prepare their small craft at night and sail off across the channel. *Captains of the Clouds* (1942) concerns Canadian bush pilots of the northwest who enlist in the Royal Canadian Air Force. They are motivated by a radio broadcast of Sir Winston Churchill's speech following the battle of Dunkirk. In the epic production *The Longest Day* (1962), about the Normandy invasion, Peter Lawford, as a Scottish officer, reminds his men of the Dunkirk evacuation just before they hit the beaches. "Most of you have had your feet wet before—Dunkirk, Dieppe, Norway," he says solemnly. "We all know what it means to be driven into the sea. In a few hours from now we're going back from the sea, and this time we're going to stay."

On at least one occasion Dunkirk became the subject of criticism. In *The Devil's Brigade* (1968) Canadian officer Cliff Robertson attempts to enlighten William Holden, the American senior officer of the newly formed brigade, of the virtues of his Canadians. "Many of the Canadian units fought at Dunkirk," he explains, "so it might be possible that you may want to learn a lesson from their combat experience." "Yes, I might," Holden replies, "if you had won at Dunkirk. You lost. I'm training this outfit to win. Good night, major." ■

E

Eagle and the Hawk, The (1933), Par. *Dir.* Stuart Walker; *Sc.* Bogart Rogers, Seton I. Miller; *Cast includes:* Fredric March, Cary Grant, Jack Oakie, Carole Lombard, Sir Guy Standing.

Fredric March portrays a conscience-stricken pilot in the Royal Flying Corps during World War I who cannot adjust to the death and slaughter of the conflict. After a brief encounter with Carole Lombard, whom he meets while on leave in London, he returns to duty. He cracks psychologically after flying too many missions and seeing many of his fellow aviators killed in battle. After drinking too much and growing sick of the futility of the war, he retires to his quarters and commits suicide. Cary Grant, as a fellow airman who has not as yet earned his wings, salvages March's reputation. He takes March's body up in a plane, stages a crash and riddles the ship with bullets to make it appear as if the air ace has died in combat. Grant's thoughtful act was to be repeated three years later by Franchot Tone in *Suzy* (1936), a World War I spy drama. This time around, Tone performs the deed for none other than Grant. Some of the footage was borrowed from previous air dramas, including *Wings* (1927), *Lilac Time* (1928) and *The Dawn Patrol* (1930).

The story digressed from the familiar air adventure films that were popular during the early sound period following the enormous success of the silent epic, *Wings*, which launched the cycle. Where such films as *Hell's Angels*, *Young Eagles* and *Hell in the Heavens* stressed individual combat, derring-do in the face of danger and sacrifice—all accepted elements of escapist adventure, *The Eagle and the Hawk* focused on a pilot who, after seeing his comrades go down in flames, could no longer bear the brutality and horrors of war. March gives a stirring speech against war and its cost in human lives before he takes his own life. Grant's actions at the end add a cynical note to the already downbeat theme. ■

Eagle and the Hawk, The (1950), Par. *Dir.* Lewis R. Foster; *Sc.* Geoffrey Homes, Lewis R. Foster; *Cast includes:* John Payne, Rhonda Fleming, Dennis O'Keefe, Thomas Gomez.

Agents of Napoleon III, as part of their plot to make Maximilian the emperor of Mexico, attempt to instigate the followers of Juarez to declare war on Texas in this action drama set in 1863. John Payne stars as a Texas Ranger who is assigned to escort a government agent, played by Dennis O'Keefe, into Mexico. O'Keefe's job is to foil the impending attack on the Lone Star state, and when he is killed before he can accomplish his mission, Payne carries on for him. Rhonda Fleming, as the wife of the chief conspirator, falls in love with Payne and assists him in exposing her husband's plot to the principal Mexican general (Thomas Gomez). ■

Eagle Squadron (1942), U. *Dir.* Arthur Lubin; *Sc.* Norman Reilly Raine; *Cast includes:* Robert Stack, Diana Barrymore, John Loder, Eddie Albert, Nigel Bruce, Leif Erickson.

This World War II drama tells the story of a group of American fliers who volunteer to fight alongside the British before the United States entered the war. The film covers their exploits in the air war against Nazi planes and targets and their lives while off duty. Robert Stack, who heads the handful of Americans, falls in love with Diana Barrymore between assignments. He also accompanies a Commando raid on the French coast and returns with a captured enemy aircraft of advanced design. The film also shows the devastation caused by Nazi air raids on England. John Loder, Eddie Albert, Leif Erickson and Jon Hall portray American airmen in Stack's squadron. For authenticity, the British government provided producer Walter Wanger with actual air combat footage as well as detailed sequences of British raids in Nazi-occupied Europe. Quentin Reynolds, the American war correspondent, provides the patriotic foreword which introduces the American pilots and their motivation for forming the Eagle Squadron. American movie audiences were already sympathetic toward Britain's lone struggle and moved by the horrors of the war and the ruthlessness of the Nazis through such films as *Mrs. Miniver*, released earlier the same year.

The first of three Eagle Squadrons came into existence in September 1940. The American fliers, wearing an eagle patch on their left sleeve, saw action over Europe and the Mediterranean. They downed more than 70 German planes and sustained 100 losses, including those killed, captured or missing in action. All three squadrons were transferred to the Eighth Air Force in September 1942. The fliers were permitted to take their British Spitfire fighter planes with them. ∎

Eagle's Wings, The (1916), Bluebird. *Dir.* Rufus Steele; *Sc.* Maude Grange; *Cast includes:* Grace Carlyle, Vola Smith, Herbert Rawlinson, Charles Hill Malles, Charles Gunn.

Chiefly a World War I preparedness film advocating a stronger industrial base for the U.S., the drama re-anacts Pancho Villa's raid across the Mexican border in 1916 on Columbus, New Mexico, which resulted in the deaths of several American civilians. The Mexican bandit-general, embittered by President Wilson's support of Pancho's foes, decided to attack American property and citizens on both sides of the border. Wilson reacted quickly by sending General Pershing and troops on a punitive expedition into Mexico the same year. ∎

Earhart, Amelia. See *Flight for Freedom* (1943). ∎

Early, Jubal A. See Battles of Shenandoah Valley. ∎

Easter Uprising. See Irish Rebellions. ∎

Edge of Darkness (1943), WB. *Dir.* Lewis Milestone; *Sc.* Robert Rossen; *Cast includes:* Errol Flynn, Ann Sheridan, Walter Huston, Nancy Coleman.

A World War II drama about a Nazi-occupied Norwegian town whose inhabitants rise up against the invaders, the film traces the growth of a typical resistance movement. Errol Flynn and Ann Sheridan portray two local leaders of the underground who organize the other townspeople following a series of brutal acts by the Nazis. One particularly dramatic scene occurs in a church where a wounded survivor of another town reveals how its people, aided by weapons delivered by British planes, revolted against their oppressors. The townspeople listen quietly and vote for direct action. Loyalty and nationalism run high in the community. The town doctor, played by Walter Huston, condemns his brother-in-law for collaborating with the Nazis; the physician's daughter (Ann Sheridan) publicly denounces her own brother as a traitor. By the end of the film, when fresh German troops enter the Norwegian town, all they find are the bodies of the former Nazi occupiers. The civilian population has vanished. The women and children escaped in fishing boats to England while the men retreated to the mountains to continue the struggle to free their land. The film ends with President Roosevelt's words: "If anyone wonders why this war is being fought, let him look to Norway . . . And if there's anyone who has doubts of the democratic will to win, again I say, let him look to Norway."

Segments of the film recall two similar works that were released the same year. The conflict of wills between an elderly retired Norwegian schoolteacher (Morris Carnovsky) and a German officer parallels scenes in *This Land Is Mine*, released the same year, in which a French schoolteacher (Charles Laughton) speaks out for liberty, civil disobedience and the rights of man. In *Edge of Darkness* Carnovsky enlightens the young officer on why the New Order is doomed to failure. "What you don't understand is that the individual man must stand against you like a rock," the old scholar states. The German beats him. "We are not animals," the teacher continues, unafraid, "we are men. That is the foundation of law. You cannot win."

The Moon Is Down, also released the same

A local priest of a Nazi-occupied Norwegian village helps the badly beaten Morris Carnovsky, a symbol of defiance against totalitarian brutality. *Edge of Darkness* (1943).

year, also deals with Norwegian resistance, Quislings and Nazi brutality in a peaceful village. In fact, the name of Quisling is referred to several times, always with derision and disgust by the proud Norwegians who eventually take up arms against their occupiers and kill them all. ■

Edson, Merritt A. "Red Mike." See *Marine Raiders* (1944). ■

Eichmann, Adolf. See *Operation Eichmann* (1961). ■

Eight Iron Men (1952), Col. *Dir.* Edward Dmytryk; *Sc.* Harry Brown; *Cast includes:* Bonar Colleano, Arthur Franz, Lee Marvin, Richard Kiley.

A squad of G.I.s, who have sought refuge in a deserted, shell-scarred house, struggle to rescue a fellow soldier pinned down by machine-gun fire in this World War II character study of men under stress. The group exchange robust stories and wisecracks, make futile attempts to save the trapped man

and fantasize about their sex lives as they wait for further orders. Bonar Colleano portrays the infantryman who dreams of women ready for conquest. He is also the one who quietly goes out to rescue his buddy. ■

84 Charlie Mopic (1989), New Century/ Vista. *Dir.* Patrick Duncan; *Sc.* Patrick Duncan; *Cast includes:* Richard Brooks, Christopher Burgard, Nicholas Cascone, Jonathan Emerson, Byron Thames.

A Vietnam War drama, the film tells its bitter-sweet story from the point of view of an army cameraman who accompanies a six-man reconnaissance squad. Despite the familiar plot cliches about a squad on a specific mission, director Patrick Duncan realistically conveys the camaraderie of the men. They refer to each other as "brothers" and huddle together in moments of quiet. When one is killed, another covers his fallen buddy's body tenderly. The cameraman's point of view is refreshing and perhaps more truthful in capturing the Vietnam War experience than several other films of the genre that burst upon the screen in the late 1980s. The term "mopic" in the title refers to "motion picture." ■

Eisenhower, Dwight David (1890–1969).

An early scene in the epic World War II drama, *The Longest Day* (1962), shows General Eisenhower at a critical meeting discussing with his staff whether the western Allies should go ahead, despite bad weather, with a previously postponed invasion of Normandy. He listens to the comments and then makes the final decision that the invasion is on. That scene captured the essence of one of Eisenhower's great talents—his ability to work with and lead a diverse group of military men in the complex undertakings of modern war.

From the time he graduated from West Point in 1916 to World War II, Eisenhower was just another bright but hardly distinguished army officer. His brilliant performance in the army maneuvers of 1941 led to his appointment in Washington as army chief of operations. His work there led to a number of higher posts.

He took command of U.S. forces in Europe early in 1942, only a few months after America's entry into World War II, and headed American units in the North African landings (November, 1942). In 1943 he became chief of all Allied forces in North Africa and later that year directed the invasions of Sicily and Italy. By the end of the year, Eisenhower was appointed supreme commander of the Allied Expeditionary Force in Britain. He had to work with such strong personalities as Britain's General Montgomery and France's General DeGaulle. Eisenhower's aptitude for directing large, complex operations played a great role in the success of the Normandy invasion (June, 1944) and ultimate defeat of Nazi Germany in Europe. His abilities and popularity ultimately led to postwar appointments as army chief of staff and supreme commander of N.A.T.O., followed by election to two terms as U.S. President (1952–1960).

Unfortunately for the movie-going public, Hollywood never made a full-length film biography of Eisenhower, unlike the lavish treatment afforded to his contemporary—MacArthur (with whom Eisenhower clashed repeatedly)—and to some underlings such as Patton. Eisenhower was a complex, administratively brilliant military leader with a warm personality, but not one who had the marked eccentricities or grandiose egos of some of his contemporaries. Consequently, Hollywood may not have deemed him a worthwhile box-office gamble. Besides the large-scale film about Normandy mentioned above, Eisenhower appeared in person in the opening sequence of the documentary *The True Glory* (1945). He introduces the story of how the combined Allied effort brought about the defeat of the Axis in Europe from D-Day to the fall of Berlin. ■

El Alamein, Battles of. See Alamein, Battles of El. ■

El Alamein (1953), Col. *Dir.* Fred F. Sears; *Sc.* Herbert Purdum, George Worthington Yates; *Cast includes:* Scott Brady, Edward Ashley, Robin Hughes, Rita Moreno.

Scott Brady portrays a civilian who maintains and supplies tanks to the British African forces in this World War II drama. He and a tank crew lose their way in the desert and rest at a nearby oasis which they discover is a supply depot for General Rommel's tanks. They fight off repeated Nazi attacks and manage to destroy the dump before they are rescued. The story is told in flashback as Brady, ten years later, returns to visit the place of the battle.

This is another low-budget action drama that has little to do with the battle mentioned in its title. Another film that exploits a famous battle in its title is *Battle of the Coral Sea* (1959), with Cliff Robertson. In this instance, the action takes place on an island on the eve of the battle. ■

El Salvador: Another Vietnam (1981), Icarus. *Dir.* Glenn Silber, Tete Vasconcellos.

A documentary about the civil strife in El Salvador, the film makes a strong case for its premise that American foreign policy in that Central American country is again leading us down the road to another Vietnam. The similarities include the now familiar stages of economic aid, the sending of advisers and the support of an oppressive military regime supposedly tough on Communism. Once again, the film suggests, the U.S. has become entangled in a complex struggle between a right-wing government and a resistant peasantry that see themselves as freedom fighters. The work consists of a compilation of newsreel film borrowed from numerous countries, including Canada, Holland, France, Mexico,

Great Britain and the U.S., as well as several interviews with religious and political figures. ∎

Eleni (1985). See Greek Civil War. ∎

Elizabeth I (1533–1603). As Queen of England (1558–1603), the daughter of Henry VIII and Anne Boleyn ruled through a period that saw England's fortunes rise from a low point to one of eminence in colonization, trade, naval power and literature. During her reign she engaged in a long period of undeclared war with Spain, whose monarch, Philip II, at one time a suitor in marriage, resented her support of Protestant forces in France and the Lowlands. She encouraged Sir Francis Drake to attack Spanish treasure ships and settlements, particularly in the New World. *The Sea Hawk* (1940), with Flora Robson as Elizabeth, depicts the court intrigues of Spain and England and has Philip describing her as "barren and treacherous." In *Seven Seas to Calais* (1963) Elizabeth (Irene Worth) is seen as a clever, conniving ruler who enjoys material possessions, especially those stolen from Spain. "We are both pirates," she says jokingly to Sir Francis Drake, her chief source of income.

The defeat of the Spanish Armada in 1588 raised both her and England's prestige. Though she never married, Elizabeth, in her earlier years, used the lure of marriage as a diplomatic tool. She had domestic favorites such as Robert Dudley, Earl of Leicester, and Robert Devereux, Earl of Essex, a volatile military and court leader whom Elizabeth had executed for reportedly being involved in a plot to usurp the powers of the throne. Michael Curtiz's lavish historical drama, *The Private Lives of Elizabeth and Essex* (1939), focuses on this affair. Bette Davis and Errol Flynn portray the title characters. ∎

Empire films. Hollywood produced several adventure dramas with British colonial backgrounds. Known as "empire films" and reaching their peak in the 1930s, they were distinguished by their use of local color, pageantry and national heroism. Columns of stalwart troops patrolled the vast deserts of the Sudan or defended the rugged terrains and borders of India. Exotic places like the Khyber Pass, Khartoum and Omdurman and legendary names such as Kitchener and Gordon lent authenticity and a heightened sense of anticipated excitement to each film. Experienced career officers brought English law and order to these regions, knew their enemy and understood the role of empire. They rode tall at the head of their columns. Colonial governors and commanders of remote outposts, usually played by such perennial character actors as C. Aubrey Smith and Henry Stephenson, dealt firmly with rebellious leaders who incited the natives. These professional soldiers, like the films themselves, exemplified imperial England's belief that it was destined to take up the "white man's burden." They also symbolized the individual's call to service.

What the American studios' stake in this genre was, aside from entertainment, can only be conjectured. Were these films a reflection of American values as well as British? Was America, consciously or otherwise, sanctioning imperialism and racism? Upon closer scrutiny there appears to be an affinity between American and British attitudes. Empire films delineated the white man's superiority over other races which were seen as barbaric and treacherous. The plots and themes promoted imperialism or, to a lesser degree, paternalism, as the only proper form of government for these peoples. The films, with their conventional heroes and villains and their themes of honor and glory, suggested a common bond between England and the U.S.

The military problems of insurrection and external dangers that faced outnumbered British troops in their far-flung empire were similar to those that U.S. troops encountered in the 1800s by American Indian uprisings in the West, Southwest and Mexico. The social attitudes of a class-structured society were more than implied in these films. Like the colonial natives who virtually never joined the English for tea, the American Indian or Mexican rarely socialized with the whites. As a result of the empathy they created for England, empire films contributed to the pro-British propaganda that swept through America when World War II erupted.

Duty and honor were two of the mainstays of these dramas. In *Four Feathers* (1915) an English officer's honor comes into question when he resigns his commission instead of marching off to war in the Sudan with the rest of his regiment. To prove to his comrades and fiancee that he is not a coward, he journeys alone to North Africa where, by performing heroic acts, he wins back his respect.

The film was remade as another silent in 1929. England finally produced its own stirring Technicolor adaptation of the A. E. W. Mason novel in 1939.

The British officer was expected to uphold the traditions of the service even if it meant undergoing physical torture as seen in *Lives of a Bengal Lancer* (1935), starring Gary Cooper, Franchot Tone and Richard Cromwell. In this tale of India, Cromwell, as a young English lieutenant and son of the regiment's colonel, is duped by a bellicose native chieftain who holds the officer captive. The colonel, suspecting a trap, refuses to send his troops out to rescue his son. Cooper and Tone, as the boy's comrades and fellow officers, take it upon themselves to try to rescue him but are captured. All three are subjected to torture before the climactic battle restores the honor of England. The film was so successful that its major plot elements became the basis for two subsequent diverse adventures. In *Storm Over Bengal* (1938), a minor empire entry, Cromwell once again portrays a youth who is forced to redeem himself by saving the regiment. The father-son theme was repeated in *Geronimo* (1939), a routine western.

Service for the British soldier often meant more than sacrifice and personal danger. If his family accompanied him, it meant that their lives, too, were often at risk. The first half of *The Charge of the Light Brigade* (1936), starring Errol Flynn, deals with a brutal massacre of women and children at a British outpost in India by the villain Surat Khan, a fictitious leader played by C. Henry Gordon. His only motivation for the slaughter is that England has cut off his annual stipend. Later, the light brigade, made up chiefly of fathers and husbands of the victims, exact their revenge on the Khan at Balaklava in a suicidal but glorious charge.

The British ability to influence and persuade occasionally extended to their young. In *Wee Willie Winkie* (1937), another fictitious Khan residing in the mountains of India, this time played by Caesar Romero, is about to wage war upon the British. He is ultimately convinced by the charming Shirley Temple, as the granddaughter of the English colonel, to end his hostilities against the British outpost.

The themes of honor and duty dominate *The Sun Never Sets* (1939), a drama set in Africa where a would-be dictator (Lionel Atwill) plots a world war. Douglas Fairbanks, Jr. and Basil Rathbone, as English brothers steeped in the tradition of honor and duty to family and country, serve as territorial commissioners. They manage to foil Atwill's plans. Perhaps the most popular empire film of this period is *Gunga Din*, also released in 1939. Blending comedy and romance, the plot involves a mad leader of thousands of followers of the Thuggee cult who wage war upon the British presence in India. The title character, a lowly water boy played by Sam Jaffe, sacrifices his life to save the British forces about to march into an ambush.

Even when the English gentleman was not in his own country's uniform, he brought the values of his native land with him. Percival Wren's novel of the French Foreign Legion, *Beau Geste*, was filmed three times, as a silent in 1926, and as sound versions in 1939 and 1966. The most memorable adaptation was director William Wellman's 1939 film starring Gary Cooper. Again, English honor was the subject. Cooper, to save his family's reputation, steals a counterfeit diamond and disappears into the ranks of the Legion. When some malcontent Legionnaires decide to mutiny, Cooper refuses to take part, claiming he took an allegiance to the French flag and to the corps.

By the early 1940s the action and scope that were so prevalent in empire films were transferred to the combat dramas of World War II. Following the global conflict, attempts were made to resurrect the old empire films with such features as *King of the Khyber Rifles* (1953), starring Tyrone Power; *Khyber Patrol*, starring Richard Egan; *Bengal Brigade*, starring Rock Hudson; and *Charge of the Lancers*, starring Paulette Goddard and Jean-Pierre Aumont (all three released in 1954). But the old spark that ignited the genre began to flicker. Besides, the attitudes and tastes of the American audiences had changed. Twenty years later director John Huston turned out *The Man Who Would Be King* (1975), starring Michael Caine and Sean Connery. The brash adventure film of derring-do captures some of Rudyard Kipling's atmosphere of the days when the sun would never set on the British Empire. But it was too late. The spark was gone. ∎

Empire of the Sun (1987), WB. *Dir.* Steven Spielberg; *Sc.* Tom Stoppard; *Cast includes:* John Malkovich, Miranda Richardson, Nigel Havers, Christian Bale.

Director Steven Spielberg's visually attractive drama of World War II concerns a young boy's forced and sudden maturation. The film opens in 1941 in Shanghai during the Sino–Japanese War with Japan poised for battle against the U.S. and Britain. Christian Bale portrays Jim, a rich, spoiled 11-year-old who is fascinated by airplanes. His parents are part of an English community isolated from the economic and social privations of the local natives. When Shanghai is suddenly overrun by the Japanese in 1942, he becomes separated from his parents as the trio attempt to leave the crowded city. After his futile search for his mother and father among the city's chaos, he returns to his empty house. But the ransacked, once-stately home provides no solace except for a few cans of food that he finds there. When the food runs out and he realizes his parents are not returning, he ventures forth into the unfamiliar city.

He is now forced into a lonely and friendless world where he must learn to survive on his own. Hungry and exhausted, he tries to surrender to the Japanese troops who ignore him. Suspicious of a Chinese street urchin, Jim runs through the streets and back alleys. But the older boy catches him, beats him and steals his shoes. He then meets an American drifter (John Malkovich), also a victim of the conflict, who is busy scavenging for food. The drifter takes the boy to his squalid quarters that he shares with a fellow American. The trio, about to loot Jim's abandoned house, are caught by the Japanese and placed in a prison camp that is adjacent to a Japanese air field.

Jim's experiences in the camp during the next four years take their toll upon his innocence and his remembrances of things past. He idolizes the American, who manages to set up a comfortable existence for himself by wheeling and dealing with other inmates and the guards. Jim learns well the intricate ways of survival from his mentor and becomes the camp's chief scavenger, stealing and trading with consummate skill. But he retains his own sense of values. He helps an elderly English couple who had known his parents and who have taken him in. He befriends the camp doctor who continues the boy's schooling with private lessons. He cleverly ingratiates himself with the otherwise brutal camp commandant. Although he witnesses many horrors during his confinement, including the beatings and deaths of other prisoners, he is most affected by two incidents—the accidental killing of a Japanese boy whom he has befriended and his disillusionment in his American idol. The man escapes from camp without taking Jim after promising the boy he would not abandon him. Jim, who has cast off his childhood when he finally tosses his suitcase filled with cherished items of his past into a river, is finally reunited with his parents.

Spielberg presents an epic and sad picture of a youngster turned scavenger and compelled to shed his youth to survive. Other American war movies have explored the effects of war on children (*Journey for Margaret, Tomorrow the World*, etc.), but few have examined so closely the emotional and psychological impact of loss upon one child brought on by war as this film. The boy's fantasies about flying replace his thoughts about his family while the faces of his parents recede into the vague past. ■

Enchanted Cottage, The (1924, 1945). See Veterans. ■

End of the Trail (1936). See Spanish-American War. ■

Enemy, The (1928), MGM. *Dir.* Fred Niblo; *Sc.* Willis Goldbeck; *Cast includes:* Lillian Gish, Ralph Forbes, Ralph Emerson, Frank Currier, Karl Dane.

In an unusual move for the period, MGM released this film, based on a play by Channing Pollack, that presents World War I from the point of view of the enemy. The sympathetic hero and heroine are Austrian newlyweds, played by Lillian Gish and Ralph Forbes. The church bells have not stopped ringing when war is declared. A military band is heard playing martial music. Forbes answers his country's call to arms. Soon Gish has a child, but times are hard and food is scarce. She ends up in a brothel to earn enough to feed her baby. When the war ends, Forbes returns home, but the baby has died.

The many squalid scenes of Gish's existence at home and her husband's miserable life in the trenches, often juxtaposed with scenes of parades and splendid young men in spotless uniforms suggest the film's antiwar theme. It anticipates the early sound classic, *All Quiet on the Western Front*, another work that presents the war from the German side. Both show the cruelty and stupidity of war

French hostages are about to be executed in front of a church, symbolizing the Nazi contempt for religion. *The Enemy General* (1960).

and the human suffering it causes, regardless of nationality.

D.W. Griffith covered similar ground several years before Niblo's film. After having made a handful of overpowering anti-German dramas during World War I, Griffith also turned out *Isn't Life Wonderful?* in 1924, one of the earliest films to evoke sympathy for the German people who, plagued with political unrest and hunger, were paying the price of their aggression. ■

Enemy Agents Meet Ellery Queen (1942). See Detectives at War. ■

Enemy Below, The (1957), TCF. *Dir.* Dick Powell; *Sc.* Wendell Mayes; *Cast includes:* Robert Mitchum, Curt Jurgens, Al Hedison, Theodore Bikel.

A duel between the captains of an American destroyer and a Nazi U-boat provides the basis for this tense drama set during World War II. Robert Mitchum, as the commander of the destroyer escort, is a battle-hardened pursuer of submarines. Curt Jurgens, as Mitchum's German counterpart, desperately attempts to escape the destroyer. Both captains maneuver their vessels expertly until Jurgens launches a torpedo that damages the destroyer. Mitchum then tricks the German commander into surfacing and rams the submarine. Another American destroyer comes to the rescue of both crews.

Since the film was made more than two decades after the war, the character of the German captain differs from that of Nazi officers depicted in the war films made during the conflict. Jurgens is shown as an anti-Nazi German reluctantly doing his duty as a veteran military officer. ■

Enemy General, The (1960), Col. *Dir.* George Sherman; *Sc.* Dan Pepper, Burt Picard; *Cast includes:* Van Johnson, Jean Pierre Aumont, Dany Carrel, John Van Dreelen.

Spies and counterspies dominate this action drama set during World War II. Van Johnson, as an American agent in the Office of Strategic Services, is assigned to smuggle a Nazi officer out of Europe and escort him safely to England. The German, played by John Van Dreelen, has a record of murder and other crimes. He was responsible for the death of Johnson's fiancee and other innocent French citizens. When Johnson, who considers his assignment repugnant from the start, discovers that the Nazi is actually a counter-spy planning to give the Allies false information, he kills him. ∎

Enemy of Women (1944), Mon. *Dir.* Alfred Zeisler; *Sc.* Alfred Zeisler, Herbert O. Phillips; *Cast includes:* Claudia Drake, Paul Andor, Donald Woods, H. B. Warner.

A highly fictional account of the life of Joseph Goebbels, Hitler's minister of propaganda, is presented in this routine World War II drama. Paul Andor portrays Goebbels who, in the 1920s, is seen as a hard-working young playwright. He is attracted to a struggling actress (Claudia Drake) who rejects him. During the following years he advances in rank within the Nazi party, a loyal disciple of Hitler. When he discovers Drake playing minor roles in a small stock company, he uses his power to promote her career. Fearing his influence, she escapes to Austria where she marries her true love (Donald Woods). Goebbels continues to pursue her, but she is killed in an air raid. ∎

Enemy to the King, An (1916), Vitagraph. *Dir.* Frederick A. Thomson; *Sc.* H. W. Bergman; *Cast includes:* E. H. Sothern, Edith Storey, Rowland Buckstone, Fred Lewis.

Famed stage actor E.H. Sothern portrays de Launay, a loyal friend to Henry of Navarre, in this adventure drama. The villainous Duke of Guise, in control of matters in Henry's absence, desperately seeks to capture the insurgent de Launay. He uses Julie de Varion, whose father he holds prisoner, to bring in his enemy. Ultimately, de Launay escapes the duke's many traps and henchmen and confronts him in his own castle. Following a duel to the death, the duke succumbs and de Launay wins the hand of Julie, played by Edith Storey. Sothern played the same role on the stage twenty years before this early silent version was released. ∎

English Civil War. See *The Exile* (1948). ∎

Enola Gay. See *Above and Beyond* (1952). ∎

Ensign Pulver (1964). See War Humor. ∎

Epic war dramas. The epic war film, which emerged during the period of World War I, had to wait until movie companies broke out of their narrow strictures of producing only one- or two-reel dramas. Film pioneer and visionary D.W. Griffith was the first American director to realize the potential of the new medium as a means of presenting more fully developed plots as well as spectacle, but he had trouble with his superiors when he attempted to expand his early films from one to two reels. One of his 1911 Civil War dramas was made in two parts, "His Trust" and "His Trust Fulfilled," in the event that the heads of his film company, Biograph, objected to a two-reel film. His suspicions were justified. Each half was released separately.

The genre is marked by certain characteristics. Sons and relatives die bravely but in vain, often at the hands of relatives on opposite sides of the conflict. Parents who, in the early stages of the war are caught up in the fervor of nationalism, realize too late the stupidity and futility of the conflict. Several characters often express a generally cynical view of world politics. But in Hollywood the failed optimism of the older generation soon gives way to a vague optimism in the young who find new strength in love. Often, the plot of the epic film spans several years. These attributes generally define the epic, a term incorrectly applied to films with large casts or overblown production costs. Epic dramas encompass a variety of wars and political events to illustrate the effects of the conflict on families and loved ones. Both the 1917 and 1935 versions of Charles Dickens' novel *A Tale of Two Cities* cover the events of the victimized Manette family and the aristocratic Darnays before and during the French Revolution. The tale of love, revenge and redemption is played out against the dark forces of the Reign of Terror. Another epic which uses the Revolution as background is Griffith's *Orphans of the Storm* (1921). Peasants and aristocrats mingle and clash with each other as two young innocents, raised as sisters, fall into villainous hands. One sister who is blind is exploited by a beggar family while the other is abducted by a lecherous marquis for his own pleasures. Again, the Reign of Terror threatens their reunion and happiness.

Griffith's *America* (1926), which chronicles the major events of the American Revolution, and *The Birth of a Nation* (1915), his

Civil War masterpiece, marked him as a leading artist in the development of the epic. The latter film relates the experiences of two families, the Stonemans who reside in the North and the Camerons in the South. The war brings only devastation, degradation and corruption to the South. The symbolic final scene shows the union of both sides as the Southern officer embraces his Northern fiancee while a double exposure envisions the rise of cities emerging in a united land. Victor Fleming's *Gone With the Wind* (1939), perhaps the most popular epic ever made, concerns two families during the Civil War period, the O'Haras and the aristocratic Wilkses. The conflict eventually brings about the destruction of a Southern way of life that will affect future generations.

World War I was represented by several respectable epic films. Rex Ingram's *The Four Horsemen of the Apocalypse* (1921) traces the events of the French and German branches of the Desnoyers family. When the war erupts, young men from both factions march off to battle and are killed. Only the parents remain to reflect upon the holocaust which brought War, Famine, Disease and Death—the Four Horsemen of the Apocalypse. In Frank Lloyd's *Cavalcade* (1933) the Marryots, an English family, suffer through the Boer War, World War I and the Jazz Age. The final optimistic scene ends with a toast to England—and nationalism—with the hope that the country will rise again to greatness in its search for peace. John Ford's *The World Moves On* (1934) follows two families from the 1880s to the rise of Mussolini and Hitler. The Warburtons are English while the Girards have branches in both France and Germany. The patriarch of each family perishes when their ship is torpedoed in World War I by their German cousin. Years later, the matriarchal head of the Warburtons ultimately turns to pacifism when she learns of rumors of another world conflict.

The epic approach was used in several films using World War II as a background. The 1962 pale remake of *Four Horsemen of the Apocalypse*, with Glenn Ford, updates the story of two families whose sons fight on opposite sides during World War II. Otto Preminger's *In Harm's Way* (1965) may be best described as a minor epic. The film concerns the lives and romances of U.S. Navy personnel before and during World War II in the Pacific. Steven Spielberg's *Empire of the Sun* (1987), about a young English boy's experiences in a Japanese internment camp during World War II, may also be considered a minor epic.

Although Hollywood has sporadically produced other epics in the post-World War II period concerning other historical or contemporary wars, such as *Exodus* (1960), about Israel's struggle for independence, the Korean and Vietnam conflicts have yet to be given this epic treatment. *Inchon* (1981), about the landing in the title city during the Korean War, is not generally considered a Hollywood production but a joint Korean and American film associated with Reverend Moon. ∎

Escape (1940), MGM. *Dir.* Mervyn LeRoy; *Sc.* Arch Oboler, Marguerite Roberts; *Cast includes:* Norma Shearer, Robert Taylor, Conrad Veidt, Nazimova, Felix Bressart, Albert Basserman.

Norma Shearer, as the mistress of a Nazi general, helps an American (Robert Taylor) get his mother out of Germany in this pre-World War II drama set in 1936 and based on a popular novel by Ethel Vance. Taylor, a naive American, journeys to Nazi Germany to locate his missing mother. She had returned earlier to her native homeland to settle some real estate accounts but had been arrested and sentenced to death for wanting her funds in United States dollars. Taylor is frustrated by the bureaucracy he encounters in his search for information. A chance meeting with Shearer, a countess whose lover is a ruthless general (Conrad Veidt), brings Taylor a spark of hope. Through other convoluted sources he learns that his mother is in a concentration camp awaiting execution. An escape is planned and carried out.

Although released before America's entry into the war and during a period when the U.S. remained officially neutral, the film was another in a series of anti-Nazi Hollywood works that helped to underscore the harshness and brutality of Hitler's regime, a belief that many Americans already shared as a result of newspaper articles and personal experiences that daily filtered out of Nazi-occupied lands. The opening scenes show Taylor's mother being held in a concentration camp awaiting her death sentence. A young doctor who had operated on her visits the aging actress and boasts of the power and goals of the new Germany. "Our children will thank us for the world we are making for

Robert Taylor (l.) experiences the dehumanizing, Kafkaesque bureaucracy of Nazi Germany. *Escape* (1940).

them," he exclaims. His patient remains un-impressed. "For a world filled with the seed of a new hate?" she responds. "For a world in ruins?" Taylor's mother is played by Alla Nazimova, whose screen debut occurred almost a quarter of a century earlier in *War Brides* (1916), a powerful antiwar drama released before America's entry into World War I. In 1944 she portrayed Paul Henreid's mother in another wartime drama, *In Our Time*. Conrad Veidt, a native of Germany, had fled that country with his Jewish wife in 1929. He portrayed Nazis in several Hollywood features (*All Through the Night, Casablanca*) before his death in 1943. ■

"Escape From Andersonville" (1909). See Prisoners of War. ■

Escape From East Berlin (1962). See Cold War. ■

Escape From Fort Bravo (1953), MGM. *Dir.* John Sturges; *Sc.* Frank Fenton; *Cast includes*: William Holden, Eleanor Parker, John Forsythe, William Demarest.

The North-South conflict engulfs a southwest cavalry fort in this Civil War drama. William Holden portrays a strict Union cavalry captain at an Arizona outpost housing Confederate prisoners. John Forsythe plays a Confederate captain among the prisoners, some of whom are plotting to escape. Eleanor Parker, as a Southern sympathizer, helps Forsythe and his men to break out. Holden and one of his lieutenants pursue the four escapees and Parker. When he overtakes his prisoners, both groups are attacked by a war party of Mescaleros. Ultimately, the cavalry arrives in time to save those who survived the hail of arrows.

In the years following World War II, several westerns involving the U.S. Cavalry began to appear in which Union and rebel troops temporarily put aside their differences and joined forces to fight hostile Indians who were threatening other whites. As exemplified in such films as the above as well as *The Last Outpost* (1951) and *Major Dundee* (1965), this subgenre had its own unique conventions: the commanding officers of each side were usually bitter enemies; they competed for the affections of the female lead; both units fought with equal courage; and the Apaches were often the warring tribe. ∎

Escape From Hong Kong (1942). See Spy Films: the Talkies. ∎

Escape in the Desert (1945), WB. *Dir.* Edward A. Blatt; *Sc.* Thomas Job; *Cast includes:* Philip Dorn, Helmut Dantine, Jean Sullivan, Alan Hale, Irene Manning. A Dutch pilot hitchhiking across America encounters a group of Nazis who have escaped from a prisoner-of-war camp in the desert. The film is based on Robert E. Sherwood's play, *The Petrified Forest*, which was adapted for the screen in 1936. In the original, a gang of killers, led by Humphrey Bogart, takes refuge in a remote desert diner where fate also brings hiker-author Leslie Howard. In the present World War II action drama, Helmut Dantine, as the vicious leader of the Nazis, holds hostages to effect his escape while Philip Dorn portrays the flier, the humane European. Eventually, a shoot-out between the escaped prisoners and a posse resolves the problem. Jean Sullivan provides the romance in this weak drama.

The Unwritten Code (1944) also dealt with German prisoners of war. A Nazi spy (Roland Varno) plots to free German prisoners interned in the U.S. Assuming the identity of a British officer who was killed in action, he enters the U.S. as an Allied hero. ∎

Escape to Glory (1940), Col. *Dir.* John Brahm; *Sc.* P. J. Wolfson; *Cast includes:* Pat O'Brien, Constance Bennett, John Halliday, Melville Cooper, Alan Baxter.

Pat O'Brien portrays a hard-drinking drifter in this drama that takes place on the eve of World War II. A handful of Americans aboard a British freighter are heading home to avoid the impending conflict in Europe. When the vessel is at sea, the passengers receive word that war has erupted. A Nazi submarine surfaces and threatens the ship. Two passengers, a fugitive murderer and his double-crossing prisoner, a corrupt district attorney, board a lifeboat loaded with depth charges and ram the submarine. Alan Baxter, as the avenging criminal, finds redemption while John Halliday portrays his victim who is forced into the lifeboat. Constance Bennett serves as the romantic interest in this well-structured little

drama. The film was originally released under the title *Submarine Zone*. ∎

Espionage Agent (1939), WB. *Dir.* Lloyd Bacon; *Sc.* Warren Duff, Michael Fessier, Frank Donaghue; *Cast includes:* Joel McCrea, Brenda Marshall, Jeffrey Lynn, George Bancroft, Stanley Ridges.

A generally conventional World War II spy drama, the film stars Joel McCrea as a career diplomat who discovers that his wife, played by Brenda Marshall, is a German spy. The plot is steeped in espionage and planned sabotage as McCrea and his wife discover a German briefcase aboard a train bound for Berlin with plans to dynamite the major centers of American industry when and if necessary. Much time is spent in explaining the vital work of the State Department, an otherwise obscure branch of the American government. George Bancroft portrays an American foreign correspondent reporting on European events. According to the film, Congress revised the nation's laws concerning espionage as a result of the findings of the two principal characters. ∎

Eternal Sea, The (1955), Rep. *Dir.* John H. Auer; *Sc.* Allen Rivkin; *Cast includes:* Sterling Hayden, Alexis Smith, Dean Jagger, Ben Cooper, Virginia Grey.

A biographical drama of the career of Admiral John M. Hoskins, the film stars Sterling Hayden in the role of the dedicated commander. Events cover two wars, World War II and the Korean conflict. During the former, Hoskins loses a leg when the U.S.S. *Princeton*, an aircraft carrier, is sunk in the Pacific. He battles with his superiors to remain in active service, taking command of the new *Princeton*. He helps to establish the carrier as a viable ship for the latest jet planes. Hoskins witnesses the results of his efforts in the highly successful employment of the navy jets during the Korean War. Alexis Smith plays his loving wife. ∎

Eve of St. Mark, The (1944), TCF. *Dir.* John M. Stahl; *Sc.* George Seaton; *Cast includes:* Anne Baxter, William Eythe, Michael O'Shea, Vincent Price, Ruth Nelson, Ray Collins.

A World War II drama of a young farmer inducted into the army, the film, a tribute to the common soldier, depicts the youth's idyllic life before Pearl Harbor and his experiences in the war during the battle of Corregidor. The young soldier (William Eythe) is shown during peacetime with his loving parents (Ray Collins and Ruth Nelson) and his girlfriend (Anne Baxter). With the advent of war, Eythe answers his country's call and is sent overseas. The plot then focuses on him and his comrades under attack on Corregidor by the Japanese.

Based on the realistic stage play by Maxwell Anderson, the film retains much of the natural dialogue and the patriotic speeches of the fighting men although the ending has been changed. In the original, Eythe and his company are killed in a delaying action. The film, however, ends on a more sanguine tone, suggesting that the men somehow make it to safety. ■

Ever in My Heart (1933), WB. *Dir.* Archie Mayo; *Sc.* Bertram Millhauser; *Cast includes:* Barbara Stanwyck, Otto Kruger, Ralph Bellamy, Ruth Donnelly, Frank Albertson.

A tear-jerker about a happily married couple before World War I, the film depicts how world events can affect the lives of two innocent people. Barbara Stanwyck portrays an American who marries a professor of German background (Otto Kruger). When war breaks out, American anti-German sentiment turns against the otherwise close couple. Kruger is hounded because of his heritage and returns to Germany where he becomes a spy for his homeland. The following year Stanwyck, while serving as a Red Cross nurse in a canteen in France, learns that he has become a spy. When he is sentenced to face a firing squad, Stanwyck instead poisons their wine without his knowledge. They die in each other's arms.

This was one of the few films about the war to show the plight of German-Americans who had to face a daily barrage of anti-German propaganda. During the war years, newspaper accounts and films continually told of German atrocities that befell the Belgian populace, all of which incited the American public against their fellow citizens of German heritage. ■

Executioners, The (1961), Continent Films. *Dir.* Felix Podmanitzky; *Sc.* Joe J. Heydecker, John Leeb.

A documentary focusing on the Nazi atrocities during World War II, the film traces the careers of the principal defendants in the Nuremberg Trials. Sequences gathered from newsreels range from the horrors of almost endless corpses at the infamous Nazi death camps to the tranquil shots of Eva Braun, Hitler's mistress, swimming in the nude. The film, narrated by Jay Willke, covers the rise and fall of the Third Reich. ■

Exile, The (1947), UI. *Dir.* Max Ophuls; *Sc.* Douglas Fairbanks, Jr.; *Cast includes:* Douglas Fairbanks, Jr., Paule Croset, Henry Daniell, Maria Montez, Nigel Bruce.

This historical drama concerns Charles II's exile from England. Douglas Fairbanks, Jr. portrays the youthful Charles Stuart. The monarch leader of the Cavaliers takes up temporary residence in Holland out of harm's way of the Roundheads. While biding his time for the Restoration, young Charles falls in love with a commoner (Paule Croset), a pretty Dutch innkeeper, and indulges in skirmishes with the Roundheads. Henry Daniell, as an assassin, is sent by Cromwell to eliminate Charles. Robert Coote plays an actor who impersonates the exiled king in this highly romanticized view of history. Paule Croset, who made her screen debut in this costume drama, later changed her name to Paula Corday.

The film is set during the English Civil War (1642–1648) which resulted from conflicts between Charles I and Parliament. When members of Parliament demanded more power and church reform, Charles reacted by attempting to arrest the leaders. Each side proceeded to raise its own army. In 1644 the king was defeated by Parliament's troops who were joined by the Scots. After forming an alliance with the Scots, Charles and his royalists marched off to war a second time and was beaten in 1648 by Oliver Cromwell's army. Charles I was then tried and executed. His exiled son, Charles II, was made king of the Scots and unsuccessfully invaded England. He then remained in exile until Cromwell's death (1658) and was eventually proclaimed king of England in 1660. ■

Exile Express (1939). See Spy Films: the Talkies. ■

Exodus (1960), UA. *Dir.* Otto Preminger; *Sc.* Dalton Trumbo; *Cast includes:* Paul Newman, Eva Marie Saint, Ralph Richardson, Peter Lawford, Lee J. Cobb, Sal Mineo.

Based on Leon Uris' popular novel, the

film traces the major events in the birth of the State of Israel. Paul Newman portrays a determined leader of the Jewish underground known as the Irgun. Eva Marie Saint, as a widowed American who works as a nurse for the Jewish refugees on Cyprus and later in Palestine, falls in love with Newman. Ralph Richardson, as a British general, is sympathetic to the Jewish cause. Lee J. Cobb, as Newman's father and a leader of the Jewish people in Palestine, believes in achieving national goals through peaceful negotiations. His more radical brother, on the other hand, adopts violent means against the British, including the blowing up of the Hotel David along with many British officers.

The action sequences include a prison break organized by members of the Jewish underground who free political prisoners and skirmishes with Arab forces who oppose the United Nations' partitioning of Palestine. The highlight of the film concerns a Greek freighter which is transporting more than 600 Jewish refugees bound for Palestine. When the British attempt to seize the ship and turn it back, the passengers go on a hunger strike and vow to blow themselves up if the British try to board the vessel. The determination of these homeless refugees who survived the death camps of Nazi Germany makes international headlines and touches the conscience of the world. World opinion turns against the British, who finally permit the Jewish to disembark. The film, like its source, is heavily tilted in Israel's favor although the superficial script, which practically ignores the existence of the Palestinians as a political entity, tries to justify some of the Arabs' discontent with the U.N. decision. ■

Extraordinary Seaman, The (1969). See War Humor. ■

F

Face in the Fog, A (1922). See Detectives at War. ∎

Face in the Rain, A (1963). See Spy Films: the Talkies. ∎

Face of War, A (1968), Commonwealth United. *Dir.* Eugene S. Jones.

A Vietnam War documentary, the film follows the exploits of a U.S. Marine Corps company for three months as its members struggle with the elusive enemy and the hostile terrain. The work steers away from ideological views, showing, instead, the dull, daily routine of the foot soldier as he slogs through the swamp and faces enemy fire. At regular intervals he witnesses the death of his buddies. But the war grinds on as he quietly follows orders and returns to the swamps to search out the foe. Other sequences depict the miserable plight of the Vietnamese people caught in the middle of the conflict. The film, made in black-and-white, underscores the dismal existence of the soldier in particular and the effects of war in general. This is in sharp contrast to the color television coverage of the conflict that was transmitted by way of the network nightly news to millions of American homes. ∎

Face Value (1927). See Veterans. ∎

Fail Safe (1964), Col. *Dir.* Sidney Lumet; *Sc.* Walter Bernstein; *Cast includes:* Dan O'Herlihy, Walter Matthau, Frank Overton, Henry Fonda.

The likelihood of accidental nuclear war is explored in this tense drama set chiefly within Strategic Air Command's compound. Proud of the infinite variety of "fail-safe" features built into the complex system, the military and political leaders unexpectedly face the frightening prospect of all-out war when the system fails and an American bomber with a nuclear payload heads toward the Soviet Union. Since it cannot be called back, the President (Henry Fonda) gets on the "hot line" to inform his Russian counterpart that this is not a sneak attack. He even tries to help the Soviets down the plane. But the bomber pierces Russian defenses and drops its nuclear weapon on Moscow. Fonda, to prevent a nuclear war, is forced to drop a similar bomb on New York City to pacify the Russians. Walter Matthau, as a Pentagon official obsessed by technology, urges full-scale war rather than divulge military data to the Soviets. Based on the novel by Eugene Burdick and Harvey Wheeler, the film is a grim reminder of the precarious future mankind has carved for itself as a result of the nuclear arsenal it has amassed. ∎

Fall In (1943). See Service Comedy. ∎

Fall of a Nation, The (1916), National Films. *Dir.* Bartley Cushing; *Sc.* Thomas Dixon; *Cast includes:* Arthur Shirley, Lorraine Huling, Flora MacDonald, Percy Standing.

A preparedness drama depicting the invasion of the United States by Germany with the help of a traitor, the film quickly became a popular success despite its dramatic deficiencies and inept acting. A millionaire, obsessed with the desire for power, secretly plots with Germany to land troops and weapons on American shores. Major cities fall to the invaders who commit a variety of atrocities upon the defenseless citizens. A prologue shows the birth of the republic as well as numerous battle scenes, all realistically staged, and extols the benefits of democracy while condemning the European political regimes of kings and royalty. In its preparedness zeal, the drama berates such antiwar critics as a thinly veiled William Jennings Bryan, played by Percy Standing, as well as religious leaders who countenance neutrality. In the film a naive, almost simple-minded minister is assigned to try to restrain the invaders by greeting them with kindness. He is quickly taken prisoner. Thomas Dixon, the screenwriter, was also the author of the novel and play, *The Clansman*, which was the basis for D.W. Griffith's 1915 masterpiece, *The Birth of a Nation*.

Although the film was attacked by many movie critics and Washington politicos, it scored at the box office. It was released almost on the heels of *The Battle Cry of Peace* (1915), another strong preparedness drama. Both helped to turn the tide against the pacifist movement (not an especially strong force even at its peak) which was supported by such productions as *Civilization* (1916). Pacifism, *The Fall of a Nation* suggested, was akin to disloyalty and cowardice. ∎

"Fall of Black Hawk, The" (1912), American. *Dir.* Joseph Sullivan, William Lee; *Sc.* Homer F. Dowd; *Cast includes:* Harry Lonsdale, Zelma Barber, Charles E. Gould, David Fischer.

Based on actual historical incidents, this short silent drama concerns the Black Hawk War of 1832. Chief Black Hawk, in an attempt to reclaim lands once belonging to Indians, leads the Sauk and Fox tribes on raids against white settlers. The film depicts the slaughter of many whites before the warring tribes are defeated.

According to historical records, Chief Black Hawk, on April 6, 1832, led a large war party from the Sauk and Fox tribes across the Mississippi River into Northern Illinois to regain ceded territory in Illinois and Wisconsin. Successful at first, the Indians were later badly defeated at the Battle of Bad Axe (August 2) by a combined force of 1,300 regulars and Illinois militia under Colonel Zachary Taylor and Brigadier General Henry Atkinson. Chief Black Hawk fled and hid with the Winnebagoes and then returned to surrender on August 27. Both Jefferson Davis and Abraham Lincoln served in the military during the war. ∎

Fall of the Roman Empire, The (1964), Par. *Dir.* Anthony Mann; *Sc.* Ben Barzman, Basilio Franchina, Philip Yordan; *Cast includes:* Alec Guinness, Sophia Loren, Stephen Boyd, James Mason.

This large-scale production captures the grandeur and weaknesses of Rome, the latter ultimately leaving the empire susceptible to invasion by barbarian forces. Alec Guinness, as Marcus Aurelius, the elderly and respected leader of Rome, fails to disinherit his worthless son, Commodus, played by Christopher Plummer, who succeeds his father to the throne. Stephen Boyd, as a noble Roman Tribune loyal to Commodus, refuses to take the reins of empire. The sadistically inclined Commodus proceeds to carry out a reign of terror, including crucifixions, the burning of estates and general mayhem. Meanwhile, the Senate, filled chiefly with vain and skeptical men, does nothing to improve the conditions of a society grown dissolute and corrupt. Sophia Loren, as Lucilla, provides the romantic interest. Outstanding battle sequences of clashing armies as well as action scenes of gladiators in life-and-death struggles add some vitality to the film. ∎

Fall of the Romanoffs, The (1917), A. H. Woods. *Dir.* Herbert Brenon; *Sc.* Herbert Brenon; *Cast includes:* Edward Connelly, Alfred Hickman, Conway Tearle, Charles Craig.

The two-hour silent drama tells the story of the last days of the Czar. The film attempts to cover all the important locations and incidents relevant to Nicholas II's demise and the rise of the Bolsheviks, including scenes of Kerensky addressing the Duma, the winter palace of the Emperor and his Czarina and their apartments, the wastelands of Siberia and a lavish festival laid out for Rasputin at the winter palace as mobs gather outside just before the fatal overthrow.

Contemporary American films about the collapse of czarist Russia and the rise of Bolshevism sought and found simplistic causes. Two most often alluded to were German duplicity and conspiracy and Rasputin's satanic power over the Czar and Czarina. Leaders of the insurrection generally were not treated sympathetically by Hollywood studios. Neither were the Russian mobs who stormed the estates and palaces of their former masters and cried out for revenge. ∎

Fallen Sparrow, The (1943), RKO. *Dir.* Richard Wallace; *Sc.* Warren Duff; *Cast includes:* John Garfield, Maureen O'Hara, Walter Slezak, Patricia Morison, Martha O'Driscoll.

The Spanish Civil War serves as an impetus for this suspenseful spy drama starring John Garfield as a former member of the Lincoln Brigade and veteran of that conflict. He had been captured and tortured during the war. It seems that he had gained possession of a Nazi battle flag lost in battle by a German battalion. Certain high officials, who are willing to kill for it, want the standard returned. Unable to extract the whereabouts from Garfield, they allow him to escape, hoping he will lead them to the flag. In New York his close friend is murdered, and he links the death to the Nazis, particularly to their sadistic leader, played by Walter Slezak. Maureen O'Hara provides the romantic interest until Garfield learns that she is working for the Nazis. He turns her over to the F.B.I. and remarks to a nearby detective: "Another sparrow has fallen."

Very few Hollywood films dealt with the controversial Spanish Civil War. Those that did, such as *Blockade* (1938), steered clear of specific social and political causes, opting instead for some nebulous statements about destruction. *The Fallen Sparrow*, released during World War II, remains an anti-Nazi drama rather than an attack on Franco's Fascism. ∎

False Faces, The (1919), Par. *Dir.* Irvin Willat; *Sc.* Irvin Willat; *Cast includes:* Henry B. Walthall, Mary Anderson, Lon Chaney, Milton Ross.

Henry B. Walthall stars as writer Louis Joseph Vance's fictional hero, "The Lone Wolf," in this World War I spy drama. The film opens somewhere in France in the trenches where Walthall makes his way back to Allied lines. Learning that a network of German spies will accelerate its activities in the United States, he sails for America to foil the plot. There is much knavery aboard the vessel involving a wounded war hero and his sister who is actually an English operative carrying a secret message. German spies then make an attempt on Walthall's life, but he manages to survive. He then helps to round up the secret agents, including their leader,

played by Lon Chaney, and recovers the message that has fallen into the hands of the chief spy. Mary Anderson, as a British agent, also provides the romance in this suspenseful tale.

Aside from the opening combat sequences, the film has scenes of German submarine warfare while the hero crosses the Atlantic. The plot structure is reminiscent of a conventional serial with its melodramatic events unfolding quickly and economically. ∎

Fane, Commander Francis D. See *Underwater Warrior* (1958). ∎

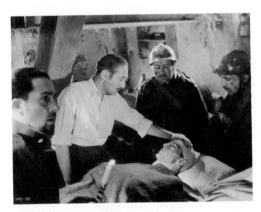

Adolphe Menjou, in one of war's few acts of humanity, attends to his wounded friend (Gary Cooper). *A Farewell to Arms* (1932).

Farewell to Arms, A (1932), Par. *Dir.* Frank Borzage; *Sc.* Benjamin Glazer, H. P. Garrett; *Cast includes:* Gary Cooper, Helen Hayes, Adolphe Menjou, Mary Philips, Jack Larue.

Ernest Hemingway's World War I novel of the tragic romance between a lieutenant and a nurse was the basis for this film starring Gary Cooper as Frederic Henry, the American officer, and Helen Hayes as Catherine, the English nurse who dies during a Caesarean operation. Henry, an ambulance driver in the Italian army, meets Catherine with whom he has a casual relationship. Later, when he is wounded, she nurses him back to health. Realizing how much they love each other, they decide to wed. By the time he returns to duty, Catherine is pregnant. The Italian army collapses during its retreat from Caporetto, and Henry, disgusted by and disillusioned with the war, deserts and returns to Catherine. She and their child die in childbirth. Henry, all alone now, is dazed by the calamity of their idyllic love, oblivious to the Austrian surrender and the subsequent Armistice.

Adolphe Menjou portrays an Italian officer and Henry's friend. He voices the futility of the war early in the film when he comments to a fellow officer: "What if we take the mountains to the north? Behind them are more mountains and behind those are more mountains yet." The most powerful scenes are those that depict the Italian retreat. The dogs of war are unleashed against civilians and soldiers alike as indiscriminate shelling as well as bombing and strafing from enemy planes take their toll among the wounded and refugees who crowd the roads.

When the film was released, the studio provided two endings, one that followed the book and another that ended happily, aimed at satisfying another segment of the public. Hemingway protested this practice but to no avail. The author was not the only one to remonstrate against the film. The Italian ambassador at the time objected to the way in which the Italian forces were pictured during the famous retreat. Hayes, a successful stage actress, was praised for her portrayal of Catherine, which some critics consider as the best performance of her career. The film was remade twice—in 1951 as *Force of Arms* and again in 1957 under its original title. Both failed at the box office despite competent directors, large productions and major stars. ∎

Farewell to Arms, A (1957), TCF. *Dir.* Charles Vidor; *Sc.* Ben Hecht; *Cast includes:* Rock Hudson, Jennifer Jones, Vittorio De Sica, Alberto Sordi, Mercedes McCambridge.

Ernest Hemingway's bold romantic novel of World War I once again comes to the screen. This latest adaptation offers more frankness ("I've never felt like a whore before"), offers scenes of visual beauty and has the benefit of color. Rock Hudson, as Frederic Henry, an American ambulance driver with the Italian army, falls in love with nurse Catherine Barkley, played by Jennifer Jones. In this version, they escape together to Switzerland where Jones dies in childbirth.

The dialogue at times captures the futility and horror of the war. "What's happening with the mountain?" Hudson inquires while recovering from his wounds. "Have we taken it yet?" "Ha," his doctor friend laughs cynically, "50,000 Italians are now freezing triumphantly on its top." Later, another doctor,

showing the strains of operating on too many wounded, comments: "What a shame to waste young lads as targets." Musing upon the German military strength, a major explains: "It isn't that they're better men. They have a better war machine. They've been building it gun by gun for many years while we Italians have been practicing civilization. Now, of course, civilization is not very useful."

One of the highlights of the film is the Italian retreat from Caporetto, a sequence charged with despair and chaos. The mud-filled road is crowded with military and civilian vehicles and rain-soaked refugees clinging to their children. On the banks are corpses strewn on barbed wire and bodies of civilians too weak to complete the journey. The pathetic sequence in which Hudson's friend, the half-crazed Rinaldi (Vittorio De Sica), is hastily sentenced to be shot by Italian officials for his mutterings about the stupidity of the war is especially affecting. Jones' agonizing childbirth scene is another poignant highlight. This screen version adheres more closely to the author's work. ∎

Farewell to the King (1989), Orion. *Dir.* John Milius; *Sc.* John Milius; *Cast includes:* Nick Nolte, Nigel Havers, Frank McRae, Gerry Lopez, Marilyn Tokuda, John Bennett Perry. Nick Nolte portrays an American soldier who tries to protect his adopted island tribe from twentieth-century evils in this awkward World War II adventure drama. After escaping capture by the Japanese, Nolte disappears into a Pacific island jungle where natives find him. The film then advances three years to show Nolte as the accepted king of the tribe. A confirmed pacifist and isolationist, he is determined to keep his people out of the war.

The Allies, however, have other plans. A handful of Commandos, led by Nigel Havers, parachute into this semi-paradise. Their mission is to seek native support against the Japanese. Nolte wants no part of the war—until the Japanese slaughter some of his villagers. He then turns his rage against the invaders, giving the enemy no quarter. "History cannot be avoided," Havers remarks to Nolte earlier in the film. But this theme is lost among the scenery, action and cumbersome flashbacks. Based on Swiss author Pierre Schoendoerffer's 1970 novel, the drama presents a fictionalized account of the exploits of Allied troops who fought together with various tribes against the Japanese. ■

Farragut, David Glasgow. See *The Southerners* (1914). ■

Fastest Guitar Alive, The (1967). See Musicals. ■

Father Goose (1964), U. *Dir.* Ralph Nelson; *Sc.* Peter Stone, Frank Tarloff; *Cast includes:* Cary Grant, Leslie Caron, Trevor Howard, Jack Good.

Cary Grant portrays a slovenly rum-soaked drifter who is conscripted by the Australians to serve as a plane-spotter on a remote South Sea island in this World War II comedy. Trevor Howard, as an Australian officer, forces Grant to help the war effort against the Japanese by doling out only one bottle of gin at a time whenever Grant cooperates. Grant's life becomes more complicated when he is saddled with seven girls and their supervisor, the very prim Leslie Caron, who are marooned on a nearby island after escaping from New Guinea. Caron ultimately ends up marrying Grant. Some battle sequences occur near the end of the film when an American submarine sinks an enemy gunboat that is pursuing Grant. ■

Federal Fugitives (1941). See Spy Films: the Talkies. ■

Fetterman Massacre. See Sioux Wars; *Tomahawk* (1951). ■

Field of Honor, The (1917), U. *Dir.* Allen Holubar; *Sc.* Elliott J. Clawson; *Cast includes:* M. K. Wilson, Louise Lovely, Allen Holubar, Sidney Dean, Helen Wright.

Two men in love with the same young woman march off to battle when the Civil War begins. M.K. Wilson, as the beau who wins the hand of Louise Lovely, proves to be a coward during the fighting. Allen Holubar portrays the other young man who is rejected. Because of his feelings for the young bride, he protects the reputation of Wilson, whom he thinks has been killed in action. Later, Wilson reappears and causes complications in the convoluted plot. Large-scale battle sequences highlight the film, which was based on a story written by the U.S. Minister to Belgium. ■

Fields of Honor (1918), Goldwyn. *Dir.* Ralph Ince; *Sc.* Irvin Cobb; *Cast includes:* Mae Marsh, Marguerite Marsh, George Cooper, John Wessell.

The hardships of a French immigrant family unfold against the background of World War I in this slow-paced drama. Mae Marsh portrays a young Frenchwoman who, along with her sister (Marguerite Marsh) and brother (George Cooper), emigrate to America, the "land of promise." Mae meets a young American artist (Vernon Steele) who quickly falls in love with her and proposes marriage. His family, suspicious of Mae, takes him on a trip to California where, they hope, he will forget about Mae. Meanwhile war breaks out and the brother returns to France to enlist. Mae's sister marries a German and leaves with him for Berlin. Both young men are killed in battle. Mae's sister, despondent, takes her own life. May eventually finds happiness in her adopted country when the artist returns to her.

The film leaves the impression that Europe is a decadent world dominated by wars and early death—a view that many Americans may well have held after becoming mired in World War I. The United States, on the other hand, is pictured as a young land filled with hope and promise. ■

55 Days at Peking (1963), AA. *Dir.* Nicholas Ray; *Sc.* Philip Yordan, Bernard Gordon; *Cast includes:* Charlton Heston, Ava Gardner, David Niven, Flora Robson, John Ireland.

The brutal Boxer Rebellion threatens a Peking outpost occupied by Europeans in this historical drama. Garrisoned by only a few hundred outnumbered but brave soldiers, those in the compound hold out against a siege that lasted for 55 days. David Niven portrays the chief of the British embassy who, as a matter of principle, refuses to surrender to the Boxers and convinces the other Europeans within the walls to do likewise. Charlton Heston, as an American major, manages to woo a widow (Ava Gardner) as the momentous events unfold around them. This widescreen production, filmed in Spain, captures the violence of the rebellion in the many battle sequences while playing down the political background. Little is explained about the commercial exploitation by such nations as Great Britain, the U.S., Russia, France and Japan of a backward country like China. Therefore, the film offers little sympathy for the rebels. ■

Fight for Peace, The (1938), Warwick. *Dir.* Don Bartlett.

An antiwar documentary composed of newsreel footage, the film presents an anti-Fascist slant. Included are sequences pertaining to World War I, the Russian Revolution, Japan's attack on China, Italy's takeover of Ethiopia, Hitler's move into Austria and the Spanish Civil War. The film, narrated by radio announcer David Ross, focuses on the rise of Mussolini and Hitler. Much of the footage has appeared elsewhere. ■

Fighter, The (1952), UA. *Dir.* Herbert Kline; *Sc.* Aben Kandel, Herbert Kline; *Cast includes:* Richard Conte, Vanessa Brown, Lee J. Cobb, Frank Silvera.

A Mexican patriot becomes a professional boxer to raise money for a revolution aimed at overthrowing the Mexican dictator Diaz in this drama based on Jack London's story, "The Mexican." Richard Conte, in the title role, crosses the border into the U.S. where a group of Mexican guerrillas are busy planning the revolution. Conte wishes to join them. His family and fiancee, along with others of his village, have been slain by Diaz's troops. When Conte learns that the guerrillas need weapons, he challenges the top contender in a boxing bout with the stipulation that the winner gets the entire purse. He defeats his opponent and uses the money to purchase the guns. Lee J. Cobb portrays the guerrilla leader. Vanessa Brown, as a member of the revolutionary group, provides the romantic interest.

The film is more concerned with character motivation than with revolutionary ideology, and rightly so, since it is based on London's hard-hitting story. Although London espoused socialism and was influenced by Marx, this was not one of his political works. Besides, the Mexican Revolution was better served by Elia Kazan's poignant *Viva Zapata!*, released several months before *The Fighter*, with Marlon Brando in the title role. ■

Fighter Attack (1953), AA. *Dir.* Lesley Selander; *Sc.* Simon Wincelberg; *Cast includes:* Sterling Hayden, J. Carrol Naish, Joy Page, Kenneth Tobey.

A downed U.S. pilot during World War II joins up with Italian guerrillas to destroy a Nazi supply depot in this action drama. Sterling Hayden portrays the airman based in Corsica who parachutes to safety over Italy. Following a narrow escape from pursuing enemy soldiers, he is found by Italian partisans and brought to their mountain hide-out. Once there, he convinces their leader (J. Carrol Naish) to help him locate a hidden German supply dump and destroy it. Following the success of the mission, he returns to his air base on Corsica. The film is told in flashback during a visit Hayden makes to the area after the war. In the last scene he is reunited with a guerrilla fighter (Joy Page) he had fallen in love with during the conflict. ■

Best friends Robert Stack (c.) and Edmond O'Brien have a falling out when the latter takes command. *Fighter Squadron* (1948).

Fighter Squadron (1948), WB. *Dir.* Raoul Walsh; *Sc.* Seton I. Miller; *Cast includes:* Edmond O'Brien, Robert Stack, John Rodney, Henry Hull.

Heroics and familiar incidents abound in this routine World War II drama about a group of fighter pilots. Edmond O'Brien portrays a rebellious air ace who clashes with his superiors about battle tactics and rigidity of regulations. When his squadron leader is reassigned elsewhere, O'Brien is moved into that position. Suddenly he becomes a stickler for regulations, alienating his best friend (Robert Stack). The obligatory action sequences are present, including dogfights with German planes, a solo rescue of a downed American pilot and the fighter squadron's participation in the Allied invasion of Omaha Beach on D-Day. The wise-cracking American is represented by one pilot who, while strafing a Nazi train, announces to his fellow airmen: "Hey, I've been working on the railroad." Rock Hudson, in his first screen appearance, has a small role as a pilot.

Although the plot provides more than its share of romantic heroics, it also brings out some realities of the air war over Europe. Several references mention America's heavy losses of planes and men while replacements consist of quickly trained youth barely out of their teens. The film opens with a foreword that acknowledges the use of stock footage. This is evident in at least one example in which studio shots are sloppily intercut with actual war footage. Early in the film a damaged fighter marked with a "B4" on its fuselage crash-lands. When the base ambulance arrives to help the pilot out, the markings on the plane read "O7." This film was the first to use excerpts from color newsreels shot during the war. ■

Fighting American, The (1924), U. *Dir.* Tom Forman; *Sc.* Harvey Gates; *Cast includes:* Pat O'Malley, Mary Astor, Raymond Hatton, Warner Oland.

Pat O'Malley portrays an all-American fullback who becomes entangled in a Chinese revolution in this comedy adventure. Expelled from college for neglecting his studies and evicted from his home for his carefree life, Bill Pendleton (O'Malley) journeys to China and meets a girl missionary whom he had known and proposed to at college. A Chinese general, leading an insurrection against the present regime, desires the girl and leads her into his tent. Bill, fighting his way through the revolutionaries, arrives in time only to discover an innocent scene in the general's quarters. It seems that the general, recognizing Bill's pin that the girl was wearing, is a member of the same fraternity as Bill.

The background of this slight film has some basis in fact. China, torn by civil strife, was often in the headlines in the 1920s and became the subject of several Hollywood action dramas and adventures. ■

"Fighting Blood" (1911), Biograph. *Dir.* D. W. Griffith; *Sc.* D. W. Griffith; *Cast includes:* Robert Harron, Florence LaBadie.

D.W. Griffith directed this exciting one-reel drama with an unfailing eye for visual action and camera angles. The story is set in the Dakotas during the 1880s where a pioneer family is besieged in their little cabin by Apaches on the warpath. The oldest son, played by Robert Harron, had earlier grown tired of the patriarch's militant control and left home. Later, when he observes his family under attack, he rides to the nearby army outpost and returns with the cavalry who quickly dispense with the Indians.

Griffith was later to use a similar situation in his Civil War masterpiece *The Birth of a Nation* (1915). Civilians, trapped in a cabin and bravely fighting off a troop of black soldiers, are saved at the last minute by the Ku Klux Klan. In both films he heightened the sympathy level by showing children cowering in fear, raised the emotional impact by adding close-ups of their faces and increased suspense by cross-cutting between the siege and the rescuers. ■

Fighting Bob (1915), Metro. *Dir.* John W. Noble; *Sc.* Edward Rose; *Cast includes:* Orrin Johnson, Olive Wyndham, Edward Brenon, Miss Redwing.

An action drama set in a fictitious South American country, the story concerns the title character, played by Orrin Johnson, who tries to help the natives establish a democracy. He proceeds to teach them about the voting process. Meanwhile, several battles erupt, precipitated by those who oppose the changes. Olive Wyndham provides the romantic interest. The action sequences are handled realistically.

At the time of the film's release, several countries south of the border could have served as inspiration for the plot, since they were undergoing general unrest and threats of insurrection. Honduras was faced with a civil war in 1911. Both political parties in Panama in 1912 called upon the U.S. to supervise elections beyond the Canal Zone. A revolution threatened Nicaragua in 1912. Finally, the U.S. Navy in 1914 intervened in the Dominican Republic's revolution by establishing a neutral zone. ■

Fighting Coast Guard (1951), Rep. *Dir.* Joseph Kane; *Sc.* Kenneth Gamet; *Cast includes:* Brian Donlevy, Forrest Tucker, Ella Raines, John Russell, Richard Jaeckel.

A tribute to the U.S. Coast Guard during World War II, this routine drama traces the activities of a handful of shipyard workers who enlist in this branch of service. The men, angered by the sneak attack on Pearl Harbor by the Japanese, enlist in the Coast Guard. The film carries them through their training and into action in the South Pacific. Brian Donlevy portrays the no-nonsense commander who bears the wrath of Forrest Tucker, a burly shipyard worker who enlists but fails officer training. Tucker ultimately proves his worth by performing heroically under fire. Ella Raines provides the romantic interludes for Tucker, who wins her love when he returns as a hero. Several battle scenes derive from newsreel footage shot during World War II. ∎

"Fighting French, The" (1942). See "The March of Time." ∎

Fighting Guardsman, The (1945), Col. *Dir.* Henry Levin; *Sc.* Franz Spencer, Edward Dein; *Cast includes:* Willard Parker, Anita Louise, Janis Carter, John Loder.

An aristocrat in France under Louis XVI takes up the cause of the downtrodden in this routine costume drama based on a novel by Alexander Dumas. Willard Parker portrays the conscience-stricken nobleman who socializes with the aristocracy while secretly leading a band of rebels just prior to the French Revolution. The revolutionists steal the king's gold and distribute it among the needy. Anita Louise, as another aristocrat, provides the romantic interest for Parker, whom some of his band suspect when they learn of his interest in Louise. However, the Revolution solves the problems of the principal players in this overly familiar Robin Hood plot. ∎

Fighting Kentuckian, The (1949), Rep. *Dir.* George Waggner; *Sc.* George Waggner; *Cast includes:* John Wayne, Vera Ralston, Philip Dorn, Oliver Hardy.

John Wayne stars as the hero of this drama concerning a French colony in Alabama about to be cheated out of its land in the days following the War of 1812. Wayne, returning with a troop of Kentucky riflemen who just fought with Andrew Jackson against the British, resigns from his troop to help the French settlers against a gang of outlaws. It seems that the U.S. government issued land to French officers who fought with Napoleon. Wayne falls in love with the daughter of a French general. Oliver Hardy provides the comic relief in this unusual historical drama in conventional western trappings. ∎

Fighting Lady, The (1944), Louis de Rochemont. *Sc.* John Stuart Martin, Eugene Ling.

Filmed by servicemen of the U.S. Navy, this World War II documentary tells the story of an aircraft carrier on duty in the Pacific. The film ranges from the drab daily routines of the sailors and pilots to the deadly combat missions in the air. Several scenes show aerial combat with the enemy. Photographed in color, the documentary captures both the dullness of days at sea as the men go through familiar drills and the anxieties felt by those on board as the carrier presses on into enemy waters. ∎

Douglas Fairbanks, Jr. crosses swords with some of Ireland's traitors. *The Fighting O'Flynn* (1949).

Fighting O'Flynn, The (1949), UI. *Dir.* Arthur Pierson; *Sc.* Douglas Fairbanks, Jr., Robert Thoeren; *Cast includes:* Douglas Fairbanks, Jr., Helena Carter, Patricia Medina, Richard Greene.

In this romantic adventure Douglas Fairbanks, Jr. portrays the title character who comes home to Ireland to claim a castle willed to him by a late relative and wins the love of the viceroy's daughter while saving his country from a French invasion. Fairbanks, a soldier of fortune and a likable rogue, dashes about with panache and humor, somewhat in the acrobatic tradition of his father, as he foils the plans of a traitorous officer (Richard Greene). Greene is attempting to clear the way for Napoleon to gain control of Ireland from where he intends to invade England.

The woman Fairbanks falls in love with (Helene Carter), who is in danger and about to confide in him, asks: "Are you loyal to your king?" "My king?" he questions. "I'm an

One of many World War II documentaries photographed in combat zones, this film was made aboard an aircraft carrier in the Pacific. *The Fighting Lady* (1944).

Irishman, and every Irishman is his own king." Later, during a conversation with Greene, Fairbanks, who has uncovered his rival's plot, is asked the price of his silence. "An Irishman silent?" Fairbanks laughs. This tone continues through most of the plot of this lilting adventure. ■

Fighting Roosevelts, The (1919), FN. *Dir.* William Nigh; *Sc.* Charles Hanson Towne, Porter E. Browne.

A biographical drama based on the life of President Theodore Roosevelt, the film emphasizes particular highlights in his active life. These include his strong protest to the German ambassador during a problem with Nicaragua, the battle of San Juan Hill and his experiences as a police commissioner. Incidents in his early life as a child, as a cowboy and as a member of the State Assembly are also shown. There is no mention of any of the controversies in which he became entangled, such as that with big business. Roosevelt authorized the script upon which the film is based. ■

Fighting Seabees, The (1944), Rep. *Dir.* Edward Ludwig; *Sc.* Borden Chase, Aeneus MacKenzie; *Cast includes:* John Wayne, Susan Hayward, Dennis O'Keefe, William Frawley.

This action drama tells the fictionalized story of the development of the navy's construction battalions during the early months of World War II and how the members were converted into an effective fighting unit. John Wayne portrays a volatile construction chief who is impatient with military regulations. "We're not fighting men anymore," a naval officer (Dennis O'Keefe) warns Wayne about the Japanese, "we're fighting animals." After Wayne's civilian crew takes a beating at the hands of the Japanese, he defies the U.S. Navy's orders not to participate in combat and leads his men in battle the next time the enemy attacks. Unfortunately, his crew, untrained in combat techniques, is again beaten. He then joins O'Keefe in training four battalions of workers in the skills of warfare. The unit of worker-fighters, now part of the navy, becomes known as the Construction Battal-

195

ion or "Seabees." When Wayne and his command return to the South Pacific, they are ready to take on a Japanese force that attacks them. Although they are greatly outnumbered, the Seabees manage to save the depot they have built while inflicting heavy casualties on the enemy. Wayne goes to his death defending the oil drums needed by the American fleet.

Released during the war, the film offers the usual obligatory propaganda of the period. O'Keefe, who has competed with Wayne for the affections of Susan Hayward throughout the film, makes the final eulogy to Wayne and the Seabees at a dress parade: "Your deeds speak for themselves and will continue to do so—from the shores of the Pacific to the Arctic, from the coasts of Europe to the distant strands of Asia—memorials on which will be described in blood and fire your own immortal challenge—'We build for the fighters—we fight for what we build.'" As the film closes, the soundtrack presents an all-male chorus singing "The Song of the Seabees." ■

Fighting 69th, The (1940), WB. *Dir.* William Keighley; *Sc.* Norman Reilly Raine, Fred Niblo, Jr., Dean Franklin; *Cast includes:* James Cagney, Pat O'Brien, George Brent, Jeffrey Lynn, Alan Hale, Frank McHugh.

James Cagney portrays a fresh army recruit from Brooklyn in this World War I drama of the famed Fighting 69th outfit. He plays a wise guy whose bragging and strutting facade crumbles under fire. His cowardice in the trenches causes the deaths of several of his comrades. Father Duffy, played by Pat O'Brien, helps to bring about a change in Cagney, who has been court-martialed and faces a firing squad. Freed from his confinement by enemy shelling, he redeems himself admirably when he volunteers to join his outfit under fire. His major and the rest of the men who are in the midst of an advance are pinned down by an artillery barrage and machine-gun fire. Meanwhile, the barbed wire in front of them has not been cut. Cagney uses a mortar to blast a gap in the wire and blow up the German machine-gun nest, thereby allowing his fellow soldiers to move forward and rout the enemy. When a German soldier hurls a hand grenade into his shell hole, Cagney sacrifices his own life by throwing himself onto it to save the life of his sergeant (Alan Hale). The film ends with a prayer by Father Duffy: "Oh, heavenly Fa-

ther, I beseech you the prayer of this, America's lost generation. They loved life, too, Lord. It was as sweet to them as to the living today. They accepted privation, wounds and death that an ideal might live . . . America, the citadel of peace—peace forever more . . ." The story is based on the actual New York Irish regiment that fought and distinguished itself in France with the Rainbow Division as the 165th Infantry of the American Expeditionary Forces. Other famous members of the regiment included "Wild Bill" Donovan, played by George Brent, who headed the outfit, and Joyce Kilmore (Jeffrey Lynn) the noted poet who was killed in battle. See also William J. "Wild Bill" Donovan. ■

Fighting Sullivans, The. See *The Sullivans* (1944). ■

Firefly of France, The (1918). See *Lafayette Escadrille.* ■

Fires of Faith (1919), Lasky. *Dir.* Edward James; *Sc.* Charles Whittaker; *Cast includes:* Eugene O'Brien, Catherine Calvert, Helen Dunbar, Theodore Roberts, Charles Ogle, James Neill.

A dramatic account of the history of the Salvation Army, the film begins with the organization's birth in England in the 1860s and continues with its work in World War I. Catherine Calvert portrays a Salvation Army worker who, along with another woman, goes to the front to help the doughboys. Here they meet two soldiers and fall in love. The war experience enriches all four of the principals who return home safely. Several battle scenes are pictured, some of which are taken from newsreels. The profits from the film were turned over to the organization by the film studio. See also Salvation Army. ■

First Blood (1982). See *Rambo: First Blood Part II* (1986). ■

First Comes Courage (1943), Col. *Dir.* Dorothy Arzner; *Sc.* George Sklar; *Cast includes:* Merle Oberon, Brian Aherne, Carl Esmond, Fritz Leiber.

A World War II drama about resistance fighters in Nazi-occupied Norway, the film centers around a Norwegian (Merle Oberon) whose romance with a Nazi officer is only a ploy on her part to extract military information which is transmitted to England. A British Commando (Brian Aherne) sent to Norway is captured and meets Oberon, whom he had met before the war. A Commando strike force comes to the rescue of the pair, but Oberon volunteers to remain and continue her spy work. A slight twist in an otherwise routine spy drama occurs when the German officer and Oberon marry. After Aherne kills the husband, Oberon decides that her status as a widow of a Nazi officer will help her covert activities. ■

First Forty Days, The (1950), U.S. Army.

A Korean War documentary produced by the U.S. Signal Corps, the film tells the story of the foot soldiers flown into Korea soon after the Communist invasion. Events deal with the tough job these infantrymen, together with other United Nations forces, had in holding on to their beachhead against overwhelming odds. Eventually, the U.S. was able to provide additional troops and supplies to turn back the enemy. The film chiefly deals with the American troops, giving little or no footage to the U.N. forces or the South Korean soldiers. ■

"First in War" (1932). See Nicaraguan Civil War. ■

First Special Aviation Project. See James H. Doolittle. ■

First Texan, The (1956), AA. Dir. Byron Haskin; Sc. Daniel B. Ullman; Cast includes: Joel McCrea, Felicia Farr, Jeff Morrow, Wallace Ford, Abraham Sofaer, Jody McCrea.

Sam Houston leads Texas in its fight against Mexican rule in this historical drama. The film covers Houston's departure from Tennessee and his journey to Texas, the fall of the Alamo, his strategic retreat as he shrewdly lures General Santa Anna into the heart of Texas and the climactic Battle of San Jacinto. Disinterested at first in the stormy political climate of that territory, he ultimately becomes the major force behind the state's independence and emerges as its first president. The rousing battle in which the Mexican general is defeated and captured is the highlight of the film. The plot allows for several historical figures to appear, including, among others, Davy Crockett (James Griffith), Jim Bowie (Jeff Morrow) and Stephen Austin (Dayton Lummis). ■

Gene Hackman and Chad Everett as two marines battling more than the Japanese. *First to Fight* (1967).

First to Fight (1967), WB. Dir. Christian Nyby; Sc. Gene L. Coon; Cast includes: Chad Everett, Marilyn Devin, Dean Jagger, Gene Hackman, Bobby Troup.

A Medal of Honor marine hero loses his nerve when he returns to battle in this World War II action drama. Chad Everett, as a U.S. Marine sergeant, is promoted to second lieutenant, decorated for bravery on Guadalcanal in 1942, is sent back to the States to receive his decoration and then goes on tour to sell war bonds. While on leave he meets and marries the tour hostess (Marilyn Devin) whom he promises that he will not volunteer for active duty.

The second half of the film deals with his frustration at not being back in action. When his wife releases him from his pledge to her, he returns to the Pacific front. He freezes up once he hits the beach during the invasion of Saipan and again when his unit comes under heavy shelling. Gene Hackman, as his sergeant, attributes his loss of nerve to his new role as husband. Before their assault on a Japanese stronghold, Hackman remarks: "This time do us a favor. Stick around for the show." Others in his unit think Everett is a coward. "There goes Fearless Freddie," one marine quips to another. Eventually, Everett resumes his true character as the exemplary fighting man. Dean Jagger, as Everett's colonel, advances the young marine from sergeant to lieutenant. The plot allows for two lengthy action sequences, one on Guadalcanal at the beginning of the film, and the second on Saipan at the conclusion. ■

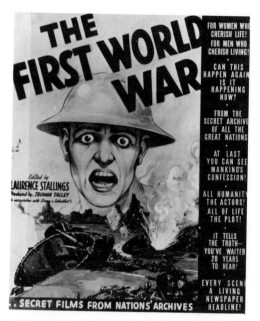

Lobby card dramatizes the documentary *The First World War* (1934), edited by playwright Laurence Stallings.

First World War, The (1934), Fox. *Sc.* Laurence Stallings.

A documentary about the Great War edited by playwright Laurence Stallings, the film makes intelligent use of old newsreels as it traces the tragic conflict back to the 1890s. Scenes of leaders pinning medals on the wounded are juxtaposed with scenes of the slaughter at the front. Stallings gathered film footage from various nations and sources, including the British War Museum. Although some of the war material has been seen in other documentaries, the ironic approach to the subject and the new sequences make for a stark realization of the senselessness of the hell that the fighting men had to go through.

Many historical figures appear on screen, including the Archduke Franz Ferdinand, whose assassination precipitated the conflict; Kaiser Wilhelm during the prewar years; Emperor Franz Josef; and the Russian royal family accompanied by Rasputin. The nighttime bombardment of London by German zeppelins, hand-to-hand fighting in the trenches and the sinking of the cruiser *St. Stephen* in the Adriatic are some of the action sequences. Actor Pedro de Cordoba narrated the film. ■

First Yank Into Tokyo (1945), RKO. *Dir.* Gordon Douglas; *Sc.* J. Robert Bren, Gladys Atwater; *Cast includes:* Tom Neal, Barbara Hale, Marc Cramer, Richard Loo, Key Luke.

Tom Neal portrays an American soldier who volunteers to pose as a spy to help rescue an American engineer held captive in Japan in this low-budget World War II spy drama. Army Intelligence selects Neal because he has lived in Japan before the war. They give him a face-lift to make him look Japanese and send him off to enemy territory. Neal not only rescues the engineer (Marc Cramer) but his girlfriend (Barbara Hale) as well. A nurse on Bataan, she was captured and imprisoned by the Japanese when the peninsula fell. The familiar obligatory scenes of Japanese atrocities that marked many war films of that period are present. This time they are committed against American prisoners of war. A shot of the atom bomb exploding ends the story. This was a last-minute addition since the film was made before the bomb was announced and released a month or so after the war. According to the original script, the U.S. needed the engineer for his invention of a new type of gun that would bring the war to a speedier end. Last-minute editing changed the weapon to the atom bomb, thereby making this the first film to deal with the A-bomb. ■

Five Branded Women (1960), Par. *Dir.* Martin Ritt; *Sc.* Ivo Perilli; *Cast includes:* Silvana Mangano, Vera Miles, Barbara Bel Geddes, Jeanne Moreau, Richard Basehart.

Yugoslavian guerrillas battle Nazi invaders in this grim World War II drama of resistance. Van Heflin portrays a partisan leader. Richard Basehart, as a German officer, is ultimately captured by the guerrillas. Harry Guardino plays a member of the resistance. Director Martin Ritt depicts the partisans as cold and ruthless fighters, traits they believe are essential to defeat the enemy. The film, shot in Europe, includes an abundance of action sequences. ■

Five Fingers (1952). See Spy Films: the Talkies. ■

Five Graves to Cairo (1943), Par. *Dir.* Billy Wilder; *Sc.* Charles Brackett, Billy Wilder; *Cast includes:* Franchot Tone, Anne Baxter, Akim Tamiroff, Erich von Stroheim.

A suspenseful World War II drama set in

North Africa in 1942 after the fall of Tobruk, the film stars Franchot Tone as a British corporal, the lone survivor of a tank crew, who seeks refuge in a hotel in a North African town. German troops, led by Field Marshal Rommel (Erich von Stroheim), arrive almost at the same time. Tone impersonates a German agent in an effort to get Rommel's plans for his African campaign. The anxious hotel owner (Akim Tamiroff) is worried that Tone will be discovered by the Nazis. Fortunio Bonanova, as a happy-go-lucky Italian general whom the Germans treat with scorn, dismisses the insults. "Can a nation that belches understand a nation that sings?" he remarks. Anne Baxter, as a French maid whose brother is a prisoner in Germany, at one point is willing to betray Tone to help her brother. Tone, who is about to leave for British-held Cairo with Rommel's strategic plans, pleads the Allied cause. "It's not one brother that matters," Tone reminds her, "it's a million brothers. It's not just one prison gate . . . It's all their gates that must go." After he leaves, the Nazis execute her. When Tone returns to the hotel several months later following General Montgomery's counterattack, he learns of her death. Tamiroff leads him to the cemetery where she is buried. "We're after them now," he says, kneeling at her grave, "British, French and American. We're after them now, coming from all sides. We're going to blast the blazes out of them!"

The film, made in the middle of the war, certainly has its obligatory propaganda although director-writer Billy Wilder and cowriter Charles Brackett have tried not to stereotype Rommel as just another villain. He is shown treating captured British officers with respect at a dinner party. But this may have been to promote his own vanity rather than to display any signs of warmth. The didactic speeches, villainous German lieutenant, exaggerated courage of Baxter and the buffoonish portrayal of the Italian general dominate the work and mark it as a product of its time. ■

Five Man Army (1970), MGM. *Dir.* Don Taylor; *Sc.* Marc Richards, Dario Argento; *Cast includes:* Peter Graves, James Daly, Bud Spencer, Marc Lawrence.

An action drama filmed in Spain, the story deals with five social outcasts who are brought together to steal a gold shipment for Mexican revolutionaries, circa 1913. Peter Graves leads the five-man army with a firm hand. Known as "The Dutchman," he is not unlike the legendary Flying Dutchman, a wanderer without a home. James Daly, as an over-the-hill dynamite expert, calls Graves a "man without a country." The two had been friends for years but had drifted apart. Daly philosophizes that the mission is doomed and that the small pathetic band that Graves has assembled will all be killed. When Graves questions him why he agreed to go along, Daly, who sees men like himself and Graves as anachronisms, replies: "We are already dead."

Constructed in the form of a caper drama, the film covers familiar territory and brings to mind elements of *The Professionals* (1966), *The Dirty Dozen* (1967) and *The Wild Bunch* (1969) but lacks their style. The plot concerns the intricate preparations and execution of taking over a heavily guarded military train carrying the gold. The mission is accomplished after much killing and a few minor setbacks, ending with the half-million dollars in gold being turned over to the revolutionary army. Several scenes depict the Mexican troops as brutal with their officers particularly ruthless in their treatment of prisoners and the peasantry. Although the film takes place during a period of turmoil in Mexico, historical events or leaders remain murky and are never mentioned. ■

Five Steps to Danger (1957). See Cold War. ■

Fixed Bayonets (1951), TCF. *Dir.* Samuel Fuller; *Sc.* Samuel Fuller; *Cast includes:* Richard Basehart, Gene Evans, Michael O'Shea, Richard Hylton, Skip Homeier.

This Korean War drama concerns a platoon of Americans who remain behind to fight a rear-guard action while the rest of the regiment pulls back. The second film made about the conflict by director-writer Samuel Fuller (*The Steel Helmet* was released earlier the same year), it projects a similar cold and tough surface. "Somebody's got to be left behind and get their rifles wet," the general in charge of the operation announces.

Richard Basehart, as a gun-shy young corporal, is unable to kill the enemy. As the small patrol gets picked off one by one, Basehart finds himself in charge and is able to muster up enough courage to throw off his psychological fears. Gene Evans portrays a

Lobby card shows Richard Basehart (r.) with his hands full during the Korean War. *Fixed Bayonets* (1951).

veteran sergeant as does Michael O'Shea in this suspenseful and gritty tale of men under stress. Evans had the same kind of role in the earlier film.

Fuller sprinkles the action with wisecracking and hard-edged dialogue. "Morale is high but ammo is low," a general quips. "Only three things you have to worry about in the infantry," comments a soldier, "your rifle and your two feet." There is no time to mourn for fallen comrades among the small force battling overwhelming odds. "Strip him of everything we can use, roll him in a blanket and bury him," the order goes out as each defender is killed. Fuller's vision of war reveals a grim picture of tough, brave men fighting to survive. ∎

Flame and the Arrow, The (1950), WB. *Dir.* Jacques Tourneur; *Sc.* Waldo Salt; *Cast includes:* Burt Lancaster, Virginia Mayo, Robert Douglas, Frank Allenby, Nick Cravat.

Resistance to tyranny and Hessian ruthlessness in Lombardy is the subject of this romantic costume drama set during the Middle Ages. Burt Lancaster portrays a dashing acrobatic hero, a local mountaineer who leads his people in a victorious revolution against a local tyrant (Frank Allenby). Diminutive Nick Cravat, former circus partner of the star, plays Lancaster's loyal comic assistant who aids him in his acrobatic stunts. Virginia Mayo, as the niece of the despised despot, provides the romantic interest.

The film is loosely based on events during the Wars of the Lombard League (1167–1183) and the Holy Roman Empire-Papacy Wars of 1228–1241 and 1243–1250. During the former, Holy Roman Emperor Frederick I Barbarossa organized several military incursions into Italy, hoping to gain control over the Lombard cities in the north as well as the Papacy. In the first of the Papacy Wars, Holy Roman Emperor Frederick II, who had renewed the empire's interest in Lombardy, defeated the Second Lombard League, newly reunited to resist the invader, at the Battle of Cortenuova in 1237. Following Pope Gregory IX's death in 1241, the new pope, Innocent IV, proved a more formidable opponent to

Frederick, whom he distrusted. Innocent fomented rebellion in Lombardy. ∎

Flame of Calcutta (1953), Col. Dir. Seymour Friedman; Sc. Robert E. Kent; Cast includes: Denise Darcel, Patric Knowles, Paul Cavanagh, George Keymas.

The daughter of a murdered French official who was stationed in India engages in guerrilla fighting against the guilty prince whose ambitions include the ousting of the British East India Company in this action drama set in the mid-1700s during the Seven Years' War. Denise Darcel portrays the brave daughter who challenges the authority of the treacherous local prince (George Keymas). Patric Knowles, as a British army captain, finds time to woo the vengeful daughter while foiling the plans of the villain. Several battle sequences involve Knowles leading his men against the prince's troops.

The European war between France and England spread to India when Joseph-Francois Dupleix, of the French East India Council, schemed to use his Indian allies against Britain's more powerful position on that continent. Britain's Robert Clive attempted to drive out French trading stations in Bengal. Meanwhile, a Moslem leader loyal to the French, captured Calcutta in his own long-range plan to expel the British from India. Clive's troops, made up of English soldiers and Indian sepoys, eventually defeated the Indian ruler. France and England each had loyal Indian leaders and troops. ∎

Flame of the Desert (1919), Goldwyn. Dir. Reginald Barker; Sc. Charles Logue; Cast includes: Geraldine Farrar, Lou Tellegen, Alec Francis, Edythe Chapman.

Espionage and rebellion pervade this romantic drama set during the Sanusi Anti-British Revolt in colonial Egypt. Lady Isabella (Geraldine Farrar), an Englishwoman, falls in love with a sheik (Lou Tellegen), who is actually an English lord in disguise. His acceptance by other Egyptian leaders places him at their conference tables where he is able to learn of their plot to overthrow British rule. Farrar follows the bogus sheik to Egypt and becomes embroiled in the uprising which is quickly suppressed by the alert British. She is rescued by the lord and is awarded a medal, which is presented by the man she loves. Farrar is surprised to discover that the sheik is an Englishman. ∎

Flames of Chance (1918). See Spy Films: the Silents. ∎

Flaming Frontier, The (1926), U. Dir. Edward Sedgwick; Sc. Edward Sedgwick; Cast includes: Hoot Gibson, Anne Cornwall, Dustin Farnum, Ward Crane, Noble Johnson.

Another historical drama about the Indian uprising that led to Custer's defeat at Little Bighorn, the film stars Hoot Gibson as a pony express rider and a scout for the famous Indian fighter. Gibson gets an appointment to West Point where he meets Lawrence Stanwood, a senator's son, played by Harold Goodwyn. Meanwhile, a group of unscrupulous Washington businessmen plot to steal land from the Indians, causing the various tribes to unite. The corrupt power brokers, in an attempt to hurt Senator Stanwood, involve his son in a scandal, for which Gibson takes responsibility and is dismissed from the Point. He returns to the West. Before Colonel Custer and his troop are wiped out by the Indians, young Stanwood, an officer with the colonel, confesses everything and a dispatch is sent off exonerating Gibson. Other historical figures portrayed in the film are General Grant and Sitting Bull. Several battle scenes are poorly staged, including the fight at Little Big Horn.

As a matter of historical record, no one from Custer's command escaped although in this film version Gibson manages to survive to be reinstated in the army with a commission. ∎

Flat Top (1952), Mon. Dir. Lesley Selander; Sc. Steve Fisher; Cast includes: Sterling Hayden, Richard Carlson, Bill Phipps, John Bromfield, Keith Larsen.

Sterling Hayden portrays a stern flight commander who takes over a squadron of fighter pilots aboard an aircraft carrier in this World War II tale. As the new men land, he observes one flier who is flagged off. The pilot disobeys the order and brings his plane in. Hayden promptly grounds him indefinitely, a decision that results in a clash with his executive officer (Richard Carlson). The junior officer believes in going easy with the men, treating them affectionately. Hayden, on the other hand, is determined to train them to accept discipline and work as a team. The chief mission of the carrier and the fighter pilots is to join the main fleet in the South Pacific and support MacArthur's return to the Philippines. After several combat flights, Carlson realizes Hayden was right and admits this, whereupon he is told that he has been promoted to flight commander. Keith Larsen portrays the grounded flier who eventually returns to the skies in a heroic attempt to stave off Japanese planes from attacking the carrier while the main squadron is supporting an invasion. Generally effective battle sequences include the bombing and strafing of Japanese ships and airfields and several dogfights. The clash between Hayden and Carlson is highly reminiscent of that between John Wayne and Forrest Tucker in *Flying Leathernecks*, released one year earlier. ∎

"Fleet That Came to Stay, The" (1945), Office of War Information.

The battle of Okinawa is the subject of this short World War II documentary made by U.S. Navy, Marine and Coast Guard cameramen. Aside from demonstrating naval support of the marines who landed and fought the Japanese, the film highlights the deadly attack of the kamikaze, or suicide pilots, sent out to destroy or cripple the U.S. Navy. Scenes show fanatical Japanese pilots aiming their planes at the decks of American ships as anti-aircraft fire fills the skies. Although most of the planes go down in flames, some manage to escape the wall of anti-aircraft fire and hit American ships and transports.

More than 4,000 Japanese planes were destroyed, but the cost was high in the number of American ships that were sunk or damaged and the number of casualties suffered. "It was suicide," the narrator announces. "But it would be the pattern from now on to the very finish . . . a struggle between men who want to die and men who want to live." ∎

Flight (1929), Col. *Dir.* Frank Capra; *Sc.* Frank Capra; *Cast includes:* Jack Holt, Lila Lee, Ralph Graves, Allan Roscoe, Harold Goodwin.

An air drama set in Central America, the film stars Jack Holt as a tough American sergeant who takes a young airman, another American (Ralph Graves), under his wing. Lila Lee provides the love interest for Holt, who at one point suspects Graves of interfering with his romance. Although the plot concerns the use of airplanes in battling bandits in a fictitious country, the action, especially the use of air power, resembles the then current Nicaraguan Civil War of the mid-1920s

when that country was plagued with revolution and the anti-government forces of Augusto Sandino. The government was forced to rely on military aid from the U.S., which responded with marines, ships and air support. ∎

Flight Command (1940). See Preparedness. ∎

Flight for Freedom (1943), RKO. *Dir.* Lothar Mendes; *Sc.* Oliver H. P. Garrett, S. K. Lauren; *Cast includes:* Rosalind Russell, Fred MacMurray, Herbert Marshall, Eduardo Ciannelli.

Rosalind Russell portrays an American aviatrix in this drama that begins in the early 1930s and moves to the early years of World War II. She meets another flier (Fred MacMurray), and they fall in love in spite of her instructor's warning to stay away from aviators. Later, she is enlisted by the U.S. Navy to purposely crash somewhere in the Pacific so that American ships can photograph Japanese military installations while they search for her.

The film is a fictionalized amalgam of two famous women aviators, Amelia Earhart and Jacqueline Cochran. Amelia Earhart (1898–1937), the American aviatrix, pioneered women's involvement in flight. She had several noteworthy accomplishments to her credit when she suddenly disappeared on July 2, 1937, near the South Pacific island of Howland. She was on the last third of an around-the-world flight. Unsubstantiated rumors repeatedly surfaced for many years afterward that she was forced down by the Japanese and crashed on a South Seas island because she allegedly discovered that Japan had built bases on mandated former German Pacific islands. At the time of her disappearance, Earhart and Lieutenant Commander Fred Noonan were flying a twin-engine Lockheed on the way back to the U.S.

Earhart, born in Atchison, Kansas, served as a military nurse in Canada during World War I and then did social work in Boston before taking up flying. She was the first woman to cross the Atlantic by air (1928) as a passenger on a flight from Newfoundland to Wales. She married publisher George Putnam in 1931 but continued to use her own name in succeeding aerial endeavors. In 1932 she became the first woman to negotiate a solo crossing of the Atlantic. Among her solo exploits was a flight from Hawaii to California in 1935. During the early 1930s she also served as an officer of one of the early airlines to offer regular air service between Washington, D.C. and New York. Jacqueline Cochran was the wife of RKO's board chairman Floyd Odlum. ∎

Flight Nurse (1953), Rep. *Dir.* Allan Dwan; *Sc.* Alan LeMay; *Cast includes:* Joan Leslie, Forrest Tucker, Arthur Franz, Jeff Donnell, Ben Cooper.

The film pays tribute to the U.S. Air Force nurses who served in the Korean War. Joan Leslie portrays a flight nurse who is torn between her love for a helicopter pilot (Arthur Franz) and her career. She decides to end the affair and stay with the service. Forrest Tucker, as a C-47 pilot engaged in evacuating the wounded, is also romantically interested in the flight nurse. The film includes some harrowing scenes of Chinese and North Korean Communists committing atrocities against U.N. troops in this routine drama. ∎

Fly by Night (1942). See Spy Films: the Talkies. ∎

Flying Blind (1941). See Spy Films: the Talkies. ∎

Flying Circus. See Richthofen, Baron Manfred von. ∎

Flying Fool, The (1929). See Veterans. ∎

Flying Leathernecks (1951), RKO. *Dir.* Nicholas Ray; *Sc.* James Edward Grant; *Cast includes:* John Wayne, Robert Ryan, Don Taylor, Janis Carter.

John Wayne portrays a tough commander of U.S. Marine fighter pilots in the Pacific during World War II in this action drama concerned chiefly with the battle of Guadalcanal. His executive officer (Robert Ryan) clashes with him over his rigidity. He is also resentful that he has not been recommended for promotion and assigned to command the squadron of flying leathernecks. Later, when Wayne is convinced that his exec officer has gained enough experience, he recommends him for his own command. The generally routine film uses war footage from newsreels and documentaries. Several exciting action sequences include air strikes on Japanese warships and assaults by the dreaded kami-

kaze pilots on the American fleet. Janis Carter plays Wayne's wife. J. C. Flippen, as an army sergeant, contributes some humor as a con man who can scrounge materiel, legally or otherwise, for his unit. The plot involving the conflict between the two officers was repeated the following year in *Flat Top*.

Curiously, some of the battle footage came from the Korean War, the conflict that was raging when the film was made. The actual combat sequences were so similar to those of World War II that those in charge of the production decided to use the footage. This was the first Hollywood film to do so. However, the first significant feature film of the Korean War was *The Steel Helmet* (1951). ∎

Flying Tigers. A small, outnumbered volunteer force of American fliers helping the beleaguered Chinese people fight against the Japanese invader caught the American public's attention with their daring exploits in the bleak early days of World War II. Flying outdated P-40s whose noses were painted with the gaping mouth of a long-toothed tiger shark, the American Volunteer Group in China took the popular name "Flying Tigers." General Claire Lee Chennault organized the group early in 1941 before America's entry into World War II. Although still officially neutral, the U.S. government, early in 1941, took steps to counter growing Japanese aggression in Asia by allowing Army Air Force pilots to resign or take a leave of absence to join Chennault in China's air defense. The planes they flew had been sold to China as part of America's Lend-Lease Act, designed to send help to those nations resisting the Axis.

The Flying Tigers caught Americans' fancy by their daring tactics and precision flying used to defeat numerically superior enemy air forces. The exploits of the volunteer group stood out at a time when war news was constantly depressing for most Americans who saw the Axis nations of Germany, Italy and Japan sweeping through large areas of Asia and Europe.

The Flying Tigers successfully carried out a number of important missions. They raided enemy ground forces and supply areas, provided air cover over the Burma Road—China's only land supply link to the outside world, flew supplies over "the hump"—that section of the Himalayas bordering southern China and India—and provided air defense for Chinese troops in southwest China and Allied forces in Burma. The unit was disbanded on July 4, 1942, following America's entry into the war, and most of its personnel re-enlisted in the U.S. Army Air Force as part of the 14th Air Force under Gen. Chennault.

Two films, *Flying Tigers* (1942) and *God Is My Co-pilot* (1945), cover the unit's air actions. The latter drama is partly biographical, based on a book of the same name by one of the pilots in the group, Colonel Robert L. Scott. Both films are strong on aerial dogfights. Surprisingly, neither one emphasizes the accomplishments of Colonel "Pappy" Boyington, who became one of the more famous members of the Flying Tigers. He eventually became America's first World War II flying ace, with 28 reported "kills," before he was shot down late in the war. He survived the conflict interred in a Japanese prisoner-of-war camp.

Despite its brief history, the unit's importance to the war effort is reflected in the introduction to the film *Flying Tigers*. The movie begins with a tribute by Nationalist leader Chiang Kai-shek appearing on the screen: ". . . The Chinese people will preserve forever the memory of their glorious achievements." ■

Flying Tigers (1942), Rep. *Dir.* David Miller; *Sc.* Kenneth Gamet, Barry Trivers; *Cast includes:* John Wayne, John Carroll, Anna Lee, Paul Kelly.

This routine World War II drama pays tribute to the American volunteer pilots who journeyed to China before Pearl Harbor to help fight the Japanese. Unfortunately, the weak plot does not distinguish this film from other similar low-budget second features. John Wayne portrays the squadron commander of a handful of American airmen who daily risk their lives in combat against the Japanese for $600 per month. The thin story concerns one hot-shot pilot (John Carroll) whose self-centered attitude and casual approach to his job result in the death of a fellow flier (Paul Kelly). He redeems himself at the end, however, by smashing his plane, filled with explosives, into a Japanese supply train. The title refers to the American airmen and their ships which had a uniquely painted design on their front.

Several exciting combat sequences— chiefly done in miniature—depict Wayne and his pilots, always outnumbered, battling against enemy bombers and escort fighters.

The screen foreword states General Chiang Kai-shek's gratitude to these brave fliers: ". . . They (the Flying Tigers) have become the symbol of the invincible strength of the forces now upholding the cause of justice and humanity. The Chinese people will preserve forever the memory of their glorious achievements." ■

Flying Torpedo, The (1916), Triangle. *Dir.* Jack O'Brien, Christy Cabanne; *Sc.* Robert Baker, John Emerson; *Cast includes:* John Emerson, Spotiswoode Aitken, William E. Lawrence, Fred Butler.

A silent fantasy about a foreign invasion of America, the plot centers around the invention of a new weapon, a flying torpedo. An unnamed foreign power gains access to the model and, armed with the new destructive force, attacks the Pacific coast of the U.S., landing its troops in California. However, a resourceful American designs a similar weapon, and it is unleashed upon the invaders, driving them out of California.

An advocate of the "preparedness" school of war dramas, the film, according to its studio, received the earnest support of the government. The military provided torpedoes to be exhibited in theater lobbies and set up recruitment booths. ■

Flying Wild (1941). See Spy Films: the Talkies. ■

"Flying With the Marines" (1918), Committee on Public Information. *Dir.* S. L. Rothaphel.

This World War I propaganda documentary, made at the U.S. Marine aviation camp in Miami, Florida, shows several views of a squadron of military airplanes flying in formation. Besides witnessing scenes from the ground, the audience is taken inside the airship itself as it dives and performs other maneuvers. This was one of the first times a movie camera was placed in a military airplane to demonstrate to the public what a pilot sees from the cockpit. ■

Follow the Boys (1944). See Musicals. ■

Follow the Girl (1917). See Home Front. ■

Following the Flag to France (1918), FN.

The second documentary in the series released by the Committee on Public Information, the film begins with historical vignettes of Lafayette, George Washington and Abraham Lincoln. The remainder of the film utilizes contemporary footage of General Pershing's landing in France, American troops marching through Paris and greeting the local inhabitants, and Pershing along with members of the French military high command viewing American and French troops at the front. ∎

Fontenoy, Battle of. See *A Celebrated Case* (1914). ∎

For Better, for Worse (1919), Artcraft. Dir. Cecil B. DeMille; *Sc.* Edgar Selwyn, Jeanie Macpherson; *Cast includes:* Elliot Dexter, Gloria Swanson, Tom Forman, Sylvia Ashton, Raymond Hatton.

In this World War I romantic drama a young woman must choose between two men. One, a doctor, declines a military commission to stay at home and help heal sick children, while the other enlists to fight for his country. The girl selects the latter, thinking the doctor a coward. Although they marry, they decide to consummate the marriage when the groom returns from the war. But the husband is horribly wounded in battle, losing an arm and half his face. He sends a message back with a fellow officer that he has been killed in action. His wife then renews her friendship with the doctor. The husband, meanwhile, undergoes successful operations which restore his face, and he is given a wooden arm. Strengthened by this transformation, he returns home to his wife who is about to announce her engagement to the doctor.

This was one of the earliest post-World War I films to address the problems of those wounded in battle. Although the plot concentrates too heavily on melodramatics, the drama at least attempted to introduce some of the fears that the returning soldiers faced regarding rehabilitation and readjustment. ∎

For France (1917), Vitagraph. *Dir.* Wesley Ruggles; *Sc.* Cyrus Townsend Brady; *Cast includes:* Edward Earle, Betty Howe, Arthur Donaldson, Mary Maurice.

A patriotic drama with World War I as the chief setting, the story concerns the fighting at the front. A lone American displays his heroism as he advances to a machine gun in the heat of battle and holds numerous German soldiers at bay. There are several battle scenes and much sniping and killing until the last scene which shows the French and American flags flying side by side.

The film is not without its share of propaganda. As with similar war movies of the period, it portrays the Huns as brutal and bestial figures who specialize in taking advantage of defenseless women. One young Frenchwoman is rescued at the last moment from a lustful German by a brave American. But a peasant mother does not fare as well. She is attacked by a Prussian officer and his aide. However, an American pilot eventually avenges her death. The German aide is played by Erich von Stroheim, who tended to specialize in this type of role during and after the war. ∎

For Liberty (1917), Fox. *Dir.* Bertram Bracken; *Sc.* Bennett Cohen; *Cast includes:* Gladys Brockwell, Charles Clary, Bertram Grassby, Willard Louis.

An American artist working in France falls for a German officer until she discovers his true character in this World War I drama that takes place prior to America's entry into the war. The couple meet and become intimate in Paris. The artist, played by Gladys Brockwell, accompanies him to Berlin where she learns that he is responsible for the death of a young American. She then assists the victim's brother who is intent on seeking revenge. The brother kills the German officer just as he is about to seduce Brockwell.

The film is another in a series of propaganda war dramas that depicted the Germans as bestial figures who cannot be trusted. Most of these features, released between 1914 and 1918, portrayed French or Belgian women as defenseless victims of the Huns' lust. This entry no doubt added to the outrage of American audiences by having one of their own daughters almost compromised by a lecherous German. ∎

"For the Common Defense" (1942). See "Crime Does Not Pay." ∎

For the Freedom of the East (1919), Goldwyn. *Dir.* Ira M. Lowry; *Cast includes:* Lady Tsen Mei, Robert Elliott, Lei Mon Kim, Herbert Horton Pattee.

China becomes the goal of a political chess game between the U.S. and Germany in this World War I drama. An American diplomat (Robert Elliott) attempts to prevent China from joining the war on the side of Germany. His adversary is a German official who is very persuasive with the Chinese leaders. Lady Tsen Mei, a Chinese actress, portrays a viceroy's daughter who becomes romantically involved with Elliott. When he rejects her, she threatens to help the German in his cause. This is one of the few World War I films to use the East as background. ∎

For the Freedom of the World (1918), Goldwyn. *Dir.* Ira M. Lowry, F. J. Carroll; *Sc.* Edwin Bower Hesser; *Cast includes:* E. K. Lincoln, Romaine Fielding, Jane Adler, Neil Moran, Walter Weems.

Set during World War I, this silent drama intertwines the lives of three people. One is a brave Canadian lieutenant who is in love with a nurse whom he marries. She, in turn, has rejected another suitor she thought to be a "slacker." He joins the military and rises in the ranks. Eventually the three meet in France where the remainder of the complex plot unfolds. The lieutenant volunteers for a suicide mission in which he has to blow up some mines. The film has several extensive battle sequences. Aside from the romantic drama, the film provides plenty of propaganda for its audiences. With its condemnation of slackers and its allusions to the plight of such nations as Belgium and France, it turns into a strong cautionary tale for American audiences. They are encouraged to unite and put their trust in their government and their efforts into the war industry. ∎

For the Honor of Old Glory or Carrying the Stars and Stripes Into Mexico (1914), World.

A Mexican spy manipulates his way into the good graces of an American colonel and becomes a second lieutenant in the officer's cavalry regiment. The remainder of this silent film set during the Mexican War tells how the spy leads the colonel, his family and the regiment into a trap in Mexico. The colonel's pretty daughter is kidnaped, while battles break out between the American troops and Mexican soldiers in this not too realistic story. ∎

For the Service (1936), U. *Dir.* Buck Jones; *Sc.* Isadore Bernstein; *Cast includes:* Buck Jones, Clifford Jones, Edward Keene, Beth Marion, Fred Kohler.

An action drama about the U.S. Cavalry, Indians and a horde of brigands, the film features cowboy star Buck Jones as a government scout. He journeys to a remote stockade where he quickly solves several local problems. Clifford Jones portrays the weak son of the captain of the post who can't face death and killing. Beth Marion provides the romantic interest in this low-budget film. There is plenty of action but little basis for any specific historical events of the period. ∎

For Valour (1917), Triangle. *Dir.* Albert Parker; *Cast includes:* Richard Barthelmess, Winifred Allen, Henry Weaver, Mabel Ballin.

This silent domestic drama depicts how World War I affects an impoverished Canadian family. The sickly father, a veteran of the Boer War, can barely make ends meet with his small pension. His daughter sacrifices her simple pleasures so that her brother could look presentable when he applies for a job. When war breaks out, she persuades the boy to enlist. Once in Europe and in the thick of battle, he distinguishes himself by saving an officer's life and is presented with the Victoria Cross. However, he is seriously wounded and loses an arm. When he returns home, he finds his sister involved in some difficulty with the law, but he straightens the problem out. She, too, has made personal sacrifices for the family but has received no medal. ∎

For Whom the Bell Tolls (1943), Par. *Dir.* Sam Wood; *Sc.* Dudley Nichols; *Cast includes:* Gary Cooper, Ingrid Bergman, Akim Tamiroff, Vladimir Sokoloff, Katina Paxinou.

Hemingway's novel of the Spanish Civil War has been adapted into a romantic drama with its emphasis on the love between Robert Jordan, played by Gary Cooper, and Maria, a Spanish orphan, played by Ingrid Bergman. Jordan, an American engineering instructor, works for the Republic of Spain and is assigned to blow up a strategic bridge during an offensive against the Fascists. His journey to the mountains takes him to the camp of a band of guerrillas led by Pablo (Akim Tamiroff), a tired and drunken peasant who no longer believes in the Republic. Here Jordan meets Maria, who has been rescued by the group during a train wreck and now cooks for them. Vladimir Sokoloff plays an old loyal Republican who is reluctant to kill. When Jordan suggests that the old man will have to shoot a guard at the bridge, the peasant remarks that the soldier is only a boy. "I would kill the sentry, yes," he admits to the American, "considering the necessity of the bridge. But if I live later, I would try to live in such a way doing no harm to anyone that it will be forgiven."

When Jordan learns that the enemy has brought many troops across the bridge in anticipation of the offensive, he tries to send a message to the Republican general. But the message arrives too late, and Jordan, in an act of futility, is forced to blow up the bridge. The treacherous Pablo plans to provide enough horses for his little band's escape by killing some of the local guerrillas who have volunteered to help destroy the bridge. "We understand each other," he says, winking at Jordan. Pablo's wife is suspicious of his intentions. "No one understands you," she says, "neither God nor your mother, nor I, nor you." As the small group attempts to escape, Jordan is wounded in the leg. He volunteers to stay behind to slow down the advance of the Fascist troops while his companions and Maria make their escape.

The scene in which Robert Jordan sacrifices his life for the remnants of the guerrilla force as he mans the machine gun against the advancing troops became a familiar film icon in the 1940s—that of the brave American fighting for a noble cause against impossible odds. Other examples include Robert Taylor as the last marine in *Bataan* (1943) behind the machine gun cutting down the hordes of attacking Japanese; the remaining American soldiers in *Wake Island* (1942) battling to the end as they are overwhelmed by the invading enemy; and Humphrey Bogart in *Sahara* (1943) preventing a battalion of desperate German soldiers from reaching an oasis. ∎

Force of Arms (1951), WB. Dir. Michael Curtiz; Sc. Orin Jannings; Cast includes: William Holden, Nancy Olsen, Frank Lovejoy, Gene Evans.

A thinly disguised version of Hemingway's *A Farewell to Arms*, this World War II romantic drama stars William Holden as a sergeant on the Italian front who falls in love with Nancy Olsen, a member of the Women's Army Corps (WAC). Holden, during a brief break from the front lines, meets Olsen and they fall in love. When he returns to the fighting, he is wounded. He believes that his thoughts during the battle of returning to his love may have been responsible for his major's death. He marries Olsen but returns to the front voluntarily to redeem himself for his past actions during battle. He is again wounded. His wife finds him among a group of released prisoners of war. Frank Lovejoy plays the major in command of Holden's outfit. Several realistic battle sequences include newsreel footage of the Italian front during World War II. ∎

Forced Landing. See *Flying Blind* (1941). ∎

Foreign Agent (1942). See Spy Films: the Talkies. ∎

Foreign Correspondent (1940), UA. Dir. Alfred Hitchcock; Sc. Charles Bennett, Joan Harrison; Cast includes: Joel McCrea, Laraine Day, Herbert Marshall, George Sanders, Albert Basserman, Robert Benchley.

Hitchcock's highly suspenseful and exciting drama of political intrigue on the eve of World War II was his second American film. Joel McCrea, as an American reporter sent to Europe in August of 1939 to uncover the truth about the threat of war, becomes entangled in an international spy ring whose members are posing as part of a peace organization. He witnesses the kidnaping of a famous Dutch diplomat and the assassination of the diplomat's double. Several attempts are made on his life as he attempts to expose the leaders of the ring. George Sanders, as a fellow reporter, aids him in the search. Herbert Marshall portrays the mastermind behind the plot, while his daughter (Laraine Day), unaware of her father's ties to Nazi Germany, falls in love with McCrea.

The director has loaded the film with his usual inventive devices and witty style. McCrea's pursuit of an assassin through a crowd of umbrella-carrying onlookers is cleverly executed, as is the climactic plane crash of a transatlantic clipper. There is probably more of Hitchcock's humor in this film than in any of his other works. Robert Benchley plays a correspondent who spends half his day rewriting government press releases and the other half drinking. A humorous Latvian who understands no English appears occasionally. There is the running gag of McCrea losing a variety of hats. Much of the dialogue is witty. When McCrea is about to be arrested by Dutch authorities, he says: "I hope the chief of police speaks English." "We all speak English," the officer replies. "That's more than I could say for my country," McCrea quips.

Once war breaks out near the end of the film, the dialogue—much of it written by James Hilton—turns serious and patriotic. "This is London," a radio announcer says at the beginning of a world-wide broadcast. "We have as a guest tonight one of the soldiers of the press—one of the little army of historians who are writing history from beside the cannon's mouth." McCrea is about to go on the air, but he is interrupted by an air-raid and the lights go out. As bombs rain down on London, he addresses America from the darkened radio studio: "The lights are all out everywhere—except in America. Keep those lights burning. Cover them with steel. Ring them with guns. Build a canopy of battleships and bombing planes around them. Hello, America. Hang on to your lights. They're the only lights left in the world."

This last scene, which intensifies the immediacy of the drama, was hastily added to the film when it became obvious that air attacks over England were forthcoming. In addition, it served as effective propaganda. Few Americans who saw the film realized at the time that the British government had asked the director to stay in Hollywood and continue to turn out propaganda dramas arousing anti-Nazi sentiments. Britain also hoped that such films would prod the U.S. to enter the war. ■

Foreign Devils (1928), MGM. *Dir.* W. S. Van Dyke; *Sc.* Marian Ainslee; *Cast includes:* Tim McCoy, Claire Windsor, Cyril Chadwick, Frank Currier.

This action drama is set in China during the Boxer Rebellion with Tim McCoy portraying an officer at the American Embassy. A love affair develops between McCoy and a young Englishwoman (Claire Windsor) who foolishly leaves the safety of the settlement and goes off exploring on her own. She is taken captive by priests of a Chinese temple and is ultimately rescued by McCoy, who returns her to safety. Later, when a group of Americans are threatened by Chinese rebel forces, McCoy, the U.S. Marines and the British navy arrive in time to save them. Little information is given concerning the Boxers or the causes of the rebellion. ■

Foreign Legion. In 1831 France introduced a professional military unit made up of volunteers of various nationalities. The original purpose of this group was to enforce French authority in its colonies. Legionnaires served in Mexico in the 1860s where 63 troopers fought to the death against 2,000 Mexicans. The Legion, which lists among its distinguished veterans poet Alan Seeger and songwriter Cole Porter, fought in both World Wars. Originally stationed in Algiers, the force is currently quartered in France. Today, more than a thousand men each year join the Legion because of its mystique.

Sometimes described as an army of "professional gunmen in search of a war," the French Foreign Legion has been immortalized and romanticized in scores of American films whose principal players represent the major stars of the period. The most popular story of the elite unit remains *Beau Geste*, based on Percival Wren's story. Of the three versions (1926, 1939, 1966), William Wellman's 1939 film starring Gary Cooper with Brian Donlevy as the sadistic captain is the best known. However, all three capture in part the daily life and duties of a Legionnaire. Ouida's successful novel of the Foreign Legion also received three screen treatments. *Under Two Flags* (1916) stars Theda Bara as Cigarette, a sultry cafe entertainer who falls in love with a Legionnaire and ends up sacrificing her life for him. Priscilla Dean portrays the alluring cafe entertainer in the 1922 version. The third adaptation and first talking version (1936), directed by Frank Lloyd, features Claudette Colbert as Cigarette and Ronald Colman as her lover.

The attractive cafe entertainer has become a staple of the genre. *Morocco* (1930), starring Marlene Dietrich as a male-attired cabaret singer who falls for Legionnaire Gary Cooper and ultimately follows him into the desert, offers as much camp as romance. Jack Holt and Ralph Graves, as two rival Legionnaires in the comedy drama *Hell's Island* (1930), brawl over another cafe entertainer, Marie (Dorothy Sebastian). Hala Linda, as a cafe singer in the low-budget *Legion of Missing Men* (1937), provides the romantic interest and conflict between two brothers (Ralph Forbes and Ben Alexander).

Another convention is the testing of the

hero's courage, honor and loyalty. Warner Baxter in Victor Fleming's *Renegades* (1930) portrays a rebellious Legionnaire who temporarily joins the enemy. Myrna Loy plays a spy who meets her just end. In the routine *Desert Legion* (1953) Legionnaire officer Alan Ladd is forced to desert so that he can uncover a rebel leader hiding in the hills. Carlos Thompson in *Fort Algiers* (1953) portrays a former Legionnaire who is trying to prove that he was wrongly court-martialed. An alcoholic Englishman (Ron Randall) in *Desert Sands* (1955) demonstrates that he has the right stuff once the climactic battle between the Legion and warring Arabs begins.

Unlike American westerns, which occasionally attempt to justify the actions of hostile Indians, Legion films rarely sympathize with the desert tribes or try to explain their grievances. They generally remain unidentified although the *Beau Geste* dramas mention the Tuaregs and *Hell's Island* (1930) and the *Desert Song* films single out the Riffs. They seem to exist only as targets in a shooting gallery. Although they attack in overwhelming hordes against undermanned forts or lie in ambush to strike at small patrols of Legionnaires, they usually perish in disproportionate numbers to the soldiers. Their hostile chieftains, generally treacherous, power-crazed figures, sometimes lust for the heroines. Occasionally, they are portrayed as having been educated in the West.

The Legion has provided the backgrounds for comedies and satires as well as romantic dramas and adventure tales. Such films as *We're in the Legion Now* (1937), *Flying Deuces* (1939) with Laurel and Hardy and *Abbott and Costello in the Foreign Legion* (1950) are straight farces that depend heavily on slapstick. *The Silent Lover* (1926), a satire of the 1920s "sheik" films, stars Milton Sills as an officer in the French Foreign Legion who competes with a sheik for the heroine. Marty Feldman's *The Last Remake of Beau Geste* (1977) pokes fun at various aspects of the Legion mystique. ■

Forever After (1926), FN. *Dir.* F. Harmon Weight; *Sc.* Paul Gangelin; *Cast includes:* Lloyd Hughes, Mary Astor, Hallam Cooley, David Torrence.

Lloyd Hughes portrays a popular college football player who does not end up with his true love until after he becomes a war hero in this World War I romantic drama. Before the conflict, the young man is in love with Mary Astor but is rejected by her mother who sees little promise in Hughes as a prospective son-in-law. When he leaves town for a job following his father's death, he concedes to the officious mother's request and tells his sweetheart that the romance is over. With the advent of World War I, Hughes, now a captain, distinguishes himself in battle and is wounded. Astor appears at his bedside. Several effective battle sequences include, among others, the hero's attack on a machine-gun emplacement. ■

Forever and a Day (1943). See Propaganda Films: World War II. ■

Forgotten Men (1933), Jewel. *Dir.* Samuel Cummins.

A World War I documentary assembled chiefly from government newsreels, the film describes the events of the war in chronological order, injecting a note of pacifism. War scenes include those on land, on sea and in the air. Military officers representing eight different countries who participated in the war help to narrate the important events. The film differs from others of this type by having veterans of the various campaigns, men from different countries, describe their personal experiences in battle. One of the highlights depicts the German invasion of Belgium in which the retreating army is seen destroying bridges, railroads and anything else that would help the advancing enemy. Another startling sequence shows the first use of poison gas, resulting in British soldiers choking to death in their trenches. Included too are scenes of German air ace von Richthofen's flying circus in action, a zeppelin raid over England and the battles of the Marne, Somme and Verdun, among others. ■

Fort Algiers (1953), UA. *Dir.* Lesley Selander; *Sc.* Theodore St. John; *Cast includes:* Yvonne De Carlo, Carlos Thompson, Raymond Burr, Leif Erickson.

The French Foreign Legion faces another Arab insurrection in this routine action drama. Yvonne De Carlo portrays a French spy masquerading as a cafe singer. She is assigned to gather information concerning hostile Arab activities. She accomplishes this by developing a friendship with the principal villainous chieftain (Raymond Burr) whose plans include the destruction of strategic oil fields. Burr eventually gets wise to her, but she is rescued by another agent and her true love. Carlos Thompson, as the hero, a former Legionnaire, tries to prove that he was wrongly court-martialed. Exciting action sequences include the obligatory climactic skirmish between the Legion and the Arabs. ∎

Fort Apache (1948), RKO. *Dir.* John Ford; *Sc.* Frank Nugent; *Cast includes:* Henry Fonda, John Wayne, Shirley Temple, Ward Bond, Pedro Armendariz.

This is the first part of John Ford's cavalry trilogy set in the Southwest during the latter part of the 19th century when the soldiers rode out from their remote outposts to tame the hostile Apaches. Henry Fonda portrays a vindictive colonel who takes control of a remote fort in the Arizona desert. Resentful of his assignment following an exceptional career in the army, he is unusually inflexible with his subordinates. John Wayne as a major in Fonda's command is an experienced Indian fighter. On the other hand, the colonel's military background stems solely from his Civil War days. Their differences concerning tactics in battling the Apaches lead to their personal conflict. Seeing a chance to capture the notorious Indian chief Cochise, Fonda sends Wayne to arrange a parley. Fonda then arrives with a troop of cavalry and charges blindly toward the chieftain and his warriors. The soldiers are cut down mercilessly. Only Wayne and a handful of troopers survive. Shirley Temple, as Fonda's daughter, falls in love with a lieutenant (John Agar).

Director John Ford's images of the cavalry gallantly riding across the desolate land, the fierce and glorious battles between the soldiers and the Apaches and the details of army life at the outpost may not always be historically accurate, but he paints them as we wish them to have been. This holds true as well for one of the major themes—the need for heroes. In the final sequence, which occurs years later, Wayne, now in charge, is seen answering reporters' inquiries. Wayne goes along with one journalist's false but heroic account of Fonda's charge. Fonda may have been pompous and misdirected, but he was brave. ∎

Fort Bowie (1958), UA. *Dir.* Howard W. Koch; *Sc.* Maurice Tombragel; *Cast includes:* Ben Johnson, Jan Harrison, Kent Taylor, Jane Davi, Larry Chance.

War erupts between the Apaches and the U.S. Cavalry in this action drama when the Indians learn that some of their tribe were massacred after they surrendered. A politically appointed cavalry major (J. Ian Douglas), obsessed with furthering his own professional career, orders his detachment to gun down a band of Apaches who have turned themselves in peacefully. Apache warriors, seeking revenge, take to the warpath and annihilate the major and his men. Later, another battle ensues when the cavalry attacks its own fort to rout the hostiles who have taken possession of it. Ben Johnson, as a captain falsely accused by his colonel's wife (Jan Harrison) of having made advances toward her and who strongly opposes the colonel's methods, is sent on a perilous mission to the Apache chief. Kent Smith, as the colonel, perishes with his wife during an Indian attack. ∎

Fort Courageous (1965), TCF. *Dir.* Lesley Selander; *Sc.* Richard Landau; *Cast includes:* Fred Beir, Donald Barry, Hanna Landy, Harry Lauter, Cheryl MacDonald.

A court-martialed sergeant regains his reputation and self-respect in this routine cavalry-vs.-Indians drama. Fred Beir portrays the sergeant who is wrongfully condemned by his military superiors. When his captain, played by veteran western performer Donald "Red" Barry, is wounded in an Indian attack, Beir assumes command of the cavalry troop. The mauled soldiers eventually reach their destination but find that the defenders of the fort have all been killed. Beir, compelled to confront the hostiles, quickly organizes his men and manages to battle the Indians to a standstill. The attackers acknowledge the courage of the small garrison and withdraw. ∎

Fort Defiance (1951), UA. *Dir.* John Rawlins; *Sc.* Louis Lantz; *Cast includes:* Dane Clark, Ben Johnson, Peter Graves, Tracey Roberts, George Cleveland, Iron Eyes.

An action drama concerning clashes between the U.S. Cavalry and the Navajos and an ex-soldier's pursuit of a deserter, the film features Dane Clark as the hunted man and Ben Johnson as the man seeking revenge. Johnson, whose company of troops were killed because of Clark's desertion in battle, tracks him to his family ranch where he waits for Clark's return. Meanwhile the Navajo decide to take to the warpath rather than comply to a government decree that they relocate to a reservation. When skirmishes break out between the cavalry and the Indians, Johnson and Clark put aside their differences and join forces against the hostiles. Clark eventually loses his life in a gunfight with outlaws who are threatening his family. Peter Graves portrays Clark's blind brother. Tracey Roberts, as a young woman of questionable reputation, falls in love with Graves.

Few cavalry-vs.-Indian films depicted the Navajo as a hostile force (*Column South* (1953) was another). The wily Apaches and fearsome Comanche in the Southwest and the defiant Sioux in the plains states provided a longer and more bloody history of resistance for Hollywood screenwriters. The Navajo was one of the first great tribes to face defeat at the hands of the whites. Kit Carson with four hundred troops routed the Navajos from their stronghold in northeast Arizona and brought them under subjugation by 1867. They were moved to a reservation at Bosque Redondo where they faded from the pages of Indian military history. ■

Fort Massacre (1958), UA. *Dir.* Joseph M. Newman; *Sc.* Martin N. Goldsmith; *Cast includes:* Joel McCrea, Forrest Tucker, Susan Cabot, John Russell, Anthony Caruso.

Joel McCrea portrays a cavalry sergeant who takes command of a troop when its officer is killed in an ambush in this better-than-average revenge drama. McCrea turns into an Indian hater after his wife and two children are killed by Apaches. He leads the men in his charge into dangerous Indian country to provoke a war with the Apaches. The soldiers eventually come under attack. When McCrea, in his blind hatred, intends to shoot a harmless old Indian, a fellow soldier, played by John Russell, kills the sergeant. Only a handful of troopers survive the battle.

The film was one of several pro-Indian dramas released during the 1950s, a trend that was begun with *Broken Arrow* (1950), starring James Stewart. It is also one of the rare instances in which McCrea, almost invariably an upright hero, portrays a less than noble role. ■

Fort Ti (1953), Col. *Dir.* William Castle; *Sc.* Robert E. Kent; *Cast includes:* George Montgomery, Joan Vohs, Irving Bacon, James Seay, Ben Astar.

Rogers' Rangers join forces with the British to remove the French from Fort Ticonderoga in this routine drama set during the French and Indian War. George Montgomery portrays one of Major Robert Rogers' stalwart rangers who help to turn the tide against the French in this 17th century conflict. Meanwhile, he must contend with two females, Joan Vohs, who is suspected of being a French spy, and an Indian, played by Phyllis Fowler. Howard Petrie plays Rogers. Originally released in 3-D, the film takes advantage of the short-lived fad. Sequences include flaming arrows and other objects propelled at the viewer. ■

Fort Vengeance (1953). See Sitting Bull. ■

Fort Yuma (1955), UA. *Dir.* Lesley Selander; *Sc.* Danny Arnold; *Cast includes:* Peter Graves, Joan Vohs, John Hudson, Joan Taylor, Addison Richards.

Apaches take to the warpath when their chief is killed in this routine action drama. Abel Fernandez, as the Indian chief's son, swears revenge for his murdered father who was shot while journeying to Fort Yuma to sign a peace treaty. The young warrior plans to disguise his braves as soldiers and annihilate the defenders at the fort. He attacks a column of troopers to get the uniforms, but several escape and warn the fort. In the ensuing battle, the Apaches are defeated. Peter Graves portrays a lieutenant who hates Indians although he woos a pretty Indian played by Joan Taylor.

No doubt influenced by the superior *Broken Arrow* (1950), a trend-setting social drama cloaked in a western setting that advocated tolerance for the Indian, *Fort Yuma* suggests a similar contemporary theme. A raging conflict between Indian-hating Graves and his Indian-sympathizing scout (John Hudson) is resolved only when they are attacked by Apaches and Hudson's sister is killed. ■

Fortune's Mask (1922), Vitagraph. *Dir.* Robert Ensminger; *Sc.* C. Graham Baker; *Cast includes:* Earle Williams, Patsy Ruth Miller, Henry Herbert, Milton Ross.

A tale of South American revolution and political intrigue, the film stars Earle Williams as the son of a murdered president. Williams had been sent to the U.S. for his schooling and is now ready to right the wrongs against the corrupt regime in his native country and avenge his father's death. He manages to awaken the patriotism in enough of his fellow countrymen to overthrow the present government in this story based on O. Henry's "Cabbages and Kings."

Enough political unrest was going on south of the border at the time of the film's release to make the story timely. Several Latin-American countries were plagued with possible insurrections including, among others, Panama (1918–1920), Honduras (1919) and Guatemala (1920). American audiences may also have been attracted to this type of film since American troops were often involved. The U.S., for example, intervened in all three of these countries either to protect American interests or its legation, to maintain order or to secure a neutral zone during an anticipated revolution. ∎

Fortunes of Captain Blood (1950), Col. *Dir.* Gordon Douglas; *Sc.* Michael Hogan, Robert Libott, Frank Burt; *Cast includes:* Louis Hayward, Patricia Medina, George Macready, Alfonso Bedoya.

Another remake of Rafael Sabatini's popular story of the Irish doctor who turns pirate, this action drama takes place in the 1700s, chiefly near the coast of South America, during the unofficial sea war between England and France. Louis Hayward portrays the title character, Peter Blood, who is banished from England for giving medical aid to a political dissident. He soon turns to piracy and preys upon Spanish shipping in the Indies. ∎

Four Feathers (1915), Metro. *Dir.* J. Searle Dawley; *Sc.* J. Searle Dawley; *Cast includes:* Edgar L. Davenport, Fuller Mellish, Ogden Child, Jr., Howard Estabrook, Arthur Evers.

The first of several screen adaptations of A.E.W. Mason's popular novel, the silent drama revolves around a captain in the British army who resigns his commission when his regiment sails to Egypt. Three of his fellow officers, believing him to be a coward, send him a white feather, the symbol of cowardice. His sweetheart follows suit. To redeem himself, he journeys alone to Egypt to return each feather by performing heroic acts. The fictitious events center around the Battle of Omdurman (1898). Howard Estabrook, who plays the lead, became a highly successful screenwriter (he wrote the screenplay for

the silent remake of this film in 1929), continuing in this capacity into the late 1950s. ∎

Four Feathers, The (1929), Par. *Dir.* Merian C. Cooper, Ernest B. Schoedsak; *Sc.* Howard Estabrook; *Cast includes:* Richard Arlen, Fay Wray, Clive Brook, William Powell, Theodore von Eitz, Noah Beery.

Another silent version of A.E.W. Mason's adventure novel, the film adds striking visuals to the already popular story of an officer who resigns his commission in the British army when his regiment is ordered overseas. As in the earlier film, he receives white feathers, representing cowardice, from his closest acquaintances as well as his fiancee. The remainder of the film concerns his individual acts of bravery as he attempts to redeem himself.

Produced at such a late date for a silent film, the question arises as to why it wasn't made as a sound feature, especially since a silent version, albeit crude, already existed. The battle scenes are above average. Another entry in sound and color featuring Ralph Richardson was produced in England in 1939 and is considered by many film historians and critics to be the best version. ∎

Four Horsemen of the Apocalypse, The (1921), Metro. *Dir.* Rex Ingram; *Sc.* June Mathis; *Cast includes:* Rudolph Valentino, Alice Terry, Joseph Swickard, Brinsley Shaw, Alan Hale, Mabel Van Buren, Stuart Holmes, Jean Hersholt, Edward Connelly.

Based on the novel by Vincente Blasco Ibanez, the film chronicles the Desnoyers family, with Rudolph Valentino as Julio Desnoyers. The elder, Marcelo, has fled his native France in 1870 to avoid war. He settles in Argentina where he accumulates wealth and marries his patron's daughter. After raising two children, the family returns to France while another faction of the family moves to Germany. World War I breaks out, pitting Julio on one side of the conflict and three sons of Marcelo's sister-in-law on the other. All the young men perish in the war, leaving the parents to contemplate the Four Horsemen of the Apocalypse—War, Famine, Disease and Death.

This was the first major postwar film to treat the topic of war generally and World War I specifically from the viewpoint of some distance—without the usual patriotism and propaganda that invariably accompanied the military dramas of the period. The film reflects the author's role as a neutral observer of countries at war. ∎

Four Horsemen of the Apocalypse, The

(1961), MGM. *Dir.* Vincente Minnelli; *Sc.* Robert Ardrey, John Gay; *Cast includes:* Glenn Ford, Ingrid Thulin, Charles Boyer, Paul Lukas.

A remake of the popular 1921 silent version of the Ibanez novel, this glossy Technicolor production of a family torn by war and fighting on opposite sides failed critically and at the box office. The story is updated to World War II and offers several imaginative special-effects images of war. But the overall result lacks conviction. Glenn Ford portrays Julio Desnoyers, the role that brought fame to Rudolph Valentino. Ingrid Thulin, whose voice had to be dubbed by Angela Lansbury, plays Marguerite Laurier, Julio's mistress. She is married to a French officer (Paul Henried) who later joins the Resistance and is killed by the Gestapo. Charles Boyer is featured as Marcelo Desnoyers, Julio's father. Paul Lukas portrays the matriarch of the German branch of the family. Julio, who has tried to remain neutral and detached from the war, eventually joins the French underground and sacrifices his life for the Allied cause. ∎

442nd Regimental Combat Team. See *Go For Broke!* (1951). ∎

Four Hundred Million, The (1939), Garrison. *Sc.* Dudley Nichols; narrated by Fredric March.

A documentary about the the Sino-Japanese War, the film develops its pro-Chinese theme by utilizing three areas of footage. These include excerpts from newsreels of the conflict in the East, scenic shots of a once peaceful land and its people, and educational sequences tracing the origins and the present situation of the war. Screenwriter Dudley Nichols wrote the script that is narrated by actor Fredric March. ∎

Four Jills in a Jeep (1944), TCF. *Dir.* William A. Seiter; *Sc.* Robert Ellis, Helen Logan, Snag Werris; *Cast includes:* Kay Francis, Carole Landis, Martha Raye, Mitzi Mayfair, Phil Silvers.

Based on the personal experiences of a handful of women entertainers, the film describes the work of the United Service Organization (U.S.O.), particularly the contributions of those who traveled overseas to entertain the troops during World War II. Kay Francis, Carole Landis, Martha Raye and Mitzi Mayfair are some of the performers who play themselves in this fictionalized version of their tour. Landis and Dick Haymes provide some romantic interest, Phil Silvers and Martha Raye contribute their comedic talents and Harry James and his orchestra supply much of the music. ∎

Four Sons (1928), Fox. *Dir.* John Ford; *Sc.* Philip Klein; *Cast includes:* Margaret Mann, James Hall, Francis X. Bushman, Charles Morton, George Meeker.

This domestic drama concerns the impact of World War I on a modest German family living happily in a cottage in Bavaria. Mother Bernie (Margaret Mann) has four sons. Joseph, who has migrated to America before the war, owns a delicatessen shop and has a wife and a child. When war breaks out her three other sons enlist while Joseph joins the American troops. His three brothers are killed. The war takes its toll on the mother who finds no joy when the armistice is announced. Joseph returns home from the war and sends for his lonely mother. She arrives at Ellis Island but is detained. She is finally reunited with her remaining son and her grandchild.

Director John Ford's film, along with D. W. Griffith's *Isn't Life Wonderful?* (1924) and Fred Niblo's *The Enemy* (1928), was one of a series of features to depict the war and its effects through the eyes of the enemy. The protagonists have the same joys and fears as others, the director is quick to point out. As long as Ford concentrates on the common people, describing them as having been tricked by their power-crazed leaders, he is on safe ground. American audiences may not have been prepared to forgive Prussian militarism as exemplified by the Kaiser, but Ford's drama moved them emotionally concerning the plight of the German people. This humanistic approach reached its zenith in the highly acclaimed *All Quiet on the Western Front* (1930), in which all the principal characters were German youths innocently caught up in the spirit and fervor of World War I.

A 1940 remake updated events to World War II. It described the ravages and sufferings that are left in the wake of Hitler's onslaught in Europe. Don Ameche, as a patriotic son, moves to America while Alan Curtis portrays a Nazi sympathizer. ■

Francis (1950), U. *Dir.* Arthur Lubin; *Sc.* David Stern; *Cast includes:* Donald O'Connor, Patricia Medina, ZaSu Pitts, Eduard Franz, Howland Chamberlin.

Francis, the subject of this wartime comedy set in Burma during World War II, is a talking mule that has more common sense than most army personnel. Donald O'Connor portrays a young lieutenant who is rescued from the enemy by Francis. Patricia Medina, as a spy, provides the feminine interest while veteran screen comedienne ZaSu Pitts plays a nurse. The voice of the mule is supplied by Chill Wills. The box-office success of this one-joke comedy led to six sequels, all released between 1950 and 1956. Screenwriter David Stern based the film on his own novel. ■

"Francis Marion, the Swamp Fox"
(1914), Kalem. *Cast includes:* Guy Coombs, Marguerite Courtot.

This rousing action drama tells the story of Francis Marion, known as the Swamp Fox, and how he routed the British and rescued General Gates during the American Revolution. The film, which includes several good battle sequences, adheres very closely to the actual incidents in Marion's life. Some melodramatics have been added for dramatic effect, such as the rescue of a heroine from a burning house. ■

Franco-Prussian War (1870–1871). The Franco-Prussian War was one of those short conflicts of the late 19th century that played a significant role in shaping future events. Prince Otto von Bismarck, Prussia's chief minister, used the Franco-Prussian War to bring about the unification of Germany. In 1870 he convinced many independent German states to join Prussia in fighting a common enemy—France. Bismarck instigated the war by falsifying a dispatch from his ruler, Prussia's William I, to evoke French hostility. France responded to the bait by declaring war. German armies under General von Moltke swept into France and defeated the French at the key Battle of Sedan. Flushed by a resounding victory over France, the leading German princes agreed to unification under William, who was proclaimed Emperor on January 18, 1871. As a result of the war,

France ceded the mineral-rich provinces of Alsace and Lorraine and paid Germany an indemnity. Germany's treatment of France helped create the animosity that led to World War I in the next century.

Hollywood made very few dramas about the Franco-Prussian War. "The Standard Bearer" (1908), a short silent drama with strong action sequences of the war, concerns a French color sergeant who, although mortally wounded in battle, saves his regimental colors. *Mademoiselle Fifi* (1944), about an avidly patriotic French laundress (Simone Simon) who refuses to acknowledge the Prussian occupiers of a small village in her beloved country, suggests as much about the period of its release as it does about the Franco-Prussian War—its actual setting. Released during World War II, the film presents the conventional anti-German propaganda emanating from Hollywood studios in the 1940s. ■

Franklin, Benjamin. See *1776* (1972). ■

Fremont, John C. (1813–1890). Called "The Pathfinder," Fremont was one of the nation's more colorful, popular and controversial characters. An explorer, soldier and politician during the mid-19th century, he first achieved fame as a western explorer when, as a commissioned officer in the U.S. Topographical Corps, he was involved with and sometimes led several expeditions in the Rockies between 1838–45. Kit Carson served as his guide on two such ventures. Fremont's expeditions served as background for two films. *Kit Carson Over the Great Divide* (1925), with Arthur Hotaling portraying Fremont, fictionalized much of the two men's exploits. *Kit Carson* (1940), with Jon Hall as Carson and Dana Andrews as Fremont, recounted the historic first expedition, embellishing the facts for the sake of action and romance. Fremont was in California, following his third expedition, when the Mexican War broke out (1846). He organized a revolt of American settlers against Mexican authorities and helped create the Bear Flag Republic at Sonoma on June 14, 1846. The 1940 film gives a highly fictional account of this event, contributing much of its success to the heroics of Carson.

After the war, Fremont briefly represented California as U.S. Senator (1850–1851). He was the first presidential candidate for the newly formed Republican Party in 1856, losing to John Buchanan. During the Civil War, Fremont returned to the army with a rank of major-general and served as head of the Department of the West and later in western Virginia. Following the Civil War he failed as a railroad promoter but gained appointment as territorial governor of Arizona (1878–1883). ■

French-Algerian Wars. See Algerian-French Wars. ■

French and Indian War (1754–1763). When British troops commanded by General James Wolfe successfully climbed the imposing cliffs that rose above the St. Lawrence River to the Plains of Abraham outside Quebec one gray dawn morning in September 1759, they caught by surprise and defeated French forces defending the city. It was the last major battle in the French and Indian War. The results of the conflict greatly affected the future development of much of North America. "Seats of the Mighty" (1914), a short silent drama set in Paris and Quebec heights and featuring Lionel Barrymore, recreated the famous battle.

By losing the war, France ceased to be a major colonial power in the New World. France ceded to Britain all of its Canadian territory and all land east of the Mississippi River. Britain emerged as the dominant North American colonial empire, its culture eventually dominating the region. Britain's postwar colonial policy for ruling its North American territories eventually led to the hostility that erupted into the American Revolution in the next decade.

The French and Indian War was the North American portion of the Seven Years' War, one of a series of worldwide clashes for empire supremacy between England and France that raged through much of the 17th and 18th centuries. The dispute that pitted England against France and its Indian allies had its roots in the decisions by both European powers to enforce conflicting claims in the Ohio valley.

Films about this period were not concerned with the domestic and worldwide significance of this conflict. They depicted, with a few exceptions, military engagements and the personal interplay and problems of the often fictitious main characters. One of the earliest entries, a 1914 Kalem silent production titled *Wolfe, or the Conquest of Quebec*, concerns the decisive battle of the French and Indian War.

Winners Of The Wilderness (1927), with Tim McCoy and Joan Crawford, accurately portrays an early British defeat in the war's first important clash, the Battle of Fort Duquesne in 1755, near the present site of Pittsburgh. The film faithfully points out the naivete of British redcoats and American colonial militia under General Edward Braddock trying to fight a wilderness war in the formal colorful uniforms and parade-ground style of battle developed in Europe. The work includes Braddock's death by forest ambush in his unsuccessful attempt to drive the French out of Fort Duquesne. *Unconquered* (1947), starring Gary Cooper, illustrates the different groups that became involved in the battle, including British soldiers, Virginia militia, pioneers and Indians. *Iroquois Trail* (1950), loosely based on James Fenimore Cooper's Leatherstocking Tales, shows the impact of the war on upper New York State and the St. Lawrence Valley.

Indian allies on both sides committed atrocities. One such large-scale historical event appears in the 1920 silent version of *The Last Of The Mohicans*, featuring Wallace Beery. French General Montcalm, after capturing Fort William Henry, promises safe passage to the defeated defenders. His Indian allies treacherously set upon and massacre the retreating garrison. The sequence recurs, with the same overall stark effect, in the 1936 sound version with Randolph Scott.

Hollywood films generally fail to explain why most northeastern tribes sided with France. The Indians did not percieve the French, who had very few colonists in North America, as threats. Instead, they developed a mutually beneficial fur trade. By contrast, native tribes had good reason to fear England's 13 American colonies with a population 20 times greater than that of the French. American colonists vigorously expanded their land claims, interfering with traditional Indian hunting and passage rights. By the time of the French and Indian War, a century-old conflict between the Indians and the American colonists had existed. Many Indian leaders saw a French alliance as a means of restraining the English colonists as well as punishing them for past wrongs. ■

French Foreign Legion. See Foreign Legion. ∎

French Indo-China War (1946–1954). Vietnam had an extensive history of rebellion against French control that stemmed back into the mid-1800s when France first imposed direct colonial supervision over the southeast Asian kingdom. World War II gave Vietnamese nationalists the opportunity to press their struggle for independence even more vigorously. France, overrun by Hitler's Nazi forces in 1940, had to agree to allow Japan to move troops into Indochina in September.

Native nationalist elements under Ho Chih Minh, a Vietnamese socialist who cofounded the French Communist party in 1920 and later organized the Indochina Communist Party in 1930, conducted a war of resistance against Japanese occupation forces during World War II. At the end of the war, Ho Chih Minh refused to accept the return of French power, and on September 2, 1945, he proclaimed the existence of the Democratic Republic of Vietnam. An anti-French guerrilla war broke out (December 1946). The Communist-led nationalists, supported by aid from neighboring Communist China, became even more aggressive and successful in attacks on French military units and their non-Communist (often Catholic) native supporters. The action drama *China Gate* (1957) portrays this period and details the story of a patrol of French Legionnaires assigned to blow up a secret Communist ammunition dump.

The Communist Viet Minh armies, led by Vietnamese General Vo Nguyen Giap, dealt France a serious defeat in 1954 at the Battle of Dienbienphu in northern Vietnam. Giap's forces laid siege to the French stronghold for 56 days, pounding it with artillery and infantry. Exhausted French troops, running short of ammunition and supplies, surrendered on May 7, 1954. *Jump Into Hell* (1955) depicts these last days as the French make a brave but futile attempt to defend the fortress. The Communists are seen overrunning the French position. The French defeat at Dienbienphu ended their attempts to hold on to Vietnam.

An international conference in Geneva, Switzerland, worked out an agreement—the Geneva Accords—that went into effect in July 1954. They provided for the complete withdrawal of France from Vietnam, the temporary splitting of the region at the 17th parallel between a Communist government in the North and a non-Communist administration in the South, and the right for the native population to shift and re-settle in the region of their choice. Furthermore, the agreement stipulated that free elections would be conducted within two years to set up a government for a unified nation.

However, hostilities broke out again in 1956, when the U.S. began giving increased support to South Vietnam's anti-Communist government with the goal of making the division a permanent one to prevent the possibility of unification under the more popular Communist-dominated nationalists. What started as a Communist-fomented guerrilla war in 1956 gradually escalated into the Vietnam War by the early 1960s.

American films of the French Indo-China War have skirted the social and political issues—with one or two exceptions. In *The Quiet American* (1958) Audie Murphy, as an American in Vietnam in 1952, clashes ideologically with an English correspondent (Michael Redgrave). The writer loses his objectivity and sides with the Communists who use him as a dupe and ultimately betray him. In *Rogues' Regiment* (1948) a French colonel aboard a Saigon-bound train shows his frustration with the war. Unable or unwilling to accept the colonial struggle for self-determination, he blames the military conflict on those who are selling arms to the guerrillas and sees the dispute only as an ideological clash between Communism and democracy. "The people of French Indo-China are fighting only because they are tired of French injustice and misrule," a fellow passenger replies to the officer's simple explanation of the conflict. "No," the colonel stubbornly persists, "there are only two marching songs in the world today—the 'Internationale,' which may be theirs, and 'La Marseillaise,' which will always be ours!" ∎

French Revolution (1789–1799). King Louis XVI could not comprehend what was happening to his well-ordered and luxurious world in the summer of 1789. The supreme autocrat, Europe's most powerful symbol of a monarch who ruled by Divine Right, saw his power challenged by mobs of common people. The excesses of his bloated court, coupled with numerous costly wars including his own expensive involvement in the American Revolution, had created a massive drain on the public treasury. At the same time, a corrupt and inefficient system of taxation contributed to the growing specter of government bankruptcy. The financial crisis would soon explode into the French Revolution, an event that caused waves of political and military turmoil beyond the borders of France.

The Estates-General, led by the representatives of the common people, rejected the existing political and social system and demanded several changes. Louis' obstinate refusal to change matters resulted in widespread riots. A Paris mob on July 14, 1789, attacked the Bastille, a political prison that stood as a symbol of the tyranny of the Old Regime. Peasants in the countryside, upon hearing of the happenings in the capital, attacked the castles of many nobles, destroying records of feudal dues as a way of freeing themselves from the traditional and oppressive burden of payments. Fearing for his own safety, Louis yielded to demands for creation of a National Assembly.

The Assembly did away with all feudal privileges and set up a limited monarchy. A mob converged on the royal court at Versailles and physically transferred the royal family to Paris. Many nobles, fearing the worst, fled the country. When Louis tried to do the same, he was captured and returned to Paris. The revolutionists adopted "Liberty, Equality, Fraternity" as their cry. Danton and Marat, who controlled the Paris commune, seized all police power in 1792. By September of that year the monarchy was abolished, and the First Republic was established. Louis and his wife, Marie Antoinette, were executed in January 1793, supposedly for conspiring against the Revolution. (*Marie Antoinette* (1938) recreated several of these events.) Royalist uprisings, in turn, brought about the dreaded Reign of Terror. Robespierre, a power-crazed revolutionist, emerged as a major figure during this new burst of violence. Fearing his abuse of power, the National Convention had him guillotined as well on July 27, 1794.

Despite a new constitution and a new governing body, the Directory (1795–1799), France continued to face economic and political instability, leading to Napoleon Bonaparte's coup d'etat on November 19, 1799, that effectively elevated him to ruler of France. The French Revolution, with its ensuing Napoleonic Wars, demolished the traditional political and social fabric of Europe. It unlocked the floodgates for European liberalism and accelerated the rise of nationalism. The French Revolution has also become a symbol of extremism in which the forces of change often result in the execution of its former leaders.

Hollywood's treatment of the French Revolution has differed from its portrayals of the American and Mexican upheavals. In the latter, films tended to be more sympathetic to revolutionary leaders and often depicted the reigning establishment as corrupt or oppressive. Dramas concerning the French struggle, however, were more ambivalent and sometimes portrayed royalists and, at other times, republicans, as scoundrels. The unruly mobs often threatened the hero or heroine; revolutionary forces seemed as venal as those in power.

One of the earliest silent films that used the French Revolution as a background, D.W. Griffith's "Nursing the Viper" (1909), concerns a Royalist who takes refuge at his Republican friend's home after being pursued by a mob. He betrays his friend by making advances toward the Republican's wife. In "Gambling With Death," another 1909 short silent drama, a jilted suitor vindictively joins the Republicans so that he can lead them to the girl's father. In "The Oath and the Man" (1910), another Griffith film, an idealistic leader of a band of revolutionists guides his followers based on the teachings of Christianity. The more complex and historically oriented *Charlotte Corday* (1914) recounted the death of Marat at the hands of the title character. The film suggested that Marat was responsible for numerous executions.

As the silents grew in length, they offered more complicated plots and richer characterizations. Frank Lloyd's *A Tale of Two Cities* (1917), based on Charles Dickens' classic tale, faithfully conveyed the author's themes of love, revenge and redemption during the Revolution. The same was true of Jack Conway's 1935 version, with Ronald Colman and Elizabeth Allan. It recreated faithfully several historical events, including the storming of the Bastille. Griffith's *Orphans of the Storm* (1921) reflected the director's attitude towards the Revolution. Sympathizing with the momentous event but condemning its excesses, he depicted the abuses of the aristocrats as well as the tyrannical rule of such leaders as Robespierre. *Madame Sans-Gene* (1925), a comedy starring Gloria Swanson as a laundress whose customers include Napoleon, included several action sequences of which the storming of Versailles is a highlight.

Only a handful of sound films have concerned the Revolution. W.S. Van Dyke's *Marie Antoinette*, one of the best and most lavish, is a historical drama depicting the passing of power from a decaying French aristocracy to leaders of the common man. *Captain of the Guard* (1930), the first musical about the Revolution, starred John Boles as Rouget de Lisle, the composer of "La Marseillaise." Such historical figures as Marie Antoinette, Danton and Robespierre occasionally appeared to add a note of authenticity to an otherwise inaccurate re-enactment of historical events.

As with other genres, films of the Revolution occasionally attempted to use the upheaval as a metaphor for contemporary events. Griffith, for example, in *Orphans of the Storm*, released shortly after the Russian Revolution, stated in his opening titles that the French Revolution rightly overthrew an evil government, but we must exercise care not to exchange our good government for "Bolshevism." See also Napoleon, Napoleonic Wars. ■

Friendly Enemies (1925), PDC. *Dir.* George Melford; *Sc.* Alfred A. Cohn; *Cast includes:* Joe Weber, Lew Fields, Virginia Brown Faire, Jack Mulhall, Stuart Holmes.

A comedy drama set during World War I, this was the first full-length feature that the famous vaudeville and stage comedians, Weber and Fields, appeared in. They both portray German-Americans. Fields, a loyal patriot of his adopted country, is proud of his son who is in the army and about to be shipped to France to fight against Germany. His friend, Weber, however, remains loyal to the Fatherland and donates money to a German organization which he hopes will bring an early end to the war. He later learns that his money was used to sink a troopship of American soldiers. Fortunately, Fields' son was not aboard at the time.

Aside from its humor and love interest, the film, released years after the war, emphasizes the duties and responsibilities of foreign-born Americans and their offspring toward their new homeland. This was a real-life dilemma for many German-American citizens when the original play by Samuel Shipman and Aaron Hoffman first appeared in 1918 during World War I.

A 1942 remake updated the original story to World War II. Charles Winninger and Charles Ruggles portray the bickering German-American tycoons who differ in their loyalties to the U.S. and Germany. Winninger, who is sympathetic to Germany, is deceived into contributing to enemy saboteurs and learns too late that he has helped sink an American troop ship that was transporting his own son. ■

Friendly Persuasion (1956), AA. *Dir.* William Wyler; *Sc.* Michael Wilson; *Cast includes:* Gary Cooper, Dorothy McGuire, Marjorie Main, Anthony Perkins, Richard Eyer.

Based on the novel by Jessamyn West, the comedy drama recounts the life of an Indiana Quaker family during the Civil War. Gary Cooper and Dorothy McGuire portray the parents of a teen-age boy and girl and a younger son, all of whom are soon drawn into the war to some degree. Forbidden by their religion to raise arms against others, the men of the community have a difficult time explaining their position to a Union officer who enters their church and asks for volunteers.

Cooper's older son (Anthony Perkins) eventually decides to join the local militia to defend the community against a Confederate raiding party. "Man's life ain't worth a hill of beans unless he lives up to his own conscience," Cooper explains to his son. The daughter falls for a local Union soldier who is wounded in battle. When Perkins' horse returns to the farm, Cooper goes to the battlefield to find his wounded son and is grazed by a young Confederate sniper's bullet. Cooper then disarms the boy and lets him go. Meanwhile, a troop of Southern raiders visits his farm. McGuire gives them food and supplies. But when one trooper tries to take the family's pet goose, McGuire, losing all sense of composure, beats the man with a broom. The raiders are driven away and the family is reunited. The younger son, played by Richard Eyer, can't wait to tell his father how the mother whipped the soldier.

The bloody skirmish between the Northern defenders and the Southern invaders provides a sharp contrast to the idyllic life of the tranquil Quakers. Glowing with warmth and humor in other sequences not related to the conflict, the film captures the anguish and inner struggle of the Quakers who are confronted with the choice of retaining their identity or bearing arms against their fellow men. Cooper, as a man who has tried to live by his convictions, also displays his own doubts. When he is questioned in the church by the officer, he candidly admits that he is not sure what he will do if his farm or family are attacked by the enemy.

Screenwriter Michael Wilson may well have identified with the character played by Cooper. An unfriendly witness before the House Un-American Activities Committee (H.U.A.C.) investigating Communist influence in Hollywood during the early 1950s, Wilson was blacklisted by the studios. He was forced to submit his scripts without receiving screen credit. The screenplay for *Friendly Persuasion*, unfortunately, remains uncredited. ■

Frogmen, The (1951), TCF. Dir. Lloyd Bacon; Sc. John Tucker Battle; *Cast includes:* Richard Widmark, Dana Andrews, Gary Merrill, Robert Wagner.

This drama concerns the gutsy underwater demolition teams who functioned in the Pacific during World War II. Richard Widmark portrays a strict, dispassionate commander of one such squad and is sent to replace a former leader who was killed in action. At first the men resent him, but when he displays the right stuff by defusing a Japanese torpedo that has penetrated a ship's hospital ward and by his subsequent deeds, they change their attitude. Dana Andrew plays one of the men who at first finds it difficult to accept Widmark. Several effective sequences of the frogmen in action include their activities close to Japanese-controlled islands where they destroy underwater obstructions to landing craft and a daring underwater journey in which the team blows up an enemy submarine base. ■

From Here to Eternity (1953), Col. Dir. Fred Zinnemann; Sc. Daniel Taradash; *Cast includes:* Burt Lancaster, Montgomery Clift, Deborah Kerr, Donna Reed, Frank Sinatra, Philip Ober.

Based on James Jones' novel, the film is a scathing attack on certain aspects of America's peace-time army. The drama concentrates upon the illicit love affairs of the officers and their wives and the meaningless cruelty that some soldiers are capable of dishing out to others. The story is set in Hawaii prior to Japan's attack on Pearl Harbor. Montgomery Clift portrays Private Prewitt, a transfer to the company commanded by an impotent captain (Philip Ober) who wants the private to box for his outfit. Prewitt, who prefers bugle playing to fighting after he blinded a fellow boxer during a sparring session, refuses. The captain decides to pressure Prewitt into fighting by putting him through excessive duties, punishments and beatings.

Burt Lancaster, as Sergeant Warden, a 30-year-man, covers for the incompetent captain while having an affair with his neglected wife (Deborah Kerr). Warden takes Prewitt under his wing but can do little to prevent the abuses the private is subjected to. When he warns the private to cooperate with the captain, Prewitt again refuses, saying: "If a man don't go his own way, he's nothin'." Frank Sinatra plays Private Maggio, the fun-loving, hard-drinking buddy of Prewitt. Witnessing the harsh treatment doled out to his pal, he says to a fellow soldier: "I hate to see a good guy get it in the gut." "You better get used to it, kid," the other replies. "You're gonna see a lot of it before you die." Maggio has several confrontations with a barracks bully, Sergeant "Fatso" Judson, who is in charge of the prison stockade. Maggio ultimately gets a six-month sentence for leaving his post and ends up in the hands of Judson, whose continual brutal beatings result in the private's death. That evening, Prewitt plays taps for his buddy while the men in the barracks listen quietly, as if hearing it for the first time. Donna Reed, as a local bar girl who dreams of some day being respectable, falls in love with Prewitt and protects him after he kills "Fatso" in a back-alley knife fight.

The film ends following the Japanese attack on Pearl Harbor. These sequences have been singled out for their realistic depiction of the bombing. They capture the chaos of combat as the ground forces, caught unaware, try to organize and fight back against the strafing enemy planes. The scenes are filled with destruction and black smoke as Lancaster, the professional soldier in his own element, takes command of the situation. His cool control during battle is a tribute to the professional army.

Meanwhile Prewitt, trying to get back to his barracks, is shot and killed by guards. Lancaster studies the dead private and says to a nearby officer: "He loved the army more than any other man I ever knew." Donna Reed and Deborah Kerr, who loses her lover, Lancaster, to the army—his first love—sail back to the States.

The film won eight Academy Awards, including Best Director, Best Supporting Actor (Sinatra), Best Supporting Actress (Reed) and Best Screenplay. It helped restore Sinatra's floundering career. Ironically, it was prohibited from being shown at naval bases because of its indictment of the army. ∎

From This Day Forward (1946). See Veterans. ∎

Frontier Uprising (1961). See *Kit Carson* (1940). ∎

Frontiersman, The (1927), MGM. *Dir.* Reginald Barker; *Sc.* L. G. Rigby; *Cast includes:* Tim McCoy, Claire Windsor, Tom O'Brien, Louise Lorraine.

An action drama of early America, the film takes place in 1813 and stars Tim McCoy as an officer under Andrew Jackson, played by Russell Simpson. McCoy is assigned to make peace with the Creek Indians who are on the brink of going to war against the whites. He later falls in love with the general's ward (Claire Windsor). When she is captured by the hostiles, McCoy springs into action and performs the inevitable rescue. The troops are then assembled and ordered to wreak vengeance upon the guilty hostiles. Several effective battle sequences help to compensate for a generally weak plot. ∎

"Fugitive, The" (1910), Biograph. *Dir.* D. W. Griffith; *Sc.* J. McDonagh; *Cast includes:* Kate Bruce, Edward Dillon, Clara Bracey, Edwin August, Lucy Cotton.

In this early silent Civil War drama a Union soldier shoots and kills a Confederate youth. Later in this grim film the mother of the slain soldier saves the life of the boy from the North. Director Griffith turned out a series of one- and two-reel dramas with a Civil War background during his tenure with Biograph. He later used some of the characters and incidents from these dramas in his 1915 classic, *The Birth of a Nation.* ∎

Fugitive Road (1934), Chesterfield. *Dir.* Frank Strayer; *Sc.* Charles Belden, Robert Ellis; *Cast includes:* Erich von Stroheim, Wera Engels, Leslie Fenton, George Humbert.

Erich von Stroheim portrays an Austrian officer commanding a border garrison on the Italian frontier in this World War I romantic drama. Feared by his troops as a no-nonsense commander, he nevertheless can be quite soft-hearted and sentimental, especially in matters of romance. He becomes attracted to a Russian-Hungarian emigrant (Wera Engels) journeying to the U.S. whom he purposely detains. But when he discovers her romantic interests lie elsewhere, he gallantly assists the couple to get married before they leave for the New World. Leslie Fenton, who later switched to directing B movies, plays the young lover. George Humbert, as an Italian immigrant, provides a few moments of comedy relief. The war plays almost no role in this low-budget tale. ∎

Full Metal Jacket (1987), WB. *Dir.* Stanley Kubrick; *Sc.* Stanley Kubrick, Michael Herr, Gustav Hasford; *Cast includes:* Matthew Modine, Adam Baldwin, Vincent D'Onofrio, Lee Ermey.

Stanley Kubrick's Vietnam War film follows a squad of U.S. Marines from boot camp at Parris Island, South Carolina, to the embattled streets of Hue in Vietnam. On the surface the film appears to be composed of two separate segments, but Kubrick capably ties both together with a subtle and devastating finale. The first half, set at the marine camp, is dominated by Sergeant Hartman (Lee Ermey), a real marine turned actor in a previous film. A hard-nosed, foul-mouthed drill instructor, he drives the raw recruits toward one goal—to transform them into killers, devoid of emotion or conscience. Barking obscenities, racial insults and tirades at the young innocents and forcing them to sleep with their rifles which they have given female names, he strips the youths of any pre-conceived humaneness as he instills in them Marine Corps loyalty and pride. It is as if he were hammering out "full metal jackets," the rifle cartridges that are the field ammunition of the combat marines. He cites as model marines mass murderer Charles Whitman and assassin Lee Harvey Oswald. "These individuals showed what one marine and his rifle can do!" he boasts. The central figure of the film is Private Joker (Matthew Modine), a smart-alecky, intelligent recruit who is quickly subdued by Hartman. Private Gomer Pyle (Vincent D'Onofrio), so named by the sergeant, is an awkward, fat boy whom the instructor browbeats and terrorizes until he is transmogrified into an exemplary recruit with a penchant for raw violence, foreshadowing the events in the second part of the film.

The second half takes place during the Tet offensive in the once-beautiful city of Hue, now reduced to rubble. Joker has become a combat correspondent for a marine paper that specializes in manipulating words for bureaucratic expediency. He acknowledges that "search and destroy" missions will subsequently be known as "sweep and clear." He also symbolizes the ambivalence of the war with his peace emblem sewed on his jacket and the slogan "born to kill" painted on his helmet. "We run two types of stories here," Joker's editor-lieutenant (John Terry) briefs his writing staff. "Grunts who give half their salary to buy gooks toothbrushes and deodorants, winning hearts and minds; and combat actions that result in a kill, winning the war."

The major battle scenes have to do with a squad of grunts and their frustrations with an elusive sniper, concealed in an abandoned building, who has seriously mauled the small patrol and who turns out to be a girl. Their revelations about this enemy and the war in the final shattering scenes show how Kubrick has masterfully arranged events so that the spirit of Sergeant Hartman hovers over his disciples. The film, based on the novel *The Short-Timers* by Gustav Hasford, who was a combat correspondent during the war, has more in common with the earlier highly imaginative *Apocalypse Now* (1982) than with the starkly realistic *Platoon* (1986). ∎

"Fury in the Pacific" (1945), Office of War Information. *Dir.* Comdr. Bonney M. Powell, U.S.N.R.

The invasion of two Pacific islands is the subject of this two-reel World War II documentary released by the War Activities Committee of the motion picture industry. The film depicts the amphibious assaults on Peleliu and Angaur and the subsequent battle. Among the killed and wounded were photographers who helped to make the documentary. ∎

Future wars. Future or imaginary war movies began to appear early in the history of the film industry. Several were released before the U.S. entered World War I. They were designed to warn the nation of the dangers of unpreparedness. As cautionary tales, they were rather effective and helped move the public away from a position of pacifism. One entry during the Depression years reversed the preparedness view and preached an anti-war theme. The next major cycle of future-war films was released after World War II, during the Cold War, when the threat of nuclear conflict between the East and West seemed a strong possibility. By the 1980s the genre fell into a pattern of conventional plotting and routine action, offering little that was original or new. Films of future wars produced in the U.S. proved at least one point over the last eight decades—that they were flexible enough to encompass a wide range of viewpoints.

The Battle Cry of Peace (1915), produced by J. Stuart Blackton, envisions a defenseless America invaded by a foreign country. While pacifists are holding a conference, an enemy fleet gathers off shore. New York and Washington are bombed from the air. Enemy troops, in uniforms not unlike those of German soldiers, overrun the American defenders who are lacking in arms. Many of the sequences are quite graphic for the period. *The Fall of a Nation*, a similar film directed by Bartley Cushing, appeared the following year. The story concerns a power-hungry millionaire who plots with Germany to land troops and weapons in the U.S. The invaders capture several cities and commit terrible atrocities as they advance. In its zeal to promote preparedness, the film suggests that those who advocate a course of pacifism are akin to cowards and traitors. Thomas Dixon, who wrote the script, had also written *The Clansman*, the novel on which D. W. Griffith based his Civil War film, *The Birth of a Nation* (1915).

The early 1930s witnessed a surge of anti-war films, led by such dramas as Lewis Milestone's *All Quiet on the Western Front* and James Whale's *Journey's End*, both released in 1930. *Men Must Fight*, an antiwar drama directed by Edward Selwyn which appeared in 1933, develops its theme within the context of a future conflict, circa 1940. A Secretary of State opposes his wife's pacifist views.

Having lost her first husband in World War I, she has since become a staunch pacifist. Their son (Phillips Holmes) sides with his mother. War finally erupts between the U.S. and an unnamed foreign country. After New York is bombed, the son changes his views and enlists in the air force. To its credit, the film resists the familiar trappings of glory and heroism in its depiction of the war.

The largest output of films dealing with future wars appeared during the Cold War. Stuart Gilmore's *Captive Women* (1952), a low-budget drama set in a bombed-out New York City in the year 2000 after an atomic war, tells of small tribes of survivors struggling to stay alive. A none too optimistic view of the future, the film includes scenes of the next generation born with grotesque scars while one tribe plots foul play against the others. Atomic bombs again play a role in Alfred E. Green's offbeat *Invasion U.S.A.*, released the same year. A foreign power attacks the nation with atomic bombs, invades Alaska and captures the state of Washington. As city after city falls to the invading armies, the military leaders in the Pentagon seem helpless. The final scenes reveal that the invasion has never occurred. It is the result of mass hypnosis. A television personality (Dan O'Herlihy) makes the point that this calamity may well occur unless the citizenry awakens to the present world situation and its potential threats. The drama uses footage from the Atomic Energy Commission. Another film with the same title appeared in 1985 starring Chuck Norris and deals with Russia's invasion of Florida.

By the end of the 1950s, major studios, prominent directors and well-known screen personalities were immersed in the genre. Ranald MacDougall's *The World, the Flesh and the Devil* (1959), starring Harry Belafonte, Inger Stevens and Mel Ferrer, envisions a postnuclear world inhabited by only three survivors. They explore the uninhabited and eerily silent New York City for other human beings. The film ends optimistically, following some bickering and jealousy, as the trio leaves the city in search of other survivors. Stanley Kramer's well-received antiwar drama, *On the Beach*, also released in 1959, is perhaps the best and most ambitious of the postnuclear disaster films. It stars Gregory Peck, Ava Gardner, Fred Astaire and Anthony Perkins. A nuclear war

claims the lives of all of earth's inhabitants except for a handful in Australia. But they, too, are doomed as a radioactive cloud approaches. The film premiered simultaneously in major cities around the world.

The following decade provided several examples of these doomsday dramas. *Panic in the Year Zero* (1962), directed by and starring Ray Milland, again tells of small bands of survivors struggling to exist after an atomic war. Milland, as the husband and father of a small family, tries to keep his loved ones alive by seeking shelter in a cave and fighting off hordes of marauders. Henry Fonda portrays the President of the U.S. in Sidney Lumet's *Fail Safe* (1964), another drama which warns of the pitfalls of depending solely on nuclear weapons to maintain peace. A squadron of U.S. bombers heading for the Soviet Union is unable to be recalled. The President warns Russia, but one plane gets through and levels Moscow. To show good will, Fonda must order the destruction of an American city to avoid an all-out nuclear war. The Russians insist on New York City as the target. Fonda, whose wife is in New York, reluctantly agrees.

The genre continued into the 1980s with the addition of color. *Massive Retaliation* (1982), directed by Thomas A. Cohen, is a weak attempt to show how three couples try to survive an impending nuclear war. They retreat to their country place to wait out the coming destruction. John Milius' World War III drama, *Red Dawn* (1984), ends up as a routine war story. The film opens after Russia has destroyed most of America's defense missiles. Cuban troops land in various cities and ruthlessly crush any resistance. However, in one community several high school students led by the older brother of one of the boys escape into the mountains where they engage in guerrilla warfare against the invaders. Milius virtually reverses the roles of the combatants of the Vietnam War in which the enemy were the guerrillas and the U.S. was the invading force.

If most of these films present a bleak view of the near future, they at least establish that there is a future. They point out the dangers of relying solely on arms to secure peace and warn that advanced technology is no assurance against global conflict. They also suggest that the next war can destroy civilization as we know it. ∎

G

G.I. Honeymoon (1945). See Home Front. ■

Gabaldon, Guy. See *Hell to Eternity* (1960). ■

Gadsden Purchase (1853). See *Conquest of Cochise* (1953). ■

Gallant Blade, The (1948), Col. *Dir.* Henry Levin; *Sc.* Walter Ferris, Morton Grant; *Cast includes:* Larry Parks, Marguerite Chapman, George Macready, Victor Jory.

The unscrupulous Marshal of France aims to stir up a war with Spain to prevent an internal rebellion in this routine historical drama set in 17th Century France. Victor Jory portrays the marshal who kidnaps General Cadeau (George Macready), thereby hoping to crush the revolt. Larry Parks, as a trusted lieutenant of the beleaguered and noble general, eventually foils Jory's plans. A romance blossoms between a beautiful spy (Marguerite Chapman) in the employ of the sinister marshal and Parks, the "gallant blade" of the title. Allegedly, the events have been loosely based on historical incidents. ■

Gallant Hours, The (1960), UA. *Dir.* Robert Montgomery; *Sc.* Beirne Lay, Jr., Frank D. Gilroy; *Cast includes:* James Cagney, Dennis Weaver, Ward Costello, Richard Jaeckel.

James Cagney portrays Admiral William F. Halsey in this chiefly uninteresting biographical drama set in 1942 during World War II. The film depicts Halsey's character under stress during the period when the war with Japan in the Pacific turned in favor of the Allies. Halsey's strategy in defeating Yamamoto, the Japanese admiral, was the turning point. Dennis Weaver portrays Halsey's aide. The Japanese are depicted as three-dimensional characters as opposed to the usual stereotypes found in earlier war dramas. No battle sequences appear in this sincere tribute to the commander of the South Pacific area whose battle strategy contributed to the final victory over Japan. ■

"Gambling With Death" (1909), Vitagraph.

In this implausible short silent drama that takes place during the French Revolution, a jilted suitor joins the republicans. He then proceeds to lead a mob to the house of the girl's father. During this early period of the American film industry several companies, including Biograph, Kalem and Selig, attempted to depict historical dramas within the confines of the one- or two-reel format. Subject matter ranged from the uprisings in 19th century Colonial India with such films as "The Sepoy's Wife" (1910) to the American Civil War, as exemplified by director D.W. Griffith's 1911–1912 cycle of films of the conflict. ■

Gangway for Tomorrow (1943), RKO. *Dir.* John H. Auer; *Sc.* Arch Oboler; *Cast includes:* Margo, John Carradine, Robert Ryan, Amelita Ward, William Terry, Harry Davenport.

The effects of war on different individuals is the theme of this World War II drama. Five people, now employed in the same defense plant, tell their strange stories through flashbacks. Margo, as a French refugee, has helped to inspire the French underground in its resistance against the Nazis. Robert Ryan portrays an ex-racing driver whose accident not only ended his career but kept him out of the air force. Amelita Ward is a disillusioned beauty queen while John Carradine plays a former hobo whose patriotic fervor led him to defense work. James Bell is a former prison warden who was forced to act as the executioner during his tenure in office. ■

Gardens of Stone (1987), Tri-Star. *Dir.* Francis Coppola; *Sc.* Ronald Bass; *Cast includes:* James Caan, James Earl Jones, D. B. Sweeney, Anjelica Huston, Mary Stuart Masterson.

The film takes place in 1968 during the Vietnam War. But unlike *Platoon,* which was released several months earlier and contained graphic depictions of several violent battles, the war in the present film is shown only through television images. The setting is Fort Myer, Virginia, where a special unit of soldiers is in charge of burying the Vietnam casualties.

James Caan portrays Clell Hazard, a loyal and sensitive sergeant who has served in Vietnam and has grown to hate the conflict. He understands that it can't be won the way it is being fought. Unhappy with his present assignment that includes burying the dead that arrive daily from the front, he seeks to transfer to another camp where he can train the green recruits for the realities of Vietnam. D.B. Sweeney plays a young idealistic soldier anxious to go to Vietnam. He looks upon the experienced sergeant as his mentor. Caan's friend, a sergeant-major, and another seasoned combat veteran (James Earl Jones), tries to enlighten Sweeney about his patriotic impressions of battle. When Caan mentions that the boy believes his place during wartime is "at the front," Jones says to Sweeney: "There ain't no front in Vietnam." Jones is not as intense or philosophical about the Vietnam War as Caan is. "We're middle management," he explains to a fellow officer. "We are the heart and soul of America. We keep the wheels turning while we get ahead—while we watch our backside." Caan's girlfriend (Anjelica Huston), a Washington reporter, disagrees fiercely with him on issues relating to the war but still is able to love him. "Clell sees this war as bad judgment, as corrupt," she admits to a friend, "I see it as genocide." Sweeney finally get his wish and is eventually transferred to Vietnam as a lieutenant. A short time afterward Caan is notified that the young officer has been killed in action and that he, Caan, will preside over the military funeral.

The film, based on Nicholas Proffitt's novel, is less about the war than it is about the military as a tightly closed unit—as a source of sustenance to its members—while the country is steeped in a national tragedy. The "gardens" is the ironic euphemism the soldiers use for the cemetery where they are kept busy burying the war dead. ■

Gathering of Eagles, A (1963). See Cold War. ■

Gatling gun. See *The Siege at Red River* (1954). ■

Gay Diplomat, The (1931). See Spy Films: the Talkies. ■

Gay Retreat, The (1927), Fox. *Dir.* Ben Stoloff; *Sc.* Murray Roth, Edward P. Moran; *Cast includes:* Sammy Cohen, Ted McNamara, Gene Cameron, Betty Francisco.

Sammy Cohen, as a chauffeur, and Ted McNamara, as a butler, accompany their employer (Gene Cameron) to France in this World War I comedy. The pair's comic antics at the front include their problems with a top sergeant and their accidental capture of a German battalion for which they receive medals for bravery. Cohen returns to the U.S. with his heavyweight wife (Judy King) and a child that sports Cohen's comic features. The Jewish-Irish comedy of the featured pair first appeared in *What Price Glory?* (1926). ■

General, The (1927), UA. *Dir.* Buster Keaton, Clyde Bruckman; *Sc.* Clyde Bruckman; *Cast includes:* Buster Keaton, Marion Mack, Glen Cavender, Jim Farley.

Buster Keaton's famous Civil War comedy has a train, *The General,* as his co-hero. The plot is based on an actual incident that occurred during the Civil War, known as the Andrews Raid, in which Union soldiers, dressed as civilians, stole *The General,* a rebel locomotive. In Keaton's version, he plays Johnnie Gray, railroad man, who tries to impress his girl (Marion Mack) by enlisting in the army. But those in charge reject him because he is more useful as an engineer. His sweetheart, thinking him a coward, snubs him. However, when he learns that his train has been stolen, he springs into action. Following several hilarious incidents, our Southern hero saves his sweetheart who is held captive by the enemy, foils a Union surprise attack and captures a high-ranking Union officer.

The film has been noted for its authentic

backgrounds and its photography. Keaton's superb timing of his sight gags deserves praise as well, especially the sequence involving a loaded cannon aimed at Keaton and the one in which he has to remove railroad ties scattered on the tracks before him. In the former, the ignited cannon, originally aimed high and situated on a railway car behind him, begins to drop because of the movement of the train until the mouth of the weapon stares him in the face. But the train turns in time and the cannonball barely misses him. The railroad ties strewn across the tracks before his moving train comprise another obstacle. He removes all but the last one, which he dislodges by dropping another he is holding on the edge of the first. Both ties fall harmlessly out of the way. The marvel of the scene is in Keaton's split-second timing.

Considered by many to be Keaton's best work as well as one of the best films about the Civil War, *The General*, based on William Pittenger's *The Great Locomotive Chase*, contains the longest chase sequence in the history of film comedy. Walt Disney in 1956 used the same source for his film which retained the original title. When asked why the war in his film looked more authentic than it did in *Gone With the Wind*, Keaton replied: "They went to a novel, we went to history." See also Andrews Raid. ∎

General Crack (1929), WB. *Dir.* Alan Crosland; *Sc.* Walter Anthony; *Cast includes:* John Barrymore, Marion Nixon, Lowell Sherman, Hobart Bosworth, Jacqueline Logan.

John Barrymore, in his first full-length talking feature, plays Prince Christian, a mercenary commander who sells his military services to the Emperor of Austria in this early 18th century drama. Known as Captain Crack to his friends, Barrymore marries a gypsy and leaves her in Vienna when he rides off to battle. The emperor, meanwhile, has an affair with the young bride. A disgruntled officer witnesses this and reports what he has seen to Crack. The general swiftly concludes his military obligations so that he can wreak vengeance upon those who wronged him. Riding with his troop of 500 cavalrymen, he vanquishes his foes and dethrones King Leopold III. Several effective battle sequences as well as other action scenes enhance the production. A coronation scene is photographed in color and utilizes a wide screen for its maximum effect. ∎

General Died at Dawn, The (1936), Par. *Dir.* Lewis Milestone; *Sc.* Clifford Odets; *Cast includes:* Gary Cooper, Madeleine Carroll, Akim Tamiroff, Dudley Digges, Porter Hall, William Frawley, John O'Hara.

Set in strife-torn China, the plot of this atmospheric film concerns the conflict between an idealist gunrunner (Gary Cooper) who is trying to aid the impoverished Chinese people to free themselves of a brutal and greedy warlord, and the bandit general (Akim Tamiroff) who is planning to dominate northern China. Tamiroff captures a train with a variety of interesting characters aboard, including Cooper. Dudley Digges plays the general's underling. Madeleine Carroll, as a confidence woman who first tries to steal the money for the arms from Cooper, eventually falls for him. The final scene, in which Cooper convinces the mortally wounded warlord, who plans to kill his captives, to order his loyal troops to kill each other, is rather far-fetched. Writer John O'Hara has a minor role as a reporter. Expertly directed by Lewis Milestone, who just a few years earlier had made *All Quiet on the Western Front*, the film proved to be Paramount's biggest success of the year. ∎

"General Marion, the Swamp Fox" (1911). See Francis Marion. ∎

General Spanky (1937) MGM. *Dir.* Fred Newmeyer, Gordon Douglas; *Sc.* Richard Flourney, Hal Yates, John Guedel; *Cast includes:* Spanky McFarland, Phillips Holmes, Frank Morgan, Irving Pichel, Rosina Lawrence, Carl Switzer.

Producer Hal Roach recruited members of his successful Our Gang team to help the Confederacy in this Civil War comedy drama. Spanky plays an orphan adopted by a plantation boss (Phillips Holmes) who marches off to fight in the war. Spanky, as commander-in-chief, and Buckwheat as his assistant, organize the gang of kids into a rag-tag army that manages to outmaneuver some Union troops. When Holmes is captured and sentenced to face a firing squad, Spanky persuades the Union general (Frank Morgan) to release the condemned prisoner. Morgan is made an honorary member of the Our Gang club in this harmless feature. ∎

Genghis Khan (1167?–1221). The son of a Mongol tribal chief, Genghis (also Jenghis) Khan rose to become one of the greatest conquerors in history with an empire that stretched thousands of miles from Manchuria and northern China in the east to southern Russia in the west and included all or part of the modern states of Iran, Afghanistan and Turkestan. Originally named Temujin, he adopted the name Genghis Khan to signify his exalted position as supreme leader of the Mongols.

Using diplomacy, treachery and military tactics, he united the different nomadic Mongol tribes in what is today the Mongolian Peoples Republic (formerly Outer Mongolia). Beginning in 1213, his fiercely loyal horseborne warriors conquered the kingdom of the Chins in modern north China, including capturing their capital, the site of modern Beijing. Turning westward, he extended his conquests until he reached the Caucasus and the region of Azerbaijan. The Russians used the term "Golden Horde" to designate the westernmost khanate of the Mongol empire. Universal borrowed the evocative expression for a 1951 costume drama, *The Golden Horde*, a highly fictionalized account of the Mongolian chief's siege of Samarkand in 1220.

He followed a practice of sparing the people in those towns which surrendered without resistance but mercilessly killing all the inhabitants in communities that fought against him. The Mongols did not settle in their conquered lands. They generally preferred to remain nomadic and extract tribute from subjugated areas. Genghis Khan died while fighting to expand his control over northern China. His empire, divided among his sons and grandsons, disintegrated within a few generations.

Hollywood has not been kind to Genghis Khan. *The Conqueror* (1956), a large-scale action drama about the Mongol-Tartar conflicts with John Wayne portraying the Mongol leader, is considered by many to be one of the worst films ever made. The weak script and general miscasting turn *Genghis Khan* (1965), another fictionalized biography with Omar Sharif as the title character, into an unintentionally comical film. ∎

Genghis Khan (1965), Col. *Dir.* Henry Levin; *Sc.* Clarke Reynolds, Beverly Cross; *Cast includes:* Stephen Boyd, Omar Sharif, James Mason, Eli Wallach, Francoise Dorleac.

Omar Sharif portrays the Mongol leader who fulfills his dream of uniting his people in this routine biographical drama. The film traces his escape from slavery and his political education in China to his successful unification of the Mongols and the building of an empire that intimidated both western and eastern civilization. Stephen Boyd, as a rival tribal chieftain, kidnaps and rapes Khan's wife (Francoise Dorleac). The two finally meet in hand-to-hand combat resulting in Boyd's death. The film depicts the political intrigues involving Persia and other lands who double-deal in alliances to ward off attacks by either Boyd's troops or Khan's hordes. The inept script works against the production which otherwise adheres closely to historical facts concerning the Mongol leader's ability to unite the various tribes. ∎

Genocide (1982), Simon Wiesenthal Center *Dir.* Arnold Schwartzman; *Sc.* Arnold Schwartzman.

A documentary concerning the extermination of the European Jews by the Nazis during World War II, the film covers the plight of the Jewish people from after World War I through the years of the Second World War. Director-writer Arnold Schwartzman focuses on the rounding up of Jews in Germany, the installation of the first death camps in Poland in 1941 and the neglect of the major nations to increase their immigration quotas after they became aware of Nazi persecution of the Jews as early as 1938. Certain scenes, such as those showing nude victims being executed and their bodies piled up, have become familiar to audiences who have seen newsreels and other compilations of the holocaust, but they nevertheless remain images of horror. The soundtrack contains Jewish folk music and songs and poems written by victims of the holocaust. Orson Welles and Elizabeth Taylor each narrate different sections of the film. ∎

Gentleman From America (1923). See Service Comedy. ∎

Geronimo (1829–1909). Probably no other Indian chief has so captured the American imagination as Geronimo. The quintessential symbol of native resistance against the white man, he led an Apache band in a series of southwestern rebellions from 1871 to 1886. Although considered a renegade and murderous savage by some contemporaries because of the many innocent people killed in his raids, Geronimo usually initiated his attacks as the result of broken promises and arbitrary acts by government officials. He was acknowledged to be a wily, courageous and tenacious warrior who, before his final capture, managed to elude and inflict defeat on Mexican and American forces hundreds of times larger than his.

Films based on Geronimo's exploits blend fact and fiction so thoroughly that it is difficult to know the real person and activities. "Geronimo's Last Raid" (1912), one of the earliest and chiefly fictitious dramas, exemplifies the kinds of murderous attacks he was generally accused of. It helped set the pattern for future films of this genre. *Geronimo* (1962), starring Chuck Connors in the role of the chief, probably comes closest to portraying that segment of Geronimo's life when he took his rebellious band into Mexico and used it as a base to attack southern Arizona. The film was part of a trend that began with *Broken Arrow* (1950) in which the Indian is depicted as a victim of white officialdom. Although Geronimo himself eventually did become a prosperous farmer and celebrity in his later days, the film falsely shows most Indians gaining their rightful place in a white-dominated society during the chief's lifetime.

As a youth, Geronimo took part in raids against white settlers and military forces with two other celebrated Apache leaders, Cochise and Victorio. Geronimo initially accepted pacification and reservation life. But later, in 1876, as leader of the Chiricahua Apache, he led his forces in revolt into Mexico when the U.S. government arbitrarily abrogated previous guarantees and abolished the Chiricahua reservation and forcibly moved its residents onto the arid San Carlo reservation in New Mexico. Geronimo and his warriors hid in the Sierra Madre mountains between raids. The 1939 version of *Geronimo*, in which Chief Thundercloud plays the title role, has many action sequences showing his terrorizing of settlers but falls short as an accurate biography of the chief.

Geronimo was soon captured but he escaped again with a renegade group in 1881 and, from his base in Mexico, terrorized the Mexican state of Sonora and parts of southern Arizona. He surrendered again in 1883 to General Crook and was returned to the reservation. He escaped again in 1885 and conducted a year-long guerrilla war against Mexican and American forces in northern Mexico before his final capture by General Lester Miles in late 1886. Mexican officials claimed Geronimo's band had caused the deaths of hundreds of people in Sonora. *Tomahawk Trail* (1957) recounts one historical incident in which the Apache stole horses held by pursuing American soldiers. American troops, using a "heliograph," a sun-signaling device, closed in on Geronimo and his diminished band in wild country.

After his third and final capture, Geronimo was deported to Florida, served a term in a federal prison in Alabama and was eventually transferred to Fort Sill, Oklahoma, where he embraced Christianity and prospered as a farmer. He became a celebrity in old age, appearing in the St. Louis World's Fair and riding in President Theodore Roosevelt's inaugural procession. He dictated his autobiography in 1906. ∎

Geronimo (1939), Par. *Dir.* Paul H. Sloane; *Sc.* Paul H. Sloane; *Cast includes:* Preston Foster, Ellen Drew, Andy Devine, Gene Lockhart, Chief Thunder Cloud.

Based on the the U.S. Army's campaigns against Geronimo, an Apache chief who fought the whites in the Southwest during the late nineteenth century, the film provides plenty of action and subplots in this vigorous action drama. Preston Foster portrays an army captain at an Arizona outpost who befriends a young West Point graduate (William Henry). The lad clashes with his father, a stern general and post commander who adheres too strictly to traditional values. Gene Lockhart enacts a corrupt Indian trader who peddles guns and ammunition to the hostiles. The title character, played by Chief Thundercloud, terrorizes the nearby settlers as well as the troops until he is captured by the general's son. Ellen Drew provides the romantic element when she falls in love with the young lieutenant.

The film does little to shed light on the plight of the American Indian or to establish any plausible or realistic motivation for the attacks by the Apaches. Instead, it continues the stereotype of the Indian as savage. The conflict between the neglected son and the stern commander-father is borrowed directly from Paramount's successful adventure tale of colonial India, *Lives of a Bengal Lancer* (1935). ∎

Lobby card of Chief Thundercloud, as the title character, leading apparently out-of-shape Apaches against the U.S. Cavalry. *Geronimo* (1939).

Geronimo (1962), UA. *Dir.* Arnold Laven; *Sc.* Pat Fielder; *Cast includes:* Chuck Connors, Kamala Devi, Ross Martin, Pat Conway, Adam West.

A familiar biographical drama of superficial insight into the title character, the film focuses on the later career of the famous Apache chief. Chuck Connors portrays the great warrior leader who is betrayed by the whites, particularly a greedy cattleman, an unscrupulous government agent and a callous U.S. Cavalry captain. They manage to steal the land promised to the Apaches. Geronimo, frustrated in his efforts to get a fair deal for his people, escapes with a band of warriors from his reservation and sets up camp in Mexico from where he declares war on the U.S. This phase of Geronimo's exploits is historically accurate. Kamala Devi, as Geronimo's woman, provides the romantic interest.

The film ends on a false note with the Apaches attaining most of their goals from a U.S. Senator. History has proved otherwise. However, the Apaches are portrayed as intelligent, thoughtful dissidents idealistically seeking their place in the sun. This sympathetic treatment of the Indian continued the 1950s trend beginning with such films as *Broken Arrow* (1950), starring James Stewart. ■

"Geronimo's Last Raid" (1912), American. *Dir.* G.P. Hamilton; *Sc.* John Emerson.

An early silent drama of the Indian-vs.-cavalry conflicts, the film tells of some of the fictitious exploits of the famous Apache chief. Geronimo and his warriors capture a white man and plan to burn him at the stake. The captive's sweetheart, hiding in a barrel, saves his life by firing through a hole in the barrel and killing three of the marauders. Other action sequences include U.S. Cavalry attacks against the Apaches. The film was only one of many to help stereotype the Indian as savage. ■

Gestapo. Rule by terror was a basic tenet of the Nazi regime, and the Gestapo was the government agency that carried out that function. Its name is an acronym for the official State Secret Police—Geheime Staatzpolizei.

The agency, a feared symbol of the unlimited power of the state both within Nazi Germany and in the occupied countries during World War II, practiced unrestrained arrest, interrogation by whatever means it chose and confinement without trial in a concentration camp. In addition, through close cooperation with the S.S., the Nazi party's paramilitary force that operated concentration camps, the Gestapo could order the execution of any of its prisoners. Because of its power to wipe out all records of those whom it arrested or had executed, the Gestapo could insure that its victims would vanish without a trace.

The agency came into being in 1933 in Prussia under Hermann Goring, then Prussian state minister of the interior. It became a national organization under Heinrich Himmler in 1934, and eventually functioned as an independent national police force, starting in 1936 under Heinrich Muller, and later under Himmler's subordinate, Reinhardt Heydrich. The scope of the Gestapo was further extended during World War II to the occupied countries where numerous branch offices were located.

Interrogation by torture was common, using primitive methods such as the rack and modern techniques such as the use of electric shock treatment to sensitive body parts. *Beasts of Berlin* (1939) was one of the earliest exposés of the brutal methods the Gestapo employed to gather information, break men's spirits and terrorize its victims in general.

The Nuremberg Trials, as a result of evidence presented, collectively condemned all Gestapo agents as war criminals. The agency operated slave labor camps, caused the execution of millions of Jews and perpetrated numerous brutalities against suspected opponents of the Nazi regime. American films released during World War II relentlessly portrayed Gestapo officers and their agency as particularly ruthless and cruel toward their defenseless prisoners. In the drama *Man Hunt* (1941) the Gestapo torture an Englishman (Walter Pidgeon), demanding that he sign a confession that he was sent by the British government to kill the German dictator. That same year Martin Kosleck portrayed the quintessential Gestapo officer in *Underground*, a drama about German resistance within the Nazi state. He tortures suspects, turns brother against brother and browbeats loyal servants until they are forced to testify against their innocent employers. James Cag-

ney suffers a similar fate in *13 Rue Madeleine* (1946) as an American agent captured in Nazi-occupied territory whom the Gestapo tortures to gain information about the forthcoming Allied invasion.

Other war dramas of the period used the dreaded Gestapo as pursuers of Allied heroes and heroines. In *The Seventh Cross* (1944) a Nazi concentration camp prisoner (Spencer Tracy) escapes and is hunted by the Gestapo. In both *Paris Underground* (1945) and *O.S.S.* (1946), the Gestapo pursues women members of the French underground.

Some postwar dramas continued to stress the brutality of the Gestapo. One film, *The Great Escape* (1963), is based on a true event. It is the story of fifty Allied prisoners who have broken out of a German prison camp and are caught by the Gestapo and executed. Sometimes a Gestapo member appeared kindly, only to elicit information. In *Target Unknown* (1951), for example, Gig Young, as a German officer raised in America, poses as an understanding friend whom an American airman (Mark Stevens) confides in. The Gestapo man even criticizes the brutality of members of his organization.

Other postwar films softened the image of some members of the Gestapo as well as Germans in general. In *36 Hours* (1964) Rod Taylor, as a sympathetic German doctor working for the Gestapo, ultimately helps Garner, as an American officer, escape into Switzerland. The passage of time allows not only for revisionism of a once-feared agency but for its comic treatment as well. In Mel Brooks' *To Be or Not to Be* (1983) Charles Durning plays an incompetent local Gestapo chief who falls for the charms of Ann Bancroft.

Although many Gestapo films were made during World War II and, in some cases, may have served as propaganda to arouse the American public's zeal for prosecuting the war, portrayal of the Gestapo conducting its widespread forms of bestiality does reinforce an essential difference between democracy and an oppressive dictatorship. The screen, through its graphic images, shows far better the horrors of Nazism than the mere recital of numbers killed in Hitler's gas chambers. ■

Get Going (1943). See Washington, D.C. ■

Gettysburg, Battle of (July 1–3, 1863). The sight must have been awesome, even frightening, to a Union trooper huddled behind his breastworks on Cemetery Ridge outside the small town of Gettysburg in southeastern Pennsylvania. Looking through the haze of battle smoke and summer heat on July 3, 1863, he could see lines of Confederate foot soldiers stretching out, seemingly without end, advancing towards him in an unhurried, close-order formation. The sunlight flashed off the rifle barrels and bayonets of 15,000 men, who, with their battle flags dipped forward in the position of attack, moved closer toward the Union lines. As the Confederates approached a slope rising up toward the Union defenses, they broke into a charge.

After two days of intense but inconclusive fighting between Lee's 76,000 gray-clad troops and the 92,000 men in blue under General George G. Meade, the South decided to gamble the outcome on an infantry charge led by General George E. Pickett to break the Union lines. Union and Confederate artillery and rifle fire tore into each other's ranks as the two sides closed in combat. The fighting became hand-to-hand and the Union line was pierced in places. Northern replacements hurriedly rushed into battle helped drive back the Southerners. When the fighting was over, the Union lines had held, and Pickett's magnificent but futile and costly charge had failed to carry the day. Lee's attempt to invade the North through Pennsylvania had foundered and though the participants probably didn't realize it then, the forces of the Confederacy, from then on, could only fight a defensive war that would merely postpone their final defeat.

The South lost more than a battle at Gettysburg. It suffered a higher number and proportion of deaths and casualties which totaled 28,000 in contrast to the Union's 23,000. Stopping the Confederacy at Gettysburg meant that the North's industrial eastern cities were safe from invasion and that the war, with its attendant destruction, would continue on Southern soil.

Lincoln visited the battlefield later that autumn and delivered his brief but touching speech, a two-minute consecration of the military cemetery, that would underline Gettysburg's unique place in American history. Vitaphone produced an early sound short in 1927, "Lincoln's Gettysburg Address," with Reverend Lincoln H. Caswell, a distinguished lecturer on Lincoln, portraying the President.

Only a handful of films have dramatized the famous battle. Thomas Ince's *The Battle of Gettysburg* (1913) presented a faithful reenactment of the battle, as did *Between Two Fires*, released the following year. In 1936 MGM produced *The Battle of Gettysburg*, a documentary written by Dore Schary. ■

"Giant of Norway, The" (1939). See Refugees. ■

Gigolo (1926), PDC. *Dir.* William K. Howard; *Sc.* Marion Orth; *Cast includes:* Rod LaRocque, Jobyna Ralston, Louise Dresser, Cyril Chadwick.

World War I and its aftermath provide the background for this romantic drama. Rod LaRocque portrays the son of a weak mother and stepson of an unscrupulous English physician who eventually absconds with his wife's money. LaRocque is forced to part from his childhood sweetheart (Jobyna Ralston) when his mother insists that he accompany her and his stepfather on a trip to France. When war breaks out, the young man enlists in the French Flying Corps and is seriously injured in a plane crash. His face has to be rebuilt as a result of the injuries, and he is finally released from the hospital after the armistice. He returns to his mother, arriving in time to witness her death. Penniless and alone, he becomes a gigolo. One day Ralston and her parents enter the cafe where he is working and she recognizes him. At first he denies he is the young man she has known, but he finally admits his true identity and returns to the States with her. ■

Girl He Left Behind, The (1956). See Service Comedy. ■

"Girl Scout, The" (1909), Kalem.

A short silent film set during the Boer War, this implausible drama tells of a young Canadian woman who is determined to follow her father and brother who have volunteered to join the British struggle against the Boers in Africa. Somehow she disguises herself as a male and enlists in the army. Once in Africa, she is able, through plot contrivances, to save her father's life. There are numerous cavalry scenes in the film but no battle sequences. ■

"Girl Spy Before Vicksburg, The" (1911). See Spy Films: the Silents. ■

Girl Who Stayed at Home, The (1919),
Par. *Dir.* D. W. Griffith; *Sc.* S. E. V. Taylor, D. W. Griffith; *Cast includes:* Clarine Seymour, Robert Harron, Richard Barthelmess, Carol Dempster, Tully Marshall, George Fawcett.

World War I serves as background for this romantic drama of two young brothers who, as doughboys, are shipped to France during the conflict. Clarine Seymour portrays the title character who is in love with one of the brothers (Robert Harron). Meanwhile the other brother (Richard Barthelmess) falls in love with Carol Dempster, a French wife whose husband is away at the front. Dempster, who is harassed by the ruthless Germans and whose husband is killed in action, is rescued by Barthelmess. Each American ends up with the woman he loves.

Released immediately after the war, the film, which contains some actual shots of airplanes in battle, failed to cash in on its subject matter. Its topics of patriotism and anti-German propaganda became dated too quickly despite director D.W. Griffith's last-minute revisions that showed a German soldier killing a fellow German who is about to violate the pretty French wife. It joined the list of dozens of other similar features in the storage vaults. Also, the critics were disappointed in the plot, with one labeling the latest work by the master director as "muddled." ■

Girls of Pleasure Island, The (1953). See War Humor. ■

Glorious Revolution (1688–1689). When England's James II, a converted Catholic, fathered a son, many of his subjects were struck with fear at the thought of a Catholic heir. William of Orange, the Dutch Protestant husband of James' daughter Mary, was invited by both the Whigs and Tories to replace James. In 1688 William landed in England, and James escaped to France. Parliament in 1689 barred by law Catholic succession to the throne. The Civil War generally had been a bloodless one.

Films set in this period often referred to other locations which provided more opportunities for visual action to entertain their audiences. One exception is the historical drama *Dangerous Maid* (1923), which is set in England in 1685. Constance Talmadge portrays a headstrong young woman who, along with her family, favors the Duke of Mon-

mouth as a replacement for the current ruler. Both versions of *Captain Blood* (1924, 1935), based on Rafael Sabatini's novel and set chiefly in the Caribbean, concern James Blood, an English doctor wrongly accused of conspiring against the crown. Condemned to a penal colony, Blood escapes and turns to piracy since he cannot return to England. When James II, who had sentenced Blood to the penal colony, is overthrown and William III gains the throne, Blood is pardoned. *Fortunes of Captain Blood* (1950), also based on Sabatini's novel, with Louis Hayward as the doctor, covers much the same ground. The 1935 Michael Curtiz film, starring an energetic and dashing Errol Flynn, is generally acknowledged as the best adaptation. ■

Glory Brigade, The (1953), TCF. *Dir.* Robert D. Webb; *Sc.* Franklin Coen; *Cast includes:* Victor Mature, Alexander Scourby, Lee Marvin, Richard Egan.

Conflict arises between an American fighting unit and a Greek detachment in this Korean War drama. When the Greek soldiers appear to have given up without a struggle during their first engagement with the enemy, a wave of anti-Greek sentiment permeates the American G.I.s. Victor Mature portrays an American lieutenant of Greek heritage who leads the two units. Their mission is to gather information concerning Communist strength and activities. When the smoke clears after several ensuing battles, all of which end in the allies' favor, each group has grown to respect the other. ■

Glory Guys, The (1965), UA. *Dir.* Arnold Laven; *Sc.* Sam Peckinpah; *Cast includes:* Tom Tryon, Harve Presnell, Senta Berger, James Caan.

The U.S. Cavalry clashes again with Indians in the old West in this routine drama. Tom Tryon portrays a cavalry officer under the command of an ambitious general who disobeys orders and causes his troops to be slaughtered. Andrew Duggan, as the inept general, makes life tough for his men. Senta Berger provides the romantic interest for both Tryon and Harve Presnell, an Indian scout. Both men engage in a fist fight over her, after which they become buddies. Jeanne Cooper plays Presnell's cruel wife. James Caan portrays one of the recruits.

The film has been singled out for its different ending in which the Indians win the cli-

Lobby card of Victor Mature (c.) leading a surprisingly cheerful Greek detachment of U.N. forces during the Korean War. *The Glory Brigade* (1953).

mactic battle. This is especially unusual in a genre whose entries rarely digress from the conventional formula. The script is generally sympathetic toward the Indian, following a trend that began with *Broken Arrow* (1950) and continued into the following decades. The several action sequences are adequate in this otherwise familiar tale. ■

Go for Broke (1951), MGM. *Dir.* Robert Pirosh; *Sc.* Robert Pirosh; *Cast includes:* Van Johnson, Lane Nikano, George Miki, Akira Fukunaga.

The film pays tribute to the heroic Japanese-American soldiers who fought in France and Italy during World War II. Van Johnson portrays the commander of these members of the 442nd Regimental Combat Team. When first assigned to this unit, he recoils in disgust and voices his prejudice against the Nisei. But his attitude changes toward his troops as they go through their training and are sent overseas. His fondness for the Nisei is demonstrated when he is temporarily relieved of the command and assigned

elsewhere. Much of the story is developed with warm humor. The battle sequences are few but effective as the men of the 442nd prove their worth in battle. A particularly poignant moment comes at the climax as the Japanese-Americans under heavy fire by the Nazis relieve a besieged Texas battalion who had previously expressed their intolerance toward their saviors. The cast includes many of the Nisei heroes of the actual campaigns. The 442nd Regimental Combat Team, made up of Nisei volunteers from Hawaii and the mainland, came into being in February 1943. Its purpose was to serve as a model and provide leadership for the Japanese-American community after the war. The unit fought in Italy in 1944 and later in France. The group earned four distinguished unit citations, received more than 18,000 individual decorations and suffered almost 10,000 casualties.

Japanese-Americans had enough problems resulting from their evacuation to internment camps during the war and a general national hostility toward them as a minority group, without Hollywood's contributions. Several low-budget films attributed fictitious acts of betrayal to these otherwise loyal Americans. In *Little Tokyo, U.S.A.* (1942), for example, Preston Foster, as a police officer on duty in the Japanese-American quarter of Los Angeles known as "Little Tokyo," uncovers an espionage network. According to the F.B.I. and other government sources, not one act of espionage or sabotage was ever committed during the war by any Japanese-American. ■

John Megna, Jonathan Goldsmith and Craig Wasson, as part of an American unit assigned to defend an abandoned Vietnamese village, come under Viet Cong attack. Go Tell the Spartans (1978).

Go Tell the Spartans (1978), Avco. Dir. Ted Post; Sc. Wendell Mayes; Cast includes: Burt Lancaster, Craig Wasson, Jonathan Goldsmith, Marc Singer, Joe Unger, Dennis Howard.

A Vietnam War drama set in 1964 when American involvement consisted only of military advisers, the story concerns a group of Americans and Vietnamese mercenaries ordered to occupy Muc Wa, a small village. Burt Lancaster, as a capable, seasoned major—a hero of two previous wars—anguishes over the futility of the venture ordered by his general. One of the major's naive officers, however, is more optimistic. "We won't lose because we're Americans," he exclaims. The hamlet, abandoned by the defeated French ten years earlier and presently deserted, is surrounded by grave markers and a cemetery, over which ominously hangs a sign written in French. "'Stranger,'" a corporal reads aloud, "'when you find us here, go tell the Spartans we obeyed their orders.'" The soldier explains that the words refer to the 300 Spartans who died at the Battle of Thermopylae. Following several savage battles, the Ameri-

can general, deciding that the Muc Wa mission was pointless after all, orders the remaining American advisers to evacuate the village, leaving the Vietnamese soldiers behind. Lancaster, who voluntarily stays behind with a corporal, is killed that evening.

One of the grimmest of the dramas to come out of that war, the film, part of the first wave of Vietnam features, anticipates the highly acclaimed 1986 entry, *Platoon*, in its depiction of the frustrations of the troops, their escalating participation in atrocities, the political corruption and the ultimate military disaster. A green gung-ho second lieutenant sends back a message after the first skirmish with the Vietcong: "We have met the enemy and they are ours," ironic words that were to be repeated by wrong-headed military leaders throughout the conflict. An officer skilled in psychological warfare introduces Lancaster to an "Incident Flow Priority Indicator" that allegedly predicts, with the aid of a computer in Saigon, where the enemy will strike next. A burnt-out sergeant, forced to assume command of the outpost when the lieutenant is killed, commits suicide. "By God," the obstinate general announces in defense of his original decision to occupy Muc Wa, "we can't let those scroungy little jungle buggers chase the American Advisory Command off a post, can we?" Based on the novel *Incident at Muc Wa* by Daniel Ford, the film captures the tragedy of the war. The Americans' arrogance toward the military defeat of France and their own general ignorance of the Vietnamese are emphasized. The battle scenes are realistic, and the sequence in which the Americans are forced to abandon their fellow Vietnamese soldiers to the encroaching enemy is at once forceful and poignant. An American soldier shrugs off the incident by explaining to another: "It's their war." ■

God Is My Co-Pilot (1945), WB. Dir. Robert Florey; Sc. Peter Milne; Cast includes: Dennis Morgan, Dane Clark, Raymond Massey, Alan Hale, Andrea King.

A World War II drama about the experiences of an American fighter pilot, the film is based on the memoirs of Colonel Robert L. Scott. The studio embellished the modest story by adding some early romantic interludes, a priest who influences the flier and exaggerated heroic air battles between the

Ground crews prepare a squadron of Flying Tigers for action during World War II. *God Is My Co-Pilot* (1945).

colonel and the enemy. Dennis Morgan portrays the airman who joins General Chennault and his "Flying Tigers" in the Far East. Alan Hale, as "Big Mike" Harrigan, the missionary priest, restores the colonel's faith in religion. When Morgan muses that he is not alone in his fighter plane, Hale concurs. "Son," the missionary says, "you're not up there alone. You have the greatest co-pilot in the world." Raymond Massey enacts Chennault in this heavy-handed production.

Robert Lee Scott, one of the more publicized pilots in the Flying Tigers, of early World War II fame, registered 13 kills during the war and achieved a degree of literary prominence as well when he wrote *God Is My Co-pilot*, dealing with his exploits.

In the book Scott related his early fascination with aerial affairs, detailing how he jumped off a barn roof using an umbrella as a parachute. Born in 1908, he attended West Point and at one time flew the mail. He joined Chennault's American Volunteer Group, more popularly known as the Flying Tigers, who fought the Japanese in China before America's entry into World War II. Dur-

ing his service with the Flying Tigers, Scott shot down three enemy aircraft, including "Tokyo Joe," a Japanese ace.

Scott transferred to the U.S. Army Air Corps in the spring of 1942, following the disbanding of the Flying Tigers with America's entry into the war. He commanded the 23rd fighter group. After a tour of duty as an air instructor in the States, he returned overseas to promote the use of rocket-armed fighter planes against Japanese shipping around Okinawa and railway facilities in China. He later wrote several other books and became an anti-Communist speaker during the 1950s. Besides serving as a vehicle for showing Scott's air triumphs, the film version of *God Is My Co-Pilot* also presents his mystical and religious outlook on combat flying. ∎

Gold Chevrons (1927), Sales Pictures.

This World War I documentary is based on official war footage taken by the U.S. Signal Corps. The film covers several famous battles, including Chateau-Thierry, the Argonne and that of the "Lost Battalion." There are powerful scenes of fighting in the trenches, a

German and American dogfight in the air, men advancing and dropping as they come within range of enemy machine-guns, a cavalry attack caught by an exploding shell. There are other scenes of the wounded being carried in to the field hospitals and of captured prisoners. The film uses German newsreels effectively by intercutting these so that a battle can be shown from two points of view. Some of the footage has been used previously in other documentaries. ∎

Golden Dawn (1930), WB. *Dir.* Ray Enright; *Sc.* Walter Anthony; *Cast includes:* Walter Woolf, Vivienne Segal, Noah Beery, Alice Gentle, Lupino Lane, Marion Byron.

Based on a stage production by Oscar Hammerstein II and others, this offbeat operetta with a World War I background concerns a native uprising in East Africa against English and German forces. Meanwhile, an English regiment attempts to control the blacks. Vivienne Segal, as Dawn, is about to marry a black god as part of a ritual, when it is learned that she is white. Generally weak musical numbers continually interrupt the inept plot. Noah Beery, painted in blackface, gets to sing "The Whip Song." Other numbers include "Dawn," "My Bwana," "Africa Smiles" and "In a Jungle Bungalow." The film was shot in Technicolor. ∎

Golden Earrings (1947). See Spy Films: the Talkies. ∎

Golden Hawk, The (1952), Col. *Dir.* Sidney Salkow; *Sc.* Robert E. Kent; *Cast includes:* Sterling Hayden, Rhonda Fleming, John Sutton, Helena Carter.

The conflicts between France and Spain in the 17th century are played out in the Caribbean in this seafaring adventure drama. Sterling Hayden portrays a stalwart French privateer who rescues a female pirate (Rhonda Fleming) from his adversary's ship. Hayden holds the governor (John Sutton) of a Spanish stronghold, responsible for his mother's death. The implausible plot finds Sutton as Hayden's real father and Fleming turning to piracy to recover her lost treasure from the French. The film was adapted from the novel by Frank Yerby.

The wholly fictitious plot seems to be based on one of two wars during this period—a minor conflict between France and Spain (1683–1684) or the War of the League of Augsburg (1689–1697) in which France's overly confident Louis XIV, hungry for European conquests, single-handedly took on Spain, Austria, Holland, Sweden and England. Louis counted heavily on his 400,000-man army and 60,000 seamen. The war ended indecisively with the treaty of Ryswick (1697), but France's naval power was weakened permanently. ∎

Golden Horde, The (1951), U. *Dir.* George Sherman; *Sc.* Gerald Drayson Adams; *Cast includes:* Ann Blyth, David Farrar, George Macready, Henry Brandon.

Based on a story by Harold Lamb, this undistinguished costume drama uses the siege of Samarkand in 1220 as its background. Ann Blyth portrays a princess whose city is besieged by Genghis Khan (Marvin Miller). At first the wily princess devises a plan to set Khan's son against another rival warrior. But David Farrar, as a gallant English knight, comes to her rescue. He rallies his Crusaders to do battle against the ruthless hordes of Khan and saves the city from destruction in this routine adventure very loosely adapted from historical events. Several exciting battle scenes, including fights with the broadsword and crossbow, are highlighted.

Historically, the Mongol leader destroyed the city of Samarkand in 1221. The city, one of the oldest in the U.S.S.R. and an important depot along the "silk route," had been razed earlier by Alexander in 329 B.C. ∎

Gone With the Wind (1939), MGM. *Dir.* Victor Fleming; *Sc.* Sidney Howard; *Cast includes:* Clark Gable, Leslie Howard, Olivia de Havilland, Vivien Leigh, Thomas Mitchell, Hattie McDaniel, Evelyn Keyes, Ann Rutherford, George Reeves, Butterfly McQueen.

Margaret Mitchell's extremely popular Civil War novel became the basis for one of the most acclaimed and perennial films ever produced. There are few people who have not read the book or seen Selznick's production. In some ways it is a typical Hollywood product—expensive, boasting a large cast, shot in and around the studio and highly publicized. Criticism ranged from astounding to less than enthusiastic. But American and world audiences flocked to see the epic war film and the heroic and hapless love story of two strong-willed people. The making of the film has become almost as legendary as the film itself. Clark Gable was chosen by national referendum to play Rhett Butler while Selznick and MGM had tested more than a thousand candidates for the role of Scarlett. Norma Shearer, the studio's first choice, rejected the role. Eventually, English actress Vivien Leigh won the part, disturbing some that she was not an American and calming Southerners that at least a Northerner was not chosen. Several dozen writers worked on the script. Ironically, Sidney Howard, who wrote the major part of the screenplay, never saw the film; he died in an accident before the screening. Several directors had a hand in the work. George Cukor was taken off the project. Victor Fleming, who received full credit, had a nervous breakdown while working on the film and was assisted temporarily by Sam Wood.

The Civil War plays as significant a role in the film as does the love story. The conflict results in the destruction of a Southern way of life that was to influence future generations. It affected the two families, the O'Haras and the aristocratic Wilkses. Scenes of the war and its results remain as memorable as the principal characters. The burning of Atlanta, the high angle shot of the Confederate wounded sprawled along the streets and in the hospital and Scarlett's shooting of a Union deserter are just three such images.

Scarlett O'Hara, by far the most interesting character in the film, demonstrates a will and a strength that suggest she will attain what she goes after. Men fall in love with her not for her tenderness or romantic ideas but for her strength. She marries not for love but out of a need for the moment. Her first husband reinforces her with innocence; her second provides security; her third, Rhett Butler, represents energy and experience. Scarlett, however, remains true to Ashley, who symbolizes the past, a South that was quickly disappearing into memory. Not until Rhett walks out on her does she finally come to terms with reality, a reality that casts a shadow over her sense of tomorrow. ∎

Good Fight, The (1984), First Run Features. *Dir.* Noel Buckner, Mary Dore, Sam Sills.

A documentary about the Spanish Civil War (1936–1938), the film recalls the conflict between the Loyalists who were trying to defend their freedom and independence and the insurgent Fascists, led by General Francisco Franco. The main focus is on the Lincoln Brigade, a unit made up of more than 3,000 American volunteers who went to Spain to fight for the republic against Franco. The Americans were part of the International Brigade, composed of 40,000 volunteers representing 51 nations. The struggle was doomed almost from the start. Not only were Franco's forces better equipped, they also received help from Nazi Germany by way of bombers and from Italy through its fighter planes. Half of the American citizen soldiers perished in the war and another 700 were wounded. Those who returned home were accused of Communist leanings. Many could not find jobs.

The film, narrated by Studs Terkel, blends interviews with some of the survivors, stock footage of the war and excerpts from the 1938 film *Blockade*. The story the film unfolds is not a sentimental one but an analysis of the events. Veterans of the Lincoln Brigade, now in their seventies, offer differing views of conflict. On the one hand, it was a prelude to World War II, and in this sense it was only one lost battle in a war that ended victoriously for those who cherished freedom. On the other hand, some veterans believe, it was just another lost cause against the forces of totalitarianism. Regardless of the final outcome, the film pays tribute to those brave Americans who left the safety of their homes, jeopardized or sacrificed their lives and continued to pay a price for many years after "the good fight." ∎

Good Luck, Mr. Yates (1943). See Home Front. ∎

Good Morning, Vietnam (1987), BV. *Dir.* Barry Levinson; *Sc.* Mitch Markowitz; *Cast includes:* Robin Williams, Forest Whitaker, Tung Thanh Tran, Chintara Sukapatana, Bruno Kirby.

Robin Williams portrays an irreverent disk jockey in Saigon in this comedy drama set in 1965 during the Vietnam War. The film is loosely based on the experiences of Adrian Cronauer, whom Williams portrays on screen. Williams is assigned by the Armed

Forces Radio Service to liven up a comatose morning show by bringing chatter and music from home to the American soldiers. He not only turns the program into an instant hit but emerges as a popular Saigon personality. His iconoclastic monologues and ramblings on everything from the military to sex provide his devoted listeners with one of the few voices of sanity, a sharp contrast to a war that is escalating in numbers and violence.

His broadcasts, however, ruffle his superior officers who grow impatient with him. More comfortable with military doublespeak, they begin to censor his materal. In his spare time he works as an English teacher. He meets a young attractive Vietnamese woman whom he introduces, along with her family of twelve, to American culture by way of the film *Beach Blanket Bingo*, complete with subtitles.

The bombing of a Saigon nightclub by the Vietcong becomes the center of the film. Williams is a witness to the tragedy but is not permitted to mention it on his radio show. The comedy chiefly derives from Williams' freewheeling improvisations while in front of the microphone. This was the first film to treat the Vietnam War humorously. Some of the paradox of the war is suggested when Williams plays a recording of Louis Armstrong's "What a Wonderful World" as the camera cuts to bombings, the siege of Saigon and other combat shots. ∎

Goodbye Kiss, The (1928), FN. *Dir.* Mack Sennett; *Sc.* Mack Sennett, Jefferson Moffitt; *Cast includes:* Johnny Burke, Sally Eilers, Matty Kemp, Wheeler Oakman, Irving Bacon.

Producer-director Mack Sennett's contribution to the parade of World War I comedies that appeared after the conflict stars Johnny Burke as an American soldier in France. The war sequences and comic elements in the film switch from a Paris cafe that undergoes an air raid to the war in the trenches where a doughboy loses his nerve during his first battle. Some heroics blend into the plot when an American soldier hides in a spy's automobile, learns about an impending bombing of his unit and saves his buddies at the last moment. Sally Eilers portrays a nurse in this comedy drama that generally lacked the director's famous ingenuity for evoking laughs. ∎

Goose Step (1939). See *Beasts of Berlin* (1939). ∎

Government Girl (1943). See Washington, D.C. ∎

"Governor's Daughter, The" (1909), Kalem.

In this silent drama of the American Revolution a minister sides with the colonists and enlists as a spy. The girl he courts, the governor's daughter, breaks off her engagement to him when she learns of his sympathies. During one of his missions he is discovered and pursued by the British. He asks the governor to hide him and his request is granted. The daughter at first disagrees but allows him to stay. While the British search the house, the officer makes advances toward the girl and the minister saves her. He escapes with the officer's uniform after knocking the soldier unconscious. When the war ends, the minister returns and proposes to his sweetheart. ∎

Gown of Destiny, The (1917). See Propaganda Films: World War I. ∎

Grant, Ulysses S. (1822–1885). The supreme commander of all the Union armies in the final stages of the American Civil War never conveyed the image of a dashing, noble courtly gentleman that had become associated with his chief rival, Confederate General Robert E. Lee. Grant was a short, scruffy, stolid individual who appears to have been given to bouts of drinking, perhaps triggered by his mood swings as much as a need to relieve his own inner doubts and tensions. He was a steady plugger who did his job in the simplest and most direct way possible. His view of war, delivered to an army doctor, was to "find out where your enemy is, get at him as soon as you can, and strike him as hard you can, and keep moving on." It was a philosophy that fitted his personality and the task he faced. The unglamorous but dogged Grant had behind him the preponderant industrial and population strength of the Union. With steady pressure he could slowly strangle the South despite its tactically superior leaders.

A West Point graduate, Grant was cited for gallantry in the Mexican War but he resigned from the army in 1854 amidst unproved allegations of drunkenness. He engaged in several businesses with little success before re-entering federal military service at the start of the Civil War. His stunning victories in the west at Forts Henry and Donelson (February 1862) on the Tennessee River brought him a measure of fame because they were the first Union successes of the war. In sharp contrast to the Union's lack of success in the east, Grant continued to win battles in the west. His forces took Shiloh (April 1862) and then split the Confederacy by capturing Vicksburg on the Mississippi River (July 4, 1863). His victory at Chattanooga (November 23–25, 1863) led to his promotion to lieutenant general and supreme command of all Union land forces.

In the Wilderness Campaign (May 5–June 3, 1864) Grant initiated a war of attrition against Lee. Following his capture of the important transportation center of Petersburg (April 2, 1865), Grant continued to apply relentless pressure to Lee's army, now badly weakened, with supplies running short and cut off from the rest of the Confederacy. Lee surrendered a few days later (April 9, 1865) at Appomattox Court House.

At the surrender ceremony, the contrast in appearances between the generals could not have been sharper. Lee, tall, handsome, immaculately groomed, a flashing sword at his side, came astride his white charger to meet his victor. Grant appeared in his "working clothes," his boots dappled with mud, a private's coat with his stars tacked on thrown over a rumpled shirt and no sword. The plain man from nowhere had humbled a glamorous representative of a fading aristocracy. But plain appearance did not mean crudeness for Grant. Observers at the surrender commented favorably on Grant's gracious and sensitive treatment of his former opponent.

Grant eventually gained the presidency (1869–1877) on the basis of his war record. Though personally honest, his administration was racked by scandal by unscrupulous politicians. Back in private life, Grant became impoverished because of bad business deals, but the writing of his memoirs (1885), in a race with death, earned a large sum for his surviving family.

Grant has been portrayed in numerous films, generally those directly relating to the Civil War, but unfortunately more care has been spent on the accuracy of his physical appearance than on his character. "The Blue and the Gray or the Days of '61" (1908), "Stirring Days in Old Virginia" (1909), *With Lee in Virginia* (1913), *The Battle Cry of Peace* (1915), *Defense or Tribute?* (1916), *My Own United States* (1918), *Abraham Lincoln* (1924) and *The Warrens of Virginia* (1924) are some of the silents in which he is characterized, albeit in secondary roles, as the Union's symbol of determination.

With the advent of sound, his portrait, chiefly in cameo roles, gains more credibility, particularly in such features as *Only the Brave* (1930), *Sitting Bull* (1954), *Drum Beat* (1954) and *The Horse Soldiers* (1959). D.W. Griffith in *Abraham Lincoln* (1930) adds another dimension to Grant's character (as well as Lee's) by showing him agonizing over the long war and its toll in lives and destruction. ∎

"Gray Sentinel, The" (1913), Broncho. *Dir.* Burton King; *Cast includes:* Charles Ray, J. Barney Sherry, John Emerson, Fred Mace.

A Southern fisherman volunteers his services as a spy for the Confederates who are attempting to run a Union blockade in this Civil War drama. Eventually, he is shot trying to escape in a small boat. This silent film was one of the first to move the Civil War action from the conventional battlefield to the sea. Charles Ray, who was to emerge within a short time as one of the most popular silent screen stars, portrays the young hero. ∎

Great Day in the Morning (1956), RKO. *Dir.* Jacques Tourneur; *Sc.* Lesser Samuels; *Cast includes:* Virginia Mayo, Robert Stack, Ruth Roman, Alex Nicol, Raymond Burr.

Set in Denver in 1861, the film concerns elements from the North and South attempting to control the gold from Colorado mines for the anticipated Civil War. Robert Stack portrays a Confederate sympathizer who seems more interested in the local women than in the Southern cause. Virginia Mayo, as an easterner who owns a dress shop in town, falls for Stack. Alex Nicol plays a Union agent sent west on a secret mission. Ruth Roman, as the saloon entertainer, is also interested in Stack, who has won the watering hole in a card game from local bad man Raymond Burr. Action chiefly centers around the two political factions whose emotions continually explode into violence, foreshadowing the tragic war about to descend upon the land. ∎

Great Deception, The (1926). See Spy Films: the Silents. ∎

Charlie Chaplin, as the title character in *The Great Dictator* (1940), is challenged by medal-bedecked fellow dictator Jack Oakie (r.) while Henry Daniell looks on.

Great Dictator, The (1940), UA. Dir. Charlie Chaplin; Sc. Charlie Chaplin; *Cast includes:* Charlie Chaplin, Paulette Goddard, Jack Oakie, Reginald Gardiner, Billy Gilbert, Henry Daniell.

A flawed work, chiefly because of its didacticism, Chaplin's first all-talking film and the last to employ the character of the tramp nevertheless offers several rewards. After its preachy opening—"This is a story of a period between two World Wars—an interim in which Insanity cut loose, Liberty took a nose dive and Humanity was kicked around somewhat"—we find Charlie comically struggling with a cannon in the midst of battle during World War I. Eventually, he is wounded and suffers from amnesia. The war ends and Charlie, a barber, returns to his little shop. From this point on, Chaplin begins his attack on Fascism. He satirizes Hitler in the form of Adenoid Hynckel, a Hitler-like dictator, also played by Chaplin, who has taken over the country of Tomania. The plot allows for the barber to exchange places with Hynckel and take over the government. Chaplin performs his famous ballet scene in which, as the power-crazed dictator, he dances with a

globe of the world. Jack Oakie does a brilliant parody of Mussolini. Chaplin's comic inventiveness appears throughout this devastating satire. But the last scene, in which he abandons the barber character to present a speech on how to better the world situation, is totally out of place and weakens the impact of the work. One of the earliest Hollywood comedies to include the topics of anti-Semitism and concentration camps, the film reveals the intrusion of Chaplin's social consciousness at the expense of entertainment.

Chaplin's other satiric comedy about World War I, *Shoulder Arms* (1918), stands in marked contrast to the above work. The earlier film possesses none of the latter's bleakness and despair. There is no hint of didacticism, and its ending is upbeat. Charlie as the innocent doughboy in *Shoulder Arms* manages to survive the idiocies of war with a shrug and a smile whereas Charlie the barber finally loses his sense of humor at the end of the film as he witnesses a world gone mad. ∎

Great Escape, The (1963), UA. Dir. John Sturges; Sc. James Clavell, W. R. Burnett; *Cast includes:* Steve McQueen, James Garner, Richard Attenborough, James Donald, Charles Bronson, Donald Pleasence, James Coburn.

This prisoner-of-war film, a large-scale production running almost three hours, recounts the story of a mass escape by Allied prisoners from a German prison camp during World War II. P.O.W.s with records of repeated attempts at escaping from their German captors are sent to a new maximum-security camp where the commandant states: "We have, in effect, put all our rotten eggs in one basket, and we intend to watch this basket very carefully." As soon as the inmates are settled in at their new camp, British officer Richard Attenborough and a handful of others begin to make plans for a large-scale breakout.

The remainder of the film deals with the meticulous preparations required—digging three different tunnels, making civilian clothes, forging passports and other papers and assigning a variety of jobs to other prisoners. Attenborough's intentions are to free 250 prisoners, thereby forcing the Germans to take soldiers from other war duties to hunt for the escapees. Eventually 76 prisoners break out and scatter over the countryside. Fifty are caught by the Gestapo and executed, and others are rounded up and returned to the camp. Only three make it across the border. At the end of the film a recaptured Canadian officer (James Garner), learning of the tragic fate of the fifty, asks the senior British officer (James Donald): "Do you think it was worth the price?" "It all depends on your point of view," Donald replies.

Steve McQueen, as a recalcitrant American prisoner who has made 17 previous escape attempts, is continually confined to the "cooler," or solitary confinement. His motorcycle ride with German troops in hot pursuit is one of the highlights of the film. Charles Bronson, as a Polish patriot fighting with the British, is in charge of digging the tunnels. James Garner, the Australian officer, is the "scrounger" of the camp, capable of obtaining everything from cameras for passport photos to wood for bracing the tunnels. In one of the more poignant scenes, he volunteers to stay with Donald Pleasence throughout the escape. Pleasence, the "forger" of the camp, has lost his eyesight in creating the numerous counterfeit documents.

The film, from the book by Paul Brickhill, is based on a true incident. The actual camp, Stalag Luft III, was opened in 1942 and originally boarded several hundred prisoners. The captives spent much of their time planning escapes. In March 1944, 76 prisoners escaped, much to the embarrassment of the Germans. Fifty of those caught were executed on Hitler's orders. These deaths stunned the remaining prisoners. However, the Normandy invasion brought a new surge of hope to the men. *The Great Escape* is a tribute to the ingenuity, resourcefulness and courage of the prisoners who believed it was their duty to escape. In fact, the film is dedicated to "the fifty" who were brutally executed. ∎

Great Guns (1941), TCF. *Dir.* Monty Banks; *Sc.* Lou Breslow; *Cast includes:* Stan Laurel, Oliver Hardy, Sheila Ryan, Dick Nelson, Edmund MacDonald, Kane Richmond.

Laurel and Hardy portray a gardener and chauffeur who enlist in the army when their employer does likewise in this below-average service comedy. The duo become entangled in their usual messes before events get straightened out. The comic antics of the team are below par most of the time. Stan and Ollie had left producer Hal Roach for whom they turned out most of their best work and signed with 20th Century-Fox where they had little control over their material. Dick Nelson and Sheila Ryan provide the romantic subplot in this forgettable comedy. ∎

Great Impersonation, The (1921), Par. *Dir.* George Melford; *Sc.* Monte Katterjohn; *Cast includes:* James Kirkwood, Ann Forrest, Winter Hall, Alan Hale.

In this spy drama set just prior to World War I and based on E. Phillips Oppenheim's popular novel, James Kirkwood portrays the dual roles of Sir Dominey and Leopold Von Ragastein. The German secret service sends its agent, who looks very much like Sir Dominey, to replace the Englishman. Ann Forrest provides the romantic interest. Two sound versions of the story appeared, one in 1935 starring Edmund Lowe, and another in 1942 with Ralph Bellamy in the dual role. ∎

Great Impersonation, The (1935), U. *Dir.* Alan Crosland; *Sc.* Frank Wead, Eve Greene; *Cast includes:* Edmund Lowe, Valerie Hobson, Wera Engels, Lumsden Hare, Spring Byington, Frank Reicher.

A remake of the 1921 version of E. Phillips Oppenheim's novel, this adaptation contains a major alteration. Instead of identifying particular countries such as Germany, the film describes the villains as members of an international cartel, merchants of death who foment conflicts around the world so that they can sell their munitions. Edmund Lowe portrays the dual role of Englishman and spy who exposes the sinister ring, including the brains behind the organization (Charles Waldron).

At the time the film was released, newspapers carried stories of a mysterious international figure who amassed great wealth from the sale of weaponry and who lived a luxurious life in Europe. Also, several documentaries about World War I released in the 1930s, such as *Dealers in Death* (1934), began condemning the munitions makers and government leaders for making secret deals during the conflict. ∎

Great Impersonation, The (1942), U. *Dir.* John Rawlins; *Sc.* W. Scott Darling; *Cast includes:* Ralph Bellamy, Evelyn Ankers, Aubrey Mather, Edward Norris.

E. Phillips Oppenheim's popular novel is updated to World War II in this third version of the spy drama. Ralph Bellamy portrays the dual role of an Englishman and a German. Both meet somewhere in Africa before the outbreak of war. Then only one is followed to assume an important post in England during the war. But which one? Finally, the audience learns that he is the true Englishman. He is given false plans to turn over to agents in Germany. The film adds a subplot involving Rudolf Hess to the original story in which Bellamy dispatches Hess on his notorious journey by plane to Scotland. Evelyn Ankers plays Bellamy's English wife in this suspenseful tale. ∎

Great Love, The (1918), Par. *Dir.* D. W. Griffith; *Sc.* D. W. Griffith; *Cast includes:* Lillian Gish, Robert Harron, Henry B. Walthall, Gloria Hope.

Director D.W. Griffith's World War I romantic drama is set chiefly in war-torn England where German spies are plotting the destruction of a munitions factory. Lillian Gish, who plays the daughter of a rector, is the love object of a soldier (Robert Harron). But Gish is cajoled into marrying Sir Roger (Henry B. Walthall), a despicable character who recently abandoned a young woman with whom he had had a child. Both were killed in an air raid. Meanwhile, Harron foils a German plot to guide enemy zeppelins to the munitions target. He then kills Sir Roger, thereby rescuing Gish from an unsavory marriage.

World War I movies made in America almost invariably dealt with only the three major allies—England, France and the U.S.—particularly in their choice of principal characters. Belgium was used chiefly as an innocent and helpless symbol of Germany's depravity and aggression. Italy, which seemed inconsequential in Hollywood's view, provided very few heroic characters. In terms of social background, spy dramas and sophisticated characters, the studios preferred England over France. American movie audiences were already familiar with English types and probably felt comfortable with these settings. The above film is typical in its employment of English society. Griffith used left-over on-location footage from his earlier World War I drama, *Hearts of the World.* ∎

Great Sioux Massacre, The (1965), Col. *Dir.* Sidney Salkow; *Sc.* F. C. Dobbs; *Cast includes:* Joseph Cotten, Darren McGavin, Philip Carey, Julie Sommars, Nancy Kovack.

This action drama depicts the events that culminated in Custer's defeat at Little Big Horn. Philip Carey portrays the flamboyant hero-on-horseback who, according to this script, is openly critical of political corruption within the Indian agency. Custer is then recalled to Washington where his superiors plan to curtail his verbal attacks. Meanwhile, another politician promises to make Custer a national hero if he would take a firmer stand against the Indian. When he returns to duty, Custer's new attitude toward the tribes infuriates Sitting Bull, chief of the Sioux. In the ensuing conflict, Custer, seeking personal glory in defeating the Sioux, is overly hasty in leading his 251 men against the hostiles and finds himself surrounded and overwhelmed by Sitting Bull's braves.

Joseph Cotten portrays a heavy-drinking major and former Confederate officer. Darren McGavin plays a captain loyal to Custer. Michael Pate, as Sitting Bull, is forced to take up arms against the soldiers following a series of mistreatments. Julie Sommars, as Cotten's daughter, provides the romantic interest for McGavin in this better-than-average retelling of Custer's Last Stand. ∎

Great Sioux Uprising, The (1953), U. *Dir.* Lloyd Bacon; *Sc.* Melvin Levy, J. Robert Bren, Gladys Atwater; *Cast includes:* Jeff Chandler, Faith Domergue, Lyle Betger, Peter Whitney.

Tensions mount between the Sioux and the U.S. Cavalry in this western with a Civil War background. An unscrupulous rancher (Lyle Betger) who supplies horses to the Union, including those his men rustle from other small ranchers as well as steal from the Sioux, instigates the cavalry to attack the Indians to cover his theft of the tribe's sacred mounts. Meanwhile, a Confederate officer who is part Cherokee calls a war council of Chief Red Cloud of the Sioux and leaders of other tribes in an attempt to have them join the South in its war against the North. Jeff Chandler, as a former army medic who has set up shop as a horse doctor in the town, has his work cut out for him talking the Indian chiefs out of going to war and bringing Betger to justice. The cavalry commander apologizes to Red Cloud and promises to pay for all the stolen horses. Faith Domergue, as a rival horse dealer, provides the romantic interest for both Betger and Chandler. The entirely fictitious and routine plot has almost nothing to do with the actual Sioux wars of the period. ∎

Great Trek. See South African War. ∎

Great Waldo Pepper, The (1975). See Veterans. ■

Greater Glory, The (1926), FN. *Dir.* Curt Rehfeld; *Sc.* June Mathis; *Cast includes:* Conway Tearle, Anna Q. Nilsson, May Allison, Ian Keith, Lucy Beaumont, Jean Hersholt.

This World War I drama set chiefly in Vienna explores the effects of war on an average family. The focal character is an elderly aunt (Lucy Beaumont). As the war grinds on, the family is reduced to poverty, forcing several of its members to react less than nobly. One of the nieces, Fanny (Anna Q. Nilsson), becomes the mistress of a crude war profiteer. Another niece (May Allison) is separated from the man she loves. Other members of the once-comfortable clan include a musician, a physician, a professional soldier and a professor. The ravages of war are somewhat tempered by the power of love by the time the plot winds down.

The cast of thousands, lavish costumes and impressive sets were all designed to present an epic in the fashion of *The Four Horsemen of the Apocalype* (1921), also written by June Mathis. The lengthy production was eventually cut from its original 30 reels to 11 but still was unable to match the power of its predecessor. ■

Greatest Power, The (1917). See Propaganda Films: World War I. ■

Greatest Thing in Life, The (1918), Par. *Dir.* D. W. Griffith; *Sc.* S. E. V. Taylor, D. W. Griffith; *Cast includes:* Lillian Gish, Robert Harron, Adolphe Lestina, Elmo Lincoln.

Robert Harron portrays an aesthete who dislikes everyone else but himself and the daughter of a tobacco dealer (Lillian Gish). When the girl's father decides to return to his native France, she accompanies him. World War I breaks out and Harron enlists. Once in the trenches he learns the meaning of love and comradeship. A fellow doughboy risks his own life to save that of Harron. Later, he and a black soldier are cut off from their unit. His comrade gives him the last of the water when he sees that Harron is dying of thirst. A changed person, he meets Gish in France during the war and they renew their close friendship.

The film won the respect of the critics for its artistic merits, especially the work of C.W. Bitzer, Griffith's loyal cameraman. But the director's next war drama, *The Girl Who Stayed at Home*, released after the conflict, was criticized by the reviewers for its confused plot. ■

Greco-Persian Wars. See Thermopylae. ■

Greek Civil War (1944–1949). This conflict marked the beginning of Cold War tensions in Europe between pro-Communist and anti-Communist elements. Following the liberation of Greece from the Axis by British forces in 1944, fighting broke out on December 3, 1944 between Communists and anti-Communist groups for control of the country. The British negotiated a truce under an interim government and set up a plebiscite to determine the nature of the postwar Greek government.

The Communists refused to accept the results of the vote that restored the monarchy under King George II and fighting broke out again in May 1946. Communist rebels received support from the bordering totalitarian socialist nations of Yugoslavia, Albania and Bulgaria. Heeding the Greek government's appeal for aid, Britain and the U.S. sent help. The U.S. sent large amounts of military and economic aid under the Truman Doctrine in the first instance of an American Cold War program designed to meet a perceived growing Communist threat in post-World War II Europe.

Between 1947 and 1949, the Greek government gradually narrowed the area under rebel control to a Communist-dominated region along the nation's northern border. Yugoslavia, in the meantime, had split away from the Eastern bloc, dominated by the Soviet Union, and ceased aiding the Greek rebels. The Communist movement collapsed by mid-October, 1949, and some of its followers fled into the European Communist zone. The Communists, however, left a legacy of bitterness in Greece, because of charges they abducted young children who disappeared into the Soviet satellite world.

Relatively few American films have dealt with this period of Greek history. In the film *Guerrilla Girl* (1953) a former Greek officer (Helmut Dantine) returns to his homeland after World War II only to find it threatened by a Communist takeover. It depicted, in part, some of the turmoil that afflicted strife-torn Greece during the Civil War. Peter Yates' *Eleni* (1985), based on the nonfiction work by

Casualties mount as an American military base in Vietnam comes under heavy attack from Viet Cong forces. *The Green Berets* (1968).

Nick Gage, concerns the search by a reporter (John Malkovich) for the truth about the assassination of his mother (Kate Nelligan) by the Communists during the Civil War. The film explores in part the controversy of the missing children. The reporter discovers that his mother—Eleni—was executed by a local Communist chieftain for helping children to flee the Communist zone. ∎

Green Berets, The (1968), WB. *Dir.* John Wayne, Ray Kellogg; *Sc.* James Lee Barrett; *Cast includes*: John Wayne, David Janssen, Jim Hutton, Aldo Ray.

A cliché-ridden Vietnam War action drama of the special forces unit known as the Green Berets, the film, based on a novel by Robin Moore, features John Wayne as a hard-fighting colonel with the familiar warm spot underneath his tough exterior. The story, with its unabashed heroics and stereotyped good guys and "heavies," has more in common with World War II than Vietnam. The

undermanned force defends a base against overwhelming odds as the barbaric Vietcong, who are depicted as rapists and torturers, attack in full fury. Later, the Green Berets manage to kidnap a Vietcong general. Jim Hutton, as a happy-go-lucky soldier, steals supplies from other outfits. David Janssen, as a cynical correspondent, is against America's involvement in Vietnam. He soon sees the error of his thinking and eventually picks up a weapon to join in the struggle against the sadistic foe. By the end of the film, Wayne stands on the Vietnam shore looking out toward the U.S. as the sun sets (only in a Wayne movie could the sun set in the East) and muses, referring to a South Vietnamese orphan, "This is what the war is all about."

This was the only major film about the war produced by Hollywood during the conflict. It had the full cooperation of the State and Defense Departments. But despite Wayne's heroics, the romanticized special forces unit and the spirited theme song "The Ballad of the Green Berets," it made few converts for the cause. Critics attacked its simplistic politics while antiwar factions protested the film, which nevertheless ended up with large grosses at the box-office. ∎

Green Temptation, The (1922), Par. Dir. William Desmond Taylor; Sc. Monte Katterjohn, Julia Crawford Ivers; *Cast includes:* Betty Compson, Theodore Kosloff, Neely Edwards.

This World War I drama depicts how the conflict affected one person's life for the better. Betty Compson portrays a dancer with a troupe of French street players who are actually a gang of thieves. As the players charm their audience, other members of the gang pickpocket the onlookers. Although she rises in the world of entertainment and appears in fashionable Paris theaters, she continues to ply her trade until the police eventually close in on her. But she escapes in time and enlists as a nurse when war erupts. While caring for the wounded at the front, she decides to shed her past life and start anew. She journeys to the U.S. after the Armistice where her past catches up to her. Invited to a swanky party by a wealthy American who had met her while he was recuperating from a war wound, she meets a former member of her old gang (Theodore Kosloff). He exposes her past when she refuses to assist him in stealing some valuable jewels. Kosloff is killed trying to escape. The American rejects her when he learns of her shady past, but an Englishman, another one of her former patients, proposes marriage. ∎

Guadalcanal, Battle of (August 7, 1942– February 19, 1943). The invasion of Guadalcanal in the Solomon Islands marked the first successful American land offensive in the Pacific theatre in World War II. The Guadalcanal campaign initiated the American strategy of "island hopping" to secure bases from which to carry the war to the Japanese home islands. The documentary *Victory at Sea* (1954) explains the U.S. plan in its Guadalcanal sequence.

The landing of Major-General Alexander Vandegrift's 1st Marine division, without opposition, caught the Japanese by surprise. But the next day, Japan began a large-scale land-naval-air counterattack to drive the Americans off the island. The Japanese, at one point, had nearly 50,000 troops facing 18,000

U.S. Marines and their support elements. The invasion is recreated in *Marine Raiders* (1944), a routine action drama starring Pat O'Brien as a tough marine major and Robert Ryan as a captain. O'Brien's part is based on Colonel Merritt Edson's exploits.

The fighting, under jungle conditions, was among the most vicious in the war and often resulted in hand-to-hand combat. Much of the early fighting, such as that at the Battle of Bloody Ridge, was over control of an unfinished Japanese airfield. The marines seized the field, completed it and renamed it Henderson Field. The airstrip played an important part in American forces retaining control of the air over the island and nearby waters. This bitter and bloody phase of the battle has been realistically depicted in *Guadalcanal Diary* (1943).

The Japanese twice failed to penetrate marine positions in counterattacks. One enemy commander, after seeing his force decimated by aerial bombardment and encircling ground forces, burned his regimental colors and committed hara-kiri. Edson's Raiders (dramatized in *Marine Raiders*) and Carlson's Raiders (portrayed in *Gung Ho!*, released in 1943), both elite Marine battalions, were among the units that received praise for their actions against the enemy.

A series of American naval actions around Guadalcanal hindered Japan's attempt to supply and reinforce its garrison. Army units under General Alexander Patch replaced the marines in December. By the end of the six-month campaign, which resulted in an American victory, the Japanese had lost 25,000 men, 600 airplanes and 24 ships. American losses were 1,490 dead, nearly 5,000 wounded, 55 missing and 24 vessels sunk or damaged. The U.S., though it lost the same number of ships as Japan, did not suffer as much destruction in tonnage.

Several other films have dealt with the ordeal on Guadalcanal. *Pride of the Marines* (1945), based on a true story, stars John Garfield as a marine who is blinded while fighting off a Japanese attack. *Flying Leathernecks* (1951), starring John Wayne, deals chiefly with U.S. Marine fighter pilots during the battle. *The Thin Red Line* (1964) and *First to Fight* (1967), the latter about a Guadalcanal Medal of Honor hero who temporarily loses his nerve during battle, are both fictitious tales that use Guadalcanal for their settings. ∎

William Bendix (r.c.) teases a fellow marine about to shave for the first time. *Guadalcanal Diary* (1943).

Guadalcanal Diary (1943), TCF. *Dir.* Lewis Seiler; *Sc.* Lamar Trotti; *Cast includes:* Preston Foster, Lloyd Nolan, William Bendix, Richard Conte, Anthony Quinn.

An eloquent World War II drama of a marine unit assigned to take an island from a cunning and unyielding enemy, the film dispenses with excessive heroics and concentrates on the fears and anxieties of each man as he goes about the dirty business of fighting a war. There are realistic scenes of the Japanese bayoneting the wounded, wiping out a unit of marines stranded on a beach, and resorting to all sorts of treacherous tactics as they strive to hold back the Americans from capturing the island. The marines are just as determined as the foe and eventually are victorious, but they pay a heavy price as they move out and leave the mopping up to the army.

The film has several light moments, some provided by character actor William Bendix, to relieve the grimness of battle. In one scene the marines gather around a portable radio to listen to a World Series ball game, but the radio goes dead just as the score is to be announced. In another scene a young marine imitates the sounds of a turkey to lure the Japanese out of hiding. "Are you Sergeant York or Gary Cooper?" a pal asks. The first man fires his rifle, hits his target and quips: "Scratch one squint-eye." The screenplay is based on the book by Richard Tragaskis.

Upon its release, the drama was hailed by many for its realism. However, it contained many of the conventional trappings of similar films of the period. The marines, while at sea before the assault, sing "Rock of Ages." There is the usual ethnic mix, including a leather-

neck from Brooklyn. Younger men write home to their mothers while others brag of their romantic exploits back in the States. Patriotic dialogue in the guise of sincerity seeps in at appropriate moments. "I ain't no hero," Bendix confesses during a heavy enemy bombardment. "I'm just a guy. I'm here because someone sent me and I just want to get it over with and go home as soon as I can."

Historically, it took the marines, who were short of supplies and replacements, three months of bitter fighting to secure the island. The battle itself, a particularly bloody one, lasted from August 1942 to February 1943. ■

"Guerrilla, The" (1908), Biograph. *Dir.* D. W. Griffith; *Sc.* D. W. Griffith; *Cast includes:* Arthur Johnson, Mack Sennett, Harry Solter, George Gebhardt.

This was D.W. Griffith's first of a series of one-and two-reel Civil War films that he turned out for Biograph and that he made in his first year as film director. The drama deals with a loyal black servant who rides to the rescue of his master. Even after his horse is shot, the rider gets through with the message entrusted to him. Although a simple and crude film by later standards, it whetted the director's appetite to return to the war and use it as background for ten more short films and, finally, for his 1915 masterpiece, *The Birth of a Nation*. He also repeated his use of a faithful black servant as a main character in two other short Civil War dramas—"His Trust" (1911) and "His Trust Fulfilled" (1911). ■

Guerrilla Girl (1953), UA. *Dir.* John Christian; *Sc.* John Byrne, Ben Parker; *Cast includes:* Helmut Dantine, Marianna, Irene Champlin, Ray Julian.

A former Greek officer who fled Athens when it was controlled by the Nazis returns after the war only to be threatened by Communist revolutionaries seeking to take over the country. Helmut Dantine portrays the officer who, with his fiancee, escapes from the Germans with the help of a band of gypsies. During the journey, one of the gypsy girls and Dantine have an affair. When the Nazis are ousted from Greece, Dantine returns to his homeland where he is singled out for assassination by Communist forces. His former gypsy lover notices his name on the death list and attempts to warn him. They are both shot and die in a final embrace in this low-budget film produced in Europe. This is one of the few dramas dealing with the Greek Civil War. ■

Guerrilla warfare. See Resistance. ■

Guevara, Dr. Ernesto "Che" (1928–1967). See *Che!* (1969). ■

Guilty of Treason (1949). See Cold War. ■

Gun Runners, The (1958), UA. *Dir.* Don Siegel; *Sc.* Dan Mainwaring, Paul Monash; *Cast includes:* Audie Murphy, Eddie Albert, Patricia Owens, Everett Sloane.

Based on Ernest Hemingway's *To Have and Have Not*, the drama stars Audie Murphy as a down-on-his-luck captain who hires out his cabin cruiser to smuggle guns to Cuban rebels. Eddie Albert, as a smooth-talking gangster, rents Murphy's boat for his gun-running enterprise. Everett Sloane plays Murphy's rum-soaked assistant, a role handled earlier by Walter Brennan in the 1944 version of the Hemingway tale. Patricia Owens portrays Albert's sexy wife. By the end of the film, Murphy reforms and turns on the dealers of death. In a climactic gun battle he kills the gun runners.

The film is played for action, avoiding any political discussion involving the revolt against Cuban dictator Machado. Its lower production values place it below Howard Hawks' production of *To Have and Have Not*, starring Humphrey Bogart and Lauren Bacall, a film which curiously switched locales from Cuba to Martinique. ■

Gun That Won the West, The (1955), Col. *Dir.* William Castle; *Sc.* James R. Gordon; *Cast includes:* Dennis Morgan, Paula Raymond, Richard Denning, Chris O'Brien.

The U.S. Cavalry brings the Springfield rifle into play against the Sioux in this routine outdoor drama. Determined to construct a string of forts in Wyoming to help protect railroad workers, the government assigns two Indian scouts, the famous Jim Bridger (Dennis Morgan) and his pal (Richard Denning) to renew their old friendship with Red Cloud, chief of the Sioux. They do their best, but when an attack upon the troops erupts, the army uses the new rifles to defeat the Indians. Michael Morgan plays a hostile who leads his warriors against the soldiers. Some of the battle scenes were borrowed from other

films. Ironically, it was not the Springfield rifle that earned the description "the gun that won the West," as implied in the title, but the Winchester. ■

Stalwart Randolph Scott (r.), as a no-nonsense U.S. Marine colonel, directs his fighting troops. *Gung Ho!* (1943).

Gung Ho! (1943), U. *Dir.* Ray Enright; *Sc.* Lucien Hubbard; *Cast includes:* Randolph Scott, Grace McDonald, Alan Curtis, Noah Beery, Jr., J. Carrol Naish.

This World War II film depicts the selection, training and the first offensive action of a select group of U.S. Marines. Randolph Scott portrays the tough and dedicated colonel in charge of the special hand-picked unit slated to attack Japanese-held Makin Island. Before the actual raid occurs, the film gets bogged down in a romance in which two marines (Noah Beery, Jr. and David Bruce) compete for the affections of Grace McDonald. The battle scenes are realistic and bloody as the tough and specially trained American troops exact a heavy toll on the enemy. The title comes from a Japanese expression meaning "work together."

Randolph Scott portrayed Evans F. Carlson (1896–1947), the officer who had led the actual raid on Makin Island on August 17, 1942. Carlson, who served as technical adviser for the drama, had been an observer with the Chinese Army in 1937. He recommended in 1941 that a special U.S. Marine unit be formed based on that of the British Commandos. The 2nd Marine Raider Battalion, depicted in the film, became known as Carlson's Raiders and was originally made up of 200 specially selected men. The special force did reconnaissance work on Makin on August 17, 1942 and saw combat on Guadalcanal in September.

Makin Island was finally captured by American troops in the latter part of 1943, previous to the film's release. Based on a factual account as written by marine Lieutenant W. S. Le Francois, the film has come under heavy fire by several film historians and critics in more recent times for its sanguinary, jingoistic training and approach to war. They particularly take exception to making patriotic heroes of the violent types that made up the special force depicted on the screen. ▪

Gunga Din (1939), RKO. *Dir.* George Stevens; *Sc.* Joel Sayre, Fred Guiol; *Cast includes:* Cary Grant, Victor McLaglen, Douglas Fairbanks, Jr., Sam Jaffe, Eduardo Ciannelli, Joan Fontaine.

Based on Rudyard Kipling's immortal poem, the film enlarges the story of the lowly water carrier into an epic adventure filled with exciting battles on India's frontier, spectacle and comedy. The plot concerns two English sergeants (Cary Grant and Victor McLaglen) who try to prevent their pal (Douglas Fairbanks, Jr.) from leaving the service to marry his sweetheart (Joan Fontaine). Meanwhile, an uprising of the Thuggees, a religious cult of murderers who strangle their victims, threatens British troops governing the region. Fairbanks, who enjoys a good fight, decides to stay on temporarily to join his friends, whom he suspects of trickery. The trio ultimately are captured, along with Gunga Din, by the leader of the fanatical sect (Eduardo Ciannelli). Din, the "regimental beastie" and waterboy (Sam Jaffe), sacrifices his life to save the regiment when he blows his bugle from atop the enemy's stronghold to warn the advancing army.

Kipling's poem is based on an incident during the siege of Delhi in 1857. His famous lines ending with "You're a better man than I am, Gunga Din," narrated by a British soldier, may pay tribute to the native waterboy, but the lines that follow raise questions about the poet's racism. When Kipling wrote "An' for all 'is dirty 'ide, 'E was white, clear white, inside, When 'e went to tend the wounded under fire!," was he expressing his own views or describing the attitudes of the common, uneducated soldier? Did Kipling embrace the belief accepted by many in that period that the native servants' obedience and

reverence should extend to their laying down their lives for their white masters?

The film has become a classic among colonial adventure yarns. George Stevens replaced Howard Hawks as the director when the latter was dismissed by studio heads for bringing in a previous film over budget. Ironically, Stevens followed suit, making *Din* the most costly project in RKO's history. But he was redeemed when the picture scored a hit both critically and commercially. The film was remade in 1961 as *Sergeants Three*, starring Frank Sinatra, Dean Martin and, in the Sam Jaffe role, Sammy Davis, Jr. But it failed to capture the chemistry of the original.

The Thuggees or Thugs, originally believed to be descended from Indian Muslim tribes, developed into a Hindu religious sect of organized gangs that strangled victims for their wealth. The sect was active in India from the 1300s until its extinction in the mid-1800s. The organization took its name from the Sanskrit terms "sthag" (to conceal) and "sthaga" (cheat). The modern English word "thug," or one who uses physical force in a robbery or crime, is derived from the group's activities.

The film portrays some of the murderous activities of the Thuggees and their worship of Kali, the Hindu God of destruction. However, tying the Thuggees in with a specific Indian uprising, the Sepoy Mutiny of 1857–1858, may be an example of Hollywood altering history to make an interesting film. The Thuggees had been largely brought under control by the combined forces of the British and friendly Indian Princes during the 1830s, two decades prior to the revolt. Only about 340 members of the sect were still registered in 1852. There is no record of its members taking an active, organized role against British army units in the uprising. It appears that Hollywood jammed the two periods together in the interests of a rousing tale. ▪

Guns of August, The (1964), U. *Sc.* Arthur H. Tourtellot.

A documentary based on Barbara Tuchman's book about that fateful August in 1914 when the world erupted in a senseless war, the film meticulously uses newsreel footage to cover the events that led to the slaughterhouse and those personalities who were partially responsible for World War I. Pictured here, among other inept dignitaries, are the senile Franz Josef of Austria and the inexperienced King George V of England. The grim battle sequences prove once again that the cost of war in human misery and lives is always high. ■

Guns of Fort Petticoat, The (1957), Col. *Dir.* George Marshall; *Sc.* Walter Doniger; *Cast includes:* Audie Murphy, Kathryn Grant, Hope Emerson, Jeff Donnell.

Audie Murphy, as a Union officer, returns to Texas during the Civil War to prevent the massacre of a Texas town in this offbeat action drama. He abandons his army command when his inept superior officer wantonly slaughters a band of Indians at the Sand Creek Massacre. Realizing that the Indian braves will seek revenge, he rides to the Texas town where the women, whose men are away fighting the war, are defenseless. He gathers the women into a mission, trains them to use weapons and defeats the attacking Indians. ■

Guy Named Joe, A (1943), MGM. *Dir.* Victor Fleming; *Sc.* Dalton Trumbo; *Cast includes:* Spencer Tracy, Irene Dunne, Van Johnson, Ward Bond, James Gleason.

Spencer Tracy portrays a reckless American pilot who is killed while on duty in England and returns as a spirit in this World War II fantasy. Appearing in the ethereal world of other dead fliers, he meets The Boss, who assigns him the task of helping young pilots on earth. Tracy returns to the world of the living and guides a young American flier (Van Johnson) into the life of Tracy's former sweetheart (Irene Dunne). When the couple take to each other, Tracy at first shows signs of jealousy but soon realizes they have their own lives to lead. Tracy adds some wit to his role, but the film turns too somber most of the time. The title is attributed to a remark made by General Chennault, who organized the Flying Tigers in 1941: "Boys, when I'm behind the stick, I'm just a guy named Joe." ■

H

Hail, Hero! (1969), NC. *Dir.* David Miller; *Sc.* David Manber; *Cast includes:* Michael Douglas, Arthur Kennedy, Theresa Wright, John Larch, Charles Drake.

The Vietnam War provides the background for this domestic drama of a college student who leaves school to enlist in the service. Michael Douglas, in his film debut, portrays the student whose moral views about war contrast sharply with those of his parents. Although descending from a long line of war heroes, Douglas differs from them in principle. He volunteers to fight in a war that he doesn't believe in against a people he does not consider his enemy. His parents, played by Arthur Kennedy and Theresa Wright, have never understood their son and have communicated with him only on the most superficial level. At first they are bewildered by his reasoning. But by the end of the film they are swayed to his way of thinking about the war. Charles Drake portrays a pretentious politician.

The film was one of the earliest entries to question the national policy concerning the Vietnam War. Allegedly directed at the growing youth audience and taking advantage of the contemporary "generation gap" that emerged as a result of the conflict, the film attempted to speak for the alienated of the 1960s. ■

Hail the Conquering Hero (1944), Par. *Dir.* Preston Sturges; *Sc.* Preston Sturges; *Cast includes:* Eddie Bracken, Ella Raines, Bill Edwards, Raymond Walburn, William Demarest.

Considered by many as Preston Sturges' best satirical comedy, the World War II film pokes gentle fun at several institutions of American life. An army reject (Eddie Bracken), reluctant to face his family and friends, is encouraged by a group of compassionate marines to temporarily play the role of a homecoming hero. The conspiracy gets out of hand as Bracken is compelled to challenge the incumbent mayor. Finally, the bogus hero confesses all and is forgiven and accepted by his neighbors. Beneath the warm humor lurks the director's trenchant attacks on politics, hero worship, small-town life and the military. Events are helped considerably by an excellent supporting cast of comic character actors, a familiar Sturges trademark. William Demarest plays a sympathetic marine. Franklin Pangborn, as a prissy emcee, tries to organize the homecoming ceremonies for Bracken. Sturges was at his peak when he made this film, the last of seven for Paramount, but his career and popularity came to an abrupt end within the next few years. ■

Hale, Nathan (1775–1796). He was only 21 years of age when, facing execution by hanging by the British as an American spy, he said the words which enshrined him as a hero and martyr in the cause of the American revolution: "I regret that I have but one life to give for my country."

Born in Coventry, Connecticut, Hale worked briefly as a schoolteacher after graduating from Yale (1773). Soon after the American Revolution began, Hale joined the Connecticut militia where he received a commission as captain. He took part in the siege of Boston and then joined William Heath's brigade when they left to go to New York to serve with George Washington.

Hale, on September 21, volunteered for an especially dangerous mission—to penetrate British lines on Long Island as a spy and report on the strength and disposition of enemy forces. His disguise as a Dutch schoolteacher failed to prevent his capture and he was hanged, without a trial, the next day.

Except for a few early silent films, Hale has not fared too well as a popular screen subject. The earliest film about the patriot was Edison's 1911 one-reeler titled "The Death of Nathan Hale." This was followed by a 1913 experimental color drama, *Nathan Hale. The Heart of a Hero* (1916), a film biography of Hale, covers several of the above highlights of his life, including his employment as a teacher, his joining the militia and his eventual capture while working as a spy for the rebels. By the 1940s he was relegated to a symbol of patriotism in *Joe Smith, American* (1942), a World War II spy drama in which Robert Young, as an airplane draftsman captured and tortured by spies, conjured up images of Hale to sustain him from revealing military secrets. ■

Half Shot at Sunrise (1930), RKO. *Dir.* Paul Sloane; *Sc.* James Creelman; *Cast includes:* Bert Wheeler, Robert Woolsey, Joan Rutherford, George MacFarlane, Roberta Robinson.

A World War I comedy starring the stage comedy team of Wheeler and Woolsey, the film has the boys romp through Paris and the battlefield in their zany, wisecracking style. To elude the M.P.s, Wheeler and Woolsey don officers' uniforms during their unofficial leave from the front lines. In one sequence they pose as waiters in a posh restaurant. "Do you have any wild duck?" a customer inquires. "No," Woolsey responds, "but if you like, we'll bring you a tame one and aggravate him." Later, a customer complains: "I can't eat this duck. Send for the manager." "It's no use," Woolsey replies. "He won't eat it either." In the final moments of the film there is a battle sequence that turns serious as Wheeler, concerned that Woolsey has been gone too long in "no man's land," goes over the top to rescue his friend.

Although the comics had made three previous films, this was their first starring vehicle. Studio heads rarely trusted vaudeville comedy teams to carry an entire film during the early sound period. Their studio was relatively lavish in its production costs for the film. A French village was built for the comedy. ■

Half Way to Shanghai (1942). See Spy Films: the Talkies. ■

Halls of Montezuma (1950), TCF. *Dir.* Lewis Milestone; *Sc.* Michael Blankfort; *Cast includes:* Richard Widmark, Jack Palance, Reginald Gardiner, Robert Wagner, Karl Malden.

This World War II drama pays tribute to the heroism of the U.S. Marines who fought in the Pacific. The film follows the exploits of a marine lieutenant (Richard Widmark), who suppresses his own fears by taking pills, and the men in his command. After they land on an enemy-held island, Widmark is ordered to take Japanese prisoners for questioning about the location of rocket launchers before the marines make a full-scale assault. Widmark, with a small patrol, accomplishes the mission but not without the loss of some of his men.

The film presents the usual "types" found in similar combat films, including a green leatherneck, a tough kid from the wrong side of the tracks, an ex-fighter and, for comic relief, a marine who is obsessed with building his own still. Karl Malden plays "Doc," a pharmacist's mate and confidant to the lieutenant. Reginald Gardiner portrays an unorthodox sergeant and translator. Jack Webb, as a combat correspondent, reads Doc's words aloud to Widmark and the surviving marines after Malden is killed in action: "We all ask ourselves the question why it is that some of us are killed while others remain. The only answer is our faith in the wisdom of a supreme being. If He has chosen us to live, there must be a reason . . . Perhaps He has saved us because we are needed as witnesses to remind each other, our folks, folks everywhere, that war is too full of horror for human beings . . . We must keep our country strong, courageous and wise in spirit, be unafraid in the knowledge that we are on God's side."

Like other World War II action films made after the conflict, the drama softens the image of the Japanese. Their true enemy is not the Americans but their own Japanese military officers. The troops seem more than willing to give up, but they fear their officers, professionals who live by the Bushido code and consider surrender a disgrace. ■

Halsey, William F. (1882–1956). The son of a U.S. Navy officer, Halsey won the Navy Cross in World War I. Vice-Admiral Halsey was at sea aboard the aircraft carrier *Enterprise* when the Japanese attacked Pearl Harbor on December 7, 1941. An aggressive commander, he took the offensive against the enemy by raiding several Pacific islands. His task force helped to launch Lt. Col. Doolittle's B-25s in their famous raid on Tokyo. Ill at the time of the Battle of Midway, he was unable to participate in that important sea fight.

He became the subject of several controversies during the remainder of the war. At the Battle for Leyte Gulf (October 23–26, 1944), he allowed Japanese carriers, used as decoys, to draw his ships away from San Bernardino Strait, permitting enemy battleships and cruisers to pass through. He was later brought before two courts of inquiry and criticized for his actions in two typhoons which resulted in loss of lives and ships.

By mid-1945 the aircraft of his Third Fleet were pounding Japan's cities. After the U.S. dropped two atomic bombs, Japan capitulated. Halsey participated in the surrender ceremonies aboard the *Missouri* on September 2. He returned to the States to a hero's welcome and continued on active duty until April 1947.

Three films portray Halsey during World War II. *The Gallant Hours* (1960), a restrained biography of the admiral, stars James Cagney as Halsey. In *Tora! Tora! Tora!* (1970), which recreates the attack on Pearl Harbor, Admiral William F. Halsey's ships are assigned to sea duty to avoid their possible entrapment at Pearl Harbor. *Midway* (1976), with Robert Mitchum as Admiral Halsey, concerns the critical air-sea battle that became the turning point in the Pacific during World War II. ■

Ham and Eggs at the Front (1927), WB. *Dir.* Roy Del Ruth; *Sc.* Darryl F. Zanuck; *Cast includes:* Tom Wilson, Karl Dane, Heine Conklin, Myrna Loy.

A World War I comedy with racist overtones, the film features a white cast made up in blackface. Two pals, played by Tom Wilson and Charlie Conklin, go through training together and end up in the trenches where they intercept an enemy message by mistake. Myrna Loy, also in blackface, is sent as a spy to retrieve the information. The script contains the typical barracks and front-line gags, but they are presented entertainingly.

The black stereotypes highlighted in the film (e.g., every player in a poker game has four aces and a razor) may be repugnant to audiences today, but they were generally accepted at the time the film was released. The stage for decades featured minstrel shows and, as late at the 1920s and 1930s, audiences applauded the talents of Al Jolson, Eddie Cantor and other blackface performers. ■

Hamburger Hill (1987), Par. *Dir.* John Irvin; *Sc.* Jim Carabatsos; *Cast includes:* Anthony Barrile, Michael P. Boatman, Don Cheadle, Dylan McDermott, Courtney Vance.

Based on an actual battle during the Vietnam War, the film recreates the repeated attacks upon Hill 937, which serves as a symbol of the futility and senselessness of the war in this grim and bloody drama. The hill, located in the Ashau Valley in Vietnam, became the target of the 101st Airborne Division in May of 1969, when troops continually stormed it and suffered heavy losses after each assault. The human drama focuses on one of these squads of 14 young grunts, youths who seem more at home behind the wheel of their cars or on a beach with their dates than attacking an obscure hill thousands of miles from home. Plagued by racial discord, individual clashes, an indifferent home-front and a belligerent media as well as a stubborn enemy, they fortify themselves against the almost suicidal task before them by recalling their pride in being members of the 101st, the "Screaming Eagles."

As if to outdo the realism of its contemporary companion films, *Platoon* (1986) and *Full Metal Jacket* (1987), this entry enhances its battle sequences with dismemberment and mutilation. The men are picked off one at a time as they struggle up the hill. Only four members of the squad survive the battle.

Dylan McDermott portrays a tough, compassionate sergeant who early senses the reality of the war. "We did good today, didn't we?" one of his squad asks proudly after his first battle. "One of my people got killed," the sergeant replies quietly, "that's all that happened." Courtney Vance plays a bitter black medic who sees only black soldiers being killed in a "white man's" war. "Take the hill," he pleads before he dies in the embrace of two white soldiers. Several didactic references to the antiwar movement back in the States tend to weaken the drama. Stripped of any metaphorical meaning, the film ends up as just one more harrowing chapter in the Vietnam experience.

After ten days of fierce assaults upon the

hill and heavy casualties—as much as 70 percent—the American troops finally dislodged the North Vietnamese regulars. Ironically, the position was abandoned one month later. ■

Hancock, John (1737–1793). The first signer of the Declaration of Independence (July 4, 1776), Hancock, a Harvard graduate and leading Boston merchant, was among the foremost figures in Massachusetts to organize American resistance to British trade and tax policies that led to the American Revolution. He took part in early demonstrations against the Stamp Act, and became chairman in 1770 of the Boston committee, formed after the Boston Massacre, to demand the removal of British troops from Boston.

The attempt by British troops to seize Hancock, as president of the Massachusetts Provincial Congress, and Sam Adams, along with colonial military supplies at Concord led to the Battle of Lexington and Concord which started the American Revolution. During the American Revolution, Hancock served as both a member and president of the Continental Congress for several years. After the war, he served nine terms as governor of Massachusetts and briefly again as president of the Continental Congress.

Few Hollywood films paid tribute to this American patriot. Two historical dramas, however, did include him among other historical figures—*Cardigan* (1922) and D.W. Griffith's silent epic of the American Revolution, *America* (1924). ■

"Hand of Uncle Sam, The" (1910), Essanay. *Dir.* Emile Chautard; *Cast includes:* J. Warren Kerrigan.

An early example of gunboat diplomacy, this spy drama concerns an American in a foreign country who is wrongly accused of spying. He is about to face a firing squad when the American consul demands a fair trial. Meanwhile, the Secretary of War sends a torpedo boat to the rescue. In the end the young man is saved and the real traitor is sent to his death. ■

Hands Up (1926), Par. *Dir.* Clarence Badger; *Sc.* Reginald Morris; *Cast includes:* Raymond Griffith, Marion Nixon, Virginia Lee Corbin, Mack Swain, Montagu Love.

Raymond Griffith portrays a Southern spy in this Civil War comedy. He is assigned to stop a much-needed gold shipment from reaching President Lincoln. Meanwhile, Lincoln has sent a Union officer to make sure the shipment gets through. Probably one of Griffith's best films, the work contains several good visual gags, an Indian attack on a stagecoach and a wild chase in a western mining town where Union soldiers pursue the elusive Griffith. Suddenly peace is declared and the hunt for Griffith ends. Meanwhile, two daughters of a mine owner fall in love with Griffith, who, inspired by the Mormons, rides off with the sisters in a stagecoach headed for Salt Lake City. The film takes liberties with its portrayals of historical figures, including Lincoln, Allan Pinkerton (who created the first U.S. spy service) and Brigham Young. See Allan Pinkerton. ■

Hangmen Also Die (1943), UA. *Dir.* Fritz Lang; *Sc.* John Wexley; *Cast includes:* Brian Donlevy, Walter Brennan, Anna Lee, Gene Lockhart, Dennis O'Keefe.

One of the strongest indictments against the Nazi regime to come out of wartime Hollywood, this World War II propaganda drama is a fictionalized account of the assassination of the Nazi executioner, Reinhardt Heydrich, known by his victims as the Hangman. Brian Donlevy plays the Czech doctor whom the Prague underground assigns to kill Heydrich. After the assassination, Donlevy, now wounded, seeks temporary refuge in the home of a professor (Walter Brennan) and his daughter (Anna Lee). When her father, along with hundreds of other Czech citizens, is taken as hostage, the daughter plans to turn Donlevy over to the Nazis. But she relents, realizing that he represents the free spirit of the people. Donlevy escapes while the underground frames a local Quisling (Gene Lockhart) for the killing.

Although the drama is based on actual incidents, it loses some credibility as a result of the stereotyped, heavy-handed treatment of the German characters. Several other dramas about Heydrich appeared during the war years. See also Reinhardt Heydrich. ■

Hanoi Hilton, The (1987), Golan-Globus/Cannon. *Dir.* Lionel Chetwynd; *Sc.* Lionel Chetwynd; *Cast includes:* Michael Moriarty, Jeffrey Jones, Paul La Mat, Stephen Davies, Lawrence Pressman.

For no apparent reason, a string of Vietnam War films appeared in the late 1980s. *The Hanoi Hilton* focuses on American prisoners of war rather than on the combat of that conflict. Lawrence Pressman portrays a no-nonsense American colonel who maintains discipline among his fellow prisoners, all kept in Hoa Lo Prison in Hanoi. The captives are chiefly steadfast officer fliers who endure cruel and inhuman torture designed to break their spirit and make them confess to spurious war crimes. After Pressman's death, a U.S. Navy pilot (Michael Moriarty) assumes command of the men and continues the former officer's resistance. The prison commandant (Aki Aleong), who failed to get a confession from Pressman, is determined to break Moriarty.

A politically active American actress (Gloria Carlin), sympathetic to the North Vietnamese cause, visits Hanoi and tries to convince the prisoners to collaborate with their captors. The men find her naive and tell her that she is being manipulated. A vain figure, she ignores their charges. (The character is based on the political activities of actress Jane Fonda, whose vocal stance against the war and whose visit to North Vietnam earned her the wrath of many veterans' groups.) After several years of unrelenting humiliation and horror, the surviving prisoners are released at the end of the war.

Aside from director-writer Chetwynd's controversial views—the betrayal of the P.O.W.s by wrong-headed liberals back home and that those who fought the war did so with the most noble intentions—the film has only a slight connection to the Vietnam War. It has more in common with such earlier prisoner-of-war dramas as *The Purple Heart* (1943) than it does with *Platoon* (1986) or *Full Metal Jacket* (1987). The characterizations of the commandant and several of the prisoners are little more than stereotypes reminiscent of old war movies. ∎

Happy Land (1943). See Propaganda Films: World War II. ∎

Hard-Boiled Haggerty (1927), FN. Dir. Charles Brabin; Sc. Carey Wilson; Cast includes: Milton Sills, Molly O'Day, Arthur Stone, Mitchell Lewis.

A World War I comedy drama, the film stars Milton Sills as Haggerty, an American air ace. After one of his many dogfights in which he downs another German plane, he and his mechanic (Arthur Stone) journey without leave to Paris where Sills meets his true love (Molly O'Day). He suddenly decides to give up his wild life. But his conversion doesn't last long. When a major suggests that O'Day's reputation isn't all that it should be, Sills strikes his superior. At his court martial the girl confirms the major's story. After the war Sills learns that the person the major knew was actually O'Day's sister and that O'Day was trying to protect the unfortunate girl's reputation. The couple are finally reunited. Several air battles add the proper amount of action to the film. Arthur Stone supplies some comedy relief. ∎

Harpers Ferry. Twice in American history this small West Virginia town, located about 60 miles northwest of Washington, D. C., has been the focus of national attention. On October 16–18, 1859, a group of abolitionists under John Brown raided the federal arsenal there to gain arms for a planned slave revolt. The raid, covered in *Santa Fe Trail* (1940) and *Seven Angry Men* (1955), failed to inspire a slave uprising but did strain already tense relationships between the North and South on the eve of the Civil War. Brown was eventually caught and hanged for his act.

During the Civil War Confederate forces under General Thomas "Stonewall" Jackson captured the town following a battle, on September 13–15, 1862, that resulted in the surrender of about 12,000 Union soldiers, the largest number of Northern troops taken in any engagement of the war.

Harpers Ferry was originally settled in 1747 by Robert Harper who set up a ferry and mill at the site. The federal government purchased a tract of land from Harper's heirs in 1796 at the urging of President George Washington to construct an armory. At the start of the Civil War, the village, with its Unionist sympathies, became part of the new state of West Virginia that had seceded from Virginia, a leading state in the Confederacy. ∎

Havoc (1925), Fox. Dir. Rowland V. Lee; Sc. Edmund Goulding; Cast includes: Madge Bellamy, George O'Brien, Walter McGrail, Eulalie Jensen.

Two friends, officers in the British army during World War I, fall in love with the same young woman, a hard-hearted flirt, in this romantic drama. George O'Brien and Walter McGrail, as the buddies, compete for the affections of Eulalie Jensen. When she chooses O'Brien over McGrail, the latter, in a fit of jealousy, assigns his fellow officer to a perilous mission in the front lines. O'Brien survives the ordeal but is blinded during the fighting. McGrail, realizing too late the extent of his actions, commits suicide. When the war ends, the unfeeling flirt rejects the sightless hero. But O'Brien finds true love and kindness with McGrail's sister. Also, as if by some miracle, he regains his sight. ■

Hayes, Ira. See *The Outsider* (1961). ■

Heads Up (1926), FBO. *Dir.* Harry Garson; *Sc.* Rob Wagner; *Cast includes:* Maurice "Lefty" Flynn, Kathleen Myers, Kalla Pasha, Jean Perry, Milton Gross, Harry McCoy.

Another excursion into a fictitious South American country on the verge of revolution, this comedy drama stars the athletic "Lefty" Flynn as the "Americano." A wealthy American in the South American country on a lark, Flynn becomes involved in its political turmoil when a traitorous general who has designs on the president's office also desires the man's pretty daughter. Flynn resolves the situation following a battle with a troop of soldiers loyal to the unscrupulous general.

Scores of American film comedies and dramas have exploited the political instability in countries south of the border. Continual newspaper stories of revolts and U.S. intervention in many of these lands no doubt contributed to the popularity of these films. Countries plagued with unrest or possible insurrections at the time the above film was released include, among others, Panama (1918–1920), Honduras (1919) and Guatemala (1920). In all three cases, the U.S. sent troops either to protect American interests or its legation, to maintain order or to secure a neutral zone during an anticipated revolution. ■

Heart of a Hero, The (1916), World. *Dir.* Emile Chautard; *Cast includes:* Robert Warwick, Gail Kane, Alec Francis, George McQuarrie.

A fictionalized biographical drama of Nathan Hale's role in the American Revolution, the film is set just prior to and during the rebellion. Hale (Robert Warwick) is a schoolteacher when hostilities erupt in Concord between the British and the colonists. He organizes a company of volunteers to join the Minute Men. Gail Kane portrays a young woman with whom Hale falls in love. When

he volunteers to serve as a spy against the British, she pleads with him not to go. Her appeals are futile. He accomplishes his mission but is captured and sentenced to hang.

Released during World War I but one year before America's entry into the conflict, the film anticipates the numerous patriotic dramas that were to appear within the next two or three years. Besides having all the right propaganda elements— heroism, duty and self-sacrifice, the film starred Robert Warwick, a stalwart and earnest actor who was popular on the stage before he entered films. ■

Heart of Humanity, The (1919), U. *Dir.* Allen Holubar; *Sc.* Allen Holubar; *Cast includes:* Dorothy Phillips, William Stowell, Walt Whitman, William Welsh.

Dorothy Phillips portrays a Red Cross nurse in this earnest World War I drama. She leaves her home in Canada and follows her husband, an airman fighting in the skies over France. Once in France she not only has to attend to the wounded soldiers and care for pitiful orphans, but she must fight off the lustful desires of a sinister Prussian officer, played by Erich von Stroheim, who tears her dress as she escapes his clutches. She is rescued at the last moment by her flier husband. Several battle sequences, including hand-to-hand combat and the destruction of villages and hospitals, enhance the production.

The drama has been singled out by several film historians for its antiwar elements. Those sequences focusing on the helpless orphans—the innocent victims of war—are especially effective. Von Stroheim was particularly brutal as the villainous Hun who, in one scene, tosses an infant out of a window. At the end of the film the couple take some of the war orphans home with them. The peaceful fields of Canada stand in sharp contrast to the battle-scarred fields of France, a reminder of the discord of a world at war. ■

"Heart of Lincoln, The" (1915), Gold Seal. *Dir.* Francis Ford; *Sc.* W. W. Young; *Cast includes:* Francis Ford, Grace Cunard, Ella Hall, William Quinn.

This Civil War drama opens before the hostilities with a Southern colonel and his daughter Betty visiting a Northern colonel in Washington. At a party which Lincoln attends, he is attracted to Betty's charms. Later in the evening the two colonels get into an argument and Betty's father leaves for home, taking her with him. War breaks out and the two officers meet once again, this time in battle. Betty's mother falls ill and sends a message to her husband. But the home is occupied by Union troops and the Southern colonel must don a Union uniform to pass the guards. He is captured and sentenced to death as a spy. Betty calls on the President who intervenes in the colonel's behalf.

Francis Ford, John Ford's mentor and older brother, directed and acted in several historical films during the early silent period, including "The Invaders" (1912), "When Lincoln Paid" (1913) and *Washington at Valley Forge* (1914). Some of these films featured his wife, Grace Cunard. He portrayed George A. Custer in "Custer's Last Raid" (1912). During the 1920s he directed westerns and action dramas. ■

Heart of Maryland, The (1915), Tiffany. Dir. Herbert Brenon; Sc. Herbert Brenon; Cast includes: Mrs. Leslie Carter, William E. Shay, Matt Snyder, Herbert Brenon, J. Farrell Mac-Donald.

The popular stage actress Mrs. Leslie Carter, who starred as Maryland Calvert in the original stage production of David Belasco's play, repeated her role in this Civil War drama. The war stands between her and the man she loves. She is a Southerner, and he is from the North. Following a series of obstacles, they are finally reunited after the armistice. Mrs. Carter originally played the role for twenty years before the release of this silent film. ■

Heart of Maryland, The (1927), WB. Dir. Lloyd Bacon; Sc. C. Graham Baker; Cast includes: Dolores Costello, Jason Robards, Myrna Loy, Warner Richmond, Charles Bull.

Dolores Costello portrays a Southerner who falls in love with a young soldier (Jason Robards) from the North in this Civil War drama, the second film version of Belasco's play. Following several plot complications filled with too many coincidences and the eventual armistice, the lovers get together. Charles Bull portrays Abraham Lincoln in this film which has, among its few virtues, a rousing climax in a bell tower. The earlier screen version appeared in 1915. ■

Heart Trouble (1928), FN. Dir. Harry Langdon; Sc. Arthur Ripley, Gordon Bradford; Cast includes: Harry Langdon, Doris Dawson, Lionel Belmore, Madge Hunt.

Harry Langdon stars as a simple-minded soul whose desire to enlist in the army is continuously frustrated in this World War I comedy. Even his repeated pleas to a recruiting officer result in failure. Circumstances, by way of plot manipulation, however, provide him with a golden opportunity to save the officer's life as well as destroy an enemy munitions supply. Doris Dawson provides the romantic interest for the silent screen comic in this below-par film. ■

Heartbreak (1931), Fox. Dir. Alfred Werker; Sc. William Counselman; Cast includes: Charles Farrell, Madge Evans, Hardie Albright, Paul Cavanaugh, John Arledge.

Charles Farrell portrays an American airman in this chiefly implausible World War I romantic drama. He takes his plane without permission into enemy territory to visit his love. The story is set in Italy and Austria. Farrell, as an attaché of the U.S. Embassy in Vienna, joins his country's air corps and is sent to Italy. But he has left behind the woman he loves, an Austrian countess (Madge Evans). In an air battle with an enemy, he downs the plane and learns that the mortally wounded pilot is the brother of the countess. Distraught over the incident, he steals a plane and crosses into Austria to visit his love. When he returns to his own lines, he is charged with desertion. He ends up in jail for the duration of the war. After the armistice, the couple are reunited. ■

Heartbreak Ridge (1986), WB. Dir. Clint Eastwood; Sc. James Carabatsos; Cast includes: Clint Eastwood, Marsha Mason, Mario Van Peebles.

Clint Eastwood portrays a tough, battle-hardened sergeant who has served in Korea, the Dominican Republic and three tours in Vietnam in this drama that pays homage to the U.S. Marines. Considered an over-the-hill sergeant, Eastwood, a Medal-of-Honor winner, pushes his men hard, swears with ease and woos his ex-wife with the same degree of passion he exerts to his military responsibilities. But he is also capable of displaying a tender nature below his leathery facade. His long record of rebelliousness and off-duty brawls in town anger his new major. "Characters like you," the commanding officer exclaims, "are an anachronism. You should be sealed in a case which reads 'Break glass only in the event of war.'" The major warns Eastwood to toe the mark in his battalion, continually harping upon his age. "I ask for marines and division sends me relics."

The overzealous drilling to which Eastwood subjects his men seems brutal at times. "It's my will against yours," he announces upon his first encounter with his new platoon, "and you will lose." But he knows his methods will pay off when the men go into battle. And the men perform well when they are called upon to invade Grenada in 1983. The film avoids the political issues of the Grenada invasion, except, perhaps, for one ironic note. As the marines charge up a hill and part the underbrush, they gaze upon a sign that reads: "St. George's University Medical School." Instead, the film focuses on the marines as professionals performing what they have been trained for. In the tradition of the war films of the 1940s, *Heartbreak Ridge* conveys a degree of humanity and a sense of humor lacking in many contemporary works about military life. ■

Hearts and Minds (1974), WB-Col. Dir. Peter Davis.

An incisive documentary about the Vietnam War, the film depicts the stages in which the U.S. became entangled in the conflict. Director Peter Davis, who does not attempt to rationalize America's involvement in that war-torn land, employs actual footage of various battles and other scenes, including those of the Vietnamese people caring for their wounded and burying their dead. It soon becomes clear that he believes the participation of such a great power has turned into a debacle. The documentary includes excerpts from old Hollywood films that sharply define the forces of good and evil—delineations more comprehensible to American audiences than the ambiguities raised by the Vietnam conflict. Interviews with American participants, politicians and Vietnamese peasants serve to underscore the dilemma. Although the film is pacifist in its total effect, it is not overly didactic in its presentation. The words of policy makers representing all sides of the controversy and the diverse remarks of the soldiers speak for themselves. ■

Hearts in Bondage (1936), Rep. *Dir.* Lew Ayres; *Sc.* Bernard Schubert, Olive Cooper; *Cast includes:* James Dunn, Mae Clarke, David Manners, Charlotte Henry, Henry B. Walthall.

A Civil War drama leading up to the famous battle between the *Merrimac* and the *Monitor*, the film founders in the areas of romance and characterization. The action sequences of the fight between the two ironclad ships (expertly done with miniatures) are satisfactory but too short. James Dunn portrays a Union naval officer who is dishonorably discharged but ultimately redeems himself when he serves upon the *Monitor*. He wins the heart of Mae Clarke. David Manners, as Clarke's brother and a Confederate naval officer, is killed in battle. Charlotte Henry is cast as a sympathetic heroine who loses her loved one in the war. Several historical figures are impersonated in the film, including President Lincoln, Jefferson Davis and John Ericsson, the designer of the *Monitor*.

The American Civil War battle between the Union's *Monitor* and the Confederate *Merrimac* (March 9, 1862), marked history's first recorded battle between ironclad warships. The engagement took place off Hampton Roads near the entrance to Chesapeake Bay, Virginia.

The Confederacy, in the spring of 1862, attempted to crack the Union's successful blockade by armor-plating a former sunken wooden steamship, the *Merrimac*, that the South had captured from the Union. Adding a metal ram to its prow and outfitting it with guns, the South renamed the vessel the *Virginia* and planned to use it against a federal fleet patrolling the entrance to Chesapeake Bay outside Norfolk, Virginia. The armored warship, on its first voyage on March 8, sank the *Cumberland* and burned the *Congress*.

The North, meanwhile, had quickly built its own version of an ironclad, the tiny *Monitor* with a revolving turret mounted on a low flat deck. Its design earned it the nickname "Yankee cheesebox on a raft." The *Merrimac*, steaming out the next day to attack the grounded Union flagship *Minnesota*, came up against the *Monitor* which had hurried down to Virginia. The five-hour battle before huge crowds ashore ended in a draw although the *Merrimac* was forced to return to Norfolk for repairs. It was later burned and destroyed by the South to prevent its capture when Norfolk fell to the Union on May 10, 1862. ■

Hearts of the World (1918), World. *Dir.* D. W. Griffith; *Sc.* M. Gaston de Tolinac; *Cast includes:* Robert Harron, Lillian Gish, Ben Alexander, Dorothy Gish, Adolphe Lestina, Josephine Crowell.

Griffith's World War I drama centers around two Americans, a young man (Robert Harron) and a young woman (Lillian Gish), living in France when war erupts. The young man decides to fight for France. The village in which the two lovers have resided becomes the target of fighting, bombing and a list of atrocities by the brutal Germans. There are numerous battle sequences in this lengthy film. Griffith develops his story of love and war in his typical leisurely pace, introducing many characters and events that depict the naturalness of love and its counterpart, the horrors of war. Much of the footage was shot in Europe during the conflict.

One of the more striking scenes concerns the fate of Lillian Gish at the hands of a lecherous German officer played by Erich von Stroheim. He was cast in this type of role so often (*For France* (1917), *The Heart of Humanity* (1919), *Three Faces East* (1930), *The Lost Squadron* (1932) and *Five Graves to Cairo* (1943) in which he portrayed a lustful General Rommel) that he earned the title "the man you loved to hate." Another scene shows Robert Harron, as her boy friend, willing to shoot her rather than have her suffer at the hands of the invaders.

The film also hints at Griffith's capacity for change and growth. Perhaps to atone for the alleged racist sequences in his Civil War epic *The Birth of a Nation* (1915), the director pauses long enough in one battle scene to depict a white soldier tenderly kissing a fallen black fellow soldier. Years later, Griffith was to make another shift concerning his portrayal of the Germans. In *Isn't Life Wonderful?* (1924) he showed deep sympathy for the German people who were suffering a series of hardships in the wake of World War I, portraying them more as victims than as initiators of the devastation. ■

Heaven Knows, Mr. Allison (1957), TCF. *Dir.* John Huston; *Sc.* John L. Mahin, John Huston; *Cast includes:* Deborah Kerr, Robert Mitchum.

A Roman Catholic nun and a marine corporal are stranded on a South Pacific island in this World War II drama. Robert Mitchum, as a U.S. Marine on a reconnaissance mission, washes ashore when his submarine abandons him to escape Japanese depth charges. He finds the island abandoned except for Deborah Kerr, a nun accidentally left behind. The two strangers quickly join forces in their attempt to stay alive and avoid capture by Japanese troops who invade the island and set up a small weather station. Mitchum and Kerr, forced to take refuge in a cave, become concerned for each other's welfare as he forages for food at night and when she becomes ill with fever. The lonely marine, growing fond of his companion, thinks he is in love and proposes marriage. Although Kerr has not yet taken her final vows, she tactfully rejects his display of affection.

This tender story tests the moral strengths of two lonely people cast together by circumstance. Mitchum, an orphan, equates his entrance into the marines to Kerr's joining the Church. "I'm a marine, all through me, a marine like you're a nun," he explains. "You got your cross, I got my globe and anchor . . . I got the corps like you got the Church." When the U.S. Marines invade the island and overrun the Japanese, Mitchum knows his close relationship with Kerr has come to an end. "I wish you every happiness," he says sadly. "No matter how many miles apart we are," she replies, "and no matter if we never meet again, you will be my dear companion always—always." ■

Held by the Enemy (1920), Par. *Dir.* Donald Crisp; *Sc.* Beulah Marie Dix; *Cast includes:* Lewis Stone, Jack Holt, Agnes Ayres, Wanda Hawley.

A Civil War drama based on William Gillette's play, the film stars Lewis Stone as a captain in the Confederate army while Jack Holt portrays a Union colonel. Several suspenseful battle sequences help to expand the original stage version. Lewis Stone had a long and distinguished career with MGM, gaining popularity during the 1930s and 1940s as Judge Hardy, Mickey Rooney's unruffled father in the "Andy Hardy" films. Jack Holt starred in numerous action and adventure dramas during the next two decades and continued in films as a character actor into the 1940s. Director Donald Crisp, who had worked as an actor for D.W. Griffith before World War I, eventually gave up directing to emerge as one of the screen's great character actors during the silent and sound periods. ■

Helen of Troy (1955), WB. *Dir.* Robert Wise; *Sc.* John Twist, Hugh Gray; *Cast includes:* Rossana Podesta, Jack Sernas, Sir Cedric Hardwicke, Stanley Baker, Robert Douglas.

The Trojan War provides the background for this lavish costume drama filmed in Italy. Paris, a Trojan prince (Jack Sernas), is sent to Sparta on a peace mission between Greece and Troy. He meets and falls in love with Helen (Rossana Podesta), unaware that she is the Queen of Sparta. When he fails to bring about the desired peace, he abducts Helen. The Greeks, enraged at her kidnaping, march off to war against the Trojans. The film provides spectacular battle sequences with large armies on each side. The long siege is not broken until the Greeks introduce the famous wooden horse which secretly holds their soldiers. Once inside the Trojan fortress, they open the gates for the Greek army. Many famous figures appear as part of the main plot or as peripheral characters, including, among others, Achilles, Menelaus, Agamemnon, Ulysses and Ajax. The script portrays the Greeks as the aggressors more interested in plunder than in the rescue of their queen.

Although the Trojan War (c. 1200 B.C.) is often considered a myth as a result of its inclusion in Homer's *Iliad*, with its overtones of disputes among the Gods, the story appears to be based on a real incident, the war between the Greek city-states and Troy, in Asia Minor. A number of supporting archaeological proofs and the inclusion of several history figures in the story give it credence.

Troy at that time seems to have been in dispute with many Greek city-states over the question of regional dominance and control of trade through the Dardanelles. In Homer's epic, the war began as a result of the kidnaping of Helen, wife of Sparta's King Menelaus, by Paris, son of Troy's King Priam, all of which was recounted fairly accurately in the film. Though the Greeks besieged Troy for nine years and laid waste to the surrounding area, the Trojans held out behind their city walls. In the tenth year, the Greeks triumphed as a result of a ruse—the wooden horse.

The myth became the basis for several statements and beliefs, including the idea of being tricked or lulled by a false gift, the fear of being weakened or defeated by an enemy within, and the role of Cassandra—one who warns of disaster—who, in the myth, tries but fails to convince the Trojans not to accept the gift horse. ■

Hell and High Water (1954), TCF. *Dir.* Samuel Fuller; *Sc.* Jesse L. Lasky, Jr., Samuel Fuller; *Cast includes:* Richard Widmark, Bella Darvi, Victor Francen, Cameron Mitchell.

A former U.S. Navy officer is hired by a group of concerned scientists from different nations to command a submarine whose mission is to prevent a nuclear war from erupting. It seems that a plot is afoot to implicate the U.S. in a nuclear incident somewhere in the Arctic, thereby inciting retaliation. Richard Widmark portrays the commander whose undersea vessel battles a Chinese Communist submarine. He and his crew ultimately foil the unseen enemy's plan to start World War III by shooting down a captured American bomber as it ascends to drop its atomic device. ■

Hell Below (1933), MGM. *Dir.* Jack Conway; *Sc.* Laird Doyle, Raymond Schrock; *Cast includes:* Robert Montgomery, Walter Huston, Madge Evans, Jimmy Durante, Eugene Pallette.

A World War I submarine drama, the film stars Robert Montgomery as an undisciplined officer. Angry when his buddy is abandoned by his submarine commander (Walter Huston) who takes his vessel below to avoid an approaching fleet of German destroyers, Montgomery releases all four torpedoes at the enemy ships. Two are destroyed, but the others then go after the sub. The captain orders Montgomery to his quarters as the undersea vessel attempts to withstand the attack. A gas leak results in the death of several crew members. Huston manages to save the sub. Later, Montgomery is dishonorably discharged from the service. To complicate matters, he is in love with Huston's daughter (Madge Evans), whose husband returns after being wounded in battle. In an act of redemption and self-sacrifice, and to step out of the couple's life, Montgomery takes out another sub loaded with explosives and blows up an enemy fortress.

The incident in which Montgomery sacrifices his life is similar to that in *Today We Live*, released the same year, in which Robert Young rams a torpedo boat into a German bat-

American pilot Warner Baxter (behind Conchita Montenegro) and French fliers seek safety from a German air attack during World War I. *Hell in the Heavens* (1934).

tleship. In both cases, their noble sacrifice is motivated partly by their willingness to give up the woman they love. The film strains plausibility in several incidents, particularly the outcome of Montgomery's court martial. His disobeying of the captain's orders during battle which resulted in damage to the ship and the deaths of his fellow seamen would have resulted in a harsher punishment than mere discharge.

Comic relief is provided by Jimmy Durante, who plays the dentist and cook aboard the sub, and Eugene Pallette, one of the crew, who incurs Durante's wrath. "What's the matter with the ham?" Durante argues. "It's imported from the States." "They must have towed it all the way over. It's salty," Pallette protests. "That's the way you cure ham," Jimmy explains. "If that ham was cured, it had a relapse," Pallette cracks. ▪

Hell in the Heavens (1934), Fox. *Dir.* John Blystone; *Sc.* Byron Morgan, Ted Parsons; *Cast includes:* Warner Baxter, Conchita Montenegro, Russell Hardie, Andy Devine.

A World War I airplane drama set in France, the film stars Warner Baxter as an American volunteer replacement in the French Flying Corps. He is determined to down a German ace who is wreaking havoc with the squadron. The airman, known only as "the Baron" (Arno Frey), is finally captured by Baxter, who also finds time to romance a local French maiden (Conchita Montenegro). The usual stunt flying sequences include several adequate air battles involving Spads and Fokkers. ▪

Hell in the Pacific (1968), Cin. *Dir.* John Boorman; *Sc.* Alexander Jacobs, Eric Bercovici; *Cast includes:* Lee Marvin, Toshiro Mifune.

Lee Marvin and Toshiro Mifune are the only performers in this World War II story of two adversaries stranded on a remote Pacific island. Marvin, as an American soldier, unintentionally intrudes upon Mifune, a Japanese soldier who has been surviving on the beach. At first they threaten each other. Marvin is desperate for some of Mifune's water.

Shipwrecked American soldier Lee Marvin and Japanese counterpart Toshiro Mifune learn to co-exist in the World War II allegory *Hell in the Pacific* (1968).

But the suspicious Japanese warrior refuses to share it with his enemy. A struggle ensues in which the water container is knocked over. Ultimately, each learns to cope with the other's presence. They decide to build a raft together to escape from the island. After days aboard their flimsy raft, they land on another island that has been abandoned by both Japanese and American troops. Recollections of the war at first intrude upon their relationship. They then settle down to a peaceful but temporary coexistence until each wanders off in opposite directions and to an uncertain future. The allegorical implications concerning the nature of rivalry, war and coexistence make the film an interesting, if somewhat drawn out, effort. ∎

Hell Is for Heroes (1962), Par. *Dir.* Don Siegel; *Sc.* Robert Pirosh, Richard Carr; *Cast includes:* Steve McQueen, Bobby Darin, Fess Parker, Harry Guardino, James Coburn.

A ten-man squad of G.I.s is assigned to defend a position along the Siegfried Line usually requiring a company of defenders in this World War II action drama. Steve McQueen, as a cynical loner and angry soldier, has made the war a personal battle after he is stripped of his NCO rank. "People do the same all over the world," he remarks. "Go with the time." Comedian Bob Newhart, in his film debut, plays a G.I. who does a telephone monologue meant to confuse the Germans. Harry Guardino portrays an indecisive sergeant.

The handful of men must make the Germans believe that the Americans represent a much larger force. When the final attack on an enemy pillbox occurs, McQueen is mortally wounded in the assault. He rises from the ground Phoenix-like and throws himself and an explosive charge into the opening where he is consumed by the ensuing flames. The film concludes during the battle with the ground covered by dying men. The action scenes are harrowing in their realism in this tough little drama. ∎

Hell Squad (1958), AI. *Dir.* Burt Topper; *Sc.* Burt Topper; *Cast includes:* Wally Campo, Brandon Carroll, Fred Gavlin, Greg Stuart.

The Tunisian desert during World War II provides the background for this action drama. A patrol of American soldiers becomes lost in the vast sands. As they struggle to find their main outfit, they encounter German troops whom they engage in battle. Wally Campo portrays the lone survivor who ends up wounded and in the middle of an enemy mine field. Meanwhile, he trains his rifle on a Nazi officer (Brandon Carroll) who possesses a map of the mine field and who is desperate for water. ∎

Hell to Eternity (1960), AA. *Dir.* Phil Karlson; *Sc.* Ted Sherdeman, Walter Roeber Schmidt; *Cast includes:* Jeffrey Hunter, David Janssen, Vic Damone, Patricia Owens.

Jeffrey Hunter stars in this biographical drama based on the exploits of war hero Guy Gabaldon during World War II. A California orphan, Gabaldon is taken in and raised by a Nisei family before Pearl Harbor. When war erupts, he joins the U.S. Marines and is sent to the Pacific where he distinguishes himself by convincing hundreds of well-entrenched Japanese to surrender. His knowledge of Japanese is the key. The film in part explores his mixed feelings toward the Japanese. David Janssen portrays his battle-hardened buddy. Vic Damone plays another fellow marine. Patricia Owens provides the romantic and sexual interest in several frank scenes. Realistic action sequences include the invasion of Saipan and subsequent battles. ∎

Hellcats of the Navy (1957), Col. *Dir.* Nathan Juran; *Sc.* David Lang, Raymond Marcus; *Cast includes:* Ronald Reagan, Nancy Davis, Arthur Franz, Robert Arthur.

A routine submarine drama set during World War II, the film stars Ronald Reagan as the commander of a sub who is forced to sacrifice one man to save the lives of others. Reagan is assigned to gather information about the mine fields in the Tsushima Strait and Sea of Japan. He abandons a frogman (Harry Lauter) when the undersea vessel comes under danger of being exposed. Others aboard think their captain had personal reasons for not rescuing Lauter. However, he successfully completes his mission. Nancy Davis (Nancy Reagan), as a nurse, provides the romantic interest. ■

Hell's Angels (1930), UA. *Dir.* Howard Hughes; *Sc.* Howard Estabrook, Harry Behn; *Cast includes:* Ben Lyon, Jean Harlow, James Hall, John Darrow, Frank Clarke.

Director Howard Hughes was reported to have spent $4,000,000 on this World War I airplane epic. The film concerns two English brothers (Ben Lyon and James Hall) who enlist in the Royal Flying Corps when war breaks out. At one point they are both interested in the same woman (Jean Harlow) until Lyon realizes she is unfaithful to his brother. Several highly effective war sequences include a battle over London between a zeppelin and British fighter planes. A German soldier, educated in England, directs the bombs to fall harmlessly into a lake instead of onto their original targets. The Germans aboard the craft ask for volunteers to jump so that the ship can escape the pursuing English fighter planes. One British flier plows his plane into the massive dirigible. Later in the film a dogfight occurs between dozens of British and German planes led by Baron von Richthofen.

The story of the two brothers, one weak and cowardly, the other highly honorable, resumes during the massive air battle over Germany. The boys are flying in a bomber out to destroy a munitions factory. They succeed in their mission but are shot down. When they are captured, the weak one succumbs when his life is threatened, forcing his brother to shoot him so that he does not reveal any pertinent information.

The air spectacle, which was first shot as a silent film, took three years to make. Hughes scrapped the silent version with its synchronized track of sound effects and started from scratch. The film, often compared with William Wellman's *Wings* (1927), rivaled the silent epic in its action sequences. Both, however, were hampered with banal stories, according to critics. The tremendous success of each depended on its adventurous war theme and action sequences. Neither made any pro-

found comment on the nature of war although Lyon in *Hell's Angels* does cry out against the useless sacrifices. However, since he is more a coward than an observer of life, his comments may easily be dismissed. Hughes did not have the assistance of the military establishment, with its vast resources of equipment and troops, as director Wellman had had. Instead, he rounded up all the stunt pilots he could locate. There were 79 airmen involved in staging the spectacular airplane sequences. ■

Hell's Holiday (1933), Superb Pictures.

A World War I documentary narrated by Eugene Dennis, the film is one more attempt to tell the story of the war from its inception to the armistice, ending only in a superficial treatment of the conflict. There are several graphic scenes of corpses, wounded soldiers, bombed-out villages and war-weary prisoners. But the major part of the film shows only the firing of cannon and machine guns. Much of the footage, some of which is unclear, has come from official government sources. ■

Hell's Horizon (1955), Col. *Dir.* Tom Gries; *Sc.* Tom Gries; *Cast includes:* John Ireland, Maria English, Bill Williams, Hugh Beaumont, Larry Pennell.

The story of a single bombing mission provides the basis for this weak Korean War action drama. John Ireland, as the captain of the American bomber, is dispatched from his base in Okinawa to destroy a vital bridge over the Yalu River. At first the plane has the advantage of cover provided by bad weather, but when the sky clears the plane comes under attack from enemy fighters. The bomber ultimately makes it back to base with an empty fuel tank. Bill Williams portrays Ireland's co-pilot. Tensions mount among the crew members who voice a dislike for their captain in this familiar story. ■

Hell's Island (1930), Col. *Dir.* Edward Sloman; *Sc.* Jo Swerling; *Cast includes:* Jack Holt, Ralph Graves, Dorothy Sebastian, Richard Cramer, Harry Allen.

Jack Holt and Ralph Graves portray two rival Legionnaires in this comedy drama. They brawl over Marie, a cafe entertainer (Dorothy Sebastian). During a skirmish between troops of the Foreign Legion and the Riffs, Holt is wounded in the back and thinks that Graves shot him. He is taken to a hospital while

Graves, in an altercation with his sergeant, knocks him down. Graves is court-martialed and sentenced to ten years on Hell's Island. Marie convinces Holt to leave the Legion and work as a guard on the island. Holt learns that the bullet removed from his back came from a Riff rifle, not from that belonging to Graves. He helps Graves to escape with Marie, while he is once again shot in the back.

The story is a composite of other films, including such Foreign Legion entries as *Beau Geste* (1926). The principal characters closely resemble the popular rivals, Captain Flagg and Sergeant Quirt, from *What Price Glory?* (1926). ■

Henry, Patrick (1736–1799). It was not as a fighter in the field but as a colonial orator, with the ability to create and deliver speeches of such emotional intensity that they moved others to action, which made Patrick Henry a leading figure in the American Revolution. He was among those early colonial leaders who advocated resistance and finally rebellion against English colonial policy. He first achieved prominence when, as a member of Virginia's House of Burgesses, he spoke out against the Stamp Act in 1765, contending that Virginia had legislative autonomy and the right to nullify acts by the British parliament. He warned England's George III, "Caesar had his Brutus—Charles I, his Cromwell—and George the third, ('Treason!' shouted the Speaker of the Assembly)—may profit by their example. . . . If this be treason, make the most of it." This phase of his career is faithfully recreated in the historical drama *The Howards of Virginia* (1940), with Richard Gaines portraying Henry.

When Governor Lord Dunsmore dissolved the colonial legislature because of growing resistance to royal policies, Henry emerged as leader of a group of representatives who met clandestinely and urged forming a continental congress and the raising of armed forces. One speech (March 23, 1775) ended with the ringing declaration, "Is life so dear, or peace so sweet, as to be purchased at the price of chains and slavery? Forbid it, Almighty God! I know not what course others may take, but as for me, give me liberty or give me death!"

Hollywood films, unfortunately, have transformed this passionate orator into a statuesque museum piece in which he appears in cameo roles rather than as a leading character. This is especially true in such historical dramas as *Cardigan* (1922), *America* (1924), *Janice Meredith* (1924) and *The Howards of Virginia* (1940). In *John Paul Jones* (1959), however, he is given slightly more prominence and allowed to make his famous speech in Virginia. ■

Her Country First (1918). See Propaganda Films: World War I. ■

Her Country's Call (1917). See Propaganda Films: World War I. ■

Her Debt of Honor (1918). See Spy Films: the Silents. ■

Her Father's Son (1916), Par. *Dir.* William Desmond Taylor; *Sc.* Anne Fielder Brand; *Cast includes:* Vivian Martin, Alfred Vosburgh, Herbert Standing, Helen Jerome Eddy, Joe Massey.

Vivian Martin portrays a young Southerner who poses as a man after her father's death in this domestic drama set before and during the Civil War. Her uncle, whom she goes to live with, had written a letter to her father stating that he would accept his nephew as one of his heirs. Dressed in men's attire, she is able to fool her uncle (Herbert Standing) and her cousin (Helen Jerome Eddy). When war erupts and a handsome young lieutenant visits the uncle's home, complications arise for the heroine. She eventually reveals her true identity and a romance blossoms. Several suspenseful battle sequences occur in which the young officer participates. ■

Her Man o' War (1926), PDC. *Dir.* Frank Urson; *Sc.* Charles Logue; *Cast includes:* William Boyd, Jimmie Adams, Jetta Goudal, Robert Edeson, Frank Reicher.

Two American soldiers (William Boyd and Jimmie Adams) volunteer to act as deserters in this World War I drama. Their mission is to find a route behind enemy lines to a big gun that is preventing an Allied attack. The men are accepted by the Germans and assigned to work on farms near where the gun is installed. But Boyd's real mission is exposed, and he is sentenced to face a firing squad. A local farm girl who has fallen in love with him contacts the American troops and he is saved. ■

Her Sister's Secret (1946), PRC. *Dir.* Edgar G. Ulmer; *Sc.* Anne Green; *Cast includes:* Nancy Coleman, Margaret Lindsay, Philip Reed, Felix Bressart.

A World War II romantic drama about a mother's love for a child born out of wedlock, the film stars Nancy Coleman as a young girl who falls in love with a soldier (Philip Reed) during a New Orleans Mardi Gras. Her lover is sent overseas while she finds herself pregnant with his child. Her sister (Margaret Lindsay) offers to raise the baby as her own. Just as Coleman is about to give up her child, Reed returns in time to profess his love and save the traumatic situation. ■

Here Come the Jets (1959), TCF. *Dir.* Gene Fowler, Jr.; *Sc.* Louis Vittes; *Cast includes:* Steve Brodie, Lyn Thomas, Mark Dana, John Doucette.

The problems of a Korean War veteran are depicted in this low-budget drama. Steve Brodie, as an alcoholic war hero, is given a chance to salvage his life when he is offered a job as a jet test pilot. At first the veteran has trouble passing a series of tests on a flight simulator. His mock flight results in his emotional breakdown. However, he soon surmounts his problems and participates in the launching of a jumbo jet plane. ■

Here Come the Marines (1952). See Service Comedy. ■

Here Come the Waves (1944). See Musicals. ■

Hero, The (1923). See Veterans. ■

Hero of Submarine D-2, The (1916), Vitagraph. *Dir.* Paul Scardon; *Sc.* Cyrus Townsend Brady; *Cast includes:* Charles Richman, James Morrison, Anders Randolf, Charles Wellesley.

In this silent drama an American naval officer (Charles Richman) discovers that a fleet of U.S. battleships is about to be destroyed by an unnamed enemy. His only chance to save the warships is to gain entry to the enemy vessel. To accomplish this, he allows himself to be fired out of one of the torpedo tubes of a submarine. He then boards the enemy ship and prevents the detonation of a series of mines intended for the American fleet. Released before America's entry into World War I, the film gave its nervous audiences,

torn at the time between pacifism and preparedness, views of some of America's fighting power while suggesting the resourcefulness and potential heroism of the nation's servicemen. ■

Heroes All (1931), RKO. *Sc.* Emile Gauvreau, Major General John J. Bradley.

A documentary about World War I, the film chiefly utilizes excerpts from war footage produced by the U.S. government during the conflict. Sound effects have been added as well as some narration by a reporter. Sequences of various allies of the U.S. on different war fronts include those of Russian soldiers as well as Italian troops fighting in the Alps. Others depict American troops crashing through German positions with the enemy in full retreat. These are followed by shots of enemy prisoners. ■

Heroes for Sale (1933). See Veterans. ■

Heroes of the Alamo (1938), Col. *Dir.* Harry Fraser; *Sc.* Roby Wentz; *Cast includes:* Lane Chandler, Ruth Findlay, Roger Williams, Edward Piel, Rex Lease.

This low-budget film depicts the heroic stand made by Davy Crockett, Stephen Austin, William Travis and the handful of other Texans at the Alamo who fought to the death against overwhelming odds. Mexico's General Santa Anna unleashes his troops against the little rag-tag army of defenders until every one of them is killed. Lane Chandler stars as Crockett while Ruth Findlay, who plays the wife of one of the Americans, remains alive to remind Sam Houston to "Remember the Alamo." The film is weak on characterization and plot although the battle scenes are adequate. The stand at the Alamo has become one of Hollywood's most often photographed historical topics along with Custer's battle at Little Big Horn. ■

Hess, Dean. See *Battle Hymn* (1956). ■

Hessians. See "1776, or Hessian Renegades" (1909). ■

Hey, Rookie (1944). See Musicals. ■

Heydrich, Reinhardt (1904–1942). He was better known to his victims as "Heydrich the Hangman" for his atrocities in Nazi-occupied countries during World War II, especially in

General Santa Anna's Mexican troops crush American resistance in Texas. *Heroes of the Alamo* (1938).

Czechoslovakia. Heydrich was appointed second-in-command to Himmler in the Gestapo and S.S. His assassination by Czech patriots in 1942 so angered the Nazis that a large number of hostages were summarily executed and the village of Lidice destroyed. The Nazi reign of terror failed to break the spirit of the Czech people and only further fueled the determination of the Allied nations to crush the Axis powers.

His infamous activities have been described in a handful of films, chiefly World War II propaganda dramas. In *Hangmen Also Die* (1943), a fictionalized account of the assassination of Heydrich, Brian Donlevy plays the Czech doctor whom the Prague underground assigns to kill the Hangman. *Hitler's Hangman*, released the same year, recounts the story of Czechoslovakian resistance to Nazi oppression, the assassination of Heydrich (John Carradine) and the Nazi reprisals which led to the destruction of the village of Lidice. *One Inch From Victory* (1944), chiefly a World War II documentary about the battle of Russia, also covers Reinhardt Heydrich's funeral and Hitler's attendance at his burial in Berlin. *Operation Daybreak* (1976) is another re-enactment of the assassination of

Heydrich by Czech freedom fighters parachuted into Czechoslovakia by the British and the resultant destruction of Lidice by the Germans. ■

Hidden Code, The (1920). See Spy Films: the Silents. ■

Hidden Enemy, The (1940). See Spy Films: the Talkies. ■

Hiding Place, The (1975), World Wide. Dir. James F. Collier; Sc. Allan Sloane; Cast includes: Julie Harris, Eileen Heckart, Arthur O'Connell, Jeannette Clift.

Based on the autobiography of Corrie ten Boom, the film depicts the exploits of her Christian family's efforts to save many Jews during World War II. Corrie (Jeannette Clift) and her younger sister (Julie Harris) live with their watchmaker-father in the Dutch town of Haarlem that the Germans have invaded. Their father (Arthur O'Connell) opposes the persecution of the Jews and devotes himself to their rescue. Together with his daughters and other townspeople, they manage to save many Jews from extermination. Eventually the family is caught and sent to a German concentration camp. Corrie was the only member of the heroic family to survive. The well-meaning film was produced by the Billy Graham Evangelistic Association. ■

High Barbaree (1947), MGM. *Dir.* Jack Conway; *Sc.* Anne Chapin, Whitfield Cook, Cyril Hume; *Cast includes:* Van Johnson, June Allyson, Thomas Mitchell, Marilyn Maxwell.

Two downed American pilots adrift in the Pacific rely on their memories as civilians to sustain them in this World War II drama. The story is told through flashbacks after Van Johnson and Cameron Mitchell ditch their airplane. Johnson tells his buddy about his uncle (Thomas Mitchell), a seafaring man who appears periodically and regales Johnson as a lad with tall tales of the sea including an imaginary island called High Barbaree. June Allyson is seen during the flashbacks as Johnson's sweetheart. The film has little to do with World War II except as a frame for the past. ■

"High C's" (1930). See War Humor. ■

Highest Law, The (1921), Selznick. *Dir.* Ralph Ince; *Sc.* Lewis Allen Browne; *Cast includes:* Ralph Ince, Robert Agnew, Margaret Seddon, Aleen Burr, Cecil Crawford.

Abraham Lincoln (Ralph Ince) is forced to choose between army regulations and the law of humanity, "the highest law," in this Civil War drama. The film opens with two World War I veterans who, on Memorial Day in 1920, meet an older veteran of the Civil War sitting on the base of a Lincoln statue. He tells them the following story. A young Union soldier, whose two brothers have been killed in the war, receives a letter that his mother is very sick. Denied official leave, he takes off to visit his dying mother without permission. He is later arrested and charged with desertion. Meanwhile, Secretary of War Stanton tries to convince Lincoln that the boy must be punished if army discipline is to be maintained. The President replies that he will follow the dictates of his conscience. When the story again shifts to the present, the audience learns that the man seated at the base of Lincoln's statue was that young soldier. ■

Highest Trump, The (1919). See Spy Films: the Silents. ■

"Highlander's Defiance, The" (1910), Selig.

In this silent Boer War melodrama, Scotsmen volunteer for the British army and are sent to South Africa. The main characters, two brave young men, distinguish themselves in battle and advance through the ranks until they command their own post. Under siege by Boer soldiers, the young heroes refuse to surrender and the entire unit is wiped out. Back home in Scotland the women mourn for their sons and sweethearts.

One curious note about the film is that the men are transported to Africa by battleship instead of a troop ship, contrary to the custom of the period. During these early years of the movie industry, Selig, as well as other studios including Kalem and Biograph, turned out several one- and two-reel historical war dramas ranging from Britain's colonial conflicts in India to America's own Civil War. ■

Hillbilly Blitzkrieg (1942). See Service Comedy. ■

His Buddy's Wife (1925), AE. *Dir.* Tom Terris; *Sc.* T. Howard Kelly; *Cast includes:* Glenn Hunter, Edna Murphy, Flora Finch.

A World War I romantic drama, the film stars Glenn Hunter as a soldier who promises his wartime buddy that he will take care of his mother and wife. The friend is killed in France and Hunter travels to the dead soldier's farm to make good on his pledge. The mother eventually passes away while Hunter and the widow fall in love. On the day that they are about to be married, the husband returns. It seems that he wasn't killed but was captured by the enemy and held prisoner. Hunter steals away, resolving the conflict between his strong love for the woman and his loyalty to his friend.

The film is a weak adaptation of a popular theme that had already become a cliché by the mid-1920s. ■

His First Command (1929). See Service Comedy. ■

His Foreign Wife (1927), Pathe. *Dir.* John P. McCarthy; *Sc.* Albert De Mond; *Cast includes:* Greta von Rue, Edna Murphy, Wallace MacDonald, Charles Clary.

A doughboy returns home from World

War I with his German war bride only to face his father's bigotry. Wallace MacDonald portrays the young American who, with his brother, enlists and is sent to the front lines in France. MacDonald's brother is killed in action. When the war ends, MacDonald remains behind as part of the army of occupation and falls in love with a young German (Greta von Rue). They marry and return to his home town. His father, still embittered about the loss of his other son and the war in general, cannot forgive the Germans. At a town gathering at which the father is to present his son with a medal, the war hero denounces his father's hypocrisy and prejudice. The father later realizes his mistake and accepts his daughter-in-law. ■

His Forgotten Wife (1924), FBO. *Dir.* William A. Seiter; *Sc.* Will Lambert, Del Andrews; *Cast includes:* Warner Baxter, Madge Bellamy.

A domestic drama of a soldier who loses his memory in battle during World War I, the film depends too heavily on coincidence. Warner Baxter portrays an American doughboy who is wounded while fighting in France during the war. Having no memory of his past or even his name, he recuperates at a military hospital where he falls in love with his nurse. They marry and return to the U.S. where they seek employment as domestics at a Long Island estate. It so happens that he had once owned this home and left it to his fiancee. When she learns of his marriage, she takes off with some valuable bonds that belong to her ex-lover but is apprehended by Baxter's wife. Loss of memory has become a familiar convention of war dramas, along with the unexpected return of a husband previously reported killed in action. ■

His Master's Voice (1925), Lumas. *Dir.* Renaud Hoffman; *Sc.* Henry McCarty; *Cast includes:* George Hackathorne, Marjorie Daw, Mary Carr, Will Walling.

George Hackathorne portrays a village weakling in this routine drama who develops into manhood as the result of his World War I experiences. The hero, wounded in battle, is saved by Thunder, a brave canine who rescues him in time to connect the wires of a mine which saves the battle. He falls in love with and marries a member of the Red Cross, returns to his home town and licks the local bully. Marjorie Daw provides the romantic interest. The film contains an ample supply of action footage. The only unique aspect of this minor drama is that the entire tale is told from the viewpoint of the dog to one of his puppies. ■

"His Trust" (1911), Biograph. *Dir.* D.W. Griffith; *Cast includes:* Wilfred Lucas, Dell Henderson, Clare McDowell, Edith Haldeman.

A faithful black servant is assigned to protect the wife and little daughter of his Southern master who rides off to battle in this Civil War drama. When the master is killed in action, friends return with their fallen comrade's saber and present it to the widow. The servant then mounts it over the mantel. Later, Union troops raid the village and set fire to the widow's home, but the servant rescues the child and rushes back into the flames to retrieve his former master's sword. He takes the widow and child to his own humble cabin. The few battle scenes are effective, considering the year the drama was made.

The film was the first of two parts, both of which Griffith planned to have released as a two-reeler. But his superiors at Biograph rejected his proposal and released the films, each of which contained a complete story, separately. The second part is titled "His Trust Fulfilled." ■

"His Trust Fulfilled" (1911), Biograph. *Dir.* D.W. Griffith; *Cast includes:* Wilfred Lucas, Claire McDowell, Gladys Egan, Dorothy West, Harry Hyde.

The second half of a two-part drama (the first was titled "His Trust"), the film begins four years later. The Civil War has ended. The faithful black servant, still loyal to his deceased master, has been paying the bills for the education of his master's daughter. When he runs out of funds, he considers stealing but soon rejects the temptation. Fortunately, an English relative arrives in time to make the payments and fall in love with the girl. As the newly married couple leave for England, the servant tearfully looks on and is content in the knowledge that he has fulfilled his master's wishes.

As repulsive as the theme may be to today's audiences, Griffith innocently attempted to ennoble his main character by bestowing upon him the qualities of trust and loyalty. Little did he realize he was portraying blacks (white actors made up in blackface) as stereotypes. Nor was he the first. As early as 1900, short comedies such as "A Bucket of Cream Ale" and "A Nigger in the Wood Pile" had already established blacks as abject servants and the victims of pranks. ∎

Hitler (1962), AA. *Dir.* Stuart Heisler; *Sc.* Sam Neuman; *Cast includes:* Richard Basehart, Cordula Trantow, Maria Emo, Martin Kosleck.

This weak drama focuses on the Nazi dictator's private life. Richard Basehart portrays Der Fuhrer as a dull, colorless figure haunted by impotence and an Oedipus complex. Cordula Trantow plays his niece. Maria Emo, as Eva Braun, has to deal with Hitler's sexual inadequacies. Martin Kosleck portrays Goebbels. Other historical figures include Himmler, Goering and Rommel, but they add little to the plausibility of the film. Stock newsreel footage is used from time to time to show the progress of the war and world events. ∎

Hitler, Adolf (1889–1945). The Nazi German state that Adolf Hitler had boasted would last a thousand years crumbled around him in the spring of 1945, barely a dozen years after its creation. The Russians, only a few blocks away from the Fuhrer's last redoubt, forced the Nazi leader to face the reality that his dream for a new world order was close to collapse.

On the early afternoon of April 30, 1945, a few days past his 56th birthday, Hitler bid farewell to some of the members of his loyal entourage. A broken and sick man, unable to comprehend why his schemes for final victory had failed to materialize, he withdrew into the suite that he shared with his new wife and former mistress, Eva Braun Hitler. A short time later the sound of a single shot cracked through the air. A small group, including Martin Bormann and Joseph Goebbels, opened the door to find Hitler's body, blood oozing from his head, sprawled on the sofa. He had shot himself in the temple. Next to him lay Eva's corpse, dead from suicide by poison.

Following previously mandated instructions, both bodies were taken outside, doused with gasoline and set afire. The end had come to a man who easily ranks as the 20th century's dominant figure—a coldly cruel, demanding, highly emotional, evil political genius who had done more than any other person to unleash history's most destructive war on the western world. At the peak of his short reign, he had conquered more of Europe than any other individual in history. His death soon brought an end to World War II in Europe.

As befits an individual of such historical importance, Hitler became a subject of more documentaries, dramas, comedies and cartoons than any other World War II figure. Some were blatant propaganda films while others were commercial exploitations. A few attempted to explore the man and his motives. One of the earliest films about Hitler, the semi-documentary *Hitler's Reign of Terror* (1934) traces his rise to power.

Hitler was a failed artist and rabid, impoverished German nationalist living in Vienna when he volunteered to fight for Germany in World War I rather than the polyglot Hapsburg Austro-Hungarian empire of which he was a native. Gassed and temporarily blinded near the end of the war, he won the Iron Cross for bravery. He returned to active service in peacetime and in 1920 was ordered by the army to investigate a small German Workers' Party in Munich. Hitler became intrigued by the group's ideas which fit his philosophy—a mixture of nationalism, anti-marxism, anti-Semitism, disgust with Germany's floundering new democratic government and a burning desire to avenge Germany's recent defeat and subsequent ill treatment by the western allies. He joined the party, renamed it the National Socialist German Workers' Party (Nazi), and soon became its most prominent speaker and leader.

The Nazis, by 1923, sensing a wave of German discontent from economic hard times, attempted to seize the government of Bavaria. The Munich Putsch (November 8, 1923) failed, and Hitler spent a short time in jail where he wrote *Mein Kampf*, his political treatise. With the advent of a worldwide Depression around 1930, the Nazis gained enough strength to become the second biggest party in Germany. Through a combination of political alliances and threats, Hitler quickly silenced and ultimately outlawed the opposition. He further solidified his control over the party and the nation by killing and jailing those whom he felt were a threat to him, including among his victims some of his early supporters. *The Hitler Gang* (1944) highlights many major events in the dictator's life, including his participation as a corporal in World War I where he is wounded and diagnosed as paranoid, his beer hall gatherings, his jail term during which he writes *Mein Kampf*, his rise to power, his suppression of all opposition, his rantings against religion and the 1934 purge. Bob Watson, who virtually made a career during the war years portraying Hitler, impersonates the dictator.

His internal policies as Nazi dictator included the use of concentration camps, originally set up to house political prisoners and later used extensively to eradicate millions of "undesirables" such as Jews, Slavs and Gypsies. He renounced the Versailles Treaty and in 1935 started Germany on a military rebuilding program. Between 1935 and 1939, Hitler remilitarized the Rhine basin, annexed Austria and Czechoslovakia, made alliances with other Fascist regimes in Italy and Japan and began World War II in Europe with the invasion of Poland (September 1, 1939).

He easily vanquished Poland through his concept of a new style of warfare, the Blitzkrieg, a swift and coordinated attack of air and mechanized ground forces to quickly overwhelm the enemy. In the following spring of 1940 the Nazi war machine humbled Denmark, Norway, Holland, Belgium, Luxembourg and France. The documentary "Plan for Destruction" (1943) concerns Hitler's avaricious appetite for his neighbors' lands. Only a badly weakened Britain remained as his European foe. Confident of his infallibility, he was stung by Britain's gallant stand against massive Luftwaffe attacks and its destruction of the Nazi invasion fleet on the French coast. Seeking new areas to conquer, Hitler made what many historians feel was his biggest mistake of the war when he turned eastward, in June 1941, to invade Russia.

A series of German defeats beginning in late 1942 and continuing into 1943 marked the beginning of Hitler's collapse. His reputation as a military genius suffered because of his military blunders in Russia and elsewhere. After the Allied invasion of Normandy (June 6, 1944), a number of German generals, including the famous Erwin Rommel, realized that Hitler's policies would lead to the complete destruction of the nation. They unsuccessfully tried to assassinate the dictator (July 20, 1944). *The Desert Fox* (1951), a biographical drama about Erwin Rommel, includes Luther Adler's portrayal of an emotional and ranting Hitler who is guided in his military decisions by astrology.

It delves, as well, into the generals' plot against the dictator. The breaching of Hitler's western defense line and the invasion of Germany from both east and west by 1945 made total Allied victory only a matter of time.

Hitler, at the end of his career, had fully retreated into a world of fantasy. He refused to accept responsibility for the monumental defeat and destruction he had brought on Germany. Instead, he blamed the people and his generals for letting him down. In his maniacal fanaticism he turned against the generals who had stood by him. A few days before his death he ordered a full scale counterattack to drive the Russians out of Berlin, though where the sizable force for such a mission would come from was left unsaid.

His distorted sense of reality showed in his final testament in which he absolved himself for causing the war and blamed the conflict on the Jews. "It is untrue that I, or anyone else in Germany, wanted war in 1939," he said. "It was desired and instigated solely by those international statesmen who were either of Jewish descent or worked for Jewish interests."

Among the dozens of films that attempted to shed some light on Hitler's personality and goals, the documentary form generally provided the most insight. One early example, *The Unknown Soldier Speaks* (1934) begins at the famous tomb of the Unknown Soldier and depicts events in the rise of Hitler and Mussolini. "Inside Nazi Germany" (1938), a "March of Time" entry, emphasizes how the Nazi dictatorship controls its citizens through propaganda and censorship and how it perceives religious groups as the last bastions of resistance. "Peace—by Adolf Hitler" (1941) was meant to warn prewar America of the dictator's treachery and impending danger.

Postwar documentaries, with the help of confiscated Axis newsreel footage and a broader perspective of past events, continued to study the war and analyze its architect. *Will It Happen Again?* (1948) traces Hitler's rise, the growth of Nazism and Germany's ultimate incursions into its neighbor's lands, bringing devastation and death. *After Mein Kampf* (1961), another documentary, shows Hitler ranting and raving at German rallies. *Smashing of the Reich* (1962) covers the rise and fall of the Third Reich. *The Black Fox* (1963) covers much of the same material but also emphasizes his support by the German people who believed he would bring economic recovery to the nation. Various scenes depict several of Hitler's assistants in action as well as images of the death camps.

Dramas portraying the dictator ranged from the conventional stereotype to a figure who was highly volatile and demented. In *The Strange Death of Adolf Hitler* (1943), an inept exploitation drama, Hitler's double is mistaken for the dictator and assassinated. *Hitler* (1962), a weak drama about the Nazi dictator's private life, has Richard Basehart portraying him as a dull, colorless figure haunted by impotence and an Oedipus complex.

Hitler became the butt of several comedies even before the U.S. entered the war. In Charlie Chaplin's flawed work, *The Great Dictator* (1940), the comedian satirizes the German leader in the form of Adenoid Hynckel, a Hitler-like dictator, played by Chaplin, who has taken over the country of Tomania. The plot allows Charlie, as a Jewish barber, to exchange places with Hynckel and take over the government. The Three Stooges lent their low-brow comic talents to several satirical comedy shorts about Hitler, including "You Nazty Spy" (1940) and "I'll Never Heil Again" (1941). In the fantasy *The Devil With Hitler* (1942), the Devil tries to tempt Adolf to perform a good deed. "Herr Meets Hare" (1945) and "The Ducktators" (1942) were only some of the cartoons that focused on Hitler. Such postwar comedies as *On the Double* (1961), with Danny Kaye, and *Which Way to the Front?* (1970), with zany Jerry Lewis, continued to deride Hitler.

If any criticism could be leveled at Hollywood's attempts to present a picture of Hitler, it is that they generally failed to analyze the motives and inner drives that drove him to such excesses. That failure, however, is not Hollywood's alone, for even the Nazi dictator's nearest associates remarked that he was difficult to know. Perhaps his message of hate and violence and his legacy of colossal inhumanity, so vividly captured on film, are sufficient. ■

Hitler—Beast of Berlin. See *Beasts of Berlin* (1939). ■

Hitler—Dead or Alive (1942), Ben Judell. *Dir.* Nick Grinde; *Sc.* Sam Neuman, Karl Brown; *Cast includes:* Ward Bond, Dorothy Tree, Warren Hymer, Paul Fix, Bob Watson.

In 1942 newspapers carried an unusual item. An American businessman offered a $1 million reward for the capture of Hitler, dead or alive. This implausible film is based on that premise. Three former jailbirds, played by Ward Bond, Warren Hymer and Paul Fix, accept the contract. By various means they reach Berlin disguised as musicians, ready to play at one of Hitler's affairs. The German leader is played by Bob Watson, who impersonated Hitler throughout the war years in several films. Sometimes it is difficult to tell the intentions of the work—whether it is satire or drama. ■

Hitler Gang, The (1944), Par. *Dir.* John Farrow; *Sc.* Francis Goodrich, Albert Hackett; *Cast includes:* Robert Watson, Roman Bohnen, Martin Kosleck, Victor Varconi, Sig Ruman.

A World War II drama depicting the rise of Hitler and the subsequent growth of the Nazi regime, the film highlights the important events in the German dictator's life. Beginning with Hitler's participation as a corporal in World War I where he is wounded and diagnosed as paranoid, the plot moves to his enlistment of Rudolf Hess, Himmler, Goebbels and Goering, all the while showing his betrayal of those groups that employed him. The film dramatizes his beer hall gatherings, the putsch and his jail term during which he writes his famous book, *Mein Kampf*. These incidents are followed by his rise to power, his suppression of all opposition, his rantings against religion and the 1934 purge. Bob Watson, who virtually made a career during the war years portraying Hitler, once again impersonates the dictator. Several fine character actors, many of them German refugees from Nazi-occupied Europe, play Hitler's underlings. ■

Hitler's Children (1942). See Propaganda Films: World War II. ■

Hitler's Hangman (1943), MGM. *Dir.* Douglas Sirk; *Sc.* Peretz Hirshbein, Melvin Levy, Doris Malloy; *Cast includes:* Patricia Morison, John Carradine, Alan Curtis, Ralph Morgan.

This World War II drama tells the story of Czechoslovakian resistance to Nazi oppression; the assassination of Heydrich, Hitler's infamous executioner; and the Nazi reprisals which led to the destruction of the village of

Der Fuhrer (Robert Watson) plots with one of his henchmen (Roman Bohnen) as others pay strict attention. *The Hitler Gang* (1944).

Lidice. Alan Curtis, as a leader of the Czech underground, returns to Lidice from England by parachute to organize the villagers against their occupiers. Patricia Morison, as Curtis' childhood sweetheart, joins him in his cause. John Carradine portrays Heydrich the Hangman, as he was better known to his victims.

At first the villagers, fearing for the safety of their families, are hesitant to rise up. But after several atrocities committed by the Nazis, they retaliate with acts of sabotage. After Heydrich's men kill the local priest, some of the citizens assassinate the Hangman. One particularly poignant sequence deals with the rounding up of the townspeople following the assassination. The men are lined up for execution, the women are taken away to prison camps and the children of the victims are sent elsewhere. After the men are executed, the Germans destroy the village. The film is based on a true story written by Emil Ludwig and Albrecht Joseph. Eleanor Roosevelt reportedly suggested that it be made into a feature movie. Poetess Edna St. Vincent Millay contributed several verses es-

pecially written for the film. The last scene pictures the ghosts of those shot down in cold blood. Each recites several lines of Millay's poem, ending with the following:

"I'm telling you not to eat or drink/One morsel of food, one swallow of drink Before you think, before you think/What is best for your country./Keep your country free from the foe you hate;/Catch him, catch him, do not wait.

The story of Heydrich's murder was the subject of other films, including *Hangmen Also Die*, released earlier the same year. ∎

Hitler's Reign of Terror (1934), Samuel Cummins. *Dir.* Mike Mindlin; *Cast includes:* Cornelius Vanderbilt, Jr., Edwin C. Hill.

One of the earliest American films to cover the rise of Adolf Hitler, the film is an inept hybrid of documentary and semi-fiction. Cornelius Vanderbilt, Jr. was unable to get most of his footage out of Germany, so he narrates on screen his alleged interviews with important German personages, including the Nazi leader himself. Several scenes have been staged or re-enacted. But there is some revealing footage of the torturing of Jews and the burning of books outlawed by the Nazi party. Other sequences fit into the realm of a travelogue. The film ends with two interviews, one with Helen Keller, whose books were part of the Nazi conflagration, and the other with a congressman who warns of the growing number of Bundists, or Nazi sympathizers, in America. ■

Hold Back the Night (1956), AA. *Dir.* Allan Dwan; *Sc.* John C. Higgins, Walter Doniger; *Cast includes:* John Payne, Mona Freeman, Peter Graves, Chuck Connors, Audrey Dalton.

John Payne portrays a U.S. Marine officer during the Korean War who has been carting around a bottle of Scotch since World War II, which he intends to open only on a very special occasion. He ultimately offers it to his men as a reward for fighting their way back to their lines while under almost continuous fire from the Communists. The marine company heroically battles the enemy while using the bottle as a symbol of their goal. Mona Freeman plays Payne's wife in this routine action drama. ■

Hollywood Canteen (1944). See Musicals. ■

Holocaust. Nazi Germany's deliberate and organized attempt to destroy an entire race of people was a unique phenomenon in the history of mankind. Historians may continue to ponder over how the Holocaust was possible. Others will persist in questioning how other nations and groups reacted to the threat as well as the implementation of the mass killings. The consequences of the Holocaust are still evolving. They may be witnessed in Israel's attitudes toward their neighbors and the Palestinians. They affect Austria and Kurt Waldheim, former secretary general of the United Nations. They raise questions of collective guilt and denial in many countries. Most of all, they haunt the survivors and their children.

The American film industry has seldom come to grips with the full story of the Holocaust. Excluding documentaries, only a handful of dramas have alluded to the death camps, deportation and extermination. Some of the earliest films to approach the topic of anti-Semitism and all of its ramifications did so within the framework of farce, a technique which in itself raises questions of propriety in treating so grave a subject as the Holocaust.

Charlie Chaplin in *The Great Dictator* (1940), which he also wrote and directed, satirizes Hitler in the form of Adenoid Hynckel, a Hitler-like dictator, also played by Chaplin, who has taken over the country of Tomania. The plot allows for Charlie the barber, the dictator's look-alike, to exchange places with Hynckel and take over the government. In one sequence an adviser to Hynckel recommends attacks against the Jews as a means of quelling the food-hungry citizens. The same councilor at another point suggests to his leader that he will emerge as world ruler after "wiping out the Jews." Other scenes show Jews being harassed in their ghetto that is eventually set on fire. The film acknowledges the existence of concentration camps when a ghetto resident says that others have "gone there." Chaplin's final speech—an overly long and didactic plea for peace and brotherhood in the world—distracts from the comic and satirical intentions of the work.

Ernst Lubitch's satirical black comedy *To Be or Not to Be* (1942), concerning a troupe of mediocre actors led by Jack Benny, takes place in Nazi-occupied Poland. Several critics attacked the film as "tasteless" and "callous" for treating the destruction of Warsaw humorously. Others acknowledged the work simply as anti-Nazi propaganda and dismissed some of the offbeat humor as ill-timed. One of the comic highlights is the oft-repeated line—"So they call me Concentration Camp Ehrhardt?"—spoken with delight and pride by a buffoonish Nazi officer (Sig Ruman). Another sequence has a Jewish actor performing Shylock before an audience of Nazi officers. Leo McCarey's comedy drama *Once Upon a Honeymoon*, released the same year, is an odd combination of events, blending the devastation of Czechoslovakia, Poland and France with the frivolous desires of a young woman looking for a titled husband. Once again, critics complained about its lack of taste in finding humor in war and destruction.

Very few dramas dealing with the plight of Jews and other Holocaust victims appeared in the early 1940s. Frank Borzage's domestic drama of prewar Nazi Germany, *The Mortal Storm* (1940), illustrates the oppressive road that Germany had already taken. When a Jewish professor, lecturing at a German university, refuses to contradict science which states that all blood is similar, he is placed in a concentration camp.

Post-World War II films focused slightly more sharply on the horrors perpetrated by Hitler's Germany upon the innocent. *The Diary of Anne Frank* (1959), directed by George Stevens and based on the Pulitzer prize-winning Broadway production, was in turn taken from the published diary of a young death camp victim. The film, about the lives of a family of Dutch Jews living in hiding, supplements the stage play by adding actual footage taken at the infamous death camps. In Otto Preminger's *Exodus* (1960) the gas chambers of the death camps are referred to in a poignant scene. The Israeli underground questions a prospective young member (Sal Mineo) about his experiences in one of these camps. The youth reveals indirectly that at age 12 he was digging graves for the victims. This gains him acceptance into the secret cadre. *Judgment at Nuremberg* (1961), directed by socially conscious Stanley Kramer, deals with questions about individual responsibility for war crimes committed by the state. Victims of sterilization and other medical experiments testify before the tribunal, conjuring up frightening images of Nazi atrocities. *The Pawnbroker* (1965), a disturbing film directed by Sidney Lumet, blends the present life of an embittered Holocaust survivor (Rod Steiger) living in New York with flashbacks of his experiences during the war. These memories of things past but not forgotten include a scene in which dogs pursue a Jewish concentration camp prisoner as Steiger looks on helplessly; one in which a crowded trainload of Jews journeys to the inevitable gas chambers; and another, more horrifying one, in which Steiger is forced to watch the rape of his wife by a Nazi official. Alan J. Pakula's *Sophie's Choice* (1982) offers a sensitive study of a Polish-Catholic survivor of a Nazi death camp who is forced to choose which of her children will survive. Meryl Streep, as the title character, has a love affair with a New York Jew, played by Kevin Kline. Periodically, the camera presents close-ups of Sophie, who then recollects her tormenting experiences at Auschwitz. The flashbacks, shot in a softer color tone, signify a distant past, another world.

Several combat dramas of World War II made after the conflict include sequences in which advancing G.I.s enter the camps after the Germans flee. The films show how differ-ent soldiers—a German officer, an American-Jewish G.I. and a gentile American infantry-man—react upon first witnessing the victims of the camps. In Edward Dmytryk's *The Young Lions* (1958), based on Irwin Shaw's novel, Marlon Brando, as a disillusioned German officer, stumbles upon one of these camps. Seeing the wretched victims of the camp and hearing the commandant complain that he is too shorthanded to kill the remaining prisoners are the final assaults upon Brando's conscience. He smashes his machine gun in a rage and staggers down a hill. Several scenes later, an American G.I. (Dean Martin) comforts his buddy, a fellow soldier of Jewish heritage (Montgomery Clift), who has just witnessed the human remnants of the camp and is so struck with disbelief that he cannot speak. Writer-director Samuel Fuller related some of his own World War II experiences in *The Big Red One* (1980). Mark Hamill, as a foot soldier, is reluctant to kill the enemy until he witnesses a Nazi concentration camp and its pitiful survivors hastily abandoned by the retreating Germans. He finds a German hiding in one of the ovens and empties his weapon into the soldier.

Several postwar dramas, although not war films, were produced as a result of the Holocaust. *Gentleman's Agreement* (1947), based on Laura Z. Hobson's book, deals with anti-Semitism in America and stars Gregory Peck as a writer who poses as a Jew to experience first-hand some of the indignities American Jews face daily. *Crossfire*, a murder mystery released the same year, concerns a paranoid bigot (Robert Ryan) who, under questioning as a murder suspect, admits his hatred of Jews when he talks about "Jewboys who lived on easy street during the war while white people fought in the front-line trenches."

Documentaries of the Holocaust, stripped of the artifices of melodrama, romantic subplots and other ingredients of feature films, perhaps came closest to the truth in their depictions of the misery and death that stalked the camps. Based on newsreel footage from both Allied and Axis countries, these black-and-white images of corpses piled high, mounds of victims' clothes and eyeglasses and emaciated survivors, brought to light the incomprehensible slaughter that the Nazi regime carried out with extreme proficiency. After the war, these documentaries began to emerge from many European countries—

France, Czechoslovakia, the Soviet Union, Poland, Great Britain, Belgium and West Germany.

The U.S. added to this growing body of work over the next four decades. *After Mein Kampf* (1961), which mixes newsreel footage with excerpts from dramas, includes actual scenes of the death camp victims. *The Executioners*, released the same year, traces the careers of the principal defendants in the Nuremberg trial and focuses on the Nazi atrocities. The plight of the Jewish people in Europe between the two world wars and their eventual extermination are the subjects of *Genocide* (1982). Other titles include *Nuremberg* (1946), *Will It Happen Again?* (1948), *The Memory of Justice* (1976), *The Avenue of the Just* (1978), *Image Before My Eyes* (1980), and *Who Shall Live and Who Shall Die?* (1981).

Using a variety of techniques including interviews with civilians, military personnel and survivors as well as actual footage, most of these films cover similar topics. Several former Nazis remain unrepentant; a few even think that the medical experiments performed at the camps were justified; others insist they were just following orders. Some younger Germans believe that much of the footage shot at the camps was fabricated by the Allies; others state that their parents could never accept the enormity of the Nazi crimes. Questions of national and individual guilt are raised and examined. A few documentaries, such as *Who Shall Live and Who Shall Die?*, accuse the major powers of failing to ease their immigration quotas when they learned of Jewish persecution as early as 1938. Some films show Holocaust survivors returning after the war to visit their villages only to find them decimated or re-inhabited by others with no memory of the past.

The Holocaust has been presented in various forms ranging from feature films to television mini-series to documentaries. Film dramas have simplified the social and historical complexity of the Holocaust. Television dramas, with their pretty faces and commercial interruptions every ten minutes, have trivialized it. Only documentaries have come closest to the truth. The final story of the horror has yet to be told. See also Concentration Camps. ■

Holy Roman Empire-Papacy Wars. See *The Flame and the Arrow* (1950). ■

Home front. War films of the home front may not provide the action, continuing confrontation with death or large-scale battles of combat films, but they show another face of war. Movie studios have used the home front for romantic tales, spy stories, domestic and social dramas, comedies and musicals. Films with these settings are often more economical since they permit a smaller cast and can utilize conventional sets. Aside from providing entertainment—their original purpose—films of the home front very often carry their own propaganda value. Wives and sweethearts may be seen manning the war plants; children collect scrap for the war effort; parents pray for their sons in uniform and place stars in their windows; all are shown conserving food and other items necessary for victory. In summary, these films—rife with patriotism and propaganda—give evidence to a united civilian front against the enemy.

Perhaps one of the earliest wars to be used as background for a film concerning the home front was the Crusades. In such dramas as *The Adventures of Robin Hood* (1938) the battlefields are never seen. Instead, the story describes the turmoil at home as Prince John attempts to usurp the throne of his brother, King Richard, who is away fighting in the Crusades. Robin Hood (Errol Flynn) and his outlaws are forced to take up arms to defend their king's interests. Director D.W. Griffith turned out several home-front dramas of the Civil War between 1908 and 1911. The restrictions of budget, cast and length of each film (one reel) may have had much to do with his choice of subject. In such films as "His Trust" and "His Trust Fulfilled," both made in 1911, Griffith tells a simple but dramatic story of a Southern officer riding off to war and leaving his faithful black servant to protect the master's wife and child. The Civil War provides the background for several screen versions of John Greenleaf Whittier's poem, "Barbara Frietchie."

The bulk of home-front films made by Hollywood studios concerned the two world wars. World War I saw a flood of spy dramas and comedies, often featuring female performers in the lead roles. Florence La Badie in *War and the Woman* (1917) is falsely accused of betraying her country. She turns in her own stepfather when she learns he is the traitor. In *Follow the Girl* (1917) a Swedish immigrant maid (Ruth Stonehouse) becomes entangled with foreign agents plotting against the U.S. The film underscores the responsibilities of all citizens to their nation during wartime. Vivian Martin in *Her Country First* (1918) organizes a young women's aviation auxiliary which helps to capture a handful of German spies. Gloria Swanson appeared in three films in 1918 in which she naively becomes entangled with foreign spies. Not learning her lesson in the first two, in which she narrowly escapes, she pays with her life in the third.

One interesting drama to show women in a different role is *War Brides* (1916). A strongly pacifist work, the film stars Alla Nazimova as a defiant subject who refuses to follow her king's decree to produce children for the military. She shoots herself in the king's presence as a protest against his inhuman command. In the domestic drama *For Valour* (1917) an impoverished Canadian family suffers at home during the war while the son is away at the front. In *The Charmer*, released the same year, Ella Hall portrays a refugee child who makes an impassioned plea to those at home for self-sacrifice as their most important contribution toward winning the war.

Home-front comedy was provided by such popular screen personalities as Douglas Fairbanks and Mary Pickford as well as a host of lesser-known actors and actresses. In the charming *Johanna Enlists* (1918), directed by William Desmond Taylor, for instance, Mary Pickford, as a young girl who daydreams of romance and handsome pursuers, has her fantasies come true when an army regiment takes up residence near her father's farm. She snares a handsome captain (Douglas MacLean).

A popular theme in many World War I films pertained to the slacker. There was little subtlety in these propaganda tales with such titles as *The Slacker* (1917) and *Mrs. Slacker* (1918). In both of these, the sweetheart or wife learns of her man's devious attempts to avoid the draft and has to shame him into doing his duty. The slacker in World War II films was generally overlooked. One minor film, *Good Luck, Mr. Yates* (1943), handles the theme in an interesting, if undeveloped, way. Jess Barker, as a teacher at a military academy, receives little respect from his students because he is not in uniform. Rejected from military service because of a punctured eardrum, he takes a job at a shipyard where he has an opportunity to play hero during a fire.

Home-front films during World War II consisted of comedies, musicals and dramas of various types. *Margin for Error* (1943), in which a Jewish cop (Milton Berle) is assigned to guard the German Consulate, provides little in the way of laughs. Ann Sothern in *Swing Shift Maisie* (1943) more or less represented the emerging role of women. She works in an airplane factory, falls in love with a flier (James Craig) and has time to sing "The Girl Behind the Boy Behind the Gun." Another comedy that reflected conditions at home is *Rationing* (1944), starring Wallace Beery and Marjorie Main. The plot deals with black market meat. In *G.I. Honeymoon* (1945) Gale Storm and Peter Cookson portray newlyweds whose honeymoon is interrupted by military demands and officious civilians.

Musicals like *Star Spangled Rhythm* (1942) and *Stage Door Canteen* (1943) cheered up servicemen on leave as well as civilians at home. *Reveille With Beverly* (1943), an inept musical strictly for "hepcats," features Ann Miller as a radio disc jockey who runs a wake-up program aimed at G.I.s in a nearby army camp. Guest stars include Frank Sinatra, the Mills Brothers and the orchestras of Duke Ellington and Count Basie. Child stars did their patriotic duty in films like *Johnny Doughboy* (1943). "Spanky" McFarland and "Alfalfa" Switzer of the "Our Gang" comedies, Jane Withers and Bobby Breen join the "Junior Victory Caravan," a troupe of young performers who entertain at army camps. A slightly different approach is used in *Thumbs Up*, released the same year. Brenda Joyce, as an obscure American singer in a second-rate London nightclub, gets a job in a war factory when she learns that a producer plans to recruit talent from there. The other workers shun the American when they discover her motives. By the end of the film she realizes she was wrong to use the war for selfish reasons. In *You Can't Ration Love* (1944) college girls solve their wartime problem of a shortage of males by rationing their dates. Co-eds at Adams College rate their fellow male students on a scale of 1 to 30, with Johnnie Johnston playing unattractive chemistry major "Two-Point" Simpson. One of the girls (Betty Rhodes), as a prank, decides to transform him into a popular Sinatra-like crooner.

Dramas often revealed how family members coped with various wartime problems. In *Mrs. Miniver* (1942), which emphasizes home-front England, a family suffers a series of hardships including air raids, a direct hit on its home and the loss of its daughter-in-law. But the family remains strong and courageous, gaining the sympathy of American audiences. *The Human Comedy* (1943), adapted from William Saroyan's novel, tells the tearful story of a family in an idyllic American town. A teen-age son (Mickey Rooney) supports the family while his older brother (Van Johnson) is away at the front. *Happy Land* (1943), with a similar Norman Rockwell setting, tells of a father (Don Ameche) who has to come to terms with the loss of his sailor-son. Wartime conditions prevent a soldier and his sweetheart from getting married through most of *Army Wives* (1944). Paulette Goddard faced another problem in *I Love a Soldier* (1944). She turns down G.I. Sonny Tuft's marriage proposal on the grounds that his thoughts about his bride would endanger his soldiering.

The war provided an opportunity for local criminals to find new and lucrative rackets. Rubber, for example, became a rationed commodity, leading to a profitable black market in tires. Monogram, a studio that specialized in B movies, released *Rubber Racketeers* in 1942, starring Ricardo Cortez and Rochelle Hudson. Irate defense workers, whose pal is killed by a defective tire, smash a ring of tire bootleggers led by Cortez. *X Marks the Spot*, released the same year by Republic, another second-string studio, also deals with rubber racketeering. Warner Brothers made its contribution to the tire bootlegging theme in 1944 with *The Last Ride*, a routine crime drama featuring Richard Travis, Charles Lang and Eleanor Parker. *Allotment Wives* (1945), with Kay Francis and Otto Kruger, exposes a racket in which scheming women marry soldiers and sailors for their allotment checks. The war also brought forth unscrupulous war profiteers. *All My Sons* (1948), the most powerful of these dramas, concerns a plant owner (Edward G. Robinson) who allows defective airplane cylinders to be shipped out. They lead to the deaths of several American airmen. Robinson, meanwhile, lets the blame fall on his innocent partner.

As in World War I, spy comedies and dramas were a popular genre during the Second World War. Of a more serious nature were such dramas as *They Came to Blow Up America* (1943) and *The House on 92nd Street* (1945). The latter, unfolding in semi-documentary style, concerns Nazi spies who are trying to steal the secret of the atomic bomb.

Home-front films of the 1970s and 1980s included nostalgic journeys back to World War II in such comedies as *1941* (1979) and romantic dramas as *Yanks* (1979) and *Swing Shift* (1984). One noteworthy aspect of these films was their liberal use of popular songs of the period. The Vietnam War had its share of home-front tales. In *Hail, Hero!* (1969) Michael Douglas portrays a college student who enlists to fight in a war he doesn't believe in. This was one of the earliest films to question the national policy concerning the conflict. Wives whose husbands are listed as missing in action in Vietnam are the subject of *Limbo* (1972). The film explores their anxieties and shattered lives. Finally, the documentary *The War at Home* (1979) traces the turmoil of the 1960s that resulted from the Vietnam War and includes speeches of some of the leading political figures of the period. See also Washington, D.C. ■

Night fails to hide the racial bigotry simmering in some G.I.s as Frank Lovejoy (l.) tries to comfort James Edwards, one of its victims. *Home of the Brave* (1949).

Home of the Brave (1949), UA. Dir. Mark Robson; Sc. Carl Foreman; Cast includes: James Edwards, Douglas Dick, Steve Brodie, Jeff Corey, Lloyd Bridges.

Based on the successful play by Arthur Laurents, the film version depicts the torment of a black G.I. in World War II who endures more pain from the prejudice of his fellow soldiers than from the enemy. The setting is a Japanese-occupied island in the South Pacific where five soldiers are assigned a dangerous mission. The black soldier

(James Edwards) is brought back in a state of psychological shock. The doctor learns that Edwards, after a long period of personal racial abuse, especially from one fellow soldier (Steve Brodie), has cracked under the final blow—the death of his one loyal white pal.

The film was the first Hollywood feature to tackle the problem of racial bigotry and set the pattern for similar dramas. Although producer Stanley Kramer, in collaboration with the director and screenwriter, altered the original play by having a black instead of a Jewish soldier as the central character, the effect—the emotional and psychological damage upon the victim—is the same. Kramer used an all-male cast, many of whom were virtually unknown performers, to present his tale of racism in the armed service. ■

Homecoming (1948), MGM. *Dir.* Mervyn LeRoy; *Sc.* Paul Osborn; *Cast includes:* Clark Gable, Lana Turner, Anne Baxter, John Hodiak, Ray Collins.

A World War II romantic drama told chiefly in flashback, this routine film stars Clark Gable as an army doctor and Lana Turner as his nurse. Gable, a successful and smug surgeon in civilian life, falls in love with Turner while both are serving in the army. The affair lasts through the North African campaign to the Battle of the Bulge. Turner enlightens Gable about life, love and responsibility with such thoughts as the following in which she explains the present war: "People didn't care what went on over there until the murderers got so far that the whole world was in danger. If we had a little simple humanity at the very start, it might have been stopped." She succumbs to war wounds, and he returns to his waiting wife. John Hodiak portrays Gable's confidant and fellow physician. Anne Baxter plays Gable's wife. ■

Honest Man, An (1918). See Propaganda Films: World War I. ■

Honor First (1922), Fox. *Dir.* Jerome Storm; *Sc.* Joseph F. Poland; *Cast includes:* John Gilbert, Renée Adorée, Hardee Kirkland, Shannon Day.

A World War I drama of twin brothers in the French army, the film stars John Gilbert in the dual role of Jacques, a private, and Honore, a lieutenant. During a battle, the brothers' unit is ordered to attack. Honore turns tail while Jacques leads the men to victory. Mistaken for his officer-brother, Jacques is decorated for bravery. He accepts the honor and the leave that goes with it. He journeys to Paris where he meets his cowardly brother who plots against Jacques' life. Ironically, it is Honore who is killed. Jacques then falls in love with Honore's wife whose marriage, she confesses, had been an unhappy one. ■

"Honor of His Family, The" (1910), Biograph. *Dir.* D. W. Griffith; *Sc.* Frank Woods; *Cast includes* Henry B. Walthall, James Kirkwood, William J. Butler, Gus Pixley.

In this silent Civil War drama a young man of the South answers the call to arms. His father, too old to enlist, fights the war vicariously through his son, who is an officer. During a major battle, the boy turns coward and flees to his home. The patriotic father, disgusted with his son's actions and the dishonor he has brought upon the family, shoots the boy and returns the body to the battlefield. He positions the corpse with sword in hand, facing the enemy.

This is one of director Griffith's rare morbid dramas. Although many of his films, especially his Civil War cycle, include scenes of violence and killing, the characters don't usually physically move corpses around. The theme of cowardice recurs in several of his works, including "The House With Closed Shutters," another Civil War film also released in 1910. During his years with Biograph, Griffith directed a cycle of one-reel Civil War dramas, all of which served as preparation for his epic drama of that conflict, *The Birth of a Nation* (1915). ■

Hook, The (1963), MGM. *Dir.* George Seaton; *Sc.* Henry Denker; *Cast includes:* Kirk Douglas, Robert Walker, Nick Adams, Enrique Magalona.

Each of three American soldiers is faced with the dilemma of obeying military orders or following his own conscience in this tense Korean War drama that takes place aboard a Finnish freighter. Their superiors order the trio to kill a prisoner in their custody. But out of the context of battle, the man's death seems uncalled for. Kirk Douglas portrays a tough, battle-hardened sergeant who is one of the men faced with carrying out the brutal assignment. Nick Adams, another soldier involved in the situation, follows Douglas, who

War's corruption filters down to children as American paratrooper Rock Hudson leads a young guerrilla band in World War II Italy. *Hornet's Nest* (1970).

once helped Adams out of a scrape. Robert Walker, as the last member of the trio, is a young scholarly type incapable of executing the unusual order.

The film ends on a tragic and ironic note when the crew and passengers receive news that the war has ended. The prisoner, who does not understand English, escapes from his quarters and hides below deck. He tries to set the ship afire but fails. Douglas and Walker pursue him but can't make him understand that an armistice has been signed. Douglas confronts the cornered prisoner, who is holding a razor and speaking in Korean. Catching him off guard, Douglas disarms him and in the ensuing struggle, kills him. Walker then translates the man's last words. "He was trying to say, 'I can't do it.'" The Korean is buried at sea. ■

Horizontal Lieutenant, The (1962). See War Humor. ■

Hornet's Nest (1970), UA. *Dir.* Phil Karlson; *Sc.* S. S. Schweitzer; *Cast includes:* Rock Hudson, Sylva Koscina, Sergio Fantoni.

Rock Hudson stars as an American paratrooper in this implausible action drama set in Italy during World War II. He leads an unlikely group of guerrillas consisting of Italian children whose parents were killed by the Germans. They help him to accomplish his mission—the destruction of a vital dam. Sylva Koscina, as a captured German doctor, provides the romantic interest. Sergio Fantoni portrays a German soldier. Hudson at first is reluctant to use the young fighters, but they persuade him otherwise. A macabre twist occurs when one of the older boys, played by Mark Colleano, is transformed into a ruthless killer. But the plot, on the whole, keeps to the path of a routine action drama without delving too deeply into the theme of the effects of war and violence on children. Plenty of action occurs when the boys and Hudson battle Nazi troops. ■

Horrors of War (1940), Merit.

A documentary compiled from newsreel footage as well as from feature films, the film speaks out against America's entry into World War II. Its major premise is that an accelerated industrial growth resulting from a war economy is bound to involve the nation in military conflict, pointing to World War I as an example. The film, one of the last anti-war documentaries to be released during World War II, provides numerous battle sequences from the 1914–1918 war. ■

Horse Soldiers, The (1959), UA. *Dir.* John Ford; *Sc.* Lee Mahin, Martin Rackin; *Cast includes:* John Wayne, William Holden, Constance Towers, Althea Gibson, Hoot Gibson.

John Wayne, as a battle-hardened Union colonel, leads his troop of cavalry on a raid behind enemy lines in this Civil War drama based on an actual incident. A humane army surgeon (William Holden) accompanies the troops. Constance Towers, as a Southern belle who overhears Wayne's plans for the raid when the Union officers occupy her home, is taken along as a prisoner and provides the romantic interest for both Wayne and Holden. By the end of the film Towers and Wayne fall in love with each other.

Director John Ford's penchant for humor appears in several forms. It is displayed in Holden's repeated sardonic comments concerning Wayne's apparent impulsiveness to engage in battle. It also emerges in the scene in which an elderly headmaster of a Southern military academy proudly but foolishly leads his eager young boys in a march against the Union cavalry. Wayne, of course, sounds the retreat.

Two major battle sequences add to the excitement of this outdoor action drama. In an early portion, Wayne's troops surprise a trainload of rebel soldiers who have come to rescue a town under siege by his cavalry. In the ensuing battle the brave but foolhardy Southerners are slaughtered in their head-on attack. The film ends with another engagement between Wayne's troops and the enemy. With a column of Southern soldiers approaching from the rear and an enemy force before him on the other side of a creek, he leads a desperate but heroic charge across a wooden bridge and wipes out the rebel resistance. Holden, who acts as Wayne's foil, volunteers to remain behind to care for the wounded as the advancing Confederate column approaches. Meanwhile, Wayne blows up the bridge and leads his troops to safety.

Aside from some bloody scenes of wounded troopers and one amputation operation, Ford embellishes the action with his romantic views of war, heroism and glory—distributing these elements equally between the North and the South. The brave Southern citizens of Newton Station make an abortive stand against the invaders. Long shots of Wayne and his troops riding along the horizon in silhouette are quite effective. His men, at times, appear overly chivalrous toward their adversaries. We seem to be more in Ford country than in the thick of the Civil War.

In April of 1863, General Grant assigned Colonel Benjamin Grierson to journey 300 miles into Confederate territory to demolish the rail link between Newton Station and Vicksburg. Grierson and his three cavalry regiments, a force of 1,700 men, succeeded in their mission; they rode 600 miles in a little more than two weeks and returned safely to Union lines. ■

Hoskins, John M. See *The Eternal Sea* (1955). ■

Hostages (1943), Par. *Dir.* Frank Tuttle; *Sc.* Lester Cole, Frank Butler; *Cast includes:* Arturo de Cordova, Luise Rainer, William Bendix, Oscar Homolka, Katina Paxinou, Paul Lukas.

A drama of the Czechoslovakian underground during World War II, the film features William Bendix as a leader of the freedom fighters caught up in the intrigues of a handful of greedy Nazis. When a Nazi officer is drowned, 26 Czech hostages are rounded up. Several Nazis, who want to share the wealth of one of the prisoners, a German collaborator, claim the officer was murdered so that the hostages would be shot. Meanwhile, Bendix escapes and sabotages Nazi munitions storage areas. Paul Lukas portrays a Gestapo officer. Luise Rainer plays the daughter of the collaborator. The grim film is based on a novel by Stefan Heym which in turn was drawn from actual incidents. ■

Hotel Berlin (1945), WB. *Dir.* Peter Godfrey; *Sc.* Jo Pagano, Alvah Bessie; *Cast includes:* Helmut Dantine, Andrea King, Raymond

Underground leader Helmut Dantine (r.), realizing the power and authority of a uniform in World War II Germany, poses as a Nazi officer with help from Andrea King. *Hotel Berlin* (1945).

Massey, Faye Emerson, Peter Lorre, George Coulouris, Henry Daniell.

A World War II melodrama set in 1945 during the final days of the Nazi regime, the film, inordinately steeped in propaganda, is an adaptation of the novel by Vicki Baum, who also wrote *Grand Hotel.* The once elegant hotel, a metaphor for the decline of Nazi Germany, has been damaged by periodic Allied air raids. Elevators don't work, the general structure requires additional support and guests are herded below into shelters at regular intervals. A sense of impending defeat permeates the atmosphere of the hotel.

Helmut Dantine, as an underground leader, has escaped from a concentration camp and seeks shelter in the hotel where some of his conspirators are employed. Meanwhile, in another room, Nazi officers plan their escape to the U.S. where they intend to prepare for World War III. "This time we shall be anti-Nazis," one explains, "poor refugees who have escaped from Germany . . . Americans forgive and forget easily. But we must spread rumors and create dissension and distrust." Andrea King, who portrays a successful stage actress, at first helps Dantine to elude the Gestapo but eventually informs on him to protect her own future. Her lover (Raymond Massey), a high-ranking German officer involved in an assassination plot against Hitler, is given 24 hours to "do the honorable thing." An unrepentant Nazi to the end, he says to a fellow officer: "We have lost this war. Tell those who come after us they must prepare better for the next one. We must never lose

again." Peter Lorre portrays a German Nobel prizewinner and professor who has been brainwashed to cooperate with the Third Reich but ultimately returns to the underground to help turn out anti-Nazi propaganda. Steven Geray, as the chief hotel clerk, adds some comic relief, particularly when he is drafted. A pathetic figure in his new uniform, he looks at a portrait of Hitler hanging over the hotel desk and remarks: "I'd like to see him hung in a different way."

The film ends with Allied bombers again raiding Berlin as a message scrolls up the screen: "Our purpose is not to destroy the German people—but we are determined to disband all German armed forces . . . bring all war criminals to just and swift punishment— wipe out the Nazi Party and Nazi laws from the life of the German people—Germany must never again disturb the peace of the World." The signatures of Winston Churchill, Franklin Roosevelt and J. Stalin appear at the bottom. ∎

Hotel Imperial (1927), Par. *Dir.* Mauritz Stiller; *Sc.* Jules Furthman; *Cast includes:* Pola Negri, James Hall, George Seigmann, Max Davidson.

Pola Negri portrays a hotel chambermaid in this World War I drama. The hotel is nestled in a border town that is alternately occupied by Austro-Hungarian and Russian troops. She hides an Austrian soldier (James Hall) in the hotel during a Russian advance into Galicia. The Russians occupy the village, and their general (George Seigmann) makes the hotel his headquarters. He quickly takes a liking to Negri, but she falls in love with Hall. When a Russian spy appears with information about the Austrian army, Hall kills him and makes his way to his own troops. The Austrians attack and drive the Russians back. Hall returns to his love and marries her while his commander, grateful for both their brave deeds, gives Hall leave for a honeymoon.

The film presents a unique background in comparison to other World War I films by concentrating on the Austrian-Russian conflict and setting the story along the Austro-Hungarian border. This was one of the earliest war dramas not only not to use an American or Allied hero, but to focus sympathetically on a hero of the Central powers.

Historically, Russia did overrun Galicia in 1914 and occupied the eastern section for about a year. After the war, the Ukrainians declared the area an independent state, but Poland soon claimed Galicia as part of its territory, putting an end to the short-lived independent nation. ∎

Hotel Imperial (1939), Par. *Dir.* Robert Florey; *Sc.* Gilbert Gabriel, Robert Thoeren; *Cast includes:* Isa Miranda, Ray Milland, Reginald Owen, Gene Lockhart, J. Carrol Naish.

A weak remake of the 1927 film of the same title starring Pola Negri, this version of the World War I drama introduces the European personality Isa Miranda to American audiences. The international star portrays a young woman seeking revenge for the death of her sister. She works as a chambermaid at the Hotel Imperial, the same position and hotel where her sister was employed. The town has changed hands several times in the course of the war between the Austrians and Russians. Ray Milland plays an Austrian officer she finds hiding in a room. They soon fall in love. Milland manages to escape while the town is in the hands of the Russians and makes it back to his lines in time to save his army from defeat. When the Austrians retake the town, he resumes his romance with the young chambermaid who has resolved the death of her sister. Reginald Owen plays a buffoonish Russian general.

Billy Wilder's suspenseful World War II drama, *Five Graves to Cairo* (1943), starring Franchot Tone as an English officer hiding from the Germans who have occupied an Egyptian hotel and Ann Baxter as a chambermaid who falls for him, has borrowed much of its material from these earlier films. ∎

Hour Before the Dawn, The (1944). See Propaganda Films: World War II. ∎

House on 92nd Street, The (1945). See Spy Films: the Talkies. ∎

"House With Closed Shutters, The" (1910), Biograph. *Dir.* D. W. Griffith; *Sc.* Emmett Campbell Hall; *Cast includes:* Dorothy West, Henry B. Walthall, Charles West, Edwin August.

Another in the series of director D. W. Griffith's early one-reel dramas with a Civil War background, the film concerns the tragedy that befalls a Southern family because of a son's cowardice and drinking problem. When the war erupts, the young alcoholic son wins a commission and is assigned to General Lee's staff. His sister sews a flag for his regiment before the troops march to the front. The son, stricken with fear when he is sent on an important mission, begins to drink heavily. He then returns to his home and continues to hit the bottle. His sister poses as a soldier and carries out his mission for him. But she is fatally wounded protecting the flag. News reaches his mother that her son was killed in action. To avoid bringing shame to the proud family name, she closes the shutters of her home and keeps her cowardly son locked in. He remains there for many years until his death. ∎

Houston, Samuel (1793–1863). A writer of fiction would be hard-pressed to generate a story that matched the life of Sam Houston. His public career and private life alternated between the peaks of victory and public acclaim to the depths of despair and defeat. Although honored as a military hero in two wars and considered the savior of Texas independence, the "Hero of San Jacinto" died a sad and politically scorned man in the state for which he did so much. Films on Houston certainly had a rich store of events upon which to draw, and, although most focused on his accomplishments, his personal tragedies were mostly overlooked.

As a youth, Houston lived with his family in the Cherokee Indian area of Tennessee, near the present border of North Carolina. He was adopted by the Cherokee and many years later, as an adult, he returned to live with the tribe when his private life became a shambles. Houston served under Andrew Jackson in the Creek War of 1814, part of the War of 1812, and was seriously wounded in the Battle of Horseshoe Bend.

Houston, as a Tennessee lawyer, entered politics and served in Congress as a Democrat (1823–1827). He rose to Governor of Tennessee in 1827 but resigned the office in 1829 after his wife left him. Facing a serious drinking problem at this time, he left the state and drifted for the next few years. He briefly rejoined the Cherokee in their new home in Oklahoma, to which most of the tribe had been forcibly resettled from their eastern lands, then moved to Arkansas and in 1833 went to Texas to join the rapidly growing colony of Americans there.

Houston, while attending the 1836 convention that declared Texas independent from Mexico, was appointed general of the army of

Texas. His leadership soon suffered serious criticism after Texas sustained losses to superior forces at the Battles of the Alamo and Goliad. Despair with Houston's leadership mounted as he and his army retreated before pursuing Mexican forces under General Santa Anna. But at the San Jacinto River, near the present site of Houston, the Texans mounted a surprise attack in which they soundly defeated a Mexican force of 1,200 troops and captured Mexico's President and commanding general, Santa Anna. Houston's victory at San Jacinto (April 21, 1836) successfully ended the war for Texas, and he was subsequently elected the first president of the new republic.

Mirabeau Lamarr replaced Houston as President from 1838–1841 but Houston won re-election and served from 1841–1844. Following the American annexation of Texas, Houston served in the Senate for 14 years. But as sectional controversy grew and the threat of civil war became stronger, Houston's strong stand for preserving the Union, caused his defeat in 1859. He used his personal popularity to win election as governor that same year and again tried to keep Texas in the Union as secession began. The Texas legislature removed Houston from the governorship in 1861 when Texas seceded and joined the Southern confederacy. He retired from politics and died in 1863, while the Civil War still raged, as a political pariah in the state he had helped to create and with his beloved Union torn apart.

Two films showed Houston's early rise to political power in Tennessee before his military and political triumphs in Texas— *Man of Conquest* (1939) and *The Conqueror* (1917). The former has a wealth of historical personal detail such as his close relationship to the Cherokee, his rise to political prominence in Tennessee, his broken first marriage and, ultimately, his successful role as leader in the Texas rebellion. The latter covers much of the same ground in a more limited version but distorts events in his failed first marriage by having him leave his wife. Instead, she actually left him. *The First Texan* (1956) is an effective biography of that portion of Houston's life beginning with the time he left Tennessee, his military success in the war against Mexico and his election as first president of Texas.

The cinema, however, has ignored the later drama and tragedy of Houston's life. As far as Hollywood is concerned, Houston's career ends on a note of triumph and popularity. There is no mention of his loss of two public offices for his principled stand against secession. It leaves untouched his unsuccessful efforts to preserve the Union and prevent the coming wave of fratricidal warfare. There is no mention of the scorn he suffered in his final days. The entire story of his life would be a powerful parallel of ancient Greek dramatic tragedy. To paraphrase Euripides, "He whom the Gods would destroy, they first raise up." ■

How Uncle Sam Prepares (1917), Hanover.

A propaganda film advocating preparedness, the documentary opens with the figure of Uncle Sam asleep. After he is visited by the apparitions of famous personages of the past and present, he reads in the headlines of the sinking of a ship full of civilians. He suddenly springs to life. The remainder of the film shows the training of raw recruits and how they are turned into an effective fighting force for the army and navy. The film, released shortly before America's entry into World War I, also describes how food is prepared for large numbers of troops. ■

Howards of Virginia, The (1940), Col. *Dir.* Frank Lloyd; *Sc.* Sidney Buchman; *Cast includes:* Cary Grant, Martha Scott, Sir Cedric Hardwicke, Alan Marshall, Richard Carlson.

This historical drama set during the American Revolution describes in part the British oppression of the colonists and the ultimate result of the tyrannical acts—the revolt of the colonies. Cary Grant portrays a rugged backwoodsman who, with the help of his city-bred wife (Martha Scott), carves out a home in the wilderness. Years pass, and the family prospers. When conflict erupts between the colonists and the British, Grant, over the objections of his wife, sides with the patriots. His sons join in the fighting. Several historical incidents are re-enacted, including the Stamp Act riots, the Boston Tea Party and the hardships suffered by the troops at Valley Forge. Also shown are some of the major figures who helped to give birth to the fledgling nation—Patrick Henry, George Washington and Thomas Jefferson.

Based on Elizabeth Page's massive novel *The Tree of Liberty*, the drama covers only part of the original work. Much of the film was shot at the restoration village of Williamsburg, which adds to the realism of the production. However, the anti-British sentiments suggested by the film were poorly timed. In 1940, when the film was released, England was bogged down in World War II and threatened by a possible invasion from Nazi Germany. ■

Human Comedy, The (1943), MGM. *Dir.* Clarence Brown; *Sc.* Howard Estabrook; *Cast includes:* Mickey Rooney, Van Johnson, Donna Reed, Ralph Morgan, Marsha Hunt, James Craig.

A sentimental drama of an idyllic America, Mickey Rooney stars as a son who supports his family during World War II when his older brother (Van Johnson) leaves for the service. Rooney gets an after-school job at a telegraph office run by James Craig. Frank Morgan, as a telegraph operator who likes his liquor, befriends the young messenger. Jack Jenkins plays Rooney's inquisitive little brother, and Donna Reed appears as his sister. The film at times switches to Van Johnson and his army life where he becomes close friends with a fellow G.I. (John Craven). Meanwhile, the humor and tragedy of life in the small town go on. Rooney is hit with a dual tragedy when Morgan dies of a heart attack and he receives a telegram that his brother has been killed in action.

William Saroyan, who wrote the screenplay before he wrote his novel based on the script, pictures a fictional, Norman Rockell-like community steeped in patriotism and religion—a town where all the citizens are kindly, daughters accompany their mothers in singing spirituals and the young men look forward to settling in their home town. The war hardly intrudes upon the stability of this peaceful town. If this was not a realistic image of the nation, it was, at least, a picture of how many Americans envisioned themselves at the time. ■

Humming Bird, The (1924), Par. *Dir.* Sidney Olcott; *Sc.* Forrest Halsey; *Cast includes:* Gloria Swanson, Edward Burns, William Ricciardi.

A drama set in France before and during World War I, Gloria Swanson portrays a petty thief whose American lover has marched off to fight for France. The film depicts the arrival of American troops, showing thousands of doughboys marching through the streets of Paris as they prepare to take their places at the front. This World War I film was released at a time when American audiences had had their fill of war dramas although the story line has more to do with crime than war. However, the stirring scenes of the almost endless parade of American soldiers and the several scenes in the trenches almost overshadow the original plot. ■

Humoresque (1920). See Veterans. ■

Hun Within, The (1918), Artcraft. *Dir.* Chester Withey; *Sc.* Granville Warwick (D. W. Griffith); *Cast includes:* George Fawcett, Dorothy Gish, Charles Gerard, Douglas MacLean.

A domestic drama of World War I, the film centers on an American family of German descent. The father sends his son to Germany to study, but when World War I breaks out the boy joins the German army. His sweetheart back home breaks off her engagement to him and his father disowns him. When he returns as a German spy, he shoots his father during an altercation, wounding the old man. Meanwhile, the spy ring has planted a time bomb in a troop ship headed for France. An agent in the U.S. Secret Service, a new beau of the girl, helps to prevent the ship's destruction and assists in the roundup of the spy network. D.W. Griffith supervised the production of the film and wrote the screenplay under a pseudonym. ■

Hundred Days War. See Napoleonic Wars. ■

Hundred Years' War (1337–1453). France's rejection of the claim of English King Edward III to the throne of France by way of his mother Isabelle initiated this lengthy conflict. In 1337, when Edward's advisers assured him that Philip VI was weak and that he would be preoccupied with a crusade to the Holy Land, the king resumed his claim to the French throne. The English made gains at Crecy (1346) and Calais (1347) in the early stages of the war. They captured the French king and exchanged him for large land concessions. England's Richard II preferred a peaceful settlement, but the defiant French continued the conflict and soon regained their lost territory. Henry V at Agincourt (1415), using his archers and their long-bows strategically against the more heavily armored French army, temporarily halted France's gains. But Joan of Arc's victories at the siege of Orleans and the battle at Patay, which ultimately forced England to abandon the continent, ended that country's dreams of ruling France.

Few films deal with events of the Hundred Years' War. Those based on incidents in Joan of Arc's life, such as Cecil B. DeMille's *Joan the Woman* (1917), Victor Fleming's *Joan of Arc* (1948) and Otto Preminger's *St. Joan* (1957), all concern the English-French conflict, with the first two dramas providing recreations of the Battles of Orleans and Patay. ■

Hungarian Revolution (1956). Many Hungarians, chafing under rigid Soviet controls, resented the expulsion of Premier Imre Nagy, a moderate Communist nationalist, from the Hungarian Communist party in the Spring of 1956, after his failed attempt to secure some economic freedom from Soviet domination. Large scale popular discontent reached a boiling point on October 23, 1956. Riots and demonstrations broke out in Budapest in which demands were raised for free elections, economic reforms, withdrawal of Soviet forces and the reinstatement of Nagy.

Hungarian troops soon joined the rioters and helped to overthrow (October 25) the Communist government. A pro-Western, democratic administration under Nagy came into existence. Revolutionists took over public buildings and factories. Soviet troops began to withdraw on October 28, following Nagy's announcement of an agreement to do so. They were all out of the country by October 30. Nagy denounced the Warsaw Pact, a U.S.S.R.-dominated alliance of East European Communist states, and asked the U.N. to grant Hungary neutral status in the Cold War between the Communist bloc and Western-style democracies.

Soviet forces, numbering some 200,000 troops and several thousand armored vehicles, secretly regrouped on the Hungarian border and invaded the country on November 4. Despite fanatic resistance by Hungarian freedom fighters, the uprising was crushed by the end of the month. Appeals by the revolutionary government for assistance from the West and the U.N. went unheeded. A puppet hard-line Hungarian regime was installed under Janos Kadar, supported by a strong Soviet-armed presence. During the fighting,

over 100,000 Hungarians fled to the West. The brief conflict resulted in the deaths of 25,000 Hungarians and 7,000 Russians. Nagy was eventually seized and executed (1958) following a secret trial.

Unfortunately, only a few American-produced films touch upon the gallant Hungarian people who found for a short time a ray of light that brightened their hopes for independence and self-rule—only to have it obliterated by the long shadow of Soviet oppression. *The Beast of Budapest* (1958) recounts the developments that led to the uprising and depicts the ruthlessness of the Communist regime. Newsreel footage of the Russian tanks quelling the revolt adds a note of authenticity to the drama. *The Journey* (1959) concerns a group of travelers from various countries who are caught up in the political intrigue of the Hungarian revolt. Yul Brynner portrays a Soviet officer who suspects one of the travelers (Jason Robards, Jr.) of being a leader of the Hungarian revolt. ■

Hunters, The (1958), TCF. *Dir.* Dick Powell; *Sc.* Wendell Mayes; *Cast includes:* Robert Mitchum, Robert Wagner, Richard Egan, May Britt.

The Korean War, circa 1952, provides the background for this action drama of American airmen who flew their jet planes over Korea during the conflict. Robert Mitchum portrays a World War II air ace, a battle-hardened professional officer who is now squadron commander. A gutsy flier without a trace of fear, he is called "The Iceman" among his fellow airmen. He falls in love with the wife (May Britt) of one of his pilots. Lee Philips, as the wronged husband, suffers from fear of combat and starts to drink heavily. His wife beseeches Mitchum to help the younger pilot. During one of their missions, Philips is forced to bail out over enemy territory. Mitchum and another airman (Robert Wagner) join him on the ground and, together with the help of local natives, they return to their own lines. The incident makes a new man of Philips. The battle sequences concern the squadron's assignment to destroy the Communist planes in the vicinity of the Yalu River, which the Americans are not permitted to cross. ■

Huron Indians. Around the time of the American Revolution, the Hurons were living near Detroit, Michigan, and Sandusky, Ohio, where they became known as the Wyandot Indians. Though some of the tribe took part with Chief Pontiac in a combined Indian attack to drive the British out of Detroit in Pontiac's Wilderness War of the early 1760s in the Ohio Valley, they later became friendly with the British. The Hurons assisted the British in the American Revolution and the War of 1812. Few features used the Huron tribe as their main subject. However, the Hurons played somewhat important roles in films based on the works of James Fenimore Cooper, such as the silent and sound versions of *Last of the Mohicans* (1920, 1935) and *The Deerslayer* (1957). ■

Hutch of the U.S.A. (1924), Sterling. *Dir.* James Chapin; *Sc.* J. F. Natteford; *Cast includes:* Charles Hutchison, Edith Thornton, Frank Leigh, Ernest Adams.

Charles Hutchison stars as a stereotypical American hero who becomes entangled in a South American revolution. Hutch, a journalist, is sent to investigate events in Guadala where he falls in love with the ward of General Moreno. The general is planning to overthrow the president and make himself dictator. Hutch decides to join the revolution which ultimately fails. But Hutch gets the girl. Several battles occur with plenty of fighting on Hutch's part as he straightens things out almost single-handedly. There is some comic relief from Ernest Adams in this minor action film.

The continuous instability of countries south of the border gave impetus to a series of adventure dramas and satires during the 1910s and 1920s concerning revolution and general unrest. In many of these incidents it was more than one American who became involved in these entanglements. The U.S. often sent troops to such countries as Panama (1918–1920), Honduras (1919) and Guatemala (1920) either to protect American interests or its legation, to maintain order or to secure a neutral zone during an anticipated revolution. ■

I

I Cover the War (1937), U. Dir. Arthur Lubin; *Sc.* George Waggner; *Cast includes:* John Wayne, Gwen Gaze, Don Barclay, Pat Somerset.

A newsreel cameraman (John Wayne) helps to foil an Arab revolt, uncover the villainous leader and rescue a company of lancers in this romantic adventure. While on assignment in Mesopotamia, he and his assistant (Don Barclay) become embroiled in a native uprising stirred up by a revolutionary leader (Charles Brokaw). Wayne finds time to woo and win the niece of a British commandant, whose troop of lancers is threatened with annihilation by the hostile Arab rebels. The film is a low-budget affair but provides Wayne with a rare opportunity to temporarily step out of a western series he starred in for Lone Star Productions, a poverty-row studio.

Iraq had a sporadic history of domestic disturbances during the 1920s and 1930s. Universal, it seemed, used this collective background of desert turmoil as a loose pretext for *I Cover The War* (1937). The film is set during the Iraqi Rebellion of 1935. The ancient land of Mesopotamia was the basis for the modern Arab nation of Iraq after World War I. The League of Nations granted a mandate over the region to Great Britain who supported both the area's independence after centuries under Turkish control and the elevation of King Faisal to the throne. Britain had a close relationship with Faisal, and, after it relinquished the mandate in 1932, the two nations signed a treaty of friendship that included the granting of air bases to the British. Revolts broke out in 1935 against a new government organized by General Yasin Pasha el Hashimi, but they were quickly suppressed by the government.

The movie does not go into depth about the politics of the revolt other than to use the British presence in Iraq, incorrectly referred to by its pre-World War I name of Mesopotamia in the film, as a target for hostile actions by some desert tribesmen. Instead of subduing American Indians and western bad men, Wayne, this time, takes on the Arabs and comes up with the same result. ■

I Escaped From the Gestapo (1943). See Crime and War. ■

I Killed Geronimo (1950), Eagle Lion. Dir. Sam Neuman; *Sc.* Nat Tanchuck; *Cast includes:* James Ellison, Chief Thunder Cloud, Virginia Herrick.

Smugglers supply illegal rifles to hostile Apaches in this action drama. The U.S. Cavalry is assigned to capture or kill the marauding Indians as well as the smugglers. James Ellison portrays an army captain who manages to gain the trust of the outlaw gang. He also manages to capture Geronimo, played by Chief Thunder Cloud, during an Apache raid. Virginia Herrick provides the romantic interest for Ellison in this routine western. Thunder Cloud had portrayed the Apache chief previously in *Geronimo*, released in 1940.

The title represents the most inaccurate element of this chiefly fictitious plot. Geronimo spent his last years in an Alabama federal prison; was then sent to Fort Sill, Oklahoma, where he converted to Christianity and turned to farming; appeared in the 1904 St. Louis World's Fair; and dictated his autobiography in 1906. ■

I Love a Soldier (1944). See Home Front. ■

I Married a Communist (1950). See Cold War. ■

I Want My Man (1925). See Veterans. ∎

I Want You (1951), RKO. *Dir.* Mark Robson; *Sc.* Irwin Shaw; *Cast includes:* Dana Andrews, Dorothy McGuire, Farley Granger, Peggy Dow.

Dana Andrews and Dorothy McGuire portray a happily married couple whose lives, along with those of Andrews' family, are affected by the Korean War. This quiet, plausible drama captures the loves and fears of an average family as they respond to their country's mobilization. Andrews, as a veteran of World War II, is driven by conscience to answer his country's call. He decides to volunteer for this latest conflict—much to his wife's displeasure. His father, played by Robert Keith, has an especially poignant moment in the film when he reveals that he is not the World War I hero he has been masquerading as. Instead, he served as a general's toady during the war. Farley Granger, as Andrews' younger brother, is called to serve in the army. He reacts selfishly and immaturely, fretting that the war has interfered with his personal plans. Mildred Dunnock, as the mother, worries about her two sons since she has already lost one boy in action. Peggy Dow plays the draftee's fiancee.

Unlike the many home-front dramas of World War II—with their topics of rationing, the mobilization of women for defense work, housing shortages, wartime marriages, etc.— the films of the Korean conflict overwhelmingly focused on the combat aspect. Those which were not directly concerned with the fighting dealt with prisoners of war, the court martial of collaborators or related subjects set in Tokyo. ∎

I Was a Captive of Nazi Germany (1936), Malvina. *Sc.* Isobel Lillian Steele.

An anti-Nazi propaganda film, this semi-documentary concerns Isobel Lillian Steele's arrest and imprisonment in a women's prison in Germany. The film uses newsreel footage as well as staged scenes and actors to dramatize Steele's experiences as an American freelance member of the press who collaborates with an alleged Nazi official on a story about a wealthy baron and his friends. They are arrested by the secret police. Suddenly she is arrested and shipped to different prisons, always under the supervision of stern Nazi officials. Finally, under pressure of U.S. Senator Borah, she is reluctantly released. Stock footage portrays the history of Nazi Germany, but the best sequences are the ones showing the journalist's harsh incarceration. ∎

I Was a Communist for the FBI (1951). See Cold War. ∎

I Was a Male War Bride (1949). See Service Comedy. ∎

I Was an American Spy (1951), Mon. *Dir.* Lesley Selander; *Sc.* Sam Roeca; *Cast includes:* Ann Dvorak, Gene Evans, Douglas Kennedy, Richard Loo.

Ann Dvorak plays the title role in this weak drama, based on the true experiences of Claire Phillips during World War II. The film opens with the fall of Manila to the Japanese. After Mrs. Phillips' husband is killed during the Bataan death march, she joins a band of guerrillas led by Gene Evans. She then masquerades as an Italian and operates a Manila nightclub where she obtains bits of useful information which she gives to Evans. She is finally exposed and imprisoned, but Evans and his small force rescue her before she is executed. The film is based on a novel, *Manila Espionage*, by Claire Phillips and Myron B. Goldsmith and a *Reader's Digest* article. Mrs. Phillips received the Freedom Medal for her espionage activities. ∎

Ice Station Zebra (1968). See Cold War. ∎

Identity Unknown (1945). See Propaganda Films: World War II. ∎

If I Were King (1920), Fox. *Dir.* J. Gordon Edwards; *Sc.* E. Lloyd Sheldon; *Cast includes:* William Farnum, Fritz Lieber, Betsy Ross Clarke, Walter Law.

William Farnum portrays the roguish poet Francois Villon in this first screen adaptation of Justin Huntley McCarthy's popular novel and stage production. Villon, living a life of reckless abandon as a vagabond and thief who incidentally writes poems, gets an opportunity to act as the ruler of France for one week in this witty drama. Fritz Lieber plays the eccentric King Louis XI, who exhibits more than a trace of villainy in his own character. Betsy Ross Clarke, as the high-born Katherine, provides the romantic interest, while Walter Law plays a traitor. ∎

If I Were King (1938), Par. *Dir.* Frank Lloyd; *Sc.* Preston Sturges; *Cast includes:* Ronald Colman, Basil Rathbone, Frances Dee, Ellen Drew, C. V. France, Henry Wilcoxon.

Ronald Colman stars in this dramatic re-telling of the story of Francois Villon, the 15th-century poet-philosopher who was a hero and leader of the Parisian beggars, whores and pickpockets. Basil Rathbone, as a whimsical King Louis XI, appoints Villon grand constable of France. Villon accepts and meets the members of the king's court while ministering out justice with mercy and wisdom. Louis soon tires of the joke and is ready to put Villon to death when Paris is attacked by the Duke of Burgundy's forces. Villon quickly summons the rabble of Paris to defend the city and defeat the invaders. Other screen versions of the Villon tale include *The Beloved Rogue* (1928), a silent film starring John Barrymore in the title role, and two musical versions based on Rudolf Friml's operetta, *The Vagabond King*, one made in 1930 with Dennis King as Villon and the other in 1956 featuring Oreste as the beggar-poet.

The events in the film are not entirely accurate. Francois Villon (1431–1463) was already dead at the time of the Battle of Montlhery (July 13, 1465) between Charles the Bold, the last powerful Duke of Burgundy, and Louis XI. The king was forced to sign an unfavorable treaty which he later ignored. Charles was eventually defeated in 1477 in a war against the Swiss, after which Louis annexed Burgundy, a flourishing independent state whose cultural and political peak began in the late 1300s. Some historical records dispute the year of Villon's death, listing it simply as after 1463. Even so, Villon, who was exiled from France in that year, could not have participated in any military engagement. Finally, no battle or siege of Paris took place in the time period of the film. ■

If Moscow Strikes (1952). See Cold War. ■

I'll Be Seeing You (1944). See Veterans. ■

"I'll Never Heil Again" (1941). See War Humor. ■

I'll Say So (1918). See Spy Comedies. ■

Sergeant Glenn Ford, posing as a general, proves that "clothes make the man" by successfully leading G.I.s into battle. *Imitation General* (1958).

Imitation General (1958), MGM. *Dir.* George Marshall; *Sc.* William Bowers; *Cast includes:* Glenn Ford, Red Buttons, Taina Elg, Dean Jones, Kent Smith.

A sergeant (Glenn Ford) with American troops in France poses as a general in an effort to re-organize the G.I.s who are in disarray following a German offensive in this World War II comedy. Kent Smith portrays a general who believes that only an officer of his rank can restore order and confidence in the troops. He dies before he has a chance to carry out his beliefs. Ford, loyal to his commander, decides to masquerade as a general despite warnings by his buddy (Red Buttons). Nevertheless, the imitation general manages to inspire the troops and successfully leads them into battle against German machine guns and tanks. Taina Elg provides the romantic interest. ■

Immortal Sergeant, The (1943), TCF. *Dir.* John Stahl; *Sc.* Lamar Trotti; *Cast includes:* Henry Fonda, Maureen O'Hara, Thomas Mitchell, Allyn Joslyn, Reginald Gardiner.

A World War II drama of a handful of soldiers lost somewhere in the Libyan desert, the film depicts the influence of the patrol's sergeant on a shy corporal. Thomas Mitchell portrays the title character, a combat veteran of World War I who tries to teach all he knows about warfare to his corporal, played by Henry Fonda. When Mitchell is killed, Fonda is forced to take command of the remnant of the patrol. Originally consisting of 14 men, the unit is whittled down to four as they

Allied troops come under attack in North Africa early in World War II. *The Immortal Sergeant* (1943).

Japanese planes catch American defense forces at Pearl Harbor off guard on December 7, 1941. *In Harm's Way* (1965).

are confronted by the hostile desert and German soldiers. Fonda, strongly motivated by the dead sergeant, screws up enough courage and determination to get his men through to their lines as well as blow up a German camp. The first American film to dramatize the fighting in North Africa, provides vivid battle scenes, including an air attack on the patrol and several skirmishes between the Allied soldiers and German troops. The action, however, never dominates the human aspects of the story, especially the camaraderie between Mitchell and Fonda. Flashbacks provide some romantic interest between Fonda and Maureen O'Hara. ■

Impostor, The (1944), U. *Dir.* Julien Duvivier; *Sc.* Julien Duvivier; *Cast includes:* Jean Gabin, Richard Whorf, Allyn Joslyn, Ellen Drew, Ralph Morgan.

A World War II drama about the fall of France in 1940 and the emergence of Free French units in Africa, the film stars French actor Jean Gabin as a reformed criminal who turns hero. About to be executed for murder in France, Gabin escapes during a German air raid. He takes the identity and uniform of a dead soldier and enlists in the Free French forces where he is cited for bravery following his attack upon an Italian desert position. He confesses his impersonation to his officers and is broken in rank. Later, he once again distinguishes himself in battle, this time sacrificing his life by attacking a machine-gun position that is threatening his battalion. Ellen Drew provides the romantic interest in this rather slow-moving drama. This was one

of a handful of important films directed by Julien Duvivier, one of France's greatest directors, in his second trip to the U.S. ■

In Again-Out Again (1917). See Preparedness. ■

In Enemy Country (1968), U. *Dir.* Harry Keller; *Sc.* Edward Anhalt; *Cast includes:* Tony Franciosa, Anjanette Comer, Guy Stockwell, Tom Bell, Paul Hubschmid, Patric Knowles.

Allied forces, after suffering heavy losses at sea from a new type of torpedo invented by the Germans, assign secret agents to learn more about the weapon and where it is manufactured in this World War II action drama. A French intelligence officer (Tony Franciosa) assists Allied agents to infiltrate the plant where the torpedoes are made. An American air force officer (Guy Stockwell) accompanies the special force. Tom Bell plays a British explosives expert. Anjanette Comer, as a French spy, also provides the feminine interest. Paul Hubschmid portrays a Nazi Intelligence officer. Aided by the French underground, the team manages to appropriate one of the highly secret torpedoes which some of the members of the special force take back to England. Allied bombers, meanwhile, destroy the factory. ■

In Harm's Way (1965), Par. *Dir.* Otto Preminger; *Sc.* Wendell Mayes; *Cast includes:* John Wayne, Kirk Douglas, Patricia Neal, Tom Tryon, Paula Prentiss, Dana Andrews.

Director Otto Preminger blends the lives

and loves of U.S. Navy personnel with the efforts of the service to rebuild its military strength following the Japanese surprise attack at Pearl Harbor into a sprawling drama of World War II. John Wayne portrays a navy captain who falls in love with a nurse (Patricia Neal). This is the second time around for both. Kirk Douglas, as an executive officer who has lost his unfaithful wife in the Japanese raid, plays Wayne's friend. Wayne's spoiled son (Brandon de Wilde) from his first marriage is an arrogant young ensign who eventually matures when he begins to understand what his father stands for. Burgess Meredith, as a naval Intelligence officer and former Hollywood screenwriter, is Wayne's personal friend and is instrumental in Wayne's promotion.

Several effective action sequences show outnumbered American warships parrying with the Japanese Navy early in the war. These include an attack by several P.T. boats on an advancing Japanese fleet in which Wayne's son is killed in action and a battle between Wayne's handful of warships against the remains of the still superior Japanese fleet in which he loses a leg. Wayne, who earlier in the film is promoted to admiral, is put in charge of taking and securing a Japanese-held island while avoiding confrontation with the current but incompetent naval commander (Dana Andrews) in charge of operations. He outfoxes Andrews to the latter's embarrassment. The title derives from a quotation by John Paul Jones: "I wish to have no connection with any ship that does not sail fast, for I intend to go in harm's way . . ." ■

In Love and War (1958), TCF. Dir. Philip Dunne; *Sc.* Edward Anhalt; *Cast includes:* Robert Wagner, Dana Wynter, Jeffrey Hunter, Hope Lange, Bradford Dillman, Sheree North, France Nuyen, Mort Sahl.

The World War II drama focuses on three young marines who become close friends while in the service. Robert Wagner portrays a coward whose father was an alcoholic. Jeffrey Hunter plays a sergeant who comes from the wrong side of the tracks. He marries Hope Lange, who is carrying his child. Bradford Dillman plays the intellectual, the third member of the trio. He comes from a wealthy home but rejects all that his pompous father stands for. He returns home on leave to find his fiancee (Dana Wynter) an alcoholic and a tramp. Back on duty, the

Marine Sergeant Jeffrey Hunter leads his men against the Japanese on a Pacific island during World War II. *In Love and War* (1958).

marines invade a Japanese-held island. Wagner, in a heroic act, saves a fellow marine's life and receives a medal. Dillman's ideals are shattered as he grows disillusioned by the war. Hunter is killed while knocking out an enemy tank. When the war ends, Wagner visits Hunter's wife and child and is invited to visit again. We are left with the impression that he will ultimately care for his sergeant's family. Dillman returns to his Hawaiian girlfriend whom he met before leaving for overseas duty.

The first half of the film moves slowly as it develops characterization and relationships. The second half concerns the war segment which includes several brutal and realistic scenes. Comedian Mort Sahl provides the comic relief, one of the many highlights of the film. On board the troop transport he reads aloud from a handbook titled *Know Your Enemy*: "'The most fanatical of the enemy can be encouraged to surrender by offering him clean clothes, a bed and a warm meal.' Are they kidding?" a marine asks. "No," Sahl replies, "that's how I got in." On the island he suggests to a nervous marine: "Why don't you eat something?" "I keep throwing up," the soldier replies. "It's all part of nature's plan," Sahl explains. "It's protection against C rations." He answers a field telephone with: "Good morning, World War II." When Sahl is killed, both his humor and pain are laid to rest, giving them that particular poignancy which approaches that elusive boundary between comedy and tragedy. Sahl's death comes as a shock and a surprise, since rarely does the comic relief perish in Hollywood dramas. ■

"In Old Kentucky" (1909), Biograph. *Dir.* D. W. Griffith; *Sc.* Stanner Taylor; *Cast includes:* Henry B. Walthall, Kate Bruce, Owen Moore, Verner Clarges, Mary Pickford.

In this silent Civil War drama two brothers fight on opposite sides. The younger brother who has joined the Confederate cause is sent with dispatches through the Union lines and is captured by his own brother. He escapes and hides in his mother's home. The pursuing brother follows him and begins to search each room. When the Union son comes to his mother's bedroom where the fugitive is concealed, the mother threatens to shoot herself if he continues the search. He leaves quietly. The film shifts to the end of the war when the older brother, now an officer, returns home, as does the younger boy who has been wounded. They shake hands in reconciliation.

Griffith directed eleven one- and two-reel dramas which used the Civil War as background during his tenure with the Biograph studio. The reconciliation scene, a highlight and poignant moment in the film, anticipated a similar scene in the director's 1915 masterpiece, *The Birth of a Nation.* ■

In Our Time (1944), WB. *Dir.* Vincent Sherman; *Sc.* Ellis St. Joseph, Howard Koch; *Cast includes:* Ida Lupino, Paul Henreid, Nancy Coleman, Mary Boland, Victor Francen.

A World War II romantic drama set before and during the Nazi invasion of Poland, the film stars Ida Lupino as an Englishwoman who, while visiting Warsaw, falls in love with and marries Polish aristocrat Paul Henreid. His family objects to the union on social grounds since Lupino comes from a lower social class. Together, they modernize the family farm and derive a bountiful harvest which is shared with other farmers. But the Nazi invasion shatters the couple's dreams as the Polish people resort to a scorched earth policy, destroying any crops that might aid the advancing enemy. As Lupino and Henreid leave their beloved fields, they know that they will one day return.

One-time silent screen star Alla Nazimova, who appeared in the World War I drama *War Brides*, plays Henreid's mother. She also portrayed Robert Taylor's mother several years earlier in *Escape* (1940).

Just as the French war classic *Grand Illusion* (1938) depicted how World War I contributed to the collapse of the old order in Europe and the rise of democracy, *In Our Time* suggests a similar theme when Henreid defies his family with its strict class distinctions and marries Lupino. The film is also a tribute to the heroic spirit of the Polish people during the early days of the war. ■

In the Navy (1941). See Service Comedy. ■

In the Palace of the King (1923), Goldwyn. *Dir.* Emmett Flynn; *Sc.* June Mathis; *Cast includes:* Edmund Lowe, Blanche Sweet, Hobart Bosworth, Pauline Starke, Sam de Grasse, Lucien Littlefield.

The drama takes place in the royal court of Spain during the Battle of Lepanto. Philip II, who is jealous of the military victories and popularity of his warrior-brother, Don John of Austria, dispatches his brother to fight a holy war against the Moors. Although at one point the outcome of the conflict seems bleak for Don John, he manages to emerge victorious and returns to Spain. An attempt is made on the warrior's life, initiated by Philip. But Don John once again triumphs, this time winning the heroine, Dolores Mendoza (Blanche Sweet). An earlier version of the drama appeared in 1915. Directed by Fred E. Wright, the film featured E. J. Ratcliffe, Richard C. Travers, Arleen Hackett and Lewis Edgard.

There was much rejoicing throughout Christian Europe when the allied fleets of Spain, Venice, the Papal states, Malta, Genoa and Savoy, under the command of Don John of Austria, defeated a massive Turkish fleet led by Ali Pasha. The Battle of Lepanto is considered one of the greatest sea engagements in history and served to temporarily check Turkish expansion in the western Mediterranean.

War had broken out between the Turkish Ottoman empire and Venice in 1570 when the latter refused to cede Cyprus to the Turks. Spain joined Venice in the war later that year. Pope Pius V organized a Holy League against the Turks in 1571. Don John, natural brother of Spain's King Philip, was placed in command of a powerful Christian fleet of 208 galleys at Messina, Sicily. He inflicted a serious defeat upon the Turks who, out of an armada of about 230 galleys, had 50 sunk and 130 captured by the European allies. The allies liberated some 15,000 enslaved Christians. This was the last major sea engagement using oar-propelled warships.

As we can see, the film, with its focus on jealousy and court intrigue, manages to include the appropriate historical figures—such as Philip II and Don John—but then concocts a histrionic plot filled with routine derring-do and romance. ■

"In the Shenandoah Valley" (1908). See Battles of the Shenandoah Valley. ■

In the Year of the Pig (1969), Cinetree. *Dir.* Emile de Antonio.

A documentary critical of America's role in the Vietnam War, the film states its point of view through the use of stock footage, interviews and speeches. The work traces the history of the conflict from the days of French colonialism of the 1940s to the collapse of Diem's regime and the Paris negotiations. A few rare scenes from the 1930s reveal a peaceful Saigon with sidewalk cafes fashioned after Paris. There are several interviews with important figures and journalists as well as speeches by American politicians and military leaders, including Presidents Johnson and Nixon and General Le May. The film particularly finds fault with the lack of American credibility in its reports to the American people and other countries. Footage was borrowed from French, American, North Vietnamese, British, German and other sources. ■

Inchon (1981), One Way Productions. *Dir.* Terence Young; *Sc.* Robin Moore, Laird Koenig; *Cast includes:* Laurence Olivier, Jacqueline Bisset, Ben Gazzara, Richard Roundtree.

This inept large-scale action drama recounts the landing of United Nations forces at the port of Inchon and the ensuing battle against the North Koreans. The production company, associated with Reverend Moon, is largely responsible for the emphasis on religion in the film. Laurence Olivier portrays General MacArthur who is helped spiritually as he directs the bold landing and counterattack. Ben Gazzara, as a brave marine officer, manages to find time to romance Jacqueline Bisset. Richard Roundtree portrays a tough sergeant. Discounting the poor acting and weak script, the film provides several realistically staged action sequences. The production was a joint Korean and American venture. ■

Incident at Phantom Hill (1966), U. *Dir.* Earl Bellamy; *Sc.* Frank Nugent, Ken Pettus; *Cast includes:* Robert Fuller, Jocelyn Lane, Dan Duryea, Tom Simcox, Linden Chiles.

One million dollars in gold becomes the focal point of this Civil War drama set during the last days of the conflict. Confederate troops ambush a Union wagon train, steal the gold shipment and conceal it in a cave. Five Union soldiers, two of whom are officers (Robert Fuller and Tom Simcox), are assigned to recover the treasure. The captured rebel leader, Barlow (Dan Duryea), agrees to take them to the gold in return for his release. Following several Indian attacks and some treachery from the rebel, the troopers kill Barlow and recover the gold. Little of the Civil War comes across in this minor drama, the conflict serving only as a gimmick to initiate the plot. Jocelyn Lane, as a woman of experience, joins the search party and provides the romantic interest. ■

"India at War" (1942). See "The March of Time." ■

Indian Fighter, The (1955), UA. *Dir.* Andre de Toth; *Sc.* Frank Davis, Ben Hecht; *Cast includes:* Kirk Douglas, Elsa Martinelli, Walter Abel, Walter Matthau, Eduard Franz.

Kirk Douglas, as the title character, leads a wagon train through hostile Sioux country in this adventure drama filmed on location in Oregon. The plotting provides for a suspenseful Indian assault on a frontier stockade. The war is brought to a halt when Douglas hands over several unscrupulous white men to Red Cloud, the Sioux chieftain (Eduard Franz). Italian actress Elsa Martinelli, as a pretty Indian, provides the romantic interest. Walter Abel plays the captain of the military outpost. Walter Matthau, in one of his rare role as a "heavy," enacts a troublemaker who stirs up hatred between the Sioux and the soldiers. ■

Indian Mutiny of 1857–1858. The uprising of Indian soldiers against their British rulers was brought under control only when the British employed a large army against the sepoys and fiercely punished those they considered rebels. The mutiny was attributed to two general causes. The Indian soldiers objected to biting open British cartridges greased with animal fats. This was brought out in *King of the Khyber Rifles* (1953) with

Tyrone Power and *Bengal Brigade* (1954) starring Rock Hudson. A British colonel aptly explains the blunder in the latter film. "The first cartridges that were made for the new rifles were greased with a concoction of beef and pork fat. As the Hindus considered themselves damned if they eat beef and the Moslems are no better off if they eat pork, with one master stroke of stupidity we very nearly succeeded in alienating the entire Indian army."

The second cause was more deeply rooted in the abuses of the East India Company, including excessive taxation, removal of Indian leaders and the introduction of unpopular land-reform laws, none of which are dealt with in the films. The British eventually replaced company control with government rule. The mutinous troops, fearing that the British intended to end the Mogul Empire, captured Delhi and declared the elderly Mogul as their rightful emperor. The sepoys gained control of other cities as well. Following the slaughter of 200 British women and children at Cawnpore in 1857, British forces sought vengeance. Atrocities were committed by both sides until the natives were finally defeated in June 1858.

Several early silent films dealt directly with the mutiny. "The Sepoy's Wife" (1910), a short drama, concerns an English regimental physician who saves the life of a sepoy's child. This act is repaid when the child's mother rescues the doctor's family as well as the besieged fort during the Indian Mutiny. *The Campbells Are Coming* (1915), directed by Francis Ford, concentrated directly on the battles between the British and natives. The film conveyed much of the horror and violence of the brief but bloody war. *The Beggar of Cawnpore* (1916), starring H.B. Warner as a doctor addicted to morphine, includes several large-scale battles between the rebellious sepoys and British troops. ■

Indian Uprising (1952), Col. *Dir.* Ray Nazarro; *Sc.* Kenneth Gamet, Richard Schayer; *Cast includes:* George Montgomery, Audrey Long, Carl Benton Reid.

Apache chief Geronimo once again goes on the warpath when unscrupulous whites seek out gold deposits found on Indian land in this outdoor drama. George Montgomery portrays a U.S. Cavalry captain assigned to keep peace between Apaches and settlers. When an Indian uprising erupts, in which

Geronimo (Miguel Inclan) swears to wipe out the army post, Montgomery goes into action and squashes the potential massacre. The Apache chief is captured. Audrey Long provides the romantic interest. Joe Sawyer and John Call, as army sergeants, supply some comic relief. Several lively skirmishes and full-scale battles enliven this otherwise routine tale. ■

Indian wars (1675–1890). No other series of events in American history has produced a human tragedy of such extended proportions and mutual cruelty as the Indian wars. From colonial times until the end of the 19th century, white-Indian contact often resulted in violence of the most personal and vengeful nature. Hollywood for decades emphasized with almost metronomic consistency the antagonism that existed between the cultures. At the same time it colored historical events with stereotypes, distortion and outright misinformation under the guise of entertainment.

The most important cause of this conflict was a contest for control of the land. North American Indians, most of whom were seminomadic hunters and gatherers, depended completely on nature to supply their basic necessities, tools and simple comforts. The size and number of spreading white settlements greatly interfered with the Indians' traditional relationship to the land and their very survival.

Part of the difficulty stemmed from the different attitudes of the two cultures towards land ownership. Indians practiced communal land ownership and held land in reverence as the source of life. Land was not viewed as a commodity that could be sold. Especially in early property dealings between whites and the natives, many Indians believed they had merely granted permission to settlers to share the land's bounty rather than give its exclusive use to one side. The great Shawnee chief, Tecumseh, expounded this view in 1810. Indians, he said ". . . consider the land their common property . . . for it never was divided, but belongs to all. Sell a country! Why not sell the air, the clouds and the great sea, as well as the earth? Did not the Great Spirit make them all for the use of his children?" These issues were rarely addressed in Hollywood's numerous cavalry-vs.-Indians films.

Ignored or blatantly broken treaties often

initiated a dispute. *Tomahawk* (1951), an otherwise unexceptional film, clearly dramatized the point that a string of broken treaties and other abuses precipitated the Sioux uprising of the late 1800s. Geronimo led the Chiricahua Apache into war against U.S. forces in 1876 when the federal government abolished a treaty guaranteeing his tribal reservation. Furthermore, the government directed his tribe to move to another, more arid, location outside their traditional hunting grounds. Not until after World War II, when Hollywood began to explore the theme of racial prejudice in general, did film studios emphasize the long chain of broken agreements to which Indians were subjected.

In some cases corrupt dealings led to other problems. A few Indian chiefs were occasionally "mellowed" by liquor into agreeing to cede portions of a tribe's territory. In other instances, the written terms of a treaty did not agree with the verbal declarations made to Indian leaders. Hollywood showed how whites used alcohol to exploit and incite some braves in such films as Fritz Lang's *Western Union* (1941), John Ford's *Fort Apache* (1948), Lloyd Bacon's *The Great Sioux Uprising* (1953) and Nathan Juran's *Drums Along the River* (1954).

But the story of the Indian wars is more than simple Indian-white conflict. In a number of instances, Indians became the willing allies of white forces in clashes with other tribes. The Mohicans of lower New England and upstate New York supported the English colonists in conflicts with other tribes. Crazy Horse, despite his history of antagonism towards whites, volunteered to send Sioux warriors to assist the army in fighting the Nez Perce. Sometimes, rival Indian tribes became enmeshed in a larger conflict between white nations as happened in the French and Indian War where the Iroquois supported the English and the Algonquins sided with the French. The many film versions of James Fenimore Cooper's novels of early America reflect this.

In general, a number of stereotypes appear in films about Indian warfare. Many dramas depict natives as treacherous attackers who waylaid wagon trains and ambushed U.S. troops. But movies usually failed to go into the causes of these raids which were often a response to encroachment into Indian territory. Early American films such as *Call of the Blood* (1913) generally portrayed unprovoked Indian attacks upon settlers and pio-

neer wagon trains. Hollywood produced both fictitious and historical large-scale Indian killings of whites such as the Fetterman Massacre (1866), shown in *Tomahawk*. However, savagery and butchery were not restricted to one side. Few films portray equally vicious attacks by the army that tore into the camps of peaceful Indians and conducted an orgy of indiscriminate killing. Two exceptions are Ralph Nelson's *Soldier Blue* (1970) and Arthur Penn's *Little Big Man* (1970).

Sometimes, as in the Battle of Wounded Knee (1890), accumulated tension and suspicion caused an incident to explode into an unintended battle. The early silent film *The Adventures of Buffalo Bill* (1914), virtually the only screen re-enactment of the clash, failed to show the slaughter of Indian women and children. William "Buffalo Bill" Cody, who acted as producer, claimed the film was historically accurate.

Hollywood, in the post-World War II era, reflected a changing national mood toward minorities. Stereotypes became unpopular for several reasons. Veterans of different ethnic, religious and racial backgrounds returned from military service with a greater sense of equality. In addition, the 1950s witnessed a rise in the black civil rights movement. Hollywood, reflecting this social transformation, developed a greater sensitivity in its portrayal of minorities. The film industry demonstrated greater balance in depicting the causes of Indian-white conflict. Delmer Daves' *Broken Arrow* (1950), with James Stewart, began a trend that showed Indians as victims of injustice rather than the conventional savage transgressor.

Movies tended to feature a very narrow and selective group of Indian leaders—Geronimo, Cochise, Crazy Horse and Sitting Bull—with varying degrees of historical inaccuracy. Geronimo even met an untimely death in the routine western *I Killed Geronimo* (1950), though in real life he became a celebrity who rode in the presidential parade of Theodore Roosevelt, authored a biography and died peacefully at the age of 80 early in the twentieth century.

In contrast, Tecumseh, considered by his white foes and military historians as a military and political genius with tremendous powers of oratory, appears only briefly as a screen character. Similar superficial treatment was accorded to Iroquois chief Joseph Brandt, who played a prominent role in the

American Revolution by aligning his Mohawks to the British. Chief Pontiac of the Ottawas, who headed a powerful campaign against whites in the Ohio valley, is poorly represented in the weak drama *Battles of Chief Pontiac* (1952). Other Indian leaders, such as Broken Hand in *White Feather* (1955), Yellow Hand in *The Plainsman* (1936) and Acoma in *New Mexico* (1951) received inadequate treatment on the screen.

While portraying the cavalry in a generally heroic role, Hollywood neglected to bring out the superb military leadership of such war chiefs as Chief Joseph of the Nez Perce, the Apache's Geronimo and Chief Kintpuash (Captain Jack) of the Modocs. They each eluded, held off and sometimes defeated well-equipped forces many times the size of their bands. Contrary to their screen image, Indians generally suffered far fewer casualties than U.S. troops did.

Movies usually characterized Indian leaders as having limited speaking ability and incapable of handling a complex concept. They are also shown as overly dignified and somber. In reality, Indian leaders sometimes expressed their views in almost Shakespearean eloquence. One wonders what the effect on a general audience would be if it heard the actual words of Chief Joseph making his final surrender speech and finishing with the phrase, "I shall fight no more, forever." Or Crazy Horse's dying words to his guards after having a bayonet plunged into his midsection: "Let me go, my friends. You have hurt me enough." Or Tecumseh's needling comment to General Harrison during negotiations over a land treaty: "How can we have confidence in the white people? When Jesus Christ came upon the earth, you nailed Him to a cross and killed Him . . . I shall now be glad to know what is your determination about the land."

The most outstanding Indian leaders spoke this way because they came out of an oral, pre-written culture in which a chief gained his position by a combination of war deeds and the ability to influence others through speechmaking. He could not order braves into battle, he could only persuade them to follow his leadership.

"History," according to a French philosopher, "never embraces more than a small part of reality." In Hollywood's version of the history of the Indian wars, even that small part of reality too often turned into a crafted falsehood to satisfy the gods of entertainment and prejudice. See also specific Indian chiefs, tribes, wars and battles. ■

Informer, The (1935), RKO. *Dir.* John Ford; *Sc.* Dudley Nichols; *Cast includes:* Victor McLaglen, Heather Angel, Preston Foster, Wallace Ford, Margot Grahame.

Director John Ford turned out a forceful and poignant drama of the Irish Rebellion, based on Liam O'Flaherty's novel. The film tells the tragic story of Gypo Nolan (Victor McLaglen), a slowwitted drifter who betrays his friend Frankie (Wallace Ford), a fugitive patriot. He turns him in to the British forces in exchange for a handful of money. Frankie is killed trying to escape and Gypo, in a vain attempt to forget what he has done, foolishly spends the money in a night of drunken revelry. He is accused of betrayal by a rebel court and finally confesses. He escapes his captors but is soon tracked down and mortally wounded.

Ford, who had made *The Lost Patrol* the previous year with McLaglen and screenwriter Nichols, used simple sets, creative lighting and fog to give the film a stark, unreal atmosphere that underscores the hellish night the tormented Gypo spends before his conscience overtakes him. The director employed extensive biblical images and allusions (pieces of silver, Judas) as he carefully developed his characters. The film won Oscars for Best Actor, Director, Screenplay and Musical Score. O'Flaherty's novel was previously filmed in England in 1929 as a silent feature. ■

"Inside Nazi Germany" (1938). See "The March of Time." ■

Inside North Vietnam (1967), Felix Greene. *Dir.* Felix Greene.

A documentary about the effects of the Vietnam War on the people of North Vietnam, the film, blatantly opposed to America's policy, points out that the U.S. bombing has resulted in many dead and wounded civilians as well as in the destruction of their homes and villages. Other scenes attempt to show the North Vietnamese as serene and appealing people as they go about their daily routines working in the rice fields and repairing bridges and roads. A captured American pilot, in an interview, voices his disapproval of his country's policies concerning the war.

The film pulls out all emotional stops as it holds the camera on a child wounded during a bombardment. ■

Inside the Lines (1918, 1930). See Spy Films: the Silents. ■

"Insurrection, The" (1915), Lubin. *Dir.* George Terwilliger; *Sc.* George Terwilliger; *Cast includes:* Ormi Hawley, Earl Metcalfe, Herbert Fortier.

A weak silent drama about Mexico and its continuous revolutions, the story tells how the U.S. Navy takes control of the chief town. The insurrectionists plan to kill several American sailors, but the plot fails. A slight romance is intertwined in this short film.

The film is based on actual events. The arrest of a few American sailors by Mexican troops expanded into an incident of international importance and almost led to war between the two countries. When an American admiral demanded that the officer responsible be disciplined and the stars and stripes be raised and saluted, Mexico's President Huerta refused. President Wilson fumed at the response and ordered the shelling of Veracuz. U.S. Marines then invaded the port. More than a dozen lost their lives. ■

International Lady (1941). See Spy Films: the Talkies. ■

International Settlement (1938), TCF. *Dir.* Eugene Forde; *Sc.* Lou Breslow, John Patrick; *Cast includes:* Dolores Del Rio, George Sanders, June Lang, Dick Baldwin.

The drama blends newsreel footage of the Sino-Japanese War with the plot of gunrunners and hijackers in strife-torn China. George Sanders portrays an American adventurer who poses as a smuggler so that a shipment of illegal contraband can be freed, but he ends up getting captured by hijackers. The Japanese bombing of Shanghai saves him from his captors. The gunrunners are busy shipping arms and ammunition to China although the film takes no side concerning political issues. Dolores Del Rio appears as the heroine of this low-budget action feature. ■

International Squadron (1941), WB. *Dir.* Lothar Mendes; *Sc.* Barry Trivers, Kenneth Gamet; *Cast includes:* Ronald Reagan, Olympe Bradna, James Stephenson, William Lundigan, Joan Perry.

A World War II drama about an American pilot who ferries Lockheeds across the Atlantic to England, the film stars Ronald Reagan as a conceited flier responsible for the deaths of two fellow airmen. He joins the Royal Air Force, learns the value of teamwork and abandons his recklessness. Between flights, he finds time to romance a French driver (Olympe Bradna) for the R.A.F. Reagan redeems himself when he is killed on a dangerous mission to destroy a munitions dump somewhere in France. The low-budget film is a remake of the studio's *Ceiling Zero* (1936), which starred James Cagney and Pat O'Brien. ■

Into No Man's Land (1928), Commonwealth. *Dir.* Cliff Wheeler; *Sc.* Elsie Werner; *Cast includes:* Tom Santschi, Betty Blythe, Josephine Norman, Crawford Kent.

The film is a drama about a big-time gang leader (Tom Santschi) whose daughter falls in love with the local district attorney. To avoid arrest and embarrassment to his daughter, Santschi enlists in the army and is sent overseas to France. He returns after being wounded in battle, but his daughter does not recognize him because of his scars. The D.A., his son-in-law, however, identifies him as the gang leader. Several thrilling battle sequences of the war enhance the film. ■

Intolerance (1916), Wark. *Dir.* D. W. Griffith; *Sc.* D. W. Griffith; *Cast includes:* Mae Marsh, Fred Turner, Robert Harron, Sam De-Grasse, Bessie Love, Eugene Pallette, Constance Talmadge, Elmer Clifton.

Griffith, encouraged by the critical and commercial success of *The Birth of a Nation* (1915), directed an even more ambitious drama. The film, which runs almost four hours, is comprised of four stories, each exploring the theme of intolerance—Christ's conflict with Rome and the Pharisees, the massacre of St. Bartholemew in France, the fall of Babylon and the struggle between workers and capitalists in twentieth-century America. The film ends with apocalyptic visions of battle scenes, weapons of war, the destruction of a city—until bands of angels stop the chaos and slaughter. The scene then shifts to children playing in the sunshine while the weapons of destruction, partially covered by flowers, decay in the background.

Griffith was able to tie all four stories together through his central theme as well as his secondary motif—"love's struggle throughout the ages." His massive sets stunned the audiences of his day and are still impressive after decades of film spectacles. Some of the scenes in the "Babylon" sequence utilized more than 15,000 extras. But his simpler images were just as effective; e.g., the opening one that is the same as that which closes the film—the timeless image of a woman rocking a cradle.

While *The Birth of a Nation* directly influenced Hollywood in respect to the numerous spectacles that were to follow, *Intolerance* would have more far-reaching effects. Its mature subject matter, emotional intensity and artistic integrity inspired filmmakers both in America and in other countries, including Sergei Eisenstein in the Soviet Union. ∎

Introduction to the Enemy (1975), IPC Films. *Cast includes:* Jane Fonda, Tom Hayden.

A pro-North Vietnamese documentary starring the husband-and-wife team of Tom Hayden and Jane Fonda during their journey to that country, the film results in a simplistic view of the war issues. Scenes focus on the ruins left in the wake of American bombers and the work of the people in trying to rebuild their land. Fonda and Hayden conduct a series of interviews with different North Vietnamese citizens. In one scene the American couple are seen playing frisbee as the natives look on. The film was sponsored by the Indo-China Peace Campaign. ∎

Invaders, The (1929), Big Productions. *Dir.* J. P. McGowan; *Sc.* William Sterret; *Cast includes:* Bob Steele, Edna Aslin, Thomas Lingham, Bud Osborne.

An action drama of cavalry days in the old West, the film stars cowboy actor Bob Steele. He and his sister are rescued after an Indian attack on their wagon train—he by a colonel and the girl by the Indians. Years later Steele, a lieutenant under his stepfather, falls in love with the colonel's daughter. His sister is the adopted daughter of an Indian chief. When the soldiers try to move the natives to a reservation, a battle ensues as the Indians attack the fort. At the end, the brother and sister reunite. Several rousing action sequences add some life to this familiar tale. ∎

Invaders From Mars (1953). See Science Fiction Wars. ∎

Invasion of the Body Snatchers (1956). See Science Fiction Wars. ∎

Invasion U.S.A. (1952). See Future Wars. ∎

Invisible Agent (1942). See Spy Films: the Talkies. ∎

Iowa Under Fire (1924), Pictorial Sales Bureau.

A documentary of Iowa troops during World War I, the film traces their training, landings in France and England, several battles and eventual journey home. The doughboys saw action in several battles, including those at Alsace, Chatteau-Thierry and Argonne. After the Armistice the troops are seen entering Germany. This was one of a series of "Under Fire" documentaries depicting the exploits of troops from different states. ∎

Iraqi Rebellion of 1935. See *I Cover the War* (1937). ∎

Ireland in Revolt (1921), American Film Co. *Dir.* Captain Edwin F. Weigle.

A silent documentary of the contemporary conflict in Ireland, the film was shot by Captain Edwin Weigle, a member of the U.S. Signal Corps, under the sponsorship of the Chicago *Tribune*. Scenes include the capture of a nationalist by the Black and Tans, a raid on a suspected I.R.A. headquarters and the burned-out houses of either collaborators or rebels that mark the streets of Belfast as a reminder of the turmoil. Early scenes show the beauty of Irish landscapes and a land of peace as a contrast, underscoring the irony and tragedy of the sequences that follow. The film succeeds in remaining neutral in its selection of visual material and titles. ∎

Irish rebellions. England's influence in Ireland goes back to the twelfth century when Pope Adrian granted control over Ireland to England's Henry II. There have been numerous Irish rebellions through the centuries against efforts to impose British rule. The dispute also took a religious turn in the 1500s as Irish nationalists fought attempts by the British crown to impose Protestantism on an overwhelmingly Catholic Irish culture. The British, after putting down an Irish rebellion in the 17th century, sought to populate the northern counties (Ulster) with Scottish and English Protestants. As a result, a religious civil war has existed between paramilitary forces representing the two groups.

One uprising, perhaps motivated by the French Revolution, occurred in 1798. *Captain Lightfoot* (1955), starring Rock Hudson and Barbara Rush, presents a superficial treatment of this revolt. Although Britain offered home rule to the island in the mid-1800s, the Catholic majority continued to support the idea of independence. In 1905 the Sinn Fein ("Ourselves Alone") nationalist movement was born and its leaders insisted on an independent Irish state. However, the Protestant minority, concentrated in Ulster, were unwilling to be ruled by a Catholic state, and preferred to retain their ties with England. By 1914 each group had organized its own paramilitary unit.

Catholic Irish nationalists initiated the 1916 Easter Uprising with the aim of securing independence. They took control of part of Dublin and declared Ireland a republic. But superior British forces compelled the dissidents to surrender within a week. The British executed the rebel leaders and carried out widespread arrests. John Ford's *The Plough and the Stars* (1937), a weak, stagy adaptation of Sean O'Casey's play, is set during the Easter week uprising and conveys some of the anxieties of the rebels and their families.

Britain partitioned Ireland in 1922 as part of a new home rule bill, into a predominantly Protestant Ulster in the north and the Catholic Irish Free State in the south as self-governing entities in the British Empire. The Irish Republican Army, chiefly representing Catholic nationalists, refused to accept the partition and has since waged an intermittent guerrilla war against British forces in the North. The Ulster Defense Force, a Protestant paramilitary organization, in turn, conducted acts of terrorism against suspected nationalist supporters. The Irish Free State (1922–37) declared its independence in 1937 and became the nation of Eire. The two factions are still locked in conflict in Ulster where the Catholic minority claims it is the victim of economic discrimination.

Whether because of the large and influential Irish population in the U.S. or some vague similarity between the Irish cause and that of the American Revolution, films of the Rebellion are generally sympathetic toward the nationalists. Not unlike some American Civil War dramas, a few films involve a plot in which lovers represent opposing sides. *Beloved Enemy* (1936), starring Merle Oberon as the titled daughter of a British dignitary and Brian Aherne as a noble leader of the Irish rebels, condemns the senseless slaughter on both sides. Occasionally a love triangle is introduced as in *Whom the Gods Destroy* (1916) where two close friends, one an Irish patriot and the other an officer in the English navy, are in love with the same young woman.

Others movies concern betrayal, greed, hatred and violence. One such dramatic gem, John Ford's *The Informer* (1935), tells the story of Gypo Nolan (Victor McLaglen), an oafish drifter who, for a handful of money, betrays his friend Frankie (Wallace Ford), a hunted patriot. *Shake Hands With the Devil* (1959), starring James Cagney as a ruthless rebel leader, is a tense drama about an idealist who, once he has turned killer, finds he cannot end his thirst for violence.

At least two documentaries dealt with the Irish Rebellion— *Ireland in Revolt* (1921), which remains neutral in its study of the strife-torn country, and *World in Revolt* (1934), covering several conflicts including the Irish troubles. ∎

Iron Curtain, The (1948). See Cold War. ∎

Iron Glove, The (1954), Col. *Dir.* William Castle; *Sc.* Jesse Lasky, Jr., DeVallon Scott, Douglas Heyes; *Cast includes:* Robert Stack, Ursula Thiess, Richard Stapley, Charles Irwin.

A Scottish prince attempts to gain the English throne of King George I in this 18th century drama. Richard Stapley portrays James Stuart, the Scottish pretender, who ends up not with the crown but with a pretty wife and heir. Robert Stack plays his loyal and principal swordsman in his struggle for power. Ursula Thiess provides the romantic interest in this action film. Alan Hale, Jr. plays Stack's Irish sidekick. ∎

Iron Major, The (1943), RKO. *Dir.* Ray Enright; *Sc.* Aben Kandel, Warren Duff; *Cast includes:* Pat O'Brien, Ruth Warrick, Robert Ryan, Leon Ames.

Pat O'Brien portrays the once-famous football coach, Frank Cavanaugh, in this biographical drama. The film traces Cavanaugh's coaching career at Holy Cross, Dartmouth and Fordham, where his pep talks and high moral standards inspired hundreds who played for and worked with him. During World War I he is sent to France where he is killed in action. Ruth Warrick plays his wife. Robert Ryan portrays his priest and former teammate. Leon Ames enacts his confidant in this routine story about one of America's popular heroes whose final words epitomize his life: "Fight for what you believe in and believe in three things—love of God . . . love of country . . . and love of family." ∎

Iron Triangle, The (1989), Scotti Brothers. *Dir.* Eric Weston; *Sc.* Eric Weston, John Bushelman, Larry Hilbrand; *Cast includes:* Beau Bridges, Haing S. Ngor, Johnny Hallyday, Liem Whatley, James Ishida.

Just as *All Quiet on the Western Front* (1930) gave a human face to the enemy by unfolding World War I through the point of view of a German soldier, *The Iron Triangle* attempts a similar theme through a Viet Cong guerrilla during the Vietnam War. Ho (Liem Whatley), an idealistic 19-year-old Vietnamese soldier, captures Capt. Keene (Beau Bridges) who is on a scouting mission. But Ho has clashes with Khoi (James Ishida), an ambitious Communist Party official who dislikes Ho as much as dislikes the American captain.

The remainder of the drama concerns the relationships between these men during their journey north. Ho, who wishes to get full credit for the capture and to protect Keene from Khoi's sadistic aims, breaks away with his prisoner from the overzealous party member. Soon Ho and Keene form a bond as they grow to respect each other. "We couldn't have been more different," Keene says at one point during a voice-over, "but maybe we couldn't have been more alike." Ho suddenly fades into the jungle, leaving his captive free to return to his unit. The film, which attempts to bring out the humanity on both sides of a conflict, reportedly is based in part on the diary of a Viet Cong soldier. ∎

Iroquois Trail, The (1950), UA. *Dir.* Phil Karlson; *Sc.* Richard Schayer; *Cast includes:* George Montgomery, Brenda Marshall, Glenn Langan, Reginald Denny.

The French and Indian War provides the background for this weak outdoor drama about treacherous Indian guides, British and French soldiers and heroes and heroines. Set in the St. Lawrence and Hudson valleys where the British and French battle for con-

trol of this territory, the plot concerns a British Indian guide (Sheldon Leonard) who betrays his superiors. George Montgomery portrays Hawkeye, a loosely drawn character based on James Fenimore Cooper's famous frontiersman. In this film he is a trapper raised by the Indians. He works as a scout for the British against the French, who killed his brother. Monte Blue plays Sagamore, his Indian companion. Brenda Marshall provides little more than the romantic interest while Marcel Gourmet portrays General Montcalm. Several rousing battle sequences enliven an otherwise tired plot. ∎

Is Paris Burning? (1966), Par. *Dir.* René Clement; *Sc.* Gore Vidal, Francis Ford Coppola; *Cast includes:* Jean-Paul Belmondo, Charles Boyer, Leslie Caron, Kirk Douglas, Glenn Ford.

Set during the liberation of Paris, this sprawling World War II drama, shot in Paris with an international cast, concerns Nazi Germany's plans to burn the city. Meanwhile, the plot attempts to thread together isolated stories of various characters caught up in the uprising of the French resistance. The Germans, threatened by the partisans and a possible Allied invasion of the city, are ordered by Hitler to destroy Paris. The German commander (Gert Frobe), who must make the ultimate decision, believes that the destruction would serve no purpose.

The battle for Paris is seen from several viewpoints. The wife of a man about to be deported tries desperately to save her husband. Disagreements flare up between different factions of the underground. A Swedish consul (Orson Welles) brings off a temporary truce so that political prisoners can be rescued. French soldiers use an old woman's apartment to attack a German machine-gun position. Resistance fighters battle Nazi troops for control of streets and buildings as a French tank unit storms the city and joins the fighting.

The film is based on the book by Larry Collins and Doninique Lapierre. The title comes from a telephone call which an impatient Hitler, awaiting news of his command, supposedly made. ∎

Isn't Life Wonderful? (1924), UA. *Dir.* D.W. Griffith; *Sc.* D.W. Griffith; *Cast includes:* Carol Dempster, Neil Hamilton, Helen Lowell, Erville Alderson.

German officers personify Nazi order, regimentation and respect for authority as they agree to carry out Hitler's plan for the destruction of the City of Light. *Is Paris Burning?* (1966).

Director D.W. Griffith's affecting drama of an impoverished family struggling to survive in postwar Germany underscores the economic havoc and political instability of the nation and much of Europe as a result of the conflict. An indigent professor and his family are forced from their home. One son, a student, works as a waiter in the evenings. Another is employed in a shipyard, but his poor health as a result of his war experience brings his job to an end. Members of the family are each reduced to eating one potato daily. The title stems from a remark made by Carol Dempster, as the fiancee of Neil Hamilton, who portrays one of the sons. After a crop of potatoes they have harvested in a back lot is stolen from them, she says: "I still have you, so isn't life wonderful?" Shot at various locations in Germany, the film was one of several produced in the early 1920s that were sympathetic toward the German people. This is in sharp contrast to the stream of anti-German features released during World War I and immediately after which depicted the country as barbaric. "Years of war and hell,"

protests a German who is reduced to filching potatoes for his hungry family, "beasts they have made us." By placing the blame for the conflict on the Kaiser and his military advisers, these films exonerated the German people, portrayed as dupes of their maniacal leaders.

Griffith was one of the many directors who turned out anti-German propaganda films during the war years (*Hearts of the World*, etc.). However, anti-German sentiment in postwar America was still rather strong, so many of the films that advocated the slightest sympathy suffered at the box office. The nation was not ready to forgive Germany, no matter how compassionately the screen portrayed its suffering citizens and the chaos that was engulfing them. ∎

Israel's War of Independence (1948–1949). The creation of the state of Israel by the U.N. on May 14, 1948, brought both joy and heartache to the new nation. By partitioning the ancient land of Palestine into Jewish and Arab states, the U.N. ignited a long-simmering dispute into a full scale war between the two peoples. Surrounding Arab countries, refusing to accept partition, invaded Israel on the day of the U.N. announcement.

The war had its roots in the rise of nationalistic Zionism in the late 19th century, a movement meant to create a modern Jewish national state in the historical biblical lands of the Jews. Britain's *Balfour Declaration*, issued during World War I, favored the proposal. In the period immediately following World War I, Britain encouraged Jewish immigration into Palestine, a region taken from the defeated Turks and placed under British control as a League of Nations mandate. Jews settled in western Palestine in increasing numbers starting in the 1920s. The influx escalated during the 1930s and 1940s as many European Jews fled Hitler's persecution while others came as war-displaced persons. *Sword in the Desert* (1949), Hollywood's first attempt to dramatize the Israeli-Arab conflict, focused on World War II refugees trying to enter British-controlled Palestine.

Palestinian Arabs, supported by Arab nationalists in neighboring Middle Eastern states, intensified their attacks begun in the 1920s on growing Jewish communities in the area. Caught in a continuing civil war between Arabs and Jews, Britain, shortly after World War II, first attempted to stop Jewish immigration. But as the influx continued, Britain turned the problem over to the U.N. with the suggestion that Palestine be partitioned. The U.N. decision resulted in full-scale war as Jews and Arabs each sought to reinforce what they believed was a legitimate claim to the same land. *Exodus* (1960), based on Leon Uris' popular novel, depicted the birth of Israel and, like *Judith* (1966), concerned refugees from Europe trying to get to Jewish-controlled areas in Palestine on the eve of partition.

Armies from the surrounding Arab nations of Lebanon, Syria, Jordan, Iraq and Egypt invaded Israel. Jordan seized Eastern Palestine, (also known as the West Bank of the Jordan River), and Egypt took the Gaza Strip on the Mediterranean coast. Both areas were overwhelmingly Arab-populated. Israeli troops, however, not only pushed invading Arabs out of the area originally granted to Israel by the U.N. but, through conquest, enlarged their state by almost half. *Cast a Giant Shadow* (1966), based on the experiences of Colonel David (Mickey) Marcus, an American Jew who fought in Israel's War of Independence, had many action sequences of the Jews battling the Arabs in that conflict. *Judith* re-enacted battles between the Israelis and Syrian troops.

Though Israel signed an armistice with most of the Arab states in early 1949, real peace eluded the region. About 500,000 Palestinians who settled in refugee camps continued to agitate for the return of their homeland and supported guerrilla attacks against Israeli citizens and institutions. The Palestinians received both open and covert assistance from other Arab leaders. The problem resulted in several later wars between Israel and its Arab neighbors in the next few decades.

American films on the conflict have tended to lean in Israel's favor with only superficial attempts to present the Arab or Palestinian point of view. Portrayals of British administrators and troops vary greatly. In *Exodus* they were chiefly unsympathetic representatives of a system that sought to prevent the downtrodden and homeless from reaching their promised homeland. *Sword in the Desert* depicted them as unfortunate pawns caught in the middle of an unsolvable dilemma. In *Judith*, as represented by Jack Hawkins, they were seen as sympathetic to the Israeli cause. ■

Ivanhoe (1952), MGM. *Dir.* Richard Thorpe; *Sc.* Noel Langley; *Cast includes:* Robert Taylor, Elizabeth Taylor, Joan Fontaine, George Sanders, Emlyn Williams, Robert Douglas.

Robert Taylor stars as the title character in this historical drama filled with spectacle and action. He portrays Sir Walter Scott's brave Saxon leader who battles to extricate King Richard from Austrian incarceration and to restore him to the throne of England. Elizabeth Taylor co-stars as Rebecca, the daughter of a Jewish merchant who raised the ransom for Richard's release. Ivanhoe is in love with Joan Fontaine, who portrays the ward of his father. Meanwhile, Rebecca falls in love with Ivanhoe. The romance is set against a backdrop of court intrigue which results in a series of action sequences including duels and the siege of a castle.

MGM, Robert Taylor and director Richard Thorpe combined their talents once again in 1955 for the adaptation of another Scott novel, *Quentin Durward*. This film, like the former, was produced in England but was not as commercially successful. ∎

Iwo Jima, Battle of (February 19–March 24, 1945). The picture of an American flag being planted atop captured Mount Suribachi on Iwo Jima by four U. S. Marines is probably the most dramatic photograph of American troops at a moment of victory to emerge from World War II. The scene, now immortalized in a statue, symbolizes the dauntless spirit and exultation of success of Americans in battle. The incident took place on February 23 in the midst of one of the most difficult engagements encountered by American troops anywhere in World War II.

The attack on Iwo Jima, under the direction of Admiral Nimitz, was part of a strategy designed to gain forward bases to carry the war to Japan. Also, the Japanese air base on the island had caused heavy losses to American bombers hitting the Japanese homeland. The eight-square-mile island was the most heavily fortified position to be attacked by Allied forces in the war. It was a bristling fortress defended by over 22,000 enemy troops in concealed gun emplacements, caves and pillboxes, protected by interlaced minefields. The fortifications enabled the Japanese to survive without serious losses several days of preliminary air and naval bombardment.

The 3rd, 4th and 5th U.S. Marine divisions participated in the month-long assault, suffering 6,891 killed and 18,070 wounded. Japanese losses are just one indication of how tenacious was the defense. Only 212 enemy troops surrendered while 21,000 were confirmed killed and uncounted others died in sealed caves. The struggle to wrest the island from Japanese control was so intense and costly that Admiral Nimitz commented afterward: "On Iwo Jima, uncommon valor was a common virtue."

Several war films refer to Iwo Jima. "To the Shores of Iwo Jima" (1945), a World War II documentary shot in color, covers the story of the battle, including the pre-invasion bombardment and the use of flame-throwers to dislodge the stubborn Japanese. *Sands of Iwo Jima* (1949), starring John Wayne as a hard-bitten sergeant, tracks a platoon of marines from boot camp to the invasion of the Japanese-held island. It recreates rather realistically some of the bloody fighting that occurred on the island. Three survivors of the historic flag-raising on Mount Suribachi appear in the drama. *The Outsider* (1961), a biographical drama of the World War II hero Ira Hayes (Tony Curtis), shows some of the fighting on Iwo Jima and re-enacts the raising of the stars and stripes on top of Suribachi by Hayes and four other U.S. Marines. ∎

J

Michael O'Shea, as the title character and American correspondent during the Russo-Japanese War, gets a lesson in censorship from a Japanese officer. *Jack London* (1943).

Jack London (1943), UA. *Dir.* Alfred Santell; *Sc.* Ernest Pascal; *Cast includes:* Michael O'Shea, Susan Hayward, Osa Massen, Harry Davenport, Frank Craven, Virginia Mayo.

Michael O'Shea gives a vivid portrayal of the popular author who led a lusty and adventurous life in this highly fictional biographical drama. Since the film was made during World War II, the screenplay emphasizes the Russo-Japanese War and graphically depicts the Japanese penchant for ruthlessness and desire for world conquest. London, as a guest of the ambitious Captain Tanaka, learns of Japan's plans for the proposed takeover of England and the U.S. "The rising sun has a destiny," the captain confides to the writer, "her expansion is inevitable. The taking of Korea is only the first step—the first act of the drama. But the play is on, the curtain is up and it will ring down upon a Japanese world."

Jack London, as a correspondent during that conflict, witnesses Russian prisoners senselessly slaughtered by Japanese machine-gun fire. When he scoops more experienced correspondents on the Russo-Japanese War, they at first resent his actions. Then one suggests that they commend him with a toast from one of his own books. "Here's to the man on the trail at night," a reporter quotes. "May his grub hold out; may his matches never misfire." According to the script, London tries to warn the U.S. of Japan's potential for treachery, but the country, at peace with Japan and doing billions of dollars of business with the empire at the time, views his theories as too provocative. "Those sawed-off little runts in their papier-maché island," his editor scoffs, "why, we could lick them with one hand tied behind our back."

The film rarely touches upon London's early idealistic writing which conveys the author's interest in social and economic reform. The script is based upon *The Book of Jack London*, written by his wife, Charmian London, who is portrayed on screen by Susan Hayward. ∎

Jacknife (1989), Kings Road. *Dir.* David Jones; *Sc.* Stephen Metcalfe; *Cast includes:* Robert De Niro, Ed Harris, Kathy Baker.

Robert De Niro and Ed Harris portray ex-Vietnam War pals in this drama that explores in part the isolation and despair of some of the veterans of that bitter conflict. Set in a small, industrial Connecticut town, the plot concerns De Niro's unexpected visit to his buddy who is living with his unmarried teacher-sister (Kathy Baker). De Niro, emotionally maladjusted, confides that he is getting help from a veterans' encounter group. Harris, on the other hand, relies on his heavy drinking to forget his war experiences. A former high-school star athlete, he now spends his time bad-mouthing his sister. Baker disapproves of De Niro but soon begins to have an affair with him. ■

Jackson, Andrew (1767–1845). Jackson was already the old west's leading military hero when, as a major general of militia, he arrived in New Orleans early in December 1814, charged with the biggest responsibility of his career in the War of 1812. He had only a few weeks to prepare the defense of the city that controlled the entrance to the Mississippi River valley against a British invasion force already on its way. He immediately declared martial law to control New Orleans' predominantly anti-American Creole population. His force of 5,000, about half of whom were poorly armed and untrained militia, piled up cotton bales, timbers and earth to form a defensive breastwork along an abandoned canal several miles south of the city.

On January 8, 1815, British Major General Sir Edward Pakenham personally led his full force of 7,500 battle-seasoned veterans, fresh from fighting Napoleon in Europe, in three assaults against the Americans. When the sides finally separated, Pakenham and his two senior generals were dead, as were more than 2,000 of his troops. Another 500 British soldiers were captured. Jackson had lost seven killed and six wounded in the Americans' greatest victory of the war. Other than reinforcing Jackson's stature as a military man, the battle had no bearing on the war. Peace had already been signed two weeks earlier in Europe, but news had not yet reached the U.S. by ship. Jackson's stand at New Orleans, coming after his victories in the Creek War (1813–1814) and his seizing of a British-Indian base at Pensacola in Spanish Florida (November 7, 1814), earned him the popularity to become President for two terms (1829–1937). He was liked by farmers, backwoodsmen and city workers because, besides his military prowess, he was the first president with a commoner's background.

A man of action, accomplishment and the common touch, he is a proper subject for the screen, but Hollywood failed to fully exploit the potential of this unaffected American hero. The only attempt at a film biography appeared in 1913, with "Andrew Jackson," directed by Allan Dwan. Jackson is portrayed briefly in *My Own United States* (1918), a World War I patriotic compilation of highlights in American history. Director Cecil B.

DeMille in *The Buccaneer* (1938) treats General Andrew Jackson, who is not the main character, with more depth as he enlists the aid of the pirate Jean Lafitte to help fight against the British in the Battle of New Orleans. He is seen as crusty, shrewd and beloved by civilian and soldier alike. In *Man of Conquest* (1939) Jackson (Edward Ellis) is portrayed as mentor to Sam Houston, whose rise in Tennessee politics is attributed to Jackson's guiding hand. Cecil B. DeMille, in *Land of Liberty* (1939), a patriotic documentary about the history of the United States, eulogizes Jackson and his victory at the Battle of New Orleans. Charlton Heston plays a shrewd, tough-minded Jackson who accepts Lafitte's help out of a sense of expediency in *The Buccaneer* (1958), a remake of the 1938 film. ■

Jackson, Thomas J. "Stonewall" (1824–1863). Morally righteous, stern and demanding, he brought an almost religious fervor to his participation in the American Civil War. General Thomas "Stonewall" Jackson was, unquestionably, Lee's best lieutenant among Southern generals. Jackson allegedly got his nickname during the First Battle of Bull Run (Manassas Junction) on July 21, 1861. At one point in the fight a Southern officer, seeing his lines crumbling under a Union attack, pointed to Jackson and his Virginia troops holding firm on a crest. "There is Jackson standing like a stone wall. Rally behind the Virginians!" exclaimed the officer. The sobriquet became part of the Jackson legend.

A West Point graduate, he served in the Mexican War and was a professor of military science at Virginia Military Institute. Jackson took part in a number of important battles during the Civil War. He developed a reputation for coolness under fire and successful use of tactical surprise. Besides First Bull Run, Jackson saw action in the Shenandoah Valley (March–June 1862) where he consistently humbled larger enemy concentrations, Second Bull Run, Antietam (the war's bloodiest battle), Fredericksburg and Chancellorsville.

He died following his brilliant victory at Chancellorsville. While in front of his lines organizing the pursuit of the enemy, Jackson received a mortal wound accidentally inflicted by one of his own men. Without doubt, the loss of Jackson hurt Lee's conduct of the war. "Under Southern Stars," a 1937 film short, concerns Jackson on the evening before his fatal charge at Chancellorsville.

Most of the films in which Jackson is portrayed are early silents, including "To the Aid of Stonewall Jackson" (1911), "With Stonewall Jackson," also 1911 and "The Bugler of Battery B" (1912). Although generally crude in production values, these short dramas tend to be more historically accurate than later war films of the conflict that are based on nondescript battles and fictional characters. ∎

James, Jesse. (1847–1882). As a member of a family of Southern sympathizers in Missouri who was subjected to rough treatment in the local strife that accompanied the American Civil War, Jesse, at age 15, joined William Quantrill's band of Confederate guerrillas in 1862. Several films, including *Jesse James* (1927), depict this phase of his life. He developed into a valued marksman and took part in many of the band's raids in the Kansas-Missouri area. Henry King's *Jesse James* (1939), with Tyrone Power as the famed outlaw, portrays the abuses his family suffered, but the time period of the film is set after the war.

Allowed to go free after the war as a surrendered soldier, he and his brother Frank headed a gang of outlaws that became famous as western bank and train robbers. In response to a $10,000 reward for the capture of Jesse, dead or alive, by Missouri's Governor Crittenden, Jesse was shot and killed by two members of his group who had turned against him. His brother Frank eventually surrendered and, after being tried twice and acquitted each time, lived quietly as a Missouri farmer until his death in 1915.

Although Jesse James' screen exploits have generally been confined to the more popular western genre, some films have included the Civil War as part of the plot. *Jesse James Under the Black Flag* (1921), in which Jesse James, Jr. portrays his father, begins in 1863 when young James joins Quantrill's guerrilla forces in an attempt to avenge the Union soldiers' mistreatment of his family. He takes an oath of allegiance to the Black Flag, the raiders' banner. In the sequel *Jesse James as the Outlaw* (1921) James, again played by Jesse James, Jr., is depicted as a Civil War veteran who returns home to Missouri to live in peace but is falsely accused of robbing a

bank. Hounded by the law, he is forced to take up a life of crime. *Jesse James* (1939), starring Tyrone Power in the title role, is probably the best film biography of the noted badman. The story opens with battle sequences of the Civil War. Upon their return home following the end of the conflict, the James brothers have a run-in with corrupt railroad men and are forced to become outlaws. *Kansas Raiders* (1950), starring Audie Murphy as Jesse in a highly fictionalized rendering of historical events, focuses on his exploits with Quantrill's Raiders. All the films virtually portray him as a sympathetic, if violent, character. ∎

Janice Meredith (1924), MGM. *Dir.* E. Mason Hopper; *Sc.* Lillie Hayward; *Cast includes:* Marion Davies, Harrison Ford, W. C. Fields, Ken Maynard, Maclyn Arbuckle, Spencer Charters.

In this historical romance of the American Revolution, Marion Davies plays the title character, a daughter of a wealthy New Jersey landowner, who falls in love with a bond servant (Harrison Ford). Actually, he is a British lord who has aligned himself with George Washington and the colonial cause. Davies is then sent away to relatives in Boston where she learns that the British are planning to march to the Concord arsenal. Her timely warning allows Paul Revere to alert the countryside. She later becomes entangled in a series of subplots but is eventually rescued by Ford. Following the end of hostilities, President George Washington attends their wedding.

Besides several action sequences, such as the Battles of Lexington and Concord, Trenton and Yorktown, the film depicts famous historical events, including Paul Revere's midnight ride, Patrick Henry's speech in Virginia, Washington's crossing the Delaware and the Boston Tea Party. Among the famous contemporary figures that appear on screen, other than those already mentioned, are Benjamin Franklin, Alexander Hamilton, Marie Antoinette and Lafayette. W.C. Fields appears in a minor role as a comic British sergeant while future cowboy star Ken Maynard impersonates Paul Revere. ∎

Japanese War Bride (1952). See Veterans. ∎

Jesse James (1927), Par. *Dir.* Lloyd Ingraham; *Sc.* Frank M. Clifton; *Cast includes:* Fred Thomson, Nora Lane, Montagu Love, Mary Carr, James Pierce.

A highly fictional account of the famous bandit's exploits during and after the Civil War, the action drama opens with Jesse James as a member of Quantrill's raiders during the conflict. At one point he is almost caught as a spy but manages to escape. When the war ends, James learns that his mother has been hurt by Union sympathizers and is about to be evicted from the town. He returns to seek revenge on those who have mistreated his mother but ends up as an outlaw. Although the film includes the characters of Frank, Jesse's brother, and Bob Ford, the man who betrayed the bandit, the plot has little historical accuracy. ∎

Jet Attack (1958), AI. *Dir.* Edward L. Cahn; *Sc.* Orville H. Hampton; *Cast includes:* John Agar, Audrey Totter, Gregory Walcott, James Dobson.

An American jet pilot, downed behind enemy lines during the Korean War, not only escapes but rescues a captured scientist in this action drama. John Agar portrays the heroic pilot who, along with two buddies (Gregory Walcott and Nicky Blair), is shot down over North Korea. Audrey Totter, as a Soviet nurse, volunteers to help the suspicious Americans. When they learn that an American scientist is being held captive nearby, they decide to rescue him. They make their escape in a Communist plane. ∎

Jet Pilot (1956). See Cold War. ∎

Jim Bludso (1917), Triangle. *Dir.* Tod Browning, Wilfred Lucas; *Cast includes:* Wilfred Lucas, Olga Grey, George Stone, Monte Blue.

Wilfred Lucas portrays the title character, a Northerner who marries a Southern woman. When the Civil War breaks out, he enlists in the Union army. His wife (Olga Grey) resents her husband's choice of sides and runs off with a riverboat gambler who later abandons her. Jim is saved by a black man during a battle and takes his rescuer home with him when the war ends, employing him as a helper on his riverboat. When Jim meets up with the gambler and learns the whole story, a fight ensues. The film is based on the Pike County poems of John Hay. ∎

Joan of Arc (1412–1431). Enemy armies threatened the reign of France's Charles VII during the early 15th century. The British, who challenged his right to the crown, occupied part of his nation in the Hundred Years' War (1337–1453). He had to contend as well with the hostile Burgundians who allied themselves with the foreign forces. In the midst of these troubles, a deeply religious French peasant girl declared she heard voices and saw visions of saints beckoning her to free her country from British rule. Joan, self-confident and dressed in men's attire, convinced Charles VII, the dauphin of France, to entrust her with troops.

She proceeded to Orleans which had been under siege by the British since 1428. Joan inspired the French soldiers to follow her and, though wounded by an arrow, led an offensive that routed British forces on May 7, 1429. The battle was recreated fairly effectively in Victor Fleming's otherwise stagy *Joan of Arc* (1948), starring Ingrid Bergman as Joan. Following several other victories, Joan encouraged Charles to go to Reims and receive the crown. This event was re-enacted in Cecil B. DeMille's 1917 *Joan the Woman*. Then, disobeying her king, she stormed Paris in a failed attempt to capture the city.

Captured by the Burgundians in 1430, she was ransomed to the English who turned her over to Church authorities for trial. She was charged with practicing witchcraft and heresy. Charles, now king of France, could have negotiated her release but elected to do nothing. In 1431, at age 19, Joan was burned at the stake by secular authorities as a relapsed heretic. For four short months she enjoyed military glory that restored Charles to the throne of France. But some of her own actions contributed to her downfall. Her bold choice of breeches and boots, suggesting her rebellion against male domination, eventually worked against her. More importantly, her claims of saintly visions and voices—not accepted by Church authorities—led to charges of heresy and her ultimate death.

American films concerning the Maid of Orleans were generally inept productions that failed to capture the high drama and historical importance of the life of the real Joan. Cecil B. DeMille's highly romanticized *Joan the Woman* (1917), one of the earliest dramas about the "girl patriot", recounted how Joan (Geraldine Farrar) led the French army to victory and saved the throne of Charles VII. Otto

Preminger's *St. Joan* (1957), with Jean Seberg in the title role, presented a weak adaptation of George Bernard Shaw's play.

Hollywood occasionally altered the character of Joan to fit contemporary circumstances. For example, in *A Little Patriot* (1917), a World War I comedy, the plot centered on little Baby Marie who is strongly influenced by stories of Joan of Arc. Comedienne Mabel Normand, as an orphan in *Joan of Plattsburg* (1918), another World War I film, fantasizes that she is a 20th-century Joan of Arc and prevents the sale of government documents to the enemy. In the World War II drama *Joan of Paris* (1942) Michele Morgan portrayed a young French patriot who, inspired by Joan of Arc, her patron saint, rescues downed Allied pilots. ∎

Joan of Arc (1948), RKO. *Dir.* Victor Fleming; *Sc.* Maxwell Anderson, Andrew Solt; *Cast includes:* Ingrid Bergman, Jose Ferrer, Francis L. Sullivan, J. Carrol Naish, Ward Bond.

Ingrid Bergman portrays the Maid of Orleans in this biographical drama. The film covers her early years from her humble life as a peasant girl to her rise as France's greatest heroine. "Our strength is in our faith," she commands with conviction. Several stirring sequences include her appeal to the Dauphin to lead the French armies to victory, the battle of Orleans, her ultimate disillusionment and the tragic trial in which she is charged with heresy and condemned to death. Francis Sullivan plays Pierre Cauchon, her fierce and bellowing persecutor. Jose Ferrer portrays the impotent and indecisive Dauphin. The film is not without humor. "There must be no swearing in the army," Joan demands as she stubbornly tries to reorganize the French forces. "You want our army to be dumb?" a general (Ward Bond) replies, balking at the order.

Loosely based on Maxwell Anderson's literate play, *Joan of Lorraine*, the film avoids the intellectual foundations of the original. Instead, it focuses on the spectacle surrounding the heroine's triumphs and tragedies which result in part in a series of static scenes. ∎

Joan of Paris (1942), RKO. *Dir.* Robert Stevenson; *Sc.* Charles Bennett, Ellis St. Joseph; *Cast includes:* Michele Morgan, Paul Henreid, Thomas Mitchell, Laird Cregar, May Robson.

This World War II drama tells about one crew of downed British fliers who try to escape from Nazi-occupied France to England. Paul Henreid, as a French patriot and flier, helps four fellow R.A.F. airmen by contacting British Intelligence, all the while placing his own life in danger. Michele Morgan, as a young French barmaid inspired by her patron saint Joan of Arc, helps Henreid and the others escape. She later pays with her life for helping the Allied fliers. Thomas Mitchell portrays a priest who harbors the men temporarily. May Robson plays a British agent who is killed by the Gestapo. Laird Cregar, as a shrewd Gestapo officer, relentlessly pursues Henreid, hoping to capture the entire bomber crew. A romance develops between Henreid and Morgan but does not distract from the drama.

Americans largely unfamiliar with the perilous but strategic role of the French Underground, especially those members of the Paris unit (as represented by Robson), received a fairly unromanticized picture of their efforts in this film. ∎

Joan of Plattsburg (1918). See Joan of Arc. ∎

Joan the Woman (1917), Par. *Dir.* Cecil B. DeMille; *Sc.* Jeanie Macpherson; *Cast includes:* Geraldine Farrar, Raymond Hatton, Hobart Bosworth, Wallace Reid, Charles Clary.

A romantic version of the life of Joan of Arc, this silent film stars Geraldine Farrar as the "girl patriot." The story describes how this simple French country girl led an army to victory and saved the throne of Charles VII. The film includes a love story and several battle scenes in the DeMille style of large numbers of extras seen in long shots as well as in close-ups of hand-to-hand fighting. ∎

Joe Smith, American (1942). See Propaganda Films: World War II. ∎

Johanna Enlists (1918). See Home Front. ∎

John Paul Jones (1959), WB. *Dir.* John Farrow; *Sc.* John Farrow, Jesse Lasky, Jr.; *Cast includes:* Robert Stack, Marisa Pavan, Charles Coburn, Erin O'Brien, Macdonald Carey.

Robert Stack, as the title character in *John Paul Jones* (1959), personifies the young nation's courage and daring as he battles the British during the American Revolution.

Robert Stack portrays the title figure in this biographical drama set chiefly during the American Revolution. The film traces John Paul Jones' life from his Scottish boyhood when he ran away to sea, to his gaining a captain's position and his arrival in the American colonies on the eve of the rebellion. Jones' efforts to fight alongside the colonists are first met with distrust. The plot allows for the introduction of several historical figures, including a charming Benjamin Franklin (Charles Coburn), a stalwart Patrick Henry (Macdonald Carey) and an enigmatic George Washington. Other figures in small roles are Catherine the Great (Bette Davis) and Louis XVI (Jean Pierre Aumont). Erin O'Brien and Marisa Pavan provide the romantic interests for the hero. The highlight of the film is the exciting sea battle between Jones' *Bonhomme Richard* and Britain's *Serapis*.

One of the greatest naval commanders in American history, John Paul Jones is famous for his daring exploits in the American Revolution and the phrase, "Sir, I have not yet begun to fight." The statement was his response to the demand that he surrender dur-

ing the memorable clash between his vessel and the more heavily armed British warship.

The engagement between Jones' ship, named in honor of Benjamin Franklin, and the *Serapis* that took place off the English coast on September 23, 1779, illustrated Jones' tenacious and defiant character as a wartime sea captain. Though outgunned by the enemy vessel, Jones closed in on his target. A blistering sea duel that lasted for several hours found the *Bonhomme Richard* on the verge of sinking with its deck ripped up, fires raging and its hold filling with water. He refused a call to surrender. Instead, he lashed the two ships together and, after a hand-to-hand deck battle, captured the other craft. Jones and his crew sailed off in the *Serapis* when his boat sank.

Born in Scotland, Jones fled to the American colonies in 1773 after killing a seaman during a mutiny on a ship he commanded in the Caribbean. He was was given a commission in the fledgling American navy late in 1775. He captured 16 prizes as commander of the *Providence* and was promoted to captain the following year. Jones used French ports

Timothy Bottoms is about to experience the horrors of World War I. *Johnny Got His Gun* (1971).

as a base to carry the war to the waters around Britain, first as captain of the *Ranger*, and later with the *Bonhomme Richard*. His raids on British shipping were partially responsible for British merchants pressuring their government to seek peace with their former colonies. ∎

Johnny Doesn't Live Here Any More (1944). See Washington, D.C. ∎

Johnny Got His Gun (1971), Marketing & Distribution Co. *Dir.* Dalton Trumbo; *Sc.* Dalton Trumbo; *Cast includes:* Jason Robards, Timothy Bottoms, Marsha Hunt, Diane Varsi.

An antiwar drama based on Dalton Trumbo's 1939 novel, the film tells about a youth who goes off to World War I and returns as a basket case. Timothy Bottoms portrays the soldier who has had his arms, legs and face blown off. The chief medical officer concludes that the quadriplegic is "decerebrated," incapable of emotions or thought. But the doctor is proved wrong when the youth articulates his feelings in a series of affecting flashbacks. A nurse (Diane Varsi) realizes that Bottoms still has thoughts and can express them. She communicates with him by forming letters on his bare chest, moving him so that he can feel the warmth of the sun. He replies by tapping out messages with his head, using the Morse Code. When he requests of his superiors to leave the hospital, they instead lock him away in a dark room. The military, it seems, cannot afford to expose the physical horrors of war to the public. Even the nurse's humane attempt to put the lad out of his misery is foiled. Jason Robards portrays the father. Kathy Fields plays the boy's prewar sweetheart.

Trumbo, who had been blacklisted as a writer as a result of the House Un-American Activities Committee investigating Communist influence in Hollywood, could not get his downbeat novel sold to any studio until the Vietnam era. Marsha Hunt, who portrays Bottoms' mother in the film, was another victim of the infamous blacklist. ∎

Johnny Ring and the Captain's Sword (1921), Temple. *Dir.* Norman L. Stevens; *Sc.* Russell H. Conwell; *Cast includes:* Ben Warren, Frank Walker.

Reportedly based on the true experiences of a Philadelphia minister, this religious drama recounts his conversion to Christianity as a result of certain incidents that occurred during the Civil War. Russell H. Conwell (Ben Warren), a Union captain during the war, was honored by his fellow townspeople with a special sword. The officer, an avowed atheist, has a young religious orderly Johnny Ring (Frank Walker) who cares for the sword but is not allowed to read the Bible by his superior. The boy, however, prays for the captain. During a battle the orderly is mortally wounded trying to save the precious sword. Meanwhile Conwell has advanced to colonel and is himself seriously wounded in battle. In terrible pain, he promises that if God permits him to live, he will do His work in the name of the dead orderly. ∎

Johnny Tremain (1957), BV. *Dir.* Robert Stevenson; *Sc.* Tom Blackburn; *Cast includes:* Hal Stalmaster, Luana Patten, Jeff York, Sebastian Cabot.

The American Revolution forms the background for this historical drama about a young apprentice to a silversmith who gets entangled in the political intrigues of the colonists. Hal Stalmaster, as the young lad, becomes an eyewitness to the major events of the period, including the Boston Tea Party, Paul Revere's Ride and the Battles of Lexington and Concord. Based on the novel by Esther Forbes, the film depicts the struggle of the colonists in the New World for recognition and representation. Walter Sande portrays Paul Revere, Rusty Lane plays Samuel Adams and Ralph Clanton enacts General Gage. ∎

Join the Marines (1937). See Service Comedy. ∎

Jolt, The (1922). See Crime and War. ∎

Young Hal Stalmaster (l.), as the title character in *Johnny Tremain* (1957), joins other American colonists during the Battle of Lexington and Concord.

Jones, John Paul. See *John Paul Jones* (1959). ■

Journey, The (1959), MGM. Dir. Anatole Litvak; Sc. George Tabori; *Cast includes:* Deborah Kerr, Yul Brynner, Robert Morley, E. G. Marshall, Jason Robards, Jr.

Several travelers from various countries are caught up in the political intrigue of the Hungarian revolt of 1956 in this drama. Prevented by Russian troops from boarding their Budapest-to-Vienna plane, the group is forced to take a bus from Budapest to the Austrian border. The simple 100-mile journey out of strife-torn Hungary turns out to be a venture fraught with danger for the passengers. When they arrive at the border, they are delayed by a Russian officer (Yul Brynner) who suspects one of the travelers (Jason Robards, Jr.) of being a leader of the Hungarian revolt.

A romantic triangle develops when Brynner becomes infatuated with a pretty Englishwoman (Deborah Kerr) who in turn is in love with Robards. She soon finds herself strangely fascinated by the Russian, who can be both cruel and romantic, clever and unso-phisticated. Robards, an angular figure obsessed by his passion for freedom, is actually a rebel leader. Not usually one to easily abandon his duty or surrender that which he desires, Brynner ultimately allows the lovers and the rest of the passengers to cross the border to safety. ■

Journey for Margaret (1942), MGM. Dir. W. S. Van Dyke II; Sc. David Hertz; *Cast includes:* Robert Young, Laraine Day, Fay Bainter, Nigel Bruce, Margaret O'Brien.

Robert Young and Laraine Day portray a childless couple in this sentimental, unpretentious World War II drama about war orphans. On assignment in England as a correspondent, Young is accompanied by his wife. They experience a Nazi bombing raid that results in her inability to bear children. He visits a home for parentless children as part of an assignment and grows fond of two orphans (William Severn and Margaret O'Brien) whom he and his wife adopt and take to America. During a poignant scene in a recently bombed street in which an English mother gazes in disbelief at her dead child,

Young cries out: "All right, you're mad now—mad at stink, mad at smoke, mad at Nazi bombs that murder little children! Oh, God, let me stay mad! Give me the wisdom, give me the strength, to stay mad!"

When he finally gets the adopted orphans to the shores of New York City, Peter, the little boy who has experienced only blackouts, asks upon seeing the city ablaze with lights: "What's it got lights on for?" Sirens begin to sound, signaling another blackout, and the lights begin to go out. "Will they go on again?" little Margaret asks. Her adopted parents reassure her that they will. The film, drawn from war correspondent W. H. White's factual account of his experiences, helped to bring home to American audiences the plight of children in wartime. Along with *Mrs. Miniver*, released the same year, it emphasized the effects of the conflict on Britain's home front rather than on the battlefield. Both films contributed much to America's pro-British attitudes. ■

Journey Into Fear (1942). See Spy Films: the Talkies. ■

Journey to Shiloh (1968), U. *Dir.* William Hale; *Sc.* Gene Coon; *Cast includes:* James Caan, Michael Sarrazin, Brenda Scott, Don Stroud, Paul Peterson, Harrison Ford.

A pretentious action drama of seven buddies who travel across the country to enlist in the Confederate army, the film gets bogged down in too many artificial episodes. The journey becomes a rite-of-passage for the young innocents from Texas as they experience life, love and death. The film tries too hard to introduce scenes dealing with racism and the horrors of war. James Caan portrays the leader of the impulsive group. Michael Sarrazin, as one of the volunteers, discovers the inglorious face of war. Harrison Ford, of later *Star Wars* fame, hardly distinguishes himself as one of the young Texans. Veteran character actors Noah Beery and Rex Ingram have bit parts in this inept tale. ■

Journey's End (1930), Tiffany. *Dir.* James Whale; *Sc.* J.M. March; *Cast includes:* Colin Clive, David Manners, Ian Maclaren, Anthony Bushell.

Author R.C. Sherriff and director James Whale translated some of their front-line experiences during World War I into a successful stage play which originally opened in London. Whale came to Hollywood where he directed the screen version of this antiwar drama about a group of English officers who experience the dehumanization of the conflict. Colin Clive portrays Major Stanhope, the main character, whose three years in the trenches and whose job it is to send young soldiers to face death have resulted in his spiritual and psychological ruin. He bolts down whiskey for temporary escape. David Manners, as Raleigh, a young Englishman and green lieutenant, is proud to be assigned under Stanhope's command until he discovers the change in his former school-hero idol.

The film is practically a literary reproduction of the play and may account for its failure at the box office. To its credit, the screen version did not add a love story, glorious battle sequences or a happy ending. A few external scenes were inserted to show the war that was raging above the dugout where the principal players are quartered. Some of these additions are more effective than others, especially the opening shot showing a handful of soldiers quietly moving and stumbling over the wounded land as they head for their trenches. Other scenes are simply literal translations that contribute little to the general conflict or its antiwar theme.

The film, whose thematic intentions were similar to those of *All Quiet on the Western Front* released the same year, did not do as well at the box office or with the critics as Milestone's more visually satisfying and creative antiwar drama. One reason may have been its staginess, since most of the film takes place inside a dugout. Both entries set a new trend in realism in war movies. *Journey's End*, however, still retained vestiges of national honor and sacrifice as expressed by some of its characters. These romantic elements were completely absent in *All Quiet on the Western Front*. ■

Juarez (1939), WB. *Dir.* William Dieterle; *Sc.* John Huston, Wolfgang Reinhardt, Aeneas MacKenzie; *Cast includes:* Paul Muni, Bette Davis, Brian Aherne, Claude Rains, John Garfield, Donald Crisp.

Paul Muni portrays the title character in this historical drama of political intrigue, romance and revolution in Mexico in the mid-1800s. The complex plot concerns an attempt by France's Napoleon III to bring Mexico under French domination by placing his puppet, Maximilian, on the throne of Mexico, the tragic love story between Maximilian and Carlotta, and Juarez's political struggle to free Mexico from foreign entanglements and forge a democratic state. Benito Juarez, a native Indian and elected head of the Mexican republic, is first defeated by French troops but he continues to fight a guerrilla war to rid his country of foreign invaders.

Maximilian (Brian Aherne), although kept in power by French troops, believes in fair play and pleads unsuccessfully for Mexican unity. A tragic pawn in French politics, he is abandoned by France and resigns himself to defeat and eventual court martial. Bette Davis, as Carlotta, his wife and empress of Mexico, returns to France to beg for military and financial aid for her husband but is refused.

Historically, the United States, at first preoccupied with its own Civil War, chiefly ignored the conflicts of its southern neighbor. But when the U.S. Civil War ended, the U.S. government aided Juarez by pressuring France to remove its troops from Mexico. While Carlotta pleaded her lost cause to Napoleon, her husband was captured by Juarez and executed.

The film provides several brief battle scenes, but the political events and the problems of the individual characters dominate the drama which is based on Bertita Harding's novel, *The Phantom Crown*, and Franz Werfel's play, *Juarez and Maximilian*. Warner Brothers spared little expense in the production, emphasizing authenticity, massive and numerous sets and a large cast. The film was not the financial success the studio had hoped for. Several critics found fault with some of the dialogue ("You were right in setting me on the road to my manifest destiny") and Muni's somber performance and heavy make-up. Also, the cinematic story never allows the principal characters to confront each other—it has them deal through intermediaries.

The film was released at a time when the dark forces of totalitarianism threatened large parts of the world. The studio, known for tackling topical themes, used the drama to extol the struggle by oppressed people against an externally imposed dictatorship. The film also served as a warning to European despots to stay out of the Americas.

Benito (Pablo) Juarez (1806–1872), president of Mexico from 1857 until his death in office in 1872, is revered by the people of his nation as a courageous fighter for liberal reform. It was through his efforts that Mexico started to change from a semi-feudalistic society dominated by a conservative triumvirate of the upper class, the military and the clergy, to a more democratic federal republic with greater economic and political rights for the masses.

On becoming President in 1857, Juarez ended judicial immunities for the clergy and military in civil matters. Driven out of the capital by French forces intent on placing Maximilian in power, Juarez still had a strong following among the common people and, as shown in the film, successfully conducted a guerrilla war. Following the collapse of Maximilian's government, Juarez was re-elected president in 1867 and 1871.

There is, unfortunately, room for serious criticism of the film, despite its many good points as historical drama. For example, it loses sight of its theme. It is as concerned with developing a feeling of sympathy for the well-intentioned Maximilian as it is with exploring the character of Juarez. Secondly, the title is deceptive because the film is far from a full biography of the Mexican leader. It covers only that portion of Juarez's life concerning his conflict with Maximilian, a period of not quite four years. Perhaps, in comparing *Juarez* to the gross distortions of history commonly served up by Hollywood, we should be thankful for this cinematic morsel and keep criticism in restrained perspective. ∎

Judgment at Nuremberg (1961), UA. *Dir.* Stanley Kramer; *Sc.* Abby Mann; *Cast includes:* Spencer Tracy, Burt Lancaster, Richard Widmark, Marlene Dietrich, Judy Garland, Montgomery Clift.

Stanley Kramer's intelligent production of the German war crimes trial of 1948 focuses on the issues of the responsibility and accountability of those who administer the laws of a state. Spencer Tracy, as the presiding judge, portrays a simple New England judge who is compassionate and objective as he strives to reach the proper balance between justice and political expediency. Burt Lancaster, as a former world-renowned jurist and one of four defendants representing the German judiciary during the Nazi regime, at first is silent during the trial. He then speaks out, charging those guilty (including himself) who explained away or disregarded the long list of barbarous crimes committed by the Nazis. He particularly condemns those who had the power or the ability to denounce the crimes. Montgomery Clift plays a feeble-minded victim of Nazi sterility experiments. Judy Garland portrays a German citizen who had been falsely accused of having had an affair with an elderly Jew—for which she was imprisoned and the man sentenced to death. Marlene Dietrich plays the stately widow of a German general who was hanged for war crimes. Richard Widmark, who, as the prosecutor, has been relentless in bringing accused war criminals to justice in a string of trials, buckles under pressure from superior officers who, for political reasons, want him to ease up on his demands for harsh sentences.

Events unfold through the point of view of Tracy, who observes and listens in and out of the courtroom as American military officers and politicians and German civilians attempt to influence him. A U.S. Senator suggests that the West, in its struggle against Communism, needs the support of the German people while an officer asks that the trials be accelerated and light sentences be handed down. But in his final decision at the trial he is firm in his convictions about placing responsibility. "This trial has shown," he states publicly, "that under a national crisis, ordinary men— even able and extraordinary men— can delude themselves into the commission of crimes so heinous that they beggar the imagination." He finds the four defendants guilty. Later, the defense attorney (Maximilian Schell) remarks privately to Tracy: "In five years the men you sentenced to life imprisonment will be free." "It is logical in view of the times in which we live," Tracy replies, referring to growing East-West tensions, "but to be logical is not to be right. And nothing on God's earth can ever make it so."

The film manages to raise the issues of individual accountability of war crimes carried out under state orders and the extent of guilt on the part of those who do not speak out against these crimes. In the final scene Tracy, at the request of Lancaster, visits the former judge in his cell. "These millions of people," Lancaster confides, "I never knew it would come to that. You must believe it." "It came to that," Tracy explains, "the first time you sentenced a man to death you knew to be innocent." ■

Judgment House, The (1915). See South African War. ■

Judith (1966), Par. *Dir.* Daniel Mann; *Sc.* John Michael Hayes; *Cast includes:* Sophia Loren, Peter Finch, Jack Hawkins, Hans Verner.

An American-produced film with a chiefly British cast, the drama concerns the search of a Jewish ex-wife for her Nazi war-criminal husband against the backdrop of Israel's War of Independence. Sophia Loren, as a woman who was betrayed by her husband and sent to Dachau, joins forces with the Haganah, the Jewish underground, who also seeks her husband for other reasons. Loren wants revenge, but the Israelis want her husband, a former tank expert now employed by the Arabs, for his military knowledge of an impending battle.

Peter Finch, as a kibbutz leader and member of the underground, helps her to find her former husband who is ultimately killed. Jack Hawkins, as a British major, is sympathetic to the Israeli cause and assists Finch and Loren. Suspenseful sequences include the smuggling of a boatload of Jewish refugees into the territory and battles between the Israelis and Arabs, especially the Syrians. ■

Julius Caesar (1953), MGM. *Dir.* Joseph L. Mankiewicz; *Sc.* Joseph L. Mankiewicz; *Cast includes:* Marlon Brando, James Mason, John Gielgud, Louis Calhern, Edmond O'Brien, Deborah Kerr.

This film adaptation of Shakespeare's play captures the bard's exploration of conspiracy, assassination and authoritarianism by emphasizing the personal drama of those involved in Caesar's murder and its aftermath rather than the pageantry of the tale. Filmed in black and white, the screen version portrays Brutus (James Mason) as a rational idealist concerned more with a democratic Rome than with crowning Caesar (Louis Calhern) king. Ambitious Cassius (John Gielgud) draws Brutus into a conspiracy to assassinate Caesar. Brutus, governed by a noble soul that cannot tolerate an autocatic Caesar ruling Rome, joins the group of conspirators and assists in killing the soldier-hero. A vengeful Mark Antony (Marlon Brando) gives an emotional eulogy over the corpse of Caesar that incites the crowd against Brutus, who tries to appeal to their reason. Brutus, Cassius and the other conspirators are then forced to flee for their lives as Antony, Octavius Caesar and Lepidus take over the reigns of government.

Other highlights in the film include the as-

The surrender of besieged French forces at the ill-fated battle at Dienbienphu during the French Indo-China War reflects the rise of post-World War II nationalism. *Jump Into Hell* (1955).

sassination scene in which mortally wounded Caesar stumbles toward his friend Brutus, who delivers the final, fatal thrust, and the emotional scene showing the split between Cassius and Brutus at the Battle of Philippi. The battle scenes are brief but effective.

Producer John Houseman in an interview stated that he tried to parallel events in the play with those of the 20th-century politics, particularly Nazi Germany. The black-and-white photography, he said, was meant to suggest the World War II newsreels. ■

Jump Into Hell (1955), WB. *Dir.* David Butler; *Sc.* Irving Wallace; *Cast includes:* Jack Sernas, Kurt Kasznar, Arnold Moss, Peter Van Eyck, Marcel Dalio.

This drama of the French Indo-China War depicts the last days at Dienbienphu as the French make a brave but futile attempt to defend the fortress. Arnold Moss, as the fort commander, sends a message to France for additional officers to help defend the position against the Communists. Jack Sernas, Kurt Kasznar, Peter Van Eyck and Norman

Dupont portray the volunteer officers who parachute into the besieged fortress. After 56 days of fierce fighting, the Communists overrun the French position. Sernas and Dupont are the only survivors of the volunteers who manage to escape. Although the combat sequences (some of which were borrowed from newsreels) add interest to a story that is weak in characterization, the limited production values of the film fail to establish that more than 10,000 French troops participated in the battle. ■

Jumping Jacks (1952). See Service Comedy. ■

Jungle Patrol (1948), TCF. *Dir.* Joseph Newman; *Sc.* Francis Swann; *Cast includes:* Kristine Miller, Arthur Franz, Ross Ford, Tom Noonan, Gene Reynolds.

This World War II action drama concerns a handful of American fighter pilots in the Pacific. Assigned to contain the Japanese until a permanent air base is completed, the eight gallant airmen have taken a heavy toll of enemy aircraft without sustaining any losses.

The personal drama and tension evolves from this fact as each wonders who among them will be the first casualty. Kristine Miller provides the feminine interest as an entertainer who visits the remote airstrip near Fort Moresby. The air battles chiefly are heard but not seen in this low-budget production. ■

Junior Army (1942). See Spy Films: the Talkies. ■

K

Kaiser, The. See Wilhelm II. ■

Kaiser, the Beast of Berlin, The (1918), U. *Dir.* Rupert Julian; *Sc.* Elliot J. Clawson, Rupert Julian; *Cast includes:* Rupert Julian, Allan Sears, Lon Chaney, Walter Belasco, Elmo Lincoln.

Virtually an *auteur* film (Rupert Julian directed, co-wrote the screenplay and played the title role), this propaganda drama emphasizes the weaknesses in the character of Kaiser Wilhelm. According to the plot, he is a self-deluded, vain figure who considers himself larger than life and seems obsessed with a desire for conquest. The film also suggests that his lust was not confined entirely to politics. In one scene he is shown fondling a young woman's hand. Some of the highlights of the film include the emperor's conspiring with his military leaders; his conference with the American ambassador, James Gerard, concerning the sinking of the *Lusitania*; his meeting with von Nagel, the U-boat captain responsible for the atrocity; and scenes of the invasion of Belgium. The film also emphasized the atrocities allegedly committed by the Germans against the Belgian people. Since a steady stream of news releases reported these outrages—real or imagined— during the course of the war, audiences rarely doubted their accuracy. The film, which drew upon information from a book titled *Wilhelm II and His Consort*, added to the enmity hurled at the Kaiser not only on screen but in its advertising. "Warning—" an ad for the film read, "Any person throwing mud at this poster will *not* be prosecuted." Ambassador Gerard wrote an account of his experiences among the German leaders in his book *My Four Years in Germany* which was made into a feature film with that title in 1918. ■

Kaiser's Finish, The (1918), WB. *Dir.* John Joseph Harvey, Clifford B. Saum; *Sc.* John Joseph Harvey; *Cast includes:* Earl Schenck, Claire Whitney.

Earl Schenck portrays the Kaiser's illegitimate son who was raised in the U.S. in this patriotic World War I drama. Schenck, who can easily be mistaken for the Kaiser, turns agent and journeys to Germany to assassinate the Crown Prince and his son. The film cleverly blends its scenes with actual newsreel inserts of the Kaiser inspecting the front lines. At times, it is difficult to discern which portions are fictitious and which are real. The film added fuel to America's hatred of the Kaiser, a feeling brought about four years earlier by Germany's show of militancy as reflected by a series of international confrontations. One particular scene suggests that he be lynched in Times Square. This was one of Warner Brothers' first entries into the burgeoning film industry and helped launch the studio into its eventual success. ■

Kaiser's Shadow, The (1918). See Spy Films: the Silents. ■

Kamikaze. Kublai Khan's fleet, sailing to invade Japan in 1281, was destroyed by a typhoon that the Japanese called a "kamikaze" (divine wind). In the late stages of World War II, Japan took this idea of a divine wind that annihilates the enemy and applied the name to a suicide corps of pilots who crashed their explosive-laden aircraft into American targets, mostly ships.

Americans first encountered suicide air strikes by the Japanese Special Attack Corps in late October 1944, during the invasion of Leyte in the Philippines. The Japanese originally planned to use kamikaze attacks as a temporary device against carriers supporting the invasion and thus deprive Americans of air cover over the region. The attacks, however, were so successful in damaging American sea power that the concept was expanded to other areas of the Philippines and Okinawa. At Okinawa a force of 1,815 Japanese planes carried out well-planned and highly organized suicide raids.

The Japanese expanded the number of kamikaze attacks from bases in Kyushu during the early part of 1945. By late June of that year, close to 1,500 kamikaze planes had sunk 26 American ships and damaged 164. Japanese records indicated that close to 3,000 kamikaze planes took part in raids before the war ended. There were plans to defend Japan, in the probability of an American invasion, through widespread use of this method of warfare.

American wartime propaganda portrayed kamikaze pilots as drugged or hypnotized and not fully cognizant of the nature of their mission. This was not the case. According to Japanese sources, the pilots volunteered and considered it a sacred honor to give their lives in defense of the emperor and homeland. The dropping of two American atomic bombs in August 1945 suddenly ended the Pacific war and prevented further and more widespread use of kamikaze attacks.

War dramas did not include kamikaze sequences until after the conflict. For variety, Hollywood pitted diverse American warships against the suicide planes. The film *Task Force* (1949), a tribute to the mighty aircraft carrier, depicts a lively battle between a carrier and a swarm of kamikazes. *Okinawa* (1952), a drama about a U.S. destroyer supporting the island invasion and fighting off the kamikaze, borrowed Japanese newsreels showing the ceremonial rites kamikaze pilots underwent before their suicide missions. *Away All Boats* (1956) presents a harrowing kamikaze attack upon a U.S. attack transport off the coast of Okinawa. As a result, the captain (Jeff Chandler) is mortally wounded. *Flying Leathernecks* (1951), starring John Wayne as commander of a squadron of marine pilots, also includes sequences of the kamikaze in action. One American film, *Out of the Depths* (1946), took a different approach. The plot concerns a U.S. submarine that rams a Japanese aircraft carrier loaded with kamikaze planes. Occasionally documentaries, such as "The Fleet That Came to Stay" (1945) and

Kamikaze (1962), covered the deadly battles between the U.S. Navy and the Japanese pilots. ■

Kamikaze (1962), Brigadier. *Sc.* Perry Wolf.

A documentary about the World War II battle in the Pacific, the film covers the days before the attack on Pearl Harbor and ends with the dropping of the atom bombs. Aside from the desperate suicide attacks of the Japanese planes against the U.S. Navy, the work points out in several sequences that America ignored several signs that foretold of the sneak attack on Pearl Harbor. The action shots of the kamikaze pilots hurtling themselves almost with complete abandon at the warships still have a chilling effect on the viewer. ■

Kansas Pacific (1953), AA. *Dir.* Ray Nazarro; *Sc.* Dan Ullman; *Cast includes:* Sterling Hayden, Eve Miller, Barton MacLane, Henry Shannon.

Southern sympathizers try to obstruct the western progress of the Kansas Pacific railroad in this pre-Civil War drama. The film is set in Kansas in 1860 on the eve of the conflict. Those who side with the South want to prevent the rail lines from linking the various forts. The North assigns an army engineer (Sterling Hayden) to put an end to the fighting between the two adversaries. Eve Miller provides the romantic interest in this tale of two emotionally charged, brawling factions. ■

Kansas Raiders (1950), U. *Dir.* Ray Enright; *Sc.* Robert L. Richards; *Cast includes:* Audie Murphy, Brian Donlevy, Tony Curtis, Marguerite Chapman, Dewey Martin.

A highly fictionalized account of Quantrill's murderous raids during the Civil War, the film adds up to just another routine western. The undistinguished script brings together some of the most infamous outlaws joining the notorious leader in a series of chases and skirmishes. Audie Murphy portrays Jesse James, Brian Donlevy impersonates Quantrill, Tony Curtis plays one of the Dalton boys, and Dewey Martin and James Best are featured as the Younger brothers.

One of the few historical events the film recreates is the pillaging of Lawrence, Kansas, in 1862. However, the film then reverts to fiction as it telescopes Quantrill's exploits. It shows Union troops, led by Richard Arlen, putting an end to Quantrill's career in a gun battle. Actually, Quantrill continued for another two years, executing a series of raids. He was finally killed in 1865 in Kentucky when he ran into a Union patrol. ∎

Keep 'Em Flying (1941). See Service Comedy. ∎

Keep 'Em Rolling (1934). See Dogs in War. ∎

"Keep 'em Sailing" (1942). See "Crime Does Not Pay" Series. ∎

Keep Your Powder Dry (1945), MGM. *Dir.* Edward Buzzell; *Sc.* Mary C. McCall, Jr., George Bruce; *Cast includes:* Lana Turner, Laraine Day, Susan Peters, Bill Johnson.

The role of women in war is the subject of this World War II drama. As in its counterpart, the male-dominated war film which often is composed of a unit of recruits from different walks of life, this film similarly focuses on a group of volunteers in the Women's Army Corps or WACs. The women are shown going through a variety of training programs. Lana Turner, as a wealthy socialite, joins up only as a means to claim an inheritance. Laraine Day, as a young woman from a military family, wishes to carry on its tradition. Ultimately, the two women clash (a dispute that existed off-stage as well). Jean Peters portrays a young bride who enlists after her husband has been sent overseas. After the film had been completed, Peters suffered a spinal injury during a hunting accident that left her unable to walk until her death in 1952. ∎

Kelly's Heroes (1970), MGM. *Dir.* Brian G. Hutton; *Sc.* Troy Kennedy Martin; *Cast includes:* Clint Eastwood, Telly Savalas, Don Rickles, Carroll O'Connor, Donald Sutherland.

This World War II comedy drama includes battle scenes, a bank heist, satire, a group of fun-loving G.I.s, suspense and a lot of smart-alecky talk. In other words, the film aims for wide appeal and succeeds much of the time. Its weaknesses lie in its routine plot elements (American soldiers as super-heroes), cliché dialogue ("We're all nuts or we wouldn't be here," "You never stick your neck out for nobody") and irritating anachronisms (anti-establishment attitudes and hippies). Clint

Sergeant Don Rickles weighs part of a captured Nazi gold cache while Clint Eastwood looks on in the offbeat comedy drama *Kelly's Heroes* (1970).

Eastwood, an independent-minded American soldier, learns from a captured German officer that $16 million in gold bullion is stored in a bank behind enemy lines. With the help of his platoon, his reluctant sergeant (Savalas), an overage hippie tank commander (Sutherland) and a self-serving hustler (Rickles), Eastwood sets out against near-impossible odds to relieve the Nazis of the treasure.

Although the plot and much of the heroics are implausible, the lengthy film (over two hours) is helped along by its large-scale production, frequent action sequences, humorous situations and interplay among the odd characters. In fact, one character, Sutherland, sporting a beard and, appearing invariably out of uniform, is called "Oddball." He believes in positive and negative "waves," plays music over a loudspeaker while engaged in battle ("We play music very loud. It kind of calms us down.") and occasionally fires cartridges of paint from his tank instead of deadly shells ("We have our own ammunition. When we fire it, it paints beautiful pictures."). Carroll O'Connor furnishes some broad satire as a loud-mouthed, gung-ho general who mistakes the small cadre of bank robbers for a brave unit of fighting heroes who have taken the initiative to break through German lines. Rickles is particularly funny in his complaints about the discomforts of the war and splitting the take too many ways. Another bit of satire occurs when Eastwood, Savalas and Sutherland approach a German Tiger tank western style, as if going to a shoot-out, while the soundtrack supplies music similar to that of spaghetti-westerns.

The absurdity of the anachronisms—the

offbeat hippie-character of Sutherland and the soundtrack emitting 1960s-type songs (both reminiscent of *M*A*S*H* released one year earlier)— weakens the overall comedy. The anti-patriotic attitudes of the key figures and the dealings with a German officer concerning his split of the gold are further anachronisms that jar the viewer's acceptance of the story on its own terms. The film, shot in Yugoslavia, has more in common with the anti-establishment convictions of the Vietnam War years than it does with the period in which it is supposedly set. ∎

Key, Francis Scott (1779–1843). The War of 1812 had been going badly for the U.S. in the summer of 1814. Following the defeat of an American force of 7,000 at Bladensburg, Maryland, the British marched unopposed into the national capital and burned large areas of the city, including the White House and many government buildings. A British fleet than sailed up Chesapeake Bay to take Baltimore.

Francis Scott Key, a lawyer and poet, went out to meet the approaching enemy force, seeking to negotiate the release of a friend who had been captured at Bladensburg. The British detained Key during the night of September 13–14 while they began to shell Fort McHenry, one of the strongholds defending Baltimore harbor, in preparation for an assault on the city. When, after a night of bombardment, Key saw the American flag still flying over the fort, he immediately poured his emotions into a poem he called "The Defense of Fort McHenry." The poem soon appeared anonymously in handbill form and a few days later was printed in the *Baltimore Patriot*.

The title was changed to "The Star Spangled Banner" sometime in October, 1814. It soon became popular throughout the nation as a song using a well-known British tune, "To Anacreon in Heaven." An Act of Congress (1931) designated the song as the official national anthem. The attack on the fort and Key's inspired poem were the subjects of several early silent one-reel films, including "The Stars and Stripes" (1910), "The Star Spangled Banner" (1911), "The Stars and Stripes Forever" (1913), "The Star Spangled Banner" and a two-reel Edison production "The Birth of the Star Spangled Banner" (both 1914). ∎

Key, The (1934), WB. *Dir.* Michael Curtiz; *Sc.* Laird Doyle; *Cast includes:* William Powell, Edna Best, Colin Clive, Hobart Cavanaugh, Halliwell Hobbes, Henry O'Neill.

The Irish Rebellion provides the background for this drama of a romantic triangle set in 1920. William Powell portrays a British army captain who boasts of his indiscretions. He resumes an earlier affair with his former flame (Edna Best) who is presently married to a captain in British Intelligence (Colin Clive). When the husband sees the two lovers together, he goes on a drinking spree and is taken hostage by the rebels. The revolutionaries offer Clive in exchange for their leader (Donald Crisp) who is about to be hanged. Powell manages to provide an exciting climax to this well-made film.

There is sufficient coverage of the struggle between the Irish revolutionaries and the Black and Tans, including street battles and snipers, to show the horrors and futility of the endless killing that has plagued both Ireland and England for decades. The film has been singled out for its excellent use of atmosphere. ∎

Kharkov trial. See *We Accuse* (1945). ∎

Khyber Patrol (1954), UA. *Dir.* Seymour Friedman; *Sc.* Jack DeWitt; *Cast includes:* Richard Egan, Dawn Addams, Raymond Burr, Patric Knowles.

Warring native tribes, supplied with weapons from the Russians, seek to control the Khyber Pass in this action drama set in Afghanistan in the 1890s. Richard Egan portrays an audacious captain in the British Lancers. His unorthodox methods, both in battle and discipline, affect the morale of his troops. But when he leads his men to victory in their battle against the hostile natives, he vindicates his approach. Paul Cavanaugh plays the general of the Lancer regiment. Dawn Addams, as the commander's daughter, provides the romantic interest for both Egan and Patric Knowles, a lieutenant under Egan. Several exciting action sequences enliven this otherwise routine drama.

The film is reminiscent of those screen adventures of the 1930s which took British imperialism for granted and extolled the glories of British militarism. *Khyber Patrol*, like its predecessors, offers no justification for the British presence in so remote an area or any social or political motivations on the part of the natives who may wish self-rule. Rebel leaders are treated as villainous criminals who, so often easily tricked by a half-clever British officer, must be suppressed. ▪

Kim (1950), MGM. *Dir.* Victor Saville; *Sc.* Leon Gordon, Helen Deutsch, Richard Schayer; *Cast includes:* Errol Flynn, Dean Stockwell, Paul Lukas, Robert Douglas.

Based on Rudyard Kipling's novel, the film tells of a young orphan boy's adventures in late nineteenth-century British-ruled India. Dean Stockwell portrays the youth of the title. The son of Irish parents, Kim's mother died when he was born, and his father, a sergeant in an Irish regiment, died several years later. The boy was left in the care of a half-caste woman. Raised in the streets of India, Kim became knowledgeable in the customs of the land. He later masquerades as a native to help British Intelligence unmask a villainous Czarist Russian who has been plotting to conquer India.

Errol Flynn, sporting a red beard, portrays Mahbub Ali, a horse merchant, who in reality is a member of British Intelligence. Using Kim to deliver a message to a British officer, he eventually introduces the boy to the methods of the secret service. He employs Kim, disguised as a native, as a horse boy. They both become entangled in the plot which ends with Kim's helping the British.

Paul Lukas plays an elderly lama whom Kim, the street urchin, takes a liking to. The lama is seeking a sacred river, and Kim joins him on his journey. As they travel together, the old man imparts his wisdom to the young lad. He later leaves a sum of money for Kim's education.

The film captures much of the sweep and spectacle of Kipling's novel and was attained by cleverly blending location footage with studio shots. Although the story unfolds at a leisurely pace, it has spurts of action, including a native uprising. The plot concerning Russian spies was not an afterthought or conciliatory move by the studio in response to the Cold War; it is part of the original work. ▪

King of the Khyber Rifles (1953), TCF. *Dir.* Henry King; *Sc.* Ivan Goff, Ben Roberts; *Cast includes:* Tyrone Power, Terry Moore, Michael Rennie, Guy Rolfe.

Tyrone Power portrays a half-caste captain in the British army in India. The drama takes place in 1857 when the colonial troops were confronted by the rebellious Afridi tribesmen. Power is assigned to the Khyber Rifles, a troop of natives. Michael Rennie plays the English general in charge of the outpost. Terry Moore, as his daughter, provides the romantic interest. After several skirmishes with the warring tribe, Power leads the climactic charge of the Khyber Rifles who are armed only with knives in a desperate battle with the Afridis. The native soldiers refuse to use the new Enfield rifles, believing that the bullets are greased with pig fat. See Indian Mutiny of 1857–1858. ▪

King Richard and the Crusaders (1954), WB. *Dir.* David Butler; *Sc.* John Twist; *Cast includes:* Rex Harrison, Virginia Mayo, George Sanders, Laurence Harvey, Robert Douglas.

England's King Richard summons the knights of Europe for the Third Crusade and, together, they invade the Holy Land in quest of the Holy Grail. Richard (George Sanders) faces a monumental challenge since he has to struggle against the crafty Saladin, sultan of the Moslem forces, as well as with the selfish aspirations of several members of his entourage. Saladin (Rex Harrison) tries to persuade the king's cousin, Lady Edith (Virginia Mayo), to marry him so that the sanguinary war will end. Laurence Harvey, as the Scot, Sir Kenneth, is Richard's loyal friend. Robert Douglas plays Sir Giles Amaury, the treacherous and ambitious knight. Action sequences include jousts between the knights themselves and battles between the Crusaders and Saladin's hordes. The story is based on Sir Walter Scott's novel, *The Talisman.* ▪

Kings Go Forth (1958), UA. *Dir.* Delmer Daves; *Sc.* Merle Miller; *Cast includes:* Frank Sinatra, Tony Curtis, Natalie Wood, Leora Dana.

France during World War II provides the background for this romantic drama. Natalie Wood, as an American living in Paris, is of mixed blood. Her mother (Leora Dana) is white and her father, now dead, was black. Tony Curtis portrays an American soldier who possesses an abundance of charm but little tolerance. He woos Wood, who falls in love with him. When she tells him of her background, he bluntly rejects her. Frank Sinatra, as another soldier who also likes her, learns of Curtis' callous treatment towards Wood and promises to kill him.

Europe's knights prepare their troops to invade the Holy Land. *King Richard and the Crusaders* (1954).

Their personal differences are temporarily laid aside when they are assigned to a perilous mission. Upon entering a German-occupied town, the two Americans observe a large enemy supply depot and transmit the information to their headquarters. As they attempt to escape, Curtis is mortally wounded. Sinatra holds his former rival in his arms and forgives him. When Sinatra discovers that the Germans plan to move out under the cover of darkness, he calls for American artillery to blast the village. During the shelling Sinatra is hit and loses an arm. When the war ends, he returns to Wood who is busy running a school for war orphans. The film, with its limited number of action sequences, is a routine war romance except for the topic of miscegenation. ■

Tony Curtis and Frank Sinatra, as G.I.s in France during World War II, are assigned to a dangerous mission. *Kings Go Forth* (1958).

Kings of the Sun (1963), UA. *Dir.* J. Lee Thompson; *Sc.* Elliott Arnold, James R. Webb; *Cast includes:* Yul Brynner, George Chakiris, Shirley Anne Field, Richard Basehart.

The ancient Mayans' search for a new home after their defeat in battle serves as the subject of this fascinating drama. Yul Brynner stars as the chief of an Indian tribe who sympathizes with the plight of homeless Mayans and invites them to join his people. George Chakiris portrays the young Mayan king while Shirley Anne Field, as a young Mayan woman, provides the romantic interest. Ultimately, both tribes must defend their homes against the Mayans' former savage enemies who attack these peaceful peoples. ∎

Kiowa War of 1874. This militant Indian tribe that lived in the forbidding canyons of northern Texas, along the tributaries of the Red River, was badly decimated in a campaign by U.S. troops during the Red River Indian War of 1874–1875. Beginning in the late 1860s, a number of western tribes such as the Comanche, Cheyenne and Kiowa had been put on reservations in Oklahoma and Texas. Many of the Indians broke out of confinement and began attacking white settlements. General William Tecumseh Sherman led a detachment of cavalry and infantry in a series of pitched battles against the Indians during the winter of 1874–1875, principally in the Red River valley, that decisively broke the strength of the hostiles. The Kiowa War represented one important phase of the mission. Sherman sent six columns against them, attacking from different directions. In one battle, soldiers descended the steep walls of the Palo Duro Canyon to attack a village of sleeping Kiowas. The Indians were routed and pursued for several miles until many were caught. Their ponies were rounded up and killed. Though some Kiowas continued to show sporadic resistance to white control and reservation life, this was the last great battle for the once proud tribe.

Only a handful of Indians-vs.-cavalry films concern the Kiowa tribe, none of which deals specifically with the actual events of the Kiowa War. The films do, however, underscore the ferocity of the Kiowas. In *Two Flags West* (1950), for instance, the largely fictitious plot has the Union enlisting the aid of captured Confederate soldiers who journey west to help defend the territory against warring Kiowas. In *War Arrow* (1954), a film with even less respect for historical fact, the tribe is so successful in its raids that a U.S. Cavalry outpost has been unable to protect the territory. The government is forced to send an officer to the cavalry outpost who trains a band of Seminole Indians to battle and finally defeat the Kiowas. ∎

Kiss Barrier, The (1925), Fox. *Dir.* R. William Neill; *Sc.* E. Magnus Ingleton; *Cast includes:* Edmund Lowe, Claire Adams, Dina Miller, Marion Harlan, Thomas Mills.

A romantic drama set in France during World War I, the film stars Edmund Lowe as a stage actor fighting in France as a flier. After his plane is shot down, he meets a pretty nurse from whom he steals a kiss. When the war ends, he returns to the stage but is unable to forget his brief meeting with the nurse. He later discovers that she is the niece of his long-time friend. He pursues her, determined to make the relationship permanent while others in the plot provide complications for the would-be lovers. The war scenes, although they provide plenty of action, do not ring true in many instances. The nurse, for example, has been assigned too close to the trenches and the actual conflict, a fact unsubstantiated by the actual war. ∎

Kiss Them for Me (1957), TCF. *Dir.* Stanley Donen; *Sc.* Julius Epstein; *Cast includes:* Cary Grant, Jayne Mansfield, Suzy Parker, Leif Erickson, Ray Walston.

Three naval air aces enjoy an unofficial four-day leave from the Pacific front in this comedy set during World War II. Cary Grant, as one of the trio, maneuvers the leave for himself and his buddies with the intention of adding some romance to his love-starved life. He woos and falls in love with Suzy Parker. Another pilot (Ray Walston) enters politics and wins the election. The third member of the team, Larry Blyden, has been unsuccessful with women. When they receive news that their aircraft carrier has been sunk, they decide to return to duty.

The film, based on a stage version of the novel *Shore Leave* by Frederic Wakeman, touches upon the subject of war profiteering, an issue also included in the play. But for the most part, the film concentrates chiefly on comedy. ∎

Kit Carson (1940), UA. *Dir.* George B. Seitz; *Sc.* George Bruce; *Cast includes:* Jon Hall, Lynn Bari, Dana Andrews, Harold Huber, Ward Bond, Renie Riano, Clayton Moore.

Jon Hall portrays the title character in this action drama set in the 1840s that concludes with a fictionalized account of the birth of the California Republic. The tale is based on the historic first transcontinental crossing by the U.S. Cavalry led by Captain John C. Fremont. Carson, as a wagon train guide, leads a group of settlers to California and is accompanied by Fremont and his troops who are seeking the shortest route to the Mexican-controlled province. The cavalry and settlers join forces to fight off raiding Shoshones while Carson and Fremont, in their spare moments, compete for the attention of Lynn Bari.

Both men are treated as revered and heroic figures. Carson is an omniscient guide whose wit and wisdom make him a natural leader as well as a romantic western hero. "I never was much for houses," he says, rejecting the restraints of civilization for the great outdoors. "You can't see through the walls." Fremont, on the other hand, is the culture hero who defends social structure and the roots of community. "When they write the history of the West," a young pioneer says just before going to his death, "your name is going to stand out awfully big."

Once in Monterey, the American settlers and ranchers are threatened by Castro, an ambitious Mexican general who suspiciously resembles Santa Anna and dreams of becoming the emperor of Mexico. Carson and his two loyal pals, played by Harold Huber and Ward Bond, hold off the invading army at a hacienda until the Americans and Fremont and his soldiers counterattack. Meanwhile, the ranchers hastily declare California a republic and raise a flag with the picture of a bear. "I wasn't present at the birth of this new republic," General Castro states arrogantly after seeing the new flag, "but I'll certainly be present at its death."

The film is similar in plot and theme to *Kit Carson Over the Great Divide* (1925), a silent action drama also featuring Carson and Fremont. Both have the trappings of an ordinary western but blend epic action with historical background. *Frontier Uprising*, a remake of the 1940 George Bruce story and screenplay, appeared in 1961 with James Davis and Nancy Hadley in the featured roles. Basic plot elements remained intact although the characters' names were changed completely.

Historically, Capt. Fremont brought about the conflict between the Americans and the Mexicans by violating international agreements. His actions, which were contrary to his orders, precipitated the Bear Flag War. The frontiersman and army scout Kit Carson, who had been a member of Fremont's expeditions, became embroiled in the Bear Flag conflict. However, the flag with the emblem of the bear was raised for the first time in Sonoma, not in Monterey, and was taken down after only a few days. It was Commodore John Drake Sloat who raised the American flag over Monterey while proclaiming California part of the U.S. See also Bear Flag War, Kit Carson. ∎

Knights of the Round Table (1953), MGM. *Dir.* Richard Thorpe; *Sc.* Talbot Jennings, Jan Lustig, Noel Langley; *Cast includes:* Robert Taylor, Ava Gardner, Mel Ferrer, Anne Crawford, Stanley Baker, Felix Alymer.

Adapted from Sir Thomas Malory's *Le Morte D'Arthur*, the film traces Arthur's rise as leader of England, the founding of the Round Table, the internal wars between dissident knights and Arthur's followers and his eventual death. These events are portrayed with sweep and action in MGM's tradition of lavish spending on costumes and sets. Robert Taylor portrays Lancelot, a loyal follower of King Arthur. Queen Guinevere (Ava Gardner) falls in love with Lancelot prior to her marriage to Arthur. Arthur (Mel Ferrer) is forced to banish his friend Lancelot when the treacherous Modred charges Lancelot with having an affair with the king's wife. Stanley Baker, as the ambitious and envious Modred, plots the fall of Arthur so that he may become ruler.

The legendary story begins after the Roman legions have departed from England, leaving that country to engage in a series of internal wars. Arthur, with the help of Merlin (Felix Alymer), gains the throne when he is able to remove the fabled sword Excalibur from its anvil. He unites the various factions and brings an uneasy peace to the strife-torn land. Modred, who seeks the crown for himself, stirs up discontent among some of the knights. But he must first remove Lancelot, Arthur's greatest champion and Modred's most formidable obstacle. The action sequences involve several hand-to-hand combats as well as large-scale battles between Modred's forces and the armies of Arthur and his loyal knights. Cavalry charges of lancers and long lines of archers firing their arrows into the enemy are particularly effective. ∎

Korea Patrol (1951), Eagle Lion. *Dir.* Max Nosseck; *Sc.* Kenneth G. Brown, Walter Shenson; *Cast includes:* Richard Emory, Al Eben, Benson Fong.

A low-budget Korean War drama, the film depicts the ordeals of a six-man patrol sent out to destroy a strategic bridge before the enemy is able to use it for its advance. Richard Emory portrays the lieutenant in charge of the operation while Benson Fong plays a South Korean scout. Only three men survive to carry out the mission. The film, one of the earliest to use the Korean War as its background, employs stock footage in several places, particularly in scenes showing the United Nations' role in the war and in several battle sequences. ■

Korean War (1950–1953). The weather throughout much of the Korean peninsula on that fateful early Sunday of June 25, 1950, was rainy and windy. But as daylight approached, South Koreans faced something much more serious, the sudden invasion of their country by powerful North Korean Communist forces. At 4:00 A.M. North Korean units crossed the 38th parallel separating the two states and shattered a tenuous world peace that had existed for only five years since the end of World War II. Wielding a military force that completely overshadowed that of the South in numbers as well as in quality of equipment—South Korea, for example, had no tanks or fighting aircraft—the North had taken a gamble to unify the peninsula by force and bring the whole region under Communist domination.

The ensuing war recorded a remarkable number of "firsts." It was the first outright clash between Communist and non-Communist states that turned the Cold War into a shooting war. The conflict marked the first instance that a large portion of the non-Communist world united, under the leadership of the U.S., to repel aggression. For the first time in modern American history the U.S. had to settle for less than total victory in war. It marked the emergence of the widespread use of jets and helicopters. Also, "brainwashing" became part of the English language to describe the first use of techniques developed by the Communists to psychologically break down prisoners. Finally, the war resulted in the longest armistice in American history. No peace treaty was ever signed; an armed truce has been in existence since 1953.

The roots of the Korean War lay in an administrative decision made by the victorious allies at the end of World War II. At that time the Soviet Union and the U.S. agreed to temporarily divide Korea at the 38th parallel, roughly across the middle of the peninsula, so that U.S. forces could take the surrender of Japanese troops in the south while the

U.S.S.R. would handle the surrender of enemy units in the north. That temporary administrative line, however, soon became a rigid political barrier as the Soviet Union repeatedly rebuffed U.N. attempts to unify the country under a freely elected government. Instead, the U.S.S.R. created a militarily powerful Russian-backed Communist dictatorship in the North. When U.S. occupation troops withdrew from South Korea in 1949, the leaders of North Korea made plans to invade the South.

The Korean War soon escalated into a bigger conflict. In a few days the U.S. rushed poorly equipped troops to assist in the defense of South Korea and, at the same time, called for other U.N. countries to do the same. By the end of the war almost two million Americans had seen service there, and a total of 22 U.N. countries had contributed fighting and non-combat forces. Communist China later entered on the side of North Korea and changed a virtual U.N. victory into a stalemate.

North Korea quickly swept southward following the invasion and captured the South Korean capital of Seoul in five days. In two months of steady conquests, the aggressors pushed U.N. troops to the southern tip of the peninsula into a small and beleaguered defense perimeter around the South Korean port of Pusan. The situation for U.N. forces seemed at their bleakest when General Douglas MacArthur, who had been put in charge early in the conflict of all U.N. troops, launched a surprise amphibious assault at the west coast port of Inchon (September 15, 1950) deep behind enemy lines.

The daring U.N. invasion, unexpected at that location, soon resulted in the recapture of Seoul and cut enemy supply lines to strand the bulk of Communist forces far to the south. The U.N. quickly advanced, recovering all its lost territory and taking tens of thousands of Communist prisoners. MacArthur continued to drive forward into North Korea to unify the nation under U.N. control. The American public was exhilarated by the prospect of a short war ending with a resounding defeat for the forces of aggression.

But as U.N. troops in November 1951 approached the Yalu River, North Korea's border with China, Communist China launched a massive attack on forward U.N. elements with 300,000 troops. The assault forced the U.N. into a massive retreat back into South Korea. The Communists recaptured Seoul, marking the city's third exchange of control within seven months. A large contingent of U.S. Army and Marine units, trapped near the Chosen Reservoir and outnumbered by as much as 6 to 1, had to battle their way out of encirclement. They negotiated a 13-day, 75-mile fighting retreat southward through windswept, mountainous terrain in sub-freezing weather to reach the evacuation port of Hungnam. Their successful withdrawal ranks as one of the high points of courage in American military annals. *Retreat, Hell!* (1952), with Frank Lovejoy, re-enacts this grim action and includes the unit commander's phrase, "Retreat, Hell! We're just advancing in another direction."

The U.N. finally stemmed the Communist advance and, in a counteroffensive in the spring of 1951, drove most of the Communist forces back into North Korea. The U.N. retook Seoul for the last time in the see-saw conflict. Heavy fighting continued for control of strategic high ground in central Korea. For most of the remaining two years of war, hostilities alternated between static warfare with opposing forces in heavily barricaded positions to limited offensives by each side. The U.N. military command changed its strategy from seeking to gain ground to a policy of inflicting heavy losses on the Communists through repeated air and artillery bombardment in hopes of weakening the enemy's resolve to continue the war.

An armistice was signed in July 1953, following two years of negotiations that were often interrupted over the problem of repatriation of prisoners. The fighting ended with opposing armies facing each other in the vicinity of the 38th parallel. The see-saw nature of the war savaged the country to a degree rarely equaled in modern combat.

Never acknowledged as an official war—it was called a "police action" by the U.S. government—the Korean conflict, nevertheless, was a major dispute as evidenced by the casualty figures. The U.N. suffered 118,515 killed and another 264,591 wounded, which included U.S. losses of 53,629 dead and 103,284 wounded. Less than a third of the 10,218 Americans taken prisoner returned alive from Communist captivity. An estimated 500,000 South Korean civilians died from causes directly attributed to the war. The Communists had 1,600,000 battle-related

casualties, the majority of whom were Chinese. The Communist Chinese tactic of using human-wave infantry assaults against rapid-firing and powerful weapons resulted in their wholesale slaughter that shocked the western world. In addition, another 400,000 Communist troops had non-battle casualties, principally from weather, disease and inadequate supplies. North Korea suffered an estimated 3 million civilian casualties.

It was a unique war in its effect on domestic American politics. The conflict resulted in a corrosive public dispute—whether it should be broadened or limited to Korea— between the U.N. Commander-in-Chief, General Douglas MacArthur, a popular American World War II military leader, and President Truman. The President, supported by his military staff, advocated that fighting be contained to Korea and fired MacArthur on April 11, 1951. By this act he enforced the principle that civilian authority in a democracy always takes precedence over the military. The MacArthur controversy and ultimate battlefield stalemate eroded public support for the President, and he declined to run for re-election in 1952.

American films of the war often echoed those of World War II. There were dramas about various branches of the service. *Battle Flame* (1959) and *Marines, Let's Go!* (1961) paid tribute to the leathernecks. *The Bridges at Toko-Ri* (1954) and *Battle Taxi* (1955) extolled the bravery of helicopter rescue teams. *Sabre Jet* (1953) and *The Hunters* (1958) recounted the exploits of U.S. fliers. *Battle Circus* (1953) told of the work of field medical units while the more popular *M*A*S*H* (1970) handled the same theme with black humor and irreverent satire.

The story of the individual combat soldier was captured in several films, including *Fixed Bayonets* (1951), *Korea Patrol* (1951) and *Combat Squad* (1953). But perhaps the bleakest aspect of the war was the treatment of American prisoners shown in dramas such as *The Rack* (1956) and *The Hook* (1963) which attempted to recreate some of the horrors inflicted upon those who were captured and the after-effects.

The better-quality films like *Retreat, Hell!* and *Pork Chop Hill* (1959) were generally realistic and uncompromising in their depictions of the war. However, most of the more than 60 films dealing with the Korean conflict treated enemy soldiers and their officers as one-dimensional characters—ruthless, fanatic figures bent on inflicting pain—similar to the portrayals of the Japanese and Nazis in World War II films. Curiously, postwar films did not soften the character of the North Korean troops, as has happened in movies about German soldiers. ■

Kremlin Letter, The (1970). See Cold War. ■

Kukan (1941), William Alexander. *Sc.* Ralph Schoolman.

Chiefly a travelogue of a reporter's journey from Hong Kong to Tibet, with significant pauses at such places as Chungking and Mongolia, the documentary also brings out the brutality of the Japanese in their acts against the Chinese people. Especially disturbing is the merciless bombing of Chungking by waves of Japanese planes. The city is seen as a blazing hell. The film depicts the perseverance and courage of the Chinese as they struggle against the invaders. The Chinese word "kukan" means courage. ■

Kultur (1918), Fox. *Dir.* Edward J. Le Saint; *Sc.* Fred Myton; *Cast includes:* Gladys Brockwell, William Scott, Georgia Woodthorpe, Willard Lewis.

A fictitious re-enactment of the events leading up to World War I provide the background for this tragic love story. Early scenes show the Kaiser plotting for war. Meanwhile, his emissary, Baron von Zeller, is sent to convince the Crown Prince's father, Franz Josef, to cooperate. René, a French Intelligence officer, is assigned to Vienna and told to gain the confidence of a countess, played by Gladys Brockwell, who is close to Franz Josef. They soon fall in love with each other. Archduke Ferdinand, suspicious of Brockwell's influence, orders her to leave Vienna. A fanatic is then dispatched to assassinate the archduke at Sarajevo. When the assassin is captured, von Zeller orders him to say he is a Serbian. "We shall have no difficulty in proving Serbia responsible for the crime," the Baron remarks. He then orders the countess to betray the Frenchman, whom he is suspicious of. Instead, she helps her lover to escape with plans of Germany's invasion. When von Zeller and a handful of soldiers enter her apartment, she admits to assisting the spy and is immediately shot. ■

L

La Follette, Robert Marion. See *Over the Top* (1918). ▪

Ladies Courageous (1944), U. *Dir.* John Rawlins; *Sc.* Norman Reilly Raine, Doris Gilbert; *Cast includes:* Loretta Young, Geraldine Fitzgerald, Diana Barrymore, Anne Gwynne.

This leisurely paced World War II drama pays tribute to the women who ferried airplanes from the U.S. to England. Loretta Young portrays the earnest officer in charge of the WAFS, or Women's Auxiliary Ferrying Squadron. Her job is to keep her pilots' thoughts on delivering the planes. When she is not occupied with straightening out the personal problems of some of her charges, she is busy battling Washington officials to accept the unit as an official branch of military service.

The film explores some of the various reasons why some of the young women joined the group. Geraldine Fitzgerald, for example, plays Young's publicity-seeking sister and member of the team. When she cracks up a plane, she almost causes the discontinuation of the entire squadron. Several romances emerge between the girls and the servicemen they meet. ▪

Ladies of Washington (1944). See Washington, D.C. ▪

Lady From Chungking (1943), PRC. *Dir.* William Nigh; *Sc.* Sam Robins; *Cast includes:* Harold Huber, Anna May Wong, Mae Clarke, Rick Vallin.

Chinese guerrillas battle Japanese troops in this routine drama set during the Sino-Japanese War. Anna May Wong portrays the guerrilla leader who organizes the Chinese peasant farmers against the brutal occupying forces. Harold Huber, as the Japanese officer in charge of the troops, has a weakness for the opposite sex. This leads to his downfall as he becomes enamored of the guerrilla leader who pries military information from him. The film reveals its budget in its cheap sets and small cast. ▪

Lady Has Plans, The (1942). See Spy Comedies. ▪

Lady in Ermine, The (1927), FN. *Dir.* James Flood; *Sc.* Benjamin Glazer; *Cast includes:* Corinne Griffith, Einar Hansen, Ward Crane, Francis X. Bushman.

The drama takes place in the 1800s during the Austrian invasion of Italy. Corinne Griffith portrays Mariana, who marries Adrian, an Italian soldier, on the eve of the invasion. The Italian army marches off to meet the attack but goes in the wrong direction. Meanwhile the Austrians arrive, and their general meets Mariana and takes a fancy to her. The remainder of the film is concerned with how she manages to escape his clutches. There is little action or interest in the war itself. The film should not be confused with *That Lady in Ermine*, a 1948 musical fantasy directed by Ernst Lubitsch.

Austria and Italy twice engaged in short wars during the mid-19th century. The two conflicts (1859, 1866) were important to the growth of an Italian national state. In the first instance the Italian state of Piedmont, a leader in the movement for Italian unification, joined France to attack and defeat Austria. Less than a decade later, Italy allied with Prussia against Austria in the Seven Weeks War (June 20 to October 12, 1866). Austria, in both cases, lost territory in what is today northern Italy. *The Lady In Ermine* (1927), which has no historical significance, uses this background of Austro-Italian conflict for a fictional romantic drama without specifying which of the two wars served as the backdrop to the story. ■

Lafayette, Marquis de (1757–1834). A French aristocrat, military leader and statesman, Lafayette gained tremendous esteem in the hearts of the American people of his time for his part in the American revolution. With no military experience beyond a purchased captain's commission in the French Dragoons, Lafayette at age 20 came to the U.S. at his own expense and presented himself in 1777 to representatives of the American Congress in Philadelphia with a request for a commission as a major general. Lafayette may have sought an opportunity to join the American cause not simply because of his zeal for liberty but as an opportunity to avenge the loss of his father who had been killed by the British in the French and Indian War.

He convinced Congress to allow him to serve without pay. Assigned as an aide to Washington, Lafayette and the American leader developed a close relationship. The young Frenchman took part in the Battle of Brandywine Creek (September 9–11, 1777) where he received a minor wound and shared the hardships of winter at Valley Forge (1777–1778). Later as a divisional commander he served with distinction at the Battles of Barren Hill and Monmouth. During a trip to France (1779–1780), he helped arrange substantial French aid for the Americans. He played a major role in both planning the battle and in the actual fighting against Lord Cornwallis at Yorktown (1781), the engagement that marked the successful end of the Revolution for the young republic.

He returned to France at the conclusion of the American conflict. On his 1784 visit to the U.S., Lafayette was given a hero's welcome, and several states granted him permanent citizenship. In 1824 he returned again to the U.S. on the invitation of Congress as "guest of the nation." His last visit resulted in an outpouring of unparalleled welcome by crowds who looked upon him as one of the last dominant figures of the American Revolution.

As was the case with several other noted historical figures of that period, Lafayette's screen image was chiefly one of cameo roles in silent historical dramas; e.g., *Washington at Valley Forge* (1914) and *Janice Meredith* (1924). In the latter film he received almost as much screen exposure as a comic sergeant played by W. C. Fields. In *Following the Flag to France*, a 1918 World War I documentary, the figure of Lafayette appears only symbolically as a freedom fighter. ■

Lafayette Escadrille. In April 1916, while the U.S. was still neutral in World War I, a small contingent of American pilots volunteered to fight as a unit in the French Air Force against Germany. The Americans, in a romantic historical gesture, adopted as part of their name that of the French hero, the Marquis de Lafayette, who played an important role in the American Revolution. The unit saw considerable action and suffered heavy casualties as part of the French air fleet. Following the entry of the U.S. into the war, the air group transferred to the Army Air Force in January 1918 and became the 103rd Pursuit Squadron.

Of the dozens of World War I films concerning airmen, only a handful pertain to the French squadron. Virtually all were romantic dramas featuring an American ace who performed heroic deeds. *A Romance of the Air* (1918), the first to mention the Escadrille, recounts Lieutenant Bert Hall's true experiences with the flying group and was based on his book *In the Air*. Donald Crisp's *The Firefly of France*, released the same year, concerns an American flier (Wallace Reid) who journeys to France to enlist in the Escadrille. In *Captain Swagger* (1928) an American airman (Rod La Rocque) brings down a German ace responsible for the loss of many allied pilots. William Wellman's *Legion of the Condemned* (1928) resembles the plot of a typical Foreign Legion film more than an air drama. Gary Cooper portrays an American flier with the Escadrille who, because of personal problems, volunteers for suicide missions. Wellman, who directed the trend-setting airplane drama *Wings* (1927), also turned out the inept drama *Lafayette Escadrille* in 1958, not a very fitting final tribute to the famous squadron or the American eagles who volunteered in the early days of the Great War. ■

Lafayette Escadrille (1958), WB. *Dir.* William A. Wellman; *Sc.* A. S. Fleischman; *Cast includes:* Tab Hunter, Etchika Choureau, Bill Wellman, Jr., Jody McCrea.

An American pilot, fighting for the French during World War I, has a German plane on his tail. *Lafayette Escadrille* (1958).

The American volunteer air squadron provides the background for this weak romantic drama set during World War I. Tab Hunter portrays an American who escapes to Paris from a home dominated by an overly strict father. He falls in love with a French prostitute (Etchika Choureau) before volunteering for the Escadrille. The quick-tempered American hits a French officer who has struck him first and is thrown into prison. His American buddies help him to escape. Later, when the U.S. has entered the war, Hunter, who has remained in hiding, joins the American pilots. The film, supposedly based on director William Wellman's experiences during the Great War, provides only a few action sequences. It concentrates chiefly on the romance between Hunter and Choureau, who decides to change her ways. ■

Lafayette, We Come! (1918), Affiliated. *Dir.* Leonce Perret; *Sc.* Leonce Perret; *Cast includes:* E.K. Lincoln, Dolores Cassinelli, Ernest King, Ethel Winthrop.

A World War I drama, the film concerns an American youth (E.K. Lincoln) who, while studying music in France before the war, meets a young Frenchwoman (Dolores Cassinelli). He returns to America, joins the army and is sent to France where he is wounded in battle. He later renews his acquaintance with the young woman whom he discovers has dealings with German spies. But all ends well when he learns that in reality she is an American double agent. The title refers to the remark, "Lafayette, we are here!," allegedly made by one of General Pershing's aides at the tomb of Lafayette following the arrival in France of the first American Expeditionary Forces. ■

Lafitte, Jean (1780?–1854?). Lafitte (also spelled Laffite) was a shadowy character whose real-life exploits as a buccaneer and patriot became the basis for legend. There is no accurate information about his early life before he achieved prominence as the leader of a pirate colony on the Baratarian coast, near New Orleans, from 1810–1814. He attacked Spanish ships in the Caribbean and sold the booty, including slaves, in New Orleans.

During the War of 1812, the British tried to secure Lafitte's assistance for an impending attack on New orleans by offering him $30,000 and a captain's commission in the navy. Lafitte turned the information over to the American governor of the territory. The governor refused to believe the buccaneer and, instead, sent an American force against the colony. Though the Baratarians suffered some losses in the attack, the buccaneer persisted in trying to aid the U.S. He next offered his services to General Andrew Jackson, charged with the defense of New Orleans, in return for a full pardon for him and his colony. All these events were depicted in Cecil B. DeMille's *The Buccaneer* (1938) with Fredric March as Lafitte.

Jackson accepted Lafitte's offer. The Baratarians distinguished themselves as artillerymen and helped to repel the British at the Battle of New Orleans (January 8, 1815). Two films recount Lafitte's exploits during this period. *The Buccaneer* is a fairly accurate version of historical events. Anthony Quinn's 1958 remake, also titled *The Buccaneer*, featured Yul Brynner in the role of a well-dressed, urbane Lafitte and Charlton Heston as Jackson.

President Madison granted full pardon to the Baratarians in 1817. Though accepted as a hero and loyal ally, the lure of buccaneering proved too strong for Lafitte. In 1817 he moved his colony, numbering about a thousand men and their families, to an island off the coast of Texas that is now the site of Galveston. His group resumed preying on shipping in the gulf where some of his men also attacked American vessels. The U.S. government sent another punitive naval expedition against him in 1821. Lafitte put together a select crew for his favorite ship, *The Pride*, and sailed away. Little is known about the remainder of his life. Perhaps Byron's lines best sum up the colorful buc- caneer's career:

He left a corsair's name to other times,
Linked with one virtue and a thousand crimes. ∎

Lancer Spy (1937). See Spy Films: the Talkies. ∎

Land of Liberty (1939), MGM. *Sc.* Jeanie Macpherson, Jesse Lasky, Jr.

Cecil B. DeMille edited this patriotic documentary about the history of the U.S. Using excerpts of films from more than 50 motion picture companies, this compilation covers many significant moments in the nation's rise and development, including, among others, the American Revolution, the battle at the Alamo, the War of 1812, the Civil War, the building of the railroad and the growth of America in the twentieth century. The film, which opened at the 1939 World's Fair in New York, shows various historical figures of which Andrew Jackson, Lincoln and Roosevelt are but a few. Re-edited in 1941 for general theatrical release, it included allusions to World War II and emphasized freedom of race, creed and religion. ∎

Lash, The (1931). See Bear Flag Republic Revolt. ∎

Last Blitzkrieg, The (1958), Col. *Dir.* Arthur Dreifuss; *Sc.* Lou Morheim; *Cast includes:* Van Johnson, Kerwin Mathews, Dick York, Larry Storch, Lise Bourdin.

Van Johnson portrays a German lieutenant in this World War II drama of a squad of Nazi soldiers who infiltrate behind the lines posing as American soldiers. The men are singled out because of their expertise in speaking English. Their mission is to link up with American units and demoralize the Allies and cause confusion. Johnson slowly turns against the Nazi regime and is especially repulsed by their sadistic tendencies as exemplified by one of his own soldiers (Kerwin Mathews). The Americans eventually learn of his masquerade and make him a prisoner. In the final scenes he goes to his death helping his enemies in battle by annihilating a group of German soldiers. This is one of the handful of war films made after the conflict

Sterling Hayden, as Jim Bowie, just before the fall of the Alamo. *The Last Command* (1955).

in which a German is both the main character and a sympathetic figure. ∎

Last Command, The (1955), Rep. *Dir.* Frank Lloyd; *Sc.* Warren Duff; *Cast includes:* Sterling Hayden, Anna Maria Alberghetti, Richard Carlson, Arthur Hunnicutt, Ernest Borgnine.

The battle of the Alamo provides the basis for this action drama starring Sterling Hayden as James Bowie. At first Bowie, a friend of General Santa Anna (J. Carrol Naish) and a rich landowner, prefers moderation in dealing with Mexico. When he returns to his home in Mexico, he has his last friendly meeting with the general. "People nowadays just don't take to one-man rule," Bowie warns the ambitious Mexican. "Most people are like I am," he continues, "and you'll never make me follow you by force." The hypocritical general ignores his friend's pleas to end the oppression of the Texans. "I do not wish to be a dictator, a tyrant," the general says half-heartedly. "I wish to be a gracious page in history." But when Bowie departs, the general issues orders to an army officer to occupy San Antonio.

Fed up with the general's ruthless actions, Bowie joins the other Texans at the old mission and becomes their leader in their fight against their oppressors. The siege that lasted twelve days is depicted in a series of suspenseful and exciting sequences. Richard Carlson, as William Travis, the passionate lawyer, at first opposed Bowie. Arthur Hunnicutt plays Davy Crockett, whose good humor and tall stories regale the other defenders. Ben Cooper, as a young Texan whom

Bowie uses as a courier, becomes the only survivor of the siege. ∎

Last Flight, The (1931), FN. *Dir.* William Dieterle; *Sc.* John Monk Saunders; *Cast includes:* Richard Barthelmess, John Mack Brown, Helen Chandler, Elliott Nugent, Walter Byron.

A drama of four American pilots injured in World War I, the film explores their friendship, their individual fears and their different methods of suppressing the horrors of their experiences. Having reconciled themselves to the fact that they can never go home to their parents or the conventional values of their society, they decide to remain in France after the war where they indulge in drinking and other pleasurable pursuits.

Richard Barthelmess plays a flier whose hands were burned. He uses both hands for such commonplace functions as holding a glass. Another (David Manners) was wounded in one eye. Elliott Nugent, as a third member of the group, has difficulty staying awake. The fourth airman (John Mack Brown) is high-strung and hostile. Helen Chandler, as a wealthy young woman and 1920s flapper, joins the quartet and displays a romantic interest in Barthelmess. The latter is the only flier to survive, the others losing their lives in mundane incidents.

Although similar films about wartime camaraderie and the problems of ex-servicemen were to follow (*The Lost Squadron* (1932), for example), very few would capture the psychological complexities of this almost forgotten drama. ∎

Last Frontier, The (1955), Col. *Dir.* Anthony Mann; *Sc.* Philip Yordan, Russell S. Hughes; *Cast includes:* Victor Mature, Guy Madison, Robert Preston, James Whitmore, Anne Bancroft.

Tensions mount at a frontier outpost plagued by a deranged colonel, a ruthless sergeant and threats of Indian attacks in this drama set during the 1860s. Victor Mature portrays one of three unsuccessful trappers who sign up as scouts for the post commander, played by Robert Preston. Mature then proceeds to woo the colonel's wife (Anne Bancroft). Guy Madison plays a captain. Peter Whitney, as the brutal sergeant, is hated by the men. Preston organizes a large-scale assault on the Indians and is killed in the ensuing battle. ∎

Last Man, The (1916), Vitagraph. *Dir.* William Wolbert; *Cast includes:* William Duncan, Corinne Griffith, Mary Anderson, Otto Lederer.

A domestic drama set on a remote army post in Montana and in the Philippines, the film centers on an army major's failed marriage and new-found love. William Duncan, as the officer who returns from the Philippines after the Spanish-American War, discovers that his wife (Mary Anderson) is having an affair with a young lieutenant. Following the couple's divorce, she marries her lover. The major meets and falls in love with a local girl of the mountains (Corinne Griffith). When he is reassigned to the Philippines, he takes the young woman along as a nurse. The lieutenant also is ordered to the islands and takes his wife along. The remainder of the film deals with live jungle battles during the Moro uprising and the former wife's fruitless efforts to win her husband back, the latter resulting in friction between the two officers. ∎

Last of the Comanches (1952), Col. *Dir.* Andre DeToth; *Sc.* Kenneth Gamet; *Cast includes:* Broderick Crawford, Barbara Hale, Johnny Stewart, Lloyd Bridges.

A small U.S. Cavalry force fights its way to safety after the Comanches attack a western town in this drama. The cavalrymen, under command of their sergeant (Broderick Crawford), are joined by a group of stagecoach passengers also seeking to escape the murderous hostiles. The two groups take refuge in an abandoned mission which contains the only water available for miles. The Indians, who keep the whites under siege, also are desperate for water and plan to wipe out the few defenders. But the cavalry arrives in time to end this routine film.

The sequences involving the water have been lifted from *Sahara* (1943), a World War II action drama starring Humphrey Bogart. Set in North Africa during a British rout by German forces, an entire German column, also desperate for water, advances to a known oasis only to find it controlled by a handful of allied soldiers. The defenders plan to hold the oasis as a means of slowing down the German advance. ∎

Last of the Mohicans, The (1920), APR. *Dir.* Maurice Tourneur; *Sc.* Robert Dillon;

Cast includes: Harry Lorraine, Wallace Beery, Barbara Bedford, Albert Roscoe, Lillian Hall.

Based on James Fenimore Cooper's novel set during the French and Indian Wars, the film recounts most of the important incidents of the original work. One major change is the emphasis on the characters of Uncas, the young Mohican; Cora, General Munro's daughter; and Magua, the traitorous Indian and deadly enemy of both the British and the Mohicans. Hawkeye, Cooper's heroic figure in the Leatherstocking Tales, has a less important role in the film version. Action sequences include the massacre of British troops and their families by the Hurons after General Montcalm promises safe conduct if they surrendered and the final hand-to-hand combat between Uncas and Magua. Wallace Beery portrays a vicious and frightening Magua. An earlier abbreviated screen version of the novel, also titled "The Last of the Mohicans," appeared in 1911.

Director Tourneur's visual style enhances the film. He carefully selected California locales that closely resembled the Northeast where the story is set. He also handled the romance between Uncas and Cora discreetly.

Last of the Mohicans, The (1936), UA.

Dir. George B. Seitz; *Sc.* John Balderston; *Cast includes:* Randolph Scott, Binnie Barnes, Heather Angel, Henry Wilcoxon, Bruce Cabot, Robert Barrat, Phillip Reed.

The first sound adaptation of James Fenimore Cooper's novel of the French and Indian War, this version stars Randolph Scott as Hawkeye, the celibate colonial scout; Binnie Barnes and Heather Angel as Alice and Cora, the daughters of Colonel Munro; Henry Wilcoxon as the aloof British major assigned to protect the sisters; Bruce Cabot as the treacherous Magua; Robert Barrat as Chingachgook, the proud, stoic Mohican chief; and Phillip Reed as his obedient son, Uncas, the "last of the Mohicans." The episodic film provides plenty of suspense and action as Hawkeye and his two Mohican friends lead the small party of the sisters and the major to safety while Magua plots a series of obstacles.

An acceptable adaptation of the novel, the film makes several deletions as well as some minor alterations, such as the additional romance between Hawkeye and Alice, the way

Buster Crabbe portrays Magua, a treacherous Iroquois in *Last of the Redmen* (1947), yet another version of James Fenimore Cooper's tale, *The Last of the Mohicans.*

in which Uncas and Cora die and the transformation of Cora's racial origin. Cooper has Cora's father explain that her mother was a West Indian. Since this is not mentioned in the film, the budding romance between Uncas and Cora seemed bold for the 1930s. But like most interracial affairs concocted in Hollywood, this one ends in disaster. When Uncas is killed by Magua, Cora jumps to her death. In the novel the young couple are killed by Hurons.

Seitz was an experienced director of action dramas since the silent period. He effectively substituted California locales for the colonial Northeast and gave the film a sense of vigorous action, especially in the massacre sequence at Fort William Henry. ∎

Last of the Redmen (1947), Col. Dir.

George Sherman; *Sc.* Herbert Dalmas, George H. Plimpton; *Cast includes:* Jon Hall, Michael O'Shea, Evelyn Ankers, Julie Bishop, Buster Crabbe.

Based on James Fenimore Cooper's novel, *The Last of the Mohicans,* the film strays from the original work as it tells of the journey of British General Munro's children from Fort Edward to Fort William Henry to join their father. Jon Hall portrays Major Heyward, an English officer who accompanies the two pretty daughters and a 12-year-old son. Magua, a malcontent Iroquois warrior (Buster Crabbe), plots to capture them but is foiled by Hawkeye (Michael O'Shea), a loyal British scout, who is accompanied by his friend and the last of the Mohicans, Uncas.

Confederate troops join Union forces to battle the Apache during the Civil War. *The Last Outpost* (1951).

Although set at the time of the French and Indian War, the film contains little mention of the conflict. Instead, it focuses on several battles between the Indians and the British colonials. Several more accurate versions of Cooper's famous novel have been brought to the screen. ∎

Last Outpost, The (1935), Par. *Dir.* Louis Gasnier, Charles Barton; *Sc.* Phillip MacDonald; *Cast includes:* Cary Grant, Claude Rains, Gertrude Michael, Kathleen Burke, Colin Tapley.

Cary Grant and Claude Rains portray two British officers assigned to the Middle East in this World War I drama dominated by a routine romantic triangle. They assist each other during battle but are in love with the same woman. Grant falls in love with his nurse while he is recuperating from a previous battle. He later learns that she is the wife of a British Intelligence officer (Rains) who has saved Grant's life. Rains returns to his wife after a three-year absence, but her love for

him has vanished. Several effective action sequences include native uprisings, a realistic and brutal retreat of hordes of natives fleeing from a savage Kurdish attack and a rousing, climactic last-minute rescue of a beleaguered Sudanese outpost. ∎

Last Outpost, The (1951), Par. *Dir.* Lewis R. Foster; *Sc.* Geoffrey Homes, George W. Yates, Winston Miller; *Cast includes:* Ronald Reagan, Rhonda Fleming, Bruce Bennett, Bill Williams.

Two brothers on opposing sides during the Civil War join forces temporarily to fight the Apaches in this routine drama set in the West. Ronald Reagan portrays a Confederate officer in charge of a guerrilla band that raids Union supply lines. Bruce Bennett, as his brother and a Yankee officer, is sent west to stop the raids. His instructions include arming the Apaches and using them to fight the Confederate raiders. Reagan, suspecting the Indians will turn against all whites, tries to stop the move but fails. When the Apaches attack the fort of Union troops and settlers, Reagan and his cavalry come to the aid of the besieged post. The Southerners then depart and return to the South. Rhonda Fleming provides the romantic interest for Reagan in his first starring western. The film sometimes appears under the title *Cavalry Attack.* ■

Last Parade, The (1931), Col. *Dir.* Erle C. Kenton; *Sc.* Dorothy Howell; *Cast includes:* Jack Holt, Tom Moore, Constance Cummings, Gaylord Pendleton.

Two buddies who enlist in World War I and see action together in France wind up on opposite sides of the law in this drama based on a story by Casey Robinson. Jack Holt portrays a wisecracking news reporter before he joins the army while Tom Moore plays a policeman who enjoys his pal's humor. During a battle, Holt saves Moore, who becomes entangled in some barbed wire, but loses an eye during the rescue. Both men end up in a field hospital where they meet and fall in love with Constance Bennett.

After the armistice, the friends, with their entire unit, proudly parade through the streets of New York. Holt, unable to find work, turns to a life of crime and rises to gang leader. Moore, on the other hand, advances to detective. Eventually, Holt is brought to justice for the murder of a rival gangster (Robert Ellis) and sentenced to death. Moore and Bennett are permitted to accompany their friend to the death chamber, the "last parade." ■

Last Plane Out (1983), Jack Cox Prod. *Dir.* David Nelson; *Sc.* Ernest Tidyman; *Cast includes:* Jan-Michael Vincent, Julie Carmen, Mary Crosby, David Huffman.

An American journalist takes the audience through the final days of Nicaragua's Somoza regime in this inept semi-documentary drama. Jan-Michael Vincent portrays Jack Cox, a long-time reporter of Latin-American activities, who manages to interview spokespersons from both sides of the revolution. However, the rebel forces think he is a C.I.A. agent and warn him to leave strife-torn Nicaragua. The remainder of the film deals with melodramatic events as Cox, whose life is on the line, attempts to escape while carrying on an affair with a female rebel leader. In the chaotic background, Somoza's government is collapsing. Lloyd Battista plays the beleaguered Anastasio Somoza. Julie Carmen, as

Cox's romantic interest, has to choose between the rebel cause and her love for the journalist in this low-budget film. ■

Last Rebel, The (1918), Triangle. *Dir.* Gilbert Hamilton; *Sc.* G. E. Jenks; *Cast includes:* Walt Whitman, Belle Bennett, Lillian Langdon, Joe Bennett.

A romantic drama with a Civil War background, the film concerns two lovers, a boy from the North and his sweetheart from the South. With the outbreak of the war, the boy joins the Union army. The girl marries a Southerner. Fifty years have passed and the girl, now dead, leaves a granddaughter who is about to lose the family home. The Northerner, who now has a grandson, for sentimental reasons, sends the young man to buy the house. Although he arrives too late to prevent the sale, he is able to save the young woman from poverty by marrying her. ■

Last Ride, The (1944). See Home Front. ■

Last Starfighter, The (1984). See Science Fiction Wars. ■

Last Time I Saw Archie, The (1961), UA. *Dir.* Jack Webb; *Sc.* William Bowers; *Cast includes:* Robert Mitchum, Jack Webb, Martha Hyer, France Nuyen, Joe Flynn, James Lydon.

Robert Mitchum portrays a crafty private during World War II who convinces others that he is a general on special assignment in this routine comedy. A talented con man, Mitchum poses as an Intelligence officer who is pursuing a Japanese agent. The film continues his shady career into his civilian life. Director Jack Webb plays Mitchum's buddy. Screenwriter William Bowers based his tale on his own army experiences. Incidentally, the real Archie, on whom the title character was fashioned, sued the studio. ■

Last Train From Madrid, The (1937), Par. *Dir.* James Hogan; *Sc.* Robert Wyler, Louis Stevens; *Cast includes:* Dorothy Lamour, Lew Ayres, Gilbert Roland, Karen Morley, Anthony Quinn.

The drama combines the *Grand Hotel* framework of bringing together a variety of characters in a tense situation with the Spanish Civil War as background. However, little of the conflict comes through either in the dialogue or the action, except for some street fighting. The conflict serves as a frame for an assortment of principals who board a train in Madrid that is bound for the safety of Valencia. Lew Ayres portrays an American reporter, Helen Mack a prostitute and Anthony Quinn a Spanish captain.

The studio decided to take a neutral stand on the issues of the war in this inept drama. However, this was the first Hollywood film to use the Spanish Civil War as backdrop for its drama. *Blockade*, starring Henry Fonda and Madeleine Carroll, appeared the following year. The overcautious studio emphasized the romantic element and avoided any specific political or social issues concerning the war. Despite its heedful approach, the innocuous film was attacked by both factions of the political spectrum. ∎

Lava Beds War. See Modoc War of 1872–1873. ∎

Leatherneck, The (1929). See Court-Martial Films. ∎

Leathernecks Have Landed, The (1936), Rep. *Dir.* Howard Bretherton; *Sc.* Seton I. Miller; *Cast includes:* Lew Ayres, Isabel Jewell, Jimmy Ellison, James Burke, J. Carrol Naish.

An action drama with China as a backdrop, the film stars Lew Ayres as a fighting marine who is drummed out of the corps when he is held responsible for the death of his friend. The incident was provoked by an unscrupulous Russian, played by J. Carrol Naish. The Leathernecks manage to defeat hordes of Chinese bandits in their rescue of a handful of Americans. The film involves gun running and contains several action sequences, some of which were borrowed from newsreel footage and smoothly interspersed into this low-budget release. ∎

Lee, Robert E. (1807–1870). April 18, 1861, must have been a day of deep, searing anguish for Virginia-born Robert E. Lee. His native state announced its secession from the Union and, with war seeming imminent, President Lincoln offered him the post of field commander of all Union land forces. Many military historians claim Lee was the outstanding general of the American Civil War and that the conflict may not have turned into such a long, blood-letting struggle if he had been field general of the Union army. Subsequently, as commander of the

Army of Northern Virginia, Lee was credited with keeping superior enemy forces unbalanced and in check for most of the conflict.

His decision to resign from the Union army was difficult because he was personally against slavery and the idea of secession. But when Virginia broke with the Union, Lee said: "I must side either with or against my section. I cannot raise my hand against my birthplace, my home, my children." Films have failed to explore this personal drama.

In his first major Civil War engagement he ended McLellan's threat to Richmond, the Confederate capital, in the Seven Days Battle (June 25–July 1, 1862). He defeated General Pope at Second Bull Run (August 29–30, 1862), was stopped in his first Northern drive at Antietam (September 17) in the bloodiest engagement of the war, rebounded to defeat General Burnside at Fredericksburg (December 13) and followed that with a victory over General Hooker at Chancellorsville (May 2–4, 1863). His audacious plan to invade the North and encircle Washington led to his defeat by considerably superior enemy forces at Gettysburg (July 1–3, 1863), the turning point of the war. Several of these battles have been re-enacted in silent films, including *The Battle of Bull Run* (1913), *The Battle of Gettysburg* (1913, 1936) and *Between Two Fires* (1914).

Though Lee repulsed Grant's frontal assaults in the Wilderness Campaign (May–June, 1864), he was too weak to press an offensive. Grant's long, successful siege of Petersburg (July 1864–April 1865) forced Lee to retreat. Badly outnumbered, his troops depleted and cut off, he surrendered to Grant at Appomattox Court House (April 9, 1865), ending the war.

Like his counterpart, General Grant, Lee has been portrayed in numerous silent and sound films but only as a minor character. He is shown chiefly as a commanding and sympathetic figure. "The Blue and the Gray or the Days of '61" (1908), "Stirring Days in Old Virginia" (1909), "The Road to Richmond" (1910), *With Lee in Virginia* (1913), *Abraham Lincoln* (1924) and *The Warrens of Virginia* (1924) are some of the silents. He is also portrayed directing his troops during battle in D.W. Griffith's Civil War classic *The Birth of a Nation* (1915).

With the advent of sound, he was represented in fewer films. These include, among others, *Only the Brave* (1930) and *Seven An-*

gry Men (1955). One noteworthy and poignant portrait of Lee appears in Griffith's
Abraham Lincoln (1930). He is depicted as a
crushed soul on the eve of his surrender. ▪

Leech, The (1922). See Veterans. ▪

Legion of Missing Men (1937), Mon. *Dir.*
Hamilton MacFadden; *Sc.* Sherman Lowe,
Harry O. Hoyt; *Cast includes:* Ralph Forbes,
Ben Alexander, George Regas, Hala Linda.

Another adventure drama about the French
Foreign Legion, this inept low-budget film
adds another element to the familiar formula—songs. Veteran actors Ralph Forbes
and Ben Alexander portray brothers much in
the vein of the earlier *Beau Geste*. Hala Linda,
as a cafe singer, provides the romantic interest and conflict as she warbles "You Are My
Romance" to Forbes, the older brother. The
film provides some action sequences, but
they are chiefly borrowed from stock footage,
betraying the low production values of the
drama. ▪

Legion of the Condemned (1928), Par.
Dir. William Wellman; *Sc.* John Monk Saunders, Jean de Limur; *Cast includes:* Gary Cooper, Fay Wray, Barry Norton, Lane Chandler,
Francis MacDonald.

A World War I aviation drama turned out
by the same director as *Wings*, released a year
earlier, the film concerns a group of American airmen in the Lafayette Escadrille who
continually volunteer for suicide missions
because of some personal incident in their
past lives. Gary Cooper, one of the fliers, was
in love with an attractive young woman (Fay
Wray) whom he had seen at a gathering with
a German officer. Disillusioned, he joined the
other members of the Legion. What he didn't
know was that she was a French spy ordered
to develop a friendship with the German. He
volunteers for the next assignment—dropping a spy behind enemy lines. The spy turns
out to be the young woman he is trying to
forget. She explains all and the mission proceeds, with Cooper scheduled to return for
her at a specific time. She is caught and used
as bait to capture the pilot. When he comes
for her he is seized as well. His fellow pilots
attack, drop bombs and rescue both the hero
and heroine.

Wellman, the director, utilized some of the
footage of his previous air epic. The story,
however, is different, if weaker. Cooper's mo-

French Legionnaires on the attack against warring
desert tribes. *Legion of the Doomed* (1958).

tivation for joining the "legion of the condemned" seems silly in terms of the film's
concept and the reasons given by his fellow
pilots. Co-screenwriter Jean de Limur, a
former member of the Escadrille, had been
credited with shooting down seven enemy
aircraft during the war. ▪

Legion of the Doomed (1958), AA. *Dir.*
Thor Brooks; *Sc.* Tom Hubbard, Fred Eggers;
Cast includes: Bill Williams, Kurt Kreuger,
Dawn Richard, Anthony Caruso.

Another tale of the men of the French Legionnaires and their battles against the desert
sands and rebellious tribes, this action drama
is below average in its routine plot. Bill
Williams portrays a soldier who ultimately
gives a good account of himself in the famous
Legion. But he manages to fall in love with
his commander's wife (Dawn Richard). Kurt
Kreuger enacts the sadistic post commander
and husband. The tedious and familiar plot
provides some relief with an occasional skirmish between the soldiers and the warring
natives. ▪

Leonidas. See *The 300 Spartans* (1962). ▪

Lepanto, Battle of. See *In the Palace of the
King* (1923). ▪

Lest We Forget (1918), Metro. *Dir.* Leonce
Perret; *Sc.* Leonce Perret; *Cast includes:*
Hamilton Revelle, Rita Jolivet, L. Rogers Lyt-
ton, Kate Blancke, Emil Roe.

A large-scale production based on the sinking of the *Lusitania* and its aftermath, the unabashedly propagandistic drama pleads for
revenge. The film stars Rita Jolivet, one of the
actual survivors. Scenes include the salon of
the vessel with the passengers dressed in

evening clothes, the inside of a submarine with a view of a torpedo speeding toward the ill-fated ship, people rushing to the decks, others jumping overboard, children swimming helplessly. The film later shows scenes in the trenches where an American joins a Canadian unit fighting against the Germans so that he can avenge the one he loves. Released during World War I, the production contains an abundance of patriotic elements, including much flag-waving. A doughboy, for instance, salutes the flag while in the trenches as another fatally wounded soldier embraces Old Glory in his arms. Concluding with a cry for revenge, it evokes images of the Statue of Liberty and the spirit of Edith Cavell, the English nurse who was executed by the Germans. The propaganda element was so persuasive that during one of Rita Jolivet's appearances in Connecticut, she was able to raise more than $250,000 in sales of Liberty Bonds. After the armistice, the German consul in Geneva, Switzerland, objected so strongly to the film being shown there that several scenes had to be cut from the production. ∎

Let It Rain (1927). See Service Comedy. ∎

Let's Get Tough! (1942). See Spy Films: the Talkies. ∎

Letter to Evie, A (1945), MGM. *Dir.* Jules Dassin; *Sc.* De Vallon Scott, Alan Friedman; *Cast includes:* Marsha Hunt, John Carroll, Hume Cronyn, Spring Byington.

A World War II comedy drama, the film concerns a young girl (Marsha Hunt) who puts a letter into the shirt pocket of an unknown G.I. Selecting a large-size shirt, she envisions the man of her dreams writing to her. A G.I. (John Carroll) known for his female conquests, receives the letter but turns it over to his diminutive buddy, Hume Cronyn, who corresponds with Hunt. He also sends her a picture of Carroll. When the boys hit New York, the expected complications arise as Cronyn attempts to protect his secret love from his wolfish pal in this entertaining tale. The film is a remake of *Don't Write Letters* (1922), starring Gareth Hughes as the shy doughboy. ∎

Lexington and Concord, Battle of (April 19, 1775). It was a cold, spring day, and though the sun shined brightly, a steady east wind gave a bite to the air. Late in the afternoon, a rag-tag column of 70 armed Minute Men under Captain John Parker had formed on the Lexington town green facing the road that ran past Lexington from Boston to Concord. Alerted by Paul Revere shortly past midnight that the British were coming, the moment of confrontation had arrived.

Facing the colonial militia were an estimated 600–800 British troops in ordered ranks under Major John Pitcairn. They had been on the way to Concord to destroy a supply of colonial arms and ammunition when their path was barred by the small unit of colonial militia.

"Stand your ground," said Parker to his militiamen. "Don't fire unless fired upon. But if they want a war, let it begin here."

The British commander came forward and ordered the Colonials to lay down their arms and disperse. Realizing the hopelessness of the odds, Parker ordered his men to leave, and some Americans began to drift away.

Suddenly a shot rang out from the British lines, followed by a series of volleys at the retreating Americans. The Colonials responded with a few scattered shots, and the British answered with a charge that scattered the militia. The Americans suffered eight dead and ten wounded to one wounded British private. It was hardly a skirmish, much less a battle. But as Captain Parker had prophesied before he himself was cut down, it was the start of open warfare between the colonies and Britain.

The British advanced to Concord where they seized some American supplies, but on resuming their return march to Boston, the second phase of the battle took shape. American militia swarmed into the area as word of the fighting spread. An estimated 4,000 Colonials attacked from the woods and from behind buildings and fences, all along the route of the retreating British. By the time the beleaguered column reached Boston, the British casualty list showed 73 killed, 174 wounded and 26 missing. The Americans had 93 casualties which included dead, wounded and missing. Colonial forces immediately closed in on Boston, the main British base in New England, to begin a siege that would last almost a year. The American Revolution had begun.

The battle played a prominent role in a handful of historical films. One of the earliest, *The Heart of a Hero* (1916), a fictionalized biography of Nathan Hale, had Hale witness the skirmish between the colonists and British troops at Concord. *Cardigan* (1922) depicted the battle as well as the retreat of the British soldiers. In *Janice Meredith* (1924), another drama of the American Revolution, the battle was one of several historical events re-enacted on screen. Finally, in *Johnny Tremain* (1957), a youth during the Revolution becomes an eyewitness to major events, including the initial battle. ■

Leyte Gulf, Battle for. American and Japanese naval and air force units fought three consecutive sea battles (October 23, 1944– October 26, 1944) to secure control of Leyte Gulf, essential for supporting the landings by American troops on the Philippine Island of Leyte. Japan precipitated the action by using part of its fleet as a decoy to lure an American carrier force away from the Gulf of Leyte. This would allow a second Japanese fleet to overwhelm the amphibious elements supporting the American invasion and strand the American ground forces already on shore.

Though badly defeated at the Battle of Surigao Strait, the decoy force retreated and succeeded in attracting Admiral Halsey's naval units in pursuit away from the Gulf. However, in two immediate follow-up encounters with other converging Japanese units in Battles off Samar and Cape England, enemy naval units were badly mauled.

The Battle for Leyte Gulf stands out for at least two reasons. As a result of extensive losses, the Japanese fleet was finished as a viable naval force for the remainder of World War II. In addition, the engagement involved the greatest concentration of personnel and vessels in history. A total of 282 ships and about 185,000 sailors and pilots took part. The Japanese lost 10,500 sailors and airmen, 500 planes, and 29 ships, including four carriers, plus sustaining damage to those vessels that escaped. American losses were 2,800 killed, 1,000 wounded, six ships and 200 aircraft.

Few films covered this World War II action. *Brought to Action* (1945), a World War II documentary, covers the October 1944 second sea battle of the Philippines off Leyte. *Raiders of Leyte Gulf* (1963), a low-budget action drama, exploits the battle in the title but has little to do with actual events. Small forces of American soldiers and Filipino guerrillas

battle the Japanese who overwhelmingly outnumber them. ■

Lieutenant Wore Skirts, The (1956). See Service Comedy. ■

Life and Times of Rosie the Riveter, The (1980), Connie Field. *Dir.* Connie Field.

A documentary about the contributions of women to the war industry during World War II, the film entertainingly depicts the variety of jobs they performed and how they were callously mistreated when the conflict ended. Using excerpts from newsreels and other documentaries of the war years, director Connie Field reveals how the wives, sisters and sweethearts of men fighting the war were persuaded to pick up the tools of light and heavy industry and carry on the essential work in the factories and shipyards. Some unpleasantries are also exposed, such as the racist attitudes of some employers, unions and fellow workers who tried to halt the employment of black women or, when they were hired, to prevent them from sharing the shower facilities with the white workers. Interviews with several women who served their country on the home front in these war industries bring out how they were quickly discarded when the men returned from the front to claim their old jobs. Although they were once again relegated to their homes and kitchens, the film suggests that the role of women was changed forever after their experiences on the assembly line proved they could compete favorably with their counterparts. The title is from the popular song of the 1940s and a film from that decade. ■

Life of General Villa, The (1914), Mutual. *Dir.* Christy Cabanne; *Cast includes:* Raoul Walsh.

General Pancho Villa, engaged in armed rebellion while the film was made, liked motion pictures so much that he allowed American cameramen to accompany him on his raids and photograph executions of prisoners. Of course, he also enjoyed the $500 in gold he received each month while the picture was being shot. Raoul Walsh, later to become a major Hollywood director, played Villa as a young man. Part of the plot concerns Villa's motivation for turning into a rebel. After his sister is raped by an army officer, Villa kills the man and escapes into the mountains. The story then traces his career as bandit and revolutionary. The film includes exciting action sequences as the camera follows Villa and his men in actual battles.

This crude biography is one of the earliest examples of a movie studio influencing actual events. Villa's practice was to execute his prisoners early in the morning before full daylight. Because the lighting was poor, the cameramen requested that the shootings occur later in the day. Villa agreed. ■

Lifeboat (1944), TCF. *Dir.* Alfred Hitchcock; *Sc.* Jo Swerling; *Cast includes:* Tallulah Bankhead, William Bendix, Walter Slezak, John Hodiak, Henry Hull, Heather Angel, Hume Cronyn.

A World War II drama about survivors adrift in a lifeboat after their freighter has been torpedoed and shelled by a German U-boat, the film examines the depths of Nazi depravity. The submarine captain, portrayed by Walter Slezak, is rescued by the inhabitants of the lifeboat although some vote to throw him overboard. John Hodiak, as an American crew member of the torpedoed freighter, is suspicious of the Nazi. But they all share their food and water with him. In return, he secretly steers the boat toward German waters while professing the doctrines of Nazi superiority. When all are asleep, he disposes of one of the passengers (William Bendix), an American seaman who has lost a leg. Eventually, the others learn that he was the captain of the U-boat that sank their ship. When they discover what he has done to the wounded seaman and his other deceptions, they turn on him, pummel him and throw him overboard. John Steinbeck wrote the story for Hitchcock.

The film is representative of the propaganda and patriotism that Hollywood specialized in during the war. The American and British occupants of the lifeboat, including a black steward (Canada Lee), display their humanity and democratic values in their treatment towards the Nazi and in rationing their food and water supplies equally. They take a vote each time an important decision is to be made. The German, on the other hand, embodies the characteristics of the stereotypical enemy—he is brutal, treacherous, almost inhuman. "You can't treat them as human beings," an industrialist (Henry Hull) concludes at the end of the film. "You've got to exterminate them!" Several critics faulted Hitchcock's character portrayals by pointing

out that the Nazi was more articulate about his political beliefs than were the contentious representatives of democracy.

The film also touches upon several other points. The effectiveness of Germany's submarine fleet in interrupting the flow of war materiel across the Atlantic is suggested in Bendix's frustration. "This is the fourth time I shipped out since the war and I ain't got no place yet," he says. "I wish I could make the complete round trip just once." The film condemns the evils of capitalism, as personified by Hull, while extolling the virtues of the common man, as represented by Hodiak, Hume Cronyn, Bendix and Lee. "Remember the boom we had after the last war?" Hull, the rich, lonely industrialist muses. "The boom after this war will make the last one look like a flurry." A rich, spoiled journalist (Tallulah Bankhead), who calls the black steward "Charcoal," lives only for her sensual pleasures and "earthly possessions," including her diamond bracelet and fur coat, until she falls in love with Hodiak. Meanwhile Hodiak, the ideal American as viewed during World War II, suspects the enemy, demonstrates leadership qualities, treats the other survivors equally and fantasizes about improving the lot of factory workers. The seaman, Bendix, has changed his name from Schmidt to Smith. "They make me ashamed of the name I was born with," he avows, referring to the Nazis. The idealization of the common man emerges as a recurrent theme in World War II films released during the conflict. ■

Life's Greatest Problem. See *Safe for Democracy* (1918). ■

Light, The (1919), Fox. *Dir.* J. Gordon Edwards; *Sc.* Adrian Johnson, Charles Kenyon; *Cast includes:* Theda Bara, Eugene Ormonde, Robert Walker, George Renevant.

Theda Bara portrays a loose woman who inhabits the cheap dance halls of Paris during World War I. She breaks with her Apache lover when she meets a young sculptor who would like her to pose for him. But he goes to the front lines, is blinded and returns to Paris. She meets him and accompanies him to a country house where she helps him regain his strength. Her lover traces her to the country, and she is forced to kill him. The blind soldier, who "sees" into her soul and finds only good there, defends her. ■

Light of Victory, The (1919), Bluebird. *Dir.* William Wolbert; *Sc.* Waldemar Young; *Cast includes:* Monroe Salisbury, Bob Edmond, Fred Wilson, Fred Kelsey.

A young alcoholic officer in the U.S. Navy (Monroe Salisbury) is entrusted with important documents in this World War I drama. He goes into a sleazy bar, gets drunk and loses the papers to German spies. His fellow officers find him and suggest that he take his own own life. When he refuses, they abandon him on a Pacific island. He soon finds employment with the Germans, supplying information to those aboard an enemy submarine. Eventually he is shot in the back by Germans. The young American's repentance—a final salute to his country's colors before he dies— comes too late. ■

Light That Failed, The (1916), Pathe. *Dir.* Edward Jose; *Cast includes:* Robert Edeson, Jose Collins.

This is the first American film version of Rudyard Kipling's first novel. An artist-correspondent returns to England from the Sudan to continue his career as an artist. He meets Maisie, his childhood sweetheart, who fails to stand by him when she learns he is going blind. He struggles alone to finish his masterpiece before completely losing his eyesight. After Maisie rejects him, he returns to Egypt where the Sudanese Revolt of 1881, led by the Mahdi, is raging. He deliberately allows himself to be mortally shot by the enemy.

This early silent film adaptation takes certain liberties with the original work. In the artist's visit to a sleazy Port Said bar, for example, the film version has him brawling with several toughs, while in the novel he spends part of the evening drawing the face of a local prostitute. Also, in the final scenes of the film, instead of his dying almost instantly by a stray bullet, he is seen wandering about the battlefield for an extraordinarily long time before he is killed. ■

Light That Failed, The (1923), Par. *Dir.* George Melford; *Sc.* F. McGrew Willis, Jack Cunningham; *Cast includes:* Percy Marmount, Jacqueline Logan, Sigrid Holmquist, David Torrence, Mabel Van Buren.

In this second screen adaptation of Kipling's novel, the ending has been completely changed. Instead of the main character returning to Egypt and deliberately getting himself killed rather than continuing to live without his sight and rejected by Maisie, the film version, in its quest for a "happy ending," has him remain helplessly dependent upon Maisie. Other alterations occur involving characters and incidents. There are some early battle scenes in the Sudan during the Sudanese Revolt of 1881. ■

Light That Failed, The (1939), Par. *Dir.* William A. Wellman; *Sc.* Robert Carson; *Cast includes:* Ronald Colman, Walter Huston, Muriel Angelus, Ida Lupino, Dudley Digges.

Another film version of Kipling's novel of a melancholy artist who goes blind as a result of a war wound, this adaptation stars Ronald Colman in the role of the painter, Dick Heldar. Ida Lupino plays Bessie, the prostitute, who poses for Heldar and who, in a fit of rage, destroys his painting. Walter Huston, as the artist's friend, helps him to adjust to his future life of darkness. But Heldar, whose passion is art, rejects this bleak prospect, preferring instead to die on the battlefield during the Sudanese Revolt of 1881. ■

Lights Out in Europe (1940), Arthur Mayer. *Dir.* Herbert Kline; *Sc.* James Hilton.

A World War II documentary showing the effects of war in general and totalitarianism in particular, the film employs excerpts of contemporary newsreel footage. Nations who have fallen victim to Nazi terror are the chief subjects. Scenes include the wounded in Poland and the children in London being evacuated to the relative safety of the countryside. Fredric March performs the narration that was written by English novelist James Hilton. ■

Lilac Time (1928), FN. *Dir.* George Fitzmaurice; *Sc.* Carey Wilson; *Cast includes:* Colleen Moore, Gary Cooper, Burr MacIntosh, George Cooper.

A World War I airplane drama, the film stars Gary Cooper as Captain Philip Blythe of the British Royal Flying Corps who falls in love with Colleen Moore. But the war interferes with their romance, especially in the person of the dreaded Red Ace of Germany who has shot down more British planes than any other flier. The Red Ace downs Blythe's airship and the captain is wounded. But he in turn has destroyed the Ace's red airplane which falls in French territory. Action sequences include numerous air battles as well as the bombing and strafing of towns. Gallant young men are sent up to their almost certain death to meet German planes with orders not to return until all the enemy planes are destroyed. In one engagement only two of a group of seven fliers return.

This was one of several World War I movies made during and after the conflict to feature British airmen as the principal characters. These dramas usually emphasized the derring-do of the pilots, gallant warriors who faced death unflinchingly. In the above film, they offer the following salute: "Here's to us flying in the Heavens at five, and frying in Hell at six." ■

Limbo (1972), U. *Dir.* Mark Robson; *Sc.* Joan Silver, James Bridges; *Cast includes:* Kate Jackson, Katherine Justice, Stuart Margolin, Hazel Medina.

Long before Chuck Norris in *Missing in Action* and Sylvester Stallone in his "Rambo" films took up the cause of those American soldiers considered officially as missing in action in Vietnam but whom others believe are being held as prisoners by the North Vietnamese, this little drama tackled the controversial and human problem of M.I.A.s. The film concentrates on several wives whose husbands have not returned from Vietnam. Kate Jackson portrays a young woman who has been married for only two weeks before her husband left for the war and is now reported missing. She is presently having an affair with another man. Katherine Justice, as the rich wife of a husband who is reported killed in action, refuses to accept the mounting evidence of his death. Hazel Medina appears as another wife whose husband is missing in action. Kathleen Nolan's husband had been interned for several years before she learns of his death. The film concentrates on the human drama rather than the controversial issues that dominated the war. ■

Lincoln, Abraham (1809–1865). The bombardment by Confederate artillery of Fort Sumter, guarding the harbor of Charleston, South Carolina, placed the 16th president of the U.S. in a situation he had hoped to avoid—the tearing asunder of the Union in civil war. No other President before or since had ever faced such a calamity.

He had said many times he would not interfere with slavery where it existed and that his primary goal was to preserve the Union in peace. Nonetheless, the South perceived his election in 1860 as the beginning of a drive by Northern radical Republicans to eliminate slavery. The South's response—secession and the seizure of all federal forts and property within the Confederacy, and finally the attack on a federal fort—had forced upon him no choice but to use military might to preserve the integrity of the Union.

During the war, Lincoln had to withstand attacks by extremists in the North. These included some who wanted to grind the South into total submission and Copperheads who espoused peace at almost any price. In addition, he had to contend with a group of border states, such as Maryland and Kentucky, where sentiment for the South was strong. He fluctuated between policies of force, diplomacy and occasional inaction in dealing with these states, keeping most of them in the Union. He was roundly criticized as a dictator for acts such as suspending the constitutional right of Writ of Habeas Corpus to jail suspected enemies of the Union.

It was in his forceful conduct of the military side of the war—some historians went so far as to call it meddling—that he showed his determination and seriousness of purpose to crush the rebellion. He went against the advice of his cabinet and ordered the provisioning of Fort Sumter, an act that the South considered hostile and that led to its decision to subdue the military post by shelling and seizure. Once fighting began, Lincoln issued a call to state militias for federal service and announced a naval blockade of the South.

He achieved fame for his Emancipation Proclamation (January 1, 1863) and several speeches. The Gettysburg Address (November 19, 1863) was delivered at the battlefield military cemetery of the engagement that is considered the turning point of the war. In his second inaugural speech he appealed for postwar harmony with the phrase that the nation ". . . must finish the work we are in . . . with malice toward none, with charity for all."

Lincoln was assassinated shortly after Lee's surrender, shot by John Wilkes Booth, a crazed actor and Southern sympathizer, in Ford's Theatre (April 14, 1865) in Washington, D.C. This incident has been re-enacted on screen several times, most effectively in D.W. Griffith's classic Civil War epic *The Birth of a Nation* (1915).

He has been portrayed in numerous silent

and sound films and, unlike many of his contemporaries, several biographical dramas. Virtually all have depicted him with compassion and sympathy— almost a tragic figure. Most of the Civil War dramas showed him only as a minor character. Actor Frank McGlynn virtually made a career of impersonating him on screen. The most effective interpretations have been those by Walter Huston (*Abraham Lincoln*), Henry Fonda (*Young Mr. Lincoln*) and Raymond Massey (*Abe Lincoln in Illinois*).

Some of the silents in which he is portrayed include *With Lee in Virginia* (1913); *The Heart of Lincoln* (1915), which recounts an incident in which he intervenes to save the life of a young man accused of spying; *Defense or Tribute?* (1916), a World War I documentary that invokes the image of Lincoln; *The Crisis* (1916), which recreates the siege of Vicksburg; *The Lincoln Cycle* (1917), which dramatizes his prewar years; *My Own United States* (1918), a patriotic panorama of highlights in American history; *Following the Flag to France* (1918), a World War I documentary; *Abraham Lincoln* (1924); and *The Heart of Maryland* (1927), a romantic war drama.

Characterizations of Lincoln continued into the sound era and include such dramas and biographies as D.W. Griffith's *Abraham Lincoln* (1930), which gave a generally even-handed picture of the North and South as well as Generals Grant and Lee; *Are We Civilized?* (1934), an antiwar drama that invokes historical precedents (through the use of excerpts from old features and newsreels) to show the folly of war; *Hearts in Bondage* (1936), which includes the famous battle between the *Merrimac* and the *Monitor*; "Lincoln in the White House" (1939), a patriotic short; and *Land of Liberty* (1939), Cecil B. DeMille's patriotic documentary about the history of the U.S. ∎

Lincoln Cycle, The (1917), Charter. *Cast includes:* Benjamin Chapin.

This silent biographical film covers the life of Abraham Lincoln from his boyhood until he reached the presidency and issued the first "call to arms" in anticipation of hostilities between the North and the South. There are scenes of Lincoln as a boy overpowering a local bully, of his conflicts with his father and of the firing on Fort Sumter. ∎

"Lincoln in the White House" (1939), WB. *Dir.* William McGann; *Sc.* Charles Telford; *Cast includes:* Frank McGlynn, Dickie Moore, John Harron, Raymond Brown.

A patriotic short, part of a series initiated by Warner Brothers in the midst of world tensions between democratic nations and oppressive regimes, the film depicts the human side of the sixteenth President as he wrestles with the Civil War and clashes with his cabinet. He is shown commuting a Union soldier's court martial, playing with his son (Dickie Moore) and reciting the Gettysburg Address. ∎

"Lincoln's Gettysburg Address" (1927). See Battle of Gettysburg. ∎

Little American, The (1917), Artcraft. *Dir.* Cecil B. DeMille; *Sc.* Jeanie Macpherson; *Cast includes:* Mary Pickford, Jack Holt, Hobart Bosworth, James Neill, Ben Alexander, Walter Long, Raymond Hatton.

The most popular screen star of the period, Mary Pickford, better known as "America's Sweetheart," did her share to help sway the nation against Germany with her role in this World War I propaganda film. The story opens prior to the war. Mary, in the title role, is adored by two admirers, one French and the other German. When hostilities break out, each suitor returns to his own homeland to fight for his country. Meanwhile, Mary crosses the Atlantic in an ocean liner. The vessel is torpedoed by a German U-boat and she is rescued. Working as a nurse in a French villa, she meets her French admirer who warns her to leave before the advancing German army arrives. She decides to stay to help the wounded. The Germans arrive and commit almost every possible atrocity upon the civilians. One of the invading soldiers is her German admirer, and he saves her from falling into the hands of the others. When he renounces his country and its leaders for the horrors they have caused, he is arrested with Mary, who is accused of spying, and both are sentenced to death. A French bombardment of the village saves the couple.

By using one of America's most popular screen stars—the embodiment of American innocence and virtue—the studio had no problem in fomenting anti-German propaganda. The script places her in a situation bordering on rape when a lecherous Prussian officer takes a sexual interest in her. Earlier films depicted French and Belgian maids as the objects of the carnal desires of the bestial Germans. Exposing American girls, particularly Little Mary, to these horrors, was almost too much for American audiences to bear.

When audiences protested the ending, which shows Mary kissing her German lover through the wire fence of a prison camp, the studio quickly changed it. The new ending has Mary returning to the States where she waits for the Frenchman. The film had been completed before America's entry into the war, and the writers did not anticipate the extent of the public's anti-German hostility. ■

Little Big Horn (1927), Oxford. *Dir.* Harry L. Fraser; *Sc.* Carrie E. Rawles; *Cast includes:* Roy Stewart, John Beck, Helen Lynch, Edmund Cobb.

The film is another re-enactment of Custer's defeat at the hands of the Sioux. John Beck portrays the famous general who, with a handful of his troops of the 7th Cavalry, fought the hostiles to the last man. Much of the drama is taken up with the preparations of the Indians as they assemble for the historic attack. A weak love story featuring Roy Stewart and Helen Lynch is woven into the plot which includes several rousing battle sequences. ■

Little Big Horn (1951), Lippert. *Dir.* Charles Marquis Warren; *Sc.* Charles Marquis Warren; *Cast includes:* Lloyd Bridges, John Ireland, Marie Windsor, Reed Hadley, Jim Davis.

Custer's debacle at the hands of the Sioux provides the background for this recreation taken from a page of American history. A handful of U.S. Cavalry troops are sent to warn General Custer of a possible ambush. As they travel through perilous territory swarming with war parties, the men are picked off one by one by concealed hostiles. When it seems that they have reached their objective, they are suddenly overwhelmed by a large force of Indians and are wiped out to the last man. A personal conflict arises between the captain (Lloyd Bridges) of the ill-fated squad, and a lieutenant (John Ireland) under his command. The captain, who suspects that his marital problems stem from Ireland's interference, assigns the lieutenant to hazardous missions. Marie Windsor plays the captain's wife in this low-budget film. ■

Little Big Man (1970), NG. *Dir.* Arthur Penn; *Sc.* Calder Willingham; *Cast includes:* Dustin Hoffman, Faye Dunaway, Martin Balsam, Richard Mulligan, Chief Dan George.

Dustin Hoffman gives a rich characterization of Jack Crabb, a 121-year-old survivor of the early pioneer days and Indian wars of the West. Based on Thomas Berger's popular novel, the film traces Crabb's and his sister's capture and upbringing by Indians after their parents are killed by hostiles of another tribe to his eventual witnessing of arrogant General Custer's planned massacre of the Indians, a scheme that ironically resounds in his own defeat.

Carol Androsky portrays his masculine sister Caroline who happily settles down with an Indian husband. Chief Dan George, as an eccentric chief, befriends Hoffman and provides the young man with advice. Faye Dunaway, as a preacher's wife, seduces Hoffman. Her sexual prowess leads her into prostitution. Richard Mulligan plays a pompous Custer. Martin Balsam, as an itinerant swindler, reappears from time to time, each of which physically reveals another perilous brush with death. The loss of a limb and an eye and the suffering of other deformations do not deter his abounding spirit. The film leans chiefly toward satire as it depicts Hoffman in a series of misadventures as well as his encounters with such historical figures as Wild Bill Hickok and Custer. Penn's incisive directing underscores the pitiful Indian extermination while maintaining an ironic and humorous tone. ■

Little Bighorn, Battle of. See George Custer, Sioux Wars. ■

Little Miss Hoover (1918), Par. *Dir.* John S. Robertson; *Sc.* Adrian Gil-Spear; *Cast includes:* Marguerite Clark, Eugene O'Brien, Alfred Hickman, Forrest Baldwin.

Marguerite Clark portrays a patriotic young woman determined to help her country by increasing food production in this World War I comedy. She persuades her grandfather, with whom she is living, to help her start up a chicken farm. Many of the farm workers are less than enthusiastic until Clark instills in them a spark of patriotism. A wounded veteran (Eugene O'Brien) is assigned by the government to visit farmers and encourage them to produce more. He establishes himself near the Clark poultry farm.

Appearing out of uniform, he is mistaken for a slacker and is almost lynched by the community.

Released only weeks after the armistice, the film may have lost some of its immediacy in terms of its original purpose. However, war-ravaged Europe found itself with a critical food shortage when hostilities ceased. The film, therefore, may well have served as a stimulus for American farmers to produce more. ■

Little Patriot, A (1917). See Children in War. ■

Little Tokyo, U.S.A. (1942). See *Go for Broke* (1951). ■

Little Wildcat (1922). See Crime and War. ■

Little Yank, The (1917), Triangle. *Dir.* George Seigmann; *Sc.* Roy Summerville; *Cast includes:* Dorothy Gish, Frank Bennett, A.D. Sears, Robert Burns, Fred Turner.

Dorothy Gish portrays the title character in this romantic drama set in Civil War times. The plot includes several battles and the employment of spies. General Grant is portrayed in one humorous sequence in which he temporarily halts hostilities so that a soldier can cross no-man's land. ■

Lives of a Bengal Lancer (1935), Par. *Dir.* Henry Hathaway; *Sc.* Waldemar Young, John Balderson, Achmed Abdullah, Grover Jones, W. S. McNutt; *Cast includes:* Gary Cooper, Franchot Tone, Richard Cromwell, Sir Guy Standing, Kathleen Burke, Monte Blue.

A rousing adventure set in Great Britain's colonial India, the film centers around a father-son conflict at a remote military outpost. Colonel Stone (Sir Guy Standing), a traditional soldier and no-nonsense commandant of the post, treats his newly arrived son, a lieutenant (Richard Cromwell), as just another officer. The young officer, hurt by the impersonal greeting, allows himself to be duped by a belligerent native chief who then holds the colonel's son captive. Two fellow officers (Gary Cooper and Franchot Tone) go to the boy's rescue and are also captured and tortured. The colonel's son cracks under the pressure and betrays the corps but later redeems himself in the truest tradition of the service. Douglass Dumbrille, Akim Tamiroff

and J. Carrol Naish provide the native villainy.

The film, which used only the title of Francis Yeats-Brown's book, provides sufficient action and well-staged battle scenes in this epic adventure that has been equated with the romantic tradition of Kipling. The stunning exterior shots were made on location. Politically, the film is heavily sympathetic towards Britain's colonial policies, giving short shrift to either the aspirations or grievances of the local natives. Inspiring such action films as *The Charge of the Light Brigade* (1936), starring Errol Flynn, and *Wee Willie Winkie* (1937), starring Shirley Temple, *Lives of a Bengal Lancer* was instrumental in establishing a genre to be known later as empire films. Its box-office success motivated the studio to repeat the plot about the neglected young officer-son and the martinet commander-father in its release of *Geronimo* (1939), which resulted in just another routine western. See also Empire Films. ■

Lone Eagle, The (1927), U. *Dir.* Emory Johnson; *Sc.* Ralph Blanchard; *Cast includes:* Raymond Keane, Barbara Kent, Nigel Barrie.

Raymond Keane portrays Lieutenant William Holmes, a British flier, in this World War I airplane drama. When Holmes' guns jam during a dogfight, he avoids battle with the German planes and heads back to base. His fellow pilots don't believe his story and brand him a coward, especially since one of the men in the squadron took the machine-gun bursts from an enemy plane meant for Holmes. Later, when a German ace who is seeking revenge for his brother's death challenges the British officers to a duel, Holmes volunteers. Although his plane is shot up, he manages to down his rival. The film ends with the armistice. The aerial photography and the battle scenes are not as effective or realistic as those in William Wellman's *Wings* (1927). ■

Lone Wolf, The (1924). See Detectives at War. ■

Lone Wolf Spy Hunt, The (1939). See Detectives at War. ■

Long Voyage Home, The (1940), UA. *Dir.* John Ford; *Sc.* Dudley Nichols; *Cast includes:* John Wayne, Thomas Mitchell, Ian Hunter,

American troops hit the beaches of Normandy in World War II. *The Longest Day* (1962).

Barry Fitzgerald, Wilfred Lawson, Mildred Natwick.

John Wayne stars as a seaman aboard a tramp steamer during wartime in this sea drama based on four one-act plays by Eugene O'Neill which were updated to World War II. The film follows the vessel with its cargo of high explosives from the West Indies to its destination at an American port. During the journey the crew members face the deaths of a few of their mates and an attack from a Nazi airplane before they reach land. Director John Ford concentrates on characterization, bringing out the reasons some of the men take to the sea. Wayne is reserved as a sailor who is saving to purchase a farm in Sweden. ∎

Longest Day, The (1962), TCF. *Dir.* Ken Annakin, Andrew Marton, Bernhard Wicki, Gerd Oswald; *Sc.* Cornelius Ryan, Romain Gary, James Jones, David Pursall, Jack Seddon; *Cast includes:* John Wayne, Robert Mitchum, Henry Fonda, Robert Ryan.

The invasion of Normandy provides the subject of this World War II semi-documentary epic consisting of one of the largest casts of star performers (over 40 major screen personalities) ever assembled for a war drama. Based on the book by Cornelius Ryan, who wrote the screenplay, the film covers the D-Day landing from several perspectives, including that of the Germans. On the horizon the German defenders witness the largest armada ever assembled in history. The night before the actual invasion, American paratroopers are dropped behind enemy lines. Some units overshoot their destination and are killed before they reach the ground. British Commandos, meanwhile, who are sent in by gliders to another area, also meet with similar disaster. Some of the gliders crash, killing all aboard.

On board the troop ships the next morning, officers address their men before they hit the beaches. "Most of you have had your feet wet before—Dunkirk, Dieppe, Norway," a Scottish officer (Peter Lawford) says solemnly. "We all know what it means to be driven into the sea. In a few hours from now we're going back from the sea, and this time we're going to stay." On another ship a leader of the French Commandos speaks to his unit.

"We've been fighting everywhere for four years—in Abyssinia, Libya, Egypt, Crete. But this time we are going to fight on French soil . . . in our fields . . . in our villages . . . under the eyes of our own people."

Following the expected bombardment of the beaches and their immediate environs, the Allies launch their attack troops. Some divisions get bogged down on the beaches and take heavy casualties while others move forward. The film shifts from one beach to another to show the problems the Allied officers and men encounter. Robert Mitchum, as one of the officers on Omaha Beach, manages to organize the troops in a breakthrough while another officer (Eddie Albert) is killed during the advance. John Wayne, as a paratrooper colonel, gathers up the remnants of several units to wrest a French town from the Germans. Other scenes depict the pressures on German officers who fail to get tank support from their high command.

Hollywood's war dramas usually single out the Americans as largely responsible for the major victories—with the expected protests from former Allies. But this film underscores the contributions of other countries. British Commandos, for example, take a vital bridge; French units doggedly battle to occupy a key town; French partisans blow up strategic railroad tracks hours before the invasion. The large-scale production manages to capture some of the human drama of frustration and slaughter on both sides as the cost in human lives mounts. Richard Burton, as a seriously wounded British soldier, sums up the invasion, and perhaps all wars, near the end of the film. "Here we are," he says to a G.I. separated from his outfit while a dead German soldier lies motionless nearby. "I'm crippled, you're lost and he's dead." However, the last line of the film, reflecting the military success of "the longest day" and general Allied optimism, is reserved for Mitchum, who is still on the battered beach. "Ride me up the hill, son," he says quietly to a G.I. ■

Losers, The (1970). See Vietnam War. ■

Lost at the Front (1927), FN. *Dir.* Del Lord; *Sc.* Frank Griffin; *Cast includes:* Charlie Murray, George Sidney, Natalie Kingston, John Kolb, Max Asher.

Charlie Murray, as Muldoon, an Irish cop, and George Sidney, as August Krauss, a German-American bartender, star in this World War I comedy. Krauss, who thinks he has a secret weapon that can cause random explosions, enlists in the service to help bring the war to a speedy conclusion. His friend, Muldoon, joins up later in an attempt to locate Krauss and tell him that the U.S. has entered the war. The two buddies become involved in a series of hilarious escapades, including a drinking bout with Russians and a shower house which is used to fumigate women prisoners. ■

Lost Battalion, The (1919), McManus.

This World War I semi-documentary re-enacts the famous battle in which six American companies of the 77th Division advanced into the Argonne Forest and held out for six days against overwhelming odds. The film begins in September 1917, when the division was first formed. Various scenes depict the wives and sweethearts of the doughboys saying farewell to their loved ones. The story continues in France and the Argonne, where the battalion, under the command of Major Whittlesey, is encircled by the enemy. After a furious six-day battle with the munitions and food of the beleaguered Americans almost exhausted, the 308th, commanded by Major McKinney, fought its way through the German lines and lifted the siege of the "Lost Battalion." Several of the men who participated in the actual event appeared in the film.

Aside from depicting the bravery and endurance of American troops under fire, the film emphasized the various racial and social groups that made up the battalion. "Out of this mixed . . . and 'despicable mass' was to be forged a thunderbolt to be hurled against the proudest army in Europe," a title card proudly exclaimed. This ideal "democratic army," so effective as propaganda, became a standard device in the genre and was to be employed in war films for the next seven decades. See also *Gold Chevrons*. ■

Lost Command (1966), Col. *Dir.* Mark Robson; *Sc.* Nelson Gidding; *Cast includes:* Anthony Quinn, Alain Delon, George Segal, Michele Morgan.

Anthony Quinn stars as the commander of French paratroopers assigned to the Algerian conflict after seeing action in Indo-China. Having risen from the ranks following the deaths of several of his superiors in the Indo-China conflict, Quinn has no patience with

Anthony Quinn (c.), personifying French colonialism, surrenders his French paratroopers to the Vietnamese at the end of the Indo-China War. *Lost Command* (1966).

incompetence within his own troops or with his superiors. A tough commander, he has the ability to temper his sternness with tenderness. George Segal, as an Algerian who has fought alongside Quinn in Indo-China, emerges as a terrorist leader when his parents are murdered. Alain Delon, as another co-fighter of Quinn's, resigns from the military when he realizes the corrosive effects and the futility of the war. Maurice Ronet, as a foil character to both Quinn and Delon, is ruthless and sadistic but proficient as a soldier under Quinn. Michele Morgan provides the romantic interest for Quinn. The Algerian struggle for independence, which receives a balanced treatment, furnishes the impetus for the characters.

The Algerian War of 1954–1962 ignited in open warfare in 1954 when National Liberation Front, created by Algerian Muslims, rebelled against French domination. The rebels attacked French military posts and European property. France sent in troops to quash the dissidents in 1957 after turning down their request for independence. Charles de Gaulle,

who took office as France's president in 1958, suggested a compromise plan of self-determination to the Algerians. By 1960 he proposed a cease-fire. A shaky cease-fire took hold in 1962, and on July 1 the Algerians voted for independence. France acknowledged the results of the national referendum two days later. ∎

Lost Patrol, The (1934), RKO. *Dir.* John Ford; *Sc.* Dudley Nichols; *Cast includes:* Victor McLaglen, Boris Karloff, Wallace Ford, Reginald Denny, J. M. Kerrigan, Billy Bevan, Alan Hale.

Based on the story *Patrol* by Phillip MacDonald, the film centers on a British patrol during World War I that strays into the Mesopotamian desert. When their officer is killed by unseen Arabs, the soldiers seek refuge at an oasis where most of the action unfolds. Victor McLaglen plays the sergeant of the doomed men who get picked off one at a time by the concealed enemy. McLaglen is the sole survivor when a relief column rides to the oasis. In one poignant scene a young

Boris Karloff (c.) prays for a fallen comrade as Sgt. Victor McLaglen (l.) looks on in this scene that fore-shadows the futility and hopelessness of *The Lost Patrol* (1934).

soldier confides to McLaglen why he elected to start at the bottom rather than accept a commission from an influential uncle in the war office. "I'm glad I'm here," the young idealist admits. "You're around fine soldiers . . . the kind of soldiers I read about in Kipling . . . and here I am. I'm part of it now. The funniest thing is they're so modest. They don't even see the glory in it, do they?" The next morning he is found dead—killed while on guard duty. The drama includes several fine characterizations, including Boris Karloff as a religious fanatic who crosses over the edge of sanity. In his last scene he wanders, half-crazed and carrying a large crucifix, into the desert where he is soon cut down by an enemy bullet.

Director John Ford made the realistically grim film, his first major critical and commercial success, on location in the Yuma desert in about fourteen days. It has gained a reputation over the years, emerging as a minor classic. It was a remake of a 1929 English film of the same name and starred Victor McLaglen's brother, Cyril McLaglen. Ironically,

Victor McLaglen served with the British in Mesopotamia during World War I. RKO remade the film in 1939, changed the location to the West, substituted Indians for the Arabs and retitled it *Bad Lands*. ∎

Lost Squadron, The (1932). See Veterans. ∎

Love and Death (1975), UA. *Dir.* Woody Allen; *Sc.* Woody Allen; *Cast includes:* Woody Allen, Diane Keaton, Harold Gould, Alfred Lutter.

Woody Allen's anachronistic period comedy parodies Russian literature and foreign film directors like Eisenstein and emulates such comics as Charlie Chaplin, Bob Hope and Groucho Marx. In this romp about a declared coward during the Napoleonic Wars, Allen once again touches upon some of his favorite themes—marriage, male-female relationships, self-deprecation, and his love of films. The plot concerns the bumbling battlefield exploits of Allen and, later, his attempt, provoked by his cousin (Diane Keaton) to assassinate Napoleon.

The comedy depends heavily on Allen's verbal humor. In bed at night, he reaches out to his wife. "No, not here," she says. In another scene a woman asks Allen, "It must be lonely at the front. How long has it been since you made love to a woman?" "What's today?" Allen ponders, "Monday, Tuesday? Two years." Later, the same woman admits, "You're the greatest lover I ever had." "Well," explains Allen, "I practice a lot when I'm alone." "Sex without love is an empty experience," Diane Keaton says. "Yes," Allen replies, "but as empty experiences go, it's one of the best." Woody also has a chance to direct his lines to the audience. "Some men are heterosexual; some men are bisexual; some men don't think about sex at all—they become lawyers." Later: "There are worse things than death. If you've ever spent an evening with an insurance salesman, you know exactly what I mean." And: "If it turns out there is a God, I don't think He's evil. The worst thing you can say about Him is that He's basically an underachiever." ■

Love and Glory (1924), U. *Dir.* Rupert Julian; *Sc.* Elliott Clawson, Rupert Julian; *Cast includes:* Charles De Roche, Madge Bellamy, Wallace MacDonald, Ford Sterling.

This romantic drama was filmed previously in 1916 as *The Bugler of Algiers*. The plot, laid in France during the 1860s, concerns two friends, Pierre, who loves Gabrielle, and her brother, Anatole. When trouble erupts in Algeria, the two pals answer their country's call to arms. Gabrielle receives word that the two have been killed in action. They return to their village and find she is gone. Their search for her proves futile. Fifty years later the two men, who have remained friends all this time, start off for Paris where Anatole is to receive a belated war medal. The trip proves too difficult for Anatole who dies along the way. Pierre decides to continue the journey and accept the medal for his friend. To his surprise, he meets Gabrielle there and the two lovers are reunited. The film includes several battle sequences with the Arabs.

The two versions, both set in the wake of the Algerian–French Wars of the mid-1800s, differ in one major aspect. In the 1916 film Pierre assumes Anatole's identity so that the ceremony is not canceled. ■

Love and the Law 1918. See Spy Films: the Silents. ■

"Love and War" (1909), Edison.

This short silent drama depicts a ballroom scene on the eve of the Battle of Waterloo. Wellington receives a message concerning the advancing enemy, and the officers prepare to engage the enemy. One British officer says farewell to his loved one at the ball. Later, a scene reveals the young man who is mortally wounded following the conflict. Although Hollywood made several dramas pertaining to the Napoleonic Wars, this is one of the few American films to dramatize the Battle of Waterloo or to highlight the figure of the Duke of Wellington. ■

Love in a Hurry (1919). See Spy Films: the Silents. ■

Love in the Desert (1929), RKO. *Dir.* George Melford; *Sc.* Harvey Thew; *Cast includes:* Olive Borden, Noah Beery, Hugh Trevor, Frank Leigh.

A part-silent, part-talking drama, the film stars Olive Borden as an Arabian chief's daughter. She falls in love with an American (Hugh Trevor) on vacation. When he is kidnaped by a tribe of warriors, Borden releases him. But this provokes a desert war. The film, a weak melodrama that appears to be based entirely on a fictitious conflict, has several small desert battles. It was re-released in a second version that included a prologue and an epilogue laid in New York. ■

Love Letters (1945), Par. *Dir.* William Dieterle; *Sc.* Ayn Rand; *Cast includes:* Jennifer Jones, Joseph Cotten, Ann Richards, Anita Louise, Cecil Kellaway.

A victim of amnesia is cured by love in this World War II romantic drama. Jennifer Jones, as an Englishwoman whose fiance is a British officer (Robert Sully) on the Italian front, receives deeply moving love letters from him which she cherishes. The letters, however, were written by a fellow officer (Joseph Cotten). When the fiance returns, the couple are married. But his wife soon learns that her husband is not the sensitive soul who wrote the beautiful letters but an obnoxious cad who beats her. An elderly aunt murders him, and his widow is accused of the crime. The shock of the event brings on a case of amnesia. The officer-friend enters the scene to unravel the situation and fall in love with the widow. ■

Love Light, The (1921), UA. Dir. Frances Marion; Sc. Frances Marion; Cast includes: Mary Pickford, Fred Thomson, Evelyn Dumo, Edward Phillips.

Mary Pickford, "America's Sweetheart," portrays a young Italian lighthouse keeper who lives in a small fishing village in this World War I romantic drama. Her two brothers have been lost in the war. One day she discovers a man washed up on the shore. He poses as an American sailor, but in reality he is a German spy. Pickford falls in love with him and they marry. When she learns the truth that he was sent to transmit messages about Allied shipping to the Germans, she rejects him. She hides him from the authorities until she discovers that it was his signal to a German submarine that led to her brother's death. She then reveals his whereabouts, and he is killed. Later, she finds contentment and love with a former beau who has lost his sight in the war. Fred Thomson, a former army chaplain who was later to become a popular screen cowboy, plays the German spy. Edward Phillips portrays the blind lover. ■

Love Thief, The (1916), Fox. Dir. Richard Stanton; Sc. Ben Cohn; Cast includes: Alan Hale, Frances Burnham, Gretchen Hartman, Edwin Cecil.

Based on Mexican revolutionary leader Pancho Villa's raid in 1916 on Columbus, New Mexico, the drama involves American border troops, a romance between an officer and his California sweetheart and the attempts of Mexican guerrillas to buy arms from Americans. Alan Hale portrays a cavalry captain who is ordered to patrol the border. He leaves behind his fiancee (Frances Burnham). Gretchen Hartman and Edwin Cecil, as two guerrillas from below the border, seek to buy weapons for their army from Burnham's guardian. When the U.S. Secret Service learns of this, the arms dealer and his ward escape to Mexico where they are captured by the guerrillas and sentenced to death. The captain and the American troops ride to the rescue.

During this unstable period in Mexico, the U.S. at first recognized the forces of Pancho Villa as the legitimate representatives of the people. But by 1915 President Wilson re-jected Villa and recognized Carranza, another revolutionary leader and Villa's major adversary. In a desperate ploy to defeat his enemy, Villa attacked Columbus, hoping the U.S. would be drawn into armed conflict against Carranza's forces. Instead, President Wilson sent an expeditionary force under General Pershing into Mexico to hunt down Villa. But the punitive expedition failed. One of the benefits derived from the incident was the unusual number of cameramen assigned by film companies to cover the action. Much of the resultant footage ended up in documentaries, feature films and serials of the period. ■

Lure of the Islands (1942). See Spy Films: the Talkies. ■

Lusitania. The British luxury liner *Lusitania* was sunk without warning by a German submarine, the U-20, in May 1915, with the loss of 1,198 lives, 128 of whom were American citizens. The German attack was part of an all-out submarine war designed to force Britain out of the conflict by cutting her vital supply lines. Although the German embassy, through notices in American newspapers on the day the ship sailed, had warned prospective passengers to stay off the vessel because it was a potential target once it reached the war zone, the incident became a rallying cry against German barbarity and probably turned many Americans, who were still neutral, against the Central Powers. The sinking resulted in controversy which continued for many years after the war ended. The Germans charged that the vessel was a "floating arsenal" carrying war materiel to England. Colin Simpson, in his exhaustive book, *Lusitania*, substantiates this claim and suggests that the British intentionally sacrificed the ship to accelerate America's entry into the war.

Several films of the period used the catastrophe for propaganda purposes. One of the most popular was Leonce Perret's *Lest We Forget* (1918), starring the French actress, Rita Jolivet, who had been a passenger on the doomed vessel. Winsor McCay, the famous cartoonist, turned out "The Sinking of the Lusitania" in 1918. The animated one-reeler pulled no punches in its many provocative titles. "The babe that clung to his mother's breast," one such title exhorted, "cried out to the world to avenge the most violent cruelty ever carried out on an innocent and unsuspecting nation."

Other films released during World War I alluded to the sinking in a variety of ways. Thomas H. Ince's pacifist film *Civilization* (1916) employs a situation similar to that of the *Lusitania* but does not use the actual name of the vessel. In Rupert Julian's *The Kaiser, the Beast of Berlin* (1918), a World War I propaganda film that characterizes Kaiser Wilhelm as a power-crazed, self-deluded, vain figure, he is seen meeting with Capt. von Nagel, the commander of the submarine responsible for the tragedy. *Lest We Forget*, mentioned above, presents the most detailed and graphic depiction of the sinking. Two documentaries about World War I, *Pershing's Crusaders* (1918) and *The Big Drive* (1933), refer to the British vessel as part of their coverage of the conflict. ∎

M

MacArthur (1977), U. Dir. Joseph Sargent; Sc. Hal Barwood, Matthew Robbins; Cast includes: Gregory Peck, Ed Flanders, Dan O'Herlihy, Marj Dusay, Sandy Kenyon.

Gregory Peck portrays one of the most popular and controversial military leaders of the century in this sympathetic biographical drama. The film covers the years from MacArthur's World War II command at Corregidor in 1942 until his removal as general during the Korean conflict ten years later.

He is reluctant to leave his troops at Corregidor and does so only under a direct order from President Roosevelt. As he leaves the island he pledges to his own men and to the natives that he will return. Stationed in Australia, he is disappointed to learn that no provisions have been made to relieve the besieged "rock," and its abandonment will haunt him through most of the film. Fond of quoting his father, also a general, and regaling others with anecdotes from his own experiences, MacArthur holds no truck with surrender or defensive tactics. When his fellow Allied commanders explain their strategy for the defense of Australia, he objects strenuously and persuades them to bring the war to the enemy by attacking New Guinea. Later in the war his egomania leads him to another disappointment when he learns that the Japanese have surrendered following the dropping of two atomic bombs on their homeland. He had made extensive preparations for the invasion of Japan. The film next covers the period of MacArthur's successful efforts to bring Japan into the family of democratic nations. One poignant scene shows a Japanese statesman explaining to the general that he wishes the new constitution to state that Japan will be prohibited from ever having armed forces. MacArthur is visibly moved by these words.

From the moment that President Truman assumes his office following the death of Roosevelt, he comes into conflict with the general who is personally negotiating with Chiang Kai-shek. Truman travels to Hawaii to meet with MacArthur, who is late for the conference. "They probably had to get him down off his cross," the President quips. As the general approaches from a distance, Truman says: "He's not in uniform—he's in costume." But the comment, although funny, does not ring true. When MacArthur arrives, he is simply dressed in an open-collar shirt and khaki slacks. In several scenes Truman, conferring with his aides, refers to MacArthur as "His Majesty."

The conflict gains momentum at the outbreak of the Korean War. MacArthur pushes for an invasion of North Korea and gets his way, assuring the President and others that Communist China will not interfere. When the Chinese invade and drive the Americans back, MacArthur calls for a full assault on China and issues statements to the press attacking the present administration's ineptness. At this point Truman recalls the general. MacArthur returns to America to a hero's welcome and is shown making his famous speech to Congress. "Old soldiers never die," he says softly, his voice almost breaking, "they just fade away. Like that old soldier, I close my military career of 52 years and quietly fade away."

Several battle sequences of World War II and the Korean War punctuate the film although the story is more introspective, concentrating on MacArthur's character and his inner conflicts rather than external events. ■

MacArthur, Douglas (1880–1964).

MacArthur was unquestionably a military genius, one of the greatest American generals of his time. But his character was seriously flawed. His biographers and contemporaries noted he was arrogant, petty, egotistical and, at least in his earlier years, dominated by an authoritative mother.

The third son of General Arthur MacArthur, a career officer who won the Medal of Honor at the age of 20 in the American Civil War, Douglas was strongly supported—perhaps even driven—by his doting mother to set high standards for himself. He completed his studies at West Point with the third highest grades in the academy's history. In the following years, he won the admiration of the nation for his military accomplishments in three wars.

MacArthur first achieved prominence in World War I as a front-line commander of the 42nd (Rainbow) Division where he was nicknamed "The Fighting Dude" for his dashing manner and unorthodox dress. Wounded several times and cited for bravery on a number of occasions, he became, as a brigadier-general, the youngest American division commander at the time.

Between World Wars I and II, he served as superintendent of West Point, army chief-of-staff and military adviser to the Commonwealth government of the Philippines. The one blot upon his record in this period occurred during the Depression when he commanded the troops that drove the Bonus Marchers, World War I veterans seeking economic aid during the depression, out of Washington, D.C. Early in World War II, MacArthur organized the dramatic but unsuccessful American defense of Bataan and Corregidor in the Philippines. Later, he devised and led the American strategy of island-hopping that resulted in America's recapture of the Pacific islands and ultimate victory over Japan. Numerous photos and newsreels show MacArthur wading ashore at various points in the Philippines to dramatize his pledge to return. President Truman later accused his flamboyant general of "playing to the galleries." President Eisenhower, who at one time served as an aide to MacArthur, also

alluded to the latter's flamboyance by saying "I studied dramatics under him."

MacArthur's military career came to an end during the Korean War, a conflict that represented both one of his highest achievements and his downfall. His direction of the Inchon invasion in September 1950 took the U.N. from the edge of defeat at the hands of North Korea to almost total annihilation of the enemy. However, his attempt to unify Korea by military force brought China into the war. His further advocacy of carrying the war to China brought him into conflict with American policy of containing the war to Korea and led to his dismissal by President Truman. The President emphasized the importance in a democracy of maintaining civilian control of the military. MacArthur later returned to the U.S. as a military hero. He made a brief and unsuccessful attempt to seek the Republican nomination for the 1952 presidential campaign.

MacArthur has been portrayed in relatively few films. Joseph Sargent's 1977 biographical drama *MacArthur* gives a fairly straightforward and accurate picture of the general's military career and his clashes with President Truman. *Inchon* (1981), produced under the guidance of Reverend Moon, depicts General MacArthur (Laurence Olivier) as being helped spiritually while he directs the bold landing and counterattack at Inchon during the Korean War. The film was criticized for its inept script and acting. *They Were Expendable* (1945), a World War II action drama about American torpedo boats in the Pacific, depicts MacArthur's (Robert Barrat) departure from the Philippines in the dark days of 1942. Director John Ford embellished the sequence with an overabundance of reverence, defining the general in heroic, almost mystical, terms. ■

Mad Parade, The (1931), Par. *Dir.* William Beaudine; *Sc.* Henry McCarthy, Frank Conklin; *Cast includes:* Evelyn Brent, Irene Rich, Louise Fazenda, Lilyan Tashman, Marceline Day, Fitzi Ridgeway.

A World War I drama about women in battle, the film has an all-female cast except for a few extras. The plot follows the experiences of eight nurses near the trenches. The conflicts have more to do with their personal dramas than with the actual war around them. Two women fight over the same soldier. Another intimidates a fellow nurse, threatening to expose her for breaking the rules. The former is murdered by a hand grenade. Another, depressed over losing her man to another, walks off into no man's land to die. Like the soldiers around them, those who survive have been hardened by the horrors of the war. ■

Madam Spy (1918). See Spy Films: the Silents. ■

Madam Who? (1918), W. W. Hodkinson. *Dir.* Reginald Barker; *Cast includes:* Bessie Barriscale, Edward Coxen, Howard Hickman, Joseph J. Dowling.

A young Confederate woman, willing to sacrifice her life for the South, engages in the dangerous act of espionage in this Civil War spy drama. Bessie Barriscale portrays the brave Southerner who, when accused of being a traitor, determines to find the real spies. She succeeds in her mission after cleverly outmaneuvering several Union officers. In one particularly dramatic scene, she battles a drunken villain (Howard Hickman). Although chiefly a spy tale, the film provides a few battle scenes near the conclusion. ■

Madame Sans-Gene (1925), Par. *Dir.* Leonce Perret; *Sc.* Forrest Halsey; *Cast includes:* Gloria Swanson, Warwick Ward, Charles De Roche, Emile Drain, Madeleine Guitty.

Gloria Swanson stars as the title character in this historical comedy of the French Revolution adapted from the 1893 play by Victorien Sardou and Emile Moreau. Swanson portrays a laundress in France during the turbulent 1790s. Her customers include two soldiers, a sergeant whom she marries after the revolution and the future Emperor Napoleon. The sergeant becomes a duke while Gloria, as his duchess, becomes an embarrassment to the court because of her coarse ways. Bonaparte's sisters urge their brother to command a divorce, but Gloria cleverly dissuades her husband from the action by reminding him—and Napoleon—of their unpaid laundry bills. Emile Drain portrays Napoleon. Several background scenes were photographed at the Palace of Versailles and its immediate vicinity. Action sequences, including an attack upon the palace by revolutionary troops, are dispersed through the film. ■

Madame Spy (1934). See Spy Films: the Talkies. ■

Mademoiselle Fifi (1944), RKO. *Dir.* Robert Wise; *Sc.* Josef Mischel, Peter Ruric; *Cast includes:* Simone Simon, John Emery, Kurt Kreuger, Alan Napier.

The plot of this little tale, adapted from two stories by Guy De Maupassant, chiefly concerns a coach journey of French aristocrats, businessmen and a laundress (Simone Simon) during the Franco-Prussian War. France has been overrun in part and occupied by enemy troops. To protect their property and profits, the upper-class coach passengers have compromised their patriotism and made accommodations with the Prussian occupiers. The young laundress, an avid patriot, refuses to collaborate with the Prussians. When the coach stops at an inn, Simon refuses to dine with an arrogant Prussian officer who then prevents the travelers from continuing their journey. The other passengers cajole Simon to compromise her patriotism so that they may continue to their destinations.

John Emery, as a cowardly revolutionist, at first respects and supports Simon's defiance but joins the others against the laundress. Stirred by the young Joan of Arc, he later redeems himself by openly defying the Prussians. Kurt Kreuger, as the villainous Prussian officer billeted in Simon's village and sarcastically nicknamed "Mademoiselle Fifi," is ultimately killed by the laundress.

Critics and viewers were quick to draw parallels between the ruthlessness of the Prussians during the Franco-Prussian War and the Nazis during World War II, when the film was released. French collaboration with the Germans was of major concern in France and its colonies, and the film reflected this controversy. The drama also underscored the hollow triumph of an invading army forced to face a hostile population. After the officer's death, a fellow officer questions the Prussian presence in France. "Are we the winners? What kind of victory is this? What good does it do us?" ■

Madero, Francisco Indalecio (1873–1913). A Mexican statesman who fought for democracy and social reforms, Madero served as president of Mexico from 1911 to 1913 after leading a successful revolution against Porfirio Diaz, dictator from 1876 until his overthrow. Madero, hampered by internal strife and opposition to his proposed reforms, could not bring about the social changes he desired. He was overthrown by General Victoriano Huerta, a former supporter who had served under Diaz. After his arrest by the new regime, Madero was killed, allegedly trying to escape. Huerta became president in 1913 but was forced to resign one year later as a result of his unpopular reactionary administration.

Madero has generally been portrayed sympathetically, if not entirely accurately, by Hollywood. In "A Prisoner of Mexico" (1911), for example, General Madero is seen leading the cavalry to rescue the hero and heroine in this fictional account of the turmoil in Mexico. *Barbarous Mexico* (1913), a documentary about the first year of the Revolution, traces Madero's early setbacks against Diaz and his eventual inauguration as the new president. In *Viva Villa!* (1934) he is described as idealistic but ineffectual. Pancho Villa (Wallace Beery), a hero to his people during the revolution, is almost mesmerized by Madero's gentleness and disbands his army when Madero asks him to. In "Madero of Mexico" (1942), a one-reel drama produced by MGM as part of the "John Nesbitt Passing Parade" series, he is described as the prime mover of the Revolution who ultimately gave his life in the struggle for freedom. *Viva Zapata!* (1952) again portrays a well-intentioned Madero who is overwhelmed by the political intrigue that surrounds him. Following a bitter struggle in which the revolutionary forces triumph, Zapata (Marlon Brando) appeals to Madero to institute long-delayed and promised land reforms. But the new president, surrounded by self-serving politicians and military officers, hesitates, stating that such matters take time. *Villa Rides* (1968) adds another dimension to the character of President Madero, describing him as a tragic figure who dreams of peace but is forced to wield raw power to expedite his policies. ■

Magnificent Doll (1946), U. *Dir.* Frank Borzage; *Sc.* Irving Stone; *Cast includes:* Ginger Rogers, David Niven, Burgess Meredith, Horace McNally, Peggy Wood.

In this fictionalized biography of Dolly Madison, the gallant patriot who saved important government documents from falling into the hands of the British during the War of 1812, the film strays from fact for the sake of fancy. Ginger Rogers temporarily turns in her dancing shoes to portray Dolly and recite the virtues of America each chance she gets. The story begins with her early life on her family plantation in Virginia. David Niven portrays the traitorous Aaron Burr whose love for Dolly influences him to abandon his claims to the presidency. Burgess Meredith plays the idealistic James Madison.

Dolly Madison (1768–1849) served as official hostess for both her husband and Thomas Jefferson. A charming and graceful figure, she gained a wide reputation for her skill and elegance at entertaining. She is also portrayed in Cecil B. DeMille's *The Buccaneer* (1938), a biography of the pirate Jean Lafitte. As the Americans beat a hasty retreat from the capital before the rapidly advancing British troops, Dolly dashes back into a government building to save the Declaration of Independence. ■

Maid of Belgium, A (1917), World. *Dir.* George Archainbaud; *Sc.* Adrian Gil-Spear; *Cast includes:* Alice Brady, Louise de Rigney, George MacQuarrie, Richard Clarke.

A young Belgian wife loses her memory as a result of German atrocities she witnesses in this World War I drama. An American couple, driving through a Belgian village that has been bombarded by the Germans, find a lone survivor, a young woman (Alice Brady) who has lost her memory. Because World War I is still raging, and the couple are childless, they decide to adopt her and take her to America. Once they are back home, the wife learns that their ward is pregnant. It seems that she had been married to a Belgian viscount who went to war and is now visiting the U.S. The separated pair are finally brought together.

As with other war films of the period, this drama was quick to portray the Germans as a brutal and bestial race by placing the cause of the heroine's loss of memory on the invaders' rape and pillage of Belgium. The movie studios, however, did not initiate this view (although they successfully exploited it); they only reflected the news releases during the war which often carried such stories—real or fabricated. ■

Major Dundee (1965), Col. *Dir.* Sam Peckinpah; *Sc.* Harry Julian Fink, Oscar Saul, Sam Peckinpah; *Cast includes:* Charlton Heston, Richard Harris, Jim Hutton, Senta Berger.

A mixed unit of Union and Confederate soldiers crosses into Mexico to rescue three

Charlton Heston, as the title character in *Major Dundee* (1965), prepares to lead volunteer Confederate prisoners against hostile Indians during the Civil War.

white children captured by Apaches in this action drama set during the Civil War. Charlton Heston portrays the title character, an obsessed Union officer relegated to command a prison camp after his irregular actions at the Battle of Gettysburg. Following a murderous raid by Apaches upon the local civilians, Heston, short of manpower, asks for volunteers among the Confederate prisoners to help bring back the children and wipe out the band of hostiles who have crossed into Mexico. Richard Harris, as a Southern captain, promises to lead some of his troops only "until the Apache is taken or destroyed." The punitive expedition also includes a handful of black soldiers and several civilians. The remainder of the film consists of mounting tensions between Heston and Harris, former friends, and of skirmishes and a major battle with the hostiles in which all the Confederates and Apaches are killed.

The drama underscores Sam Peckinpah's propensity for violence which is the director's vision of western realism. This is especially prevalent in two sequences—the skirmish between the Americans and Maximilian's French lancers residing in Mexico and the final battle with the Apaches. Another Peckinpah trademark is his interest in having his characters personalize the battle or war that engulfs them. Heston, for example, made the Civil War a personal fight and was banished to a remote prison outpost; the six black Union soldiers have to prove their worth; and Harris makes his fight a personal one between him and Heston who chooses to fight for the Union. Peckinpah differs from John Ford in his handling of similar material

such as the U.S. Cavalry and the Indian wars. Peckinpah's west is less romantic, more gritty and graphically more violent than Ford's, which is a land steeped in glory and tradition. ■

Makers of Men (1925), Bud Barsky Corp. *Dir.* Forest Sheldon; *Sc.* William E. Wing; *Cast includes:* Kenneth MacDonald, William Burton, Clara Horton.

A slender World War I drama about how the military service can help its recruits when they return to civilian life, the film stars Kenneth MacDonald as a young man with a nervous affliction. Recoiling at every loud or sudden sound, he is judged a coward at home by his sweetheart and the local bully. When war is declared, he answers his country's call to arms. His sergeant not only helps him to overcome his affliction but is responsible for the young man becoming a hero in battle. When he arrives home, he wins a fight with the bully and eventually gains the love of the girl he left behind. ■

Malaya (1949), MGM. *Dir.* Richard Thorpe; *Sc.* Frank Fenton; *Cast includes:* Spencer Tracy, James Stewart, Valentina Cortesa, Sydney Greenstreet, John Hodiak.

The U.S. government, desperate for rubber during the early part of World War II, hires two adventurers to smuggle tons of it out of Japanese-held Malaya. Two old buddies, a convicted smuggler (Spencer Tracy) and an unscrupulous and cynical journalist (James Stewart) reunite to buy the rubber hidden from the Japanese by various plantation growers. Stewart's reasons for taking on the dangerous task are more noble than Tracy's. "He got stopped at Wake Island," Stewart explains, referring to his dead brother. "I thought I'd take it the rest of the way." Tracy, at the beginning, accepts the assignment as a way of getting out of prison. They arrive in Malaya posing as two shipwrecked Irish sailors and contact Tracy's acquaintance, the "Dutchman," a cafe owner (Sydney Greenstreet) who arranges the details. After transporting most of the rubber to a hidden American cargo ship, Tracy and Greenstreet suggest they stop. Stewart, however, decides to make one more haul although they all suspect the Japanese are lying in ambush. He is killed while taking his boats up the river. Tracy then takes over the last shipment as if paying a debt to his dead pal and also kills the Japanese officer in charge of the ambush. The drama is based on an actual incident during the war.

The dialogue is well above average for this type of adventure film, with Greenstreet getting most of the good lines. When the Japanese officer enters his cafe, the Dutchman warns the two Americans: "You'd better let me do the talking. The only thing that stands between you and eternity is my vocabulary." Near the end of the film, Tracy announces to the Dutchman that his former partner was a fool. "He's dead for something," Greenstreet replies. "When I'm dead it will be for nothing, just as it will be for you . . . He believed in something." ∎

Mamba (1930), Tiffany. *Dir.* Al Rogell; *Sc.* Tom Miranda, Winifred Dunn; *Cast includes:* Jean Hersholt, Eleanor Boardman, Ralph Forbes, Joseph Swickard, Claude Fleming.

The drama is set in East Africa on the eve of World War I. A relaxed harmony exists between English and German soldiers stationed in the jungle until the European war erupts. Jean Hersholt portrays a German trader, a bestial wretch who beats the natives and lusts for any women within his grasp. He buys a white woman (Eleanor Boardman) whom he intends to marry and take back to Germany. As he is about to leave, he is notified that he has been called for military duty by his country. Ralph Forbes, portraying a German captain, falls for Boardman and interferes with Hersholt's plans. Meanwhile the rebellious Zulus attack a small fortress of whites who are saved by the British troops and Forbes. Hersholt is brutally killed by the natives while Forbes rescues the heroine. The film was one of the earliest to be shot entirely in Technicolor. ∎

Man at Large (1941). See Prisoners of War. ∎

Man From Dakota, The (1940), MGM. *Dir.* Leslie Fenton; *Sc.* Laurence Stallings; *Cast includes:* Wallace Beery, John Howard, Dolores Del Rio, Donald Meek, Robert Barrat.

Based on McKinlay Kantor's novel about the Civil War, the film tells of the escape of two Union soldiers from a Confederate prison. Wallace Beery plays a lethargic sergeant while John Howard portrays his captain. The two fugitives maneuver their way through enemy lines in time to save the Union army from an impending rout. Beery, as the title character, redeems himself at the end with a heroic act. Dolores Del Rio, as a young Russian refugee, joins the two Union soldiers after killing a fellow Russian who was with the Confederate troops. The implausible story is helped along by likable Beery and plenty of action. ∎

Man From the Alamo, The (1953), U. *Dir.* Budd Boetticher; *Sc.* Steve Fisher, D. D. Beauchamp; *Cast includes:* Glenn Ford, Julie Adams, Chill Wills, Hugh O'Brian, Victor Jory.

This action drama concerns one of the defenders of the Alamo—the only survivor—who was chosen by lot to slip through Santa Anna's lines so that he could warn the defenders' families of the Mexican general's advance. Glenn Ford portrays the lone survivor who discovers the families have been slaughtered by a renegade band masquerading as Mexican troops. Other settlers label him a coward, forcing him to prove he is not a deserter. He tracks down the raiders and their leader (Victor Jory) and avenges the heroes of the Alamo. The film plays loose with historical facts, which show that there were no survivors of those who entered the Alamo as defenders. ∎

Man From Wyoming, The (1930), Par. *Dir.* Rowland V. Lee; *Sc.* John V. A. Weaver; *Cast includes:* Gary Cooper, June Collyer, Regis Toomey, Morgan Farley.

Gary Cooper portrays a Wyoming construction worker who, along with his buddy, enlists in the army when the U.S. enters World War I. In France he meets an American socialite (June Collyer) who is serving in the ambulance corps. They fall in love and marry. Later, after he returns to the front, she receives news that he has been killed in action. To forget her sorrow, she engages in wild parties at her family mansion. Cooper, who was only wounded, returns and frowns upon her behavior. When he offers to take her back to Wyoming, she turns him down. He returns to the front lines in disgust. When the war ends, she returns to the town where they were married. They meet once again and resume their marriage. ∎

Man From Yesterday, The (1932), Par. *Dir.* Berthold Viertel; *Sc.* Oliver H. P. Garrett; *Cast includes:* Claudette Colbert, Clive

Brook, Charles Boyer, Andy Devine, Alan Mowbray.

A husband presumed killed in the war returns to find his wife in love with another man in this World War I drama. During a Paris air raid, army officer Clive Brook marries Claudette Colbert. He leaves the next day for the trenches where he is gassed and then captured by the enemy. He spends the remainder of the war in a German prison camp. Meanwhile, a doctor (Charles Boyer) proposes marriage to Colbert after they are informed that her husband is dead. Brook returns and Boyer sends Colbert back to her man. But Brook realizes she loves the doctor and bows out of the picture. The film provides very little action pertaining to the war. ■

Man Hunt (1941), TCF. *Dir.* Fritz Lang; *Sc.* Dudley Nichols; *Cast includes:* Walter Pidgeon, Joan Bennett, George Sanders, John Carradine, Roddy MacDowall.

A suspenseful and far-fetched tale about an attempt to assassinate Hitler, the film stars Walter Pidgeon as a British big-game hunter whose expertise in the hunt brings him into direct confrontation with the Gestapo. He decides to enter Germany surreptitiously and gain access to Hitler's private lair to prove to himself that he could knock off the dictator if he wanted to. Just as he gets the Nazi leader in his sights, he is captured by guards. The Gestapo torture Pidgeon, demanding that he sign a confession that he was sent by the British government. He manages to escape and eventually reach England where, ironically, he is now the one who is stalked by Nazi agents. Director Fritz Lang's suspenseful film ends with Pidgeon's decision to return to Germany, this time to finish off his prey. The film was remade as a British television production in 1976 starring Peter O'Toole and titled *Rogue Male*, the original title of Geoffrey Household's novel. ■

Man I Killed, The (1932), Par. *Dir.* Ernst Lubitsch; *Sc.* Ernest Vajda, Samson Raphaelson; *Cast includes:* Lionel Barrymore, Nancy Carroll, Phillips Holmes, Lucien Littlefield. ZaSu Pitts.

A former French soldier (Phillips Holmes) visits the family of a German soldier whom he killed in battle in this post-World War I drama. The father (Lionel Barrymore) of the slain youth has not gotten over the loss of his son. Neither has his wife nor the boy's fiancee who now lives with the bereaved family. When Holmes sees the emotional condition of the family, he cannot bring himself to tell them his true reason for the visit. Instead, he says he was a friend of their son. They slowly accept Holmes as part of the family—almost a surrogate son. When the girl learns the truth, she tells him not to destroy the little peace the parents have attained from his stay.

In the village, meanwhile, a rejected suitor of the fiancee stirs up hatred for the French intruder. When some of the men of the village complain about Holmes to Barrymore, the father berates them for their prejudice—the same hatred that caused the previous war and took so many innocent lives. The film, originally titled *Broken Lullaby*, handles its pacifist theme with intelligence and quiet dignity. The taking of human life, the film suggests, is wrong even when it is sanctioned by the state. It is one of the few Hollywood dramas to focus on the agony of parents who have lost a son in battle. In its quiet tone, realistic setting and avoidance of national glory and honor, the work has much in common with such antiwar films as the trendsetting *All Quiet on the Western Front* (1930). Lubitsch's controlled direction, owing much to such directors as Eisenstein and Pudovkin, adds to the power of the story, especially in such scenes as the one in which the father stands in the same street the young men marched down on their way to battle. As he stands there thinking of that fateful day, the only sound is that of marching feet. Holmes, who gave a sensitive portrayal as the young French soldier, was killed in 1942 while serving with the Royal Canadian Air Force in World War II. This was a very unusual film for Lubitsch, who is better known for his sophisticated romantic comedies. ■

Man I Married, The (1940), TCF. *Dir.* Irving Pichel; *Sc.* Oliver H. P. Garrett; *Cast includes:* Joan Bennett, Francis Lederer, Lloyd Nolan, Anna Sten, Otto Kruger, Maria Ouspenskaya.

Joan Bennett stars in this World War II drama about an American who visits Nazi Germany with her German-American husband and their child. Previously apolitical, she is repulsed by the regimentation and eventual oppression of the Nazi regime. On the other hand, her husband becomes fascinated by the glory and power of the "new order" and joins the party. He plans to divorce his American wife and raise his young son as a Nazi when he learns from his father that Lederer's mother was a Jewess and that the child's life would be in danger.

Although the film contains plenty of anti-Nazi propaganda, it presents its characters intelligently, especially in its portrayal of the German people. They are depicted not as ruthless monsters but as those who are hypnotized and misled by jingoistic spectacles to forfeit freedom of thought and belief in exchange for a false sense of security. ■

Man in the Gray Flannel Suit, The

(1956), TCF. *Dir.* Nunnally Johnson; *Sc.* Nunnally Johnson; *Cast includes:* Gregory Peck, Jennifer Jones, Fredric March, Marisa Pavan, Lee J. Cobb.

Gregory Peck portrays a Madison Avenue executive whose conscience finally persuades him to tell his wife of an affair he has had during World War II, the result of which bore him a son. His confession almost causes the marriage to fall apart. His wife (Jennifer Jones) is infuriated when she hears about the affair. The film includes a series of flashbacks of Peck's experiences as a paratrooper during the war as well as his liaison with his wartime love (Marisa Pavan). ■

Man Must Live, A (1925). See Veterans. ■

Man of Conquest (1939), Rep. *Dir.* George

Nicholls, Jr.; *Sc.* Wells Root, E. E. Paramore, Jan Fortune; *Cast includes:* Richard Dix, Gail Patrick, Edward Ellis, Joan Fontaine, Victor Jory.

Richard Dix stars as Sam Houston in this historical drama about the creation of the state of Texas. The story begins with Houston's rise in Tennessee politics under the guiding hand of Andrew Jackson (Edward Ellis) and continues with his governorship, his unsuccessful marriage and his participation in the Texas War of Independence. Vivid battle sequences include those of the Alamo and at San Jacinto, both of which adhere fairly closely to historical facts. Joan Fontaine portrays Houston's indifferent first wife. Gail Patrick plays the second love interest in his life. The major figures at the Alamo, Davy Crockett, Stephen Austin and Jim Bowie, are played by Robert Barrat, Ralph Morgan and Robert Armstrong, respectively. C. Henry

Gordon gives another of his villainous portrayals as Santa Anna. ■

Man on a Tightrope (1953). See Cold War. ■

Man Who Reclaimed His Head, The

(1934), U. *Dir.* Edward Ludwig; *Sc.* Jean Bart, Samuel Ornitz; *Cast includes:* Claude Rains, Joan Bennett, Lionel Atwill, Baby Jane, Henry O'Neill.

Claude Rains portrays a ghost writer for a publisher (Lionel Atwill) and contributes a series of antiwar editorials to his employer's paper in this World War I domestic drama set in France. Meanwhile, Atwill makes advances toward the writer's wife (Joan Bennett). When war breaks out, Atwill switches allegiances to the munitions makers. Rains, in disgust, joins the army where Atwill's influence places the soldier in dangerous situations at the front. Rains manages to survive and, returning home unexpectedly, witnesses his former employer trying to force his wife into a compromising position. He then kills the publisher.

The subjects of pacifism and suspect munitionions makers were not unique during the period when the film was released. Both topics had been themes in films (*All Quiet on the Western Front*, released in 1930) or in newspapers which exposed secret deals during World War I between arms manufactures in France and Germany. Rains played a similar role the following year in *The Last Outpost* in which he again appeared as a soldier with marital problems. This time his rival was Cary Grant. ■

Man Who Was Afraid, The (1917), Es-

sanay. *Dir.* Fred E. Wright; *Sc.* H. Tipten Steck; *Cast includes:* Bryant Washburn, Ernest Maupain, Margaret Watts, Frank Raymond.

A young man would like to follow his older brother into military service, but his mother stops him. Labeled a "slacker" by some and a coward by others, our young hero (Bryant Washburn) eventually disobeys his parent's wishes and joins up with the National Guard. His unit is assigned to the Mexican border where bandit raids have resulted in the deaths of several Americans. Washburn soon distinguishes himself as a hero. When he returns home, he wins the admiration of his community and the love of his sweetheart.

The film includes many battle scenes with the American troops fighting Mexicans who are portrayed in a demeaning manner.

Historically, no battles between Mexican troops and Americans resulted from any National Guard action or General Pershing's punitive expedition into Mexico in 1916. Pershing was ordered across the border in pursuit of Pancho Villa, whose raid on Columbus, New Mexico, earlier that year, resulted in the deaths of several American civilians. ∎

Man Who Wouldn't Tell, The (1918). See Spy Films: the Silents. ∎

Man Without a Country, The (1917), Jewell. *Dir.* Ernest C. Warde; *Sc.* Lloyd Lonergan; *Cast includes:* H.H. Herbert, Florence La Badie, J.H. Gilmour.

Edward E. Hale's novel received a relatively accurate treatment in this silent drama. The film begins during the early days of World War I with a young American pacifist (H.H. Herbert) who thinks his sweetheart has been lost at sea. The vessel she had been on was torpedoed by the Germans. Angered by this personal loss, he practically repeats the fateful words of Philip Nolan in Hale's novel, damning the United States and wishing never to hear his country's name again. A friend of his family hands him a copy of *The Man Without a Country* and, as he begins to read the book, the story of Philip Nolan unfolds on the screen. The young pacifist, upon finishing the novel, enlists in his country's service the next morning.

Released shortly after America's entrance into World War I, the film no doubt contributed to the patriotic mood of the country. The use of the story as a propaganda tool was not far from Hale's original intent. He wrote it as propaganda for the intensely contested presidential campaign of 1864. ∎

Man Without a Country, The (1925), Fox. *Dir.* Rowland V. Lee; *Sc.* Robert N. Lee; *Cast includes:* Edward Hearn, Pauline Starke, Lucy Beaumont, Richard Tucker, Wilfred Lucas.

The second screen version, also silent, of Edward Everett Hale's tale was more accurate to its original source than the 1917 screen adaptation that used World War I as a framework for the tragic story of Philip Nolan. The later film covers Lieutenant Nolan's naive belief in Aaron Burr's plot against the U.S. government. Nolan (Edward Hearn) is indicted as a conspirator and at the trial utters the words that were to seal his fate: "Damn the United States. I hope that I may never hear of the United States again." He is then given his unusual sentence—to remain at sea for the rest of his life, never to set foot on American soil and never to hear the name of the United States mentioned.

The film covers the incident in which Nolan distinguishes himself in a naval battle with another vessel. Action sequences include Decatur's battle at Algiers and a sea fight with a pirate ship. In the written work he dies alone after fifty years of exile, a forgotten man aboard an American ship. In this film, however, a former sweetheart (Pauline Starke), after several futile appeals to various presidents, gains a pardon for Nolan from Abraham Lincoln (George Billings). The news reaches Nolan just before his death. As the vessel reaches port, his old flame also dies and the spirits of the two lovers unite as the woman, now transformed by death to her former youth, places an American flag over Nolan's shoulders. ∎

Man, Woman and Wife (1929), U. *Dir.* Edward Laemmle; *Sc.* Charles Logue; *Cast includes:* Norman Kerry, Pauline Starke, Marion Nixon, Byron Douglas, Kenneth Harlan.

Norman Kerry portrays a World War I deserter who is listed as killed in action in this domestic drama. His wife (Marion Nixon), who considered the marriage a failure, weds a former boy friend after she receives news of her husband's death. Kerry returns home under a pseudonym and becomes a drifter. A former sweetheart (Pauline Starke) helps him to get back on his feet. Kerry then kills a local gangster who is threatening his wife's reputation and goes to prison. During a prison break, he purposely lets himself be gunned down to further protect his wife. ∎

Manchurian Candidate, The (1962), UA. *Dir.* John Frankenheimer; *Sc.* George Axelrod; *Cast includes:* Frank Sinatra, Laurence Harvey, Janet Leigh, Angela Lansbury.

Set during and after the Korean War and based on Richard Condon's novel of political assassination and Cold War paranoia, the film recounts the collective nightmare of a group of former prisoners of war. Frank Sinatra and Laurence Harvey portray army buddies who, along with other captives, have

A Chinese Communist official (with suit) is about to demonstrate how American prisoners, captured during the Korean War, can be "programmed" to kill upon command. *The Manchurian Candidate* (1962).

been brainwashed during their internment in a North Korean prison camp. Harvey has been programmed to carry out a series of assassinations. When they return to the U.S., Sinatra begins to untangle the Chinese Communist plot in which Harvey, outwardly an acknowledged war hero, is subconsciously ordered to assassinate a liberal presidential candidate during a convention at Madison Square Garden. Sinatra stops him at the last moment. Angela Lansbury, as Harvey's scheming mother, manipulates both her son and her husband, a U.S. Senator (James Gregory).

A disturbing drama in many respects, the film had been out of circulation for many years until its re-release in 1988, when it stirred new controversy. Its original release anticipated the series of traumatic assassinations which a shocked nation was soon to experience. A plot that had once seemed highly improbable was later seen in a new light. Scenes such as those in the prison camp involving brainwashing of American prisoners and that originally appeared as far-fetched had a more chilling effect years later.

The possibilities of a single figure, perhaps in the employ or under the influence of a foreign power, killing a national leader and plunging an entire country into political turmoil, unfortunately moved from the realm of fiction to tragic reality. ∎

Mangas Colorado. See Apache Wars, *War Drums* (1957). ∎

Manila Calling (1942), TCF. *Dir.* Herbert I. Leeds; *Sc.* John Larkin; *Cast includes:* Lloyd Nolan, Carole Landis, Cornel Wilde, James Gleason, Martin Kosleck.

A World War II action drama about American-Filipino guerrillas battling the Japanese invaders in the Philippines, the film stars Lloyd Nolan as the brave group's leader. The plot provides for plenty of battle sequences between the enemy troops and the "good guys" in this simplistic but effective war movie. Cornel Wilde plays an American who wants to combat Japanese propaganda by building his own radio transmitter. Nolan, shown as a woman-hater, softens up to Carole Landis, who portrays a dance-hall girl. Character actor James Gleason provides the comic relief. ∎

"March of Time, The." A series of documentaries released monthly from 1935 to 1954, the short films, approximately 15 minutes in length, covered domestic and foreign subjects. They were produced by Louis D. Rochemont under the sponsorship of *Time*, *Life* and *Fortune* magazines. Originally intended to inform its audiences about topical events in an entertaining manner by blending narrative with visual pictures, the series during the early stages of World War II sought to influence American opinion in favor of the British and against Nazi Germany and its allies. The series was noted for its skillful use of understatement and irony as it combined filmed scenes with the spoken word. During the war various segments touched upon almost every aspect of the conflict. *The Ramparts We Watch* (1942), an extended entry, gained the attention of critics and audiences alike.

The "March of Time" films were some of the first to suggest the threat of another war. One particular segment, "Inside Nazi Germany" (1938), stressed how the dictatorship controls its citizens through propaganda and censorship and how it sees religious groups as the last bastions of resistance. Joseph Goebbels is seen and heard calling for a return of German territory lost after World War I.

Once World War II began, the series brought home to American audiences the progress of the war and its related crises. "Britain's R.A.F." (1940) showed pictures of England's coastal command in readiness. "Canada at War" (1940) described that country's importance as a training ground for future fliers and as a chief source of food and other materiel for Britain.

Other entries dealt with topics aimed at the American public prior to the nation's entrance into the conflict. "Crisis in the Atlantic" (1941) covered the importance of the convoys to the war effort. "Sailors With Wings" (1941) dealt with the U.S. Navy's role in protecting the critical convoys. "America Prepares" (1941) outlined the gearing up of U.S. war-related industries and the training of its military forces. "Peace—by Adolf Hitler" (1941) was designed to warn prewar America of the dictator's treachery and impending danger.

Other films told of some of the nations caught up in the conflict and how they were faring. "Australia at War" (1941) described that country's role in England's overall war plan in the Pacific. "China Fights Back" (1941) pointed out that China has been fighting the longest against aggression. "Men of Norway" (1941) related how those Norwegians who escaped Nazi domination are aiding the war effort by transporting fuel for the British and training in Canada as pilots.

America's entry into the war only gave new impetus to the series which had been waging its own battle for years. The films continued in the same vein, underscoring the ruthlessness of the Axis powers and the necessity for a united front by the Allies. "Men of the U.S. Navy" (1942) focused on U.S. Navy recruitment and training while stressing the role the warships will play in the conflict. "America at War" (1942) traced the nation's role in World War I. "America's New Army" (1942) concerned General George Marshall's reorganization of the military. "India at War" (1942) described that country mobilizing in the struggle against the Axis powers. "Prelude to Victory" (1943) was about the Allied invasion of North Africa. "Preparation for Invasion" (1943) detailed the complexities of organizing and supporting an assault on Europe. "What to Do With Germany" (1944) suggested harsh penalties for the nation that inflicted destruction and terror upon its neighbors.

The Pacific and Japan's aggression received almost as much attention as Europe and the Atlantic. "Crisis in the Pacific" (1940) pointed out the Japanese threat in that area, particularly with its troops surrounding Hong Kong. "Battlefields of the Pacific" (1942) outlined Japan's aggressive policy in the Pacific with its vast potential benefits. "Back Door to Tokyo" (1944) emphasized the importance of keeping the Burma Road open as a supply route to China.

A few films emphasized heroic resistance movements in countries occupied by the Nazi invaders. "The Fighting French" (1942) told about the French resistance against Nazi Germany in occupied France and elsewhere. "Underground Report" (1944) traced the struggle of resistance movements in various countries occupied by Nazi Germany.

South America came under scrutiny as well. "The Argentine Question" (1942) discussed Argentina's controversial ties with the

Axis powers and her questionable neutrality. "South American Front" (1944) analyzed the different alignments of Argentina and its Fascist sympathies and democratic Brazil.

Not all of the later films were able to maintain the high standards set in the first few issues—and critics were quick to point this out. But the series, more often praised than attacked in the U.S. and abroad, were an important adjunct to the movie theater program during the war years. They laid much of the groundwork for the many excellent documentaries that were to follow. ■

Mare Nostrum (1926), MGM. *Dir.* Rex Ingram; *Sc.* Willis Goldbeck; *Cast includes:* Alice Terry, Antonio Moreno, Michael Brantford, Fernand Mailly, Hughie Mack.

Based on a novel by Blasco Ibanez, the World War I drama concerns a German spy (Alice Terry) who gains the love of a Spanish sea captain (Antonio Moreno). He abandons all for her. Eventually she meets her end before a firing squad. Her lover dies in a sea battle with a German submarine but manages to get off a final shot from a deck gun which sinks the U-boat. The film, shot largely in Spain and Italy, includes several effective scenes of submarine warfare that are not too flattering toward Germany.

Why MGM would release this type of propaganda film eight years after World War I is not clear. As for Ibanez turning out this material, the motivation is even more obscure, since Spain remained neutral during the war. ■

Margin for Error (1943). See Spy Films: the Talkies. ■

Marianne (1929), MGM. *Dir.* Robert Z. Leonard; *Sc.* Dale Van Every; *Cast includes:* Marion Davies, Lawrence Gray, Benny Rubin, Cliff Edwards.

Marion Davies stars as the title character, a young French woman, in this musical comedy with World War I as the background. Lawrence Gray portrays a doughboy who falls in love with her, but Marianne is engaged to a French soldier who has lost his sight in battle. When the blind hero chooses to enter the priesthood, Marianne is free to marry Gray. Marion Davies does several impersonations while Benny Rubin and Cliff "Ukulele Ike" Edwards provide the comedy. Half a dozen songs help to liven up an other-

wise weak production. The film was also made in a silent version with different male leads. ■

Marie Antoinette (1938). See French Revolution. ■

Pat O'Brien (c.) and Robert Ryan (r.) help defend the Guadalcanal beachhead against a Japanese counterattack during World War II. *Marine Raiders* (1944).

Marine Raiders (1944), RKO. *Dir.* Harold Schuster; *Sc.* Warren Duff; *Cast includes:* Pat O'Brien, Robert Ryan, Ruth Hussey, Frank McHugh, Barton MacLane.

A tribute to the U.S. Marine Corps, this World War II action drama focuses chiefly on marine assaults of Japanese-held Pacific islands, including the invasion of Guadalcanal by the First Marine Raider battalion. Pat O'Brien portrays a tough and competent marine major while Robert Ryan, as a captain, plays O'Brien's buddy. After their successful attack on Guadalcanal, O'Brien and his men are moved to Australia where Ryan falls in love with Ruth Hussey, a member of the Women's Auxiliary Air Force. Before the couple can marry, O'Brien, thinking his pal is making a mistake, takes Ryan back with him to the U.S. to train new troops. Upset at his former buddy, Ryan breaks off their friendship. They are soon ordered back into action to take another Pacific island. In Australia, before their assault, Ryan locates Hussey and they marry. The friendship between the two marines resumes as the men perform gallantly in the climactic invasion. Frank McHugh, as the outfit's cook, and Barton MacLane, as McHugh's chief critic, provide comic relief.

The final battle scenes, showing a joint air and sea attack, are fairly realistic and dramatic. Both battle sequences are helped by actual combat footage supplied by various branches of the service. Much of the film was shot at the U.S. Marine base at San Diego. Released during the war, the drama includes the usual conventions of the genre—the epithets hurled at the Japanese ("the little monkeys") and the women who wait and pray for their loved ones to return from battle ("Bless them all, bless every mother's son of them").

Although the film is chiefly fictional, much of it parallels the exploits of Merritt A. "Red Mike" Edson, commander of the First Raider Battalion and First Parachute Battalion in August 1942. He and his force took up a defense position on Guadalcanal and withstood an all-out Japanese attack on September 13, that threatened the tenuous U.S. beachhead. Later, he led assaults on several other Japanese-held islands in the Pacific. ■

Marines Are Coming, The (1935), Mascot. Dir. David Howard; Sc. James Gruen; Cast includes: William Haines, Esther Ralston, Conrad Nagel, Armida, Edgar Kennedy.

A minor drama set in Central America for its action, the film concerns a U.S. Marine (William Haines) who is compelled to retire but re-enlists to prove his worth. When he returns, he heroically battles a cadre of bandits and emerges triumphant. The plot also includes a romantic triangle involving two marines and a blonde. The little action that the film offers lacks energy.

Loosely based on events relating to America's incursion into Nicaragua during that country's civil war (1925–1933), the film, like a handful of others (e.g., Frank Capra's 1929 Flight), depicts the guerrilla fighter Sandino and his men as bandits. Sandino was seen by many as a nationalist and patriot. He resisted foreign intervention and fought against local militarists who had overthrown the popularly elected government. See Nicaraguan Civil War of 1925–33. ■

Marines Are Here, The (1938), Mon. Dir. Phil Rosen; Sc. Jack Knapp, J. Benson Cheney; Cast includes: Gordon Oliver, June Travis, Ray Walker, Guinn Williams.

A low-budget action drama, the film eulogizes the courage and physical prowess of the U.S. Marines. Also included is a romantic plot involving a marine (Gordon Oliver) who sees the error of his ways and quickly reforms. The film provides some action when the marines battle a stronghold of bandits. June Travis provides the feminine interest. Guinn Williams, the former cowboy star, handles the comic relief in this weak melodrama. ■

Marines Come Through, The (1943). See Spy Films: the Talkies. ■

Marines Fly High, The (1940), RKO. Dir. George Nicholls, Jr., Ben Stoloff; Sc. Jerry Cady, A. J. Bolton; Cast includes: Richard Dix, Chester Morris, Lucille Ball, Steffi Duna, John Eldridge.

Richard Dix and Chester Morris co-star in this action drama as two airborne marines stationed in a Central American country and who fall in love with the same woman (Lucille Ball). Meanwhile, a local bandit and his men are terrorizing the cocoa planters. Ball is captured by the marauding bandit chief, bringing Dix, Morris and a group of marines into action. The battle scenes are adequate in this otherwise weak film which, despite its fictional flavoring, is based on the U.S. incursion into Nicaragua during that country's civil strife. America lent air, sea and land support to that government against guerrilla forces, chiefly those of General Sandino. Director George Nicholls, Jr. was killed in an automobile crash during the making of the film, and Ben Stoloff was brought in to finish the production. See Nicaraguan Civil War of 1925–1933. ■

Marines, Let's Go (1961), TCF. Dir. Raoul Walsh; Sc. John Twist; Cast includes: Tom Tryon, David Hedison, Tom Reese, Linda Hutchins, William Tyler.

A marine platoon is temporarily removed from the battlefront and sent to Tokyo to rejuvenate the fighting spirit of the men in this unrealistic drama set during the Korean War. The usual stereotypes persist in this caliber of war tale, including, among others, the shy country boy from Texas (David Brandon), the crafty conman (Tom Tryon) and the haughty rich boy (David Hedison). Linda Hutchins provides part of the romantic interest. The early and climactic battle sequences are staged effectively and excitingly by veteran director Raoul Walsh. ■

U.S. Marines prepare to go into action during the Korean War. *Marines, Let's Go* (1961).

Marion, Francis (1732–1795). Marion and a squad of 16 men, moving through the darkness of the South Carolina woods, came upon a British and Tory force guarding about 160 American prisoners who were being taken to the main British base at Charleston. Just before daybreak on August 20, 1780, Marion and his group rushed the surprised guards and captured them all. He set the Americans free, some to rejoin the patriot army and others to return home, then melted back into the woods. It was another example in a series of exploits by Marion that had earned him the name "The Swamp Fox."

After the American defeat by British troops at Camden earlier that year, the cause looked bleak in the Carolinas for the American rebels. It appeared that the British were succeeding by focusing their strength on holding the southern colonies as a base from which to move out and put down the revolution that had been boiling for several years. Only the hit-and-run guerrilla tactics of Francis Marion, probably refined from his experience as an Indian fighter against the Cherokee (1759, 1761), kept the British from consolidating their gains.

His activities in the Carolinas, where he

headed a force of horse and foot irregulars, kept alive sympathy for the American cause in an area in which there were many Loyalists. Operating from a base near Williamsburg, he often succeeded in cutting enemy communications and eluding forces that were numerically superior by disappearing into the swamps after an engagement, to appear suddenly and strike again at a different location.

Though he was made a brigadier general of the militia in 1781, Marion continued to employ those guerrilla tactics that worked so well. He was instrumental in helping to wrest eventual control of the Carolinas from the British. Marion took part as a regimental commander in the Battle of Savannah (1779) and served under General Nathaniel Greene in the Battle of Eutaw Springs (September 8, 1781) that resulted in driving back the British to the port of Charleston.

After the Revolution, he served three terms in the South Carolina state legislature where he advocated a policy of leniency towards former Tories. He became the subject of numerous American novels and, unfortunately, only a handful of early silent films. Both "General Marion, the Swamp Fox" (1911) and

The famous "Last Supper" scene from *M*A*S*H* (1970), the irreverent black comedy set during the Korean War.

"Francis Marion, the Swamp Fox" (1914) deal with his heroic exploits against the British. ■

Marked Woman, The (1914). See Boxer Rebellion. ■

Marriage Ring, The (1918). See Spy Films: the Silents. ■

Martyrs of the Alamo. The (1915), Triangle. *Dir.* Christy Cabanne; *Sc.* Christy Cabanne; *Cast includes:* Sam DeGrasse, Walter Long, Tom Wilson, A.D. Sears, Ora Carew.

This historical drama recounts the story of the brave defenders of the Alamo and how they fought against the Mexican general Santa Anna. Several famous figures out of the pages of American history are present, including James Bowie, Davy Crockett and Sam Houston. The events been filmed numerous times, and this early version seems relatively authentic as well as being dramatically interesting. ■

M*A*S*H (1970), TCF. *Dir.* Robert Altman; *Sc.* Ring Lardner, Jr.; *Cast includes:* Donald Sutherland, Elliott Gould, Tom Skerritt, Sally Kellerman, Robert Duvall, Gary Burghoff.

Based on the novel *MASH* by Richard Hooker, this black comedy centers around a Mobile Army Surgical Hospital in Korea during the war, a military unit dealt with seriously in *Battle Circus* (1953). The tone of the film is established early during a dispassionate conversation in a field operating room. "Is he an enlisted man or an officer?" "Enlisted man." "Okay, then make the stitches bigger." The conflict revolves around the dedicated and religious Major Burns (Robert Duvall) and the pompous and equally dedicated Major O'Houlihan (Sally Kellerman) in one corner and three young surgeons, Donald Sutherland, Elliott Gould and Tom Skerritt, in the opposite corner. The young Turks declare war on the pair, which sometimes leads to the cruel humor of the film. For example, to prove that O'Houlihan, whom some have renamed "Hot Lips," is a true blonde, they rig up the shower walls so that it will collapse as she is showering. Meanwhile, almost the entire camp is seated to witness the event. Other memorable moments from this otherwise black comedy include the wiring and playback over the camp loudspeakers of the lovemaking between Duvall and Kellerman; the hilarious football game in which the opposing team is injected with a sense-dulling drug; and the "Last Supper" sequence to help the dentist, Painless Pole, overcome his fears of impotence. In an early scene the uptight nurse Kellerman, exasperated with the antics of surgeon Sutherland, wonders out loud "how a degenerated person like that ever reached a responsible position in the regular army corps." "He was drafted," a colleague answers. Altman's irreverent and witty look at the ironies of war and survival is filled with visual and sound techniques that have become his trademark. The film became a popular television series in the 1970s. ■

"Massacre, The" (1912), Biograph. *Dir.* D.W. Griffith; *Sc.* D.W. Griffith; *Cast includes:* Wilfred Lucas, Blanche Sweet, Charles West, Alfred Paget.

A dramatization of Custer's last stand, this little silent film illustrates director D.W. Griffith's attempt to present a screen spectacle, thereby expanding the dimensions of the fiction film. He hired hundreds of extras who filled the screen as cavalrymen and warring hostiles to help bring the historical event to life. He used two reels instead of the customary one to tell his story and utilized large numbers of costumes, all of which invoked the wrath of the studio's front office. The owners of Biograph were more concerned with budgets than with pioneering new forms. Foreign films, however, overshadowed the infant American movie industry in producing multiple-reel spectacles for American audiences. Griffith's early epic, considered today by several film historians as one of his formative works, faded into obscurity.

By 1911 Griffith's attitude toward the Indian was ambivalent. In such one-reelers as "The Last Drop of Water" and "Fighting Blood," the Indian can be seen attacking wagon trains of pioneers and cabins of white settlers for no apparent reason. He added lurid scenes of hostiles abusing young pioneer women, preparing to scalp infants and bludgeoning white men. On the other hand, Griffith occasionally portrayed Indians as heroes, as in "Ramona." They were virtually always played by white performers. ■

Massacre River (1949), Mon. *Dir.* John Rawlins; *Sc.* Louis Stevens; *Cast includes:* Guy Madison, Rory Calhoun, Carole Mathews, Cathy Downs, Johnny Sands.

The U.S. Cavalry is confronted with hostile Indians in this romantic adventure that stresses the romance rather than the action. Guy Madison and Rory Calhoun portray two cavalry officers at a remote outpost who compete for the colonel's daughter, played by Cathy Downs. Although the film provides several skirmishes with the hostiles, the bulk of the plot concerns the romantic entanglements of the principal characters. ■

Massive Retaliation (1982). See Future Wars. ■

Master Race, The (1944), RKO. *Dir.* Herbert J. Biberman; *Sc.* Herbert J. Biberman; *Cast includes:* George Coulouris, Stanley Ridges, Osa Massen, Carl Esmond.

Nazi leaders begin their strategy for the next war as Allied armies push toward Berlin in this World War II cautionary drama. George Coulouris portrays a high Nazi official and advocate of German supremacy who orders his military staff to go underground and cause turmoil among the liberated nations of Europe until the Nazis are strong enough to rise again. He journeys to an American-occupied Belgian village where he poses as a patriot. He soon starts to spread dissension and unrest among the villagers before he is exposed. A quotation from another war movie, *Till We Meet Again*, released the same year and in which a character prophetically states: "We are never through with the Germans," may well be the theme of the present film. ■

Masters of Men (1923), Vitagraph. *Dir.* David Smith; *Sc.* Graham Baker; *Cast includes:* Earle Williams, Alice Calhoun, Cullen Landis, Wanda Hawley, Dick Sutherland.

Cullen Landis portrays a young man who joins the U.S. Navy after he is falsely accused of theft in this romantic drama set during the Spanish-American War. Landis and a navy lieutenant (Earle Williams) are later shanghaied by a villainous captain but manage to escape after being subjected to cruel treatment aboard the captain's vessel. The two American sailors make their way back to their own warships in Santiago Harbor. War erupts between the U.S. and Spain, and Landis, performing bravely during a battle with Spanish warships, receives a commission. By the end of the film he is cleared of the theft charges against him. ∎

Mata Hari (1876–1917). Perhaps the most famous spy in World War I, Mata Hari, whose real name was Margaretha Zelle, was a Dutch dancer in the employ of the Germans beginning in 1907. As a dancer in Paris, she became the intimate of many military officers who confided in her. The French discovered her secret and executed her. Several film biographies, discussed below, have recounted her exploits. In the World War I spy drama *Stamboul Quest* (1934) Myrna Loy, as a German spy, is depicted as having caused the demise of Mata Hari who made the fatal mistake of falling in love with one of her victims. ∎

Mata Hari (1932), MGM. *Dir.* George Fitzmaurice; *Sc.* Benjamin Glazer, Leo Birinski; *Cast includes:* Greta Garbo, Ramon Navarro, Lionel Barrymore, Lewis Stone, Henry Gordon, Karen Morley.

The notorious World War I German spy who gained a reputation for sleeping with her victims is played by Greta Garbo in this early sound film. Mata Hari in this drama confines most of her operations to Paris in 1917, where she first ruins a Russian general (Lionel Barrymore) who pays with both his honor and his life as he succumbs to her charms and sexuality. Another potential victim, Ramon Navarro, as a naive Russian lieutenant, proves more difficult for the spy. Although she manages to steal important secrets entrusted to him, she falls in love with the handsome young officer. She shoots Barrymore when, in a jealous rage, he threatens to denounce her young lover as a traitor. She is exposed as a German agent and sentenced to face a firing squad. Lewis Stone plays the ruthless head of a German spy ring in Paris.

Although the film is based on true incidents, it is very similar to *Dishonored*, another World War I spy drama released the previous year, in which Marlene Dietrich, as a notorious spy, also places love before duty at the cost of her own life. In both cases the female star dominates the familiar plot. ∎

Mata Hari (1985), Cannon. *Dir.* Curtis Harrington; *Sc.* Joel Ziskin; *Cast includes:* Sylvia Kristel, Christopher Cazenove.

Another version of the legendary spy, the film opens in Paris in the spring of 1914 before World War I. Two close friends, one a Frenchman and the other a German officer, meet the beautiful dancer, Mata Hari (Sylvia Kristel), in a museum and both fall in love with her. When war breaks out, the German returns to Berlin and Mata Hari travels by train to Berlin to appear on stage. She is framed for a murder that occurs in one of the railway cars and is forced to spy for Germany. When she returns to Paris, she is arrested as a spy and volunteers her services as a double agent for the French. She becomes involved in a plot to blow up a cathedral filled with important members of the military but disconnects the charge in time. The French who catch her in the act of dismantling the bomb, associate her with the spies and sentence her to death by a firing squad. At her trial she admits that whatever she has done, she did for love. A few battle scenes are included, but the bulk of the work focuses on her affairs with different men, including the two friends she met in the museum. ∎

Mau Mau Uprising. See *Something of Value* (1957). ∎

Mauldin, William Henry "Bill." See *Up Front* (1951). ∎

Maximilian (Ferdinand Maximilian Joseph) (1832–1867). When Emperor Maximilian of Mexico died before a firing squad on June 19, 1867, outside Queretaro, Mexico, several hopes died with him. His death ended his naive and contradictory goals of establishing a liberal Mexican monarchy based on conservative support and foreign arms. Also finished was the grandiose scheme of French Emperor Napoleon III to rebuild a French empire in the New World.

Maximilian's story is faithfully covered in the Warner Brothers film *Juarez* (1939) with Brian Aherne as the emperor and Paul Muni as Juarez, the Mexican revolutionary who defeated him. The drama captured much of the historical and personal conflict of a turbulent period in Mexico's history. Though Juarez is the central character in the film, it does render a very sympathetic portrayal of Maximilian.

The Austrian Archduke Ferdinand Maximilian came to the throne of Mexico as a result of the machinations of Mexican conservatives and Napoleon III of France, a nephew of the French military leader. Mexicans opposed to the liberal reforms of Juarez convinced both Maximilian and Napoleon III that a strong monarchy would gain the support of many Mexicans tired of the disorder that plagued their country. Napoleon saw an opportunity to extend his influence in North America and offered the throne to Maximilian. Maximilian was crowned Emperor of Mexico in 1864 after French troops had driven Juarez and his republican forces out of the capital. *Juarez* shows the native Mexican leader continuing his struggle in a guerrilla war.

Maximilian's collapse was due as much to events outside Mexico as to his inability to rally popular support. The U.S., which had been involved in its own Civil War at the time, considered France's action as a violation of the Monroe Doctrine. With the end of the American Civil War in 1865, the U.S. threatened military intervention in Mexico unless France withdrew. Meanwhile, Napoleon III faced the growing threat of a European war and withdrew his troops from Mexico by March 1867. Though given the opportunity to leave with them, Maximilian determined to stay with his small native army and fight for his beliefs. The battle scenes in *Juarez* between Republican and Monarchist forces, although brief, convey his bold but hopeless effort.

Juarez easily defeated the military remnants of his monarchist opponents. Maximilian was captured and executed after a military trial. Again, *Juarez* portrays him as a tragic figure resigned to his fate. Meanwhile, Maximilian's wife Carlotta had returned to Europe to beg aid for her husband. With its concern for historical accuracy, the drama pictures her pleading to Napoleon III in Paris for support for her husband. Failing to prevent her husband's execution, she lost her sanity. She died in 1927.

Several other films deal with this turbulent period but in a fictitious and superficial manner. In *The Eagle and the Hawk* (1950), an action drama set in 1863, agents of Napoleon III, as part of their plot to make Maximilian the emperor of Mexico, attempt to instigate Juarez's followers to declare war on Texas. *Stronghold* (1952), a contrived love story involving Americans in Mexico, has no connection to historical events. George Macready portrays Maximilian in *Vera Cruz* (1954), a cynical and fictitious tale about trust and betrayal during the Juaristas' attempts to free their country from the emperor's grip. ∎

May Blossom (1915), Par. *Dir.* Allan Dwan; *Cast includes:* Gertrude Morgan, Russell Bassett, Marshall Neilan, Donald Crisp.

A conventional romantic drama with a Civil War background, the film concerns May Blossom, the pretty daughter of a lighthouse keeper, who marries a young man, Richard Ashford, against her father's wishes. He had another potential husband in mind, Steve Harland, a young fisherman. Ashford is arrested by Union troops as a spy. Harland witnesses the scene but does not tell May, who thinks he has drowned. Harland and May marry. One year later Ashford returns and, when he learns the truth, he enlists in the army and dies in battle. ∎

McAuliffe, Anthony C. See *Battleground* (1949). ∎

McConnell Story, The (1955), WB. *Dir.* Gordon Douglas; *Sc.* Ted Sherdeman, Sam Rolfe; *Cast includes:* Alan Ladd, June Allyson, James Whitmore, Frank Faylen.

Alan Ladd portrays Captain Joseph McConnell, Jr., America's first three-time jet ace, in this biographical drama. McConnell achieved recognition in World War II as a navigator who flew 25 missions, gained distinction as a flier during the Korean War and later built a reputation as a military test pilot. The film begins with McConnell serving in the army as a soldier in the medical corps. Although he had taken private flying lessons, he managed only to emerge as a navigator in the air force during the Second World War. When the Korean conflict erupted, he was recalled to duty as a pilot with the rank of captain and soon established himself as a jet ace. He was later killed while testing an experimental jet plane at Edwards Air Force Base. June Allyson provides the romantic interest as the hero's sweetheart while James Whitmore portrays his commanding officer and friend. ∎

McHale's Navy (1964). See Service Comedy. ∎

McHale's Navy Joins the Air Force (1965), U. *Dir.* Edward J. Montagne; *Sc.* John Fenton Murray; *Cast includes:* Joe Flynn, Tim Conway, Bob Hastings, Gary Vinson.

A sequel to the previous year's *McHale's Navy*, this weak comedy involves the misadventures of Tim Conway, an ensign who masquerades as an air force officer following a hangover. Joe Flynn, as the frenetic captain, is obliged to play along with the ploy. Conway eventually manages to cause the sinking of several Japanese warships and emerges as a hero. Tom Tully plays a no-nonsense general. Ernest Borgnine, the star of the earlier entry, does not appear in this feature based on the popular television series. ∎

McKenzie Break, The (1970), UA. *Dir.* Lamont Johnson; *Sc.* William Norton; *Cast includes:* Brian Keith, Helmut Griem, Ian Hendry, Patrick O'Connell, Caroline Mortimer.

The commandant of a prisoner-of-war camp in Scotland during World War II engages in a deadly battle of wits with a captured German U-boat commander in this action drama. Brian Keith, as an undisciplined British Intelligence officer and a heavy-drinking Irishman, is assigned to take charge of and investigate a poorly run prison camp. The U-boat commander (Helmut Griem) is a strong leader and expert strategist who organizes the discipline and riots of his fellow inmates, all according to his plan of escape. On another level, he transforms the camp into a microcosm of Nazism, complete with anti-Semitic outbursts and patriotic songs. Keith allows the German officer and a handful of his men to escape, hoping that they will lead him to a German submarine. The last part of the film centers on a suspenseful pursuit of the German prisoners as they head for their rendezvous.

The film concentrates chiefly on the two main characters, each possessing a strong will which brings them into continual confrontation. Keith, with his anti-authoritarian views and a host of other eccentricities, is the antithesis of Griem, the quintessential screen Nazi—a ruthless, power-hungry disciplinarian with little regard for human life who is willing to sacrifice the lives of some of his own men to reach his goals. ∎

Me and the Colonel (1958), Col. *Dir.* Peter Glenville; *Sc.* S. N. Behrman, George Froeschel; *Cast includes:* Danny Kaye, Curt Jurgens, Nicole Maurey, Akim Tamiroff.

Two unlikely traveling companions, stranded in Paris in 1940, decide to flee the city when the Germans invade France in this comedy drama based on a play by Franz Werfel. A pompous Polish colonel (Curt Jurgens) reluctantly accepts to ride with Jacobowsky (Danny Kaye), a humble Polish Jew who happens to have a car. The remainder of the plot deals with their narrow escapes, capture and final escape from the Nazis as the enterprising Jacobowsky concocts a variety of helpful schemes. Meanwhile, the anti-Semitic colonel undergoes a change of attitude. "I think I like that fellow Jacobowsky," he admits at the end of the journey.

The central interest is the growing relationship between the two men who engage in several humorous interchanges. As they leave Paris, they stop to pick up the colonel's female companion (Nicole Maurey) who begins to fall for Kaye. This puzzles the colonel who considers himself the consummate lover. He romantically delivers to a bevy of European women his charmer line: "In the cathedral of my heart a candle will always burn for you." On one occasion this prompts Kaye to quip: "That must be the best lit cathedral in Europe." ∎

Medal for Benny, A (1945), Par. *Dir.* Irving Pichel; *Sc.* Frank Butler; *Cast includes:* Dorothy Lamour, Arturo de Cordova, J. Carrol Naish, Charles Dingle.

A satire about a ne'er-do-well who becomes a World War II hero, the film stars J. Carrol Naish as the dead boy's father. The story is set in a Mexican-American community of a southern California fishing village where the local dignitaries fight each other to present the posthumous medal to the hero's father. They also see an opportunity to promote business for their town. When they learn that the father resides in a squalid section of town, they relocate him to a more lavish but temporary home. When he discovers the motives of the self-serving politicians, Naish returns to his own shack where army officials and others finally present him with the medal.

The film provides several opportunities for biting satire as the various town officials scramble to cash in on the award ceremony.

The bank president epitomizes the hypocrisy of his cronies when he answers an out-of-town call. "Do I know the Martins!" he exclaims. "Why, the Martins are some of the best people we've got—fine old California family." In another scene a local booster wants a spirited news photo of Naish outside his new dwelling. "See all that country?" he says in a vain effort to inspire the elderly fisherman. "Try to imagine that your ancestors owned it." "They did," Naish says innocently. The film ends with Naish's humble speech at the ceremony: "A man is only what he grows out of—his family, his friends and his home . . . Maybe it is good for the country that she must depend for life on all kinds of people and men like my son." ■

Meet Boston Blackie (1941). See Detectives at War. ■

Meet the Prince (1926), PDC. *Dir.* Joseph Henabery; *Sc.* Jane Murfin, Harold Shumate; *Cast includes:* Joseph Schildkraut, Marguerite De La Motte, Vera Steadman, Julia Faye.

The Russian Revolution provides the background for this comedy drama featuring Joseph Schildkraut as an exiled Russian prince currently residing in a dilapidated tenement on New York's Lower East Side. Dozing off while on his fire escape, the former prince dreams of better days in Russia in his lavish palace. But the times are turbulent—labor strikes threaten the country; revolution erupts. The prince flees his homeland with his sister after he kills a peasant who has been chasing her. He awakens from his dream to find himself in tenement surroundings. ■

Melody of Love (1928), U. *Dir.* A. B. Heath; *Sc.* Robert Arch; *Cast includes:* Walter Pidgeon, Mildred Harris, Jane Winton, Tommy Dugan.

Walter Pidgeon portrays a songwriter who discovers true love in this World War I romantic drama. Before he is sent overseas to fight in the trenches, Pidgeon falls in love with a chorus girl (Jane Winton). In France he meets a singer (Mildred Harris) who falls for him. Pidgeon is wounded at the front and loses the use of his right arm. He returns to the States where his sweetheart rejects him. The French singer journeys to the U.S. and is employed in a cabaret. The wounded veteran accidentally sees her entertaining and, in his surprise at finding her, regains the use of his arm. He then realizes she is the one he really loves. This was Universal's first all-talking feature and was made with equipment borrowed from William Fox.

Having Marshall recover from his handicap so suddenly and miraculously was rather gimmicky for the year the film was released. Earlier films with a similar theme handled the problem of rehabilitation much more realistically. In *The Leech* (1922), for example, a World War I veteran who has lost an arm undergoes special training which enables him to get a job. His rehabilitation is more plausible and does not detract from the plot. ■

Memphis Belle (1944), War Activities Committee. *Dir.* Lt. Col. William Wyler.

A tribute to the U.S. Army Eighth Air Force, this World War II color documentary depicts the perils American fliers face on their bombing raids over Europe. *Memphis Belle* is the name of one of the Flying Fortresses that flew 25 missions over German-occupied territory. The film shows the strategic planning of missions, encounters with enemy opposition and the return to base of damaged planes and wounded airmen. ■

Marlon Brando, as a World War II infantry lieutenant, is wounded in action somewhere in Europe. *The Men* (1950).

Men, The (1950), UA. *Dir.* Fred Zinnemann; *Sc.* Carl Foreman; *Cast includes:* Marlon Brando, Teresa Wright, Everett Sloane, Jack Webb.

This post-World War II drama of the physical, psychological and sexual difficulties of a paralyzed veteran was to change the nature of acting in Hollywood films. Marlon Brando

Remnants of an infantry platoon pause between battles during the Korean War. *Men in War* (1957).

gives a sensitive and believable performance as one of several paraplegics at a Veterans' Administration hospital who at first refuses to adjust to civilian life. The patients are told that their condition is irreversible; they are encouraged to accept the reality of their handicap and carve out a constructive future.

A lieutenant in the infantry, Brando had been shot while leading his men in battle. When he learns the extent of his wounds, he withdraws from the world outside the hospital and breaks off his engagement to his fiancee (Teresa Wright). But she continues to visit him. Encouraged by her love, he reluctantly consents to marry her. But the marriage ends in disaster. Brando is sensitive about his wife's stares and thoughts. Wright appears nervous at the sound of his wheel chair moving around their new home. A confrontation results and Brando storms out and returns to the hospital. Both face numerous problems as each has to make allowances for the other's shortcomings.

Everett Sloane plays the understanding and sympathetic doctor who at times becomes frustrated by his own failures and those of modern medicine. Brando, trying to understand his own wrecked life, seeks his help from Sloane. The doctor has no easy answers, but tries to make Brando accept reality and return to his wife.

The paraplegic Vietnam veteran (Jon Voight) in Hal Ashby's *Coming Home* (1978) has much in common with Brando's character—both face emotional and psychological problems in their adjustment to society. Their basic difference is in the target of their rage. Brando's bitterness is personal—he cannot understand why he is crippled. "What did I do?" he asks his doctor. "Why did it have to be me?" Voight's rage is directed against the war in Vietnam and leads him to chain himself and his wheelchair to a fence in protest against the conflict. ∎

Men in War (1957), UA. *Dir.* Anthony Mann; *Sc.* Philip Yordan; *Cast includes:* Robert Ryan, Aldo Ray, Robert Keith, Philip Pine, Vic Morrow.

This routine Korean War drama with realistic overtones follows the exploits of an infantry platoon fighting its way back to its headquarters. A war-weary lieutenant (Robert Ryan) in charge of the platoon must surmount enemy snipers and machine guns. He appropriates a jeep driven by a sergeant

(Aldo Ray) who is taking his battle-shocked colonel to a field hospital. Ray, resentful of the interference, at first resists. When the rag-tag platoon reaches its battalion headquarters, the men discover that their comrades have been annihilated and the Communists control the hill. The lieutenant and the sergeant put aside their differences and lead the men in a bloody attack to recapture the position. They win their prize although most of their men have been killed. The two survivors then pay tribute to their fellow soldiers. ■

Men Must Fight (1933), MGM. *Dir.* Edgar Selwyn; *Sc.* C. Gardner Sullivan; *Cast includes:* Diana Wynyard, Lewis Stone, Phillips Holmes, May Robson, Ruth Selwyn, Robert Young.

An antiwar drama set sometime in the near future, the film concerns a family whose mother remains a pacifist when war erupts. Diana Wynyard plays the matriarch whose lover (and the father of her son) was killed in France during World War I. Her present husband, the Secretary of State (Lewis Stone), supports the current war. Phillips Holmes, portraying the son, eventually changes his views and joins the other young Americans who march off patriotically to defend their land.

The latter segment of the film prophetically predicts war in 1940, except in this fictional conflict New York suffers an air raid. The Empire State Building, symbol of the nation's pride and the century's progress, is bombed and crumbles to the ground. The pacifist theme is suggested only through dialogue during the first half of the film and chiefly through the mother. In an ironic sense Phillips Holmes, who had starred in a previous antiwar film *The Man I Killed* (1932), was killed in World War II while serving with the Royal Canadian Air Force.

The film anticipates the actual isolationist-interventionist controversy which raged in America from 1939 to 1941 and its inevitable aftermath. The pacifist mother and son are attacked verbally, and their home is damaged by those who oppose their views. Once the enemy bombs rain down on the U.S. in the film—as with Japan's attack on Pearl Harbor—the hysteria of war quickly drowns out the voices of pacifism. ■

Men of Bronze (1977), Men of Bronze, Inc. *Dir.* William Miles.

This documentary reveals the story of a black regiment of American soldiers in World War I. The film points out that government officials were hesitant about using these troops to fight the Germans. Assigned to mundane jobs in the rear line in France, the black troops were finally attached to the French Army and fought bravely. The bigotry and racism on the part of Washington bureaucrats and the military brass of the war years and the postwar period are clearly depicted in their attitudes toward and handling of the black regiment. The black doughboys were ardently cheered when they returned home, but the U.S. government delayed a proposed battlefield monument in France honoring them and the 4,000 casualties the regiment suffered. Nevertheless, the tone of the film is never bitter. Instead, director William Miles and the surviving veterans he interviews treat the subject lightheartedly. The unit was first known as the Fifth New York and later became the 369th Infantry Regiment. ■

"Men of Norway" (1941). See "The March of Time." ■

Men of Purpose (1926), Veterans Film Service. *Sc.* Hoey Lawlor.

A documentary about World War I, the film uses official newsreel footage from various countries, including the U.S. and Germany. It covers the war beginning with the assassination of Archduke Ferdinand in Sarajevo, Serbia, on June 28, 1914. Titles explain that this scene, the only one in the film, is a dramatization of the actual event. The story of the war continues with the German invasion of Belgium, scenes of wounded soldiers, shellings and bombardments and others showing some of the famous figures of the period, including the Kaiser, Czar Nicholas, King Albert, President Wilson and Eddie Rickenbacker. From German cameramen came scenes of vessels sinking as a result of submarine attacks. There are glimpses of the famous battle in the Argonne forest. Another title states that the war took 9,000,000 lives. ■

Men of the Fighting Lady (1954), MGM. *Dir.* Andrew Marton; *Sc.* Art Cohn; *Cast includes:* Van Johnson, Walter Pidgeon, Louis Calhern, Dewey Martin, Keenan Wynn.

This Korean War drama centers on the exploits of a U.S. aircraft carrier somewhere off Korea. Jet planes from the carrier, in support of U.N. land troops, make their daily attacks on Communist positions. Van Johnson portrays a jet pilot. In the climactic suspenseful sequence, he guides a blinded fellow pilot (Dewey Martin) safely onto the deck of the *Fighting Lady* by "talking" him in. Frank Lovejoy, as a lieutenant commander, believes in low-level bombing, resulting in criticism from both his superiors and fellow officers. Keenan Wynn, as a highly decorated airman, is fatally wounded during one of the air strikes. Walter Pidgeon, as a sympathetic flight surgeon, relates the exploits of these navy fliers to author James Michener (Louis Calhern), who has come aboard the carrier looking for a good story.

The film, which has plenty of aerial action sequences—many of which are borrowed from actual combat footage, often reverts to war-movie clichés in the sky and on the ground. Pidgeon, the flight surgeon, has a plaque on his wall quoting part of John Donne's meditation, "No Man Is an Island," which the camera focuses in on again at the conclusion. This is supposed to be the theme of the film. The pilots outwardly boast that they're going to look out for "number one" first. But in a crisis, they are quick to help their buddies. Lovejoy provides the conventional wisecracks. "Due to technical difficulties," he announces from his cockpit after knocking out a North Korean supply train, "the Wonton Limited will be a few minutes late." Some of the officers voice their disillusionment with the war. "You and Shakespeare couldn't make this dirty little war romantic," Pidgeon says to Michener. Another comments: "The bombs alone cost more than any target they'll hit." Still others question the value of hitting the same target each morning, a particular rail line, which is restored each afternoon. The film is based on magazine articles written by Michener ("The Forgotten Heroes of Korea") and U.S. Navy Commander Harry A. Burns ("The Case of the Blind Pilot"). ■

Men of the Hour, The (1918), Cosmofotofilm.

A documentary concerning the training of a typical soldier and sailor, this World War I propaganda film contains numerous details in the life of a serviceman. Each half of the film follows the recruit from the enlistment office, to the training camp and to the final stages that show him ready for combat. The naval section displays submarines, torpedo boats and the firing of torpedoes. ■

Men of the Sky (1931). See Musicals. ■

"Men of the U.S. Navy" (1942). See "The March of Time." ■

Merrill's Marauders (1962), WB. *Dir.* Samuel Fuller; *Sc.* Milton Sperling, Samuel Fuller; *Cast includes:* Jeff Chandler, Ty Hardin, Peter Brown, Andrew Duggan.

This World War II action drama depicts the exploits of Brigadier General Frank D. Merrill and his volunteer group of American soldiers who fought in Burma in 1942 and helped the British to keep the Japanese out of India. Jeff Chandler portrays the determined and tough leader of the Marauders. Ty Hardin plays his sensitive young lieutenant. There is plenty of action as the men harass and raid strategic Japanese positions, including a railroad station. In spite of the heroics, the film, made in the Philippines, attempts to bring out the idea that war is anything but glamorous.

The plot is constructed in such a manner as to underscore the terrible ordeal the soldiers must face and the inordinate pressure placed on the leader. After the men successfully carry out their mission—a raid on a Japanese supply dump, General Stilwell meets with Merrill and requests that he now lead his exhausted troops to Shadzup and then help to take Myitkyina. When Merrill objects, his superior says: "Your job is to do the impossible." They manage to take their next objective after a bloody fight, but the men are physically and psychologically exhausted. "I've taken my last order from that butcher," exclaims one soldier. Merrill, suffering from a bad heart, persuades the remnants of his command to push on. As they do, he collapses and dies. His lieutenant, who earlier criticized Merrill for not caring about the men, now assumes command. "Come on, move," he orders. Merrill's death motivates the bedraggled, almost disoriented soldiers to proceed.

Jeff Chandler, who died before the film was released, had starred in numerous war and action dramas. This, his last work, is a fitting tribute to his commanding screen image and talent.

The special forces unit, the 5307th Composite Provisional Unit, known as Merrill's Marauders, was organized by General Frank D. Merrill (1903–1955) from volunteers stationed in the South Pacific. Originally designed for long-range penetration tactics, they were supervised by Major-General Wingate and trained in India. During the first half of 1944 they completed five major engagements and dozens of minor ones. They were cited for their highly successful capture of the Japanese airfield dramatized in the film. The Marauders were disbanded in August 1944, and reorganized into an infantry regiment until August 1945.

General Joseph W. Stilwell (1883–1946), who was a U.S. staff officer in France during World War I and served two tours of duty in China in the 1920s and 1930s, was assigned to Chiang Kai-shek and headed U.S. forces in that region. He commanded the Chinese 5th and 6th Armies in Burma in 1942 before being forced out by Japanese forces. He was then appointed as deputy commander of the Allied Southeast Asia Command in 1943. ■

Merry-Go-Round (1923), U. *Dir.* Rupert Julian; *Sc.* Harvey Gates; *Cast includes:* Norman Kerry, Mary Philbin, Cesare Gravina, Edith Yorke, George Hackathorne.

Norman Kerry portrays a Viennese count and captain in Emperor Franz Josef's Royal Guards who falls in love with the daughter of a poor puppeteer in this romantic drama set on the eve of World War I. Kerry, dressed in civilian clothes, meets the young woman (Mary Philbin) at an amusement park, where she plays a hand organ for her father's act. Kerry poses as a necktie salesman. Later, when she learns his true identity and that he is promised to a noblewoman, she is emotionally crushed. When war erupts, Kerry is sent into battle where he is reported killed. Philbin, broken-hearted, consents to marry a hunchback. Kerry unexpectedly returns, and the prospective bridegroom gives the girl up so that she can wed the man she really loves.

The film has few action sequences, concentrating more on the romantic plot. Erich von Stroheim, who was originally hired to direct the film, was replaced by Rupert Julian following financial disputes with the producer. However, several scenes strongly suggest von Stroheim's influence. ■

Message to Garcia, A (1936), TCF. *Dir.* George Marshall; *Sc.* Gene Fowler, W. P. Lipscomb; *Cast includes:* Wallace Beery, Barbara Stanwyck, John Boles, Alan Hale, Herbert Mundin.

A fictional rendition of the experiences of Lieutenant Andrew Rowan in Cuba during the Spanish-American War, the film is based on his book and Elbert Hubbard's popular essay. The drama recounts Rowan's assignment to convey President McKinley's message to General Garcia. John Boles, as Rowan, endures a variety of dangers and tortures as he relentlessly journeys through jungle and shark-infested areas. He is captured at one point and tortured by a spy (Alan Hale). Wallace Beery portrays a slovenly, amoral sergeant who reluctantly assists Boles. Barbara Stanwyck, miscast as the daughter of a Cuban patriot, provides some romantic interest in this otherwise routine tale.

Lt. Andrew S. Rowan's journey became world famous when Elbert Hubbard, editor of *The Philistine*, a monthly magazine, wrote in the March 1899 issue of the lieutenant's experience, using it as a symbolic sermon. He embellished the incident to underline how one determined individual views his task and accomplishes it. The essay became so popular that the issue sold out immediately, reprints by the millions were circulated during World War I and the article was translated into more than a dozen languages. Meanwhile, Rowan resigned from the army after serving in the Philippines in 1909 and wrote a book about his actual experiences, which were chiefly ignored or altered in the screen version. However, the film provides sufficient action and the winning personality of Beery. ■

Mexican Revolution (1910–1921). Although dictator Porfirio Diaz's regime, which ran from 1876 to 1910, brought foreign investment and material growth to Mexico, social conditions deteriorated. Foreign corporations, encouraged by Diaz as a means of modernizing Mexico, were concerned more with profits and export of the country's resources and less with its social and economic development. This resulted in the suppression of the working class and labor movements and alienation of the middle class, including ranchers, professionals and businessmen. Francisco Madero led a successful revolution in 1910–1911 which unseated Diaz. *Barbarous Mexico* (1913), an early documentary, covers this phase of the Revolution and includes Madero's flight to the U.S. following an unsuccessful coup, his return and capture of the city of Juarez and his inauguration as president. Madero's attempts at nationalization and modernization met stiff resistance. He failed to bring about the much-needed reforms and, although originally supported by revolutionary leaders such as Victoriano Huerta, Venustiano Carranza and Pancho Villa, he was overthrown in 1913 by General Huerta. Huerta's reactionary rule lasted only one year. He was opposed by Carranza, Villa and Emiliano Zapata, who sought some form of democracy and land reforms.

It was during Huerta's regime that the U.S. invaded Mexico's port city of Veracruz, an act that raised eyebrows around the world. The arrest of a few American sailors by Mexican troops expanded into an incident of international importance and almost led to war between the two countries. When an American admiral demanded that the officer responsible be disciplined and the stars and stripes be raised and saluted, President Huerta refused. President Wilson fumed at the response and ordered the shelling of Veracruz. U.S. Marines then invaded the port. More than a dozen lost their lives. The drama *Soldiers of Fortune* (1919), although set in a fictitious Central American country, obliquely refers to this entire incident.

Before the above incident, the U.S., under President Wilson, in an attempt to protect its own citizens' private property in Mexico and re-establish order and stability below its border, supported Huerta's government. It sent him large shipments of arms to be used against his opponents. The revolutionists, in turn, obtained their own arms from private merchants across the border. They gained control of central Mexico and toppled Huerta's short-lived regime. Carranza became president (1914–1920) and effected several reforms, including national ownership of land deposits and restoration of agricultural lands from foreign control to small farmers.

Villa and Zapata, more interested in a decentralized state and local self-government, grew disillusioned with Carranza. Villa, with his army of emancipated peasant farmers, and Zapata, leading his loyal Indian followers, occupied northern Mexico and temporarily took possession of Mexico City. The U.S. once again took sides against the revolutionists and backed Carranza and his two major supporters—the middle class and the elite. Villa, enraged at America's support of Carranza, took reprisals against American property in Mexico and in 1916 carried out raids across the border into U.S. territory. This resulted in a punitive expedition by General "Black Jack" Pershing in 1916–1917 against the revolutionist leader. *The Eagle's Wings* (1916) re-enacts the attack on Columbus, New Mexico, and *The Love Thief* (1916), in part, concerns Pancho Villa's raid and the subsequent skirmishes between U.S. and Mexican troops.

With U.S. warships entering several Mexican ports and the enormous arms supplied to his government troops, Carranza was able to defeat the revolutionists. Villa was forced into exile and assassinated in 1923. Zapata was insidiously murdered in 1919 by an agent of Carranza. In 1920, following a coup, Alvaro Obregon was made president. He served until 1924 and effected educational reforms.

The Mexican Revolution was a multifaceted struggle. On one level, it was a proletarian revolt whose highly organized members were able to bring about effective, large-scale strikes; they also considered themselves superior to the rural peasants. On another level, it was an agrarian struggle—led by Villa and Zapata—for self-government, decentralization and land reform. Finally, it was a national revolution aimed at transforming Mexico into a modern state that advocated private property. Initiated by Madero, it was continued by Carranza and Obregon. This was the revolution that succeeded. To a large degree, it was as much anti-American as it was national in its goals.

Virtually all American films about the Revolution tend to side with those forces who have opposed the establishment— usually depicted as corrupt and oppressive, particularly toward the peasantry. They also ignore any references to U.S. intervention. They range from action dramas to sympathetic biographies of some of the major participants. *The Life of General Villa* (1914), one of the earliest attempts to portray the Mexican leader on screen, covers the events that led to his becoming a revolutionist and his eventual battles with government troops. However, the definitive film of his exploits, *Viva Villa*, appeared in 1934, with Wallace Beery playing the title character. The plot depicts Villa's fondness for the idealistic but impotent Madero. In *The Fighter* (1952) Richard Conte, as a Mexican patriot, turns professional boxer to raise money for the Revolution. The film points out the ruthlessness and oppressive nature of the Diaz regime. That same year Elia Kazan's *Viva Zapata* came to the screen with a screenplay by John Steinbeck. Marlon Brando portrays Zapata as a reticent but strong leader who, after his assassination, emerges as a mythical hero. The script plays down his Indian heritage. *Wings of the Hawk* (1953) again dramatizes the brutality of the Diaz regime. Van Heflin, as an American engineer whose mine is confiscated by the Federales, joins the revolutionists under Villa. Pancho Villa is again the subject of the biographical drama *Villa Rides* (1968), starring Yul Brynner as Villa. Loosely based on the Mexican revolutionist's exploits, he is seen as defender of the peasants' human rights but not averse to putting to death numerous opponents whom he arbitrarily labels "traitors." Madero is pictured as a tragic figure while Huerta is portrayed as a treacherous politico.

Several films show American soldiers of fortune ultimately joining the cause of the revolutionists. Robert Mitchum, as a mercenary gun runner in *Bandido* (1956), intends to steal arms from a competitor and sell them to the revolutionists. Peter Graves in the routine action drama *Five Man Army* (1970) leads a group of American "experts" in the theft of a gold shipment from a government train. The loot is then turned over to Mexican revolutionists. Government troops are again depicted as ruthless toward prisoners and peasants. Perhaps the best film in this subgenre is the action drama *The Professionals* (1966). An exciting tale about four hardened adventurers (Lee Marvin, Burt Lancaster, Robert Ryan, Woody Strode) hired by a railroad magnate to bring back his kidnaped wife from a revolutionary leader, the quartet reveal both romantic and cynical traits during their journey. They ultimately side with the Mexican leader whom the wife loves. Although some of the dialogue is pretentious ("We stay because we believe, we leave because we are disillusioned, we come back because we are lost, we die because we are committed"), much of it deals with the nature of revolution. ∎

Mexican War (1846–1848). When Mexican and American troops clashed on April 15, 1846, in a disputed border region in present-day southern Texas, it marked the beginning of a war that both nations seemed to desire. Mexico was still bitter from a double blow to its territory and national pride—the loss of Texas in 1836 in a revolution by American settlers and the subsequent U.S. annexation of Texas in 1845. The U.S., caught in the fever of "Manifest Destiny"—a belief in the righteousness of expansion to the Pacific—had already been rebuffed in a bid to buy Mexico's northern region of upper California and public feeling ran strong to take the area by force. High government officials on both sides believed they could win a war between the two nations.

The actual opening clash came about when the U.S. and Mexico both sent troops into the region between the Rio Grande and Nueces Rivers to bolster conflicting claims on the southern boundary of Texas. The war itself was a short and victorious one for the U.S. California came under American control in less than three months as the result of a revolt by American settlers under Captain John Fremont and the arrival of a U.S. naval squadron under Commodore John Sloat. A highly fictitious re-enactment of the uprising, known as the Bear Flag Republic Revolt, was staged in *Kit Carson* (1940), with Fremont and Carson directing the settlers and outsmarting the Mexican troops. *Frontier Uprising* (1961), a weak remake, covered much the same ground.

Brigadier-General Stephen Kearny led a column of troops into New Mexico where he occupied Santa Fe, the administrative headquarters of the area, and continued into southern California to buttress U.S. forces there. Another expedition under General Zachary Taylor moved south from the Rio Grande into Mexico and won important battles at Palo Alto, Monterey and Buena Vista. Taylor defeated Mexican forces under dictator General Santa Anna.

A third expedition under General Winfield Scott made a successful landing at the Gulf of Mexico port of Veracruz—the first major amphibious operation in American history. After a bitterly contested drive inland, Scott captured Mexico City on September 14, 1847.

In the Treaty of Guadalupe Hidalgo (1848) Mexico formally ceded nearly one-third of its territory, a sparsely populated northern region, to the U.S. in return for $15 million. The area eventually became all or part of the states of California, Arizona, New Mexico, Texas, Colorado, Wyoming and Utah. The American dream of Manifest Destiny had been realized. The U.S. now stretched from the Atlantic to the Pacific and was poised on the threshold of recognition as the "colossus of the north" by the nations of the western hemisphere. Hollywood films have hardly exploited this relatively short conflict that added such a vast territory to the U.S. One of the reasons might have been a dearth of popular stories, novels or plays—a major source of movie plots—based on the war. The few movies that did show this period are about the revolt of the Californians against Mexico. One of the earliest dramas, *For the Honor of Old Glory* (1914), concerned a fictitious plot about a Mexican spy setting a trap for an American colonel, his daughter and his troops. In *A California Romance* (1923), a comedy about a Spaniard (John Gilbert) who is reluctant to take up arms against the Americans, the U.S. Cavalry charges in to California to suppress a revolt. In *California* (1927) an American cavalry officer (Tim McCoy) defends American settlers against hostile Mexican forces. *Pirates of Monterey* (1947) with Maria Montez showed American settlers in California fighting against Mexican control of that territory. ∎

Michael Strogoff (1910), Edison. *Dir.* J. Searle Dawley; *Sc.* J. Searle Dawley; *Cast includes:* Mary Fuller, Charles Ogle.

This silent version of Jules Verne's novel about a dedicated Russian courier during the Russo-Turkish War (1877–1878) is the earliest known adaptation. It was made at Thomas A. Edison's New York studio. Little is known about the production values although the two leading players became popular screen actors within a few short years. ∎

Michael Strogoff (1914), Selig. *Dir.* Lloyd B. Carleton; *Sc.* Benjamin Kotlowsky; *Cast includes:* Jacob Adler.

Based on Jules Verne's novel about a loyal and determined Russian courier during Russia's conflicts with the Tartars (Russo-Turkish War of 1877–1878), the film starred the popular Yiddish stage actor Jacob Adler in the title role. Adler plays Czar Alexander II's personal messenger who is entrusted with secret plans that will defeat the belligerent

Tartars in an impending attack. He goes through a series of harrowing experiences, including being blinded by the enemy, before he delivers the important message.

The novel underwent many film adaptations during the next decades, including two silent versions, one French and the other German, as well as a 1937 American sound remake, *The Soldier and the Lady* starring Anton Walbrook, followed by another foreign adaptation in 1960 with Curt Jurgens. ∎

Midnight Lovers (1926), FN. *Dir.* John Francis Dillon; *Sc.* Carey Wilson; *Cast includes:* Lewis Stone, Anna Q. Nilsson, Chester Conklin, John Roche, Gale Henry.

A simple misunderstanding almost breaks up a marriage between a British flying ace and his disillusioned wife in this slight romantic drama with a World War I background. Lewis Stone portrays the airman who is wrongfully accused by an officious aunt of being unfaithful. Married for only two weeks, Stone reports back to his squadron. When he returns to his bride (Anna Q. Nilsson), she demands a divorce. But their personal problems are solved by the end of the film. There are some minimal sequences concerning the war. Silent screen comic Chester Conklin provides the comedy relief. ∎

Midway, Battle of (June 3–6, 1942). This important World War II air and sea battle between U.S. and Japanese warships in which the U.S. was to emerge victorious became the turning point in the Pacific war. The battle for Midway resulted in the loss of four Japanese aircraft carriers, the damage of 28 other warships and the destruction of 300 enemy planes.

Before the critical battle, Japan was on the offensive. It had hoped to capture Midway and use it as a base to threaten Pearl Harbor. A more important goal of the Japanese was to force the numerically inferior U.S. Navy into the open in the defense of Midway. The Japanese were certain they could destroy or seriously cripple the remaining U.S. resistance in the Pacific. However, one critical advantage fell to Admiral Nimitz, commander of the Pacific Fleet. Intelligence had broken the Japanese code. American task forces maneuvered into position to meet the enemy fleets. "The Battle of Midway" (1942), a documentary, depicts the bloody air, sea and land battles that resulted in victory for U.S. forces over those of Japan. *Wing and a Prayer* (1944) tells about U.S. Navy strategy prior to the Battle of Midway. When word arrives that the battle has begun, both ships and planes attack the Japanese navy with all their fury. *Task Force* (1949), starring Gary Cooper, deals with the Battle of Midway as well as other events, and includes several stirring World War II battle sequences, especially those involving Midway and the ensuing kamikaze attacks. *Midway* (1976) recreates the vital battle in detail, showing the strategy and fighting from the points of view of both participants. Actual historical figures, including Commander Nimitz, Admiral Halsey and Admiral Yamamoto, are portrayed in this large-scale production. ∎

Midway (1976), U. *Dir.* Jack Smight; *Sc.* Donald S. Sanford; *Cast includes:* Charlton Heston, Henry Fonda, James Coburn, Glenn Ford, Hal Holbrook.

The critical air-sea battle that became the turning point in the Pacific during World War II provides the subject matter for this weak drama that is redeemed only by its exciting action sequences. Many of the battle shots have been borrowed from actual newsreel footage. The film utilizes a special-effects system called Sensurround that enhances the sound of exploding bombs and planes crashing upon the decks of aircraft carriers. The Battle of Midway was the last great sea battle although each side depended heavily on aircraft to supplement the firepower of its warships which never came within sight of their counterparts.

Charlton Heston, as a navy captain, has problems with his son (Edward Albert) who is in love with a young Japanese-American (Christina Kokubo). Henry Fonda portrays Pacific Fleet Commander Chester W. Nimitz. Glenn Ford plays an admiral brought in at the last moment to command a carrier. Toshiro Mifune appears as Admiral Yamamoto, commander of the Japanese fleet. Robert Mitchum plays Admiral Halsey.

The film, whose first half covers the Battle of the Coral Sea, underscores the point that great victories (as well as defeats) depend as much on luck as they do on bravery and skill. At each turn of events in the deadly cat-and-mouse game between the Japanese and American carriers, each side counts heavily on its scout planes to locate the enemy before its counterparts do. One Japanese patrol plane,

for instance, spots an American carrier but is unable to relay its location because of a faulty radio. Also, military commanders on both sides must evaluate the accuracy of vague intelligence reports about the enemy's whereabouts as well as outguess their adversaries' next move.

Like other epic war movies produced after World War II such as *The Longest Day* (1962) and *Tora! Tora! Tora!* (1970), the film presents both sides of the battle, showing conferences aboard Japanese ships as well as meetings aboard American vessels. Secondly, the film treats the enemy as three-dimensional characters filled with the same fears and anxieties as their counterparts, unlike the propaganda-oriented films released during the war. ∎

Mighty, The (1930), Par. *Dir.* John Cromwell; *Sc.* William S. McNutt, Grover Jones; *Cast includes:* George Bancroft, Esther Ralston, Warner Oland, Raymond Hatton, Dorothy Revier.

A professional gangster (George Bancroft) is drafted into the army to fight in World War I. He dodges the draft at first but is finally seized and physically taken into service. He is quickly sent to the trenches in France where he distinguishes himself in battle, wins several medals and is made a major. During one scene a young officer is fatally wounded and dies in Bancroft's arms. When he returns from the war, he visits the family of the dead soldier and falls for the officer's sister. The town gives him a hero's welcome and offers him the police commissioner's job. It seems that an organized gang is menacing the community. A pal from his old crime days shows up, forcing him to choose between his former life and that offered by the town and the young woman he loves.

Following World War I, several silent features employed the theme of regeneration. A series of films appeared in which the main character, a former criminal, is converted by his combat experience. Some of these doughboys, after receiving medals for bravery, exchanged their army uniforms for those of law enforcement officers. This transition from war to crime was a relatively simple matter for the screenwriter who shifted the action of the war drama to the violence of the gangster genre. See Crime and War. ∎

Minesweeper (1943), Par. *Dir.* William Berke; *Sc.* Edward T. Lowe, Maxwell Shane; *Cast includes:* Richard Arlen, Jean Parker, Russell Hayden, Guinn Williams.

An Annapolis graduate (Richard Arlen) has wrecked his life and career because of his gambling habit in this low-budget World War II drama. But his ties to the service and his country are dormant, not dead. When war breaks out, he enlists in the navy using a pseudonym and is assigned to a mine-sweeper. It seems the Japanese have developed a new and highly effective mine that threatens American and Allied shipping. The situation allows Arlen to redeem himself. Jean Parker provides the romance. Guinn Williams, of cowboy fame, adds some comic relief to an otherwise routine story. ∎

Ministry of Fear (1944). See Spy Films: the Talkies. ∎

Miniver Story, The (1950). See *Mrs. Miniver* (1942). ∎

Minute Men. A term used to describe those members of American colonial militias who were ready on a minute's notice to report for duty with their arms. The name was probably first used in 1774 in Massachusetts to designate that portion of the militia pledged to provide immediate armed support. The patriots who took part in the Battle of Lexington and Concord (April 19, 1775) at the start of the American Revolution against Britain were Minute Men.

Three films highlight their contributions to the rebellion. The earliest, a one-reel 1911 Edison release, is titled "The Minute Men." *The Heart of a Hero* (1916), a biographical drama of Nathan Hale's role in the revolution, depicts the Battle of Concord and Hale's organizing of a company of volunteers to join the Minute Men. In *Cardigan* (1922), an historical romance set before and during the American Revolution, the fictional title character is permitted entry to the secret meetings of the Minute Men where he meets several rebel leaders before he decides to join them in their struggle for liberty. ∎

Miss Jackie of the Army (1917). See Spy Films: the Silents. ∎

Miss V From Moscow (1943). See Women and War. ∎

Missing (1918), Par. *Dir.* James Young; *Sc.* J. Stuart Blackton, James Young; *Cast includes:* Thomas Meighan, Sylvia Breamer, Robert Gordon, Ola Humphrey, Winter Hall.

A romantic drama set in England during World War I, the film concerns two sisters, Hester and Nell. Hester arranges a marriage for her younger sister to a wealthy gentleman, but Nell falls in love and marries a young officer who is shortly sent to France. Nell learns that her husband has been listed as missing in action. For one year she receives no word about his being captured or wounded. Her sister intercepts a telegram that he is in a hospital suffering from loss of memory. Still determined to have Nell marry the wealthy suitor, she says nothing. Nell receives the second telegram and goes to see her husband. She helps him to recover by singing their favorite song to him. ∎

Missing in Action (1984), Cannon. *Dir.* Joseph Zito; *Sc.* James Bruner; *Cast includes:* Chuck Norris, M. Emmet Walsh, Lenore Kasdorf, James Hong.

A former colonel (Chuck Norris) with the U.S. special forces in Vietnam, sets out to prove that the Vietnamese are still holding American prisoners years after the end of the war. He accompanies a special U.S. committee invited to Vietnam to hear the Communist high command pronounce that no such prisoners exist. Norris, after sneaking out of the guarded Saigon hotel at night by climbing down its facade like a human fly, learns the whereabouts of the prison camp. He later sets out with a former army buddy and a small arsenal of sophisticated weapons to free the Americans.

The film begins with a flashback of a battle sequence somewhere in the jungles of Vietnam. Enemy soldiers are in hot pursuit of Norris and a group of American soldiers. The fighting is fierce with heavy losses on both sides. Most of the men escape in helicopters, but Norris is captured after fighting a rear guard action. This early introduction of Norris as super-hero sets the tone for the following action sequences, particularly the climactic battle between Norris and a horde of Vietnamese who fail to prevent him from fleeing with the rag-tag group of American prisoners. He lands the helicopter in front of the conference building and, together with the former prisoners, forces his way into the meeting room filled with dignitaries and reporters just as the chief Vietnamese delegate is concluding that there is no evidence that his country is holding any Americans. ■

Missing in Action 2: The Beginning
(1985), Cannon. *Dir.* Lance Hool; *Sc.* Arthur Silver, Larry Levinson, Steve Bing; *Cast includes:* Chuck Norris, Soon-Teck Oh, Steven Williams, Bennett Ohta.

Another in the string of violent action dramas using the Vietnam War as background but providing little or no discussion of the topic the genre purports to be about, this entry stars Chuck Norris who undergoes almost every conceivable punishment as a prisoner of the Vietnamese. Norris portrays a tough colonel who joins a helicopter crew on a routine rescue mission. During a heavy battle, the 'copter is hit and the crew captured. The camp commandant, a sadistic Vietnamese officer who deals in opium as a sideline, keeps Norris and his men alive for only one purpose. For the next several years he administers a variety of psychological and physical tortures to get Norris to sign a confession that accuses the U.S. of war crimes. Eventually, Norris escapes and wreaks havoc on the camp and those in charge.

To give a sense of urgency and authenticity to the problem of Americans who may still be held captive in Vietnam, the opening scenes include newsreel shots of President Reagan addressing a large crowd. "We write no last chapters," he announces, "we close no books, we put away no final memories. An end to America's involvement in Vietnam cannot come before we have achieved the fullest possible accounting of those missing in action." Following this, the remainder of the film offers only violence and action. *Braddock: Missing in Action III*, directed by Aaron Norris and starring Chuck Norris, appeared in 1988. ■

"Mission Accomplished" (1943), Office of War Information.

A one-reel World War II documentary produced by the U.S. government for showing in commercial theaters, the film depicts the mission of one Flying Fortress over Europe from its inception. The crew is first seen at a briefing session. The camera then follows the bomber on its raid over Nazi-held territory until its successful return to its base. ■

Mission Batangas (1968), Manson Films.
Dir. Keith Larsen; *Sc.* Lew Antonio; *Cast includes:* Dennis Weaver, Vera Miles, Keith Larsen.

This weak, low-budget action drama, set in 1942 during World War II, concerns rescuing the gold of the Philippine government before it falls into the hands of the invading Japanese. Dennis Weaver portrays an American flier who ends up as the hero. Vera Miles, as a nurse, sacrifices her life during the mission, as does an American officer (Keith Larsen). Most of the routine action consists of jungle pursuits in which those who are trying to save the gold try to elude Japanese troops and headhunters. The film was shot on location in the Philippines. ■

Mission to Moscow (1943), WB. *Dir.*
Michael Curtiz; *Sc.* Howard Koch; *Cast includes:* Walter Huston, Ann Harding, Oscar Homolka, George Tobias, Gene Lockhart, Frieda Inescort.

One of the most barefaced propaganda films to come out of World War II, the drama, based on the memoirs of former Ambassador to Russia Joseph E. Davies, gives a convincing argument about Russia's sincerity and paints that country as a true freedom-loving ally. Stalin (Mannart Kippen) is pictured as an avuncular figure exuding warmth and kindness. The real villains, according to Stalin, are the Trotskyites, Chamberlain and the American isolationists. The purge trials of 1937 are explained away in the film by excerpts of confessions and transcripts that allegedly prove that those convicted were actually agents in league with Japan and Germany seeking to weaken the Russian government. The Nazi-Soviet pact, the film rationalizes, was the result of British Tory leaders who forced Stalin into the infamous agreement so that Russia would have time to build its military strength. Walter Huston portrays Davies while other performers impersonate a host of historical figures whose actual names are used throughout the drama.

The film, plagued with controversy from the date of its release, failed in its purpose. Contemporary dissenters declared the work "fourth term propaganda," referring, of course, to President Roosevelt's sanction of having himself impersonated in the opening scenes in which he sends Davies forth on his mission. Others objected to the simplistic rationalizations of the purge trials and the

Hitler-Stalin pact. Still others criticized the image of the Senate as a clique of war profiteers. "Not only can we do business with Hitler," one member declares, "but we can make a nice profit doing so." Warner Brothers reportedly became entangled in the film as the result of a phone call from President Roosevelt, who suggested the project as a means of keeping Stalin in the war by improving his image with the American public.

During the late 1940s the film was again the subject of controversy. Members of the House Un-American Activities Committee, seeking to ferret out Communist influence in Hollywood, pointed directly to this film as an example of Red infiltration into the popular arts. Screenwriter Howard Koch was blacklisted from the industry in 1951. The work remains today as a milestone in American propaganda; an unofficial government-sponsored film saturated with distortions, lies and omissions of facts.

Although it contains no combat scenes, the film deals with a very real problem that evolved during World War II—how to make Stalin, one of the Allied leaders, more palatable to the American public. He was known for his cruelty toward his own people as a result of the Communist political purges of the 1930s and the wholesale slaughter of private farmers (Kulaks) even earlier. Despite the howls of criticism leveled at the film, it did contribute to the softening of Stalin's image. ■

Mister Roberts (1955), WB. *Dir.* John Ford, Mervyn LeRoy; *Sc.* Frank Nugent, Joshua Logan; *Cast includes:* Henry Fonda, James Cagney, William Powell, Jack Lemmon, Betsy Palmer.

Henry Fonda portrays Lieutenant Roberts, an officer aboard a cargo ship that ferries supplies through relatively safe waters in the Pacific in this World War II comedy. Roberts yearns for the action of the war, but all his requests for transfer are disapproved by his vindictive and neurotic captain (James Cagney). The captain, who makes life difficult for those aboard his vessel, cares more about the condition of his palm tree than he does about the welfare of his crew. Having received the tree as a gift from an admiral for "delivering more toothpaste and toilet paper than any other ship," Cagney values this prized possession above all else. It ultimately becomes the target of the men's hilarious conspiracy

against Cagney. William Powell portrays the ship's sympathetic doctor. Jack Lemmon, as Ensign Pulver, is a schemer who makes empty threats aimed at the captain. Fonda played the same role in the stage production before doing the film.

The humor of the film, although not as risqué as in the stage version, derives as much from the dialogue as it does from situation and character. When sailors aboard the vessel discover the nurses' quarters on a nearby island, they quickly apply their binoculars for a better view. "Look," one excited seaman cries, "there goes a sea gull!" In another scene, Fonda and Powell pitch in to make Lemmon's evening with a nurse a success. "All right," Powell says, "Doug and I made the scotch. The nurse is your department." ■

Mobile Bay, Battle of. See *The Southerners* (1914). ■

Mockery (1927), MGM. *Dir.* Benjamin Christensen; *Sc.* Benjamin Christensen; *Cast includes:* Lon Chaney, Barbara Bedford, Ricardo Cortez, Mack Swain.

Lon Chaney portrays an ignorant peasant in this story of the Russian Revolution. Tatiana, a Russian countess disguised as a peasant woman on her way to a military encampment, offers the lowly Chaney, seen gnawing on a bone, food and a job if he will pose as her husband. He agrees and eventually is given a servant's position. When the Revolution begins, he lusts for the countess and hunts for her through the rooms of her estate. But soldiers arrive in time to save her. She protects him when they question his presence. Later, he risks his life to save her when the situation is reversed and the peasants plot to kill her. Scenes of the revolution are limited in this film that concentrates on the character of Chaney. Benjamin Christensen was one of the most famous directors of the Danish silent screen. ■

Modoc War of 1872–73 (also known as the Lava Beds War). See *Drum Beat* (1954). ■

Mohawk (1956), TCF. *Dir.* Kurt Neumann; *Sc.* Maurice Geraghty; *Cast includes:* Scott Brady, Rita Gam, Neville Brand, Lori Nelson, John Hoyt.

The Mohawk Valley erupts in violence when white and Indian troublemakers have their way in this drama of early pioneer days. A half-crazed settler (John Hoyt) thinks all of the valley is his domain and is willing to kill any Mohawks who trespass. His actions ignite a war between the tribe and the settlers. Neville Brand portrays the leader of a band of warring Indians. Peace is finally restored through the wisdom of a Mohawk chief (Ted de Corsia) and a visiting artist (Scott Brady). Rita Gam plays a Mohawk princess with whom Brady falls in love. ■

Mohawk Indians. The Mohawks were the easternmost tribe in the Iroquois confederation. They resided in the Mohawk Valley in a section of upper New York State occupied by present-day Albany, Saratoga and Ticonderoga. The semi-legendary Hiawatha is believed to have been a Mohawk chief who brought peace and a confederate form of government to the five Iroquois "nations." The Mohawks were among the most sophisticated of eastern Indians. They lived in permanent, communal, wood-and-brush "long houses" within palisaded villages.

The Mohawks had suffered from raids in the 1600s by the Algonquins who periodically swept east and south from the eastern Great Lakes. As a result of this animosity, the Mohawk aided the Dutch in the Algonquin War (1641–1645) when the latter attacked spreading Dutch settlements in the Hudson Valley, Manhattan and Staten Island. When England captured Dutch holdings in New York, the Mohawk transferred their allegiance to the English in a mutual alliance against the French and Algonquin partnership.

In the late 1600s, the Mohawks stood by their commitment to the English by refusing to join an Indian uprising known as King Philip's War, directed against English settlements in lower New England. During the French and Indian War (1754–1763) the Mohawk assisted the English in fighting the French and Algonquins. When the American Revolution broke out, most Mohawks sided with the English. Chief Joseph Brant led his warriors, in concert with Tory Rangers, on raids against pro-revolutionary settlements in upper New York and the northern Alleghenies of Pennsylvania. D.W. Griffith's silent epic *America* (1924) includes a climactic battle showing the Mohawk Indians attacking the colonists during the American Revolution. As a result of England's loss of the 13

colonies, most of the tribe left New York State with Brant and migrated to Canada where they have a reservation today at Brantford, Ontario.

Chief Brant is portrayed in Walter D. Edmonds' historical novel *Drums Along the Mohawk* but is omitted from the film version released in 1939. Very few feature films with Indians as their subject deal with the Mohawk tribe. An early silent one-reeler, "A Mohawk's Way," produced by Biograph in 1910, treats the tribe in a very general way. The simple plot concerns an Indian family who seeks help from a white doctor for their sick child. When the doctor, who hates Indians, shuns the distraught family, his wife goes to the village, administers the proper medicine and saves the child's life. *Mohawk* (1956), a routine settlers-vs.-Indians action drama starring Scott Brady and Rita Gam, is historically vague. ■

Mohican Indians. During early colonial times the Mohicans (also spelled Mahicans) resided in New York's upper Hudson Valley, north of the Catskills, and in southwestern Connecticut around the Thames River. They were generally friendly with the English colonists, whom they assisted on several occasions in conflicts with other tribes. The Mohicans supplied scouts and warriors to the forces of the New England Confederation in King Philip's War (1675–1676), which broke the power of anti-white Indians in New England. They also helped English colonists in upper New York State in fighting the French and their Indian allies in the French and Indian War (1754–1763). This aspect of the tribe's history has been covered on screen in numerous films based on Cooper's Leatherstocking Tales, a series of five novels about Indians and settlers in early America.

Movie audiences have become familiar with members of the tribe chiefly through adaptations of Cooper's novels. *The Last of the Mohicans* became the basis for several silent and sound features and one serial. Columbia titled its inferior 1947 version of the novel *Last of the Redmen*, hopefully out of reverence for Cooper. His novel *The Deerslayer* was another of his works that Hollywood adapted several times, including a 1923 silent version and two talkies, one released in 1943, the other in 1957. Generally, all the films adhered to Cooper's romantic depiction of the Indian, especially the characters Chingachgook and Uncas, as having a code of honor and morality. ▪

"Molly Pitcher" (1911). See Pitcher, Molly. ▪

***Monitor* and *Merrimac*, Battle of the.** See *Hearts in Bondage* (1936). ▪

Montgomery, Bernard M. (1887–1976). One biographer characterized the famous English general (also known as Montgomery of Alamein) as immodest, outspoken to the point of insensitivity, egotistical, domineering and vindictive. He won battles through caution, meticulous planning, and by building superior power over the enemy instead of through daring tactics.

Montgomery first achieved prominence during World War II when he took over as field commander of the struggling British Eighth Army in the Egyptian-Libyan desert in August 1942. He defeated Rommel's vaunted Africa Corps at the second Battle of El Alamein (October 23-November 4, 1942) and sent Axis forces reeling permanently back into Libya. It was Britain's first major land victory of the war. The Allied triumph ended an Axis bid to conquer Egypt and the Suez Canal and sever the Allied supply line through the Mediterranean.

The Desert Fox (1951), which dramatized Montgomery's triumph over Rommel at Alamein, presented a sympathetic portrait of the Nazi Panzer commander. *El Alamein* (1953), whose title would lead one to anticipate a chronicle of that important desert clash, was a superficial action drama involving minor fighting over a Nazi supply dump. It did not even include Montgomery as a character. The film interspersed newsreel footage for its desert fighting sequences. Billy Wilder's *Five Graves To Cairo* (1943), a better-than-average wartime spy story, at least mentioned the importance of Montgomery's victory at Alamein.

Following the Axis defeat in North Africa in the spring of 1943, Montgomery commanded British forces in the British-American invasion of Sicily. His rivalry with American General George S. Patton emerged during this campaign in the race to capture Messina and complete the conquest of Sicily. *Patton* (1970), a large-scale and thorough study of that controversial American general,

not only portrayed that rivalry but gave a creditable vignette of the Montgomery ego.

Montgomery's later service in World War II included command of the British Eighth Army in Italy, head of the English 21st Army Group for the invasion of Normandy and eventual promotion to Field Marshal during the fighting on the western front in the drive to conquer Germany. He accepted the surrender of German forces on May 4, 1945. In peacetime he commanded all British occupation forces in Germany and later became Deputy Supreme Allied Commander in N.A.T.O. ▪

"Mooching Through Georgia" (1939). See War Humor. ▪

Moon Is Down, The (1943), TCF. *Dir.* Irving Pichel; *Sc.* Nunnally Johnson; *Cast includes:* Sir Cedric Hardwicke, Henry Travers, Lee J. Cobb, Dorris Rowden.

A World War II propaganda drama, the film depicts Norway's struggle against Nazi occupation. It transcends one nation's fight against oppression and injustice; it emerges as a metaphor for every nation that has had to fight against an invading enemy. Resistance is met with punishment; acts of sabotage are met with the executions of hostages. But the struggle of the determined guerrillas increases. Sir Cedric Hardwicke portrays a Nazi colonel who doubts some of his own methods used against the citizens to combat resistance. He believes that for every hostage that is killed, ten new vindictive enemies will rise up. The film is based on John Steinbeck's popular novel that in turn was adapted for the stage.

Norway's actual resistance against the Nazis was well known during World War II and was reported in Allied newspapers throughout the occupation period. The character of George Corell, played by E. J. Ballantine, was based on the real-life pro-Nazi Norwegian leader, Vidkun Quisling, who betrayed his country. ▪

Moran of the Marines (1928), Par. *Dir.* Frank Strayer; *Sc.* Sam Mintz, Ray Harris; *Cast includes:* Richard Dix, Ruth Elder, Roscoe Karns, Brooks Benedict.

A U.S. Marine private (Richard Dix) gets mixed up with a Chinese bandit in this action drama set in the 1920s during China's civil strife. Dix plays a carefree drifter who, after serving ten days on a work gang for fighting in a gin mill, joins the marines. But the service does not mollify his recklessness. He gets into hot water again while stationed in China when he makes a pass at his general's daughter. However, he wins her heart when he rescues her from the local Chinese bandit. See also Chinese Civil Wars. ∎

More the Merrier, The (1943). See Washington, D.C. ∎

Morgan, John Hunt (1825–1864). A Confederate general, he became famous for his raids during the Civil War. Operating chiefly behind Union lines, he and his raiders captured a Northern Garrison in Huntsville, Alabama, in 1862. He was rapidly promoted to brigadier general. He was captured by the Union on one of his forays later that year but managed to escape. Transferred to a different command, he was killed in action in Greenville, Tennessee.

His daring exploits into enemy territory made exciting screen material. *The Chest of Fortune*, released in 1914 by Kalem, was the first to appear. It portrayed Morgan and his raiders as cold-blooded murderers who butcher a Northern officer and his family. Other action melodramas include *Morgan's Raiders* (1918), *The Little Shepherd of Kingdom Come* (1920) and *Morgan's Last Raid* (1929) although the figure of Morgan was never the main character. ∎

Morgan's Last Raid (1929), MGM. *Dir.* Nick Grinde; *Sc.* Bradley King, Harry Braxton; *Cast includes:* Tim McCoy, Dorothy Sebastian, Wheeler Oakman, Allan Garcia, Hank Mann.

Tim McCoy portrays a Southern captain who decides not to take up arms against Tennessee, his home state, when it secedes from the Union. Dorothy Sebastian, as the young woman he loves, accuses him of being a traitor. Later, he joins John Morgan and his raiders, a unit of the Confederates. During one of their raids, McCoy rescues Sebastian who, of course, forgives him. The film was one of four westerns McCoy made for MGM before he moved on to other studios where he became a popular cowboy star. ∎

Morgan's Raiders (1918), Bluebird. *Dir.* Wilfred Lucas; *Sc.* Bess Meredyth; *Cast includes:* Violet Mersereau, Edward Burns, Barbara Gilroy, Frank Holland.

In this Civil War drama a young Southern belle falls in love with a Union captain. With the outbreak of the war the girl's father joins John Morgan and his Confederate raiders. When a messenger is shot and killed, Morgan asks for a volunteer to take the dead soldier's place. The girl volunteers and, dressed in men's clothing, carries the message across Union lines. Later in the film she is captured and eventually rescued by Morgan's raiders. At the end of the drama she is reunited with her lover from the North. ∎

Moritori (1965). See Vietnam War. ∎

Moro War (1901–1913). The Moros, a large group of Muslim tribes that inhabit the island of Mindanao in the Philippines, were the targets of American military campaigns shortly after the U.S. drove the Spaniards out of the region in the Spanish-American War (1898). The Moros had a reputation as raiders and pirates among neighboring Filipinos. Furthermore, the tribespeople refused to give up their unique culture to follow an American policy that sought their assimilation into a predominantly Christian Filipino culture. The Muslims attacked U.S. troops in sporadic outbreaks beginning in 1901.

Capt. John J. Pershing first distinguished himself in American pacification campaigns against the tribe. In 1906 a band of 600 rebellious Moros on the nearby island of Jolo fled for safety to the inside of a local volcano, where they were trapped and killed by forces under General Leonard Wood. The event raised such a howl of indignation in the U.S. that public pressure gradually forced a change of policy by 1913 and allowed the Moros to peacefully continue the practice of their religion and traditions.

Only a few films dramatized the conflict between the Moros and U.S. troops. *The Last Man* (1916), a silent domestic drama, deals in part with several jungle battles during the Moro uprising. *Tides of Hate* (1917), a romantic drama concerned chiefly with a counterfeiter, his innocent wife and her true lover, also deals partially with the Moro War. The film presents several colorful battles between the Moros and American troops when the young rejected lover volunteers for service in the Philippines. *The Real Glory* (1939) takes place in 1905 after the Spanish-American War and following the withdrawal of American soldiers who leave Mindanao in the hands of native troops and several American officers (Gary Cooper, David Niven and Broderick Crawford). A Moro insurrection which threatens the peaceful outpost and surrounding villages is ultimately subdued by the quick-thinking Cooper. ∎

Morocco (1930), Par. *Dir.* Josef von Sternberg; *Sc.* Jules Furthman; *Cast includes:* Gary Cooper, Marlene Dietrich, Adolphe Menjou, Ulrich Haupt, Juliette Compton.

Gary Cooper and Marlene Dietrich co-star in this steaming romantic drama set in Morocco. Cooper portrays a soldier in the French Foreign Legion who denigrates women. Dietrich plays an entertainer who journeys to Morocco to appear in a cafe. On board the boat is Adolphe Menjou as a sophisticated continental type who offers Dietrich money and security to become his mistress. She refuses and goes on to sing at the nightclub where she meets Cooper. She slips him the key to her private quarters, confirming his opinion of all women. By the end of the film, Cooper and the other Legionnaires march off into the desert. Menjou this time proposes marriage, but Dietrich once again refuses the offer, having fallen for the tall soldier. Along with other camp followers, she walks off into the night to be close to the man she loves.

Today, much of the film is considered high camp, especially the love scenes between the two principals and the ludicrous ending in which Dietrich follows Cooper into the desert in her bare feet. This was her first American film, and she made quite a startling appearance. In her opening night at the Moroccan cafe she is dressed in male clothes—a white tuxedo complete with a top hat. During her act she approaches a pretty customer and kisses her fully on the lips. This shocks the others in the cafe. Director von Sternberg and Dietrich made seven films together, giving rise to rumors about a Svengali-Trilby relationship between the two. The film provides a minimum of action. This fits into the director's style of suggesting violence without presenting it. He also focuses on characters who have come to the end of their tether, either emotionally or physically, eventually discovering the reality of their failed lives. They

face the truth gracefully, as Dietrich does about herself and the man she loves. ∎

Mortal Storm, The (1940), MGM. *Dir.* Frank Borzage; *Sc.* Claudine West, Andersen Ellis, George Froeschel; *Cast includes:* Margaret Sullavan, James Stewart, Robert Young, Frank Morgan, Robert Stack, Bonita Granville, Irene Rich.

An anti-Nazi propaganda drama, the film opens in Germany in 1933 when Hitler was gaining recognition and power. The principal story, centering on the family of a university professor, shows the effects of National Socialism on each member as the political movement turns child against parent, friend against friend. Frank Morgan portrays the professor who loses his teaching position because he is Jewish. Margaret Sullavan, as his daughter, is in love with the independent-thinking James Stewart, who rejects the new doctrines that are sweeping his country. Robert Young portrays Stewart's friend who becomes a fervent Nazi. The young couple escape across the border, but Sullavan is struck by a bullet and dies in Stewart's arms.

The United States officially remained neutral during the European War in 1940. MGM, adhering to the government's policy, did not name Germany as the country, but listed the location of the film as "Somewhere in Europe." Neither American nor European audiences were fooled. The film, one of the earliest from a major studio to condemn the Nazi regime, helped to influence those who remained undecided in the European conflict. The director and the screenwriters were more than forthright in their indictment of Nazi Germany's political direction. ∎

Mosby, John Singleton (1833–1916). A Virginia lawyer and Confederate partisan leader during the American Civil War, he led his Mosby's Raiders against Union cavalry, supply trains and communications. His most notable achievement was the capture of Union General Edwin Stoughton behind Union lines at Fairfax Courthouse in 1863. The daring leader later served as U.S. consul in Hong Kong from 1878 to 1885. He also served with the Justice Department from 1904 to 1910 as an assistant attorney.

His wartime exploits appeared on film as early as 1909 in "The Old Soldier's Story." In 1910 77-year-old Mosby played himself in "All's Fair in Love and War." The plot concerned his daughter's activities as a Confederate spy although she was allegedly wed to a Union officer at the time. The film was remade in 1913 as "The Pride of the South," a Broncho release with Joseph King in the role of Mosby. ∎

Mothers of Men (1920), Rep. Dir. Edward Jose; Sc. Henry Warner, De Witte Kaplan; Cast includes: Claire Whitney, Lumsden Hare, Gaston Glass, Martha Mansfield.

Of French and Austrian heritage, a young woman (Claire Whitney) is raised in Vienna where she is seduced by a young officer in this World War I drama. She moves to France and stays with relatives. After the war breaks out, she discovers that the Austrian officer is a guest in her relative's home. When he threatens to expose her unless she steals military plans for him, she kills him. All ends happily when she marries a young Frenchman. ∎

Mountain Road, The (1960), Col. Dir. Daniel Mann; Sc. Alfred Hayes; Cast includes: James Stewart, Lisa Lu, Glenn Corbett, Henry Morgan, Frank Silvera.

An American major (James Stewart) is assigned to a demolition team ordered to slow down the advancing Japanese in this routine World War II action drama. Set in 1944 in war-torn China, the film traces Stewart and his eight-man force as they destroy bridges, blow up mountain passes and encounter problems with local Chinese as they carry out their mission. A Chinese colonel sends along one of his officers and a pretty war widow (Lisa Lu). At first Stewart tries to rid himself of the female burden but soon falls in love with her. The film touches upon the extreme privations the Chinese civilians suffered during the long war.

The central conflict concerns his lack of understanding of local customs and his insensitivity to problems of the unending stream of refugees who flood the roads. In the beginning of the film a superior officer asks him: "Do you know what 'command' is?" "Well," Stewart begins to reply, "the book says—" "Command is power," the officer interjects, cutting Stewart off. Later, when some local bandits ambush part of his convoy, Stewart over-reacts by leading the remainder of his team in an attack on the town where the bandits take refuge. Using his demolition supplies, he blows up most of the village to rout the bandits. The next day he admits to the widow, who tried to stop him, that he abused his power. ∎

Mr. Logan, U.S.A. (1918). See Spy Films: the Silents. ∎

Mr. Walkie Talkie (1952). See Service Comedy. ∎

Mr. Winkle Goes to War (1944), Col. Dir. Alfred E. Green; Sc. Waldo Salt, George Corey, Louis Solomon; Cast includes: Edward G. Robinson, Ruth Warrick, Ted Donaldson, Bob Haymes.

An unassuming middle-aged bank clerk (Edward G. Robinson) who is dominated by his wife becomes a full-fledged war hero in this World War II comedy drama. Desperate for servicemen in the early days of World War II, the U.S. begins recruiting men over 38. Robinson soon finds himself working for Uncle Sam. Tired of desk jobs and fascinated by mechanical objects, he volunteers for the ordnance division. He survives the ordeal of basic training and is sent overseas to a Pacific island where he is wounded while performing an act of heroism during a Japanese attack. When he returns home, he opens a repair shop. Better known for his gangster portrayals, Robinson is refreshing in this offbeat role. ∎

Mrs. Miniver (1942), MGM. Dir. William Wyler; Sc. Arthur Wimperis, George Froeschel, James Hilton, Claudine West; Cast includes: Greer Garson, Walter Pidgeon, Teresa Wright, Richard Ney, Dame May Witty.

An English middle-class family learns to persevere during war in this World War II drama that won seven Academy Awards. Greer Garson portrays the title character, a strong, brave wife and mother who witnesses her son go off to war, her daughter-in-law killed and her home and beloved village bombed in air raids. Walter Pidgeon plays her husband who is called upon to help in the evacuation of Allied troops stranded at Dunkirk. Richard Ney, as their son, signs up with the Royal Air Force as soon as war breaks out. Teresa Wright portrays Ney's wife who dies from wounds received in an air raid. Regardless of the innumerable hardships the family undergoes, they are resolute in their struggle to emerge victorious.

Several outstanding sequences exemplify

the courage and strength of a peaceful people determined not to surrender to fear or danger. In one scene Mrs. Miniver captures a downed German pilot whom she tries to help, only to be rewarded with his hysterical ravings that soon thousands of German planes will come to bomb English cities. When the citizens who own small boats are called upon to help their government, they assemble by the hundreds, their small craft forming an impressive fleet. "As you know," an officer announces, "the British Expeditionary Force is trapped between the enemy and the sea. Four hundred thousand men are crowded on the beaches under bombardment from artillery and planes. Their only chance to escape annihilation rests with you. Your destination is Dunkirk." In another sequence the townspeople continue their cherished tradition of a simple little community flower show. In the final scene, the village minister leads religious services in a bombed-out church as British planes soar overhead. His sermon stirs his congregation who have come to mourn their dead. "This is not only a war of soldiers in uniform," he reminds them, "it is a war of the people—all of the people. And it must be fought not only on the battlefield, but in the cities and in the villages . . . in the home and in the heart of every man, woman and child who loves freedom . . . This is the people's war. It is our war!" The film caused a ground swell of sympathy for Britain's plight and helped to galvanize the American public against the Axis forces. Its anticomplacency theme had done its work.

A sequel, *The Miniver Story*, appeared in 1950 with the same two stars and covered the postwar period. Directed by H.C. Potter with a screenplay by Ronald Millar and George Froeschel, the drama opens at the end of World War II. Mrs. Miniver returns from her doctor from whom she has learned that she does not have long to live. She decides to keep the news from her family. Her husband returns from Germany. Her daughter, portrayed by Cathy O'Donnell, is released from her war work in Egypt. Finally, her son returns from the U.S. When Mrs. Miniver learns that her daughter is involved with a married man, she visits him and convinces him that he is still in love with his wife. John Hodiak portrays an American officer who becomes infatuated with Mrs. Miniver. ∎

Mrs. Slacker (1918), Pathe. *Dir.* Hobart Henley; *Sc.* Agnes Johnson; *Cast includes:* Gladys Hulette, Creighton Hale, Paul Clerget.

A minor World War I drama, the film concerns a cowardly young man who rushes into marriage with his fiancee, a local laundress, to keep out of the draft when war erupts. When the wife (Gladys Hulette) learns of her husband's real reason for the hasty marriage, she insists that she will not be known as "Mrs. Slacker." She is determined to set an example for her spineless husband (Creighton Hale). An opportunity presents itself when German agents plot to destroy a nearby reservoir. When she foils their plans, her embarrassed husband enlists in the army. This was just another of numerous patriotic films of the period that helped to encourage enlistments and singled out the "slackers" as cowards. ∎

Murphy, Audie (1924–1971). The most decorated soldier of World War II, Murphy won 24 decorations, including the coveted Congressional Medal of Honor. Wounded in action three times, he once single-handedly attacked a German-occupied hill, killing 15 and wounding 35 of the enemy. On another occasion he climbed atop a burning tank destroyer and, with only its single machine gun, held off 250 Germans and six tanks.

He later entered films and appeared in 40 features, chiefly as the leading character. Director John Huston cast him against character in *The Red Badge of Courage* (1951), adapted from Stephen Crane's Civil War novel. Murphy went on to play Union, Confederate and cavalry officers as well as other heroic roles in a series of action dramas, including *Apache Rifles* (1964), *Arizona Raiders* (1965), *Battle at Bloody Beach* (1961), *The Guns of Fort Petticoat* (1957), *Column South* (1953), *The Gun Runners* (1958), *Kansas Raiders* (1950) and *Walk the Proud Land* (1956). He died at age 46 in an airplane crash in Virginia in June 1971. See *To Hell and Back* (1955), a film based chiefly on Murphy's military career. ∎

Musicals. Musicals with a war background first appeared on screen in the late 1920s with the advent of sound. The plots were thin, the productions crude and the songs forgettable. The audiences, however, found them entertaining even if the critics didn't. World War I had been over for more than a decade, so these films had little to do with patriotism or propaganda. In fact, they occasionally satirized the military aspects of the conflict.

The Battle of Paris (1929), starring Gertrude Lawrence in her screen debut as a street singer-turned-nurse, and Charles Ruggles as a Parisian pickpocket, was panned by virtually every movie critic. The inept story pokes fun at the war. Marion Davies, as a young Frenchwoman in *Marianne*, a musical comedy released the same year, is engaged to a soldier who has lost his eyesight in battle. A doughboy (Lawrence Gray) falls in love with her. Benny Rubin and Cliff Edwards provide the comedy. *Men of the Sky* (1931) was an unusual film for its time. A musical drama set during World War I, it featured Irene Delroy as a French spy who falls in love with an American flier (Jack Whiting). Both are caught by the enemy and executed.

After a few faltering starts, the war musical flourished during World War II. Like other escape genres, such as the mystery, adventure and comedy film, the musical quickly developed its own set of conventions. The plots became familiar but were secondary to the music. Entertainers are drafted or enlist into the military where they continue to ply their talents. A troupe of entertainers visits a military base where a G.I. will fall for one of the singers. A lonely soldier on leave visits a canteen where he finds romance while being entertained by name bands and performers. The films scored with the civilians who were weary of their long hours in the defense plants and those in uniform, both seeking a temporary respite from the war. Mindful of the box-office success of early entries produced by some of the minor studios, the majors pressed their top stars into the genre and surrounded them with more lavish settings.

Rookies on Parade (1941), although released months before America's entry into the war, was one of the earliest musicals with a military setting. Bob Crosby and Eddie Foy, Jr. portray songwriters drafted by Uncle Sam. They produce a musical for their army buddies which ultimately moves to Broadway. *The Yanks Are Coming* (1942) concerns a band that enlists in the army as a defiant act against their bandleader who belittles the common soldier. There are the usual patriotic songs, including "The Yanks Are Coming," "Zip Your Lip," and "There Will Be No Blackout of Democracy." In *Hey, Rookie* (1944) Larry Parks, as a stage producer caught in the draft, is delegated to organize a camp show. He manages to enlist the help of his dancing star and sweetheart (Ann Miller).

Female performers were regularly featured in war musicals. Singer-dancer Ann Miller, as an entertainer in *Priorities on Parade* (1942), chooses war work in an airplane plant over a Broadway career. She appeared in *Reveille With Beverly* the following year as a disk jockey entertaining troops at army camps—along with Frank Sinatra, Count Basie and Duke Ellington. *Sweetheart of the Fleet* (1942), with comedienne Joan Davis, features the patriotic song "We Did It Before and We'll Do It Again." An all-female band entertains in a defense plant in *Beautiful But Broke* (1944), again featuring Joan Davis. One of the songs is "Mr. Jive Goes to War." Another popular comedienne of the period was the hillbilly entertainer Judy Canova. In *Joan of Ozark* (1942) she mixes it up with Nazi agents while finding time to sing such tunes as "Lady at Lockheed."

Plots hinging on a soldier were popular. Betty Rhodes, as a radio singer in *Salute for Three* (1943), flirts with war hero Macdonald Carey to further her career—and falls in love with him. Noah Beery, Jr. portrays a G.I. who just wants to catch up on his sleep in *Weekend Pass* (1944). *A Wave, a WAC and a Marine* (1944) features members of three branches of service and the song "Gee, I Love My G.I. Guy."

All the above, released as B musicals, received second billing in movie theaters that played two features. The major studios presented their share of war musicals throughout the 1940s. Paramount offered its all-star revue, *Star Spangled Rhythm*, in 1942. Bing Crosby, Ray Milland, Bob Hope, Veronica Lake and Dorothy Lamour all help to carry a thin story about a sailor on leave who visits his father, a studio gatekeeper (Victor Moore). Warner Brothers' *Yankee Doodle Dandy* (1942), starring James Cagney as George M. Cohan, was one of the most popular patriotic musicals of the period. The studio also produced *This Is the Army* (1943). One of the film industry's major contributions to the war effort and a tribute to the fighting troops, the film was based on Irving Berlin's successful stage play that raised almost $2 million for the Army Emergency Relief Fund. The film raised much more. *Stage Door Canteen*

(1943), released by United Artists, uses a romantic framework to highlight the volunteer work of show-business personalities who entertained the men and women in the armed forces in canteens across the nation. Not to be outdone, Warners offered its own version, titled *Hollywood Canteen*, in 1944, featuring Eddie Cantor, John Garfield, Bette Davis, Joan Leslie and Robert Hutton. MGM launched *Ship Ahoy* (1942), an unusual spy musical comedy with Eleanor Powell, Red Skelton, Bert Lahr and Frank Sinatra. The plot concerns enemy agents transporting a magnetic mine aboard a ship sailing for Puerto Rico. Universal turned out its share of wartime musicals. *When Johnny Comes Marching Home* in 1943, featured the talents of Allan Jones, Donald O'Connor, Gloria Jean and Peggy Ryan. Jones portrays a returning war hero and former singer. *Follow the Boys* (1944), another Universal filmed variety show, paid tribute to show business personnel and the various organizations that entertained the fighting troops. Jeanette MacDonald, Orson Welles, Marlene Dietrich, Sophie Tucker, Ted Lewis, W. C. Fields and the Andrews Sisters were some of the performers.

By 1944 the war musical had reached its peak. Major screen stars, along with new talent, appeared in a steady stream of musical comedies. Betty Grable, as an ambitious singer in 20th Century-Fox's *Pin-Up Girl* (1944), crashes a party for a war hero, is caught and forced to entertain before all the guests. Paramount's *Rainbow Island* (1944) stars Eddie Bracken as an American sailor stranded on an island with, among others, Dorothy Lamour. The studio turned out *Here Come the Waves*, with Bing Crosby and Betty Hutton, the same year. Fox's *Something for the Boys* (1944) concerns the building of a home for army wives. It features Carmen Miranda, also known as the "Brazilian bombshell," comic Phil Silvers and Vivian Blaine. RKO's *Up in Arms*, released the same year, has singer-comedian Danny Kaye in his screen debut as a hypochondriac who is drafted into the army.

Following the armistice, war musicals diminished in popularity and all but disappeared from the screen. The genre was occasionally revived with mixed results. *The Fastest Guitar Alive* (1967), for example, uses the Civil War as background for the talents of Roy Orbison and Sammy Jackson. Julie Andrews portrays a World War I German spy who, posing as an English entertainer in *Darling Lili* (1970), falls in love with American flier Rock Hudson. The following year Walt Disney released *Bedknobs and Broomsticks*, a musical fantasy set in World War II England and starring Angela Lansbury. The special effects include bewitched suits of armor repelling a German invasion force. *Cabaret* (1972) was one of the few successful musicals of the 1970s. It concerns an American entertainer (Liza Minnelli) caught up in the amorality and hedonism of pre-World War II Berlin and the rise of Nazism.

The war musical, predominant during World War II, although dated by today's perspective, fulfilled a particular need for its audiences. The films provided an escape from the early years of the conflict when events appeared particularly bleak. They served to boost the morale of the home front and fighting forces overseas. They suggested a democratic spirit in their various plots (romances between successful entertainers and common servicemen; wealthy producers and stars drafted into service to mingle with the average recruit). Above all, they unified the nation through a popular culture of music and dance that was universally accepted by those at home and overseas. ∎

Mutiny (1952), UA. Dir. Edward Dmytryk; Sc. Philip Yordan, Sidney Harmon; Cast includes: Mark Stevens, Angela Lansbury, Patric Knowles, Gene Evans.

Set during the War of 1812 and based on an actual incident, this action drama tells the story of American patriots seeking to transport much-needed gold bullion from France. The gold, necessary to continue the war against Britain, becomes the object of a greedy and mutinous crew, led by Gene Evans. Mark Stevens portrays the zealous American patriot-captain who makes the risky voyage and faces losing the gold. Patric Knowles plays the first officer of the vessel while Angela Lansbury, as his girlfriend who also lusts for the gold, sides with the mutineers in this routine tale. ∎

My Buddy (1944). See Veterans. ∎

My Country First (1916). See Spy Films: the Silents. ∎

My Favorite Blonde (1942). See Spy Films: the Talkies. ∎

My Favorite Brunette (1947). See Spy Films: the Talkies. ∎

My Favorite Spy (1951). See Spy Films: the Talkies. ∎

My Four Years in Germany (1918), State Rights. *Dir.* William Nigh; *Sc.* Charles A. Logue; *Cast includes:* Halbert Brown, William Dashiell, Louis Dean, Earl Schenck, Karl Dane.

Based on Ambassador James W. Gerard's book of the same title, the feature film version purportedly gives a factual picture of the Kaiser and the German leaders prior to America's involvement in World War I. Halbert Brown portrays Ambassador Gerard and emphasizes how the German leaders deceived the United States as well as other countries with whom they were supposed to have had friendly relations. Interspersed with dramatic scenes, some of which show atrocities committed at German prison camps, are segments from newsreels and documentaries, all of which are designed to substantiate the conclusions drawn by the ambassador.

The studio insisted that much of the film was compiled from actual newsreel footage. In truth, it was produced in a New Jersey studio. It cost about $50,000 to make and earned more than $400,000. ∎

My Own True Love (1948). See Prisoners of War. ∎

My Own United States (1918), Froman. *Dir.* John W. Noble; *Sc.* Anthony Paul Kelly; *Cast includes:* Arnold Daly, Charles E. Graham, Duncan McRae, Sydney Bracey, Thomas Donnelly.

A sweeping, sprawling panorama of highlights in American history, the film is a patriotic tract presented in dramatic fashion.

Major American figures are depicted, including, among others, Aaron Burr, Alexander Hamilton, Thomas Jefferson, Andrew Jackson, Admiral Stephen Decatur, General Grant and President Lincoln.

Released during World War I, the film must have contributed substantially to the patriotic fervor of the period. The story begins with President Wilson presenting his declaration on democracy to Congress. ∎

My Son John (1952). See Cold War. ∎

Mystery Sea Raider (1940), Par. *Dir.* Edward Dmytryk; *Sc.* Edward E. Paramore, Jr.; *Cast includes:* Carole Landis, Henry Wilcoxon, Onslow Stevens, Kathleen Howard, Wallace Reirdon.

A naive American (Carole Landis) helps a disguised Nazi hijack a freighter in this World War II drama. The innocent-looking vessel is then used to prey upon other ships in the Caribbean as well as to sink a British cruiser. Onslow Stevens plays the German naval captain while Henry Wilcoxon portrays the deposed freighter captain who romances Landis in this low-budget film. Obvious newsreel footage is interspersed into the feature as part of the action sequences. ∎

Mystery Submarine (1950), UI. *Dir.* Douglas Sirk; *Sc.* George W. George, George F. Slavin; *Cast includes:* Macdonald Carey, Marta Toren, Robert Douglas, Carl Esmond.

A renegade German submarine remains active after World War II in this drama. Its sinister captain (Robert Douglas) uses his undersea vessel for nefarious activities, such as snatching a German scientist living peacefully in the U.S. and turning him over to an undisclosed organization. As the captain sails off to meet a tanker, his U-boat is sighted by the U.S. Navy. A series of depth charges brings the submarine to the end of its journey in this routine film. ∎

N

Naked and the Dead, The (1958), WB. Dir. Raoul Walsh; *Sc.* Denis and Terry Sanders; *Cast includes:* Aldo Ray, Cliff Robertson, Raymond Massey, Lili St. Cyr, Barbara Nichols.

Based on Norman Mailer's critically acclaimed novel, this World War II drama of a platoon of Americans fighting in the Pacific doesn't live up to the richness of its original source. Aldo Ray portrays Croft, the cruel sergeant whose wife is unfaithful. Cliff Robertson, as a lieutenant and general's aide, continually challenges his superior on such ideological issues as command and power. Raymond Massey plays the general who, impressed by his own power, parries with Robertson on the issue of officers' relationships with their men. "Make the men hate and fear you," he states. "There is no other way." But Robertson disagrees and gets the chance to test his own beliefs when he is assigned to lead a reconnaissance patrol behind enemy lines. He returns, wounded, with only two other survivors. "There's a spirit in man," he concludes, "that will survive all the reigns of terror."

Several incidents and battle sequences convey some of the power and realism inherent in the original work. In one scene, as the platoon is climbing up a mountain, a Jewish soldier (Joey Bishop) is afraid to jump across a hazardous ravine and freezes up. The sergeant, in an attempt to rile the soldier into action, calls out: "Jump, you dirty Jew!" The G.I., in a fit of rage, jumps and falls to his death. But, for the most part, the film version has weakened Mailer's incisive novel about men under pressure by adding inane dialogue and stereotyped characters. ∎

Naked Brigade, The (1965), U. Dir. Maury Dexter; *Sc.* Alfred J. Cohen, A. Sanford Wolf; *Cast includes:* Shirley Eaton, Ken Scott, Mary Chronopoulou, John Holland.

The Nazi invasion of Crete provides the background for this action drama set during World War II. The stranded daughter (Shirley Eaton) of an English archaeologist who is killed during the attack seeks refuge with a group of guerrillas until she can be rescued. Ken Scott, as the leader of a group of women guerrillas, leads them in the destruction of a Nazi ship stationed in the harbor. He attempts to woo Eaton but is quickly rejected. Mary Chronopoulou plays his jealous girlfriend in this implausible tale. Action sequences include stock war footage. ∎

Nansen, Fridtjof. See Refugees. ∎

Napoleon I (Napoleon Bonaparte) (1769–1821). Napoleon Bonaparte may have been a product of the French Revolution, with its cry of liberty, equality and fraternity, but in his personal demeanor he was as imperial and commanding as any other monarch France had known. At a coronation ceremony in 1804 that he directed must take place at the Cathedral of Notre Dame in Paris, Napoleon received the crown from Pope Pius VII and placed it upon his own head. He was now emperor of France in both the trappings of royalty and in actual authority.

Born in Corsica into a family of minor Corsican nobility who suffered economic hardships, he attended military school in France. Napoleon was a superior military strategist, driven by an ambition to conquer, and a leader of considerable personal magnetism. Despite his eventual defeat and banishment, he became a legend and an object of adoration almost immediately after his death.

Following his graduation from the military academy in 1785, He soon became a supporter of the French Revolution. He joined the radical Jacobins and spoke out against the privileges of the nobility and clergy. As a young artillery officer, he helped expel the British, who had come to the assistance of the Royalists, from the French port of Toulon (1793). Napoleon temporarily lost his army post (1794–95) when he fell out of favor with a ruling revolutionary clique. It was at this time that he became involved in a love affair with Desiree Clary, daughter of a rich businessman. Desiree's sister had recently married Napoleon's older brother, Joseph. The film Desiree (1954) presented a highly fictionalized version of this romance.

He again became the center of attention when, in a new command, he turned back a Parisian mob trying to storm the National Convention, France's revolutionary government. While in Paris, he courted and married Josephine (1796), a leading socialite. As a reward for defending the Convention, Napoleon was put in control of the French army in northern Italy. He rose to national hero when he defeated the numerically superior forces of Austrians and Italians in the 1796–1797 campaign. He used his next campaign, a failed attempt to seize Egypt, to become leader of France. Though forced to flee Egypt in defeat, he hurried back to France and successfully engineered a coup (1799) before news of the reversals reached his homeland. He became, in essence, a military dictator. As First Consul, he brought reform, order and military success to France. He won significant military victories that enlarged France's borders.

Napoleon proclaimed himself emperor in 1804 in a ceremony at Notre Dame in Paris. By 1810 he was master of most of continental Europe through conquest, alliances and a policy of placing relatives on thrones of vassal states. He further cemented his hold upon Europe by first annulling his marriage to Josephine when she failed to give him an heir, and marrying the archduchess Marie Louis, daughter of Austrian emperor Francis I. Just before his latest marriage, Napoleon had been negotiating with Russian Czar Alexander I for his daughter's hand, Catherine. The one exception to Napoleon's record of success, however, was on the Iberian peninsula where the people of Spain and Portugal conducted a guerrilla conflict (Peninsular War), aided by sizable British forces.

Napoleon's downfall stemmed from the Russian campaign in 1812 in which he lost over 90 percent of his Grand Army of a half-million troops. He fell from power on April 6, 1814, when France, its economy exhausted and its forces weakened by decades of war, surrendered to a European coalition led by England. Napoleon was exiled to the Mediterranean island of Elba. The opening sequences of Devil-May-Care (1929), a musical romance, dramatized his removal from office and his departure. He escaped, returned to the mainland and exhibited the magic hold he had on the people of France by raising a new army to rebuild his empire in the Hundred Days War.

Defeated at the Battle of Waterloo, he was exiled again to the remote Atlantic island of St. Helena where he died from a serious stomach ailment on May 5, 1821. Despite the turmoil he caused France, he was almost immediately deified for the glory and permanent positive social changes he brought to the country. Napoleon's remains were brought back to France in 1840 and, following a stately funeral procession in Paris, his body was interred beneath the dome of the Invalides.

The American screen was not so generous in its treatment of Napoleon. Very few dramas emphasized his turbulent life and many accomplishments. Clarence Brown's Conquest (1937) covered the last few years of Napoleon's life and focused on his love affair with the Polish countess Marie Walewska (Greta Garbo). The film was enhanced by Charles Boyer's absorbing portrayal of the emperor and MGM's lavish production. Henry Koster's Desiree (1954) mainly centered on a confused Napoleon (Marlon Brando) and his romance with the title character (Jean Simmons). The script undermined the decisiveness of such a major historical figure by depicting Desiree as having a strong influence over him. In King Vidor's War and Peace (1956), a much-abbreviated adaptation of Tolstoy's epic novel, Herbert Lom por trayed a brooding Napoleon who, outwitted by a Russian general, witnesses the disintegration of his Grand Army.

His overall image also suffered in films in which he was portrayed as a minor figure. In an early 1911 Edison one-reeler, "The Price of Victory," a revengeful father, whose young son is killed while serving under Napoleon, plots to kill the general. In *Are We Civilized?* (1934), a pretentious antiwar drama, the image of Napoleon is invoked to prove the folly and destruction of war. Abel Gance's French-produced epic *Napoleon* (1926) remains the definitive film about the controversial French hero. See Napoleonic Wars, Battle of Trafalgar. ∎

Napoleonic Wars (1803–1815). The Napoleonic Wars that ravaged Europe at the beginning of the 19th century had their roots in the French Revolutionary Wars (1792–1802). At first, a coalition of monarchical European powers attempted to stop France from spreading its revolutionary republican ideals by military intervention into several neighboring areas. Following Napoleon's succession to power by a coup d'état in 1799 and a brief period of peace from 1802–1803, the conflict resumed as a result of his overpowering ambition to dominate the European scene. The British, fearing Napoleon's growing might and angered by his refusal to reopen French markets, declared war on France in 1803. The conflict spread to draw in every major European state before Napoleon's final defeat in 1815.

At one point Napoleon planned to invade England, but Lord Horatio Nelson's monumental naval victory at the Battle of Trafalgar (October 21, 1805), along with other factors, spelled doom for French sea power. Two films graphically dramatized the Battle of Trafalgar, albeit from the British point of view—*The Divine Lady* (1929) and *That Hamilton Woman* (1941). Meanwhile, on land, Napoleon continued to pile up victories. He took Naples and Genoa and crowned himself King of Italy (1805). He defeated Russia and Austria at the Battle of Austerlitz (December 2, 1805). He effected additional gains in Prussia and Poland during 1806 and 1807. He made a brief peace with Russia who joined him in defeating Sweden in 1808.

Napoleon tried to weaken England, his only remaining enemy, by instituting a trade boycott. Attempts to force Spain and Portugal into the boycott, along with his scheme to place his brother, Joseph, on the throne of Spain, led to the Peninsular War (1808–1814). The British sent the Duke of Wellington and a sizable force into the Iberian peninsula to aid their Portuguese ally. Wellington won several victories between 1809–1814 and even carried the war into France. Stanley Kramer's plodding historical drama *The Pride and the Passion* (1957), starring Cary Grant as an English naval officer and Frank Sinatra and Sophia Loren as Spanish resistance fighters against the French incursion into Spain, used the Peninsular War for its background.

French relations with Russia deteriorated by 1812. Napoleon, angered at Russia's peace overtures with England, launched his Grand Army of almost 500,000 troops against Russia. The invasion marked the beginning of the end of Napoleon's record of success. Czarist forces, outnumbered and defeated in several key opening battles, retreated, but practiced a scorched-earth policy to deny Napoleon much-needed supplies. Though Napoleon captured Moscow, he found himself in a burned-out city from which many of its inhabitants had fled. Suffering from a shortage of food and war supplies, and further weakened by fatigue and the bitter Russian winter, the French retreated across Europe back to France.

Russian Cossack troops constantly harried the diminished remnants of the Grand Army. Napoleon abandoned his beleaguered force in December to hurry back to Paris to quell a reported plot against him and raise more troops. Only an estimated 20,000-30,000 French soldiers, out of an initial force of a half-million, survived the retreat. King Vidor's *War and Peace* (1956), with its spectacular battle sequences, dramatized Napoleon's debacle in Russia. In a much lighter vein, Woody Allen in *Love and Death* (1975) unleashed his satirical wit upon the image of Napoleon.

Sensing his weakness, a new coalition of Russia, Prussia, Austria and Sweden declared war against Napoleon and defeated the French leader on October 19, 1813. Napoleon abdicated and went into exile on the island of Elba. He escaped, returned to France, and, remarkably, raised a new army to rebuild his empire in the "Hundred Days War." A new allied force of almost one million troops, under the overall command of Britain's Duke of

Wellington, attacked France. Napoleon met his final defeat at Waterloo, Belgium, on June 25, 1815. "Love and War" (1909), an Edison one-reeler, focused on the Duke of Wellington and the Battle of Waterloo. Napoleon was exiled again, this time to the island of St. Helena where he died in 1821.

The Napoleonic Wars served as background for several other films, chiefly fictional dramas. *The Secret of St. Ives* (1949), a low-budget affair, concerned captured French soldiers who escape their English captors. *Captain Horatio Hornblower* (1951), starring Gregory Peck, emphasized the sea battles between the British and French navies. *Tyrant of the Sea* (1950), a low-budget action drama, portrayed Lord Nelson as a minor character and featured several rousing sea fights. *Sea Devils* (1953), with Rock Hudson and Yvonne De Carlo, was a routine spy drama that takes place during this turbulent period. See Battle of Trafalgar. ∎

Nathan Hale (1913). See Hale, Nathan. ∎

Nation's Peril, The (1915), Lubin. *Dir.* George Terwilliger; *Sc.* George Terwilliger, Harry Chandlee; *Cast includes:* Ormi Hawley, William H. Turner, Earl Metcalfe, Eleanor Barry.

A war drama extolling preparedness, the film tells of a young army lieutenant who invents an aerial torpedo. He is in love with an admiral's granddaughter who objects to his invention on the grounds that it will take human life. A spy, interested in stealing the plans for the torpedo, gains her trust by pretending to be interested in her antiwar beliefs. A group of spies captures a coastal town, but the U.S. Navy shells the area and retakes the town. The pacifist heroine realizes she was wrong and becomes a staunch supporter of preparedness.

The film is an early example of the industry's growing attack on pacifism. Using the familiar literary tool of ridicule, the writers reduced the heroine, played by Ormi Hawley, to a capricious, scatterbrained embodiment of pacifism. ∎

Naval battles. See Sea Battles. ∎

Navy Comes Through, The (1942), RKO. *Dir.* A. Edward Sutherland; *Sc.* Roy Chanslor, Aeneas MacKenzie, Earl Baldwin, John

Twist; *Cast includes:* Pat O'Brien, George Murphy, Jane Wyatt, Jackie Cooper.

This was Hollywood's tribute to the U.S. navy crews stationed aboard merchant marine ships during World War II. The film dramatizes the many scraps the fighting sailors engage in against enemy submarines and planes bent on sinking the "bridge of ships," as President Roosevelt called the steady flow of war supplies to the Allies and U.S. troops. Pat O'Brien plays the chief petty officer in charge of one of these navy crews. George Murphy, as a seaman on board the vessel, is in love with O'Brien's sister (Jane Wyatt). After joining forces in several battles against the enemy, the two sailors become friends, and O'Brien accepts Murphy as a fit mate for the gal. The chiefly routine and unrealistic plot features several exciting combat sequences, including the downing of a German bomber, the sinking of a U-boat and the capture of an enemy supply ship. The following year Lloyd Bacon's *Action in the North Atlantic*, starring Humphrey Bogart, was released and quickly overshadowed Sutherland's tribute to the merchant marine. ∎

Navy Way, The (1944), Par. *Dir.* William Berke; *Sc.* Maxwell Shane; *Cast includes:* Robert Lowery, Jean Parker, Bill Henry, Roscoe Karns, Robert Armstrong.

A former prizefighter (Robert Lowery) on the road to a championship bout resents being in the service in this low-budget World War II action drama. Believing that the war and the military have interfered with his career, he becomes rebellious and unconcerned about his duties at a naval training camp in the Great Lakes. But his attitude gradually changes when he meets Jean Parker, who provides the romantic interest in this routine tale. Her influence straightens him out as he embarks aboard his ship for sea duty. ∎

Nazi Agent (1942). See Spy Films: the Silents. ∎

Nazi Spy Ring (1942). See Spy Films: the Talkies. ∎

Nazis Strike, The (1942). See "Why We Fight." ∎

Nebraska Under Fire (1924), Pictorial Sales Bureau.

A documentary concerning Nebraskan

troops during World War I, the film covers the soldiers' experiences from their training to their departure for home after the armistice. The doughboys are seen in training camps before their debarkation in England and France. The troops are then seen participating in several battles, including those at Chatteau-Thierry, St. Mihiel and Argonne. At the war's end, they are sent into Germany before leaving for the U.S. This was one of several documentaries dealing with soldiers representing various states. ■

Negro Soldier, The (1944), U.S. War Dept. *Dir.* Col. Frank Capra; *Sc.* Carlton Moss.

The contributions and sacrifices made by blacks to this nation, from the American Revolution to the Second World War, are outlined in this World War II documentary. Individual figures range from Crispus Attucks, a hero during the 1770 Boston Massacre, to Robert Brooks, the first American serviceman to fall in World War II. The film, which makes a strong case for tolerance, continues to point out an impressive list of blacks present during other wars in the history of the U.S. The second half of the documentary emphasizes the large number of black men and women who served their country with honor during World War II. ■

Nelson, Horatio (1758–1805). Cruising eastward off the Atlantic coast of southern Spain, heading towards Cadiz, Admiral Nelson saw ahead of him the naval force he had set out to engage. A powerful Franco-Spanish fleet of 33 vessels was running in ragged style from Nelson's force of 27 ships to seek refuge in the port of Cadiz, north of Gibraltar.

Nelson ordered his fleet into two prearranged parallel battle lines and headed straight for the center of the enemy force. He then sent out his famous signal: "England expects that every man will do his duty." The English ships tore through the middle of the Franco-Spanish fleet and then turned to engage the enemy in one of history's most important naval encounters. When the fighting ended, the British had taken 18 enemy ships without losing even one of their own. Only 11 enemy vessels struggled into Cadiz. Nelson's victory at Trafalgar on October 5, 1805, sealed his reputation, already an eminent one, as Britain's foremost naval leader. The Trafalgar campaign dashed Napoleon's already dimming hopes of wresting control of

the sea from the English. *The Divine Lady* (1929) and *That Hamilton Woman* (1941), both chiefly romantic historical dramas, recreated the Battle of Trafalgar.

But Nelson's victory came at the expense of his life. He was struck by a bullet in the spine from a sharpshooter in the rigging of an enemy vessel. Before he died, he said, on receiving a favorable report of the battle, "Thank God, I have done my duty." His mortal wound marked the fourth time he had been hit in action.

Nelson had run up a string of victories before and during the Napoleonic Wars. He defeated the French at the Battle of the Nile (August 1, 1798), thereby ending Napoleon's plan to conquer Egypt. *The Divine Lady* in part reproduced the battle. In the Battle of Copenhagen (April 2, 1801), Nelson fashioned a stunning victory over a Danish fleet by deliberately disobeying orders. As he abandoned formation to engage the enemy, he received flag signals from his superior to return to position. Nelson put his telescope to his blind eye and continued with the attack, later claiming he never saw the signal.

His personal life, at times, raised criticism. Married in 1787 to a widow, Nelson later became involved in a romantic affair with Lady Emma Hamilton. Both *The Divine Lady* and *That Hamilton Woman*, the latter featuring Vivien Leigh and Laurence Olivier as the star-crossed lovers Lady Hamilton and Lord Nelson, dramatized the romance. His affair led to a permanent separation from his wife by 1801. In *Tyrant of the Sea* (1950), a routine adventure drama, the character of Lord Nelson appears in a minor role. ■

Never Let Me Go (1953). See Cold War. ■

Never So Few (1959), MGM. *Dir.* John Sturges; *Sc.* Millard Kaufman; *Cast includes:* Frank Sinatra, Gina Lollobrigida, Peter Lawford, Steve McQueen, Charles Bronson.

A World War II action drama with a revenge motif, this brutal film stars Frank Sinatra as a battle-hardened, rebellious captain of a small force of American and British troops in Burma. Following a successful mission in which he and his men wipe out a Japanese air base, he learns that another detachment of Americans has been ambushed by Chinese Nationalist mercenaries led by a local warlord operating from across the border.

Forbidden to enter China, Sinatra vows revenge and defiantly leads his troops across the border to hunt down the killers. He captures the cadre's stronghold and kills the leaders. He then discovers the belongings of dozens of G.I.s killed by the Chinese irregulars and a letter from the Chinese government giving warlords permission to raid American units and sell their supplies to the Japanese. When one of his officers is suddenly killed by a wounded warlord, Sinatra orders the execution of all the prisoners. Returning to his base in Burma, he is reprimanded by his superiors for disobeying orders and commanded to apologize to a representative of the Chinese government. When he refuses, a high-ranking general (Brian Donlevy) comes to his defense. Peter Lawford plays a medic who early in the film is at odds with Sinatra's unorthodox methods. Steve McQueen and Charles Bronson have secondary roles as soldiers loyal to Sinatra. Gina Lollobrigida, as the mistress of a secret agent of the Allies, provides the romantic interest for Sinatra when she switches lovers. Unfortunately, the dialogue she is given doesn't match her other attributes. "I kiss you," she confesses, "and the bells ring wildly in my temples." ■

Never Wave at a WAC (1952). See Service Comedy. ■

New Commandment, The (1925), FN. *Dir.* Howard Higgin; *Sc.* Sada Cowan, Howard Higgin; *Cast includes:* Blanche Sweet, Ben Lyon, Holbrook Blinn, Clara Eames, George Cooper.

A romantic drama set in France during World war I, the film stars Blanche Sweet as an American visiting France and Ben Lyon, who is also traveling abroad. They meet in a Paris cafe and fall in love. The war interrupts their romance when Lyon enlists. Wounded in action, he lands in a military hospital where the young lovers are reunited.

The film includes several elaborate battle sequences, some of which are actual combat shots made during the war. George Cooper provides the comic relief. A passionate love scene between Lyon and Sweet was singled out for its intensity by several contemporary critics. Although the production was not designed to compete in scope or theme with *The Big Parade*, it was released at about the same time and was quickly overshadowed by the acclaim bestowed upon the latter. ■

New Lives for Old (1925). See Women and War. ■

New Mexico (1951), UA. *Dir.* Irving Reis; *Sc.* Max Trell; *Cast includes:* Lew Ayres, Marilyn Maxwell, Robert Hutton, Andy Devine, Raymond Burr, Jeff Corey.

Another routine cavalry-vs.-Indians action drama, the film stars Lew Ayres as a U.S. Cavalry captain who is sympathetic to the Indians' grievances. After the violation by white men of a treaty between President Lincoln and Acuma, the Indian chief, the warriors take to the warpath. Ayres, a friend of Acuma, is assigned to take a patrol of troopers to put down the uprising. He is cut off from help by the Indians and takes cover in an abandoned Indian village on a mesa. The remainder of the film concerns the bloody battle between the two forces. Marilyn Maxwell, as an entertainer whom Ayres rescues from a stagecoach attacked by hostiles, provides the romantic interest.

Appearing only one year after the landmark film *Broken Arrow*, which set the tone for future pro-Indian dramas, the film sides with the Indians by showing how the whites wronged them. But all this is subordinated to the battle raging between the adversaries. ■

New Orleans, Battle of (January 8, 1815). Though it was the last major land battle of the War of 1812, and an overwhelming victory for the U.S. in its conflict with Britain, the engagement had no bearing on the outcome of the conflict. A treaty had been signed two weeks earlier (Treaty of Ghent, December 24, 1814), but news of the agreement took several weeks to reach the U.S. by sailing ship, well after the clash.

Prior to the Battle of New Orleans, neither side had been able to make any important gains in the conflict on land after two years of fighting. Late in 1814, Britain shifted its efforts to a new region. A force of 7,500 veteran troops under General Sir Edward Pakenham, who embarked from the island of Jamaica, were sent to seize the American port of New Orleans on the Gulf of Mexico. The British hoped, thereby, to close off American trade, both foreign and domestic. General Andrew Jackson, in command of American forces in the area, received warning of the impending British assault through Jean Lafitte, a pro-American pirate, and prepared to meet the attack.

The British landed in mid-December and made their way slowly toward the city. Jackson won time to prepare defenseworks by first stopping an advance British force in a night engagement (December 23–24) seven miles from New Orleans. A thundering artillery duel on January 1, 1815, in which the Americans were assisted by Lafitte's gunners, forced the British to delay their attack even longer and bring up reinforcements.

The decisive stage of the battle took place on the morning of January 8, when Pakenham sent his main force of 5,300 men, marching forward in close-order ranks, against Jackson's 4,500 troops, protected by breastworks, five miles outside the city. Jackson's men, many of whom were expert riflemen from Kentucky and Tennessee armed with their long rifles, put down an accurate, murderous fire that stopped two British frontal assaults. The British retreated, after suffering 2,036 killed and wounded, including the deaths of General Pakenham and two of his generals, while the Americans lost eight dead and 13 wounded. The American victory made Jackson a national hero and aided his later rise in politics that led to the presidency in the next decade. The battle became the dramatic highlight of two films, Cecil B. DeMille's *The Buccaneer* (1938) and a 1958 remake directed by Anthony Quinn. ■

Nicaraguan Civil War of 1925–1933.
General Emiliano Vargas and Adolfo Diaz seized political power in Nicaragua in a coup d'état on October 25, 1925, driving out a popularly elected government of combined conservatives and liberals. A revolt led by General Augusto Sandino broke out against the government, and his revolutionary forces seized U.S. property. American gunboats and troops helped restore order, allowing the national legislature to elect the conservative Diaz to the presidency.

However, former Vice President Juan Sacasa, who had been deposed by the coup, established a rival liberal government in which his military forces under General Jose Moncada, with Mexican military backing, battled government troops. Diaz, the American-recognized president who had been put into office by the national legislature, requested and received military assistance in 1927 from the U.S. Sandino joined in the guerrilla war against the combined forces of the Americans and the Diaz government.

U.S. envoy Henry L. Stimson, sent by President Calvin Coolidge, arranged a truce between the main Nicaraguan factions and arranged an election, under U.S. supervision, that saw the liberal Moncada elected in 1928. But Sandino refused to accept the results of the election and continued his attacks against U.S. Marines. America responded by sending planes to bomb guerrilla mountain bases.

Sandino fled to Mexico, vowing to keep fighting until the marines left the country. In 1933 U.S. troops withdrew, and the former guerrilla leader returned to Nicaragua after receiving a pledge of amnesty from the newly elected president, Juan Sacasa. Sandino was murdered in 1934 by government soldiers who had been angered by the amnesty he received.

The memory of Sandino as a populist fighter against foreign domination, particularly the U.S., has been invoked in the 1980s by the Sandinista government in Nicaragua that has been labeled as a veiled Communist dictatorship. The Sandinistas, since coming to power in 1979, have had recurring difficulties with American-backed conservative forces within the country.

A handful of American films were based on Nicaragua's civil strife during this period. Frank Capra's *Flight* (1929) stresses the role that the U.S. military, particularly its air power, played in Nicaragua without mentioning its name. The script alludes to the fictional adversary of that country's government and U.S. Marines, a thinly disguised Sandino, as a bandit rather than a nationalist resisting foreign intervention. Other action films based on America's incursion into Nicaragua during its civil war include *The Marines Are Coming* (1935) and *The Marines Fly High* (1940). Again, both films refer to the guerrillas as bandits. Finally, screen comedian Charley Chase, in a 1932 satirical comedy short titled "First in War," becomes entangled in a revolution in the fictitious country of Nicarania. ■

Nick Carter, Master Detective (1939).
See Detectives at War. ■

Night Fighters, The (1960), UA. Dir. Tay Garnett; Sc. Robert Wright Campbell; Cast includes: Robert Mitchum, Anne Heywood, Dan O'Herlihy, Cyril Cusack.

The outlawed Irish Republican Army's collaboration with the Nazis during World War

II serves as background for this drama of intrigue. Robert Mitchum portrays an Irishman who, persuaded by a close buddy, joins the underground I.R.A. in the belief that he can help rid Ireland of the British. He soon grows disillusioned with the rebel leader (Dan O'Herlihy) and informs on the group. Members of the I.R.A. capture him, but he is rescued and escapes to England. Mitchum's fiancee (Anne Heywood) voices her disapproval of his joining the rebel organization. Richard Harris plays Mitchum's friend. The film, photographed in Ireland, provides plenty of atmosphere. ■

Night People (1954). See Cold War. ■

Night Plane From Chungking (1943). See Sino-Japanese War. ■

Night Watch, The (1928), WB. *Dir.* Alexander Korda; *Sc.* Lajos Biro; *Cast includes:* Billie Dove, Paul Lukas, Donald Reed, Nicholas Soussanin, Anita Garvine.

A steamy drama set during World War I, the film is told in flashback beginning with the court-martial trial of a French captain accused of killing one of his officers. Paul Lukas portrays the captain of a warship who is on trial. His wife (Billie Dove) innocently stows away aboard the vessel in her former lover's cabin so that she can surprise her husband. Nicholas Soussanin, as an unscrupulous officer, discovers her and demands sexual favors from the stowaway, threatening that he will expose her to the captain. Her ex-lover (Donald Reed) kills Soussanin with the captain's gun to protect Dove's honor. Lukas is saved at the last moment by his wife's courtroom confession. The film, remade as *The Woman From Monte Carlo* in 1932, provides some action when the warship successfully engages the enemy in an exciting naval battle. ■

Nightingale, Florence. See *The White Angel* (1936). ■

1941 (1979), U. *Dir.* Steven Spielberg; *Sc.* Robert Zemeckis, Bob Gale; *Cast includes:* Dan Aykroyd, Ned Beatty, John Belushi, Lorraine Gary, Murray Hamilton, Christopher Lee.

A large-scale, chiefly unsuccessful comedy concerning the war scare that hit Los Angeles following the Japanese attack on Pearl Harbor, the film is overloaded with slapstick and physical comedy but short on plot and characterization. However, director Spielberg provides plenty of high-class special effects as he collapses factories, causes homes to plunge into the ocean and destroys Hollywood Boulevard. Dan Aykroyd portrays a serious-minded army sergeant. Robert Stack, as a confused general, watches Disney's *Dumbo* while anti-aircraft fire explodes above Los Angeles. Dianne Kay provides the romantic interest for Bobby DiCicco and Treat Williams.

Historically, the Los Angeles war hysteria incident occurred on February 26, 1942, not on December 13, 1941, as depicted in the film. ■

Nisei. See *Go For Broke!* (1951). ■

"No Dough, Boys" (1944). See War Humor. ■

No Drums, No Bugles (1971), Cin. *Dir.* Clyde Ware; *Sc.* Clyde Ware; *Cast includes:* Martin Sheen.

Martin Sheen portrays a deserter who does not believe in killing in this unusual Civil War drama. Living as a recluse in the hills, he hunts and fishes to survive, avoiding even taking the lives of creatures when unnecessary. He survives the entire war and, upon hearing that the conflict has ended, decides to journey home. "I did not kill," he says to himself in quiet triumph, but suddenly he slumps to the ground, seemingly unable to finish the trip. This is essentially a one-character film. Others, when they appear, do not speak. When other voices are heard, the characters are not seen. ■

No Escape. See *I Escaped From the Gestapo* (1943). ■

No Greater Glory (1934), Col. *Dir.* Frank Borzage; *Sc.* Jo Swerling; *Cast includes:* George Breakston, Jimmy Butler, Jackie Searl, Frankie Darro.

Based on Molnar's allegorical novel *The Paul Street Boys*, about the innocence and agony of boyhood, the film depicts a battle between younger students at a school and an older group of boys, most of whom are ruffians. The plot involves military strategy, courageous actions, spying and betrayal of military secrets as the two "armies" engage in hurling sand bags at each other. George Breakston plays a lad who is anxious to get into the fray. He is the only private in the Paul Street Boys army. He is also the only casualty; he succumbs to pneumonia. Jackie Searl plays a traitor in this unusual film. ∎

No Man Is an Island (1962), U. *Dir.* John Monk, Jr.; *Sc.* John Monk, Jr.; *Cast includes:* Jeffrey Hunter, Marshall Thompson, Barbara Perez, Ronald Remy.

A biographical drama of the exploits of World War II navy hero George R. Tweed, the film stars Jeffrey Hunter as the sailor who helped in the invasion of Guam. Following the attack on Pearl Harbor, Tweed remained on Guam during the Japanese occupation and from his hidden hilltop outpost signaled vital information about the enemy to the U.S. Navy. The film, made in the Philippines, includes adequate action sequences.

George Tweed (1903–1989), a U.S. Navy radio operator, eluded Japanese troops for more than two years when they overran Guam in 1941. Rather than surrender, he and several of his buddies hid in the jungle. The other men eventually were captured and killed. Tweed continued to supply the navy with information until the U.S. retook the island in 1944. He received the Legion of Merit. His exploits were described in the book *Robinson Crusoe U.S.N.*. Tweed died in a car accident on January 16, 1989. ∎

No Man's Land (1918). See Spy Films: the Silents. ∎

No Time for Sergeants (1958). See Service Comedy. ∎

None But the Brave (1965), WB. *Dir.* Frank Sinatra; *Sc.* John Twist, Katsuya Susaki; *Cast includes:* Frank Sinatra, Clint Walker, Tommy Sands, Brad Dexter.

The absurdity of war is underscored in this action drama set on an uncharted Pacific island during World War II. A plane carrying U.S. Marines crash-lands on a remote Pacific island inhabited by a small unit of stranded Japanese soldiers. Hostilities immediately break out until the Japanese lieutenant (Tatsuya Mihashi), as senior officer of his men, initiates a truce with the war-hardened pilot (Clint Walker), the senior officer of the downed marines. A cynical corpsman (Frank Sinatra) operates on a Japanese soldier and

saves his life. With the airship's radio out of commission and the small detachment of Japanese troops all but abandoned by their superiors, the leathernecks and their counterparts expect little chance of rescue. Resigning themselves to spending the remainder of the war on the island, they enter into an agreement with the Japanese to live in peace. But hostilities resume in full fury once the Americans' radio is repaired and a rescue ship appears. All the Japanese and most of the Americans are killed in a senseless final battle.

Many of the sequences are implausible as the film, Sinatra's first directorial effort, attempts to show similar characters on both sides. Each has its war-hungry advocates anxious for a scrap. Each has an understanding officer trying to save the lives of his men and avoid unnecessary killing. A young marine more interested in eating than in killing secretly exchanges cigarettes for fish with his Japanese counterpart. "Even hatred has its ritual," the Japanese officer muses following an early skirmish which claims several lives on both sides. "We and the enemy pause to bury our dead." The central irony of war is illustrated when the only source of drinking water is threatened by an impending hurricane. Both sides join together and work feverishly to build a barricade around the supply. Later, they return to killing one another. ∎

None Shall Escape (1944), Col. *Dir.* Andre de Toth; *Sc.* Lester Cole; *Cast includes:* Marsha Hunt, Alexander Knox, Henry Travers, Erik Rolf, Richard Crane.

A World War II drama about a Nazi war criminal brought to justice, this chiefly grim film, told in flashback, suggests that the results of World War I instilled a smoldering bitterness in many Germans and ultimately led to the rise of Nazism. An angry and resentful German soldier (Alexander Knox) returns from the Great War to his teaching career in a small town. His sweetheart (Marsha Hunt), unable to tolerate his vindictive outbursts, leaves him. Driven from the town after having sexually molested a female student, he rises in the ranks of the Nazi movement sweeping Germany. He is appointed party leader of the same town at the outbreak of World War II and indulges in a string of ruthless actions, including the killing of the local rabbi. This was director Andre de Toth's first major film.

A minor controversy arose decades later

between film critic Richard Schickel and screenwriter Lester Cole (who won an Oscar for this screenplay) concerning a line from the film. The former in a review in *Film Comment* (March–April 1981) of Victor Navasky's book *Naming Names*, about the House Committee on Un-American Activities and its investigation of Hollywood, alluded to a reference in the work that one of the Hollywood Ten admittedly plagiarized a quotation from the Spanish Civil War period. La Pasionara announced to the volunteers of the Lincoln Brigade: "It is better to die on your feet than live on your knees!" Cole borrowed this line for the above film, giving it to a rabbi who, along with fellow Jews, was being sent to a Nazi concentration camp and eventual extermination. Navasky mocked the quotation as sophomoric in the context of the film. Cole, in a written reply to Schickel's review, explained: "I stole it honorably; it was more eloquent than anything I could write, fit the moment perfectly and aroused the passive, broken Jews to a heroic moment of resistance." ∎

Normandy invasion (June 6, 1944). After several days of gale-force winds, driving rain and low clouds, the weather had suddenly turned clearer, though it remained windy and the seas choppy on the early morning of June 6, 1944. At 6:30 A.M., as darkness lifted, an armada of 5,000 ships began to disgorge the first waves of 154,000 Allied troops onto the beaches of Normandy, France. The long-expected invasion of Western Europe had begun. The startling panorama of innumerable Allied ships positioned off the coast is memorably depicted in *The Longest Day* (1962), perhaps the definitive film of the invasion.

The Germans, lulled by bad weather and a successful Allied plan of deception (Ultra), had been largely caught off guard. The greatest amphibious assault in history, by a combined force of Americans, British and Canadians, sought to penetrate Hitler's "Atlantic Wall," a string of in-depth fortifications facing the English channel. The date of the invasion had been dubbed "D-Day," and the entire undertaking was called "Operation Overlord."

The beginning of the invasion of Hitler's Fortress Europe had come even earlier that day when, at 15 minutes past midnight, special Allied assault teams of parachute and glider troops began dropping inland from the Normandy coastline to cut communications and create a diversion for Nazi defense forces under Generals von Rundstedt and Rommel. The Germans at first refused to attack the aerial assault troops in strength, correctly sensing a diversion. But, when von Rundstedt, at 4 A.M., decided to contain the air strike by bringing two Panzer units into battle, his orders were countermanded by his high command pending approval by Hitler, who was asleep. Again, *The Longest Day* vividly recounts these Allied thrusts.

Though fewer troops went ashore in Normandy on the first day of the invasion than the attack upon Sicily earlier in the war, the aggregate of personnel and equipment used in the assault dwarfed any previous waterborne attack. The armada was composed of 900 warships, ranging from battleships to patrol craft, and even included midget submarines. Allied air forces, numbering some 2,500 bombers and 7,000 fighters and fighter-bombers, dropped over 10,000 tons of explosives in 11,000 sorties to weaken Nazi defenses.

The main landings by American troops took place at Omaha and Utah beaches, near the Cherbourg Peninsula. The British and Canadians landed at three locations farther east at sites designated as Gold, Juno and Sword. The U.S. First Division, supported by four regimental combat teams, ran into the stiffest opposition of all at Omaha when it came against heavily fortified bluffs and sustained the heaviest losses of the landings. German artillery raked the landing craft and beach area, destroying much of the Allied armor and support equipment before it could get off the shoreline.

The Nazi high command delayed bringing armored units and reserves into Normandy. It had been tricked by false documents, double agents and other ruses into believing that the main landings would come at Calais, further north and east, at the shortest crossing point on the English Channel. The Allies further impeded German movement by coordinating guerrilla activities of the French resistance. As a result, the Allies were able to consolidate their grip at the invasion sites in several days of fighting. Hitler, incidentally, had intuitively suspected Normandy would be the main landing site, but he was not able to convince his generals to deploy their troops and defenses accordingly.

The fall of the port of Cherbourg, on June

27, led to an Allied breakout several days later that resulted in a drive that would carry to the German border in seven weeks. The Normandy invasion marked the beginning of the end of Hitler's domination of the European continent because he now had to split his forces to defend Germany caught in a "nutcracker," with the Russians advancing in the east and the Allies driving from the west.

Several films, ranging from dramas to satires, have been based on the invasion. *Breakthrough* (1950) depicts the story of one infantry company during the battle of Normandy. *The Desert Fox* (1951), a biography of Field Marshal Erwin Rommel, includes stock footage of the Normandy invasion. In *Screaming Eagles* (1956) a group of paratroopers is assigned to take and hold a strategic bridge during the invasion. In *36 Hours* (1964) a captured American officer is almost tricked by the Germans into revealing the actual invasion plans of the Allies. *The Americanization of Emily* (1964), a satirical black comedy, revolves around a demented American admiral who wants the first fighting man to be killed during the Normandy invasion to be a navy man. *Up From the Beach* (1965) involves an American infantry squad that moves inland in the wake of the invasion.

The most ambitious film about D-Day, however, is *The Longest Day* (1962), based on the book by Cornelius Ryan, who also wrote the screenplay. The sprawling semi-documentary, which boasts an impressive list of international directors and players, covers the landing from several perspectives, including that of the Germans. Other sequences describe the contributions of various Allied forces, including American paratroopers who are dropped behind enemy lines, British Commandos who are sent in by gliders to another area and French units who doggedly battle to occupy a key town.

Of the many documentaries about World War II, two stand out in their focus upon the Normandy invasion. "Beachhead to Berlin" (1944) depicts the role of the U.S. Coast Guard during the invasion of Normandy. *The True Glory* (1945) presents the story of D-Day, showing the build-up of men and supplies in England prior to the invasion, the difficulties of bringing supplies to the beaches, maintaining a beachhead and battling a stubborn, well-entrenched enemy. Breakthroughs finally occur and the vital port of Cherbourg is captured. ■

North of Shanghai (1939). See Sino-Japanese War. ■

North Star, The (1943), RKO. *Dir.* Lewis Milestone; *Sc.* Lillian Hellman; *Cast includes:* Anne Baxter, Dana Andrews, Walter Huston, Ann Harding, Jane Withers, Farley Granger.

The Nazi invasion of Russia provokes the resistance of a group of humble and noble villagers in this World War II drama. As the people of a happy village concentrate on their harvest while the young ones think of love, German planes attack, killing dozens of their neighbors. Nazi atrocities heaped upon a once-peaceful village, including using local children's blood for wounded German solders, lead to the uprising of its citizens. Arms are smuggled through the enemy lines to a band of determined mounted guerrillas who decide to return and liberate their village. A fierce and well-directed cavalry attack catches the German occupiers by surprise. Weapons are distributed to the villagers who join the guerrillas in annihilating the enemy. Anne Baxter and Farley Granger portray two high school students in love and who are soon caught up in the events of war. Dana Andrews, as Granger's older brother and a bombardier, goes to his death by smashing his crippled plane into German tanks. Walter Huston portrays the local village physician who ultimately avenges his neighbors' deaths. Erich von Stroheim, as a German officer-surgeon, justifies using the children's blood as the way of the "new order." "To me you are the real filth," Huston exclaims before shooting Stroheim. "Men who do the work of Fascists and pretend to themselves they are better than those for whom they work."

The film develops slowly as the villagers frolic at harvest time and the young dream of love. The people sing folk songs and dance. Old men tease the women. Children help with village chores. The local principal addresses the students on the last day of school, reminding them of their obligations to their country. This idyllic community is thus set up for despoiling by the Nazi invaders.

Some lines, as in other propaganda films of this genre, seem stilted and didactic. "The trouble in the world," Andrews announces casually in an obvious swipe at the Germans, "comes from people who don't know what they are and pretend to be something they're not." Later, when some farmers are killed by a German airplane, a local village elder (Walter Brennan) tries to lead the children away from the mangled bodies. "The face of war is ugly and not for the young," he explains. "We're not young anymore," Baxter replies. Anne Baxter gets to speak the final lines. "Wars don't leave people as they were," she pronounces while driving a wagon out of her burning village. "All people will learn that—and come to see that wars do not have to be. We'll make this the last war. We'll make a free world for all men. The earth belongs to us—the people—if we fight for it. And we will fight for it."

In her efforts to glorify the members of the resistance and develop her themes of patriotism and retribution, Lillian Hellman ended up with an unusually pro-Soviet screenplay. Except for scattered reviews which condemned the pro-Russian propaganda elements, this approach was acceptable and expected for its time. After the war, however, the film was singled out as a piece of pro-Communist propaganda. Many of these didactic and propaganda scenes ultimately were cut from the film for the television version which was retitled *Armored Attack*. The new version, which includes additional material and a commentator who explains that the Communists have simply replaced the Nazis, has been turned into an anti-Soviet propaganda film.

Hellman's two stage plays with World War II as background were adapted to the screen. *Watch on the Rhine* (1943) concerns a resistance leader who sacrifices his life to fight Fascism, and *The Searching Wind* (1946) deals with an uncaring family of diplomats and their crippled veteran son. ∎

Northern Pursuit (1943), WB. *Dir.* Raoul Walsh; *Sc.* Frank Gruber, Alvah Bessie; *Cast includes:* Errol Flynn, Julie Bishop, Helmut Dantine, John Ridgely, Gene Lockhart.

A Nazi submarine deposits several spies on the shores of northern Canada in this World War II drama. Helmut Dantine, as the leading enemy agent, is captured by two members of the Royal Canadian Mounted Police (Errol Flynn and John Ridgely) but manages to escape from a prisoner-of-war camp. He is determined to succeed in his original mission of sabotage.

Flynn quits the force and poses as a Nazi sympathizer in an attempt to prevent the saboteur and his underlings from accomplishing their purpose. Julie Bishop, who provides the romantic interest for Flynn, is taken hostage by the spies who distrust the ex-Mountie. After Flynn leads the agents to their objective—an abandoned mine containing crates of airplane parts—Dantine boastfully reveals his target: "One of the most vital waterways connecting the U.S. and Canada. A main artery of all war supplies going to England. Eight bombs placed with scientific precision will destroy the canal and the locks and block shipping for months. I will drop those bombs with precision."

The Germans spend the next few days assembling the bomber. Each night they lock Flynn in a room, intending to kill him before they leave. But Flynn foils their plan at the last moment by boarding the plane disguised as a crew member whom he has overpowered only moments earlier. He shoots the other Germans and bails out before the plane crashes harmlessly. Gene Lockhart enacts a Nazi agent in this action drama that makes ample use of the wintry wastelands of Canada's northwest. ∎

Northwest Africa, Allied invasion of.

Also known as Operation Torch (November 8, 1842), the invasion produced the first major setback in the West for the Axis. As American forces from the largest invasion armada in American history up to that time swarmed ashore at four locations in Northwest Africa, the voice of Free French military commander Charles deGaulle in London came over the airwaves to his countrymen in France's northwest African territories: "French commanders, soldiers, sailors, airmen, officials, colonists; rise every one of you. Help our Allies . . . The great moment has come." Operation Torch, under the command of General Eisenhower, represented the beginning of American ground participation in the war against the Axis in the West. American troops, supported by British naval and air units, landed near Dakar, Casablanca, Algiers and Oran.

Though the landings took place in French-controlled territory, they were really designed to hurt the Axis in a number of ways. Allied leaders feared that the enemy might be planning, through pressure on the Nazi-controlled puppet French Vichy government, to increase their military presence in North Africa beyond the Italian colony of Libya.

One of the objectives of the invasion was to forestall such a move.

The Allies saw additional strategic gains in a successful North African operation. At the time of the landings, Rommel's badly weakened Africa Corps was already retreating out of Egypt into Libya before General Montgomery's pursuing British Eighth Army. The invasion created a pincers move against Axis forces caught in the middle. Sweeping the enemy completely out of North Africa would produce several other beneficial results. It would supply a much-needed boost for Allied morale by marking the first time the Axis suffered defeat and lost territory in the West. Loss of their North African bases would greatly reduce Axis power in the Mediterranean and enable the western Allies to more easily send materiel to the Soviet Union using the Mediterranean-Suez route. Furthermore, Allied control of North Africa could then open up southern Europe to the possibility of invasion, especially against Italy whose people were already showing a reluctance to fight for Mussolini and Hitler.

However, Allied political and military leaders were highly concerned that the French might resist vigorously the intrusion into their colonies, and, in doing so become reluctant military partners with their Nazi conquerors. Allied authorities, such as American President Franklin D. Roosevelt, made great efforts to convince the French that the invasion was the first stage toward their liberation from Nazi control and not a conquest of French territory. Roosevelt and DeGaulle broadcast directly to the French, and leaflets were dropped by air in the invasion sectors, asking French troops not to resist. Most of the landings were unopposed except for brief but hard fighting at the port of Casablanca. Allied forces were in firm command of all the landing sites by the second day.

The invasion was mentioned early in the film *Patton* (1970), which carried scenes dealing with General Patton's role in North Africa. He commanded the western task force of Operation Torch that landed on the Moroccan coast of West Africa. The American First Division, a participant in the Oran, Algiers landing, was the subject of *The Big Red One* (1980). Its director, Samuel Fuller, served as a member of that division, and the movie is filled with his personal remembrances of the war in North Africa and later in Europe. At least a dozen films dealt with the subsequent fighting in North Africa. ∎

Northwest Passage (1940), MGM. *Dir.* King Vidor; *Sc.* Laurence Stallings, Talbot Jennings; *Cast includes:* Spencer Tracy, Robert Young, Walter Brennan, Ruth Hussey, Nat Pendleton, Louis Hector, Robert Barrat, Donald McBride.

Based on the first half of Kenneth Roberts' novel, the film tells the story of a group of early American settlers of the upper New York region who set out on an expedition to wipe out a hostile Indian village. Spencer Tracy plays Major Robert Rogers, the leader of 160 trained fighters, known as Rogers' Rangers, hardened settlers who have lost neighbors and loved ones to the savage raids of the Abenaki tribe. Accompanying the men is a young Harvard artist (Robert Young) who goes along to sketch the Indians. The stalwart group tramp through virgin forests, wade through swamps and ford rushing rivers to carry out their punitive mission.

The climactic attack is filled with suspense and excitement as the Rangers reach a hill overlooking the enemy village. They plan their strategy, wait quietly through the long night and swoop down at daybreak in a surprise attack. The aftermath is almost as eventful as the build-up to the assault. The embattled party, including the wounded and white female prisoners they have freed, must march to an English stockade where they are to receive food and supplies. Suffering from hunger, the rangers split up into four groups, some of which are ambushed and tortured to death. When the remnants of the troops, fifty in all, arrive at the fort, they find it abandoned. The film includes some stark moments, such as the one in which a half-crazed ranger carries a mysterious sack, boasting that he'll never go hungry. The bundle turns out to contain the head of an Indian. Ultimately, British reinforcements arrive.

The film ends with Tracy's blatantly anachronistic speech to his troops after they have had several weeks of rest. Determined to find his northwest passage, he announces: "We're taking a walk first for our appetites—about a thousand miles to a little fort called Detroit. Why, you rangers haven't seen any Indians yet. You're going to see the Plains Indians. You're going to see the red men of the shining mountain, and those men along the mighty River Oregon—red men that white men have never seen before. Because we're going to end up by that great western ocean itself. You're going to find a way across this continent—a Northwest passage. You'll see hardwood groves like cathedrals, corn stalks as tall as elms, rivers packed with salmon trout and grass so high the cows stand knee deep in it and give nothing but cream.''

The film does not cover the entire novel, whose title suggests its premise—that of finding a Northwest Passage through Canada. Contemporary film critics assumed—incorrectly as it turned out—that a sequel, encompassing the second half of Roberts' book, would be forthcoming. The film image of Major Rogers differs sharply from that of real life. His many brushes with the law and his lack of political convictions made him something less than the exemplary figure portrayed on screen by Tracy.

Residing in what is now Maine, Vermont and New Hampshire, the Abenaki (Abnaki) Indians, usually with French support, conducted a series of three wars between 1675–1725 against the English colonists. The Abenaki joined the Wampanoags under King Philip (King Philip's War 1675–1676) in an attempt to drive back the New England settlers in the First Abenaki War (1675–1678). The Abenaki, in three years of raids on the Maine frontier, forced the English colonists to give up some settlements. In a peace treaty signed in 1678, the colonists agreed to pay an annual tribute to the tribe.

The French, in their struggle against Britain for world colonial supremacy during much of the 1700s, supported the Abenaki in the Second Abenaki War (1702–1712) that was part of the North American phase of the conflict. Indian and French forces conducted raids along Maine's northern frontier that resulted in the killing of 300 English settlers early in the war. The Abenaki continued to raid English settlements for ten years and ceased doing so only when the tribe lost French support as a result of the Treaty of Utrecht that brought a temporary peace between Britain and France.

The Abenaki, encouraged by a French Jesuit missionary, Sebastien Rasles, to resist further encroachment by whites, launched raids that initiated the Third Abenaki War (1722–1725). The Massachusetts colonial government formally declared war on the Indians and several bloody battles took place. The missionary, Rasles, was slain during one of the battles in 1724. A peace conference in Boston the following year ended the hostilities. The tribe's bloody raids upon early English settlements were referred to in the film. See Rogers' Rangers. ■

Notorious (1946), RKO. *Dir.* Alfred Hitchcock; *Sc.* Ben Hecht; *Cast includes:* Cary Grant, Ingrid Bergman, Claude Rains, Louis Calhern.

The daughter (Ingrid Bergman) of a convicted Nazi spy assists U.S. Intelligence to expose a network of Nazis operating in post-World War II Brazil in this suspenseful spy drama. Bergman, who falls in love with her Intelligence agent contact (Cary Grant), at first hesitates to go through with her assignment because of her feelings for him. But she accepts when he leaves the decision up to her. She establishes a relationship with one of the leaders of Brazil's Nazi spy ring (Claude Rains). When he grows suspicious of her meeting with Grant, he tests her love by proposing marriage. Once again she waits for Grant to comment on the proposal, but when he remains silent she decides to go through with the marriage. Bergman, who never hears Grant protecting her honor and reputation, thinks he is uncaring. However, before she enters the American embassy with her story about the proposal, Grant has an altercation with one of the officials who refers to her as a "woman of that sort." "She may be risking her life," Grant reminds the man, "but when it comes to being a lady, she doesn't hold a candle to your wife, sir, sitting in Washington playing bridge with three other ladies of honor and virtue." The focus of the investigation concerns uranium ore deposits. Hitchcock expertly handles the suspense elements.

The film has been singled out for several of its distinct attributes. Its sensual love scenes are some of the strongest ever shown on the commercial screen up to that time. The direction and cinematography, especially the now-famous long crane shot from the top of a staircase to the close-up of a significant key in Bergman's palm, have retained their power to grip an audience. Perhaps most important is the film's ambiguous morality. Grant, as the hero, propels Bergman into the arms of the villain and then rejects her. To some degree, the audience feels more compassion for Rains, whose greater love for Bergman is requited only with betrayal. ■

Now We're in the Air (1927). See *Behind the Front* (1926). ∎

Nun and the Sergeant, The (1962), UA. Dir. Peter Adreon; Sc. Don Cerveris; Cast includes: Robert Webber, Anna Sten, Leo Gordon, Hari Rhodes.

A hard-bitten marine sergeant assembles a motley assortment of American prisoners to assist him on a perilous demolition assignment in this low-budget action drama set during the Korean War. At first the fugitives from the brig plan to escape, but each is regenerated as they help a nun who joins them along the way and a group of native schoolgirls. They manage to carry out their original mission—the blowing up of a fuel dump—after a drunken brawl and a near rape of one of the students. Robert Webber portrays the sergeant, and Anna Sten plays the nun in this routine tale. ∎

Nun's Story, The (1959), WB. Dir. Fred Zinnemann; Sc. Robert Anderson; Cast includes: Audrey Hepburn, Peter Finch, Dame Edith Evans, Dean Jagger.

A young Belgian nun (Audrey Hepburn) faces personal moral conflicts in this drama set before and during World War II. She takes her final vows following some problems, leading her Mother Superior to believe that Hepburn is not able to fully control her personal feelings. After serving in the Congo, she is reassigned to Belgium when war erupts. Although her superiors tell her to remain neutral, she joins the resistance movement after her father (Dean Jagger) is killed by the Germans. She leaves the Church with the consent of her superiors who realize that she can never wholly devote herself to the principles of the order. Peter Finch, as an agnostic doctor whom Hepburn assists during her stay in the Congo, influences her to re-evaluate her role as a nun. Peggy Ashcroft portrays Mother Superior. ∎

Nuremberg Trials (1945–1946). Organized by U.S. authorities and conducted under joint Allied control following World War II, the International Military Tribunal sought to bring to justice the numerous Nazi war criminals. The initial trial, based on the 1945 findings of jurists of the four Allied powers and endorsed by 23 nations, was unique in judicial history. The major charges against the defendants included foreign aggression; crimes against peace; war crimes against civilians and prisoners of war; and crimes against humanity, including murder, enslavement, extermination and persecution.

Hermann Goring, Rudolf Hess, Joachim von Ribbentrop, Alfred Rosenberg, Hans Frank, Julius Streicher and Franz von Papen were some of the defendants. Martin Bormann was tried *in absentia*. Robert Ley committed suicide before his trial commenced. Adolf Hitler, Heinrich Himmler and other major leaders were dead. Several, including Adolf Eichmann, fled the country or went into hiding. Following this major trial, others were conducted by the Allies and lasted until 1948. The results of the trials were mixed. Some controversy arose about their legality, chiefly concerning the issues of applying laws retroactively and having the accusers act as judges. On the other hand, the enormity of Nazi Germany's crimes was exposed before the entire world and a precedent was set for the future—international law would prevail and the international community would hold those responsible for similar crimes.

American films of the Nuremberg Trials vary from informative documentaries to weak melodramas. *Nurnberg* (1946), a documentary sponsored by the American Film Section and supervised by Pare Lorentz, presents a composed, dispassionate report of the trial, including German footage taken at the extermination camps. *The Executioners* (1961), another documentary, traces the careers of the principal defendants and includes newsreel footage of the horrors of the infamous death camps. In *The Stranger* (1946), Orson Welles' suspenseful and visually appealing drama, Welles portrays an escaped Nazi war criminal who is wanted by the Allied War Crimes Commission. *Rogues' Regiment* (1948), an earnest but more routine drama, concerns an American army officer (Dick Powell) assigned to hunt down a ruthless Nazi war criminal who has escaped justice at the Nuremberg trials and is hiding under another identity in the Foreign Legion. *Verboten!* (1959), shot in Germany, deals with a postwar Hitler youth gang. One of the vandals, exposed to films of the Nuremberg War Trials and scenes of the Nazi atrocities at the death camps, utters: "I didn't know." Stanley Kramer's *Judgment at Nuremberg* (1961), the most intelligent drama about the trials, focuses on the issues of the responsibility and

Anna Neagle, as the heroic English nurse of the title, is charged with war crimes by German officer George Sanders in the World War I biographical drama *Nurse Edith Cavell* (1939).

accountability of those who administer the laws of a state. ■

Nurse Edith Cavell (1939), RKO. *Dir.* Herbert Wilcox; *Sc.* Michael Hogan; *Cast includes:* Anna Neagle, Edna May Oliver, George Sanders, May Robson, ZaSu Pitts, H. B. Warner.

An antiwar drama that appeared too late (war was declared only days after its opening in New York), the film highlights the historical events in the remarkable life of the title character. Anna Neagle plays Edith Cavell, whose noble sacrifices include giving succor to German as well as Allied soldiers during World War I. Remaining in German-occupied Belgium, she aids prisoners of war to escape across the border. She is finally captured by the enemy and executed.

The film attacks the German military hierarchy rather than the rank-and-file occupation troops. "Leniency will only be mistaken for weakness," the German officer in charge of the Belgian city's occupation states to his subordinates as he calls for the death of the English nurse. The American ambassador's secretary pleads with the officer for Cavell's life, describing her sentence as a "crime against humanity." But the German refuses to revoke the decision. The American concludes that the defendant is a victim of the German war machine. In contrast, a German soldier selected as part of the firing squad refuses to carry out the assignment and is arrested for disobeying orders. A German officer of medium rank secretly sends a note to the American embassy notifying the ambassador that Cavell has been sentenced to death.

English director Herbert Wilcox had already made a silent version in 1928 of Nurse Cavell's war experiences, a film that also stressed antiwar sentiments. This later adaptation did not meet with great box-office success, but it contributed to RKO's image as a studio capable of turning out prestigious features. An earlier American silent version of her life was produced in 1918 titled *The Woman the Germans Shot*. ■

"Nursing a Viper" (1909), Biograph. *Dir.* D.W. Griffith; *Sc.* Frank Woods, D.W. Griffith; *Cast includes:* Arthur Johnson, Florence Lawrence, Marion Leonard, Billy Quirk.

A short silent drama set during the French Revolution, the film tells the story of a Royalist, pursued by a Republican mob, who seeks shelter at his friend's house. His friend, a former Royalist, hides the hunted man from the bloodthirsty horde. Once he is safe, the fugitive makes advances toward his friend's wife (Florence Lawrence). The husband rescues his wife just in time and turns the Royalist over to the mob. Director Griffith was later to make another, more complex, epic film about the French Revolution, titled *Orphans of the Storm* (1922). ■

O

O.S.S. See Office of Strategic Services. ■

O.S.S. (1946), Par. *Dir.* Irving Pichel; *Sc.* Richard Maibaum; *Cast includes:* Alan Ladd, Geraldine Fitzgerald, Patric Knowles, Richard Benedict.

Four agents of the American Office of Strategic Services are sent into Nazi-occupied France to blow up an otherwise inaccessible railway tunnel in this World War II spy drama. Geraldine Fitzgerald, as the female member of the team, is treated with hostility by one of the agents (Alan Ladd). The leader of the operation is captured by the Gestapo, and Ladd assumes command. When Fitzgerald proves her value to the mission, Ladd not only changes his attitude but falls in love with her. After they accomplish their objective, they are asked to remain in France to gather information for the upcoming Allied invasion. Following this, Fitzgerald is captured by the Gestapo as she and Ladd are about to make their escape. Ladd regretfully is forced to abandon her so that the vital information can be turned over to Allied headquarters. Although the film includes the typical heroics of a Ladd drama of this period—parachute drops behind enemy lines, derring-do escapes and plenty of action—the final capture of Fitzgerald adds a note of realism to the drama. ■

O.W.I. See Office of War Information. ■

"Oath and the Man, The" (1910), Biograph. *Dir.* D.W. Griffith; *Sc.* Stanner Taylor; *Cast includes:* Henry B. Walthall, Lottie Pickford, Florence Barker, W.C. Miller.

A short silent film about the French Revolution, the story tells of a principled leader of a band of revolutionists who guides his followers based on the teachings of Christianity. Veteran actor Henry B. Walthall portrays the strong-willed leader.

During his tenure with the Biograph studio, director Griffith turned out more than 200 one- and two-reel dramas and light films, several of which had military backgrounds, particularly of the Civil War. He had made another short film about the Revolution two years earlier, "Nursing a Viper." But *Orphans of the Storm* (1922) remains his best and most famous work about the French Revolution. ■

Objective Burma (1945), WB. *Dir.* Raoul Walsh; *Sc.* Ranald MacDougall, Lester Cole; *Cast includes:* Errol Flynn, William Prince, James Brown, George Tobias, Henry Hull.

American paratroopers are dropped into the Burmese jungle to destroy a Japanese radar station in this realistic World War II action drama. The well-trained soldiers, led by a tight-lipped captain (Errol Flynn), must first traverse the difficult jungle. They locate their target and destroy it. When they reach their rendezvous for pickup, they are ambushed by enemy soldiers and must move out to a second prearranged clearing. Meanwhile, they are relentlessly pursued by the Japanese. A middle-aged journalist (Henry Hull) accompanies the raiders so that he can get firsthand a realistic combat story. The film avoids much of the exaggerated heroics and flag-waving dialogue that marred other war movies of the period. The battle scenes are gritty and plausible as the outnumbered and beleaguered paratroopers fight their way out of the unfriendly terrain.

The film takes place at a time when Japan controlled Burma after their successful early invasions in the Pacific. Special forces units, such as Merrill's Marauders and Wingate's

Raiders, helped to pave the way for the Allies in their drive to regain these territories. The film met stiff resistance in Britain, whose critics objected to the major role the script attributed to U.S. forces while omitting that of the British. It was pulled from exhibition after only one week. It was not until 1952 that the feature was re-released in that country. ■

Off Limits (1953). See Service Comedy. ■

Off Limits (1988), TCF. *Dir.* Christopher Crowe; *Sc.* Christopher Crowe, Jack Thibeau; *Cast includes:* Willem Dafoe, Gregory Hines, Fred Ward, Amanda Pays, Scott Glenn.

Willem Dafoe and Gregory Hines portray plainclothes military cops hunting for an insane killer of several prostitutes in Saigon in this detective drama set during the Vietnam War. Hampered by reluctant Saigonese police officials, murdered witnesses and a sergeant (Fred Ward) of the army's Criminal Investigation Detachment who tries to cover for a suspected military officer, the two sleuths nevertheless pursue the case to its conclusion, each from a sense of conviction.

The film is rich in irony and atmosphere. It presents its ironic overtones by paralleling the story of the senseless killings of obscure hookers against the backdrop of the tragic war with its anile waste of human life. An unbalanced colonel (Scott Glenn) throws uncooperative Vietnamese captives to their deaths from a helicopter as Dafoe and Hines question him about the murders of the prostitutes. The film, with its atmosphere of the sleazy red-light section of the city and its array of low-life characters, is reminiscent of the post-World War II *film-noir* dramas. ■

Office of Strategic Services (O.S.S.). The U.S., upon entry into World War II, lacked an effective international secret service agency. President Franklin D. Roosevelt created the O.S.S. on July 13, 1942, modeled upon the British secret service known as the Special Operations Executive or S.O.E. Roosevelt appointed his friend and confidant, Col. William "Wild Bill" Donovan, who had studied the operations of the S.O.E., as its director. Intelligence operations within the U.S. and in Latin America were to remain the province of the F.B.I.

The O.S.S., because of its unorthodox methods of operation and personnel, encountered resistance from a good number of high-ranking military leaders, including General Douglas MacArthur, who refused to allow it to operate in his theatre of war in the Pacific. Colonel Benjamin Dickson of the First Army fighting in Europe, banned the O.S.S. from his area of operations. William Casey, in his history of the O.S.S. titled *The Secret War Against Hitler*, points out that spies were necessary in the region of the Ardennes since German forces maintained radio silence. Colonel Dickson's belligerence put the Allied forces at a disadvantage when Hitler suddenly unleashed his all-out offensive in the winter of 1944–1945. On the other hand, relations with some of General Eisenhower's key officers were slightly better. They welcomed O.S.S. operations behind German lines. Stewart Alsop and Thomas Braden, who later became well-known columnists, were two such members of the O.S.S. who took part in these covert and perilous activities.

O.S.S. functions fell into three areas—propaganda, the gathering and analyzing of information in areas where American forces may become involved, and secret intelligence. The last category received the major amount of glamorized publicity, particularly in such World War II dramas as O.S.S., starring Alan Ladd as a representative agent operating in France, and *13 Rue Madeleine*, starring James Cagney who also was assigned to France as an O.S.S. agent. Both films were released in 1946. The O.S.S. infiltrated operatives into enemy territory to promote sabotage, organize guerrilla resistance and conduct campaigns against enemy forces. All three of these operations were depicted in the two films. Some of its biggest successes included aiding in the capture of Corsica, coordinating guerrilla attacks in Burma that resulted in 15,000 Japanese casualties (killed and wounded) and a massive infiltration of agents into the lowlands and France to coordinate guerrilla groups in preparation for the invasion of western Europe.

Allen Dulles, who later became head of the Central Intelligence Agency, was in charge of one of the most successful bureaus of the O.S.S., located in Bern, in neutral Switzerland. Dulles and his agents penetrated Germany's Gestapo (secret police), Foreign Office and military. Through his contacts, Dulles effected the surrender of all German troops in Italy a week before the end of the war in Europe. The O.S.S. went out of existence after the war. An occasional postwar drama referred either to the work of the O.S.S. or focused on a particular agent. In *Captain Carey, U.S.A.* (1950), for example, Alan Ladd portrays a former O.S.S. agent who returns to Italy after World War II to unmask a traitor responsible for several deaths during the conflict. See also William J. "Wild Bill" Donovan. ■

Office of War Information (O.W.I.) Responsible for directing propaganda and the dissemination of official information, the O.W.I. came into being on June 13, 1942, by authorization of President Roosevelt. A popular newscaster, Elmer Davis, was in charge of the department. Assisting him were Milton S. Eisenhower and writers Robert E. Sherwood and Leo Rosten. One of its branches included the production of documentary films which were distributed to the armed forces and commercial theaters. Considered one of the more effective government agencies, it was disbanded after the war. See Propaganda Films: World War II. ■

Okinawa (1952), Col. *Dir.* Leigh Jackson; *Sc.* Jameson Brewer, Leonard Stern, Arthur Ross; *Cast includes:* Pat O'Brien, Cameron Mitchell, Richard Denning, Rhys Williams.

This low-budget World War II drama focuses on the exploits of one ship, a destroyer of the U.S. Fifth Fleet, during the battle of Okinawa. Set in 1945, the plot stresses the significant role of the navy before and during an invasion. Pat O'Brien portrays the familiar no-nonsense captain. Richard Denning plays his lieutenant, and Cameron Mitchell is in charge of the men. The crew, hailing from different walks of life, is similar to that of many other typical war films.

Most of the battle sequences have been lifted from newsreel footage, including Japanese newsreels showing the ceremonial rites of kamikaze pilots prior to their suicidal attacks. Included are sequences dealing with the deadly kamikaze attacks by the Japanese while the fleet lays down a barrage cover for the invasion of the island. Incidents are routine aboard the ship as the film unfolds its weak plot. ■

Old Ironsides (1926), Par. *Dir.* James Cruze; *Sc.* Harry and Walter Woods; *Cast includes:* Charles Farrell, Esther Ralston, Wallace Beery, George Bancroft, Johnny Walker.

The story of the *Constitution*, the fighting ship that helped to make the American navy a viable sea force, is embellished with a slight love plot in this sea drama that highlights events in the Tripolitan War. A farmboy (Charles Farrell) on his way to join his country's navy and another sailor are shanghaied aboard a vessel. The daughter (Esther Ralston) of the barque's owner, who is also aboard, falls in love with Farrell. The vessel is captured by pirates and those aboard are brought to Tripoli and sold as slaves. Four Americans, including Farrell, Wallace Beery and George Bancroft, make their escape in a small boat and are picked up by the *Constitution*.

The vessel then heads for the coast of Tripoli where she blasts the forts, sinks an enemy frigate and captures a key fort where the victors raise the American flag on foreign soil for the first time. Besides these battle scenes, the film includes Decatur's bold assault on and sinking of the *Philadelphia*, a U.S. ship which the pirates had captured and intend to use against the *Constitution*. There are also hand-to-hand fights on the decks of the ships. During one of the sea battles a master gunner (George Bancroft) sees an enemy cannonball bounce off the sides of the *Constitution* and calls her "Old Ironsides." The film portrays several historical figures, such as Stephen Decatur and Thomas Jefferson, and dramatizes the "Millions for Defense" speech in Philadelphia. See also U.S.S. *Constitution*. ■

Omdurman, Battle of (September 2, 1898). Britain reconquered the Sudan during the Sudanese War of 1896–99 as a result of a combined Anglo-Egyptian invasion under General Horatio Kitchener that decisively defeated a major Sudanese force at the Battle of Omdurman, just outside Khartoum. The British and British-influenced Egyptian government had recently lost control of the area in the Sudanese War of 1881–85 when native forces under a religious mystic called "The Mahdi," liberated the country from foreign domination.

Following several defeats in earlier engagements in the war of 1896–99, a Sudanese army of Mahdists and dervishes, totaling 40,000 men, under Khalifa Abdullah, attacked Kitchener's invading force of 26,000 at Omdurman on the Nile River. The British used machine guns and cavalry to beat back Khalifa, who retreated to Kordofan, where his forces held out for a year. Khalifa was killed in battle in 1899 and the Sudanese revolt collapsed. Kitchener's victory, which made him a national hero in Britain, avenged the defeat and death of British General Charles "Chinese" Gordon at Khartoum in 1885. As a result of Kitchener's victory, Sudan was placed under an Anglo-Egyptian government and remained a British protectorate until 1956.

Few American films used this famous battle as background. Based on A.E.W. Mason's novel, *Four Feathers* (1915) and the 1929 remake (both silent, the latter with sound effects) more or less adhered to their original source and highlighted the battle. However, the 1939 British screen adaptation of the novel remains the definitive re-enactment of the events at Omdurman. ■

On Dangerous Ground (1917). See Propaganda Films: World War I. ■

On the Beach (1959), UA. *Dir.* Stanley Kramer; *Sc.* John Paxton, James Lee Barrett; *Cast includes:* Gregory Peck, Ava Gardner, Fred Astaire, Anthony Perkins, Donna Anderson.

A cautionary tale describing the effects of nuclear war, the film traces the last days of a handful of survivors in a dying world. Following an atomic conflict, the only survivors are those living in Australia. A submarine captain (Gregory Peck) and his crew, the sole remnants of the U.S. Navy, join the Australians. Both groups are doomed, for a deadly cloud of radiation from the northern hemisphere is expected to reach them in a few months. Suicidal car races, religious gatherings and lines for pills to make the end less painful mark the end of the human race. The final ironic scene shows a gray, chilling shot of a lifeless street. The camera closes in on a banner which reads: "There is still time, brother."

Ava Gardner portrays a sad and luckless woman, a heavy drinker who falls in love with the captain who has lost his wife and son in the war. Fred Astaire, as Julian Osborn, a brilliant scientist, engages in auto-racing and drinking to help him forget that he took part in building the terrible weapons responsible for the debacle. Anthony Perkins plays an Australian naval lieutenant married to Donna Anderson.

Osborn the scientist speaks with the conscience of the human race. "The war started," he explains, "when people accepted the idiotic principle that peace can be maintained by arranging to defend themselves with weapons they couldn't possibly use without committing suicide." Science and the military are not the only forces to come under attack. The public, according to the film, was also partially to blame for its complacency. "It's unfair because I didn't do anything," Gardner complains ironically to Peck. "Nobody I know did anything." Later, someone muses: "Who would believe that human beings would be stupid enough to blow themselves off the face of the earth." The film is based on the novel by Nevil Shute. ■

On the Double (1961). See Spy Comedies. ■

Once Upon a Honeymoon (1942), RKO. *Dir.* Leo McCarey; *Sc.* Sheridan Gibney; *Cast includes:* Ginger Rogers, Cary Grant, Walter Slezak, Albert Dekker.

A World War II comedy drama, the film is an odd combination of events, blending the devastation of Czechoslovakia, Poland and France with the frivolous desires of a young woman looking for a titled husband. Ginger Rogers portrays an American dancer and husband-hunter. Cary Grant plays an American reporter with whom she ends up. But before this happy conclusion comes about, the misguided Rogers marries nobleman Walter Slezak, a Nazi agent. Grant, who knows the truth about the bridegroom, hounds the couple on their honeymoon through war-torn Europe, slowly developing a relationship with Rogers. Albert Dekker, as an amoral double agent, is living in France while spying for both the U.S. and Germany. "No income tax!" he confides proudly to Rogers regarding his chief motivation.

Several critics, who seemed more aware than those who produced this inane work of the plight of European countries being overrun by Nazi Germany, singled out the film as tasteless and unfunny. This is particularly noticeable in a Nazi concentration camp sequence involving Rogers and Grant. ■

100 Rifles (1969), TCF. *Dir.* Tom Gries; *Sc.* Clair Huffaker, Tom Gries; *Cast includes:* Jim Brown, Raquel Welch, Burt Reynolds, Fernando Lamas.

This routine action drama concerns the Yaqui uprising of 1912 against Mexico. Jim

Brown portrays an Arizona marshal who pursues a bank robber into Mexico. The dashing outlaw (Burt Reynolds) is part-Yaqui and plans to use the stolen money to buy rifles for his tribe who is suffering under the oppressive Mexican government. Raquel Welch, who provides the romantic interest, leads the Yaqui tribe in revolt. Brown temporarily joins forces with the Indians and, at the end of the film, returns to Arizona alone. The film includes plenty of battle sequences between the Yaquis and the Mexican soldiers.

Several reviewers criticized the scenes involving the romantic encounters between Brown, a black actor, and Welch, with at least one critic (from *Variety*) labeling the embracing and kissing as "tasteless." The film was hardly an interracial landmark but may have been considered shocking because of its western roots, a genre which rarely breaks new social ground.

The Yaqui Indians, located in Mexico's Sonora region, had a long history of resistance. They fought against the Spanish conquerors who sought to subjugate the tribe. Later, they carried out guerrilla warfare against Mexican troops until 1918. ■

One Inch From Victory (1944), Scoop Productions. *Sc.* Quentin Reynolds.

The battle of Russia is the chief subject of this World War II documentary composed mainly of captured Nazi newsreels. The film explains the German plan to overrun the Soviet Union in just a few weeks by simultaneously attacking Leningrad, Moscow and Stalingrad. Quentin Reynolds, a foreign correspondent who also wrote the commentary, narrates the events leading up to Hitler's decision to invade Russia, including the Nazi successes in Poland, Czechoslovakia, Norway, Belgium and France. The film covers Reinhardt Heydrich's funeral and Hitler's attendance at his burial in Berlin as well as scenes of President Roosevelt, Prime Minister Churchill and Premier Stalin at the historic Teheran Conference. See also Reinhardt Heydrich. ■

One Minute to Zero (1952), RKO. *Dir.* Tay Garnett; *Sc.* Milton Krims, William W. Haines; *Cast includes:* Robert Mitchum, Ann Blyth, William Talman, Charles McGraw.

This Korean War drama deals with the Communist thrust south of the 38th parallel and how the U.N. troops forced the enemy

Col. Robert Mitchum (c.) helps to push back the Communist invasion of South Korea. *One Minute to Zero* (1952).

back. Robert Mitchum portrays a battle-hardened colonel and professional soldier in charge of the operation. Ann Blyth plays a widowed U.N. employee who falls in love with Mitchum. William Talman, as an officer in the U.S. Air Force, is Mitchum's buddy. Charles McGraw plays a sergeant and the colonel's confidant. Action sequences include jet planes hurling rockets against the invading forces and hand-to-hand combat.

The plot, with its more than the usual number of clichés, does offer one incident of more than passing interest. In one particularly brutal scene Mitchum orders his troops to drop mortars on a column of civilians where North Korean soldiers have taken cover. Overly sensitive U.S. Army officers objected to this uncomplimentary view of American fighting forces and withheld any assistance to the production. The otherwise routine war story includes actual footage taken from newsreels as well as some special effects accomplished by the use of miniatures. ■

One Night in Lisbon (1941). See *Once Upon a Honeymoon* (1942). ■

Onionhead (1958). See Service Comedy. ■

Only the Brave (1930). See Spy Films: the Silents. ■

Operation Bikini (1963), AI. *Dir.* Anthony Carras; *Sc.* John Tomerlin; *Cast includes:* Tab Hunter, Frankie Avalon, Scott Brady, Jim Backus, Gary Crosby, Eva Six.

A U.S. Navy underwater demolition team is assigned to destroy a sunken American submarine so that the Japanese don't obtain highly secret radar equipment in this World War II drama. Tab Hunter portrays the lieutenant in charge of the operation, named "Bikini." Scott Brady plays a submarine captain. Eva Six provides the romantic interest for Hunter. Action sequences include a sea battle between Japanese warships and American planes and a submarine. ■

Operation CIA (1965). See Vietnam War. ■

Operation Cross Eagles (1959), Continental Dist. *Dir.* Richard Conte, Casey Diamond; *Sc.* Vincent Fotre; *Cast includes:* Richard Conte, Rory Calhoun, Aili King, Phil Brown.

Richard Conte portrays a lieutenant who is on a special mission in Yugoslavia to rescue a captured American officer in this routine World War II drama. Conte, with the help of local partisans, enlists the aid of three Commandos, led by Rory Calhoun, who have just completed their own mission and are waiting for their contact to take them back to their base. Conte's plan to capture a German commandant and exchange him for the American officer is almost foiled by a traitor in their midst. However, they manage to free the American, retain their prisoner and uncover the traitor. Aili King provides some romantic interest. Location shots include Trieste and Yugoslavia. ■

Operation Crossbow (1965), MGM. *Dir.* Michael Anderson; *Sc.* Richard Imrie, Derry Quinn, Ray Rigby; *Cast includes:* Sophia Loren, George Peppard, Trevor Howard, John Mills.

A special Commando unit is assigned the perilous mission of seeking out and helping to destroy a Nazi secret missile base in this tense and action-filled World War II drama. George Peppard, Tom Courtenay and Jeremy Kemp make up the special team. They parachute into Holland and masquerade as German agents when they enter Germany. After several setbacks, including the capture and death of Courtenay who is recognized by the Gestapo, Peppard and Kemp illuminate the missile stronghold for a squadron of Allied bombers. The site is destroyed, but the two Commandos sacrifice their lives in carrying out their mission. Lilli Palmer, as an underground leader, assists the Commandos. Sophia Loren, as the wife of the man Peppard is impersonating, is killed for security reasons by Palmer.

The actual Operation Crossbow concerned Allied attacks against the launching sites of Germany's V-1 flying bombs and V-2 rockets, the so-called vengeance weapons that caused havoc over London and took a terrible toll in lives—more than 6,000 before the last rocket fell on England in March 1945. The major launching pads were in Holland and France. Allied bombing raids were not entirely effective in destroying all the launch sites, some of which were difficult to locate. ■

Operation Dames (1959), AI. *Dir.* Louis Clyde Stoumen; *Sc.* Ed Lakso; *Cast includes:* Eve Meyer, Chuck Henderson, Don Devlin, Ed Craig.

An American entertainment troupe is trapped behind enemy lines in this low-budget action drama set in Communist territory during the Korean War. Chuck Henderson portrays the sergeant in charge of getting the troupe and his squad back to U.N. lines. Eve Meyer, as one of the entertainers, provides the romantic interest. Action sequences occur periodically as the group make the long trek to safety in this familiar tale. ■

Operation Daybreak (1976), WB. *Dir.* Lewis Gilbert; *Sc.* Ronald Harwood; *Cast includes:* Timothy Bottoms, Karel Curda, Joss Ackland, Nicola Pagett.

This World War II drama re-enacts the assassination of Nazi officer Reinhard Heydrich, also known as "Heydrich the Hangman" by Czech freedom fighters, and the resultant destruction of Lidice by the Germans. A special group of Czechs is parachuted by the British into Czechoslovakia for the purpose of killing the brutal Nazi administrator. Following the assassination, the Germans retaliate by destroying the town of Lidice and murdering most of its citizens. The Germans, aided by an informer, capture the members of the special force and execute them. Timothy Bottoms portrays one of the assassins. Anton Diffring impersonates Heydrich. Nicola Pagett provides the romantic interest for Bottoms in this tale based on facts. See Reinhard Heydrich. ■

Operation Eichmann (1961), AA. *Dir.* R. G. Springsteen; *Sc.* Lewis Coppley; *Cast includes:* Werner Klemperer, Ruta Lee, Donald Buka, Barbara Turner, John Banner.

A superficial biographical drama of the Nazi war criminal responsible for sending millions to their death during World War II, the film covers the war years and the aftermath in which Adolf Eichmann was pursued by Jewish agents. Eichmann (Werner Klemperer), the mass murderer, ironically rails against the injustice he must endure at his ensuing trial. Ruta Lee portrays his devoted mistress. Donald Buka plays the Israeli who relentlessly hunts for Eichmann. In an attempt to add authenticity, the writers introduce several historical figures, including Rudolf Hoess (John Banner) and Heinrich Himmler (Luis Van Rooten).

The film was released prior to Eichmann's trial, evidently designed to take advantage of the national headlines. The script, unfortunately, reveals little depth of character. The production makes use of newsreel footage showing the atrocities committed by the Nazis at the various death camps. Adolf Eichmann (1906–1962), an Austrian Nazi who supervised Germany's directives of mass deportation, torture and death at various concentration camps, was held responsible in part for the extermination of millions of Jews. He was in charge of the Gestapo's Jewish department during World War II. In 1945 he fled to Argentina. Israeli agents kidnaped him and brought him to Israel in 1960 where he was convicted of crimes against humanity and sentenced to death. ■

Operation Mad Ball (1957). See Service Comedy. ■

Operation Overlord. See Normandy Invasion. ■

Operation Pacific (1951), WB. *Dir.* George Waggner; *Sc.* George Waggner; *Cast includes:* John Wayne, Patricia Neal, Ward Bond, Scott Forbes.

The skipper of a submarine is torn between his navy career and his love for his ex-wife in this World War II drama. The captain (John Wayne) pursues both with equal vigor. His former spouse (Patricia Neal) will not take him back because of his limited devotion to her and takes up with a navy pilot (Philip Carey). Meanwhile, Wayne has more success battling the Japanese. The film provides some compelling action sequences, particularly when Wayne finds himself in the midst of the Japanese fleet. He surfaces, radios his position to headquarters and then lets loose his torpedoes. The original captain of the sub

(Ward Bond) early in the film sacrifices his life to save the vessel and crew. ■

Operation Petticoat (1960), U. *Dir.* Blake Edwards; *Sc.* Stanley Shapiro, Maurice Richlin; *Cast includes:* Cary Grant, Tony Curtis, Joan O'Brien, Dina Merrill, Arthur O'Connell.

This comedy, set during World War II in the Pacific, was one of Universal's biggest hits in 1960. The appropriate mixture of plot elements and stars helped to provide the many laughs. The captain (Cary Grant) of a damaged submarine is determined to make it seaworthy once again so that it can do battle. He pleads with his superior officer to give the *Sea Tiger* another chance. "It's like a beautiful woman dying an old maid," he explains. This sets the sexual tone of the film. His scheming junior officer (Tony Curtis) whose wheeling and dealing provide the proper equipment and supplies, also creates several complications for Grant. He writes in the vessel's log: "To paraphrase Churchill, never have so few stolen so much from so many."

During a Japanese air attack on the base, Grant inquires as to the whereabouts of Curtis. "All Mr. Holden said was that in confusion there is profit," a sailor replies. When the sub is ready to leave, the engineer has trouble getting it started. To help things along, Curtis hires an island witch doctor to perform a religious ceremony. As Grant looks on in disbelief, the sub's engines begin to work successfully. On one of their stops at an island about to be overrun by the Japanese, Grant is forced to take aboard a handful of nurses, creating further problems in the already tight quarters among the sex-starved crew. Curtis is quick to invite one of the female guests to his cabin, offering her some of his garments, to which she replies: "A girl just doesn't get into any man's pajamas." When he finally maneuvers her into a rubber raft, another officer warns the captain that they are missing. "When a girl's under 21," Grant explains to the concerned officer, "she's protected by the law; when she's over 65, she's protected by nature; anywhere in between, she's fair game."

Machinist's mate Arthur O'Connell has his own difficulties with the chief nurse, an officer, who insists on aiding him with his engines. At first he resists, then succumbs to her mechanical skills and her charms, in that order. "You're different," he confesses to her in a soft voice. "You're not a woman. You're more than that. You're a mechanic." The film includes visual gags as well, making it one of the best war comedies to come out of Hollywood. ■

Cornel Wilde (r.), as an American agent, temporarily joins the French in their fight against the Nazis. *Operation Secret* (1952).

Operation Secret (1952), WB. *Dir.* Lewis Seiler; *Sc.* James R. Webb, Harold Medford; *Cast includes:* Cornel Wilde, Steve Cochran, Phyllis Thaxter, Karl Malden.

A World War II spy drama unfolded through flashbacks, the film involves the French underground and a traitor. The story opens at a trial concerning a murder during the war. As former members of the underground and others connected with the crime testify, the chief suspect seems to be Cornel Wilde, an American agent believed killed in an airplane crash during the conflict. He suddenly appears in the courtroom and gives evidence that proves the real murderer was a Communist spy masquerading as a French patriot (Steve Cochran). Action sequences include Wilde's wartime exploits in capturing Nazi films of a jet airplane and his suspenseful escape from behind enemy lines. Phyllis Thaxter, as a member of the underground, also provides the romantic interest. The film is based on the experiences of Lt. Colonel Peter Ortiz, a World War II marine hero. ■

Operation Torch. See Northwest Africa, Invasion of. ■

Operation Vittles. See Cold War. ■

Operator 13 (1934), MGM *Dir.* Richard Boleslawsky; *Sc.* Harvey Thew, Zelda Sears, Eve Greene; *Cast includes:* Marion Davies, Gary Cooper, Jean Parker, Katharine Alexander, Ted Healy.

·Except for a few songs interspersed by the Mills Brothers, including "Sleepy Head," this routine Civil War spy drama offers few surprises. A Union actress (Marion Davies) volunteers to work for detective Allan Pinkerton as a secret agent for the North. Gary Cooper plays her counterpart, a Confederate spy. The usual love affair follows as the two try to outwit each other after Cooper discovers her real identity. At one point she saves Cooper's life. Katherine Alexander portrays Pauline Cushman, an actual spy for the Union. Ted Healy, who introduced the Three Stooges comedy team to the stage and ultimately to the screen, plays a trouper in a medicine show who is actually working for the Union secret service. This was the second Civil War spy drama for Cooper, who displayed a sense of impartiality concerning the war; in *Only the Brave* (1930) he played a Union spy who operated behind Confederate lines. After completing the film, Marion Davies left MGM to work for Paramount. See also Pauline Cushman. ■

Ordeal, The (1914), Life Photo. *Sc.* Edward M. Roskam; *Cast includes:* William H. Tooker, George De Carlton, Harry Spingler, Anne Laughlin.

With the World War I serving as background, this unusual silent drama employs an extended dream sequence as its chief plot. The son of a French farmer balks at enlisting in the army since it means leaving his sweetheart. His father, a veteran of previous wars, regales his son with tales of his heroic deeds. The boy, asleep, dreams that his family and sweetheart are in danger from German troops who have occupied his village. Operating as a guerrilla fighter, he is captured. The enemy threatens to kill his family unless he reveals the hiding place of the other rebels. One by one his family is taken out and shot. The boy finally awakens from his "ordeal."

The film, with its obvious anti-German propaganda, caused controversy during its initial preview showing. German representatives protested to authorities in Washington against the release of the feature. At least one New York theater owner withdrew the picture when he was threatened by officials (who claimed it defied President Wilson's announcement of neutrality) that he would lose his license if the film continued to be shown. ∎

Oregon Passage (1958), AA. *Dir.* Paul Landres; *Sc.* Jack DeWitt; *Cast includes:* John Ericson, Lola Albright, Toni Gerry, Edward Platt.

The U.S. Cavalry pursues Black Eagle, a Shoshone chief who rejects any overtures of peace, in this drama set in the Northwest during 1871. A lieutenant (John Ericson) clashes with his stubborn and wrong-headed commanding officer (Edward Platt) whose faulty decisions result in the slaughter of a number of troops at the hands of the hostiles. Platt suspects his wife (Lola Albright) of having had an affair with the young lieutenant. After she is captured by Black Eagle, Platt and his wife are killed during his attempt to rescue her. Ericson takes over command of the fort and defeats the Indians. The film is based in part on the true exploits of the Shoshone warrior Black Eagle. ∎

Orleans, Siege of. See Joan of Arc. ∎

Orphans of the Storm (1921), UA. *Dir.* D.W. Griffith; *Sc.* Marquis de Trolignoc (Griffith); *Cast includes:* Lillian Gish, Dorothy Gish, Joseph Schildkraut, Lucille La Verne, Monte Blue.

D.W. Griffith adapted the popular play of the period, *The Two Orphans,* by Adolph D. Ennery, and material from *A Tale of Two Cities,* and turned them into a spectacle of the French Revolution while maintaining a human story of two girls raised as sisters. Lillian Gish portrays Henriette, the daughter of a peasant couple who also raise Louise (Dorothy Gish), an orphan the father finds abandoned on church steps by a member of a family of aristocrats. A plague, which kills the parents, also blinds Louise. Henriette promises never to leave her adopted sister until her sight is restored. Unfortunate circumstances soon separate the pair. Henriette is abducted by a marquis to satisfy his lust. But she is rescued by a brave aristocrat (Joseph Schildkraut) who falls in love with her. Meanwhile, helpless Louise falls into the clutches of an unsavory beggar (Lucille La Verne) who beats her until she promises to beg in the streets.

The remainder of the film concerns different events of the French Revolution which affect the lives of the two girls. In an ending reminiscent of a Dickens novel (an author whom Griffith very much admired), preceded by the familiar Griffith last-minute rescue, the girls are once again brought together. Louise's sight is restored, and she is reunited with her real mother.

Griffith shows his mastery of the medium in handling the storming of the Bastille, the surging throngs that fill the streets and his obligatory last-minute rescue of Henriette and her lover from the Guillotine. Yet he retains control over the human elements, especially the sibling devotion between the two vulnerable innocents throughout their tribulations. The film reflects Griffith's attitude towards the Revolution. He sympathized with the momentous event but condemned its excesses. He goes through great pains to depict the abuses of the aristocrats during the first half, while later showing the tyrannical rule of such leaders as Robespierre (Sidney Herbert). One of the director's intended purposes in making this film, released only a few years after the Russian Revolution, was to present a cautionary tale to his audiences. This is made clear in the opening titles which state that the French Revolution rightly overthrew an evil government, but we must exercise care not to exchange our good government for "Bolshevism." ∎

Ortiz, Peter. See *Operation Secret* (1952). ∎

"Our Bridge of Ships" (1918), General Film.

A patriotic two-reel documentary produced by the Committee on Public Information, the film shows the enormity of America's shipbuilding industry that stretches from Maine to California. The construction of a ship is shown in its several stages, beginning with the downing of trees and the preparation of the steel to the eventual launching. Several important figures are shown throughout the documentary, including President Wilson. The film was part of a series of documentaries made by the C.P.I. during World War I. ∎

Our Fighting Forces (1917), Pathe.

A documentary promoting preparedness, the film uses facts and figures to compare the military status of the U.S. to that of other major nations. Emphasis is placed on the latest appropriations toward defense. The film, released just before America's entry into World

War I, covers both land and sea preparations and anticipated war production. ∎

Our Invincible Navy (1918), Prizma.

A World War I documentary produced by Prizma, a company that specialized in an experimental color process, the film pays tribute to the U.S. Navy. It presents a short history of the service, shows sequences of the training of officers and describes the manufacture of the big guns used by the warships. The film also depicts the construction of a typical war vessel. Demonstrations of torpedo launchings, seaplanes catapulted from cruisers and several turret guns in action helped to convince the contemporary audiences of the navy's preparedness and strength in one of the earliest detailed documentaries of this branch of military service. ∎

"Out of Darkness" (1941), MGM. *Dir.* Sammy Lee; *Sc.* John Nesbitt; *Cast includes:* Rudolph von Heinrich, Egon Brecher, Wolfgang Zilzer, Lotti Palfie.

Part of "John Nesbitt's Passing Parade" series of short dramas produced by MGM, the one-reel film eulogizes a little-known phase of Belgian resistance during World War I. The story concerns an audacious newspaper that dared to defy that country's German invaders by continuing to publish despite the enemy's threats. Although this series concentrated chiefly on figures whose ideas were spurned during their lifetime, others who went unnoticed, or still others who changed world events, Nesbitt occasionally digressed, especially during World War II, to present little tales of patriotism or propaganda. ∎

Out of Luck (1923). See Service Comedy. ∎

Out of the Depths (1946), Col. *Dir.* D. Ross Lederman; *Sc.* Martin Berkeley, Ted Thomas; *Cast includes:* Jim Bannon, Ross Hunter, Ken Curtis, Loren Tindall.

An American submarine takes on a Japanese aircraft carrier in this routine World War II drama. When the commander and crew of an American underwater vessel encounter an enemy aircraft carrier loaded with kamikaze pilots and planes ready to attack U.S. warships, they decide to act. The final scenes of this low low-budget film show the sub ramming the carrier. ∎

Out of the Ruins (1928), FN. *Dir.* John F. Dillon; *Sc.* Gerald C. Duffy; *Cast includes:* Richard Barthelmess, Marion Nixon, Robert Frazer, Emile Chautard, Eugene Pallette.

A romantic drama with a World War I background, the film takes place in France where a French lieutenant (Richard Barthelmess) deserts his post to prevent the woman he loves from marrying another man. He stays with her for several days during which time his men are killed in battle. When he returns to his command, he is court-martialed for desertion and sentenced to face a firing squad. But he is saved at the last moment when his comrades, who make up the squad, deliberately miss their target. Listed officially as dead, he returns to Paris and his fiancee. The film concentrates chiefly on the love story, showing little action of the war. ∎

Outpost in Morocco (1949), UA. *Dir.* Robert Florey; *Sc.* Charles Grayson, Paul de Sainte-Colombe; *Cast includes:* George Raft, Marie Windsor, Akim Tamiroff, John Litel.

George Raft portrays the hero in this routine colonial adventure drama about an Arab uprising against the French. Raft, a captain in the Foreign Legion, helps to crush the rebellion stirred up by a local villainous emir (Eduard Franz) while wooing the Arab leader's attractive daughter (Marie Windsor). Windsor is killed when Raft and his men attack the stronghold of the emir. Although the film was shot on location and had the assistance of the French Foreign Legion and the cooperation of hundreds of Moroccan cavalry, the plot and characters are reminiscent of several films that have covered the same ground. Akim Tamiroff portrays a fellow Legionnaire loyal to Raft. ∎

Outside In (1972), Harold Robbins International. *Dir.* Allen Baron; *Sc.* Robert Hutchinson; *Cast includes:* Darrell Larsen, Heather Menzies, Dennis Olivieri, John Bill.

A draft dodger (Darrell Larsen) opposed to the Vietnam war and residing in Canada returns to the U.S. to attend his father's funeral in this drama. He decides to remain and soon becomes entangled in the personal lives of two of his friends. One of his pals (John Bill) is a Vietnam veteran whose pro-American sympathies clash with the antiwar sentiments of Larsen. Dennis Olivieri, as Larsen's other buddy and fellow draft dodger who has served his prison sentence, takes his own life

Lobby card of French Foreign Legion defending its fort against warring Arabs. *Outpost in Morocco* (1949).

when he discovers that he is still classified 1A. Heather Menzies provides some romantic interest for Larsen. ∎

Outsider, The (1961), U. *Dir.* Delbert Mann; *Sc.* Stewart Stern; *Cast includes:* Tony Curtis, James Franciscus, Gregory Walcott, Bruce Bennett, Vivian Nathan.

A biographical drama of the World War II hero Ira Hayes, the film covers his life from the time he leaves his Pima reservation in Arizona to enlist in the marines until his tragic death ten years later. Tony Curtis portrays the American Indian who was one of the leathernecks to raise the stars and stripes on top of Mount Suribachi. After the war, Hayes was unable to handle the fame thrust upon him or come to terms with the white man's world. He began to drink heavily before his untimely death. James Franciscus plays his service buddy. Vivian Nathan portrays Hayes' mother. Hayes appeared in *Sands of Iwo Jima* (1949) as one of the marines who raises the American flag on Mount-Suribachi. Joining him on screen were René

A. Gagnon and John H. Bradley, all of whom had taken part in the actual event.

The biography, based on William Bradford Huie's *The Hero of Iwo Jima*, failed to capture the human tragedy of its main figure. What it did present to its audiences, saturated with cavalry-vs.-Indian movies, was another belated handling of the American Indian as someone other than a marauding savage. The film in this sense follows in the wake of such films as *Broken Arrow* (1950) and *The Unforgiven* (1960), Hollywood milestones that treated the native Americans as rounded characters. ∎

Outsider, The (1979), Par. *Dir.* Tony Luraschi; *Sc.* Tony Luraschi; *Cast includes:* Craig Wasson, Sterling Hayden, Patricia Quinn, Niall O'Brien.

A young Irish-American, raised on the stories of Ireland's struggles against Britain, decides to join the Irish Republican Army in this contemporary drama concerning theproblems in Northern Ireland. Craig Wasson portrays the green American who wants to fight for Irish nationalism. However, he is soon disillusioned by the conflict. Members of the I.R.A. have their own use for the recruit. They intend to have him killed by a British bullet so that they can more readily raise funds in America for their cause. The British, meanwhile, plan to frame Wasson so that one of their own informants is not uncovered. Wasson returns to the States in disgust. Sterling Hayden, as the grandfather, has regaled Wasson with the glories of the past.

The film, shot chiefly in Dublin, captures the tragedy of the conflict without sensationalizing it. Children are seen preparing incendiary bombs; British troops gun down children fleeing from an explosion and torture I.R.A. sympathizers; young Irish lads who have spent a lifetime steeped in violence turn into callous killers. ■

"Over Here" (1917), World.

A documentary showing America in the early stages of preparation for the World War I, the film reveals how a modern Arkansas army camp was constructed on a site that had been a wooded wilderness. Various scenes depict giant machines digging ditches, hordes of men constructing the shelters, a railroad link laid down in record time and, finally, the first troops marching in to their new quarters on the 3,000-acre tract. ■

Over Secret Wires (1915). See Spy Films: the Silents. ■

Over the Top (1918), Vitagraph. Dir. Wilfred North; Sc. Robert Gordon Anderson; Cast includes: Arthur Guy Empey, Lois Meredith, James Morrison, Arthur Donaldson.

Based on the World War I novel of the same name by Arthur Guy Empey, the film digresses at times from the original story. Sergeant Owen, the main character, is shown receiving decorations for his bravery on the Mexican border. Later, while in London, he enlists in the British army and is sent to the front lines in France during World War I. The film includes a plot involving a German spy who later becomes a general in the German army. There is also a suspenseful escape by airplane to the American lines by Owen and a young American woman who has been held captive by the general.

The principal character, Owen, was played by Empey himself. In the film another character, called "Folly," supposedly was fashioned after Senator Robert Marion La Follette. Folly is seen dealing with the German spy. In real life La Follette (1855–1925), who had served as congressman, governor of Wisconsin and U.S. senator, had been highly criticized for his outspoken opposition to America's entry into World War I and was censured in the Senate. However, he was never directly indicted for treason or any other war crime. ■

Over There (1917), Selznick. Dir. James Kirkwood; Sc. Eve Unsell; Cast includes: Charles Richman, Anna Q. Nilsson, Gertrude Berkeley, Walter Hiers.

A World War I drama depicting the isolation and disgrace of a coward during wartime, the film was an ideal advertisement for recruitment. A young man, sensing himself a coward, refuses to enlist when his country calls. His sweetheart breaks off their engagement and presents him with a white feather, the symbol of cowardice. His business partners and others disengage themselves from him. He finally gathers up enough courage to enlist, is sent overseas and distinguishes himself in battle where he is wounded. When he returns home he hands back the white feather, now stained with his blood, to his former girl.

Antipacifist films during the war were many, some more callous than others. This entry represented one extreme, while Douglas Fairbanks' comedy, In Again—Out Again (1917), illustrated a lighter approach. However, in the latter, Fairbanks, portraying an advocate of preparedness, does rather sharply denounce the pacifists. See Antiwar Films, Preparedness. ■

Over There (1928), Super Film Attractions.

A documentary about World War I, the film is a compilation of combat and newsreel footage taken from the official archives of the U.S. and other Allied governments. The work includes the usual bombardments, over-the-top attacks and marching troops, none of which is identified either by date or battle. At the time of its release, it was endorsed by the national chairperson of the Daughters of the American Revolution. ■

Members of the German general staff on the western front, as seen in the 1928 documentary of World War I *Over There*.

P

P.O.W. The Escape (1986), Cannon. *Dir.* Gideon Amir; *Sc.* Jeremy Lipp, James Bruner, Malcolm Barbour, John Langley; *Cast includes:* David Carradine, Charles R. Floyd, Mako, Steve James, Phil Brock.

A low-budget action drama that takes place near the end of the Vietnam War, the film stars John Carradine as a captured American colonel who strikes a deal with the camp commandant for the sake of his fellow prisoners. The North Vietnamese captain, played by Mako, senses the war is drawing to a close and would like to escape to the U.S. with his two trunks of loot. He offers Carradine his freedom if the colonel will help him get through American lines. Carradine agrees only after the captain consents to release the handful of other American prisoners.

The remainder of the film concerns incidents steeped in treachery and greed over the loot and the heroism of the colonel who rescues a besieged unit of American soldiers about to be annihilated by the enemy. The commandant waits in ambush for Carradine, who outwits the captain and kills him and his men. Charles R. Floyd portrays a slightly deranged American prisoner who attempts to steal the treasure for himself. He later redeems himself when he throws himself on a grenade, thereby saving the lives of his fellow prisoners. ■

P.T. 109 (1963), WB. *Dir.* Leslie H. Martinson; *Sc.* Richard L. Breen; *Cast includes:* Cliff Robertson, Ty Hardin, Robert Culp, Grant Williams.

The story of John F. Kennedy's experiences as a lieutenant in the U.S. Navy during World War II results in a chiefly bland, patriotic drama. Cliff Robertson portrays the young naval officer whose P.T. boat is split in two by a Japanese destroyer. Kennedy and his crew must survive on Pacific islands that are barely inhabitable. The film depicts him as a strong, dedicated officer who can handle stress and, at the same time, one who possesses warmth and a sense of humor. James Gregory plays a tough commander. Comic relief is provided by Robert Blake as a gunner's mate and Biff Elliott as a surrogate cook. The film, based on the book by Robert J. Donovan, fails to capture the charm and wit of the real Kennedy. ■

Pacifist films. See Antiwar Films. ■

Pacific Blackout (1942). See Spy Films: the Talkies. ■

Pacific Rendezvous (1942). See Washington, D.C. ■

Pack Up Your Troubles (1932). See Service Comedy. ■

"Pale Horseman, The" (1946), Office of War Information. *Sc.* Irving Jacoby.

This two-reel documentary captures the tragic aftermath of World War II as it depicts the famine and disease that have fallen upon millions of people in all corners of the globe. The film asks for American support of the hungry and sick children and adults in numerous countries. Scenes not only show the victims of war ranging from China to Europe, but show the Allied armies and the United Nations are trying to help. ■

Panama Canal. This strategically important waterway linking the Atlantic and Pacific oceans has been the subject of several Hollywood spy films. Within this genre it has been

Crew members of a PT-boat battle the Japanese in *PT 109* (1963), based on the experiences of Lieutenant John F. Kennedy.

the target of various foreign agents who were bent on stealing plans of its structure or destroying its locks. One of the earliest dramas to focus on the Panama Canal was the serial *Pearl of the Army* (1916). Silent serial queen Pearl White portrayed an intrepid lass who prevents Oriental agents from sabotaging the Canal. *The Silent Command* (1923), a spy story involving the mining of the Canal, centers on secret agents trying to steal an American navy officer's (Edmund Lowe) plans for the mine fields.

With the advent of World War II, the number of dramas about the Canal increased in proportion to its strategic significance. The films, most of which were low-budget entries, explored the determination of Axis spies to halt or at least slow down the transport of vital Allied war supplies. The plots were chiefly fictitious, but the dangers at the time seemed real to American audiences. In *Panama Patrol* (1939), for instance, Leon Ames portrays an army major who captures a spy ring operating in the Canal Zone. In *Phantom Raiders* (1940) saboteurs were busy

attacking ships in the region before master detective Nick Carter (Walter Pidgeon) puts a stop to their activities. In *Charlie Chan in Panama*, released the same year, the Hawaiian sleuth, working with U.S. Intelligence, snuffs out a plot to blow up a portion of the Canal. *The Phantom Submarine* (1941), a weak drama about a mysterious sub lurking in the waters off the Canal, features Anita Louise as a secret agent who is assigned by the U.S. Navy to learn the vessel's whereabouts and its mission. Humphrey Bogart in *Across the Pacific* (1942) portrays an American agent posing as a court-martialed army officer trying to prevent Sydney Greenstreet from bombing the Canal. *Betrayal From the East* (1945), with Lee Tracy and Nancy Kelly, concerns Japanese agents seeking a blueprint of the Panama Canal defenses. Thanks to Hollywood and the American armed forces, the Panama Canal survived World War II intact. ∎

Panama Patrol (1939). See Panama Canal. ∎

Panic in the Year Zero (1962), UI. *Dir.* Ray Milland; *Sc.* Jay Simms, John Morton; *Cast includes:* Ray Milland, Jean Hagen, Frankie Avalon, Mary Mitchel.

The drama depicts the struggle for survival following a nuclear war. After several American cities undergo an atomic attack by an unspecified foe, little remains of society except for small bands of survivors who fight each other over food and other items. Ray Milland portrays the father of a small family whose resourcefulness helps him to keep his two children and his wife alive. They temporarily seek shelter in a cave, eventually returning home to try to rebuild their lives. In the interim, they go through some harrowing experiences—the family is continually terrorized by marauding thugs, and Milland's wife (Jean Hagen) and teen-age daughter (Joan Freeman) are raped. Frankie Avalon plays Milland's son. ∎

Parachute Battalion (1941), RKO. *Dir.* Leslie Goodwins; *Sc.* John Twist, Major Hugh Fite; *Cast includes:* Robert Preston, Nancy Kelly, Edmond O'Brien, Harry Carey, Buddy Ebsen.

In the spirit of other preparedness dramas released before America's entrance into World War II, this film concerns the training of parachute troops. The plot hinges on three trainees—a former football hero (Robert Preston), the commander's son (Edmond O'Brien) and a third who provides the comic relief (Buddy Ebsen). Preston, with an air of arrogance, takes the training very casually. O'Brien at first displays cowardice but redeems himself later on. Nancy Kelly, as the top sergeant's daughter, provides the romantic interest for O'Brien and Preston.

The film was made with the cooperation of the 51st Parachute Battalion at Fort Benning, Georgia. This may be the cause for some lack of action. Evidently, the military, always hoping to get more volunteers, frowned upon any incidents that suggested accidents or any unnecessary perils involving the work of paratroopers. These sequences certainly would have added tension and excitement to the drama but might have discouraged recruits. ∎

Parachute Nurse (1942), Col. *Dir.* Charles Barton; *Sc.* Rian James; *Cast includes:* Marguerite Chapman, William Wright, Kay Harris, Frank Sully.

This World War II drama tells the story about that branch of the nursing profession who parachute to otherwise inaccessible areas to help the wounded fighting men below. The story follows the young women in their training stages, adding melodramatic elements, such as one recruit using the parachute to commit suicide. A subplot involves a German-American nurse who is alienated by the others because of her background. Marguerite Chapman portrays a trainee who falls in love with the instructor (William Wright). ∎

Parades (1972), Confron/Cinerama. *Dir.* Robert J. Siegel; *Sc.* George Tabori; *Cast includes:* Russ Thacker, Brad Sullivan, David Doyle, Lewis J. Stadien, Dorothy Chace.

The mistreatment of A.W.O.L. soldiers in army stockades across the nation provides the background for this brutal drama. The film allegedly is based on actual incidents that occurred in stockades at such noted army camps as Fort Dix, New Jersey; Fort Riley, Kansas; and Fort Jackson, South Carolina. Several graphic scenes depict the inhuman handling the inmates receive by their guards as well as their fellow prisoners. Russ Thacker, who is a featured player in this work, appeared as a deserter in another film released the same year, *AWOL*, concerning an American soldier who takes up residence in Denmark rather than fight in Vietnam. ∎

Paratroop Command (1959), AI. *Dir.* William Witney; *Sc.* Stanley Shpetner; *Cast includes:* Richard Bakalyan, Ken Lynch, Jack Hogan, Jimmy Murphy.

A paratrooper is shunned by his fellow soldiers after he accidentally causes the death of another member of the unit in this low-budget action drama set during World War II. The passage of time does not ease the friction within the unit; instead, it mounts as the men engage in various missions. The troubled paratrooper (Richard Bakalyan) ultimately sacrifices his life in a heroic act of redemption. Ken Lynch portrays the lieutenant who commands the unit. Action sequences in North Africa and Italy are adequate. ∎

Paris After Dark (1943), TCF. *Dir.* Leonide Moguy; *Sc.* Harold Buchman; *Cast includes:* George Sanders, Philip Dorn, Brenda Marshall, Marcel Dalio.

A slow-moving but realistic drama of

Nazi troops in occupied Paris round up the usual suspects. *Paris After Dark* (1943).

French resistance in Nazi-occupied Paris during World War II, the film features Philip Dorn as a French soldier recently returned from a concentration camp and whose spirit is broken. He believes it is futile to resist the indefatigable Nazis, until near the end when his conscience is re-awakened and he becomes an active member of the French underground. Brenda Marshall, as Dorn's wife, and George Sanders portray other important members of the resistance. ■

Paris Calling (1941), U. *Dir.* Edwin L. Marin; *Sc.* Benjamin Glazer, Charles S. Kaufman; *Cast includes:* Elisabeth Bergner, Randolph Scott, Basil Rathbone, Gale Sondergard, Lee J. Cobb.

A World War II spy drama set in Paris immediately after the Nazi occupation of France, the film concerns a wealthy Frenchwoman (Elisabeth Bergner) who volunteers to work with the French underground. When her mother is killed by Nazi planes as the pair try to flee from Paris, Bergner decides to return to the city and fight the invaders. An American flier (Randolph Scott) with the Royal Air Force is hunted by the Germans.

Bergner is forced to kill her ex-lover (Basil Rathbone) when he turns traitor. The main plot in this suspenseful tale depicts the heroic efforts of underground members to disrupt the German war machine. ■

Paris Green (1920). See Service Comedy. ■

Paris Underground (1945), UA. *Dir.* Gregory Ratoff; *Sc.* Boris Ingster, Gertrude Purcell; *Cast includes:* Constance Bennett, Gracie Fields, Kurt Kreuger.

This World War II spy drama concerns two women, an American and an Englishwoman, and their activities in the French underground. Constance Bennett portrays the American wife of a Frenchman in the foreign office, and Gracie Fields plays the owner of a book shop in Paris. The two women join forces and help more than 250 Allied airmen out of occupied France. Their adventures include pursuit by the Gestapo, killing of a member of the Gestapo, capture and ultimate rescue by allied troops who arrive just in time to save their lives. This routine film, which was Gracie Fields' last screen appearance, was based on the actual experiences of Etta

Shiber, who aided Allied pilots escape the Nazis. ∎

Parker, Quana. See *Comanche* (1956). ∎

Captain Claude Rains (l.), assisted by George Tobias (r.) and other loyal Frenchmen, battles to retake his freighter from pro-Nazi forces. *Passage to Marseilles* (1944).

Passage to Marseilles (1944), WB. *Dir.* Michael Curtiz; *Sc.* Casey Robinson, Jack Moffitt; *Cast includes:* Humphrey Bogart, Michele Morgan, Claude Rains, Sydney Greenstreet, Peter Lorre.

A tribute to the fighting Free French, this World War II drama stars Humphrey Bogart as one of a group of escaped convicts from Devil's Island. All have vowed to fight for their native France against the Nazis. Bogart, a former journalist who opposed the pacifists and those who appeased Hitler, was falsely imprisoned in an attempt to silence him. The plot is told in a series of complex flashbacks by Claude Rains, as a French liaison officer, to an American reporter who is writing a feature story on the Free French. Sydney Greenstreet, as a career officer who despises the Republic, supports the Fascist regime of Marshal Petain. The chief action takes place aboard a freighter which is seized by Greenstreet and a handful of mutineers. But the loyal French convicts, led by Bogart and Peter Lorre, retake the ship and shoot down a German plane. The film includes several patriotic speeches, some condemning isolationism and pacifism, others extolling the virtues of a free France and her allies. ∎

Passport to Adventure. See *Passport to Destiny* (1944). ∎

Passport to Destiny (1944), RKO. *Dir.* Ray McCarey; *Sc.* Val Burton, Murial Roy Boulton; *Cast includes:* Elsa Lanchester, Gordon Oliver, Lenore Aubert.

A London charwoman travels to Germany to assassinate Hitler in this inept World War II fantasy drama. Believing that her late husband's snake-eye charm will protect her from harm, the woman (Elsa Lanchester) journeys to Nazi Germany by stowing away on a French ship, carrying her pail and brush all the way. She manages to get hired as a cleaning woman in the Nazi chancellery by masquerading as a mute but is eventually arrested. However, an officer in the underground rescues her and flies her to safety in a German plane. An interesting sidelight occurs in the scene in which Lanchester converses with a picture of her late husband—a photograph of Charles Laughton, her real-life husband. The film was originally released as *Passport to Adventure.* ∎

Passport to Hell, A (1932), Fox. *Dir.* Frank Lloyd; *Sc.* Bradley King; *Cast includes:* Elissa Landi, Paul Lukas, Warner Oland, Alexander Kirkland, Donald Crisp.

Elissa Landi stars in this drama with a World War I background. Driven out of England because of a scandal, she ends up in a British colony where once again she meets with hard luck. She is blamed for the suicide of a British official and sent into German territory. When World War I breaks out, she marries a German commandant's son to avoid being imprisoned as an English subject. The father sends the couple to a northern province where the groom, after selling military secrets to a British agent to raise money for his wife, kills himself. Landi burns his suicide note to protect his honor and leaves for parts unknown, hoping that the postwar period will reunite her with her lover whom she met while she was married. The film reveals little of the war in Europe. ∎

Passport to Suez (1943). See *Detectives at War.* ∎

Patent Leather Kid, The (1927), FN. *Dir.* Alfred Santell; *Sc.* Adele Rogers St. Johns; *Cast includes:* Richard Barthelmess, Molly O'Day, Arthur Stone, Raymond Turner, Hank Mann.

French soldiers, led by Kirk Douglas (l.), become part of the debris of World War I. *Paths of Glory* (1957).

Richard Barthelmess plays a slacker and professed coward in this World War I drama. Meeting with some success as a prizefighter but disliked by the public because of his egotism, he finally loses a major bout by means of a setup. He is drafted into the army but boasts of his cowardice through much of his military service. His sweetheart (Molly O'Day), who volunteers as a nurse, follows him to France and effects a change in Barthelmess. He performs a series of heroic acts which result in the paralysis of his hands and feet. While hospitalized, he struggles to rise up in an effort to salute the American flag as troops march by and the band plays "The Star-Spangled Banner." He accomplishes this feat after much effort.

Although a silent film, the accompanying music in the scene in which Barthelmess struggles to salute Old Glory was scored so that the National Anthem was played at that moment. Some critics found the film excessively patriotic and in bad taste. One reviewer singled out the ludicrous scene in which the hero undergoes an operation without an anesthetic while his sweetheart-nurse assists the surgeon. ■

Pathfinder, The (1952), Col. *Dir.* Sidney Salkow; *Sc.* Robert E. Kent; *Cast includes:* George Montgomery, Helena Carter, Jay Silverheels, Walter Kingsford.

Adapted from James Fenimore Cooper's novel set during the French and Indian War, this drama stars George Montgomery as the title character. A British scout, he is assigned to spy upon a French fort. Helena Carter accompanies him as his interpreter, masquerading as a French girl. They learn that the French plan to control the Great Lakes, but they are caught when Carter's former suitor, a British traitor, exposes her. British troops come to the rescue as the couple are about to face a firing squad. ■

Paths of Glory (1957), UA. *Dir.* Stanley Kubrick; *Sc.* Stanley Kubrick, Calder Willingham, Jim Thompson; *Cast includes:* Kirk Douglas, Ralph Meeker, Adolphe Menjou, George Macready.

The insanity and stupidity of war and particularly the blundering arrogance of those in high command are the subjects of this scathing drama set in 1916 during World War I. A scheming French general (George

Macready) orders his troops to take the "ant hill," an impregnable position controlled by the Germans. At first he rejects the plan, but when he learns he is being considered for a higher post and another star, he orders the attack. When the soldiers, led by their colonel (Kirk Douglas), fail to do so because of heavy bombardment, the general orders the French artillery to fire upon his own men to prod them forward. But the enemy resistance is too great and the French fall back. Some of the men never even left the trenches. Macready, infuriated that his orders were not carried out, charges the unit with cowardice and directs Douglas to select three men for court martial. "If those little sweethearts won't face German bullets," he exclaims, "they'll face French ones!"

The colonel, a lawyer in civilian life and the only high-ranking officer who displays any compassion for his men, volunteers to defend the soldiers who are being used as an object lesson. Earlier in the film during the futile attack, a major mocks the troops for huddling together during the bombardment. "They never learn, it seems . . . gang up every time," he scoffs. "Herd instinct, I suppose—kind of a lower animal sort of thing." Douglas is quick to berate the major. "Kind of a human sort of thing, it seems to me," he replies. "Or don't you make a distinction between the two?" Douglas soon learns the futility of bucking military politics. "You are an idealist and I pity you," a general remarks, "the way I would pity the village idiot."

A corps commander (Adolphe Menjou), representing the general staff, views the war as a series of political maneuvers, power struggles and studied calculations. He manipulates Macready into ordering the attack by dangling a promotion in front of him. "Troops crave discipline," he states. "One way to maintain discipline is to shoot a man now and then." When Macready is of no further use to him, Menjou says: "France cannot afford to have fools guiding her destiny."

Although it was released the same year as David Lean's *The Bridge on the River Kwai*, another indictment of the madness resulting from war, *Paths of Glory* has more in common with Lewis Milestone's *All Quiet on the Western Front* (1930) and Howard Hawks' *The Road Back* (1937) because of its economy, its black-and-white realism, its grim battle scenes and its World War I background.

However, it is similar to Lean's film in at least one respect. Both tend to be more critical of the military than of war. In fact, its forceful antimilitary theme resulted in its being banned in parts of Europe and in theaters on American military bases. ■

Patriot, The (1916), Triangle. *Dir.* William S. Hart; *Sc.* Monte M. Katterjohn; *Cast includes:* William S. Hart, Georgie Stone, Joe Good-Boy, Roy Laidlow.

A veteran of the Spanish-American War (William S. Hart) prospects for gold on his New Mexico homestead in this drama. An unscrupulous land agent, seeing the value of the land, forces the veteran to move. Hart pleads his case in Washington but fails. Upon his return, he finds his motherless son has died. Bitter at the turn of events, he joins Mexican guerrillas who raid American towns. On one of these incursions he comes across a child the same age of his son and realizes the errors of his actions. Several exciting battle scenes follow. As the film concludes, he walks off with his newly adopted son to begin life anew.

The background of the Mexican raids was no doubt inspired by the activities of Pancho Villa during the Mexican Revolution. When the U.S. intervened on the side of President Carranza, whom Villa opposed, the revolutionary responded by raiding American border towns and killing several U.S. citizens. This resulted in a punitive expedition by General "Black Jack" Pershing in 1916 against Villa and his troops. ■

Patriot and the Spy, The (1915), Mutual. *Cast includes:* Alphonse Ethier, James Cruze, Marguerite Snow.

When a local villager in an unnamed European country marries a pretty girl, another suitor harbors feelings of jealousy and revenge in this World War I drama. At first, the remote village seems out of danger of the war, but the conflict soon spreads. The husband (James Cruze), hurt by a speeding car while rescuing one of his children, is unable to serve in the army. Later, his former rival (Alphonse Ethier), now a spy and traitor, tricks the hero into blowing up a bridge. The husband, desperately seeking a way to serve his country, is captured by the invading troops but escapes in time to find his wife (Marguerite Snow) threatened by the spy. A fight

G.I.s in World War II Europe drive forward despite heavy German resistance. *Patton* (1970).

ensues with predictable results. The war, like the country, goes unnamed in this silent drama, but the Continental setting, characters' names, battle sequences and weaponry mark it as World War I. James Cruze became a popular film director. ∎

Patton (1970), TCF. *Dir.* Franklin J. Schaffner; *Sc.* Francis Ford Coppola, Edmund H. North; *Cast includes:* George C. Scott, Karl Malden, Michael Bates, Karl Michael Vogler.

George C. Scott gives a strong and colorful characterization of General George S. Patton, Jr. in this biographical drama set chiefly during World War II. He is portrayed as a multi-faceted figure—arrogant, flamboyant, energetic, resolute, overbearing, outspoken and, at times, sensitive and introspective. The film traces his role in the war from 1943 in North Africa, when he is placed in charge of an American unit of a joint English-American force, to Germany's surrender and the time when he is relieved of his command for his outspoken views that conflicted with U.S. policy.

The famous opening poses Patton in front of a giant-sized American flag as he addresses the men under him. "I want you to remember that no bastard ever won a war by dying for his country," he begins. "He won it by making the other poor dumb bastard die for his country." He then continues about how Americans love the sting of battle and how he intends to conduct his campaigns. "I don't want to get any messages that we are holding our position. We're not holding anything. We are advancing constantly. We are not interested in holding onto anything except the enemy . . . We're going to go through him like crap through a goose."

In one sprawling sequence after another, Patton battles his way out of the North African desert and across Italy to Germany. The tank battles and movements of troops are on a large scale. The highly mechanized armies instill a certain remorse in Patton, who often alludes to the wars of the past as more personal. "God," he exclaims, "how I hate the twentieth century." At times the scene shifts to German headquarters where Rommel (Karl Michael Vogler), shown as a cautious officer, studies his counterpart's background. An aide sums up the American general's strategy for Rommel: "Patton is a romantic officer lost in contemporary times."

Patton is seen and heard as an earthy general who enjoys the smell of battle, competes with the British to arrive at an objective first and tosses about quips that often reveal his true feelings as well as his own shortcomings. When someone asks what he thinks of Morocco, he replies: "I love it. It's a combination of the Bible and Hollywood." Later in the film, during the German counterattack at Bastogne, Patton, who has volunteered to push forward with reinforcements to the besieged General McCullough, hears that the general replied to the enemy's demand that he surrender with "Nuts!" "A man that eloquent has to be saved," Patton cracks as he presses his men forward.

Karl Malden portrays an authoritative General Omar Bradley. Michael Bates, as a prissy Montgomery, acts as foil to the more dynamic Patton, who races him to objectives in Italy (Palermo and Messina). Tim Considine plays the foot soldier whom the general, who despises cowardice, slaps during his visit to a field hospital. The incident stirs up enough commotion in the States to have Patton temporarily withdrawn from duty and forced to apologize publicly to American troops. Karl Michael Vogler appears as Field Marshal Rommel. But it is the gutsy personality of Patton, who, looking over a field of battle, admits: "I love it! God help me, I love it so!" that dominates this production. The final scene equates him with Don Quixote. A long shot shows him as a small, lonely figure on a barren landscape except for a single windmill in the foreground.

A few minor historical errors appear from time to time. For example, athough Patton, according to the film, tried to get to Messina before Montgomery, the English general was not engaged in any race. His intent was to prevent the Germans from escaping. Since Patton was in a more advantageous position to effect that goal, Montgomery encouraged him to use the very route allocated to the British Eighth Army. ∎

Patton, George S. (1885–1945). Egotistical, dynamic, given to explosive profanity, both adored and hated by those he led, and easily one of the most successful tank generals of World War II— George Patton was all of these and more. A figure of sharp contrasts, he could display callous insensitivity to the plight of others as well as fall on his knees to pray and shed tears for the suffering of his soldiers. Some believed that Patton contrived a facade of toughness to cover up his own self doubts and sensitive nature.

A graduate of West Point, Patton never doubted that a military career was his singular destiny. "The only thing I am good at is military," he once wrote his father. He believed in déjà vu and reincarnation, claiming he remembered being present at great battles in ancient times. Patton was an early advocate of tank warfare, which he first experienced in World War I. In World War II he was a successful practitioner of mobile armored attacks in North Africa, Sicily and Europe's western front. His sudden, and sometimes unauthorized, dashes and changes of direction often caught both his superiors and the enemy by surprise.

Patton first achieved fame as commander of land forces in Operation Torch, the 1942 invasion of Northwest Africa that brought the first major reversal for Axis forces in the west. In the Sicilian campaign that followed, Patton climbed to still higher public esteem by his use of fast-moving armored columns to capture Messina (August 17, 1943) on the northern tip of the island. The victory trapped many thousands of Axis troops, and the port eventually served as the jumping-off point for the invasion of Italy (September 3, 1943).

It was during the Sicilian campaign, however, that his words and actions brought him his first press criticism. He slapped two American soldiers in a field hospital and gave each a tongue-lashing about the responsibilities of men in war before sending them back to their units. Though Patton later publicly apologized for his actions, the incidents led to his temporary suspension as a commander.

Following the invasion of Normandy (June 6, 1944), Patton was put in charge of the Third Army that relieved the besieged American garrison at Bastogne (December 26, 1944) in the Battle of the Bulge. His force then turned eastward in the early spring of 1945 and raced across southeastern Germany to reach the borders of Czechoslovakia and Austria, where he was ordered to stop and wait for the Russians to advance to prearranged military dividing lines. Patton chafed at his orders. He was further criticized for commenting that the U.S. should continue its advance into Russian territory and destroy the citadel of Communism, a menace he believed was at least equal to, if not greater than, that of Nazi Germany.

In the postwar occupation of Germany, Patton's actions and remarks brought more severe criticism that ultimately caused him to be removed from command (October, 1945). He was reprimanded for defending the use of ex-Nazis in administrative posts. His personal diaries, found after the war, contained blatant anti-Semitic statements. "The noise against me," he wrote, referring to the criticism, "is only the means by which Jews and Communists are attempting, and with good success, to implement the future dismemberment of Germany." Writing about displaced persons, of which his army had encountered many, he said they were not human beings "and this applies particularly to the Jews who are lower than animals."

A colorful and successful battlefield leader with a seriously flawed personality, he did not feel comfortable in a world at peace or with democratic ideals of religious tolerance and respect for individuals. Patton died on December 21, 1945, following an auto accident in Germany.

The biographical drama *Patton* (1970), starring George C. Scott as the flamboyant and outspoken general, covers most of the highlights of his World War II experiences. He may also be seen in several documentaries pertaining to the war, including *The True Glory* (1945), which traces the Allied landing at Normandy and the retreat of German forces on all European fronts. Patton appears in the sequences concerning the Battle of the Bulge—the final, desperate German counterattack. ■

Pawnbroker, The (1965), Landau. *Dir.* Sidney Lumet; *Sc.* Morton Fine, David Friedkin; *Cast includes:* Rod Steiger, Geraldine Fitzgerald, Brock Peters, Jaime Sanchez.

A Jewish pawnbroker (Rod Steiger) in New York's Harlem is haunted by horrible memories of the Nazi concentration camps. Having lost faith in God, society and his fellow human beings, he permits his shop to be used as a front for a black racketeer (Brock Peters) who exploits the community. Flashbacks provide some inkling of the nightmares he

has lived through. One such scene shows him being forced to witness the rape of his wife by Nazi soldiers. Now he survives as a loner among prostitutes and petty thieves. Jaime Sanchez plays his young assistant who stops a bullet intended for his elderly employer when some crooks try to rob the shop. Geraldine Fitzgerald, as a social worker, tries to restore his faith in humankind in this grim drama. ■

Paws of the Bear (1917). See Spy Films: the Silents. ■

Paying the Price (1916). See Washington, D.C. ■

"Peace—by Adolf Hitler" (1941). See "The March of Time." ■

Pearl Harbor attack (December 7, 1941). The American naval base at Pearl Harbor was just beginning to stir at 7:55 A.M. on December 7, 1941, in what was anticipated as being another routine peaceful Sunday morning. But the unexpected roar of overhead aircraft shattered both the day's early quiet and a tenuous peace as the first wave of 183 carrier-borne Japanese torpedo planes came in to attack. Facing hardly any opposition, they came down low and headed for the rows of American warships anchored about the harbor. After dropping specially fitted shallow-running torpedoes that tore into the hulls of the warships, the raiders executed a brief but telling aerial bombardment with armor-piercing bombs. Every one of the eight anchored American battleships suffered damage, some permanent.

About 45 minutes later, another 180 planes came over the main Hawaiian island of Oahu, that held American naval, air and army bases and the city of Honolulu, capital of the island chain. When the two attacks ended a large part of America's military power in the Pacific had been wiped out. Two battleships, the *Arizona* and the *Oklahoma*, had been sunk. Six others were temporarily put out of action. Two destroyers and a target ship were also gone, as were 261 out of a total of 481 planes, most caught on the ground in neat, closely spaced rows. At least 3,226 American military personnel died in the attack and another 1,272 were wounded. The Japanese lost

29 planes, five midget submarines and about 100 men.

American films depicting the devastating sneak attack ranged from short documentaries to lavish dramatic productions. Most gave a fairly accurate account of events, motivated as much by reasons of propaganda as out of a desire for accuracy. *December 7th* (1942), the first documentary to cover Japan's sneak attack on Pearl Harbor, was commissioned by President Roosevelt "to present accurately the story of the attack." Newsreel scenes showed Pearl Harbor before and after the assault. Another documentary, *Behind the Enemy Lines* (1945), used Japanese footage to depict the attack on Pearl Harbor and other World War II events.

Pearl Harbor inspired a host of World War II propaganda dramas. In such films as *To the Shores of Tripoli* and *Two Yanks in Trinidad*, both released in 1942, personal feuds between servicemen are put aside "for the duration" when they learn of the sneak attack. *Remember Pearl Harbor* (1942), one of the earliest films to appear following the attack, concerned two soldier-pals stationed in the Philippines when the raid plunges America into the war. The attack motivates shipyard workers in *Fighting Coast Guard* (1951) who, angered by the bombing, enlist in the military. Many low-budget action dramas such as *Submarine Raider* (1942) used Japan's strike on Pearl Harbor as a background.

Several dramas rose above the pack in graphically recreating the attack and the destruction left in its wake. One whose scenes have been singled out for their realistic portrayal of the Japanese assault was *From Here to Eternity* (1953), a drama set chiefly in Hawaii on the eve of the raid. The film ends with the Japanese attack. *Tora! Tora! Tora!* (1970), an American-Japanese co-production at a reported cost of $25 million, recreated the attack on Pearl Harbor and told of the events from both points of view. Although flawed as drama, the film has been commended for its historical accuracy.

Fortunately for the U.S., three Pacific fleet carriers were at sea when the attack occurred; otherwise American naval strength in the Pacific would have been practically non-existent for the first year of war. The sea drama *Wing and a Prayer* (1943) told about one of these carriers.

Though American military leaders had been apprised of the growing possibility of an attack, most felt the blow would fall in the Far East, particularly on the Philippines. At Pearl Harbor and its surrounding supporting military installations, the fear was more of sabotage, leading military officials to group their equipment in close formations to be more easily guarded.

However, some early warnings of the impending attack did go unheeded. An off-duty soldier manning a radar post reported seeing objects on his screen, but his observation was dismissed. The destroyer U.S.S. *Ward* had earlier spotted and destroyed a Japanese midget sub within the harbor, but no alert resulted. *Kamikaze* (1962), a documentary, pointed out that the U.S. ignored several signs that foretold the December 7 attack.

Relations between Japan and the U.S. had been steadily deteriorating for several months in the late fall of 1941. Admiral Isoruku Yamamoto, Japan's Naval Chief, had developed a plan earlier in the year that should war with the U.S. appear imminent, Japan would launch a heavy surprise first strike at Pearl Harbor. This would neutralize the only sizable Pacific force that stood in the way of further Japanese expansion. The plan was a copy of the successful tactic Japan used in overwhelming Russia in the Russo-Japanese War of 1904–1905.

As negotiations continued between the U.S. and Japan, Admiral Chuichi Nagumo sailed towards Hawaii on November 26, with a fleet under radio silence that included six carriers. Nagumo received confirming orders at sea on December 2 to proceed with the attack. The fleet approached undetected to within 275 miles north of Hawaii before launching the air strike. The following day, December 8, President Franklin D. Roosevelt, calling the incident "a day that will live in infamy," asked for and received from Congress a declaration of war against Japan. ∎

Pearl of the Army (1916). See Serials. ∎

Peninsular War (1808–1814). See Napoleonic Wars. ∎

Pershing, John Joseph (1860–1948). A graduate of West Point Military Academy, "Black Jack" Pershing, as he was known informally, had a long and colorful career in the military service and in public administration. By blending patience with force, he was able to bring the Moro tribes of the Philippines under control. He was then taken into their confidence and elected to their council. After the Moro War (1901–1913), he next gained fame as the leader of the punitive military expedition into Mexico in 1916 against Pancho Villa, following the guerrilla leader's raid on Columbus, New Mexico, earlier that year. *The Man Who Was Afraid* (1917) deals with American troops across the border clashing with Mexican bandits. Historically, however, Pershing's forces never engaged in actual warfare during the expedition.

An efficient administrator, Pershing created the Bureau of Insular Affairs. His greatest achievement came during World War I as commander-in-chief of the American Expeditionary Force. He was in charge of the fighting at Chateau-Thierry and Belleau Woods, stipulating that he was to have complete command of his troops. He received a Pulitzer Prize for his book *My Experiences in the World War* (1931). A chiefly private figure, he avoided politics and interviews for publication.

At least two films focused on the general's military exploits, the documentary *Pershing's Crusaders* (1918) and the drama *Why America Will Win*, also released in 1918. The latter describes a rather pompous general. The following year Fox released a biography of Pershing's life titled *The Land of the Free*. ■

Pershing's Crusaders (1918), FN.

Produced for the Committee for Public Information, the documentary covers various aspects of World War I. Some of the highlights include President Wilson addressing Congress, the ill-fated *Lusitania*, a German U-boat off the coast of America, the invasion of Belgium and numerous scenes of the home front and its contributions to the war effort. The propaganda film is divided into two sections—"America Preparing" and "The Stars and Stripes Over There." ■

Pettigrew's Girl (1919), Par. *Dir.* George Melford; *Sc.* Will M. Richey; *Cast includes:* Ethel Clayton, Monte Blue, James Mason, Charles Gerrard.

A Southern recruit stationed in an army camp in the North during World I falls in love with a Broadway entertainer in this wistful romantic drama. Monte Blue, as the lonely doughboy, is without a sweetheart while all his buddies at the base boast about their wives and girlfriends. As he wanders through the streets of New York, he sees a photograph of a showgirl (Ethel Clayton) in a window. He purchases it and proceeds to the theater where she is appearing. He finally manages to meet her but learns she is more interested in a rich playboy. However, she forsakes wealth for the sincere love of the soldier. The film was remade ten years later as *The Shopworn Angel* starring Gary Cooper and Nancy Carroll. ■

Phantom Raiders (1940). See Detectives at War. ■

Phantom Submarine, The (1941). See Panama Canal. ■

Philippine Insurrection (1899–1902). The Philippines, between 1896–1898, were fighting for independence against corrupt Spanish rule. When Spain and the U.S. clashed in the Spanish-American War (1898), Filipino revolutionary leader Emilio Aguinaldo returned from exile in Hong Kong and, with American support, organized a native army to help fight the Spanish. The Filipino rebels, under Aguinaldo, declared their independence from Spain (June 12, 1898) while the conflict was in progress.

However, when Spain ceded the islands to the U.S. for $20 million in the Treaty of Paris, Aguinaldo's rebel forces refused to accept American control. Instead, they declared their independence. The rebels set up a native republic under the Malolos constitution on January 20, 1899, initiating an anti-American rebellion that lasted until 1902. The film *Across The Pacific* (1926) portrays the rebel force not as a nationalist movement struggling for independence but as a minority dissident group fighting against a constitutional government backed by the U.S. In *Cavalry Command* (1963) American occupation forces in the Philippines are faced with guerrilla resistance. They capture the rebel leader who is portrayed as a fanatic who continues to oppose U.S. occupation. He eventually changes his opinion when he realizes the Americans have been helping the Filipinos by bringing in food and medical supplies.

American General Arthur MacArthur, father of Douglas MacArthur, gradually subdued most of the rebels and, with the help of Filipino scouts loyal to the U.S., captured Aguinaldo in 1901 through a trick. Though he proclaimed allegiance to the U.S. and ordered an end to the rebellion, fighting continued for another year under other native leaders until May 6, 1902. The movement for Filipino independence never died out, and the islands eventually gained total self-determination shortly after World War II. The earliest films of the conflict were newsreels made by Biograph Studio's field cameramen and released in 1900. Few American dramas have dealt with this phase of Philippine history. The two films mentioned above exemplify the point that the true story of the Philippine Insurrection has yet to be told on screen. ■

Phillips, Claire. See *I Was an American Spy* (1951). ■

Pied Piper, The (1942), TCF. *Dir.* Irving Pichel; *Sc.* Nunnally Johnson; *Cast includes:* Monty Woolley, Roddy McDowall, Anne Baxter, Otto Preminger, J. Carrol Naish.

An Englishman on vacation in southern France reluctantly agrees to take a British couple's two children back to England when the Nazis invade France in the spring of 1940. Monty Woolley stars as an irritable old codger in this heart-warming World War II drama. Woolley, who has a natural aversion to children, ends up with other dependent youngsters from various countries as he journeys across France. In one suspenseful sequence he encounters and outwits a Nazi officer (Otto Preminger) before the Englishman and his mixed brood sail for England and safety.

The film is not without its propaganda in its descriptions of Nazi brutality although, for the most part, it is understated. German planes strafe defenseless civilians. Oppressed victims living under the Nazi regime elicit fear and suspicion. A German child traveling with Woolley is relieved when she is told she no longer has to say "Heil Hitler." ■

Pigeon That Took Rome, The (1962), Par. *Dir.* Melville Shavelson; *Sc.* Melville Shavelson; *Cast includes:* Charlton Heston, Elsa Martinelli, Harry Guardino, Brian Donlevy.

An American officer during World War II is assigned to undercover work in Nazi-occupied Rome with unexpected results in this comedy. Charlton Heston portrays the Yank who communicates his strategic information about German activity by carrier pigeons—until an Italian family consumes the birds during an Easter feast. The bewildered Heston is then given German pigeons as a replacement. He proceeds to send out erroneous reports to disrupt the enemy who intercept his communications. Eventually, the Allies take Rome with little difficulty. Elsa Martinelli provides the romantic interest while Harry Guardino plays Heston's assistant. ■

Pillars of the Sky (1956), U. *Dir.* George Marshall; *Sc.* Sam Rolfe; *Cast includes:* Jeff Chandler, Dorothy Malone, Ward Bond, Keith Andes, Lee Marvin.

Jeff Chandler portrays a savvy Indian scout in this routine cavalry-vs.-Indians action drama. He tries to warn the colonel of a cavalry unit about a potential Indian uprising if the army breaks its treaty by opening a projected road and building a fort on the tribe's land. Dorothy Malone, as the wife of an army officer (Keith Andes), falls for Chandler temporarily but returns to her husband by the end of the drama. Michael Ansara, as Kamiakin, the Indian chief, leads his warriors against the soldiers. Lee Marvin plays the proverbial tough sergeant. Ward Bond plays a missionary doctor whose death leads the warring tribe to have second thoughts about their actions. An otherwise predictable film, it does contain several effective action sequences. ■

Pilot No. 5 (1943), MGM. *Dir.* George Sidney; *Sc.* David Hertz; *Cast includes:* Franchot Tone, Marsha Hunt, Gene Kelly, Van Johnson, Alan Baxter.

This World War II drama is told in flashback by the hero's buddies and begins with a political background. A young lawyer (Franchot Tone) becomes entangled in his state's corrupt political machine during a gubernatorial election. Conscience-stricken, he switches sides just in time to defeat the crooked candidate and then enlists in the air force. Tone ultimately must make another momentous decision. He is selected from among five Allied fliers to take the only plane available to bomb a Japanese aircraft carrier. To carry out the mission, he sacrifices his life by diving his plane directly into the warship. Gene Kelly, another flier and former associate of Tone's, plays the role of narrator in his second film. Others in the cast include Van

Johnson, Alan Baxter and Dick Simmons as some of Tone's comrades and Marsha Hunt as the romantic interest. ■

Pin-Up Girl (1944). See Musicals. ■

Pinkerton, Allan (1819–1884). The famous detective founded the Pinkerton National Detective Agency in 1850. Primarily involved in solving railroad crimes, the agency uncovered an assassination plot against President-elect Lincoln in 1861. During the Civil War Pinkerton gathered information about the South for the Union. His spy service was the first use of secret intelligence in the U.S.

Two Civil War films portray him busy at his work of employing agents. In *Hands Up* (1926), a silent comedy, Raymond Griffith portrays a Southern spy assigned to prevent a gold shipment from reaching President Lincoln. Meanwhile, Pinkerton sends a Union spy to make certain the shipment gets through. In *Operator 13* (1934) Pinkerton solicits the services of a Union woman (Marion Davies) to spy on the South. ■

Pirates of Capri, The (1949), Film Classics. *Dir.* Edgar Ulmer; *Sc.* Sidney Alexander; *Cast includes:* Louis Hayward, Binnie Barnes, Alan Curtis, Rudolph Serato.

Louis Hayward portrays a foppish courtier in the court of Naples in this costume drama set in 1779. But he is also Captain Sirocco, the leader of a group of revolutionaries seeking to overthrow the oppressive Queen Carolina and her ruthless military troops as well as avenge the murder of his brother by a villainous police chief. Able to gain useful information for the insurgent movement from his presence at the royal court, Hayward provides plenty of action reminiscent of Hollywood westerns. Rudolph Serato plays the evil chief of police while Binnie Barnes enacts the queen in this low-budget film made in Italy.

Louis Hayward had played a similar role as a fop who at night donned a black mask and became "The Torch," a fighter against oppression in a fictitious country in *The Return of Monte Cristo* (1946).

The Austrian archduchess Maria Carolina in 1768 married the pleasure-loving king of Naples, Ferdinand IV. Queen Maria Carolina was a strong figure who influenced her husband to get rid of his pro-Spanish advisers and replace them with British councilors.

Her actions provoked resentment from the Neapolitan group that had lost power. But there is no record of her authority being overthrown by pirates from Capri. That was probably just another example of Hollywood's distortion of history in the name of entertainment. The time frame for the movie plot, however, was a particularly disturbing one for Ferdinand, Maria Carolina and Naples. The kingdom, which eventually became the Kingdom of The Two Sicilies, suffered through several upheavals and invasions that were an outgrowth of the French Revolution and Napoleonic Wars. ■

Pirates of Monterey (1947), UI. *Dir.* Alfred Werker; *Sc.* Sam Hellman, Margaret B. Wilder; *Cast includes:* Maria Montez, Rod Cameron, Mikhail Rasumny, Philip Reed.

Set in the 1840s when California fought against Mexican rule of the territory, the routine film stars Maria Montez as a Spanish noblewoman who comes to the New World to wed her fiance (Philip Reed), a soldier of Spain stationed in California. Instead, she falls for an American (Rod Cameron), a friend of Reed's. Cameron, as a soldier of fortune, is transporting a wagon train of late-model rifles to a Mexican army detachment. Gilbert Roland, as an unscrupulous figure, leads a Mexican army against the Californians who decide to fight for their independence. A large battle ensues with the conventional rousing ending. ■

Pitcher, Molly (1754–1832). A heroine of the American Revolution whose real name was Mary Ludwig Hays, she gained fame for carrying water to Colonial troops at the Battle of Monmouth (1778). The soldiers, seeing her with her pitcher, affectionately called her Molly Pitcher. Two early silent films, both released in 1911, paid tribute to her: a Champion production titled "Molly Pitcher" and a Kalem film with Anna Q. Nilsson as the heroine, also titled "Molly Pitcher." ■

Pitt, William. See *America* (1924). ■

Plainsman, The (1936), Par. *Dir.* Cecil B. DeMille; *Sc.* Waldemar Young, Lynn Riggs, Harold Lamb; *Cast includes:* Gary Cooper, Jean Arthur, James Ellison, Charles Bickford, Porter Hall, Helen Burgess, Paul Harvey.

Cecil B. DeMille's epic western helped to restore the genre to respectability after years of neglect at the hands of poverty row studios and hack writers and directors. Although the film at times is weighted down with too many studio shots, it often has a sprawling sweep and sense of excitement. DeMille dots the production with a variety of historical figures such as President Lincoln and General Custer to add authenticity to the story. Gary Cooper portrays a stalwart Wild Bill Hickok, Jean Arthur a glamorous Calamity Jane, and James Ellison impersonates a boyish, clean-shaven Buffalo Bill Cody. The action sequences concern skirmishes with Indians, including a rousing battle in which soldiers are besieged for days by the hostiles and an unscrupulous gun runner (Charles Bickford). Porter Hall portrays the treacherous Jack McCall who fatally shoots Hickok in the back.

DeMille, like other directors and writers before him, romanticized the three major characters. Calamity Jane in real life was a homely hag. Cody, a repulsive figure according to historical records, often went unshaven and unkempt. Wild Bill Hickok underwent revision in the 1950s by historians who described him in terms ranging from a pompous bully and reprobate to an outright coward and murderer. McCall, who shot Hickok, was acquitted at first but in a second trial was found guilty and hanged.

Several Indian leaders protested strongly over the inaccurate portrayal of the Cheyenne in certain sequences. One particular bone of contention was the climactic battle in which only a small detachment of cavalry holds at bay large numbers of Indians. DeMille, refusing to let the criticism go unchallenged, came up with a military report which stated that during a battle in Colorado on September 18, 1868, 48 cavalrymen were able to hold out against 800 Cheyenne. ■

"Plan for Destruction" (1943), MGM. *Dir.* Edward Cahn.

Part of the studio's high-quality series of two-reelers titled "Crime Does Not Pay," this World War II documentary covers the geopolitical basis for Nazi Germany's avaricious appetite for its neighbors' land. The film points out how Hitler became intrigued with this theory. Veteran actor Lewis Stone does the narration. Although this highly praised series usually dealt with exposing domestic rackets, it occasionally digressed into other topics, particularly during the war years. ■

Planet of the Apes (1968). See Science Fiction Wars. ■

Plastered in Paris (1928). See Service Comedy. ■

Platoon (1986), Orion. *Dir.* Oliver Stone; *Sc.* Oliver Stone; *Cast includes:* Charlie Sheen, Tom Berenger, Willem Dafoe.

Oliver Stone's explicit and tough film about a platoon of soldiers caught up in the bloody Vietnan war in 1967 unfolds its events from the point of view of 21-year-old Chris Taylor (Charlie Sheen). Personified as the film's conscience, he has dropped out of college and volunteered, believing that his less fortunate peers could teach him about life. "Maybe from down here I can start up again and be something I can be proud of, without having to fake it, maybe . . . I can see something I don't yet see, learn something I don't yet know." His idealism ultimately turns to harsh experience. The opening scenes signal the reality of the war. As new recruits exit from the belly of a giant transport plane, they witness corpses of soldiers being wheeled across the field to be shipped home. Sheen is wounded when his platoon, out on a night ambush, is itself attacked by the enemy. Like Henry Fleming in Stephen Crane's Civil War novel, *The Red Badge of Courage*, he has earned his rite of passage.

The men eventually split into two factions. One sergeant, Barnes (Tom Berenger), a courageous and ruthless killer, leads the malevolent half, while another sergeant, Elias (Willem Dafoe), with a higher set of ideals, symbolizes the good element. The conflict between the two cliques becomes sharply apparent. The platoon, in an early scene, terrorizes a native village following the murder of one of the Americans. The brutality wreaked upon the natives makes it evident that the thin line between civilization and barbarism has been obliterated when even a compassionate soldier like Chris is fired with rage.

Stone is not as interested in the politics of the war as he is concerned with its effects upon decent young men—how it transforms them into conscienceless killers; how it turns them at times against each other. The battle sequences are grimly realistic as the men of the platoon confront diverse enemies—the North Vietnamese who are as brave and determined as the Americans, the unyielding jungle and the soldiers' own doubts and fears. Each encounter leaves the men numb and stupefied rather than exhilarated. There are no noble causes here, only a daily struggle to survive. By the end of the film, Chris, the narrator, concludes: "Those of us who did make it have an obligation to build again, to teach others what we know and try with what's left of our lives to find a goodness and a meaning to this life."

Besides the critical acclaim heaped upon the film and its director-writer, *Platoon* received its share of brickbats. Some complained it was overly critical of the average soldier who did not participate in many of the atrocities described in the film. Others felt that Stone omitted the natural comradeship that grows between those who face death each day, and therefore his depiction of the interplay among the major characters is, to a large extent, false. The film, however, remains a brutal view of the Vietnam War as seen through the eyes of someone who was there and witnessed the horror. ■

Plough and the Stars, The (1937), RKO. *Dir.* John Ford; *Sc.* Dudley Nichols; *Cast includes:* Barbara Stanwyck, Preston Foster, Barry Fitzgerald, Denis O'Dea, Eileen Crowe, Arthur Shields.

A weak, stagy adaptation of Sean O'Casey's play set during the Easter week uprising of the Irish Rebellion, the film stars Barbara Stanwyck as the despairing wife who fears for her husband's life. Preston Foster, as a revolutionary who is promoted to officer status in the rebel army, is the object of Stanwyck's concern. Although she tries very hard to keep him from participating in the battle, he joins the others and narrowly escapes death. Moroni Olsen, as an Irish general, is executed by the English in an especially poignant scene. The film failed at the box office.

The basic premise of O'Casey's work was changed. Where the playwright stressed the political futility of the Irish struggle because of the Irish penchant for speechmaking and bickering, the film script emphasized the personal conflict of the married couple in which Stanwyck, uninterested in the uprising, struggles to keep Foster from participating in the fighting. There are other changes as well. In the stage version the husband is killed in battle and the wife loses her mind. Perhaps the most disturbing change, in the minds of many viewers, was the elimination of several interesting and colorful minor characters who appeared in the original work. ■

Pontiac, Chief. See *Battles of Chief Pontiac* (1952). ■

Lt. Gregory Peck (r.), ordered to hold a strategic hill during the Korean War, prepares a bunker with the help of Woody Strode (c.) against an expected assault. *Pork Chop Hill* (1959).

Pork Chop Hill (1959), UA. *Dir.* Lewis Milestone; *Sc.* James R. Webb; *Cast includes:* Gregory Peck, Harry Guardino, Rip Torn, George Peppard, George Shibata, Robert Blake, Woody Strode.

A Korean War drama with Gregory Peck as a lieutenant, the film concerns a company of men ordered to take a hill from the Chinese Communists. The soldiers accomplish their objective despite heavy losses. Peck leads the men through the savage attack. The 25 survivors of the original 135 men do not understand the significance of Pork Chop Hill but somehow muster up enough courage to seize and hold it. At the same time that the battle is raging, a U.N. negotiating team is haggling with its Chinese counterpart over the boundaries. The Americans realize that the Chinese are stalling until their side wins the hill, aware of its insignificance. They are testing the Americans to see how many men they will sacrifice in holding the worthless objective. Meanwhile the senseless slaughter continues.

American officials, too, want to save face and decide to hold the hill. But those who are doing the fighting have doubts about their objective and the high price they are paying. Peck's fellow lieutenant is ordered to withdraw his George Company, leaving Peck and his handful of men alone to defend the hill. "Is this hill worth it?" the officer asks. "Worth what?" Peck replies. "It hasn't much military value. I doubt if any American will give you a dollar for it . . . Values change somehow, sometime. Maybe when the first man died." Their superiors back at the command post echo similar doubts. "Do we still take George Company off at 1500?" a colonel inquires of the commanding officer. "Yes. We may lose the hill, but I'm not about to spend any more men for it—not until I'm assured we don't intend to give it away tomorrow."

The drama is realistic in many respects. Besides the vivid battle scenes and high casualty rate the Americans suffer, the film does not shun away from military blunders. As the U.S. troops approach the Chinese positions in the dark of night, Americans below mistakenly turn on a series of floodlights. This exposes the American troops, who are in the open, to enemy gunfire. Later, those responsible send an apology. Love Company, supposed to protect Peck's flank, arrives late and with only ten survivors. The Korean War was the first conflict in which black troops were integrated. One black soldier (Woody Strode) freezes out of fear and is placed under watch by another black. "Why are you staring at me?" Strode asks his guard. "I have a special interest in everything you do," the soldier says. The grim film offers little comic relief. Harry Guardino supplies what little there is. One of his best lines is a comment he makes about wearing his bullet-proof vest and getting shot in the leg.

In the end, one is left with a feeling of the futility and irony of the fight for Pork Chop Hill. Even Peck, the stalwart lieutenant, deludes himself in conjuring up some abstract significance to the conflict. As the men walk slowly down from the hill after they are relieved, he says in a voice-over: "The hill was bought at the same price we commemorate [with] monuments at Bunker Hill and Gettysburg. Yet there are no monuments on Pork Chop. Victory is a fragile thing, and the battle will not linger long in our century. But those who fought there know what they did and the meaning of it. Millions live in freedom today because of what they did." ■

Powder Town (1942). See Spy Films: the Talkies. ■

Practically Yours (1944). See *Once Upon a Honeymoon* (1942). ■

"Prelude to Victory" (1943). See "The March of Time." ■

Prelude to War (1942), War Activities Committee *Dir.* Frank Capra.

Produced by the U.S. War Department, the World War II documentary presents a stirring depiction of background events that led up to the war. Using government footage and newsreel shots, Hollywood director Frank Capra, a lieutenant colonel in the Signal Corps, underscores how the U.S. unwisely depended on its two bordering oceans as security against hostile forces. The film goes back to the 1930s, showing how the aggressor nations, chiefly Germany, Japan and Italy, were preparing for World War II while America slept. The U.S. in the 1920s had already scuttled part of its World War I fleet as a gesture toward promoting peace. This propaganda film was the first in a series under the supervision of Frank Capra titled "Why We Fight." ■

"Preparation for Invasion" (1943). See "The March of Time." ■

Preparedness. The American film industry, emerging from its infancy in the 1910s, began to tackle the controversy surrounding national defense when World War I exploded in Europe. The inevitable clash between those who favored a stronger military and the proponents of pacifism drew citizens and politicians alike into the fray. A few major films by important producers and directors advocating pacifist views appeared first. But within months they were soon overshadowed by a succession of dramas, comedies and documentaries that preached preparedness. With the sinking of the *Lusitania* in 1915 and the loss of 128 American lives, public opinion shifted overwhelmingly from pacifism to preparedness. Hollywood films reflected this change. Of course, the debate became moot once America entered the war.

Some of the initial preparedness films were released as early as 1915. *The Nation's Peril*, a spy melodrama, concerns a young heroine who, as a pacifist, objects to her fiance's new invention, an aerial torpedo. After having been duped by spies who capture a coastal town, she changes her views and becomes a strong supporter of preparedness. Earlier, she is portrayed as capricious and scatterbrained. Movie studios found ridicule an effective weapon against pacifists. *Via Wireless* also involves a new weapon—a big gun designed for coastal defense. President Wilson, who supported a strong coastal defense, appears briefly in an early part of the film. J. Stuart Blackton's *The Battle Cry of Peace*, the most celebrated preparedness film of the period, depicts an invasion of a defenseless America by a European power. Foreign agents infiltrate the peace movement in the U.S. and work as lobbyists to stop funds from going to the military. Striking sequences picture the ruthless invaders slaughtering scores of workers and laying waste to Washington. Theodore Roosevelt, a strong advocate of preparedness, supported the film vigorously. Major General Wood, Roosevelt's friend, supplied the film company with more than 2,000 marines to be used as extras at no cost.

American audiences witnessed more preparedness dramas the following year. But the plots by this time had a familiar look to them. *The Fall of a Nation*, for example, repeats the idea of an invasion. Once again a foreign power (thinly disguised German troops) destroys American cities and commits unspeakable atrocities on defenseless citizens. The film, which pauses long enough to belittle political pacifists and religious champions of neutrality, suggests that those against preparedness are either disloyal or cowards. The west coast comes under attack by another foreign power in *The Flying Torpedo*. Landing troops in California, the unnamed country is finally beaten by a resourceful American who invents a weapon more powerful than the invaders' flying torpedo. Not only did the U.S. government support the film morally, it supplied torpedoes for exhibition in movie theater lobbies and set up recruitment booths there as well. *The War Bride's Secret* follows the pattern of previous films by depicting the Germans either as spies trying to steal America's military secrets or bestial soldiers defying all civilized rules of conduct. Popular screen personality Douglas Fairbanks contributed his acrobatic talents with the comedy *In Again—Out Again* (1917). He portrays a brash young man whose stand on preparedness results in his pacifist sweetheart jilting him.

Meanwhile, the documentary as a relatively new genre rose in stature during the war years before the U.S. entered the conflict. It, too, took up the cause of preparedness. *Defense or Tribute?* (1916), using newsreels and excerpts from other films made in the U.S. and abroad, traces the history of war as far back as Rome to prove that preparedness is the only solution to a nation's defense. Boasting "Quality we possess—we must have quantity," *America Prepares* (1916) shows the nation ready for any emergency. Scenes of military preparedness range from different military bases to the sea where a long column of battleships seems poised for battle. *How Uncle Sam Prepares* (1917), another propaganda film about America's ability to respond quickly to a conflict, unfolds its message by way of an allegory. Uncle Sam, seen napping, receives a visit from famous historical figures. After having read in the newspaper about the sinking of a ship full of civilians, he springs to life. *Our Fighting Forces*, released the same year, takes a more objective approach. It compares facts and figures of the military status of the U.S. with those of other major nations. The film then discusses the latest appropriations toward defense.

The pre-World War II years, including the period immediately before the U.S. was drawn into the global conflict, had its share of preparedness dramas and documentaries. Such films as *Here Comes the Navy* (1934), *Devil Dogs of the Air* (1935), *Flight Command* (1940) and *Dive Bomber* (1941), aside from providing action and fast-paced entertainment, suggested the strength of our different military branches and became recruitment posters for the service. The semi-documentary *The Ramparts We Watch* (1940), produced and directed by Louis de Rochemont, compares the state of military readiness of the U.S. in World War I with that of 1941. The film then uses Nazi propaganda footage of the invasion of Poland to show how a modern army can overrun a country poorly prepared for war.

Following World War II, the period of the Cold War produced several preparedness dramas and documentaries. Films like *Strategic Air Command* (1955), starring James Stewart and June Allyson, blended the romantic aspects of drama with the need for a strong defense against Communism. Echoing the sentiments of earlier preparedness films, Stewart, as a dedicated officer in the Strategic Air Command, explains: "This is a kind of war. We've got to stay ready to fight so that we may never have to." ■

President Vanishes, The (1934), Par. *Dir.* William Wellman; *Sc.* Carey Wilson, Cedric Worth; *Cast includes:* Arthur Byron, Janet Beecher, Paul Kelly, Peggy Conklin, Rosalind Russell, Sidney Blackmer, Douglas Wood.

This intriguing drama concerns a missing American President, a nation on the brink of war and jingoistic factions bent on joining a fictitious conflict raging in Europe. The country's pacifist leader (Arthur Byron) is determined to keep the United States out of another foreign war. A belligerent Congress is about to vote for war when news spreads that the President has disappeared. Arms manufacturers and a right-wing organization known as the Gray Shirts are suspected of abducting him. A coalition of militant businessmen, media owners and self-serving politicians encourage the Fascist Gray Shirts to usurp power. Pacifists and followers of the President are physically beaten. The President, who has deliberately vanished to avoid thrusting the nation into war and to expose his enemies, returns to office and galvanizes the country behind him and against the militarists and the strong-arm bullies. ∎

"Price of Victory, The" (1911), Edison. *Dir.* Edwin S. Porter; *Sc.* Edwin S. Porter.

A silent drama set at the time of the Napoleonic Wars, the film tells about a revengeful father whose young son was killed while serving as a drummer boy in Napoleon's service. The father then plots to kill the legendary general. Porter, a pioneer in moviemaking, directed "The Great Train Robbery" (1903), a landmark western that helped to establish the pattern for the western genre as we know it. The film, which ran only 12 minutes, remained one of the most popular films for more than a decade. Although he turned out scores of dramas and comedies, he made relatively few war-oriented or historical films. He directed "The Midnight Ride of Paul Revere" (1907), "The Boston Tea Party" and "Romance of a War Nurse," both released in 1908. ∎

Pride and the Passion, The (1957), UA. *Dir.* Stanley Kramer; *Sc.* Edna and Edward Anhalt; *Cast includes:* Cary Grant, Frank Sinatra, Sophia Loren, Theodore Bikel.

The French incursion into Spain during the Napoleonic Wars provides the impetus for this large-scale drama of people uniting to overthrow their oppressive invaders. Spanish guerrillas struggle to move a large, abandoned cannon that they intend to use against a French stronghold. The crude, emotional leader (Frank Sinatra) of a rag-tag guerrilla army is determined to rout the French from the heavily fortified city of Avila. A disciplined English navy captain (Cary Grant) is sent to Spain in 1810 to retrieve the cannon for the British in its war against Napoleon. Sinatra convinces him to help the Spanish in their battle before he takes possession of the weapon. Sophia Loren, as Sinatra's fiery mistress, helps to maintain peace between the two strong-willed men whose views on war and battle tactics differ greatly.

A French general (Theodore Bikel) doesn't understand the passion of the Spanish peasantry or why the cannon is so important to them. "How big can a cannon be?" he wonders out loud. "The people of an occupied country begin as martyrs," an aide explains. "Give them something to rally around and they explode into a new army. That is the real danger of this cannon." Later, Bikel witnesses thousands of unarmed Spaniards poised for the inevitable attack upon his heavily fortified and virtually impregnable fortress and realizes the heavy losses they will suffer. "How these Spaniards love their moment of truth, their compulsion to die—to drench the ground with their blood. Why?" "Probably because it is their ground, General," his aide replies. The film is based on C.S. Forester's novel *The Gun.*

Historically, the British sent in more than one sailor to help the Spanish in their revolt against the French under the rule of Joseph, Napoleon's brother. An entire British army helped to bring about Napoleon's first defeat on the continent. He lost 50,000 men in Spain. See Napoleonic Wars. ∎

Pride of the Army (1942), Mon. *Dir.* S. Roy Luby; *Sc.* Jay Vlahos; *Cast includes:* Billy Lee, Addison Richards, Kay Linaker, Bradley Page.

The training of dogs for military purposes is the subject of this minor World War II drama. The plot concerns little Billy Lee who donates his dog for the defense of a war plant. His father, an alcoholic as the result of war wounds, works at the plant. When saboteurs attempt to destroy the factory, Billy's dog discovers the plot while his father sacrifices his life to save the plant. The film is sometimes listed under its alternate title, *War Dogs.*

The film is based on the actual recruitment of canines during the war. Under the auspices of Dogs for Defense, Inc. and the Quartermaster General of the U.S. Army, 50,000 dogs were recruited and trained for defense and war duties. See Dogs in War. ∎

John Garfield, as blinded marine hero Al Schmid, gets support from girlfriend Eleanor Parker (l.) and Ann Todd. *Pride of the Marines* (1945).

Pride of the Marines (1945), WB. *Dir.* Delmer Daves; *Sc.* Albert Maltz; *Cast includes:* John Garfield, Eleanor Parker, Dane Clark, John Ridgely, Rosemary DeCamp, Ann Doran.

Based on the true story of Al Schmid, a marine hero who lost his sight while fighting in the Pacific, the film stars John Garfield as the young leatherneck who returns home embittered and too proud to seek help. At first he rejects his sweetheart (Eleanor Parker). But with the patience and care of a sympathetic nurse (Rosemary DeCamp), a few buddies (Dane Clark and Anthony Caruso) and others, he slowly begins to realize that he can still lead a productive life.

Released at the end of World War II, the drama presents a realistic view of the returning troops who are concerned about such items as jobs, their future and the G.I. Bill. This is particularly underscored in scenes in a navy hospital where Garfield is stationed after being wounded at Guadalcanal. He hears the men around him air their gripes and fears. However, the overall tone is optimistic. Despite the ordeal Garfield undergoes before he adjusts to his affliction, the film suggests to other servicemen in similar circumstances that they too can successfully re-enter society. ∎

"Pride of the South, The" (1913), Mutual. *Dir.* Burton King; *Sc.* Burton King; *Cast includes:* Mildred Bracken.

In this silent domestic tragedy that takes place during the Civil War, a Confederate colonel disowns his daughter when she marries a Union officer. The family is not reunited until the proud colonel's little granddaughter influences him to visit his daughter on her deathbed. The film includes many battle scenes of the war. ∎

Priorities on Parade (1942). See Musicals. ∎

Prison Ship (1945), Col. *Dir.* Arthur Dreifuss; *Sc.* Josef Mischel, Ben Markson; *Cast includes:* Nina Foch, Robert Lowery, Richard Loo, Ludwig Donath.

A Japanese vessel carrying civilian prisoners is used as a decoy to attract American submarines in this World War II action drama. When some of the prisoners aboard the ship notice how well lit it is at night, they realize the Japanese intent. They rise up against their captors but are quickly subdued. The film then depicts the typical Japanese atrocities as dozens of women and children are killed in retaliation for the mutiny. Eventually an American sub surfaces and fires upon the vessel. This time the prisoners gain control and send up a white flag. Robert Lowery and Nina Foch portray the hero and heroine who lead the revolt of the captives in this routine film.

A similar situation was to occur in *Torpedo Run* (1958), a submarine tale of World War II. Glenn Ford, as a submarine commander, learns that his wife and children, along with other American prisoners of war, are aboard a Japanese vessel that is being used as a shield for an enemy carrier. ∎

Prisoner of Japan (1942). See Spy Films: the Talkies. ∎

"Prisoner of Mexico, A" (1911), Kalem.

Exploiting the 1910 revolution in Mexico, this short action drama romanticizes the political turmoil of that country. It depicted the Americans who crossed the border to fight with the Mexicans as supporters of such leaders as Pancho Villa and Francisco Madero, patriots who are helping the nation to form a republic. General Madero is seen leading the cavalry to rescue the hero and heroine.

Historically, President Taft did not support Madero, who was eventually murdered in 1913 after Victoriano Huerta's troops stormed the National Palace. Soon another rebellion erupted with Carranza, Villa and Zapata opposing Huerta's federal troops. American politics made another turn when President Wilson took office. He did not recognize Huerta, whom he considered a usurper. The U.S., therefore, was forced to side with the rebels. ■

Prisoner of War (1954), MGM. *Dir.* Andrew Marton; *Sc.* Allen Rivkin; *Cast includes:* Ronald Reagan, Steve Forrest, Dewey Martin, Oscar Homolka.

The treatment of prisoners of war by the North Koreans forms the background of this Korean War drama. To check on a series of stories emanating from behind enemy lines about the brutal treatment of captured soldiers, U.S. Army Intelligence drops a volunteer (Ronald Reagan) into North Korea. He joins a detachment of American prisoners and witnesses first-hand a variety of atrocities executed by a Russian colonel (Oscar Homolka) and others. The men are subjected to anti-American propaganda classes, beatings and torture. Some are killed. Dewey Martin portrays a collaborator who in reality is another U.S. agent. Steve Forrest, as another prisoner, continuously resists his captors.

The film, based on actual interviews of former prisoners and documented evidence of the atrocities of the Communists, lacks credibility. Its cliché-ridden dialogue ("Every man has his breaking point") and one-dimensional characters, particularly the nasty Communists, work against the basic theme. ■

Prisoners of war. American film studios have produced numerous war films concerning individuals captured by the enemy and explored almost every conceivable angle involving prisoners. Some films depicted the interplay between the two adversaries. Others worked in a love story between a prisoner and a local female. Those designed for propaganda purposes concentrated on the brutal treatment of the captives. Still others found comedy in the situation. The approach most often used was the escape. Breaking out almost became an obligatory element of prison camp dramas and comedies. The planning and execution of an escape embellished the drama with suspense, action and the anticipated pursuit as the hero tries to return to his own lines.

America's earliest films about prisoners of war concerned the Civil War. In 1909, for ex-

ample, D.W. Griffith's short, one-reel drama "In Old Kentucky" underscored one of the tragedies of that war when a Confederate soldier is captured by his own brother who is fighting with the Union. Another one-reeler, "The Road to Richmond" (1910), told of a Union soldier who saves the life a Southern girl and is then captured by the Confederates. The girl intercedes for the prisoner, and General Lee releases him. Southern gentility and honor prevail. Three years later a similar plot unfolded when a daughter of the South falls in love with a Union officer in "The Sinews of War" (1913), directed by Thomas Ince. When he is captured, the girl's brother effects his escape. The Northerner later saves the girl's life. The "faithful black slave," already a staple on stage and on the early silent screen, played a prominent role in *Dan* (1914). The title character, a servant-slave, helps his young master, a Confederate officer, escape his Union captors. Dan remains behind in his master's place and is executed the next morning. Director D.W. Griffith the following year turned out his classic, *The Birth of a Nation*. A major portion of the plot concerns a Southern colonel, Ben Cameron, who is wounded and captured by the Union. Scheduled for execution as a spy, he is saved by pleas to an understanding President Lincoln.

Andersonville, the Confederate military prison for Union soldiers outside the village of Andersonville in southwest Georgia, was the site for one of the Civil War's most shocking tragedies. During the two years (1864–65) in which the prison and its prison hospital existed, almost 13,000 inmates died there. The North made great propaganda use of the situation. Its commander, Captain Henry Wirz, was hanged on November 10, 1865, soon after the end of hostilities, following a trial before a military tribunal. The area today is the site of a Federal cemetery and park memorializing the tragedy. Few films have used the notorious prison as background. The earliest was a superficial silent one-reeler, "Escape From Andersonville" (1909), which barely touched upon its terrible conditions. More contemporary military conflicts such as the Balkan Wars and World War I provided the movie studios with opportunities to broaden the scope of prisoner-of-war dramas. The former conflict supplied the background for *The Captive* (1915). A Turkish soldier, captured by the Montenegrins, is assigned to work on a local farm run by Blanche Sweet. The Turks attack and overrun the farm. When a drunken Turkish officer tries to rape the farm girl, the prisoner rescues her. A similar plot occurred in the World War I drama, *Barbed Wire* (1927), when a French farm girl (Pola Negri) falls in love with a German prisoner of war (Clive Brook). The film ends with a plea against national hatreds. This romantic plot was again employed in *Surrender* (1931). A French prisoner in northern Prussia (Warner Baxter) and a young German woman (Leila Hyams) living in a nearby castle fall in love.

The Great War furnished a variety of combinations of captives and captors. An Austrian in *Three of Many* (1916) is taken prisoner by an Italian, both of whom were friends before the war. *Who Goes There?* (1917) told of an American civilian in Belgium who is taken prisoner by the Germans and forced to spy for his captors. In *After the War* (1918) a former French prisoner shows his gratitude to a Prussian officer who has saved his life. An English officer (Clive Brook) is captured by the Germans and held prisoner until the end of the conflict in *The Man From Yesterday* (1932); his wife (Claudette Colbert), thinking he is dead, plans to marry someone else (Charles Boyer). A German air ace becomes a prisoner of the Americans in *Hell in the Heavens* (1934) while an American sailor (Wallace Beery) is captured by the crew of a German U-boat in *Thunder Afloat* (1939). Many World War I films involved escapes. In *An Alien Enemy* (1918) German soldiers attempt to escape from a French prison camp. The most famous canine in screen history, Rin-Tin-Tin, helps a downed American flier to escape his German captors in *Dog of the Regiment* (1927). William Boyd and Louis Wolheim, as two bickering doughboys captured by the Germans in the comedy *Two Arabian Knights* (1927), escape from their prison camp dressed as Arabs. World War II dramas continued the patterns set by the earlier films and added a few of their own. *The Cross of Lorraine* (1943) depicted the barbaric treatment of French prisoners by their Nazi captives. The grim drama *The Seventh Cross* (1944), starring Spencer Tracy, again portrayed the brutality of the Nazi captors, this time toward political prisoners in a concentration camp.

Dramas made during the war showed that the Japanese were just as cruel in their treatment of prisoners as the Germans were. In *The Purple Heart* (1944) American fliers captured after the April 1942 raid over Tokyo are tortured, tried as war criminals and sentenced to death. *Back to Bataan* (1945) in part recounted the infamous Bataan death march during which many captured American and Filipino troops perished. That same year in *Tokyo Rose* an American prisoner of the Japanese is selected for an interview with Toyko Rose, Japan's purveyor of propaganda to the G.I.s, but he manages to escape, blow up the station and capture Rose.

Other escapes occurred in such films as *Man at Large* (1941) and *Bomber's Moon* (1943). In the former, an escaped German flier from a Canadian prisoner-of-war camp becomes the object of a search by reporter Marjorie Weaver and F.B.I. agent George Reeves. In the latter, a captured American airman steals a German plane, shoots down the enemy pilot who killed his brother and heads for England. Near the end of the war, the number of prisoners was estimated at four million. Germany alone held 1.7 million Allied prisoners. The Allies, in turn, also had well over a million Axis prisoners.

Prison camp films of the conflict continued to appear long after the war ended, some of which softened or entirely ignored any references to inhuman treatment by the Germans and Japanese. An English soldier (Philip Friend) in *My Own True Love* (1948) suffers psychological scars as a result of his internment in a Japanese camp. *Stalag 17* (1953), based on the stage play, described treachery from within when captured American fliers learn that their German captors have planted a spy in their barracks. The stalag guard (Sig Ruman) is a jovial German with an unusual sense of humor. *The Great Escape* (1963), one of the more exciting and popular escape dramas, depicted elaborate plans on the part of British prisoners to break out of their German camp and create chaos within Germany, thereby diverting numerous enemy troops from combat. Frank Sinatra, as an American prisoner of war in *Von Ryan's Express* (1965), steals an enemy train and, with a number of fellow British captives, rides the rails to the Swiss border and freedom. In *The McKenzie Break* (1970) Nazi officers escape from a prison camp in Scotland but are soon apprehended by their clever commandant (Brian Keith). Allied prisoners in *Victory* (1981) plot their escape from German captivity during a soccer game with their foes.

Films of the Korean War told another story of American prisoners in the hands of Communists. The enemy employed brainwashing techniques and other hardships on their captives. Ronald Reagan in *Prisoner of War* (1954) is purposely dropped behind North Korean lines to investigate atrocities against American soldiers in their prison camps. Collaboration on the part of several prisoners results in their murders or courts martial after the war in such films as *The Rack* (1954), starring Paul Newman, and *Time Limit* (1957), starring Richard Widmark. *The Bamboo Prison* (1954) suggests that American collaborators actually were agents working for the U.S. government. The atrocities that American combat troops faced escalated in brutality by the time dramas of the Vietnam War appeared. *The Deer Hunter* (1978) described harrowing sequences of the treatment of American prisoners by the Viet Cong, including a deadly "Russian roulette" game the captives are forced to participate in for the amusement of their captors. Some of the Chuck Norris *Missing in Action* films and Sylvester Stallone *Rambo* action dramas also included brutal sequences of torture on the part of the enemy. ∎

Private Benjamin (1980). See Service Comedy. ∎

Private Izzy Murphy (1926), WB. *Dir.* Lloyd Bacon; *Sc.* Philip Lonergan; *Cast includes:* George Jessel, Patsy Ruth Miller, Vera Gordon, Nat Carr, William Strauss.

Another film debut by a Broadway Ziegfeld performer (Eddie Cantor starred in *Kid Boots* and W. C. Fields made *It's the Old Army Game*), this comedy stars George Jessel as a Jewish boy in love with an Irish girl who doesn't know his ethnic background. He joins the Fighting 69th, the Irish regiment, under the name Isadore Patrick Murphy, and is shipped to France. He finally reveals the truth in a letter to his sweetheart (Patsy Ruth Miller). When her family learns the truth, sparks begin to fly. But upon his return, his fellow doughboys come to his rescue, and the marriage takes place.

The film strikes a few false notes, especially in its handling of the theme of ethnic relations. Instead of treating it comically in tune with the rest of the plot, the film becomes didactic. There is an insert concerning the status of the Jewish war veteran; Murphy's Jewish orthodox parents don't object to his marrying out of his religion; his father makes a speech about members of all groups being the children of God. Also, some of the gags, such as the one referring to the cash register as the "Jewish organ," are more anti-Semitic than humorous. Certainly anti-Semitism was as much an issue during this period as it is today, but other films prior to this one, such as *Abie's Irish Rose*, handled the theme with more humor and less phoniness. ∎

Private Jones (1933), U. *Dir.* Russell Mack; *Sc.* Prescott Chaplin, William N. Robson; *Cast includes:* Lee Tracy, Donald Cook, Gloria Stuart, Shirley Grey, Emma Dunn, Walter Catlett.

A World War I comedy starring Lee Tracy, the film traces his changing attitudes from a slacker who doesn't believe in killing Germans to his heroic deeds once he hits the trenches in France. In the interval he is revealed at K.P. and other supposedly funny misadventures. Several character actors help the proceedings. They include Walter Catlett as a prissy canteen worker and Frank McHugh as a chef. A few war sequences are interspersed in the latter half of the film. Viewed as satire, the film may well reflect America's disillusionment with the war—at least from the vantage point of the 1930s. It poked fun at officers (the naive lieutenant), do-gooders (Y.M.C.A. workers) and those who would protect our youth from any potential immoral temptations they might encounter once "over there" (the hygiene speaker). The strongest antiwar aspect, however, was the title character, a draft dodger who merely had no desire to fight. ∎

Private Navy of Sgt. O'Farrell, The (1968), UA. *Dir.* Frank Tashlin; *Sc.* Frank Tashlin; *Cast includes:* Bob Hope, Phyllis Diller, Jeffrey Hunter, Gina Lollobrigida.

Bob Hope stars as the title character, a noncom stationed on a remote Pacific island during World War II. When a cargo ship carrying a shipment of beer is torpedoed, Hope is determined to appropriate the coveted consignment for his men to boost their sagging morale. The soldiers get the beer while Hope captures a Japanese submarine. Comedienne Phyllis Diller portrays a nurse who provides little romantic comfort for those on the island. Jeffrey Hunter plays a navy lieutenant. Gina Lollobrigida, as Hope's former flame, shows up on the island and provides the romantic interest for our dubious hero in this zany comedy. ■

Private Peat (1918), Par. *Dir.* Edward Jose; *Sc.* Charles Whittaker; *Cast includes:* Harold R. Peat, Miriam Fouche, William T. Sorelle.

Based on the true war experiences of Harold Peat, the drama covers his enlistment, his experiences on the front lines, his being wounded and his convalescence. The film, in comparing World War I casualties to those of the Civil War, presents statistics concerning the lower death rate of the wounded in the more recent conflict. During the war between the North and the South approximately 22 percent of those wounded in battle died. In World War I the figure had decreased dramatically to less than three percent. Peat's war experiences were first published under the title *Two Years in Hell and Back With a Smile.* ■

Private Snuffy Smith (1942). See Service Comedy. ■

Professionals, The (1966), Col. *Dir.* Richard Brooks; *Sc.* Richard Brooks; *Cast includes:* Burt Lancaster, Lee Marvin, Robert Ryan, Ralph Bellamy, Claudia Cardinale, Woody Strode.

An American millionaire (Ralph Bellamy) hires four soldiers of fortune to rescue his wife from a Mexican rebel leader in this action drama set in 1916 during the Mexican Revolution. Each of the hired men is an expert in his own field. A dynamite expert (Burt Lancaster) also enjoys women and alcohol. "So what else is on your mind," a friend asks him, "besides 100-proof women, 90-proof whiskey and 14-karat gold?" "Amigo," Lancaster replies, "you just wrote my epitaph." The leader of the team (Lee Marvin) is a former Rough Rider, weapons expert and tactician. A top wrangler (Robert Ryan) is in charge of the mounts. A professional tracker (Woody Strode) is also proficient in the bow and arrow.

Their trek, across a "hellhole of a desert," brings them into confrontations with bandits as well as revolutionaries led by Jack Palance. When they reach Palance's camp, they discover that their employer's wife (Claudia Cardinale) has not been kidnaped but has voluntarily run off to be with Palance, her childhood sweetheart. Following a stormy battle with Palance's men, the professionals bring her back, with Palance as their prisoner. When Bellamy orders his guards to shoot Palance, the quartet, out of their own sense of justice, object. "You haven't earned the right to shoot him," Lancaster remarks. Against the objections of Bellamy, the four "professionals" allow Cardinale to return to Mexico with her lover.

Distrustful of Bellamy, a symbol of big business and the establishment, and cynical about causes, the four men follow their own code as exemplified by Marvin, who is the conscience of the team. When Lancaster says that his word to Bellamy "ain't worth a plug nickel," Marvin reminds him: "You gave your word to me." Disillusioned with all aspects of society ranging from government to business, the professionals realize they can count only on each other.

The film makes several references to the revolution. On the walls of abandoned villages is painted "Viva Villa." When Marvin calls Cardinale a "whore," she replies: "If we can keep the revolution alive . . . for even one more day, then I will cheat and steal and even whore." But Lancaster voices a more cynical outlook. "Maybe there's only one revolution," Lancaster states, "the good guys against the bad guys. The question is, 'Who are the good guys?'" Later, in a colloquy with Palance, Lancaster muses: "When the shooting stops and the dead are buried and the politicians take over, it all adds up to one thing—a lost cause." But the pragmatic rebel leader understands the shifting nature of revolution, comparing it at first to a love affair with a beautiful woman who later becomes corrupted. "We stay because we believe, we leave because we are disillusioned, we come back because we are lost, we die because we are committed." The film, released during the Vietnam War and civil unrest that struck America, may well reflect this turbulent period. ■

Project X (1968). See Cold War. ■

Propaganda films: World War I. The first conscious use of the film medium for propaganda purposes began prior to America's entry into World War I. England, Germany and France produced compilation films based on combat newsreels and designed for home-front consumption. Some made their way to America. The U.S., including the Army Signal Corps, was ill-equipped at first to provide documentaries or even newsreels, having no official branch capable of handling such matters. The Committee on Public Information, a federal propaganda agency, was formed and eventually began turning out feature-length documentaries. The first, *Pershing's Crusaders* (1918), alludes to the ill-fated *Lusitania*, Germany's invasion of Belgium, President Wilson's address to Congress and other topical events. Later films include *America's Answer* and *Under Four Flags*.

Meanwhile Hollywood was busily engaged in the controversy between the forces of pacifism and preparedness. Such films as *War o' Dreams* (1915) and Thomas Ince's epic *Civilization* (1916) pleaded for peace while J. Stuart Blackton's *The Battle Cry of Peace* (1915) and Bartley Cushing's *The Fall of a Nation* (1916) exhorted the nation to build up its military power. The debate ended when the U.S. was drawn into the war.

With the outbreak of hostilities, the movie studios saw the potential for profit in the lurid aspects of the war while they simultaneously served their country. The C.P.I. willingly provided scripts and ideas to the studios and occasionally offered troops and lent out military equipment. A flood of dramas found their way into movie houses in America as well as in neutral countries. Films that attacked slackers, incited audiences against the brutal Huns and praised those on the home front who kept the war materiel flowing all served to feed the propaganda machine.

Those who evaded the draft drew the wrath of public opinion, thanks to such films as *The Slacker* (1917), about a wealthy young man who marries to escape the draft, and *Draft 258* (1918), about a slacker who discovers the importance of fighting for one's country. Both were directed by Christy Cabanne. In *Shame* (1917) a family is disgraced by a son who shirks his duty. The heroine in *The Service Star* (1918) shames a slacker into joining the army. In *Mrs. Slacker* (1918) a wife discovers that the only reason her husband married her was to avoid the draft. *For Valour* (1917), *The Man Who Was Afraid* (1917) and *Bud's Recruit* (1918) were other films with a similar theme. In the last, Wallis Brennan portrays a young lad who embarrasses his older brother

into joining the army in this two-reel comedy. Perhaps the genre reached its peak with *A Little Patriot* (1917), in which the child star, Baby Peggy, chides other children to spit on those suspected of being slackers.

Anti-German propaganda included denunciations of disloyal German-Americans as well as the enemy on the battlefield. In Raoul Walsh's *The Prussian Cur* (1918), a hooded gang, not unlike the Ku Klux Klan, engages in lynching German-Americans who come under suspicion of sabotage. A German-American betrays the U.S. in *The Hun Within* (1918).

But the bulk of Anti-German propaganda films during World War I concerned the brutality and general inhumanity of the Prussian military. *On Dangerous Ground* (1917), made before America's entry into the war, incensed its audiences by showing Germans torturing a French maiden who helps an American escape from enemy-occupied France. Hollywood scored its greatest propaganda success when it placed America's most popular screen star, Mary Pickford, in jeopardy in *The Little American* (1917). A lecherous Prussian officer gazes at Mary with the most dishonorable intentions. *My Four Years in Germany* (1918), a pseudo-documentary based on the writings of James W. Girard, the former U.S. Ambassador to Germany, depicts the horrors suffered by prisoners of war at the hands of the Germans. Several scenes that claim to be authentic had been shot in a studio. *The Kaiser, the Beast of Berlin* (1918) emphasizes, once again, the atrocities perpetrated by Germany upon Belgium.

Both the government and private studios supplied a series of films showing how those at home could serve the war effort. The subject matter gave actresses an opportunity to play the leading characters. Mary Miles Minter, a popular screen personality of the period, portrays a patriotic young woman in *Her Country's Call* (1917). She sets out to prove that women can replace men in war plants and shipyards, thereby releasing the workers for military service. In *Her Country First* (1918) Vivian Martin organizes a girls' aviation auxiliary. When German agents break into her home, she and her troop help to capture the spies.

Men not in uniform tried desperately to join up or served their country in other ways. Heavy-drinking William Desmond in *An Honest Man* (1918) is at first rejected from military service but later reforms under the influence of a farmer and his pretty daughter. A chemist and his female assistant (Ethel Barrymore) develop a new explosive in *The Greatest Power* (1917). The chemist, a confirmed pacifist, hesitates to give the formula to the U.S. government until it is almost stolen by foreign agents. A male dress designer in *The Gown of Destiny* (1917) who is too frail for the front lines uses the profits from his business to purchase much-needed ambulances.

Following the war, the anti-German films subsided and gave way to dramas which treated the German people sympathetically—portraying them as helpless and duped victims of a heartless military. See also Atrocity Films. ■

Propaganda films: World War II. Preceding America's entry into the Second World War, Hollywood turned out a string of military-related films that seemed more like recruitment posters than the familiar entertainment vehicles audiences had grown accustomed to. These features romanticized various branches of the service. Warner Brothers seemed to be the vanguard of this type. The titles are self-explanatory—*Here Comes the Navy* (1934), starring James Cagney; *Devil Dogs of the Air* (1935), again with James Cagney; *Submarine D-1* (1937), starring Pat O'Brien; and *Wings of the Navy* (1939), starring George Brent. Other studios were quick to follow suit. RKO, for instance, released *Parachute Battalion* (1941), with Robert Preston and Edmond O'Brien. Several films were made with the welcome cooperation of the government which furnished the facilities and staff.

World War II provided a steady outpouring of propaganda documentaries and feature films. As in the previous world conflict, the U.S. was late in developing its full propaganda potential. Private producers and studios were first on the screen with films that awakened its audiences to the European situation, aroused sympathy for Britain and incited anti-Nazi sentiment. Louis de Rochemont produced a series of 20-minute shorts under the title "The March of Time," which contributed towards turning American opinion against the Axis powers. Such entries as "Inside Nazi Germany" (1938), "Canada at War" (1939), "Britain's R.A.F." (1940), "The Ramparts We Watch" (1940) and "America Speaks Her Mind" (1941) mixed newsreel shots with staged footage.

Major studios entered the propaganda war with caution, while the U.S. maintained a policy of neutrality. Warner Brothers produced *Confessions of a Nazi Spy* (1939), starring Edward G. Robinson as a federal agent who exposes a German network of agents operating in the the U.S. It was the first American drama prior to the nation's entry into the war to attack the Nazi regime openly. Nazi officials registered protests, and pro-German forces set fire to a Milwaukee theater that exhibited the film. Director Alfred Hitchcock, who had come to Hollywood in 1939, turned out *Foreign Correspondent* in 1940, warning audiences about Nazi spies. Prewar America was not yet completely mobilized against the Nazi threat. When Chaplin released *The Great Dictator* in 1940, his satire of a dictator strongly resembling Hitler was banned by Chicago's censors as being politically biased. *Sergeant York* (1941), directed by Howard Hawks and starring Gary Cooper as the World War I hero, helped to convert American sentiment against Germany.

By late 1941, several months before America's entry into the war, a Senate subcommittee began examining allegations of "war propaganda" in Hollywood films, citing such examples as the last three listed above. The committee charged that these features gave only one side of the European conflict and, more specifically, were strongly pro-British. Other members of the Senate accused the studios of predetermining the direction of foreign policy and invoking war hysteria. The controversy faded temporarily when the Japanese attacked Pearl Harbor.

One of the strongest anti-Nazi propaganda films concerning Germany's youth was Edward Dmytryk's *Hitler's Children* (1942). The story centers on a simple love story between a German youth (Tim Holt) who falls victim to Nazi ideology and a young American (Bonita Granville) raised in Germany. More fascinating than the routine romantic plot were the portions dealing with the political indoctrination of the young, the clinics set up to sterilize "undesirable" women and the experiments in genetic control designed to produce a super-Aryan race.

Hollywood's retaliation to Japan's sneak attack took several forms. Films, often dotted with racial slurs, were quick to point out Japan's treachery in battle, its brutality toward prisoners and civilians and its utter disregard for international rules of war. With these images in mind, audiences delighted whenever one of Japan's sons bit the dust and an American fighting man followed through with a quip. "Fried Jap going down," gunner George Tobias exclaims in *Air Force* (1943) as he blasts an enemy Zero. "Scratch one squint-eye," a marine utters after shooting a Japanese soldier in *Guadalcanal Diary* (1943). John Wayne in *The Fighting Seabees* (1944) can't wait to tangle with "Tojo and his bug-eyed pals." Even wise-cracking Bugs Bunny in the cartoon "Bugs Bunny Nips the Nips" (1944) gets into the act by addressing his Japanese adversaries as "slant eyes."

The Office of War Information enlisted the services of some of Hollywood's major directors in producing several high-quality propaganda documentaries. Frank Capra, no doubt chosen for his films that often bordered on populist sentimentality, produced the "Why We Fight" series, which ran from 1942 through 1945. John Ford turned out *The Battle of Midway* (1942), the crucial sea battle that was the turning point in the war in the Pacific, and William Wyler was responsible for *Memphis Belle* (1944), the story of an American bomber and its crew that flew 25 missions over German-occupied territory. One lesser-known director, Anatole Litvak, had worked in the film industry in his native Russia, Germany, England and France before coming to America. During World War II he co-directed several documentaries with Capra, including *The Nazis Strike* (1942), *Divide and Conquer* (1943) and *The Battle of China* (1944). He also directed *Operation Titanic* (1943), *The Battle of Russia* (1943) and *War Comes to America* (1945), all documentaries.

Generally, government-sponsored propaganda films were not shown in local movie houses. Instead, the government proposed the following topics that should be included in feature films: issues of the conflict, the nature of the Axis Powers, the nature of America's allies, the production and home fronts, and the fighting troops. Hollywood was quick to respond.

Film studios also produced short subjects to help the war effort. Warner Brothers, for example, made "Service With the Colors," "Meet the Fleet," "Soldiers in White," "The Tanks Are Coming," "Here Comes the Cavalry," "Commandos of the Sky" and "Rear Gunner." The last, starring James Stewart, was suggested by a general who informed the studio that the air force was short of rear gunners. Soon after the film was exhibited, the shortage was alleviated.

The home front was the subject of numerous dramas during World War II. Although many were confined to escapist entertainment, some were propaganda vehicles. In *Joe Smith, American* (1942) Robert Young portrays an aircraft worker who is kidnaped by spies. As they torture him for information, he resists by thinking of patriotic images, including those of Nathan Hale and "The Pledge of Allegiance." Don Ameche plays a grieving father in *Happy Land* (1943). When he bemoans that his son, killed in action, never had a chance to grow up, he is visited by the spirit of "Gramps," a Civil War veteran, who reminds Ameche of the many happy moments in the boy's life. Richard Arlen, as a returning G.I. suffering from amnesia in *Identity Unknown* (1945), comforts families who have lost someone in the war. They come to understand that the spirits of those killed in action live on in the future of America.

Perhaps the most effective piece of propaganda during these early years was William Wyler's *Mrs. Miniver* (1942), which depicts the English home front, by way of a very appealing family, struggling bravely to maintain its democratic ideals while battling the evil forces of Nazism. Other propaganda dramas turned to England for their background. *Forever and a Day* (1943), the efforts of seven directors, 21 screenwriters and more than 75 popular screen personalities, glorifies the English people and their many sacrifices spanning a century of conflicts. RKO turned over the film profits to several charities. In *The Hour Before the Dawn* (1944) Franchot Tone portrays an English conscientious objector—until he discovers that his wife (Veronica Lake) is a Nazi agent.

Light comedies such as *Swing Shift Maisie* (1943) and *Rosie the Riveter* (1944) suggest the changing role of women and their important contributions to the war effort.

Government agencies supplied several documentaries stressing the integral part the home front plays in winning the war. *War Department Report* (1943) underscores how the war materiel produced in the factories at home can lead to Nazi and Japanese defeats at the front. The Office of War Information released the short subject "War Town" in 1943 to show how one city coped with a housing shortage when defense workers poured into the community.

Unlike the postwar period of the 1920s, post-World War II continued to produce propaganda films—its subject now changed to the Cold War with the Soviet Union. Official government films of the U.S. Information Service included such titles as *Red Nightmare*, *Why Korea?* (1951) and *This Is Your Army* (1954). Hollywood studios complemented these with *The Red Menace* (1949), *My Son John* (1952) and *The Green Berets* (1968). See also Atrocity Films. ∎

Proud and the Profane, The (1956), Par. *Dir.* George Seaton; *Sc.* George Seaton; *Cast includes:* William Holden, Deborah Kerr, Thelma Ritter, Dewey Martin, William Redfield.

A romantic drama set on a Pacific island during World War II, the film concerns a tough marine colonel (William Holden) and a war widow and nurse (Deborah Kerr). They meet in New Caledonia, an island used as a base for the wounded. At first sparks fly between them as she rejects his callousness. Ultimately they fall in love and she becomes pregnant. She then learns that he has an alcoholic wife back in the U.S. However, the obstacle is removed when Holden's wife conveniently dies. Several brief action sequences are interjected between the love scenes in this routine story that often resembles *From Here to Eternity* (1953). ∎

Prussian Cur, The (1918), Fox. *Dir.* Raoul Walsh; *Sc.* Raoul Walsh; *Cast includes:* Miriam Cooper, James Marcus, Patrick O'Malley, Lenora Stewart.

An anti-German propaganda film made during World War I, the drama concerns a German spy bent on initiating acts of sabotage in America. He visits a town in the West where he tries to convince a German-American to damage an airplane plant. Bristling at the suggestion, the loyal American has the agent arrested. When pro-Germans gather in the street to plan the spy's rescue, white-hooded horsemen ride into town and capture the German sympathizers. The patriotic riders force the Germans to kiss the stars and stripes and then lead them into the jail. The climactic scene resembles that of the Ku Klux Klan coming to the rescue of a Southern

town in D.W. Griffith's *The Birth of a Nation* (1915). At least one reviewer criticized the film for advocating mob violence as the means to a just end. ∎

Puppets (1926). See Veterans. ∎

Dana Andrews, as captain of a U.S. air force crew captured after the Doolittle raid on Tokyo, faces a brutal and recalcitrant enemy. *The Purple Heart* (1944).

Purple Heart, The (1944), TCF. *Dir.* Lewis Milestone; *Sc.* Jerome Cady; *Cast includes:* Dana Andrews, Richard Conte, Farley Granger, Donald Barry, Sam Levene.

A tribute to the bravery of young men during World War II who withstood torture rather than submit to enemy demands, the drama tells of an American bomber crew captured by the Japanese after their successful mission in the spring of 1942 over Japan and their mock trial. Dana Andrews plays the stalwart captain. The men represent the typical democratic crew prevalent in films made during the war. Richard Conte portrays Angelo Canelli, an Italian-American. Sam Levene plays Wayne Greenbaum, the Jewish member from New York who studied law. He reminds his pals that Japan never signed the Geneva Treaty. Kevin O'Shea is Jan Skvoznik, an unidentified Slovak. The other fliers are from various sections of the country. During the trial, a travesty of justice, prewar disaster films are projected showing innocent civilians suffering from an unnamed disaster. The Japanese prosecutor claims the raid was aimed at schools and hospitals. A corrupt Chinese governor of a local province testifies against the defendants. His idealistic son not only refutes the testimony but kills his father in the courtroom. As the boy is led away, the American prisoners stand up in his honor.

Later, the American fliers learn that the purpose of the trial is to get them to admit they came from the aircraft carrier *Hornet*. Rival army and naval officers are trying to shift the blame for the devastating raid on each other. After several Americans are physically tortured and the entire crew votes against cooperating with their captors, they are sentenced to death. Dana Andrews makes the final speech: "It's true we Americans don't know very much about you Japanese, and now I realize you know even less about us. You can kill us . . . But if you think that's going to put the fear of God into the United States of America and stop them from sending other bombers against you, you're wrong, dead wrong. They'll come by night and they'll come by day, thousands of them. They'll blacken your skies and burn your cities to the ground and make you get down on your knees and beg for mercy. This is your war, you started it . . . and it won't be finished until your dirty little empire is wiped off the face of the earth!" The defiant Americans are then marched out of the courtroom and down one of the longest corridors in screen history as the soundtrack plays the entire "Army Air Corps" song.

During the war, stories filtered out of Japanese-held territories of atrocities practiced upon prisoners. The Japanese announced that downed pilots of the April 1942 raid on Tokyo were executed following their confessions. The film is a fictional interpretation of that announcement. *Thirty Seconds Over Tokyo* (1944), starring Spencer Tracy as Doolittle, recounts the events of the first American bombing raid over Japan. The Purple Heart, a U.S. decoration originated by George Washington, was awarded to military personnel who were killed or wounded in action. Until September 1942 it was occasionally presented to those who demonstrated meritorious service. ∎

Purple Heart Diary (1951), Col. *Dir.* Richard Quine; *Sc.* William Sackheim; *Cast includes:* Frances Langford, Judd Holdren, Ben Lessy.

This light World War II drama about a group of U.S.O. entertainers in the Pacific includes musical numbers, romance and some battle scenes. The weak plot is based on

Frances Langford's newspaper columns during the war. In the film she helps a romance between a nurse (Alice Towne) and a wounded officer (Brett King). The Japanese interfere with the romances and the entertainment when they stage a surprise attack, but they are soon defeated by the stalwart American forces in this routine film. ∎

Purple Hearts (1984), WB. *Dir.* Sidney J. Furie; *Sc.* Rick Natkin, Sidney J. Furie; *Cast includes:* Ken Wahl, Cheryl Ladd, Stephen Lee, David Harris, Cyril O'Reilly.

The Vietnam War provides the background for this weak and familiar love story between a navy surgeon and a nurse. Ken Wahl portrays a cynical battlefield doctor who meets a pretty nurse (Cheryl Ladd) while performing a critical operation. A war widow reluctant to have her heart broken a second time by the loss of a serviceman, she at first rejects Wahl but later succumbs to his charms. The gritty action sequences include waves of Viet Cong troops attacking U.S. machine-gun positions, Wahl being shot down behind enemy lines and his perilous escape while helping a wounded buddy. ∎

Purple Mask, The (1955), U. *Dir.* Bruce Humberstone; *Sc.* Oscar Brodney; *Cast includes:* Tony Curtis, Colleen Miller, Gene Barry, Dan O'Herlihy, Angela Lansbury.

Tony Curtis plays a dual role in this familiar costume drama set during the French Revolution. Highly reminiscent of *The Scarlet Pimpernel*, a 1934 English film, Curtis, as the title character, is an elusive hero who champions the cause of the Royalists by kidnaping high officials of the Republic and then returning them for ransom. When he is not busy in derring-do, he masquerades as a foppish figure. After futile attempts to capture him, he surrenders to save the lives of a group of Royalists. He then fights a duel for their journey out of France and manages to leave with them. Colleen Miller, as the daughter of an imprisoned aristocrat, provides the romantic interest. Robert Cornthwaite plays Napoleon in this colorful but familiar tale. ∎

Purple V, The (1943), Rep. *Dir.* George Sherman; *Sc.* Bertram Millhauser; *Cast includes:* John Archer, Mary McLeod, Fritz Kortner, Rex Williams.

A routine World War II drama, the film

concerns an American pilot (John Archer) who is shot down behind German lines. Fritz Kortner portrays a sympathetic German schoolteacher who disagrees with the "new" Germany and helps the flier to reach Allied lines. He also conveniently provides the American with secret plans concerning North African military strategy—a move which costs him his life. Mary McLeod provides the romantic interest. ■

Pursuit to Algiers (1945). See Detectives at War. ■

Pyle, Ernie. See *The Story of G.I. Joe* (1945). ■

Q

Quana Parker. See *Comanche* (1956). ∎

Quantrill, William Clarke (1837–1865). A band of 450 men led by William Quantrill, a Confederate guerrilla leader, crossed the Missouri border into Kansas one summer night in 1863. The son of a Northern school teacher, Quantrill, who for some unknown reason had decided to aid the South in the vicious guerrilla war that raged on the Kansas–Missouri border, was bent on revenge. Several women, wives and sisters of members of his band had died in the collapse of a building in which they were detained by Federal officials for providing food and shelter for his group. Quantrill and his group decided to wreak their vengeance many times over for their personal loss.

The band first captured and killed ten farmers suspected of Northern sympathies. They then headed to Lawrence, an area noted for its rabid espousal of the anti-slavery cause. They struck the town at dawn on August 21, 1863. Within the next few hours they killed 183 men and boys and torched 185 buildings before fleeing from pursuing Federal cavalry to their sanctuary in the Missouri woods. *Quantrill's Raiders* (1958), the only film to recreate the bloody raid, fictionalizes the ending by having the guerrilla leader killed there. Historically, Quantrill survived the assault.

This wasn't the only raid executed by Quantrill, who had brought together a gang of killers that included some who would become famous as outlaws, such as the James and Younger brothers. *Jesse James Under the Black Flag* (1921), *Jesse James* (1927) and *Kansas Raiders* (1950) all have the famed outlaw joining Quantrill. Many of the outlaws joined the raiders not for political cause but

as an opportunity to commit brutal acts. In August 1862, Quantrill had captured Independence, Missouri, an event that earned him an officer's commission from a grateful Confederate general.

The band continued its destructive raids over the next two years following the Lawrence massacre despite increased Union attempts to capture the group. The imprisonment of their women, which led to the tragic building collapse and some of their deaths, was merely one of several attempts to separate the band from supporters who gave them aid.

Quantrill eventually headed eastward, reportedly seeking to assassinate Lincoln. He ran into a Union patrol in Kentucky and was killed in 1865. Some members of his group surrendered after the war ended and were allowed to go free as paroled soldiers. Among them were the James and Younger brothers who continued their lawlessness.

Other films in which Quantrill is portrayed are *Red Mountain* (1951) and *Arizona Raiders* (1965), fictitious tales of his exploits. Two Civil War westerns, *The Dark Command* (1940) and *The Desperados* (1969), have a Quantrill-like guerrilla leader committing similar raids. Walter Pidgeon portrays the leader in the former while Jack Palance plays him in the latter. ∎

Quantrill's Raiders (1958), AA. Dir. Edward Bernds; Sc. Polly James; *Cast includes:* Steve Cochran, Diane Brewster, Leo Gordon, Gale Robbins.

The violent exploits of the famous Confederate guerrilla, Quantrill, provide the basis for this Civil War action drama. Steve Cochran portrays a Confederate officer who delivers orders to the guerrilla leader about a

Union arsenal located in Lawrence, Kansas. Cochran, posing as a horse trader, enters the town first and learns that the arms have been moved elsewhere. When he returns to the raiders, Quantrill insists on attacking the town to settle an old score. Cochran objects and is kept behind while the leader and about 20 men ride out for revenge. Cochran escapes and warns the townspeople. In the battle Quantrill is killed and his men defeated.

The conclusion of the film is fictitious. Historically, hundreds of Quantrill's men raided the town and killed several hundred of its inhabitants. He survived to continue his marauding along the Kansas-Missouri border during the war. ∎

Quebec (1951), Par. *Dir.* George Templeton; *Sc.* Alan LeMay; *Cast includes:* John Barrymore, Jr., Corinne Calvert, Barbara Rush, Patric Knowles.

This historical drama concerns Quebec's unsuccessful revolt in 1837 against British rule. Corinne Calvert portrays Madame Stephanie Durossac, the silent leader of the rebellion and wife of the conspiring commander of the British troops. She is romantically involved with the fighting leader of the revolt (Patric Knowles). John Barrymore, Jr. plays their illegitimate son who is chased by various females in this inept film that offers more fiction than historical fact. ∎

Quentin Durward (1955), MGM. *Dir.* Richard Thorpe; *Sc.* Robert Ardrey; *Cast includes:* Robert Taylor, Kay Kendall, Robert Morley, George Cole.

A costume drama based on Sir Walter Scott's novel of the same name, the film stars Robert Taylor as a knight who becomes entangled in court intrigue. He journeys from Scotland to France to seek out a bride for his uncle. The dubious honor falls to Kay Kendall with whom Taylor falls in love. Meanwhile, he is forced to battle against the political plotting of King Louis XI of France (Robert Morley) and the Duke of Burgundy (Alex Clunes). There are several stirring action sequences, including hand-to-hand combat between hero and villain. The historical context of the drama concerns the conflict between Charles the Bold of Burgundy and Louis XI, both of whom eventually clashed at the Battle of Montlhery (1465).

Taylor made five films in England during this period, including the more successful

Ivanhoe (1952), based, of course, on another Scott novel, and which no doubt gave impetus to the above production. ∎

Quick and the Dead, The (1963), Beckman. *Dir.* Robert Totten; *Sc.* Sheila Lynch, Robert Totten; *Cast includes:* Larry Mann, Victor French, Jon Cedar, James Almanzar.

A squad of American G.I.s engage in a series of bloody battles against the Germans in northern Italy in this low-budget World War II action drama. Diminished in numbers by the skirmishes, the group teams up with Italian partisans. Together, they are able to stave off a superior force. The film concentrates more on action than on characterization, thereby weakening audience sympathy for those who bravely fall in battle. ∎

Quiet American, The (1958), UA. *Dir.* Joseph L. Mankiewicz; *Sc.* Joseph L. Mankiewicz; *Cast includes:* Audie Murphy, Michael Redgrave, Claude Dauphin, Giorgia Moll.

An American in Vietnam in 1952 during the French Indo-China War clashes ideologically with an English correspondent in this talky drama based on Graham Greene's novel. Greene's attack on the U.S. and its botched foreign policy has been diluted by having Audie Murphy portray a private American citizen instead of an official who believes there is an alternative between Communism and French colonialism in that part of the world. Michael Redgrave, as a cynical writer who loses his objectivity, sides with the Communists who use him as a dupe and ultimately betray him. He is partially responsible for Murphy's death by informing the Communist guerrillas that Murphy is dealing in explosives. Giorgia Moll, as Redgrave's mistress, falls in love with the American who proposes to her. Limited action sequences concern guerrilla activities against the French forces. ∎

Quiet Please, Murder (1942). See Spy Films: the Talkies. ∎

Quincannon, Frontier Scout (1956), UA. *Dir.* Lesley Selander; *Sc.* John C. Higgins, Don Martin; *Cast includes:* Tony Martin, Peggie Castle, John Bromfield, John Smith.

Tony Martin portrays the title character, an ex-army captain, in this routine outdoor drama. Having served under General Custer and witnessing a particularly cold-blooded Indian massacre executed by the general, he resigned from the military. When a secret shipment of repeating rifles en route to an army outpost disappears, Quincannon is hired to investigate the affair. Following a series of skirmishes with Indians, he exposes the traitorous post commander (Ron Randell) as the culprit who sold the rifles to the hostiles. Peggie Castle, as the sister of a soldier killed in battle, provides the romantic interest. ■

Quisling, Vidkun (1887–1945). His name has become part of the English language as a synonym for one who betrays his country. To call someone a "Quisling" is to label that person as a traitor or "fifth columnist" who supports his country's oppressor.

Quisling was originally a Norwegian army officer with a promising career on the general staff in 1911. He served in several overseas diplomatic posts as a military attaché from 1918–1921 and at one time was the peacetime minister of defense (1931–1933) in the conservative government of the Agrarian Party. Though he dabbled briefly with socialist politics, by the early 1930's he began to formulate a coherent philosophy of Nordic supremacy with anti-leftist tendencies. He founded and led the National Union Party, using it as a platform for his political ideas.

Quisling and his party did poorly in elections, and he was no longer considered a serious force in national politics by the time World War II broke out. As a result, he turned to the German Nazi party for support and even met with Nazi leaders, including Adolf Hitler and Admiral Raeder, before his coun-

try's involvement in the war. Following the Nazi invasion of Norway in the spring of 1940, the Norwegian government fled Oslo, and Quisling was appointed premier of the Nazi puppet government. He tried, with little success, to implement Nazi policies and goals.

Norway quickly developed one of the more active resistance movements among the occupied nations. The activities of the Norwegian underground are covered in films such as *Edge of Darkness* (1943), in which Errol Flynn and Ann Sheridan portray a pair of resistance leaders, and *The Moon Is Down* (1943). The latter was a philosophically deeper drama based on John Steinbeck's anti-Nazi novel of the same name that also became a Broadway play prior to the movie. The character George Correl in *The Moon Is Down* is easily recognizable as the real-life Quisling.

Both films, to varying degrees, show the cruelty of underground war and reprisals that typified life in occupied lands. Surprisingly, in *The Moon Is Down*—a film that was blatantly propagandistic—a Nazi colonel (Sir Cedric Hardwicke) who is charged with subduing the Norwegian resistance questions the morality and ultimate success of the policy he must implement.

After Norway was liberated, Quisling was captured and executed by a firing squad on October 24, 1945, for his treasonous activities. Perhaps the most derisive screen attack upon him came in a 1943 Warners cartoon, "The Fifth Column Mouse." Quisling is reduced to a mouse who betrays his fellow creatures by collaborating with a despotic cat. ■

R

Rack, The (1956), MGM. *Dir.* Arnold Laven; *Sc.* Stewart Stern; *Cast includes:* Paul Newman, Wendell Corey, Walter Pidgeon, Edmond O'Brien, Anne Francis, Lee Marvin.

Paul Newman portrays a Korean War collaborator who is being court-martialed in this drama. A war hero before he was captured by the enemy, he is defended by Edmond O'Brien, who tries to establish that the accused suffered from extreme mental torture and was not responsible for his actions. Lee Marvin, as a fellow prisoner of war, testifies against Newman. Walter Pidgeon plays the defendant's father, a colonel in the army. Ultimately Newman is found guilty.

The subject of the film was fairly topical at the time of its release. The brainwashing and maltreatment that many American soldiers had to endure while captives of the Communists were coming to light as former prisoners related their tales of horror and incidents in which some of their buddies began to collaborate with the enemy. ∎

Racket Man, The (1944). See Crime and War. ∎

Raid, The (1954), TCF. *Dir.* Hugo Fregonese; *Sc.* Sydney Boehm; *Cast includes:* Van Heflin, Anne Bancroft, Richard Boone, Lee Marvin, Tommy Retig, Peter Graves.

Based on an actual incident during the Civil War, the film recounts a Confederate raid upon a small Vermont town in 1864. The small Southern force crossed the border from Canada to surprise the Yankees. A Rebel major (Van Heflin) escapes with several others from a Union prison and journeys to Canada, where they seek a temporary haven. Heflin then plots to raid a nearby Vermont village. His purpose is twofold: to give the Union a taste of the devastation and horror that Southern civilians experienced repeatedly and to relieve pressure on General Lee by diverting Union troops north to protect their towns. A war widow (Anne Bancroft) who runs a boarding house becomes emotionally involved with Heflin. Lee Marvin portrays an impulsive Rebel soldier. Richard Boone enacts a one-armed Yankee veteran. The film is indirectly based on the article "Affair at St. Albans," written by Herbert Ravenal Sass. ∎

Raid on Rommel (1971), U. *Dir.* Henry Hathaway; *Sc.* Richard Bluel; *Cast includes:* Richard Burton, John Colicos, Clinton Greyn, Danielle De Metz.

Richard Burton portrays a British Intelligence officer in this action drama set in North Africa during World War II. A British plan to infiltrate German lines and knock out the enemy's guns at Tobruk before the British fleet arrives hinges upon a specially trained Commando unit that has been captured by the Germans. Burton allows himself to be taken prisoner so that he can free the group. But he learns too late that the men have been transferred to another base. Interred chiefly with a group of medics, he decides to enlist their aid in accomplishing the mission. The film then proceeds with a series of suspenseful escapes and skirmishes with the enemy as the newly formed assault team goes about destroying strategic targets as well as crippling Rommel's tanks by igniting his fuel supply. Some of the spectacular action sequences used in the film *Tobruk* (1966) have been cleverly intercut into this present work. ∎

Raiders of Leyte Gulf (1963), Hemisphere. *Dir.* E. F. Romero; *Sc.* E. F. Romero, Carl Kuntze; *Cast includes:* Jennings Sturgeon, Michael Parsons, Liza Moreno.

American soldiers and Filipino guerrillas join forces in preparing for MacArthur's return to the Philippines in this low-budget World War II action drama. Made in the Philippines, the film provides plenty of action sequences as the small force battles the Japanese who overwhelmingly outnumber them. Jennings Sturgeon portrays an American Intelligence officer held prisoner by the Japanese and who is freed by the guerrillas. The rebels eventually are aided by the villagers who rise up against their conquerors. ■

Raiders of the Lost Ark (1981), Par. *Dir.* Steven Spielberg; *Sc.* Lawrence Kasdan; *Cast includes:* Harrison Ford, Karen Allen, Wolf Kahler, Paul Freeman.

A light-hearted adventure yarn in the spirit of the old serials, the action-packed, incredulous drama set during World War II concerns an adventurous American archaeologist who locates a hidden chest containing magical powers. He manages to find the coveted prize before the Nazis can get their hands on it. Indiana Jones (Harrison Ford), the stalwart hero, undergoes a string of close calls before he succeeds, including being trapped in a snake pit, escaping from an exploding airplane and getting caught in a submarine base. Karen Allen, as the heroine, shares many of the dangers with Ford. The film, which cost $20 million to produce, boasts several spectacular special effects and was highly successful at the box-office. A sequel, *Indiana Jones and the Temple of Doom*, followed in 1984. ■

"Railroad Raiders of '62" (1911), Kalem. *Cast includes:* Sidney Olcott.

An early silent historical drama, this short film deals with an actual event that occurred during the Civil War. A troop of about two dozen Union soldiers, dressed as civilians, penetrate behind enemy lines and steal *The General*, a Confederate train. The leader of the raid was an officer named Andrews. The incident became the basis of Buster Keaton's silent comedy *The General* (1927) and a Walt Disney feature titled *The Great Locomotive Chase* (1956). Kalem, a studio known more for its one-reel westerns, also turned out a

series of historical dramas during this period. See also Andrews Raid. ■

Rainbow Island (1944), Par. *Dir.* Ralph Murphy; *Sc.* Walter DeLeon, Arthur Phillips; *Cast includes:* Dorothy Lamour, Eddie Bracken, Gil Lamb, Barry Sullivan.

Three American sailors in the merchant marine are stranded on a South Pacific island in this World War II musical comedy. Eddie Bracken, Gil Lamb and Barry Sullivan portray the Americans whose ship was torpedoed by the Japanese. Finding safety on a nearby island, they manage to steal a Japanese airplane. But they are forced to land on another island inhabited only by natives. Dorothy Lamour, playing an American stranded here years ago, saves their lives by having Bracken pose as a local god, whom he happens to resemble. ■

Rambo: First Blood Part II (1985), Tri-Star. *Dir.* George Cosmatos; *Sc.* Sylvester Stallone, James Cameron; *Cast includes:* Sylvester Stallone, Richard Crenna, Charles Napier.

The controversial topic of M.I.A.s, American soldiers listed as missing in action during the Vietnam War and believed by some of their families and others still to be alive and held prisoner, is exploited in this action drama set in 1985. John Rambo (Sylvester Stallone), a highly decorated Vietnam War hero, is persuaded by his former special forces commander (Richard Crenna) to return to Vietnam on a special mission. Crenna, along with a shadowy government agency, enlists him to obtain photographs of Americans held captive in a suspected Vietnamese prison camp. The head of the agency (Charles Napier) emphasizes that Rambo is not to take any military action—that he is to return to a designated site after he has taken the pictures. As Rambo departs by airplane to be parachuted into the Vietnamese jungle, the agency bureaucrat doubts that the war hero will succeed. "What you choose to call hell," Crenna reassures him, "he calls home." Rambo finds the camp and returns with one prisoner he has released. But when he reaches the rendezvous site, the rescue helicopter abandons the two men. The head of the covert agency aborts the mission rather than confront the American people with proof that some troops are indeed alive and held captive. He admits to Crenna that even if

Rambo returned with photographic proof, the pictures would conveniently have been lost. When Crenna, frustrated with the treachery and warned to keep silent about the mission, asks about the fate of Rambo, the bureaucrat smugly and sarcastically remarks: "He went home."

Rambo and the soldier are captured and returned to the camp where Vietnamese and Soviet officers torture them. But Rambo escapes and, in an extended violent blood bath, slaughters numerous enemy troops who unsuccessfully attempt to hunt him down. After destroying the entire prison camp and killing its guards, he releases the American prisoners, captures a Soviet helicopter and returns to the American base. In a rage, Rambo empties his machine gun into the sophisticated equipment used by the agency and threatens Napier to effect the freedom of other American prisoners of war. As Rambo leaves, Crenna accompanies the embittered veteran part of the way. "What is it you want?" his former commander asks. "I want what they want," Rambo says, pointing to the recently freed Americans, "and every other guy who came over here and spilt his guts and gave everything he had, wants—for our country to love us as much as we love it. That's what I want."

First Blood (1982), although preceding the above film, concerns Rambo as a Vietnam veteran who, unable to adjust to civilian life and mistreated by a local sheriff and his deputies, devastates the town. The film concentrates more on action and violence than on the plight of disoriented or alienated veterans. ∎

Rambo III (1988), Tri-Star. *Dir.* Peter Macdonald; *Sc.* Sylvester Stallone, Sheldon Lettich; *Cast includes*: Sylvester Stallone, Richard Crenna, Marc de Jonge, Kurtwood Smith.

Sylvester Stallone, as John Rambo, America's lone and vengeful super-hero, takes on the Russian forces in Afghanistan in the third entry in this action series. As the film opens, Rambo is residing at a Buddhist monastery where he is raising money for the order and helping the priests to build a temple. He then gets caught up in the Afghanistan War when his friend, Colonel Trautman (Richard Crenna), who has been training Afghan guerrillas, is captured by a nasty, sadistic Russian Colonel (Marc de Jonge). Rambo's efforts to rescue Trautman result in large-scale action

sequences filled with special effects which reveal the large budget allotted to the film.

As with the previous entries, *Rambo III* relies more on action than on dialogue, more on Rambo's wild battles than on political issues. With such lines as "That was close" and "You've tried my patience long enough," the film offers little insight into character or motivation. Even dialogue that is meant to be significant falls short. "Who are you?" the Soviet colonel asks. "Your worst nightmare," replies Rambo. The politics of the war are condensed into the remark of one Afghan freedom fighter: "What we must do is stop this killing of our women and children."

Rambo may not be eloquent or romantically inclined (there are no female leads), but he is definitely impressive in his violent battles, ultimately disposing of what seems to be half the Soviet forces in the war-torn country. Almost everything about the film is larger than life, including the way our hero handles his own wounds. He removes a spike in his side by pulling it through, then cauterizes both wounds with the use of gunpowder. One wonders how he will improve on that in the next film.

The Afghanistan War (1979–) is a painful reminder of how the complexities of internal politics, external intervention and a long, drawn-out conflict affect a land and its people. In an effort to extend its influence into that country, the Soviet Union began sending in troops in late 1979. Afghanistan was already embroiled in an internal struggle, fragmented by the emergence of its own Communist Party and the appearance of dozens of rebel leaders. The Soviets, however, added terror and devastation to a troubled land suffering from social and political unrest. A shaky Afghan Communist government needed Soviet support to curb spreading guerrilla resistance. The rebels, because of their limited resources, chose to fight a guerrilla war against superior Soviet-Afghan forces. In return, the Communists clamped down on those villages suspected of assisting the rebels as a warning to others. The government proceeded to destroy homes, families and entire villages. Approximately three million Afghans fled the ravaged land into refugee camps in northern Pakistan. But the guerrillas continued to exact a heavy price upon government and Soviet forces and equipment. Faced with a costly, endless war, mounting casualties and serious economic problems at home, Mikhail Gorbachev in 1987 elected to wind down the Soviet presence in Afghanistan. ∎

Ramparts We Watch, The (1940), RKO. *Dir.* Louis de Rochemont; *Sc.* Robert L. Richards, Cedric R. Worth; *Cast includes:* John Adair, John Summers, Julia Kent, Ellen Prescott.

Director-producer Louis de Rochemont took his film production crew to a typical New England town for this propaganda film to show the impact of World War I on the people and the community as well as to preach for preparedness. The film underscores the similarities between the problems the U.S. faced in 1917 and those the country is confronted with in 1940, specifically those of military readiness. The director includes scenes from a Nazi propaganda film, an account of the German invasion of Poland, to demonstrate how a modern army can overrun a nation ill-prepared for war. It also includes a voice-over from narrator Westbrook Van Voorhis and newsreel scenes of World War I.

The film was begun in 1939 to show how the U.S. became entangled in the First World War. But as international events changed, the film evolved as a frank propaganda work designed to rouse the American audiences out of their complacency and against the Nazis. ∎

Random Harvest (1942). See Veterans. ∎

Rangers. See Rogers' Rangers; *Darby's Rangers* (1958). ∎

"Ransomed, or a Prisoner of War" (1910), Vitagraph. *Cast includes:* Clara Kimball Young, Leo Delaney.

A short silent drama set during the Civil War, the story is concerned with a Confederate soldier who crosses Union lines to visit his son who is celebrating his sixth birthday. As the father makes his way back to his own lines, he is captured and sentenced to death as a spy. His little son intervenes by appealing to the Union general and saves his father's life. The simple little domestic drama has no battle scenes. ∎

Rationing (1944), MGM. *Dir.* Willis Goldbeck; *Sc.* William Lipman, Grant Garrett, Harry Ruskin; *Cast includes:* Wallace Beery, Marjorie Main, Donald Meek, Howard Freeman.

A World War II comedy about the black market in meat, the film centers on a local storekeeper (Wallace Beery) who deals in beef. He has a running feud with the local postmistress (Marjorie Main). Meanwhile a romance emerges between Beery's son, who is about to leave for the service, and Main's daughter. Gloria Dickson plays the female barber of the town. The comedy in this routine film depends heavily upon slapstick. ∎

Ravagers, The (1965), Hemisphere Pictures. *Dir.* Eddie Romero; *Sc.* Cesar Amigo, E. F. Romero; *Cast includes:* John Saxon, Fernando Poe, Jr., Bronwyn Fitzsimmons, Mike Parsons.

Filipino guerrillas battle their Japanese occupiers in this action drama set during World War II and shot in the Philippines. John Saxon portrays the leader of the small rebel force trying to prevent the enemy from seizing a gold shipment concealed on one of the islands. Romance blooms between Fernando Poe, Jr. and Bronwyn Fitzsimmons when the guerrillas come across a convent of young students. Several action sequences involve battles between the Filipino freedom fighters and the Japanese troops. ∎

Ravished Armenia. See Auction of Souls (1919). ∎

Real Glory, The (1939), UA. *Dir.* Henry Hathaway; *Sc.* Jo Swerling, Robert Presnell; *Cast includes:* Gary Cooper, Andrea Leeds, David Niven, Reginald Owen, Broderick Crawford, Kay Johnson.

Gary Cooper portrays a U.S. Army medical officer stationed at a remote outpost in the Philippines in this action drama. The story takes place in 1905 after the Spanish-American War and following the withdrawal of American soldiers who leave Mindanao in the hands of native troops and a handful of American officers. Suddenly a Moro insurrection threatens the peaceful outpost and surrounding villages. Gallant Cooper springs into action, along with his fellow Americans, played by easy-going David Niven and feather-brained, orchid-loving Broderick Crawford. Cooper fights off a cholera attack, a siege by the savage Moros and possible annihilation. The captain of the outpost (Reginald Owen) falls ill, placing the command on the shoulders of Cooper. In a tense sequence, he leads a handful of native troops into the jungle to dynamite a dam so that the besieged and desperate villagers can have fresh water. Andrea Leeds provides the romantic interest.

The film, despite its exotic setting and native inhabitants, is reminiscent of an old-fashioned, rousing western. However, it offers plenty of action and suspense, particularly the sequence in which the fanatical attackers literally catapult themselves over the barriers of the compound. ∎

Rebel City (1953), AA. *Dir.* Thomas Carr; *Sc.* Sydney Theil; *Cast includes:* Wild Bill Elliott, Marjorie Lord, Robert Kent, Keith Richards.

Southern sympathizers stir up trouble in Kansas in this low-budget Civil War drama. A gambler (Wild Bill Elliott) journeys to a small Kansas town to find out who murdered his father, the former owner of the local freight line. He decides to investigate the death on his own after the local Union colonel, burdened with copperhead problems, fails to help him. Ultimately he unmasks a Union captain (Robert Kent) who was responsible for the murder and heads the local troublemakers in this routine tale. ∎

Rebel in Town (1956), UA. *Dir.* Alfred Werker; *Sc.* Danny Arnold; *Cast includes:* John Payne, Ruth Roman, J. Carrol Naish, Ben Cooper, John Smith, James Griffith.

An accidental killing re-ignites tensions between a former Confederate family and the victim's Union parents in this post-Civil War drama. While a Southern father (J. Carrol Naish) and his four sons are traveling west, one of the boys, upon hearing the click of a pistol behind him, spins around and fires instinctively. He discovers too late that he has killed a child with a toy gun. The father of the dead child, a former Union officer (John Payne), wants revenge for the senseless killing. After much soul-searching on the part of both families, revenge is replaced with forgiveness. Ruth Roman plays Payne's wife. Ben Cooper, as Naish's sensitive son, defies his own father's callousness and, sympathizing with Payne, wants only to see justice prevail. John Smith plays the trigger-happy son in this suspenseful and intelligent little film. ∎

Rebellion in Cuba (1961), International. *Dir.* Albert C. Gannaway; *Sc.* Frank Graves, Mark Hanna; *Cast includes:* Bill Fletcher, Jake LaMotta, Lon Chaney, Jr., Sonia Marrero.

Released only a few short months after the Bay of Pigs debacle in which a force of anti-Castro Cuban nationals invaded the shores of that island, the film presents its own fictional tale of a similar coup. Several Americans, deeply distressed over Cuba's Communist government in such a strategic location, decide to support a revolt against Castro led by a dissident faction. Prize fighter Jake LaMotta has a featured role in this minor, low-budget drama shot on the Isle of Pines. ∎

Recompense (1925), WB. *Dir.* Harry Beaumont; *Sc.* Dorothy Farnum; *Cast includes:* Marie Prevost, Monte Blue, John Roche, George Seigmann, Charles Stevens.

This romantic drama, based on the novel by Robert Keable, takes place during World War I. The settings, realistically handled, are France, South Africa and England. A clergyman (Monte Blue) gives up his position to volunteer as a soldier in France. He meets a Red Cross nurse (Marie Prevost) and they have an affair. The former reverend's fiancee, a streetwalker, dies. Later, he goes to South Africa where he has an altercation with a slave foreman, is shot and nursed back to health by Prevost. Arriving back in England, he opens a shelter for the homeless. Prevost finally agrees to marry him. ∎

Recruitment films. Writer William Manchester in an article in the New York Times Magazine of June 14, 1987, mentions a poll that he had taken while he was in the U.S. Marines during World War II. He and some buddies asked members of a rifle company why they joined the marines. A majority alluded to the 20th Century-Fox film *To the Shores of Tripoli* (1942) with John Payne, Maureen O'Hara and Randolph Scott. The routine drama suggested that military life consisted chiefly of attractive blue uniforms, plenty of time off and a pretty nurse always on call. The U.S. government could not have made a more effective recruitment film.

Besides turning out official films enticing the youth of America into joining one of the armed services, the U.S. government has received plenty of assistance from the film industry. Sometimes a Hollywood studio would receive a request for a particular type of film from one branch of service. More often the studio, always hungry for new angles, would select the subject. This was especially true if a story line was visually attractive and evoked a fair amount of danger, such as the parachute unit or the submarine service. Many films intended purely for entertainment, however, produced a side effect. They ignited the patriotism in some young people. Others, which emphasized the ruthlessness of the enemy, angered the potential recruits. Recruitment films, whether intended for this purpose or not, range from simple documentaries to complex dramas.

One of the earliest documentaries that may have encouraged recruitment was "Troop B, 16th Cavalry, in Maneuvers" (1910), a crude one-reel silent film. However, not until World War I erupted in Europe did the recruitment film emerge as a major weapon. Documentaries designed to lift civilians out of their seats and into uniforms included *How Uncle Sam Prepares* (1917), *Our Fighting Forces* (1917) and *Our Invincible Navy* (1918).

The drama perhaps was more persuasive a tool during World War I. *The Flying Torpedo* (1916), a silent fantasy about a foreign invasion of America, motivated the military to provide torpedoes to be exhibited in theater lobbies and set up recruitment booths. *The Fall of a Nation* (1916), a didactic preparedness drama, repeats the idea of an invasion. Once again a foreign power (thinly disguised German troops) destroys American cities and commits unspeakable atrocities on defenseless citizens. The film, which pauses long enough to belittle political pacifists and religious champions of neutrality, suggests that those against preparedness are either disloyal or cowards. If the able-bodied men who attended movie theaters were not stirred by these images of their country under fire, they were assaulted from another front. *Over There* (1917), a World War I drama, depicts the isolation and disgrace of a coward during wartime. *The Volunteer* (1917), a propaganda film blatantly promoting recruitment, opens during World War I and depicts how a Quaker family reconciles themselves to their only son going off to war. Madge Evans portrays the daughter of an army officer and a mother who is a Red Cross nurse departing for the front.

Although Hollywood grew more sophisticated in equipment and story development during the 1930s and by the time Europe was embroiled in World War II, the recruitment films the studios turned out remained rather blunt. Such dramas as *Here Comes the Navy* (1934) with James Cagney and Pat O'Brien, *Devil Dogs of the Air* (1935) with Cagney and O'Brien, *Wings of the Navy* (1939) with George Brent and John Payne, and *Dive Bomber* (1941) with Errol Flynn and Fred MacMurray, not only provided action and fast-paced entertainment. They suggested the strength of our different military branches and became recruitment posters for the service. Warner Brothers produced many of these. Other studios soon joined the parade. RKO, for instance, released *Parachute Battalion* (1941), with Robert Preston and Edmond O'Brien. Several films benefited from the welcome cooperation of the government which furnished the facilities and staff.

At times, it was not a specific service but the incident in a film that provoked enlistment. Such dramas as *Wake Island* (1942), a "heroic defeat" film, told of how a small detachment of U.S. Marines stubbornly held out against overwhelming odds before they were finally overrun. Immediately after the film was released, the ranks of the marines swelled with new recruits.

The documentary became an important source for swelling the military ranks, especially once the U.S. entered the conflict. "Men of the U.S. Navy" (1942), for example, focuses on U.S. Navy recruitment and training while stressing the role the warships will play in the conflict. Film studios also produced short subjects to help the war effort. Warner Brothers, for example, made "Service With the Colors," "Meet the Fleet," "Soldiers in White," "The Tanks Are Coming," "Here Comes the Cavalry," "Commandos of the Sky" and "Rear Gunner."

The last, starring James Stewart, perhaps exemplifies the power of the film medium. A general, informing the studio that the air force was short of rear gunners, suggested the idea for the film. Soon after the film's release, the shortage was alleviated. ∎

Red Badge of Courage, The (1951),
MGM. *Dir.* John Huston; *Sc.* John Huston; *Cast includes:* Audie Murphy, Bill Mauldin, John Dierkes, Royal Dano.

Based on Stephen Crane's Civil War novel about the psychological impact of war on a young recruit, the film stars Audie Murphy as the youth. He gripes openly among his comrades about the useless drilling and the endless marching, impatient for the first fight. But inwardly he is concerned over how he will react in battle—will he show fear and run? During the first battle, an enemy attack, he becomes part of the whole; he fires his rifle into the advancing Confederates and watches them fall back. A moment of pride engulfs him; he has been tested and has come through. Suddenly the enemy mounts a cavalry charge. This time he breaks and runs, witnessing the deaths of his fellow soldiers. When he rejoins his unit, his initial fear turns to rage against the enemy. Almost unconsciously, he picks up a flag and leads his regiment in an advance. When the din of battle subsides, his buddies praise his courage as they march off. The youth is satisfied with himself. A narrator, quoting from the novel, says: "He had been to touch the great death and found that, after all, it was but the great death."

The film uses a narrator to quote passages from the original work. For instance, when the youth sees the many wounded, the narrator remarks: "He wished, too, that he had a wound—a red badge of courage." John Huston directed the film without glamour or glory, presenting instead a grim, stark depiction of men in war. Audie Murphy, cast against type, was the most decorated hero of World War II. He had a long career in films playing leads in action, adventure and western films. ∎

Red Ball Express (1952), U. *Dir*. Budd Boetticher; *Sc*. John Michael Hayes; *Cast includes:* Jeff Chandler, Alex Nicol, Charles Drake, Judith Braun, Hugh O'Brian.

The problem of supplying General George Patton's tanks with fuel and other supplies as they race toward Paris is the subject of this World War II action drama. The film focuses on the war-weary men of the Transportation Corps who work under pressure from their officers and under fire from the enemy. Jeff Chandler portrays a lieutenant who struggles to keep the trucks rolling to supply the fast-moving general. Alex Nicol, as a sergeant, clashes with a black soldier (Sidney Poitier), the latter thinking Nicol is a racist. Several effective action sequences concern battles between the men who drive the trucks to the front and the Germans. Some of the support-

ing cast subsequently carved out major careers in television, including Hugh O'Brian and Jack Kelly. Poitier, of course, went on to film stardom.

The actual Red Ball Express, improvised by transportation chief Major General Frank A. Ross, consisted chiefly of a one-way truck transport network that brought fuel and provisions to the rapidly moving Allied advance across France in 1944. Between August and September, for example, 6,000 trucks delivered 135,000 tons of supplies from Saint-Lo and Chartres. Speed limits and traffic regulations were disregarded by the drivers who often competed with other units to arrive first. ∎

Red Baron, The. See Baron Manfred von Richthofen. ∎

Red Clay (1927), U. *Dir*. Ernst Laemmle; *Sc*. Charles Logue, Frank Inghram; *Cast includes:* William Desmond, Marceline Day, Ynez Seabury, Albert J. Smith.

An early Hollywood attempt at preaching tolerance toward the American Indian, this drama, set during World War I, tells the tragic story of an Indian war hero. William Desmond portrays an Indian chief who is drafted into military service at the outbreak of the war. Meanwhile, a congressman advocates equal treatment for the native Americans. Once overseas, Desmond saves the life of the congressman's son during a battle. After the war, the son, who doesn't know the identity of his rescuer, forbids his sister (Marceline Day) from dating Desmond, who has now become a scholar and famous football player. By the end of the film, Desmond is mortally wounded. He reveals his identity to the girl's brother and dies in his arms.

The drama appeared two years after *The Vanishing American*, perhaps one of the best Hollywood features about the American Indian ever produced. Like Desmond, Richard Dix played an Indian who returned from World War I only to find his land in ruin. *Ramona* (1928), another sensitive and intelligent film about the native American, temporarily brought to an end this short cycle of dramas that depicted the Indian sympathetically. It was not until after World War II, with such films as *Broken Arrow* (1950), did Hollywood return to this theme. ∎

Red Cloud (1822–1909). A member of the Oglala Sioux, he was an outstanding warrior who attracted a large following within his tribe because of respect for his accomplishments and leadership in battle. Not actually a chief, he was, nevertheless, treated as one by both Indians and white officials because of his stature. He was involved in several well-known raids during the period of American Indian wars in the West. These included the Fetterman Massacre (1866) and the Wagon Box Raid (1867). *Tomahawk* (1951) shows Red Cloud taking part in the Fetterman Massacre.

As Indian leaders had planned, these attacks forced the federal government to abandon a string of forts (1868) protecting the Bozeman Trail that went through Sioux territory in Colorado, Wyoming and Montana. Red Cloud's attacks on the Bozeman Trail forts appear in *The Gun That Won The West* (1955).

The Indian warrior, during ensuing peace negotiations, was even invited to Washington, D.C., where he met President Grant and received a tour of the city. Later, at a speech in New York City's Cooper Union Institute, Red Cloud aroused much sympathy for the Indians by detailing the corruption and injustices his people had suffered in dealing with white officials and private citizens. His talk helped create public pressure that compelled the government to adopt an Indian policy more favorable to native tribes. The clashes between corrupt white officials and the Sioux are covered in several films, including *The Great Sioux Massacre* (1965) and *The Indian Fighter* (1955), with Red Cloud appearing in the latter. Unlike several noted contemporary Indian chiefs, Red Cloud accepted the idea of living peacefully on a reservation though he remained protective of Indian rights. He was deposed as an Indian leader in 1881 because of suspected duplicity. He led the soldiers who captured and killed Crazy Horse, one of the Sioux's most revered warrior chiefs. Red Cloud lived for most of his later years at the Pine Ridge Reservation in South Dakota, where he died at the age of 87. ∎

Red Dance, The (1928), Fox. *Dir.* Raoul Walsh; *Sc.* James Creelman; *Cast includes:* Dolores Del Rio, Charles Farrell, Ivan Linow, Boris Charsky.

A drama set in Russia prior to and during the Revolution, the film stars Charles Farrell as a Grand Duke who falls in love with a dancer, portrayed by Dolores Del Rio. Director Raoul Walsh, responsible for the film version of *What Price Glory?* (1926), created several stirring scenes of the Czar's overthrow and the general uprising.

This is one of the few films of the genre that make an attempt at justifying the Revolution. (Cecil B. DeMille in *The Volga Boatman* approached the subject to a limited degree by depicting the wide chasm between the aristocrats and the serfs who pulled the barges along the canal.) But Walsh's work is more graphic in its description of the abuses and covers more ground. Those who speak out for reform are sentenced to life imprisonment; peasant women are at the mercy of the aristocrats; the Cossacks carry out their deadly raids with impunity. ∎

Red Danube, The (1949). See Cold War. ∎

Red Dawn (1984), MGM/UA. *Dir.* John Milius; *Sc.* Kevin Reynolds, John Milius; *Cast includes:* Patrick Swayze, C. Thomas Howell, Ron O'Neal, William Smith, Charles Sheen.

Director John Milius' vision of World War III as fought in America's heartland results in a routine war drama consisting chiefly of a series of battle sequences and is hampered by weak dialogue and a feverish patriotism. When the film opens, the Russians have knocked out most of America's defensive missiles while Cuban troops land by parachute in several American towns. Abandoned by its allies, the U.S. fights on alone, bogged down in a conventional war. Both adversaries decide not to use further nuclear weapons. A high school is interrupted by the invading Cubans who indiscriminately machine-gun civilians. Several students, led by one boy's older brother (Patrick Swayze), escape by truck into the mountains after stocking up on food and rifles. Calling themselves "Wolverines," the small teen-age band of guerrillas raids and harasses the invading forces. They are soon joined by several young girls and an American pilot whose plane was shot down. Together, they destroy convoys, blow up munitions dumps and instill a general fear among the Cuban troops. Eventually, the original members of the group are killed off as other cadres take up the struggle for freedom. At least one perceptive critic noted that the film reverses the roles of the participants of the Vietnam War. This time around it is the Americans who are invaded by overwhelming outside forces and must fight a guerrilla war of resistance. ∎

Red Hot Romance (1922), FN. *Dir.* Victor Fleming; *Sc.* John Emerson, Anita Loos; *Cast includes:* Basil Sydney, Mae Collins, Edward Connelly.

The film is a farce comedy involving an unusual will and the mythical principality of Bunkonia. The story concerns young Rowland Stone (Basil Sydney) who will inherit his father's fortune only after he has proved himself by working as an insurance salesman for one year. His sweetheart, Anna Mae, is taken by her father to Bunkonia, where he has been appointed the American ambassador. Rowland decides to sell insurance in that country so that he can be near Anna Mae. He arrives in the midst of a revolution which he helps to crush with the aid of a battalion of U.S. Marines.

For a simple comedy employing broad burlesque, the film contains several unusual scenes. The troops are made up of black soldiers for no apparent reason. This was rather controversial for the period, especially since the soldiers use their rifles to control the unruly white crowds. In a courtroom scene a black bailiff addresses the spectators as "miscolored white trash." ∎

Red Menace, The (1949). See Cold War. ∎

Red Mountain (1951), Par. *Dir.* William Dieterle; *Sc.* George W. George, George Slavin, John M. Lucas; *Cast includes:* Alan Ladd, Lizabeth Scott, Arthur Kennedy, John Ireland.

A Confederate captain (Alan Ladd) joins up with the infamous Quantrill and his raiders in this Civil War action drama. Ladd journeys west to a small town that sided with the North. When he kills a stranger in a fair fight, the townspeople turn on another ex-Rebel (Arthur Kennedy) and accuse him of the crime. Ladd saves his life and both escape into the mountains. He then links up with Quantrill (John Ireland). When Ladd discovers that the renegade has dropped the Southern cause and, obsessed with his own greed, intends to stir up the Indians against the settlers, he turns against him and kills him in a bloody knife fight. The cavalry charges to the rescue against the warring Indians as Ladd walks off with the former fiancee (Lizabeth Scott) of Arthur Kennedy who died fighting

Quantrill. Historically, the film contains several inaccuracies. For example, the Confederate guerrilla leader, Quantrill, died at the hands of a Union patrol he was unfortunate enough to encounter elsewhere. ∎

Red Tomahawk (1967), Par. *Dir.* R. G. Springsteen; *Sc.* Steve Fisher; *Cast includes:* Howard Keel, Joan Caulfield, Broderick Crawford, Wendell Cory, Scott Brady.

The citizens of Deadwood fear that the Sioux will attack them next in the wake of the Indians' victory over Custer at Little Big Horn in this action drama. Howard Keel, as a captain in the U.S. Cavalry, is sent with his troop to protect the town, but he needs more rifles. Dakota Lil (Joan Caulfield) seems to be the only one who knows where Custer's soldiers have hidden a cache of weapons. Meanwhile the townspeople have internal troubles rising from unsavory gamblers. Action sequences include the fight with the local gamblers and the climactic battle against the warring Sioux. ∎

Red, White and Black, The (1970), Hirschman-Northern. *Dir.* John Cardos; *Sc.* Marlene Weed; *Cast includes:* Robert DoQui, Janee Michelle, Lincoln Kilpatrick, Rafer Johnson, Isaac Fields.

A small, independently made production, the film concerns a handful of new recruits and their experiences in the all-black 10th U.S. Cavalry regiment assigned to maintain peace in the West between the Indians and the whites. The unit had been created during the late 1800s. Rafer Johnson and Lincoln Kilpatrick portray troopers who have the difficult task of turning the raw recruits into a fighting unit. Meanwhile Johnson has developed a close friendship with the local Indian chief (Robert Dix). Later, during a battle between the cavalry and the Indians, the chief is killed. His friend's death deeply disturbs Johnson. Robert DoQui, as one of the newcomers to the regiment, has a reputation as a ladies' man. He is killed in a skirmish with the local hostiles. Janee Michelle provides the romantic interest in this meandering but interesting tale. ∎

Reds (1981), Par. *Dir.* Warren Beatty; *Sc.* Warren Beatty, Trevor Griffiths; *Cast includes:* Warren Beatty, Diane Keaton, Edward Herrmann, Jack Nicholson.

A biographical drama about the career of

John Reed, a dashing, charismatic writer during the early years of this century, the film also covers the Russian Revolution as well as Reed's love affair with Louise Bryant, another writer. Warren Beatty, who also directed and co-wrote the script, portrays the American writer whose turbulent adult life embroiled him in an array of social and political events. He covers the revolt in Russia more out of boyish fascination for the excitement and the action than for the political complexities. He finds an exhilaration in the chaos and the upheaval of social structures. Back in the U.S. he involves himself in workers' strikes and American left-wing politics during the 1920s. He later returns to Russia where he dies of tuberculosis and kidney failure. He remains the only American to be buried in the Soviet Union as a Communist hero.

Diane Keaton portrays Louise Bryant, a dentist's wife and aspiring writer who, after falling in love with Reed, follows him to Russia during the stormy period of the Revolution. Maureen Stapleton plays the famous anarchist Emma Goldman. Jack Nicholson appears as the alcoholic playwright Eugene O'Neill who has an affair with Bryant. ■

Refugees. Few films have captured the plight of the refugee in the wake of war. Perhaps this is because even fewer films have been able to convey the actual experience of war itself. Most films dealing with refugees are set during either World War I or World War II.

Refugees chiefly are portrayed peripherally in both dramas and documentaries of World War I. For example, in "The Spirit of the Red Cross" (1918), a semidocumentary depicting the field work of that noble service during the Great War, its members are seen helping numerous refugees as well as soldiers. *Under Four Flags*, an American propaganda documentary released the same year, has scenes of French refugees running from the invading Germans. In *Nurse Edith Cavell* (1939), an antiwar biographical drama of the famous nurse who was eventually shot by the Germans, the title character is seen helping Belgian refugees escape across the border into France. A silent version of her World War I experiences appeared in 1918, titled *The Woman the Germans Shot*, but it omits her work with refugees. One of the most poignant dramatizations of refugees during World War I appears in the first film version of Hemingway's novel *A Farewell to Arms* (1932). Italian refugees crowd the mud-drenched roads along with retreating soldiers and vehicles while shells and the strafings of enemy planes indiscriminately take their toll on men, women and children. The 1957 remake adds to the horror of the Italian retreat and the innocent civilians caught up in the event. Bodies are strewn about on the sides of the road; mothers cling to their children as the rain beats down, making the trek even more difficult. In all these films, the refugees play a minor role. They seldom speak of their hardships. No major character talks to them. They are simply part of the landscape. A 1939 film short, part of John Nesbitt's "Passing Parade" series produced by MGM, focuses on an almost forgotten hero. "The Giant of Norway" tells the story of Fridtjof Nansen, a humanitarian who spent most of his life assisting World War I refugees.

World War II films treated the refugees with ambivalence. On the one hand, the screen viewed them sympathetically. But some films (Herman Shumlin's 1943 *Watch on the Rhine*) showed some as spies or agents of foreign powers, especially when refugees reached American shores. *So Ends Our Night* (1941), with Fredric March, Margaret Sullavan and Glenn Ford, is one of the rare films which features the uprooted and homeless victims of European political turmoil as principal characters. March portrays a German forced to flee his country because of his ideological views. Sullavan, as a stateless Jewess, is compelled to seek refuge wherever she can find it. Ford is another homeless victim of religious persecution. The drama follows the experiences of refugees forced to cross borders at night, seeking counterfeit passports and always trying to evade the police. George Brent and Martha Scott, as Austrian emigrés in *They Dare Not Love*, released the same year, arrive in America where Scott and her father devote their time to helping other refugees. Brent, an anti-Nazi leader, volunteers to give himself up to German agents in exchange for the release of several prisoners held in Germany.

The preceding two films were made before America's entry into the war. Following Japan's attack on Pearl Harbor, the U.S. was quick to exploit the problems of refugees as part of its propaganda campaign. Several shorts began to appear in which refugees were used to remind Americans of their blessings. In "What Are We Fighting For?" (1943), part of a series titled "America Speaks," Lon Chaney portrays a complainer who criticizes various shortages, blackouts and other inconveniences—until he is confronted by refugee Osa Massen. She paints a graphic picture of life under Hitler. In the propaganda film *Gangway for Tomorrow* (1943), a French refugee and former member of the resistance (Margo) is currently in the U.S. working in a defense plant. She and other employees tell their personal stories in a series of flashbacks.

Other features dramatized the tenuous and chaotic world of the expatriate. In *Casablanca* (1943) the dispossessed of war-torn Europe, desperately seeking entry to a neutral country, try to obtain legal or illegal passports, trade or gamble their valuables at Rick's Cafe and engage in a variety of shady deals. A womanizing prefect of police (Claude Rains) is quick to seize upon the desperation of some of the more unfortunate women who cross his path. Refugee children are the focus of *The Pied Piper* (1942), a drama about a vacationing Englishman (Monty Woolley) in France when war erupts. He leads a group of orphans to safety after several harrowing experiences.

Some refugees embraced Fascism and Nazism or were duped into helping alien spies. George Coulouris, as a decadent Rumanian count living off others in Washington, is willing to trade in human lives in *Watch on the Rhine*. Socializing with high-ranking officials at the German embassy, he learns how to line his own pockets. In *Ministry of Fear* (1944), set in wartime London, Ray Milland stumbles across a network of German spies using an Austrian refugee's charitable organization as a front.

Films involving refugees as major or minor characters trickled onto the screen during the Post-World War II period. In *Arch of Triumph* (1948), a murky drama of France during the Nazi invasion, a refugee doctor (Charles Boyer) escapes to France where he saves Ingrid Bergman's life. Later, he is thrown into a concentration camp when the Germans march into Paris. Israel's struggle for independence is the subject of *Sword in the Desert* (1949) and *Exodus* (1960), both of which focus on refugees trying to enter British-controlled Palestine. In the former, an American captain (Dana Andrews) of a freighter who delivers displaced Jews to the shores of Palestine ultimately becomes involved in their problems. In the latter, more than 600 Jewish refugees aboard a Greek freighter who are forbidden to enter Palestine threaten to blow themselves up if the British come aboard. After arousing the conscience of the world, they are finally allowed to debark. *The Boy With Green Hair* (1948), an offbeat film directed by Joseph Losey, concerns a war orphan (Dean Stockwell) who, in a dream sequence, is visited by war orphans. They step out of a poster to inform him that he must plead their antiwar message.

By the late 1940s Hollywood studios, reflecting the tenor of the Cold War period, began releasing anti-Soviet films, some of which include incidents concerning refugees. In *The Red Menace* (1949), a didactic tale about the evils of Communism, a refugee from eastern Europe falls prey to false promises of the Communist party. A refugee scientist becomes the target of Soviet agents operating in the U.S. in *Walk East on Beacon* (1952), a drama about the Cold War.

Except for a few rare instances (*So Ends Our Night*), Hollywood has never made full use of the personal dramas and tragedies that surround the lives of refugees. Perhaps their stories date too quickly or are too depressing for the average audience. ∎

Regular Girl, A (1919). See Veterans. ∎

Reign of Terror (1949), Eagle Lion. *Dir.* Anthony Mann; *Sc.* Philip Yordan, Aeneas MacKenzie; *Cast includes:* Robert Cummings, Arlene Dahl, Richard Hart, Arnold Moss, Richard Basehart.

The search for a valuable diary forms the plot of this offbeat drama set during the French Revolution. When several idealistic revolutionaries learn that Robespierre (Richard Basehart) plans to form a dictatorship, they enlist the aid of a loyal companion (Robert Cummings) to pose as one of Robespierre's followers. His mission is to locate a small black book that lists the names of those destined for the guillotine. He manages to obtain the book and expose the contents, thereby foiling the intended dictator's plans. Although it includes little in the way of historical fact, the film presents an array of historical figures—Saint Just (Jess Barker), Barras (Richard Hart) and Fouche (Arnold Moss). The film has appeared on television under its alternate title, *The Black Book*. ∎

Religion and War. Religious films have generally not done well at the box-office. Yet, surprisingly, Hollywood has continued to produce them, albeit sporadically, including scores of war films with religious characters or themes. The religious war movie may take several shapes. In early silents the image of Christ was occasionally invoked on screen to stop the violence or give support to democracy and peace in general or to the U.S. in particular. Romantic dramas sometimes have the hero or heroine, seeking redemption or escape, enter the service of the Church. For example, in *Johnny Ring and the Captain's Sword* (1921), a rare religious Civil War drama based on a true incident, a wounded Union captain and avowed atheist promises that if God spares his life he will convert. He later becomes a devout minister. Religious figures were also used for symbolic purposes—to arouse hatred for the enemy, as foils for the main characters, or simply to conjure up sentimentality or sympathy.

One of the earliest uses of religion in war movies was for symbolic purposes. D.W. Griffith, in his Civil War classic *The Birth of a Nation* (1915), concludes the epic with a superimposed image of the Prince of Peace deposing the sword-wielding God of War. In Thomas H. Ince's *Civilization* (1916) the spirit of Christ appears and preaches peace and brotherly love to a bellicose ruler. When Jesus shows the king images of death and destruction, all caused by war, the man is so stirred by the visions that he ends all hostilities. That same year Griffith concluded his lengthy *Intolerance* with apocalyptic visions of war. Bands of angels finally end the scenes of chaos and slaughter which are replaced with children playing in the fields where flowers cover the decaying weapons of destruction. In *The Unbeliever* (1918) Christ's spirit appears, hovering over a World War I battlefield, in support of democracy. To balance things out, another scene depicts a rabbi attending to a dying Catholic doughboy. To support its themes that love is stronger than hate and that the U.S. represents a moral force for peace and democracy, the World War I film *The Birth of a Race* (1919) conjures up images of Adam and Eve, Noah and Christ. The 1926 version of *Ben-Hur*, directed by Fred Niblo, opens with the Star of Bethlehem appearing in the sky and the Three Wise Men journeying to the Birth of the Savior, images that

serve to introduce the theme of the rise of Christianity.

Religious symbolism occasionally emerged in war films of the 1930s and 1940s. In Edwin Carewe's pretentious antiwar drama *Are We Civilized?* (1934), a pacifist demonstrates to a bellicose leader of a fictitious state the errors of embarking on the path of war. The country suspiciously resembles Germany. The film employs a series of flashbacks of historical figures, including, among others, Christ and Moses, to make its point. A more subtle use of symbolism occurs a decade later in Fred Zinnemann's World War II drama *The Seventh Cross* (1944). When seven prisoners of a Nazi concentration camp escape, the commandant orders seven crosses mounted to trees and vows to nail one escapee to each. Six of the men are eventually caught, but Tracy, as one of the prisoners, evades his pursuers. The seventh cross remains empty. It stands as an ironic symbol of Nazi Germany's mockery of the crucifixion and religion, as well as its failure to crush the spirit of man.

Every so often a distraught screen lover, believing his or her beloved has been killed, forsakes the world by becoming a priest or nun. The most popular of these romantic tales was F. Marion Crawford's novel *The White Sister* which saw three screen adaptations—in 1915, 1923 and 1933. In each film, directed by Fred Wright, Henry King, and Victor Fleming respectively, the doleful young woman enters a convent when she learns that her lover has been killed in action. When he returns unexpectedly and pleads with her to leave the Church, she refuses. In *Marianne* (1929), a World War I musical, a French soldier who has lost his sight in battle enters the priesthood, thereby freeing his fiancee (Marion Davies) to marry another.

On occasion, wartime dramas presented a romance involving one or more members of a religious order. Hollywood walked a thin line in handling this delicate subject matter and almost invariably came through with high marks for good behavior. Two former lovers meet during World War I in *Victory of Conscience* (1916). The man, seeking redemption for ruining the young woman's reputation, has become a priest. She has given up her life on the streets to become a nun. They are both serving in France where they meet again. Before the reunion goes too far, they both are killed by a nearby shell. In Frank Borzage's *Till We Meet Again* (1944) a close relationship develops between a downed American flier (Ray Milland) in Nazi-occupied France, and a novitiate nun (Barbara Britton) who helps him to escape. A marine (Robert Mitchum) in the World War II drama *Heaven Knows, Mr. Allison* (1957) is stranded on a Pacific island with a nun (Deborah Kerr). When Mitchum, who thinks he has fallen in love with her, proposes marriage, she gently and tactfully declines his offer.

To arouse audience antipathy against a common foe, movie studios in their war films have frequently introduced religion and religious leaders as the targets of enemy attacks. In *The Hitler Gang* (1944) the Nazi dictator, portrayed by Robert Watson, is shown ranting against religion. An innocent and highly revered rabbi is sent to his death in the World War II drama *None Shall Escape*, released the same year. Otto Preminger's *The Cardinal* (1963) depicts Hitler's Brown Shirts attacking a religious assembly in Vienna in 1938 and pillaging the quarters of the Catholic Archdiocese. *Salvador* (1985) covers the killing of a priest and the brutal rape and murder of four nuns in its condemnation of government forces during the 1980–1981 turmoil in strife-torn El Salvador.

Other dramas portrayed more outspoken religious figures who elect to choose sides. In *Joan of Paris* (1942), for example, Thomas Mitchell, as a priest who works with the French underground, hides downed British airmen. In *Women in Bondage*, released the following year, a humane priest (H.B. Warner) in Nazi Germany constantly clashes with officials. Barbara Britton, as a French nun who helps downed Allied fliers in *Till We Meet Again*, mentioned earlier, is caught by the Nazis. When the local mayor (Walter Slezak) learns that they intend to send her to a German brothel, he kills her before the Germans can carry out their sentence. In Fred Zinnemann's *The Nun's Story* (1959) a Belgian nun (Audrey Hepburn) joins the resistance movement against the Nazis although her superiors warn her to remain neutral. She eventually leaves the Church.

More often than not the religious figure acts as an inspirational force for the individual or community. Pat O'Brien as the famous Father Duffy in *The Fighting 69th* (1941) never gives up hope on the cowardly doughboy (James Cagney) who finally redeems himself by sacrificing his life to save the lives of his buddies. Walter Brennan, as the village

pastor in Howard Hawks' World War I biographical drama *Sergeant York*, also released in 1941, helps young Alvin York understand the role of religion in an individual's life. Sir Cedric Hardwicke, as a minister of an English village in William Wyler's *Mrs. Miniver* (1942), stirs his congregation with his sermon following an air raid. The bomb-damaged church, like England itself, stands defiantly as British planes soar overhead. In *God Is My Co-Pilot* (1945), based on the memoirs of Colonel Robert L. Scott, a missionary priest (Alan Hale) restores the fighter pilot's faith in religion. John Lund portrays a chaplain aboard an aircraft carrier during World War II in *Battle Stations*.

Religious fanaticism has sometimes served as the subject of war films. In John Ford's World War I drama *The Lost Patrol* (1934), a tale of a squad of British soldiers stranded in the Mesopotamian desert, Boris Karloff, as a religious zealot, crosses over the edge of sanity and wanders into the desert carrying a large cross. He eventually is cut down by the enemy. The most popular religious fanatic on film is probably John Brown, as portrayed by Raymond Massey in *The Santa Fe Trail* (1941) and again in *Seven Angry Men* (1955). In both he is seen as a religious crusader and ruthless murderer who leaves a trail of death and destruction in the wake of his Kansas raids and the battle at Harpers Ferry. In a lighter vein, the romantic adventure tale *Gunga Din* (1939) depicts the exploits of three British soldiers (Cary Grant, Douglas Fairbanks, Jr. and Victor McLaglen) who tangle with the murderous Thuggee cult whose members strangle their victims.

Serious religious sequences presented problems to writers and directors alike. The scenes often were too wordy or slowed down the pace of the film. Also, studios in their attempts not to offend any denomination created religious characters who were so morally straight that they appeared unrealistic or, worse, dull and stodgy. These reasons may explain why war films often try to keep the religious aspects to a minimum or in the background. ■

Remagen. See *The Bridge at Remagen* (1969). ■

Remember (1927). See Veterans. ■

Remember Pearl Harbor (1942), Rep. *Dir.* Joseph Santley; *Sc.* Malcolm Stuart Boylan, Isabel Dawn; *Cast includes:* Donald Barry, Alan Curtis, Fay McKenzie, Sig Ruman.

An action drama that takes place on the eve of Pearl Harbor, the film stars Donald Barry and Alan Curtis as two soldier-pals stationed in the Philippines. Barry is a roughneck and troublemaker while Curtis is the more serious-minded of the pair. When news of Japan's attack on Pearl Harbor reaches the troop, Barry, who has become mixed up with a group of agents working for the Japanese, realizes the error of his ways and quickly redeems himself. Not only does he expose an espionage network, but he crashes an airplane into a Japanese troop ship. Other battle sequences include land engagements between Americans and Japanese forces in the Philippines. Fay McKenzie provides the romance in this low-budget film that was one of the earliest to appear following the attack on Pearl Harbor. ■

Rendezvous 24 (1946). See Spy Films: the Talkies. ■

Renegades (1930), Fox. *Dir.* Victor Fleming; *Sc.* Jules Furthman; *Cast includes:* Warner Baxter, Myrna Loy, Noah Beery, Gregory Gaye, George Cooper.

The French Foreign Legion is the background of this drama. Four recalcitrant Legionnaires, led by Warner Baxter, break away from the ranks and temporarily join forces with the enemy. When the friends learn about an attack on their fellow soldiers, they return to aid the Legion. All die in the final battle. Myrna Loy, who often played the femme fatale in the late 1920s, portrays a spy in this film and is the cause for much of the conflict. One of the four Legionnaires manages to shoot her before he dies. The film features a native attack across the desert sands. ■

Report From the Aleutians (1943), U.S. Signal Corps. *Sc.* Capt. John Huston.

A World War II documentary showing American troops battling the bleak Arctic elements while they maintain their fighting spirit, the film focuses on the building of an airfield on the island of Adak. Capt. John Huston, who supervised the production and wrote and narrated much of the script, depicts bombers taking off for raids on Japanese-held territories and often returning to fields drenched with water. The film concludes with the raid on Kiska. Walter Huston, the director's father, contributes to the narration in this technicolor tribute to American troops stationed in the barren and hostile landscape of the Aleutians. ■

Resistance. Films of resistance date back to the early silent period when movies were a fledgling entertainment industry. The historical periods covered in this genre range from ancient times to Nicaragua and Afghanistan in the 1980s. As with other genres, some of these films are simple action dramas that exploit the turmoil of a period while others are serious attempts to explain the social and political forces of the time. Virtually all the entries tend to reflect the collective values of American audiences as interpreted by studio moguls, directors or screenwriters. Sympathy, therefore, often lies with the oppressed underdog and their noble struggle for democratic ideals.

The French Revolution served as background for several films of intrigue and resistance. *The Fighting Guardsman* (1945), based on a novel by Alexander Dumas, features Willard Parker as a conscience-stricken aristocrat who leads a band of rebels on the eve of the Revolution. Robert Cummings, as a member of a small group of idealists in the historically fictitious *Reign of Terror* (1949), resists the schemes of Robespierre to establish a dictatorship in France. Other European countries of this period were utilized as backgrounds for the theme of resistance. In *Adventures of Casanova* (1948), set in the 1700s, the romantic hero (Arturo De Cordova) leads the Sicilian peasants in a revolt against the oppressive Austrian establishment. Historically, Casanova served as a spy for the Venetian Inquisition (1774–1782) during this period. The Irish struggle against England in 1798 provides the background for *Captain Lightfoot* (1955), a romantic action drama starring Rock Hudson as a hot-headed Irishman who joins the resistance against Britain. The resistance film moved to early Australia in *Captain Fury* (1939), an action drama starring Brian Aherne as an Irish patriot sentenced to serve a prison term "down under." He escapes with a handful of prisoners and organizes a struggle against an oppressive land baron while helping Australian ranchers who have fallen under the heel of the villain.

The resistance of the American Indian was a particularly bloody one and has been popularized by Hollywood in numerous outdoor dramas. In *Apache* (1954), based on historical incidents, Burt Lancaster portrays a defiant brave who wages a one-man war against the U.S. The government finally offers him amnesty. After 900 men, women and children of the Cheyenne tribe surrender to the U.S. Army in 1877 in *Cheyenne Autumn* (1964), their numbers dwindle to 286 as a result of lack of medicine and starvation at a barren Oklahoma reservation. The remaining Indians decide to escape, evading the pursuing troops during most of the journey. Again, the plight of these native Americans was taken from historical records.

The Irish resistance against the British in the 1920s was a popular subject of several American films. John Ford's Academy Award-winning *The Informer* (1935), starring Victor McLaglen as Gypo Nolan, explores the conscience of a traitor who turns in his best friend, a member of the resistance. One of the best of the Irish dramas, Ford avoids the heroism and romanticism that usually accompany similar films. In *Shake Hands With the Devil* (1959) James Cagney, as a Dublin university professor, is also a leader in the Irish underground. He has been fighting and killing for so long that when peace is arranged between both sides, Cagney wants to continue the killing.

America's Civil War was the basis for several films of resistance. The most controversial, D.W. Griffith's *Birth of a Nation* (1915), describes the rise of the Ku Klux Klan as a heroic movement that fought against the excesses of the Reconstruction Period. Local Southern citizens don white sheets to strike terror among local blacks as well as the carpetbaggers who have invaded the defeated South. In *Tap Roots* (1948) a group of prosperous Mississippi farmers who have abolished slavery in their section of the state decide to secede from the Confederacy. They are virtually decimated in a battle with Southern troops in this drama based on an actual incident.

Revolutions, the rise of dictators and the invasion and occupation of weaker countries by their more aggressive neighbors in the twentieth century served as fresh sustenance for the voracious Hollywood studios that were constantly searching for new and topical material. The oppressed were pictured in their old struggles against new forces in a variety of countries. Several dramas were concerned with the different upheavals in Mexico. *Viva Villa* (1934), starring Wallace Beery, depicts the unsophisticated bandit leader's struggle against the tyrannical regime of Diaz. In *The Fighter* (1952), based on a story by Jack London, Richard Conte turns professional boxer to raise money for Mexican rebels determined to overthrow the Diaz regime. His family and sweetheart have been murdered by government troops. An American engineer (Van Heflin) who has his property confiscated by the oppressive Diaz government joins the rebels in their struggle for freedom in *Wings of the Hawk* (1953). Several scenes show the peons suffering injustices at the hands of Mexican soldiers. Cuba's Machado government becomes the target of revolutionaries in *We Were Strangers* (1949). John Garfied, as a leader of a group of rebels, plots to assassinate several top government officials while they attend a funeral. Curiously, American films about World War I rarely dealt with the issue of resistance. "Out of Darkness" (1941), a one-reel drama produced as part of "John Nesbitt's Passing Parade" series by MGM, tells about a defiant underground newspaper in Belgium while under German occupation during the war.

Strife-torn China during the 1930s and 1940s served as background for several resistance dramas. Inhabitants of a once-peaceful village decide to rise up against their brutal Japanese occupiers in *Dragon Seed* (1944), starring Katharine Hepburn and Walter Huston. Chinese rebels, led by Anthony Quinn, fight off a Japanese attack against a local village in *China Sky* (1945), based on the novel by Pearl S. Buck. Hollywood made more resistance films dealing with World War II than with any other conflict. Virtually every country overrun by Nazis or Japanese had bands of partisans performing acts of sabotage, espionage and terrorism. They provided Hollywood with a steady source of dramatic material. One of the earliest in the genre was *Underground* (1941), about resistance inside Germany. Philip Dorn, as a leader in the German underground, runs a network of illegal radio stations seeking to broadcast the truth to the German people. Dorn is betrayed by his own brother, a believer in Nazi ideology.

Norway's struggle against Nazi oppression was the motive for several films. In *The Commandos Strike at Dawn* (1942) Paul Muni, as a simple fisherman, organizes the people against the invaders and finally leads a British Commando raid against the Germans. In *Edge of Darkness* (1943) Errol Flynn and Ann Sheridan are local leaders of a resistance group who kill all the Nazis in their village and disappear into the hills to continue the struggle. That same year *The Moon Is Down* was released. The fighting between the invader and the invaded grows more vicious as the Germans execute hostages for each act of sabotage. But the Norwegian guerrillas are not deterred; instead, they increase their activities. The film was based on John Steinbeck's popular novel.

Russia was best represented by *The North Star* (1943), with Anne Baxter, Dana Andrews and Walter Huston as some of the villagers who, after witnessing Nazi atrocities, become guerrilla fighters and take up arms against the invaders. *Song of Russia*, released the same year, tells of an American orchestra conductor (Robert Taylor) on tour who marries a Russian pianist (Susan Peters). When the Germans invade, the couple join the resistance against the invaders. But they are told to go to America to convey the heroic struggle of the Russian people. In *Days of Glory* (1944) Gregory Peck, as a Russian partisan, fights alongside his sweetheart, a ballerina. They both go to their deaths during a Russian counterattack.

Other European countries who defied the German invaders received similar screen tributes. Czechoslovakia under Nazi domination was the subject of several dramas. In *Hangmen Also Die* (1943), a highly fictional account of the assassination of the hated Reinhardt Heydrich, known as the Hangman, Brian Donlevy portrays the Czech assassin. Hundreds of hostages are killed by the Germans in retaliation. The film, whose script is partially attributed to Bertholt Brecht, was released only one year after the incident. *Hitler's Hangman*, another film that recounts the assassination of Heydrich, was released the same year. John Carradine plays the title character while Alan Curtis portrays a leader in the Czech underground. "To My Unborn Son" (1943), a one-reel drama from "John Nesbitt's Passing Parade" series, tells of a Czech resistance fighter who writes a letter explaining his struggle against the Nazis to a son he will never meet. Yugoslavia was represented by *Chetniks* (1943). Based on actual accounts that filtered out of Europe at the

time, the film describes the exploits of the guerrillas who ambush enemy supply columns and capture entire towns from the invading troops. Sometimes resistance fighters were faced with traitors from within, as in *Betrayed* (1954), a drama about the Dutch underground. The film depicts the story of an underground leader (Victor Mature) who causes the deaths of his fellow guerrillas. His traitorous actions come about when he learns that the underground has condemned his mother for collaborating with the Germans.

Several American wartime dramas concerned the famous French Resistance, which emerged shortly after the Germans occupied the country. It consisted of several different groups, including, among others, the French Committee of National Liberation, French Forces of the Interior (F.F.I.), the Secret Army of the Gaullists and the Army Resistance Organization (O.R.A.). The Resistance played an important role in the Allied invasion in June 1944. Michele Morgan, as a courageous young Frenchwoman in *Joan of Paris* (1942), sacrifices her own life when she and other members of the Resistance help downed British airmen to escape from Nazi-occupied territory. In *Assignment in Brittany* (1943) the Resistance helps a British agent to locate and destroy a hidden submarine base. In *Paris After Dark* (1943) a French soldier (Philip Dorn) returns from a German concentration camp with his spirit for resistance broken. But by the end of the film he joins the Paris underground in its struggle against the enemy. Charles Laughton changes from a weak-spirited French teacher to an outspoken patriot after he witnesses the abuses of Nazi occupation in *This Land Is Mine* (1943), a drama directed by Jean Renoir. Burt Lancaster in *The Train* (1964) portrays a simple train conductor who helps the French Resistance to stop a train filled with his country's art treasures headed for Germany.

The Japanese conquerors felt the might and vengeance of the brave guerrillas of the Philippines in a handful of films. *Back to Bataan* (1945), starring John Wayne and Anthony Quinn, and *American Guerrilla in the Philippines* (1950), starring Tyrone Power, are fairly representative of the courage displayed by the Filipino people. Following World War II, other conflicts contributed to the flow of resistance films. *Sword in the Desert* (1949) and *Exodus* (1960) tell of the Jewish struggle for a homeland. The background of the abortive Hungarian revolt of 1956 is explored in *The Beast of Budapest* (1956). *Lost Command* (1966), starring Anthony Quinn as a French commander assigned to the Algerian conflict, George Segal as an Algerian terrorist and Alain Delon as a soldier who grows weary of war, tries to present a balanced view of the Algerian struggle for independence. The last days of the Somoza regime in strife-torn Nicaragua is the subject of *Last Plane Out* (1983), starring Jan-Michael Vincent as an American journalist who becomes involved with a female rebel leader. A much better depiction of that country's turmoil occurs in *Under Fire*, released the same year. Nick Nolte, as an American photographer, loses his objectivity once he witnesses the brutality of the Somoza government. He begins to side with the rebels and manipulates his photographs to help their cause. *Salvador* (1985), starring James Woods as a photo journalist, recounts the brutal events in El Salvador during the early 1980s. The film openly sides with the rebels in their struggle against a ruthless regime.

Other films have dealt with open defiance. They range from *The Swamp Fox* (1914), which tells of Francis Marion's exploits during the American Revolution, to *Viva Zapata!* (1952), about open revolution in Mexico. Although the parameters often blur, these dramas tend more towards open rebellion than resistance. The latter term implies struggling with no organized governmental base, fighting without uniforms or territorial control and striking at the enemy with the ability to blend into the civilian population after the act is completed. The guerrillas in *For Whom the Bell Tolls* (1943), for instance, are able to survive in the mountains while returning to the local villages at will to obtain horses or information.

Resistance films often include the usual stereotypes of noble peasants sometimes clothed in quaint native costumes, fearless guerrilla leaders fighting the good cause and one-dimensional villains whose sadism and brutality often provoke the local population. These dramas frequently distort events and fuel negative attitudes, useful ploys during the conflict but counterproductive when the struggle has ended. Many are so dated and didactic that they are difficult to watch without laughing. But the best of the lot transcend the genre, the particular country or the specific circumstances. These few present a picture of ordinary people engaged in a heroic struggle against overwhelming odds. In today's more complex world we often look back with some regret at the passing of their simple, optimistic spirit and moral sense of right and wrong. ■

Retreat, Hell! (1952), WB. *Dir.* Joseph H. Lewis; *Sc.* Milton Sperling, Ted Sherdeman; *Cast includes:* Frank Lovejoy, Richard Carlson, Rusty Tamblyn, Anita Louise.

This Korean War film, with its grim battle sequences, traces the events of the U.S. Marines' First Battalion from the landing at Inchon, the drive north and to the infamous retreat when confronted by overwhelming odds. Frank Lovejoy portrays the hard-driving colonel who uttered the famous remark: "Retreat, hell! We're just attacking in a different direction." Lovejoy's words echo those of another officer during an earlier war. Captain Lloyd D. Williams at the Battle of Belleau Wood during World War I was asked if he was thinking about retreating. "Retreat, hell!" he replied. "We just got here."

Richard Carlson, as a captain recalled to active duty, is resentful of being plucked from his peaceful world. He at first objects to the colonel's obstinacy. Ned Young, as a tough, experienced sergeant, keeps the men in line. Rusty Tamblyn, as a young soldier, wants to become a hero. Some of the battle scenes come from newsreel footage. ■

Return From the Sea (1954), AA. *Dir.* Lesley Selander; *Sc.* George Waggner; *Cast includes:* Jan Sterling, Neville Brand, John Doucette, Paul Langton.

A sailor who usually drinks away his shore leaves meets a waitress and falls in love in this romantic drama set during the Korean War. The seaman (Neville Brand) decides to settle down with his new-found love (Jan Sterling). They make plans to start a farm. But the romance takes a temporary turn for the worse when Brand is wounded during his tour of duty. But he returns to Sterling and they are married. ■

Reunion in France (1942), MGM. *Dir.* Jules Dassin; *Sc.* Jan Lustig, Marvin Borowsky, Marc Connelly; *Cast includes:* Joan Crawford, John Wayne, Philip Dorn, Reginald Owen.

A rich French socialite (Joan Crawford) is unconcerned about world events or even the fall of her country to the Nazi invaders in this unconvincing World War II drama. Her conscience is finally awakened when she discovers that her fiance (Philip Dorn) is involved with the occupiers. She assists a downed American pilot (John Wayne) who is being pursued by the Germans. Although she becomes emotionally involved with Wayne, she decides to return to Dorn, whom she learns is manufacturing defective arms for the Germans while assembling a guerrilla army for the overthrow of the invaders.

As with similar films produced in Hollywood during the war years, including *Casablanca*, *Reunion* stressed that duty to one's country and self-sacrifice took precedence over matters of the heart and personal happiness. American audiences, who saw their loved ones march off to war, not only understood but demanded this personal sacrifice.

The major weakness in this drama is the absence of any mention of the French resistance fighters of the period—men and women who daily faced death and torture. They were not members of the French aristocracy or participants in the active Parisian social life that the principals shared in the film. ■

Reveille With Beverly (1943). See Musicals. ■

Revere, Paul (1735–1818). A leading colonial silversmith and engraver, and fervent propagandist and patriot for the American cause in Boston, Revere achieved his greatest fame because of his night ride through the countryside outside Boston warning the populace that the British were coming. His alarm helped start a chain of events that led to the first battle of the American Revolution, the Battle of Lexington and Concord (April 19, 1775). Though two other men joined him in that famous night journey, Revere's role became better known as the result of Longfellow's popular classic poem "Paul Revere's Ride."

Tension had been building for almost a decade between the American colonists and Britain over trade and political differences. Boston and the surrounding area were known as hotbeds of patriot activity. Britain's General Gage decided to send out a secret expedition from Boston on the night of April 18, 1775, to seize colonial leaders, including Sam Adams and John Hancock, and stores of colonial arms at Concord, thereby hoping to weaken and defuse American resistance. Patriots suspected the British might make a

foray into the country, so Revere organized a system to report any unusual activity by British troops in the area.

A signal was arranged to hang lanterns in the North Church steeple, two should the British go out from Boston by water and one if they took the land route. When Revere saw two lights in the steeple just before midnight, he set out to warn Adams and Hancock, who were staying at Lexington, and arouse patriot militiamen and farmers along the road that the British were coming. Revere was joined in Lexington by two other riders, Dr. Samuel Prescott and William Dawes. They all started for Concord five miles away but ran into a British patrol. Revere was captured. Dawes escaped through the woods, but Prescott got through to sound the alarm at Concord. Revere was released at Lexington.

Prior to his famous ride, Revere took part in the Boston Tea Party, served as a courier for patriot committees between Boston and New York and was an active member of the Sons of Liberty. With the outbreak of fighting, he helped the cause for revolution in a number of ways.

Revere's famous ride has been depicted in several films. One of the earliest was "The Midnight Ride of Paul Revere" (1907), a short Edison production directed by film pioneer Edwin S. Porter. Others include the silent historical dramas *The Midnight Ride of Paul Revere* (1914), *Washington at Valley Forge* (1914), *Cardigan* (1922), *America* (1924) and *Janice Meredith* (1924). Each of these features, although slightly staid, made an earnest attempt to portray historical incidents realistically.

By the 1930s Revere as a serious national hero seemed to fall out of favor in Hollywood to the extent that he was satirized in the Marx Brothers comedy *Duck Soup* (1934). Harpo re-enacts the ride which ends up in an attractive woman's bathtub. In the historical drama *Johnny Tremain* (1957), Revere was restored to his rightful place in history. The title character, a young lad, witnesses the major historical events of the American Revolution, including Revere's ride to warn the farmers. ■

Revolt at Fort Laramie (1957), UA. *Dir.* Lesley Selander; *Sc.* Robert C. Dennis; *Cast includes:* John Dehner, Gregg Palmer, Frances Helm, Don Gordon.

The start of the Civil War causes additional problems for a cavalry outpost already plagued by Indian unrest. John Dehner, as a Virginian major in charge of Fort Laramie, prepares to pull out those troops loyal to the Confederacy. He turns over the command to the captain (Gregg Palmer) who is faced by Chief Red Cloud's demand of $50,000 in gold. Once outside the fort, the major and his Southerners are attacked by the hostiles. The captain leads his troops to rescue their fellow soldiers.

Another entry in a handful of films in which cavalry troops, split in their allegiances between the North and the South, ultimately join forces to fight the Indians. In Hollywood, it seems that as bitter as the sectional hatred was, the Indians represented the greater foe. In all of these features, the officer in charge of either faction comes to the aid of his fellow officer and troops against the hostiles. Each film stops short of suggesting that the reason is a racist one. ∎

Richard I, Richard Coeur de Lion (Richard the Lion-Hearted) (1157–1199).

Ruler of England (1189–1199), he was the epitome of a medieval warrior king whose fame was based entirely on his exploits in war. He spent barely six months of his reign in England, devoting the major part of his adult life to battle, which he seemed to love and at which he excelled as a leader.

He was the third son of England's Henry II. He first gained military prominence by crushing revolts by his French barons. Richard later allied himself with Prince Philip II of France and forced his father in 1189 to submit to a demand that he, Richard, be declared heir to the throne. He succeeded to the crown of England on Henry's death later that year.

Richard evinced no interest in administering England. He left government affairs to his ministers and joined Philip in the Third Crusade. It was his exploits during this period that made Richard one of England's most beloved and famous kings—and put him into Hollywood's spotlight.

He set out to reconquer Jerusalem, which Saladin had recently retaken. En route, Richard captured the Sicilian city of Messina and the island of Cyprus, then married Berengaria of Navarre before landing in Palestine. Though he was not successful in taking Jerusalem, Richard inflicted a serious defeat on Saladin and the Moslem forces at the Battle of Acre (1191). His victory forced Saladin to agree to respect the rights and safety of Chris-

tian pilgrims. At least two films deal extensively with Richard's confrontation with Saladin. *Richard, the Lion-Hearted* (1923), with Wallace Beery in the title role, is overly concerned with a fictitious love story that pits Richard and Saladin as romantic and military rivals. Cecil B. DeMille's *The Crusades* (1935) is of more historical value, showing Richard's marriage and much graphic detail of his important victory at Acre.

After Richard returned to Europe, he became embroiled in one of the byzantine intrigues that marked European royal politics in the middle ages. He ended up being imprisoned by Austria's Leopold II who handed him over to Emperor Henry VI. Richard had to pay a large ransom, raised by his English subjects, to gain freedom. In Richard Thorpe's *Ivanhoe* (1952), from Sir Walter Scott's medieval novel, the fictitious Ivanhoe (Robert Taylor) is charged with the responsibility of raising funds to free his king with whom he had served in the Crusades. Hollywood's penchant for creating pseudo-history even tied in the legend of Robin Hood to Richard's ransom. The mythical outlaw in several films, including *The Adventures of Robin Hood* (1938) that starred the dashing Errol Flynn in the title role, robs the rich to gain funds for Richard's release.

Richard returned to England briefly in 1194 but left within a month to go to France to seek revenge on his former ally, King Philip II. Philip had been involved in an unsuccessful plot to usurp Richard's crown in favor of Richard's youngest brother John while Richard was away on the Crusades and in prison. *Ivanhoe* and *The Adventures of Robin Hood* dramatized the attempt to dethrone Richard. He was killed in a minor conflict in France five years later without having returned to England again. Though he made no lasting mark on English government, Richard, because of his military prowess, brought his country great prestige during the turbulent middle ages. ∎

Richard, the Lion-Hearted (1923), APD.

Dir. Chet Webey; Sc. Frank E. Woods; *Cast includes:* Wallace Beery, Marguerite de la Motte, Charles Gerrard.

Wallace Beery's robust performance as King Richard in the Douglas Fairbanks production of *Robin Hood* spurred those who dreamed up this feature to cast him again in the role. Adapted from Sir Walter Scott's *The*

Talisman, the story, set in the days of the Crusades, focuses on the adventures of the Lion-Hearted while Robin Hood goes about protecting the king's interests in England. The plot is not without its interesting moments. In one scene, for example, where Richard is ill, Saladin (Charles Gerrard), the King's mortal enemy who prefers to see his foe die at his hands in battle and not in bed, masquerades as a physician and comes to his aid. When Richard recovers and learns the true identity of the doctor, he gives Saladin safe passage to his own lines. In another sequence, Saladin raids Richard's camp while the King is away and encounters Lady Edith (Marguerite de la Motte), whom he immediately desires. Upon Richard's return, the Sultan is willing to promise anything as long as Richard gives him permission to marry the woman. The angry King objects strongly to the proposal. The film includes plenty of sword fights and battles. ∎

Richthofen, Baron Manfred von (1892–1918).

Silently a squad of Australian and New Zealand (ANZAC) riflemen, serving as honor guard at a military funeral, point their weapons into the air. A moment later the quiet is shattered by a ceremonial volley to a fallen fighter. Scores of British air officers had gathered around the site on April 22, 1918, to pay their last respects, not to one of their own, but to a former enemy, Baron Manfred von Richthofen, the famous "Red Baron" of the German air force and leading ace of World War I.

Such was the sense of chivalry that existed among opposing fliers on the western front in World War I. They thought of themselves as modern knights in battle, their steeds being the wood, cloth and wire flying machines that hurtled about the skies. Though their aerial jousts were grim and deadly for many, they followed an almost medieval code of respect for a beaten enemy.

When he died at age 30, von Richthofen had been credited with 80 kills, the highest number of victories achieved by any other pilot in the entire war. Most sources credit Captain A. Roy Brown, a Canadian in the British Royal Flying Corps, with shooting down Richthofen. But at least one major source contends that Richthofen, after a wild dogfight involving some 50 airplanes, was flying low when he ran into ground fire and crashed. An artillery barrage pounded the wrecked plane. His recovered body showed he had been shot in the side near his heart.

Hollywood turned out several air action films about the war ace. *Von Richthofen And Brown* (1971) details the clash between the two pilots and shows Brown ending the career of the German ace. The film, though characterized by wooden performances, does have some effective aerial fighting sequences and is faithful to history in several ways. It illustrates the chivalrous nature of World War I aerial encounters. It also shows Hermann Goering, the future Nazi air chief, in a small role as second-in-command to von Richthofen at the llth Pursuit Squadron. Goering, in real life, succeeded to squadron leader upon von Richthofen's death.

At the outbreak of World War I, Richthofen was an officer in the Prussian cavalry who saw action on both the Russian and western fronts. The rise of trench warfare in the west ended the use of cavalry, leading him to shift briefly to the infantry where he won an Iron Cross. His restlessness prompted him to apply in 1915 to the German Imperial Air Force. His first solo ended in a crash, but by 1916 Richthofen had become a combat pilot. His squadron, flying scarlet-colored Fokkers—hence the name Red Baron—became known as "Richthofen's Flying Circus" for their unusual tactics. Newspaper accounts stressed that the group developed a feared reputation for their daring forays along the front line that caused destruction to ground forces, supply lines and enemy aircraft.

Von Richthofen and the fighting style of those times were the subjects of several other films. In *Berlin Via America* (1918), a fictional American joins the Flying Circus as part of a spying mission. Howard Hughes' air epic *Hell's Angels* (1930) has the Red Baron and his Flying Circus engaged in a spectacular air battle with a squadron of British fighters in the latter half of the film. The second and more popular version of *Dawn Patrol* (1938), with Errol Flynn, David Niven and Basil Rathbone, includes a German air ace with a similar-sounding name, von Richter. ∎

Rickenbacker, Captain Edward. See *Captain Eddie* (1945). ∎

Riley of the Rainbow Division (1928).
See Service Comedy. ∎

Rio Grande (1950), Rep. *Dir.* John Ford; *Sc.* James K. McGuinness; *Cast includes:* John Wayne, Maureen O'Hara, Ben Johnson, Claude Jarman, Jr., Harry Carey, Jr., Victor McLaglen.

Part of director John Ford's U.S. Cavalry trilogy (*Fort Apache* (1948) and *She Wore a Yellow Ribbon* (1949) being the first two), the film centers on Colonel Kirby Yorke (John Wayne). He is in command of a remote outpost near the Mexican border from which hostile Apaches do their murderous raiding. His son, whom he hasn't seen in fifteen years, enlists in the cavalry and is assigned as an ordinary trooper to Yorke's outpost. Yorke's estranged wife (Maureen O'Hara) follows to take her son home. Always the dutiful officer, Yorke, during the Civil War and under General Sheridan's orders, burned down his wife's plantation, an act for which she has never forgiven him. Now, fifteen years later, he serves in the Southwest, a lonely man. After several Indian raids and other battles, he and his wife come to an understanding while their son is cited for bravery. Ford once again has embellished his film with details of military life, lively characters, sentimental humor and an emphasis on the glory and tradition of the cavalry. ■

German soldiers celebrate the end of World War I. *The Road Back* (1937).

Road Back, The (1937), U. *Dir.* James Whale; *Sc.* R. C. Sherriff, Charles Kenyon; *Cast includes:* John King, Richard Cromwell, Slim Summerville, Andy Devine, Barbara Read, Louise Fazenda.

Based on the novel by Erich Maria Remarque, the film, like the book, is intended as a sequel to his *All Quiet on the Western Front.* The story attempts to describe what happens to the soldiers who were fortunate enough to survive the horrors of the war when they return home. The veterans, old young men, come back to hunger riots and threats of revolution. Bands of thugs attack the puzzled, returning heroes. Their old uniforms, which they still wear, symbolize the cause of the economic and social strife. The impact of the soldiers' difficult "road back" and the generally somber tone is vitiated by the inappropriate use of slapstick comedy as provided by Andy Devine and Slim Summerville. The only battle sequences appear in the beginning, but, like the earlier work based on Remarque's novel, the film suggests a strong antiwar message. "You cannot take human beings and train them to be inhuman for four years and expect them to be a fit companion for normal men and women," a German ex-soldier exclaims to his sweetheart.

The film failed to come close to the artistic and commercial success of *All Quiet on the Western Front* (1930) although, like its predecessor, it stirred controversy. The Nazi consulate warned those affiliated with the production that their subsequent works might be prohibited in Germany. The last scene, showing a goose-stepping child playfully leading a mock army of little children, is both haunting and prophetic. ■

Road Through the Dark, The (1918), Select. *Dir.* Edmund Mortimer; *Sc.* Kathryn Stuart; *Cast includes:* Clara Kimball Young, Jack Holt, Henry Woodward, Eleanor Fair, Bobby Connolly.

Clara Kimball Young portrays a young French patriot who saves her village and its people in this World War I drama. She elects to become the mistress of a German aristocrat to protect the village from being destroyed and her neighbors from being slaughtered by the advancing German army. Meanwhile, for the remainder of the war, she acts as a spy for the Allies as she gathers information about enemy troops and strategy. Some critics, disturbed by the heroine's loss of innocence, questioned the moral tone of the film. ■

Road to France, The (1918). See Spy Films: the Silents.■

Road to Glory, The (1936), TCF. *Dir.* Howard Hawks; *Sc.* Joel Sayre, William Faulkner; *Cast includes:* Fredric March, Lionel Barrymore, June Lang.

This graphic World War I drama was another entry in the cycle of realistic antiwar films that began in 1930 with *All Quiet on the Western Front* and *Journey's End* and which underscored the senselessness of the conflict while avoiding, for the most part, the romantic aspects of national honor and glory. A war-weary French captain (Warner Baxter) tries to relieve his father (Lionel Barrymore), a soldier in his command, from front-line duty in the trenches. But the stubborn old man refuses to leave his post. Meanwhile, the men in the trenches hear the ominous digging of enemy axes. The Germans are in the process of undermining the French trenches. The men wait in fear for orders to evacuate their position—orders that come just in time. Other realistic moments dot this better-than-average war film, including a scene in which a French soldier, trapped in a maze of barbed wire, cries out in pain. After several of his comrades are killed trying to rescue the wounded man, Baxter coolly shoots him to put him out of his misery. Fredric March portrays a lieutenant under the command of Baxter. The romantic interest is supplied by June Lang, who plays a nurse.

The film has been singled out by film historians and critics for its brutal and realistic depiction of the war. June Lang at one point asks March why men go to war. "Do not ask me that," he replies. "Men always have died in wars and probably always will. For what reason we do not know." Other critics, however, claim that the film romanticizes militarism, patriotism and heroism, especially in the last scene in which March carries on in the proud tradition of Baxter, who has been killed in battle. March addresses the new recruits with all the nationalistic splendor he could muster.

It is a remake of a French feature, *Wooden Crosses*, that was well received in Europe but had never been released in the United States. The sequence of the undermining of the trenches, previously dramatized in another World War I film *The Doomed Battalion* (1932), is based on an actual incident that occurred during the war. Italian troops, aware of the digging, were ordered to remain at their posts and were eventually killed by the powerful explosives. An earlier film had appeared in 1926 bearing the same title, but it had nothing to do with war. ∎

"Road to Richmond, The" (1910), Selig.

A Civil War drama of two cadets who meet at West Point, the story tells of how each enlists and fights on opposite sides. The Union soldier, who had met his friend's sister while visiting their Southern home, captures his former roommate during a battle. The Confederate soldier manages to escape but because of his wound cannot destroy a bridge according to orders. His sister completes the mission for him and jumps into the river below. The Northerner, who has advanced with his troops, rescues her and is captured by the Confederates. The girl speaks to General Lee on his behalf and the captive is freed. The friendship of the two youths and the visit to the Southern home anticipate similar incidents in Griffith's *The Birth of a Nation* (1915). ∎

Roar of the Dragon (1932), RKO. *Dir.* Wesley Ruggles; *Sc.* Howard Estabrook; *Cast includes:* Richard Dix, Gwili Andre, Edward Everett Horton, Arline Judge, ZaSu Pitts, Dudley Digges.

An adventure yarn set in pre-World War II strife-torn China, the film concerns a pilot (Richard Dix) of a Chinese riverboat. He and his passengers are stranded in a village about to be overrun by a local bandit and his followers. The whites take refuge in a walled garden and hold off the attacking hordes with a lone machine gun until the paddle wheel is repaired, after which they slip away to the boat and eventual safety. The film includes sufficient action for the simple plot which in some ways suggests that of *Shanghai Express*, starring Marlene Dietrich, released earlier the same year. In fact, the heroine, Gwili Andre, has been made up to resemble the Garbo-Dietrich woman of mystery, particularly the latter personality in regard to speech and appearance. Edward Everett Horton and ZaSu Pitts provide some much-needed comic relief. ∎

Roaring Rails (1924). See World War I. ∎

Rocky Mountain (1950), WB. *Dir.* William Keighley; *Sc.* Winston Miller, Alan LeMay; *Cast includes:* Errol Flynn, Patrice Wymore, Scott Forbes, Guinn Williams.

A band of Confederate soldiers, led by their stalwart officer (Errol Flynn), meet at a western rendezvous with a gang of outlaws in this Civil War drama shot almost entirely outdoors. Meanwhile, they rescue a Northern woman (Patrice Wymore) from a group of hostile Indians and then use her as bait to capture a Union patrol. When the small force is threatened by a large number of hostiles, Flynn and his men divert the Indians and engage them in battle. They sacrifice their lives so that the woman can make it to safety. ■

Rogers' Rangers. The rangers were British contingents of mounted soldiers in Colonial America who protected designated lands against hostile Indians. Many Colonials joined the rangers who also fought in the French and Indian war. The most famous unit, Rogers' Rangers, was led by Robert Rogers (1731–1795), a colorful adventurer. He served as a scout and spy for the British in the French and Indian War. His motives were less than noble, for he was eluding prosecution as a counterfeiter. He was soon put in charge of a company of rangers and aided in the capture of Montreal (1763). He also helped to crush Chief Pontiac's rebellion. A journey to England gained the ambitious Rogers a position, upon his return, at Mackinac where he conducted several explorations into the Northwest. Accused of illegally trading with the French, he was arrested on orders of General Gage but was acquitted. He left America and worked for the Bey of Algiers in 1774. When he returned to America the following year, he was willing to join either the British or the Colonials. General Washington arrested him as a spy. While on parole, Rogers joined the British and became captain of a ranger company. He was beaten in a battle at White Plains, New York. He again journeyed to England in 1780 where he lived an obscure and impoverished existence until his death in 1795.

In King Vidor's highly fictional *Northwest Passage* (1940), based on the first half of Kenneth Roberts' book, Spencer Tracy plays Major Rogers. He leads 160 trained fighters, known as Rogers' Rangers, on a punitive expedition to wipe out an Abenaki village whose hostile braves were responsible for repeated savage raids against white settlers. In *Fort Ti* (1953), a routine drama, Rogers' Rangers join forces with the British to remove the French from Fort Ticonderoga during the French and Indian War.

The concept of the rangers was resurrected during World War II. The U.S. Army Rangers, the counterpart of the British Commandos, were organized in 1942 to carry out behind-the-lines raids as well as beach assaults. Six Ranger battalions saw action on several fronts, including North Africa, Europe, the Aleutian Islands, New Guinea, Leyte and Luzon. William Wellman's *Darby's Rangers* (1958) recounts the exploits of this special fighting unit created by Colonel William Darby in World War II. James Garner, as Darby, leads his specially trained men on a series of successful missions in North Africa, Sicily and northern Italy. ■

Rogue's March (1952), MGM. *Dir.* Allan Davis; *Sc.* Leon Gordon; *Cast includes:* Peter Lawford, Richard Greene, Janice Rule, Leo G. Carroll, John Abbott.

Russia stirs up trouble in 19th century India as a British soldier, branded a traitor, tries to prove his worth in this routine adventure drama. Peter Lawford portrays the young Englishman accused of being a turncoat. He enlists in the service to prove to his father that the charges are false. Once in India he performs honorably as well as heroically, saving his entire regiment. The highlight of this minor film that tries to mirror such past adventure dramas as *Lives of a Bengal Lancer* (1935) and *Gunga Din* (1939) is its battle sequences between the British troops and the dissident tribes. The natives are aroused by the Russian representatives of the Czar who seeks a foothold on the continent. John Abbott plays a Russian spy working within the British War Office. Janice Rule provides the slight romantic interest. ■

Rogues of Sherwood Forest (1950), Col. *Dir.* Gordon Douglas; *Sc.* George Bruce; *Cast includes:* John Derek, Diana Lynn, George Macready, Alan Hale, Paul Cavanagh.

The son of Robin Hood invokes the spirit of his famous father when the avaricious King John begins overtaxing his English subjects in this romantic costume drama. John Derek portrays the legendary hero's offspring who enlists the aid of Little John, Friar Tuck, Will Scarlett and the rest of his father's merry men to foil the new tyrant's oppression. After a series of forest pursuits and skirmishes, young Robin and his rebels persuade the king to sign the Magna Carta. George Macready portrays the villainous King John. Diana Lynn, as Lady Marianne, provides the romance. Alan Hale returns to play Little John with as much gusto as he did in the 1938 *Adventures of Robin Hood* starring Errol Flynn. ■

Rogues' Regiment (1948), UI. *Dir.* Robert Florey; *Sc.* Robert Buckner; *Cast includes:* Dick Powell, Marta Toren, Vincent Price, Stephen McNally.

An American army officer is assigned to hunt down a ruthless Nazi war criminal who has escaped justice at the Nuremberg trials. Dick Powell, in another of his tough, post-World War II dramas, portrays the clever and relentless American who pursues the trail of the Nazi to Saigon. Stephen McNally portrays the hunted, now in civilian clothes and ready to lose his identity as a common soldier in the Foreign Legion engaged in battling the Vietnamese insurrectionists. Powell eventually discovers his identity and brings him to justice. Although released several years after World War II, the film depicts the Germans in a negative light and includes a didactic narration of Nazi brutality and other crimes.

When McNally, as Martin Bruner, goes to his death at the end of the drama, the narrator announces: "The last steps of Martin Bruner upon that scaffold are a warning to the world that such men must not march again. There is no other road to justice and mankind's dream for a lasting peace." Vincent Price plays a former German passing himself off as a Dutch businessman. Marta Toren is engaged as a French spy working as a cafe singer.

Perhaps more interesting is the subplot of the French colonial war in Indo-China. Early in the film a French colonel aboard a train bound for Saigon shows his frustration with the war. Unable or unwilling to accept the colonists' struggle for self-determination, he blames the military conflict on those who are selling arms to the guerrillas while viewing the political struggle as that between communism and democracy. "The people of French Indo-China are fighting only because they are tired of French injustice and misrule," a fellow passenger replies to the officer's simple explanation of the conflict. "No," the colonel insists, "there are only two marching songs in the world today— the 'Internationale,' which may be theirs, and 'La Marseillaise,' which will always be ours!" He then leaves the compartment. ■

Rolling Thunder (1977). See Vietnam War. ■

Roman Civil Wars (49–44 B.C. and 43–31 B.C.) This period, ushered in by the rise of Julius Caesar, involved some of the ancient world's most notable individuals in a period of complex upheaval. Julius Caesar's enemies in the Roman Senate, fearing his popularity, ordered him to give up his command (49 B.C.) in Gaul after his successful campaign there and return to Rome.

Caesar refused to do so. Instead, he invaded Italy and set off a civil war against his chief rival, Pompey, backed by most of the Senate. In the six years of fighting that followed, Caesar defeated his enemies and Pompey was murdered in Egypt while attempting to flee. The films that touch upon the Roman Civil Wars usually begin after these turbulent events.

Caesar, in Egypt, successfully supported Queen Cleopatra's bid for the throne she had previously shared with her husband-brother. She became ruler of Egypt as a vassal and accompanied Caesar back to Rome. These events are dramatized in Cecil B. DeMille's *Cleopatra* (1934), with Claudette Colbert as the queen and Warren William as Caesar, and again in Joseph Mankiewicz's *Cleopatra* (1963), starring Elizabeth Taylor and Rex Harrison in the same roles.

Caesar triumphed in North Africa (46 B.C.) and in Spain the following year, eliminating the remaining Senate forces opposing him. Returning to Rome, he became a popular dictator for a year. However, a group of Senators led by Brutus and Cassius, fearing that Caesar might make himself king for life, assassinated him on March 15, 44 B.C. The plot, its execution and its ramifications are realistically retold in Mankiewicz's *Julius Caesar* (1953), based on Shakespeare's tragedy.

Caesar's death precipitated another civil war. On one side were Caesar's nephew and heir, Octavian, Mark Antony and Lepidus. Brutus and Cassius, who led the opposing forces, both committed suicide after their defeat. The ruling triumvirate of Octavian, Lepidus and Antony divided the empire among them but soon had a falling out. The Senate dismissed Lepidus from office over suspicion of his loyalty. When Octavian refused to assist Antony in the latter's war against Parthia, Antony turned for help to Cleopatra, with whom he had fallen in love.

Antony divorced his Roman wife, Octavia (Octavian's sister), and married Cleopatra, designating her and their children as his heirs. His actions aroused the ire of the Roman people and Senate who feared the possibility of being ruled by Cleopatra, a non-Roman. The two sides clashed at sea in the Battle of Actium (31 B.C.) and on land with Roman forces emerging as victors. The battle is vividly recreated in *Cleopatra* (1963).

Antony killed himself (30 B.C.) upon being falsely told that Cleopatra was dead. When informed she would be paraded as a prisoner in Rome by the victorious Octavian, Cleopatra committed suicide by holding a poisonous asp to her breast. Octavian, as Augustus, ruled the Roman world in a period of civil peace. *Serpent of the Nile* (1953), a weak recounting of the above events, conjures up a plot in which the queen of the Nile attempts to usurp the Roman throne by having Antony killed. *Cleopatra* (1963), despite its several faults, gives a more poignant picture of the doomed love affair between the queen and Antony, two tragic figures who see both their youth and their power slipping away. See Cleopatra, Julius Caesar, Mark Antony. ■

Romance of Rosy Ridge, The (1947), MGM. *Dir.* Roy Rowland; *Sc.* Lester Cole; *Cast includes:* Van Johnson, Thomas Mitchell, Janet Leigh, Marshall Thompson.

This Civil War drama, which takes place in the spring of 1865, centers on the bitter hatreds and wounds between the North and the South rather than on the conflict itself. Van Johnson portrays a traveling schoolteacher who woos the daughter (Janet Leigh) of a Missouri farmer (Thomas Mitchell), a man who harbors deep enmity towards the North. He suspects Johnson of being a Union sympathizer. But the young visitor manages to bring the two factions together by the last reel of this romantic tale. This was Janet Leigh's first screen appearance. ■

Romance of the Air, A (1918), Crest. *Dir.* Harry Revier; *Sc.* Franklin B. Coates; *Cast includes:* Bert Hall, Edith Day, Florence Billing, Stuart Holmes.

Based on Lieutenant Bert Hall's book *In the Air,* the film recounts his experiences in the Lafayette Escadrille during World War I. Hall, a flier with the famous air group, is shot down over Germany, dons a fallen enemy's uniform and convalesces in a German hospital. He meets his American sweetheart in Germany who has been trapped there when the war began. Together with a female German spy, they fly to freedom. Hall received several medals from the French, including the Croix de Guerre. He and Major Thaw allegedly were the only survivors of the original group of Americans who joined the celebrated Escadrille. The love story was added to the film version of the book. It was one of the few air war movies made by an American company during or immediately after the war. Another was *The Zeppelin's Last Raid* (1917). Interest in this genre did not develop until William Wellman's epic *Wings* appeared in 1927. ■

Rommel, Erwin (1891–1944). The word "chaotic" best describes the situation in France early in June 1940. The nation that had produced Napoleon and Foch was being hammered into the ground in a matter of weeks by a series of lightning strokes by the armored Panzer divisions of Nazi Germany. The acknowledged leader of this new form of attack—the blitzkrieg—was 49-year-old Erwin Rommel, often racing ahead of the main body of his own armored column to strike the surprised enemy. Speeding through towns far from the battle lines, villagers sometimes came out to cheer and strew flowers in the path of his 7th (Ghost) Panzer Division, thinking his force were English reinforcements coming to head off the Germans.

Rommel was a superlative World War II battlefield leader, a master tactician of tank warfare. He was Germany's most popular war hero and the general most feared and respected by the Allies. One of his adversaries in North Africa, British General Claude Auchinleck, deemed it necessary for troop morale to counter Rommel's reputation by telling his officers in a written memo: "There is a real danger that our friend Rommel will turn into a bogey-man for our troops. . . . He is not superhuman . . . it would be most un-desirable for our soldiers to attribute super-natural powers to him." (In the film *The Desert Fox* (1951) these words are read aloud by a British commander to his officers.)

As newly appointed commander of the 7th Panzer Division, Rommel used his ideas on tank tactics to spearhead the drive in early 1940 across part of Belgium and western France to the channel. He believed a leader should be up with his troops, especially as head of a fast-moving strike force, and was not above showing disdain for what he termed "armchair generals."

Rommel was posted to Libya, North Africa, in 1941 as head of the Africa Corps to salvage Italy's crumbling empire. The vast, open ter-rain there suited his tactics, and his early ex-ploits earned him the nickname "Desert Fox." Battle lines surged back and forth over hundreds of miles in desert warfare domi-nated by armor strategy. Although Rommel had a mercurial, driving temperament that re-sulted in a steady stream of dismissals of se-nior staff officers, his troops developed a close bond with him. This, too, is brought out in *The Desert Fox*.

He made several attempts to invade Egypt and sweep to the Suez Canal, but each was turned back by either superior enemy forces or failures in his supply system. The highly fictionalized *Tobruk* (1967), with Rock Hud-son and George Peppard, concerns Allied units trying to blow up some of Rommel's fuel dumps in the Sahara. In his first desert attack, beginning in March 1941, Rommel pushed the British out of Libya and into Egypt. A British counter-attack later that year sent the Africa Corps reeling back. Rommel surged forward again and defeated the British in a massive tank battle at Gazala-Bir Hakim that enabled the Axis to penetrate 250 miles into Egypt and mount the most serious threat of the war to the Suez Canal. However, faced by vastly superior forces, and restricted by supply problems and terrain that hampered his wide sweeping tank tactics, Rommel could not break the British defense at El Alamein.

The importance of stopping the Panzer leader at Alamein is brought out in *Sahara* (1943) starring Humphrey Bogart. A climactic moment occurs near the end of the film when Bogart, as an American tank commander stranded for days in the desert, asks a rescu-ing British force how the war is going. "We held them at El Alamein," comes the reply. General Montgomery, beginning in October 1942, used superior ground and air power to push Rommel back across the whole of Libya to the Tunisian border. The American-British invasion of North Africa, around the same time, forced Rommel to evacuate his troops to Europe.

Rommel is portrayed in about half-a-dozen major films; they are either devoted entirely to him or have segments dealing with his mil-itary campaigns. *The Desert Fox*, with James Mason as the Panzer leader, is a biography of his later life with a wealth of accurate detail and a sympathetic portrayal of Rommel. It covers his desert actions, an unsuccessful British Commando assassination attempt based on fact and his growing disillusion with Hitler's leadership. The last resulted in Rommel's forced suicide because of his im-plication in the generals' plot to assassinate Hitler. The film concludes with an authentic quotation by Churchill that pays tribute to Rommel after the latter's death.

The Desert Rats (1953), again with James Mason as Rommel, deals with the German tank master's first major desert defeat. Tough Australian troops, holed up in Tobruk, with-stand Rommel's 242-day siege in 1941. *Five Graves to Cairo* (1943), featuring Erich von Stroheim as Rommel, is an unusual film for its time. Though made during World War II, it resisted the usual convention of portraying German officers as cold, sadistic caricatures. Instead, it shows Rommel's attitude of re-spect for captured prisoners. In truth, Rom-mel allowed no S.S. troops in his command, the group usually associated with atrocities. He thought of war as a duel between honor-able opponents. Despite its title, the action drama *Raid on Rommel* (1971), starring Rich-ard Burton as a British Intelligence officer, has nothing to do with the German com-mander.

After the Axis had been driven out of Af-rica early in 1943, Rommel was placed, shortly later, in command of a portion of the French seacoast to resist the expected Allied invasion. This is depicted in *The Longest Day* (1962), which shows him (portrayed by Werner Hinz) strengthening the beach de-fenses and saying that the outcome of the war will be determined on these beaches.

After the invasion he was badly injured in a strafing attack and was in a hospital when the aborted German generals' plot on Hitler's

Wally Brown and Alan Carney are about to become the guests of Japanese soldiers in the World War II comedy *Rookies in Burma* (1943).

life took place on July 20, 1944. To avoid a domestic morale problem, Hitler gave Rommel a choice: either stand trial as a traitor and forfeit his family's pension benefits or secretly commit suicide. In the latter case, the German nation would be informed that he died a hero as a result of his strafing injuries. Rommel chose this course. See El Alamein. ■

Rookies in Burma (1943), RKO. *Dir.* Leslie Goodwins; *Sc.* Edward James; *Cast includes:* Wally Brown, Alan Carney, Erford Gage, Claire Carleton.

Wally Brown and Alan Carney appear in their second film as a comedy team (*Adventures of a Rookie* was their first). Using a blend of dialogue, slapstick and chase sequences, the pair try to inject comedy into a weak plot that involves the two dimwitted army privates' capture, along with their tough sergeant (Erford Gage), by the Japanese. Managing to double-talk their way out of a prison camp, they escape their captors, plod through the Burmese jungle, meet two pretty American entertainers whom they take along with them and return to their lines in a cap-

tured Japanese tank—all the while being pursued by the enemy. ■

Rookies on Parade (1941). See Musicals. ■

Roosevelt, Theodore (1858–1919). Theodore Roosevelt was Assistant Secretary of the Navy during the administration of President McKinley when the Spanish-American War broke out. He resigned his post when war was declared and, together with Leonard Wood, Roosevelt organized the 1st Volunteer Cavalry Regiment, more commonly known as "The Rough Riders." Wood was colonel of the regiment, and Roosevelt served as lieutenant colonel.

Roosevelt led the charge up Kettle Hill, part of the Battle of San Juan Hill in the Cuban campaign, in which the regiment distinguished itself. Prior to his service in Cuba, Roosevelt, a Harvard graduate, briefly practiced law, wrote historical works and held several elected and appointed offices in New York City and New York State. As Assistant Secretary of the Navy he helped prepare

American sea forces for the possibility of war before the outbreak of hostilities with Spain.

His service in the Spanish-American War and personal magnetism boosted him to the vice-presidency under McKinley in the election of 1900. He succeeded to the presidency upon McKinley's assassination (1901) and won re-election in 1904. As President, he was awarded the Nobel Peace Prize for his role in bringing an end to the Russo-Japanese War (1904–05).

His colorful personality made him a ripe subject for several films. *The Fighting Roosevelts* (1919), the only biographical feature based on his career, includes incidents from his political life as well as his exploits during the Spanish-American War. *The Rough Riders* (1927) and *End of the Trail* (1936) again allude to his role in the Battle of San Juan Hill. Warner Brothers, as part of their historical series of film shorts, produced a two-reel biography "Teddy, the Rough Rider" in 1940. He is portrayed as a minor character in other war-related dramas, including *The Copperhead* (1920) and *The Wind and the Lion* (1975). ∎

Rose of the South (1916), Vitagraph. *Dir.* Robert Scardon; *Sc.* Joseph Poland; *Cast includes:* Peggy Hyland, Antonio Moreno, Mary Maurice.

A romantic drama of the Civil War, the story is told in flashback by one of the chief participants who is now an elderly gentleman. The film includes several battle scenes. ∎

Rose of the World (1918), Par. *Dir.* Maurice Tourneur; *Sc.* Charles Maigne; *Cast includes:* Elsie Ferguson, Wyndham Standing, Percy Marmont, Ethel Martin.

Colonial India provides the background for this romantic war drama. Elsie Ferguson portrays the young wife of a British officer (Wyndham Standing) who is assigned to a remote outpost, the symbol of British rule, that is under attack by mutinous natives. A raging battle ensues, and the officer is listed as killed in action. His wife, at first grief-stricken, later recovers and marries a major (Clarence Handysides). When she reads her former husband's letters, she again falls in love with him and becomes ill. She returns to England to recover and is followed by the major and his mysterious secretary, a bearded native, who turns out to be her first husband. It seems that he was captured by the natives.

By the time he escaped and returned to British lines, he learned of his wife's marriage. Rather than ruin her chances for happiness, he decided to hide his identity and remain nearby to find out if she was really happy. Aside from the implausible plot elements, the film includes several exciting action sequences. Another film bearing the same title appeared in 1925 but had nothing to do with the above plot. ∎

Women abandon their stereotyped roles to work in war plants during World War II. *Rosie the Riveter* (1944).

Rosie the Riveter (1944), Rep. *Dir.* Joseph Santley; *Sc.* Jack Townley, Aleen Leslie; *Cast includes:* Jane Frazee, Frank Albertson, Vera Vague, Frank Jenks.

This World War II romantic comedy focuses on the problems of four defense plant workers confronted with a housing shortage. Two men and two women, working different shifts, decide to share one room at a boarding house. The situations arising from this arrangement as well as the family that owns the house provide the basis for the good-natured comedy that results. Of course, the couples pair off and fall in love. The title of this otherwise routine film became the name of a popular novelty song during the war. The title also came to symbolize both the contributions of women to the war effort and their liberation from conventional domestic roles. In fact, Sherna Berger Gluck, in her 1987 book titled *Rosie the Riveter Revisited*, explored the role of women during World War II and the government's stake in molding public opinion about women coming out of the kitchen and entering the war plants. Unfortunately, the end of the conflict brought about the end of women's new-found image of independence in the work force. But the five years that they spent in the war plants taught them that they were just as capable as their counterparts and left a permanent mark upon them and society. See also Women in War and *The Life and Times of Rosie the Riveter* (1980). ■

Ross, Betsy (1752–1836). See *Betsy Ross* (1917). ■

Rough Diamond, The (1921), Fox. *Dir.* Edward Sedgwick; *Sc.* Edward Sedgwick; *Cast includes:* Tom Mix, Eva Novak, Sid Jordan, Edwin Brady, Hector Sarno.

Tom Mix stars in this satirical film of mythical kingdoms, revolutions and gallant heroes. Mix, as a rodeo cowboy, is hired by the leader of a Latin-American country who is threatened by an insurrection. Attracted to the President's pretty daughter and anxious to show his mettle, he accepts the challenge and leads the army to victory, thereby saving the throne for the girl's father. This was a digression for the famous cowboy star who usually played his roles straight.

The threat of a Latin-American insurrection was a current topic in the newspapers of the period. Several countries could have served as inspiration for the plot. A revolution threatened Nicaragua in 1912. The U.S. Navy in 1914 intervened in the Dominican Republic's revolution by establishing a neutral zone. Panama (1918–1920), Honduras (1919) and Guatemala (1920) also were torn by threats of revolution. ■

Rough Riders, The (1927), Par. *Dir.* Victor Fleming; *Sc.* John F. Goodrich; *Cast includes:* Charles Emmett Mack, Mary Astor, Charles Farrell, Frank Hopper.

A drama depicting the events leading to the historical charge up San Juan Hill during the Spanish-American War, the film begins in Texas at a mobilization camp. A romantic angle is interjected into the historical story. Two soldiers (Charles Farrell and Charles Emmett Mack) are in love with the same girl (Mary Astor). The troops are eventually sent to Cuba where Lt. Col. Theodore Roosevelt (Frank Hopper), under the command of Colonel Leonard Wood, leads the men of the Rough Riders in their famous charge. The film is disappointing as a dramatic vehicle although it

presents the actual events rather accurately with plenty of hand-to-hand combat. ■

"Rough Seas" (1931). See War Humor. ■

Rough, Tough and Ready (1945), Col. *Dir.* Del Lord; *Sc.* Edward T. Lowe; *Cast includes:* Chester Morris, Victor McLaglen, Jean Rogers, Veda Ann Borg.

Two army buddies argue and fight over women and other matters in this routine World War II comedy drama. Chester Morris and Victor McLaglen portray the two rough-and-tumble pals who are assigned to the engineers' corps and find time to carry on their personal feud. Jean Rogers plays the major cause of their dispute. They both embark for action in the Pacific while remaining mortal enemies. However, their personal war ends when Morris rescues McLaglen during a battle against the Japanese. ■

Royal African Rifles, The (1953), AA. *Dir.* Lesley Selander; *Sc.* Dan Ullman; *Cast includes:* Louis Hayward, Veronica Hurst, Michael Pate, Steven Geray.

Louis Hayward stars as a British navy officer in this World War I drama set in East Africa. He is on the trail of a shipment of rifles and machine guns stolen from his ship, weapons sorely needed by British colonial troops but destined for a rival tribe. The Germans, who are behind the scheme, hope to tie up British troops with the native uprising. Fortunately, Hayward, with the help of an African corporal, foils the plot before the arms are widely distributed. He also finds time to woo the daughter of the chief gunrunner. The major battle between the insurgents and the colonials occurs in the final sequence of this weak film. ■

Rubber Racketeers (1942). See Home Front. ■

Run of the Arrow (1957), RKO. *Dir.* Samuel Fuller; *Sc.* Samuel Fuller; *Cast includes:* Rod Steiger, Sarita Montiel, Brian Keith, Ralph Meeker, Jay C. Flippen, Charles Bronson.

Rod Steiger portrays an embittered Confederate who retains his hatred for the Union even after the Civil War in this offbeat drama. He journeys west where he joins the Sioux tribe following a hazardous trial, a tribal ritual known as the "run of the arrow." He is accepted into the tribe and marries an Indian woman (Sarita Montiel). His hostility toward Yankees still smoldering within him, Steiger fights with the Sioux against the U.S. Cavalry. The troops have been assigned the task of building a fort close to the Sioux hunting grounds. Brian Keith, as a cavalry captain, labels the renegade "a man without a country." Ralph Meeker plays a lieutenant. Jay C. Flippen takes on the role of a Sioux scout. In the final scenes Steiger abandons his adopted people and returns to the white man's world where he sets out to make a new life for himself. ■

Run Silent, Run Deep (1958), UA. *Dir.* Robert Wise; *Sc.* John Gay; *Cast includes:* Clark Gable, Burt Lancaster, Jack Warden, Brad Dexter, Don Rickles.

Set in the Pacific during World War II, this submarine drama stars Clark Gable as the commander of the *Nerka* seeking revenge on a Japanese destroyer that sank his previous sub. Burt Lancaster, as his executive officer who expected to be given command of the sub, resents Gable. Determined to sink the enemy destroyer, Gable drills the men incessantly and avoids battle with an enemy sub. He is branded a coward by his officers and crew. "We're going to challenge the Japs to a drill," a sailor says mockingly to his fellow mates following the incident. The officers suggest to Lancaster, who has had several confrontations with Gable, that he take command. But he refuses. Later, when Gable is seriously injured in an unsuccessful attack on the destroyer and orders a second attack, Lancaster relieves him of his command. However, the executive officer soon reverses his decision and, with Gable giving orders, they both go in for the kill. In the last scene in which Gable is buried at sea, Lancaster in his eulogy announces: "Let no one here, no one aboard this boat, ever say we didn't have a captain."

Obvious comparisons may be made between the film and *Moby Dick* in terms of the revenge theme and *The Caine Mutiny* in which another captain is relieved of his command. The battle scenes are suspenseful and exciting, particularly the undersea sequence in which an enemy sub pursues the *Nerka*. Comedian Don Rickles supplies some comic relief. Director Robert Wise uses the confining quarters of the sub to capture the personal tensions and the pressures of battle.

Captain Edward L. Beach, who wrote the novel on which the film is based, served as part of President Eisenhower's staff and became a decorated navy officer. He was the commander of the U.S.S. *Triton* during its historic undersea circumnavigation of the earth. See also Submarine Warfare. ■

Russell, Harold. See *The Best Years of Our Lives* (1946). ■

Russian Revolution (1917). By early 1917, Czarist Russia was ripe for revolution. A decadent aristocracy, unfailingly inept as leaders through the first three years of World War I, faced growing domestic resentment. Anarchy spread in the form of civilian strikes and loss of government control over peasant soldiers. The Petrograd (Leningrad) army garrison, by refusing to obey orders to fire upon striking city workers in March 1917, provided the spark that released the seething discontent of the long-patient Russian people. The mass upheaval that followed completely altered the nation's traditional structure. The Russian Revolution of 1917, actually two revolutions in rapid succession, rivaled the late 18th century French Revolution in violence and long-term effects.

The Russian monarchy collapsed from a multitude of problems. Its soldiers were poorly armed and clothed and even more poorly led by their military aristocracy. Russian combat losses on the eastern front soared into the millions after only one year of fighting. A counteroffensive in the summer of 1916, meant to regain lost land, resulted in another million casualties. On the home front, soaring inflation, food shortages and breakdowns in railroad transportation all combined to create a general lack of confidence in the government. Strikes became commonplace.

At the same time war-weary soldiers deserted in growing numbers. And a growing rift over land ownership developed between the peasants, who were convinced the land belonged to those who toiled on it, and the aristocracy, who believed it owned the land by rights of inheritance and tradition. When the Duma, Russia's legislature, demanded reforms, Czar Nicholas II replied with an order for it to disband. The Duma refused to obey the Czar's command, and realizing his authority to rule had vanished, Nicholas abdicated.

A new liberal Provisional Government

tried to establish a western-style democracy. But instead of addressing land reform and other pressing economic issues, the government elected to honor the commitment to the western allies and continue in the war. Initial Russian advances soon turned into major losses of men and territory.

Germany, meanwhile, smuggled Nikolai Lenin, a refugee Bolshevik leader, into Russia to foment disorder and weaken the nation. He was joined by leading Bolsheviks, including Leon Trotsky. Demanding "Peace, Bread and Land," the Bolshevik (Communist) rallying cry attracted support from large elements of soldiers, city workers and peasants. The Communists gathered sufficient strength to overthrow the Kerensky administration on November 7, 1917. They declared a dictatorship headed by Lenin as Premier and Trotsky as War Minister.

In the Treaty of Brest-Litovsk (1918) that Germany forced on a crippled Russia, the loser ceded large ethnic areas on its western border, including Finland, Russian Poland, Estonia, Latvia, Lithuania and the Ukraine. Between 1918 and 1921 Russia faced more turmoil. Civil war raged between the Communists (Reds) and anti-Communists (Whites). Russia also had to contend with invasions by small military forces from the U.S., Britain, France and Japan. The Communists consolidated their hold on the country by a "Red Terror," a program of mass executions and imprisonment of suspected opponents. The violence easily equaled that of the "Reign of Terror" of the French Revolution.

Several American films, generally ignoring ideologies, managed to convey, artistically and intelligently, the onrushing events of that complex social and political upheaval. American studios treated the Revolution with mixed feelings. A few films generally leaned toward the peasants. Many others were more sympathetic to the upper classes and portrayed them as having been kind to their employees. The dramas were particularly critical of the unruly mobs bent on revenge and destruction. A few movies suggested the abuses of the old regime.

The Fall of the Romanoffs (1917), one of the earliest films to recreate this period and produced while the Russian revolution was still in progress, covers a number of significant incidents associated with Nicholas II's demise and the rise of the Bolsheviks. It has scenes of Kerensky addressing the Duma and

views of the winter palace of the Emperor and the Czarina. That same year another film appeared, *Under False Colors* which hinted that the Revolution had taken a wrong turn and that all that was needed to set Russia right again was a little financial backing. Jeanne Eagels, as a Russian countess, escapes with the help of an American and later becomes involved with a group of revolutionaries fighting to establish freedom in Russia. An American millionaire gladly volunteers to finance the venture.

By the 1920s films of the Revolution began to follow familiar patterns. They often concerned a romance between a peasant and a member of the aristocracy, while depicting revolutionary leaders as vengeful, violent types and aristocrats as their helpless victims. *Bavu* (1923) focuses on an illiterate and brutish peasant who rises to power in the wake of the Revolution and threatens the life of Princess Annia (Estelle Taylor). The princess flees across the border through the assistance of a former and still loyal employee. In Cecil B. DeMille's *The Volga Boatman* (1926), a peasant (William Boyd) who pulled barges along the banks in pre-revolutionary Russia, rises in the ranks of the revolutionaries and saves a princess with whom he has fallen in love. Lon Chaney, as a lowly peasant in *Mockery* (1927), risks his life to save a Russian countess who had earlier protected him from soldiers.

Occasionally, a film would reverse the role of the sexes but maintain the theme of sympathy for the nobility. In *The Scarlet Lady* (1928) Lya De Putti, as a Communist agent, is given the honor of assassinating a captured aristocrat whom she has fallen in love with. Instead, she shoots her revolutionary leader and escapes with her lover. In each of these cases, a not-so-subtle message implies that a "good" Russian is a fallen aristocrat or one who is loyal to a helpless aristocrat.

British Agent (1934), starring Leslie Howard as a staunch British anti-revolutionary in strife-torn Russia, and Kay Francis as Lenin's secretary, stands as a good example of Hollywood's anti-Communist approach by showing Revolutionary forces as ill-bred rabble who murder the innocent. Raoul Walsh's *The Red Dance* (1928) is one of the few films made during the 1920s that attempts to justify the Revolution. It is graphic in its description of the aristocrats' abuses.

Two large-scale productions portray the

turbulence of the Revolution. David Lean's *Doctor Zhivago* (1965) hints at the aimlessness of life in strife-torn Russia and includes re-enactments of the Revolution and a street massacre. Warren Beatty's ambitious *Reds* (1981), a biographical drama, concerns the career of the controversial American journalist John Reed. The writer, who finds exhilaration in the chaos, covers the Revolution more out of boyish fascination than for its political complexities.

Films of the Russian Revolution have more in common with those of the French upheaval than they do with the American insurrection. Russian and French revolutionists, who often appear as unruly mobs intent on looting and killing, have been treated with little sympathy. Their leaders are portrayed in unflattering terms. The reasons for their actions are rarely considered in any depth. On the other hand, their aristocratic victims, with their old-world grace and charm, are depicted as symbols of the past fated for annihilation by a vengeful rabble. In this respect, the American film industry seems to be more comfortable in presenting stereotypes than exploring the real causes and complexities of some social and political upheavals. ■

Russo–Finnish War (November 30, 1939–March 12, 1940). Finland has had an extensive history in modern times of struggling to preserve its independence from its giant Russian neighbor to the east. The winter war of 1939–1940 was one more manifestation of that spirit. The conflict aroused the public's sympathy in some of the large democratic western nations, whose press often presented the disputants as tiny, democratic David against a giant, dictatorial Goliath. The war came about when Finland refused to accede to the demands of Joseph Stalin, the Soviet communist dictator. He insisted the Finns give up a strategically important small portion of the Karelian isthmus and lease to the Soviet Union the Hanko Peninsula for a naval base.

The Finns fought bravely under 72-year-old Field Marshal Carl Mannerheim and even succeeded, through the use of mobile ski troops, to make minor penetrations into Soviet territory as well as inflict substantially greater losses on the enemy. Only one film in part captures the 1939–1940 winter war, *Ski Patrol* (1940). It doesn't delve into the politics of the situation and only deals with the fighting, in which Finland's use of ski troops is the basis for the story. Some inserted newsreel footage of the war gives the drama a semblance of realism. The controversial film *Mission to Moscow* (1943), which attempts to explain away most of Stalin's aggressive policies, treats the Russo-Finnish War in a similar manner. The League of Nations requested its member states to send assistance to Finland. Norway sent arms, and France and England pledged troops. However, Norway and Sweden, fearful of being dragged into the conflict, refused to allow transit through their respective nations for the French and British troops.

A late winter offensive by the Soviet Union breached Finland's defenses, known as the Mannerheim line. Faced by the overwhelming power of its adversary, Finland signed a peace treaty in which it gave up the southeastern portion of its territory and a lease of the Hanko Peninsula for a Soviet naval base. The vast majority of Finns living in the ceded area chose to accept resettlement in Finland rather than remain under Russian domination.

War resumed between the two countries from June 25, 1941 to September 19, 1944, in what is considered a continuation of the 1939–1940 winter war. Finland, isolated from contacts with the outside world, accepted military assistance from Germany and was dragged into the U.S.S.R.-Nazi Germany phase of World War II. With the impending defeat of Nazi Germany in the later stages of World War II, Finland again made peace with Russia and suffered additional minor adjustments to its national boundaries and was required to pay an indemnity. ■

Russo–Japanese War (1904–1905). The comparatively short Russo-Japanese War conflict is important because of its worldwide repercussions and its apparent foreshadowing of several of imperial Japan's future goals and tactics. By its victory, Japan signaled to the western world, and particularly those imperialist powers which had freely carved up much of Asia during the 1800s, that it intended to make its military presence a factor in eastern power politics. As a result of the war, Japan dislodged what till then had been growing Russian influence and encroachment in northern China, particularly in Manchuria, and Korea. Furthermore, by subjecting Czarist Russia to a resounding defeat, both on land and at sea, Japan became the first Asiatic country to defeat a powerful European nation. This, in turn, led to domestic unrest that resulted in a revolution against the imperial Russian system of government.

The war resulted from expansionist conflicts between Russia and Japan towards the end of the 19th century in northern China and Korea, then a Chinese satellite. The clash began on the night of February 8–9 with Japan's unexpected and successful attack on and subsequent blockade of the Russian fleet and base at Port Arthur. Later in the war, Japan's Admiral Togo inflicted a naval defeat of even greater proportions on Russia in the Battle of the Strait of Tsushima (May 27–28, 1905) off Korea's southern coast. The Russian Baltic fleet was totally annihilated after it had made a long trip from Europe to challenge Japan's control of the Yellow Sea and Sea of Japan, necessary for supplying its troops on the mainland.

The Treaty of Portsmouth, signed in Portsmouth, N.H., on September 5, 1905, ended the war and merited President Theodore Roosevelt the Nobel Peace Prize the following year for his efforts in mediating the conflict. Russia's defeat created such anger in the Russian people with the manner in which the Czarist government conducted the war that a revolution broke out two months later and forced Czar Nicholas II to grant a charter with limited democratic rights for the people.

Few American films refer to this war. *An Affair of Three Nations* (1915) concerned Japanese spies operating in Washington, D.C. *The Breath of the Gods* (1920), a drama set chiefly in Japan, dealt with a young American-educated Japanese woman who falls in love with a westerner. *Jack London* (1943) includes limited action sequences of the Russo-Japanese War. The dialogue reveals Japan's future tactics and imperialistic goals. The character Captain Tanaka probably is based on the future General Tanaka, a Japanese militarist who allegedly authored the Tanaka Memorial in the 1920s that outlined Japan's plans for expansion and conquest. Discounting the fact that the film, made during World War II, poured forth the obligatory propaganda of the period (Japan's barbaric treatment of Russian prisoners), it did have a good bit of basic historical relevance to actual events. ■

Russo–Turkish War (1877–1878). The expanding Russian empire, under Romanov Czar Alexander II, clashed with Turkey's decaying Ottoman empire over the latter's holdings in the Balkans and the Caucasus. Russian Grand Duke Nicholas commanded about 245,000 troops in an invasion of Turkey's Balkan region, and Grand Duke Michael led an army of 70,000 in a drive into Turkish territory in the Caucasus. Most of the numerous Muslim Tartar tribes in the Crimea and Caucasus, historic enemies of the Russians for several hundred years, sided with the Turks. Russia won the war which was often characterized by ineptness on both sides. In the Treaty of San Stefano (March 3, 1878) Turkey was forced to give up most of its Tartar lands in the lower Caucasus; grant independence to Serbia, Montenegro and Rumania; and allow Bulgaria to become an autonomous state under Russian control.

Only a handful of American films concern the conflict. Jules Verne's novel, about Czar Alexander II's personal courier who is entrusted with secret plans to defeat the belligerent Tartars, has undergone several screen adaptations. They include, among others, *Michael Strogoff* (1910), made at Thomas A. Edison's New York studio; *Michael Strogoff* (1914), with the popular Yiddish stage actor Jacob Adler in the title role; and *The Soldier and the Lady* (1937), with Anton Walbrook. ■

S

Sabotage Squad (1942). See Spy Films: the Talkies. ∎

Saboteur (1942). See Spy Films: the Talkies. ∎

Sabre Jet (1953), UA. *Dir.* Louis King; *Sc.* Dale Eunson, Katherine Albert; *Cast includes:* Robert Stack, Coleen Gray, Richard Arlen, Julie Bishop, Leon Ames.

This Korean War drama focuses on the U.S. jet pilots who daily flew sorties over Korea from their bases in Japan, where their lonely wives anxiously awaited their return. Robert Stack portrays a squadron leader who prefers that his wife (Coleen Gray) stay at home instead of advancing her career as a reporter. Produced in the days before the feminist movement became popular, the film has Stack's wife accept her husband's philosophy that her role as spouse is more important than her career. Meanwhile, the men go about their missions facing flack and other dangers above the skies of war-torn Korea. Richard Arlen plays the air base commander in this routine film. ∎

Sad Sack, The (1957). See Service Comedy. ∎

Safe for Democracy (1918), FN. *Dir.* J. Stuart Blackton; *Sc.* Anthony Paul Kelly; *Cast includes:* Mitchell Lewis, Ruby de Remer, Gus Alexander, Ida Darling, Helen Ferguson.

A patriotic drama with World War I as the background, the film describes a variety of slackers, Americans shirking their duty either as soldiers or workers in war-related jobs. It presents a derogatory picture of the leaders of the International Workers of the World, a radical union of the period. J. Stuart Blackton, who produced the work, interjects newsreel footage between the fictional scenes. This adds a note of authenticity. In the end, the men realize their responsibilities to the war effort and join the fight.

The theme of the film was suggested by a remark made by a military leader at the time. "Work or fight!" General Crowder demanded of the citizenry. Blackton's attack on members of the I.W.W., whose leaders he equates with alien agents, casts the drama more in the form of an anti-union tract than as a patriotic tale. The film was retitled *Life's Greatest Problem*. ∎

Safecracker, The (1958). See Spy Films: the Talkies. ∎

Sahara (1943), Col. *Dir.* Zoltan Korda; *Sc.* John Howard Lawson; *Cast includes:* Humphrey Bogart, Bruce Bennett, Lloyd Bridges, Rex Ingram, J. Carrol Naish, Dan Duryea.

Humphrey Bogart portrays an American tank commander fighting with the English in Libya in June, 1942. He and two of his tank crew are cut off from their lines. Driving through the hot, unforgiving Sahara Desert seeking to link up with the British, they pick up six stranded Englishmen, a South African, a Frenchman, a Sudanese corporal and his Italian prisoner and a downed Nazi pilot. Guided by the Sudanese soldier (Rex Ingram), they reach an old ruin and water hole that is virtually dry except for a continual trickle. They are able to replenish their water supply after spending hours gathering the droplets. The Italian prisoner (J. Carrol Naish) is placed with the German flier who bullies his fellow captive. But the Italian, who wants only to return home to his wife and child, has no stomach for the war; he

Allied soldiers, illustrating a united front against totalitarianism, capture a downed German pilot in the Libyan desert. *Sahara* (1943).

damns Hitler and Mussolini. "Italians are not like Germans," he announces to the captured flier. "Only the body wears the uniform and not the soul."

When Bogart learns that a German battalion, desperate for water, is heading for the ruin, he suggests to the group that they stay and fight, thereby detaining the enemy until help arrives. Some of the men question the odds—nine men against 500 troops. "No one minds giving his life," one British Tommy says, "but this is throwing it away. Why?" "Why?" Bogart replies. "Why did your people in London go about their business while the Germans were throwing everything they had at them? Why did the Russians make a stand at Moscow? . . . Why Bataan? Why Corregidor? Maybe they were all nuts. There's one thing they did do. They delayed the enemy and kept on delaying them until we got strong enough to hit him harder than he was hitting us." The men then elect to hold off the heavily armed German column. Bogart sends one of his tank crew (Bruce Bennett) to find the British main force and return with help. The Germans make several attempts to cap-

ture the ruin, but they are thrown back after each attack. By the time British troops arrive, only three of the grimly determined defenders are left. The incident of the siege was used in a 1952 western, *Last of the Comanches*, with besieged whites in control of the only water for miles and the attacking Indians suffering from lack of it.

Although several critics faulted the film for its inaccurate premise (no American tanks fought alongside the British at this point in the war), this did not dampen its popularity. The story is set in 1942 when the German Africa Corps pushed the British back in the Libyan desert to the line at El Alamein where they were finally stopped. This is brought out at the end when Bogart learns this fact from Bennett, who is sad that the men buried at the ruin never knew this. "Yeah," Bogart agrees and names each of their fallen comrades, "they'd want to know . . . we stopped them at El Alamein."

The film, therefore, is a testament to Allied resolve as much as it is a tough drama. The small band of American, British, Sudanese, French and South African soldiers become a microcosm of the Allied nations. They symbolize in their gallant stand against the German column the larger life-and-death struggle that was being waged around the world against the forces of totalitarianism. ■

Sailor-Made Man, A (1921). See Service Comedy. ■

Sailor Takes a Wife, The (1945). See Veterans. ■

"Sailors With Wings" (1941). See "The March of Time." ■

Saladin (1137?–1193). He was a man of many qualities who dominated his age like a giant colossus. To his Christian opponents during the Crusades, Saladin was a fierce adversary who showed a broad streak of chivalry and generosity to the defeated. To Moslems, he was the pre-eminent military leader of his time. He recaptured Jerusalem from the Christians (1187) and later prevented the Third Crusade, under England's Richard I (the Lion-Hearted) and France's King Philip II, from advancing into Moslem-controlled areas in the Holy Land. He was also a man of culture highly versed in religious theology; a patron of literature; and a builder of mosques, colleges and a Cairo aqueduct.

Born in Mesopotamia, (modern Iraq) of Kurdish background, Saladin helped his uncle defeat the Moslem rulers of Egypt. He eventually succeeded to the Sultanate of Egypt where he founded the Ayyubid dynasty. He enlarged his domain through diplomatic measures and conquest. At its peak, Saladin's empire stretched westward in North Africa to Gabes in mid-Tunis and eastward in the Middle East that today includes parts of Syria, Palestine and Yemen.

The only blemishes on an outstanding military career were his failure to conquer the Frankish-held city of Tyre in Palestine and his defeat at the Battle of Acre (1191) by Richard the Lion-Hearted's superior forces. As a result of the Battle of Acre, Saladin was forced to make concessions to the Christians. They were permitted to establish a kingdom on a small strip of land on Palestine's Mediterranean coast. Also, Christian pilgrims had the right to visit Jerusalem's holy sites. Nevertheless, his empire remained largely intact and free from further incursions by Christian

forces, most of whom went home, exhausted, after the bitter campaign.

Two films, the 1923 silent drama *Richard the Lion-Hearted* and Cecil B. DeMille's *The Crusades* (1935), touch upon his conflicts with the European Christians during the Third Crusade. The former has an almost totally fictitious plot in which the Moslem leader is both a romantic and military rival of Richard. In *The Crusades* Saladin is shown in truer historical perspective as a worthy and intelligent opponent of Richard. The film includes much historical detail about the practice of warfare during this period, particularly in the battle sequences at Acre. ■

Salute for Three (1943). See Musicals. ■

Salute to Courage. See Nazi Agent (1942). ■

Wallace Beery, as a 30-year marine veteran, helps to defend the Philippines against the Japanese invaders early in World War II. *Salute to the Marines* (1943).

Salute to the Marines (1943), MGM. Dir. S. Sylvan Simon; *Sc.* George Bruce; *Cast includes*: Wallace Beery, Fay Bainter, Reginald Owen, Keye Luke, Marilyn Maxwell.

Wallace Beery plays a 30-year marine veteran living with his wife and daughter in the Philippines in this World War II drama. Forced by his wife (Fay Bainter) to retire from the service, he becomes depressed as a result of his quiet domestic existence. Suddenly the Japanese invade the Philippines. Beery springs into action. He directs the evacuation and organizes the defenses against the enemy. His aggressive and courageous action during the battle helps to dislodge the Japanese forces, but he pays for the victory with his life. His daughter (Marilyn Maxwell) accepts a decoration honoring her father. ■

Salvador (1985), Hemdale. *Dir.* Oliver Stone; *Sc.* Oliver Stone, Richard Boyle; *Cast includes:* James Woods, James Belushi, Michael Murphy, Elpedia Carrillo, John Savage.

A journalist-photographer (James Woods) thinks he can profit from the turmoil of events during 1980–1981 in strife-torn El Salvador. A disorganized, obnoxious cameraman fired from his last job, he continually borrows money, owes favors to others, and lies his way into and out of situations. Refused loans by acquaintances for the air fare, he journeys south by car with his buddy (James Belushi), promising him women, booze and drugs. When they reach the ravaged land, they are arrested. Woods saves his and Belushi's skin by appealing to an infantry colonel whom Woods had once given good press coverage. The more abuses he experiences on the part of the military government, the deeper he becomes involved in the people's revolution. He teams up with another photographer (John Savage) and leads him to El Playon, a dumpsite for numerous victims of the "death squads." "You gotta get close to get the truth," Savage says as he takes close-ups of the corpses. "If you get too close, you die." This foreshadows Savage's own death while photographing government planes strafing and bombing a village.

Woods, in his aimless wanderings, gets a chance to meet a variety of dignitaries. The indecisive American ambassador (Michael Murphy) attempts to sum up his frustrations with this Central American country: "A pathological killer on the right, God knows what on the left, and a gutless middle." But Woods does not allow the ambassador, who opts for the present military dictator, to escape that easily. "You'll run with him because he's anti-Moscow," he charges. "You let them close down the universities, you let them wipe out the best minds in the country . . . you let them wipe out the Catholic Church, and you let them do it all because they aren't Communists." "Whatever mistakes we make down here," Murphy replies defensively, "the alternative would be ten times worse." Woods leaves the country in frustration, smuggling out incriminating pic-

tures of the brutal regime taken by Savage before his demise.

Graphic scenes of atrocities, chiefly committed by government forces, include the callous slaying of a priest and the brutal rape and murder of four American nuns. But when the revolutionaries occupy a town after a fiercely fought battle, they begin to execute their prisoners in the same way as their adversaries. An epilogue on the screen announces: "Salvador continues to be one of the largest recipients of U.S. military aid in the world." ■

Salvation Army. Founded by William Booth in 1865, the Salvation Army is a Christian association organized in military style. Using the Bible as their guide, its members, pledging absolute obedience, carry out social and missionary work. The organization, whose headquarters are located in London, began operations in the U.S. in 1880. *Fires of Faith* (1919) gives a dramatic account of the history of the organization during World War I. Catherine Calvert portrays a Salvation Army worker who, along with another woman, goes to the front to help the doughboys. In *The Spirit of the U.S.A.* (1924), a World War I drama, an idealistic young American from a farming family (Johnny Walker) joins the Salvation Army after he is rejected from military service because of an ear illness. ■

Samarkand, Siege of. See *The Golden Horde* (1951). ■

Samurai (1945), Cavalcade. *Dir.* Raymond Cannon; *Sc.* Raymond Cannon; *Cast includes:* Paul Fung, Luke Chan, David Chow, Barbara Woodell, Fred C. Bond.

A low-budget World War II propaganda drama, the film blends newsreel footage with staged sequences of atrocities to bring out its anti-Japanese theme. David Chow portrays a Japanese youth who is raised in the U.S. He turns traitor, joins the Japanese secret service and takes part in a scheme involving the Japanese invasion of California. The film was released after the war had ended and therefore lost much of its impact. ■

San Jacinto, Battle of (April 21, 1836). The revolt by American settlers in Texas to gain independence from Mexico appeared to be heading for failure until General Sam Houston, in a brilliant stroke, defeated the Mexicans in this decisive battle of the war and thus secured victory and independence for Texas.

Prior to the Battle of San Jacinto, Mexican President General Antonio Lopez de Santa Anna had already inflicted two defeats on the rebellious Texans in clashes at the Alamo and at Goliad. His forces, in both instances, massacred the defenders. American settlers fled before Santa Anna's army that penetrated deep into northern Texas in pursuit of Sam Houston's retreating forces, the only remaining rebel contingent of noteworthy size. Houston lured Santa Anna to a site near the San Jacinto River, not far from where the city of Houston now stands. Taking advantage of the Mexican siesta hour, he inflicted a crushing defeat upon an advance guard of 1,200 enemy troops and captured Santa Anna, who was attempting to conceal himself in the tall grass.

As prerequisite for his release, Santa Anna was forced to sign two treaties in which he pledged to withdraw Mexican troops from Texas and secure recognition from the Mexican government for the new republic. Santa Anna and the Mexican Congress later repudiated the treaties, claiming they were negotiated under duress. Nonetheless, Mexico ceased military operations against Texas.

On the basis of his successful wartime military leadership, Houston was elected to the presidency of the new republic and was further honored with a city named for him on a site not far from the battlefield.

The Battle of San Jacinto and Santa Anna's capture are highlighted in such films as *The First Texan* (1956), which stays close to historical facts, and in the somewhat more fictionalized silent screen drama of Houston's life, *The Conqueror* (1917). ∎

San Juan Hill, Battle of. See Spanish-American War. ∎

Sand Creek Massacre (1864). In the fall of 1864, a band of Indians who had originally been given permission to settle peacefully near Fort Lyon was driven away by a newly appointed commander. The Cheyenne, along with some Arapaho, settled into a winter camp at Sand Creek, a feeder stream of the Arkansas River in southeastern Colorado. They were shortly to become victims to one of the worst blood baths perpetrated by an

army unit in the long history of vicious Indian-army warfare.

A detachment of cavalry and artillery under Colonel John Chivington that had been on the march for five days in extreme cold discovered the Indian encampment on November 24, 1864, and charged into it. The Cheyenne chief, Black Kettle, tried to prevent violence by raising both a white and an American flag above his tepee. But in the ensuing confusion, both sides began shooting at each other. Soldiers indiscriminately started to kill members of the tribe, including warriors, women and children. By the time the fighting ceased, over 400 Indians had been killed. One of the victims was Chief Yellow Cloud, in his 85th year. The soldiers lost seven men. After confiscating the tribe's belongings, the unit marched on.

The incident provoked a general uprising of Cheyenne and other southwestern tribes. The army sent several columns against the Indians over the next four years. One of them, under Colonel George Custer, destroyed Black Kettle's camp on the Washita River in 1868. Fighting between the army and the Southern Cheyenne all but ceased after that incident, except for occasional raids.

The massacre is touched upon in at least one drama and was the basis for a particularly savage sequence in another. In *The Guns of Fort Petticoat* (1957), an unexceptional western with a Civil War background, a Union officer (Audie Murphy) leaves the army after his superior officer deliberately slaughters a band of Indians at Sand Creek. In Ralph Nelson's *Soldier Blue* (1970) one scene shows a cavalry commander (John Anderson) ignoring an Indian chief's attempt to surrender as soldiers proceed to indiscriminately slaughter men, women and children. ∎

Sand Pebbles, The (1966), TCF. *Dir.* Robert Wise; *Sc.* Robert Anderson; *Cast includes:* Steve McQueen, Richard Attenborough, Richard Crenna, Candice Bergen.

America's gunboat diplomacy in strife-torn China in 1926 provides the background for this drama. Steve McQueen portrays an individualistic machinist's mate aboard the *San Pablo*, a U.S. gunboat on duty on the Yangtze River. He falls in love with a schoolteacher (Candice Bergen) at a local mission. He plans to desert from the navy but is caught up in the wake of a Chinese revolution. He is killed while helping a handful of Americans escape

Crew members of a U.S. gunboat on the Yangtze River in the 1920s tangle with Chinese revolutionaries in *The Sand Pebbles* (1966).

to the vessel. Richard Crenna, as the captain of the American vessel, is assigned to protect American citizens working along the river. Richard Attenborough, as a sailor, becomes involved in a tragic love affair with a Chinese girl. The film depicts the personal and international conflicts of the period, including the thin line the captain and his crew must walk to prevent further escalation of tensions. ■

Sandino, Augusto. See Nicaraguan Civil War of 1925–1933. ■

Sands of Iwo Jima (1949), Rep. *Dir.* Allan Dwan; *Sc.* Harry Brown, James Edward Grant; *Cast includes:* John Wayne, John Agar, Adele Mara, Forrest Taylor.

This World War II drama follows a platoon of marines from boot camp to the invasion of the Japanese-held island of Iwo Jima. In a series of realistic war scenes, the film captures the bloody battles and the dirty job the leathernecks have of dislodging the stubborn enemy from their cover. Eventually, the marines raise the stars and stripes on top of Mount Suribachi.

John Wayne portrays Sergeant Stryker, a

U.S. Marines in World War II pay a high price in the battle for the Pacific. *Sands of Iwo Jima* (1949).

tough, experienced soldier who knows how to convert callow recruits into killers. John Agar, as the pacifist son of a famous colonel killed at Guadalcanal, at first resists Wayne's hardening process but is ultimately converted into a fighting marine. The men under Wayne, who earlier had resented his stringent training, begin to appreciate what he has taught them during their first encounter with the Japanese. After Wayne is killed by a sniper's bullet, Agar carries on in the sergeant's spirit. "Saddle up!" he announces, echoing Wayne's frequent command. "Let's get back to the war."

The film uses newsreel footage of actual battles in the Pacific but blends the shots skillfully. Three survivors of the historic flag-raising on Mount Suribachi appear in the drama. Wayne plays a tragic figure—a near alcoholic whose wife and child have left him. The script suggests that men like him are essential in war but superfluous in peacetime. He is killed unexpectedly only a few moments after the major battle is won. ■

Santa Anna, Antonio Lopez de (1794–1876). Santa Anna, as dictator–general of Mexico during the Texas War of Independence, commanded the troops who massacred nearly 200 Americans defending the Alamo. Later, he led his nation to defeat in the Mexican War.

As a general and politician, Santa Anna seemed to follow a policy of personal opportunism that placed him at the forefront of Mexican governmental affairs for over 30 years during the early period of that country's independence. That part of his career in which he clashed with Americans became grist for the Hollywood mill. He was always characterized as the "heavy," a role that mirrored much of his actual career.

Although an officer in the Spanish army, Santa Anna sided with revolutionary forces that won independence for Mexico. He showed, soon after the revolution, an opportunistic streak. He enhanced his rise in power by constantly shifting loyalties and often leading the opposition against those he had backed earlier. He became president in 1833 and a reactionary dictator in 1834.

Santa Anna helped to precipitate the Texas War of Independence when he attempted to impose greater control by the central Mexican government over the growing autonomy of its northern province of Texas, peopled largely by American settlers. *The Last Command* (1955), about the last days of the defense of the Alamo, captures his ambition and some of the hypocrisy he exhibited in dealing with representatives of the American settlers in Texas. He was portrayed as the villain of *Heroes of the Alamo* (1938), an earlier version of the defeat of the defenders of the old Spanish mission.

During the conflict, many Americans viewed Santa Anna as a murderous ogre for allowing massacres, first at the Alamo and then at the Battle of Goliad in which some 300 defenders were killed after they surrendered. Hollywood emphasized his brutality in several action dramas. *The Conqueror* (1917), a silent film, included scenes depicting both massacres. *The Alamo* (1960), an epic western directed by and starring John Wayne, covered the principal characters who led the stirring but tragic defense of the Alamo.

Santa Anna's defeat and capture at the Battle of San Jacinto, by Texan forces under Sam Houston, was the subject of some climactic scenes in *The First Texan* (1956) and *The Conqueror*.

He held and lost the presidency of Mexico several times. At one point, he was driven into exile as a result of his nation's startling defeat in the Mexican War. He returned to power, albeit briefly, as "permanent dictator" in 1853, before being overthrown for the last time in 1855 in a popular revolution led by Benito Juarez. Exiled again, he ceased being a force in Mexican politics. He was allowed to return to his country in 1874 at age 80 and died two years later. ■

Santa Fe Trail (1940), WB. Dir. Michael Curtiz; *Sc.* Robert Buckner; *Cast includes:* Errol Flynn, Olivia de Havilland, Raymond Massey, Ronald Reagan, Alan Hale, William Lundigan.

Errol Flynn portrays J.E.B. "Jeb" Stuart, a recent West Point graduate, in this pre-Civil War historical drama about the exploits of the radical abolitionist John Brown and his followers. Stuart and George Custer (Ronald Reagan), two young cavalry officers recently sent to Fort Leavenworth to help maintain order in Kansas, are assigned to guard a freight caravan. They quickly clash with Brown and his followers over a shipment of rifles. The officers are reassigned, together with a cavalry troop, to capture the fanatic Brown and his small ragtag army. They manage to locate the armed group and, following a night skirmish, drive them into the hills. Stuart comments that this is the end of Brown's force. But Custer senses the impending storm over slavery that will drench the nation in blood and tears. "Nothing will break the force of John Brown," he says to his friend, "not even death."

Some time later Brown is seen soliciting

funds from Boston abolitionists who support his plans to raise an army. Brown's trail of bloodshed and devastation ends in a violent battle at the U.S. arsenal at Harpers Ferry. Intending to arm more than a thousand followers with his newly acquired weapons, Brown is surrounded and overwhelmed by government troops.

John Brown (Raymond Massey) is presented as a religious zealot who leads bloody raids through Kansas while at the same time effects the freedom of slaves through the famed "underground railroad." Following his capture, he goes to the gallows unrepentant, convinced he was right. "I, John Brown, am now quite certain that the crimes of this guilty land can never be purged away but with blood," he announces to the solemn spectators. "Aye, let them hang me. I forgive them, and may God forgive them, for they know not what they do." Van Heflin plays one of Brown's followers who is expelled from West Point for distributing political leaflets concerning abolition. In a quarrel with Stuart, a Southerner who criticizes Heflin for misusing a harness on his horse, Heflin says scathingly: "You know how to harness Negroes—with a whip across their back!" Alan Hale and Guinn "Big Boy" Williams, as Flynn's sidekicks, provide the comic relief.

Aside from a handful of brief scenes, the film skirts the controversial issue of slavery, emphasizing instead the melodramatics of the plot. In an incident aboard a train, two proslavers try to regain custody of a family of blacks from one of John Brown's sons (Alan Baxter) who is transporting them to a free state. In a later sequence during a battle between Brown's troops and the U.S. Army, a black couple, caught in the middle, voice their confusion. In the most stereotypical speech and tone, one remarks: "If this is freedom, I don't want no part of it."

Historical inaccuracies abound, with only one authentic general incident adhered to—the capture of John Brown—but the script tampers even with this event. The film shows Brown's capture by Captain Stuart. Historically, Col. Robert E. Lee was credited with the capture. According to the screenplay, Custer, Stuart, Sheridan and Longstreet all graduated from West Point in the same class—that of 1854. James Longstreet, born in 1821 and who later proved to be a brilliant Confederate general, would have graduated at age 34. Custer, born in 1839, would have

had to be a child prodigy to finish at age 15. (Actually, he was graduated in 1861 at the bottom of his class.)

The film probably has and refers to more historical figures than any other Hollywood work. These include, aside from those already mentioned, Robert E. Lee, Phil Sheridan, Jefferson Davis and Kit Carson. Historical places and events, such as "bloody Kansas," the underground railroad, Harpers Ferry and West Point play significant roles as well. See John Brown. ■

Santiago (1956), WB. *Dir.* Gordon Douglas; *Sc.* Martin Rackin, John Twist; *Cast includes:* Alan Ladd, Rossana Podesta, Lloyd Nolan, Chill Wills, Paul Fix.

A mercenary gun runner (Alan Ladd) becomes idealistically involved in Cuba's struggle for independence against Spain in this action drama set on the eve of the Spanish–American War. Ladd falls in love with a Cuban revolutionary (Rossana Podesta) and is persuaded by her to join the good fight. Lloyd Nolan, as a competitor–smuggler, at first brawls with Ladd and then links up with him to fight the Spanish. Chill Wills, as captain of the ship that Ladd uses to run the Spanish blockade, sacrifices his life by blowing himself up with his vessel to delay the Spanish fleet from overtaking the cargo of guns. The film includes several effective action sequences. ■

Sanusi Anti-British Revolt (1915–1917). Sanusi desert tribes in Egypt revolted against the British, who at the time controlled the country. The revolution, inspired by Turkish propaganda during World War I, used Muslim kinship as a means to generate attacks on the British, who were then Turkey's enemy. The British, at first unsuccessful, eventually drove the Sanusi out of Egypt and into Libya's eastern province of Cyrenaica in 1917. The Sanusi, a militant and puritanical Muslim sect, had fought periodically since 1902 against the French, the Italians and the English to maintain control of their desert oases in Libya and Egypt.

Flame of the Desert (1919), a romantic drama of espionage and revolution in colonial Egypt, seems to be based on the Sanusi Revolt. A native uprising occurs which is quickly suppressed by the British. The film was released only two years after the fighting ended. *Burning Sands* (1922), another romantic drama also set in Egypt, concerns a desert tribe about to revolt against British rule. As with the former film, this drama also seems to draw its inspiration from the Sanusi Revolt. Several desert battles occur before the British troops crush the revolution. ■

Sap, The (1926), WB. *Dir.* Erle Kenton; *Sc.* E. T. Lowe, Jr.; *Cast includes:* Kenneth Harlan, Heinie Conklin, Mary McAllister, David Butler.

Kenneth Harlan portrays a mother's boy whose experiences in World War I indirectly help him to overcome his fears at home in this comedy drama. Parental coddling has turned Harlan into a cowardly young man. Drafted into military service and sent overseas, he wins several medals for acts of bravery which he did not actually perform. He returns home a hero but reverts to his former cowardly character when he is threatened by the local bully. His sweetheart (Mary McAllister) is disgusted with him. Believing he doesn't deserve his medals, he returns them to the War Department until he feels he has earned them. He confronts the bully determined to prove his worth. He manages to best his adversary, thereby regaining the respect of his loved one. Warner Brothers released another film with the same title three years later which had no relation to the earlier work. ■

Saracen Blade, The (1954), Col. *Dir.* William Castle; *Sc.* DeVallon Scott, George Worthington Yates; *Cast includes:* Ricardo Montalban, Betta St. John, Rick Jason, Carolyn Jones.

A son vows revenge for his father's death in this 13th century drama. Set during the turbulent times of Frederick II and a Holy Land crusade, an Italian commoner (Ricardo Montalban) seeks to even the score against an unscrupulous count (Rick Jason) and his son. The count has also stolen Montalban's woman (Betta St. John) and made her his wife. Action sequences include individual combats as well as the siege of a castle, albeit the latter is a black-and-white insert from stock footage. Whitfield Connor portrays Frederick II, Holy Roman emperor. He was eventually deposed by Pope Innocent IV despite his efforts in the Crusades. Civil war followed in both Germany and Italy. The conflict portrayed in the drama, however, has no histor-ical relevancy. The weak film is based on Frank Yerby's novel of the same title. ■

Saskatchewan (1954), U. *Dir.* Raoul Walsh; *Sc.* Gil Doud; *Cast includes:* Alan Ladd, Shelley Winters, Robert Douglas, J. Carrol Naish, Hugh O'Brian.

A Canadian mountie (Alan Ladd) prevents the American Sioux from inciting the peaceful Canadian Cree Indians to go on the warpath against the whites in this action drama. Ladd portrays a brave redcoat who was raised by the Indians. Disobeying orders, he leads his troops against the Sioux and re-arms his Cree companions to help him crush the rebellious factions and save the regiment. Ladd's superior (Robert Douglas) finally admits that Ladd was correct in going against his orders. Shelley Winters, as a fugitive from justice, provides the romantic interest in this routine plot. ■

Satan Never Sleeps (1962), TCF. *Dir.* Leo McCarey; *Sc.* Claude Binyon, Leo McCarey; *Cast includes:* William Holden, Clifton Webb, France Nuyen, Weaver Lee.

China during the 1949 revolution provides the background for this weak drama of two Catholic priests caught up in the political and social events of the period. William Holden and Clifton Webb portray the men of the cloth who are incarcerated by the local leader (Weaver Lee) of the People's Party. A young Chinese woman (France Nuyen), who is infatuated with Holden, is raped by Lee. The party leader eventually grows disenchanted with Communist ideology following the murder of his parents. When a counter-insurrection erupts, the two priests, Lee and Nuyen, who has given birth to his child, flee to Hong Kong.

One of the major weakness of the film is its depiction of the Communists as stereotypes—emotionally unstable super-villains or clowns—a problem Hollywood has always been plagued with in characterizing political adversaries. The film is based on the novel by Pearl S. Buck. ■

Savage, The (1952), Par. *Dir.* George Marshall; *Sc.* Sydney Boehm; *Cast includes:* Charlton Heston, Susan Morrow, Peter Hanson, Joan Taylor.

Charlton Heston portrays a white youth raised by the Sioux after his father was killed by the Crow Indians in this routine outdoor drama. Forced to choose between the whites and Indians in an upcoming war, he eventually sides with the whites. He explains to his foster father that the Sioux tribe should not resist since the whites, besides having superior forces and arms, have much to offer the tribe. Romantic interest is supplied by Susan Morrow as a white woman who lives at the army outpost and Joan Taylor as an Indian girl who has fallen for Heston. The film includes several adequate action sequences. ∎

Sayonara (1957), WB. *Dir.* Joshua Logan; *Sc.* Paul Osborn; *Cast includes:* Marlon Brando, Red Buttons, Ricardo Montalban, Patricia Owens, Martha Scott.

Marlon Brando portrays a battle-weary American pilot who falls in love with a Japanese actress–dancer in this drama of romance and racism during the Korean War. He is sent to Kobe in Japan to rest. His fiancee (Patricia Owens) is waiting for him. But they find they have drifted apart. Brando's buddy (Red Buttons) has married a Japanese girl, an act that invokes the wrath of his bigoted commanding officer who plans to have Buttons shipped back to the U.S. The newly married couple decide to commit suicide rather than be separated. Brando, who has also fallen in love with a Japanese (Milko Taka), resolves to marry her despite the racial prejudice of the military. The film is based on James Michener's novel. ∎

Scaramouche (1923), Metro. *Dir.* Rex Ingram; *Sc.* Willis Goldbeck; *Cast includes:* Ramon Navarro, Alice Terry, Lewis Stone, Lloyd Ingraham, Julia Swayne Gordon, William Humphrey, George Seigmann.

Based on Rafael Sabatini's novel, the historical drama is set at the time of the French Revolution. A young man (Ramon Navarro) loves a titled woman who is also desired by a marquis. A friend of the young man tells of the cruelty of the marquis who had been responsible for the death of an old man on the marquis' estate. Later the friend is also killed by the same marquis, causing Navarro to swear that he will bring the marquis to justice. The Revolution erupts and Navarro, who has been outspoken in the town square, is sought by soldiers. He escapes and joins a group of entertainers. He later encounters the marquis only to learn that the man is his father. The film includes several mob scenes and an attack by the peasants on the palace.

MGM's lavish 1952 remake, starring Stewart Granger, Eleanor Parker, Janet Leigh and Mel Ferrer, had little to do with the French Revolution. ∎

Scarlet Coat, The (1955), MGM. *Dir.* John Sturges; *Sc.* Karl Tunberg; *Cast includes:* Cornel Wilde, Michael Wilding, George Sanders, Anne Francis, Robert Douglas.

A colonial major poses as a spy for the British in an effort to uncover an actual traitor who turns out to be Benedict Arnold in this historical drama of the American Revolution. Cornel Wilde portrays the spy who masquerades as the traitor. Michael Wilding, as Major John Andre, a British officer, develops a fondness for his adversary, the American spy. Robert Douglas plays Benedict Arnold. Anne Francis provides the romantic interest. The film provides little of the armed conflict of the period, concentrating, instead, on characterization and intrigue.

No other figure in American history has become as infamous a traitor as Benedict Arnold (1741–1801). During the American Revolution he attempted to dispose of the fort at West Point, on New York's Hudson River, to the British. An intensely ambitious man, Arnold seemed to have acted out of feelings of frustration and revenge for what he felt was a lack of appreciation for his military competence and bravery.

Prior to the West Point incident, Arnold had compiled a record of near brilliance as a commander in the patriot cause. He defeated the British at Fort Ticonderoga and on Lake Champlain in upstate New York. He was wounded in an unsuccessful winter invasion of Quebec (1775–1776) and played an important role in the American victory at Saratoga (1777). Earlier in 1777, Arnold was passed over for promotion by Congress in favor of less senior and accomplished officers despite Washington's appeal in Arnold's favor. He did get his promotion to major general later in the war, but the incident seemed to have scarred him. Arnold was put in charge of American troops in Philadelphia (1778). There he married the daughter of a prominent Loyalist and first initiated contact with the enemy. Within a few weeks after being posted to the command of West Point in the summer of 1780, Arnold reopened contact with Major John Andre, an aide to British General Clinton, and delivered plans to the British officer detailing the fort's weaknesses.

Andre, however, was captured on the way to New York with the information and Arnold, upon hearing of the seizure of the courier, fled to a British warship in the Hudson River.

The British rewarded Arnold for his treachery with a commission as a brigadier general and pension payments for him and his family. For the remainder of the American Revolution, Arnold served the British for whom he led raids against the Americans in Virginia and Connecticut. After the Revolution, Arnold and his family lived in Canada and London where he died a man scorned by the people of England. ■

Scarlet Dawn (1932), WB. *Dir.* William Dieterle; *Sc.* Niven Busch, Erwin Gelsey, Douglas Fairbanks, Jr.; *Cast includes:* Douglas Fairbanks, Jr., Nancy Carroll, Earle Fox, Lilyan Tashman, Sheila Terry, Betty Gillette, Guy Kibbee.

Douglas Fairbanks, Jr. portrays an exiled aristocrat in love with a servant girl (Nancy Carroll) in this drama set during the Russian Revolution. When the Czar's troops kill their own officers and join the Revolution, Fairbanks escapes with Carroll to Constantinople. He marries her and joins his fellow expatriates in their carefree night life. He renews his affair with his mistress (Lilyan Tashman) who persuades him to tout fake jewelry to American tourists. Tiring of this existence and realizing he loves his wife, he returns with her to Russia. The film includes several scenes of the Revolution. The art director, Anton Grot, provides some elaborate and stunning sets. ■

Scarlet Lady, The (1928). See *Russian Revolution.* ■

Scarlet West, The (1925), FN. *Dir.* John G. Adolfi; *Sc.* A. B. Heath; *Cast includes:* Robert Edeson, Clara Bow, Martha Francis, Johnnie Walker, Walter McGrail, Florence Crawford.

This historical drama is set in the West of the 1870s at the time of Custer's last stand. The film focuses on an army outpost and the lives and loves of its inhabitants. During the uprisings of the hostiles, one educated Indian (Robert Edeson) falls in love with the army commander's daughter. When conflict erupts between the Indians and the whites, he sides with his heritage although he warns the outpost of an impending attack. He also saves the girl's life and realizes she is in love with

a lieutenant in her father's command. The film presents a rousing depiction of the battle at Little Big Horn, utilizing thousands of Indians who encircle Colonel Custer and his doomed men. Several Colorado civic and historical organizations assisted the production in an effort to add authenticity to the historical events. ■

Schmid, Al. See *Pride of the Marines* (1943). ■

Science fiction wars. Science fiction has been a neglected genre in the history of American films. France was the first country to explore the genre. George Melies, a French magician, applied his craft to motion pictures and turned out the celebrated short narrative "A Trip to the Moon" in 1902. The most notable sf film of the 1930s was the British production of *Things to Come*, based on the story by H. G. Wells. Relegated chiefly to serials featuring Flash Gordon and Buck Rogers—popular comic strip heroes—and low-budget films, science fiction in the U.S. did not receive wide attention from the major studios and filmmakers until the 1950s. George Pal, the producer credited with popularizing the genre, turned out several striking features, all endowed with high production values, superb special effects and color. They included *Destination Moon* (1950), *When Worlds Collide* (1951), *War of the Worlds* (1953) and *The Time Machine* (1960).

In *War of the Worlds*, directed by Byron Haskin, fearsome, almost indestructible Martian invaders leave a trail of devastation and death before they succumb to this planet's most common germs. Their own sterile world did not provide them with any protection against such an enemy. The Martians made another attack on Earth in *Invaders From Mars* (1953), directed by William Cameron Menzies. A 12-year-old boy witnesses the landing of Martian invaders who capture residents of a small California community. Helena Carter, as a city doctor, and Arthur Franz, as an astronomer, warn the military of the danger of an alien invasion. Leif Erickson and Hillary Brooke play the boy's parents.

Sometimes the alien invaders appeared in unusual forms not easily detectable but just as menacing. In *Invasion of the Body Snatchers* (1956), directed by Don Siegel, creatures resembling humans emerge from alien pods and replace their look-alike counterparts.

Meanwhile, the pods are being distributed across America. A local doctor (Kevin McCarthy) tries to escape to warn others of the "invasion." The pods drain humans of all emotions. The film has often been interpreted as an allegory of McCarthyism and the Communist paranoia of the Cold War that swept through America during the 1950s.

War is not a phenomenon restricted only to this planet. Alien worlds as well suffer from this affliction. In *This Island Earth* (1955), directed by Joseph Newman, aliens lure earth scientists to their planet to help them defend it against enemy invaders. Rex Reason and Faith Domergue, as two American nuclear scientists, are shanghaied to Metaluna, the beleaguered planet, by its leader, Exeter (Jeff Morrow). They witness the destruction of this strange world as another hostile alien force bombards it. Exeter helps the two Americans return home as he watches his own planet turned into an inferno. "A lifeless planet," he muses. "Yet, still serving a useful purpose, I hope. Yes, a sun—warming the surface of some other world—giving light to those who may need it."

Franklin J. Schaffner's allegorical *Planet of the Apes* (1968), which spawned a string of sequels, practically created its own cycle. Space explorer Charlton Heston and his crew are propelled by error 20 centuries into the future. They find themselves in a world controlled by apes who treat humans as animals. Aside from the pointed political and social satire, the film provides ample suspense, action and humor as Heston leads his fellow beings in an attempt to re-establish man's rightful position.

Some sf films warn of the inherent dangers of the military's inordinate reliance on technology. In *WarGames* (1983), directed by John Badham, Matthew Broderick portrays a bright high-school senior and computer addict. He uses his modem to change his school grades. He connects with the Norad defense system, thinking he is playing a war game called "Global Thermonuclear Warfare." At the defense base, a computer expert describes the War Operations Plan Response—WOPR—to the military: "The WOPR spends all its time thinking about World War III—24 hours a day, 365 days a year. It plays an endless series of war games. . . . The WOPR has already fought World War III—as a game." By the time Broderick realizes he has activated the master computer to engage in World War III, he has

brought down upon himself the wrath of the F.B.I. and the military establishment, the latter thinking that the Soviets have launched an attack. The computer has been programmed in such a way that it cannot be canceled or shut down. Broderick and the original designer (John Wood) strain their intellectual prowess to abort the impending disaster. At the end of the film, the computer responds to a question with: "The only winning move is not to play. How about a nice game of chess?"

The extraordinary success of George Lucas' adventure fantasy *Star Wars* in 1977 led to a new cycle of sf films which emphasized wit, imaginative special effects and elaborate sets. Blending technology with human drama, Lucas, as both writer and director, presented a highly entertaining story of intergalactic wars, rebel planets, heroic space knights and quirky robots. The plot concerns young Luke Skywalker (Mark Hamill) who sets about to rescue a captive princess (Carrie Fisher) from the clutches of a master villain (Peter Cushing) who has delusions of becoming the ruler of the universe. Lance Guest, as a whiz at arcade war games in Nick Castle's *The Last Starfighter* (1984), is recruited by an impish alien (Robert Preston) as a fighter pilot to defend the Star League of Planets against villainous invaders.

In its depictions of future or alien wars, the sf film, like the literature from which it emerged, has always been a natural medium for satirizing the weaknesses of human society and underlining its strengths. ∎

Scotland Yard (1930), Fox. *Dir.* William K. Howard; *Sc.* Garrett Fort; *Cast includes:* Edmund Lowe, Joan Bennett, Lumsden Hare, Barbara Leonard, Donald Crisp.

Edmund Lowe portrays a Raffles-type character in this formula drama set during World War I. To evade the law, which is hot on his trail, Lowe joins the British Army and is sent to the trenches in France where he is wounded in the face by shrapnel. About to have his face restored, he shows a French plastic surgeon a picture of Sir John Lasher, an English nobleman who has died in the war. Lowe returns to England and assumes his new identity, which fools the friends and relatives of the late Sir John, including his estranged wife (Joan Bennett) with whom Lowe falls in love. Meanwhile, a Scotland Yard inspector and friend of her family suspects Lowe. But the redemption of the former criminal as a result of his war experiences and new-found love results in his going straight. The film ends with the inspector bowing out of the picture. ∎

Scott, Robert Lee. See *God Is My Co-Pilot* (1945). ∎

U.S. paratroopers, on a special mission behind German lines during World War II, pause to attend to a fallen comrade. *Screaming Eagles* (1956).

Screaming Eagles (1956), AA. *Dir.* Charles Haas; *Sc.* David Lang, Robert Presnell, Jr.; *Cast includes:* Tom Tryon, Jan Merlin, Alvy Moore, Martin Milner, Jacqueline Beer.

Another behind-the-lines mission provides the motivation for this World War II action drama. A group of paratroopers is assigned to take and hold a strategic bridge during the Normandy invasion. The men parachute into German-occupied territory and battle their way to their objective. Tom Tryon, as a testy private and replacement, soon proves his worth in battle. He undergoes a transformation after fighting alongside his fellow paratroopers and particularly falling under the influence of his sympathetic lieutenant (Jan Merlin). Jacqueline Beer, as a French girl whom the G.I.s rescue from the Germans and who later proves helpful to the Americans, provides a slight romantic interest in this routine tale. ∎

Sea battles. War on the high seas seems a natural subject for the big screen. Warships battling each other to the finish, vessels riding the waves to escape the foe, Spanish galleons aflame as fighting men hurl themselves upon the enemy's deck—all are familiar images to the moviegoer. No other medium can offer the vistas, the movement and the excitement of such stories. The film stu-

dios, however, have faced certain problems with these scripts. Sea stories restrict the obligatory romance required by many in the audience. Also, the battle scenes can be costly. However, despite these temporary setbacks, movie sea battles have raged on.

The resourcefulness of American film companies has provided a wide range of historical backgrounds for these films. *Ben-Hur* (1926), directed by Fred Niblo, and William Wyler's 1959 sequel, for instance, returned to the birth of Christianity to present spectacular sea clashes between Roman and pirate fleets. Accidents and loss of lives reportedly plagued the silent version during the shooting of sea battles. The sea fights in both the 1924 and 1935 versions of *Captain Blood* take place during England's Glorious Revolution. Other pirate films, such as the 1924 and 1940 versions of *The Sea Hawk* and *Barbary Pirate* (1949), supplied plenty of action and adventure in such remote places as the Caribbean and Tripoli. The Napoleonic Wars served as background for historical sea dramas. *The Divine Lady* (1929) and *That Hamilton Woman* (1940) depicted Lord Nelson's victory at the Battle of Trafalgar. The sea adventures of the steadfast *Captain Horatio Hornblower* (1951), starring Gregory Peck in the title role, continued the tradition.

American history has its entries as well. *Old Ironsides* (1926), the story of the *Constitution*, paid tribute to the warship that helped to make the U.S. Navy a force to be reckoned with. Battles with the pirate ships of Tripoli and land forts proved the strength and determination of the new republic. The biographical drama *John Paul Jones* (1959), starring Robert Stack, included a reenactment of the historical battle between *Bonhomme Richard* and Britain's *Serapis*.

Surprisingly, few sea action dramas appeared during World War I. The U.S. government turned out several propaganda films which boasted of the nation's readiness at sea. In *Our Invincible Navy* (1918), for example, modern warships are shown releasing torpedoes and catapulting sea planes. It was not until after the armistice that a string of sea stories about the conflict began to appear. One such tale, *Convoy* (1927), blended a spy plot with several sea battles. In *Suicide Fleet* (1931) the American navy sets up a schooner as a lure for German U-boats whose captains think the lone vessel is its supply ship. Navy warships close in and blast the enemy subs out of the water. Wallace Beery, as an American tugboat captain whose vessel is sunk by a German submarine, joins the crew of a subchaser in Thunder Afloat (1939). He later manages to effect the capture of the U-boat.

The greatest number of sea battle films pertain to World War II. They cover several genres, including comedy, biography and drama. Mystery Sea Raider (1940), one of the earliest entries, concerned an innocent-looking freighter hi-jacked by the Germans and used to prey upon Allied shipping in the Caribbean. It is also responsible for sinking a British cruiser. Several films, such as The Navy Comes Through (1942) and Action in the North Atlantic (1942), the latter starring Humphrey Bogart and Raymond Massey, told about the gallant merchant marine and its perilous task of getting supplies through despite attacks from enemy submarines and planes.

War films began to concentrate on different types of warships. Stand By for Action (1942) told of a battle between an American destroyer and a Japanese battleship. In Destroyer, released one year later, a veteran of the last war (Edward G. Robinson) manages to get on board a World War II destroyer. When Japanese planes damage the vessel, he repairs it sufficiently so that it is able to ram and sink an enemy submarine. The British–Canadian escort warship used chiefly to protect convoys was the center of focus of Corvette K-225 (1943), starring Randolph Scott as skipper. Minesweeper (1943) related how that type of vessel protected Allied shipping. The PT boat was the subject of interest in They Were Expendable (1945), starring John Wayne and Robert Montgomery.

Films about the mighty aircraft carrier seemed to get a budget from the studio almost as large as the vessel itself. One of the earliest, Wing and a Prayer (1944) told about U.S. Navy strategy prior to the Battle of Midway. One carrier is to act as decoy and make the Japanese believe that the American fleet is scattered throughout the Pacific and too weak to fight. Pilots, to their frustration, are ordered not to return enemy fire. Finally, word arrives that the battle has begun, and both ships and planes attack the Japanese navy with all their fury. Task Force (1949), starring Gary Cooper and released after the war, paid tribute to the aircraft carrier. It also dealt with the Battle of Midway and other events. A highly rated documentary, The Fighting Lady

(1944) traced the daily routines of the men aboard an aircraft carrier, the U.S.S. Yorktown, and some of the battles they fought in.

After the war Hollywood continued to make sea dramas about the conflict. They ranged from low-budget films that relied heavily on newsreel footage for combat sequences to large-scale spectaculars with international casts. Fighting Coast Guard (1951), which belongs to the former category, concerned shipyard workers who enlist in the U.S. Coast Guard following Japan's sneak attack on Pearl Harbor and see action in the Pacific. John Wayne, as a submarine captain in Operation Pacific (1952), finds himself in the middle of a Japanese fleet before he reports its location to his base. Okinawa (1952), another low-budget action drama, focused on a destroyer and its role in the invasion of this strategic, Japanese-held island. Okinawa also played an important role in Away All Boats (1956). Jeff Chandler portrays the captain of an attack transport that participates in several invasions in the Pacific, including Makin, and comes under attack by the dreaded kamikaze. Filmmakers returned to life aboard an aircraft carrier in Battle Stations (1956), a routine drama of limited budget and action. The Battle of the Coral Sea (1959) was more concerned with crew members of a submarine on a reconnaissance mission in the Pacific who are captured by the Japanese than with the battle mentioned in the title.

One oddity was a joint U.S.–Italian production, Under Ten Flags (1960), with Van Heflin. He portrays a sympathetic German captain who helms the Atlantis, a Nazi raider disguised as a friendly freighter. When unwary Allied cargo ships come within range of the seemingly harmless vessel, the Atlantis uncovers its guns and sinks the surprised prey. Charles Laughton, as a Churchill-like chief of British naval operations, finally succeeds in having the German ship destroyed.

Some of the big-budgeted spectacles include In Harm's Way (1965), Tora! Tora! Tora! (1970), and Midway (1976). The first, directed by Otto Preminger and starring John Wayne, Kirk Douglas and Patricia Neal, concerned the efforts of the navy to rebuild its Pacific fleet following the Pearl Harbor debacle. It featured several effective combat sequences. Tora! Tora! Tora!, an American–Japanese co-production that reportedly cost $25 million, recreated the attack on Pearl Harbor and covered the events from both points of view. The film was singled out for its historical accuracy. *Midway*, another blockbuster, starred Charlton Heston, Henry Fonda, James Coburn and Glenn Ford in a disappointing re-enactment of the critical air–sea battle that became the turning point in the Pacific war. Like *Tora! Tora! Tora!*, the film presented both sides of the battle by shifting from the Japanese commanders to the American officers. ■

Sea Chase, The (1955), WB. *Dir.* John Farrow; *Sc.* James Warner Bellah, John Twist; *Cast includes:* John Wayne, Lana Turner, David Farrar, Lyle Bettger, Tab Hunter.

John Wayne plays an anti-Nazi German captain of a freighter determined to bring the vessel home in spite of insurmountable odds in this World War II drama. The British navy pursues the elusive ship from Australia to the North Sea where it is finally sunk. Lana Turner, as a Nazi spy aboard the freighter, provides the romantic interest. David Farrar portrays a British naval commander resolved to capture the German vessel, particularly when he learns that one of its passengers is a ruthless Nazi (Lyle Bettger) who cold-bloodedly killed several shipwrecked fishermen. Wayne, as the hard-driving captain, eludes his pursuers for most of the perilous journey. ■

Sea Devils (1953). See Spy Films: the Talkies. ■

Sea Hawk, The (1924), FN. *Dir.* Frank Lloyd; *Sc.* J. G. Hawks; *Cast includes:* Milton Sills, Enid Bennett, Wallace Beery, Lloyd Hughes, Wallace MacDonald.

Rafael Sabatini's novel received special treatment in this large-scale silent screen adaptation. The film includes several action-packed sea battles as well as other exciting sequences. Milton Sills portrays Sir Oliver, an Englishman in love with Rosamund (Enid Bennett). Oliver's young brother kills Rosamund's brother and Oliver is accused of the crime. The younger brother, to protect himself, has Oliver sold into slavery to the Moors. His disappearance causes his fiancee and others to believe him guilty. The ship on which Oliver is held prisoner is captured by a Spanish vessel and he is chained to the oars of the Spanish galley. Later, the ship in turn is taken in battle by the Moors and Oliver joins them in their plunder of Spanish vessels. After gaining his own ship, he becomes known as the Sea Hawk and constantly preys upon Spanish galleons. He returns to England at last where he learns that his fiancee is about to be married to his brother. More complications set in until his brother confesses the killing, thereby exonerating Oliver. ■

Sea Hawk, The (1940), WB. *Dir.* Michael Curtiz; *Sc.* Howard Koch, Seton I. Miller; *Cast includes:* Errol Flynn, Brenda Marshall, Claude Rains, Donald Crisp, Flora Robson, Alan Hale.

Although Warner Brothers borrowed the title from Rafael Sabatini's novel, which was made into a rousing silent epic in 1924, the studio came up with a new screenplay. The important Moorish plot and characters were discarded and replaced by the court intrigues of Spain and England. The film opens in 1585 with Philip II of Spain verbalizing his delusions of grandeur. "Only northern Europe holds out against us. Why?" he rhetorically questions a handful of his closest confidants. "The reason is a puny, rough-bound island as barren and treacherous as her queen." As he rises, his shadow spreads across a map of the world. "With England conquered, nothing can stand in our way," he explains. "One day before my death we shall sit here and gaze at this map upon the wall. It will have ceased to be a map of the world. It will be—Spain." With this, he dispatches Don Alverez (Claude Rains) to England to allay the fears of Elizabeth while he continues to build the Spanish Armada for an eventual invasion of England.

In the next scene Errol Flynn, as Captain Thorpe, commander of a privateer, attacks and sinks the Spanish galleon transporting the ambassador and his niece (Brenda Marshall). After a stirring sea battle and much hand-to-hand fighting, Flynn frees the grateful English galley slaves, removes his prisoners from the sinking vessel and unloads the spoils of war. Back in England, Elizabeth publicly rebukes him for antagonizing Philip while privately condoning his plan to ambush a vast gold shipment in the New World. "Captain Thorpe, if you undertook such a venture, you would do so without the approval of the Queen of England," she says, then adding in a softer voice, "but you would take with you the grateful affection of Elizabeth."

The land attack on the Spanish caravan is a

fiasco. Having been warned of the ambush, the Spanish capture Flynn and his sailors who are sentenced to a life term in the Spanish galleys. But Flynn and his men eventually effect an escape and return to England to deliver captured plans that reveal Spain's true intentions.

The film has several humorous moments as well as epic sweep and action. As the English pirates go about their business of plundering the Spanish ship, the English maid (Una O'Connor) to the ambassador's niece says apologetically: "My lady, these are not typical Englishmen." "You're quite right," interjects a bony-cheeked, toothless, long-nosed pirate, "they're not all as handsome as we are." When Alan Hale, Flynn's first mate, labels Spain as a heathen nation, O'Connor says: "Spain is an old country with a very rich history. In fact, there is much in Spain that we English can profit by." "Well," Hale replies laughingly, "we're certainly doing the best we can." Brenda Marshall, a captive aboard Flynn's ship, rejects his advances. "I'm not in the habit of conversing with thieves," she announces. "I've been admiring some of the jewels we found in your chest," Flynn replies, "particularly the wrought gold. Aztec, isn't it? I wonder just how those Indians were persuaded to part with it."

Historically, Philip did consider England as a thorn in his side. Elizabeth was aiding the Netherlands, which Philip found difficult to conquer. Although the king of Spain had successfully beaten the Turkish fleet, he feared England's sea power. When he finally launched his mighty Armada against Elizabeth in 1588, the attack ended in failure. It was the greatest sea battle in the history of sailing ships. The film was also accurate in the type of warships used by each country. Spain used galley slaves to help maneuver the large galleons and employed soldiers aboard its vessels. England, on the other hand, carried no troops aboard her vessels and used no oarsmen; the ships were lighter and faster, depending rather on wind and sail for their maneuverability.

Perhaps the change from the original plot was an attempt to portray a strong and determined England beset by new threats. Philip's remarks about the "puny, rough-bound island" and "with England conquered, nothing can stand in our way" certainly hint at this. The final speech by Elizabeth about her country's preparedness to defend itself against any foe suggests that the abortive attempt by the Spanish Armada to invade Britain may have been a metaphor for Nazi Germany's dreams of conquest. ∎

Seabees. The Seabees, or the U.S. Navy Construction Battalion, were established in January 1942. The unit was formed to handle construction and maintenance in combat zones. Near the end of World War II the outfit boasted more than 240,000 men. Admiral Halsey paid tribute to the Seabees by describing the bulldozer— along with the submarine, airplane and radar—as one of the four critical weapons in the Pacific war.

The Fighting Seabees (1944), starring John Wayne as a volatile construction chief, dramatizes the development of the navy's construction battalion during the early months of World War II and how its members were converted into an effective fighting unit. The film quotes the Seabees motto: "We build for the fighters—we fight for what we build" and ends with the "Song of the Seabees." In *Blood and Steel* (1959), a low-budget action drama, four American sailors, members of the U.S. Navy's Construction Battalion, are assigned to explore a Japanese-held island in the Pacific for use as a future air base. ∎

Sealed Cargo (1951), RKO. *Dir.* Alfred Werker; *Sc.* Dale Van Every, Oliver H. P. Garrett, Roy Huggins; *Cast includes:* Dana Andrews, Carla Balenda, Claude Rains, Philip Dorn.

A fishing-boat captain off the coast of New England uncovers a German supply ship filled with torpedoes in this tense World War II drama. Dana Andrews, as the skipper, rescues an innocent-looking Danish vessel that has been shelled by a U-boat. Its captain (Claude Rains), claiming to be Danish, is the only survivor. Andrews and one of his crew members (Philip Dorn) suspect the captain's story and the derelict ship. After the ship is towed to port, the two seamen examine the ship more closely while Rains is ashore. They discover a secret compartment below filled with torpedoes.

Unable to contact military authorities from the isolated village, Andrews and his crew decide to sail the ship away from the village and blow it up. They enlist the aid of other local fishermen in their plan. Meanwhile the German captain's crew, put ashore by submarine, boards the square-rigger. Andrews and his men engage the Germans in battle and overpower them. The American captain takes the vessel out to sea and detonates a timing device wired to the torpedoes. The explosion destroys several submarines that have surfaced for supplies. Carla Balenda, who provides the romantic interest, is caught up in the Nazi plot when she is taken hostage by the Germans. ■

Sealed Verdict (1948), Par. *Dir.* Lewis Allen; *Sc.* Jonathan Latimer; *Cast includes:* Ray Milland, Florence Marly, Broderick Crawford, John Hoyt, John Ridgely.

A U.S. Army prosecutor of Nazi war criminals falls in love with the ex-mistress of one of the defendants in this romantic drama set in post-World War II Germany. When the prosecutor (Ray Milland) learns that the Nazi (John Hoyt) may take his own life before the sentence and thus become a martyr to other unrepentant Nazis, he prevents the attempted suicide by dislodging a poisonous vial from a scar in the defendant's cheek. Florence Marly portrays the heroine suspected of being a Nazi sympathizer who in reality is a patriot gathering evidence against Hoyt. ■

Search, The (1948), MGM. *Dir.* Fred Zinnemann; *Sc.* Richard Schweizer, David Wechsler; *Cast includes:* Montgomery Clift, Aline MacMahon, Jarmilla Novotna, Wendell Corey.

A mother's desperate search for her lost child in the wake of World War II is the subject of this poignant drama. But the film, made in the American zone of Germany, explores a larger problem caused by the global conflict—the tragedy of the shattered lives of those innocent children who were left homeless and abandoned. A sensitive and kindly American G.I. (Montgomery Clift) finds a nine-year-old Czech boy (Ivan Jandl) who has been living among the debris and rubble of the city. Having been beaten in the past by the Germans, the child remains suspicious and uncommunicative toward Clift. In time, the boy begins to trust the soldier who has given him shelter and plans to take him home to America. When Clift takes the boy to a United Nations relief agency to obtain the proper papers for the journey, the boy's mother, who works there caring for other homeless children, recognizes her lost child. Aline MacMahon plays a dedicated worker with the U.N. agency. Wendell Corey, as

Clift's sympathetic buddy, warns him of not growing too fond of the child. The New York Film Critics selected the drama as one of the ten best pictures of 1948. ■

Search and Destroy (1981), Film Ventures. *Dir.* William Fruet; *Sc.* Don Enright; *Cast includes:* Perry King, Don Stroud, Tisa Farrow.

A Vietnamese official seeks revenge on four American soldiers ten years after they abandoned him to the Viet Cong in this weak action drama. The American soldiers left the official (Park Jong Soo) behind when he refused to help a wounded American soldier. Now in America, Soo, whose gloved hand covers the torture he underwent in the clutches of the Communists, hunts down each of the four veterans. One of the hunted men (Perry King) finally triumphs over the assassin. Tisa Farrow provides the romance for this revenge tale set chiefly at Niagara Falls. ■

Searching Wind, The (1946), Par. *Dir.* William Dieterle; *Sc.* Lillian Hellman; *Cast includes:* Robert Young, Sylvia Sidney, Ann Richards, Dudley Digges, Albert Basserman.

Based on Lillian Hellman's stage play about the dangers of not heeding the lessons of past wars, the film depicts the story of an indecisive American diplomat who fails to comprehend the significance of events that have occurred between the two world wars. Robert Young portrays the diplomat who misinterprets the rise of Fascism in Italy as well as the spread of Nazism in Germany. He marries the wrong woman (Ann Richards) whose social ties are with the corrupt and arrogant of Europe while his true love, an idealistic journalist (Sylvia Sidney), still carries a torch for him. Douglas Dick, as Young's son, symbolizes the next generation that must reject the failed values of the past. The literate screenplay, also written by Hellman, provides a fascinating look into the world of Europe in the 1920s and 1930s. The film, however, failed at the box office. ■

Seas Beneath, The (1931), Fox. *Dir.* John Ford; *Sc.* Dudley Nichols; *Cast includes:* George O'Brien, Marion Lessing, Mona Marie, Walter C. Kelly, Walter McGrail.

A World War I sea drama, the film tells about a U.S. Navy "mystery" ship, disguised as an innocent schooner, that lures German submarines into a trap. George O'Brien portrays an American captain who falls in love with a German spy (Marion Lessing). Lessing's brother is the commander of the infamous U-172, a German submarine, and her true lover is an officer aboard her brother's vessel. O'Brien's concealed gun crew, together with a U.S. submarine, eventually sink the U-boat. O'Brien watches as the spy, her brother and her fiancee, rescued from the water, are taken away as prisoners of war.

The first half of Ford's rambling film offers little in the way of action. Instead, he explores the camaraderie among the sailors, engages in some humorous situations and presents a ritualistic burial at sea. The American seamen seem naive while on leave in a foreign port—easy prey for several female spies who have little trouble obtaining information from them. On the other hand, the German officers, posing as civilians in the same port, appear sophisticated and organized in espionage work. ■

"Seats of the Mighty" (1914). See French and Indian War. ■

Second in Command, The (1915), Metro. *Dir.* William J. Bowman; *Cast includes:* Francis X. Bushman, Marguerite Snow, William Clifford, Lester Cuneo.

A wealthy English major is hopelessly in love with a young woman who rejects his attentions in this romantic drama with the Boer War for the background. Instead, she loves another major (Francis X. Bushman). The rejected officer invents a story that the one she loves does not care for her, but she still rejects the persistent suitor. When the Boer War breaks out, both men are sent to South Africa where they win praise for their acts of heroism. The deceitful officer confesses to the other what he has done. Both return to England, and Bushman marries the girl. ■

Secret Agent of Japan (1942). See Spy Films: the Talkies. ■

Secret Code, The (1918). See Spy Films: the Silents. ■

Secret Game, The (1917), Par. *Dir.* William C. DeMille; *Sc.* Marion Fairfax; *Cast includes:* Sessue Hayakawa, Jack Holt, Florence Vidor, Raymond Hatton.

In this World War I spy story Sessue Hay-

akawa portrays a secret agent on the trail of spies in Los Angeles who are leaking information to the Germans. Japanese warships are acting as convoys to American transport ships on their way to Russia, and the Germans want the exact route of the convoy. Hayakawa helps to transport Americans by way of Siberia to the Russian front. He falls in love with a white woman but commits suicide, thereby permitting her to return to her true (white) hero. ■

Secret Invasion, The (1964), UA. *Dir.* Roger Corman; *Sc.* R. Wright Campbell; *Cast includes:* Stewart Granger, Raf Vallone, Mickey Rooney, Henry Silva, Mia Massini.

A British officer leads a handful of volunteer convicts on a special assignment in Nazi-occupied Yugoslavia in this World War II action drama. Stewart Granger has the thankless task of supervising this motley crew of experts whose mission is to rescue an Italian general held prisoner in a Nazi stronghold. Raf Vallone portrays a former gang leader; Mickey Rooney, a dynamite expert; and Henry Silva, a sharpshooter. They portray some of the criminals who, if successful during the mission, are promised a pardon. The small force links up with two partisans (Peter Coe and Mia Massini). After they succeed in their mission, they learn that they have only rescued the prisoner's double. The film, which ends tragically with only one member of the special force surviving, provides plenty of action. The plot device of using prisoners for a dangerous mission anticipates the more popular World War II action drama, *The Dirty Dozen* (1967). ■

Secret of St. Ives, The (1949), Col. *Dir.* Philip Rosen; *Sc.* Eric Taylor; *Cast includes:* Richard Ney, Vanessa Brown, Henry Daniell, Edgar Barrier.

Set during the Napoleonic Wars, the plot of this historical drama concerns a group of French soldiers captured by the British. The captives are imprisoned in Edinburgh Castle where one of the Frenchmen (Richard Ney) leads a daring escape and journeys across England accompanied by his English girlfriend (Vanessa Brown). They encounter the typical problems inherent in this type of drama. He is eventually caught but manages to elude execution. Henry Daniell portrays a villainous English officer in this low-budget film that is based on a story by Robert Louis Stevenson. ■

Secret of Santa Vittoria, The (1969), UA.
Dir. Stanley Kramer; *Sc.* William Rose, Ben Maddow; *Cast includes:* Anthony Quinn, Anna Magnani, Virna Lisi, Hardy Kruger.

A northern Italian village, in a collective act of defiance and resistance, conceals one million bottles of wine from the Germans in this World War II drama. When the villagers learn that some of the retreating Nazis intend to sack their town of all its wine, its only product and therefore its only means of survival, the citizens decide to hide the wine in an ancient cave. Anthony Quinn portrays a heavy-drinking, irresponsible fool who is selected as mayor when he erases a pro-Mussolini slogan from a water tower. The new position motivates Quinn, who soon sobers up, displays a sense of dignity and matches wits with the Nazi captain (Hardy Kruger) who arrives to claim the booty. The officer, disappointed at not finding the large supply of wine but convinced it exists, threatens Quinn's life. But the mayor and the townspeople retain their silence. As the detachment of Germans leave, the mayor presents the captain with one bottle as a gift. "Are you sure you can spare it?" the officer says sardonically. "There are one million more where this came from," Quinn calls out. The film, based on Robert Crichton's novel, features Virna Lisi and Sergio Franchi who provide the romantic interest. ■

Secret Orders (1926). See Spy Films: the Silents. ■

Secret Service (1919), Par. *Dir.* Hugh Ford; *Sc.* Beulah Marie Mix; *Cast includes:* Robert Warwick, Wanda Hawley, Theodore Roberts, Edythe Chapman, Raymond Hatton, Guy Oliver.

Based on William Gillette's famous Civil War spy play, this silent film drama stars Robert Warwick as the Union secret service agent who is assigned the task of helping to bring about the fall of Richmond. A romance develops between him and a young Southern woman (Wanda Hawley). Guy Oliver portrays the role of an elderly black. Playwright Gillette portrayed the role of the Union officer on stage. This film marked Robert Warwick's return to the screen following his military service in World War I. ■

Secret Service (1931), RKO. *Dir.* J. Walter Ruben; *Sc.* Bernard Schubert; *Cast includes:* Richard Dix, Shirley Grey, William Post, Jr., Fred Warren.

A sound version of William Gillette's Civil War play, the film stars Richard Dix as a Union captain who journeys into Confederate territory to gather information. Dressed in the enemy's uniform, he comes across a wounded son of the South. He carries the boy home and is invited to stay with the family. He then becomes romantically involved with the boy's sister (Shirley Grey). His love for her results in his being torn between his duty to the North and his devotion to Grey. She finds it difficult to believe that he is a spy when she sees him caught and taken away. ■

Secret War of Harry Frigg, The (1968), U. *Dir.* Jack Smight; *Sc.* Peter Stone, Frank Tarloff; *Cast includes:* Paul Newman, Sylvia Koscina, Tom Bosley, Andrew Duggan.

Paul Newman portrays a slow-witted G.I. assigned to rescue a handful of allied generals held captive by the Germans and Italians in this World War II comedy. James Gregory portrays the American general who devises the scheme and has Newman masquerade as a general so that the five officers he is to free will follow his orders. Tom Bosley and Andrew Duggan play two of the incarcerated generals who have to contend with the incompetent hijinks of their rescuer. Sylvia Koscina, the only woman in the cast, provides the romantic interest for Newman in this weak comedy. ■

Secrets of Scotland Yard (1944). See Spy Films: the Talkies. ■

Security Risk (1954). See Cold War. ■

See Here, Private Hargrove (1944). See Service Comedy. ■

Seminole (1953), U. *Dir.* Budd Boetticher; *Sc.* Charles K. Peck, Jr.; *Cast includes:* Rock Hudson, Barbara Hale, Richard Carlson, Anthony Quinn, Hugh O'Brian, Lee Marvin.

West Point graduate Rock Hudson is assigned to an army post in his native Florida in this drama involving conflicts between the U.S. Cavalry and the Seminole. Richard Carlson, as an ambitious, inflexible major, is bent on forcefully removing the Seminoles from the Everglades. Hudson's suggestions of accomplishing this through peaceful means only anger his belligerent superior. Although he is sympathetic to the Indians, especially to their chief, Osceola (Anthony Quinn), who happens to be his boyhood friend, Hudson guides Carlson and a troop of soldiers into the swamp for a surprise attack. But Carlson's plan to massacre the Seminole backfires, and his command is wiped out. Hudson, wounded in the battle, is saved by Quinn but later is court-martialed for the murder of the Indian chief. As he is about to face a firing squad, another Seminole saves his life by admitting to the killing. Barbara Hale provides the romantic interest while Lee Marvin serves as a loyal sergeant to the major.

Set in 1835 in Florida's Everglades, the film recounts the familiar plot of a power-crazed army officer more interested in killing Indians than on seeking peace ("I live by the book, I fight by the book," the major declares). It follows the trend-setting pro-Indian film *Broken Arrow* (1950), which laid much of the blame for the Indian wars on the doorstep of the U.S. government. Carlson early in the film explains to Hudson that the government wants all the Florida tribes off the rich land and resettled in the West. The major is shown as completely unsympathetic toward the peaceful Seminoles. Beaten in battle, he arranges for a parley under a flag of truce with their chief and then beats him mercilessly and locks him up. The script has Colonel Zachary Taylor presiding at the court martial, an obvious attempt to garner a note of authenticity for the tale. ■

Seminole Uprising (1955), Col. *Dir.* Earl Bellamy; *Sc.* Robert E. Kent; *Cast includes:* George Montgomery, Karin Booth, William Fawcett, Steve Ritch.

A band of defiant Seminoles flee their Florida reservation and head west in this outdoor drama set in the 1850s. George Montgomery portrays a cavalry lieutenant assigned to capture them and return them to Florida. Steve Ritch plays the elusive chief of the renegades. Karin Booth, as the post commander's daughter, provides the romantic interest. At one point, she is captured by the Seminoles and eventually rescued by Montgomery. The battle sequences in this routine plot lack originality and excitement. Some of this footage has been borrowed from earlier films. ■

Seminole wars. The Seminole Indians, a branch of the Creek nation that settled in Spanish Florida early in the 1700s, engaged in three wars with U.S. troops in the 1800s. American military expeditions against the tribe in the early 1800s led to tensions with Spain and Britain and played a major role in Spain's decision to sell Florida to the U.S.

The Seminole grew stronger during the 1700s and early 1800s by taking in runaway black slaves and remnants of other tribes. The U.S. Army's practice of pursuing slaves across the border into Spanish Florida and Seminole territory brought retaliation by the tribe which ambushed and scalped an American force. General Andrew Jackson, without specific authorization, led 3,000 soldiers in a punitive expedition that resulted in the First Seminole War of 1817–1818. Jackson seized Spanish forts at Pensacola and St. Marks and captured several Indian chiefs and two British traders. His invasion and subsequent order to execute the prisoners raised a furor within the American, Spanish and British governments. Jackson's incursion convinced Spain it could not defend its colony from American forces. In 1819 President John Quincy Adams negotiated a treaty by which Spain ceded all its territory east of the Mississippi River for $5 million. The U.S. could now deal directly with the "Seminole Problem."

The Treaty of Paynes Landing (1832), signed by several Seminole chiefs, required the tribe to relocate west of the Mississippi. However, chief Osceola and a large band refused to acknowledge the treaty and withdrew into Florida's Everglades. There they successfully eluded U.S. troops in a bitter and costly seven-year struggle known as the Second Seminole War (1835–1842). Seminole resistance crumbled after Osceola was lured with a promise of safe conduct to a peace conference. When he arrived for the parley, he was treacherously seized and put in jail in North Carolina where he died. Most of the tribe, except for a small group that stayed in the Everglades, moved west of the Mississippi to what is now Oklahoma. The Second Seminole War was the army's most expensive conflict in its history of Indian engagements. It cost between $30 and $40 million, the lives of about 2,000 whites and the annihilation of thousands of Indians and tribal villages.

The Third Seminole War occurred in

1855–1858 when the U.S. government tried to root out those Seminoles who remained in the Everglades and conducted raids against whites encroaching on ancestral lands. The American government eventually paid most of the remaining Florida Seminoles to go to a reservation in Oklahoma. However, a few stayed behind in the swamps and did not make peace until 1934. Their descendants live on a small reservation in Florida. *Seminole* (1953) combined some of the more significant historical incidents of the Second and Third Seminole Wars and the ignominious capture of Osceola. The lively film was accurate, in spirit if not in fact, to the actual events. *Seminole Uprising* (1955), on the other hand, went counter to fact. Washington politicians, by using military force, were seeking to drive the Indians out of Florida onto western reservations. The film, however, dealt with the government's efforts to have the Seminole return to Florida. ■

Sepoy Mutiny. See Indian Mutiny of 1857–1858. ■

"Sepoy's Wife, The" (1910), Vitagraph. *Cast includes:* Maurice Costello, Clara Kimball Young.

A silent drama set in India, the story takes place during the Indian Mutiny of 1857–1858. An English regimental physician saves the life of a sepoy's child. This act is repaid when the child's mother saves the doctor's family as well as the besieged fort. The battle scenes are realistic and exciting in this short film. ■

Sergeant Mike (1945), Col. *Dir.* Henry Levin; *Sc.* Robert Lee Johnson; *Cast includes:* Larry Parks, Jeanne Bates, Loren Tindall, Jim Bannon.

The use of dogs in battle is the subject of this World War II action drama. Larry Parks portrays a soldier who is transferred from his machine-gun unit to the K-9 Corps, composed of dogs trained for various military tasks. At first unhappy about his new assignment, he accepts it when he learns that one of the canines, Sergeant Mike, belongs to a boy whose father was killed in action. Mike and his mate Pearl prove indispensable in uncovering Japanese machine-gun nests and conveying dispatches in the action sequences. Jeanne Bates provides the romantic interest in this canine tale. See also Dogs in War. ■

Sergeant York (1941), WB. *Dir.* Howard Hawks; *Sc.* Abem Finkel, Harry Chandlee; *Cast includes:* Gary Cooper, Walter Brennan, Joan Leslie, George Tobias, Stanley Ridges.

A film biography of perhaps the greatest American hero of World War I, the drama stars Gary Cooper in the role of Alvin York, a humble Tennessee backwoodsman whose religious beliefs result in an internal struggle between his patriotism and pacifism. Raised in the mountains as a farm boy, he is strongly influenced by his environment where he also develops his expertise with a rifle. He uses these talents to great advantage when he is shipped to France, along with countless other doughboys, to fight the Germans. The battle sequences depict his exploits in single-handedly killing 20 enemy troops and bringing about the surrender of 132 others in the Argonne sector. He is awarded the Distinguished Service Cross, Medaille Militaire, Croix de Guerre and America's highest decoration, the Congressional Medal of Honor. Marshall Foch was to describe York's deed as "the greatest thing ever to be accomplished by any private soldier in all the armies in Europe."

The film is concerned as much with York's dilemma about killing as with the war sequences. Walter Brennan plays the village pastor who helps the young hero, at first a carefree rowdy, to understand the role of religion in one's life. Joan Leslie, as a local villager who loves York, furnishes the romantic interest. Margaret Wycherley, as his strong-willed mother, embodies the fierce, independent spirit of these mountain people, especially in one scene before breakfast. "Dear Lord," she says, leading the family prayer, "we thank Thee for this food and that we are beholden to nobody." George Tobias, as "Pusher," one of his army buddies who is ultimately killed in action, adds some humor as a former New York City subway worker. Later, in remembrance of his fallen comrade, Cooper, on a visit to New York, asks to ride on the Bronx Express.

Director Howard Hawks presents a dignified and noble portrait of a poor but proud and valiant rural people whose virtues are embodied in York. The simple dialogue he uses belies the depth of his character. "I'm as much agin killin' as ever," he confesses to his superior officer following his heroic exploits, "but when I heard those machine guns . . . well, them guns was killin' hundreds, maybe thousands, and there weren't nothin' anybody could do but to stop them guns." Later, he is offered thousands of dollars to endorse certain commercial products. "I ain't proud of what I done over there," he replies, rejecting the offers. "What we done in France is something we had to do. Some fellers done it ain't a-comin' back. So, the way I figure, things like that ain't for buyin' and sellin'."

The real-life Alvin York held back permission to film his life for 20 years, preferring to remain anonymous as a farmer and educator. When Warner Brothers promised to tell his story with integrity and dignity, as well as with a lucrative donation to his educational work, he finally relented. The film, released during World War II, has been singled out for its strong propaganda content at a time when the U.S. was building up its military forces. York as a mythical figure not only inspired patriotism in many young Americans but was alluded to in several other war films. In *Guadalcanal Diary* (1943) a marine lures Japanese soldiers into his gunsight by imitating a turkey gobble. A buddy asks: "Are you Sergeant York or Gary Cooper?" In the Korean War film *Pork Chop Hill* (1959) a lieutenant (Gregory Peck) asks one of his brave but reckless soldiers, "Who do you think you are, Sergeant York?" ■

Serials. The movie serial, at one time one of Hollywood's most reliable staples, witnessed its last chapter in 1956, another victim of television's encroaching domination. But before its demise, the genre poured forth hundreds of titles and emcompassed many genres, including westerns, detective stories, mysteries, and spy and war dramas. The serials with either World War I or II as background were concerned with such usual conventions as superweapons, secret formulas and spies. The heroes ranged from men of action to more vulnerable but steadfast women and children. When the final, long-awaited twelfth or fifteenth chapter finally appeared on screen, all breathed a sigh of relief. America was once again safe from peril, the spies were under lock and key and the secret weapon was in the hands of the government to be used effectively against its menacing enemies.

A variety of military branches flashed across the screen during the World War I period. *Neal of the Navy* (1915) featured William Courtleigh and Lillian Lorraine in 14 exciting chapters. *Pearl of the Army* (1916) starred the silent serial queen Pearl White as the intrepid lass who prevents Oriental agents from sabotaging the Panama Canal.

Germany posed the largest threat to the U.S., according to the serials. In *Wolves of Kultur* (1918) Charles Hutchinson and Leah Baird track down the German designer of a new and powerful torpedo. Jane Vance, as the title character in *A Daughter of Uncle Sam* (1918), bravely battles German agents for 12 chapters. *The Eagle's Eye* (1918), an epic serial in 20 chapters, added a touch of paranoia to the threat of enemy agents by suggesting that hundreds of German spies were running rampant across America. The nation's youth were given a chance to serve their country in *Boy Scouts to the Rescue* (1918). They ferret out a nest of German agents.

Japan won second place as the next largest threat to the country's security. Besides *Pearl of the Army*, mentioned earlier, *The Secret of the Submarine* (1916), a 14-chapter serial, has Japanese agents planning to steal a device which allows a submarine to remain submerged indefinitely. The coveted invention draws oxygen from sea water.

An actual incident precipitated *Patria* (1916), an anti-Japanese and anti-Mexican serial which was financed by William Randolph Hearst. The influential publisher, who owned a large ranch in Mexico, was enraged when Pancho Villa raided his property and distributed his 60,000 head of cattle to the peons. Hearst ordered his editors to lash out against Mexico, claiming it had a secret alliance with Japan to invade the U.S. The serial *Patria* echoed this threat. Dancer Irene Castle, as an American heiress, provides secret funds designed to prepare America against an enemy attack. It depicts the Japanese so repulsively that President Wilson was prompted to send a note to those responsible, complaining that the film was "extremely unfair to the Japanese . . ."

Following the Armistice, our heroes and heroines kept busy battling power-crazed master villains (*Drums of Fu Manchu*), tracking down gangs of kidnapers (*The Clutching Hand*), taming the wilderness (*Custer's Last Stand*), hunting for lost treasure (*The New Adventures of Tarzan*), braving the perils of the jungle (*Darkest Africa*), protecting the skies from airborne criminals (*Mystery Squadron*) and traveling in space to save our planet (*Flash Gordon*). All these exploits proved valuable training for the next world conflict and the threat of totalitarianism.

Once again the enemies chiefly were imported from Germany and Japan. (Italy, the third Axis power, was virtually nonexistent in World War II serials.) Masks often hid the identities of villains as well as heroes, both of whom fought relentlessly to gain control of superweapons, secret formulas and other vital information. The masked *Spy Smasher* (1942), starring Kane Richmond, fights against a Nazi leader called the Mask. In *King of the Mounties*, released the same year, Allan "Rocky" Lane battles the enemy in Canada's backwoods. Don Terry, as the intrepid seaman Don Winslow, clashes with the Germans in two serials, *Don Winslow of the Navy* (1942) and *Don Winslow of the Coast Guard* (1943). It took both to subdue the dangerous Scorpion (not to be confused with Tom Tyler's arch-rival of the same name in *The Adventures of Captain Marvel*), who is bent on crippling America's defenses. The fun-loving juvenile delinquents, better known as the Dead End Kids or the Little Tough Guys, turn patriotic when they collide with enemy agents in *Junior G-Men of the Air* (1942) and *Adventures of the Flying Cadets* (1943). Ruth Roman, as the *Jungle Queen* (1945), helps to quell a tribal revolt, incited by Nazi agents, against the Allies. Lloyd Bridges as *Secret Agent X-9* (1945) does his share for the war effort by rounding up a gang of Nazi saboteurs.

While German agents were being bested by these stalwart defenders of the American way, Japanese spies faced the same fate. Rod Cameron in *G-Men vs. the Black Dragon* (1943) pursues Haruchi, a nefarious figure who ultimately is killed in a ball of flame when his speedboat smashes into a Japanese submarine. Another nasty Oriental agent, Sakima, meets a violent death at the hands of William Forrest as *The Masked Marvel* (1943). The famous comic-book hero, The Batman, in a 1943 serial of the same name, takes on Dr. Saka (J. Carrol Naish), another wicked Japanese agent whose diabolical inventions almost end the masked hero's career.

Fistfights and chases were the mainstay of the serials. (Budgets did not permit battle sequences of the war. When establishing shots were required, e.g., the U.S. Navy fleet in the *Don Winslow* serials, stock footage was used.) With all their frenetic action, serials hardly had time for messages or preaching. But the opposing wartime ideologies were clearly embodied in the principal characters. Since the heroes emerged from the country's popular culture, e.g., the comics, radio and pulp fiction, and the villains were so plainly identifiable, the propaganda and patriotic elements were never far off. ■

Serpent of the Nile (1953), Col. *Dir.* William Castle; *Sc.* Robert E. Kent; *Cast includes:* Rhonda Fleming, William Lundigan, Raymond Burr, Jean Byron, Michael Ansara.

Cleopatra, queen of the Nile, plots to usurp the throne of Rome in this implausible costume drama. Mark Anthony (Raymond Burr), who has gained power following the assassination of Caesar, falls for the charms of the treacherous Egyptian queen. Although she agrees to his suggestion for an alliance between their two countries, she simultaneously schemes to have him killed so that she can assume power in Rome. William Lundigan, as Burr's lieutenant and a loyal Roman, foils Cleopatra's dream of conquest by calling upon Roman legions to defeat the Egyptians. Cleopatra, acknowledging her downfall, takes her own life. ■

Service comedy. Comedies that center on military life before, during or after hostilities—but do not thrust the hero or heroine directly into combat—have been just as popular as war comedies. Many film comics or comedy teams have made at least one service comedy. Although produced simply as entertainment vehicles, the films often reflect certain attitudes toward military life, authority figures or the enemy.

During World War I few comedies of the conflict appeared; those were somber times, and movie studios and the public considered it in bad taste to poke fun at the war. Charlie Chaplin was the first major comedian to break this taboo with his satirical and very funny *Shoulder Arms* (1918). While the industry looked on cautiously, the film became a critical and financial success. With the war now over, the studios filled the movie houses with comedies about the past conflict and military life.

The film *23 1/2 Hours' Leave* (1919), starring Douglas MacLean and set during World War I, was one of the earliest service comedies and set the pattern for others to follow. Using well-proven conventions of stage comedy, such as farce and mistaken identity, the plot concerns a fun-loving sergeant stationed at an army camp who meets the general's daughter but doesn't know this until it is too late. Other comedies took place during the war. *Paris Green* (1920) has Charles Ray as a doughboy on a 24-hour leave in Paris. *Tin Hats* (1926) follows the misadventures of Conrad Nagel and two buddies who arrive in France during the last days of the war. Comic Sammy Cohen, as a doughboy in *Plastered in Paris* (1928), is transformed into a kleptomaniac after being struck in the head. *Riley of the Rainbow Division*, also released in 1928, features Creighton Hale and Al Alt as doughboys who end up in the guardhouse on their wedding day. In *Dugan of the Dugouts*, another 1928 comedy, Danny O'Shea joins up because his sweetheart likes a particular sergeant. In *Cock of the Air* (1932) Chester Morris, as an Allied air force officer, is chased by Billie Dove. *Pack Up Your Troubles* (1932) stars Laurel and Hardy as bungling doughboys who care for a dead buddy's little girl.

Other service comedies, such as *Gentleman From America* (1923), take place immediately after the war. Hoot Gibson and Tom O'Brien portray doughboys who remain behind in France after the Armistice. They become embroiled in the local politics of a mythical kingdom, incite a revolution and save the local heroine from a forced marriage. In *Buck Privates* (1928), as in other films of this type, a rivalry develops between two servicemen over a girl—here, Malcolm MacGregor and Eddie Gribbon battle it out for Lya de Putti. In *Wife Savers*, released the same year, Wallace Beery and Raymond Hatton, stationed in Switzerland, become rivals for the affection of Sally Blane. Comic character player ZaSu Pitts does a clever parody of the Renée Adorée role from the World War I epic *The Big Parade* (1925) in which Adorée follows the lorry carrying John Gilbert back to the front. Raoul Walsh's *The Cockeyed World* (1929), another postwar comedy, continues the rivalry begun in *What Price Glory?* (1926) between Victor McLaglen and Edmund Lowe. But comic El Brendel has the best gag. An army officer studying the local maps of a French province, bellows the now-famous order, "Bring me the lay of the land." Brendel, as a dimwitted marine, responds by presenting the local prostitute.

Two additional elements emerge in *A Sailor-Made Man* (1921), starring Harold Lloyd as the title character—rejection by a loved one and last-minute heroics. Lloyd, as a rich but idle playboy, is snubbed by his sweetheart, so he joins the navy. His tour of duty takes him to the Orient where his former sweetheart is vacationing. When she is taken prisoner by a local rajah, Lloyd springs to her rescue. Hoot Gibson in *Out of Luck* (1923) joins the navy after an unfortunate circumstance separates him from his sweetheart. Following a series of misadventures and gags aboard ship, Gibson saves the captain's life and returns to his sweetheart. In *His First Command* (1929) William Boyd, as a millionaire's son, enlists in the army to be near a young woman who has caught his eye. A convenient act of heroism makes him an officer and permits him to win the girl.

Two other characteristics which were to become basic to the service comedy—the dreaded, bullying sergeant and the defiant hero's conversion—show up in *Tell It to the Marines* (1926). Lon Chaney, as a tough sergeant, treats new recruit William Haines gently until Haines signs on the dotted line. Then Haines feels the wrath of the sergeant fall upon him. The new marine does some goldbricking, fakes illness, and gets thrown into the brig. However, he develops into a true marine on board ship and during a conflict with Chinese bandits.

Several service comedies were built around a melodramatic plot. In *Let It Rain* (1927) Douglas MacLean, as a marine sergeant, becomes involved with a gang of criminals. Joe E. Brown, as a wacky navy man in *Son of a Sailor* (1933), is redeemed when he accidentally causes the capture of a spy. In *Join the Marines* (1937) the leathernecks battle hostile natives, an incident which allows hero Paul Kelly to win the girl. This blend of melodramatics and comedy continued into World War II with such films as *Hillbilly Blitzkrieg* (1942), in which Bob Duncan, as cartoonist Billy De Beck's comic strip character Private Snuffy Smith, guards a secret weapon.

World War II service comedies began to appear before America's entry into the conflict. At first, such veteran comic actors as Bob Hope and Jimmy Durante were featured. Then a new crop of performers burst upon the screen, led by vaudevillians Bud Abbott and Lou Costello. Bob Hope, as a reluctant rookie in *Caught in the Draft* (1941), fails in his attempts to avoid the draft. Once in uniform, he becomes a sort of hero when he saves his buddies during maneuvers. He also gets to woo Dorothy Lamour. Old-timer Jimmy Durante teamed up with Phil Silvers in *You're in the Army Now* (1941). As two bungling vacuum cleaner salesmen, they enlist in the army by mistake. Durante, realizing his error too late, tries to prove he is crazy to the physician during his medical examination. "Give me a gun! Send me to the front line of battle!" Durante shouts. The doctor passes him. The film includes the jingoistic song, "I'm Glad My Number Came Up," about the joys of being among the first to be called for duty. In *Top Sergeant Mulligan* (1941) two salesmen join the army to avoid a tax collector. Frank Faylen and Charles Hall play the recruits who end up under the heel of Nat Pendleton as their sergeant. Moonfaced William Tracy and tough-guy Joe Sawyer teamed up for a series of low-budget service comedies, including *Tanks a Million* (1941), *About Face* (1942), *Fall In* (1943) and *Yanks Ahoy* (1943), where they manage to capture a Japanese submarine. Comic character players Leo Carrillo and Andy Devine appeared in a series of low-budget comedy dramas, including *Top Sergeant* (1942), in which they portray trouble-prone corporals.

The most popular team was Abbott and Costello. They hopped from one branch of service to another—*In the Navy, Keep 'Em Flying,* both 1941. Their funniest comedy remains *Buck Privates,* also 1941, their first service comedy. The duo are at their most hilarious and vibrant in contrast to their later work, which was heavily derivative and repetitious. The talented Andrews Sisters sing "Boogie Woogie Bugle Boy" and "I'll Be With You in Apple Blossom Time." The film anticipated the patriotic songs and plots that were soon to become obligatory elements of this genre. It provides a subplot about the spoiled son of a millionaire ultimately shedding his haughtiness and accepting the joys of democracy. A sequel, *Buck Privates Come Home,* appeared in 1947.

Service comedies continued to appear throughout the war years by both major and small studios whose pundits tried to emulate the success of Bud and Lou. A young Jackie Gleason, in his first major role, joined Will Durant as a potential comedy team in *Tramp, Tramp, Tramp* (1942). They portray barbers who are losing business because of the draft. When they try to enlist, they are rejected. During his army examination, Gleason is asked to read an eye chart. "I can't," he says.

"You mean you can't see that chart?" asks the doctor. "I can't read," replies Gleason. Wally Brown and Alan Carney, another pair of comics packaged to compete with Abbott and Costello, turned out *The Adventures of a Rookie* (1943) and *Rookies in Burma* (1944), but the films did not generate any audience enthusiasm. In *Abroad With Two Yanks* (1944) William Bendix and Dennis O'Keefe, as two army pals, fight over the same woman. The film is often reminiscent of the Capt. Flagg–Sgt. Quirt comedies.

Some plots came from other media, including the novel and the comic strip. Robert Walker portrayed the hapless title character in *See Here, Private Hargrove* (1944), based on Marion Hargrove's comical book about life at an army camp. A sequel, *What Next, Corporal Hargrove?,* appeared in 1945. Meanwhile, Cartoonist Billy De Beck's popular comic strip, "Snuffy Smith," was transformed into a low-budget film titled *Private Snuffy Smith* (1942) with silent screen comedian Bud Duncan as the dwarfish, bulbous-nosed title character. Snuffy, a hillbilly who joins the army, is hounded by his sergeant (Edgar Kennedy). A sequel, *Hillbilly Blitzkrieg,* appeared the same year.

The postwar years brought several new faces to the genre. Abbott and Costello, the reigning comedy team of the 1940s, were replaced in the next decade by Dean Martin and Jerry Lewis, who also contributed to service comedies with *At War With the Army* (1951) and *Jumping Jacks* (1952). Later, when the team split up, Lewis went on to make other films, including his portrayal of a misfit soldier in *The Sad Sack* (1957), based on George Baker's popular cartoon strip. Tab Hunter, as a spoiled collegiate draftee in *The Girl He Left Behind* (1956), devotes all his energies to getting out of the army. The film is based on a novel by Marion Hargrove.

A handful of old reliables appeared in service comedies after the war. Bud and Lou in *Abbott and Costello in the Foreign Legion* (1950) journey to Algiers to convince a former wrestler to return to the U.S. They soon become entangled in an intrigue between local natives and the Legion, which they are tricked into joining. The Bowery Boys engage in their usual slapstick antics in *Here Come the Marines* (1952), which finds the gang in uniform at a U.S. Marine camp. Mickey Rooney, who had been in films since the late 1920s, appeared in *Off Limits* (1953) with Bob Hope. Hope, as a manager–trainer, offers to turn Rooney, another draftee, into a pro fighter when he learns that Rooney's aunt is the sexy Marilyn Maxwell. Rooney followed this zany comedy with another, *Operation Mad Ball* (1957), albeit in a minor role. Enlisted men plan a covert wild party in a French hotel under the noses of their officers. Jack Lemmon masterminds the entire scheme. One surprising post-World War II farce, *I Was a Male War Bride* (1949), has Cary Grant in drag. He portrays a French army officer who, hampered by immigration quotas, masquerades as a war bride so that he can accompany his wife, an officer in the WACs, to the U.S.

Screen comediennes appeared in several postwar service comedies. Rosalind Russell in *Never Wave at a WAC* (1952) joins the Women's Army Corps to advance her personal ambitions in this comedy about life in the WACs. Her problems arise when she remains an ordinary private instead of receiving the commission she expected because her father is a senator. In *The WAC From Walla Walla* (1952) singer–comedienne Judy Canova, hailing from a western military-oriented family, joins the Women's Army Corps through an accident. She soon becomes embroiled with enemy agents. Goldie Hawn carried on the tradition as a Jewish American Princess who finds army life full of surprises in *Private Benjamin* (1980).

The genre continued through the Korean War with such entries as *Mr. Walkie Talkie* (1952), another Tracy–Sawyer service comedy in which the two feuding sergeants continue their antics in Korea, and *The Lieutenant Wore Skirts* (1956), with husband Tom Ewell trying to get his wife Sheree North discharged from military service.

Hollywood has occasionally returned to World War II for its comedy settings. *You're in the Navy Now* (1951), originally titled U.S.S. *Teakettle*, has Gary Cooper as an inexperienced lieutenant on an experimental small vessel. Andy Griffith, who had scored a hit as a hayseed soldier in Mervyn LeRoy's *No Time for Sergeants* (1958), repeated his hayseed role a few months later in *Onionhead* as a frustrated lover in the U.S. Coast Guard. *McHale's Navy* (1964) continued the zany antics of the crew of a PT boat first made famous as a television series. *Biloxi Blues* (1988), based on Neil Simon's play and personal experiences during World War II, ex-

emplifies the elements of the genre. Matthew Broderick portrays the hapless young recruit from Brooklyn. His misadventures include his unorthodox basic training, his bouts with the heat of Mississippi, his struggle with his tough sergeant (Christopher Walken) and the joys of love.

Aside from the upbeat endings inherent in comedy films, the genre sparks another kind of optimism. The protagonist, usually a misfit, outsider or reluctant soldier, often surmounts his or her problems by showing the right amount of resilience and determination—characteristics that reflect the American character, especially during adversity. The movie audience, while rooting for this underdog, not only feels mentally and physically superior to the zany, bumbling protagonist but may also be reaffirming its own values. See also War Humor. ■

Service Star, The (1918), Goldwyn. *Dir.* Charles Miller; *Sc.* Charles A. Logue; *Cast includes:* Madge Kennedy, Clarence Oliver, Maude Turner Gordon, Mabel Ballin.

An unattractive young woman (Madge Kennedy) longs for a beau in uniform in this World War I comedy drama. Envious of her friends, all of whom have boyfriends in the service, she fabricates a story about her being secretly married to a flier who has become famous as a war hero in France. Her only mistake was to use the name of a real hero. The boy's mother, learning of the specious marriage, invites Kennedy to live with her. The girl then discovers the real son, who is afraid of firearms, living there in secret while another, the real hero, has assumed his name. When a stranger threatens to blackmail Kennedy, the alleged coward comes to her rescue and is wounded in the fight. But the altercation has ended his fears and given him the courage to enlist under the hero's name. ■

Seven Angry Men (1955), AA. *Dir.* Charles Marquis Warren; *Sc.* Daniel R. Ullman; *Cast includes:* Raymond Massey, Debra Paget, Jeffrey Hunter, Larry Pennell.

John Brown's crusade to liberate the slaves provides the subject of this Civil War drama. Raymond Massey portrays Brown as a ruthless murderer, a religious fanatic who cares little about the number of lives that are lost as he tries to get Kansas to join the Union as a free state. His son (Jeffrey Hunter) falls in love with Debra Paget and marries her. Leo

Gordon plays Reverend White, a minister who resists the preachings of Brown. The film climaxes with the famous battle at Harpers Ferry, Virginia, where John Brown is captured by Colonel Robert E. Lee. Massey had played the religious crusader in an earlier film, *Santa Fe Trail* (1940), starring Errol Flynn as "Jeb" Stuart. ∎

Seven Days' Leave (1930), Par. *Dir.* Richard Wallace; *Sc.* John Farrow, Dan Totheroh; *Cast includes:* Gary Cooper, Beryl Mercer, Daisy Belmore, Nora Cecil, Arthur Hoyt, Arthur Metcalfe.

Gary Cooper portrays a Scottish soldier on leave in this sentimental drama. An elderly spinster (Beryl Mercer) has longed for a son. She persuades Cooper to pose as her son and shows him off to all her friends. Although the film, based on J. M. Barrie's "The Old Lady Shows Her Medals," takes place during World War I, it contains no war or battle scenes. The humanity of the film is quite effective. ∎

Seven Graves for Rogan. See *A Time to Die* (1983). ∎

Seven Seas to Calais (1963), MGM. *Dir.* Rudolph Mate; *Sc.* Filippo Sanjust, George St. George, Lindsay Galloway; *Cast includes:* Rod Taylor, Keith Michell, Irene Worth.

Rod Taylor stars as Sir Francis Drake, one of England's legendary seamen, in this adventure drama made in Italy. The film traces some of the major events in Drake's career. As the story opens, he mysteriously receives a map of Spain's settlements in the New World and those where her treasures are stored. Following his raids on Spanish wealth in the New World, he thwarts a Spanish plot to assassinate Queen Elizabeth and place Mary of Scotland on the throne of England. Finally, he is seen as the principal architect in the defeat of the Spanish Armada.

Irene Worth plays Elizabeth, a clever, conniving ruler who enjoys material possessions, especially those stolen from Spain. "We are both pirates," she says jokingly to Drake, her chief source of income. Umberto Raho, as King Philip of Spain, grows frustrated with Elizabeth's political intrigues and delays in signing a peace treaty. "I sometimes think," he confides to his advisers, "the Lord sent us Queen Elizabeth as a trial to expiate our sins and to make us worthy of the life to come."

Keith Michell, as Drake's handsome and loyal aide and confidant, and his French fiancee (Hedy Vessel) provide the only romantic interest in the film. Drake, the loner and adventurer, prefers the sea. The last scene pictures him once again steering his ship toward the horizon as his young friend, who chooses to remain in England, watches his captain sail off on some new adventure. Quoting Drake, he says to his fiancee at his side: "To endure to the end of a voyage, to reach land and taste of its comforts, to have the courage to go to sea again—that is the true glory." The script focuses more on action and escapism than on historical accuracy.

Sir Francis Drake (1543–1596), the epitome of an English Elizabethan sea corsair, did more than any other individual to establish England's naval traditions. Besides circumnavigating the globe (1577–1580), he was England's most eminent sea raider in the naval war against Spain. He was knighted by Queen Elizabeth in 1580.

From 1572 to 1595 Drake regularly attacked Spain's shipping, its New World colonies and ports on the Iberian mainland. In one daring raid in 1587, he attempted to forestall the intended invasion of England by the Spanish Armada. He attacked part of the enemy fleet in its own port of Cadiz and destroyed 33 ships. Drake advanced to vice-admiral and played a major role in the destruction of the Armada in the epic Channel battles that took place in the summer of 1588.

He was believed to be the originator of the plan to send fire ships against the Armada, anchored for repairs and provisions in the French port of Calais after sustaining losses in the initial engagement with the English. The scheme seriously weakened and disorganized the Spanish fleet. It also set the stage for the almost total destruction of the fleet a few days later in an engagement off the coast of Gravelines, a battle in which Drake played a key part. He died in 1795 and was buried at sea. ∎

Seven Weeks War. See *The Lady In Ermine* (1927). ∎

Seven Women (1965), MGM. *Dir.* John Ford; *Sc.* Janet Green, John McCormick; *Cast includes:* Anne Bancroft, Sue Lyon, Margaret Leighton, Flora Robson, Eddie Albert.

An American mission in northern China

comes under attack by Mongolian barbarians in this drama set in 1935. Margaret Leighton portrays the rigid head of the mission inhabited by women and one male teacher (Eddie Albert), a frustrated minister. A newly arrived doctor (Anne Bancroft) with a modern ideology clashes with Leighton over moral and medical issues. Bancroft swears, smokes, drinks and dresses in men's clothing, all of which disturbs the mistress of the mission. Her outspoken remarks at the dinner table shock the others who are more accustomed to their sedate, cloistered life. "Well," she addresses the only man at the table, "how does it feel to be the only rooster in this hen house?"

When the bandits seize control, they murder and rape some of the Chinese inhabitants after locking the white women in a nearby building. Bancroft is forced to submit to their chieftain (Mike Mazurki) to get her instruments returned so that she can help a fellow worker who is about to give birth. Later, she volunteers to stay with the chief if he will let the women leave. After they depart, Bancroft poisons her drink and that of the leader. The undistinguished plot of the film is reminiscent of several B movies popular in the 1930s. ■

Seven Women From Hell (1961), TCF. Dir. Robert Webb; Sc. Jesse Lasky, Jr., Pat Silver; Cast includes: Patricia Owens, Denise Darcel, Cesar Romero, Margia Dean.

Several female prisoners break out of a Japanese prison camp in New Guinea and are pursued by the enemy in this weak World War II drama. Patricia Owens, as an ornithologist, defies her captors and is determined to avoid recapture. Margia Dean, as another escapee, was a waitress before the war. Cesar Romero portrays a plantation owner who cooperates with the Japanese. The women finally make it to safety when they run into American troops. "Yanks!" they exclaim with joy. "Broads!" the soldiers shout out in reply. ■

1776 (1972), Col. Dir. Peter H. Hunt; Sc. Peter Stone; Cast includes: William Daniels, Howard Da Silva, Ken Howard, John Cullum, Roy Poole.

America's first Congress debates the issue of independence from England in this musical based on the Broadway play. While George Washington and his ragtag army battle against the British in New York,

members of the Continental Congress in Philadelphia struggle over severing the colonies' ties with their mother country. John Adams (William Daniels), the loudest rebel of the lot, antagonizes many with his haughty and bullying methods as he pushes for revolution. Benjamin Franklin (Howard Da Silva), the sophisticated and witty diplomat, quietly uses his savvy to support as well as temper the fiery Adams. Franklin's aphorisms are injected at appropriate moments. When someone suggests that they are advocating treason, Franklin quips: "Treason is a charge invented by winners to hang losers." Thomas Jefferson (Ken Howard), the reserved Southern diplomat, reluctantly joins Adams and Franklin.

The representatives overcome their first hurdle concerning independence, with Franklin making the most eloquent plea. "We've spawned a new race here," he announces, "more violent, more enterprising, less refined. We're a new nationality—we require a new nation." But they are soon confronted with another major controversy—slavery. When Jefferson in his Declaration of Independence condemns the practice of slavery, the Southern delegates, led by Edward Rutledge of South Carolina (John Cullum), protest vehemently. Rutledge presents a stinging condemnation of the North and its hypocrisy, singling out the slave traders and the bankers. A compromise is reached when Adams and Jefferson, following the advice of Franklin, agree to delete the anti-slavery clause. The film depicts these early Americans as humans instead of mythical heroes. They fight for their ideals and anguish over their compromises. The film also suggests how fragile the birth of the nation was, considering the tremendous regional conflicts that dominated the colonies two centuries ago.

Franklin (1706–1790) was already 69 years old when the American Revolution started with the Battle of Lexington and Concord in 1775. At an age that most people would consider quiet retirement, he reached a new peak of accomplishment, this time as a fighter for independence on the political and diplomatic front. His activities in support of the Revolution followed a lifetime of multiple achievements as publisher, inventor, scientist, founder of cultural and educational institutions, representative in the Continental Congress and government administrator as postmaster-general.

Franklin made several important contributions to the success of the Revolution, and his value to the cause of independence easily equaled that of any patriot military leader except for Washington. Though he and two other commissioners sent by Congress to Canada (1776) to procure assistance failed in that mission, Franklin returned to help draft the Declaration of Independence and become a signer.

He went to France (1776–1785) as part of a delegation that succeeded in gaining loans for the rebelling colonies and a treaty of alliance. The French played a major role in the defeat of Britain. In fact, France had a larger force, including troops and naval strength, at the final battle of Yorktown than the Americans.

Franklin was on the commission that negotiated a favorable peace treaty with England (1783) in which the young nation received all of Britain's former North American territory east of the Mississippi River and south of Canada. ∎

"1776, or Hessian Renegades" (1909), Biograph. *Dir.* D. W. Griffith; *Sc.* D. W. Griffith, Frank Woods; *Cast includes:* Owen Moore, Billy Quirk, Mary Pickford.

The American Revolution is the background of this short silent drama about a youth assigned to carry a dispatch for the Continental Congress. Pursued by Hessians, he hides in his father's house. The soldiers enter the home and search for the messenger. The captain, suspecting the boy is in a hamper, discharges his weapon into the basket, killing the boy. The father rouses his neighbors who take the carousing Hessians by surprise and kill them.

The Hessians were mercenary troops from the German state of Hesse. The princes of Hesse improved their own finances by hiring out troops to various nations during the 1700s. An estimated 17,000 Hessian mercenaries fought alongside the British from 1776 to 1783 during the American Revolution.

Hessian mercenaries were active in a number of important engagements in the American war for independence. The first Hessian troops, numbering around 9,000 in a force of 32,000 headed by English General Howe, made their appearance at the Battle of Long Island (August 27, 1776), in present-day Brooklyn. It was the first major battle of the revolution involving George Washington as the American commander and large concentrations of troops on both sides. A Hessian garrison at Trenton was targeted by George Washington on December 26, 1776, for the first successful American attack of the war. His main force of 2,400 crossed the ice-choked Delaware River and overwhelmed a surprised contingent of 1,400 ill-prepared defenders in an hour of confused street fighting. Hessian troops were included in the army of General Burgoyne that drove south from Canada into New York State in the summer of 1877 in a brilliantly conceived plan that ultimately failed to split the colonies. Burgoyne's surrender at Saratoga marked the first time a British army surrendered to colonial forces. Many Hessians, captured during the war, remained to settle in the U.S. after the cessation of hostilities. ∎

Seventh Cross, The (1944), MGM. *Dir.* Fred Zinnemann; *Sc.* Helen Deutsch; *Cast includes:* Spencer Tracy, Signe Hasso, Hume Cronyn, Jessica Tandy, Agnes Moorehead.

A somber, realistic World War II drama portraying the ruthlessness of the Nazis, the film, set in 1936, explores the disintegration of human values in pre-World War II Germany. It also suggests that not all Germans were ardent Nazis. Spencer Tracy portrays a prisoner in a Nazi concentration camp who, along with six other inmates, manages to escape. The commandant orders seven trees stripped bare and crosses mounted on them for the seven who have escaped. He vows to nail the escapees to the crosses after they are captured and tortured. Six of the men eventually are killed or caught, but Tracy, as the seventh, eludes the Gestapo who pursue him relentlessly. He returns to his home town where several inhabitants bravely risk their own lives to assist him. Their acts soften his own cynicism. As a result of his defiance and will to remain free, the seventh cross, an ironic symbol of Nazi Germany's mockery of religion, continues to stand empty. ∎

Seventh Heaven (1927), Fox. *Dir.* Frank Borzage; *Sc.* Benjamin Glazer; *Cast includes:* Janet Gaynor, Charles Farrell, Ben Bard, David Butler.

A romantic drama set during World War I, the film stars Janet Gaynor and Charles Farrell in the lead roles as lovers whose lives are disrupted by the war. One of the most dramatic and stirring scenes in the film concerns the French mobilization with its parade of automobiles, trucks and taxi cabs, all packed with troops, moving toward the front lines to help stem the German advance at the Marne. Otherwise there is little action in this film in which the love theme dominates.

The script makes a superficial attempt to portray war as hell. Titles such as "War is hunger!," "War is panic!," "War is lust!," and "War is death!" are eventually replaced on screen by the romance motif. Another scene, in which a French soldier likens the lethal flame-thrower to an innocuous water hose he used as a civilian, endeavors to depict the ironies of war as well as how war ultimately blunts human emotions. The prevailing love story, however, constantly defeats these half-hearted forays into antiwar territory. ∎

Shadow in the Sky (1951). See Veterans. ∎

Shadow of Terror (1945), PRC. *Dir.* Lew Landers; *Sc.* Arthur St. Claire; *Cast includes:* Richard Fraser, Grace Gillern, Cy Kendall, Emmett Lynn, Kenneth McDonald.

A routine World War II spy drama involving secret plans for the atomic bomb, the film features Richard Fraser as a research scientist who is assaulted and tossed out of a moving train. His papers are stolen by spies eager to get their hands on his new weapon. Grace Gillern, as the romantic lead, helps him to recover. Snapping out of a case of amnesia, he manages to save his plans for the bomb.

The original film never makes reference to the atom bomb by name or to the nature of the scientist's plans. The drama was finished before the two bombs were dropped over Japan. Seeing a way to exploit the atomic bomb, the studio secured government footage of test results of the new and powerful explosive and spliced it to the end of the film. A narrator then announced that this was the secret of Fraser's papers. Thus the studio was able to scoop other companies with its "topical" drama. ∎

Shadows Over Shanghai (1938). See Sino-Japanese War. ∎

Shake Hands With the Devil (1959), UA. *Dir.* Michael Anderson; *Sc.* Ivan Goff, Ben Roberts; *Cast includes:* James Cagney, Don Murray, Dana Wynter, Glynis Johns, Michael Redgrave.

The Irish Rebellion of 1921 provides the background for this tense drama about an fi-ery rebel who, once he has turned killer, finds that he cannot end his thirst for violence. James Cagney portrays a Dublin university professor who is also a leader in the Irish underground. Don Murray, as one of his students and a World War I American veteran, joins the movement. An idealist whose father who was killed while fighting for Irish freedom, Murray eventually takes up arms against the British.

The rebels engage in a series of kidnapings and killings, including the taking of a hostage—the daughter of a British dignitary. Later, one of the leaders of the cause, Cagney's superior (Michael Redgrave), announces that the movement has worked out a compromise with the British that will lead to peace, but the embittered Cagney rejects the plan and vows to continue the civil war. When a rebel sympathizer dies in a British prison, Cagney decides to assassinate the hostage. But Murray shoots him before he can carry out the cold-blooded murder. Dana Wynter, as the hostage, also provides the romantic interest in this grim and generally realistic tale of strife-torn Ireland. ∎

Shanghai Bound (1927), Par. *Dir.* Luther Reed; *Sc.* John Goodrich, Roy Harris; *Cast includes:* Richard Dix, Mary Brian, Charles Byer, George Irving, Jocelyn Lee.

Richard Dix portrays an American freighter captain on the China coast in this action drama set during the Chinese civil strife of the 1920s. A local bandit chieftain, bent on uniting the population against all white intruders, has gained control of a port. Dix manages to rescue a handful of westerners whose car is destroyed and chauffeur killed by rioters. He takes the party aboard his vessel and sails down river toward Shanghai. The whites are attacked at sea but are saved in the nick of time by a U.S. warship. Mary Brian provides the romantic interest in this minor but action-filled tale. ∎

Shanghai Express (1932), Par. *Dir.* Josef von Sternberg; *Sc.* Jules Furthman; *Cast includes:* Marlene Dietrich, Clive Brook, Anna May Wong, Warner Oland, Eugene Pallette.

This romantic drama unfolds chiefly aboard a train, the Shanghai Express, during a revolution. Shanghai Lily, played by Marlene Dietrich, is that city's most notorious white prostitute. "It took more than one man

A peaceful Irish village belies the violence of the Irish Rebellion of 1921 when the British Black and Tans capture a rebel. *Shake Hands With the Devil* (1959).

to change my name to Shanghai Lily,'' she boasts with a note of cynicism. She meets her ex-lover (Clive Brook), who is now a British army officer, aboard the train. Cool and dispassionate toward each other at first, they slowly rekindle their former relationship. Suddenly the train ride is interrupted by a rebel warlord (Warner Oland) and his revolutionary forces. Seeking a hostage whom he can exchange for the return of one of his lieutenants captured by the government, he settles on Brook. When Oland threatens to burn out his captive's eyes, Dietrich volunteers to become the Chinese general's mistress. After he is freed, Brook misunderstands her decision, thinking she has again betrayed him, until another passenger explains Dietrich's sacrifice. Brook returns to rescue his love, Oland is killed by a Chinese girl and the train journey resumes. The film was released at an opportune time to help its box-office sales. Newspapers carried numerous stories of China's military struggle against both Communist and Japanese forces. A pale, updated remake with the Sino–Japanese War as background appeared in 1943 under the title

Night Plane From Chungking. See also Chinese Civil Wars. ■

Shawnee Indian Wars (1774, 1794–1795, 1811–1814). This warlike North American tribe emigrated among several eastern states before settling in Ohio in the mid-1700s. The tribe had an extensive record of conflict with settlers during the American colonial period. In Lord Dunsmore's War (1774), Virginia's colonial governor, the Earl of Dunsmore, had to dispatch a force under General Andrew Lewis to subdue a Shawnee uprising on the Virginia–Kentucky border. Lewis decisively defeated the tribe on October 10, and the Indians sued for peace.

General Anthony Wayne defeated the Shawnee at the Battle of Fallen Timbers in 1794. As a result of the Treaty of Greenville (1795), the Indians were forced to surrender their land in northwest Ohio. *Daniel Boone, Trail Blazer* (1957), a routine film set in the late 1700s, presents the Shawnee, after being stirred up by British soldiers and a French renegade, as hostile to white settlers.

The tribe moved again to Indiana where

they located their main village on the Tippecanoe River. Many were rabid followers of
their great war chief Tecumseh. A charismatic Indian leader of the early 1800s, he
urged the formation of a confederation of
tribes as a means of resisting further white
encroachment. In 1811 General William
Henry Harrison defeated the Shawnee at the
Battle of Tippecanoe. His victory helped him
in his bid for the presidency.

The Shawnee assisted British forces in the
War of 1812. In *Brave Warrior* (1952), the plot
incorrectly has a U.S. government agent (Jon
Hall) preventing the Shawnee from joining
the British. Hall ultimately gains the confidence and assistance of Tecumseh (Jay Silverheels). Historically, Tecumseh was consistently hostile to the fledgling nation. In
fact, he helped inspire the fight against the
U.S. in the Creek War of 1813. General Andrew Jackson, leading the Tennessee militia
and friendly Cherokee warriors, defeated a
large force of Indians at the Battle of Horseshoe Bend (March 27, 1814). The Shawnee
were forced to make further moves westward
across the Mississippi during the 1800s before finally settling on a reservation in Oklahoma, where some of their descendants live
today. ∎

John Holland and Eleanor Boardman take a grim
view of World War I. *She Goes to War* (1929).

She Goes to War (1929), UA. Dir. Henry
King; *Sc.* Mrs. Fred De Grace; *Cast includes:*
Eleanor Boardman, John Holland, Alma
Rubens, Glen Waters, Al St. John.

A World War I comedy drama emphasizing
the woman's role during the conflict, the
film, mostly silent with some dialogue, stars
Eleanor Boardman as a spoiled socialite who
journeys to France in search of excitement.
She finds work in a service canteen. Meanwhile her cowardly fiance (Edmund Burns),
another member of the idle rich, shirks his
responsibilities as a soldier. When the time
comes for his outfit to move up, he avoids
going. Boardman, wishing to learn about the
war first-hand, disguises herself and goes in
his place. Circumstances permit her to save
the command as well as to fall in love with
another soldier, a strong-willed lieutenant
(John Holland) who is more worthy than her
former beau. Much of the plot is implausible.
Several effective battle scenes include an allied tank advance through a flaming barrier.
There are poignant moments, too, such as the
one in which a soldier, thinking of his
mother, dies in the arms of another canteen
worker.

Alma Rubens, who provides much of the
comedy, was a heroin addict who died of
pneumonia two years after the film was released. This was her last screen
appearance. ∎

She Wore a Yellow Ribbon (1949), RKO.
Dir. John Ford; *Sc.* Frank Nugent, Laurence
Stallings; *Cast includes:* John Wayne, Joanne
Dru, John Agar, Ben Johnson, Harry Carey, Jr.,
Victor McLaglen.

Life on a remote army post in the Southwest where the U.S. Cavalry is assigned to
monitor the restless Apaches forms the background of this drama. John Wayne portrays a
captain who is about to retire but remains
long enough to prevent an Indian uprising.
Victor McLaglen, as his loyal sergeant, contributes much of the comic relief, including
an old-fashioned saloon brawl. Placed under
arrest, he is warned by his fellow soldiers to
come along peacefully. "I've never done anything peacefully in my life," he announces as
he begins the fray.

Director John Ford provides sufficient
details about the daily lives of the men in the
cavalry to give the film a ring of authenticity.
He also gives a realistic picture of the women
who braved the hardships of life on an army
post and the dangers that they and their
loved ones faced. Besides these injections of
accurate army-post life, Ford presents
through his personal vision his strongest
tribute to the U.S. military. The film, whose
visual beauty was inspired in part by the

western paintings of Frederic Remington, won cameraman Winton Hoch an Academy Award for Best Color Cinematography. ∎

Shell 43 (1916), Triangle. *Dir.* Reginald Barker; *Sc.* C. Gardner Sullivan; *Cast includes:* H. B. Warner, Enid Markey, Jack Gilbert, George Fisher.

A World War I spy drama, the film includes numerous trench and battle sequences as well as a suspenseful story. A British spy (H. B. Warner) poses as an American war correspondent. He has a German pass that allows him to move freely on the battlefield. In the final scene the heroic agent sacrifices his own life to knock out a strategic location. Knowing it will mean his own death, he secretly telephones a message to British headquarters to "shell Pit 43."

One of the early war movies to feature a British subject as hero, American film studios seemed to have their own hierarchy of national hero during the conflict. Americans were featured in the largest number of entries, followed by the British and then the French. For some unknown reason, other Allies, such as the Italians and Belgians, provided few screen heroes or heroines. ∎

Shenandoah (1913). See Battles of Shenandoah Valley. ∎

Shenandoah (1965), U. *Dir.* Andrew V. McLaglen; *Sc.* James Lee Barrett; *Cast includes:* James Stewart, Doug McClure, Glenn Corbett, Patrick Wayne, Rosemary Forsyth.

A strong-willed Virginia patriarch attempts to keep his family untouched by the Civil War that rages around his farm in this drama set in 1863. James Stewart portrays a widower who struggles unsuccessfully to keep his six sons and one daughter safe from the ravages of war. But Stewart and his family soon become steeped in the conflict when his 16-year-old son is mistakenly taken prisoner as a Confederate soldier and his prize horses are almost confiscated. He sets out with some of his sons to rescue his boy. During the search one of his sons is killed by a Confederate sentry while another, who has remained to care for the farm, is murdered by a looter. Following several action sequences, Stewart and his family, after failing to find the boy, return home. Stewart goes to his wife's grave site on his farm and tries to make sense of the turbulence around him. "It's like all wars, I

suppose," he concludes as if addressing his wife. "The undertakers are winning it, the politicians will talk a lot about the glory of it and the old men will talk about the need of it. But the soldiers—they just want to go home." Meanwhile the boy, who has escaped from a prisoner-of-war camp, returns to the town church where he is greeted by his family. The film, which depicts some of the tragedies of the war, became the basis for a successful Broadway musical of the same name. ∎

Shenandoah Valley, Battles of (July 2–October 19, 1864). During the American Civil War the Shenandoah Valley was a potential dagger for the Confederacy aimed at the heart of the Union. From the western side of Virginia's Blue Ridge Mountains, the valley ran in a southwest-to-northeast direction into western Maryland and southern Pennsylvania. The valley, at its northern end, skirted the western approaches to Washington, D.C., and Baltimore, and pointed at the North's eastern industrial heartland.

Confederate General Robert E. Lee, under increasing pressure from Grant near Richmond in early 1864, sent an army under General Jubal Early up the Shenandoah Valley in July to force Grant to relinquish some of his troops for the defense of the Union capital and southern Pennsylvania. Early, by July 11, had crossed the Potomac and advanced to within five miles of Washington. A hastily assembled Union army composed of elements of Grant's force that had been hurried from Virginia, together with troops of walking wounded and army clerks scraped together from the national capital, stopped the Confederates. But as long as the South had troops in the area, they would be a constant menace to the North's nerve-center.

Grant picked General Philip H. Sheridan, a hard-driving cavalry officer who had made a name for himself in the western campaign, to put an end to the Southern threat. Sheridan, often marshaling his troops at the front on horseback, defeated Early at Winchester (September 19) and Fisher's Hill (September 22). Sheridan turned an almost sure loss into a victory at Cedar Creek (October 19) to drive his opponent back into Virginia. He then emulated Sherman's scorched-earth policy further south and proceeded to lay waste to most of the rich Confederate farmlands of the Shenandoah Valley, thus denying the resources of that region to the enemy for the balance of the war.

Jubal A. Early (1816–1894), an 1837 graduate of West Point, was a competent Union army officer during the Seminole War (1837–38) and Mexican War (1846–48) who achieved a degree of fame as a Confederate commander during the Civil War. Though he was personally against secession, his sense of duty to his native state compelled him to fight for the South. Early saw action in a number of engagements in Virginia, including the First Battle of Bull Run (1861) and later at Gettysburg (1863). He achieved his greatest prominence as head of an invasion force in the Shenandoah valley.

Several early silent films dramatize the battles and highlight Sheridan's ride from Winchester to Cedar Creek, including "Sheridan's Ride" and "In the Shenandoah Valley," both released in 1908; another film titled "Sheridan's Ride" made by a different studio in 1912; and *Shenandoah* (1913), which also focuses on General Early. ■

Sheridan, Philip H. (1831–1888). The Union's leading Cavalry general, Sheridan was equally popular with General Grant, his military superior, and with his troops. Grant considered Sheridan the ideal general who always stressed attack, no matter what the odds or conditions, as the way to shorten and win the Civil War. Sheridan's soldiers responded to his front-line approach to leadership in which he made inspiring battlefield gallops to urge on and support his men.

His major contribution was his decisive defeat of General Jubal Early in a series of battles for control of Virginia's Shenandoah Valley during the summer of 1864. His victory denied to the South the use of the long, broad valley as an invasion route into the North. Additionally, Sheridan, by scorching the valley, neutralized the area's agricultural importance to the Confederacy. "Sheridan's Ride" (1908), "In the Shenandoah Valley" (1908), "Sheridan's Ride" (1912) and *Shenandoah* (1913) all relate to his battles during the summer of 1864.

He also took part in the last engagement of the Civil War when his forces, circling behind Lee's retreating army, cut Southern communications lines and then repelled Lee's desperate counterattack to break out of growing encirclement at Five Forks (April 1, 1865), near Petersburg, Virginia. Lee surren-

dered his rapidly weakening army on April 9 to end the war. Sheridan is also characterized in *Custer of the West* (1968) as a feisty figure as portrayed by Lawrence Tierney. ■

"Sheridan's Ride" (1908, 1912). See Battles of Shenandoah Valley. ■

Sherlock Holmes and the Secret Weapon (1942). See Detectives at War. ■

Sherlock Holmes in Washington (1943). See Detectives at War. ■

Sherman, William Tecumseh (1820–1891). He was, next to Ulysses S. Grant, probably the Union's most successful and best known Civil War general. His famous march through the South undertaken in the summer of 1864 cut a swath of devastation deep behind enemy lines, resulting in the capture and burning of Atlanta and seizure of the port of Savannah. Sherman believed in destroying an enemy's economy. "War is cruel and you cannot refine it," he said to Atlanta officials who protested the wholesale destruction by fire of their city by Sherman's troops. The recreation of the burning of Atlanta plays an important role in the epic Civil War film *Gone With the Wind* (1939). His destructive trek through the South is depicted in several films, including *When Sherman Marched to the Sea* and Griffith's Civil War masterpiece, *The Birth of a Nation*, both released in 1915.

Prior to that campaign, Sherman, a West Point graduate who had served in the Mexican War, participated in a number of important engagements, including the First Battle of Bull Run, Shiloh, Grant's Vicksburg campaign that split the Confederacy at the Mississippi River, and Chattanooga. He set out on his drive to the sea from Chattanooga, Tennessee, in May, 1864, with about 60,000 men and few supplies with instructions to live off the land. He used flanking tactics and maneuvering rather than a series of stand-up battles to gradually force back General Johnston's Confederate forces deeper into Georgia. The capture of Atlanta, an important rail and supply center, on September 2, 1864, was a severe blow for the South. Sherman's troops set fire to most of the city before embarking two months later on the rest of their drive to the sea.

After taking Savannah, Sherman turned northward into the Carolinas to lay waste some of the South's richest farmland. His mission was not to seek battle but to destroy the South's will to resist. Many years later, he said, "I am tired and sick of war. Its glory is all moonshine. It is only those who have neither fired a shot nor heard the shrieks and groans of the wounded who cry aloud for blood, more vengeance, more destruction. War is hell." After the Civil War, Sherman succeeded Grant as commander of the army, a position he held until his retirement in 1884. ∎

"Sherman Said It" (1933). See War Humor. ∎

She's in the Army (1942). See Women and War. ∎

Shifting Sands (1918). See Spy Films: the Silents. ∎

Shiloh, Battle of. The battle that took place on April 6–7, 1862, in the southwest corner of Tennessee in the early stages of the American Civil Was was important for several reasons. It was the goriest engagement of the conflict up to that time with combined casualties of 24,000 out of a total of slightly over 100,000 troops that took part from both sides.

Also known as the Battle of Pittsburg Landing, it witnessed the emergence of Union General Ulysses S. Grant as a victorious leader in a major engagement. Furthermore, the Union victory drove the Confederacy out of the border state of Tennessee and firmed up support for the North in neighboring Kentucky. In addition, it opened the way to a successful drive down the Mississippi Valley that was to result, before the year's end, in the splitting of the Confederacy. Grant's success in the west, at a time when the Union was unable to secure a major advantage in the east, made him prominent among Lincoln's generals.

After winning two earlier engagements at Fort Donelson and Fort Henry on the Tennessee–Kentucky border, Grant pursued the Confederates southward towards Shiloh. A surprise attack at Shiloh by Southern General Albert Johnston caught Grant unprepared and near defeat. But Johnston's death during the first day of the fight and the arrival of reinforcements during the night enabled Grant the following day (April 7) to resume the attack and force the enemy to retreat. The battle illustrated Grant's qualities of dogged perseverance and his penchant for attack that were eventually to gain him command of the Union armies.

Considering its importance, the battle is the subject of relatively few features. *The Battle of Shiloh*, the only film devoted entirely to the conflict, appeared in 1913. *So Red the Rose* (1935), a generally weak romantic drama of a Southern family and starring Margaret Sullavan and Randolph Scott, includes a credible but short recreation of the bloody results of the battle. *Journey to Shiloh* (1968), with James Caan, Michael Sarrazin and Harrison Ford (in his pre-*Star Wars* days), is a pretentious rite-of-passage action drama of seven friends who journey from Texas to join the Confederates at Shiloh. ∎

Ship Ahoy (1942). See Musicals. ∎

Ship Comes In, A (1928), Pathe. *Dir.* William K. Howard; *Sc.* Julien Josephson; *Cast includes:* Rudolph Schildkraut, Louise Dresser, Robert Edeson, Milton Holmes.

An immigrant's faith in America never wavers as he undergoes one adversity after another in this patriotic drama set during World War I. Rudolph Schildkraut portrays the Hungarian immigrant who happily works as a janitor in a government building. An anarchist cousin tries to influence him, but he will have none of this chatter against the land that he has adopted. When his time comes to receive his citizenship papers, he is so overjoyed that he has his wife bake the judge a cake. However, his villainous cousin conceals a bomb in the cake. It explodes and wounds the judge. Schildkraut is arrested and jailed. Meanwhile the unfortunate victim loses his son in the war. He is eventually released and returns to his janitorial duties.

The use of European immigrants as main screen characters was carried over from the previous decade when such films as Charlie Chaplin's *The Immigrant* were popular, especially in the cities which housed large populations of foreigners. It is doubtful whether the children of these immigrants, who made up a large portion of the movie audience during the 1920s, would be as absorbed by the subject matter as their parents seemed to be. ∎

Shock (1934), Mon. *Dir.* Roy J. Pomeroy; *Sc.* Madeline Ruthven; *Cast includes:* Ralph Forbes, Gwen Gill, Monroe Owsley, Reginald Sharland, David Jack Holt.

Ralph Forbes portrays a British officer in the World War I drama who is reassigned to the front lines following his marriage to Gwen Gill. He volunteers for a dangerous mission and suffers shell shock. He returns home and is nursed by his wife. An officer whom he helped at the front causes some marital problems for Forbes, but all is resolved after the war. Battle scenes are effective although rather limited. ■

Shootin' for Love (1923). See Veterans. ■

Shopworn Angel, The (1929), Par. Dir. Richard Wallace; Sc. Howard Estabrook, Albert LeVino; *Cast includes:* Nancy Carroll, Gary Cooper, Paul Lukas, Emmett King.

A remake of the 1919 silent feature *Pettigrew's Girl*, this part-sound version co-stars Gary Cooper as a naive soldier from Texas who falls in love with a Broadway entertainer (Nancy Carroll). Cooper, on leave from his army camp, meets and almost immediately falls for the showgirl. But she seems more interested in her affair with a millionaire (Paul Lukas) and the material gifts he bestows upon her. "That's what good little girls get for doing what their mommas told them not to," she boasts, displaying some of her diamonds. When Cooper is about to leave aboard a transport for France and the front lines, Carroll has a change of heart and realizes she cares more for the soldier.

The plot was to be adapted two more times by MGM, which purchased the script from Paramount, for *Shopworn Angel* (1938) starring Margaret Sullavan and James Stewart and *That Kind of Woman* (1956) with Sophia Loren and Tab Hunter. ■

Shoshone Indians. A tribe of North American plains Indians residing in Wyoming, the Shoshone (or Shoshoni) were badly decimated in the late 1700s by a smallpox plague. This was probably the result of contact with white people, since the Indians, having never encountered the disease before, had never developed any immunity toward it. The Shoshone, along with several other plains tribes, were the natural enemy of the Sioux. In fact, well into the 1870s, Shoshone braves acted as scouts for the U.S. Cavalry in its battles against the Sioux.

Hollywood made few films about the Shoshone, concentrating instead on those tribes with a longer and more colorful military history, such as the Apache. Anthony Mann's *Devil's Doorway* (1950) presented an articulate statement about the plight of the Indian. Robert Taylor, as a Shoshone chief who won the Congressional Medal of Honor in the Civil War, returns to his Wyoming ranch only to have it taken from him by others. He is informed that, since the law does not consider him an American citizen, he cannot own land. *Oregon Passage* (1957) is based in part on the true exploits of the Shoshone warrior Black Eagle. The U.S. Cavalry pursues the Shoshone chief who rejects any overtures of peace in this drama set in the Northwest in 1871. ■

Charlie Chaplin (c.), caught up in the complexities of World War I, pauses for a moment. *Shoulder Arms* (1918).

Shoulder Arms (1918), FN. Dir. Charlie Chaplin; Sc. Charlie Chaplin; *Cast includes:* Charlie Chaplin, Edna Purviance, Sydney Chaplin, Jack Wilson, Henry Bergman, Albert Austin, Tom Wilson, John Rand, Park Jones, Loyal Underwood.

A fantasy–comedy set during World War I and considered Chaplin's best film to date, this three-reeler contains much satire as well as conventional gags. It tells the story of one average doughboy's daily life in the trenches—as envisioned by Chaplin. But he simply doesn't make a very good soldier because can't seem to get instructions straight. During guard duty he dreams of city night life and good times, shown in split-screen. One of the highlights of the film occurs when Charlie is assigned to spy on the enemy. He camouflages himself inside a tree trunk in the middle of no-man's land until a German soldier, sent to gather some wood for a fire, begins chopping at Chaplin's disguise. Charlie knocks him down as he does others who follow their comrade. Finally, another enemy gets wise and chases Charlie into a forest. Another very engaging sequence is his capture of 13 German soldiers. When someone asks how he managed this feat, he replies: "I surrounded them."

Chaplin's original purpose was to make a five-reel film which he intended to exhibit as a full-length feature. Hollywood pundits cautioned him against this as well as warning him about poking fun at the war which was still raging in Europe. The comedian compromised on the length—but not the subject matter—by omitting early domestic scenes of Charlie as civilian. Today's audiences may find the film rather dated. Digressing from his more familiar universal themes, Chaplin focused on trench life, lice, mud, food packages, superstitions such as three soldiers using the same match, stereotyped German soldiers and other contemporary items relating to the war.

The film caused some controversy for its star. Several of his critics wanted to know why he didn't enlist in the service when war broke out, or why he didn't return to his native England to join up with his fellow countrymen. In fact, he was rejected by his draft board due to ill health. Aside from its strong antiwar sentiment, the film underlines the camaraderie that exists among the common soldiers. ■

Side Show of Life, The (1924), Par. *Dir.* Herbert Brenon; *Sc.* W. J. Locke; *Cast includes:* Ernest Torrence, Anna Q. Nilsson, Louise Lagrange, Maurice Cannon, Neil Hamilton.

Ernest Torrence portrays a clown in a French circus when World War I breaks out. He enlists to fight with the British and soon rises to the rank of colonel. During a battle he saves the life of a captain who invites the former clown to stay at his home during his leave. He receives news that he has been made a brigadier general. As he is about to celebrate his new promotion, an armistice is declared. All that is left for the clown is to return to his former work. He locates his former partner, a young woman, and together they perform their old act. But his heart is not in it, and the audience shows its disapproval with catcalls and other derogatory exclama-

tions. His partner returns from his dressing room and holds up his Legion of Honor Cross, announcing the last rank he had held. The audience applauds while the clown apologizes for his poor performance. A fellow soldier offers him an opportunity to start life over with a new career in Australia. ■

Siege at Red River, The (1954), TCF. *Dir.* Rudolph Mate; *Sc.* Sydney Boehm; *Cast includes:* Van Johnson, Joanne Dru, Richard Boone, Milburn Stone.

The Civil War provides the background for this action drama set in the West. Two Confederate soldiers (Van Johnson and Milburn Stone) masquerade as pitchmen of a medicine show. Hidden in their wagon is a Gatling gun recently stolen from Union troops. While they are transporting it west, an outlaw (Richard Boone) steals it from them and sells it to hostile Indians who use it to attack a Union outpost. Johnson decides to help the besieged fort. Then news of General Lee's surrender arrives and all rejoice. Joanne Dru plays a Union nurse who at first rejects Johnson's amorous advances.

The Gatling gun, the first practical machine gun, was invented by Richard Jordan Gatling (1818–1903), an American inventor, around 1862. He demonstrated an early model that same year to the Union Army. A number of other multi-firing weapons were in existence in the U.S. prior to Gatling's device, but none operated as successfully. The first model consisted of a single barrel with a rotating chamber into which was placed a paper cartridge and percussion cap.

Around the same time Gatling was developing his weapon, a new brass cartridge made its appearance that Gatling incorporated into a revised gun design. The weapon, automatically loaded and fired by an operator turning a hand crank, could deliver up to 3,000 rounds per minute.

The device, although used in limited fashion by the Union Army near the end of the Civil War, was not officially accepted by the Army Ordinance Department until 1866. It became a standard military weapon for many years following the American Civil War (1861–1865) and was used effectively against Indians in the later stages of the American Indian Wars. The American slang term "gat," for pistol, was derived from a shortened corruption of the inventor's name. ■

Sign of the Pagan (1954), U. *Dir.* Douglas Sirk; *Sc.* Oscar Brodney, Barre Lyndon; *Cast includes:* Jeff Chandler, Jack Palance, Ludmilla Tcherina, Rita Gam.

Attila the Hun sweeps across Europe and is ready to loose his barbarian horde upon Rome in this costume drama. Jack Palance portrays Attila, who fears the Lord more than he does the Roman legions. Jeff Chandler, as a centurion general, is delegated to defend Rome against the Scourge of God. Ludmilla Tcherina, as a princess, appoints Chandler to his new post. Attila's daughter (Rita Gam) is killed by him when she converts to Christianity. Attila ultimately is stopped by the spirit of this relatively new religion which he hesitates to defy. The film was originally released in 3-D.

As king of the Huns from 445–453, Attila was sometimes referred to as the "Scourge of God" for his attacks upon the Eastern and Western Roman empires. Previously he was co-ruler of the Huns from 434–445 with his brother Bleda whom he had murdered. Attila ruled an empire that stretched roughly from the Caspian Sea in the east to the Baltics and Alps in the west. For a number of years, he received tribute from the Eastern Roman emperor, Theodosius II. However, claiming that Theodosius failed to continue his payments in 441, Attila invaded Rome's Balkan provinces and ravaged sections of present-day Yugoslavia, Bulgaria, Greece and Turkey. In the peace treaty that followed, Attila doubled the amount of tribute he received from the eastern empire. Attila also received some payments from the western empire.

In 450 Attila became involved in a dispute over the selection of a Frankish chieftain in the western empire. Relations between the western empire and the Huns became even more strained when Honoria, the sister of the western emperor, Valentinian, secretly offered herself in marriage to Attila and he demanded half of the western empire as her dowry. Attila led an army estimated at half a million troops and invaded Gaul and northern Italy in 451–452. He was defeated at Chalons, in present day France in 451. He never attempted to take Rome, probably because of a shortage of provisions and a spreading plague among the Hun forces.

He was preparing to attack the Eastern empire in 453, claiming that the new ruler, Marcian, had refused to continue paying tribute agreed to by his predecessor. However, Attila died in 453 of a nasal hemorrhage during a wedding celebration of his latest marriage. His empire was split up among his sons. ∎

Silent Command, The (1923). See Panama Canal. ∎

Silent Lover, The (1926), FN. *Dir.* George Archainbaud; *Sc.* Carey Wilson; *Cast includes:* Milton Sills, Natalie Kingston, William Humphrey, Arthur Carewe, Viola Dana, Charlie Murray, Montagu Love.

A satire of the "sheik" films, this broad comedy stars Milton Sills as an officer in the French Foreign Legion who competes with a sheik for the heroine (Natalie Kingston). Other more unlikely Legionnaires include screen comic Charlie Murray as O'Reilly and Arthur Stone as Greenbaum, two incompetents whose respective dialects add to the humor.

The sentimental and romantic desert films of the 1920s were highly popular with movie audiences although several critics continually attacked them on various grounds. This burlesque, and Ben Turpin's wildly funny *The Shriek of Araby* (1923), were two of the rare spoofs of the genre. ∎

Silk-Lined Burglar, The (1919). See Detectives at War. ∎

Silver Car, The (1921), Vitagraph. *Dir.* David Smith; *Sc.* Wyndham Martin; *Cast includes:* Earle Williams, Kathlyn Adams, Geoffrey Webb, Eric Mayne, Emmett King.

A melodrama set during World War I, the film concerns two young men, an American and an Englishman, both of whom enlist in the army to escape their past. The American is an international thief with a price on his head, while the other has committed forgery. Both meet in the service and, while under heavy attack and not expected to survive, they confess their crimes to each other. They come through the battle in one piece, and the American seeks out his companion, meets the fellow's sister and becomes entangled in political intrigues. ∎

Since You Went Away (1944), UA. *Dir.* John Cromwell; *Sc.* David O. Selznick; *Cast includes:* Claudette Colbert, Jennifer Jones, Joseph Cotten, Shirley Temple, Monty Woolley, Lionel Barrymore.

The trials and tribulations of an American family during World War II are explored in this perceptive and idealized domestic drama. Claudette Colbert, as the heroic wife of a captain, struggles to raise her family while her husband is gone. Jennifer Jones and Shirley Temple play her two daughters. In one sequence they journey to New York where they hope to see their husband and father before he leaves for overseas duty. But they arrive too late. On board a train home they meet a fellow passenger, an elderly gentleman who says he has a daughter the same age as Jennifer Jones. When Colbert asks where she is, the strangers replies: "I don't know. You see, she was at Corregidor."

Later, Colbert receives the dreaded telegram: "Your husband reported missing in action." Following her initial collapse, she regains her strength and resolves to go on. She obtains work as a welder while her daughters become infatuated with soldiers Guy Madison and Robert Walker. On Christmas Eve she receives a phone call. "He's coming home, he's coming home!" she shouts while running up the stairs to her daughters.

Although some of the scenes seem cloying today, and too many characters are overly good-natured, the film remains a panoramic view of life on the home front during the war years. There are poignant scenes of rehabilitation centers and psychiatrists' offices, all designed to help the returning soldier adjust to civilian life while his family waits patiently for his recovery. Other scenes include a dance at an army camp and a painful farewell at a train station. The film received several Oscar nominations, but only Max Steiner's musical score won an Academy Award. ∎

"Sinews of War, The" (1913), Broncho. *Dir.* Thomas Ince; *Sc.* Thomas Ince; *Cast includes:* Charles Ray, Joe King, Mildred Bracken.

The Civil War furnishes the background for this silent romantic drama of a daughter of the South (Mildred Bracken) who falls in love with a Union officer (Charles Ray). When he is captured by Confederate troops, the girl's brother helps him to escape. Later, the grateful officer comes to the girl's rescue and saves her life. The film includes several battle sequences of the war. ∎

Sino–Japanese War (1937–1945). When Chinese and Japanese troops exchanged shots on July 7, 1937, near the Marco Polo Bridge not far from Beijing, the clash provided Japan with an opportunity to do what its military leaders had been planning for some time—launch a full-scale invasion of China. Japan had been following a policy of aggression towards China since World War I, including the invasion and conquest of Manchuria in 1931. Between 1934–1937, Japan continued to expand its presence in northern China. As Asia's leading military and industrial power, Japan felt confident it could quickly carve another slice out of backward and strife-torn China, as it did in Manchuria a few years before.

Some historians consider this conflict, which the Japanese referred to as the "China Incident," to be the opening shot of World War II. The documentary *The Four Hundred Million* (1939), with its pro-Chinese theme, traces the origins of the Sino–Japanese War. The number of participants expanded in 1941 to include the U.S., Britain and their allies when Japan bombed Pearl Harbor, Hawaii, and brought the U.S. into World War II. Steven Spielberg's visually evocative *Empire of the Sun* (1987) concerns western nationals in China who were captured by the Japanese as the war spread.

Japanese forces, though less numerous than their opponents, had superior equipment and leadership. Japan had the world's third largest navy and the only capable air force in Asia. Their planes rained considerable destruction upon Chinese cities. *Shadows Over Shanghai* (1938), a low-budget drama, includes actual footage of the destruction of Shanghai. *North of Shanghai* (1939), a spy drama with James Craig and Betty Furness, includes sequences of the bombing of Chinese cities and the war in general. In slightly more than a year of fighting, Japan controlled all of China's main ports, such as Canton and Shanghai, and had captured a number of important cities.

Chiang kai-Shek, China's Nationalist leader, was forced to move his capital inland twice because of Japanese conquests. The fall of Nanking (December 13, 1937) resulted in several days of widespread slaughter and rape of its inhabitants that historians refer to as the "Rape of Nanking." The 1943 documentary *Battle of China* graphically describes Japanese brutality in Nanking along with its coverage of the Sino–Japanese War in general.

Surprisingly, Chiang's government did not collapse, despite the enormity of China's early defeats. The Nationalists, as they did in Shanghai, moved inland whatever industry they could and continued in the war. A sizable Chinese Communist movement under Mao dze-Dung, though it had clashed repeatedly with the Nationalists in the past, now stressed the battle against a common enemy. It fielded its own forces against Japan as well as giving assistance to Chiang's troops.

Neither Japan nor China officially declared war. Both preferred this state of affairs because it allowed them to continue receiving supplies from the U.S. whose 1937 Neutrality Law prohibited trading with nations at war. Japan, however, had the advantage; all her ports were open while she controlled her enemy's ports. China was forced to bring supplies overland from Russia, her major source, over the Burma Road and from French Indo-China. Russian assistance halted in 1941 when Russia and Japan signed a neutrality pact. The Burma Road was also closed at times.

Between 1939 and 1941, relations between Japan and the U.S. deteriorated. The latter, fearing continued Japanese militarism, warned Japan repeatedly to stop its aggression and finally stopped selling her scrap steel and aviation fuel. Additionally, in 1941, the U.S. allowed American military pilots to join General Claire Chennault's Flying Tigers, a volunteer air force helping China. When the U.S. came into the war as a result of Japan's bombing of Pearl Harbor, American pilots played a major role in flying supplies "over the hump" (the Himalayas), and American truckers ran supply convoys over the reopened British Burma Road.

Hollywood during World War II produced several films using the Sino–Japanese conflict as background. All were sympathetic to the Chinese while showing the Japanese as ruthless aggressors. The main characters often were Americans of heroic stature who either believed in the Chinese struggle or were ultimately converted to the Chinese cause. *A Yank on the Burma Road* (1942) tells of an American (Barry Nelson) hired by the Chinese to lead a truck convoy carrying medical supplies to Chungking. Action sequences include Chinese forces battling and defeating Japanese troops encamped in the nearby hills. When Alan Ladd's truck in the drama *China* (1943) is strafed by the Japanese, he decides to join the Chinese. A particularly brutal scene depicts three Japanese soldiers raping a young Chinese woman. *Night Plane From Chungking* (1943), a routine spy drama, features Robert Preston as an American pilot working for the Chinese army.

A few films concerned the struggles of Chinese guerrillas during the war. In *Lady From Chungking* (1943), for example, a guerrilla leader (Anna May Wong) organizes Chinese peasant farmers against the Japanese oppressor. In *China Sky* (1945) a Chinese patriot (Anthony Quinn) leads his gallant fighters against a Japanese invasion of their village. The film is based on the novel by Pearl S. Buck.

Hollywood gave short shrift to the Chinese phase of World War II. China struggled and suffered the longest against Japan while tying down the bulk of enemy ground forces. However, far fewer films depicted this part of the conflict as compared to the number about the European war. This may have resulted from considerably fewer Americans being involved in China than in the western theatre. An additional reason may be the European orientation of our population and culture. See Flying Tigers, World War II. ■

Sins of Man (1936), TCF. *Dir.* Otto Brower, Gregory Ratoff; *Sc.* Samuel Engel, Fred Kohner, Ossip Dymov; *Cast includes:* Jean Hersholt, Don Ameche, Allen Jenkins, J. Edward Bromberg, Ann Shoemaker.

Jean Hersholt portrays a poor church bell ringer in an Austrian village in this sentimental drama that spans 20 years. While he is in America, his village is wiped out by the Italians during World War I. The story jumps two decades, showing Hersholt as a weak old man employed as a porter. He hears a symphonic recording that reminds him of the bells of his old village and learns that the conductor is his formerly deaf son whom he thought was lost in the war. The young man, under a new name and the present toast of Milan, had regained his hearing during the conflict. Father and son are reunited. ■

Sioux Wars (1862–1891). The names and events are familiar to most Americans— chiefs Sitting Bull and Crazy Horse, Custer's Last Stand, the Battle of Wounded Knee. All are part of a well-known legacy of the Sioux

Indians to American history. It was, however, a bitter legacy of hatred on both sides. "We must act with vindictive firmness against the Sioux," said General William Tecumseh Sherman who was sent west to help contain the Indians after the war. He later advocated ". . . their extermination, (including) men, women and children."

The Sioux were one of the largest Indian nations north of the Rio Grande. More than any other tribe, their way of life became the basis for the stereotyped Indian. Their culture was built around fearless warriors who were adept horse-riders, life in tepee villages and buffalo hunting. They had a semi-nomadic tradition, a sense of reverence for their hunting grounds and a record of violent resistance to the white man's rule.

The Sioux controlled an area that included the present-day prairie states of Wisconsin, Minnesota, Iowa and North and South Dakota. Though the U.S. and the tribe made several treaties before 1862, the two sides fought four major wars between 1862 and 1891 over white encroachment upon treaty territory and unscrupulous practices by white traders.

A portion of the tribe under Chief Little Crow rebelled in 1862 over mistreatment by whites. The Sioux first ambushed an army unit from Fort Ridgely on the Minnesota River, then attacked the fort itself. The hostiles went on to cut a destructive swath through the Minnesota territory, indiscriminately killing men, women and children. They massacred some 800 settlers and soldiers before being subdued. Minnesota Governor Henry H. Sibley, leading a volunteer force, defeated the Sioux, under Little Crow, in several battles during 1862 and 1863 in present-day North Dakota. A farmer shot and killed Little Crow in 1863. After General Alfred Sully had inflicted additional defeats on the tribe in 1864, a short-lived peace followed.

The Dakota Sioux were back on the warpath from 1865 to 1868 because of a growing parade of wagon trains and miners through their land. They regularly attacked army units and working parties sent to build forts to protect the Bozeman Trail that ran through their lands from Fort Laramie, Wyoming, to Montana's gold-mining areas. One such attack resulted in the Fetterman Massacre (1866).

Chief Red Cloud, after notifying the government his tribe would not tolerate the construction of forts on tribal lands, enforced his warning with an attack on a work party from Fort Kearny, Wyoming. When Captain William Fetterman was sent with a rescue force to help the besieged workers, Red Cloud and 1,500 warriors wiped out the army unit of 83 men in an ambush. The massacre was re-enacted in the 1951 drama *Tomahawk*. The film also accurately pointed out the Sioux's growing discontent with a series of broken treaties by the U.S. government and the incursion of whites into Indian territory.

In the following summer (August 2, 1867) another encounter— the Wagon Box Raid— took place near Fort Kearny. About 1,000 Sioux, mostly Oglalas, attacked a party of woodcutters guarded by a squad of soldiers. The whites gathered for defense inside a corral made of wagon boxes that had been removed from their wheels and kept the encircling Indians at bay. Though whites considered the encounter a victory for having driven off the hostiles under Chiefs Crazy Horse and Hump, the Indians had nevertheless made their point that the Bozeman Trail was unsafe. The battle was recreated in *Tomahawk*.

A public outcry over the constant fighting forced the U.S. to create an Indian Peace Commission to seek ways to end the disputes. In 1868 Chief Red Cloud signed a treaty to cease fighting in return for a promise by the government to abandon the Bozeman Trail and its line of protective forts. The Sioux, as part of the agreement, pledged to give up some land and accept settlement on a reservation by 1876. Peace existed for eight years.

Hostilities broke out again in 1876–1877 in a series of actions sometimes called the Great Sioux Uprising. The discovery of gold on Sioux land in the Black Hills of South Dakota brought an influx of prospectors who eluded the army's attempts to stop the intrusion. The Sioux attacked trespassers. At the same time, some bands refused to go to their designated reservations set up by the peace treaty of 1876. The incidents leading to hostilities and the uprising itself were the subjects of several films. *They Died With Their Boots On* (1941), for instance, dramatized the rush of gold seekers to the Black Hills which resulted in indiscriminate killings on both sides. *The Great Sioux Massacre* (1965) suggested that corrupt Washington politicians were responsible for the unduly harsh treatment of the Sioux and the ensuing defeat of Custer and his troops.

The government sent military expeditions to defeat the tribe. General George Crook destroyed Chief Crazy Horse's camp. Another expedition under General Alfred Terry, including the 7th Cavalry under Lt. Col. George Custer, swept westward from the Dakotas into southeastern Montana. Custer's unit, an advance heavy scouting force, was wiped out at the Battle of Little Bighorn River (June 25, 1876). Generals Crook and Terry eventually defeated the Sioux, and Chief Sitting Bull fled to Canada. Most were forced to accept life on a reservation. Custer's defeat has been re-enacted more often than any other historical battle. Films range from such early silent one- reelers as "Custer's Last Fight," released in 1912, to *Custer of the West* in 1967.

Constant pursuit by the army and massive slaughter of the buffalo herds by troopers and hunters during the 1870s weakened the Sioux. Many accepted confinement on reservations where they received annual payments and food from the federal government in return for giving up most of their hunting grounds. The surrender of their two last and most famous fighting chiefs, Crazy Horse (1877) and Sitting Bull (1890), both of whom were killed while reportedly resisting arrest on a reservation, further debilitated the tribe. The scarcity of big game on the reservations made them fully dependent on the federal government. Red Cloud saw nothing wrong in accepting free food and annuities. "The white man," he said, "owes us a living because they took our lands away from us."

In 1890–1891, economic and religious issues led to a new confrontation that culminated in the Battle of Wounded Knee. The Sioux had found reservation life increasingly difficult because of spreading disease, crop failures and poverty. Many were attracted to a new religious belief that predicted an Indian Messiah would come to unite all the tribes in an earthly paradise. Part of the belief involved the "Ghost Dance," a ritual that produced trances and mass frenzy. Some dancers, believing they were immune to bullets, became more defiant of the soldiers. When troopers tried to stop the dance and seize the arms of the participants, fights broke out.

The army decided to arrest those who might incite another rebellion. Among those killed for resisting arrest was Chief Sitting

Bull, who had returned from Canada and accepted a pardon. The army soon quashed the revolt, but not before the 7th Cavalry had gotten its revenge for Custer's defeat by massacring the Indians at Wounded Knee. The battle became the climactic highlight of *The Adventures of Buffalo Bill* (1914), with William Cody playing himself. It also played a part in *Soldier Blue* (1970), which gave a more accurate account of the massacre. The carnage ended with 150 Indians killed and another 50 wounded, including women, old men and children. The army reportedly lost 25 dead and 39 wounded. It wasn't a large battle, but its importance far outweighed the size of the conflict. It was the last major engagement between Indians and whites. The Sioux, as well as all the other tribes, realized their way of life had been crushed forever. See also Battle of Wounded Knee, Crazy Horse, George Custer, Sitting Bull. ∎

Sirocco (1951), Col. *Dir.* Curtis Bernhardt; *Sc.* A. I. Bezzerides, Hans Jacoby; *Cast includes:* Humphrey Bogart, Marta Toren, Lee J. Cobb, Everett Sloane.

The conflict between the French and Syrians in Damascus in 1925 provides the background for this drama of intrigue. Humphrey Bogart portrays a mercenary gunrunner for the natives. Lee J. Cobb, as the head of French Intelligence, eventually catches up to Bogart and his illegal activities. He makes a deal with Bogart to help him meet with the rebel leader so that he can negotiate a settlement to the war. When Cobb is captured by the enemy, Bogart shows signs of redemption when he carries the ransom money for the Frenchman's release. After Cobb is set free, the Syrians decide they have no further use for Bogart, so they plot his murder. Marta Toren, as Cobb's mistress, becomes romantically involved with Bogart. She sees in him a chance to escape from Damascus and start a new life for herself.

The film is loosely based on historical events. A minor Muslim sect in the French mandate of Syria, the Druses rebelled against French control and mistreatment by the French-supported native governor. The revolt, lasting two years, spread as the Druses received widespread support from other native groups that also resented French domination of their homeland under the League of Nations mandate stemming from the Treaty of Versailles.

At one point, the Druses forced French troops to evacuate the Syrian capital of Damascus. The French resorted to heavy air, tank and artillery bombardment to subdue the revolt. Despite many displays of Druse bravery that even included cavalry charges against tanks, the rebellion collapsed in June 1927, and rebel leaders fled to the British mandate in Palestine. ∎

Sitting Bull (1831–1890). By July 1881, the only surviving great fighting chief of the once-mighty Sioux nation, Sitting Bull, realized he had to surrender to the white man to keep his diminishing band alive in the face of growing hunger and weakness. All the other Sioux war chiefs had given up or been killed. Following the tribe's defeat in the Sioux War of 1876–1877, he had fled into Canada with a small group of followers rather than submit to reservation life. When game became scarce in the poor hunting grounds north of the border, Sitting Bull's band returned to the U.S. in the summer of 1881 to accept the restrictions of reservation life.

However, Sitting Bull's pride would not permit him to make the final personal gesture of surrender—turning his weapon over to an army officer at Fort Budford, Montana. The Indian chief, then 50 years old, passed his rifle to his eight-year-old son and ordered the child to hand it to General Nelson A. Miles. Sitting Bull's fighting days were finished but not his resistance to continuing white attempts to take more land from his tribe.

The man who was to become one of the most famous American Indian chiefs was born into the Hunkpapa band of the Teton Sioux in present-day South Dakota. He first resisted the army in 1863 over inroads by whites into Sioux hunting grounds that were starting to decimate the buffalo herds, the mainstay of the plains Indians' way of life. The Sioux made peace with the army in 1868 on promises of a guaranteed reservation around the North Platte River.

The discovery of gold in the Black Hills area of the reservation by Col. George Custer in 1874 brought in large numbers of gold miners. After the army tried but failed to contain the intruders, the Sioux began attacking whites. *The Great Sioux Massacre* (1965) treated the Sioux sympathetically, showing Sitting Bull (Michael Pate) taking up arms only after he suffered a series of abuses.

The army in 1876 mounted a campaign under General George Crook to defeat the Indians and place them on a reservation. Sitting Bull organized a massive force of Sioux, along with some allied Cheyennes and Arapahoes, that together numbered more than 10,000. The Indian force defeated Crook at the Rosebud River in June. The following month the Indians wiped out Crook's advance scouting column under Col. George Custer at the Battle of the Little Bighorn River.

Indian victories could not stop the unrelenting pressure of superior army forces that continued to pursue the natives through the following winter. As hunger spread, more chiefs surrendered in exchange for guarantees of rations and payments to their people, except for Sitting Bull, who fled to Canada in May 1877. He remained there until the summer of 1881 when he returned with promise of a pardon. The low-budget action drama *Fort Vengeance* (1953) accurately pictured Sitting Bull (Michael Granger) and his Sioux braves in Canada but then concocted a plot showing the tribe on the warpath and their chief stirring up the Blackfeet against the whites.

Upon his return, he lived at the Standing Rock agency where he unsuccessfully counseled his people not to sell their tribal lands. Sitting Bull toured with Buffalo Bill's Wild West Show in 1885 and was received as a hero by white audiences. This phase of his life is depicted in Robert Altman's *Buffalo Bill and the Indians* (1976), with Frank Kaquitts portraying an enigmatic Sitting Bull who persists in his search for historical truth. In the late 1880s Sitting Bull seemed to encourage the spread of a new religious movement among his people that preached the coming of an Indian Messiah. It included a ritual "Ghost Dance" that warriors believed made them safe from bullets. Soldiers and Indian police, fearing that he might use this belief to incite another rebellion, went to his cabin on nearby Grand River to arrest him. He resisted and died in the ensuing scuffle on December 15, 1890, along with seven of his followers and several policemen.

His death resulted in a number of Indians fleeing the agency. Fearing the combined effects of Sitting Bull's death and the frenzy induced by "Ghost Dancing," General Nelson Miles gave orders to round up and disarm the Indians in his territory. This led to the army's tragic and blundering massacre of the Indians at the Battle of Wounded Knee on December 29, 1890. It was the last major conflict between whites and Indians in the United States.

Sitting Bull has been portrayed on screen in silent and sound films by black, Indian and white performers. Noble Johnson, a black actor, played him twice, in the comedy *Hands Up!* (1926) and the drama *The Flaming Frontier* (1926), with a poorly staged version of Custer's last stand. Chief Yowlache played the Sioux leader in *Sitting Bull at Spirit Lake Massacre* (1927), and Chief Thunderbird impersonated him in *Annie Oakley* (1935). J. Carrol Naish played the Chief in the 1950 musical *Annie Get Your Gun* and again in *Sitting Bull* (1954), a highly fictionalized biography. Although the 1954 film captured little of the warrior's exploits and stature, it was appreciated by Indians for its sympathetic treatment, authentic costumes and use of native language. See also Battle of Wounded Knee, Crazy Horse, George Custer, Sioux Wars. ∎

Sitting Bull (1954), UA. *Dir.* Sidney Salkow; *Sc.* Jack DeWitt, Sidney Salkow; *Cast includes:* Dale Robertson, Mary Murphy, J. Carrol Naish, Iron Eyes Cody.

The difficulties of maintaining peace with the Indians provide the background of this outdoor drama. Dale Robertson portrays a U.S. Cavalry major, demoted for defending the rights of Indians, who struggles to keep the fragile peace between the Sioux and the whites. He comes under attack from his superiors when he refuses to fire upon several Indians who have left the reservation but is saved by President Grant, his former commander during the Civil War. Grant then assigns Robertson to set up a pow-wow with Sitting Bull (J. Carrol Naish), chief of the Sioux. But Colonel George Custer's unauthorized attack upon the Indians results in the outbreak of hostilities. Robertson is arrested for helping the Indians but is saved by Sitting Bull who enters the stockade to defend the major.

Almost none of the events depicted in the film is based on historical records. The figure of Sitting Bull plays a more prominent role in *The Great Sioux Massacre* (1965). However, the film, which was shot in Mexico, was appreciated by American Indians who praised the production for its authentic costuming,

its use of Indian language and its generally sympathetic treatment of the Indian. Ironically, the only authentic Indian in the production was Iron Eyes Cody, who portrayed Crazy Horse. The others were impersonated by Mexicans. ∎

Sitting Bull at Spirit Lake Massacre (1927), Sunset. *Dir.* Robert N. Bradbury; *Sc.* Ben Allah; *Cast includes:* Bryant Washburn, Anne Schaeffer, Jay Morley, Shirley Palmer, Chief Yowlache.

A low-budget action drama recounting Sitting Bull's revengeful exploits against the whites, the film includes plenty of excitement in the battle sequences as well as a romantic subplot involving Bryant Washburn as a brave army scout and Anne Schaeffer as a minister's daughter. Chief Yowlache portrays Sitting Bull. The drama relies little on historical facts for the incidents concerning the Sioux chief. ∎

Situation Hopeless—But Not Serious (1965), Par. *Dir.* Gottfried Reinhardt; *Sc.* Silvia Reinhardt; *Cast includes:* Alec Guinness, Michael Connors, Robert Redford, Anita Hoefer.

Alec Guinness stars as a humble German clerk who holds two American fliers prisoners for years after the end of World War II in this little comedy. Michael Connors and Robert Redford, as the two airmen, bail out over Germany during the war and seek refuge in Guinness' cellar. The room had been made into an escape-proof shelter by Guinness' mother before the war. Guinness develops a liking for his two prisoners and keeps them locked up for another six years after the war. The Americans finally gain their freedom but think that Germany has won the war. This, of course, leads to some very comical situations. Robert Redford made his film debut in this odd, satirical film that pokes fun at Germans as well as Allied occupation troops. ∎

Ski Patrol (1940), U. *Dir.* Lew Landers; *Sc.* Paul Huston; *Cast includes:* Philip Dorn, Luli Deste, Stanley Fields, Samuel S. Hinds, Edward Norris.

A weak drama designed to exploit the Russo–Finnish War of the period, the film stars Philip Dorn as a Finnish soldier who, with his ski troops, attempts to defend a mountain that has been mined by the Russians. The film includes several minor battles between soldiers of the two adversary countries, including footage from newsreels spliced between other scenes in this low-budget drama. The tragic war had ended by the time the film was released. Russia, who had precipitated the confrontation, had overwhelmed the tiny country, whose soldiers fought bravely but were ill-prepared for a full-scale conflict with its more powerful neighbor. Although a minor drama, it has the distinction of being one of the rare films to have the Russo–Finnish conflict as its subject. It is a remake of *The Doomed Battalion* (1932), set in the Austrian Tyrol during World War I. ■

Ski Troop Attack (1960), Filmgroup. *Dir.* Roger Corman; *Sc.* Charles Griffith; *Cast includes:* Michael Forest, Frank Wolff, Wally Campo, Richard Sinatra, Sheila Carol.

A small patrol of American soldiers journey behind German lines to destroy a vital bridge in this routine action drama set during World War II. The major conflict of the film concerns a battle-hardened sergeant's hostility towards a green lieutenant in charge of the ski patrol. Frank Wolff portrays the malevolent sergeant while Michael Forest plays the innocent officer in this low-budget film that provides sufficient skirmishes between the Americans and the Nazi troops. ■

Sky Commando (1953), Col. *Dir.* Fred F. Sears; *Sc.* Samuel Newman; *Cast includes:* Dan Duryea, Frances Gifford, Touch Conners, Michael Fox.

The World War II background of a stern commanding officer during the Korean conflict helps to explain his character in this routine drama. Dan Duryea portrays the misunderstood officer whose allegedly unjustifiable orders are held responsible by a jet fighter pilot for the loss of the flier's brother. The angry airman is then told of Duryea's exploits during the last war. Duryea was an unpopular commander of a photo reconnaissance squadron. His own co-pilot (Touch Conners) despised him. It was only during a mission over the oil fields of Rumania that his men realized his worth and his bravery. The low-budget film provides enough action sequences, some of which have been borrowed from actual combat footage, to keep the story moving. ■

Sky Devils (1932), UA. *Dir.* Edward Sutherland; *Sc.* J. M. March, Edward Sutherland; *Cast includes:* Spencer Tracy, William "Stage" Boyd, George Cooper, Ann Dvorak, Billy Bevan.

A World War I comedy starring Spencer Tracy and George Cooper, the film follows the escapades of two men from their civilian days to their careers in Uncle Sam's Air Force in France. Tracy and Cooper, as civilians, had their problems with William "Stage" Boyd (not the actor who played Hopalong Cassidy), who has now become their sergeant, to the two pals' regrets. Tracy is the center of interest who gets into and out of scrapes. He and his buddy are as inept as pilots as they were as lifeguards in civilian life. "I bring down one more of our planes," one of the pair quips, "and I'll be a German ace." Ann Dvorak provides the romantic interest. Some of the dialogue was written by Robert Benchley. There is plenty of action as the fliers engage a swarm of enemy planes in air battles. There is also the almost obligatory destruction of a German ammunition center as seen in previous air dramas such as *The Dawn Patrol* (1930). As Tracy and Cooper return from this successful mission, they accidentally destroy their own airport as well. The flimsy story is carried chiefly by the comedy and principal players. ■

Sky Hawk (1929), Fox. *Dir.* John Blystone; *Sc.* Llewellyn Hughes; *Cast includes:* Helen Chandler, John Garrick, Gilbert Emery, Lennox Pawle.

The film is a World War I air drama climaxing in a battle over London between a zeppelin and a lone British flier. John Garrick plays Jack Bardell, a pilot with the Royal Flying Corps. He borrows a plane without permission to say goodbye to his sweetheart and on his return wrecks the airship and is temporarily paralyzed in his legs. Condemned by his fellow fliers, Bardell purchases a damaged plane and has his mechanic restore it. When the German zeppelin appears, he takes his plane up to meet the threat. A dramatic and exciting battle ensues in which Bardell finally brings down the enemy dirigible. The last scene shows Bardell flying off with his bride on their honeymoon.

The film makes excellent use of miniatures during the climactic air battle, a set that allegedly cost the studio $250,000 to build. That was quite excessive for the period.

Bardell's mechanic, who supplies some comic relief, is played by Billy Bevan, the former silent-screen comedian. He continued to appear in supporting roles, including other war-related films such as *Another Dawn* (1937), starring Errol Flynn. ■

Sky Murder (1940). See Detectives at War. ■

Slacker, The (1917), Metro. *Dir.* Christy Cabanne; *Sc.* Christy Cabanne; *Cast includes:* Emily Stevens, Walter Miller, Leo Delaney, Daniel Jarrett.

Walter Miller portrays the title character in this strongly patriotic silent drama, one of the earliest films to use the term "slacker." His sweetheart (Emily Stevens) persuades him to do his share, and before long he is off to France along with thousands of others. Historical images are conjured up, showing scenes of America's glorious past and its famous heroes. These include Paul Revere's famous ride, Nathan Hale's death and General Lee's surrender at Appomattox.

The term "slacker," as applied to healthy young men who shirked their duty to their country when the "call to arms" went out, was very common during World War I. One of the initial goals of the government's newly formed Committee on Public Information, with its voice of propaganda in the film industry, was to instigate the public to come down hard on those who evaded the draft. Patriotic fervor was at its peak when the film was released, and the *The Slacker* certainly contributed its share. See also Propaganda Films. ■

Slaughterhouse Five (1972), U. *Dir.* George Roy Hill; *Sc.* Stephen Geller; *Cast includes:* Michael Sacks, Ron Leibman, Eugene Roche, Sharon Gans, Valerie Perrine.

Based on Kurt Vonnegut's bizarre fantasy, *Slaughterhouse Five, or the Children's Crusade,* the film traces the misadventures of Billy Pilgrim during World War II and its aftermath. Michael Sacks, as Billy, a not-too-bright 20th-century Everyman and born loser, often ends up in the wrong place at the wrong time. Drafted into the army, he falls into the hands of the Germans and spends the remainder of the war in a prison camp in Germany where he experiences the horrors of the Dresden bombing. To escape the catastrophes of his lowly life, Billy engages in "time-tripping," or journeys through time and space to an imaginary planet called Tralfamadore.

After the war, the plot picks up Billy's civilian life as an optometrist and his marriage to an overweight wife (Sharon Gans). The following years are not too kind to Billy. His son, one of two children, spends his time desecrating cemeteries and then joins the Green Berets. Meanwhile, Billy continues his travels to his secret planet where he ends up with a sexy movie actress (Valerie Perrine)—evidently a reward handed down by the Fates for his sterile existence.

The film is an awkward and confused mixture of comedy and drama, especially in terms of the Dresden bombing and Billy's nervous breakdown, as it tries to suggest Vonnegut's concern with man's inhumanity. ■

Smashing of the Reich (1962), Brigadier. *Sc.* Perry Wolf.

A documentary about the rise and fall of the Third Reich, a regime that Hitler one prophesied would last a thousand years, the film emphasizes the significant role played by air power in the collapse of Nazi Germany's dream of conquest. Although composed of the usual period footage employed in other documentaries on World War II, the work includes some sequences that have not been seen before. Several moments are worth watching again; e.g., the Allied liberation of the death camps, the French guerrillas helping to rid Paris of the German troops and the fateful meeting of the American soldiers with their Russian counterparts at the Elbe River. ■

Smiles (1919). See Spy Comedies. ■

Smilin' Through (1922), FN. *Dir.* Sidney A. Franklin; *Sc.* Sidney A. Franklin, James A. Creelman; *Cast includes:* Norma Talmadge, Wyndham Standing, Harrison Ford, Alec B. Francis.

A tragedy in the past almost wrecks the lives of two lovers in this romantic drama set during World War I. Harrison Ford (not related to the popular actor of *Star Wars* fame) portrays a young man in love with the niece (Norma Talmadge) of a man embittered by an incident that had occurred twenty years earlier. On the uncle's wedding day a former suitor of his bride-to-be fired a gun at him. The bullet killed the girl instead. Ford is the son of the murderer. When war erupts, Ford is sent to France where he is seriously wounded. The uncle encourages his niece to believe that Ford is in love with someone else. When he realizes the suffering he has caused, he brings the lovers together and dies. His spirit reunites with that of the girl who was to be his bride. ■

Smoke in the Wind (1975), Frontier. Dir. Joseph Kane; Sc. Eric Allen; Cast includes: John Ashley, John Russell, Myron Healey, Walter Brennan.

The end of the Civil War brings hatred and violence instead of peace to an Arkansas community in this postwar drama. Set in the Ozarks in 1865, the film depicts the bitterness that some ex-Confederate soldiers and Southern sympathizers displayed towards their neighbors who fought for the Union. The story focuses on the proud and respected Mondier clan, a family of farmers whose men elected to join the Yankee cause. John Russell, as Cagle Mondier, the patriarch, explains his reasons to his two sons. "I saw the niggers stripped naked, strapped to cedar logs. I've seen these niggers under the blacksnake whips . . . I said, 'My God, someday I'm gonna do something about settin' them free.'" As the father and his two sons return home from the war, they are ambushed by Mort Fagan (Myron Healey), a Southern sympathizer, and his vindictive gang. The elder Mondier is killed. The remainder of the plot deals with the sons' attempts to bring Fagan to justice and restore law and order to the land. John Ashley portrays Whipple Mondier, the principal character and son who winds things up. Veteran character actor Walter Brennan, in his last screen role before his death, has a minor part as a local storekeeper. An almost endless series of killings and ambushes follows the father's death, some of which appear senseless in this low-budget film shot on location in Arkansas. ■

Sniper's Ridge (1961), TCF. Dir. John Bushelman; Sc. Tom Maruzzi; Cast includes: Jack Ging, John Goddard, Stanley Clements, Gabe Castle.

This low-budget action drama, set during the last days of the Korean War, focuses on an emotionally unstable captain and a defiant, battle-weary corporal. As the men under the captain's command nervously wait for the ex-

American soldiers battle furiously during the last days of the Korean War. *Sniper's Ridge* (1961).

pected cease fire, the gung-ho officer (John Goddard) decides to organize a perilous mission. Suddenly, Goddard steps on a mine. It is the type that explodes the instant the foot is removed. Jack Ging, as the corporal, saves the captain's life and is seriously wounded. The action sequences are realistic and suspenseful in spite of the skimpy budget. ■

Snob Buster, The (1925), Rayart. Dir. Albert Rogell; Sc. Forrest Sheldon; Cast includes: Reed Howes, Gloria Grey, Wilfred Lucas, George Tobias.

Reed Howes portrays a rich snob whose experience in the front lines in France during World War I takes much of the conceit out of him. After the war, he returns to the same environment filled with the same pretentious people. Finding the situation intolerable, he leaves and teams up with a group of rough characters from a local boxing gym. He also meets and falls in love with the pretty owner of a local eating place, played by Gloria Grey. After some brawling with the group's leader, he settles down with his sweetheart. ■

So Ends Our Night (1941), UA. Dir. John Cromwell; Sc. Talbot Jennings; Cast includes: Fredric March, Margaret Sullavan, Frances Dee, Glenn Ford, Anna Sten, Erich von Stroheim.

A drama about the religious and political refugees of Nazi persecution, the film depicts their hardships as they travel from one European country to another during the late 1930s seeking asylum. Without a homeland and with little hope, they travel by night across borders to avoid police or deportation. Counterfeit passports, coveted symbols of survival, are available but at a high price. Fredric March portrays a German refugee forced to flee because he is at odds with his government. Margaret Sullavan plays a homeless Jewess. Glenn Ford, as the son of an Aryan father and Jewish mother, is another drifter hounded by religious persecution. He and Sullavan meet and eventually fall in love. The trio are driven out of each country as it falls to the Nazis. March secretly returns to Germany to visit his wife on her deathbed. Meanwhile, the two lovers reach Paris where they find temporary shelter.

The grim and realistic drama is based on Erich Maria Remarque's novel *Flotsam*. It was released while America still maintained an uneasy peace with Germany. This may explain why no mention of Hitler's name appears in the two-hour film. ∎

So Proudly We Hail! (1943), Par. *Dir.* Mark Sandrich; *Sc.* Allan Scott; *Cast includes:* Claudette Colbert, Paulette Goddard, Veronica Lake, George Reeves, Barbara Britton, Walter Abel.

This World War II drama of a group of heroic nurses who suffer through the siege of Bataan earned four Academy Award nominations. Merging the women's film with the combat drama, *So Proudly We Hail* is graphically realistic in its presentation of the horrors of war. A wounded soldier during the battle of Bataan has both legs amputated as his mother, a senior nurse, witnesses the operation. Another nurse (Veronica Lake), who has lost her loved one at the hands of the Japanese, walks into the enemy's midst concealing a live hand grenade. She sacrifices her own life while taking several Japanese soldiers with her. The film illustrates that American nurses have often suffered through the same bombardments, strafings and general dangers that confronted the soldiers. ∎

So Red the Rose (1935), Par. *Dir.* King Vidor; *Sc.* Laurence Stallings, Maxwell Anderson, Edwin Justus Mayer; *Cast includes:* Margaret Sullavan, Walter Connolly, Janet Beecher, Robert Cummings, Randolph Scott, Elizabeth Patterson.

This Civil War drama centers on the romantic and domestic problems of a Southern family. Walter Connolly portrays a patriarchal plantation owner who is called to fight against the Union when his only son and heir is killed in battle. Randolph Scott plays a Southerner who sympathizes with Lincoln and the Union's cause. The film depicts the Confederate women as the traditional "belles of the South" and the men as gallant officers while painting the invading Union soldiers as brutish invaders who burn and pillage. This sympathy for the Southern cause is carried further to the benign treatment of the slaves by their kindly masters. In fact, when their masters ride off to do battle against the Union liberators bent on freeing the blacks, the slaves eagerly cheer them.

The film failed at the box office and had repercussions during the next few years concerning Civil War stories. They became anathema to most of the studios who, recalling the expensive disaster of *So Red the Rose*, ultimately rejected *Gone With the Wind*, much to their dismay. ∎

Soldier and the Lady, The (1937), RKO. *Dir.* George Nicholls, Jr.; *Sc.* Mortimer Offner, Anthony Veiller; *Cast includes:* Anton Walbrook, Elizabeth Allan, Margot Grahame, Akim Tamiroff, Fay Bainter, Eric Blore.

Based on *Michael Strogoff*, Jules Verne's novel of czarist Russia during the Tartar revolt of 1870, the film stars international actor Anton Walbrook in his American debut. He portrays Michael Strogoff, courier to the czar, who is sent on a special mission by Czar Alexander II to the Czar's brother. Carrying the plans for the defeat of the Tartars, Strogoff suffers a series of harrowing experiences before he completes his mission. Others try to prevent him from completing his rendezvous, including an attractive spy (Margot Grahame) who works for the Tartar leader (Akim Tamiroff). After narrowly escaping a Tartar attack upon a barge and almost being permanently blinded by the Tartar chieftain, he reaches the Czar's brother in time for the Russian troops to defeat the enemy hordes in a spectacular battle.

American, French and German silent versions of the novel had appeared previously. The earliest feature was a Selig production released in 1914 starring Jacob Adler, a popular actor of the Yiddish stage. RKO purchased the rights to the 1926 French adaptation and skillfully inserted many of the more exciting action scenes into the 1937 film. ∎

Soldier Blue (1970), Avco. *Dir.* Ralph Nelson; *Sc.* John Gay; *Cast includes:* Candice Bergen, Peter Strauss, Donald Pleasence, John Anderson.

A violent drama of America's mistreatment of the Indian, the film stars Candice Bergen as a former captive of the Cheyenne who learns to understand their suffering. Bergen and a cavalryman, played by Peter Strauss, are the only survivors of an Indian attack on a paymaster's wagon and its armed guard. As an idealistic and patriotic young soldier, Strauss rejects her tales of atrocities practiced by whites. The remainder of the plot, set during the 1860s, deals with their attempts to return to the army post. On their journey they meet Donald Pleasence, who portrays a trader about to sell guns to the Cheyenne in exchange for the gold they stole from the wagon.

When the pair arrive at the outpost, Bergen learns that the commander is about to attack her Indian village. She rides on ahead to warn the tribe. The ensuing slaughter of the Indians by the cavalry, in spite of the Indian chief's attempt to surrender by offering a white flag of truce and the Stars and Stripes, is a particularly bloody sequence. After the braves are killed, the cavalry proceeds to annihilate the women and children. The soldiers engage in rape, mutilation and scalping. Strauss, at first staring in disbelief, tries to help the Indians but is put in irons. Allegedly based on two actual incidents in America's past—the Sand Creek massacre in 1864 and the battle at Wounded Knee in 1889—the massacre, as suggested by the film, has been equated with that at My Lai during the Vietnam War. ■

"Soldier Man" (1926), UA. *Dir.* Mack Sennett; *Sc.* Mack Sennett; *Cast includes:* Harry Langdon.

Silent film comedian Harry Langdon portrays a doughboy left behind at the end of World War I in this comedy set in a fictitious country. He wanders the abandoned battlefield searching for any sign of life and eventually becomes embroiled in a local revolution. Mistaken for the missing king, whom he resembles, he is placed upon the throne. The queen, who has been trying to murder her husband, directs her efforts at the bemused Langdon. This was one of the moon-faced comic's last short films before his move into features and his ultimate demise as a screen star. Fairly representative of his comedic talents within a well-plotted story, the film displays some of the traits that made Langdon popular—his childlike innocence, his gentle moments of fascination with a new object and his bewildered gaze. ■

Soldiers of Fortune (1919), Realart. *Dir.* Allan Dwan; *Cast includes:* Norman Kerry, Pauline Starke, Anna Q. Nilsson, Melbourne McDowell, Wallace Beery, Wilfred Lucas.

An action drama set in a South American republic, the film centers on an American civil engineer (Norman Kerry). Alverez, the country's president, is being threatened by a dissident army general, Mendoza (Wallace Beery). Kerry manages to divert a shipment of guns meant for Mendoza and, with a group of his mining laborers, holds off the revolutionaries. There are scenes of American naval forces landing fighting troops and several other battles.

Although the plot centers around an unnamed South American country, the film was released during the Mexican Revolution of 1910–1921, a conflict whose political and military ramifications concerned the U.S. In 1913 the U.S. was not only shipping arms to dictator Victoriano Huerta in his struggle against the revolutionaries Carranza, Villa and Zapata, but sent its navy to several Mexican ports including Veracruz. Gen. John J. Pershing in 1916 led a punitive expedition into Mexico against Villa. *Soldiers of Fortune*, therefore, reflects these antirevolutionary sentiments. Almost two decades later, Beery would play another revolutionary leader in one of his most popular roles—that of the patriotic Mexican bandit Pancho Villa in *Viva Villa!* (1935). By this time Hollywood, or at least screenwriter Ben Hecht, had a revised opinion of Villa. Emiliano Zapata received the same sympathetic treatment in Elia Kazan's *Viva Zapata!* (1952), with John Steinbeck providing the screenplay. ■

Soldier's Plaything, A (1930), WB. *Dir.* Michael Curtiz; *Sc.* Perry Vekroff; *Cast includes:* Lottie Loder, Harry Langdon, Ben Lyon, Jean Hersholt.

Ben Lyon portrays an irresponsible drifter and gambler in this comedy drama who, when World War I erupts, has no interest in the conflict. Harry Langdon, as Lyon's timid buddy, decides to enlist in the army. Lyon becomes entangled in a fight with a man over the affections of a woman. When the man falls from a balcony, Lyon, thinking he has killed his rival, quickly enlists along with his pal to escape the revenge of the victim's friends. While overseas, Lyon meets a young German woman with whom he falls in love and promises to marry. After the war, he returns to the U.S. to face any charges before marrying. He learns that the man he thought he killed is very much alive, so he returns to his fiancee overseas. ∎

Soldier's Story, A (1984), Col. *Dir.* Norman Jewison; *Sc.* Charles Fuller; *Cast includes:* Howard E. Rollins, Jr., Adolph Caesar, Dennis Lipscomb, Art Evans.

Set at a black army base in the South during World War II, the drama ostensibly concerns the murder of a black sergeant and the ensuing investigation. But beneath this plot surface looms the tragic story of the different paths blacks take in accommodating themselves in a world dominated by whites. Howard E. Rollins, Jr. portrays a proud black officer sent from Washington to investigate the crime. Racial tensions mount as white officers resent the black attorney's intrusion into their domain and his outspoken manner. As in other films of this genre, both sides are forced to come to terms with their own prejudices as the facts become unraveled. The murdered sergeant, played by Adolph Caesar, is revealed in flashbacks as a repulsive, tough leader, a World War I veteran who despises those in his black squad who refuse to better themselves. Consumed with self-hate, he derides other blacks who discredit their race. Caesar had appeared in the same role in the stage production titled *A Soldier's Play*. The film concludes with the lawyer shaking hands with the white officer who had earlier given Rollins a difficult time. The work also stands out as a rare Hollywood example of a drama in which blacks are allowed to tell their own story. ∎

Soldiers Three (1951), MGM. *Dir.* Tay Garnett; *Sc.* Marguerite Roberts, Tom Reed, Malcolm Stuart Boylan; *Cast includes:* Stewart Granger, Walter Pidgeon, David Niven, Robert Newton.

The title refers to three fun-loving, reckless troopers in Her Majesty's army in India during a native uprising in this comedy based on Rudyard Kipling's stories. The trio, consisting of Stewart Granger, Robert Newton and Cyril Cusack, are in constant hot water with their colonel (Walter Pidgeon) for their brawling and drinking escapades. But when a group of British soldiers come under attack by a band of warring natives, Granger turns hero as he leads his two comrades in battle and saves his besieged comrades. David Niven plays Pidgeon's aide in this broadly comic romp. ∎

Some Won't Go (1969), Education Through Communication, Inc. *Dir.* Gil Toff; *Sc.* Paul W. Decker, Jr.

A documentary of the war resisters during the Vietnam War, the film treats the moral and political issues superficially. Scenes of students and others burning their draft cards and encounters with the law underline some of the turbulence of the period. Almost completely abandoning any objectivity, the work emphasizes through many voices the conclusion that the war is immoral. The film includes interviews with people from various walks of life, including lawyers, those who have settled in Canada to escape the draft, religious leaders and black militants. ∎

Something for the Boys (1944), TCF. *Dir.* Lewis Seiler; *Sc.* Robert Ellis, Helen Logan, Frank Gabrielson; *Cast includes:* Carmen Miranda, Michael O'Shea, Vivian Blaine, Phil Silvers.

Three cousins convert a broken-down plantation into a home for army wives in this World War II musical comedy. Carmen Miranda, Vivian Blaine and Phil Silvers play the relatives who come up with the idea of restoring their inherited property to help the servicemen of a nearby army camp. They put on variety shows to raise the necessary money in this light-hearted film that was based on the Broadway play by Herbert and Dorothy Fields. ∎

Something of Value (1957), MGM. *Dir.* Richard Brooks; *Sc.* Richard Brooks; *Cast includes:* Rock Hudson, Dana Wynter, Wendy Hiller, Sidney Poitier.

The violent Mau Mau uprising in Kenya, East Africa, provides the background for this drama. Sidney Poitier portrays Kimani, a young black native forced into violence by the abuses of British colonialism. Rock Hudson, as Kimani's boyhood friend, fights on the side of the colonists but dreams of a better future for both races. He maintains that the whites must demonstrate a belief in equality and show understanding toward other cultures. The raids by the fanatical Mau Maus prove bloody and violent as they slash their way through the isolated plantations. Hudson finally gets Poitier to surrender. And it is Hudson's black assistant who voices the idea of moderation when he comments: "I want the same thing for us as he does. Only I think there's a different way of getting it." The film, based on Robert C. Ruark's novel of the same name, was photographed chiefly in Africa.

The Mau Mau terrorists of the 1950s were determined to drive the whites out of Kenya. Composed chiefly of Kikuyu tribesmen, the Mau Mau were finally subdued in 1956 by the British following substantial killings on both sides. The Mau Mau uprising contributed to Kenya's ultimate independence. ∎

Somewhere I'll Find You (1942), MGM. *Dir.* Wesley Ruggles; *Sc.* Marguerite Roberts; *Cast includes:* Clark Gable, Lana Turner, Robert Sterling, Patricia Dane, Reginald Owen.

World War II becomes only a backdrop for this romantic, sometimes steaming, drama starring Clark Gable and Lana Turner. Gable plays a war correspondent who tries to save his younger brother (Robert Sterling), also a newspaperman, from the charms of another journalist (Lana Turner), whom Gable thinks is not on the level. He makes a play for her and she responds, thereby disillusioning Sterling. Later, when she is reported missing somewhere in Indochina, the brothers start out to find her. They learn that she is helping war orphans. This convinces the cynical Gable that she is all right. Meanwhile, Sterling enlists in the service and is killed in action as Gable turns in a war scoop. Although the film skips around to various war zones like the Philippines and Indochina, the conflict is secondary to the hot romance of the two leads.

Gable lost his wife, Carole Lombard, who was killed in an air crash, while he was making the film. Production had to be halted for several weeks. Following its completion, he enlisted in the U.S. Army Air Force. ∎

Somewhere in France (1915), Par. *Dir.* Donald Thompson.

A documentary covering several battles and other sequences during World War I, the film was shot personally by Donald Thompson. His were the only scenes of the retreat from Mons where French troops, along with Thompson, were under fire for one week. A daring and aggressive American cameraman, he ignored personal danger to capture on film sequences of the war that no other cinematographers were able to get.

There were other risks for cameramen at the time. Fearing infiltration by spies as well as unfavorable reports on the progress of the war, the military and government officials banned photography by independents, and the penalties were harsh. Thompson was finally wounded at Verdun. He was later appointed as one of the official cameramen of the French government. ∎

Somewhere in France (1916). See Spy Films: the Silents. ∎

Somewhere in the Night (1946). See Veterans. ∎

Son of a Sailor (1933). See Service Comedy. ∎

Son of Lassie (1945), MGM. *Dir.* S. Sylvan Simon; *Sc.* Jeanne Bartlett; *Cast includes:* Peter Lawford, Donald Crisp, June Lockhart, Nigel Bruce.

A sequel to *Lassie Come Home*, this World War II drama follows the canine adventures of Laddie, who joins his master, a flier in the Royal Air Force. Peter Lawford, who plays the pilot, takes Laddie with him on a mission. Lawford's plane is hit, forcing the two to bail out over Nazi-controlled Norway. Laddie, separated from his master, survives bombings, snipers, dangerous rapids and other obstacles in his search for Crawford. They are reunited with the help of the underground. June Lockhart provides the romantic interest while Donald Crisp portrays the flier's father. ∎

Song of Love, The (1924), FN. *Dir.* Chester Franklin, Frances Marion; *Sc.* Frances Marion; *Cast includes:* Joseph Schildkraut, Norma Talmadge, Arthur Edmund Carewe, Laurence Wheat.

The drama, set in French-ruled Algeria, stars Norma Talmadge as a dancer who attracts the fancy of a belligerent tribal chief. He is bent on driving the foreigners from North Africa in a holy war. A French secret agent (Joseph Schildkraut) is dispatched to defuse the explosive situation. He not only foils the Arab leader's plans but wins the love of Talmadge as well. There are several action sequences between the native dissidents and the colonials.

Aside from the obvious and hackneyed romantic elements of the film, the bellicose tribal chief suggests the real-life exploits of Abd el-Kader, an Algerian Muslim leader. Attempting to stem the flow of French colonists into his homeland, he led a holy war against them in the mid-1800s. After defeating the French in two wars, he was finally beaten in a third engagement by an overwhelmingly superior force. See Algerian–French Wars (1830–1847). ∎

Song of Russia (1943), MGM. *Dir.* Gregory Ratoff; *Sc.* Paul Jarrico, Richard Collins; *Cast includes:* Robert Taylor, Susan Peters, John Hodiak, Robert Benchley.

The brave struggle of the Russian people against Nazi domination is the background of this romantic drama set during World War II. Robert Taylor portrays an American conductor on tour in Russia in 1941. He falls in love with and marries a brilliant Russian pianist (Susan Peters). Suddenly Germany invades Russia and a conflict of loyalties develops between the lovers. Taylor is devoted to his music while Peters is concerned for her people who are about to be overrun by the ruthless forces of Nazism. Robert Benchley, as Taylor's manager, provides some comic relief. In spite of the talented cast, the film remains an embarrassment in its ludicrous attempts to show similarities between Americans and Russians. "I can't get over it," Taylor remarks during a tour of Moscow, "everyone seems to be having such a good time." Later, he says to Peters: "You could be an American girl."

Robert Taylor enlisted in the navy after completing the film. Along with other similar works, the drama was destined during the next decade to be singled out by the House Un-American Activities Committee investigating Communist influence in the film industry. Members cited it as an example of pro-Russian propaganda disseminated by Communist sympathizers working in Hollywood. ∎

Song of the Flame (1930), FN. *Dir.* Alan Crosland; *Sc.* Gordon Rigby; *Cast includes:* Alexander Gray, Bernice Claire, Noah Beery, Alice Gentle, Bert Roach.

Adapted from an operetta by Oscar Hammerstein II and others, the film is a romantic drama with the Russian Revolution as background. Alexander Gray portrays a Russian prince in love with a peasant girl (Bernice Claire). She writes a rousing song which so moves the people that they make her one of their leaders during the Revolution. This gives her the opportunity to save the prince's life when she leads the storming of his estate. After she escorts him safely to the border, he returns and rescues her.

The local Red leader is pictured as a greedy hypocrite who is more interested in his personal lust than in freedom and justice for his people. The aristocrats, however, are described sympathetically. Musical numbers, written by George Gershwin, Harry Akst and others, include "Cossack Love Song," "Song of the Flame," "Liberty Song" and "When Love Calls." ∎

Sonny (1922), FN. *Dir.* Henry King; *Sc.* Frances Marion, Henry King; *Cast includes:* Richard Barthelmess, Margaret Seddon, Lucy Fox, Herbert Grimwood.

The son of a blind woman is killed in battle during World War I and a fellow soldier (Richard Barthelmess) volunteers to impersonate him in this drama. Barthelmess, who looks like the dead boy's double, agrees to take the son's place for the sake of the mother. The film, which is based on a stage play, includes several battle scenes in its first half. ∎

Sons o' Guns (1936), WB. *Dir.* Lloyd Bacon; *Sc.* Jerry Wald, Jules Epstein; *Cast includes:* Joe E. Brown, Joan Blondell, Beverly Roberts, Eric Blore, Wini Shaw.

Joe E. Brown portrays a Broadway entertainer in this World War I comedy who mistakenly gets swept up into the conflict. Having to wear a doughboy's uniform in his latest show, the song-and-dance man finds himself in a military parade and then in military service somewhere in France. He is locked up for releasing a flock of carrier pigeons but escapes disguised as an English officer. Brown then is sent into battle to knock out a machine gun nest. He ends up capturing an entire German regiment single-handedly. The film, which often has to strain for laughs, includes several songs and the talents of Joan Blondell as a French girl and comic character actor Eric Blore as a butler. ∎

Sophie's Choice (1982). See Holocaust. ■

Soul of Bronze, The (1921), Houdini Picture Corp. *Sc.* Henry Roussell; *Cast includes:* Harry Houdini.

The famous magician, Harry Houdini, portrays a jealous French suitor who causes the death of his rival, a captain in the French army, in this World War I drama. Houdini, as an engineer at a cannon works, arranges for the captain to fall into the molten bronze used for casting a special big gun designed by the officer. When war arrives, the engineer enlists and takes part in several battles. Severely wounded during a German attack, he is drawn by a vision to a cannon. It happens to be his rival's cannon. The dying engineer musters up enough strength to fire the weapon and repel the assault before he dies. The captain's spirit then drapes the French flag over the hero's body. ■

South African War (1899–1902). Britain's desire for expanding its African empire and its lust for gold were the causes of this conflict, commonly known as the Boer War, between Britain and the Boer republics of Transvaal and the Orange Free State. Though Britain won the war and integrated the area into its South African holdings, there still exists a deep antipathy between the two main groups, British and Dutch, who reside there. The differences are evident in the divisive politics of the Union of South Africa in which its chief parties represent different cultures and values.

The Boers were descended from the Dutch who settled in the Cape region of South Africa beginning in the mid-1600s. After Holland ceded the area to Great Britain in 1815, the Boers resented British rule which brought greater British immigration and the abolition of slavery. The Dutch Africans made a mass migration northward known as the Great Trek (1835–1840), covered in the film *Untamed* (1955), starring Tyrone Power and Susan Hayward, to found the republics of The Transvaal and The Orange Free State.

The discovery of gold in 1886 in the Transvaal attracted British prospectors and migrants. To protect themselves from the growing economic power of the newcomers, the Boer government denied citizenship to the British and taxed them heavily as "outsiders." Encouraged by Cecil Rhodes, a powerful figure in South African politics who envisioned the spread of British power in Africa, Britain sent troops to enforce the political and economic rights of the British in the Boer republics. When Britain turned down a Boer demand to withdraw its troops, the Dutch republics declared war on October 12, 1899.

Though initially successful, the Boers were eventually defeated when Britain increased its forces to nearly 350,000 against 60,000 Boer troops. Nevertheless, Britain experienced great difficulty in controlling their enemy's hit-and-run guerrilla tactics and even resorted to the use of concentration camps as detention centers for Boer families. An estimated 20,000 civilians died in these camps. Two British officers who enhanced their reputation in this war were Lord Kitchener, who conducted the anti-guerrilla campaign with the use of fortified strong points and detention centers, and Colonel Baden-Powell, later founder of the Boy Scouts.

Only a handful of American films focused on the conflict. The first to appear on American screens were newsreels, released by Biograph in 1900, showing actual scenes of the war. "The Highlander's Defiance" (1910), *The Boer War* (1914) and *The Second In Command* (1915), early American silent dramas based on this conflict, depicted the struggle from the British point of view. J. Stuart Blackton's *The Judgment House* (1915), chiefly about a love triangle, included battle sequences only in its second half. All emphasized the bravery exhibited by British troops without going into the causes of the conflict. One drama, however, indicted Britain's policies and personal actions of its troops. *Torn Allegiance* (1984) showed the destruction wrought on Boer farms by British policy that mandated "search and destroy missions" against suspected guerrilla strongholds and the homes of Boer sympathizers. In one scene a British officer vents his hatred of the Boers and their guerrilla tactics by raping one of their daughters. It's a powerful story of how those on both sides of a struggle can turn violent.

As a result of its victory, Britain annexed the area and a few years later combined their South African colonies into a self-governing dominion known as the Union of South Africa. The Nationalists, who gained control of the government following World War II, advocated a policy of racial separation and subjugation of non-whites known as Apartheid—

the cause of much turmoil in modern South Africa. ■

"South American Front" (1944). See "The March of Time." ■

South of the Equator (1924). Bud Barsky. *Dir.* William James Craft; *Sc.* Robert Dillon; *Cast includes:* Kenneth McDonald, Eugene Corey, Virginia Warwick.

In this below-average action drama, the daughter of an ousted president of a South American country journeys to the U.S. to seek weapons and assistance. Kenneth McDonald, as a robust American hero, comes to the damsel's aid. Accompanied by his black servant who serves also as comic relief, he straightens things out in the country in question. The film provides plenty of action by way of several battle scenes and fights before order is restored.

Another in a series of films dealing with revolution south of the border, this drama is reminiscent of *The Rough Diamond* (1921), *The Dictator, Do and Dare* and *Fortune's Mask*, all released in 1922. Unfortunately, the actual unrest in many of these countries during this period involved more than one or two Americans. The U.S. repeatedly was forced to send in troops to such countries as Haiti, the Dominican Republic, Honduras, Mexico and Guatemala to protect American property or establish a neutral zone during their revolutions. ■

South Sea Woman (1953), WB. *Dir.* Arthur Lubin; *Sc.* Edwin Blum; *Cast includes:* Burt Lancaster, Virginia Mayo, Chuck Connors, Arthur Shields.

Two stranded U.S. Marines and a blonde spend the beginning of World War II on a Pacific island in this comedy drama. The film, unfolding in flashback, opens on the eve of Pearl Harbor in Shanghai. Burt Lancaster, as one of the leathernecks, attempts to prevent his fellow marine (Chuck Connors) from marrying a local photographer (Virginia Mayo). In so doing, the buddies are too late to ship out with their unit. When they and the girl journey by way of a Chinese junk trying to catch up with the ship, they end up on an island controlled by a Vichy Frenchman. The two marines masquerade as deserters, ultimately freeing French prisoners, sinking an enemy destroyer and disrupting a Japanese invasion. ■

Southern Yankee, A (1948), MGM. *Dir.* Edward Sedgwick; *Sc.* Harry Tugend; *Cast includes:* Red Skelton, Brian Donlevy, Arlene Dahl, George Coulouris.

Red Skelton portrays a bungling bellhop and Union spy who in turn poses as a Confederate spy in this Civil War comedy. He gets entangled in his usual predicaments in this farcical film. Brian Donlevy plays a war profiteer while Arlene Dahl provides some romantic interest. Silent screen comedian Buster Keaton, who made the classic Civil War comedy, *The General* (1927), helped to create several of the comic routines for Skelton.

Sylvan Simon, who actually directed the film, was taken off the credits by the studio when he objected to reshooting minor scenes unnecessarily. According to an interview with Red Skelton, the studio, fearful of bringing in the picture under budget, ordered more retakes. The executives were afraid that the bankers would insist that future films adhere to this lower budget. Director Edward Sedgwick was then assigned the task of taking the comedy over the budget. ■

"Southerners, The" (1914), Edison. *Dir.* John Ridgely, John Collins; *Cast includes:* Richard Tucker, Mabel Trunelle, Bigelow Cooper, Herbert Prior, Julius A. Mood, Jr.

When a young man living temporarily in the South confesses to his sweetheart that his loyalties are with the North, she ends the relationship. The Civil War breaks out and the Yankee joins Captain Farragut aboard the *Hartford*. The young man successfully runs the Confederate blockade and distinguishes himself in battle. By the end of the film he and his sweetheart renew their romance. Several battles occur in this silent film, including the bombardment of Fort Morgan and the Battle of Mobile Bay.

"Damn the torpedoes! Go ahead!" Those were the immortal words of Admiral David Farragut (1801–1870) on August 5, 1864, as he led his flotilla of Union warships past the blazing Confederate guns of Fort Morgan guarding Mobile Bay, Alabama. Farragut's twin goals were to close down the last Southern port of any appreciable size so as to tighten even more the Union's naval blockade of the Confederacy and destroy the anchored enemy fleet protected by the artillery at Fort Morgan.

As his ships started their run into the harbor

Union soldier Red Skelton expresses surprise when he is chosen as a spy to infiltrate Confederate lines during the Civil War. *A Southern Yankee* (1948).

on a hot summer morning, they came under a murderous barrage from both the fort and enemy fleet that lay waiting. Confusion spread among the Union's lead vessels as several went down. Farragut, already 63 years old, climbed high into the rigging of his flagship, the U.S.S. *Hartford*, to peer ahead into the smoke of battle to see why progress had ceased. When word came to him that torpedoes, as mines were called then, were creating problems in maneuvering, he exploded in his famous command and by sheer will power, drove his force forward to successfully engage and destroy the enemy flotilla. Farragut's victory ended the port's value to the South. The bypassed fort surrendered soon after.

Promoted to vice-admiral for his victory at Mobile Bay, Farragut had two years earlier used a similar around-end tactic to neutralize the land defenses of New Orleans and help the Union capture the South's leading Gulf port. ■

Spanish–American War (1898). A powerful explosion rent the night air in Havana harbor, capital of Cuba, on February 15, 1898.

The battleship U.S.S. *Maine*, sent to protect Americans and their considerable property in Cuba during that region's ongoing revolution against its Spanish masters, had mysteriously blown up at anchor and went to the bottom, killing 260 crewmen. The tragedy, for which no cause was ever discovered, was blamed on Spain by a hysterical American press as exemplified by the "yellow journalism" of William Randolph Hearst.

The U.S. public's sympathies had already been aroused on the side of the Cubans by often sensational newspaper reports of atrocities committed by Spanish officials attempting to quash the revolt. Americans clamored for retribution, including war against Spain. Swept along by a wave of public emotion, President McKinley and the Congress declared war on April 25, 1898. The ensuing conflict became the shortest war on record for the U.S. As a result of its victory the U.S. entered the age of overseas imperialism by acquiring colonial possessions on two continents and gaining status as a world power.

Though incidents in Cuba had sparked the start of war, actual fighting between Spain and the U.S. started in Asia. Commodore George Dewey, commanding the American Asian fleet, slipped into Manila Bay on May 1 and shelled the Spanish naval squadron there. Within hours the one-sided battle was over with Spain losing all of its ships and 170 men while the U.S. force lost one sailor— due to heatstroke. American land forces under General Wesley Merritt arrived two months later and, aided by Filipino rebels under Emilio Aguinaldo, captured Manila and gained control of the islands. Several films focused on this aspect of the war and its aftermath, including *The Last Man* (1916), *Across the Pacific* (1926), *The Real Glory* (1939) and *Cavalry Command* (1963). Some of these also dealt with the Moro uprising.

In Cuba, meanwhile, an American fleet under Admiral William T. Sampson sank every vessel in a Spanish naval squadron that attempted to break through a blockade at Santiago de Cuba on July 3. General William R. Shafter's invasion force of 17,000 took Santiago, after hard fighting, on July 17. His troops included the Rough Riders, a volunteer cavalry regiment led by Colonel Leonard Wood and Lt. Colonel Theodore Roosevelt. The Rough Riders distinguished themselves in an attack up strategically important Kettle Hill as part of the Battle of San Juan Hill, overlooking Santiago.

Surprisingly, few films dealt with the sea battles of the war. *Masters of Men* (1923) depicted part of the naval engagement between Spanish and American warships at Santiago Harbor. Even fewer films dramatized the Cuban Revolution that precipitated the war. "The Dawn of Freedom" (1910) covered this period, but only superficially. American film studios did consider the Battle of San Juan Hill and the dashing Roosevelt tailor-made subjects for the screen. As early as 1909 the industry responded with "Up San Juan Hill," which included detailed battle scenes. The biographical drama *The Fighting Roosevelts* (1919) highlighted the same battle. *The Denial* (1925) had its hero killed while fighting with the Rough Riders. *End of the Trail* (1936), with Jack Holt, began with battle sequences of Roosevelt and the Rough Riders but soon settled into a conventional western. Victor Fleming's *The Rough Riders* (1927) presented the most accurate account of the famous regiment's exploits. One film, *A Message to Garcia* (1936) starring Wallace Beery, concerned the general fighting in Cuba.

Meanwhile, another American army under General Nelson A. Miles landed in Puerto Rico and easily had control of the island by the time an armistice was declared on August 12, 1898. Captain Henry Glass took the island of Guam by merely firing a volley at the Spanish who had no cannon shells. Uninhabited Wake Island was annexed by American troops on the way to the Philippines.

In the Treaty of Paris (December 10, 1898), Spain gave independence to Cuba and ceded to the U.S. the territories of Guam, the Philippines and Puerto Rico. The U.S. paid Spain $20 million for the Philippines.

Of all the dramas about the war, perhaps "Tearing Down the Spanish Flag" (1898), a brief movie running only a few minutes, was the most unusual. It was a landmark film— probably the first American war movie and America's first propaganda film. It was produced on the roof of the Morse Building on Nassau Street in New York City. Director–writer J. Stuart Blackton played a stalwart soldier who removes the Spanish colors and hoists the American flag. Contemporary audiences, impressed with the work, believed it was actually made in Cuba during combat. ■

Spanish Armada. On July 12, 1588, a Spanish fleet of 130 vessels sailed from Corunna on Spain's western coast charged with the mission of invading England. The upstart British, under Queen Elizabeth I, for some time had been challenging the power of Spain's Philip II both in Europe and on the sea lanes leading to the New World. The heavily armed Spanish flotilla, probably the largest assemblage of sea power that western Europe had ever seen, carried 8,500 seamen and galley slaves, plus 19,000 troops, all under the command of the Duke of Medina Sidonia. The English navy, under the overall command of Lord Howard of Effingham, beat the Armada in a series of engagements that began off Plymouth on the English coast on July 21. The battle continued for the next several weeks. At one point near the coast of Flanders, the English sent blazing ships into the anchored enemy fleet being reprovisioned. English warships then closed in to destroy part of the disorganized Spanish force that had cut loose and was drifting aimlessly before unfavorable winds. The Armada fled from further attacks by sailing completely around the British Isles to return to Spain.

England's victory stemmed from a number of factors. They included superior seamanship, lighter and faster ships, the use of broadside firing techniques, proximity of friendly ports for repairs and provisioning, and weather conditions that handicapped the combat maneuverability of the bulkier Spanish vessels. The remains of the Armada struggled back into Spanish ports during August and September after losing 63 ships and thousands of men. The battle ended Spain's dominance as a sea power and enhanced both Britain's image as mistress of the seas and her ambitions for an overseas empire.

The defeat of the Spanish Armada, though important to world history, is the subject of only a few American films. In *The Sea Hawk* (1940) Philip II dispatches an envoy to England to allay the fears of Queen Elizabeth while he continues to build the Spanish Armada for an eventual invasion of England. Sir Francis Drake (Rod Taylor), one of England's legendary seamen, is seen in *Seven Seas to Calais* (1963) as the principal architect in the defeat of the Spanish Armada. ■

Spanish Civil War (1936–39). Following the ousting of King Alfonso XIII and the formation of a republic in 1931, Spain was beset with political and economic strife. Separatist movements, particularly in Catalan, and constant strife between right and left wing extremists weakened attempts by a centrist republican government to deal with Spain's mounting economic problems associated with a spreading world depression. After the election of 1936 in which a leftist Popular Front won control of the government, the right-wing Falangist (Fascist) party, headed by General Francisco Franco, conspired to organize a military coup.

The revolt began with an uprising of army officers at Melilla in Spanish Morocco (July 17, 1936) that triggered similar movements by garrisons in a number of cities including Cadiz and Seville. The army rebels were supported by a majority of other military forces, large elements of the clergy, the upper class, monarchists and those opposed to socialism. The rebels had the support of a large contingent of Moorish troops.

The Spanish Civil War, besides creating a generation filled with internal bitterness, also developed into an international battleground for rival ideologies and a testing ground for arms and tactics to be used shortly in World War II. Fascist Italy under Mussolini and Nazi Germany under Hitler immediately sent "volunteers" to aid Franco's "nationalists." The Soviet Union rendered assistance to republican forces who were known as Loyalists. Though Britain, France and the U.S. followed an official policy of neutrality, volunteers from those countries formed international brigades to assist the Loyalists. These brigades fought extensively in defense of the besieged capital of Madrid. The 1984 documentary *The Good Fight*, using interviews and stock footage, covered the role of the Lincoln Brigade, made up of more than 3,000 American volunteers, in the war.

The insurgents, under a military junta headed by Franco, gradually overwhelmed Loyalist government forces. About 200,000 Loyalists fled over the French border. Those sailors in the fleet who had remained loyal to the republic sailed to Bizerte, Tunis, where they were interned by France. The end came with the capitulation of Madrid on March 28, 1939, after a 28-month siege. Franco's government set up special tribunals which tried and executed hundreds of captured Loyalist leaders, despite pleas from the democratic world to exercise moderation. The executions continued well into the 1940s. Hundreds of thousands of political prisoners were retained as special "labor battalions." Franco, who celebrated his victory with a parade through Madrid (with Mussolini's Italian Black Shirts in front and Hitler's Condor Legion in the rear), ruled as dictator into the 1970s.

The cost of the war in lives to Spain was estimated to be 700,000 slain in battle, 30,000 assassinated or executed and about 15,000 killed by air raids. The war introduced the use of extensive aerial bombardment and armor by Fascist forces and ominously foreshadowed the intense devastation of modern warfare in World War II.

The conflict also created some internal dissent within the U.S., which officially followed a policy of neutrality and placed an embargo on arms shipments to both sides. However, a small but vocal part of the American public sympathized with the Loyalists and saw the dispute as one between democracy and the growing threat of Fascism. Hollywood, fearful of losing the pro-Franco Spanish and some Latin-American markets, sidestepped the whole political issue of the war. In addition, a sizable segment of the U.S.

public looked upon the Loyalists as a Communist front.

Contemporary films using the war as background—*Last Train From Madrid* (1937), a *Grand Hotel* on wheels, and *Blockade* (1938), which raised a storm of protest—were so cleansed of any controversy that a viewer had difficulty in identifying the war or the different factions. Dramas made after the conflict, such as *For Whom the Bell Tolls* (1943), offered more insight into some of the issues and participants. *Confidential Agent* (1945), based on Graham Greene's novel of intrigue, stars Charles Boyer as a war-weary idealistic representative of Republican Spain sent to England to prevent the Fascists from purchasing coal. He is followed and hounded by Fascist agents bent on stopping him from completing his mission. In *Behold a Pale Horse* (1964) Gregory Peck portrays a former guerrilla fighter in the Spanish Civil War of the late 1930s. Although it is twenty years later, he continues to fight the war with forays into Spain from France. Hollywood felt safer treating the controversial war from a distance.

When World War II erupted, the studios almost immediately began to describe some of their fictitious heroes as veterans who fought against Franco and the Fascists. Ray Milland in *Arise, My Love* (1940) is a flier who fought for the Loyalists. Humphrey Bogart in *Casablanca* (1942) fought on the side of the Loyalists before opening his cafe to become the most famous saloonkeeper in the annals of film. Dennis Morgan in *The Desert Song* (1943), an updated version of the famous operetta, is an American expatriate in Morocco who earlier fought against Franco. John Garfield, tortured by the Fascists during the Spanish Civil War, remains a target of his enemies, now aligned with Nazi agents, upon his return to New York in *The Fallen Sparrow* (1943). Paul Lukas in *Watch on the Rhine* (1943) is a resistance leader against the forces of Nazism who earlier fought against Franco in Spain. Although many of these stalwart American champions of freedom no doubt fought with the Lincoln Brigade, this fact was virtually never mentioned in the films. ■

Spartacus (1960), U. *Dir.* Stanley Kubrick; *Sc.* Dalton Trumbo; *Cast includes:* Kirk Douglas, Laurence Olivier, Jean Simmons, Charles Laughton, Tony Curtis, Peter Ustinov.

Universal turned Howard Fast's novel of a Roman slave who struggled for freedom and dignity against a tyrannical system into an intelligent spectacle. Kirk Douglas, as the title figure yearning for freedom, leads a revolt of the slaves who are caged and groomed to fight each other for the entertainment of Roman dignitaries. Laurence Olivier portrays a sadistic patrician general who delights in the mortal combats and is not adverse to slitting the throat of a gladiator (as he does in one particularly gory scene). Peter Ustinov plays a wily operator who trades in gladiator slaves. Tony Curtis, as a houseboy slave to Olivier, joins the ragtag band of runaway slaves. Woody Strode plays a slave who, as a gladiator, reluctantly participates in a fight to the death with Spartacus. Jean Simmons provides the romantic interest for Douglas and lustful desires of Olivier.

The climactic and tragic battle between the courageous army of slaves and the Roman legions is both stirring and spectacular. Universal allegedly assembled 8,000 Spanish soldiers and had them impersonate Roman legionnaires. Following this sequence, Olivier crucifies hundreds of surviving slaves along the Appian Way.

This was screenwriter Dalton Trumbo's first screen credit since his imprisonment for refusing to answer questions before the House Un-American Activities Committee. The film was 31-year-old Stanley Kubrick's fifth directorial effort. ■

Spider and the Rose, The (1923), Principal. *Dir.* John McDermott; *Sc.* Gerald C. Duffy; *Cast includes:* Alice Lake, Gaston Glass, Richard Headrick, Noah Beery, Otis Harlan.

In this tale of old California in the days when it was ruled by Mexico, Gaston Glass portrays the son of the territorial governor who joins a revolutionary force. The governor's assistant, Mendoza, a treacherous despot, forces the governor to rule with an iron fist, thereby arousing the ire of the people. Mendoza manages to arrest the rebels and appoint himself governor. Meanwhile Glass, as the rightful governor's son, frees the prisoners and they overthrow Mendoza and his troops. ■

Spies (1929). See Spy Films: the Silents, Spy Films: the Talkies. ■

Spirit Lake Massacre. See *Sitting Bull at Spirit Lake Massacre* (1927). ■

Spirit of '17, The (1918), Par. Dir. William Taylor; Sc. Julia Ivers; Cast includes: Jack Pickford, G. H. Geldert, Edythe Chapman, L. N. Wells, Charles Arling, Virginia Ware.

A group of twelve-year-old boys, hungry for excitement and adventure, uncover a plot by German spies to stir up dissent among miners in this patriotic drama set during World War I. The goal of the enemy agents is to have the mine put out of commission, thereby crippling American war production. Young Jack Pickford (Mary's brother) plays the leader of the youngsters. He calls upon the residents of a veterans' home to help him capture the alien agents. Based on a story by Judge Willis Brown of the Chicago Juvenile Court, the film was advertised as a "red, white and blue story . . . vibrant with patriotism."

Several World War I dramas dealing with the home front focused on the importance of labor in the war effort. In *The Road to France* (1918) the hero breaks up a German plot to foment a strike at a shipyard. *Safe for Democracy* (1919) attacks members of the International Workers of the World, a radical union of the period, equating them with foreign agents bent on subverting war production. ∎

"Spirit of '76, The" (1905). See American Revolution. ∎

Spirit of '76, The (1917), Continental. Dir. Frank Montgomery, George Seigman; Sc. Robert Goldstein; Cast includes: Adda Gleason, Doris Pawn, Jane Novak, Howard Gaye.

An inflammatory anti-British depiction of the American Revolution, the film includes such scenes as an English soldier bayoneting a child during a re-enactment of the savage Wyoming Valley Massacre by the redcoats. Writer Robert Goldstein, who was also the producer, was plagued with a continuous series of setbacks. The U.S. entered World War I on Britain's side, and many thought it inappropriate to exhibit the film at this time. Chicago officials stopped its showing in July 1917 on grounds of its violence. Goldstein objected, claiming that all the incidents were based on actual facts. The injunction was lifted only after several reels were removed.

Later that year Goldstein took the film to Los Angeles where he again met with resistance, this time under the Espionage Act. After a lengthy trial he was fined $5,000 dollars and sentenced to twelve years in a federal penitentiary for inciting mutiny among the military forces. An appeal failed, the judge stating that the film might have aroused the armed forces. President Wilson intervened and reduced the sentence. Goldstein was released in 1921 after being imprisoned for almost two years and continued to exhibit the film during the postwar period to regain some of the production costs. ∎

"Spirit of the Red Cross, The" (1918), American Film Industry. Dir. Jack Eaton; Sc. James Montgomery Flagg; Cast includes: Ray McKee, Peggy Adams.

An American doughboy (Ray McKee) is sent to France with his regiment. He leaves behind his girlfriend (Peggy Adams), who volunteers as a Red Cross nurse and is also assigned to duty overseas. McKee is wounded in battle and is about to pass out. He regains consciousness in time to see a German soldier advancing towards him as he goes about bayoneting the wounded. McKee kills the enemy soldier. Later, he awakens in a field hospital where his sweetheart nurses him back to health. The film, produced by the motion picture industry, emphasizes the services performed by the Red Cross with refugees as well as with those in uniform. ∎

Spirit of the U.S.A., The (1924), FBO. Dir. Emory Johnson; Sc. Emilie Johnson; Cast includes: Johnnie Walker, Mary Carr, Carl Stockdale, Dave Kirby, Mark Fenton.

Johnnie Walker, as an idealistic son of a farming family, joins the Salvation Army when he is rejected by the military as a result of an ear infection in this drama. Meanwhile, Walker's lazy brother, who reluctantly enlisted in the army after being prodded by his wife, is killed in action. The heartless widow decides to evict the parents of her deceased husband from their home. But they are rescued in time by Walker, who returns to the farm in the nick of time to set things right. ∎

Sporting Venus, The (1925), MGM. Dir. Marshall Neilan; Sc. Frank Geraghty; Cast includes: Blanche Sweet, Ronald Colman, Lew Cody, Hank Mann.

Blanche Sweet and Ronald Colman portray star-crossed lovers in this World War I romantic drama that hangs too heavily on a simple misunderstanding. The film is set in Scotland where Sweet, as Lady Gwendolyn, falls in love with a local villager (Colman) who lives in the shadow of her family castle. When war breaks out and he is about to leave for the front, she pledges to wait for him. Two years later, while Colman is on leave in London, a jealous prince informs him that Lady Gwendolyn is no longer interested in him. Colman meets her on his last night before he returns to the war and treats her with detachment. After he leaves, Sweet, who thinks her lover no longer cares for her, promises to marry the prince. But she finds out just in time that the prince is an impoverished fortune hunter. ■

Springfield Rifle (1952), WB. *Dir.* Andre DeToth; *Sc.* Charles Marquis Warren, Frank Davis; *Cast includes:* Gary Cooper, Phyllis Thaxter, David Brian, Paul Kelly.

A Union officer (Gary Cooper) masquerades as an outlaw to find out who is stealing government horses in this Civil War action drama. A western cavalry post is plagued by a gang of rustlers who steal the mounts as they are being shipped to Union troops and sell them to the South. A Union colonel contrives a plan that cashiers Cooper out of the service on charges of cowardice. Cooper's wife (Phyllis Thaxter) and son are not aware of the scheme that allows Cooper to join the outlaws and eventually round up the miscreants, particularly the commander of the army post (Paul Kelly), who is in reality a Southern sympathizer. David Brian plays the leader of the rustlers. The title refers to the new model of rifle that Cooper tests during his exploits and that was to become standard army issue. The film, set in 1864, describes the origins of the Army Intelligence Department. ■

Spuds (1927), Pathe. *Dir.* Larry Semon; *Sc.* Larry Semon; *Cast includes:* Larry Semon, Edward Hearne, Kewpie Morgan, Hugh Fay, Dorothy Dwan.

Larry Semon plays "Spuds," a much-abused private in this World War I comedy. His sergeant continually growls at him and has Larry before a mountain of potatoes. It seems that the private will be peeling spuds for the duration. On occasion Larry performs some brave deeds in battle but is never credited with them. In one incident a payroll truck disappears and Larry's captain is suspected of the theft. Larry accidentally comes across the missing vehicle and retrieves it from the Germans. ■

Spy, The (1914), Universal. *Dir.* Otis Turner; *Sc.* Otis Turner; *Cast includes:* Herbert Rawlinson, Edna Maison, Ella Hall, William Worthington.

Based on James Fenimore Cooper's novel about the American Revolution, the silent drama tells the story of a member of George Washington's household who works as a spy for the Commander-in-Chief. To protect the young man as he journeys back and forth across British lines, even Washington's own men do not know of the subterfuge. When they capture him, they think he is spying for the British and plan to execute him at one point in the story. The film has several rousing battle scenes. ■

Spy, The (1917). See Spy Films: the Silents. ■

Spy comedies. The spy comedy became popular during World War I and has continued to entertain audiences until the present day. Except for Charlie Chaplin's *Shoulder Arms* (1918) and a few others, war comedies did not begin to appear until after the conflict. Major and minor studios offered their top screen personalities and many minor talents to the spy comedy genre. The popular Lee Sisters appeared in several spy comedies. In *Doing Their Bit* (1918) they are sent to America from Ireland to live with an uncle who owns a munitions plant. They soon help to expose a group of spies who are plotting against the factory. *Smiles* (1919) had the children help in the capture of more foreign agents. George Walsh portrays a navy reject in *I'll Say So* (1918) who gets mixed up with some German spies on the Mexican border.

Spy comedies became a Hollywood staple during World War II. *All Through the Night* (1941), starring Humphrey Bogart, is a comedy drama about spies and hoodlums in New York City. The plot involves Nazi agents who plan to blow up a battleship in a local harbor. The East Side Kids in such low-budget entries as *Bowery Blitzkrieg* and *Flying Wild*, both released in 1941, and *Junior Army* and *Let's Get Tough!*, (both 1942), engage in their usual low comedy as they clash with foreign agents. MGM's singing star Jeanette MacDonald and Robert Young journey to the Mideast in *Cairo*, a 1942 spy spoof, where MacDonald opens a secret pyramid by reaching the note of high C. In *Call Out the Marines* (1942) Victor McLaglen and Edmund Lowe repeat their familiar roles as Captain Flagg and Sergeant Quirt (using different names)—a pair of brawling leathernecks. In *The Lady Has Plans* (1942) Paulette Goddard is mistaken for a spy who has been temporarily tattooed with secret plans. Nazi and British agents attempt to undress her in an effort to gaze upon the alleged secrets.

By 1943 leading comedians of stage, screen and radio were making spy comedies. Laurel and Hardy in *Air Raid Wardens* (1943), rejected by the draft board, manage to stumble upon and capture a nest of Nazi agents. Stan and Ollie again become entangled in intrigue in *The Big Noise* (1944) when some spies plot to steal a super-bomb. *Margin for Error* (1943), with its original premise of assigning Jewish policemen to guard a German consulate in New York, features Milton Berle as one of the officers. Bob Hope brought his one-liners and his portrayal of the reluctant hero to a string of successful comedies, including *My Favorite Blonde* (1942), *They Got Me Covered* (1943), *My Favorite Brunette* (1947) and *My Favorite Spy* (1951).

Spy comedies starring major comics continued well into the postwar years. Danny Kaye as a G.I. in *On the Double* (1961) is called upon to pose as a British general whom he happens to resemble. Kaye becomes entangled with the general's chauffeur (Diana Dors) who turns out to be a German spy. ∎

Spy films: the silents. Plots about spies, double agents, enemy aliens and international intrigue have been with us since the birth of the American movie industry at the turn of the century. Ranging from crude silent one-reelers to sophisticated romantic dramas, spy films cover a variety of wars and world conflicts and take place in many countries. They generally contain the usual ingredients of other dramas—romance, adventure, suspense and, to a lesser degree, political intrigue. As a genre, they follow certain conventions. Heroes or heroines match wits with master spies who control a network of underlings. Secret weapons, military plans or important figures are the typical targets of unscrupulous domestic or foreign agents. Often, the fate of a nation hangs in the balance.

The themes of war, loyalty, greed and paranoia dominate the spy drama. Events may point to preparedness as the safest road for a nation, even if agents must steal another country's military plans. These films test the loyalties of their heroes and heroines. Agents are always on the prowl for the weak who are willing to accept money in exchange for information. National fear may set off a chain of unlikely events that seem to infringe upon one's freedoms—all for national security reasons, as in the spy films that emerged during the Cold War of the 1950s.

American spy films have ranged far and wide in their attempt to bring entertainment to their audiences. One of the earliest spy dramas, "The Hand of Uncle Sam" (1910), concerns an American in an unnamed foreign country who is accused of spying. He is rescued from a firing squad at the last minute when the Secretary of War sends a torpedo boat to the rescue. The real spy is captured and put to death. Several pre-World War I spy movies used the Civil War as background. In the one-reel short, "The Girl Spy Before Vicksburg" (1911), a daughter of the South disguises herself as a member of a Union convoy and destroys a powder wagon. A fisherman in "The Gray Sentinel" (1913) volunteers to act as a spy for the Confederates who are trying to run a Union blockade. Civil War films involving intrigue continued into the sound era. *Only the Brave* (1930), for example, tells of a Union captain (Gary Cooper) who volunteers as a spy. He purposely allows himself to be caught with false plans designed to mislead the Confederate general staff. In *Secret Service* (1931), based on William Gillette's popular Civil War play, Richard Dix, as a Union captain, dons a Confederate uniform to spy upon the enemy. The drama also appeared as a silent film in 1919.

Almost as many spy dramas about World War I were produced as those about the second global conflict. In *My Country First* (1916), one of the earliest, a Kaiser-like German spy attempts to steal the formula for a powerful explosive. *Somewhere in France* (1916) was one of the earliest World War I dramas to feature a female spy. After stealing secret plans from her French lover, Louise Glaum rapidly advances within the ranks of German Intelligence. Dustin Farnum, as a U.S. Secret Service agent in *The Spy* (1917), journeys to Berlin to obtain a book which lists all the secret agents operating in America. He succeeds in finding the book and turns it over to the proper authorities but is later caught and sentenced to death. *Paws of the Bear* (1917), a romantic spy drama set chiefly in Belgium, concerns a young Russian agent (Clara Williams) and an American agent (William Desmond).

Sometimes spies were uncovered most unexpectedly and in the most unlikely places. Jack Mulhall, as an American prisoner of war interned in a German camp in *Flames of Chance* (1918), discovers that a letter from the States, when held near a candle, contains secret writing. Enemy agents in America, he realizes, are sending messages via this route to Germany. In *No Man's Land* (1918) a German agent on a remote Pacific island uses a wireless to feed information about Allied shipping to enemy raiders.

According to American films, the home front was no guarantee of safety from enemy machinations. As early as 1915 *Over Secret Wires* depicts German spies contacting submarines about American shipping off the coast of Oregon. By 1916 foreign agents were working in Washington trying to steal the formula for a high explosive, according to the drama *Paying the Price*. In *Miss Jackie of the Army* (1917) Marguerita Fischer, as the young heroine, overhears spies planning to blow up a troop train. Director Francis Ford in *Who Was the Other Man?* (1917) also portrays a stalwart secret service agent in hot pursuit of the "Black Legion," a nefarious group of saboteurs. Dorothy Dalton, as the promiscuous wife of an English captain in *The Dark Road* (1917), has an affair with an art connoisseur who in reality is a German spy. He learns from her husband's letters about secret troop movements and relays the information to his headquarters. German spies set out to steal the plans for a new American rifle in *The Kaiser's Shadow* (1918) until they are foiled by U.S. Secret Service agent Thurston Hall and French spy Dorothy Dalton.

The year 1918 was a banner one for spy films with domestic backgrounds. Gloria Swanson, in such films as *The Secret Code*, *Shifting Sands* and *Wife or Country*, specialized in roles which depict her as a vulnerable female who is forced to spy for German agents. A similar fate fell upon Peggy Hyland, as a Senator's wife in *Her Debt of Honor*. A German agent (Frank Schiller), after having an affair with her, tries to gain vital information for his own country. In *The Border Wireless* William S. Hart foils the plans of German agents to relay the location of General Pershing's troop ship on its way to France. Tom

Mix, another cowboy star, uncovers a plot by German spies to take over a tungsten mine in *Mr. Logan, U.S.A.* Policeman Glenn White in *Love and the Law* stumbles across a plot by foreign agents to blow up a troop train. America's shipbuilding industry becomes the target of German spies in *The Road to France*. Jack Mulhall in *Madam Spy* impersonates a female agent so that he can capture a gang of spies. German agents attempt to destroy the sugar plantations of Hawaii in *The Marriage Ring*, with Enid Bennett, Robert McKim and Jack Holt. A pacifist wife in *Stolen Orders* steals secret information from her admiral husband to further the cause of her organization. In the romantic drama *Suspicion* the lonely wife of a research scientist unknowingly has an affair with a German spy. England is the setting for *The Man Who Wouldn't Tell*, a drama involving the British secret service. In *Claws of the Hun*, with Charles Ray, German spies attempt to steal highly secret papers from an American munitions plant. Lewis Stone, as an English officer in *Inside the Lines* (1918), prevents the Germans from blowing up Gibraltar and crippling a large part of the English navy anchored there. Ralph Forbes appeared in a 1930 remake.

The war may have ended in 1918, but the conflict continued in the steady stream of spy dramas and comedies that appeared during the next two decades. Carlyle Blackwell, as an American secret agent in *Love in a Hurry* (1919), poses as a muleteer aboard a tramp steamer. In reality a New York millionaire who had unknowingly sold precious war materiel to German agents, he vows to expose the entire gang. *The Highest Trump* (1919), one of the earliest war films to focus on the use of airplanes in combat, featured Earle Williams playing a dual role. *Dangerous Days* (1920) takes place on the eve of World War I. German agents are bent on subverting the production of American munitions manufacturers. In 1921 the first of three screen versions of E. Phillips Oppenheim's popular novel *The Great Impersonation* appeared. A German agent who closely resembles an Englishman travels to Britain to replace his lookalike. A variation of the plot occurs in *Nazi Agent* (1941) starring the distinguished veteran actor Conrad Veidt. He appears in the dual role of twin brothers, one a loyal German-American and the other a Nazi spy. In *The Hidden Code* (1920) the inventor of a high explosive tattoos the secret formula on his daughter's shoulder. *Secret Orders* (1926) concerns enemy agents in the U.S. trying to learn about troop sailings. In *The Great Deception*, released the same year, an Englishman (Ben Lyon) educated in Germany becomes a double agent working for England. The plot anticipates *The Counterfeit Traitor* (1962), starring William Holden and Lilli Palmer.

It is difficult to measure the effects of these films on American audiences. They must have created a good deal of suspicion toward certain foreigners and left some negative impressions of the potential vulnerability of the nation's secrets. ■

Spy films: the talkies. The advent of sound no doubt helped the spy genre which depends on dialogue more than the combat film. World War I dramas about male and female spies, often having to choose between love and duty, began to appear. George O'Brien, as an English spy in *True Heaven* (1929), falls in love with Lois Moran, a German agent. In *This Mad World* (1930) Basil Rathbone, as a French spy, decides to visit his mother living behind German lines. He falls in love with a German officer's wife who informs on him. Marlene Dietrich, as a street walker, is persuaded to pose as a German spy in *Dishonored* (1931). However, her new career is short-lived when she falls in love with an enemy agent (Victor McLaglen) and effects his escape. A military court sentences her to death for placing love before duty. "Could you let me die in a uniform of my own choosing?" she requests of a visiting priest. "Any dress I was wearing when I served my countrymen, not my country," she explains. In *The Gay Diplomat* (1931) Ivan Lebedeff portrays a handsome Russian officer. His reputation with women inspires Russian intelligence to assign him to Bucharest to track down a female spy.

This romantic theme continued throughout the 1930s. Greta Garbo starred in *Mata Hari* (1932), based on the exploits of the most famous female spy. She succumbs to the same fatal flaw as Dietrich and pays the same heavy price. Constance Bennett, as a Russian agent in *After Tonight* (1933), falls in love with Austrian counterspy Gilbert Roland. In *Madame Spy* (1934) Fay Wray, as a Russian agent, marries the chief of the Austrian diplomatic service. *Lancer Spy* (1937), with

George Sanders and Dolores Del Rio, provides a noteworthy culmination to the espionage dramas of World War I since it contained many of major elements of the genre. In a reversal of the Oppenheim plot mentioned above, Sanders plays a dual role—an English agent who doubles for a captured German officer and is sent to Germany. Dolores Del Rio, as a German spy, falls in love with him.

Upon a second viewing, the World War I spy dramas of the 1930s appear uniquely romantic and charming as the female spies more often than not choose love over duty. The settings and atmosphere are often inaccurate. The gowns and hair styles, especially, seem more in tune with the Depression era than with the World War I years. The cat-and-mouse games between the male spy and his female counterpart from the enemy country appear quaint by today's standards.

Only a handful of pre-World War II spy dramas came to the American screen. *Cipher Bureau* (1938) features Leon Ames as the head of the counter-espionage cipher bureau. The agency is set up to foil hostile nations from sending secret messages to their agents in the U.S. In *The Spy Ring* (1938), with William Hall and Jane Wyman, unidentified enemy agents plot to steal the U.S. Army's latest anti-aircraft weapon.

World War II spy dramas began with a powerful, forthright exposé of German infiltration in the U.S. *Confessions of a Nazi Spy* (1939) stars Edward G. Robinson as an F.B.I. agent who helps to unravel the web of spies. That same year Anna Sten played a European refugee in *Exile Express* pursued by foreign spies who need her to decipher a secret formula. Director Alfred Hitchcock the following year turned out *Foreign Correspondent*, starring Joel McCrea, Laraine Day and George Sanders. More sophisticated but just as anti-German as its predecessors, the plot concerns an American reporter (McCrea) who becomes entangled in international intrigue in Europe. In *Flying Blind* (1941), with Richard Arlen and Jean Parker, foreign agents try to steal a newly developed transformer for use in fighter aircraft.

As soon as America entered the war, Hollywood studios cast their major stars in a variety of spy plots set in foreign lands. The atmospheric *Journey Into Fear* (1942), with Joseph Cotten, Dolores Del Rio and Orson Welles, spins a tale of intrigue involving munitions smuggling and Nazi spies aboard a vessel bound for Turkey. In *Berlin Correspondent* (1942) Dana Andrews, as an American radio correspondent in Berlin, comes into possession of highly secret Nazi war information. Robert Cummings in Alfred Hitchcock's suspenseful *Saboteur* (1942) portrays an innocent factory worker who is accused of destroying an aircraft plant. He eludes the police and pursues Norman Lloyd, the real saboteur, across the continent to clear his own name. Joan Crawford and Fred MacMurray, as American newlyweds honeymooning in Europe in the implausible but entertaining *Above Suspicion* (1943), are asked to spy for the Allies. That same year George Raft in *Background to Danger* matched wits with Nazi and Russian agents in Turkey. Fritz Lang's *Ministry of Fear* (1944), about spies operating in England, overflows with intrigue, paranoia and deception—characteristics of *film noir*. Ray Milland, as a helpless victim, echoes another characteristic of the genre: "I wonder if you know what it means to stand all alone in a dark corner." *The Conspirators* (1944), set in Lisbon, features Hedy Lamarr as a young French woman married to a German official. Paul Henreid portrays a Dutch guerrilla leader hunted by the Nazis.

The low-budget studios, usually concerned with economics, found that spy stories were cheaper to produce than combat films which required larger casts, more special effects and larger sets. Most of these dramas pertained to the home front. Low budget films, which also came from the major studios, continued throughout the war years and beyond. J. Edward Bromberg in *The Devil Pays Off* (1941) uncovers a plot involving a shipping tycoon who plans to sell his fleet to a potential enemy of the U.S. *Underground Agent* (1942) features Bruce Bennett as a government agent trying to prevent defense plant secrets from falling into enemy hands. *Black Dragons* (1942) features Bela Lugosi as a Nazi doctor bent on a trail of revenge after he is betrayed by the Axis powers. In *Busses Roar* (1942), featuring Richard Travis, a saboteur is foiled in his attempt to ignite an oil field as a signal to a Japanese submarine. *Spy Ship* (1942), with Craig Stevens and Irene Manning, concerns a network of spies who trade American military secrets about American ship departures to the enemy. In *Spy Train* (1943) Richard Travis steps off the bus and boards a train with fellow passengers, including Nazi

agents. The flag-waving *Submarine Alert* (1943) features Richard Arlen as a foreigner and Wendy Barrie as a federal agent. Both help to prevent enemy agents from signaling a Japanese submarine off the Pacific coast. These dramas followed the conventions of the genre, rarely offering anything innovative in plot or theme.

Some of these B features were set elsewhere although they were all made in Hollywood's back lots. Often the exotic sets were more appealing than the routine plots. *Secret Agent of Japan* (1942), with Preston Foster and Lynn Bari, concerned espionage in an international settlement in Shanghai. Jon Hall dons a cloak of invisibility in *Invisible Agent* (1942) to create havoc among Nazi and Japanese leaders in Berlin. Special agent Robert Lowery in *Lure of the Islands* (1942) investigates enemy activity somewhere in the Pacific. The Pacific was also the setting of *Prisoner of Japan* (1942) where Japanese agents operating from an island threaten American warships. Leo Carrillo, Andy Devine and Don Terry teamed up in *Danger in the Pacific* (1942) to locate Nazi arms hidden on another island. The trio teamed up again for *Escape From Hong Kong* (1942), about German spies and an undercover agent (Marjorie Lord) working for British Intelligence in Hong Kong. In *Half Way to Shanghai* (1942), set in 1942 Burma, Nazi agents attempt to get maps of Chinese defenses and ammunition depots. *Secrets of Scotland Yard* (1944), with Edgar Barrier, explored some of the methods employed by the Yard to break enemy codes. *Storm Over Lisbon* (1944), with Vera Hruba Ralston, Richard Arlen and Erich von Stroheim, told a familiar tale filled with the usual spies and other assorted villains.

Espionage at home was a popular subject for dramas from both major and minor studios. As early as 1940 foreign agents in *The Hidden Enemy* are trying to steal American secrets, specifically a metal three times lighter than aluminum. Charles Farrell, as a G-man, poses as a Nazi agent in *The Deadly Game* (1941) so that he can round up a spy network. Saboteurs cause a series of fatal plane crashes in *Federal Fugitives* (1941) before Neil Hamilton puts a stop to them. Teenagers do their share at home in *Down in San Diego* (1941) by breaking up a spy ring at a naval base.

The home front as the setting for World War II spy dramas reached its peak in 1942.

In *Dangerously They Live* hospital intern John Garfield rescues a recently arrived British agent (Nancy Coleman) from the clutches of Nazi spies. In *The Dawn Express*, also known as *Nazi Spy Ring*, Nazi agents attempt to steal the secret of a new type of gasoline known as "Formula 311" in this low-budget drama. A high explosive is the prize sought by secret agents in *Powder Town*, starring Edmond O'Brien as an eccentric scientist. Hollywood is the background for *Foreign Agent*, a 1942 drama in which Nazi spies have a double mission in the film capital. They desire the plans for a special light filter and attempt to persuade citizens to resist the war effort. Hitchcock's influence can be seen in several spy dramas in which an innocent person gets involved in a spy ring. Both Richard Carlson in *Fly by Night* (1942) and Robert Preston in *Pacific Blackout*, released the same year, face this dilemma.

As World War II continued to dominate the headlines and the thoughts of all Americans, movie audiences began to tire of war films and preferred escapism. Hollywood replied by producing fewer combat and spy films. *They Came to Blow Up America* (1943) concerns eight German saboteurs who are put ashore off Long Island, ultimately caught and brought to trial. In *Appointment in Berlin* (1943) George Sanders, secretly enlisted into the British secret service, poses as a German collaborator and journeys to Berlin. Character actors J. Carrol Naish and John Carradine were enemy agents in several low-budget films, including *Waterfront* (1944), in which they both appear at their meanest as employees of the Nazis. *The House on 92nd Street* (1945), considered by many critics as one of the best spy dramas to emerge from World War II, reveals in semidocumentary style the story of how the F.B.I. prevented major military secrets, including the formula for the atomic bomb, from falling into the hands of Nazi agents operating in New York City.

Some wartime features combined the crime genre with the spy film. In *Dangerous Partners* (1945), for example, James Craig and Signe Hasso portray a couple who try to bilk an insurance company out of an inheritance, which is also coveted by a Nazi spy. *Quiet Please, Murder*, another crime-spy film with George Sanders, has Nazis involved with counterfeit copies of rare books. *Sabotage Squad* concerns a bookie, rejected by the draft, who sacrifices his life to prevent the destruction of an airplane factory. Finally, crime dominates the subject matter of *Main Street After Dark* (1944), a cautionary tale of a gang of pickpockets and small-time crooks who prey upon unwary servicemen. The crime–spy blend continued into the postwar period with such films as *The Safecracker* (1958), directed by and starring Ray Milland. Portraying the title character, Milland is released from an English prison by British Intelligence and assigned to steal a list of Nazi agents from a Belgian chateau.

At times, the heroes of these home-front spy dramas were servicemen. In *The Marines Come Through* (1943) Wallace Ford plays a leatherneck hero who prevents Nazi agents from stealing a secret bombsight.

As with World War I spy movies, those of the Second World War continued well into the postwar period. *Cloak and Dagger* (1946), starring Gary Cooper as an American scientist and Lilli Palmer as an Italian partisan, involves Nazi Germany's experiments with atomic energy. That same year *O.S.S.*, starring Alan Ladd, and *13 Rue Madeleine*, with James Cagney, describe how American secret agents operated behind German lines during the war. Ray Milland, as a British agent in the wartime romantic drama *Golden Earrings* (1947), seeks refuge with a gypsy caravan. Marlene Dietrich, as a gypsy, falls in love with him. The highly entertaining and urbane *Five Fingers* (1952), starring James Mason as a suave valet to the English ambassador in Turkey and free-lance spy who sells photographed secrets to the Nazis, added a fresh approach and a sense of realism to the spy drama. *The Counterfeit Traitor* (1962), another highly acclaimed espionage drama, stars William Holden as an American businessman who poses as a Nazi sympathizer for British Intelligence. Lilli Palmer, as an idealistic anti-Nazi agent who falls in love with Holden, is captured and executed by the Germans. *A Face in the Rain* (1963) featured Rory Calhoun in the familiar plot about an American agent who parachutes behind enemy lines and is pursued by Nazis.

Occasionally films dealt with unrepentant postwar Nazis. In *Rendezvous 24* (1946) unconverted Nazi scientists after the war experiment with atomic energy which they plan to use to blow up major cities. *The Devil Makes Three* (1952), with Gene Kelly as a U.S. Intelligence agent, concerns a secret plot hatched in postwar Germany to resurrect the Nazi party.

Spies played major roles in films about foreign revolutions and other wars. In *Conspiracy* (1939), which obliquely extols the virtues of democracy, an American (Allan Lane) gets mixed up with a revolution in a Central American country where the dictator is finally deposed. *The Fallen Sparrow* (1943), starring John Garfield, deals with events that occurred during the Spanish Civil War. Two years later Charles Boyer starred in *Confidential Agent*, another tale of intrigue about the Spanish Civil War. The Korean War figures in *Tokyo File 212* (1951), a story about Communist spies operating in Tokyo and influencing the outcome of the war.

Historical films were apt topics for spying. Jon Hall in *Brave Warrior* (1952) portrays an American agent whose mission is to ferret out those who are inciting the Indians to side with the British on the eve of the War of 1812. George Montgomery, as a British scout in *The Pathfinder* (1952), is assigned to spy on a French fort during the French and Indian War in this adventure based on James Fenimore Cooper's novel. The Napoleonic Wars furnish the backdrop for *Sea Devils* (1954), starring Yvonne De Carlo as a British spy and Rock Hudson as a smuggler. Hudson eventually rescues De Carlo, and they both escape with the plans for a French invasion.

Almost invariably (except for occasional entrepreneurs like James Mason), screen spies in most films from the early silent era through the early post-World War II decades were steadfast in their determination to serve their country, regardless of the many dangers. They sometimes were diverted by romantic interludes but returned ultimately to their assigned tasks. Enemy agents, just as dedicated to their causes, were relentless in their pursuits. Propaganda intruded often—by way of dialogue, speeches and incidents—as the heroes and heroines carried the war relentlessly to the enemy's back yard.

The movie spy, as exemplified by the James Bond character created by Ian Fleming, has changed over the years. He has advanced from amateur to professional. World events and shifting values have made him cynical and ruthless. His weapons have become more sophisticated and deadly. More ambivalent and complex than his earlier counterpart, he is capable of suddenly switching sides, engaging in immoral or unethical practices or simply concluding a case by following his own private morality. In essence, he embodies the moral relativism and incongruities of modern twentieth-century man. "Have you noticed," a Soviet spy (Paul Scofield) muses to his American counterpart (Burt Lancaster) in *Scorpio* (1973), "that we are being replaced by young men with . . . a dedication to nothing more than efficiency? . . . Hardware men with highly complex toys and, except for language, not an iota of difference between the American model and the Soviet model." See also Detectives at War, Women and War. ■

Spy Ring, The (1938). See Spy Films: the Talkies. ■

Spy Ship (1942). See Spy Films: the Talkies. ■

Spy Train (1943). See Spy Films: the Talkies. ■

Square of Violence, The (1963), MGM. *Dir.* Leonardo Bercovici; *Sc.* Eric and Leonardo Bercovici; *Cast includes:* Broderick Crawford, Valentina Cortesa, Branko Plesa, Bibi Andersson.

A joint U.S.–Yugolavian production, the drama concerns an anti-Nazi partisan who is faced with a moral dilemma. Broderick Crawford, as the Yugoslavian resistance fighter, tosses a bomb which kills 30 German soldiers. The Nazis, in retaliation, round up 300 civilian hostages, place them in a square and threaten to kill them all unless the partisan surrenders. Crawford is torn between giving himself up to be tortured into revealing other members of the resistance or remaining silent, in which case 300 innocent people will lose their lives. His superiors order him to take refuge. Instead, he decides to turn himself in. As he does so, his fellow partisans gun him down. The incensed Germans then proceed to kill all the hostages. The film, although set in Yugoslavia, is based on an actual World War II incident in Rome. Branko Plesa, a popular Yugoslav actor, portrays a Nazi officer, Crawford's adversary. ■

Stage Door Canteen (1943). See Musicals. ■

Stagecoach (1939), UA. *Dir.* John Ford; *Sc.* Dudley Nichols; *Cast includes:* John Wayne, Claire Trevor, Andy Devine, John Carradine, Thomas Mitchell, George Bancroft, Donald Meek.

Director John Ford blends western themes with that of *Grand Hotel* by placing a handful of diverse characters together in a stressful situation as a stagecoach journeys from one frontier town to another. The Apaches, led by Geronimo, have broken out of their reservation and are on the warpath. Some of the passengers include a prostitute (Claire Trevor) who has been evicted from the previous settlement, an escaped convict (John Wayne) bent on avenging his family's murder, a pompous banker (Berton Churchill) who has absconded with the town's deposits, an alcoholic doctor (Thomas Mitchell), a dissolute gambler (John Carradine) who ironically retains a trace of Southern chivalry and a prissy whiskey drummer (Donald Meek). Each of the passengers reacts differently to the eventual Indian attack (one of the best action sequences ever put on film).

The western as a film genre was practically dead or, at its best, relegated to poverty-row studios until *Stagecoach* rode upon the screen. There then followed a string of "big" westerns by most of the major studios. Ford for the first time utilized Monument Valley for his setting, capturing its sweep and stark beauty. Many of his major themes appear in this film—his romantic approach to American history with emphasis on glory and tradition, his belief in the importance of one's heritage and the relationship between man and his environment. ■

Stalag 17 (1953), Par. *Dir.* Billy Wilder; *Sc.* Billy Wilder, Edward Blum; *Cast includes:* William Holden, Don Taylor, Otto Preminger, Robert Strauss, Harvey Lembeck.

Director Billy Wilder blends comedy with drama in his film about captured American air crews in a German prisoner-of-war camp during World War II. William Holden portrays a cynical sergeant whom the others in his barracks suspect of being an informer. Two American prisoners have been killed trying to escape and another exposed for sabotaging a troop train. After he is beaten up by his fellow prisoners, Holden fixes his sights on learning the identity of the real informer. He discovers that an American-educated German spy has been planted in the barracks and

is secretly passing information to the camp commandant. When Holden explains to the others how they have been betrayed, they decide to use the informer as a decoy while Holden and a lieutenant make their escape. That same night the men toss the informer out of the barracks. Before he has a chance to identify himself, the guards shoot him down. Meanwhile, during all the confusion, the two Americans cut through the barbed wire and fade into the darkness of the night.

The film provides plenty of comedy, contributed chiefly by Robert Strauss, who plays "Animal," and Harvey Lembeck, as Harry Shapiro, to relieve the tense moments. In the final sequence Shapiro can't figure out why Holden would put his own life in danger. "I'd like to know what made him do it," he wonders out loud. "Maybe he wanted to steal our wire cutters," Animal replies. "Did you ever think of that?" Otto Preminger stepped out of his usual director's role to portray the arrogant camp commandant. Sig Ruman, as Schultz, the imitable guard, also adds to the humor. The prisoners frequently make him the butt of their jokes. "How do you expect to win the war with an army of clowns?" he asks. "We sort of hope you'll laugh yourselves to death," a prisoner quips. Peter Graves plays the German-born informer who wins the confidence of the Americans. Don Taylor portrays a captured lieutenant whom the Gestapo want for blowing up a train while he was waiting to be assigned to a prison camp. Director and co-screenwriter Wilder adapted the work from the successful stage play. ■

Stamboul Quest (1934), MGM. *Dir.* Sam Wood; *Sc.* Herman Mankiewicz; *Cast includes:* Myrna Loy, George Brent, Lionel Atwill, C. Henry Gordon, Mischa Auer.

Myrna Loy portrays one of Germany's most dangerous spies in this sophisticated World War I drama. Responsible for the demise of Mata Hari, who made the fatal mistake of falling in love with one of her victims, Loy scoffs at the thought of committing the same error. George Brent portrays an American medical student who loses his heart to Loy. He follows her to Turkey where she has been assigned to uncover an officer (C. Henry Gordon) who is collaborating with the British. She resists Brent's charms at first but soon succumbs.

However, her liaison with the Turkish officer stands in the way of their romance. Brent criticizes her country's tactics. "I know what war is," he reassures her. "You go out and fight. You shoot and get shot. That's what war is. You don't use women as weapons." Loy refuses to give up her assignment. When he asks her whether that includes having an affair with the officer, she replies that she is not sure. Her superior (Lionel Atwill), aware that Brent's jealousy is interfering with her mission, steps in. He informs her that Brent has been killed by a firing squad. Loy, thinking herself responsible for her lover's death, has a mental breakdown and spends the remainder of the war in a convent. While she is recovering, Brent visits her and the two lovers are reunited.

The film is unique in at least two respects. Not only does the drama evoke sympathy for a German spy, it also allows the same German spy to triumph. These were unthinkable elements in Hollywood during and immediately following World War I (with one eye on its lucrative foreign markets) and almost as disconcerting in the period dominated by the rise of Nazism in Germany. A foreword points out the differences between espionage and counter-espionage, concluding that where the former may be glamorous, the latter work is not. The character portrayed by Myrna Loy was based on the exploits of Anna Maria Lesser, Germany's actual top woman spy during World War I, also known as "Fraulein Doktor." A film of this title, released in 1969, as well as several others, have been made of her wartime adventures. ■

Stand By for Action (1942), MGM. *Dir.* Robert Z. Leonard; *Sc.* George Bruce, John Balderston, Herman J. Mankiewicz; *Cast includes:* Robert Taylor, Brian Donlevy, Charles Laughton, Walter Brennan, Marilyn Maxwell, Henry O'Neill.

This World War II sea drama tells the story of an old destroyer used by America in the last war. The ship is assigned to a convoy and is involved in picking up survivors of a torpedoed vessel and a heroic battle against a Japanese battleship. Robert Taylor plays a cocky navy lieutenant who comes through in a pinch when his captain (Brian Donlevy), a veteran of World War I, is wounded in action. Taylor is responsible for the detroyer's victory over the enemy battleship.

The film was released at an appropriate time. The U.S. had had a series of successful naval engagements against the Japanese in the Pacific, so the incidents depicted on screen seemed more realistic than just another propaganda film containing exaggerated deeds of bravery. Also, the scenes of the ordinary seamen caring for infants retrieved from the lifeboats of torpedoed vessels balanced the action sequences with a sense of humanity and tenderness. ■

"Standard Bearer, The" (1908), Unique.

A drama of heroism and patriotism set during the Franco–Prussian War, the plot concerns a French color sergeant who saves the regimental colors. The film opens with the sergeant parting from his wife and child as he leaves with his regiment to engage the enemy. A large battle ensues and the sergeant is mortally wounded. He manages to conceal his unit's standard before the enemy troops capture him. Once in the enemy field hospital, he gets permission to have his family visit him. He secretly passes the regiment's colors to his wife. Later, dressed in widow's attire, she turns the shattered banner over to the survivors of her husband's regiment. The film was praised by contemporary critics for its well-staged battle sequences. ■

Standing Room Only (1944). See Washington, D.C. ■

"Star Spangled Banner." See Francis Scott Key. ■

Star Spangled Rhythm (1942). See Musicals. ■

Star Wars (1977). See Science Fiction Wars. ■

"Stars and Stripes Over There, The" (1918). See "Pershing's Crusaders." ■

Start the Revolution Without Me (1970), WB. *Dir.* Bud Yorkin; *Sc.* Fred Freeman, Lawrence J. Cohen; *Cast includes:* Gene Wilder, Donald Sutherland, Hugh Griffith.

The French Revolution provides the background for this zany comedy with Gene Wilder and Donald Sutherland each portraying a set of twins. One pair of mismatched twins (Wilder and Sutherland) who are raised as peasants become involved with their counterparts, a pair of aristocrats. Hugh Griffith portrays an eccentric Louis XVI, who is suspicious of his wife, Marie Antoinette (Billie Whitelaw). The film, a blend of satire and slapstick, includes scenes that employ title cards reminiscent of silent films while others involve brawls and chases. Some of the dialogue is funny. In one scene a cowering prisoner chained to a wall of his cell receives a visit from his sadistic tormentor. "I know you," the fearful victim cries. "You're the scrounge of Corsica!" "That's scourge, you idiot!" the pompous visitor corrects the pathetic soul. ∎

State Department—File 649 (1949), Film Classics. *Dir.* Peter Stewart; *Sc.* Milton Raison; *Cast includes:* William Lundigan, Virginia Bruce, Jonathan Hale, Richard Loo, Philip Ahn.

An American vice-consul clashes with a Mongolian war lord in north China in this adventure drama. William Lundigan portrays the member of the U.S. Foreign Service who witnesses the capture of a Chinese village by a marauding Mongolian horde led by Richard Loo. The war lord, thirsty for power, dominates the surrounding countryside while waiting for the Chinese government to recognize him. Meanwhile, Lundigan has surreptitiously sent a message to American officials in Nanking. He also manages to cause the death of Loo, thereby throwing the bandit army in disarray. ∎

Steel Claw, The (1961), WB. *Dir.* George Montgomery; *Sc.* Ferde Grofe, Jr., Malvin Wald, George Montgomery; *Cast includes:* George Montgomery, Charito Luna, Mario Bari.

George Montgomery portrays a tough U.S. Marine captain in this routine action drama set in the Philippines during World War II. Having lost a hand in battle, he designs a steel claw as a replacement. The plot centers on his efforts to rescue an officer held by the Japanese. He soon discovers the prisoner is dead and has to battle his way to safety. He is helped by native guerrillas. Meanwhile, he manages to rescue a wounded Filipino girl. ∎

Steel Fist, The (1952). See Cold War. ∎

Steel Helmet, The (1951), Lippert. *Dir.* Samuel Fuller; *Sc.* Samuel Fuller; *Cast includes:* Gene Evans, William Chun, James Edwards, Robert Hutton, Steve Brodie.

The first significant film to deal with the

Steve Brodie (l.) confronts Gene Evans (r.) during the Korean War. *The Steel Helmet* (1951).

Korean War, the drama focuses on an American infantry patrol assigned to set up an observation post in a Buddhist temple. Lacking the heroic and romantic clichés of many other war movies, the film captures the chaotic and confused situations that arise during such a simple detail as the one these men must perform. The patrol is led by an experienced but insecure and overbearing lieutenant (Steve Brodie). They are joined by a young Korean who speaks American slang, a gruff and resourceful sergeant (Gene Evans) whose own squad has been brutally wiped out and a black corpsman (James Edwards) who is lost. When the Korean boy is killed by the enemy, the sergeant cracks under the strain. Others in the patrol, who under stress of battle act bravely, nevertheless betray their ineptness as soldiers. The men and incidents apparently reflect the progression of the war itself, but this little film is hampered by its low budget.

When this odd mixture of troops, which also includes a Japanese-American soldier, enter the temple, they find an English-speaking North Korean major there and take him prisoner. The officer studies his captors and tries to cause dissension. "I just don't understand you," he addresses the black soldier. "You can't even eat with them unless it's during a war." He then works on the Japanese-American. But in both cases his efforts are to no avail. Director–writer Fuller's soldiers may be bewildered and apolitical, but they are also tough and loyal. Later, when the prisoner passes an insulting comment, the distraught sergeant shoots the unarmed major.

Years after the release of the film a cult developed around the work of director Samuel Fuller, a veteran of World War II who was awarded the Silver and Bronze stars and the Purple Heart. His ardent followers singled out this tough, realistic film as one of his best, seeing in it a strong statement of how the war altered many of America's values. ∎

Steele, Lillian. See *I Was a Captive of Nazi Germany* (1936). ∎

Step by Step (1946), RKO. *Dir.* Phil Rosen; *Sc.* Stuart Palmer; *Cast includes:* Lawrence Tierney, Anne Jeffreys, Lowell Gilmore, George Cleveland, Jason Robards.

Another post-World War II drama about a group of unrepentant Nazis attempting to restore the party to its former glory, this low-budget film features Lawrence Tierney and Anne Jeffreys as an innocent couple being pursued by the F.B.I., police and secret agents. Tierney, as a marine veteran, and Jeffreys, as a secretary to a senator, are accused of stealing secret government documents. They flee from the police and government agents and hide out in a motel managed by George Cleveland, who contributes some comic relief. Meanwhile several Nazis, played chiefly by Lowell Gilmore and Jason Robards, want the coveted documents that have accidentally fallen into Tierney's possession. The remainder of the film consists of chases and other action sequences before the plot is unraveled. ∎

Stilwell, Joseph W. See *Merrill's Marauders* (1962). ∎

"Stirring Days in Old Virginia" (1909), Selig.

A Civil War drama set in the spring of 1865, this short silent film revolves around a Confederate captain assigned to a secret mission while Union troops are camped on his Virginia plantation where his wife resides. The film includes realistic battle scenes as well as portrayals of Generals Grant and Lee. ∎

Stolen Orders (1918). See Spy Films: the Silents. ∎

Storm at Daybreak (1933), MGM. *Dir.* Richard Boleslawski; *Sc.* Bertram Millhauser; *Cast includes:* Kay Francis, Nils Asther, Walter Huston, Phillips Holmes, Eugene Pallette.

Based on historical events of World War I, the film begins with the assassination of Archduke Francis Ferdinand and his wife at Sarajevo and ends after the armistice. Walter Huston portrays the mayor of a Serbian village who learns that his best friend, a Hungarian officer (Nils Asther), is in love with his wife (Kay Francis). Asther and Francis first meet when he suspects her of harboring Serbian deserters from the Hungarian army. Huston finally sacrifices his life to protect his wife and the man she loves.

The film, which concentrated more on the romantic triangle than on the war, was one of the earliest cinematic attempts to illustrate the traditional hatred between Serbia and Hungary, one of the causes of the conflict. Hollywood rarely use the Balkans as background for World War I dramas, either during the conflict or after the Armistice. ∎

Storm Over Bengal (1938), Rep. *Dir.* Sidney Salkow; *Sc.* Garrett Ford; *Cast includes:* Patric Knowles, Richard Cromwell, Rochelle Hudson, Douglas Dumbrille, Colin Tapley.

An action drama about native uprisings in 19th century India, the film stars Patric Knowles, Richard Cromwell and Rochelle Hudson as the principals. Following an intricate plot of political machinations, the film provides ample battle sequences at the finale as British forces suppress the rebel troops on the northwest frontier. Richard Cromwell portrays a green and petulant recruit who fouls up in the early scenes but redeems himself when he later saves his regiment. Douglas Dumbrille, as a treacherous tribal chief, leads his army in a revolt against the British. Knowles plays Cromwell's older brother.

The story, setting and characters are suspiciously similar to those of *Lives of a Bengal Lancer* (1935), which also had Richard Cromwell as an inexperienced young trooper stationed in India on the eve of an uprising and forced to redeem himself after he betrayed the corps. And once again Douglas Dumbrille is called upon to threaten the British Empire. The film was another entry—albeit a weak one—in the genre that came to be known as empire films, dramas that sympathized with England's colonial policies and romanticized the dangers on the far-flung frontiers. They reached the height of their popularity during the 1930s. See Empire Films. ∎

Storm Over Lisbon (1944). See Spy Films: the Talkies. ∎

Jack Holt (r.), as a mercenary flier for Bolivia in its war with Paraguay, receives orders from his major (Antonio Moreno). *Storm Over the Andes* (1935).

Storm Over the Andes (1935), U. *Dir.* Christy Cabanne; *Sc.* Al DeMond, Frank Wead, Eve Greene; *Cast includes:* Jack Holt, Antonio Moreno, Mona Barrie, Gene Lockhart.

An action drama set in South America, the film features Jack Holt as an American mercenary pilot employed by Bolivia in its struggle with Paraguay, a conflict that became known as the Chaco War. Holt, between dogfights, finds time to woo his major's wife, resulting in the enmity of his superior officer for the reckless American captain. Several adequate air action sequences are included.

The film hoped to exploit contemporary headlines. Designed chiefly for entertainment purposes and escapist audiences, it touches upon no political or controversial issues concerning the conflict. See Chaco War. ∎

Story of Dr. Wassell, The (1944), Par. *Dir.* Cecil B. DeMille; *Sc.* Alan LeMay, Charles Bennett; *Cast includes:* Gary Cooper, Laraine Day, Signe Hasso, Dennis O'Keefe.

Cecil B. DeMille's lavish production of the biographical drama about the famous doctor-hero of World War II stars Gary Cooper in the title role. Told through a series of flashbacks, the film shows Dr. Wassell's life as a country doctor in Arkansas, his prewar experiences in China and his heroic work as a navy doctor during World War II. Ordered to abandon the seriously wounded during the evacuation of Java, Dr. Wassell instead disobeyed his orders and brought out twelve American soldiers to the safety of Australia. He was awarded the Navy Cross for his courage and became the topic of a radio speech by President

Roosevelt. Several effective battle scenes add realism to film. Laraine Day provides the romantic interest as the young woman the doctor first meets in China. The film was based on incidents in Commander Corydon M. Wassell's life and a novel by James Hilton. ∎

Story of G.I. Joe, The (1945), UA. *Dir.* William Wellman; *Sc.* Leopold Atlas, Guy Endore, Philip Stevenson; *Cast includes:* Burgess Meredith, Robert Mitchum, Freddie Steele, Wally Cassell.

Burgess Meredith portrays the famous war correspondent Ernie Pyle from whose viewpoint is told the story of the average foot soldier in this World War II drama. The film follows an infantry company from the fighting in North Africa to the battlefields in Italy. Pyle marches and lives with the G.I.s, depicting their daily hardships and joys with sympathy and understanding. The soldiers accept the likable reporter as one of their own; they sense his warmth and concern for them. The film avoids the conventional heroics and didactic speeches of the genre as it pictures the men battling the mud, rain and boredom as well as the enemy. "It sounds kind of silly," says one weary G.I., "but when I'm resting like this I get a kick out of just being alive."

Robert Mitchum plays a sturdy and competent lieutenant who is eventually promoted to captain. When he is killed near the end of the film, his men and Pyle look on in silence as his body, slung over a mule, is unceremoniously placed among other fallen soldiers. The company of infantrymen quietly look at their fallen comrade, then march off toward Rome.

Ernie Pyle (1900–1945) did not live to see the completed film. He was killed by a Japanese sniper on Ie Jima, a remote Pacific island. Pyle, who won the Pulitzer Prize for his poignant and realistic accounts of the common soldier, was the best-loved correspondent among the G.I.s. A basically shy reporter who had been popular before the war for his homely articles and columns, he shared the war's hardships with the men he wrote about. The incident in the film of the captain killed in action came from Pyle's writings. He wrote of one of the many soldiers who passed by the body of Capt. Henry Waskow of Belton, Texas: "He too spoke to his dead captain, not in a whisper but awfully tenderly, and he said: 'I sure am sorry, sir.'" When the film, based on his widely published articles and book, *Here Is Your War* (1943), was proposed to him, Pyle requested that Meredith portray him. Although the film was tremendously popular with American audiences, it was criticized in England for omitting any reference to the large part played by British fighting forces in North Africa and Italy.

During the last few months of the conflict, several war movies such as *The Story of G.I. Joe* and *A Walk in the Sun*, also released in 1945, began to appear which treated men in battle with more realism and which omitted the obligatory propaganda and heroics so familiar to the genre. ∎

Strange Death of Adolf Hitler, The
(1943), U. *Dir.* James Hogan; *Sc.* Fritz Kortner; *Cast includes:* Ludwig Donath, Fritz Kortner, Gale Sondergaard, George Dolenz.

Hitler's double is mistaken for the German dictator and assassinated in this weak World War II exploitation drama. Ludwig Donath plays the dual role of Hitler and his counterpart, the latter a poor Viennese soul who is forced to masquerade as the Fuhrer. Ironically, the double's wife, played by Gale Sondergaard, decides to kill the Nazi leader but mistakenly ends up shooting her own husband. The sensational events are devoid of any reality. ∎

Strange Holiday
(1946), PRC. *Dir.* Arch Oboler; *Sc.* Arch Oboler; *Cast includes:* Claude Rains, Bobbie Stebbins, Barbara Bate, Gloria Holden.

Claude Rains portrays an American family man on vacation in a remote area who returns to his city to find it occupied by Nazis in this World War II fantasy drama. He is exposed to the usual Nazi beatings and other atrocities before he awakens and discovers it was all a dream. The speeches and incidents in this didactic film all underscore one's appreciation for an America that we all take for granted. Propaganda aside, the film presents some originality within its low-budget strictures. Gloria Holden plays his wife. ∎

Stranger, The
(1946), RKO. *Dir.* Orson Welles; *Sc.* Anthony Veiller; *Cast includes:* Edward G. Robinson, Loretta Young, Orson Welles, Philip Merivale.

An escaped Nazi war criminal is wanted by the Allied War Crimes Commission in this suspenseful World War II drama. Edward G. Robinson, as a U.S. government agent, tracks down the mass murderer (Orson Welles) to a small New England village where Robinson employs psychological warfare against him. Welles, who has gone under cover as a professor and highly respected member of the peaceful community, marries a highly respected local resident (Loretta Young). He is temporarily threatened with exposure when another former Nazi arrives to visit him. "I'll stay hidden until the day that we strike again," the unrepentant Welles confides to his friend. But when he learns that all war crimes charges against the man were dropped suddenly and that he was followed to the village, Welles suspects a trap. He kills his friend to avoid any links to him.

Robinson's suspicions about Welles are confirmed, especially when he discovers the body of the murdered man. Welles' wife, meanwhile, knows nothing of her husband's past and refuses to believe the charges when she is told. The cat-and-mouse game between the hunter and the hunted continues until the wife learns that Welles has planned to kill her. In a melodramatic climax Welles, attempting to hide from the authorities, is impaled by a moving statue in a clock tower. ∎

Strategic Air Command
(1955). See Cold War. ∎

Streets of Shanghai
(1928), Tiffany. *Dir.* Louis Gasnier; *Sc.* J. F. Natteford; *Cast includes:* Pauline Starke, Kenneth Harlan, Margaret Livingston, Eddie Gribbon, Jason Robards.

Kenneth Harlan portrays a U.S. Marine in love with a worker (Pauline Starke) at a mission in China in this romantic adventure film. A villainous Chinese also has an interest in Starke. When he and his henchmen attack the mission, a battle breaks out. The marines eventually prove victorious in this low-budget feature. ∎

Strong Man, The
(1926). See War Humor. ∎

Stronger Than Death
(1920), MGM. *Dir.* Herbert Blache; *Sc.* Charles Bryant; *Cast includes:* Nazimova, Charles Bryant, Charles W. French, Margaret McWade.

Alla Nazimova portrays a half-breed dancer entertaining in colonial India in this romantic drama. A major (Charles Bryant), the son of a cruel colonel in charge of a British garrison, falls in love with Nazimova. At a banquet she is told by doctors that if she dances again, she will die. But she decides to dance, holding the audience enthralled. Meanwhile, an uprising takes place. The young major, accompanied by troops, arrives in time and rescues Nazimova.

The film deals in part with the social attitudes of the British toward the Indians. The colonel's rape of a virgin of the temple of Vishnu symbolizes the abuses of some British officers in regard to native women. These may have been reasons enough to inflame the rebellious spirit of the populace. ■

Stronghold (1952), Lippert. *Dir.* Steve Sekely; *Sc.* Wells Root; *Cast includes:* Veronica Lake, Zachary Scott, Arturo de Cordova, Alfonso Bedoya.

Mexico's struggle against Emperor Maximilian provides the background for this routine romantic drama. The owner (Veronica Lake) of wealthy silver mines in Mexico, is captured by bandits during her return from the U.S. The leader of the kidnapers (Arturo de Cordova) intends to use the ransom silver to support the peon revolution. Captive and captor soon fall in love, with Lake embracing the revolutionists' cause. Meanwhile Zachary Scott, as the manager of the mine, helps to capture the bandit leader who is then sentenced to death. But he is saved by the peon uprising. The film was shot in Mexico. ■

Stuart, James E. B. "Jeb" (1833–1864). The South's most successful and daring cavalry commander, and one of the American Civil War's most famous military leaders, "Jeb" Stuart electrified the nation on more than one occasion by his end-runs around Union forces. However, the dashing, bearded cavalry chief, because of his tendency to go off on raids, may have contributed heavily to the defeat of Confederate forces at the all-important Battle of Gettysburg (July 1–3, 1863). Prior to the battle Stuart was absent for several days on a mission of his own creation. This deprived Lee of the "eyes" and mobility he badly needed to fight the Union troops sent to stop the Confederate advance. Stuart's attempt to rejoin Lee at Gettysburg was checked by Union cavalry several miles from the main battle scene.

Stuart distinguished himself in the war's early stages. He saw action at both Battles of Bull Run, Fredericksburg and Chancellorsville. He died on May 12, 1864, as a result of wounds suffered at the Battle of Yellow Tavern after his unit had been lured away from Lee's main army and defeated by Union General Phil Sheridan. Stuart is portrayed in an obscure 1912 silent Civil War film, *The Battle of Pottsburg Ridge*; a spy drama, *Operator 13* (1934); and a large-scale pre-Civil War western, *Santa Fe Trail* (1940), with Errol Flynn as a dashing and heroic Stuart battling the abolitionist John Brown. ■

Submarine Alert (1943). See Spy Films: the Talkies. ■

Submarine Base (1943). See Submarine Warfare. ■

Submarine Command (1951), Par. *Dir.* John Farrow; *Sc.* Jonathan Latimer; *Cast includes:* William Holden, Nancy Olsen, William Bendix, Don Taylor.

A naval officer suffers mental anguish when he is forced to take his submarine down while leaving his wounded commander on deck to perish. William Holden plays the officer who abandons his captain so that he could save the vessel and crew from enemy attack. William Bendix, as a torpedoman aboard the sub, at first condemns Holden for his actions. Holden's sweetheart (Nancy Olsen) helps him overcome his feelings of guilt in this drama that opens during World War II and ends in the midst of the Korean War. It is during this latter conflict that Holden, still tortured by his conscience, finally redeems himself in a sea battle. ■

Submarine Patrol (1938), TCF. *Dir.* John Ford; *Sc.* Rian James, Darrell Ware, Jack Yellen; *Cast includes:* Richard Greene, Nancy Kelly, Preston Foster, George Bancroft, Slim Summerville.

A comedy drama about the men who handled the sub-chasers, small wooden craft employed to hunt U-boats, the film stars Richard Greene as a chief petty officer. He woos a freighter captain's daughter (Nancy Kelly). Her father, a two-fisted sailor (George Bancroft), transports munitions to foreign ports. Several effective action sequences include sea battles during World War I.

The small craft, which were light and maneuverable, were put into service in 1917. They were used by the U.S. Navy during

World War I to fight the threat of German submarines when the military realized it could not produce enough destroyers to do the job. The four boats used in the making of the film were all that were left of the small fleet and were docked at Annapolis where director John Ford received permission to use them. ■

Submarine Raider (1942), Col. *Dir.* Lew Landers; *Sc.* Aubrey Wisberg; *Cast includes:* John Howard, Marguerite Chapman, Bruce Bennett, Warren Ashe.

The Japanese attack on Pearl Harbor provides the background for this low-budget action drama. The plot concerns an American submarine on patrol somewhere in the Pacific and its vain effort to signal the military authorities of the impending Japanese raid. Later, the undersea vessel encounters a Japanese aircraft carrier and sinks it with three well-aimed torpedoes. John Howard portrays the hero. His sweetheart (Marguerite Chapman) is being held captive aboard the enemy carrier in this routine yarn that depends too heavily upon obvious models in the battle sequences. The film is based both on an actual incident and the first American victory of World War II.

A similar situation arises in *Torpedo Run* (1958), another submarine tale of World War II. Glenn Ford, as a submarine commander, learns that his wife and children, along with other American prisoners of war, are aboard a Japanese vessel that is being used as a shield for an enemy carrier. Determined to sink the carrier, he attacks. The torpedoes miss their target but sink the prison ship. ■

Submarine Seahawk (1959), AI. *Dir.* Spencer G. Bennet; *Sc.* Lew Rusoff, Owen Harris; *Cast includes:* John Bentley, Brett Halsey, Wayne Heffley, Steve Mitchell.

A recently appointed submarine commander loses the respect of his crew when he repeatedly avoids contact with enemy ships in this suspenseful action drama set in the Pacific during World War II. At one point, one of the officers (Brett Halsey) tries to take control of the undersea craft when the captain is not present. Eventually, the men realize the value of the captain's tactics—to pursue the Japanese ships until they lead him to more substantial targets—the major warships of the Imperial fleet. John Bentley portrays the overly patient commander. The action sequences, chiefly made up of stock footage

and special miniature effects, are quite satisfactory for this low-budget film. ■

Submarine warfare. On the night of September 6–7, 1776, American Sergeant Ezra Lee slowly and quietly moved his one-man submarine, the "American Turtle," under the surface of New York bay using a hand operated screw propeller. The young American nation had turned to a newly designed wooden submersible to weaken England's naval blockade of New York harbor. Lee intended to attach a timed underwater charge to the hull of the anchored H.M.S. *Eagle* and sink the British warship. However, he could not penetrate the metal sheathing covering a portion of the ship's hull beneath the water line, so he had to release the weapon and leave. The charge went off, and though it did not result in any damage, the explosion raised sufficient alarm to cause the *Eagle* to move farther out to sea. Such humble beginnings spawned the rise of submarine warfare.

A number of improvements combined to make the submarine into a formidable weapon by the start of World War I when it was first used extensively and successfully. American film studios discovered the value of using submarines in their stories in the early 1900s. Several early silent comedies that appeared before World War I utilized the submarine as a prop.

The first realistic film of submarine warfare was *Behind the Door* (1919). A revenge drama, the plot concerned an American naval officer who kills a German U-boat commander who has raped and killed the American's wife. Other films released during the war involved submarines peripherally. Some centered on the sinking of the *Lusitania*. Others had German submarines lurking off the U.S. coast awaiting signals from spies.

Germany, during World War I, made the most effective use of the new weapon. In just one month, April 1917, she sank 430 Allied and neutral ships totaling 852,000 tons. The foreword to *Thunder Afloat* (1939), which concerned the threat of German subs off the Atlantic coast, stated that U-boats sank more than 80 American ships around that time. *Mare Nostrum* (1926), based on a novel by Blasco Ibanez, focused on Germany's ruthless use of the submarine. Germany's stepped-up unrestricted undersea warfare, designed to starve out England and cut the flow of supplies to Allied forces on the continent, was a major factor in causing the U.S. to enter the war on the Allied side in 1917.

To counter Germany's threat, the Allies developed several anti-submarine methods such as using warships to protect convoys, employing destroyers as sub hunters, laying mines and dropping depth charges. *Convoy* (1927), basically a World War I spy drama, dealt with the threat of German U-boats to Allied shipping. John Ford's *Submarine Patrol* (1938) and *Thunder Afloat*, already mentioned, both concerned American sub chasers assigned to pursue German U-boats.

German subs in World War I often surfaced at first to confront a lone merchant vessel before sinking it by gunfire. Realizing this, British ships used deception to lure a sub to the surface, where it was comparatively helpless, and then proceeded to shell it. Merchant vessels carried hidden guns and occasionally even flew the flag of a neutral. In both *Suicide Fleet* (1931) and John Ford's *The Seas Beneath* (1931) innocent looking schooners are used to lure German U-boats to their destruction. U-boats countered by sinking both neutrals and enemy ships without warning.

Subs played an equally important role in World War II. Germany devised "wolf pack" attacks on convoys. A single U-boat shadowing a convoy would radio other subs for assistance, and after a "wolf pack" had formed, they would attack the convoy from several directions. Using such methods, the Germans, by March 1943, seriously handicapped England's seaborne supply system. *Action in the North Atlantic* (1943), a tribute to the U.S. Merchant Marine in World War II, exemplified the problems of convoys as one ship after another falls prey to the dreaded wolf pack. The Allies countered with more heavily armed convoys, sound-sensing devices and escort carriers.

The submarine played a major role in effecting the outcome of World War II. British subs operating principally from Malta in the Mediterranean sank as many as half the Axis supply ships heading for Rommel's forces in North Africa. It weakened him to such an extent that he was forced to stop his advance toward the Suez canal. In the Pacific the U.S. made the submarine its principal weapon in cutting Japan's extended supply lines. American subs sank enemy ships faster than they could be replaced by Japanese shipyards. Japan lost 1,153 ships to subs, totaling nearly 5 million tons, a figure that represented nearly 60 percent of Japan's sea losses.

Before the U.S. entered World War II, undersea vessels appeared rather unoriginally in films as gimmicky plot devices. In one, *Escape to Glory* (1940), a melodramatic low-budget feature that takes place at the beginning of the war, two American passengers aboard a British freighter threatened by a surfaced Nazi U-boat board a lifeboat loaded with explosives and ram the submarine. Mitchell Leisen's *Arise, My Love*, released the same year, began in whimsy and ended with a patriotic message. Ray Milland and Claudette Colbert, as two American passengers, are returning home from Europe when their ship is suddenly torpedoed by a Nazi U-boat. They then vow to help defeat Germany. *Submarine Base* (1943), a conventional spy story, involved the destruction of a secret base.

As the submarine increased in importance, Hollywood felt impelled to give this method of warfare more serious treatment. One of the best undersea dramas made during the war years and the first war film produced in Technicolor was *Crash Dive* (1943), starring Tyrone Power. Filled with plenty of suspense and action—though burdened with a routine romantic triangle—the plot takes an American sub into battle against a German Q-boat, an armed ship masquerading as a merchant vessel, and on a raid on a German mine-laying base.

Other films were quick to follow. *U-Boat Prisoner* (1944), a routine drama with an implausible plot (although allegedly based on an actual incident), told of an American who poses as a Nazi spy. After being picked up by a German U-boat he overpowers several members of the crew. In *Destination Tokyo*, released the same year, the captain of an American submarine (Cary Grant) is assigned to deliver a meteorologist to the shores of Japan where he can gather weather information for the upcoming Doolittle raid over Tokyo.

The postwar period brought forth several more submarine films concerning the conflict. One major change in several of these dramas was their more sympathetic treatment of the Germans. Another was their emphasis on character development. Curt Jurgens in *The Enemy Below* (1957) plays a German U-boat captain devoid of the stereotyped characteristics often attributed to Nazi officers. Engaged in a deadly cat-and-mouse game with the captain of an American destroyer (Robert Mitchum), Jurgens displays the same emotions as his counterpart as he attempts to outmaneuver his foe.

As in other genres, submarine dramas sometimes echo earlier works. *Submarine Command* (1951) repeated an incident that had occurred in *Hell Below* (1933). William Holden, as an officer, abandons his wounded captain on deck when he is forced to take the submarine below. *Hellcats of the Navy* (1957) used the same idea. This time around it is Ronald Reagan, as a captain, who is forced to sacrifice one man to protect his crew and mission when his submarine is threatened.

The submarine presents serious problems for its crew, especially in war. Close confinement for extended periods may lead to antagonisms between crew members. Clashes often occurred between officers or officers and crew. In *Run Silent, Run Deep* (1958) an embittered officer (Burt Lancaster) who is passed over as commander of a sub for a new captain (Clark Gable) is encouraged by a disgruntled crew to take over of the vessel. He relieves Gable of command but later returns it to him as they both join forces against a Japanese destroyer. An unhappy crew reappeared in *Submarine Seahawk* (1959). The men grow frustrated with their captain who avoids contact with the enemy until they learn he is waiting for the smaller vessels to lead him to the major Japanese warships. In *Up Periscope* (1959) crew members, including demolitions expert James Garner, criticize their martinet captain (Edmond O'Brien) for adhering too closely to military procedures.

The genre is not without its lighter entries, however. *Operation Petticoat* (1960), one of the funniest war films ever made, stars Cary Grant as commander of a damaged sub trying to get his boat repaired. Tony Curtis portrays Grant's scheming junior officer. ■

Submarine Zone. See *Escape to Glory* (1940). ■

Sudanese War of 1896–1899. See Battle of Omdurman. ■

Suicide Attack (1951), Classic Pictures. Dir. Irving Lerner; Sc. Louis Pollack.

A World War II documentary compiled from captured Japanese war footage, the film traces the aggressive military policies of Japan beginning with its attack on Pearl Harbor on Dec. 7, 1941. The ensuing sequences showing its army and navy enveloping Pacific islands prove that the fanatical Japanese were a formidable enemy. The film attempts to establish that Hedeki Tojo dominated and guided the belligerent spirit of Japan. He was executed in 1948 for war crimes. ■

Suicide Battalion (1958), AI. Dir. Edward L. Kahn; Sc. Lou Rosoff; Cast includes: Michael Connors, John Ashley, Jewell Lian, Russ Bender, Bing Russell.

This routine action drama centers around a behind-the-lines mission in which a team is sent into the Japanese-held Philippines to destroy American documents left behind during a hasty retreat. Michael Connors portrays the major in charge of the volunteers. He brings off the assignment successfully after some skirmishes with the enemy. Jewell Lian plays a war correspondent in this low-budget film that incorporates war newsreel footage for some of the action sequences. ■

Suicide Fleet (1931), RKO. Dir. Al Rogell; Sc. Lew Lipton; Cast includes: William Boyd, Robert Armstrong, James Gleason, Ginger Rogers.

A World War I comedy drama starring William Boyd, the film deals with a duel between a mystery schooner and three German submarines. Boyd and two of his buddies (Robert Armstrong and James Gleason) run various booths at an amusement park before they join the navy. Ginger Rogers plays Boyd's sweetheart. The main war action concerns a strange German schooner the U.S. Navy discovers. The crew members burn the ship, but the navy thinks it is a contact ship for German U-boats. Boyd volunteers to run a similar schooner the navy sends out as a lure. The ship is blown up when the German submarines realize it is a counterfeit, but the U.S. warships close in to sink the enemy subs.

Although the original story was written by H.A. Jones, a commander in the U.S. Navy, there is no evidence that such a ploy was used by the American forces during World War I. Character actor James Gleason and William Boyd, who evidently made a good team, appeared in another World War I film the same year, *Beyond Victory*. Two years earlier, Gleason wrote the comedy dialogue for *The Flying Fool*, another Boyd drama with a World War I background. ■

Sullivans, The (1944), TCF. *Dir.* Lloyd Bacon; *Sc.* Mary C. McCall, Jr.; *Cast includes:* Anne Baxter, Thomas Mitchell, Selena Royle, Edward Ryan, John Campbell, James Cardwell, John Alvin, George Offerman, Jr.

Based on the real-life story of the five Sullivan brothers who were killed in action during World War II, the film covers the boys' lives from their childhood years until their tragic death. Thomas Mitchell plays their sympathetic and sometimes stern father. Selena Royle portrays their compassionate and understanding mother. The brothers decide to enlist in the navy following Japan's attack on Pearl Harbor, and since they have always done things together, they request to serve aboard the same ship. During a naval battle off the Solomon Islands their ship is seriously hit and the powder magazine explodes, killing many of the crew including the five Sullivans. The last scene shows the launching of a new destroyer named the U.S.S. *The Sullivans* in honor of the brothers. As the grief-stricken but proud parents look on, the naval officer in charge addresses the huge crowd: "As this ship slides down the ways, it carries with it a special armor all its own— the flaming and undaunted spirit that is the heritage of its name. The Sullivan boys are gone. The U.S.S. *The Sullivans* carries on . . . May her destiny be as glorious as the name she bears."

When the report of the tragedy appeared in newspapers, it stunned the nation. The film, which captures the spirit of the five youths and the agony of the family when they receive the news, also registers the patriotic fervor of the period. When the Sullivan family gathers around their radio to hear about the fateful bombing of Pearl Harbor, the father remarks in disgust about the Japanese envoys: "Those two guys have been in Washington a week, handshaking the President." "They knew all the time," adds one son. "Sure," comments another, "they must have known." A third son comments that the war will be over in a few weeks. "They can't fight," he says, referring to the Japanese. "They close their eyes when they fire off a gun." The radio commentator gives details of the men killed and damage to the American fleet. Later, when the boys are in the service, the parents proudly display the well-known banner in their window that shows a member of the family is serving in the armed forces. The Sullivans' emblem contains five stars.

On a mantle are five framed photographs of their sons in uniform. In the last sequence, as the ship bearing their name is launched, Mrs. Sullivan says to her husband: "Our boys are afloat again." ∎

Sultan's Daughter, The (1944), Mon. *Dir.* Arthur Dreifuss; *Sc.* M. M. Raison, Tim Ryan; *Cast includes:* Ann Corio, Charles Butterworth, Tim Ryan, Edward Norris.

A World War II musical involving American bands, chorus girls and German agents, the film stars Ann Corio in the title role. Charles Butterworth plays her sultan-father who tries to stop his daughter from dealing with Nazi agents. It seems they want to buy out her oil properties. Edward Norris portrays an American entertainer stranded in the desert. Fortunio Bonanova plays a scheming underling of the Sultan who is in league with the German agents in this routine but harmless tale. ∎

Sun Never Sets, The (1939), U. *Dir.* Rowland V. Lee; *Sc.* W. P. Lipscomb; *Cast includes:* Douglas Fairbanks, Jr., Basil Rathbone, Barbara O'Neill, Lionel Atwill, Virginia Field.

Douglas Fairbanks, Jr. and Basil Rathbone co-star in this drama about honor and duty to family and country. The pair play brothers whose ties to their native England bring them into government service. Rathbone, a commissioner stationed in Africa at a British colonial outpost, is assigned as special investigator. His brother joins him as the new commissioner. Lionel Atwill portrays a crazed would-be dictator who controls a powerful radio transmitter in Africa which he uses to disrupt world governments. The brothers ultimately foil Atwill's plans to start a world war as British airplanes bomb his secret lair in this implausible tale. ∎

Sunday Dinner for a Soldier (1944), TCF. *Dir.* Lloyd Bacon; *Sc.* Wanda Tuchock, Melvin Levy; *Cast includes:* Anne Baxter, John Hodiak, Charles Winninger, Anne Revere, Connie Marshall.

An impoverished family plans a Sunday dinner for a serviceman in this heartwarming World War II comedy drama. The parentless children, supervised chiefly by their big sister (Anne Baxter), live with their grandfather (Charles Winninger) on a humble barge. Support comes solely from his meager pension. Since all the wealthier families invite a soldier from a nearby military base for dinner, the barge family intends to do the same. Humorous situations arise as they attempt to raise money to buy a chicken, get their barge in order and make other preparations. A simple romance emerges between Baxter and John Hodiak, the guest for the afternoon. ■

Sundown (1941), UA. *Dir.* Henry Hathaway; *Sc.* Barre Lyndon; *Cast includes:* Gene Tierney, Bruce Cabot, George Sanders, Harry Carey, Sir Cedric Hardwicke, Joseph Calleia, Carl Esmond.

Bruce Cabot and Gene Tierney star in this World War II adventure drama set at a remote British outpost in East Africa. Cabot plays a dedicated and idealistic local administrator who understands and is respected by the local natives. George Sanders is assigned to help Cabot learn where and how a neighboring tribe is getting arms. It seems that the Nazis are intent on fomenting trouble for the British. Gene Tierney, as a sultry Eurasian owner of a string of trading posts, is working as a British agent. She learns that a mineralogist who is a Nazi spy traveling under a false Dutch passport is the chief supplier of the weapons and decides to accompany him to his secret supply depot. Cabot follows, learns where the hiding place is and sends back word to Sanders. The climax is a rousing battle in which Sanders is mortally wounded. "People of all Churches pulling together— that's strength—that's all we need," he says to Cabot before he dies. Rationalizing his choice of the army as a career rather than the Church, he concludes: "They're both the basis of civilization. The Church holds it together and the army defends it."

The scene then shifts to a bomb-damaged church in England where Sanders' father, a bishop (Sir Cedric Hardwicke), speaks to his congregation, which includes Tierney and Cabot. "Mourn not for the brave," he says. "They live in the indestructible splendor of all eternity." He continues with a patriotic plea for victory:

Fly high your flag upon the hill,
Keep bright your faith and hold until
Our England wins, and win she will.
Who waits with faith waits with victory.

The film was made before the U.S. had entered the war and during England's darkest hour. World War II had entered its second year, and the sympathies of the American public, who saw one nation after another crumble before the Nazi war machine, were clearly with the British. *Sundown* was Hollywood's—and America's—tribute to a brave, embattled nation that stood alone like a bastion against the forces of dictatorship that swept across Europe. ■

Sure-Fire Flint (1922). See Veterans. ■

Surrender (1927), U. *Dir.* Edward Sloman; *Sc.* Alexander Brody; *Cast includes:* Mary Philbin, Ivan Mosjukine, Nigel de Brulier.

In this romantic drama set in a Jewish village during World War I and, later, during the Russian Revolution, the film centers on the love between a young peasant woman (Mary Philbin) and a Russian prince. She is the daughter of a Rabbi who is respected in his village which lies between Austrian and Russian troops. When the villagers learn that she has spent the night with the gentile, they stone her. Following the war and Revolution, the lovers are reunited when he returns as a loyal comrade. Her father, in the meantime, has died. The film contains scenes of World War I as well as of the Revolution. ■

Surrender (1931), Fox. *Dir.* William K. Howard; *Sc.* S. N. Behrman, Sonya Levien; *Cast includes:* Warner Baxter, Leila Hyams, Ralph Bellamy, William Pawley, C. Aubrey Smith, Alexander Kirkland.

Warner Baxter portrays a French soldier who is a prisoner of war in a German camp located in northern Prussia in this World War I drama. Nearby is a castle inhabited by a proud father who dreams of hearing that his four soldier–sons will be part of the force that captures Paris. The fiancee of one of the sons also lives at the castle. Baxter and the young woman (Leila Hyams) soon become involved in a love affair. The situation becomes more complex when the camp commandant (Ralph Bellamy) also shows an interest in the young woman. When her fiance returns wounded from the war, he cries out against the horrors of the conflict.

Little is shown of the war itself although its ineffable horrors are suggested by a German son to his father. "Everything was different in your days," the young soldier explains. "You fought with music playing and flags flying— gloriously— magnificently. The war we're fighting is different—entirely different . . . A war impossible to describe to you." The film, with its prisoners of war, castle setting, French–Prussian class consciousness and antiwar theme, anticipates the French classic, *Grand Illusion* (1938), directed by Jean Renoir. ∎

Surrender—Hell! (1959), AA. *Dir.* John Barnwell; *Sc.* John Barnwell; *Cast includes:* Keith Andes, Susan Cabot, Paraluman, Nestor De Villa.

Philippine resistance against Japanese occupation serves as the background for this action drama based on the true experiences of Lieutenant Donald D. Blackburn during World War II. Keith Andes portrays the American officer who flees from the Japanese when they first invade and becomes a resistance leader among the inhabitants of a local village. Later he retreats once again into the hills where he organizes the headhunters into an effective fighting force. Together, they overrun several provinces and rout the Japanese troops. Finally, he and his band of warriors aid in the recapture of the Philippines by General MacArthur. The Filipino actress, Paraluman, provides some sexy scenes in this low-budget but action-oriented film shot on location. ∎

Suspicion (1918). See Spy Films: the Silents. ∎

Suzy (1936), MGM. *Dir.* George Fitzmaurice; *Sc.* Dorothy Parker, Alan Campbell, Horace Jackson, Lenore Coffee; *Cast includes:* Jean Harlow, Franchot Tone, Cary Grant, Lewis Stone, Benita Hume.

Jean Harlow becomes entangled with two husbands in this implausible World War I romantic spy drama. When her English husband (Franchot Tone) is shot by a German spy, Harlow leaves for Paris thinking Tone is dead. She meets a French air ace (Cary Grant), falls in love and marries him. Grant, who turns out to be unfaithful, is killed by the same spy. Suddenly Tone reappears on the scene. To save his wife's reputation, he crashes an airplane into the quarters where Grant's body is lying, thereby making it appear that the Frenchman died in battle.

Several effective air sequences appear in the film, some of which have been lifted from other features. The incident involving the plane crash has also been borrowed. It is reminiscent of one in *The Eagle and the Hawk*

(1933), another World War I air drama. In the latter, Grant takes the body of air ace Fredric March, who has committed suicide, up in a plane and crashes it to make it seem as though March was killed in action. ∎

"Swamp Fox, The." See "Francis Marion, the Swamp Fox" (1914). ∎

Swat the Spy (1918). See Spy Films: the Silents. ∎

Swing Shift (1984), WB. *Dir.* Jonathan Demme; *Sc.* Rob Morton; *Cast includes:* Goldie Hawn, Kurt Russell, Christine Lahti, Fred Ward, Ed Harris.

A weak World War II drama focusing on the wives and sweethearts of the men who marched off to fight, the film stars Goldie Hawn as a sailor's wife who has an affair with a factory co-worker. Ed Harris portrays her husband who answers his nation's call following the Japanese attack on Pearl Harbor. Hawn takes a job in a defense plant where many of her male counterparts are resentful of the incursion of women into their domain. She meets a safety-control inspector (Kurt Russell) whom she finally dates after months of refusing his advances. Meanwhile, her best friend and neighbor (Christine Lahti) is also carrying on with nightclub owner Fred Ward. By the end of the film, Harris, who knows about his wife's infidelity, nevertheless returns to Hawn. The best parts of the production are the close friendship between Hawn and Lahti and the sentimental images and music that evoke the war years. The film is not so much a passionate story of betrayed love as it is about women who must learn to survive emotionally and economically in a hostile, man's world. ∎

Swing Shift Maisie (1943). See Home Front. ∎

Sword in the Desert (1949), U. *Dir.* George Sherman; *Sc.* Robert Buckner; *Cast includes:* Dana Andrews, Marta Toren, Stephen McNally, Jeff Chandler.

Hollywood's first crack at presenting the Middle East conflict between the Arabs and the Jews, the drama centers on a boatload of displaced persons seeking entry into Palestine. Dana Andrews portrays an American captain of a freighter who lands the homeless refugees on Palestine's shores. They are greeted by a group of settlers who take them to their small villages following a skirmish with the British. At first, Andrews is skeptical and neutral, refusing to take sides in the Palestine war. His only interest is in the business arrangement. Later, his sympathies change as he allies himself to the Jewish cause. Marta Toren plays a Jewish patriot and broadcaster who operates out of a secret radio station. Jeff Chandler portrays a Jewish leader.

The film avoids pointing to any villains although it is chiefly pro-Jewish. The Arabs are barely mentioned while the British are depicted as fair, cautious not to inflict harm upon women and children and doubtful about their stern actions toward the refugees. "This isn't a Jewish, British or Arab problem," their commander says, "it's a problem of all mankind." ■

Swordsman, The (1947), Col. Dir. Joseph H. Lewis; Sc. Wilfrid H. Pettitt; Cast includes: Larry Parks, Ellen Drew, George Macready, Edgar Buchanan.

Highland clans battle each other in this romantic drama set in Scotland during the 18th Century. Larry Parks portrays the young and handsome son of the MacArden clan who, home on vacation from Oxford, falls in love with the pretty daughter of the Glowans (Ellen Drew). The Romeo–Juliet plot leads to clashes between the feuding clans, bitter enemies for generations. George Macready, heir-apparent of the Glowans, fuels the flames of hate in this routine tale. ■

T

Tale of Two Cities, A (1917), Fox. *Dir.* Frank Lloyd; *Sc.* Frank Lloyd; *Cast includes:* William Farnum, Jewel Carmen, Charles Clary, Herschel Mayall, Rosita Maratini, Josef Swickard.

Charles Dickens' classic tale of love, revenge and redemption during the French Revolution is treated with integrity in this silent adaptation. Charles Darnay and Sidney Carton are in love with the same woman, Lucie, the daughter of Dr. Alexandre Manette, recently released by the revolutionists from imprisonment. But certain sinister and revengeful forces seek to destroy his family when his daughter marries Darnay, a member of an aristocratic family which he has denounced. The ending of the film has been altered slightly from the original novel. ■

Tale of Two Cities, A (1935), MGM. *Dir.* Jack Conway; *Sc.* W. P. Lipscomb, S. N. Berman; *Cast includes:* Ronald Colman, Elizabeth Allan, Edna May Oliver, Reginald Owen, Donald Woods, Basil Rathbone, Blanche Yurka, Henry B. Walthall.

This MGM adaptation of Dickens' novel of redemption set during the turmoil and violence of the French Revolution and the Reign of Terror captures the sweep and spectacle of the historical events, including the frenzied storming of the Bastille and the mob in all their ferocity at the guillotine. Ronald Colman portrays the pathetic Sidney Carton who sacrifices his life so that Lucie Manette may live happily with Charles Darnay with whom she had a child. Basil Rathbone plays the Marquis St. Evremonde, the arrogant and unscrupulous symbol of the hated aristocracy. Blanche Yurka portrays Madame DeFarge, the vindictive and cruel revolutionary who has sworn to destroy the descendants of the Evremondes, including Darnay, the aristocrat's nephew who has renounced his uncle's philosophy, and Lucie and her child.

The Paris mob scenes allegedly consisted of 17,000 extras in this epic production. This was the first sound adaptation of the Dickens novel. There were two silent versions, one made in Hollywood in 1917 and the other, released in 1925, of British origin. Other adaptations followed, including a British entry released in 1958 and a television version made in 1980. ■

Tampico (1944), TCF. *Dir.* Lothar Mendes; *Sc.* Kenneth Gamet, Fred Niblo, Jr., Richard Macauley; *Cast includes:* Edward G. Robinson, Lynn Bari, Victor McLaglen, Robert Bailey.

A routine World War II espionage drama, the film stars Edward G. Robinson as the captain of an oil tanker. Victor McLaglen portrays his first mate. During their journey in the Gulf of Mexico, their vessel rescues a group of survivors whose ship was torpedoed by a German U-boat. Lynn Bari, as one of the survivors, provides the romantic interest. The plot then continues in Tampico where espionage activities seem to run rampant. ■

Tanaka Memorial. The infamous Tanaka Plan, or Tanaka Memorial, uncovered in the 1920s, included detailed maps and other information that revealed Japan's secret plans involving a future war with China, Korea and the U.S. It even told of Japan's plot to bomb America's naval base at Pearl Harbor. The papers were stolen in 1927 and released to the international press. The plan was so outlandish at the time that no one treated it seriously.

Several films refer to the Tanaka Memorial. In *Jack London* (1943), a romanticized biography of the American writer's experiences chiefly in the Russo-Japanese War, a fictitious Captain Tanaka boasts to Jack London about Japan's future goals. Although the Memorial is not named, the officer outlines a plan to conquer China, spread across the Pacific and eventually go to war with the U.S. Frank Capra's World War II documentary, *The Battle of China* (1944), alludes quite frequently to the Tanaka Memorial. The film traces Japan's military steps as outlined in the plan, beginning with the invasion of Manchuria in 1931. "In order to conquer the world," the narrator states, paraphrasing the plan, "we must first conquer China." The Tanaka document also is the focus of attention in *Blood on the Sun* (1945), a World War II drama starring James Cagney as a hardboiled American newspaper editor in pre-World War II Japan. The papers fall into Cagney's hands while Japanese agents try desperately to retrieve them. ■

Tangier Incident (1953). See Cold War. ■

Tangle, The (1914), Vitagraph. *Dir.* Harry Lambart; *Cast includes:* Darwin Karr, Naomi Childers.

A silent drama set during the Spanish-American War, the film concerns Jack Bradley, a young cavalry lieutenant, and his sweetheart who rejects him to marry a colonel when she finds a picture of another female in the lieutenant's pocket. She learns too late that the photograph is that of Jack's sister. Still in love with him, she arranges to meet him secretly. Both men are sent to battle and her husband, mortally wounded, forgives Jack and his wife. Although the misunderstanding on the girl's part is silly, the film includes realistic battle scenes. ■

Tank Battalion (1958), AI. *Dir.* Sherman A. Rose; *Sc.* Richard Bernstein, George W. Waters; *Cast includes:* Don Kelly, Marjorie Hellen, Edward G. Robinson, Jr., Frank Gorshin.

The exploits of a four-man tank crew in enemy territory form the background of this low-budget Korean War action drama. Don Kelly portrays the tank commander who battles the Communists while his tank waits for repair parts to arrive. Marjorie Hellen, as a nurse who falls for Kelly, provides the chief romantic interest. The action sequences prove adequate for this type of story. ■

Tank Commandos (1959), AI. *Dir.* Burt Topper; *Sc.* Burt Topper; *Cast includes:* Robert Barron, Maggie Lawrence, Wally Campo, Donato Farretta.

A low-budget action drama set in Italy during World War II, the plot concerns a squad of G.I.s who are assigned to blow up a bridge that is being used by German tanks. The problem is that the bridge is concealed under water. Robert Barron portrays the battle-hardened lieutenant in charge of the demolition squad. Wally Campo plays the squad's translator when the soldiers encounter Italian civilians. Maggie Lawrence provides the romantic interest. Donato Farretta, as an Italian boy who leads the men to the underwater bridge, adds human interest. The film provides ample action sequences. ■

Tank warfare. By the summer of 1916 the adversaries in World War I on Europe's western front had settled into debilitating trench warfare. Britain's General Douglas Haig, prompted by this stalemate, decided to use for the first time a secretly developed weapon—the tank—in a British offensive beginning September 15, 1916, as part of the First Battle of the Somme.

The armored, tracked vehicles with their mounted weapons that came clanking across the scarred battlefield caught the Germans by surprise, and the British recorded immediate substantial gains. However, that initial tank attack failed to produce a major breakthrough for several reasons. Too few were used to make a lasting impact on the fighting. They were mechanically so unreliable that only 11 of 47 were fit for service. Their top speed of less than 5 miles per hour, coupled with a limited fuel supply, severely restricted their range. Lacking sufficient infantry support, the tank attack failed to hold new ground. The weapon had been used prematurely without prior serious thought on how to tactically exploit its advantages. It wasn't until World War II that the tank, as a result of mechanical improvements and newly developed tactics, became a formidable land weapon.

American war films released during World War I virtually ignored tanks. The new weapon occasionally appeared in postwar dramas and documentaries about the conflict. For instance, *She Goes to War* (1929), a World War I comedy drama emphasizing the woman's role in war, included, among other effective battle scenes, an allied tank advance through a flaming barrier.

German military theoreticians, between the two World Wars, devised a form of attack in which tanks, because of their speed and firepower, would be the keys to success in any future war. They believed that fast-moving armor, coordinated with self-propelled artillery and air support, could deliver a quick, overpowering punch—the famous "blitzkrieg"—through enemy lines and race over large sections of territory. Their tactics proved highly successful, especially at the beginning of World War II. Meanwhile, the U.S. in the 1930s, began converting its horse troops to armored units. *Army Girl* (1938), with Madge Evans and Preston Foster, concerned the U.S. Cavalry's transition from the use of horses to tanks. The film included a race between a tank and mounted troops. In *The Bugle Sounds* (1941) Wallace Beery, as an old-time cavalry sergeant, resists the transition from mount to mechanization in this sentimental service drama sprinkled with comedy.

Germany successfully implemented the idea of coordinated armor and air attacks on a limited scale in the Spanish Civil War (1936–1939) that helped Spain's Fascists under General Franco overthrow a liberal democratic government. Following the outbreak of World War II in 1939, Germany's subjugation of Poland in four weeks showed the success of such thinking.

In the spring of 1940, German Panzer (armored) units under Generals Guderian and Rommel repeated their triumphs by breaking through Allied lines on the western front. Fast-moving armor used enveloping tactics to isolate the British and Belgians on the channel coast, cutting them off from the main French army. Only Britain's miraculous evacuation at Dunkirk prevented an almost total destruction of that country's ground forces. Germany's armor played a decisive role in the ensuing defeat of France.

The U.S., Britain and Russia hurriedly made tank warfare an important part of their tactics. The British and Americans even designed sea-going vessels to handle tanks on invasions, the LCT—Landing Craft for Tanks. The main U.S. tank in World War II, the M-4—christened the General Sherman by the British—played a significant role on North African desert battlefields, where they were introduced in 1942, in turning back Rommel's vaunted Africa Corps.

Many American war films of the period included tank action in North Africa. *At the Front in North Africa* (1943) showed a tank battle and focused on those G.I.s who manned the tanks in the artillery duels with their German counterparts. In *Sahara* (1943), probably the best drama about a tank and its crew, an American tank commander (Humphrey Bogart) and a handful of Allied soldiers hold an oasis against a German battalion desperate for water. Postwar combat films continued to use the region for their plots. *The Desert Fox* (1951) and *The Desert Rats* (1953) emphasized Rommel's tank battles against the British. *Raid on Rommel* (1971) concerned a British assault team in North Africa assigned to destroy strategic targets and cripple Rommel's tanks by igniting his fuel supply.

Later in the war, following the Allied Normandy invasion, tanks spearheaded the drive over the roads and fields of France. The Soviet Union, which produced more than 100,000 Joseph Stalin tanks in several models, relied heavily on tank-led counteroffensives across the broad Russian plains against the Nazi invaders. The documentary *The True Glory* (1945), which emphasized the importance of the tank in the battle for Europe, showed the frustration of a British tank crew halted outside of Metz because of lack of fuel. In that respect the film underscored the tank's major weakness—its dependence on a steady fuel supply. Rommel in North Africa was handicapped by Allied air and submarine attacks on his supply lines that cut his fuel reserves.

The training of tank crews was part of the story in *The Tanks Are Coming* (1951), about a tough tank sergeant who molds U.S. tank crews into an effective fighting force. In *Battle of the Bulge* (1965) tank battles dominated the action sequences as the superior German Tiger tanks initially subdue their American counterparts. *Is Paris Burning?* (1966) showed Resistance fighters battling Nazi troops for control of Paris streets and buildings as a French tank unit storms the city and joins the fighting. *The Bridge at Remagen* (1969) included a heated battle between the U.S. 9th Armored Division and German forces over a vital bridge the Allies need to cross the Rhine.

Tank warfare during World War II was highlighted in other films as well. *Patton* (1970), a biographical drama of one of the most successful and controversial tank generals of World War II, included large-scale tank battles. Tanks served as comedy props in *Kelly's Heroes* (1970) with probably the oddest tank crew in American film history. They play music through loudspeakers and fire cartridges of paint from their tank instead of deadly shells. In one satirical scene, Clint Eastwood, Telly Savalas and Donald Sutherland approach a German Tiger tank western style, as if going to a shoot-out. *The Big Red One* (1980), about the exploits of the U.S. First Infantry Division in North Africa and Europe, included sequences of German tanks overrunning American positions and scattering the troops, underscoring the fragility of life at the front when foot soldiers are confronted with armor.

During the Korean War (1950–1953) tanks had contrasting roles. In the conflict's opening stages North Korea successfully spearheaded its invasion with late-model Russian tanks that featured heavy armor and a sloped design that easily withstood machine gun fire and light anti-tank weapons. American troops at first reported many instances when their anti-tank "bazooka" rockets, left over from World War II, bounced off enemy tanks or failed to penetrate thick frontal armor. Heavier anti-tank weapons and projectiles with greater velocity helped overcome that problem.

In the later stages of the Korean War, when battle lines stabilized, tanks were often used as stationary, semi-permanent, front-line artillery in support of the infantry. In general, the mountainous terrain and relatively few good roads in Korea restricted the tank's chief effectiveness, its mobility. However, several films did depict tank action in Korea. In *Dragonfly Squadron* (1954), for example, Communist tanks push south ready to create havoc, but U.S. planes take to the skies and blast the enemy. In the Vietnam War (1956–1975) extensive rice paddies and jungles hampered tank movement to a great extent.

Hollywood has featured the tank in other conflicts. *Trouble in Morocco* (1937), a routine tale about the Foreign Legion, had several furious battle sequences, including the use of tanks brought in to rescue besieged Legionnaires. In *Judith* (1966), set during Israel's War of Independence, the Israelis want to capture a former Nazi tank expert who is working for the Arabs. *The Beast of Budapest* (1958) used newsreel footage of the Russian tanks crushing the Hungarian Revolt of 1956. ∎

Tanks a Million (1941). See Service Comedy. ∎

Tanks Are Coming, The (1951), WB. *Dir.* Lewis Seiler; *Sc.* Robert H. Andrews; *Cast includes:* Steve Cochran, Philip Carey, Mari Aldon, Paul Picerni.

Set in 1944 in France, this World War II drama focuses on the U.S. Third Armored Division's advance on the German border from St. Lo. The human story concerns a tough tank sergeant who replaces a platoon sergeant who was killed in battle. Steve Cochran portrays the unorthodox replacement who likes to do things his own way despite the objections of his lieutenant, played by Philip Carey. Cochran soon molds the tank crews into an effective fighting force although they have to face the superior Tiger tanks of the Nazis in this routine tale. The battle sequences utilize actual war footage at times. ∎

Tap Roots (1948), UI. *Dir.* George Marshall; *Sc.* Alan LeMay; *Cast includes:* Van Heflin, Susan Hayward, Boris Karloff, Julie London.

The Dabney clan of Mississippi and a group of neighboring farmers have prospered and abolished slavery in their corner of the state. Determined to secede from the rest of the state as well as from the Confederacy, they raise their own army. The brave but ill-equipped force is decimated in a pathetic battle by the superior Southern troops. A journalist of doubtful parentage (Van Heflin) falls in love with the strong-willed daughter (Susan Hayward) of the Dabneys in this weak Civil War drama. The Dabneys are willing to take on the Confederate Army to protect their plantation and remain neutral during the conflict between the North and South. Julie London plays Hayward's younger passionate sister. Boris Karloff, as an Indian, is a loyal friend to the family.

The film was adapted from the novel by James Street, which, in turn, was based on an actual incident during the war. Southern troops were forced to crush a seditious Mississippi community that professed its independence and neutrality. The lopsided battle occurred at Lebanon Valley where the defenders were slaughtered. ∎

Taras Bulba (1962), UA. *Dir.* J. Lee Thompson; *Sc.* Waldo Salt, Karl Tunberg; *Cast includes:* Tony Curtis, Yul Brynner, Christine Kaufmann, Sam Wanamaker, Brad Dexter.

Gogol's epic story of the Setch, the military brotherhood of the Cossacks, provides the basis for this inept 15th-century adventure drama. Yul Brynner portrays the title character, a proud, strong Cossack leader who raises his two sons as fearless warriors. Tony Curtis, as Andrei, Bulba's first son, is defiant of his father. Long sequences of Curtis' romancing of a young Polish woman (Christine Kaufmann) slows down the action and detracts from the author's original story. When Curtis attempts to rescue Kaufmann from the Polish town that has come under siege by his father's army, Brynner shoots him. Perry Lopez plays Bulba's other son.

The best moments in the film, however, are the action sequences, especially those depicting hundreds of horsemen thundering across the landscape as Cossacks and Polish troops clash in battle. The outdoor shots were staged in Argentina where the Pampas substituted for the Russian Steppes. Curtis and Kaufmann were a real husband-and-wife team from 1963 to 1967. ∎

U.S. Marines prepare to invade another Pacific island during World War II. *Tarawa Beachhead* (1958).

Tarawa Beachhead (1958), Col. *Dir.* Paul Wendkos; *Sc.* Richard A. Simmons; *Cast includes:* Kerwin Mathews, Julie Adams, Ray Danton, Karen Sharpe.

A U.S. Marine is haunted by a murder he witnessed of a fellow leatherneck at the hands of an officer in this drama set in the Pacific during World War II. At first Kerwin Mathews, as the young marine torn between his belief in justice and loyalty to the Corps, remains silent. Later, however, before the invasion of Tarawa, he decides to file charges against the guilty officer (Ray Danton). Further complications arise when the officer marries the sister of Mathews' wife while they are on leave in New Zealand. Danton dies heroically during the marine attack. When the commanding officer, who is preparing to name Danton for the Medal of Honor, asks Mathews about the dead hero, the idealistic marine replies: "Nobody knows anybody. That's a fact." ∎

Target Hong Kong (1952). See Cold War. ∎

Target Unknown (1951), UI. *Dir.* George Sherman; *Sc.* Harold Medford; *Cast includes:* Mark Stevens, Alex Nicol, Robert Douglas, Don Taylor, Gig Young.

This World War II drama explores some of the methods used by German Intelligence to extract military information from unsuspecting Allied prisoners of war. The film begins with an exciting American bombing raid over German-held territory. One of the bombers is hit, and the captain (Mark Stevens) orders the crew to bail out. The men are captured and taken in for interrogation supervised by a clever German colonel who believes significant information can be assembled from small bits of seemingly unimportant facts. When Stevens suspects their ploy, the Germans decide to switch tactics and use his own character traits against him. "An earnest soldier . . . patriotic," concludes one officer. "With pride in his country and his weapons," adds another. "That pride may very well be the chink in his armor."

The Nazis eventually learn from their captors that a major fuel dump is the next target. They order the fuel moved and every available fighter plane to meet the allied bombers. As Stevens and his crew are being shipped to a permanent prison camp, he and two comrades escape, contact the French underground and transmit a message to England warning of the German trap. Gig Young, as a German officer raised in America, poses as an understanding sympathizer whom Stevens confides in. He even criticizes the brutality of the Gestapo. "Those Gestapo men," he confides to Stevens, "they put no signatures to the Geneva Convention." To gather more information, the German command places another English-speaking German posing as a fellow American prisoner in captivity with Stevens. When Stevens learns his identity, he calls the Nazi a "traitor." "You're the traitor," the German explains. "You and that stupid crew of yours. You know what you've done? You've given us a first-rate briefing on your Cambrais raid." ∎

Target Zero (1955), WB. *Dir.* Harmon Jones; *Sc.* Sam Rolfe; *Cast includes:* Richard Conte, Peggie Castle, Charles Bronson, Richard Stapley, Chuck Connors.

An American patrol attempts to link up with its main company in this routine Korean War drama. Richard Conte portrays a battle-hardened lieutenant in charge of the small patrol. Joining them are three British soldiers and their American tank as well as a United Nations employee, played by Peggie Castle. When this motley group reach their destination, they discover that the company has been annihilated. They dig in to defend the ridge while U.N. troops plan a major advance. The American and British soldiers, who earlier were at odds, develop a healthy respect for each other during their skirmishes with the enemy. Richard Stapley, as a British sergeant, dislikes the Yanks since one of them took advantage of his sister during the last war. Charles Bronson plays an American sergeant. ∎

Tarzan Triumphs (1943), RKO. *Dir.* William Thiele; *Sc.* Roy Chanslor; *Cast includes:* Johnny Weissmuller, Johnny Sheffield, Frances Gifford, Stanley Ridges.

Nazi paratroopers take over a hidden jungle city in this World War II drama, an entry in the popular Tarzan series. Tarzan, with the help of local natives, battles the ruthless invaders and eventually overcomes them in this routine film. The jungle man's son, Boy, is captured by the invaders and has to be rescued by Tarzan. Meanwhile, Cheetah gets into the usual mischief. The last chase sequence is rather interesting as Tarzan pursues the commanding officer, the last Nazi, into the jungle and leads him into an inhabited lion trap. The last scene is typical of the humor of this series. As a Berlin radio operator tries to make contact with the doomed Nazi unit in Africa, Cheetah picks up the microphone and utters some sounds. The German at the other end announces: "It's the Fuhrer!"

The Tarzan series, previously produced by MGM, was dropped by the studio and temporarily taken over by RKO. Maureen O'Sullivan, who usually played Jane, was unavailable at the time to fulfill the role. The female interest was therefore supplied by Frances Gifford, who plays the white princess of a lost civilization. Other participants of the series, such as Boy, played by Johnny Sheffield, and Cheetah, remained intact. ∎

Tarzan's Desert Mystery (1943), RKO. *Dir.* William Thiele; *Sc.* Edward T. Lowe; *Cast includes:* Johnny Weissmuller, Johnny Sheffield, Nancy Kelly, Otto Kruger.

Nazi agents attempt to foment trouble for a peaceful sheik in this World War II entry in the "Tarzan" series. Tarzan, Boy and Cheetah travel across a desert in search of a rare medicine when they meet an American entertainer (Nancy Kelly). She is on her way to warn the sheik about the Nazi plot. Other complications arise when Tarzan is accused of stealing a prize horse and Kelly is jailed on a murder charge. But the king of the jungle resolves all by the end of the film. Otto Kruger plays a Nazi agent in this routine story. ∎

Gary Cooper (r.) takes command of an aircraft carrier during World War II. *Task Force* (1949).

Task Force (1949), WB. *Dir.* Delmer Daves; *Sc.* Delmer Daves; *Cast includes:* Gary Cooper, Jane Wyatt, Wayne Morris, Walter Brennan, Julie London, Jack Holt.

A tribute to the aircraft carrier and to those for fought for its production, the film relates the struggle of a small group of naval air officers who, through the 1920s and 1930s, attempt to persuade their superiors to develop naval air power as a major military force. After years of frustration and the development of the modern aircraft carrier, the young Turks get their chance to prove their strategy during World War II. Gary Cooper portrays the outspoken junior officer who so exasperates the navy bureaucracy with his outbursts that, to teach him a lesson, his superiors at first banish him to a desk job in the Panama Canal and later pass him over when they dole out promotions. His patient wife (Jane Wyatt) encourages him to stay in the navy when he considers a lucrative offer to enter private industry. Walter Brennan plays a crusty admiral and Cooper's immediate superior and lifelong friend.

Several effective World War II battle sequences include those involving the Battle of Midway and the ensuing kamikaze attacks. Although produced four years after the war, the film manages to interject patriotic speeches more apropos of the movies released during the conflict. Cooper, who has slowly advanced from a navy flight lieutenant to captain of his own carrier, addresses his crew following a message he has received informing him of the end of the war. "To our dead shipmates," he broadcasts through the ship, "to all those who died, who are even more of a part of this victory than any of us, our eternal thanks for keeping us a nation of free men—for giving us a nation to come back to." Returning to America and his wife who is waiting for him on shore, he witnesses a squadron of jet planes flying in precision formation. "I was proud to see these jets," Cooper's voice announces from the soundtrack in the final scene, "and I knew it wouldn't end there. Something new would follow, something better; it always has—it always will." ■

Taste of Hell, A (1973), Boxoffice International. *Dir.* Neil Yarema, Basil Bradbury; *Sc.* Neil Yarema; *Cast includes:* John Garwood, Lisa Lorena, William Smith, Vic Diaz, Lloyd Kino.

John Garwood, who also produced this low-budget drama set in the Philippines during World War II, portrays an American soldier who joins the guerrillas in their struggle against the Japanese occupiers. A sadistic Japanese officer orders his troops to machine-gun Garwood and the Filipinos after they surrender. But the American, seriously wounded, escapes. Another American soldier (William Smith) manages to dislodge the Japanese troops, and Garwood, in a fit of revenge, cuts

off the officer's head. Lisa Lorena, as a local villager, provides the romantic interest for both Americans. The film substitutes violence and bloodshed for substance. ■

Taza, Son of Cochise (1954), UI. *Dir.* Douglas Sirk; *Sc.* George Zuckerman; *Cast includes:* Rock Hudson, Barbara Rush, Gregg Palmer, Bart Roberts.

The death of Cochise, leader of the Apaches, sparks a revival of hostilities between the tribe and the U.S. Cavalry in this action drama. Taza (Rock Hudson), the son of the famous Apache chief, promises his dying father that he will honor the hard-earned treaty with the whites. Meanwhile, his younger brother (Bart Roberts) joins Geronimo (Ian MacDonald), who has come to the reservation for a respite, in waging war upon the whites. General Crook heads the horse soldiers attacked by the dissidents. Taza comes to the soldiers' aid before they are all but annihilated. Barbara Rush, as a pretty Indian maiden, provides some romantic interest. Most critics, who found the film unexceptional, praised the highly effective Utah locales chosen for the setting.

Historically, General Crook was eventually forced to resign for failing to capture Geronimo and his small dissident band of Apaches who escaped from their hated reservation. A dispute arose over his use of Apache scouts to help track Geronimo. Washington bureaucrats thought the scouts were unreliable and feeding Crook misinformation. He was replaced by General Nelson A. Miles. ■

"Tearing Down the Spanish Flag" (1898), Vitagraph. *Dir.* J. Stuart Blackton; *Sc.* J. Stuart Blackton; *Cast includes:* J. Stuart Blackton.

A landmark film, this short recreation of the fighting in Cuba during the Spanish-American War is probably the first American war movie ever made. It is also considered by screen historians as America's first propaganda film. Blackton, an ex-Englishman with a background in journalism and cartooning, produced the film on the roof of the Morse Building located on Nassau Street in New York City. He plays a stalwart soldier who removes the Spanish colors and hoists the American flag. That is virtually all there is to the film, which lasts but a few short minutes. However, it captured the attention of the public. Contemporary audiences, impressed with the work, believed it was actually made in Cuba during combat. ■

Tecumseh. See *Brave Warrior* (1952). ■

"Teddy, the Rough Rider" (1940). See Theodore Roosevelt. ■

Tell It to the Marines (1926). See Service Comedy. ■

Tempest (1928), MGM. *Dir.* Sam Taylor; *Sc.* C. Gardner Sullivan; *Cast includes:* John Barrymore, Camilia Horn, Louis Wolheim, George Fawcett.

The romantic drama opens in Russia prior to World War I and the fateful Revolution. John Barrymore portrays a sergeant in the Czar's cavalry who rises to the rank of lieutenant in spite of his peasant background. His general, who looks with favor upon him, secures the commission for Barrymore. At an affair he dances with the General's daughter, a Russian princess, who rejects his advances because of his humble birth. He gets drunk and by mistake wanders into her quarters and falls asleep. When the girl discovers him, she summons her father who is outraged. Barrymore receives a five-year prison term and is stripped of his rank. When World War I erupts, all the prisoners except Barrymore are sent to the front. His superior officer, jealous of Barrymore's affections toward the general's daughter, keeps him in solitary confinement. Revolution breaks out and Barrymore is released. The general is executed and his daughter imprisoned. Barrymore is accused by the revolutionaries of being a traitor for giving succor to the dying general. He rescues the former princess and escapes with her across the border to Austria. Louis Wolheim portrays a Russian soldier who befriends Barrymore and helps the couple escape the turmoil of the Revolution. There are no battle scenes of World War I, but the few sequences of the nominal trials and hasty executions of the aristocrats convey the chaos that swept across revolutionary Russia. ■

Ten Gentlemen From West Point (1942), TCF. *Dir.* Henry Hathaway; *Sc.* Richard Maibaum; *Cast includes:* George Montgomery, Maureen O'Hara, John Sutton, Laird Cregar, John Shepperd.

This historical drama recounts how the famous military academy came into being. The title refers to those who remained in the first class after the other candidates dropped out. George Montgomery portrays a cadet who comes to the school from Kentucky dressed in buckskins. The inhabitants of the old fort, including the commander (Laird Cregar), frown upon the experiment. After the young officers receive their training, the detachment is ordered west where an Indian uprising has occurred. The fledgling officers employ military strategy in quelling the insurrection while saving Cregar's life, making him a quick convert to the establishment of West Point. The fictitious elements dominate the plot, leaving little room for the facts concerning the growth and role of the school. To provide some degree of authenticity, the film cites an impressive list of graduates, including Generals Grant, Lee, Pershing and MacArthur. ■

Ten Tall Men (1951), Col. *Dir.* Willis Goldbeck; *Sc.* Roland Kibbee; *Cast includes:* Burt Lancaster, Jody Lawrence, Gilbert Roland, George Tobias.

Burt Lancaster portrays a sergeant in the Foreign Legion in this action adventure. When he learns that the Riffs plan an all-out attack, he volunteers, along with ten convicts in the Legion jail, to prevent the assault. He leads his motley crew across the desert and captures a sheik's daughter (Jody Lawrence), thereby crushing the impending attack. A romance soon sprouts between the captive and Lancaster. For his brave actions, Lancaster wins a decoration.

The film includes plenty of humor, especially as practiced by comic character player George Tobias, one of the Legionnaires. In one scene he is assigned to guard the captured desert princess. He observes the fiery daggers in her eyes, which are then translated into raging imprecations. "She hates with her tongue as well as her eyes," he says to his comrades. "She hates with everything. She is a real woman." ■

Ten Years' War. See *The Bright Shawl* (1923). ■

Tender Comrade (1943), RKO. *Dir.* Edward Dmytryk; *Sc.* Dalton Trumbo; *Cast includes:* Ginger Rogers, Robert Ryan, Ruth Hussey, Patricia Collinge, Mady Christians.

A drama of the women left behind to grieve for their men who march off to war, this overly sentimental World War II film stars

Ginger Rogers as a wife who loses her husband (Robert Ryan) in battle. Rogers, who works in a defense plant, suggests that she and three other servicemen's wives pool their resources, move from their individual rented rooms into a more spacious house and share everything for the duration. The dialogue includes a string of patriotic speeches. Rogers has a baby, but her bliss is short-lived; she receives a telegram informing her that Ryan has been killed in action. Years later, the film was singled out by the House Un-American Activities as an example of pro-Communist propaganda produced by Hollywood. Ignoring references to the pro-American speeches in the film, the committee instead emphasized the sharing and communal living of the war wives, including such seemingly harmless dialogue as "share and share alike." Director Dmytryk and screenwriter Trumbo, two of the "Hollywood Ten," were censured by members of the committee for their pro-Communist leanings. ■

Tents of Allah, The (1923), AE. *Dir.* Charles Logue; *Sc.* Charles Logue; *Cast includes:* Monte Blue, Mary Alden, Mary Thurman, Macey Hallam.

This drama of intrigue, revenge and desert warfare takes place in North Africa. The niece of the American consul in Tangiers is kidnaped and taken into the desert. The sultan permits this act to occur because years ago one of the women of his harem was taken from him by an American officer. U.S. Marines land from a nearby battleship, rescue the young woman and capture a Berber who was guarding her. The Berber turns out to be the son of the American officer who stole the sultan's woman. More intrigue and plotting follow until all is set right. ■

Teresa (1951). See Veterans. ■

Texas War Of Independence (1835–1836). It was only a matter of time before the rising tide of early 19th century American settlers streaming westward would lap at the boundaries of the sparsely populated and weakly defended area in northern Mexico that now comprises the American southwest. The Texas War of Independence, in which American colonists in Texas broke away from Mexico, was the first of two armed clashes between the two cultures for control of the region. Originally, Mexico encouraged some

American emigration into Texas to improve the region's economy and check the warlike Indians who controlled large parts of northern Mexico.

Stephen Austin, following up a plan devised by his father, brought in the first group of settlers in 1822. According to an agreement with Mexico, they would be all Roman Catholic and were expected to become Mexican citizens. Attracted by the region's fertile soil and mild climate, the American colony flourished. By 1830 an estimated 20,000 Americans, many of them Southern slave holders, had moved into Texas.

Friction over several issues soon developed. Mexico had recently outlawed slavery, but Texans refused to give up their chattel. Fearing the growing power of the tightly knit American colony, Mexico sought to reinforce its control by limiting American immigration in 1830. Between 1832 and 1833, the Mexican government denied petitions from the settlers for local autonomy and a redress of grievances. Austin was arrested by the Mexican government and accused of treason when he went to Mexico City to try to negotiate peacefully the differences with the government of General Santa Anna. *The Last Command* (1955) dramatized the meeting but substituted Jim Bowie for Austin in the talks with Santa Anna.

Skirmishes broke out in late 1835. Mexico's dictator president, General Santa Anna, led a force of several thousand into Texas in February 1836 to crush the growing revolution. On February 23, 1836, he began a siege of the Alamo, a former Spanish mission in San Antonio that had been turned into a fort by a force of 187 Americans under the joint command of William B. Travis and James Bowie. While the Alamo was under attack, Texas declared its independence at a convention in Washington-on-the-Brazos that also appointed Sam Houston commander of Texas forces.

Santa Anna, at first, was successful in engagements against small units of Texans. His troops overwhelmed the Alamo's defenders, all of whom were killed in the final assault on March 6. Another 300 Americans under Captain James Fannin were massacred at Goliad on March 27 after surrendering. The Texas revolt and Mexican massacres aroused the sympathy of Americans. Many of them crossed the border to volunteer their military services.

Sam Houston permanently turned the tide

of the war by delivering a crushing blow to the Mexicans at the Battle of San Jacinto (April 21, 1836). Santa Anna was captured after the battle trying to hide in the tall grass. As a prerequisite for his release, the Mexican leader had to sign a pair of treaties that affirmed the independence of Texas and guaranteed its borders. The Mexican Congress later repudiated the treaties but ceased military action against Texas.

Most films about this period center on leaders and heroes of the Texas revolution and the main battles such as the Alamo and San Jacinto. Several, including *The Conqueror* (1917) and *The First Texan* (1956), are semi-biographical characterizations of Sam Houston. The heroic defenders of the Alamo get much of the attention. *The Alamo* (1960), which John Wayne both directed and starred in as Davy Crockett, probably is the most famous film of this group.

However, the movie industry has overlooked the contributions of Stephen Austin. The individual who is sometimes referred to as "the father of Texas" is portrayed chiefly as a minor character. As mentioned above, even his attempt as a Texas representative to peacefully resolve any differences was denied by Hollywood.

A number of films, primarily action dramas, favored the Texans who are shown heroically fighting against overwhelming forces to preserve the rights and traditions they felt were being denied. *Heroes of the Alamo* (1938) and *The Last Command* pay tribute to the defenders of the old mission. *The Conqueror, The First Texan* and *Man of Conquest* (1939), the last starring Richard Dix as Houston, all deal with the decisive victory at San Jacinto.

Semi-historical films, even allowing for fictional liberties, are important since they portray major events and personalities. The action films do a creditable job in showing the heroism of the Americans in Texas and the beastly practices of the Mexicans. However, the causes of the War for Texas Independence, as seen in these dramas, are so utterly prejudiced in favor of the American colonists that they do a gross disservice to the understanding that history is supposed to foster.

It would be interesting to conjecture what the reaction of the average movie-goer would be to a film about this period that presented the causes of the conflict from a more balanced and unbiased view. Such a drama, for example, might characterize early Texans as lawbreakers who sought to retain the institution of slavery despite Mexican laws against it. The settlers could truthfully be presented as a group who refused to accept the laws, culture and language of the country that welcomed them. In reality, the colonists agitated to transplant into their new country an influence that the Mexican government viewed as alien at the least, and subversive at the worst.

Might such a film even be banned in Texas? ■

That Hamilton Woman (1941), UA. *Dir.* Alexander Korda; *Sc.* Walter Reisch, R. C. Sherriff; *Cast includes:* Vivien Leigh, Laurence Olivier, Alan Mowbray, Sara Allgood, Gladys Cooper.

Vivien Leigh and Laurence Olivier portray the star-crossed lovers Lady Emma Hamilton and Lord Admiral Nelson in this handsomely produced biographical drama. The story, told in flashback, traces Lady Hamilton's amorous career from the lover who betrayed her early in her life, to her marriage to British Ambassador Sir William Hamilton (Alan Mowbray) and to her scandalous illicit affair with Lord Nelson.

Several sea battles are interjected into the romantic plot, including the lengthy climactic Battle of Trafalgar, where Nelson is killed in action. The battle was painfully staged using miniatures which at times appear quite obvious. Produced during World War II, the film makes several parallels between the Napoleonic wars of the early 1800s and its contemporary period, all of which underscore to advantage England's important role in world affairs. ■

That Nazty Nuisance (1943), UA. *Dir.* Glenn Tryon; *Sc.* Earl Snell, Clarence Marks; *Cast includes:* Bobby Watson, Joe Devlin, Johnny Arthur, Jean Porter, Ian Keith.

The three Axis dictators get their just deserts in this World War II farce. Hitler, Mussolini and a Japanese ruler named "Suki Yaki" travel to a mythical oriental kingdom where they are intercepted by American survivors of a torpedoed merchant ship. Henry Victor plays a crew member who impersonates a magician and causes the downfall of the unholy trio. Bobby Watson once again impersonates Hitler while Joe Devlin portrays the Italian dictator. Ian Keith, as the ruler of the kingdom, refuses to sign any treaties with the dictators. ■

Then There Were Three (1961), Parade. *Dir.* Alex Nicol; *Sc.* Frank Gregory, Allan Lurie; *Cast includes:* Alex Nicol, Frank Latimore, Barry Cahill, Sid Clute.

A handful of American soldiers, separated from their main unit, attempt to make it back to their lines in this suspenseful World War II drama set in Italy. One of the G.I.s, however, is actually a Nazi spy assigned to kill an important Italian guerrilla leader. Suspicions are tossed around as the Americans try to discover which one of their number is the German. The plot is eventually foiled in this low-budget but tightly directed film. ∎

There Is No 13 (1974), Unset. *Dir.* William Sachs; *Sc.* William Sachs; *Cast includes:* Mark Damon, Margaret Markov, Harvey Lembeck, Jean Jennings.

This small drama attempts to capture the torment and suffering that has become a permanent part of the Vietnam veteran's psyche in the wake of the war. Consisting chiefly of narrative and flashbacks and flashforwards, the film depicts the physical and psychological horrors that the soldiers faced daily during the conflict and have now become nightmares to many of them. Mark Damon portrays the main character, and it is his thoughts, dreams and fears that we become privy to. The title refers to his next love affair that he dreams about but can never attain in this introspective film. ∎

There's Something About a Soldier (1944), Col. *Dir.* Alfred E. Green; *Sc.* Horace McCoy, Barry Trivers; *Cast includes:* Tom Neal, Evelyn Keyes, Bruce Bennett, John Hubbard.

This low-budget World War II film examines the rigorous training of officers for the Anti-Aircraft Artillery Command. One cocky candidate (Tom Neal) takes his training lightly. But when he falls for Evelyn Keyes and comes under the influence of a veteran (Bruce Bennett) who fought the Nazis in the deserts of North Africa, his attitude changes. The film chiefly takes place at Camp Davis, North Carolina. ∎

Thermopylae, Battle of (480 B.C.). The Battle of Thermopylae, during the Greco-Persian Wars (500–479 B.C.), has become a symbol in the western world of courage and supreme sacrifice in war. A small force of about 1,000 men, comprised of 300 Spartans and 700 Thespian allies, under Spartan King Leonidas, fought to their death against an overwhelming force of 180,000 Persians at the pass of Thermopylae in central Greece. The outnumbered defenders attempted to slow down the Persian advance, thereby giving the Greek city-states time to marshal their defense.

The Persians, under Xerxes, marched into Greece when their demands for tribute had been rejected by most of the Greek cities. Persia eventually lost the wars, and, as a result, the ancient western Mediterranean was saved from the spread of oriental despotism and came under the growing influence of Greek humanistic philosophy, individualism and democratic ideals.

The film *The 300 Spartans* (1962) captures the single-minded heroism of Leonidas and his troops, along with their famous message, "Oh, stranger, tell the Spartans that we lie here obedient to their word." It presents, as well, some of the intrigues and jealousies that marked ancient Greek politics and became the basis for the disunity and internal warfare between the city-states that characterized the history of ancient Greece. The battle was alluded to in a more recent film, *Go Tell the Spartans* (1978), starring Burt Lancaster as an American military commander, and set at a remote jungle outpost during the Vietnam War. A nearby cemetery holds the remains of French soldiers who were killed in the French Indo-China War (1946–1954). A crude sign above the site, foreshadowing the present plight of the American garrison, contains the words: "Stranger, when you find us here, go tell the Spartans we obeyed their orders." ∎

They Came to Blow Up America (1943). See Spy Films: the Talkies. ∎

They Came to Cordura (1959), Col. *Dir.* Robert Rossen; *Sc.* Ivan Moffat, Robert Rossen; *Cast includes:* Gary Cooper, Rita Hayworth, Van Heflin, Tab Hunter, Richard Conte.

This action drama explores the meaning of true courage as it depicts the exploits of five candidates for the Congressional Medal of Honor. Set in 1916 during a punitive expedition of American troops against the forces of Pancho Villa in Mexico, the film stars Gary Cooper as an army officer assigned to escort the five heroes back to the U.S. Rita Hay-

American troops attack one of Pancho Villa's Mexican strongholds. *They Came to Cordura* (1959).

worth, as the spoiled daughter of a discredited politician, joins the small group. By the end of the journey the alleged heroes have shown feet of clay as they crack under pressure of the long trip and engage in attempted rape, murder and treachery.

Cooper, as a disgraced coward in battle, has been assigned the task of Awards Officer so that he can learn about bravery. Ironically, he is the one who maintains order and discipline and brings the psychologically broken men home. True courage, the film suggests, stems from quiet reason, not necessarily from momentary accident. The heroes marked for distinction are played by actors Van Heflin, Richard Conte and Tab Hunter. ■

They Dare Not Love (1941). See Refugees. ■

They Died With Their Boots On (1941), WB. *Dir.* Raoul Walsh; *Sc.* Wally Kline, Aeneas MacKenzie; *Cast includes:* Errol Flynn, Olivia de Havilland, Gene Lockhart, Regis Toomey, Stanley Ridges.

A highly romanticized version of the saga of Colonel George A. Custer, the film stars Errol Flynn as the flamboyant cavalry officer who engraved a permanent place for himself in the pages of American history. The story follows Armstrong's career from his West Point days, through the Civil War and to his fateful stand at the Little Big Horn. He meets his sweetheart and future wife (Olivia de Havilland) while he is a cadet at the Point. After distinguishing himself in battle during the Civil War, he is assigned to a frontier outpost where unrest is brewing among the Indians. A peace treaty is signed, but unscrupulous land grabbers and greedy gold hunters cause a general uprising of the Sioux. Custer leads his famed Seventh Cavalry to join forces with General Terry but is trapped and massacred along with 264 troopers by the Sioux before he reaches the general. The famous battle of Custer's Last Stand is both suspenseful and stirring. Custer, with both guns blazing, is in the center of his unmounted troops. He and his men gallantly fight on, hopelessly surrounded and outnumbered.

Historically, the battle was futile, but the legend has since replaced the facts. The film contains other historical inaccuracies. The presence of General Winfield Scott (Sydney Greenstreet), as the commander of the Union army at Gettysburg, is one example. He had been replaced two years earlier. But Raoul Walsh's fast-paced direction of the action sequences, together with Flynn's dashing portrayal of Custer leading several rousing cavalry charges against Lee's forces, however erroneous, and his gallant stand at Little Big Horn, almost exonerate the film from any liberties it has taken with fact. ■

They Gave Him a Gun (1937). See Crime and War. ■

They Got Me Covered (1943). See Spy Films: the Talkies. ■

They Live in Fear (1944), Col. *Dir.* Josef Berne; *Sc.* Michael Simmons, Sam Ornitz; *Cast includes:* Otto Kruger, Clifford Severn, Pat Parrish, Jimmy Carpenter.

A World War II propaganda drama that calls for tolerance toward refugees, the film centers on a young emigrant who escapes to America to free himself of Nazi oppression. Ironically, the boy finds the same intolerance in his newly adopted home. Clifford Severn portrays the teen-ager persecuted with threats to his family who has remained behind. Otto Kruger appears as the only principal adult in this tale about oppressive forces in the U.S. A unique theme for its time, especially in pointing out that not all Germans were Nazis, the story is not developed sufficiently to lift it out of its low-budget status. ■

They Made Her a Spy (1939). See Spy Films. ■

They Met in Bombay (1941), MGM. *Dir.* Clarence Brown; *Sc.* Edwin Justus Mayer, Anita Loos, Leon Gordon; *Cast includes:* Clark Gable, Rosalind Russell, Peter Lorre, Jessie Ralph.

A World War II adventure drama that begins in Bombay and ends in Hong Kong, the film stars Clark Gable and Rosalind Russell as two competing international jewel thieves after the same treasure. Russell lifts the valuable jewel while Gable attempts to take it from her. But they are forced to flee Bombay as the police close in. They land in Hong Kong where Gable dons a Canadian officer's uniform as a disguise. He is quickly summoned into action to evacuate civilians from a town where he leads a British detachment in a battle against Japanese troops. Receiving the Victoria Cross for his wound and his bravery, he returns the jewel and enlists legitimately in the military service. The battle scenes are limited in this entertaining but implausible tale. ■

They Raid by Night (1942), PRC. *Dir.* Spencer G. Bennet; *Sc.* Jack Natteford; *Cast includes:* Lyle Talbot, June Duprez, Victor Varconi, Charles Rogers.

This World War II action drama involves the rescue of a Norwegian chief of staff from a Nazi concentration camp. Three Commandos drop by parachute into Nazi-occupied Norway and, following several close calls and one casualty, complete their mission. One Commando, a native of Norway, seeks out a local doctor when the chief they came to free is wounded. His former fiancee turns him in to the Nazis who torture him. He tells of the escape. Another Commando, the leader of the group, also is caught but manages to escape in this weak film.

Hollywood was quick to exploit the heroic activities of the British Commandos as soon as news of the crack unit reached U.S. shores. Films of their exploits continued throughout the war and into the postwar period. When this film was released, the famed group had accomplished a successful raid on Dieppe, an event that was heralded in the Allied press. However, the plot of this film does the Commandos an injustice. See also Commandos. ■

They Were Expendable (1945), MGM. *Dir.* John Ford; *Sc.* Frank Wead; *Cast includes:* Robert Montgomery, John Wayne, Donna Reed, Jack Holt, Ward Bond, Marshall Thompson.

This World War II drama recounts the exploits of the men who deployed their nimble little U.S. torpedo boats against the Japanese in the Pacific. The story opens prior to the attack on Pearl Harbor. Robert Montgomery, as a navy lieutenant in command of a squadron of PT boats based in Manila Bay, strongly believes that the boats are highly maneuverable and can serve as an effective attack force. Navy brass, however, are more skeptical and ignore Montgomery's small fleet. John Wayne plays Montgomery's assistant who doesn't appreciate the small boats until after the Japanese invade the Philippines. The torpedo boats gear up for action and inflict heavy damage on Japanese cruisers and supply vessels. A dramatic highlight is the departure of General MacArthur (Robert Barrat) from the Philippines in one of these boats in the dark days of 1942. The story concludes when the two officers and several members of their team are flown back to the U.S. to train future PT boat crews.

These light wooden craft became an important factor in delaying the enemy while the Americans retreated from the Philippines. The crews, the "expendables" of the film title, often put their lives on the line in near suicidal missions. The theme of expendability, with its ramifications of the futility of war, was more pronounced in the original book than in the film although director John Ford managed to capture traces of it in various scenes. The nurse (Donna Reed) who is left behind on Corregidor and the men who could not be taken off the "rock" in time are just some examples of those who are "expendable" during war.

The film, released two months after Japan's surrender, was based on William L. White's book of the same name. The author did indepth interviews with the three major participants of the events depicted in the film. John Bulkeley, who spearheaded the deployment of PT boats in the Pacific and was a close friend of John Ford, was played by Montgomery. Commander Kelly, Bulkeley's second in command, was portrayed by Wayne. Donna Reed had the role of the real-life nurse, Beulah Greenwalt. MGM was plagued with lawsuits from two of the above participants. Kelly claimed that Wayne's impersonation of him hurt his reputation and asked for $50,000 in damages. The court awarded him $3,000. The real-life nurse charged that Donna Reed's portrayal of her "cheapened her character." She fared better than Kelly, receiving $290,000. ■

Thin Red Line, The (1964), AA. *Dir.* Andrew Marton; *Sc.* Bernard Gordon; *Cast includes:* Keir Dullea, Jack Warden, James Philbrook, Ray Daley.

This World War II action drama attempts to explore the psychological strains that men suffer during combat. The film, based on the novel by James Jones, concerns the clash of two marines during the invasion of Guadalcanal. Keir Dullea, as an enterprising young private, dislikes his battle-hardened sergeant who exhibits a brutal streak. They eventually resolve their differences. The battle sequences are realistic and excitingly staged as the leathernecks struggle to take the island from the stubborn Japanese. ■

Thirteen Fighting Men (1960), TCF. *Dir.* Harry Gerstad; *Sc.* Robert Hamner, Jack Thomas; *Cast includes:* Grant Williams, Brad Dexter, Carole Mathews, Robert Dix.

Union and Confederate troops fight over a box of government gold worth $50,000 in this superficial action drama set during the final days of the Civil War. The predictable element of greed bears down on and creates discord among the handful of Northern soldiers assigned to guard the gold. Grant Williams portrays a major while Carole Mathews provides the romantic interest in this low-budget tale. ■

13 Rue Madeleine (1946), TCF. *Dir.* Henry Hathaway; *Sc.* John Monks, Jr., Sy Bartlett; *Cast includes:* James Cagney, Annabella, Richard Conte, Frank Latimer, Walter Abel.

A suspenseful World War II drama of espionage involving the O.S.S. (Office of Strategic Services), the film tells of one of its chief agents (James Cagney) who parachutes into France to learn about Germany's rocket-launching sites. Richard Conte, as a Nazi spy who has secretly trained with the O.S.S. under Cagney, captures him and tortures the American to learn the true location of the forthcoming Allied invasion. Meanwhile the London espionage office makes plans to destroy the Gestapo headquarters where Cagney is being held, hoping to kill him before he is forced to talk. The final scenes show a defiant Cagney undergoing brutal interrogation at the hands of Conte's henchmen as Allied bombs fall on the infamous 13 Rue Madeleine. ■

30 Seconds Over Tokyo (1944), MGM. *Dir.* Mervyn LeRoy; *Sc.* Dalton Trumbo; *Cast includes:* Spencer Tracy, Van Johnson, Robert Walker, Phyllis Thaxter, Tim Murdock, Robert Mitchum, Don Defore.

This World War II drama details Colonel James Doolittle's bombing raid on Japan, including the early training, preparations, eventual mission and in some cases the circuitous trek home of the crews who participated in the event. Spencer Tracy, as the resolute Doolittle, gives a convincing performance, as do most other members of the cast, including Van Johnson as Captain Ted Lawson, who, with Bob Considine, co-authored the book on which the film is based.

The film is less propagandistic than most war movies of the period. In fact, the screenplay, from the pen of Dalton Trumbo, emphasizes the humanity of the events rather than the violence. (Only three years after he wrote this movie, Trumbo was jailed for refusing to testify before the House Un-American Activities Committee investigating Communist influence in Hollywood.) On board the aircraft carrier that will subsequently transport the bombing crews to within 670 miles of their target, Robert Mitchum, a fellow pilot, confides to Johnson: "You know, I don't hate Japs, yet. It's a funny thing. I don't like them, but I don't hate them." To which Johnson replies: "I don't pretend to like the idea of killing a bunch of people, but it's a case of dropping a bomb on them or their dropping one on Ellen (his wife)." A few scenes later, Colonel Doolittle himself echoes these human sentiments. "You are to bomb the military targets assigned to you and nothing else," he announces to the crews at the final briefing session. "Of course, in an operation of this kind you cannot avoid killing civilians . . . If any of you have any moral feelings about this necessary killing . . . if you feel you might afterwards think of yourself as a murderer, I want you to drop out."

Similar in structure to *Wing and a Prayer*, released only four months earlier, and other films of this genre, the drama brings together good-natured young men from all parts of the country. They talk of their girlfriends back home and their postwar dreams. Whenever they assemble, they break into songs like "Deep in the Heart of Texas," "The Eyes of Texas" and "There's a Long, Long Trail A-Winding." There are poignant scenes of the men leaving their loved ones behind and of Van Johnson's return after losing a leg and his reunion with his wife (Phyllis Thaxter). *The Purple Heart* (1944), to some degree, is a sequel in that it portrays the story of one of Doolittle's bomber crews who are captured, tortured and subsequently sentenced to death by the Japanese.

Doolittle's audacious raid of 16 army B-52s from the carrier *Hornet*, only 131 days after Pearl Harbor, exacted little destruction upon the Japanese war machine. But it raised Allied morale and embarrassed the Imperial armed forces, compelling them to assign large numbers of fighter planes to protect their cities. All but one of the 16 bombers either crashed or had to be abandoned. Seventy-one of the 80 crew members who took part in the attack returned safely. ■

36 Hours (1964), MGM. *Dir.* George Seaton; *Sc.* George Seaton; *Cast includes:* James Garner, Eva Marie Saint, Rod Taylor, Werner Peters, John Banner.

A captured American officer is tricked by the Germans into revealing the actual invasion plans of the Allies in this suspenseful World War II drama set on the eve of the Normandy invasion. James Garner, as the American, is drugged and made to believe that he has been suffering from amnesia for six years. He discovers the Nazi scheme after he mentions Normandy but proceeds to confuse the landing place in the minds of his captors. Eva Marie Saint portrays a German nurse who falls in love with Garner. Rod Taylor, as a sympathetic German doctor who believes he can get the vital information from Garner without using torture as advocated by a Gestapo officer (Werner Peters), ultimately helps Garner and Saint escape into Switzerland. The film is partially based on "Beware of the Dog," a short story by Roald Dahl. ■

This Above All (1942), TCF. *Dir.* Anatole Litvak; *Sc.* R. C. Sherriff; *Cast includes:* Tyrone Power, Joan Fontaine, Thomas Mitchell, Henry Stephenson, Nigel Bruce.

Based on Eric Knight's World War II novel, the film takes place in England during the fall of 1942, a particularly critical period for the embattled nation that had just experienced Dunkirk and was about to endure the German Blitz. Aristocratic Prudence (Joan Fontaine), who displays her patriotism by volunteering her services as a nurse, falls in love with Clive (Tyrone Power), a member of the lower classes. After suffering through the battle of Flanders and Dunkirk, the disillusioned lover deserts from the army. However, his love of country and his desire to reclaim his self-respect propel him to complete his obligations.

The rigid English class structure and the conflict between pacifism and responsibility, as developed through the major characters and incidents, come under close examination in this wartime drama. Like *Mrs. Miniver*, released the same year, the film won the sympathy of American audiences for the embattled British—in spite of Joan Fontaine's long speech defining and exalting her resolute land. "England," she exclaims almost reluctantly, "it's Monty and the boys coming up the road from Doual . . . helping the weaker men into the boats instead of getting in themselves . . . That's England too; knowing that we'll never give in, knowing that we won't be beaten . . ." ■

This Is Korea! (1951), Rep.

A U.S. Navy-produced documentary supervised by John Ford, the film tells the part played by the Seventh Fleet and the First Marine Division in the Korean War. The cameras follow the advance of the marines through Seoul as well as their retreat from the north. The narration explains why American troops are battling in these remote regions. Since it was made with the cooperation of the air force and the Eighth Army, the film, produced in Trucolor, stresses the roles of these branches of service as well. ■

This Is the Army (1943). See Musicals. ■

This Is Your Army (1954). See Propaganda Films: World War II. ■

This Island Earth (1955). See Science Fiction Wars. ■

This Land Is Mine (1943), RKO. Dir. Jean Renoir; Sc. Dudley Nichols; Cast includes: Charles Laughton, Maureen O'Hara, George Sanders, Walter Slezak, Kent Smith.

Charles Laughton portrays a French teacher in this World War II propaganda film. Early in the drama he is ridiculed by his own students for his cowardice during an air raid. Witnessing the abuses of the Nazi occupiers of his once peaceful French town, he is transformed from a weak-mannered figure of derision to a conscience-stricken tower of strength as he defies the enemy invaders. In a dramatic courtroom scene Laughton, on trial for a murder he never committed, speaks out in defense of liberty and civil disobedience. While back in his classroom he reads aloud to his students from "The Rights of Man."

Other characters are also sharply drawn. George Sanders, as a collaborator, thinks his actions will contribute to stability. In contrast, Kent Smith portrays a patriot whose acts of sabotage against the brutal occupiers symbolize the true spirit of the oppressed community. Maureen O'Hara, as Smith's sister who strongly believes that knowledge is the best weapon against totalitarianism, helps Laughton to muster up enough courage to defy the Nazis. Walter Slezak plays a German major whose intellect tells him that the abuses his regime heaps upon hostages will ultimately destroy him and the Third Reich. In this struggle between brute force and world of ideas, the film suggests, the latter will win out in the end. ■

This Mad World (1930). See Spy Films: the Silents. ■

This Man's Navy (1945), MGM. Dir. William A. Wellman; Sc. Borden Chase; Cast includes: Wallace Beery, Tom Drake, James Gleason, Jan Clayton, Selena Royle.

Wallace Beery portrays a tough but good-natured chief petty officer in the navy's blimp service. His continuous bragging gets him into trouble in this World War II comedy drama. When he boasts that he has a foster son, he is compelled to produce the boy. Tom Drake, another navy man, poses as his son, and together they prove an indefatigable team as they battle enemy submarines with their lighter-than-air craft. Comic character actor James Gleason plays Beery's sidekick in this routine film. ■

Those Without Sin (1917), Par. Dir. Marshall Neilan; Sc. George D. Price; Cast includes: Blanche Sweet, Tom Forman, C. H. Geldert, Guy Oliver, James Neill.

Blanche Sweet portrays a Southerner in this Civil War drama set in the South. She is entrusted on a secret mission but is captured by Union troops. When an unsavory Northern colonel threatens harm to her family unless she gives herself to him, she reluctantly consents. The colonel then allows her family to escape. ■

Thousand Plane Raid, The (1969), UA. Dir. Boris Segal; Sc. Donald S. Sanford; Cast includes: Christopher George, Laraine Stephens, J.D. Cannon, Gary Marshall.

An American squadron commander convinces his superiors to send out a thousand bombers in a massive attack on one of Germany's major industrial centers in this World War II drama. Christopher George portrays the dour colonel whose concept of saturation daytime bombing meets stiff resistance from top brass until a general (J.D. Cannon) finally supports his idea. To the colonel's dismay, Allied officials select a key airplane construction center deep in enemy territory and heavily protected by anti-aircraft defenses and German fighter planes. George, a tough officer with an abrasive approach, has other problems. His stern attitude and constant criticism of the performance of his pilots strain his relationships with most of his men as well as his sweetheart (Laraine Stephens). Gary Marshall portrays an undisciplined British air ace assigned to instruct George's men on German fighter tactics. The action sequences of the B-17 raid, some of which have been culled from newsreel footage, are effective. The film points out that this was the first air strike to employ such a large number of bombers.

The actual raid was carried out against Cologne on May 30, 1942, and was designed to prove the effectiveness of strategic bombing. The attack, which took place at night, was organized into three phases. The first group of planes would light up the target. The second wave of bombers, the major force of aircraft, was to follow within the hour. Finally, the next group would bomb fifteen minutes later. The entire operation was to take an hour and a half. The 900 bombers that reached Cologne caused heavy damage over one-third of the target area. ■

Thousands Cheer (1943), MGM. *Dir.* George Sidney; *Sc.* Paul Jarrico, Richard Collins; *Cast includes:* Kathryn Grayson, Gene Kelly, Mary Astor, John Boles.

MGM takes a strong democratic stand in this World War II patriotic musical salute to America. The studio assembled many of its stars and entertainers, including Judy Garland, Mickey Rooney, Eleanor Powell, Red Skelton, three bands and conductor Jose Iturbi to put on a spectacular show before an enthusiastic audience of G.I.s. The obligatory romance between a private (Gene Kelly) and the colonel's daughter (Kathryn Grayson) forms the thin story frame and reflects the democratic overtones of the film. Both perform their musical numbers along with the other entertainers. John Boles, as a genial colonel, and Mary Astor, as a free spirit, play Grayson's estranged parents whom she tries to unite. The large-scale production begins with an overture of stirring martial music and ends with the glorious, idealistic "United Na-

tions on the March," performed by hundreds of singers and musicians before a backdrop of flags of many nations surrounding a prominent "V" for victory.

MGM, in its zeal to turn out an upbeat piece of wartime escapism, presents a democratic vision of present and future America that seems to exclude racial and religious minorities in its principal players and mass assemblages. However, talented Lena Horne is permitted to sing at an all-white army base. ■

Three Came Home (1950), TCF. *Dir.* Jean Negulesco; *Sc.* Nunnally Johnson; *Cast includes:* Claudette Colbert, Patric Knowles, Florence Desmond, Sessue Hayakawa.

Life in a brutal Japanese prison camp during World War II is the subject of this drama. Claudette Colbert plays the American wife of Patric Knowles, a British administrator. Although they were civilians, the couple and their young son were rounded up by Japanese troops in their advance through the Pacific islands. The film, which depicts the harsh treatment they and other prisoners suffered under their captors, attempts to show that some Japanese were ruthless while others simply go about their business of carrying out their orders. Colbert in particular suffers severe hardship as she tries to keep her son alive. She meets secretly with her husband and withstands a beating by her captors. Sessue Hayakawa portrays the camp commandant, a graduate of an American university. ■

Three Comrades (1938), MGM. *Dir.* Frank Borzage; *Sc.* F. Scott Fitzgerald, Edward Paramore; *Cast includes:* Robert Taylor, Margaret Sullavan, Franchot Tone, Robert Young.

Based on Erich Maria Remarque's novel, the film depicts the story of three veterans who return from World War I only to face instability, riots and economic hardship. The three comrades (Robert Taylor, Franchot Tone and Robert Young) open an automobile repair shop and taxi service. Taylor plays the romantic lead, a young German who is more interested in falling in love with Margaret Sullavan than in the stormy politics of the time. But the specter of the war hovers over Germany. "The war has become the center of everybody's life," Sullavan remarks, "a wheel that everything turns on." Franchot Tone concerns himself with car engines and the happiness of his companions, while Robert Young, the idealist of the trio who is "fighting for reason in a madhouse," joins a shadowy group of dissidents who advocate peace and stability. Taylor marries Sullavan, who is ill with tuberculosis. Meanwhile, Young is killed trying to rescue an elderly leader of his organization from a mob of militants. Shortly after, Taylor's wife succumbs to her illness. The two remaining comrades, Taylor and Tone, disillusioned by the preceding events and faced with a bleak future, decide to leave Germany.

The film was the last work in Remarque's war trilogy, the others being *All Quiet on the Western Front* (1930) and *The Road Back* (1937). The third part contained a stronger romantic angle than the earlier films which were bleaker and stronger in their antiwar sentiments. Also, the former works, which concerned World War I, created more controversy both domestically and internationally, particularly the unrelenting realism of war in *All Quiet on the Western Front* and the utter despair and disillusionment of the returning veterans in *The Road Back*. ∎

Three Faces East (1926), PDC. *Dir.* Rupert Julian; *Sc.* C. Gardner Sullivan, Monte Katterjohn; *Cast includes:* Jetta Goudal, Robert Ames, Henry Walthall, Clive Brook, Edythe Chapman.

Based on the play by Anthony Paul Kelly, the film concerns a network of German spies operating in London during World War I, the chief of whom poses as a butler employed in the home of an important British war official. Jetta Goudal portrays a female spy who develops a romantic interest in a young British officer (Robert Ames). Clive Brook plays the master spy. The film, which was remade in 1930 and again in 1940 under the title *British Intelligence*, includes several brief battle scenes.

By the 1920s, Hollywood studios were softening their image of the German. In war films released during the conflict and immediately after, enemy officers as well as their underlings almost invariably engaged in rape and pillage, burned and bayoneted babies and enslaved the children of captive nations. In all three versions of *Three Faces East* and many other war dramas released after the armistice, the Germans were depicted as suave and sophisticated, often undetectable in manner and dress from the heroes. ∎

Three Faces East (1930), WB. *Dir.* Roy Del Ruth; *Sc.* Oliver H. P. Garrett; *Cast includes:* Constance Bennett, Erich von Stroheim, Anthony Bushell, William Courtney.

This World War I spy drama, a remake of a 1926 silent film based on a 1918 melodrama, stars Constance Bennett as a British agent who maneuvers her way into German headquarters to learn the identity of a leading spy working in England. Erich von Stroheim is the master German spy working as a butler of Dutch descent in the home of Sir Winston Chamberlain. Menacing submarines off the coast of England and secret radio transmitters threaten American ships heading toward England. The climactic scene is also a surprising one. Bennett shoots the butler in the back as he attempts to send information to a German submarine. This is one of the earliest instances of a hero or heroine shooting a villain in the back. A third film version appeared in 1940 titled *British Intelligence* starring Margaret Lindsay. ∎

300 Spartans, The (1962), TCF. *Dir.* Rudolph Mate; *Sc.* George St. George; *Cast includes:* Richard Egan, Sir Ralph Richardson, Diane Baker, Barry Coe, David Farrar, Donald Houston.

Filmed in Greece, this action drama provides a large cast, stirring battle sequences and epic sweep. But it is short on characterization and subtleties. The story centers on the famous Battle of Thermopylae in 480 B.C. While a huge Persian army under Xerxes (David Farrar) advances against the Greek city-states, the various politicians hesitate to act and are more interested in their religious festivals than in the defense of Greece. Only Leonidas, a Spartan general (Richard Egan), senses the impending danger and leads his private guard, 300 Spartans, against the invading hordes when Sparta's politicians refuse to mobilize the army. Also seeing the upcoming battle as a way of uniting the different factions into one nation is Themistocles (Sir Ralph Richardson), an Athenian politician and orator who pledges to support Leonidas with the entire Athenian fleet. Leonidas is determined to hold the enemy at a strategic pass while the main Spartan army, together with troops from other city-states, march to meet the Persians. But reinforcements never come. The brave warriors, hopelessly outnumbered, fight to the death. They leave behind a message that has become as famous as the battle itself: "Oh, stranger, tell the Spartans that we lie here obedient to their word."

The film paints the Spartan military as too single-minded in their cause. The plot and dialogue ring with glory in war, honor in death and heroism in battle. *Go Tell the Spartans* (1978), an antiwar film set in Vietnam, makes ironic use of the historic battle on several occasions.

Leonidas (?–480 B.C.), king of Sparta during the Greco-Persian Wars (500–449 B.C.), and his small Greek force fought bravely against numerically overwhelming Persian invaders at the Battle of Thermopylae (480 B.C.). This bold stand was immortalized by the historian Herodotus. The actions of Leonidas and his troops, all of whom fought to the death rather than surrender, have become a symbol for unflinching bravery in a hopeless situation.

The Persian king Xerxes set out to punish the Greek city-states for refusing to perform an act of submission (giving earth and water). He invaded Greece with an army of 180,000. The Greeks planned to have the army hold off the Persians, preventing them from entering the Greek isthmus, while the Grecian navy defeated the Persian fleet, thus forcing the invader to retreat. Leonidas headed a force of 5,000 Greeks entrusted to the defense of the strategic pass at Thermopylae. Most of his army fled before the superior strength of the Persians, except for 300 Spartans and 700 Thespians. The defenders held out for three days before being annihilated. John Ruskin once wrote that the epitaph they left behind was the noblest group of words uttered by man. ■

Three Legionnaires (1937), General. *Dir.* Hamilton MacFadden; *Sc.* George Waggner; *Cast includes:* Robert Armstrong, Lyle Talbot, Fifi D'Orsay, Anne Nagel, Donald Meek, Stanley Fields.

Two American doughboys (Robert Armstrong and Lyle Talbot) get caught up in the turbulence of the Russian Revolution in this comedy. Siding with the Cossacks, the pair become entangled in misadventures involving a phony Communist general and several females. Similar to the fighting buddies in *What Price Glory?* (1926), Armstrong portrays a tough, wise-cracking sergeant while Talbot is more inclined to wooing the women. Donald Meek, apparently the third

member in the title, appears as a scientist whom the pair convince to impersonate an American general in this zany film. ■

Three of Many (1916), Triangle. *Dir.* Reginald Barker; *Sc.* Reginald Barker; *Cast includes:* George Fisher, Clara Williams, Charles Gunn.

Three close friends living in a New York City boarding house are affected by World War I in this silent drama. A girl and one of the young men are Italian, while the third member is of Austrian descent. The young Italian returns to his homeland as does the Austrian, each to fight for his own country. The girl, a nurse, volunteers her services. The war rages in a small town in which she is stationed, and she has a chance to see both of her male friends. When the Austrian is captured by his Italian friend, the latter allows him to escape. ■

Russian volunteer nurses in World War II attend to a wounded soldier. *Three Russian Girls* (1944).

Three Russian Girls (1944), UA. *Dir.* Fedor Ozep, Henry Kesler; *Sc.* Abel Kandel, Dan James; *Cast includes:* Anna Sten, Kent Smith, Mimi Forsythe, Alexander Granach.

A tribute to the Russian nurses who volunteered in World War II to serve their fellow countrymen behind the lines, the film conveys their bravery by way of a romantic drama involving one such nurse and an American engineer. Anna Sten plays the chief nurse in charge of a group of volunteers in the spring of 1941 who are assigned to a field hospital near the front. Kent Smith portrays an American engineer who is seriously hurt in a plane crash. As he recuperates under Sten's care, they both fall in love. The

Russian troops are forced to retreat under heavy attack from the Nazis, but during sub-zero winter weather the Russians launch a brilliant counterattack against the invaders. Meanwhile, Smith recovers sufficiently to part from his loved one. They promise to meet again after the war. The battle scenes are striking and exciting.

The film, a remake of the Russian original, *Girl From Stalingrad*, contains footage of the training of Russian nurses and a soundtrack enhanced by several spirited patriotic Russian songs. This is one of the few wartime dramas to depict Russians and Americans working together for a common cause. ∎

Three Sisters, The (1930), Fox. *Dir.* Paul Sloane; *Sc.* George Brooks, James M. McGuinness; *Cast includes:* Louise Dresser, Tom Patricola, Kenneth MacKenna, Joyce Compton.

The drama concerns an Italian family of a mother and her three daughters during World War I. One daughter dies in childbirth after learning that her husband was killed in battle. Another marries a musician and lives in Austria. The third daughter moves to America with her husband and opens a small business. The mother (Louise Dresser) loses contact with her two daughters and is forced to wash dishes in a sleazy restaurant in another town. The American couple have been sending money to the mother, but a supposed friend of the family never gave it to the destitute woman. Eventually the two sisters meet in the U.S. and, with their families, journey to Italy where they are reunited with their mother. Little in the way of war scenes is provided in this film whose central theme is that of motherly love. ∎

Thuggees or Thugs. See *Gunga Din* (1939). ∎

Thumbs Up (1943). See Home Front. ∎

Thunder Afloat (1939), MGM. *Dir.* George B. Seitz; *Sc.* Wells Root, Harvey Halslip; *Cast includes:* Wallace Beery, Chester Morris, Virginia Grey, Douglass Dumbrille, Carl Esmond.

A tugboat captain (Wallace Beery) is determined to get the German U-boat that sank his vessel in this World War I comedy drama. Beery, who has his eye on a lucrative towing contract, cajoles his rival tugboat operator (Chester Morris) into joining a fleet of sub

Wallace Beery swears vengeance against the German submarine that sank his tugboat during World War I. *Thunder Afloat* (1939).

chasers. But Beery loses his tug to a German submarine, so he joins the navy. His many years at sea earn him a captain's rank, and he is put in command of a sub chaser, part of a small fleet under the supervision of Morris, his former rival. Beery, an old, undisciplined sea dog, has difficulties following military routine. After he disobeys orders, his superiors strip him of his command and relegate him to the rank of ordinary seaman. Later, on board a fishing trawler designed to locate U-boats, Beery is captured by the enemy. He manages to tap out a signal while he is held captive in the sub, leading to its capture by Morris and his fleet of sub chasers. Virginia Grey, as Beery's daughter, provides the romantic interest in this entertaining but conventional tale which often resembles *What Price Glory?* (1926) in the rivalry of the two male leads.

An obviously fictitious melodrama, the film was broadly based on actual occurrences during World War I. German submarines did make several raids along the Atlantic coast in 1918. The film states in its foreword that more than 80 American ships were sunk by German subs off the Atlantic coast. Released in 1939 when German U-boats again began to appear in the headlines, the film no doubt struck a topical chord with its audiences. ∎

Thunder in the East (1953), Par. *Dir.* Charles Vidor; *Sc.* Jo Swerling; *Cast includes:* Alan Ladd, Deborah Kerr, Charles Boyer, Corinne Calvert, Cecil Kellaway.

An adventurer–mercenary (Alan Ladd) is willing to sell guns to either side during an insurrection set in a fictitious state in India.

While waiting to make the sale, he falls in love with the blind daughter (Deborah Kerr) of a British minister. When he learns that more British citizens want to leave than there are ways to transport them, he raises the price of the seats on his plane. Meanwhile, the maharaja's pacifist adviser (Charles Boyer) refuses to release the guns which are about to be used against the rebel forces. As the plane leaves, Ladd decides to stay and fight with the besieged group at the palace. When the rebels attack, Boyer relents and joins Ladd in fighting off the enemy. ■

Thunder of Drums, A (1961), MGM. *Dir.* Joseph M. Newman; *Sc.* James Warner Bellah; *Cast includes:* Richard Boone, George Hamilton, Luana Patten, Arthur O'Connell, Charles Bronson.

A young and inexperienced lieutenant clashes with his commanding officer in this action drama about the U.S. Cavalry set in the Southwest in 1870. George Hamilton portrays the stubborn green officer who, anxious for action against the hostiles, rebels against his battle-hardened commanding officer (Richard Boone). Meanwhile, marauding Apaches have been pillaging the ranchers. Luana Patten, as Hamilton's old flame, rekindles their previous romance although she is engaged to another cavalry officer who conveniently is killed in a skirmish with the hostiles. By the end of the film Hamilton has learned much about life and responsibility and the Indians have been defeated. ■

Thunderbirds (1952), Rep. *Dir.* John H. Auer; *Sc.* Mary C. McCall, Jr.; *Cast includes:* John Derek, John Barrymore, Jr., Mona Freeman, Gene Evans.

Hollywood salutes the National Guard, particularly Oklahoma's "Thunderbird" division, in this routine World War II drama. The men of the unit are activated and go through the customary training period before embarking for overseas duty. John Derek and John Barrymore, Jr. portray two pals in the outfit who vie for the same young woman (Eileen Christy). The division participates in several battles, including Salerno, Anzio and Sicily, ultimately fighting in France and Germany. The film uses some actual newsreel footage for the war sequences. Ward Bond plays Barrymore's father whom the son believes died heroically in World War I. Instead, Bond was cashiered out of West Point

and enlisted in the guard to acquit himself. Mona Freeman plays an army nurse interested in John Derek. ■

Thunderbolt (1945), War Activities Committee. *Dir.* Lt. Col. William Wyler; *Sc.* Lester Koenig.

A World War II documentary, the film covers the use of the Thunderbolt fighter aircraft during the Allied drive in Italy. Part of the 57th Fighter Group stationed in Corsica, the planes, fitted with 500-pound bombs, were employed to destroy enemy supply lines, thereby weakening their armies sufficiently to allow the British and American forces to advance. The airplanes were equipped with automatic 16mm cameras by the Signal Corps. Director William Wyler, besides capturing excellent combat footage using this technique, provides sufficient human interest as he shows the young Americans who fly these planes at work and at play. ■

Tibbetts, Colonel Paul. See *Above and Beyond* (1952). ■

Tides of Hate (1917). See Moro War. ■

Tiger Fangs (1943), PRC. *Dir.* Sam Newfield; *Sc.* Arthur St. Claire; *Cast includes:* Frank Buck, June Duprez, Duncan Renaldo, J. Farrell MacDonald.

Frank Buck leads a United Nations team into the Malayan jungles to investigate an outbreak of man-eating tigers in the region in this low-budget World War II film. They discover the particularly deadly creatures have been drugged by Nazi agents to prevent the production of rubber, essential to the Allied war effort. June Duprez, as a biologist, provides the romantic interest while Dan Seymour portrays the heavy in more ways than one in this routine tale.

Historically, the film is implausible in its premise. The rubber-producing areas mentioned in the plot had already fallen into Japanese hands early in the war. Therefore, it was highly unlikely that any plantations had to be prevented by the enemy from producing the vital war materiel for Allied countries or that scientists representing the United Nations would have been sent into enemy territory. ■

Till I Come Back to You (1918), Par. *Dir.* Cecil B. DeMille; *Sc.* Jeanie Macpherson; *Cast includes:* Bryant Washburn, Florence Vidor, George Stone.

This weak World War I drama concerns an American captain (Bryant Washburn), a Belgian wife (Florence Vidor) and her husband (G. Butler Clunbough), a Prussian army officer. As repulsive and abusive as her husband is in this romantic triangle, the wife decides to remain loyal to her marriage vows. George Stone plays a Belgian youth. Otherwise expertly directed by DeMille, the story is ruined by a succession of implausible situations.

The film as propaganda is unique in depicting the Prussians' mistreatment of children. Belgian youngsters are transported to Germany to be used as slave labor in munitions factories. Besides being beaten and deprived of food, the children are subjected to German propaganda. This was strong stuff in arousing the sensitivities of American audiences. The title alludes to King Albert's promise to return to his subjects, the heroic Belgian people. ■

Till the End of Time (1946), RKO. *Dir.* Edward Dmytryk; *Sc.* Allen Rivkin; *Cast includes:* Dorothy McGuire, Guy Madison, Robert Mitchum, Bill Williams, Tom Tully.

Based on Niven Busch's *They Dream of Home*, a novel of postwar readjustment, the film covers the homecoming of three World War II Marines and a young widow whose husband was killed in battle. Guy Madison portrays a young veteran who drifts aimlessly from one job to another after deciding he is too old to return to school. Meanwhile, his parents are planning a marriage for him. Robert Mitchum, as an ex-Marine suffering from a head injury, dreams of owning a small ranch. His plans go awry following a ruinous experience in Las Vegas. Bill Williams portrays a former boxer who has lost both legs in the war. He has lost faith in himself and any hope for a future until he joins his pal Mitchum in a bar-room brawl. They tangle with a group of racists preaching hate and who ironically call themselves American War Patriots. Dorothy McGuire as the young widow helps Madison to regain his confidence. This sometimes didactic film has often been equated with *The Best Years of Our Lives*, released the same year. ■

Till We Meet Again (1936), Par. *Dir.* Robert Florey; *Sc.* Edwin Justus Mayer, Brian Marlow, Franklin Coen; *Cast includes:* Herbert Marshall, Gertrude Michael, Lionel Atwill, Rod LaRocque.

Two lovers who are separated by the war end up as secret agents on opposite sides in this World War I spy drama. Herbert Marshall portrays an English actor who is in love with a Viennese actress (Gertrude Michael). The war interferes with their wedding as each is called to duty to act as a spy. The film includes a few brief scenes of the war itself, but these are chiefly stock shots from the archives. The couple, who engage in the usual cat-and-mouse game of espionage, are permitted at the end of the film to escape to neutral territory to continue their romance. The film has been noted for its accurate period atmosphere, an element often neglected in the Hollywood spy dramas of the 1930s. ■

Till We Meet Again (1944), Par. *Dir.* Frank Borzage; *Sc.* Lenore Coffee; *Cast includes:* Ray Milland, Barbara Britton, Walter Slezak, Lucile Watson.

A downed American flier is aided by the French underground and a novitiate nun in this World War II romantic drama. Ray Milland portrays a happily married pilot who is given important documents by the French resistance to take back to England. An unworldly convent girl (Barbara Britton) poses as his wife to help him get through Nazi lines. An affectionate relationship develops between the two as Milland explains his deep love for his wife and Britton begins to understand more about life outside the Church. Later, she is caught by the Nazis who plan to send her to a German brothel. A local French mayor and collaborator (Walter Slezak), horrified by the brutal decision, kills her before the sentence can be carried out. ■

Timbuktu (1959), UA. *Dir.* Jacques Tourneur; *Sc.* Anthony Veiller, Paul Dudley; *Cast includes:* Victor Mature, Yvonne de Carlo, George Dolenz, John Dehner.

Another familiar drama of the conflict between French colonial troops and the Arabs, the weak film, set in 1942, features Victor Mature as an American gunrunner supplying arms to the Arab warriors. But when he meets pretty Yvonne de Carlo, as the wife of a French colonel (George Dolenz), he decides to switch allegiances. Posing as a friend of the local emir (John Dehner), Mature gains the tribal leader's confidence and finally betrays him to the French colonel, who is killed while leading the climactic attack upon the rebel stronghold. His death leaves the desert path open for the renegade American and the late colonel's widow. ■

Time for Killing, A (1968), Col. *Dir.* Phil Karlson; *Sc.* Halsted Welles; *Cast includes:* Glenn Ford, George Hamilton, Inger Stevens, Paul Petersen, Max Baer.

A peace-loving Union major turns vindictive when his missionary wife is raped in this Civil War revenge drama. Glenn Ford, as a major at a Utah prison stockade, reluctantly pursues a group of Confederate prisoners who have escaped. With the war soon coming to an end, he sees no point to their recapture since they are heading home. The fugitives are under the command of an embittered captain (George Hamilton). He cannot face defeat, and decides to wipe out a squad of Union soldiers and kidnap the major's wife (Inger Stevens) who is being escorted elsewhere. His purpose is to score a string of "successes" or victories before he returns home. When he later learns that the war has ended, he withholds the news from his men so that they can continue to fight. "Just because Lee surrendered," he confides to one of his men who enjoys killing, "it doesn't mean we have to." He then rapes his captive and leaves her behind, thereby assuring that the major will come after him. When Ford learns what has happened, and at his wife's insistence, he decides to cross the Mexican border to pursue Hamilton. Although his wife knows about Lee's surrender, she doesn't tell her husband. When Ford catches up with the escapees, a violent battle ensues in which almost all of the participants are killed. ■

Time Limit (1957), UA. *Dir.* Karl Malden; *Sc.* Henry Denker; *Cast includes:* Richard Widmark, Richard Basehart, Dolores Michaels, June Lockhart, Carl Benton Reid.

An American officer, suspected of collaborating with the Communists while he was being held as a prisoner during the Korean War, is destined for court martial in this forceful drama, the only film that actor Karl Malden ever directed. The sympathetic colonel (Richard Widmark) who is to prosecute the case meticulously probes the details for the truth. He must also resist pressure from his superior

officer who prefers that the trial be treated superficially and expedited quickly. Richard Basehart portrays the major who is accused of collaborating with the enemy. The true story is finally blurted out by a lieutenant (Rip Torn). The prison camp commandant, enraged when an informer is murdered by his fellow American prisoners, threatens to kill 16 Americans. Torn between his human compassion and his military duty, the major turns traitor to save the lives of the American prisoners, knowing full well the consequences of his act.

An interesting twist occurs when the American collaborator who is murdered turns out to be the son of a general, Widmark's superior. The general condemns his dead son's weakness. "Every man has his limit, sir," Widmark says, trying to comfort the distraught father. "There's no crime in being human." But the general remains steadfast. "I cannot forgive cowardice, especially in my own son." When Basehart, as the boy's major, takes up the defense of the son, trying to prove that the boy was heroic until pushed to his breaking point, the general is still unmoved. "The choice you had to make in that prison camp," the general explains, "is no different than the choice that confronts every military leader—the decision involving the life and death of his men. You are a sensitive man, a humane man. I sympathize with that man. But you are also a soldier. And as a soldier you have failed, just as my son failed." ■

Time to Die, A (1983). See Veterans. ■

Time to Love and a Time to Die, A (1958), U. *Dir.* Douglas Sirk; *Sc.* Orin Jannings; *Cast includes:* John Gavin, Lilo Pulver, Jock Mahoney, Don DeFore, Keenan Wynn.

Life in Germany under Hitler's regime provides the background for this romantic drama. An idealistic German hero (John Gavin) returns on furlough from the Russian front in 1944 and witnesses the same devastation to his town and other parts of Germany that he has seen in other countries. He learns that his parents are missing. He meets and hastily marries Lilo Pulver. Life in Germany during the war is explored through a series of incidents and their related characters. Privileged officials enjoy luxuries while others go hungry. An officer of a concentration camp delights in regaling others in his latest methods of torture. A Jewish citizen seeks shelter in a Catholic church.

When Gavin returns to the Russian front, he is appalled by the bestial behavior of his fellow soldiers toward the Russian peasants. He shoots one soldier who is about to kill three Russians. One of the men whom he has just saved then turns on Gavin and kills him—adding to the insanity and irony of the war. Gavin dies clutching a letter that informs him he is about to become a father. Its tragic ending is similar to that in *All Quiet on the Western Front* (1930), which has its young disillusioned hero killed while reaching for a butterfly. Erich Maria Remarque, whose novel served as the basis for the film, plays a small role as a high school teacher.

Some viewers may take issue with certain ideas presented in the film. The Germans are not inherently evil people, it is suggested. The fault lay in the political and social system as well as with those who went about doing their duty without questioning it. After all, the film implies, the average German suffered almost as much as those people whose countries were bombed, burned and invaded.

Nazi discipline and conformity within Germany differed from the picture party officials painted, according to German historian Detlev J.K. Peukert's book, *Inside Nazi Germany*. Especially among the working class and the youth, dissent manifested itself in nonconformist behavior, rejection of official Nazi groups, protests about working conditions and objections of Nazi attitudes toward the churches. However, there was little outcry from these quarters against the horrors perpetrated upon political and religious victims. ■

Tin Hats (1926). See Service Comedy. ■

To Be or Not to Be (1942), UA. *Dir.* Ernst Lubitsch; *Sc.* Edwin Justus Mayer; *Cast includes:* Jack Benny, Carole Lombard, Robert Stack, Lionel Atwill, Felix Bressart, Sig Rumann.

With Mel Brooks' 1983 adaptation of Lubitsch's black comedy available, it is interesting to take another look at the original. It was made during the early, bleak years of World War II, not the best occasion to release a farce about the fall of Poland. The film encountered another dark cloud. One of its stars, Carole Lombard, died before its release. The story concerns a troupe of Polish actors, led by a vain actor (Jack Benny) and his wife (Lombard), who are in Warsaw when the Nazis invade. When their theater is closed by the invaders, the players become involved in espionage and a final escape to freedom. Mayer's witty and tight script and Lubitsch's expert direction overcome minor criticisms of the film. Benny gives the finest performance of his film career and Lombard is as beautiful and sparkling as ever. The supporting actors contribute much to the dark humor. Sig Rumann, as a Nazi officer, pans Benny's performance of *Hamlet*: "What he did to Shakespeare, we are doing now to Poland." Felix Bressart is excellent as an old-time actor. Lubitsch was criticized at the time for his insensitivity in making this film that may have seemed in bad taste then. Today's audiences will wonder what all the fuss was about. ■

To Be or Not to Be (1983), TCF. *Dir.* Alan Johnson; *Sc.* Thomas Meehan, Ronny Graham; *Cast includes:* Mel Brooks, Anne Bancroft, Tim Matheson, Charles Durning, Jose Ferrer.

A remake of the Ernst Lubitsch black comedy about a troupe of Polish performers under Nazi occupation, the film retains the basic plot but adds color, several musical numbers and the Brooks style of wit and slapstick. Mel Brooks repeats Jack Benny's original role as Bronski, the head of the theatrical company. Anne Bancroft, as his wife (and his spouse in real life), takes up a backstage romance with a Polish pilot (Tim Matheson). Charles Durning plays an incompetent local Gestapo chief who falls for the charms of Bancroft. Jose Ferrer portrays a German spy posing as a Polish patriot.

Some additions to the original include the song "Sweet Georgia Brown" sung in Polish and the Nazi persecution of a homosexual backstage dresser. Whether Brooks improved on the original film may depend on the individual's appreciation of the director's sense of humor. ■

To Each His Own (1946), Par. *Dir.* Mitchell Leisen; *Sc.* Charles Brackett, Jacques Thiery; *Cast includes:* Olivia de Havilland, John Lund, Mary Anderson, Roland Culver.

Olivia de Havilland portrays an unwed mother in this sentimental drama that spans a quarter of a century and two world wars. The child is the result of a short romance during

World War I between de Havilland and a war hero (John Lund) who is soon killed in action. Not to embarrass her druggist-father, she reluctantly gives up her son to a caring couple. However, she is permitted to bestow her love on him as his "aunt" without ever revealing their true relationship.

Years pass without the natural mother and the son meeting again until World War II when she meets the boy again. This time he is in uniform and a pilot like his real father. (John Lund also portrays the son.) He falls in love with a young woman and invites his "aunt" to the wedding. By the end of the film, a friend of both brings the son and mother together. At the affair the son approaches de Havilland and announces: "I believe this is our dance, Mother." The story opens in war-torn London during World War II but contains flashbacks to World War I. De Havilland won an Academy Award as Best Actress. ∎

To Have and Have Not (1944), WB. *Dir.* Howard Hawks; *Sc.* Jules Furthman, William Faulkner; *Cast includes:* Humphrey Bogart, Walter Brennan, Lauren Bacall, Hoagy Carmichael.

Howard Hawks' World War II drama about the resistance of the Free French against the Vichy government in Martinique stars Humphrey Bogart as Harry Morgan. Morgan, who operates a fishing boat, gets mixed up with smuggling resistance leaders for the Free French to the Caribbean island. At first, he is reluctant to get involved politically. "I don't understand what kind of war you're fighting," he remarks to one of the resisters. Later, when Vichy officials, led by character actor Dan Seymour, start pushing him around, he takes a stand against them.

Bogart gets unusually strong support from others in the cast, especially Lauren Bacall in her first screen role. As "Slim," a sultry cafe singer who falls for Bogart, she manages to steal more than one scene from her future husband. The now famous "whistle" scene has become a screen classic. Her singing was dubbed by Andy Williams. Walter Brennan has the role of Bogart's alcoholic sidekick. Hoagy Carmichael, as a cafe entertainer, contributes some singing and piano playing.

The film in many respects is reminiscent of *Casablanca*. It even has some of the same actors (Bogart, Dan Seymour, Dalio) and similar dialogue. "I'm glad you're on our side," a French patriot says to Bogart, echoing the words of Paul Henreid, the freedom fighter in *Casablanca*. Henreid's defiant and optimistic conviction that, even if all the leaders are caught, "thousands will rise in their places," is repeated in the later film by another resistance leader. "There's always someone else. That is the mistake the Germans always make with people they try to destroy. There will be always someone else." Hoagy Carmichael replaces Dooley Wilson as the ubiquitous cafe piano player and singer. Bogart repeats his personification of a neutral America that, when confronted with injustice and tyranny, will side with the forces of liberty. Even the melodramatic ending in which Bogart kills one of the pursuing officials and helps a resistance leader and his wife escape their pursuers is unabashedly duplicated.

Nelson Rockefeller, in charge of the American Affairs Committee at the time, learned about Hawks' production, which was based on Ernest Hemingway's novel. To stave off any objections from the Latin-American countries, he persuaded Hawks to switch the setting from Florida-Cuba to Martinique. Hawks and Warners agreed and also changed the author's original premise which dealt with the smuggling of Chinese into the U.S. ∎

To Hell and Back (1955), U. *Dir.* Jesse Hibbs; *Sc.* Gil Doud; *Cast includes:* Audie Murphy, Marshall Thompson, Charles Drake, Gregg Palmer, Jack Kelly.

Audie Murphy, the most decorated soldier in American history, plays himself in this biographical drama. The film not only covers his exploits during World War II, it depicts his earlier hard life in Texas where he and his mother were often strapped for money. Serving in North Africa and Europe during the war, he rose from private first class to company commander, was wounded three times and was credited with killing more than 200 German soldiers. He earned 24 decorations, including the Medal of Honor. For the most part, the film avoids the usual heroics, often depicting Murphy and his buddies as scared G.I.s. The several battle sequences are realistic, particularly those near Anzio. Marshall Thompson portrays one of Murphy's army pals. See also Audie Murphy. ∎

To Hell With the Kaiser (1918), Screen Classics. *Dir.* George Irving; *Sc.* June Mathis; *Cast includes:* Laurence Grant, Olive Tell, Betty Howe, John Sunderland, Frank Currier.

The film is a fanciful drama about Kaiser Wilhelm, his family and his dreams of placing his sons at the seat of government in the major nations of the world, including the U.S. Scenes are shown of the invasion of Belgium with the Kaiser leading the troops. At a local church where the defenseless civilians have sought sanctuary, the mother superior is shot dead when she objects to the Germans' attempt to enter. The Kaiser announces that he will have first choice of the women. The victim happens to be an American woman. When her father protests, he, too, is murdered by a German soldier. Following a plot involving intrigue, revenge and suspense, the film shows the Kaiser in Hell.

Several critics attacked the plot as ridiculous and the film as a whole in bad taste. But it was only one of many propaganda dramas to blame the war solely on the Kaiser, portraying him as a demented leader with delusions of grandeur. "Remember," he says to an underling, "we must find that pretext for war that is to make me ruler of the world." Only after the armistice were American films pertaining to the war ready to seek out other causes or persons, such as the military establishment and armaments dealers, responsible for the numerous deaths and large-scale devastation. ■

"To My Unborn Son" (1943). See Resistance. ■

To the Shores of Hell (1966), Crown International. *Dir.* Will Zens; *Sc.* Will Zens, Robert McFadden; *Cast includes:* Marshall Thompson, Kiva Lawrence, Richard Jordahl, Richard Arlen.

One of the earliest films to use the Vietnam conflict as background, the drama stars Marshall Thompson as a U.S. Marine major who penetrates Viet Cong territory to rescue his brother. Robert Dornan, as Thompson's brother and a physician, is being held prisoner by the enemy and compelled to aid their wounded soldiers. Richard Jordahl, as a local priest, assists the two brothers to escape by helicopter. He is killed during the action. Unusual for the period, the film was shot on location in Vietnam. ■

"To the Shores of Iwo Jima" (1945), Office of War Information.

A World War II documentary shot in color, the film recounts the dramatic story of the bloody battle for Iwo Jima. Scenes range from the initial bombardment of the island to the struggle of the marines to dislodge the stubborn Japanese by using flame-throwers and other weapons. The 26-day battle is considered the toughest in the history of the U.S. Marines. Several of the combat cameramen were among the killed and wounded. ■

To the Shores of Tripoli (1942), TCF. *Dir.* Bruce Humberstone; *Sc.* Lamar Trotti; *Cast includes:* John Payne, Maureen O'Hara, Randolph Scott, Nancy Kelly, William Tracy.

John Payne plays a spoiled member of the rich who competes against Randolph Scott for the affections of Maureen O'Hara in this drama about the training and duties of the U.S. Marines. The bickering between the two servicemen comes to a halt when they learn of the Japanese bombing of Pearl Harbor. They both embark to the front by the end of the film, ready to answer their country's call in this film released shortly after America's entry into World War II. The plot allows for scenes of target practice at sea and other activities in which this service branch is usually engaged. William Tracy and Maxie Rosenbloom supply the comic relief. ■

Tobruk. This port city on the Mediterranean Sea in Libya's Eastern province of Cyrenaica was the site of four battles in World War II, reflecting its strategic importance. It was the most heavily fortified area in Libya while the region was a colony of Fascist Italy. Tobruk had a zone of defense composed of underground bunkers, barbed wire, anti-tank ditches and booby traps that stretched around a perimeter of about 30 miles.

After Mussolini took Italy into World War II and started a short-lived drive into Egypt aimed at capturing the Suez Canal, British forces under Generals O'Connor and Wavell counter-attacked and took the port in one day on January 21, 1941. Rommel and his Africa Corps, sent to Libya to bolster Italy's crumbling control, sought to recapture the city and use it as a main supply port for a new attack into Egypt. Tough Australian troops successfully held out in a siege that lasted for 242 days from April to December 1941. The Australians, supplied by sea, prevented Rommel from penetrating into Egypt by blocking his main coastal supply road. The movie *The Desert Rats* (1953) graphically depicts this siege and its final relief by a British column.

A special elite British force infiltrates General Rommel's lines to wreak havoc among German troops. *Tobruk* (1966).

Early in 1942 Britain depleted its North African army to send troops to fight the Japanese, now participating in World War II in Asia. Rommel moved swiftly to exploit the weakness and retook the city in one day on June 21, 1942. Tobruk fell for the last time, to the British Eighth Army under General Montgomery, on November 13, 1942. By this time, Rommel was consistently plagued by insufficient supplies because of Hitler's emphasis on the Russian campaign. *Tobruk* (1967), starring Rock Hudson, is a superficial action drama that has almost no relevance to the important events that befell that city. It is chiefly about the destruction of one of Rommel's supply dumps. ■

Tobruk (1966), U. *Dir.* Arthur Hiller; *Sc.* Leo V. Gordon; *Cast includes:* Rock Hudson, George Peppard, Nigel Green, Guy Stockwell, Heidy Hunt.

This World War II action drama concerns a special British force made up of Commandos and German-born Jews on a special mission to destroy General Rommel's fuel supply and hold a key position at Tobruk until the British navy arrives. The plan calls for the Jews, who speak German fluently, to pose as Nazi soldiers and the British as prisoners of the "Nazis" so that they can infiltrate German lines. Hudson stars as an English major. George Peppard portrays the Jewish commander while Nigel Green plays the colonel in charge of the column of 90 men. The plot provides for plenty of action as the infiltrators, using flame-throwers and other weapons, destroy the fuel dump and battle the German defenders in this rousing tale.

The film includes a subplot involving the anti-Semitic feelings of Hudson and Green which are manifested in their attitudes toward Peppard. Unfortunately, this dramatic potential is never fully realized. ■

Today We Live (1933), MGM. *Dir.* Howard Hawks; *Sc.* Edith Fitzgerald, Dwight Taylor; *Cast includes:* Joan Crawford, Gary Cooper, Franchot Tone, Roscoe Karns.

A love triangle mixes awkwardly with aerial warfare and sea battles in this World War I drama. Richard (Gary Cooper), an American pilot in England during the war, falls in love with Diana (Joan Crawford). Diana, her brother (Franchot Tone) and Ronnie (Robert Young), a friend since childhood, maintain a close relationship. All assume Young and Crawford will marry someday. While Young is away at flying school, Crawford receives a false report that he has been killed. She soon falls in love with Cooper. Young returns, causing a stalemate in the romantic triangle. While out in a boat with his friend Tone, Young is blinded. Cooper sympathetically bows out, but Young realizes that Crawford loves the American. When Cooper volunteers to bomb a German warship, Young and Tone use a torpedo boat to beat the American to the attack. However, their torpedo fails to eject, so they ram their vessel into the enemy, sinking the dreadnought and sacrificing their lives.

The romantic plot is similar to that of previous war dramas, including *Wings* (1927) and *The White Sister* (1932). The air and navy battles excite more interest than the love triangle. Director Howard Hawks, who had made another air drama, *The Dawn Patrol* (1930), used footage from Howard Hughes' epic war film *Hell's Angels* (1930). Cooper, one of the major Hollywood stars during this period, was borrowed from Paramount and had already appeared in a string of successful war films, including *Wings*, *Lilac Time* (1928) and *A Farewell to Arms* (1932). ∎

Tokyo File 212 (1951). See Spy Films: the Talkies. ∎

Tokyo Rose (1945), Par. *Dir.* Lew Landers; *Sc.* Geoffrey Homes, Maxwell Shane; *Cast includes:* Lotus Long, Byron Barr, Osa Massen, Don Douglas.

A World War II action drama, the film concerns the famous female broadcaster and an escaped G.I.'s plan to capture her. Byron Barr portrays an American prisoner of war who is selected by the Japanese for a radio interview with Tokyo Rose, a purveyor of propaganda for the Japanese. He escapes from his captors during the excitement of an air raid and finds time to destroy the radio station. He manages to contact the Japanese underground whom he convinces to assist him in kidnaping Rose. They succeed in their mission following several close scrapes with soldiers and reach the coast where an American submarine is scheduled to pick them up in this implausible yarn. ∎

Tomahawk (1951), U. *Dir.* George Sherman; *Sc.* Silvia Richards, Maurice Geraghty; *Cast includes:* Van Heflin, Yvonne De Carlo, Alex Nicol, Preston Foster, Jack Oakie.

The Sioux clash with the U.S. Cavalry during the great Sioux uprising of the 1800s in this routine action drama. According to this film, set in South Dakota in and around Fort Phil Kearny, the insurrection was to a large extent the result of the cruel and callous actions of an army lieutenant (Alex Nicol). However, other causes are suggested as well, including a chain of broken treaties by the white man and an influx of settlers invading Sioux territory. Van Heflin portrays the legendary Jim Bridger, an Indian scout sympathetic to the Indians. Preston Foster plays a cavalry colonel and Yvonne De Carlo an entertainer and the romantic interest of Heflin. Jack Oakie, as Heflin's assistant, provides some comic relief. Two famous battles are reenacted—the Fetterman Massacre and the Wagon Box Massacre. The film points out that the Springfield-Allen breech-loading rifle, with its rapid fire, was used for the first time against the Sioux. ∎

Tomahawk Trail (1957), UA. *Dir.* Lesley Selander; *Sc.* David Chandler; *Cast includes:* Chuck Connors, John Smith, Susan Cummings, Lisa Montell.

A sergeant is forced to assume command of a cavalry troop threatened by warring Apaches in this action drama. Chuck Connors plays the sergeant whose commanding officer seems mentally incompetent. The troopers lose their mounts to the Apaches during a skirmish and must make their way back to their fort on foot. When they arrive at the outpost, they discover it has been overrun by the Indians, and all the defenders have been killed. Connors, the battle-hardened soldier that he is, takes over and organizes the men to fight off the next impending attack. The deranged lieutenant threatens to have Connors court-martialed, but the sergeant continues to lead the men to victory in this low-budget production. ∎

Tomorrow Is Forever (1946). See Veterans. ∎

Tomorrow the World (1944), UA. *Dir.* Leslie Fenton; *Sc.* Ring Lardner, Jr., Leopold Atlas; *Cast includes:* Fredric March, Betty Field, Agnes Moorehead, Skippy Homeier.

A 14-year-old German boy (Skippy Homeier) arrives in America to live with his uncle (Fredric March), a liberal professor, in this World War II drama about Hitler's effective indoctrination of a generation of youngsters. The boy realizes March's philosophy is similar to that of his father who was killed by the Nazis. Conditioned by his German mentors to reject such ideas, he becomes a menace to March and his Jewish fiancée (Betty Field) as well as to the other children in the community. Finally, through care and affection, especially as displayed by his young American cousin (Joan Carroll), he bursts into tears for the first time and is brought around to accept more humane values.

This powerful wartime drama, based on the play by James Gow and Arnaud D'Usseau, deals with one of Hitler's legacies—the German youth who were indoctrinated with Nazi ideology during the height of the Third Reich. One may ask: "Were they perpetrators or victims?" Former members raised under the Hitler Youth claim they had been seduced and deceived by evil elements of the Third Reich. The young refugee in the film symbolizes one of the postwar problems the Allies would have to face—the de-Nazification of Hitler's Germany. In an opinion poll taken in Germany six months after the war, more than 50 percent believed that National Socialism was an acceptable political doctrine that had been ineptly carried out. ∎

Tonight We Raid Calais (1943), TCF. *Dir.* John Brahm; *Sc.* Waldo Salt; *Cast includes:* John Sutton, Annabella, Lee J. Cobb, Beulah Bondi, Blanche Yurka.

A German munitions plant is the target of an Allied air strike in this World War II drama. An English agent (John Sutton) is assigned to infiltrate Nazi lines and illuminate the factory so that Allied bombers can destroy it. A French girl (Annabella) is reluctant to help the British, whom she blames for her brother's death during an R.A.F. attack on French ships. But once she witnesses the brutality of the Nazis, who kill her parents, she realizes who the true enemy is. French farmers, led by Blanche Yurka, fire the fields near the plant, thereby lighting the way for R.A.F. in this routine film. ∎

Too Fat to Fight (1918), Goldwyn. *Dir.* Hobart Henley; *Cast includes:* Frank McIntyre, Florence Dixon, Harold Entwistle, Jack McLean.

This patriotic World War I comedy, based on a story by Rex Beach, concerns a patriotic young American who is rejected by his draft board because of his obesity. Frank McIntyre portrays the principal character who is desperate to do his share but cannot get into uniform until he pulls some political strings. "I'm too fat too fight and too immoral for the Y.M.C.A.," he muses, "but I'd give a leg to be with the boys over there." He is finally sent overseas where he distinguishes himself in battle although he is wounded. Florence Dixon portrays his sweetheart.

The film was released immediately after the armistice, so the propaganda sequences, as well as scenes of American troops landing in Europe, seemed unimportant to the story or the audience. Americans very quickly grew tired of this type of film that promoted enlistment and falsified the ease with which one could achieve medals in the trenches. ∎

Too Late the Hero (1970), Cin. *Dir.* Robert Aldrich; *Sc.* Robert Aldrich, Lukas Heller; *Cast includes:* Michael Caine, Cliff Robertson, Henry Fonda, Ian Bannen.

A U.S. Navy officer is assigned to cooperate with a British Army unit in destroying a Japanese radio installation in this World War II drama. Cliff Robertson portrays the seaman, an expert at Japanese translation. Harry Andrews plays the leader of the British team. Following several skirmishes with the enemy, the infiltrators manage to blow up the radio station. The team, however, suffers heavy losses from Japanese bombers, leaving only a few survivors. They include a sarcastic medic (Michael Caine); Robertson, who proves cowardly during a crisis; and three others. By the end of the film, after being hounded by a Japanese patrol, only Caine and Robertson survive the ordeal and approach their base. The attitudes of both men have changed for the better, the film suggests. Suddenly, quite unexpectedly, distant gun bursts from the pursuing Japanese kill Robertson. ∎

Top Sergeant (1942). See Service Comedy. ∎

Top Sergeant Mulligan (1928), Anchor. *Dir.* James Hogan; *Sc.* Francis Fenton; *Cast includes:* Donald Keith, Gareth Hughes, Wesley Barry, Lila Lee.

A World War I comedy, the film centers on an entertainer (Wesley Barry) who, while trying to recruit young men for the service, finds himself in the army. Sergeant Mulligan (Donald Keith) makes Barry's life miserable. Once in France, Barry and another doughboy (Wade Boteler) become romantically involved with a French girl who is actually a male German spy. They are assigned to capture the enemy agent but are themselves caught. They are shipped to Berlin where they accidentally catch the spy they were originally sent to get. But the war has ended, and when they return to their unit with their captor, all they get for their troubles is heckling from their fellow soldiers. ■

Top Sergeant Mulligan (1941). See Service Comedy. ■

Tora! Tora! Tora! (1970), TCF. *Dir.* Richard Fleischer, Toshio Masuda, Kinji Fukasaku; *Sc.* Larry Forester, Hideo Oguni; *Cast includes:* Martin Balsam, Joseph Cotten, E.G. Marshall, Jason Robards.

An American–Japanese joint production, this World War II dramatic spectacle recreates the attack on Pearl Harbor. The story of the bombing on Dec. 7, 1941, is told from both points of view, the Japanese Navy high command and the American military. The film points out that while the Japanese were unified as to the purpose of their sneak attack, many of the American leaders were unprepared and uncertain of Japan's intentions.

E.G. Marshall, as an Army Intelligence officer, continually tries to warn his superiors about Japan's goals, but he is ignored. Martin Balsam portrays Admiral Kimmel, Commander-in-Chief of the Pacific fleet. Jason Robards plays General Walker Short, the army's Hawaiian commander. Joseph Cotten appears as cabinet member Henry Stimson.

The American studio reportedly spent 25 million dollars on the production, and it shows in the careful recreation of the air attacks upon the docked American fleet and other strategic targets. The action sequences include the use of newsreel footage, large sets and models. The film is divided into two parts, the preparations for the assault on that fateful Sunday morning and the attack itself.

The production has been cited for its historically correct details. Admiral William F. Halsey's ships are assigned to sea duty to avoid their possible entrapment at Pearl Harbor. A commanding general orders the army fighter planes not to be dispersed; their tightly packed formation on the ground gives the Japanese an attractive target. A civilian flier on a Sunday morning joy ride suddenly finds himself in the middle of a squadron of Japanese fighters. ■

Torn Allegiance (1984), Overseas Filmgroup. *Dir.* Alan Nathanson; *Sc.* Alan Nathanson; *Cast includes:* Trevyn McDowell, Jonathan Morris, Ronald France, Marius Weyers.

This action drama depicts some of the tragedy and conflict that occurred during the Boer War, also known as the South African War. The British troops, who "search and destroy" civilian farms, are treated less sympathetically than the Boers. The Dutch guerrillas are seen protecting the farmers who fall under the oppression of the British. One especially brutal British officer carries his hatred of his adversaries to the point of raping the adolescent daughter of a Boer sympathizer. Action sequences include a battle between the Dutch fighters and the British. ■

Torpedo Alley (1953), AA. *Dir.* Lew Landers; *Sc.* Sam Roeca, Warren Douglas; *Cast includes:* Mark Stevens, Dorothy Malone, Charles Winninger, Bill Williams.

A tribute to the undersea service, this routine Korean War drama which begins in 1945 stars Mark Stevens as a former World War II pilot who was saved by an American submarine when he was forced to ditch his plane in the Pacific. He re-enlists in the service following an unsuccessful stint as a civilian. Haunted by the past in which he holds himself responsible for the deaths of his two crew members during the last war, he finally overcomes his problem during the Korean conflict.

Sufficient action sequences keep the story moving. A climactic skirmish involves Stevens and Douglas Kennedy. They volunteer to go ashore and blow up a North Korean tunnel. Both men are wounded as they make their way back to their sub. Dorothy Malone provides the romantic interest for Stevens and Douglas Kennedy, the submarine commander who had rescued Stevens in the last war. The ending shows a fleet of submarines successfully returning to base as a voice-over provides a superfluous eulogy: "And on they go, these giant-killers and the officers and men who man them—a daily example of devotion to duty, vigor, stamina and valor—the fighting submarines of the United States Navy." ■

Torpedo Boat (1942), Par. *Dir.* John Rawlins; *Sc.* Maxwell Shane; *Cast includes:* Richard Arlen, Jean Parker, Mary Carlisle, Phil Terry, Dick Purcell.

A weak action drama with World War II in a very distant background, the film concerns the invention of a new high-speed torpedo boat. Richard Arlen and Phil Terry portray two buddies who design the innovative and lethal craft. Jean Parker and Mary Carlisle, as a nightclub singer, provide the romantic interests in this low-budget film. Action is restricted chiefly to the testing of the torpedo boat. ■

Torpedo Run (1958), MGM. *Dir.* Joseph Pevney; *Sc.* Richard Sale, William Wister Haines; *Cast includes:* Glenn Ford, Ernest Borgnine, Diane Brewster, Dean Jones.

A U.S. submarine commander relentlessly pursues the largest aircraft carrier in the Japanese navy in this World War II action drama. Glenn Ford portrays the determined skipper who chases the well-protected carrier into Tokyo Bay as well as in other Pacific locations. He has another reason to sink the enemy vessel. His wife and children, captured by the Japanese in Manila, were placed aboard an enemy ship along with other American prisoners. The ship was used as a shield for the carrier. Ford learns the news of his family but decides to take a crack at the carrier anyway. His torpedoes miss their target but sink the prison ship. The Japanese do not pick up the survivors; instead, they wait for the sub to surface so that they can sink it. Ford is powerless to help those Americans splashing around in the water. Later, he avenges the prisoners and his loved ones by scoring several direct hits on the Japanese carrier and sending it to its watery grave. Ernest Borgnine, as Ford's chief executive officer and friend, turns down a command of his own so that he can help Ford sink the carrier.

Other World War II-related submarine dramas share similar plots and themes. In *Prison Ship* (1945), for example, a Japanese vessel carrying civilian prisoners of war is used as a decoy to lure American submarines. *Submarine Raider* (1942), based on an actual incident, comes closer in content. U.S. submarine captain John Howard sinks a Japanese carrier that was holding his sweetheart prisoner. ■

Tracks (1976). See Vietnam War. ■

Trafalgar, Battle of. See Napoleonic Wars; Horatio Nelson. ■

Train, The (1964), UA. *Dir.* John Frankenheimer; *Sc.* Franklin Coen, Frank Davis, Walter Bernstein; *Cast includes:* Burt Lancaster, Paul Scofield, Jeanne Moreau, Michel Simon.

The art treasures of France become the object of a tense chase in this World War II drama set in 1944. Members of the French Resistance, who have probably never set foot in an art museum, attempt to stop a train carrying their country's heritage to Germany where the enemy hopes to convert the paintings and other objects into funds to support the war. The film establishes its tribute at the beginning. Among the opening credits is the following dedication: "To those French railway men, living and dead, whose magnificent spirit and whose courage inspired this story."

Burt Lancaster, as an uneducated station conductor with no interest in art, refuses to endanger his life for such a cause until a good friend (Michel Simon) is killed by the Germans. He then joins his fellow Frenchmen in halting the train. Paul Scofield portrays the Nazi colonel in charge of transporting the works of art to Germany. He is an arrogant, cultured figure obsessed with getting the train to Berlin. When he finally confronts Lancaster, who has foiled the officer's scheme, he berates the uncultured Frenchman as common and ignorant. The simple conductor, lacking in social graces, doesn't comprehend the officer's insults and simply replies by shooting the German. ■

Tramp, Tramp, Tramp (1942). See Service Comedy. ■

Travis, William Barrett (1809?–1836). William Travis was a comparatively young man, under 30 years of age, when he made his mark on the history of Texas as com-

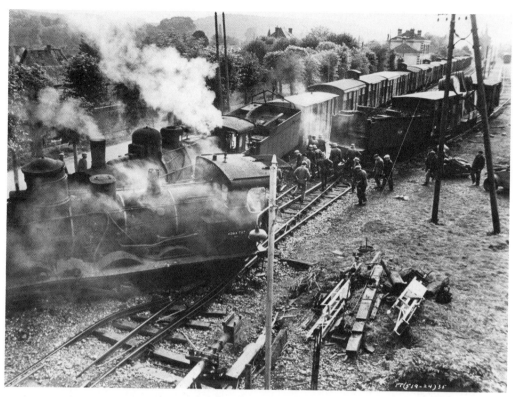

German officers examine the sabotage of French underground members who are trying to prevent their country's art treasures from being shipped to Berlin. *The Train* (1965).

mander of a small group of defenders at the Battle of the Alamo in 1836. Their actions became a symbol of courage and heroism when they fought to the last man against overwhelming forces under Mexico's General Santa Anna.

Born in Edgefield County, South Carolina, Travis moved to Claiborne, Alabama, where he practiced law. He went to Texas, then a Mexican province, in either 1831 or 1832 and soon became prominent in the large community of American colonists who were already agitating for more home rule. Travis was one of those who advocated separation from Mexico.

At the start of the revolution, he was recognized for his leadership qualities and organizational ability by being appointed a colonel in the army of Texas and placed in charge of forces defending the Alamo, a former Spanish mission in San Antonio. He was joined at the Alamo by Colonel James Bowie, who became co-commander, and Davy Crockett. The defenders, numbering less than 200, turned down an offer to surrender from the Mexican dictator-general, Santa Anna,

who, after having some of his forces defeated in earlier skirmishes with the Texans, assaulted the Alamo with 3,000 troops in the first stage of a concerted drive into Texas to crush the revolt. Following a 12-day siege, from February 23 to March 6, Travis and the surviving defenders were killed in the final assault.

Travis' heroic role is covered in such films as the low-budget action drama *Heroes of the Alamo* (1938); John Wayne's *The Alamo* (1960), a large-scale production in which Laurence Harvey plays Travis as a strong leader; and in *The Last Command* (1955), featuring Richard Carlson as Travis. In the last drama, Travis is rightfully depicted as a passionate and eloquent lawyer, but contrary to accepted historical sources, the film tends to subordinate Travis' role as a leader to that of James Bowie in the defense of the Alamo. ■

Treason (1917), U. *Dir.* Allen Holubar; *Sc.* Allen Holubar; *Cast includes:* Allen Holubar, Lois Wilson, Dorothy Davenport, Joseph Girard.

Allen Holubar and Lois Wilson portray the

hero and heroine in this obscure war drama that takes place during World War I. The story allows for several battle scenes, including the bombardment of trenches and other military installations. Critics found some of the action sequences implausible, particularly one in which a telegrapher's dugout is struck by three shells followed by the telegrapher digging himself free. The film represents one of the earliest examples of actual combat footage being combined with studio shots. ∎

Treasure of Pancho Villa, The (1955), RKO. *Dir.* George Sherman; *Sc.* Niven Busch; *Cast includes:* Rory Calhoun, Shelley Winters, Gilbert Roland, Joseph Calleia.

Rory Calhoun portrays a soldier-of-fortune who joins some of Pancho Villa's forces fighting against federal troops during the Mexican Revolution. But his interests are far from idealistic; he plans to steal a gold shipment, meant for the rebel cause, for himself. Gilbert Roland plays a revolutionary who remains loyal to Villa. Shelley Winters, as the daughter of an American mining engineer, sympathizes with the rebels after her father is killed by government troops. The plot unfolds in flashback as Calhoun and Roland are pursued by federal troops who want to retrieve the gold. The film ends with Roland's death and Calhoun's exploding a mountain to bury the gold before he rides off into obscurity. The events have little to do with historical incidents or the famed guerrilla leader who never appears on screen but whose name is often alluded to. ∎

Tripoli (1950), Par. *Dir.* Will Price; *Sc.* Winston Miller; *Cast includes:* John Payne, Maureen O'Hara, Howard da Silva, Philip Reed, Grant Withers.

This light costume drama is loosely based on the conflict between a young United States and the pirates of Tripoli during the early 1800s. John Payne portrays an American marine lieutenant and Maureen O'Hara a French countess out to snare a rich husband. Payne and a detachment of marines are assigned to attack by land a harbor that is preventing the capture of Tripoli. He is aided by a local bandit leader (Howard da Silva) who commands his own troops. Under Payne's command, the attackers manage to lay siege to the city. Historically, the land attack on

Tripoli failed while the U.S. naval blockade was partially successful. ∎

Tripolitan War (1800–1805). U.S. merchant ships, along with vessels of other Christian nations, were often the prey in the 1700s of Muslim pirates. The marauders operated in the western Mediterranean from bases in the North African Barbary states of Algiers, Morocco, Tripoli and Tunis. In 1794 alone, Algerian buccaneers seized more than a dozen American ships and took 119 American prisoners. For decades, many western nations, including the U.S. by the late 1790s, paid regular tribute to the leaders of the Barbary States to ensure safe passage for shipping and prevent either the enslavement of sailors and citizens that the pirates had captured or the necessity of paying ransom to obtain freedom for the prisoners. These acts of piracy on the part of the Barbary States are dramatized in *Yankee Pasha* (1954), with Jeff Chandler as an American storming a Moroccan stronghold to free beautiful Rhonda Fleming and other Americans held captive by an Arab chieftain.

The cost of "protection" for the U.S. was substantial. For example, in a treaty signed with the Dey of Algiers in 1795, the U.S. had to pay $642,500, part of it as ransom, in cash and gifts, and pledge to make an annual payment in naval supplies worth $21,600. Similar treaties for lesser amounts were also concluded with the other North African Muslim states. But the treaties were often ignored by individual Barbary pirates and their rulers, who continued to sanction sporadic attacks and raise new demands for payments.

Open warfare between the U.S. and the Barbary States broke out in 1800. The Pasha of Tripoli, after having his demand for increased tribute rejected, chopped down the American flag in front of the consulate, expelled the American Consul and declared war in 1801 against the U.S. President Jefferson decided to send a naval squadron to blockade Tripoli. The naval blockade was partly successful, but an American overland raid on the city failed.

Commodore Edward Preble, commanding another squadron in 1803–1804, renewed the blockade even more vigorously and even attacked shipping and fortifications in Tripoli harbor. However, during a storm, the American frigate *Philadelphia* ran aground, and the ship and its whole crew were seized. The

Jack Holt (white cap, dark jacket) and the Foreign Legion prepare to use the latest weapons against enemy tribes. *Trouble in Morocco* (1937).

Philadelphia was refloated by its captors, who began to outfit it for their own use. But on a dark night of February 16, 1804, Lieutenant Stephen Decatur, leading a band of men, boarded the captured ship and destroyed it by fire. It was the boldest stroke of the war. The blockade was pressed with greater intensity, and Tripoli was assaulted and bombarded several times during August 1804. Decatur's exploits during this engagement are re-enacted fairly accurately in the silent epic *Old Ironsides* (1926). *The Man Without a Country* (1925) and *Tripoli* (1950) depict other skirmishes with the Barbary pirates.

In 1805 Tripoli signed a peace treaty with the U.S. that ended the payment of American tribute. The U.S., still a newcomer among western nations, gained prestige as a naval power as a result of the war. However, other Barbary States continued to exact payments from the U.S. until the Algerine War (1816). See also Stephen Decatur. ■

Trojan War. See *Helen of Troy* (1953). ■

"Troop B, 16th Cavalry, in Maneuvers" (1910), Edison.

This early silent film shot at Fort Myers concerns various riding exercises of American troops. The film is more of a newsreel than a true documentary since it suggests little in the way of a point of view. The U.S., far behind the European nations in the production of war documentaries, did not release any until well into World War I. ■

Trouble in Morocco (1937), Col. *Dir.* Ernest Schoedsack; *Sc.* Paul Franklin; *Cast includes:* Jack Holt, Mae Clarke, C. Henry Gordon, Harold Huber, Victor Varconi.

Jack Holt portrays a foreign correspondent who ends up in the Foreign Legion by mistake in this action drama. The mix-up occurs when he becomes involved with an ex-mobster (Paul Hurst) who is seeking refuge in the Legion. Although his original assignment was to track down gunrunners in Morocco, Holt finds himself fighting desert tribes. Mae Clarke plays a rival correspondent. Several furious battle sequences include the use of tanks brought in to rescue the besieged Legionnaires. ∎

True Glory, The (1945), Office of War Information. *Dir.* Carol Reed, Garson Kanin; *Sc.* Eric Maschwitz, Gerald Kersh.

A World War II documentary about how the combined efforts of the Allies brought about the defeat of the Axis powers in Europe, the film tracks the battles from the personal viewpoints of various fighting personnel, animated maps and newsreel footage. General Dwight D. Eisenhower introduces the film for a few moments, praising the cooperation of the Allied nations.

The film begins in England as thousands of American troops pour into the island in preparation for the Normandy invasion. Sequences of D-Day follow, showing the difficulties of bringing supplies to the beaches, maintaining a beachhead and battling a stubborn, well-entrenched enemy. Breakthroughs finally occur and the vital port of Cherbourg is captured. Throughout, the focus is on the combined efforts of troops from other nations, including the French Underground fighting in the streets of Paris, Polish forces in the North and British, Canadian and American forces on the beaches battling their way inland. At one point, the rapidly advancing Allies run out of fuel and other supplies. The frustration of a British tank crew, halted outside of Metz because of lack of fuel, exemplifies the critical problem. The film also covers the Battle of the Bulge—the final, desperate German counterattack—and the gallant American stand at Bastogne, as well as the eventual linking up of Allied and Russian soldiers in Germany. A final frame shows a handful of Allied soldiers from many lands in front of their national flags. ∎

True Heaven (1929). See Spy Films: the Talkies. ∎

Tweed, George R. See *No Man Is an Island* (1962). ∎

12 O'Clock High (1949), TCF. *Dir.* Henry King; *Sc.* Sy Bartlett, Beirne Lay, Jr.; *Cast includes:* Gregory Peck, Hugh Marlowe, Millard Mitchell, Dean Jagger.

A World War II drama about the brave young American bomber crews who flew their planes during the hazardous daylight raids over Europe in 1942, the film deals with the morale problem of the men and the officer who tries to improve their lot. When heavy losses and poor morale plague a bomber group stationed in England, the general in command (Millard Mitchell) replaces its current commander (Gary Merrill) with General Frank Savage (Gregory Peck), a symbolically appropriate name. Merrill, the high command concludes, has become too involved with his men, more concerned about their safety than with winning the war. General Savage is assigned to restore confidence in the men as well as to find the "maximum effort" of the individual combatant. He succeeds on both counts, but he himself cracks under the pressure. He falls victim to the same intense anxieties as did his predecessor.

Determined to eliminate the human, emotional factor from each man's life, Savage addresses all the men of the bomber group in a large assembly hall. "Stop making plans," he says. "Forget about going home, consider yourselves already dead. Once you accept that idea, it won't be so tough." To minimize close relationships, he switches the men's sleeping arrangements. "A crippled airplane has to be expendable," he announces. "The only thing which is never expendable is your obligation to the group— this group—this group." Hugh Marlowe at first portrays a "deadbeat" officer who deliberately avoids all responsibility of command. Accusing him of "cowardice" and "desertion of post," Savage reassigns him as an ordinary pilot in charge of a crew of shirkers to a plane dubbed "Leper Colony." Marlowe, in an effort to reform, turns to his crew of slackers and, in the same tone as that of his superior, warns: "We've got a blowtorch turned our way and nobody is gonna shove me into it. Is that clear?"

At the end of the film, Savage goes into a state of shock; his immediate staff look on in horror and disbelief. One officer asks the field medical chief the cause of the general's condition. "Did you ever see a light bulb burn out," the physician begins to explain, "how bright the filament is just before it lets go? I think they call it 'maximum effort.' " ∎

23 1/2 Hours' Leave (1919). See Service Comedy. ∎

Two Arabian Knights (1927), UA. *Dir.* Lewis Milestone; *Sc.* James T. O'Donohue, Wallace Smith; *Cast includes:* William Boyd,

Louis Wolheim, Mary Astor, Ian Keith, Boris Karloff.

A World War I comedy with William Boyd and Louis Wolheim, the film begins in the trenches in France and then shifts to Arabia. Boyd plays a clever private and Wolheim a tough sergeant. The two American soldiers' hatred for each other is so strong that their arguing in the midst of battle results in their being captured by the Germans. Wolheim is placed in control of the prisoners at the camp. The two decide to put aside their differences and become friends. Among the allied prisoners are several Arabians. The two yanks disguise themselves as Arabs and are shipped to Arabia. The two friends then get mixed up with Mary Astor, whom they rescue from the villainous Michael Vavitch. Milestone won an Oscar for Best Comedy Direction, the first and only time this category was ever recognized by the Motion Picture Academy. ∎

"Two Down and One to Go" (1945), Office of War Information.

A World War II documentary explaining the overall military strategy of the Allies in bringing the conflict to an end, the three-reel film details the plans for the war in the Pacific against Japanese forces. With Germany and Italy out of the battle (hence, the title), General George Marshall and other commanders discuss and outline how the military forces will be reduced and the global war ended in an orderly manner.

This documentary, as well as others, began to meet stiff resistance from theater owners who objected to their movie houses being used for "educational" propaganda. Their theaters were designed for entertainment, not showplaces for government films, they insisted. General Marshall was compelled to send the following telegram to major film houses across the nation concerning the above film: "It is important that this message be seen by the maximum number of people in the shortest possible time." ∎

Two Flags West (1950), TCF. *Dir.* Robert Wise; *Sc.* Casey Robinson; *Cast includes:* Joseph Cotten, Linda Darnell, Jeff Chandler, Cornel Wilde, Dale Robertson.

Confederate prisoners of war volunteer to man Union outposts in the West in this Civil War western drama. A suave, genial Southern colonel (Joseph Cotten) and his troop ac-

cept his Union captors' terms to journey west and help protect the territory against hostile Kiowas. His reasons are twofold: to escape the inhuman conditions of the prison camp and perhaps to find a way to return to the South where he and his men can rejoin their army. Cornel Wilde portrays a Yankee officer who escorts the prisoners to a fort commanded by an insensitive, crippled officer (Jeff Chandler). Chandler, a strict, misdirected disciplinarian, is a foil to Cotten. As the Confederates are about to make their escape to their own lines, they learn that the Indians have attacked the fort. They decide to return and help their Union brothers. Chandler, who had precipitated the assault by killing the Indian chief's son in cold blood, surrenders himself to the hostiles in an effort to save the others under his command. ∎

Two-Man Submarine (1944), Col. *Dir.* Lew Landers; *Sc.* Griffin Jay, Leslie T. White; *Cast includes:* Tom Neal, Ann Savage, J. Carrol Naish, Robert Williams.

Enemy agents attempt to force the secret of the penicillin drug from Americans in this implausible World War II drama. Japanese and Nazi spies combine their sinister talents and harass a group of American researchers working in the Pacific. Ultimately, the nefarious agents are foiled as they go to their deaths aboard a submarine. Tom Neal and Ann Savage portray the hero and heroine in this low-budget film. ∎

Two Tickets to London (1943), U. *Dir.* Edwin L. Marin; *Sc.* Tom Reed; *Cast includes:* Michele Morgan, Alan Curtis, C. Aubrey Smith, Barry Fitzgerald.

A fugitive tries to clear his name in this weak drama set in England during World War II. Accused of treason by navy officials for aiding enemy submarines in the sinking of troop transports, the former first mate (Alan Curtis) escapes his captors during a train wreck. With the help of another passenger whom he saves (Michele Morgan), he heads for London to prove his innocence. All is resolved by the end of the routine film, including the romance between the hero and heroine. Dooley Wilson portrays an entertainer, similar to his role in *Casablanca*, and livens things up with his singing. ∎

Two Weeks to Live (1943). See War Humor. ∎

Two Yanks in Trinidad (1942), Col. *Dir.* Gregory Ratoff; *Sc.* Sy Bartlett, Richard Carroll, Henry Segall; *Cast includes:* Pat O'Brien, Brian Donlevy, Janet Blair, Donald MacBride.

Two American racketeers end up in the army in Trinidad and capture a Nazi agent in this routine service comedy drama that takes place on the eve of Pearl Harbor. A tough hoodlum (Pat O'Brien) joins the army to avoid a fellow gangster (Brian Donlevy) after a falling out between the two former friends. Donlevy and two of his cronies follow O'Brien into the service where the two adversaries continue their feud. When they hear that the Japanese have attacked Pearl Harbor and then discover a plot by a Nazi spy involved in the transportation of oil, the two rivals join forces to foil the enemy. Comic character actor Donald MacBride plays their harassing sergeant. ■

Tyrant of the Sea (1950), Col. *Dir.* Lew Landers; *Sc.* Robert Libott, Frank Burt; *Cast includes:* Rhys Williams, Ron Randell, Valentine Perkins, Doris Lloyd.

This sea drama is set during the Napoleonic Wars but has little to do with the conflict between England and France aside from a few sea fights. A tyrannical English captain (Rhys Williams) forces his men to mutiny. Meanwhile, the vessel encounters a French ship and a battle ensues, including hand-to-hand combat as the British sailors board the enemy's vessel. Ron Randell portrays the young hero who woos the captain's daughter (Valentine Perkins). The plot allows for several adequate sea battles in this low-budget film. To give the events a semblance of authenticity, the character of Lord Nelson appears in a minor role. ■

U

U.S.S. Teakettle (1951). See Service Comedy. ∎

U-Boat Prisoner (1944), Col. *Dir.* Lew Landers; *Sc.* Aubrey Wisberg; *Cast includes:* Bruce Bennett, Erik Rolf, John Abbott, Robert Williams.

An American poses as a Nazi spy in this seemingly implausible World War II action drama that reportedly is based on the actual experience of Archie Gibbs, a seaman detained aboard a German submarine. Gibbs (Bruce Bennett) assumes the identity of a Nazi whose ship is sunk. He is picked up by a German U-boat whose officers believe his story. Gibbs is then quartered with a group of prisoners whom he takes into his confidence. He overpowers some of the submarine crew, causes a torpedo to be destroyed and saves the prisoners. The film contains an abundance of patriotic dialogue. ∎

Ugly American, The (1963). See Cold War. ∎

Ulzana's Raid (1972), U. *Dir.* Robert Aldrich; *Sc.* Alan Sharp; *Cast includes:* Burt Lancaster, Bruce Davison, Jorge Luke, Richard Jaeckel.

Burt Lancaster portrays an aging frontier scout called upon to help a green army lieutenant (Bruce Davison) hunt down a marauding Apache leader in this action drama. The inexperienced officer, thanks to the old scout, matures as the film reaches its climactic battle. Jorge Luke portrays a friendly Apache who, as a scout, assists Lancaster. Ulzana (Joaquin Martinez) leads his war party against unsuspecting ranchers and other whites, leaving a bloody trail of rape and pillage. Richard Jaeckel plays a tough sergeant in this familiar cavalry-vs.-Indians story.

A particularly violent drama, the film attempts to debunk the romantic view of the 19th-century frontier by depicting it realistically as an inherently savage land inhabited by marauders who place little value on human life. The brutal sequences and some of the dialogue that accompanies them are designed to affect the young lieutenant's maturation.

Historically, the actual raid by Ulzana and ten of his warriors in 1885 lasted only four weeks. But it was an almost impossible feat, considering that the braves, starting from Mexico, crossed the border into unfriendly territory, traveled 1,200 miles, lived off the land, exhausted more than 200 horses and mules and were hounded by numerous troops of the 4th and 10th Cavalry and companies of Indian scouts. Ulzana left a trail of 38 dead, chiefly white miners and ranchers, before he returned to the mountains of Mexico. He lost only one brave. He surrendered voluntarily, along with members of his tribe, one year later to General Crook, who worked out a compromise treaty with the Apaches. However, General Phil Sheridan in Washington ignored Crook's treaty and accepted the Apache return to their reservation under his own terms of unconditional surrender. Crook, who gave his word to the Indians, felt slighted and resigned; he was promptly replaced by General Nelson Miles. ∎

Unbeliever, The (1918), Edison. *Dir.* Alan Crosland; *Cast includes:* Raymond McKee, Marguerite Cortot, Karl (Erich) von Stroheim and several members of the U.S. Marine Corps.

A young marine volunteer fighting in the

trenches of France during World War I undergoes certain changes in his beliefs. He holds that some men are superior to others. Witnessing the slaughter of the war, he doubts that there is a God. Finally, he laughs at the thought of "loving thine enemy." However, his further experiences in battle, including one in which his buddy dies in his arms, bring about a new outlook. "You've taught me to judge people as people," he admits to the mortally wounded doughboy. The egalitarian theme occurs again when an enraged German soldier kills his Prussian superior and shouts: "Down with militarism! Long Live Democracy!"

Aside from its pronouncement concerning the equality of all men, the film develops a religious theme as well. Christ appears, hovering over the battlefield in support of democracy. Another scene shows a rabbi attending to a dying Catholic soldier. Religious symbolism was rarely used in war films after this feature was released. The film also includes several action scenes and a love story. Erich von Stroheim appears as the ruthless Prussian officer killed by an underling after the officer destroys the violin of a sensitive soldier, a role that von Stroheim was to be associated with for the next several decades. The American government not only sanctioned the production but permitted some scenes to be filmed at a Virginia military post and provided a substantial part of the cast through the use of actual military personnel. ∎

Uncertain Glory (1944), WB. *Dir.* Raoul Walsh; *Sc.* Laszlo Vadnay, Max Brand; *Cast includes:* Errol Flynn, Paul Lukas, Jean Sullivan, Lucile Watson, Faye Emerson.

A criminal finds redemption in this offbeat World War II drama. About to be guillotined for murder, the condemned man (Errol Flynn) is saved at the last moment by an air raid of Allied planes. In the confusion he escapes his executioners. Later, he is captured by a French police inspector (Paul Lukas). Persuaded by the highly moral policeman, the fugitive volunteers to impersonate a saboteur wanted by the Nazis and turns himself in as such. He thus saves the lives of 100 French hostages about to be executed by the Germans. ∎

"Uncivil Warbirds" (1946). See War Humor. ∎

"Uncivil Warriors" (1935). See War Humor. ∎

Uncle Sam of Freedom Ridge (1920), Levey. *Dir.* George A. Beranger; *Sc.* Margaret Prescott Montague; *Cast includes:* George McQuarrie, William D. Corbett, Paul Kelley, Helen Flint.

A strong antiwar drama and advocate of President Wilson's League of Nations, the film tells the story of a West Virginia mountain man and true patriot who sends his son to answer his nation's call to arms when World War I erupts. Convinced that his boy is fighting for Wilson's cause—to make the world safe for democracy—the father accepts the news of his son's death with a sense of comfort and resignation. Later, when he realizes the cause has been betrayed by those who are resisting the movement to abolish all wars through the League of Nations, the father sacrifices his own life. He wraps himself in his cherished flag that has always flown over his cabin and shoots himself in protest. ∎

Uncommon Valor (1983), Par. *Dir.* Ted Kotcheff; *Sc.* Joe Gayton; *Cast includes:* Gene Hackman, Roger Stack, Fred Ward, Reb Brown.

The father of a Vietnam War casualty organizes a special private fighting force ten years after his son is reported missing to help him infiltrate Vietnam in search of his son and other Americans held captive. Refusing to believe that his son is dead, the father (Gene Hackman) enlists the aid of an oil millionaire (Robert Stack) whose son is also missing, and proceeds to recruit and train a half-dozen tough ex-servicemen. Much of the film is devoted to drilling the small band for their eventual perilous mission. At one point at his specially prepared private training base, Hackman addresses his small assault team. "You men . . . are thought of as criminals because of Vietnam," he says. "You know why? Because you lost . . . They want to forget about you, you cost too much, and you don't turn a profit . . . We're the only hope those P.O.W.s have, so we're going back there."

The last part of the drama concerns the small invasion force's attempts to free the captured Americans. Hackman and his crew face several setbacks. U.S. government officials, who claim they are negotiating with the

Vietnamese, think that he will hamper their efforts and try to stop him. The C.I.A. informs the Bangkok police who confiscate Hackman's small arsenal. But he and his team proceed to their target. In a bloody firefight with a horde of prison guards, the Americans manage to rescue the captives. Hackman learns that his son has died earlier, but he is content with the success of the mission.

The film contains more intelligent dialogue and better characterization than other similar action dramas that were to follow, particularly the "Rambo" series with Sylvester Stallone and the "Missing in Action" trilogy with Chuck Norris. These later works digressed from any hint of reality. They emphasized violence, action and superweapons; turned their heroes into virtual superbeings; and gave the impression that the enemy, especially the Viet Cong, were incompetent fighters and monomaniacal sadists. ■

Unconquered (1947), Par. *Dir.* Cecil B. DeMille; *Sc.* Charles Bennett, Fredric Frank, Jesse Lasky, Jr.; *Cast includes:* Gary Cooper, Paulette Goddard, Howard Da Silva, Boris Karloff.

An adventurous Virginia militiaman (Gary Cooper) journeys to the Allegheny frontier in this 18th-century colonial action drama filled with clichés. The area is aflame with hostile Indians who have been stirred up by a villainous renegade (Howard Da Silva). They hold Fort Pitt under siege until more troops arrive. Battles ensue among the settlers, British soldiers and various tribes. Boris Karloff plays an Indian chief. Paulette Goddard portrays an indentured servant recently arrived from England who experiences a series of narrow escapes including a torture stake and a hazardous journey by canoe. Directed by DeMille, the film was panned by the critics but was successful at the box office.

DeMille's attempts to add authenticity to his drama by dropping such historical names as Colonel George Washington, the Seneca Indians and Fort Pitt do not exonerate him from certain historical inaccuracies. Although Washington was involved in earlier fighting on the side of the British during the French and Indian War, it is highly unlikely that he was anywhere in the vicinity of Fort Pitt at the time the film takes place. Also, the Comanche, mentioned as one of the tribes that besieged the fort, never journeyed that far east. ■

Under Crimson Skies (1920), U. *Dir.* Rex Ingram; *Sc.* Harvey Thew; *Cast includes:* Elmo Lincoln, Harry Van Meter, Mabel Ballin, Nancy Caswell.

A drama about gun-smuggling, mutiny and revolution in South America, the film stars Elmo Lincoln as the hero who doesn't swing into action until late in the film. A greedy and brutal villain beats his wife and child, causes mutinies and sells guns to revolutionaries. The film includes several lively battle sequences and fistfights. Elmo Lincoln gained fame as being the first to portray Tarzan on the screen.

Unrest in South America and other lands south of the border was a popular film subject for dramas and satires during the silent period. Newspaper stories featuring continual instabilities in those countries and the intervention of U.S. troops in Haiti, the Dominican Republic, Panama, Honduras, Guatemala and Mexico did not pass unnoticed by movie studio moguls who translated these two factors into potential box-office receipts. ■

Under False Colors (1917), Pathe. *Dir.* Emile Chautard; *Cast includes:* Jeanne Eagels, Frederick Warde, Robert Vaughn, Anne Gregory.

Jeanne Eagels portrays a Russian countess in this drama set during the early days of the Russian Revolution. She escapes with the help of an American. The ship she is on is torpedoed, but again she manages to escape. She assumes the identity of an American woman, a fellow passenger who perishes as a result of the sinking. The remainder of the film concerns her involvement with a group of revolutionaries fighting to establish freedom in Russia and an American millionaire, played by Frederick Warde, who is financing the struggle.

American film studios were quick to exploit the Russian Revolution as a screen topic. This drama no doubt was one of the earliest and set the generally anti-revolutionary tone for those films to follow. D.W. Griffith, for example, several years later in his 1921 historical drama about the French Revolution, *Orphans of the Storm*, uses his opening titles to warn his audiences against "Bolshevism." ■

Under Fire (1957), TCF. *Dir.* James B. Clark; *Sc.* James Landis; *Cast includes:* Rex Reason, Henry Morgan, Steve Brodie, Peter Walker.

Four American soldiers are on trial for desertion during combat in this World War II courtroom drama. Rex Reason, as the defense attorney, finally proves that the men were actually lost and not deserters. Steve Brodie portrays the prosecutor. Henry Morgan, Jon Locke, Gregory LaFayette and Robert Levin play the G.I.s facing the court martial in this low-budget film. ∎

Under Fire (1983), Orion. *Dir.* Roger Spottisoode; *Sc.* Ronald Shelton, Clayton Frohman; *Cast includes:* Nick Nolte, Gene Hackman, Joanna Cassidy, Jean-Louis Trintignant, Ed Harris.

Set chiefly in Nicaragua in 1979, the drama centers around three journalists. A professional still photographer (Nick Nolte) is loyal only to his immediate assignment. A senior correspondent for *Time* (Gene Hackman) dreams of becoming a television anchor man earning $10,000 per week with a home in Long Island. A reporter for Public Radio (Joanna Cassidy) leaves her lover, Hackman, and takes up with Nolte.

The story opens in 1979 in Chad where the three principals are covering the conflict in that African country and then shifts to Nicaragua the same year. Nolte and his fellow journalists are now covering the war between President Somoza's troops and the revolutionaries. But the film is concerned with this conflict only superficially. The director's real interest lies in exploring the moral ambiguities to which correspondents are particularly vulnerable. At first Nolte is objective almost to a fault. "I don't take sides," he replies when asked where his sympathies lie, "I take pictures." Eventually he begins to sympathize with the rebels. He grows fond of a young revolutionary who dreams of becoming a baseball player. Suddenly the boy is shot in the back while joking with Nolte. In his search to photograph their elusive leader, Rafael, Nolte discovers that the man is dead. The rebels ask him to photograph him as though he were alive. This would give impetus to the revolution and end the war quickly, thereby saving many lives. At first Nolte rejects the idea but then agrees. The faked picture is released internationally. He soon learns that this is not the first time his pictures involved him in the war. It seems that a French double agent has been using Nolte's human interest shots to finger other rebel leaders who have since been assassinated.

Nolte believes he is indirectly responsible for these killings. The film ends with Somoza leaving for Florida while the people take to the streets to celebrate their victory.

The film is a frank treatment of reporters under pressure— of how they may easily become victims of the worst sin of their profession, falsifying their stories. It also suggests strongly the involvement of the U.S. and the C.I.A., often represented by wrong-headed individuals. An American public relations man working for Somoza continually justifies the dictator's actions. "We're backing a Fascist government again," Hackman utters. "Look," the publicity man protests, "there are fascists and there are fascists. Let's not go throwing names around." Nolte encounters another American from time to time. He is a mercenary whom Nolte met in Chad and who is now fighting for Somoza. He was the hired killer who shot the young rebel, an act that drove Nolte to side with the revolutionists.

When Hackman is cold-bloodedly killed by Somoza's troops, Cassidy mourns openly in view of a native woman. "Fifty thousand Nicaraguans have died and now one Yankee," the woman says to the reporter. "Perhaps now Americans will be outraged at what is happening here." "Perhaps they will," Cassidy agrees. "Maybe we should have killed an American journalist 50 years ago," the woman adds. ∎

Under Four Flags (1918), CPI.

One of a series of documentaries produced by the Committee on Public Information, the film, made by members of the U.S. Signal Corps, describes the defeat of Germany by the combined efforts of French, British, Italian and American forces. Segments include French refugees running from the German invaders, the landing of American troops in France and the celebration of the armistice in New York City. ∎

Under Ten Flags (1960). See Sea Battles. ∎

Under the Black Eagle (1928), MGM. *Dir.* W. E. Van Norn; *Sc.* Bradley King; *Cast includes:* Ralph Forbes, Marceline Day, Marc MacDermott, Bert Roach.

This World War I drama deals with a young man (Ralph Forbes) who is torn between the woman he loves (Marceline Day) and his abhorrence of war. A pacifist in his convictions, he cannot bring himself to participate in his country's conflict until the final portion of the film. There are several battle sequences of the war as well as a dog performing various feats and contributing comic relief. The principal characters are German, so the war is presented from the enemy's point of view, a perspective not introduced to American film audiences until the 1920s. ∎

"Under the Star Spangled Banner" (1908), Kalem.

An early cavalry-vs.-Indians silent drama, the short film tells the elemental story of a lone family traveling west in a covered wagon. Suddenly, the migrants are attacked by a band of hostiles. U.S. soldiers, stationed at a nearby army post, come to the rescue and drive the hostiles off. Kalem, as well as other movie studios such as Biograph and Selig, during this early period in U.S. film history produced several one- and two-reel historical dramas. Many used the cavalry-vs.-Indians conflict and the American Civil War for their backgrounds. Director D.W. Griffith, working for Biograph, turned out a cycle of one-reelers of the Civil War through 1913, preparing him for his classic *The Birth of a Nation* (1915). ∎

Under Two Flags (1916), Fox. *Dir.* J. Gordon Edwards; *Sc.* George Hall; *Cast includes:* Theda Bara, Herbert Hayes, Stuart Holmes, Stanhope Wheatcroft.

This was the first screen version of Ouida's popular novel about the Foreign Legion and the alluring Cigarette, the Algerian cafe entertainer with whom the men fell in love and over whom they often fought. Herbert Hayes plays an exiled Englishman who joins the Legionnaires in Algeria after some difficulties at home. Cigarette (Theda Bara) falls in love with him. Hayes becomes embroiled in a duel with his superior officer who then has the Englishman arrested for striking an officer and sentenced to death by firing squad. Bara obtains a pardon, races to her lover's rescue and arrives in time only to receive the bullet meant for her lover.

The second screen version, released in 1922 and directed by Tod Browning, stars Priscilla Dean as Cigarette, who falls in love with Legionnaire James Kirkwood, an exiled Englishman. Filled with atmosphere and local color, this adaptation adds more action and changes the climax. When the soldiers in their stronghold are attacked and outnum-

bered by desert tribesmen, Cigarette leads the relief column to the besieged Legionnaires.

The third adaptation and first talking version (1936), directed by Frank Lloyd, features Claudette Colbert as Cigarette, the Algerian daughter of the Foreign Legion regiment, who falls in love with Legionnaire Ronald Colman. Victor McLaglen portrays a major who is also in love with Colbert while Gregory Ratoff handles the comic relief. This time it is Colbert who leads the rescuers to the besieged soldiers fighting for their lives in the desert fort. ∎

Underground (1941), WB. *Dir.* Vincent Sherman; *Sc.* Edwin Justus Mayer, Oliver H. P. Garrett; *Cast includes:* Jeffrey Lynn, Philip Dorn, Kaaren Verne, Mona Maris, Peter Whitney.

Another in a series of Hollywood dramas intended to expose the ruthlessness of the Nazi regime, the film pays tribute to a small band of Germans who resist their government's policies. Philip Dorn, as a leader in the German underground, broadcasts from temporary mobile radio stations to bring the truth to the German people. Jeffrey Lynn portrays a dedicated Nazi soldier who inadvertently turns in his own brother to the Gestapo. Realizing too late the realities of what Nazism represents, he replaces his brother in the underground as Dorn goes to his death. The film presents the usual anti-Nazi propaganda of the period, including allusions to the dreaded concentration camps and didactic speeches. "Freedom will prevail," Lynn exclaims in a final illegal broadcast, "and peace on earth will reign when this medieval darkness will be only a memory. . . . This is our fight: to bring light where there is darkness." The following quotation from Shakespeare hangs on the wall of the brothers' home and suggests the theme of the drama:

> What stronger breastplate than a heart untainted!
> Thrice be he armed that hath his quarrel just,
> And he but naked, though locked up in steel,
> Whose conscience with injustice is corrupted. ∎

Underground Agent (1942). See Spy Films: the Talkies. ∎

"Underground Report" (1944). See "The March of Time." ∎

Underwater Warrior (1958), MGM. *Dir.* Andrew Marton; *Sc.* Gene Levitt; *Cast includes:* Dan Dailey, Claire Kelly, James Gregory, Ross Martin.

Culled from the exploits of U.S. Navy Commander Francis D. Fane, this drama covers the wartime experiences of the frogmen during both World War II and the Korean conflict. Dan Dailey portrays the commander who is dedicated to the undersea unit in the days preceding the Second World War and who meets stiff opposition from skeptical superiors. His wife (Claire Kelly) prefers having her man spending more time at home. The film includes several good underwater action sequences. ∎

Unguarded Women (1924). See Veterans. ∎

United We Stand (1942), TCF. *Sc.* Prosper Buranelli.

A World War II documentary, the film emphasizes how political and internal schisms can lead nations down a path of disaster. It traces events from World War I to the Japanese attack on Pearl Harbor, underscoring dissensions within countries, the rise of Nazism in Germany, civil war in Spain, the Japanese invasion of China, the fall of Czechoslovakia and the entrance of England and France into the war against Germany. The film also parallels the militarism and brutality of Japan with that of Germany, including invasions of neighboring lands and sneak attacks. Noted commentator and foreign correspondent Lowell Thomas narrates the documentary. ∎

Unknown Love, The (1919), Pathe. *Dir.* Leonce Perret; *Sc.* Leonce Perret; *Cast includes:* E.K. Lincoln, Doris Parker, Root Elliott.

A patriotic young woman (Doris Parker) "adopts" an American soldier fighting in France as a pen pal in this World War I romantic drama. Treating the correspondence lightly, the doughboy sends a photograph of a fellow soldier to her. When she learns that he has been wounded, she persuades an American naval officer who is in love with her to hide her aboard his vessel that is embarked for Europe. At sea the ship is attacked by a German submarine and the officer is mortally wounded. When she finally arrives at the hospital where the wounded soldier is recuperating, he confesses to her that he sent another's picture. But she explains she has grown fond of the inner person who wrote the letters, not the outward appearance. Several action sequences include actual newsreel shots that add realism to the fighting. ∎

Unknown Soldier, The (1926), PDC. *Dir.* Renaud Hoffman; *Sc.* James J. Tynan; *Cast includes:* Charles Emmett Mack, Marguerite de la Motte, Henry B. Walthall, Ethel Wales, Claire MacDowell.

Charles Emmett Mack portrays a factory worker who volunteers to go to France to fight for his country in this World War I romantic drama. He meets an American entertainer who journeys overseas to perform for the troops and they get married. But the minister who conducts the ceremony is really a deserter. Mack is sent to the front lines, so his wife cannot inform him of the illegal ceremony. He is wounded in action, suffers from shell-shock and is hospitalized for two years while his wife gives birth. Finally, his mother locates him and brings the couple together. The film includes scenes of battle and life in the trenches as well as newsreel shots of the placing of the Unknown Soldier in his grave at the Arlington National Cemetery. ∎

Unknown Soldier Speaks, The (1934), Lincoln Productions. *Sc.* Robert Rossen.

A documentary using footage from World War I, the film tries to show how the ideals that the men in the trenches fought for, as symbolized by the Unknown Soldier, have been at best forgotten and at worst betrayed. Through the use of a narrator (Alan Bunce), the story begins at the famous tomb and traces contemporary events to the rise of Hitler and Mussolini. One interesting sidelight is the segment showing black soldiers at the front during World War I. Although the film uses familiar newsreel shots, the point of view is fresh and intelligently handled. Robert Rossen, who wrote the script, emerged as an important screenwriter and director during the 1940s and 1950s. He wrote screenplays for several films with war themes, including *They Won't Forget, Edge of Darkness,*

A Walk in the Sun and *They Came to Cordura.* ■

Unpardonable Sin, The (1919), Garson. *Dir.* Marshall Neilan; *Sc.*; George K. O'Neill; *Cast includes:* Blanche Sweet, Matt Moore, Wesley Barry, Mary Alden, Wallace Beery.

A World War I drama that depicts the ruthlessness of the Germans who invaded Belgium, the film centers on a mother and her two daughters (both played by Blanche Sweet). While one of the young women is away in the U.S., the remaining sister suffers the personal and physical atrocities of the enemy. The horror of the experience takes its toll when both the daughter and the mother perish. Meanwhile, the other daughter returns to Belgium to search for her family and barely escapes in time before she is subjected to similar abuses at the hands of the Germans. Wallace Beery plays the villain who performs the outrage on the daughter.

At least one contemporary critic (the *New York Times*) questioned the wisdom of perpetuating anti-German feeling months after the Armistice. Propaganda films became a staple during the war, of course. When the conflict came to its almost abrupt end, most movie studios were able to edit out the more graphic anti-German sequences. Some films in which these sequences were central to the plot and theme were released after the war without cutting. Portraying the Germans as bestial creatures bent chiefly on satisfying their lecherous desires began during the early stages of the war and had its roots in several press releases emanating from European sources. The female victims almost invariably were Belgian or French. After the U.S. entered the conflict, American film studios began to turn out several features which substituted American women as the object of German lust. These films undoubtedly served a dual purpose; they fed the ravenous wartime propaganda machine and personalized the war for many in the audience. See Propaganda Films: World War I. ■

Untamed (1955), TCF. *Dir.* Henry King; *Sc.* Talbot Jennings, Frank Fenton, Michael Blankfort; *Cast includes:* Tyrone Power, Susan Hayward, Richard Egan, John Justin.

This period drama recounts the story of the great Boer trek through hostile Zulu territory in an effort to establish the Dutch Free State. Tyrone Power portrays a Dutch pioneer trying to carve out his destiny in South Africa. Susan Hayward plays the wife of an Irishmanwhom she convinces to begin a new life in South Africa. When her husband dies, she has an affair with Power and bears him a son while he goes off to fight with the Boers. The highlight of the battle sequences occurs early in the film when the Boer wagon train is attacked by the Zulus. The action sequences were shot in South Africa. ■

Until They Sail (1957), MGM. *Dir.* Robert Wise; *Sc.* Robert Anderson; *Cast includes:* Jean Simmons, Joan Fontaine, Paul Newman, Piper Laurie, Charles Drake.

New Zealand women, whose men are away at war, take up with Yanks in this World War II romantic drama. The film centers on the romances of four sisters. Jean Simmons, as a widow of one month, falls in love with Paul Newman, a U.S. Marine stationed nearby. Joan Fontaine, Piper Laurie and Sandra Dee play the other sisters. The story emphasizes the loneliness of the wives and sweethearts as well as that of the Americans so far from home. *Yanks*, a similar film released in 1979, concerned American soldiers and their English girlfriends during the same war. ■

Unwritten Code, The (1944). See *Escape in the Desert* (1945). ■

Up From the Beach (1965), TCF. *Dir.* Robert Parrish; *Sc.* Howard Clewes; *Cast includes:* Cliff Robertson, Red Buttons, Irina Demick, Marius Goring, Slim Pickens.

An American sergeant (Cliff Robertson) becomes involved with French civilians in the wake of the Normandy invasion in this weak drama set during World War II. Robertson moves inland with the remainder of his squad following the invasion and liberates a French farmhouse where more than twenty civilians were being held as hostages by several German soldiers. Red Buttons, as a Jewish-American soldier, is placed in charge of the former Nazi commandant of the village (Marius Goring). Irina Demick, as a French resistance fighter, provides the romantic interest for Robertson. Slim Pickens plays a strait-laced artillery colonel who keeps ordering Robertson to take the civilians back to the beach where those in charge want no part of civilians. Robertson soon mellows as supervisor and sympathetic protector of the French people in his care. ■

Up Front (1951), UI. *Dir.* Alexander Hall; *Sc.* Stanley Roberts; *Cast includes:* David Wayne, Tom Ewell, Marina Berti, Jeffrey Lynn, Richard Egan.

Willie and Joe, those two sardonic and war-weary infantrymen that Bill Mauldin made famous in his caustic cartoons, are the lead characters in this World War II comedy. Tom Ewell portrays the angular Willie while David Wayne plays his acerbic buddy. Incidents place the pair at the front lines and in Naples where, while A.W.O.L. and attempting to keep one step ahead of the M.P.s, they become embroiled in a black market caper which results in a courtroom sequence. They manage to inject their verbal humor during their misadventures, thereby capturing some of their character from the original cartoons. But much of the film is reminiscent of the typical service comedy. Jeffrey Lynn portrays their green lieutenant.

A sequel, *Back at the Front* (1952), featured Tom Ewell as Willie and Harvey Lembeck replacing David Wayne as Joe. The two G.I.s are recalled to active duty and shipped to Japan where they become entangled with a gang of smugglers selling arms to North Korea.

William Henry Mauldin, who saw service in Italy during World War II, became the most popular U.S. Army cartoonist of the war. His work, featuring his lovable characters Willie and Joe, was published in *Stars and Stripes*, the official weekly army newspaper, and captured the dour humor of life at the front. ■

Up in Arms (1944), RKO. *Dir.* Elliott Nugent; *Sc.* Don Hartman, Allen Boretz, Robert Pirosh; *Cast includes:* Danny Kaye, Dinah Shore, Dana Andrews, Constance Dowling.

Danny Kaye, in his film debut, plays a hypochondriac who is drafted into the army in this World War II musical comedy. He is shipped to the Pacific war zone along with his pal (Dana Andrews). Meanwhile, their two girlfriends (Dinah Shore and Constance Dowling), who have signed up as nurses, are aboard the boys' transport. Once on land, incompetent Kaye is taken prisoner by the Japanese. He manages not only to escape but to

capture an entire enemy unit that he leads-back to American lines. There are comic scenes involving Kaye before his induction, aboard the transport and on the Pacific island.

The entire ensemble, including the then popular Goldwyn Girls, performs a major production number, the patriotic "All Out for Freedom," as the Yanks embark for the Pacific. "We didn't have anything like this in the last war!" one old-timer, ogling the buxom beauties, remarks. "We don't have anything like it in this one either," a younger soldier responds. The film is loosely based on Owen Davis' stage play, *The Nervous Wreck*, which in turn was adapted as a 1930 musical comedy film titled *Whoopee* starring Eddie Cantor. ■

Crew members of a U.S. submarine prepare for action against the Japanese during World War II. *Up Periscope* (1959).

Up Periscope (1959), WB. *Dir.* Gordon Douglas; *Sc.* Richard Landau; *Cast includes:* James Garner, Edmond O'Brien, Andra Martin, Alan Hale.

A demolitions expert clashes with a by-the-book submarine commander in this action drama set in the Pacific during World War II. James Garner portrays a light-hearted frogman and explosives specialist whose perilous mission involves obtaining an important code from a Japanese-held island. Edmond O'Brien, as the martinet captain, is rebuffed by his crew and challenged by Garner for his narrow approach to military procedures. He finally relents when he has to rescue Garner from the island after he completes his mission. The film includes several suspenseful and exciting sequences, particularly those concerning Garner alone on the enemy island. ■

"Up San Juan Hill" (1909), Selig. *Dir.* Frank Boggs; *Cast includes:* Hobart Bosworth, Betty Harte, Thomas Santchi.

A short silent drama of the Spanish-American War, the film recounts the popular story of a message sent from President McKinley to General Garcia in Cuba. There are detailed action sequences of the famous battle of San Juan Hill. Another, more highly fictitious version of the event appeared in 1936 titled *Message to Garcia*, with John Boles as the determined messenger and Wallace Beery as his roguish assistant. ■

V

Vagabond King, The (1930, 1956). See *If I Were King.* ■

Valley Forge. Few armies in history have withstood the conditions encountered by George Washington's force during the winter encampment of 1777–1778 and survived to fight and win. When the American army went into its winter quarters in the hills outside Philadelphia in December 1777, its strength was around 9,000 men. By late winter, the toll from disease, near starvation, insufficient clothing and shelter, the weather and desertion had reduced its number to near 6,000.

Several colonial leaders commented on the abject state into which the Continental Army had fallen. Washington later told another officer, "You could have tracked the army . . . to Valley Forge by the blood of their feet." General Greene wrote, "One half of our troops are without breeches (pants), shoes and stockings; and some thousands without blankets." He estimated a quarter of the army was unfit for duty because they were barefoot and almost naked. Lafayette, in his memoirs, wrote, "The army frequently remained for whole days without provisions, and the endurance of both soldiers and officers was a miracle. . . ."

The efforts of Quartermaster General Greene to secure supplies and organize a system of distribution in the late winter had the army beginning to recover its health by early spring. Meanwhile, 47-year-old Baron Frederick von Steuben, a German volunteer soldier-of-fortune serving without pay, began in March 1778 to instruct the army in a general drill program which included for the first time the use of the bayonet.

The Americans took to von Steuben's instructions and rallied to hold the British to a standoff in the first battle after Valley Forge at Monmouth, New Jersey (June 27–28 1778). Later, the patriots captured Stony Point with a bayonet charge without firing a single shot.

The winter at Valley Forge represented a low point in strength and morale for the colonial cause. The American army showed it would not give up the struggle for independence, despite brutal and disheartening conditions, and emerged as a stronger and more confident fighting force. A handful of Hollywood films depicted the hardships the troops suffered at Valley Forge. One of the earliest, *Washington at Valley Forge* (1914), a small, four-reel epic, re-enacted other historical incidents as well, including Paul Revere's ride. Francis Ford, the older brother of director John Ford, directed and wrote the script and portrayed Washington. In the historical drama *The Howards of Virginia* (1940), with Cary Grant and Martha Scott, Valley Forge provided the background for the fictional Howard family and their involvement in major events of the American Revolution. ■

Valley of the Sun (1942), RKO. *Dir.* George Marshall; *Sc.* Horace McCoy; *Cast includes:* James Craig, Lucille Ball, Sir Cedric Hardwicke, Dean Jagger.

An unscrupulous Indian agent cheats the tribe under his jurisdiction, causing the young braves to go on the warpath in this familiar action drama. James Craig portrays a brave frontiersman who befriends the exploited Indians. A local rancher (Sir Cedric Hardwicke) attempts to bring peace to the land. Dean Jagger plays the corrupt agent. Lucille Ball, as Jagger's love object who switches over to Craig, provides the romantic interest.

The film attempts a note of authenticity by introducing two historical figures, Geronimo, a young restless brave played by veteran western actor Tom Tyler, and Cochise, played by Antonio Moreno, a popular character actor of the 1930s. Both warriors were to figure prominently in subsequent westerns although the former already had his biography transferred to the screen in *Geronimo* (1939). The basic idea of a frontiersman who is sympathetic to the Indians and befriends Cochise was to be used more skillfully less than a decade later in the landmark film of white-Indian relationships, *Broken Arrow* (1950), starring James Stewart as the white man and Jeff Chandler as the Apache chief. ■

Vanishing American, The (1925), Par. *Dir.* George B. Seitz; *Sc.* Ethel Doherty; *Cast includes:* Richard Dix, Lois Wilson, Noah Beery, Malcolm McGregor, Charles Stevens.

Richard Dix portrays an American Indian leader in this drama that depicts the plight of his people. Based on the novel by Zane Grey, the film describes how corrupt Indian agents exploit and cheat the reservation Indians. Dix falls in love with the white teacher (Lois Wilson) at the Indian school. He gets into a brawl with one of the crooked white men over the teacher and is forced to hide in the hills. When World War I breaks out, he enlists and distinguishes himself in battle. Returning to his reservation, he discovers his tribe has been pushed off their land which was stolen by unscrupulous whites. The Indians, who are slowly dying, decide to rise up and attack the whites. Dix rides to warn them. When his braves arrive, he goes out to dissuade them from fighting, but one of his tribe kills him. This was one of the earliest films to treat the Indian sympathetically and seriously. ■

Vanishing American, The (1955), Rep. *Dir.* Joseph Kane; *Sc.* Alan LeMay; *Cast includes:* Scott Brady, Audrey Totter, Forrest Tucker, Gene Lockhart, Jim Davis, Lee Van Cleef.

Although this second screen adaptation of Zane Grey's novel was shot on location in Utah in an effort to add realism to the production, its intrusive present-day dialogue detracts from the authenticity of the tale. Scott Brady portrays the author's Navajo hero who falls in love with a white woman (Audrey Totter) who has come west to take charge of her inheritance. This time around

Gene Lockhart portrays the unscrupulous Indian agent. Forrest Tucker, as a scheming Indian trader, tries to control all the water rights on Navajo land. Besides having to fend off the greedy whites, Brady has to contend with hostile Apaches who are killing his people. Unlike the earlier version, the Navajo leader survives to win the hand of the woman he loves. ■

Vanquished, The (1953), Par. *Dir.* Edward Ludwig; *Sc.* Winston Miller, Frank L. Moss, Lewis R. Foster; *Cast includes:* John Payne, Coleen Gray, Jan Sterling, Lyle Bettger.

A Confederate veteran returns home after spending time as a prisoner of war in a Union camp in this post-Civil War drama. The veteran (John Payne) has secretly been assigned to expose corruption in his home town, a condition brought about by the infamous Reconstruction Period. He soon learns that the civil administrator (Lyle Bettger), who has moved in to Payne's former mansion, is behind most of the crooked dealings. To gain proof against Bettger, Payne signs up as his tax collector, much to the dismay of his girlfriend (Coleen Gray) and the other townspeople. After the usual setbacks and typical fights and shoot-outs, Payne straightens out the local problems. ■

Vera Cruz (1954), UA. *Dir.* Robert Aldrich; *Sc.* Roland Kibbee, James R. Webb; *Cast includes:* Gary Cooper, Burt Lancaster, Denise Darcel, Cesar Romero, George Macready.

A former Confederate officer and an American outlaw become entangled in Mexican politics and the Juaristas' attempt to rid their country of Maximilian in this cynical action drama filled with amoral characters. Gary Cooper, as the officer, and Burt Lancaster, as the outlaw, hire themselves out to guard a countess (Denise Marcel) on her journey from Mexico City to the port at Vera Cruz. However, each of the Yankees schemes to steal the gold that she is carrying. Since the Juaristas also want the gold for their struggle, several skirmishes occur along the journey. Cooper eventually switches sides and joins the revolutionists, resulting in a shoot-out with Lancaster. Cooper ends up with a pretty guerrilla fighter (Sarita Montiel). George Macready portrays the French-supported emperor of Mexico, Maximilian. Cesar Romero plays one of his officers sent along to protect the gold and the countess. ■

Veracruz, U.S. invasion of. See Mexican Revolution. ∎

Verdun, Battle of (February–September 1916). Milton Mayer in his book *If Men Were Angels* wrote of those who fought at Verdun: "Two million healthy young men . . . had been . . . handed the triumphant product of the Age of Man, the machine gun. . . . One million of them dutifully killed the other million, and when the million were dead a few hundred yards of mud and blood had changed hands a half dozen times and Death was the winner again. Mass man had met his mass master and human dignity its denudation."

Verdun, a vital fortress in northwest France, was the scene of one of the longest and most sanguinary battles of World War I. In a calculated plan to exhaust the French, Germany mounted an offensive against the fortress on February 21, 1916. Despite heavy losses on both sides, the French defenders held on to most of their territory. The British came to the aid of the French who regained most of the lost ground by December. Of the two million men who participated in the bloody clash, one million lost their lives.

No American war drama, released either during the war or in the postwar period, uses the battle as its centerpiece. Three documentaries, however, capture some of the horrors of the battle. *Somewhere in France* (1915) covers the fighting at Verdun and several other battles of World War I. Donald Thompson, who personally shot the film, was wounded at Verdun. *The Big Drive* (1933), which depicts the major events of World War I, has sequences from major battles, including Verdun. *Forgotten Men* (1933), assembled chiefly from government newsreels, shows veterans of the various campaigns—men from different countries—describing their personal experiences in battle, including that of Verdun. ∎

Veterans. In virtually every postwar period, Hollywood has romanticized the role of the returning soldier. Many postwar films, especially those related to World Wars I and II, deal with a wounded veteran whose return home is filled with apprehension. Sometimes the fear is justified when he faces the mixed reactions of his loved ones. And more often than not, Hollywood provides him with a happy ending. Two of the most prevalent screen disabilities have been blindness and the loss of a limb.

In the case of the former, the hero usually has his sight restored by some miraculous cure, as in *Havoc* (1925). Milton Sills suddenly regains his sight after being blinded in World War I in *I Want My Man*, also released in 1925. But his good fortune creates a problem for his beautiful wife (Doris Kenyon) who has convinced him when he was blind that she, too, has a handicap, a disfigured face. Earle Metcalfe, as the World War I hero of *Remember* (1927), has his sight restored after he accidentally falls down a flight of stairs. In *Pride of the Marines* (1945), a World War II drama based on the true story of Al Schmid, he is blinded while resisting a Japanese attack on Guadalcanal. John Garfield, as the marine hero, at first doesn't want to return to his fiancee. He later realizes that the war was necessary and that his fellow Americans respect the sacrifices made by so many. Arthur Kennedy in *Bright Victory* (1951) portrays a World War II veteran blinded in battle by a sniper's bullet who finally learns to adjust to civilian life.

Veterans dealing with their physical wounds gave Hollywood ample opportunity to exploit not only their anguish, struggle and ultimate victory over their handicaps but the frustrations of their faithful sweethearts who encouraged their loved ones in their hour of crisis. A former concert violinist (Gaston Glass) in *Humoresque* (1920) receives an arm wound in World War I and is unable to continue his career. When he tells his sweetheart about his misfortune, she faints. As he helps her, he realizes that he can move the afflicted arm. *The Leech* (1922), a weak World War I drama, provides the story of not one, but two, wounded veterans—brothers who are former baseball idols. One loses an arm and the other returns with a permanent leg injury. The former goes through a special government training program which helps him to obtain a job while his embittered brother decides simply to collect all the financial benefits coming to him. The highly rated World War II drama *The Men* (1950) takes the audience through several stages of the rehabilitation of a paraplegic (Marlon Brando). Jon Voight, as a Vietnam veteran in *Coming Home* (1978)—a film that explores how society deals with its veterans—suffers from the same injury as that of Brando. Voight, a disillusioned soldier, is crippled as a result of the war. Bruce Dern, as

Jane Fonda's gung-ho husband, returns from the conflict a psychologically disturbed officer. Dern's disintegration ends in his suicide. Voight chains himself and his wheelchair to a fence as a protest against the war.

Regardless of the hero's physical condition at war's end, he often finds true love in the form of his childhood sweetheart who has remained faithful, the sister of a buddy, the wife of a dead comrade or a dedicated nurse. An American (David Powell) flying for the French in World War I in *Back to Life* (1925), returns to find he has been accused of embezzlement and his wife remarried. Powell's wife, to protect the name of her husband who has been reported killed in action, marries a man who has accused Powell of theft. His face changed by plastic surgery after being wounded, Powell is finally reunited with his true love. In *Face Value* (1927) Gene Gowing's facial disfigurement does not deter his prewar sweetheart from following him to France after World War I to tell him of her love. In both the silent (1924) and sound (1945) versions of *The Enchanted Cottage*, the love of the facially disfigured hero (Richard Barthelmess, Robert Young) for a homely young woman transforms them, in at least their eyes, into attractive people. In both versions of *The Dark Angel* the blind hero, to spare his sweetheart the burden of caring for him, leaves her; but she finds him and they are reunited. One of the rare exceptions occurs in the popular World War I epic *The Big Parade* (1925) starring John Gilbert. He comes home minus one leg. After finding adjustment among his family and prewar sweetheart difficult, he returns to France to his pretty French lass he fell in love with during the conflict. The most moving and powerful story concerning a physically handicapped veteran appeared in *The Best Years of Our Lives* (1946). Harold Russell (who had lost both hands in World War II) portrays a sailor whose hands have been replaced with prosthetic devices. His reluctant and fearful return home to his parents and sweetheart is one of the most poignant sequences ever captured on screen.

Another popular affliction Hollywood exploited in its war films is amnesia. In *His Forgotten Wife* (1924) Warner Baxter suffers from loss of memory while fighting in France during World War I. He marries his nurse and returns to the U.S. with the expected complications. In *Closed Gates* (1927) John Harron loses his memory and is taken to a sanitarium near his home where a loyal family maid helps to identify him. He regains his memory once he is exposed to familiar objects from his past. *Across the Atlantic* (1928) features Monte Blue as a World War I flier who loses his memory during the conflict and is presumed dead. He regains his memory years later while flying at high altitude. One of the most successful films of this type, *Random Harvest* (1942) concerns a World War I combatant (Ronald Colman) who loses all remembrances of his past as a result of wounds suffered on the battlefield. John Hodiak, as a World War II marine, suffers from amnesia as the result of battle wounds in *Somewhere in the Night* (1946). One romantic drama, *Bonnie Annie Laurie* (1918), provides its audience and Scottish heroine (Peggy Hyland) with two afflicted lovers—an American officer suffering from loss of memory and a Scotsman who lost his sight as a result of the war. Both, of course, recover.

Sometimes the soldier is mistakenly reported killed in action when in reality he is recuperating from wounds in a hospital or prisoner-of-war camp. This causes various complications for his sweetheart who usually falls in love with someone else. Claudette Colbert, Clive Brook and Charles Boyer face this dilemma in *The Man From Yesterday* (1932). After Colbert's husband is reported dead, a doctor (Boyer) falls in love with her. Brook returns home, realizes his wife is in love with the doctor and bows out of the scene. Colbert was to suffer this trauma again in *Tomorrow Is Forever* (1946) when her husband (Orson Welles), disfigured and crippled in World War I, allows himself to be listed as killed in action. Twenty years later, after she has remarried and raised a family, she comes face-to-face with Welles again. Greer Garson in *Desire Me* (1947) portrays a French widow whose husband is reported killed in World War II. He returns five years later just as she is about to marry his army buddy. Occasionally, the wife in these films senses that her first love is not dead, as Merle Oberon does about Fredric March in *The Dark Angel* (1935). In *Puppets* (1926) the wounded fiance, who has lost his hearing, returns to find his cousin in love with his fiancee, both of whom thought the hero dead. After a fight between the rivals, the veteran's hearing is miraculously restored. June Collyer in *A Man From Wyoming* (1930) tries to forget about her doughboy husband's death by indulging in parties. When her husband (Gary Cooper) returns wounded but very much alive, he reprimands his wife for her odd behavior.

Films occasionally focused on veterans with psychological and emotional problems. Joseph Cotten in *I'll Be Seeing You* (1944) portrays a shell-shocked sergeant who has problems adjusting to civilian life. Dana Andrews in *The Best Years of Our Lives* (1946) is hit with both barrels when he returns from World War II. His wife turns out to be a tramp, and his drab drug store job results in further anxieties. *Cornered* (1945) has Dick Powell, as a Canadian soldier, pursuing an escaped Nazi war criminal who is also responsible for the murder of Powell's French bride. Similarly, Edward Albert as an ex-G.I. in *A Time to Die* (1983) hunts down six Nazis responsible for his wife's death. In *Act of Violence* (1948), another postwar revenge drama, Robert Ryan, an ex-G.I. who spent time in a prisoner-of-war camp, stalks Van Heflin, a weak fellow soldier who informed on his buddies. Ralph Meeker, as a psychotic World War II veteran in *Shadow in the Sky* (1951), poses problems for the family of his married sister, who takes him to her home. In *Cease Fire* (1985) a Vietnam veteran, haunted by his harrowing war experiences, is unable to cope with civilian life.

Some veterans who have returned from war without physical or psychological wounds are confronted with other problems. Thomas Meighan in *Civilian Clothes* (1920) returns from World War I only to find his wife disenchanted when she sees him without his uniform. A similar problem faces Robert Walker in *The Sailor Takes a Wife* (1945) when he returns home to June Allyson. Questionable restorative powers, often attributed to love, bless Hoot Gibson in *Shootin' for Love* (1923). He returns from World War I as a shell-shocked veteran who cannot tolerate loud noises. By the end of the film his condition suddenly disappears following an explosion and the rescue of his sweetheart. Gaston Glass sees his civilian life come apart when he is unable to repeat his heroic battlefield image for his wife and friends in *The Hero* (1923). *From This Day Forward* (1946), with Joan Fontaine and Mark Stevens, explores the postwar problems of a married couple, including the husband's experiences at government employment agencies. Bill Williams, as a dazed sailor in *The Clay Pi-*

geon (1949), has recently recovered from a coma in a military hospital only to find himself accused of betraying fellow prisoners of war. John Ericson, as a World War II veteran, and Pier Angeli, as his Italian bride, face a wall of prejudice when they return to his home town in *Teresa* (1951). Similarly, *Japanese War Bride* (1952) depicts the prejudice and other difficulties a couple face when a Korean War veteran (Don Taylor) brings his Japanese wife home to California.

A few veterans find that their jobs have been filled by others or that no work is available. A World War I veteran (Johnnie Hines) has trouble finding a steady job in the comedy *Sure-Fire Flint* (1922). Some former air aces are forced to seek employment in the only field they know—flying. Once again they endanger their lives, but this time for money. Such films as *The Flying Fool* (1929), *The Last Flight* (1931), *The Lost Squadron* (1932), *Lucky Devils* (1933) and *The Great Waldo Pepper* (1975) depict the exploits of former World War I aces, now cynical and embittered, engaged in such varied pursuits as barnstorming for air circuses or stunting for Hollywood war dramas. Broadway entertainer Elsie Janis portrays a World War I nurse and entertainer in *A Regular Girl* (1919) who organizes a movement to find jobs for unemployed veterans.

In some instances the veteran turns to crime. A captain in *A Man Must Live* (1925) returns from World War I shell-shocked and is forced to sell drugs to survive. Franchot Tone, a veteran of the same war in *They Gave Him a Gun* (1937), also resorts to crime. *My Buddy* (1944), one of the last films to deal with the plight of World War I veterans, has Donald Barry as an unemployed ex-doughboy entering the world of crime to help his widowed mother.

On the other hand, some films feature the main character as a criminal before he puts on Uncle Sam's khakis only to be transformed into an upstanding citizen when he returns to civilian life. In *Cradle of Courage* (1920), for example, William S. Hart, as a prewar drifter and hooligan, returns from World War I a hero only to be rejected by his mother. She thinks he has gone soft and accuses him of disgracing the family tradition!

Hollywood studios during postwar periods often simply exploit the inherent sympathy evoked by a returning soldier and place him in a plot that has very little to do with his past combat experiences. Frank Mayo, as a returning veteran in *Afraid to Fight* (1922), is under strict orders not to exert himself during his recuperation period. He does not defend himself when a local bully beats him up. However, he exacts his revenge later on. Buck Jones in *Boss of Camp 4* (1922) portrays a veteran who obtains employment as a road laborer, becomes embroiled in a few fistfights, foils a plot to stop the road construction and saves the life of the boss's daughter. In *Unguarded Women* (1924) Richard Dix, as a World War I veteran, resolves to repay a debt to a fallen comrade. He attempts to help the widow of his buddy. Many post-World War II films reflect this approach. Alan Ladd, as an ex-serviceman in *The Blue Dahlia*, returns from the war and learns that his unfaithful wife has been murdered. In *Hot Cargo* two veterans visit their dead comrade's home and remain to save his failing business. Johnny Weissmuller in *Swamp Fire*, in one of his rare non-Tarzan roles, plays a nerveshattered sailor who returns from combat to work as a freighter pilot. All three films were released in 1946.

In its concentration on the veteran as a misunderstood hero, post-World War I Hollywood contributed to the development of a new film genre—the social drama—which reached its peak in the 1930s during the Depression. In *I Am a Fugitive From a Chain Gang* (1932) Paul Muni, as a jobless Congressional Medal-of-Honor winner, is framed for a robbery and sentenced to the abuses of a Georgia chain gang. *Heroes for Sale* (1933) traces the transformation of a wounded veteran (Richard Barthelmess) from unsung war hero to pitiful hobo who joins the rag-tag army of the poor during the 1930s. Romanticizing the plight of the ex-soldier probably resulted in mixed feelings for both the adamant antiwar advocates and those who preached rearmament. The studios—consciously or unconsciously—avoided the political issues of pacifism, militarism, preparedness and other topics related to the nature of war itself. These films often underscored the disillusionment and loss of idealism on the part of the returning veteran who had to contend with an ungrateful nation. However, with the rise of Fascism and Nazism in the mid-1930s and the emergence of the Cold War in the late 1940s, the above arguments about the impact of these films became moot. The war cycle of films, with its cautionary, patriotic and propaganda themes, was to be repeated as new generations geared up for the next world conflict. ■

Via Wireless (1915), Pathe. *Dir.* George Fitzmaurice; *Cast includes:* Gail Kane, Bruce McRae, Paul McAllister.

A patriotic drama set during World War I, the story concerns a U.S. Navy lieutenant and an architect, rivals in the invention of a big gun that the War Department is interested in for coastal defense. The architect sabotages the officer's gun so that it fires with disastrous results. Following several melodramatic incidents, the villain is exposed.

The film was not without its propaganda value at a time when the American public was in the midst of a heated debate between advocates of pacifism and those who cried out for preparedness. President Wilson appears briefly in an early portion of the film as an advocate of appropriate coastal defenses. ■

Vicksburg, Battle of (May 19–July 4, 1863). When the Battle of Vicksburg began, it appeared that General Grant and his Union forces would have an easy victory. The Confederates, after several defeats in the west, had fallen back to the city on the Mississippi River, seemingly disorganized and dispirited.

But Confederate engineers had done a good job constructing strong redoubts and lines of trenches on the hilly plateau upon which the city was situated. Southern troops resisted ferociously. In one Union attack, the Rebels rolled shells with lit fuses down an embankment onto the advancing enemy. A Union company in that engagement had all but one soldier either killed or wounded in an abortive attempt to storm the Confederate defenses.

Though the Confederates held out for six weeks, Vicksburg was destined to fall. The city was cut off from supplies as Grant had encircled it with his own trenches. Toward the end of the six-week siege, Southern troops were eating mule meat, the flesh of their own pack animals. At the same time, Union warships controlled the Mississippi River, and the besieged troops were subjected to intense shelling from both naval and army artillery. The strain of battle also showed on Grant. He reportedly went on an alcoholic binge at one point but was saved from disgrace by a junior officer who smuggled his superior back to the general's tent in an ambulance.

When the Confederate flag finally came down on July 4, Grant had effectively cut the Confederacy in half. The Union now held all the major Mississippi crossings and ports except one, Port Hudson, to the south in Louisiana. That town fell soon afterward when its defenders heard of Vicksburg's capitulation. The Union now controlled the entire length of the Mississippi from New Orleans northward. Along with the city, Grant took 31,000 prisoners and thousands of small arms and cannons. His victory at Vicksburg helped him gain overall command of the Union armies the following year.

Vicksburg has been alluded to in several Civil War films. "The Girl Spy Before Vicksburg" (1911), one of the earliest, is a short one-reel silent that tells little about the battle. *The Crisis* (1915), which includes portrayals of several historical figures including Lincoln and General Sherman, has as one of its highlights a re-enactment of the siege of Vicksburg. John Ford's *The Horse Soldiers* (1959), starring John Wayne, is based on an actual Civil War incident. In April of 1863, General Grant assigned Colonel Benjamin Grierson to journey 300 miles into Confederate territory to demolish the rail link between Newton Station and Vicksburg. Grierson and his three cavalry regiments, a force of 1,700 men, succeeded in their mission; they rode 600 miles in a little more than two weeks and returned safely to Union lines. ■

Victorio. See *Apache Drums* (1951). ■

Victors, The (1963), Col. *Dir.* Carl Foreman; *Sc.* Carl Foreman; *Cast includes:* George Hamilton, George Peppard, Eli Wallach, Vince Edwards, Rosanna Schiaffino.

A powerful depiction of the effects of war on both the victor and the vanquished, this sprawling World War II drama is penetrating in its point of view. The story follows an American infantry company from the Italian campaign to the collapse of Germany and the occupation period in Berlin. The G.I.s range from those who care about an abandoned dog or a refugee cowering in fear from a bombardment to those who brutally beat up fellow soldiers whose skin is black. George Hamilton, as a gentlemanly infantryman, is shunned by a young woman (Romy Schneider) who prefers the more glib, coarser Americans. He later beds a young German whose parents give her to him in return for food. George Peppard, as another G.I., has an affair with one of the major dealers in the Belgian black market. Eli Wallach plays a sergeant who shows compassion for his men and for the victims of war. He lands in a hospital after part of his face is blown away. The action sequences are stark and realistic. They range from the execution of an American deserter while the soundtrack plays Christmas music to the destruction of a German pillbox by a war-scarred French soldier who refuses to acknowledge the enemy's white flag. ■

Victory (1981), Par. *Dir.* John Huston; *Sc.* Evan Jones, Yabo Yablonsky; *Cast includes:* Sylvester Stallone, Michael Caine, Pele, Max Von Sydow, Daniel Massey, Carole Laure.

An international cast was assembled for this implausible World War II drama about a soccer game between Allied prisoners of war and their German captors. The film takes place chiefly in a prison camp inside German territory. The German high command initiates the competition for propaganda purposes. Max Von Sydow, as a German major and soccer enthusiast, says to his commanding officer: "In all these years we have never beaten England." Michael Caine, as Captain John Colby, an English soccer coach, agrees for several reasons. All members of the team will be given better diets, including meat, eggs and fresh vegetables. Above all, he has a chance of getting a handful of former East European players out of slave labor camps—at least, temporarily. While the team practices for the big game to be held in a Paris stadium, an American prisoner (Sylvester Stallone) escapes and agrees to contact the Paris underground about effecting the escape of the entire team. He meets with the French Resistance and plans are made to rescue the players during half-time. But Stallone must return to instruct the team. At first he balks, then reluctantly agrees to get caught.

The game takes place as scheduled, but at the moment set for the escape, the team decides to stay to try to beat the Germans, who are leading with a score of 4–1. The referees are all Germans, and they have received their orders to call each play in favor of the Fatherland. "We cannot afford to take a chance," a German officer says to the disappointed Von Sydow. "We must win." Once again, Stallone postpones his escape. The Allied team plays brilliantly and ties the game with a final score of 4-4. The French spectators, ecstatic over the comeback, swarm over the playing field, encircle each player and sweep the entire team out of the stadium. The German guards, unable to control the huge crowds, look on helplessly.

There is at least one effective note of irony in the film. As the German officers at the French stadium await the Allied team, they deliberate over which team should get which dressing room. One officer asks Von Sydow: "Germany is the home team, wouldn't you agree?" "Politically, historically?" he replies. "I'd rather not make that decision." ■

Victory at Sea (1954), NBC. *Sc.* Henry Salomon, Richard Hanser.

Based on the National Broadcasting Company's 26-part television series, the 97-minute documentary captures the significant highlights of the original 13 hours in its presentation of the global sea war between the Allies and the Axis Powers. The film early establishes Japan's reliance on its Imperial navy as World War II spreads from the Pacific to the Arctic and to the Mediterranean. The surprise attack at Pearl Harbor sent the U.S. Navy reeling, and it was not until eight months after that bombing that the U.S. went on the offensive at Guadalcanal. The film also covers the British battles in the Mediterranean, Germany's submarine warfare in the Atlantic, the collapse of Italy and the Normandy landing.

Alexander Scourby's narration is both literate and informative as the focus shifts from one war zone to the next. Japan's early victories in the Pacific are soon offset by the heavy toll the Allies exacted from its ships and men. Japan lost six million tons of vital supplies and equipment, including 1,300 ships. One of the more fascinating scenes shows a ship capsizing and suddenly exploding, hurtling both crew and debris toward the sky. Also effective is Japan's devastating kamikaze attack on American ships in its last-ditch effort to stem the allied advances in the Pacific. The film ends with the dropping of the atom bombs and the liberation of the Nazi death camps in Europe. In the latter sequence the camera moves from one emaciated victim to another. "Man vilified, man broken," the narrator announces. "This is society at its blackest depth, the human cost that no statistics can ever suggest." The final shots are of

American servicemen sailing home. "The ships that sailed away to war and death," Scourby summarizes, "bring back their millions to peace and life. To these men and to their allies, free men everywhere owe their victory on land, their victory in the air, their victory at sea." ■

Victory of Conscience, The (1916), Par. *Dir.* George Melford, Frank Reicher; *Sc.* Margaret Turnbull; *Cast includes:* Lou Tellegen, Cleo Ridgley, Elliot Dexter, Laura Woods Cushing.

A World War I drama of redemption, Lou Tellegen at first portrays a bon vivant who lures a naive country girl to Paris. But when she discovers his intentions, she leaves him and becomes an entertainer in an underworld cafe. Meanwhile her former lover physically attacks Tellegen who then suffers from amnesia. When he recovers, he joins the priesthood and has an opportunity to save the luckless young woman from her immoral life. She enters a convent. When war breaks out, he enlists in the army and, during a retreat, volunteers to stay behind near a field hospital where the young woman he had rescued is now engaged as a nurse. Both are killed when a shell explodes near them. ■

Victory Through Air Power (1943), UA. *Dir.* H. C. Potter.

Walt Disney produced this World War II animated documentary that advocates the principles set out by Major Alexander P. de Seversky in his best-seller on how to beat the Nazis and the Japanese Empire through the use of airplanes. The film begins with a history of aviation and proceeds to show how air power was used effectively by Nazi Germany. The final sequences outline how the Allies could use this same strategy to defeat the Axis powers. Live sequences of de Seversky are included to add authenticity to the presentation. The film is dedicated to Billy Mitchell, who first promoted the idea that air power can be a highly effective force during combat.

Historically, the film is more noteworthy for its creativity than for the major's ideas and prophecies, which included that the war would last well into 1948. He also argued that Japan and Germany were better situated geographically than the Allies were. By the end of 1943, many of his theories were proven wrong.

Major de Seversky served in the Imperial Russian Air Force during World War I and lost a leg in combat. In the U.S. during the 1930s, he developed a series of modern aircraft designs. During World War II he co-designed the famed P-47 fighter escort, known as the Thunderbolt. His ideas of air warfare, which he updated from an Italian theorist, were published in his book, *Victory Through Air Power*. The Allied war strategy, however, took a different turn and never utilized his major theses. ∎

Vietnam War (1956–1975). Six American military advisers to the government of South Vietnam, officially the Republic of Vietnam, were watching a movie on the evening of July 8, 1959, in a camp outside Bienhoa. During an intermission, when the lights were switched on, a burst of automatic gunfire came through an open window and cut down two of the soldiers along with several South Vietnamese. They were the first American casualties of the thousands that would eventually die in the U.S. phase of the Vietnam War.

At the time of their deaths, the two were part of a limited U.S. advisory presence that began in 1956. Until 1961, American troops never numbered more than the 700 allowed by the Geneva Accords (1954), the agreement that had split Vietnam at the 17th Parallel into a Communist-dominated regime in the North and a quasi-democratic U.S.-backed administration in the South.

Following France's defeat in the French Indo-China War of 1946–1954 and the withdrawal of its troops from its former colony, the U.S. increased its economic and military support to an anti-Communist government in the South in the hope of stopping the spread of Communism. Elections for a unified Vietnamese government, part of the Geneva Accords, were never held; American and South Vietnamese officials feared that the Communists would easily win. A Communist-inspired guerrilla war broke out anew in 1956 and the conflict slowly turned into a military and political pit of quicksand for the U.S., pulling the nation ever deeper into the dispute.

Retaliation and escalation by each side grew so that by 1968 the war had become "Americanized" with slightly more than 500,000 U.S. troops in Vietnam. By the end of the struggle, America had suffered 56,552 dead and was split domestically into a polar-ized citizenry, highlighted by massive anti-war demonstrations and student riots against continued involvement. Vietnam itself sustained close to four million dead and wounded, including soldiers and civilians, that represented almost 10 percent of its population. The war was a perplexing tragedy for all.

In response to growing Communist activity, the U.S. in 1961 increased its military presence and allowed American soldiers acting as advisers to join in the fight when their units were attacked. American military involvement escalated again in 1964. Following a reported attack by the North Vietnamese on two American destroyers in the Gulf of Tonkin, President Johnson ordered the bombing of North Vietnam. The arrival of 3,500 U.S. Marines to guard the air base at Danang in 1965 marked the first time that American ground troops were officially committed to combat.

The war spread beyond Vietnam into Cambodia and Laos when the Communist North Vietnamese used these areas as supply dumps and as part of the Ho Chi Minh trail to send supplies and reinforcements to the fighting in the South. Except for a few key battles, most American actions were "search and destroy" missions that featured fighting under harsh jungle conditions, often surrounded by a populace that sympathized with and harbored the enemy. *Platoon* (1986) graphically depicted this phase of the war.

In 1968 the U.S. Marine base at Khe Sanh came under heavy attack. The documentary *Dear America: Letters From Vietnam* (1988) highlighted the assault on Khe Sanh. That same year the Communists demonstrated their strength by conducting powerful, sustained raids against a large number of cities, including Hue and Saigon, as part of the Tet offensive. *Full Metal Jacket* (1987) focused on the Tet offensive. The U.S. tried to separate the Communist troops from the peasants by moving the South Vietnamese into villages ringed by barbed wire. During much of the war, South Vietnam's government underwent a number of military coups.

By 1969, the U.S. could no longer ignore growing antiwar dissatisfaction at home, and newly elected President Richard Nixon instituted a policy of "Vietnamization," turning over more of the conduct of the war to the South Vietnamese while undertaking a phased withdrawal of American forces. A tenuous cease-fire existed between 1973–1974, but as American strength declined, the Communists, in January 1975, launched a concerted drive to take over the last areas still under control of the South Vietnamese government. Remaining American officials and forces fled by sea and air. *The Deer Hunter* (1978) captured some of the chaos during these last days. On April 30, 1975, the government of South Vietnam surrendered unconditionally to the Communists.

The conflict left in its wake bitter memories of a nation torn asunder, an ally abandoned, a U.S. withdrawal seen as less than honorable and brave young men returning home to be ignored and even ostracized. The American people were more than anxious to forget the debacle and those who fought in it.

Because of the extensive television coverage of the Vietnam War, the conflict was often referred to as the country's first "living room war." While the war raged, Hollywood's major studios were reluctant to tackle such a controversial and unpopular conflict. Major filmmakers, instead, continued to produce large-scale productions about World War II, a "safer" and more popular war. Except for a few isolated films like *The Green Berets* (1968), which some critics suggested had more in common with World War II than with the conflict in Southeast Asia, the Vietnam War remained ignored by the big studios until the late 1970s.

But the effects of the Vietnam War upon society could not be ignored for long, especially in such a popular art form as the film. Growing feelings of cynicism and disillusionment, instead of being directed toward the Vietnam experience, emerged in films about World War II. "I sometimes wonder which side God is on," John Wayne ponders in *The Longest Day* (1962). In *The Bridge at Remagen* (1969) a conscience-stricken German officer (Robert Vaughn), who refuses to blow up a strategic bridge until all his troops are safely across, is sentenced to death for his actions. "Who is the enemy?" he asks before he is shot.

Hollywood reduced the noble causes of World War II to an exercise in pure violence and brutality in *The Dirty Dozen* (1967), suggesting perhaps, that war is best fought by convicted rapists and murderers. The enemy became less clear and had many faces. British Intelligence agents in *Moritori* (1965) threaten to turn in a German Jew (Marlon Brando) to the Nazis unless he spies for them.

Vietnam War-related films from independent and smaller studios were the first to touch upon certain controversial aspects of the conflict. The C.I.A.'s involvement in Vietnam was explored in two films. A relatively young Burt Reynolds, portraying a C.I.A. agent in *Operation CIA* (1965), is sent to Saigon during the Vietnam War to investigate the murder of a fellow agent. The implausible action drama *The Losers* (1970), rife with anti-American commentary, had the U.S. government hiring a motley gang of motorcyclists to rescue a C.I.A. agent whom the North Vietnamese were holding captive in Cambodia. *AWOL* (1972) featured Russ Thacker as an American deserter who escapes to Denmark where he works with other expatriates to end the war. In the violence-oriented action drama *Rolling Thunder* (1977) William Devane, as a Vietnam war veteran, leaves the violence of war only to find it at home when he witnesses the murder of his wife and son and sets out to find the killers.

By the late 1980s the Vietnam experience on film had fallen into two major categories—the action drama filled with violence, revenge and cartoon-like characters, and the realistic drama which attempted to portray the physical hardships, psychological trauma and general horror that young Americans had to live through in Vietnam. Both became popular with audiences for different reasons and sparked discussion and criticism.

The action dramas, as represented by such performers as Sylvester Stallone (*Rambo: First Blood Part II*) and Chuck Norris (*Missing in Action*, Parts I–III), had their super-heroes, using an arsenal of exotic weapons that included bows and explosive arrows, wreaking havoc on Vietnam prison camps and sadistic guards. They suggested to those back home that the struggle is far from over. In these lurid tales, the hero battles against overwhelming odds and emerges victorious. The plots and heroics had more in common with World War II movies of the 1940s than with the actual Vietnam encounter.

Realistic films of the war tried to evoke the look and feel of the Vietnam experience, sometimes through surrealistic sequences. Francis Ford Coppola in *Apocalypse Now* (1979) turned to Joseph Conrad's writings to explore the "heart of darkness" in each of us as he unfolds the horrors of the Vietnam War through a series of bizarre and frightening visions. *Platoon* hinted at the ambiguities of the war. It also covered the atrocities perpetrated by battle-weary and frustrated grunts who witness their buddies blown to bits by a vicious and often unseen enemy. Furthermore, it underscored the idea that the war was fought mostly by Americans who were poor or not clever enough to avoid the draft—young-old men who cared more about surviving than fighting for a cause. *Hamburger Hill* (1987) stressed the futility of the conflict by showing repeated attacks on the same hill. A month after the hill is captured, at a high cost in American lives, it is abandoned.

Even those dramas set partly or entirely in the States attained a high degree of realism by focusing on dialogue, characterization or the mood of the period. In *Coming Home* (1978) Jon Voight, as an embittered paraplegic veteran, encounters new enemies at home—the Veterans' Administration and a society that has turned its back on those who fought, bled and died in the war. *The Deer Hunter* (1978) traced the Vietnam exploits of three blue-collar workers and their friends who are completely overwhelmed by the meaning of the war. Its use of Russian roulette in two long, tension-filled scenes, served as a metaphor for the hideousness and senselessness of war and became a much-debated issue among critics and viewers alike. *Combat Shock* (1986) featured Ricky Giovinazzo as an ex-soldier haunted by nightmares of his part in a Vietnam massacre not unlike that at MyLai. *Full Metal Jacket*, Stanley Kubrick's personal and haunting vision of the war, emphasized the themes of dehumanization and aggression that accompany war. The opening scenes in boot camp in which a single-minded sergeant devotes himself to turning a group of raw recruits into killing machines were both harrowing and provocative.

The Vietnam experience had finally touched the conscience of Hollywood in the 1980s as shown by the sudden explosion of films on the subject. Some handled their subject matter artistically, if brutally. The better ones suggested the uniqueness of the war, the failure of our leaders to see the hopelessness of it all and the frustrations and anguish of those who fought in Southeast Asia. The complexities of the conflict at home and abroad have only begun to be explored. More than 50 documentaries and Vietnam War-related dramas were released from the beginning of the conflict through the 1980s. Others are sure to follow. Some will approach the subject intelligently and sensitively; others no doubt will exploit the topic. Hopefully, a few will provide fresh insight into what many feel was an American tragedy. ■

Vikings, The (1958), UA. *Dir.* Richard Fleischer; *Sc.* Calder Willingham; *Cast includes:* Kirk Douglas, Tony Curtis, Ernest Borgnine, Janet Leigh, James Donald, Alexander Knox.

The violent raids of the Vikings upon England's Kingdom of Northumbria during the eighth and ninth centuries provide the background of this action drama. Kirk Douglas portrays the brutal leader of the dreaded Vikings. Tony Curtis, as a Viking slave, in reality is the son of an English queen and the half-brother of Douglas. In a clash between the two, Curtis directs his falcon to attack the Viking leader. The creature gouges out one of Douglas' eyes. As a result, Curtis is thrown into a pit from which he escapes. Janet Leigh, as the daughter of an English ruler, is promised to the English king but is captured by Douglas who desires her. However, she falls in love with Curtis in this convoluted plot. Several bloody battles, excitingly staged, have little to do with historical events.

Proficient shipbuilders and seafarers, the Vikings were Scandinavian pirates who carried out raids in Europe and Britain in the 8th to 11th centuries. Once they began establishing colonies in Europe, they affected the social and political growth of the continent by promoting feudalism. The Vikings were steeped in mythology which influenced their religion and literature. Few American films explored this historical period. The highly fictional 1928 silent drama *The Viking* dealt with the voyages of Eric the Red and Leif Ericson to Greenland and the New World. ■

Villa, Francisco "Pancho" (1877–1923). The popular revolutionist had been a bandit before he joined Francisco Madero's revolution in 1910 against the dictator Diaz. He later allied himself to Venustiano Carranza who, together with Emiliano Zapata, opposed and ultimately overthrew Huerta, who in turn had replaced Madero. Carranza, Villa and Zapata sought some form of democracy and land reforms. Carranza became president (1914–1920) and effected several reforms but not enough to satisfy his former allies. Villa and Zapata, more interested in a decentralized state and local self-government, grew disillusioned with Carranza and took up arms against him. When the U.S. intervened on the side of Carranza, Villa responded by raiding American border towns in 1916 and killing several U.S. citizens. This resulted in a punitive expedition by General "Black Jack" Pershing that same year against the revolutionary leader. But Villa remained active until 1920. In 1923 he was assassinated.

Hollywood turned out several sympathetic biographies of Villa. *The Life of General Villa* (1914), one of the earliest attempts to portray the Mexican leader on screen, covers the events that led to his becoming a revolutionist and his eventual battles with government troops. However, the definitive film of his exploits, *Viva Villa*, appeared in 1934, with Wallace Beery playing the title character. The plot depicts Villa's motivations for turning against the ruthless Mexican regime and his fondness for the idealistic but impotent Madero. *Villa Rides* (1968), starring Yul Brynner as Villa, is loosely based on the Mexican revolutionist's exploits. He is seen as defender of the peasants' human rights but a brutal foe of those he considers traitors. See also Mexican Revolution. ∎

Villa Rides (1968), Par. *Dir.* Buzz Kulik; *Sc.* Robert Towne, Sam Peckinpah; *Cast includes:* Yul Brynner, Robert Mitchum, Grazia Buccella, Charles Bronson, Diana Lorys.

Yul Brynner portrays the legendary Mexican bandit leader Pancho Villa in this biographical drama set in strife-torn Mexico at the turn of the century. Villa is portrayed as a defender of human rights although he is not averse to ordering the deaths of numerous adversaries he quickly labels "traitors." Alexander Knox portrays President Madero, a tragic figure who dreams of peace but is forced to wield raw power to expedite his ends. Herbert Lom plays the treacherous General Huerta, Villa's heavy-drinking superior officer. Robert Mitchum, as an American pilot and soldier-of-fortune, allies himself with the bandit leader. Charles Bronson plays one of Villa's sadistic aides who enjoys killing. Grazia Buccella provides the amorous attraction for Mitchum. Action sequences include large-scale battles between Pancho Villa's ragtag army and government troops. Both sides are particularly vicious, a film trend which may have begun in *Alvarez Kelly*, released two years earlier. This Civil War drama depicted both the South and the North as ruthless.

Much of *Villa Rides*, obviously, is pure fiction. Aside from the inclusion of historical figures, one of the more accurate portrayals is that of Villa as a fighter for the rights of villagers. Like Zapata and other leaders, Villa was part of the agrarian revolution that sought, through local self-rule, to restore village rights to lands, forests and waters. This was only one phase of the Revolution of 1910–1921. The aims of these legendary chiefs ultimately failed in favor of a larger, national revolution initiated by Madero and continued by Carranza. It swept across Mexico and resulted in a modern, centralized state. ∎

Villon, Francois. See *If I Were King* (1938). ∎

Virginia City (1940), WB. *Dir.* Michael Curtiz; *Sc.* Robert Buckner; *Cast includes:* Errol Flynn, Miriam Hopkins, Randolph Scott, Humphrey Bogart, Frank McHugh, Alan Hale.

Errol Flynn stars in this Civil War western in which he prevents a wagon train of gold from reaching Confederate lines. Miriam Hopkins plays a Confederate spy who poses as a saloon singer in Virginia City and who falls in love with Flynn. Randolph Scott portrays a Southerner who is in charge of the operation of moving the gold through Union lines. Alan Hale, as Flynn's sidekick, provides the usual comic relief. The conventional plot provides plenty of hard riding and gunplay. ∎

Viva Max! (1969), CU. *Dir.* Jerry Paris; *Sc.* Elliot Baker; *Cast includes:* Peter Ustinov, Pamela Tiffin, Jonathan Winters, John Astin, Keenan Wynn.

An eccentric Mexican general and his ragtag platoon recapture the Alamo in this weak, zany comedy set in the present. Under the guise of marching in a holiday parade, Peter Ustinov, as the upstart general, leads his Mexican troops across the border into Texas. John Astin portrays his sergeant. Pamela Tiffin, as a revolutionary college student, is disillusioned with the physical appearance of this general who has dared to challenge the establishment. An incompetent American force, led by the bungling Jonathan Winters and Harry Morgan, is dispatched to rout the invaders from the historic site. ■

Viva Villa! (1934), MGM. *Dir.* Jack Conway; *Sc.* Ben Hecht; *Cast includes:* Wallace Beery, Leo Carrillo, Fay Wray, Donald Cook, Stuart Erwin, George E. Stone.

A chiefly fictional biography of the legendary bandit and guerrilla leader, the film begins in the turbulent 1880s with a foreword that describes Mexico's present ruler, Diaz, as a tyrant. Peons are evicted from their land and homes and whipped if they protest. It is under such conditions that Pancho Villa as a boy sees his father beaten to death. Wallace Beery portrays Villa, who has grown up and, leading a band of outlaws, seeks revenge against the government. Francisco Madero, leader of the revolutionary forces bent on ousting the Diaz regime, meets with Villa and penetrates the bandit's tough exterior with visions of a free Mexico. Villa is impressed with Madero and, putting aside his personal vengeance, promises the political leader to fight alongside the rebel generals.

Ben Hecht's script, mixing some fact and plenty of fiction, tends to glorify Villa, painting him more as a patriotic hero than a lawless marauder that contemporary newspaper accounts labeled him. There are several effective battle sequences as well as a few brutal ones. In one scene Beery orders an adversary, a corrupt general, to be smeared with honey and devoured by ants. Villa's second-in-command (Leo Carrillo) seems to enjoy the battles and the slaughter. Stuart Erwin portrays an American journalist who follows Villa's tempestuous career while exploiting the newsworthiness of the Mexican bandit. A hero to his people during the revolution, Villa disbands his army when Madero, the new President, asks him to. Villa senses he is no longer the fighting patriot whose exploits dominated the front pages. "I ain't news no more?" he asks Erwin, somewhat crestfallen. "You're better than news," Erwin replies. "You're history!" After Madero is assassinated, Villa returns from exile in the U.S. and raises another peasant army. He defeats those in power and rides into Mexico City in triumph. The film ends with his assassination by a disgruntled aristocrat.

No mention is made of America's political entanglements in the affairs of Mexico during this period. There is no reference, for example, to the unsuccessful punitive expedition against Villa, led by General Pershing and ordered by President Wilson, following the bandit leader's raid in New Mexico. The reporter whom Erwin plays is allegedly based on the real-life Hearst correspondent John W. Roberts, who accompanied the Mexican leader on his campaigns. The role was originally assigned to Lee Tracy, whose public drunkenness in Mexico compelled the studio to cancel his contract. ■

Viva Zapata! (1952), TCF. *Dir.* Elia Kazan; *Sc.* John Steinbeck; *Cast includes:* Marlon Brando, Jean Peters, Anthony Quinn, Joseph Wiseman, Arnold Moss.

John Steinbeck's strong screenplay and Elia Kazan's expert direction reveal the problem of the futility of revolution where leaders are corrupted by the power that places and keeps them in office. A biographical drama of Emiliano Zapata, covering the years 1908–1918, a period which overlaps the Mexican Revolution of 1910–1921, the film stars Marlon Brando as the Mexican revolutionary leader and hero. The exiled political leader, Madero, played by Harold Gordon, appoints Zapata, a peasant farmer, one of his generals.

Following a bitter struggle in which the revolutionary forces triumph, Zapata appeals for the long-delayed land reforms. But Madero, now the President of Mexico, hesitates, stating that such matters take time. "You know what this is, General?" Madero asks evasively, displaying an impressive map. "This is your ranch." "I did not fight for a ranch," Zapata insists, rejecting the bribe. Sensing that Madero is a pawn in the hands of his military advisers, the disillusioned Zapata leaves for home. Madero, fearing an armed peasantry, requests that Zapata and his men surrender their weapons. "And who will enforce the laws?" Zapata asks. "The regular army, the police," the President replies. "They're the ones we just fought and beat!" Zapata cries out in frustration. Anthony Quinn (who won an Oscar as Best Supporting Actor), as Zapata's emotional brother, becomes corrupted by the wars and killings and turns into a drunken bully.

When Madero is assassinated, Zapata joins forces with Pancho Villa and is handed the reins of government. But he resigns, finding the office too burdensome. The military officers, fearing that Zapata is a threat to their power, plot his assassination. Zapata rides into an ambush and is gunned down by a hail of buttets. The film suggests that political power lies directly with the people themselves. Zapata, too honest to cope with the duplicity of venal politicians and corrupt self-seekers, is disillusioned by individual leaders. "You always look for leaders," he admonishes his people, "strong men without faults. There aren't any. There are only men like ourselves. There are no leaders but yourselves. A strong people is the only lasting strength."

The film captures the spirit of the real-life Mexican leader. Like Pancho Villa, Zapata dreamed of and fought for self-rule in a decentralized Mexico where villagers, especially the Indians he represented, would have the rights to their lands and waters restored to them. These ideals, manifested in successful but local revolutions within Mexico, were soon replaced by a larger, national revolt which culminated in a centralized national modern state. ■

Vive La France (1918), Par. *Dir.* R. William Neill; *Sc.* H. H. Van Loan; *Cast includes:* Edmund Lowe, Dorothy Dalton, Frederick Starr, Thomas Guise.

In this World War I drama Dorothy Dalton portrays a French actress working in America whose parents have been murdered by the Germans during their invasion of France. She returns to her native country and is captured and tortured by a brutal, sadistic German captain. Edmund Lowe portrays a French cinematographer with whom she had worked in the past but who is now fighting with the French forces. ■

Voice in the Wind (1944), UA. *Dir.* Arthur Ripley; *Sc.* Frederick Torberg; *Cast includes:* Francis Lederer, Sigrid Gurie, J. Edward Bromberg, J. Carrol Naish.

The tragic life of a Czech concert pianist is depicted in this bleak World War II film. Francis Lederer portrays a musician who defies the Nazi invaders who have recently occupied his country. Although the German authorities have banned the playing of Smetana's "Moldau," Lederer decides to play it anyway and is condemned to a concentration camp. His sweetheart (Sigrid Gurie) leaves the country before he is arrested. On the way to the camp, he manages to escape and ends up working for two unscrupulous brothers who engage in smuggling. Eventually he is reunited with his wife who is seriously ill. The despondent pianist is mortally wounded during a knife fight. The two lovers die in each other's arms. ■

Voice of Terror, The (1942). See Detectives at War. ■

Volga Boatman, The (1926), PDC. *Dir.* Cecil B. DeMille; *Sc.* Lenore J. Coffee; *Cast includes:* William Boyd, Elinor Fair, Victor Varconi, Julia Faye, Theodore Kosloff.

William Boyd portrays the title character in this drama set just before the Russian Revolution. As a serf destined, along with a handful of others, to pull barges along the banks, Boyd leads the men in the "Song of the Volga Boatman," which promises them freedom and a better life. Princess Vera (Elinor Fair), on a picnic with Prince Dimitri (Victor Varconi), one pleasant afternoon, wanders over to the boatmen on their short break and becomes interested in Boyd, who treats the aristocrats with scorn. Later, at the height of the Revolution, Boyd is promoted by a Red general because of his work in organizing the boatmen. As the leader of a cadre of civilian fighters, he storms the home of Princess Vera and her father and sentences her to death. But when he is alone with her, he has a change of heart and saves her life. Some of the highlights of the film include the shelling of a palace where a huge wall crashes down on a group of aristocrats and a scene in which several surviving noblemen and women, all of whom are dressed in their evening clothes, are tied to a barge and forced to pull it to the Red army's headquarters. The film was remade in 1938 in France with French and Russian talent. ■

Volunteer, The (1917), World. *Dir.* Harley Knoles; *Sc.* Julia Burnham; *Cast includes:* Madge Evans, Montagu Love, Carlyle Blackwell, Kitty Gordon, Evelyn Greeley.

A propaganda film promoting recruitment, the drama opens during World War I and depicts how a Quaker family reconciles themselves to their only son going off to war. Madge Evans portrays the daughter of an army officer and a mother who is a Red Cross nurse departing for the front. The film anticipates a similar situation in *Friendly Persuasion* (1956), a Civil War drama starring Gary Cooper as the patriarch of a Quaker family seeking to retain its beliefs during the conflict. ■

German soldiers assist Allied prisoners of war from a burning train during World War II. *Von Ryan's Express* (1965).

Von Richthofen and Brown (1971), UA. *Dir.* Roger Corman; *Sc.* John and Joyce Corrington; *Cast includes:* John Phillip Law, Don Stroud, Barry Primus, Karen Huston.

This weak World War I action drama traces the spectacular military career of Germany's famous air ace, Baron Von Richthofen, and the parallel story of the Canadian flier who eventually shot him down. John Phillip Law portrays the Baron who finds his niche as his country's top flier. "It's the hunt I find most satisfying," he replies to a question about how he feels while in combat, "and finally the kill." His counterpart, Roy Brown, a former Canadian wheat farmer who sees the war as just another job that has to be done, runs into conflict with his fellow airmen who see themselves as noble knights. When they offer a toast to Von Richthofen, Brown refuses to join them. "We believe that men can become enemies without becoming beasts," his major explains. "Those who survive will find they still have need of those traditions that separate gentlemen from savages." Unmoved

by these words, Brown replies: "I'll save my wine for the next 'gentleman' your German knight blasts out of the sky."

As the war grows more violent—and especially when one of their buddies is shot in the back while leaving his plane—the British pilots begin to understand Brown's attitude toward the conflict. "I'm just a technician," Brown responds to a newspaper reporter. "I change things. Put a plane and a man in it in front of me and I change them to wreck and a corpse." Meanwhile, Von Richthofen maintains the traditions of combat as it relates to the past. "You were seen strafing medical personnel," he fumes at a young Hermann Goering, an overly enthusiastic flier (Barry Primus). "I did my duty," the pilot replies scornfully. "You're not a soldier, you're an assassin!" the Baron returns. "I make war to win," Goering protests. "It doesn't matter how." The film includes an abundance of aerial dogfights with aircraft that seem authentic. But the overall effect of the work is less than satisfying. ■

Von Ryan's Express (1965), TCF. *Dir.* Mark Robson; *Sc.* Wendell Mayes, Joseph Landon; *Cast includes:* Frank Sinatra, Trevor Howard, Raffaellla Carra, Brad Dexter, Sergio Fantoni.

This World War II drama centers around a mass escape of hundreds of Allied prisoners of war. Frank Sinatra plays an American colonel whose plane has been shot down over Italy. He is taken to a prison camp under the control of Italians. Since he is the senior Allied officer (the previous British commander died under harsh treatment), he reluctantly assumes command and makes several radical changes that irk a high-strung British major (Trevor Howard). The Italian guards, hearing that Allied troops are advancing, abandon their posts during the night, leaving the prisoners free. Sinatra leads them into the hills, but German troops quickly round them up and put them aboard a train for Austria. Sinatra, Howard and a handful of other prisoners break through the floorboards of their car, succeed in capturing the train and divert it to the Swiss border and freedom.

The film provides a fair number of tense moments as the train pulls into various stations where the escaped prisoners must impersonate German officers. They are faced with other obstacles—a German troop train following in hot pursuit and enemy planes sent to cut off the escape of the captured train. Friction between Sinatra and Howard emerges early in the film when the British major accuses the American of collaborating with the enemy. He calls Sinatra, whose name is Ryan, "von Ryan." Bits of humor are interjected from time to time, notably from the British chaplain (Edward Mulhare). When the prisoners capture the train, they find the German officer's mistress aboard. She is a young Italian girl dressed only in a negligee. "What are you doing here, my child?" the chaplain asks in surprise and innocence. "You are a pragmatist," Howard quips as the other officers smile. Later, the chaplain, who speaks fluent German, is persuaded by Sinatra and Howard to impersonate the German officer in charge of the trainload of prisoners, resulting in some humorous moments. ■

W

WAC From Walla Walla, The (1952). See Service Comedy. ■

Wackiest Ship in the Army, The (1960), Col. *Dir.* Richard Murphy; *Sc.* Richard Murphy; *Cast includes:* Jack Lemmon, Ricky Nelson, John Lund, Chips Rafferty, Tom Tully.

A broken-down sailing ship is resurrected for a secret mission in the South Pacific in this World War II comedy. The skipper of the foundering vessel, a navy lieutenant (Jack Lemmon), is assigned to train the new crew of misfits and make the U.S.S. *Echo* seaworthy within a few days. After seeing the craft, he balks at the assignment but is manipulated into accepting it by his superior officer. Ricky Nelson plays his naive ensign. Mike Kellin portrays the humorous chief mate who has difficulties learning the essential nautical terms. Eventually Lemmon grows fond of the *Echo* and its motley crew, defending both when other officers pass derogatory remarks.

The mission of the *Echo* is to transport an Australian scout to a Japanese-occupied island where he will spy on enemy ship movements. Lemmon and his men encounter enemy troops, including a Japanese officer, a graduate of U.C.L.A. During the ensuing skirmish, the *Echo* is struck by enemy fire and sinks. The crew escapes in a small boat. The film maintains its comic tone throughout while keeping the seriousness of the war at a minimum. It may not be as funny as a similar feature, *Operation Petticoat*—directed by Blake Edwards and starring Cary Grant and Tony Curtis, released a year earlier—but it provides enough humorous situations to make it an acceptable comedy. The plot is based on an actual event that occurred during the war. ■

Wagon Box Raid. See Sioux Wars, *Tomahawk* (1951). ■

Wake Island (1942), Par. *Dir.* John Farrow; *Sc.* W. R. Burnett, Frank Butler; *Cast includes:* Brian Donlevy, Robert Preston, Macdonald Carey, Barbara Britton, William Bendix, Albert Dekker.

The film is a respectable tribute to the 385 American marines who perished defending Wake Island in the first weeks of World War II. Brian Donlevy plays the cool-headed commander of the brave defenders who undergo continuous air raids and shellings as the Japanese pound the island. The small detachment of leathernecks then braces itself as the Japanese land troops on the island. When the enemy requests that the defenders surrender, the hard-bitten Donlevy scornfully replies: "Tell 'em to come and get us!" Wave after wave of enemy troops attack the tenacious marines who resist until they are finally overrun by the invaders.

Robert Preston and William Bendix, as two good-natured, bickering marines, add comic relief throughout, even during the devastating bombardment. Preston cries out that the enemy are blowing them to bits. "What d'ya care?" Bendix challenges his buddy in pugnacious Brooklynese. "It ain't your island, is it?"

Earlier in the film Bendix, remarking about sergeants, says: "The dumber those guys are, the more stripes they get." "Then you ought to look like a zebra," Preston quips. Albert Dekker plays a pugnacious civilian construction engineer who resents military interference but soon joins Donlevy in defending the island against the Japanese. A fighter pilot (Macdonald Carey) whose wife has been killed during the Japanese attack on Pearl

Japanese invasion forces storm the beaches of American-held Wake Island during the early days of World War II. *Wake Island* (1942).

Harbor volunteers to go after an enemy cruiser heading for the island. He sinks the ship and returns to Wake although he is mortally wounded. However, the plot generally avoids excessive heroics and flag-waving, relying instead on characterization and factual events.

The Japanese eventually took the island but paid a high price. They lost four warships and hundreds of troops. To Americans back home, those who fell defending Wake Island became instant heroes. The U.S. and other members of the Allied forces were to experience a series of these "heroic defeats" during the early stages of the war while they geared up for their all-out offensive against the Axis powers.

This was America's first combat film to be released following the nation's entry into World War II. Before the film was distributed nationally, Americans were receiving news of a series of Allied setbacks on different fronts. Paramount actually delayed finishing the film, anticipating a military turnaround. When events failed to improve, the studio decided to complete the film despite the gloomy times. Several screen historians attribute the rise in U.S. Marine Corps enlistments at the time to this film. ■

Walk a Crooked Mile (1948). See Cold War. ■

Walk East on Beacon (1952). See Cold War. ■

Walk in the Sun, A (1945), TCF. *Dir.* Lewis Milestone; *Sc.* Robert Rossen; *Cast includes:* Dana Andrews, Richard Conte, George Tyne, John Ireland.

This World War II drama tells the story of a platoon of G.I.s assigned to take a German-held farmhouse soon after they hit the beach at Salerno. Dana Andrews portrays the sergeant who takes charge when his lieutenant is killed and another sergeant cracks up emotionally. As the men advance through the morning toward their destination, they reveal their joys and fears as well as their boredom and anxieties. They have an encounter with German armored vehicles and meet up with two Italian soldiers fleeing from the Germans. When they reach their target which is heavily defended with enemy machine guns, they attack and capture the farmhouse but not without heavy losses. It is noon.

Director Milestone, who gave the film a distinct visual style, demythologizes the war as he presents a realistic and at times artistic portrayal of men about to enter combat. They act more like civilians than soldiers as they stumble their way through the war. There are no heroics, only young men who want to survive. They don't indulge in patriotic speeches; they wonder about their chances of getting through the day and crack jokes about anything. When the Italian prisoners are given some K-Rations, one G.I. (Richard Conte) quips: "When they get a load of this, they'll wish Italy never got out of the war."

The film contains much irony, beginning with the title which belies the hardships and losses that befall the platoon. On board the landing craft in the opening scenes, one soldier sardonically quotes: " 'The gentle waters of Mare Nostrum'. That's good." Another G.I. frequently is heard saying, "Nobody dies," a desire every soldier harbors but knows is false. Another, a farm boy in civilian life, runs some soil through his fingers. "The soil is no good, no good at all." "Maybe too many soldiers walked on it," a buddy suggests. "They've been walking on it for a long time." The soundtrack provides a deceptively simple folk-type song which is heard between sequences:

It was just a little walk
In the warm Italian sun
But it was not an easy thing
And poets are writing
The tale of that fight
And songs for the children to sing . . .

The war at times takes on a surrealistic look as the men cling to their remembrances of home. This "normalcy" of their civilian life contrasts with the insanity of battle. The film has been singled out as one of the few war films released during the last months of the conflict to present a different, more realistic, view of men in battle. In this respect, it has been equated with *The Story of G.I. Joe*, also released in 1945. ∎

Walk the Proud Land (1956), U. *Dir.* Jesse Hibbs; *Sc.* Gil Doud, Jack Sher; *Cast includes:* Audie Murphy, Anne Bancroft, Pat Crowley, Charles Drake.

This biographical drama recounts the ex-periences of John Philip Clum, an Indian agent at an Arizona Apache reservation in the mid-1870s. Audie Murphy portrays the idealistic agent who introduces the Apaches to self-rule. The film later shows Clum effecting the surrender of the infamous Apache warrior, Geronimo. He was the first white man to do so. The film, based on a biography by Woodworth Clum, is short on action. Anne Bancroft plays an Apache widow who falls in love with Clum. Pat Crowley, as the agent's eastern fiancee, has difficulties adjusting to frontier life. ∎

Wandering Fires (1925), Arrow. *Dir.* Maurice Campbell; *Sc.* Warner Fabian; *Cast includes:* Constance Bennett, Wallace MacDonald, George Hackathorne, Henrietta Crosman.

A weak romantic drama that takes place during World War I, the film stars Constance Bennett as a woman who sacrifices her reputation to clear the name of a dead soldier. It seems that the young man stayed with her the night before he was to sail for France. He is reported killed in action, but the authorities declare him a traitor until Bennett confesses that he was with her on the night in question. Suddenly he shows up in a shell-shocked state. In a short time his memory is restored. ∎

Wanted for Murder (1918), Chatham. *Dir.* Frank Crane; *Sc.* S. Jay Kaufman; *Cast includes:* Elaine Hammerstein, Mrs. Walker, Lillian Hall, Charles Raven.

Released only a few weeks after the Armistice, this World War I drama was already dated in its anti-German propaganda and its patriotic fervor. The film emphasizes the alleged atrocities committed by the Germans upon civilian populations. The French heroine (Elaine Hammerstein), in love with an American soldier, barely escapes the clutches of an enemy soldier before she is brought to America by her doughboy hero. Another scene shows the Kaiser questioning Hindenberg as to why the German armies have not taken Paris. "We did not know America had a Pershing," he explains. There are several well-staged battle sequences.

The film continued the trend—begun even before America entered the war—of placing the entire blame for the conflict on Kaiser Wilhelm and portraying him as a bestial creature and war criminal. In a dream sequence the hero envisions himself inundating Berlin with posters of the Kaiser, charging him with murder. Hollywood during the postwar period enventually allowed Wilhelm, who had abdicated, to slip into obscurity. ∎

War Against Mrs. Hadley, The (1942), MGM. *Dir.* Harold S. Bucquet; *Sc.* George Oppenheimer; *Cast includes:* Edward Arnold, Fay Bainter, Richard Ney, Jean Rogers, Sara Allgood.

Fay Bainter portrays a wife and mother who stubbornly clings to the past and whose refusal to face reality confines her to a world of loneliness in this World War II propaganda drama. At first selfishly disallowing the war effort to interfere with her personal comforts, she eventually has a change of heart when she learns that another mother, whom she has shunned, has lost a son in battle. Edward Arnold portrays a War Department official who has fallen in love with her. Richard Ney plays her son whom she manages to alienate. He joins the military and becomes a public hero. Jean Rogers plays Bainter's daughter, and Van Johnson has a small role as Rogers' husband.

Chiefly a character study of Mrs. Hadley, the film unfolds a series of incidents that reveal her particular traits. The widow of a Republican newspaper publisher, she resents the wife of the new owner who has turned the conservative daily into a liberal paper. She objects to her daughter's marriage to Johnson, who is not on a social par with the family, thereby losing any close relationship that may have existed with her child. She turns away her only admirer as well as her only lifelong female companion. Only when she willingly abandons her social snobbery, and with the help of those who are close to her, does she find true peace and friendship. Several films produced during the war years preached the lowering of social barriers and the joys of democracy, including the Abbott and Costello service comedy *Buck Privates* (1941). ∎

War and Peace (1956), Par. *Dir.* King Vidor; *Sc.* Bridget Boland, Robert Westerby, King Vidor, Irwin Shaw, et. al.; *Cast includes:* Audrey Hepburn, Henry Fonda, Mel Ferrer, Vitorio Gassman, John Mills, Herbert Lom, Oscar Homolka.

Tolstoy's epic novel of Russian life during the Napoleonic Era is given Hollywood's grand treatment in this production. Henry Fonda stars as Pierre Bezukhov, the illegitimate son of a wealthy Russian count. He falls in love with Natasha Rostov (Audrey Hepburn), the daughter of his friend, but feels unworthy of her because of his background. He is then duped into marrying the scheming Helene (Anita Ekberg). Pierre's best friend, Prince Andrei, who is wounded in battle against Napoleon's troops, returns home. After Andrei's wife dies in childbirth, Pierre, to help his friend recover from his depression, introduces him to Natasha. The two soon fall in love. But before they can marry, the prince is ordered to return to the army to help resist the advancing French army. Pierre accompanies him to the war, more as an observer than as a participant.

The remainder of the film concerns the clash of the two armies, the battle of Borodino, the Russian evacuation of Moscow and Napoleon's tragic withdrawal to France. Interrelated with these historical events are incidents in the lives of the principal characters. Pierre, after seeing the slaughter of so many men at Borodino, vows to assassinate Napoleon but fails. He is taken prisoner. Andrei returns from battle mortally wounded. Natasha's younger brother dies in the war. Meanwhile, the brooding Napoleon (Herbert Lom) is outraged that no Russian dignitaries have surrendered the city to him. His men have turned into a rabble army. The Russian general (Oscar Homolka), who decided to evacuate Moscow rather than sacrifice the lives of his troops, waits for Napoleon's inevitable retreat. The French general decides to return to France while he still has a semblance of an army, but they are not used to the Russian winters. During their retreat thousands perish from the cold as well as harassment from Russian attacks. The Russian general, by strategically retreating, saves Russia and his army. Pierre returns to Natasha, who says: "You are like this house—you suffer, you show your wounds, but you stand."

The sweep and spectacle of the film cannot compensate for its weaknesses, such as the miscasting of Henry Fonda, and its international cast which results in a strange conglomeration of accents (British, American, Russian, Italian). But there are powerful moments which suggest Tolstoy's purpose—to show that the continuity of life in history is endless; that youth and age and war and peace are so intertwined that they eventually influence others and ultimately the framework of history. ■

War Arrow (1953), U. *Dir.* George Sherman; *Sc.* John Michael Hayes; *Cast includes:* Maureen O'Hara, Jeff Chandler, John McIntyre, Suzan Ball, Noah Beery.

Maureen O'Hara portrays a widow living at a remote cavalry outpost in this action drama. Jeff Chandler, as a major, arrives to help the commander (John McIntyre), whose fort is undermanned. The troops are losing their battle against the Kiowa raiders. Chandler meets the widow and immediately makes a play for her while he trains a group of peaceful Seminoles to help fight the hostiles. Other officers ridicule his plan, but within a short time his little band has been taking its toll on the Kiowas. Chandler learns that they are led by a renegade army officer, O'Hara's husband, whom everyone thought had been killed. The outpost is attacked by Indians of several tribes, but Chandler, the cavalry and the spirited Seminoles win the day. O'Hara's husband is killed in the battle, leaving her free to leave for Washington with Chandler. The film provides numerous action sequences as the major's well-trained Seminoles fight the Kiowas.

There is little historical evidence that the Seminoles were used by the U.S. against the Kiowa. They were settled in Oklahoma Territory following the Seminole Wars, the second of which was a costly battle in terms of casualties for American troops. Although they were practically neighbors of the Kiowa, who occupied the southern Great Plains, there are no records of battles between the two tribes. The Kiowas, as depicted in the film, were one of the fiercest and most savage tribes in American history, responsible for killing more white settlers than any other group of Indians. They were an amalgam of several smaller tribes, one of which was the Kiowa Apache. ■

War at Home, The (1979), Catalyst Film. *Dir.* Glenn Silber, Barry Alexander Brown; *Sc.* Elizabeth Duncan.

A documentary concentrating chiefly on events during the 1960s at the University of Wisconsin at Madison, the film chronicles the turmoil on the American home front during the Vietnam War years. Such major political figures as Presidents Kennedy, Johnson and Nixon give their views on the war, as do Hubert Humphrey, Ted Kennedy, Wayne Morse and Eugene McCarthy. In its focus on Madison and the campus, the film depicts the chaos on the school grounds and the roles of activists, local politicians and the police chief. Much of the footage was borrowed from a local television station. ■

War Brides (1916), World. *Dir.* Herbert Brenon; *Sc.* Herbert Brenon; *Cast includes:* Alla Nazimova, Gertrude Berkeley, Charles Hutchinson, Charles Bryant.

A silent film with a strong pacifist theme, the story takes place in a mythical country where the king orders the women of the land to produce more children as future soldiers. The international star, Nazimova, portraying a factory worker, rebels against the senseless decree. "No more children for war!" she cries out and shoots herself in the presence of the king as a protest against his inhuman command. Other women rise up, vowing not to have any more births until war is outlawed. The star reportedly received $1,000 per day for one month for her performance in this loosely based adaptation of *Lysistrata*.

The handful of pacifist dramas that appeared during the early war years were overwhelmed by those which advocated preparedness. Germany's sinking of the British liner, the *Lusitania*, in May 1915, with the loss of 128 American lives, did not help the pacifist cause. America's entry into the war in 1917 put an end to the pacifist cycle. ■

War Bride's Secret, The (1916), Fox. *Dir.* Kenean Buel; *Sc.* Mary Murillo; *Cast includes:* Virginia Pearson, Glen White, Walter Law, Robert Vivian.

A routine love triangle dominates this World War I drama. Walter Law portrays a devoted husband who is so concerned with his wife's (Virginia Pearson) welfare that he is willing to give her up to another man to make her happy. Concerning the war, the film concentrates on its anti-German theme and the need for preparedness by depicting the Germans as rapists and murderers. These sentiments were not unique at the time of the film's release. A string of anti-German dramas pictured the Prussians either as secret agents bent on stealing America's secrets or bestial soldiers willing to discard all civilized rules of conduct.

With its melodramatic title, it obviously tried to capitalize on the success of Herbert Brenon's *War Brides*, starring the internationally famous performer Alla Nazimova, and released several months earlier. However, it differs from the latter work which took a strong pacifist stance in its approach to the world conflict. ∎

War Comes to America (1945). See "Why We Fight." ∎

War Correspondent (1932), Col. *Dir.* Paul Sloane; *Sc.* Jo Swerling; *Cast includes:* Jack Holt, Ralph Graves, Lila Lee, Victor Wong.

This action drama is set in strife-torn China in the 1920s as bandits and warlords challenge the government. Jack Holt plays a mercenary pilot fighting against the insurgents. Ralph Graves portrays a war correspondent broadcasting the daily events while arguing with Holt. When Lila Lee, as a woman of easy virtue who has seen the light, is captured by a villainous warlord, Holt goes to her rescue, followed by Graves. They free her while they fight off hordes of the leader's troops. Holt loses his life during the battle, leaving the heroine to Graves. There is plenty of action in this B-feature, including a dogfight between Holt and four enemy aircraft. See also Chinese Civil Wars. ∎

War Department Report (1943), U.S. War Department.

A World War II propaganda documentary produced by the War Department, the film stresses the contributions of the home front if victory is be be attained. By showing a series of battle sequences in which the narrator points out the large amount of war materiel consumed by Allied forces, the film underscores the need for more production from the defense plants back home. The narrator is quick to state that the Germans have encountered serious setbacks in Europe and their war industry has been under constant attack from the air while Japan also is suffering heavy losses in the Pacific. The voice-over continually drives home the message that these victories require high production quotas. The film was targeted for showing to 10 million workers at their war plants around the nation. ∎

War Dogs. See *Pride of the Army* (1942). ∎

War Drums (1957), UA. *Dir.* Reginald Le Borg; *Sc.* Gerald Drayson Adams; *Cast includes:* Lex Barker, Joan Taylor, Ben Johnson, Larry Chance, Richard Cutting.

Lex Barker, as the heroic and honorable Apache chief Mangas Colorado, leads his people in an uprising against white oppression in this action drama that travels along a well-worn path. The chief only breaks his treaty with the U.S. government after the whites bring injury to members of his tribe. Ben Johnson, as a white friend of Mangas Colorado, intercedes in the Indians' behalf. They are allowed to live in peace in the mountains away from white justice. Joan Taylor, as a half-breed Mexican whom the chief marries, refuses to settle for the traditional Indian wife's role, preferring instead to ride at his side. He therefore trains her in the art of warfare. The film continues in the tradition of pro-Indian dramas which became extremely popular in the 1950s.

Except for his Mexican wife (one of three, the others were Indian), there is little here that conveys the long, colorful and violent life of this chief who was able to unite several branches of the Apache. Mangas Colorado became chief of his tribe in the late 1830s, only after his chief and many of his people were massacred during an act of treachery. The Apaches were invited to attend a banquet by local Mexican miners and American trappers and traders at Santa Rita, a Mexican village. When they were assembled in a large group, a white man discharged a cannon aimed at the Apaches, killing a large number. The remainder scattered for cover as Mexicans and others picked off the survivors with their rifles. Several hundred Indians were killed. Shortly after, Mangas Colorado exacted his revenge on the inhabitants. He spent the next 25 years avenging other wrongs by raiding and killing Mexicans, white men and other Indians. He was finally captured and murdered at age 70, but only through a treacherous ploy. In 1863 a soldier under a flag of truce offered to discuss a treaty with him. As he entered the white men's camp, he was surrounded by a circle of rifles. That night an officer ordered his two guards to kill him. The two soldiers fired their rifles into the unarmed chief, then shot him with their revolvers. ∎

War Horse, The (1927), Fox. *Dir.* Lambert Hillyer; *Sc.* Lambert Hillyer; *Cast includes:* Buck Jones, Lois Todd, Lloyd Whitlock, Stanley Taylor.

Western screen star Buck Jones stars in this World War I drama of a cowboy who follows his horse to France. It seems that "Silver Buck" was shipped by mistake along with a string of horses to be used by the army. Jones enlists, finds his horse and meets a pretty ambulance driver with whom he falls in love. While at the front, Jones has the opportunity to save several fellow doughboys from a German ambush. The film contains plenty of action during the war sequences. ∎

War humor. Comedy films with a wartime setting, as well as service comedies which take place during peacetime, have always been a popular genre with the general movie audiences. Almost every comedian and comedy team has made at least one of these films.

World War I set the stage and tone for this type of film. The hero was usually an inept common soldier oblivious to military conventions and who, by either good luck or some inspired stroke of genius, was able to redeem himself by performing a heroic deed. Sergeants became the usual butts of jokes and pranks while officers were often deflated. However, the war comedy was slow in coming during this conflict. Most of the product turned out by the studios was on the melodramatic side, swelling with patriotism and propaganda. Atrocity films like D.W. Griffith's *Hearts of the World* were intended to stir the emotions of its audiences, not to evoke laughter.

Eventually, major producers such as Mack Sennett and such film stars as Charlie Chaplin began to turn their comedic talents toward war humor. In "An International Sneak" (1918), a spoof of the spy genre popular at the time, Chester Conklin plays an espionage agent. "Shoulder Arms" (1918) follows a recruit (Charlie Chaplin) from training camp to the front lines, where he encounters tough sergeants, uninhabitable trenches and hostile Germans. Producer Al Christie's "Shades of Shakespeare" (1918) pokes fun at the propaganda films of the period. "Kicking the Germ Out of Germany" (1918) stars Harold Lloyd as a spy and features comedienne Bebe Daniels as a nurse. Larry Semon captures a spy in "Huns and Hyphens" (1918). Cross-eyed Ben Turpin impersonates

the Kaiser in "Yankee Doodle in Berlin" (1919) while Douglas MacLean was featured in *23 1/2 Hours Leave* the same year.

Other film personalities participated in the genre with equal fervor. Billie Burke in "Arms and the Girl" (1917) plays an impish American in France who rescues a fellow American from a German firing squad through the use of humorous pranks. On the home front Mr. and Mrs. Sidney Drew turned out a little comedy in 1917 titled "The Patriot," which deals with conserving food. Director King Vidor's "Bud's Recruit" (1918) tells the story of a younger brother who tries to enlist in the service, thereby embarrassing his older brother into doing his duty.

The first half of the 1920s saw very few war films—comedies or dramas. Either Hollywood forgot about the Great War or the public grew tired of the genre. But with the release of several blockbusters like *The Big Parade* and *What Price Glory?*, war comedy returned with a vengeance. Harry Langdon starred in the comedy short "Soldier Man" (1926) and *The Strong Man* (1927), the latter having battle scenes only at the beginning. Wallace Beery was teamed with Raymond Hatton in a series of war comedies, beginning with *Behind the Front* (1926). Semon returned in *Spuds* (1927), comics Karl Dane and George K. Arthur starred in *Rookies* (1927) and George Sidney and Charlie Murray made *Lost at the Front* (1927). Even Broadway entertainer George Jessel turned out two vehicles, *Private Izzy Murphy* and *Sailor Izzy Murphy*, both released in 1927. Comic Monty Banks joined the flying corps in "Flying Luck" (1928). Ernest Hilliard and J.P. McGowan portrayed two army buddies in *Devil Dogs* (1928), an inept farce that borrowed heavily from similar films.

Comedies set during World War I lingered on into the 1930s. Moran and Mack starred in *Anybody's War* (1930); Buster Keaton in *Dough Boys* (1930), reportedly based on his own war experiences; and the comedy team of Wheeler and Woolsey in *Half-Shot at Sunrise* (1930), about the boys' misadventures in Paris and at the front. Laurel and Hardy appeared in *Pack Up Your Troubles* in 1932 while wide-mouthed Joe E. Brown made *Sons o' Guns* in 1936. The only film the Marx Brothers made that came close to a war comedy was *Duck Soup* (1933), about a fictitious conflict between two mythical kingdoms. At the close of the decade the Ritz Brothers made their contribution to the genre in *Pack Up Your Troubles* (1939), and, like Stan and Ollie's war comedy of 1932, took the title from the popular World War I song. The introduction of sound to these wartime comedies permitted more risqué dialogue, the addition of a handful of songs and comics who began their careers on stage to display their talents. The careers of some silent screen comedians, particularly those of Keaton and Langdon, suffered with the advent of sound.

Several major film studios during the 1930s turned out comedy shorts, ranging from two to four reels. Several used World War I as their background. MGM, for instance, released a series of comedies starring Charley Chase, three of which—"High C's" (1930), "Rough Seas" (1931) and "Sherman Said It" (1933)—concerned his misadventures during and immediately after the war.

World War II gave rise to a relatively new generation of comedians who turned to the conflict as a source for humor in the 1940s. The decade started with Charlie Chaplin's *The Great Dictator* (1940), with its opening scenes taking place during a World War I battle. Abbott and Costello, the top comedy team of the decade, starred in *Buck Privates* (1941), *In the Navy* (1941), and *Buck Privates Come Home* (1947). Bob Hope made *Caught in the Draft* (1941), while that same year Jimmy Durante and Phil Silvers were featured in *You're in the Army Now*. Radio personalities Lum and Abner (Chester Lauck and Norris Goff) in *Two Weeks to Live* (1943) brought their homespun humor to the screen in this tale involving a Nazi spy ring. Danny Kaye, as a hypochondriac in *Up in Arms* (1944), nevertheless manages to snare a Japanese unit while he is on duty in the Pacific. Minor comic actors also participated in the steady stream of war comedies, including William Tracy in *About Face* (1942), which led to several sequels, and the young Robert Walker in *See Here, Private Hargrove* (1944), an episodic story about a recruit's humorous misadventures in the army. A sequel, *What Next, Corporal Hargrove?*, appeared the following year.

Comedy shorts, a popular staple of most theater programs during the 1930s and 1940s, sometimes delved into such war-related topics as combat and spies. The Three Stooges lent their low-brow comic talents to several, including "You Nazty Spy" (1940), a takeoff on Hitler; "I'll Never Heil Again" (1941), an-

other satire of the Nazi dictator; "Back From the Front" (1943), with the trio as merchant seamen tangling with Nazis; and "No Dough, Boys" (1944), in which the boys pose as Japanese spies. Former silent screen comic Harry Langdon in "Blitz on the Fritz" (1943), although rejected by the military, does his share by exposing a spy ring.

A few comedy films of the period were attacked for their bad taste. Ernst Lubitsch's *To Be or Not to Be* (1942), starring Jack Benny and Carole Lombard, treated lightly the Nazi invasion of Poland. *Once Upon a Honeymoon* (1942), with Ginger Rogers, Cary Grant and Walter Slezak, blended the devastation of Czechoslovakia, Poland and France with the frivolous desires of a young woman looking for a titled husband. Several critics singled out the film for its insensitivity, particularly in a Nazi concentration camp sequence. *Practically Yours* (1944), with Claudette Colbert and Fred MacMurray, concerned a World War II hero whose reported death causes a nation to mourn—until he is resurrected. Critics considered the subject matter, especially the light tone of the film, to be in poor taste at a time when many households were being informed that a loved one was missing or killed in action. *One Night in Lisbon* (1941), starring Madeleine Carroll and Fred MacMurray, also tried to mix screwball comedy and romance with wartime events.

World War II comedies continued well into the postwar era. Dean Martin and Jerry Lewis, the most popular comedy team of the 1950s, appeared in *At War With the Army* in 1950, their first starring film. The following year they made *Sailor Beware*. Lewis went on to star in one of his funniest films, *Don't Give Up the Ship* (1959), in which he misplaces a battleship during wartime. Bill Mauldin's wartime cartoon characters, Willie and Joe, were brought to the screen in *Up Front* (1951), starring David Wayne and Tom Ewell, and in the sequel, *Back at the Front*. In *The Girls of Pleasure Island* (1953) three innocent lovelies raised on a South Pacific island by their father learn about romance when 1,500 U.S. Marines land. Director John Ford launched *Mister Roberts* in 1955, about life on a cargo ship during World War II, starring James Cagney as an oddball captain, Henry Fonda as an officer yearning to get into the action of the war and Jack Lemmon as a scheming braggart. In 1957 Glenn Ford starred *Don't Go Near the Water*, a weak comedy about a U.S. Navy public relations unit in the Pacific that spends all its time pacifying congressmen, creating glorified stories for the civilians back home and distracting inquisitive reporters. Andy Griffith repeated his Broadway role as the innocent hayseed in *No Time for Sergeants* (1958). One of the funniest postwar films, *Operation Petticoat* (1959), starred Cary Grant as the skipper of a damaged submarine in the Pacific and Tony Curtis as his resourceful officer.

The genre continued sporadically during the next decade. Jim Hutton, as a bungling American officer in *The Horizontal Lieutenant* (1962), is ordered to bring in a defiant Japanese soldier, the last symbol of resistance on a U.S.-occupied Pacific island. *Ensign Pulver*, a pale sequel to *Mister Roberts*, appeared in 1964 with Robert Walker as the title character and Burl Ives as the captain. In *The Extraordinary Seaman* (1969), set in the Philippines during World War II, David Niven portrays a World War I ghost relegated to linger aboard his vintage ship until he clears his family honor.

The Korean conflict and the Vietnam War years offered few war or service comedies, but one classic emerged in 1970. *M*A*S*H* concerns two uninhibited, offbeat surgeons (Elliott Gould and Donald Sutherland) who find their own methods of maintaining their sanity at a field hospital in Korea. *Good Morning, Vietnam* (1987) appeared in the wake of a series of grim dramas which depicted the Vietnam conflict with a realism seldom attained in previous films of that war. Starring Robin Williams as a brash, offbeat Saigon disk jockey at odds with the military brass but loved by the grunts, it became the first Vietnam War comedy.

Occasionally, war humor turned to the Civil War. The most popular silent comedy about the war between the states is Buster Keaton's *The General* (1927), based on an actual incident. In 1948 Red Skelton starred in the farcical *A Southern Yankee* in which the comic poses as both a Union and Confederate spy. Keaton, in his declining years, returned to the Civil War as an aging veteran in a Columbia sound short "Mooching Through Georgia" (1939). The ubiquitous Three Stooges appeared in two shorts, "Uncivil Warriors" (1938), in which they play Union spies, and "Uncivil Warbirds" (1946), in which they are targets of both factions.

War humor has changed drastically since the early silent comedies of World War I. It began with relatively "safe" subjects, such as the home front, slackers, the enemy, young innocents getting mixed up with spies and traitors. The comedy depended heavily on sight gags, slapstick and, occasionally, characterization. With Chaplin's bold satire, *Shoulder Arms*, war humor began to poke gentle fun at the military establishment, a trend that continued into the service comedies of the 1930s and the war humor of the 1940s. The post-World War II years perpetuated the images of the bungling recruit (hillbilly or city slicker), the dumb sergeant and the incompetent officer as the butts of innumerable jokes. Sometimes the main character was a con man of persuasive talents. But little changed in the way of emphasis. The comedy was apolitical; the satire gently anti-military.

There were very few comedies about the Korean and Vietnam Wars, conflicts which the public was not too comfortable with. *M*A*S*H*, set during the Korean War but made during the Vietnam conflict, is more in tune with the latter in terms of the film's irreverent main characters and anti-authoritarian spirit. In suggesting the insanity of war, the film changed the course of war humor while reflecting the attitudes of many Americans toward war in general and Vietnam in particular. It was one of the earliest films to satirize the institution of war as well as the military. *Good Morning, Vietnam* has taken a similar path. ∎

War Hunt (1962), UA. *Dir.* Denis Sanders; *Sc.* Stanford Whitmore; *Cast includes:* John Saxon, Robert Redford, Charles Aldman, Sydney Pollack.

The Korean War serves as background for this drama about the impact that war has on those who continually live with death and violence. The offbeat plot concerns an American G.I. who becomes obsessed with killing even after the cease fire. John Saxon, as the soldier twisted by war and driven by a desire to kill, continues to go on nightly forays with a stiletto in pursuit of his prey. Robert Redford, in his first screen role, portrays a fellow soldier who witnesses the tragic change in his buddy. Tommy Matsuda, as a young Korean orphan, idolizes Saxon and accompanies him on his raids. Redford, concerned about the boy's future, tries to redirect his attention. In the end, Saxon becomes the prey when his fellow soldiers are forced to hunt him down and kill him before he jeopardizes the tenuous cease-fire. Sydney Pollack, who plays one of the soldiers, soon abandoned his acting career to become a major Hollywood director. ■

War Is a Racket (1934), Eureka. *Dir.* Samuel Cummins, Jacques Koerpel; *Sc.* Vincent Valentini; *Cast includes:* Harry K. Eustace, Herschel Mayall, Gertrude Clemens, Frank Jaquet.

Using stock war footage, several actors and narration by A. L. Alexander, this hybrid semi-documentary antiwar drama poses the title in question form and interviews people in various walks of life. Newsreel excerpts show victims of submarine torpedoes as well as other war implements. An armaments maker, a minister, a wife, a mother whose son was lost in the last war and a veteran are questioned as to whether war is a racket. The pacifist message emerges stronger than the presentation itself in this inept film. ■

War Is Hell (1964), AA. *Dir.* Burt Topper; *Sc.* Burt Topper; *Cast includes:* Tony Russell, Baynes Barron, Burt Topper.

The dehumanizing effects of war on those who are directly involved in battle is the subject of this Korean War drama which is introduced by Audie Murphy. The plot concerns one soldier, played by Tony Russell, whose obsession with glory and medals takes him over the edge. He and three of his comrades are assigned to knock out a North Korean pillbox. They accomplish their mission, but Russell's fellow soldiers are killed in the battle. He returns to his unit and states that he destroyed the objective alone. When his lieutenant questions his claim, Russell shoots the officer and takes over command of the remaining troops. He accompanies them on several fierce assaults against the enemy, including attacks conducted after a cease-fire has been announced. ■

War Lord, The (1937). See *West of Shanghai* (1937). ■

War Lord, The (1965), U. *Dir.* Franklin Schaffner; *Sc.* John Collier, Millard Kaufman; *Cast includes:* Charlton Heston, Richard Boone, Rosemary Forsyth, Maurice Evans, Guy Stockwell.

The Duke of Normandy (Charlton Heston) is ordered to protect a Druid village against

Charlton Heston (l.), as the Duke of Normandy, is assigned to protect an llth-century Druid village. *The War Lord* (1965).

invaders in this 11th-century drama. To satisfy his desire for a pretty village bride, Heston summons the custom of the lord's right to the first night. The bride (Rosemary Forsyth) then refuses to return to the irate groom (James Farentino) who turns for help to the Frisian invaders. Heston's brother (Guy Stockwell) eventually turns against Heston and is killed by him in battle. Richard Boone plays the War Lord's loyal aide. The film contains authentic sets and costumes and includes several effective battle sequences. The dialogue, however, leaves something to be desired. Such lines as "I hate your knightly guts" do little to enhance this slow-paced drama. ■

War Lover, The (1962), Col. *Dir.* Philip Leacock; *Sc.* Howard Koch; *Cast includes:* Steve McQueen, Robert Wagner, Shirley Anne Field, Gary Cockrell.

A World War II pilot stationed in England allows his concern for his macho and heroic image to affect his relationships with women. Steve McQueen, as the title character, is an American pilot of a B-17 participating in continual bombing raids over Germany. He and Robert Wagner, another Yank, are in love with the same young woman (Shirley Anne Field). Wagner is able to give love and communicate his feelings, qualities lacking in McQueen. The aerial action sequences are more interesting than the romantic plot in this film based on John Hersey's novel. ■

War Nurse (1930), MGM. *Dir.* Edgar Selwyn; *Sc.* Becky Gardiner, Joe Farnham; *Cast includes:* Robert Montgomery, Robert Ames, June Walker, Anita Page, ZaSu Pitts.

This World War I drama depicts the experiences of a group of nurses near the front lines. The young women who volunteer—some are only in their teens—do so for various reasons. Several are bored with their lives, others boast about meeting a variety of young men, a few welcome the opportunity to travel abroad. A nun blesses a class of student nurses who volunteer to serve in France. "You are mere children," she announces, "yet youth has its part in war."

Once overseas and thrown into the gory routine of caring for the maimed young men laid out before them, the nurses begin to show emotional stress. One echoes the thoughts of the others when she cries out that she cannot look at another wounded soldier. "You'll learn to look at men without arms or legs, without faces," a head nurse enlightens her, "and you'll smile. Why? Because they need you."

Anita Page portrays a nurse who has an affair with a married soldier. While pregnant with his child, she witnesses his death from battle wounds. She is critically hurt when a wall collapses after a shelling. June Walker, as another nurse, brings her baby to her just before she dies. Robert Montgomery, one of the first wave of movie stars to emerge from the early sound period, plays a brash soldier who spends all of his off-duty time attempting to seduce Walker.

Woven into all this sordidness is a strong antiwar theme. There are numerous shots of wounded soldiers in this film of unrelieved suffering and grimness. The cries of the wounded and dying fill the wards; young men die in the arms of the young nurses; an almost endless stream of injured soldiers pour into the already crowded hospital.

The film was based on the frank confessions of an anonymous American nurse who had worked with a French detachment during the war, but most of the more daring incidents did not appear on screen. Some controversy followed the release of the drama. Understandably, various nursing groups protested the depiction of some of their counterparts on the screen although a foreword appears on screen stating that the story depicts the experiences of only some nurses. ■

"War o' Dreams" (1915), Selig. *Dir.* E. A. Martin; *Sc.* W. E. Wing; *Cast includes:* Bessie Eyton, Edwin Wallock, Lillian Hayward.

An unsuccessful inventor, whose daughter marries an officer, finally gets a chance to demonstrate his new explosive before a military committee. His invention is accepted, and that night he has a dream about the destructive powers of his invention. He witnesses the pain on the faces of the parents whose sons have died amid the modern inventions of war. When he awakens he decides not to sell his explosive to the military.

When this drama was released, America was in the midst of a controversial storm concerning the war in Europe. Some advocated a strong pacifist stand while others spoke out for preparedness. Antiwar films, such as the above, began to appear, as well as other features that cautioned what could happen to the nation if it remained defenseless. ■

War of 1812 (1812–1814). The War of 1812, sometimes referred to as the Second War of American Independence, was, from the outset, one of the most unpopular conflicts in the history of the U.S. When President James Madison called for a formal declaration of war against Great Britain on June 18, 1812, the congressional vote for war was 74–49 in the House and 19–13 in the Senate. Only the Vietnam War (1956–1975) caused such division within our nation.

The U.S., though neutral, had been hurt by the Napoleonic Wars (1803–1815), principally between England and France. Both combatants interfered with American trade. Britain, however, with a larger navy, stopped more American ships and heavily curtailed U.S. trade with France. The British also impressed seamen from American ships into the British navy, claiming they were deserters. In addition, westerners suspected the English of inciting and arming hostile Indians in the upper Ohio valley to attack frontier settlements. *Brave Warrior* (1952), set on the eve of the war, concerned a government agent (Jon Hall) assigned to prevent the Indians from joining the British cause.

Western settlers wanted war as a means of ending the Indian menace. Southerners saw an opportunity to seize western Florida from Spain, Britain's ally. Finally, a group of politicians among the "War Hawks" believed the U.S. could easily conquer eastern Canada while Britain was occupied with France. However, industrial New England and the maritime states, despite their losses at sea, profited from the war trade and continued to sell supplies to the enemy while the U.S. was fighting England.

The war on land did not go well for either side. Several British attempts to invade the U.S. from Canada failed, as did American thrusts into Canada. The British sent a fleet up Chesapeake Bay that temporarily captured and burned the national capital (August 24–25, 1814), forcing the government to flee. *Magnificent Doll* (1946), a fictionalized biography of Dolly Madison, dramatized these events. But an attempt to take Baltimore a few weeks later was staved off, inspiring Francis Scott Key to compose the words to the "Star Spangled Banner" in memory of the defense of Fort McHenry, defending Baltimore harbor.

The biggest and final land engagement of the war, the Battle of New Orleans (January 8, 1815), resulted in General Andrew Jackson's one-sided and spectacular victory for the U.S. But it had no bearing on the peace because the Treaty of Ghent had already been signed. Unfortunately, news of the treaty took several weeks to reach America. The battle was highlighted in two films, Cecil B. DeMille's *The Buccaneer* (1938) and its 1958 remake in color, directed by Anthony Quinn and starring Yul Brynner as the pirate Lafitte and Charlton Heston as Jackson. Lafitte, who was the main character in these two films, and his pirate forces greatly assisted Jackson.

The small American navy recorded some victories. Captain Oliver Perry defeated a British fleet on Lake Erie (September 10, 1813), and Captain Thomas Macdonough prevented a British squadron from gaining control of Lake Champlain (September 11, 1814). The British frigate *Shannon* captured the *Chesapeake* (June 1, 1813), leading to the immortal words of American Captain James Lawrence: "Don't give up the ship." The *Constitution*, which earned the title *Old Ironsides* in one engagement, recorded several notable victories under Captains Isaac Hull and William Bainbridge over British warships. Captain Stephen Decatur, who had distinguished himself in the Tripolitan War (1800–1805), took a number of prizes in the War of 1812. Edward Dmytryk's *Mutiny* (1952), an otherwise minor film set during the War of 1812, recounted the building of one of the earliest submarines by the U.S. that torpedoed a British warship.

The peace treaty did not address the causes of the war, and neither side gained territory by the conflict. American films do not explore the causes or go into the politics of the peace treaty. Unfortunately for historical enlightenment, one could easily receive the impression after viewing films on this topic that the U.S., in the role of a "David," succeeded in slaying the British "Goliath" for a second time in its early history. More accurately, both sides had become weary of fighting and realized that neither could achieve anything by continuing the war. See also Stephen Decatur, Andrew Jackson, Jean Lafitte, Francis Scott Key, U.S.S. *Constitution*. ∎

War of the Worlds (1953). See Science Fiction Wars. ∎

"War on the Plains" (1912), New York Motion Picture Co. *Dir.* Thomas Ince; *Sc.* Thomas Ince, William Eagleshirt, Ray Myers; *Cast includes:* Francis Ford, William Eagleshirt, Ray Myers.

An early silent western photographed on location at the Santa Ynez canyon, the drama features cowboys, Indians, prairie schooners, stagecoaches—the basic elements that were soon to become familiar to audiences around the world. Several reviewers of the period praised this two-reel work, calling it "true to life." Ince, the director, stated in a magazine article that this film was the forerunner of the western genre. That same year he had other two-reel westerns to his credit, including "The Indian Massacre" and "The Battle of the Red Men." ∎

War Paint (1926), MGM. *Dir.* W. S. Van Dyke; *Sc.* Charles Maigne; *Cast includes:* Tim McCoy, Pauline Starke, Charles French, Chief Yowlache, Karl Dane.

This was Colonel Tim McCoy's first big film, and it established him as a western performer to be reckoned with. He plays the chief scout at an army post. Iron Eyes, chief of the Arapahoes, seeks revenge on the cavalry outpost after being arrested. Breaking free, he leads an attack on the fort while the commander and most of the troopers are away on a mission. McCoy escapes the Indian siege, returns with a horde of friendly Indians and routs the hostiles.

Although the plot contains the conventional trappings of this genre of western, the film was one of the earliest to give motivation to the Indians' discontent. Most other films up to this time presented hostile Indians stirred up by a crazed leader, the promise of liquor, or some other immoral goal. This work suggests that certain whites may have been responsible for the hostilities between the races, that the native Americans rose up out of their justified fears of annihilation. Also, McCoy aimed at authenticity by having real Indians play featured parts and by his speaking to them in their own sign language. McCoy was a real-life hero, having served as a colonel in both World Wars and earning the Bronze Star in the latter. ■

War Paint (1953), UA. *Dir.* Lesley Selander; *Sc.* Richard Alan Simmons, Martin Berkeley; *Cast includes:* Robert Stack, Joan Taylor, Charles McGraw, Keith Larsen.

A detachment of the U.S. Cavalry faces difficulties in presenting a peace treaty to an Indian chief in this action drama set in Death Valley (where the film was shot). Earlier attempts by representatives of the U.S. government to enter Indian territory for the purposes of discussing peace were met with ambush by a tribe that harbors bitter hatred and distrust for white people. Robert Stack portrays a brave cavalry lieutenant who undertakes the perilous mission of leading his patrol into the same forbidding land to contact the hostile chief. Several action sequences are interjected throughout the film before Stack accomplishes his task. ■

War Party (1965), TCF. *Dir.* Lesley Selander; *Sc.* George Williams, William Marks; *Cast includes:* Michael T. Mikler, Davey Davison, Donald Barry, Laurie Mock.

The Comanches take to the warpath in this action drama set during the Indian wars of the 1870s. The Indians, who manage to trap a large cavalry unit, also control the only pass available for a rescue party. A column of troops starts out by way of a longer route to rescue the trapped men. Meanwhile Michael T. Mikler, as the Indian scout Johnny Hawk, learns from an Indian girl (Laurie Mock) that the pass is open. Confirming that the story is true, he leads a small patrol to tell the relief column of the shorter route. Several skirmishes with the Comanches ensue. Hawk, in a one-on-one fight, kills their chief. The remainder of the patrol finally reach the column who then ride to rescue the besieged troops. ■

"War Time Sweetheart, A" (1909). Selig.

A romantic Civil War drama set in the vicinity of Frederickstown, Maryland, the film concerns two young men vying for the love of a local judge's daughter. Battles between Union and Confederate troops and suspenseful chases fill out the simple story in this short silent film. ■

"War Town" (1943), Office of War Information.

A one-reel World War II documentary, the film shows the problems involved with finding housing for numerous defense workers who migrate to a town that is heavily geared for the production of war materiel. In this instance, Mobile, Alabama, is the town in question. The film shows how the community leaders attempt to handle the situation. ■

"Warfare in the Skies" (1914), Vitagraph. *Dir.* Frederick A. Thomson; *Sc.* Frederick A. Thomson; *Cast includes:* Earle Williams, Edith Storey.

A young aviator of an unnamed European nation falls in love with an American girl who also attracts the attention of a nobleman, another flier. When a revolution threatens the nation, both rivals enlist on the side of the Loyalists, but the nobleman switches allegiances to the rebels and proceeds to drop bombs from his airplane. The young patriot takes his plane aloft and crashes into the traitor's airship. The wounded hero is captured by the revolutionary forces and hospitalized. When his sweetheart is captured as a spy and faced with a firing squad, our young hero once again takes to the air and rescues her.

This was one of the earliest films about air warfare to be released during World War I although the story did not deal directly with that conflict. J. Stuart Blackton, one of the triumvirate who controlled Vitagraph, was later to turn out several strong war movies. If his works seem anti-German, it is probably because Blackton was born in England. Convinced that his original homeland was fighting to save civilization, he believed that the U.S. should support Britain. ■

WarGames (1983). See Science Fiction Wars. ■

Warkill (1967), Balut Productions. *Dir.* Ferde Grofe, Jr.; *Sc.* Ferde Grofe, Jr.; *Cast includes:* George Montgomery, Tom Drake, Conrad Parham, Eddie Infante.

A brutal American colonel leads Filipino

troops against the Japanese in this action drama set in the latter part of World War II. George Montgomery stars as the hard-bitten officer who does not believe in taking prisoners. His outfit is assigned to rout out pockets of Japanese resisters. Montgomery employs a variety of techniques to accomplish his mission, including dumping half-starved rats into caves used as hide-outs by the enemy and sending dogs to flush out the stubborn foe. Tom Drake portrays a correspondent who has idolized the colonel and has often written of his heroic deeds. When he finally meets Montgomery and witnesses the warrior in action, Drake quickly becomes disillusioned with his hero. "In every man there is a beast, and it's only this war that makes us animals," the colonel explains to the idealistic reporter. Drake recoils from the man he once considered a hero, and only when he stumbles upon the atrocities committed by the Japanese does he finally grasp the meaning of the horrors of war and what Montgomery was trying to say. ∎

Warpath (1951), Par. *Dir.* Byron Haskin; *Sc.* Frank Gruber; *Cast includes:* Edmond O'Brien, Charles Stevens, Forrest Tucker, Harry Carey, Jr., Polly Bergen.

A lawyer turns gunslinger and hunts down the killers of his fiancee in this revenge drama played out against the larger conflict between the U.S. Cavalry and the Indians. Edmond O'Brien portrays the hunter who pursues three bank robbers who shot his young woman during one of their escapades. He joins up with the cavalry when he suspects a strong-arm sergeant (Forrest Tucker) as one of the outlaws. Tucker warns one of his cohorts, a local storekeeper (Dean Jagger). The plot has the three men captured by Indians with Tucker sacrificing his life for the other two. Jagger also redeems himself when he gives his life in an attempt to warn General Custer of an impending trap. Polly Bergen, as Jagger's daughter, provides the romantic interest. James Millican plays Custer. The film includes several rousing battles between the cavalry and the Indians. ∎

Warrens of Virginia, The (1915), Par. *Dir.* Cecil B. DeMille; *Sc.* William DeMille; *Cast includes:* Blanche Sweet, House Peters, James Neill, P. E. Peters, Mabel Van Buren.

A New Yorker, visiting the prewar South, falls in love with Agatha, the daughter of General Warren, in this silent Civil War film based on a play by William DeMille. War breaks out and the Yankee becomes a lieutenant in the Union army. He returns to Virginia carrying false information which falls into the hands of the general. Acting upon the bogus dispatch, the general sends out a column of men and wagons of war materiel, both ambushed by Union troops. Warren and his daughter treat the lieutenant, who had once been their guest, with disdain. But after the war ends, the lovers reunite. An early work of director Cecil B. DeMille, it reflects little of his spectacle and excesses which were to dominate many of his later films. ∎

Warrens of Virginia, The (1924), Fox. *Dir.* Elmer Clifton; *Sc.* William DeMille; *Cast includes:* George Backus, Robert Andrews, Wilfred Lytell, Martha Mansfield.

A remake of the above film, both of which were based on the play by William C. DeMille, the Civil War drama takes place just before Lee's surrender and is set near the Warren home. The same basic plot unfolds, that of a young Southern woman (Martha Mansfield) who falls in love with a Northerner (Wilfred Lytell). Although this version differs from the 1915 film in its introduction of the historical figures of Generals Grant and Lee, they remain subordinate to the main love story. Mansfield, a promising film personality who had appeared in several other silent features, died after her dress caught fire during the production of the film. ∎

War's End (1934), Smythe Production. *Dir.* Thomas J. Dickson; *Sc.* Steward B. Moss.

A World War I documentary culled from official U.S. government newsreel archives, the film depicts the history of the war from its beginning to the day of the armistice, particularly underscoring the role of the American troops in bringing about the end to the conflict. The story follows the men in the trenches from one major battle to the next and the usual dangers they face. Thomas J. Dickson, who assembled the footage, was a colonel and chief chaplain with the First Division. ∎

Washington, George (1732–1799). Eulogized as "First in war, first in peace, and first in the hearts of his countrymen" by a congressional resolution at the time of his death on December 14, 1799, at Mount Vernon, Virginia, the statement is but one example of the great esteem in which Washington was held by his contemporaries.

He was a physically imposing man for his times, standing several inches over six feet. He had an aura of dominance and command that his aide, Lafayette, in his private correspondence, called "majestic." In retrospect, Washington's personality and character were very much what the new nation needed to mold a ragtag army into a fighting force that could stand up to a professional and often numerically superior British military machine, and then lead the country politically in its initial administration under the Constitution.

Washington received his first military experience in the French and Indian War (1754–1763). As a lieutenant colonel in the Virginia militia, he led his troops to victory over a small French unit that had encroached into the Ohio valley. His familiarity with the area resulted in an appointment the following year as aide to General Edward Braddock, who was charged with mounting a major British drive against French bases in the region. Braddock was defeated and killed in a combined French and Indian ambush. Washington, who had two horses shot from under him, won recognition for organizing a retreat out of the wilderness. His exploits with the British were re-enacted in a Vitagraph release in 1916 titled *Washington Under the British Flag*, one of a series of historical films produced by the studio.

In 1759, the same year he married a widow, Martha Curtis, he won election to the Virginia House of Burgesses where he soon became a leader in the resistance to British colonial policies. As a delegate to the 1st and 2nd Continental Congress, he favored the use of armed force and complete separation from the mother country.

Washington, upon receiving command of the Continental Army, (June 15, 1775), took over the siege of Boston and forced the British to evacuate their troops. He had a mixed record as a military leader during his first three years. He failed to forestall a British attack on New York by his defeat at the Battle of Long Island (Brooklyn Heights) and was forced to retreat first into Manhattan, then Westchester and finally New Jersey. Victories at Trenton and Princeton in the winter of 1776–1777 were followed by defeats at Brandywine and Germantown and the temporary loss of the national capital, Philadelphia, requiring the central government to flee.

Washington's army suffered through semi-starvation and large-scale desertions at Valley Forge in the winter of 1777–1778. It was at this time that he almost lost his command because of the machinations of a clique in Congress and the military that favored Gen. Horatio Gates for commander-in-chief. With the defeat of the rival group, Washington became more secure in his position.

In perhaps his greatest tactical stroke he helped to bring about a successful conclusion of the American Revolution. He took his troops in a rapid march south from the Hudson Valley to the Virginia Tidewater area to trap Lord Cornwallis and the main British army at Yorktown. Cornwallis' surrender (October 19, 1781), following a blockade by a combined American–French land and naval force, effectively ended hostilities.

Retiring to Mount Vernon, Washington was called back to public life on several occasions. He was elected the nation's first President (1788), serving for two terms. He died in 1799.

Along with such figures as Abraham Lincoln, Generals Grant and Lee and Davy Crockett, Washington has been portrayed in numerous films. The four-reel historical drama *Washington at Valley Forge* (1914) mixed a melodramatic fictional plot with historical events. Unfortunately, he appeared only as a cameo or minor character in most other films, often overshadowed by fictional heroes and heroines, as in *Janice Meredith* (1924) in which he is seen at the end performing a wedding ceremony of the two leads. Other films of this type include *America* (1924), *Are We Civilized?* (1934), *The Howards of Virginia* (1940), *Unconquered* (1947) and *When the Redskins Rode* (1951). He was a minor character in such biographical dramas as *Betsy Ross* (1917) and *John Paul Jones* (1959). Sometimes his image was invoked to support propaganda dramas or documentaries, as in *The Battle Cry of Peace* (1915) and *Following the Flag to France* (1918). ■

Washington at Valley Forge (1914), U.

Dir. Francis Ford, Grace Cunard; *Sc.* Francis Ford, Grace Cunard; *Cast includes:* Francis Ford, Grace Cunard.

A silent drama about General Washington

during the American Revolution, the film covers a lot of territory. It depicts some of the causes leading to the uprising of the colonies, several battles and an incident at an inn in which a local heroine (Grace Cunard) overhears a plot to kill the general, played by director–screenwriter Francis Ford (John's older brother), while he is asleep. She exchanges rooms with him, thus sacrificing her own life to save that of the commander-in-chief.

An epic of sorts within its own limitations (four reels), the film re-enacts several historical incidents, including Paul Revere's ride and the heroic actions of the Minute Men. It also introduces some of the major figures of the American Revolution, including Lafayette. ■

Washington, D.C. The nation's capital has been the focus of several wartime comedies, spy films and dramas. Some features concentrated on the country's early conflicts. In *Barbary Pirate* (1949), for instance, about America's troubles with Mediterranean principalities, hero Donald Woods uncovers a traitor in Washington who has been supplying the pirates with information concerning the cargo of American ships. Cecil B. DeMille's *The Buccaneer* (1938), a biographical drama about the exploits of Jean Lafitte during the War of 1812, opens with the burning of Washington by the British. In *Abraham Lincoln* (1924), which highlights the American Civil War, one stirring sequence shows hordes of men pouring into Washington from different sections of the nation in answer to Lincoln's call for volunteers.

Hollywood generally viewed Washington businessmen and politicians with a jaundiced eye when it came to Indian affairs. Such films as *The Flaming Frontier* (1926) and *Seminole Uprising* (1955) showed unscrupulous tycoons and callous politicos who, through the use of military force, plotted to steal land from the Indians.

Washington became the setting for films about both imaginary and actual wars during the 20th century. *The Battle Cry of Peace* (1915), an early preparedness film about a fictitious war, envisions a defenseless America invaded by a foreign country. New York and Washington are bombed from the air. Once America entered World War I, film studios depicted Washington as a hotbed of spy activities. For example, Kitty Gordon, as an ad-

venturess in *As in a Looking Glass* (1916), is blackmailed by foreign agents into stealing secret government plans from a Washington official. According to the drama *Paying the Price* (1916), foreign agents were already working in Washington trying to steal the formula for a high explosive even before America's entry in the war.

World War II brought profound changes to Washington, transforming the city from a provincial southern town ensconced in its comfortable casual pace to a bustling, overcrowded, wheeling-and-dealing political nerve center. This transformation, so aptly described in David Brinkley's 1988 book *Washington Goes to War*, was reflected in films set in the capital during the war. They encompassed both comedies and spy dramas, sometimes blending the two genres. *Careful, Soft Shoulders* (1942), a comedy set in wartime Washington, stars Virginia Bruce as a bored socialite who gets mixed up with Nazi agents. However, most comedies about wartime Washington narrowed their themes to the confusion and crowded conditions that beset the capital. *Government Girl* (1943), a weak World War II satire, dealt with these hectic and confused living conditions. *The More the Merrier* (1943) starred Jean Arthur as an office worker in the crowded capital. Middle-aged Charles Coburn, arriving in town, has difficulties in locating living quarters and rents half of Arthur's apartment and proceeds to play Cupid. *Get Going* (1943), with Robert Paige and Grace McDonald, concerns wartime Washington's shortages of available males and housing. *Johnny Doesn't Live Here Any More* (1944) features William Terry as an inductee who turns over his apartment to the alluring Simone Simon— with the predictable results. *The Doughgirls* (1944), also set in crowded Washington, primarily concerns three young women (Ann Sheridan, Alexis Smith and Jane Wyman) and their romantic misadventures. *Standing Room Only* (1944), a comedy starring Fred MacMurray and Paulette Goddard, again concerns teeming Washington.

Low-budget World War II spy dramas occasionally used the capital as their background. In *The Lone Wolf Spy Hunt* (1939) Warren William as the title character foils a Washington spy network bent on stealing secret antiaircraft plans. In *Pacific Rendezvous* (1942) Lee Bowman, as a navy officer and code expert, captures a Nazi spy ring operating in the capital. Sherlock Holmes and Dr. Watson (Basil Rathbone and Nigel Bruce) travel to the U.S. to take on an international spy ring in *Sherlock Holmes in Washington* (1943). *Ladies of Washington* (1944) has Anthony Quinn as an enemy agent trying to extract secrets from government worker Sheila Ryan.

Virtually all the above films were made in Hollywood studios, but the stock footage used as establishing shots and backgrounds gave movie audiences, many of whom in those less-traveled times seldom ventured beyond their state, various views of their capital. The climactic scene of *They Made Her a Spy* (1939), a routine drama about enemy agents operating in the U.S., takes place atop the Washington Monument. "Every time I look out at Washington," a chatty elevator operator admits, "I kind o' get the feeling that all this is permanent, that it's strong, that it's here to stay." He undoubtedly reflected the wartime patriotic spirit of many filmgoers who, while sitting in darkened theatres, saw the same grand vistas. ■

Washington Under the British Flag
(1916). See George Washington. ■

Wasted Lives
(1923), Second National Film. *Dir.* Clarence Geldert; *Sc.* William B. Laub; *Cast includes:* Richard Wayne, Catherine Murphy, Winter Hall, Lillian Leighton.

Richard Wayne portrays a dedicated doctor who devotes most of his time to a children's hospital until World War I takes him away in this domestic drama. He leaves his wife (Catherine Murphy) behind and sails for France. News arrives that he has been killed at the front. His mother withdraws her financial support of the hospital. Meanwhile, a former suitor asks the widow to be his wife. When the doctor's mother is seriously hurt in an accident, her son unexpectedly appears and saves her life. All is set right with his return. ■

Watch on the Rhine
(1943), WB. *Dir.* Herman Shumlin; *Sc.* Dashiell Hammett, Lillian Hellman; *Cast includes:* Bette Davis, Paul Lukas, Geraldine Fitzgerald, Lucile Watson, Beulah Bondi, George Coulouris.

Based on Lillian Hellman's anti-Fascist play, this World War II drama stars Paul Lukas as Kurt Muller, an anti-Nazi resistance leader and Bette Davis as his strong-willed and devoted wife. They journey to prewar America from their native Germany only to encounter elements of Fascism in this seemingly peaceful land. Lukas, a former engineer, forsakes his career and personal safety to fight against tyranny. A veteran of the Spanish Civil War where he fought against Franco, he now struggles against the forces of Hitler. When a fellow passenger aboard a train asks him what his trade is, he replies, "I fight against Fascism." Bette Davis, as his patient and loving wife, understands his passion and reassures him that she has never had any regretful moments. Lucile Watson plays Davis' doughty and headstrong mother who has been insulated from world politics. "Well," she remarks after a harrowing encounter with a Fascist guest in her own home, "we've been shaken out of the magnolias." George Coulouris plays a Rumanian count and blackmailer. A parasite swept to American shores from the backwash of European decadence, he willingly trades in human lives to fill his pockets.

Herman Shumlin, who directed the stage version as well as the film, underscores the theme that Fascism may permeate the most tranquil American home. "You don't know what it's like to be frightened," Muller says to his wife's family in America. "Unfortunately, you'll have to learn." His wife later echoes a similar warning. "The world has changed, and some of the people in it are dangerous. It's time you knew that." Shumlin pays tribute to men like Kurt Muller, who have the courage to fight totalitarianism regardless of the dangers. When Muller once again prepares to go to Germany where there is a price on his head, his mother-in-law asks, "Must it always be your hands?" "For each man his own hands," Muller explains. "Each can find his own excuse." The film, however, seems overly didactic by today's standards, especially some of Muller's long speeches to his son as he is about to depart. ■

Waterfront
(1944). See Spy Films: the Talkies. ■

Waterloo, Battle of.
See Napoleonic Wars. ■

Waterloo Bridge
(1931), U. *Dir.* James Whale; *Sc.* Benn W. Levy, Tom Reed; *Cast includes:* Mae Clarke, Kent Douglass, Doris Lloyd, Enid Bennett, Bette Davis.

A London streetwalker (Mae Clarke) falls

in love with a Canadian soldier in this World War I romantic drama. The prostitute doesn't reveal her nocturnal activities to the soldier (Kent Douglass) who falls in love with her and proposes marriage. During a weekend at his family estate, she confesses all to her lover's aristocratic mother who encourages the girl to break off the relationship for the boy's sake. Clarke is later killed during an air raid. Bette Davis portrays the soldier's sister. The film is based on Robert E. Sherwood's stage play, which saw two other screen adaptations, one in 1940 and another, retitled *Gaby*, in 1956. ■

Waterloo Bridge (1940), MGM. *Dir.* Mervyn LeRoy; *Sc.* S. N. Behrman, Hans Rameau, George Froeschel; *Cast includes:* Vivien Leigh, Robert Taylor, Lucile Watson, Virginia Field, Maria Ouspenskaya.

A remake of the 1931 romantic drama set in England during World I, this version of the Robert Sherwood play stars Vivien Leigh as a young ballet dancer who falls in love with a British officer (Robert Taylor). They make plans for their marriage during his next furlough, but after he leaves she receives news that he has been killed in action. Completely crushed, she becomes a streetwalker. But Taylor is very much alive and sees her at the railway station where she is trying to pick up men. The romance is renewed, but she decides to commit suicide rather than embarrass his prestigious family.

This new screen version begins with a flashback. It shows Taylor, gray-haired and older, returning to Waterloo Bridge where he had first met Leigh. World War II has begun and he is once again on his way to France to fight. He has stopped at the bridge to recall another war when a spirited dancer and a young officer were once very much in love. ■

We Accuse (1945), Irvin Shapiro. Sc. John Bright.

A compilation of German, Soviet and American newsreel footage, the documentary covers the events leading up to the Kharkov trial. Kharkov, a Russian city long under the occupation of the Nazis, suffered 300,000 casualties, many the result of atrocities committed by the brutal invaders. Four defendants, a German captain, a lieutenant, a private and a confessed traitor, were held responsible by the Soviets for the deaths. Included are scenes of some of the victims, followed by the

hanging of the four who were found guilty. The film, narrated by Everett Sloane, contains several lively battle sequences, some of which have appeared in earlier documentaries. ■

We Americans (1928), U. *Dir.* Edward Sloman; *Sc.* Edward Sloman, Alfred A. Cohn; *Cast includes:* George Sidney, Patsy Ruth Miller, George Lewis, Eddie Phillips.

Social prejudice threatens a romance in this domestic drama with a World War I background. Three young Americans, whose lives are somewhat intertwined, enlist when war erupts. John Boles portrays the son of an important family in society. He is in love with the daughter of Russian-Jewish immigrants. Eddie Phillips plays an Italian-American who is engaged to the daughter of German immigrants. George Lewis, as the brother of Boles' sweetheart, completes the trio.

During a battle, Lewis is killed saving Boles' life while Phillips loses a leg. The two survivors return home where Phillips marries his fiancee. Boles meets resistance from his family when he tells of his plans to marry his loved one. But once they meet the girl's parents and learn of the dead son's sacrifice, Boles' parents accept the romantic union. ■

We Are the Marines (1942), TCF. *Dir.* Louis de Rochemont; *Sc.* James L. Shute, J. T. Everett, J. S. Martin, John Monks, Jr.

This World War II documentary, a collaborative effort between "The March of Time" series and The U.S. Marine Corps, depicts the history, training and battles of the marines. The film covers this branch of service during its delicate period in China and Shanghai before the bombing of Pearl Harbor as well as its gallant defense of the islands in the Pacific. The documentary ends with the preparations and final assault of a marine unit on another island in the Pacific. Besides being a stirring work of propaganda praising the achievements of the Marine Corps, the film, narrated by Westbrook Van Voorhis, made a strong case for enlisting in this service. ■

We Were Strangers (1949), Col. *Dir.* John Huston; *Sc.* Peter Viertel, John Huston; *Cast includes:* Jennifer Jones, John Garfield, Pedro Armendariz, Gilbert Roland, Ramon Novarro.

The overthrow of Cuba's Machado dictatorship forms the background for this suspense drama. Revolutionaries plot to assassinate the top government leaders. They plan to dig a tunnel to the center of a large Havana cemetery where the politicians will assemble for a funeral. John Garfield portrays the leader in charge of the small band of diggers. But a twist of fate interferes with the scheme when the family of the deceased changes the site of the burial. Garfield is then killed in a shootout with the military police as the revolution erupts. Jennifer Jones plays a conspirator whose brother was murdered by the corrupt regime. Pedro Armendariz portrays a despotic policeman who relentlessly stalks the rebels. ■

Wead, Frank W. See *The Wings of Eagles* (1957). ■

C. Aubrey Smith, the perennial protector of Britain's far-flung empire, issues orders to his sergeant major (Victor McLaglen). *Wee Willie Winkie* (1937).

Wee Willie Winkie (1937), TCF. *Dir.* John Ford; *Sc.* Ernest Pascal, Julien Josephson; *Cast includes:* Shirley Temple, Victor McLaglen, C. Aubrey Smith, June Lang, Michael Whalen, Caesar Romero.

Based on a story by Rudyard Kipling, the film stars Shirley Temple who applies her charms to both her grandfather, a colonel at a British outpost in India, and his adversary, a native chieftain about to declare war upon the soldiers. When she hears of the impending danger, Shirley decides to visit the enemy stronghold and convince Khoda Khan (Caesar Romero) to seek peace instead. Victor McLaglen plays a sergeant-major who is mortally wounded while on a scouting mission. Director John Ford provides plenty of action, color and sentimentality in this outdoor ad-

venture of colonial India. See also Empire Films. ■

Welcome Home, Soldier Boys (1972). See Crime and War. ■

We'll Bury You (1962). See Cold War. ■

West of Shanghai (1937), WB. *Dir.* John Farrow; *Sc.* Crane Wilbur; *Cast includes:* Boris Karloff, Beverly Roberts, Ricardo Cortez, Gordon Oliver, Vladimir Sokoloff, Sheila Bromley.

Boris Karloff plays a menacing war lord in this drama set during the early 1930s in strife-torn China. Holding a handful of Americans captive, he is as likely to kill one as invite another to join him in conversation— such is the inscrutable mind of General Wu Yen Fang. The prisoners argue and fall in love with each other while awaiting their death or release. Finally, government troops catch up with Karloff and end his career in front of a firing squad. The film, which focuses on melodrama rather than the social and political issues of China, contains adequate suspense and includes action sequences of battles between the bandit leader's underlings and government forces.

Based on Porter Emerson Browne's play *The Bad Man*, the film had been made twice before (1923, 1930) under that title and in a Latin American setting. Originally released under the title *The War Lord*, the film anticipated Karloff's "Mr. Wong" detective series that was launched the following year for Monogram studios. See also Chinese Civil Wars. ■

West Wind (1915). See Cheyenne Wars. ■

We've Never Been Licked (1943), U. *Dir.* John Rawlins; *Sc.* Norman Reilly Raine and Nick Grinde; *Cast includes:* Richard Quine, Noah Beery, Jr., Anne Gwynne, Martha O'Driscoll, William Frawley.

Richard Quine plays a double agent in this World War II drama of intrigue and deception. As a student at Texas A & M and the son of a military officer who has graduated from the famous agricultural and mechanics university, Quine becomes unpopular with fellow students when he takes up the Japanese cause. He is dismissed from the school when officials learn that he has given Japanese agents a secret formula. Quine returns to Japan where he had lived for a number of years and broadcasts Japanese propaganda to the U.S. and elsewhere. Quine, however, is secretly sending military information to American Intelligence. Having the trust of Japanese officials, he joins a bombing mission, overpowers the pilot and aims the plane into a Japanese aircraft carrier at the cost of his own life.

Large segments of the film were shot on the campus of Texas A & M, with its thousands of students participating in several scenes. The plot is similar to that of *Appointment in Berlin*, released the same year, in which George Sanders flees to Germany, gains the trust of the Nazis and secretly broadcasts military information to England. He also loses his life in the last scenes. ■

"What Are We Fighting For?" (1943), U. *Dir.* Erle C. Kenton; *Sc.* Paul Huston; *Cast includes:* Lon Chaney, Osa Massen, Robert Paige, Samuel S. Hinds.

A one-reel propaganda short produced during World War II as part of a series called "America Speaks," the film was intended to enlighten the average American citizen about the importance of freedom. Lon Chaney portrays a complainer who is critical of blackouts, wartime shortages and other inconveniences. A local air raid warden (Samuel S. Hinds) confronts him with a refugee (Osa Massen) who extols the virtues of democracy. ■

What Did You Do in the War, Daddy? (1966), UA. *Dir.* Blake Edwards; *Sc.* William Peter Blatty; *Cast includes:* James Coburn, Dick Shawn, Aldo Ray, Harry Morgan, Carroll O'Connor.

An American company of G.I.s is assigned to capture an Italian town in this satirical comedy set in 1943. The Italian troops stationed in the town are more than willing to submit to the Americans. When the Italian commander asks the American captain if he's ready to surrender, the Yank exclaims: "Hell, no! Do you surrender?" "Of course," the Italian replies. He agrees under one condition— that his Italian troops first have their wine festival and soccer game. The war-weary Americans join the happy-go-lucky Italians in their festivities while communicating to headquarters that the enemy is offering resistance.

James Coburn, as a sharp lieutenant, con-tinually comes to the aid of his eccentric and inexperienced captain (Dick Shawn) who manages to foul up every assignment. Carroll O'Connor portrays an American general while Harry Morgan plays a major who gets lost in the catacombs. The film takes on an anti-heroic tone. Some of the comedy material seems repetitive. ■

What Next, Corporal Hargrove? (1945). See Service Comedy. ■

Doughboys Edmund Lowe and Victor McLaglen argue over Dolores Del Rio. *What Price Glory?* (1926).

What Price Glory? (1926), Fox. *Dir.* Raoul Walsh; *Sc.* James T. O'Donohoe; *Cast includes:* Victor McLaglen, Edmund Lowe, Dolores Del Rio, William Mong, Phyllis Haver, Leslie Fenton, Sammy Cohen.

Based on the stage play by Laurence Stallings and Maxwell Anderson, the film version of the World War I comedy drama emphasizes the rivalry between two marines, Captain Flagg (Victor McLaglen) and Sergeant Quirt (Edmund Lowe), and plays down the antiwar sentiments of the original. Flagg and Quirt brawl over women, show contempt for officers, and fight each other as well as the enemy. The story begins in China, shifts to the Philippines and finally moves to France during the war, and in each location the two fight with and swear at each other. They treat the war as secondary, a minor annoyance, to their personal feud. Their bravery on the field of battle remains unchallenged, however, each time they are called upon to fight. In France the object of their affection is the young and pretty Charmaine (Dolores Del Rio). Beneath their continuous rivalry they are brothers in arms. So when Flagg marches off, Quirt, who has won Charmaine, drops her and cries out: "Hey, Flagg, wait for baby!"

Although the film, as mentioned earlier, tempered most of the antiwar strains of the stage production, enough was left in to suggest the author's feelings. "Civilization dedicated to destruction—fields of production drenched with blood," reads an early title that denounces war. "There's something rotten about a world that's got to be wet down every thirty years with the blood of boys like those," Captain Flagg declares caustically when his unit suffers casualties later in the film. But these insertions only tended to obfuscate the work's point of view concerning war.

The battle scenes, at times, are quite shocking. One shows a group of soldiers standing in a trench being buried alive when a mine explodes. Another realistic scene depicts a pathetic shell-shocked comrade, played by Leslie Fenton. Viewers who are adept at reading lips will either be amused or horrified at the amount of swearing done by the principals. Playwright Stallings had another work turned into a successful World War I film. His story, "Plumes," became the basis for the epic *The Big Parade*, released the previous year. ■

What Price Glory? (1952), TCF. *Dir.* John Ford; *Sc.* Phoebe and Henry Ephron; *Cast includes:* James Cagney, Corinne Calvert, Dan Dailey, William Demarest, Robert Wagner.

Director John Ford has emphasized the comedy and the action in this second film version of the stage play by Maxwell Anderson and Laurence Stallings. This time around, James Cagney portrays Captain Flagg while Dan Dailey plays the crowing Sergeant Quirt, two marines in France during World War I. They scowl at each other and brawl over women, especially Charmaine (Corinne Calvert), whose affections are open to any friend of France. They leave for the front where Quirt is wounded. When he returns, he continues his wooing of Charmaine. Before he can marry her, the outfit once again marches off to battle. ■

"What to Do With Germany" (1944). See "The March of Time." ■

When Hell Broke Loose (1958), Par. *Dir.* Kenneth G. Crane; *Sc.* Oscar Brodney; *Cast includes:* Charles Bronson, Richard Jaeckel, Violet Rensing, Robert Easton.

An American soldier in Germany during World War II helps to foil an assassination plot against General Eisenhower in this drama. Charles Bronson, as a reluctant G.I. who only entered the service to beat a prison rap, meets a young German woman (Violet Rensing) with whom he falls in love. She reveals to him, and later to American authorities, that her brother (Richard Jaeckel), a member of the Nazi underground, is part of a plot to kill the American military leader.

The film uses a familiar device of many World War II dramas. English-speaking Nazi soldiers, dressed in American uniforms, infiltrate Allied lines. Bronson had appeared in several earlier features in minor roles under his real name, Charles Buchinsky. This was one of his earliest films in which he received top billing. ■

When Johnny Comes Marching Home (1943). See Musicals. ■

"When Lovers Part" (1910), Kalem.

A silent romantic drama of the Civil War period, the film tells of a young suitor who is scorned by his sweetheart's father. When war breaks out, the two men enlist. The father is killed in battle. The young soldier returns to his sweetheart and the romance is rekindled. ■

When Men Desire (1919), Fox. *Dir.* J. Gordon Edwards; *Sc.* Adrian Johnson; *Cast includes:* Theda Bara, Fleming Ward, G. Raymond Nye, Florence Martin.

A young American woman is trapped in Germany when war breaks out in this World War I drama. Theda Bara, better known as the epitome of the vamp than as a vulnerable heroine, stars as the American who barely eludes the lasciviousness of a Prussian officer. While the majority of war movies released during the conflict depicted French or Belgian maids as the object of the enemy's lust, a handful managed to intensify the already existing anti-German feeling by placing the pride of American femininity in jeopardy. ■

When the Lights Go On Again (1944), PRC. *Dir.* William K. Howard; *Sc.* Milton Lazarus; *Cast includes:* Jimmy Lydon, Barbara Belden, Grant Mitchell, Dorothy Peterson.

The problems that wounded soldiers have to face when they return home are explored in this low-keyed but sincere World War II drama. Jimmy Lydon plays a U.S. Marine who is suffering from shell-shock. On his train-ride home he dreams of his life before the war. The film covers this period in flashback while the remainder of his story tells of his rehabilitation through the cooperation of his community and his loved ones. Barbara Belden portrays his patient and understanding sweetheart. Jimmy Lydon was better known for his portrayal of the title character in the popular "Henry Aldrich" comedy films of the 1940s. ∎

When the Redskins Rode (1951), Col. *Dir.* Lew Landers; *Sc.* Robert E. Kent; *Cast includes:* Jon Hall, Mary Castle, John Ridgely, Pedro de Cordoba.

The French and Indian War provides the background for this drama. The story takes place in 1753 in Virginia. The British, who are trying to enlist the aid of the Delaware Indians to fight against the French, are having difficulties because of the interference of a French spy (Mary Castle). She charms Jon Hall, the son of the chief of the Delawares (Pedro de Cordoba), as part of her plot. But Hall soon learns of her real intentions in this routine tale. In an attempt to give the plot a semblance of authenticity, the script writers have added the figure of George Washington, who is portrayed by James Seay. Several action sequences involve skirmishes between the hostiles and the militiamen. ∎

When Willie Comes Marching Home (1950), TCF. *Dir.* John Ford; *Sc.* Mary Loos, Richard Sale; *Cast includes:* Dan Dailey, Corinne Calvert, Colleen Townsend, William Demarest.

Director John Ford's World War II satire on heroism stars Dan Dailey as a local hero who is the first to enlist after Pearl Harbor. But when he is stationed at a local base near his home town, his friends think he is a slacker. He finally gets a chance to see action when he is assigned as a gunner on a B-17 bomber. During a flight over England, the crew is told to bail out. Dailey, who has been asleep, finally parachutes out over France where he joins up with the underground. Corinne Calvert plays the sensual leader of the French Resistance. He returns to England with some top secret films and then to the U.S. where his superiors brand him a hero. When he returns home, no one believes his fanciful story until the army verifies his overseas experiences. Comic character actor William Demar-

est portrays Dailey's father who has never forgotten his own experiences in World War I. ∎

Which Way to the Front? (1970), WB. *Dir.* Jerry Lewis; *Sc.* Gerald Gardner, Dee Caruso; *Cast includes:* Jerry Lewis, Jan Murray, John Wood, Steve Franken.

Jerry Lewis stars in this weak comedy set during World War II. He plays a neurotic tycoon who is rejected by the draft board. Determined to do his share in the conflict, he hires a trio of other 4-Fs and, with several of his servants, organizes a motley guerrilla unit. They journey to Italy aboard his yacht where Lewis manages to capture a Nazi general, impersonates a German officer and does a Chaplinesque dance with Hitler. Other popular personalities of the period who appear in this generally unfunny film include Sidney Miller, Kay Ballard, Paul Winchell and Jan Murray. ∎

"While America Sleeps" (1939). See "Crime Does Not Pay." ∎

White Angel, The (1936), WB. *Dir.* William Dieterle; *Sc.* Mourdaunt Shairp, Michael Jacoby; *Cast includes:* Kay Francis, Ian Hunter, Donald Wood, Nigel Bruce, Donald Crisp, Henry O'Neill.

A biographical drama of Florence Nightingale, that stalwart figure who fought the prejudices of her period to introduce hospital and sanitation reforms, the film centers on her work during the Crimean War. Based on Lytton Strachey's account of Nightingale's life, the screen version digresses enough to present a good share of historical inaccuracies. Kay Francis portrays the nurse who tries to help the endless procession of the war's casualties. Some of the most effective scenes are those at Scutari Hospital in the Crimea. Donald Crisp plays a traditional, close-minded bureaucrat who resists innovation and change. Montagu Love portrays the stodgy undersecretary of war who denies assistance to the struggling nurse.

The actual events in Florence Nightingale's life prove to be more exciting than the ones painted on the screen. While caring for wounded British soldiers as a nurse during the Crimean War, she began to introduce hospital procedures that brought her world-wide fame. She is considered the founder of modern nursing as a result of her contributions and innovations in the training and techniques of nursing and hospital administration. The White Angel is only a partial biography that focuses principally on her work in the Crimean War. The movie gains a sense of realism with scenes at the hospital in Scutari, which she founded to tend to the war-wounded.

Born in Florence, Italy, she started visiting hospitals in 1844 while still in her early 20s. In 1850 she was with the nursing sisters of St. Vincent DePaul in Alexandria, Egypt. She continued her training the following year at the institute for Protestant deaconesses at Kaiserwerth, Germany. In 1854, shortly after the start of the Crimean War, she organized a unit of women nurses to serve in the Crimea where she set up model hospitals at Scutari and Balaklava to handle the heavy influx of wounded soldiers. British newspapers chronicled her dedicated and untiring service to the wounded and made her a public figure. In 1860 she used money from a testimonial war fund in her honor to start the Nightingale School and Home for training nurses at St. Thomas Hospital, London. She also wrote extensively on the subjects of nursing care and hospital administration. She was the first woman to be awarded the Order of Merit by the British government.

Florence Nightingale died in 1910 at age 90, having lived long enough to witness the acceptance of many of her innovations as standard procedures in hospitals around the world. The film shows her receiving a brooch from a grateful Queen Victoria. On it is inscribed: "Blessed Are the Merciful." ∎

White Black Sheep, The (1926), FN. Dir. Sidney Olcott; Sc. Jerome Wilson, Agnes Pat McKenna; Cast includes: Richard Barthelmess, Patsy Ruth Miller, Constance Howard, Erville Alderson.

Richard Barthelmess portrays the aimless son of an English army officer who has given up on the boy in despair. The son joins the army using a pseudonym and is sent to North Africa. The Arabs, who plan a revolt against the British garrison, capture Barthelmess. His commanding officer thinks he has deserted. Barthelmess escapes and returns with information that saves the garrison, now under the command of his father. The film offers little in the way of action. ∎

White Cliffs of Dover, The (1944), MGM. Dir. Clarence Brown; Sc. Claudine West, Jan Lustig, George Froeschel; Cast includes: Irene Dunne, Alan Marshal, Van Johnson, Frank Morgan, C. Aubrey Smith, Dame May Whitty.

Irene Dunne portrays a young American who, while vacationing in England, meets and marries an aristocrat, only to lose him in World War I. The drama unfolds in flashback as Dunne, working for the Red Cross in World War II, reflects back to 1914 and the major events in her life in England—her whirlwind courtship, American troops arriving in Europe in 1917, her last meeting with her husband in Dieppe, his death during the last days of the war and her father suggesting that she take her young son to America to keep him out of the next conflict.

When the film returns to the present, she sees her own son, critically wounded in action, brought into a hospital. She later comes to his bedside where he recalls an American soldier's last words before he was killed. "He said that God would never forgive us . . . if we break the faith with the dead again." Outside the hospital American troops are again marching in the streets alongside English troops. As she watches the young soldiers, her critically wounded son quietly slips away. "They'll help bring peace again," she says, still looking out of the window and unaware that he has died, "a peace that will stick." Alan Marshall plays her husband while Roddy McDowall portrays the son as a young boy. Peter Lawford has the role of the son as a young man. Frank Morgan enacts her stubborn American father.

The film, based on the poem "The White Cliffs" by Alice Duer Miller, underscores the strong ties that exist between both nations. The marriage between the young American woman and the Englishman becomes a symbol of the two nations uniting in a single cause. Released during World War II, the film singled out the Germans as the aggressors, preparing well in advance for this conflict. This is established in the scene in which Dunne's young son invites two German boys—fellow students—to his home. The time period is the early 1930s. When one mentions that the estate will make a good airfield, Dunne's father provokes the boys to elaborate. They admit that Germany never acknowledged the armistice of World War I—that the next war will end differently.

Elated over their earlier success with Mrs.

Miniver (1942), the moguls at MGM attempted to repeat that achievement. Although the film probably helped to win over more Americans to the British cause, it never attained the popularity of the former work. Neither did other Hollywood features with similar themes and backgrounds, such as *This Above All* (1942) and *Forever and a Day* (1943). ■

White Feather (1955), TCF. *Dir.* Robert Webb; *Sc.* Delmer Daves, Leo Townsend; *Cast includes:* Robert Wagner, John Lund, Debra Paget, Jeffrey Hunter.

This well-intentioned drama concerns the Cheyennes who, like other neighboring tribes, are being forced to move from their home in Wyoming to new lands to the south. Set during the late 1870s following the end of the major Indian wars, the story focuses on the Cheyenne chief's proud son (Jeffrey Hunter) who stubbornly resists the new treaty offered by the U.S. government and signed by Hunter's father, Chief Broken Hand (Eduard Franz). The chief realizes the treaty is unfair but knows resistance would mean the slaughter of many of his people. Robert Wagner, as a surveyor who befriends Hunter and tries to convince him to accept the new treaty, manages to prevent wholesale bloodshed between the two adversaries. Wagner and Hunter's sister (Debra Paget) fall in love and ride off together at the end of the film. John Lund, as the even-tempered cavalry colonel of Fort Cheyenne, tries to maintain the uneasy peace in his district.

The film is one of several of this genre released during the 1950s that elicits sympathy for the Indian while portraying the whites as the belligerents. The Washington representative is shown as unduly callous toward the Cheyenne; the local gold prospectors wait anxiously to occupy the Indian lands; the surly owner of the fort trading post incites the local whites to kill the Indians and claim their land. Sympathy for the two male leads is made more palatable by employing Hunter and Wagner, two popular young stars of the 1950s. ■

White Sister, The (1915), Essanay. *Dir.* Fred E. Wright; *Sc.* E. H. Calvert; *Cast includes:* Viola Allen, Richard Travers, Thomas Commerford, Emilie Melville.

F. Marion Crawford's popular romantic novel was adapted to the stage and saw three screen versions in as many decades. Actress Viola Allen, who successfully portrayed the title character on stage, also starred in this, the first, screen adaptation. Set in Italy prior to World War I, Allen meets and falls in love with a handsome young lieutenant (Richard Travers). When her father dies suddenly, her villainous aunt destroys the will and Allen is left with nothing. Meanwhile, her beau is assigned to Africa where he is reportedly killed. Stricken with grief, Allen enters a convent. When the lieutenant returns unexpectedly and finds his sweetheart in a convent, he proposes marriage. But she turns him down. Later, he is wounded in an explosion and sent to the convent hospital where he refuses to consent to an operation unless Allen marries him. ■

White Sister, The (1923), Inspiration Pictures. *Dir.* Henry King; *Sc.* George V. Hobart, Charles E. Whittaker; *Cast includes:* Lillian Gish, Ronald Colman, Gail Kane, J. Barney Sherry.

This romantic drama set in Italy during World War I was the second screen version of F. Marion Crawford's novel. Lillian Gish plays a bereaved young woman who enters a convent when she learns that her lover (Ronald Colman) has been killed in Africa. Colman, as Captain Severi, her dashing hero, returns and tries unsuccessfully to convince her to leave the Church. There is very little in the way of battle scenes of the war although the film includes a sequence of Mt. Vesuvius erupting. Much of the production was photographed in Italy, lending a naturalness to the setting. The film was Ronald Colman's most important role up to this time and helped to launch his screen career as a major star. He had been a stage actor who had appeared in several other silents with little success. ■

White Sister, The (1933), MGM. *Dir.* Victor Fleming; *Sc.* Donald Ogden Stewart; *Cast includes:* Helen Hayes, Clark Gable, Lewis Stone, Louise Closser Hale, May Robson, Edward Arnold.

A third film version and first sound adaptation of F. Marion Crawford's novel, the World War I romantic drama this time around stars Helen Hayes as Angela, the woman who forsakes the world when she thinks her lover has been killed in battle. Clark Gable plays the heroic captain who returns too late to dissuade Hayes from spending her life in a nunnery. This version of the popular story contains much more war footage, including air battles and Gable's escape from a prison camp. ■

Who Goes There? (1917), Vitagraph. *Dir.* William P. S. Earle; *Sc.* Robert W. Chambers; *Cast includes:* Harry Morey, Corinne Griffith, Arthur Donaldson, Mary Maurice.

The drama takes place in Belgium during World War I. An American of Belgian descent (Harry Morey) is captured by the Germans and forced to bring back from England a female spy (Corinne Griffith) who has a secret code. If he does not return with her, a group of Belgian hostages will be killed. He carries out the mission but turns over the code to British agents. On the journey back to Belgium he and the spy fall in love although she is betrothed to the German officer (Arthur Donaldson) who sent Morey to England. ■

Who Shall Live and Who Shall Die? (1981), Blue Light. *Dir.* Laurence Jarvik.

A documentary criticizing the American Jewish leadership for not doing more to save European Jewry from the Nazi death camps, the film chiefly employs interviews with heads of wartime committees and refugee boards in a variety of countries to prove its premise. One of the major points brought out is that little was done on the parts of American Jews or the U.S. government when, in the early 1940s, reports began to trickle out of Europe about the plight of the Jews. In defense of President Roosevelt, whom the film charges with turning over the refugee problem to an indifferent State Department instead of the more able and concerned Secretary of the Treasury Henry Morganthau, some of those interviewed explained that the U.S. had committed all its energy and resources to fighting the war, giving the refugee situation minor priority status.

Even before it was officially released, the film came under attack by Jewish spokespersons who argued that those European Jews who were caught in Hitler's web were beyond the reach of both American Jewish organizations and the Allied Armed Forces. ■

Who Was the Other Man? (1917). See Spy Films: the Silents. ■

Whom the Gods Destroy (1916), Vitagraph. *Dir* William P. S. Earle; *Sc.* J. Stuart Blackton; *Cast includes:* Marc MacDermott, Alice Joyce, Harry T. Morey.

The story takes place during the Irish insurrection and concerns two close friends, one an Irish patriot and the other an officer in the English navy. Each fights with bravery and distinction for his own cause in the midst of Ireland's struggle for freedom. And both are in love with the same young woman (Alice Joyce). The film is loosely based on a contemporary incident concerning Sir Roger Casement, whom the English courts had found guilty of treason. In the screen version he is portrayed by Marc MacDermott.

A storm of controversy immediately followed its release. Pro-Irish organizations objected to its treatment of Irish patriots as betrayers of their country. Riots flared up at some theaters where the film was being shown. ■

Why America Will Win (1918), Fox. *Dir.* Richard Stanton; *Sc.* Adrien Johnson; *Cast includes:* Harris Gordon, Olaf Skavlan, A. Alexander, R. A. Faulkner.

A World War I propaganda film, the drama includes famous personages of the period to help establish authenticity. General Pershing is portrayed as a rather boring and pompous figure. The Kaiser appears and is destroyed by a bolt of lightning. But the main thrust of the story deals with the Allied treatment of Germany after the war. It argues for a demilitarized Germany, severe reparations and forced occupation.

The film was not alone in its censorious attitude toward Germany. Other releases suggested equally tough retribution. *Why Germany Must Pay* (1919) hinted that Belgium should annex parts of German territory as war reparations. *My Four Years in Germany* (1918) warned that a way should be sought to prevent Germany from ever again gaining political and military power. *The Kaiser's Finish* (1918) advocated a public hanging for the Kaiser in Times Square. *After the War* (1918) championed war trials and executions of German military leaders. Other films had different solutions, all equally interesting and unique. ■

"Why Korea?" (1951), TCF. *Sc.* Joseph Kenas, Ulric Bell.

This half-hour Korean War documentary

attempts to present the reasons why the U.S. elected to send troops to Korea. The film goes back to 1931 and Japan's incursion into Manchuria as well as to other invasions by belligerent countries in its search for explanations. Any aggression that is ignored threatens all peaceful nations, the narrator suggests. The film is composed of newsreels and other documentary footage. ∎

Why This War? (1939), Jewell. *Dir.* Samuel Cummins.

An antiwar documentary focusing on World War I, the compiler, Samuel Cummins, underscores those he holds responsible for the senseless slaughter and devastation. They include the imperialists, the munitions profiteers and the military. The film covers a period of 25 years, including the causes of World War I, sequences of the various battles, postwar ramifications, the Munich Pact, Germany's march into Austria and Roosevelt's speech on neutrality. Few punches are pulled in the narrator's attack on the horrors of war. The documentary, composed of newsreel footage from several countries, ends with an indictment of war by a mother whose son was killed in the 1914–1918 conflict. ∎

"Why We Fight." A series of documentaries produced during World War II for the U.S. Army, the films were supervised by Col. Frank Capra, former Hollywood director temporarily assigned to Special Services during the war. The series was intended for screening by American servicemen so that they would have a better understanding of the events that led up to the war and learn how other allied nations are fighting back on the home front and in the field. General George C. Marshall, aware that most G.I.s had little knowledge of the political and social issues related to the war, asked Capra to make a series of films that would explain the war in simple terms to this citizens' army. Several of the films were shown in commercial theaters during the conflict. Footage was gathered from a variety of sources, including newsreels, the U.S. Signal Corps, other Allied nations and captured enemy films. Individual entries varied in length from less than one hour to 80 minutes.

It has been estimated that by 1945 more than 45 million servicemen and civilians saw the films. The series, distributed to war plants throughout the nation, did not gain immediate entry to commercial movie houses. Originally, private theater owners were resistant to showing the documentaries, claiming that they were too long. Also, Lowell Mellett, in charge of the Motion Picture Bureau of the Office of War Information, at first balked against their distribution to the general public, holding that the fervor and prejudice of the films infringed upon the criteria for domestic propaganda set down by the O.W.I. Opposition soon crumbled against mounting pressure, including that of Secretary of War Henry Stimson and Army Chief of Staff General George Marshall, and the films received wider public distribution.

Prelude to War (1942), the first in the series, was a hard-hitting attack on each of the Axis Powers, equating their leaders to gangsters. *The Nazis Strike* (1942) was a horrifying exposé of Germany's bombing of Warsaw and the executions that occurred in the wake of Nazi occupation. *The Battle of Russia* (1943) was directed by Anatole Litvak, who used footage from Russian newsreels to convey the heroism of the Soviet people in their stand against the Nazi invaders. Other titles in the series include *Divide and Conquer* (1943), *The Battle of Britain* (1943), *The Battle of China* (1943), and *War Comes to America* (1945).

Credits for the series are difficult to establish since so many talents participated on various assignments. Capra, in charge of the entire unit and project, began to hire civilian and military personnel in 1942. They included, among others, Edgar Peterson, a civilian filmmaker of documentaries; Anatole Litvak, a Hollywood director; Anthony Veiller, a screenwriter; Sam Briskin, a general manager who had been with Columbia. Eric Knight, Leonard Spigelgass, Alan Rivkin, William L. Shirer, James Hilton, John Gunther, Claude Binyon, Carl Foreman and Irving Wallace were some of the other writers. Composer Dmitri Tiomkin scored most of the films. Walt Disney's studios provided any necessary animation, and Walter Huston and Anthony Veiller narrated most of the entries. See individual title entries. ∎

Wife or Country (1918). See Spy Films: the Silents. ∎

Wife Savers (1928). See Service Comedy. ∎

Wife Takes a Flyer, The (1942), Col. *Dir.* Richard Wallace; *Sc.* Gina Kaus, Jay Dratler; *Cast includes:* Joan Bennett, Franchot Tone, Allyn Joslyn, Cecil Cunningham.

A broad spoof on Nazi officialdom and German occupation, the film stars Joan Bennett as a Dutch woman seeking a divorce and Franchot Tone as a downed British flier who poses as Bennett's eccentric husband. Allyn Joslyn portrays a Nazi major in charge of occupation forces in Holland who moves into Bennett's house where Tone is hiding. Situation and verbal comedy, much aimed at poking fun at the Nazis, carry the film. Ultimately, Tone "borrows" a German plane and escapes with Bennett to England. ■

Wild Blue Yonder, The (1951), Rep. *Dir.* Allan Dwan; *Sc.* Richard Tregaskis; *Cast includes:* Wendell Corey, Vera Ralston, Forrest Tucker, Phil Harris, Ruth Donnelly.

A tribute to the men who flew the B-29 Superfortresses during World War II, the film tells the routine story of two officers who disagree on the capabilities of the bomber while competing for the same woman. Wendell Corey, as a daring air force captain, believes the B-29 is able to withstand more stress under combat conditions while Forrest Tucker, who portrays a major behind a desk, thinks otherwise. Corey takes the ship through its paces, sometimes endangering his crew. Meanwhile, he woos Vera Ralston, the object of both men's interest. During a mission against the Japanese in which both men are aboard the same bomber, Corey is wounded when the plane is hit. Tucker, who brings the plane home, sacrifices his life when he attempts to pull a wounded crew member from the burning wreckage. The film, whose basic elements have often appeared in other similar war movies, includes little in the way of action sequences. ■

Wilhelm II (Kaiser) (1859–1941). Emperor of Germany and King of Prussia when the German empire was at its peak, Wilhelm was a belligerent and superficial ruler whose autocratic policies played a major role in precipitating World War I. Great Britain, perceiving his emphasis on building a large navy as a threat, became a suspicious rival, despite the close ties between both ruling families. (Wilhelm's mother was an English princess, and Britain's Queen Victoria was his grandmother.) Wilhelm was an autocratic ruler

who seemed more comfortable with his military aides than civilian advisers.

Before World War I Wilhelm was entangled in several crises, most notably the Moroccan Crisis of 1906, which brought Europe's major powers to the edge of war. He acted on several occasions without fully understanding the consequences. His handling of the Austrian–Serbian crisis in 1914 that developed into World War I may have been an example of his impetuous approach to international affairs. He granted a "blank check" to Austria in its confrontation with Serbia over the assassination of Austrian Archduke Francis Ferdinand. This encouraged Austria to seek military and territorial revenge for the killing. When Russia, as Serbia's ally, and France, as Russia's ally, announced their intent to mobilize, the alarmed Wilhelm immediately declared war on both Russia and France. This started the chain reaction that led to a major conflict.

After four years of fighting, President Wilson called for his abdication as a requirement for peace negotiations. Under pressure from both military and civilian leaders, and with revolution spreading in his country, the Kaiser fled to Holland in 1918 and eventually abdicated. The symbol of German aggression and militarism, he became the target of Allied posters and propaganda films during the war.

Not surprisingly, Wilhelm does not fare well in American films. *The Zeppelin's Last Raid* (1917) suggested that the struggle among the German people for democratic ideals was crushed by their oppressive and war-crazed Kaiser. *The Kaiser, the Beast of Berlin* (1918) portrayed Wilhelm as a self-deluded, vain figure who considers himself larger than life and seems obsessed with a desire for conquest. *The Kaiser's Finish* (1918), a semi-documentary drama, added fuel to America's hatred of the Kaiser. One particular scene suggests that he be lynched in Times Square. *Kultur* (1918), a fictitious re-enactment of the events leading up to World War I, showed the Kaiser plotting for war. *My Four Years in Germany* (1918), based on U.S. Ambassador James W. Gerard's book, emphasized how the Kaiser and other German leaders deceived the U.S. and other countries. In *Why America Will Win* (1918) the Kaiser appears and is destroyed by a bolt of lightning. *Wanted for Murder* (1918), again placed the entire blame for the conflict on Kaiser Wilhelm, portraying him as a bestial creature and war criminal. In *Beware!* (1919) one sequence shows the Kaiser facing a war-crimes trial.

Not only dramas attacked the Kaiser. Fantasies and comedies held him up to scorn and ridicule. *To Hell With the Kaiser* (1918), a fanciful drama, blamed the war solely on the Kaiser. In "The Bond" (1918), a one-reel propaganda short, Charlie Chaplin pummels the Kaiser with an oversized mallet. Cross-eyed Ben Turpin impersonates the Kaiser in "Yankee Doodle in Berlin" (1919).

A few postwar films shifted responsibility for the war onto Germany's leaders. *Isn't Life Wonderful?* (1924), for example, placed the blame for the conflict on the Kaiser and his military advisers, thereby exonerating the German people who are portrayed as dupes of their maniacal leaders. ■

Will It Happen Again? (1948), Film Classics.

Hitler's rise to power is once again the subject in this documentary produced for the Navy Club of the United States. Using footage from newsreels and that made by the U.S. Signal Corps and other branches of our military services as well as captured German newsreels of World War II, the film traces the growth of Nazism and its ultimate incursions into its neighbor's lands, leaving in the wake devastation and death. Grim scenes of concentration camps and informal shots of Hitler and his mistress Eva Braun at his mountain retreat exemplify the range of material covered in this World War II documentary. The film ends with the suggestion that Communist Russia may be emerging as the new scourge. ■

Wind and the Lion, The (1975), UA. Dir. John Milius; Sc. John Milius; Cast includes: Sean Connery, Candice Bergen, Brian Keith, John Huston.

The Moroccan chief (Sean Connery) of a revolutionary force kidnaps some American citizens and provokes an international incident in this adventure drama set in 1904. Candice Bergen plays one of his captors whose attitude toward the Berber leader changes from anger to sympathy when he is betrayed. Brian Keith, as an ambitious Theodore Roosevelt, exploits the situation for his own political advantage. John Huston plays Roosevelt's secretary of state. The film, supposedly based loosely on an actual incident,

includes several battle sequences although the plot is principally concerned with international power plays and the relationship between captive and captor. ■

Winding Stair, The (1926), Fox. Dir. John Griffith Wray; Sc. Julian La Mothe; Cast includes: Alma Rubens, Edmund Lowe, Warner Oland, Mahlon Hamilton.

An officer in the Foreign Legion (Edmund Lowe) is cashiered from the service and eventually vindicated in this romantic drama set prior to and during World War I. As a Legionnaire, he is assigned to suppress a native insurrection in the hills. Believing this is only a ploy on the part of the natives to attack a Moroccan town—a suggestion which his superiors reject—he deserts his post and returns to the town to rescue his sweetheart (Alma Rubens) and others from an attack. He is then drummed out of the corps on grounds of desertion. Later, when World War I begins, he trains a platoon of natives and, under a pseudonym, heroically leads them in battle. France honors his brave deeds by restoring his citizenship. Chester Conklin provides the comic relief. ■

A determined Charles Bickford, as captain of a U.S. aircraft carrier, issues orders to his pilots to strike at the Japanese navy. *Wing and a Prayer* (1944).

Wing and a Prayer (1944), TCF. Dir. Henry Hathaway; Sc. Jerry Cady; Cast includes: Don Ameche, Dana Andrews, Charles Bickford, William Eythe, Sir Cedric Hardwicke.

A U.S. aircraft carrier acts as decoy in this World War II drama that unfolds prior to the Battle of Midway. In a navy war room a solemn and determined admiral, played with conviction by Sir Cedric Hardwicke, outlines

U.S. naval strategy to a group of top-ranking officers. The key part of the plan, to have one aircraft carrier appear in four different locations as though it were four different carriers, will become the plot of this well-conceived film. The Japanese, who plan to invade Midway, must be made to think the U.S. Pacific fleet is an ineffectual fighting force. "Every time one of our pilots encounters a Jap plane, he will return to the carrier as if he couldn't stomach a fight," the admiral explains. "By sending this one carrier on such a mission, we hope to convince the enemy that our fleet is scattered, our fighting morale shattered. Actually, we shall be waiting for them in force near Midway."

Charles Bickford portrays the captain of the selected carrier, while Don Ameche is his hard-nosed air officer. Dana Andrews plays the commander of a squadron of torpedo planes that will bear the brunt of the naval strategy. The pilots suffer repeated losses and have to turn and run each time they see the enemy. In a particularly disturbing scene, Ameche refuses to break radio silence to assist a lost pilot. Finally, the new orders arrive. Bickford reads the long-awaited message over the intercom system to all hands aboard the carrier. "The main Jap fleet is headed for Midway. They're going in for the kill. And so are we. We're through running away. We're through pulling our punches. Our mission is accomplished, and from here on in we fight!"

Director Hathaway makes effective use of silhouettes on board the carrier, actual battle footage and an overall semi-documentary style in this tightly structured and moving war drama based on actual events. Japanese naval power was severely weakened at the Battle of Midway on June 4–7, 1942, one of the crucial battles that turned the tide in favor of the Allies. ∎

Winged Victory (1944), TCF. *Dir.* George Cukor; *Sc.* Moss Hart; *Cast includes:* Mark Daniels, Lon McCallister, Don Taylor, Jeanne Crain, Edmund O'Brien, Red Buttons, Judy Holliday.

This World War II tribute to the gallant men who fly America's airplanes tells the story of six young Americans from all walks of life who join the American Air Force. Leaving behind their loved ones, they train for the coveted moment when they will win their wings. One of the men flunks out, another becomes a father and is killed during a flight before he learns the news. The major roles are played by men in the service. Based on the successful Broadway play by Moss Hart, this earnest and patriotic film captures the dramatic and tender moments in the lives of the young fliers and their wives and sweethearts. ∎

Wings (1927), Par. *Dir.* William Wellman; *Sc.* Hope Loring, Louis D. Lighton; *Cast includes:* Clara Bow, Charles Rogers, Richard Arlen, Gary Cooper, Jobyna Ralston, El Brendel.

The first World War I drama devoted almost entirely to the air war, the film stars Charles Rogers and Richard Arlen as two young aviators who go through training camp together and, eager to see action, are soon sent to France. At first there is tension between the two recruits over a home-town girl (Jobyna Ralston) who prefers Arlen but doesn't want to hurt Rogers' feelings. On their first dawn patrol an exciting air battle occurs during which the two buddies are pitted against the deadly Captain Kellerman and his "Flying Circus," an obvious allusion to Baron von Richthofen. Later, both become decorated heroes. During one mission Arlen is shot down over German territory but survives. He commandeers an enemy plane and heads for his own airfield. Rogers, thinking his buddy has been killed, searches out enemy targets to avenge Arlen's death. After wreaking havoc on the enemy, he spots Arlen's plane and shoots it down, believing its pilot is a German. When he lands, he discovers the tragedy. After the war, he visits Arlen's parents and receives their forgiveness. The last scene shows him reunited with the girl next door (Clara Bow).

The script is not without its excessive sentimentality, particularly in the scene of Arlen's departure for military service. His elderly father is confined to a wheelchair; his mother partially faints as he is about to leave; Arlen takes his little toy teddy bear that he has had since childhood as a good-luck piece; and even the family dog enters to see him off. In another sequence, young Gary Cooper, as a veteran airman who is about to share quarters with the two heroes, leaves his chocolate bar on his cot as he goes for another routine flying exercise. He crashes his plane and is killed. His two bunkmates are ordered to gather up his possessions. They proceed to do so but avoid handling the bar of chocolate.

U.S. aircraft take part in the St. Mihiel offensive during World War I in the first major air drama *Wings* (1927).

Action sequences include well-staged dogfights, realistic scenes of trench warfare, strafings of troops by planes and the aerial bombing of a village. A re-enactment of the St. Mihiel offensive, which was shot from both the ground and the air, cost Paramount $250,000. It was reconstructed near San Antonio with the help of the 2nd Infantry Division's Army Engineers. The government readily loaned servicemen and equipment as long as the studio insured the thousands of troops for $10,000 each and agreed to allow government officials to approve the finished film. Paramount gladly accepted the terms.

If the air duels seem convincing, then writer John Monk Saunders, who submitted the original story, and director William Wellman must take much of the credit. The former was a pursuit pilot in the war while the latter flew with the Lafayette Flying Corps and the Army Air Service. Also, no rear projection shots were used in the combat sequences. Instead, cameras were mounted on the planes and cameramen were placed in dozens of aircraft to simulate the effect of realism.

The shooting star that Rogers paints on his car and, later, on his fighter plane was actually the insignia of the 22nd Aero Pursuit Squadron during the war, according to an October 9, 1988, *New York Times* interview with A. Raymond Brooks, one of the surviving air aces who flew with that squadron in World War I.

The film, together with Lindbergh's successful nonstop flight across the Atlantic the same year as the release of *Wings*, fired the imagination of the public about airplanes and initiated a rush of airplane films from Hollywood as well as foreign studios. In fact, an opening title card in the film presents a tribute by Lindbergh to those who flew in the war. Although the planes used in the making of *Wings* were not models, neither were they of the same vintage as those employed during the war. ■

Wings for the Eagle (1942), WB. *Dir.* Lloyd Bacon; *Sc.* Byron Morgan, B. H. Orkow; *Cast includes:* Ann Sheridan, Dennis Morgan, Jack

Carson, George Tobias, Russell Arms, Don Defore.

The topics covered in this patriotic World War II drama range from draft-dodging to responding to the call of duty. Dennis Morgan portrays an airplane factory worker who becomes essential to the operation of the plant. He is delighted with his position since his purpose is to avoid the draft. When the Japanese attack Pearl Harbor, however, he realizes his duty and enlists in the air force. Character actor George Tobias plays an alien who loves his adopted country but loses his job at the plant until, in a patriotic scene, he is sworn in as a U.S. citizen. When Tobias' son, who once worked at the factory, is killed in battle, Morgan promises to shoot down two enemy planes for him. He is shown near the end fulfilling his pledge. The film also stresses the importance of the home front and the factory workers toward the war effort. ■

Wings of Eagles, The (1957), MGM. *Dir.* John Ford; *Sc.* Frank Fenton, William Wister Haines; *Cast includes:* John Wayne, Dan Dailey, Maureen O'Hara, Ward Bond.

A biographical drama of the life of Commander Frank W. Wead, the film stars John Wayne as the man who won several naval honors and wrote a string of war stories, many of which found their way to the screen. "Sprig" Wead, who is shown successfully fighting an incapacitating illness, helped to promote the concept of navy air power after World War I. Following the attack on Pearl Harbor, he re-enlisted and advanced the concept of jeep carriers, vessels that provided the larger carrier with aircraft. Dan Dailey plays a navy mechanic who is Wead's confidant. Maureen O'Hara portrays Wead's wife. Ward Bond, as a film director, modeled his character after director John Ford. ■

Wings of the Hawk (1953), U. *Dir.* Budd Boetticher; *Sc.* James E. Moser; *Cast includes:* Van Heflin, Julia Adams, Abby Lane, George Dolenz.

This action drama is set in Mexico during the Diaz regime and the Mexican Revolution. The legendary Pancho Villa is busy organizing his guerrillas to resist the despised Federales under President–dictator Diaz. Meanwhile Van Heflin, as an American engineer who has his gold mine taken from him by a colonel of the Federales, decides to join a local group of insurrectionists. Here he meets Julia Adams, who plays a tough bandit. The remainder of the film consists of chases and skirmishes, including a climactic explosion. Some scenes depict the peons suffering injustices at the hands of Mexican soldiers. ■

Wings of the Navy (1939). See Recruitment Films. ■

Wings Over the Pacific (1943), Mon. *Dir.* Phil Rosen; *Sc.* George Sayre; *Cast includes:* Inez Cooper, Edward Norris, Montagu Love, Robert Armstrong.

A World War I veteran and his pretty daughter have their idyllic life on a Pacific Island disrupted by events of the Second World War in this weak drama. Montagu Love plays the old-timer who witnesses the intrusion of his peaceful island by a German pilot (Henry Guttman) and an American navy flier (Edward Norris). Guttman finds oil on the island and relays the information to the Japanese. Meanwhile, Norris falls in love with the veteran's daughter (Inez Cooper). Robert Armstrong portrays a Nazi agent. Hero Norris ends up defeating the Japanese and Nazi elements in this low-budget film.

Monogram was one of several secondary studios that helped to fill the movie screens of wartime America with action and spy "quickies." The sharp contrast between these dramas and those produced by such major studios as MGM, 20th Century-Fox and Paramount can be seen in the size of the cast, the sets and the stars. ■

Winners of the Wilderness (1927), MGM. *Dir.* W. S. Van Dyke; *Sc.* Josephine Chippo; *Cast includes:* Tim McCoy, Joan Crawford, Roy D'Arcy.

Tim McCoy stars in this historical drama of colonial America during the time of the French and Indian War. He portrays a soldier in the British army who manages several heroic feats but is unable to prevent General Braddock's death at the hands of the French and their Indian allies on his way to Fort Duquesne. Joan Crawford portrays a Frenchwoman and the romantic interest. The film includes limited battle scenes in this silent costume drama. ■

Wisconsin Under Fire (1924), Pictorial Sales Bureau.

A documentary concerning Wisconsin troops during World War I, the film tracks the doughboys' experiences from their training camps to their landings in England and France and their ultimate fighting at the front. Sequences depict the Wisconsin units engaged in some of the major battles of the conflict, including those at Alsace, Chateau-Thierry and the Argonne. The troops are shown entering Germany after the Armistice and, finally, departing from France for home. This was one of a series of documentaries released by Pictorial Sales that singled out troops from different states during the war. ∎

"With Lee in Virginia" (1913), Kaybee. *Dir.* Thomas Ince; *Sc.* Thomas Ince; *Cast includes:* Francis Ford, Anna Little, Joe King.

A Civil War drama with numerous action scenes, the story also contains a subplot involving a young woman who is forced to defend her honor by killing her attacker. A faithful black servant, to protect the girl, confesses to the act and is put to death. Actor Hugh Ford portrays Abraham Lincoln. Other historical figures who are impersonated in this silent film include Generals Grant and Lee. ∎

"With the Marines at Tarawa" (1944), U. *Dir.* Capt. Louis Hayward.

A two-reel World War II documentary about the battle for Tarawa in the South Pacific, the film follows the Second Marine Division from its boarding of the transport boats in preparation for the assault until the final victory. Following a four-hour barrage by the U.S. Navy, the marines land and begin to destroy the Japanese sand forts. Some scenes show the wounded being moved back to the ships while the battle rages to its close. Hollywood actor Louis Hayward, a captain in the marines, supervised the 15 combat cameramen, two of whom were killed while making the film. ∎

"Witness to War" (1984), New Directions/New Films. *Dir.* Deborah Shaffer.

A short documentary of the civil war in El Salvador, the film traces the experiences of Charlie Clements, a conscience-ridden American volunteer doctor working in rebel territory. Besides the wounded from the land battles, Dr. Clements had a constant flow of patients as a result of the constant bombing by government aircraft. When he returned to the States in 1983, he testified before various committees on human rights, describing America's role in El Salvador.

Dr. Clements, a 1967 graduate of the U.S. Air Force Academy, had flown cargo planes in Vietnam. He refused to fly on further missions when the U.S. denied any involvement in Laos. He was returned to the States where he addressed an antiwar rally. His captain's rank was removed and he was ordered to a military hospital for psychiatric observation. Discharged six months later, he decided to enter medical school. ∎

Wolfe, or the Conquest of Quebec (1914). See French and Indian War. ∎

Woman (1918). See Women and War. ∎

Woman Disputed, The (1928). See Women and War. ∎

Woman From Monte Carlo, The (1932), FN. *Dir.* Michael Curtiz; *Sc.* Harvey Thew; *Cast includes:* Lil Dagover, Walter Huston, Warren William, John Wray.

A romantic drama with a World War I background, the film stars Lil Dagover, a German actress and star of expressionist films brought over from Europe for her Hollywood screen debut. She plays the wife of Captain Corlax (Walter Huston), the commander of a French battleship. On board the vessel she has a romantic flirtation with an officer (Warren William) who tries to seduce her in his cabin. At that moment the Germans attack and sink the ship, but William and Dagover manage to survive. He is brought up on charges of neglecting his duty. He can only be saved by Huston's wife testifying that she was in his cabin. She does, and he is exonerated. Her husband, who is present at the trial, walks out on her. The film is a remake of Alexander Korda's 1928 feature, *The Night Watch*. ∎

Woman God Forgot, The (1917), Artcraft. *Dir.* Cecil B. DeMille; *Sc.* Jeanie Macpherson; *Cast includes:* Wallace Reid, Geraldine Farrar, Raymond Hatton, Hobart Bosworth, Walter Long.

The drama takes place about 1520, during the Conquest of Mexico by Cortez. Geraldine Farrar portrays Montezuma's daughter who is betrothed to an Aztec prince (Theodore Kosloff). A Spanish officer (Wallace Reid) falls in

Paul Muni (c.) and Louis Hayward (r.), rivals in love, join their fellow French airmen in searching the troubled skies. *The Woman I Love* (1937).

love with the Aztec princess. He is captured by Kosloff, who intends to offer him as a sacrifice to the gods. Farrar reaches the Spanish camp in time to lead Cortez's troops to Reid's rescue. The film attributes this series of incidents to the destruction of the Aztec nation. Raymond Hatton portrays Montezuma, and Hobart Bosworth plays Cortez. There are several battles in this lavish production directed in the typical DeMille style in which spectacle dominates over characterization and historical fact. ∎

Woman I Love, The (1937), RKO. *Dir.* Anatole Litvak; *Sc.* Mary Borden; *Cast includes:* Paul Muni, Miriam Hopkins, Louis Hayward, Colin Clive, Minor Watson.

A pilot with the French flying corps (Paul Muni) is unpopular with his fellow airmen who consider him a jinx. A new member of the squadron (Louis Hayward) befriends him, and events run smoothly until Hayward learns that Muni is the husband of the woman he loves (Miriam Hopkins). During a furious dogfight Hayward is killed and Muni wounded. The married couple renew their old love as Hopkins nurses her wounded husband back to health. The film includes several excellent action sequences.

The film, which failed at the box office, is a remake of a 1924 French feature (remade again in France in 1934), both based on Joseph Kessel's novel, *L'Equipage*. Anatole Litvak directed the 1934 and 1937 versions. Hollywood produced only a handful of World War I films during and after the conflict which featured a Frenchman as the protagonist. American heroes represented the largest number, followed by the British. In air dramas especially, Englishmen dominated the American screen. The situation changed when it came to the romantic interests of the war heroes, especially in such major films as *The Big Parade* and both versions of *What Price Glory*. Young and saucy Frenchwomen dominated the love plots in these films. ∎

Woman of Experience, A (1931). See *Women and War*. ∎

Woman the Germans Shot, The (1918),

Plunkett & Carroll. *Dir.* John G. Adolfi; *Cast includes:* Julia Arthur, Creighton Hale, J. W. Johnston, William Tooker.

American stage actress Julia Arthur portrays the role of nurse Edith Cavell in this World War I silent drama. The film depicts the English heroine's life from early childhood until her capture and execution by the Germans. Nurse Cavell aided wounded Allied and German soldiers in Belgium and remained at her post even when the enemy advanced and overran the dressing station where she worked. Her biography was retold in a sound version in 1939, titled *Nurse Edith Cavell.* ∎

Womanhood, the Glory of the Nation

(1917), Vitagraph. *Dir.* J. Stuart Blackton; *Sc.* H. W. Bergman; *Cast includes:* Alice Joyce, Harry T. Morey, Joseph Kilgour.

While the controversy over America's direction toward the war in Europe raged between the pacifists and those who advocated preparedness, Vitagraph released this propaganda drama supporting the latter group. Alice Joyce plays a young woman returning to the U.S. from the Orient who learns that her homeland, deficient in military forces and weaponry, has been invaded by a foreign power. She returns with the newly appointed Minister of Energies (Harry T. Morey). During her travels Joyce had met Count Dario (Joseph Kilgour), an officer of the foreign invaders and an admirer of hers. She meets him in New York and allies herself with him as a means of gaining military information. Meanwhile, Morey and his forces invent a new weapon, a "Firebug," which helps to defeat the enemy. The Count is killed by his own father for disobedience while the true lovers, Joyce and Morey, are reunited.

Action sequences include airships laying waste to lower New York City, sea battles and trench warfare. Many of these sequences were produced by using models and miniatures. This propaganda tract was one of several of the period that promoted preparedness as the proper course for the nation. ∎

Women and war. War may be a man's business, but the film studios very clearly dramatized the countless ways that the distaff side helped, directly or indirectly, to defeat the enemy. They pictured women as one more reason why the men were fighting and dying,

as nurses and ambulance drivers and in other branches of the military, as spies behind enemy lines, as replacements in war plants and as staunch patriots who were quick to rebuke their brothers and lovers who had become slackers or draped themselves in pacifism.

Films of the home front included heroines who uncovered spy rings that threatened the nation. Other dramas portrayed them as innocent dupes influenced by sophisticated enemy agents. When faced with the dilemma of choosing between country and their loved one, some women opted for the former while others stuck by their man. Whatever the heroine's frailties, the film studios were careful to eschew describing her as frivolous or cowardly.

Sometimes American film studios used the allegorical female figure to symbolize Peace or Civilization. This was particularly noticeable during World War I when the allegorical screen goddess was invoked to serve both causes—patriotism or pacifism. *The Four Horsemen of the Apocalypse* (1921) would be a prime example. Women began playing significant roles in war films as early as 1908. Julia Richards, as "Barbara Frietchie," bravely defends the American flag during the Civil War. This was the first of four adaptations of John Greenleaf Whittier's famous poem. The sister of a wounded Confederate soldier carries out his mission for him in "The Road to Richmond" (1910), another Civil War film. The Lubin studios in 1909 retreated further into history for its short film, "Brave Women of '76," which describes how the wives and sweethearts of an undefended community, whose men were busy fighting the Revolutionary War, pick up arms to resist invaders. A native heroine saves an English doctor's family and an entire British fort during the Indian Mutiny of the 1850s in "The Sepoy's Wife" (1910).

One of the most prolific roles women played in Hollywood's concept of war, especially during World War I, was that of mother. The war mother was a multi-faceted figure. In the early stages of the conflict she was seen as a staunch pacifist. Later, she grieved interminably as her son sailed off to France and the dreaded trenches. In the end, she became a strong advocate of preparedness and nationalism. In *The Battle Cry of Peace* (1915), a preparedness film about a foreign enemy invading a deficient America, a mother musters up the courage to shoot her two daughters rather than have them fall into the depraved hands of the invading hordes. *Four Sons* (1928) focuses on a World War I mother who finds no solace in the armistice after three of her sons are killed in battle. *Mrs. Miniver* (1942) became the prototype for the World War II mother. Greer Garson, as an English wife and mother, loses a daughter-in-law in an air raid and holds a downed Nazi flier prisoner until the police arrive. Her strength and fortitude never waver. Audiences saw her as a symbol of her embattled country. One of the most poignant scenes occurs in the World War II drama *So Proudly We Hail!* (1943) in which a mother, a senior nurse on Bataan before its fall, witnesses the amputation of her own son's legs.

World War I films paid tribute to women by placing them in a variety of sacrificial roles. *As in a Looking Glass* (1916) was one of the earliest World War I dramas to tell of a wife who is killed by enemy agents after she has destroyed vital papers about to fall into the wrong hands. The international personality, Nazimova, in the antiwar film *War Brides* (1916), shoots herself in the presence of her king as a protest against raising children to fight in wars. The famous stage and screen star Billie Burke endangers her own life to save a fellow American while in war-torn Belgium in *Arms and the Girl*, a 1917 comedy drama. *For Valour* (1917), a domestic drama, almost developed into a women's protest tract as it contrasts a daughter's sacrifices at home with those of her brother away at war. He returns with a medal, but she remains unsung. In *Daughter Angele* (1918) Pauline Starke, another popular actress of the period, poses as an orphan girl to gain entrance into a mansion so that she can help capture a German agent signaling to enemy submarines. *Daughter of Destiny* (1918), although set in a mythical kingdom, is blatantly anti-German. It concerns the romantic affairs of an American ambassador's daughter (Madame Petrova) whose husband is a German spy posing as an artist.

Movie studios provided a steady flow of war dramas that pointed out the pitfalls that lay in the paths of unsuspecting young women. In *The Secret Code* (1918) Gloria Swanson, as the wife of a senator, almost compromises his career by her indiscretions with German agents. Swanson once again almost becomes a pawn in the hands of a German spy in *Shifting Sands*, released the same

year. Her former landlord, an enemy agent, tries to blackmail her into stealing her husband's secret plans. Ethel Barrymore in *The Greatest Power* (1917) rebukes her lover when she discovers his pacifist sympathies and his reluctance to offer his newly developed explosive to the U.S. In *Luck and Pluck* (1919) Virginia Lee almost marries an enemy agent but is saved in time by George Walsh. Anna Q. Nilsson in *No Man's Land* (1918) blunders one step further than Virginia Lee when she unsuspectingly marries a German agent. But she is quickly rescued by her former lover (Bert Lytell). Some women were not so fortunate, especially Gloria Swanson in *Wife or Country* (1918), who should have known better from her previous two experiences discussed above. As the wife of an important official in the Justice Department, she becomes involved with German agents and eventually pays for her mistakes with her own life.

One particularly unusual film released only days before the 1918 armistice was Maurice Tourneur's *Woman*. Composed of a prologue, five episodes and an epilogue, the work explored the various roles of women as depicted in myth and history. It concluded with several novel ideas for 1918. Man's historical domination over woman, the film suggests, actually resulted in a form of slavery. Also, it was not until society realized woman's important contributions in World War I, ranging from nurse to factory worker, that it became aware of her vast capabilities.

Silent war-related films produced after World War I presented the more conventional female screen images, including that of spy or nurse. Marion Davies in *The Dark Star* (1919) portrays a secret agent in World War I and gains access to vital plans containing the locations of Turkish fortresses. Betty Compson in *New Lives for Old* (1925) volunteers to serve as a spy and is assigned to have an affair with a suspected officer who is ultimately convicted as a traitor.

The trend continued into the sound period which often added a touch of sophistication. Marlene Dietrich for a time dominated the screen as the worldly woman who faced danger with a smile, often at the cost of her own life. In *Shanghai Express* (1932) she plays Shanghai Lily, the notorious white prostitute who offers herself as mistress to a Chinese warlord so that her English lover can go free. In *Dishonored* (1931) she portrays a German spy who falls in love with the secret agent she has helped to capture. She sets him free and faces a firing squad for her act of love. Greta Garbo made a similar film one year later in which she plays the infamous and alluring spy *Mata Hari*. Myrna Loy in *Stamboul Quest* (1934) portrays Germany's master spy. She is responsible for the demise of Mata Hari who made the fatal mistake of falling in love with one of her victims.

Women were the principals in a host of similar films, including, among others, *Madame Spy* (1934) with Fay Wray, *Operator 13* (1934) with Marion Davies, and *They Made Her a Spy* (1939) with Sally Eilers. Sometimes they were prostitutes called upon to serve their country as spies, as were Norma Talmadge in *The Woman Disputed* (1928), Marlene Dietrich in *Dishonored* (mentioned above) and Helen Twelvetrees in *A Woman of Experience* (1931). Ilona Massey in *International Lady* (1941) plays a dangerous spy in this cautionary tale about the enemy within. Her unusual method of contacting Nazi U-boats and providing them with vital shipping and air force information consists of her using tonal phrasings and musical notes in her songs during her radio broadcasts. In *Spy Ship*, released the following year, Irene Manning portrays a fifth columnist who sells information of ship departures to the enemy.

World War II films added to the image of female patriotism and self-sacrifice both at home and in the front lines. An officer's wife (Claudette Colbert) in *Since You Went Away* (1945) struggles to raise her family while her husband is away fighting the war. Following in the footsteps of *Rosie the Riveter*, released the previous year, she takes a job in a defense plant as a welder. *Parachute Nurse* (1942) paid tribute to those brave nurses who jumped from airplanes to administer aid to the wounded soldiers below. Similarly, *She's in the Army* (1942) saluted the women who enlisted in the ambulance and defense units during the war years. In *Cry Havoc* (1943) a group of volunteer nurses on Bataan vote to remain behind with the wounded although they know their situation is hopeless—that they will be captured by the Japanese. That same year a nurse (Veronica Lake) in *So Proudly We Hail!*, also set on Bataan, after witnessing the death of her man at Pearl Harbor, swears vengeance upon the enemy. She sacrifices her life by carrying a live hand grenade into the midst of a group of Japanese

soldiers. A French hotel maid (Anne Baxter) sacrifices her life in *Five Graves to Cairo* (1943) to help a British soldier escape from the Nazis. *Ladies Courageous* (1944) tells the story of the women who ferried airplanes from the U.S. to England. Constance Bennett and Gracie Fields place their lives in peril when they decide to join the French Resistance and are hunted by the Nazis in *Paris Underground* (1945).

The war also produced its share of spy films with women as secret agents. Lola Lane, as a Russian agent in *Miss V From Moscow* (1943), considered one of the worst films ever made, is sent to Nazi-occupied Paris to pose as a German spy whom she happens to resemble. Virginia Bruce in *Action in Arabia* (1944) portrays a special agent bent on stopping Nazi spies from destroying the Suez Canal.

Several films such as *Rosie the Riveter*, mentioned earlier, and *Swing Shift Maisie* (1943) with Ann Sothern, depicted women filling in at the war plants in crucial positions. Unfortunately, the end of the conflict brought about the end of this new-found image of independence in the work force. But the five years that the women spent in the factories and shipyards taught them that they were just as capable as their male counterparts and left a permanent mark upon them and society. The documentary *The Life and Times of Rosie the Riveter* (1980) covers this period and these issues. Another documentary, *Women in Arms* (1981), provides a more recent description of women in battle, specifically the important role they played in bringing about the downfall of the Somoza regime. ∎

Women in Arms (1981), Hudson River. *Dir.* Virginia Schultz; *Sc.* Virginia Schultz.

A documentary about the overthrow of the Somoza regime in Nicaragua, the film by director–writer Virginia Schultz focuses on the active role that women played in ousting the dictator from his seat of power. Chiefly employing a series of interviews with women of various ages as well as military leaders, Schultz captures the spirit of the Nicaraguan people who sought to put an end to the beatings, torture and oppression they had to endure. The women describe how they fought with guns and crudely constructed bombs alongside their men. Other interviews with men attest to the contributions of their counterparts in the battle. ∎

Women in Bondage (1943), Mon. Dir.
Steve Sekely; *Sc.* Houston Branch; *Cast includes:* Gail Patrick, Nancy Kelly, Gertrude Michael, Anne Nagel, Mary Forbes.

The stern regimentation of the women in Nazi Germany is the subject of this World War II drama. Gail Patrick portrays the loving wife of a wounded German soldier who is paralyzed as a result of his wounds. She is also a section leader for German youth. The insensitive Nazi regime demands that she become a mother—regardless of her husband's condition. Meanwhile, she tries to help her servant girl who wants her marriage to be free of Nazi strictures. Patrick's utter rejection of her country's ruthless interference in the personal lives of its citizens leads her to help the Allied bombers find their targets. H.B. Warner portrays a priest whose humanity and private morality continually clash with those of the local German officials. ∎

Women in the Night (1948), Film Classics.
Dir. William Rowland; *Sc.* R. St. Clair; *Cast includes:* Tara Birell, William Henry, Virginia Christine, Richard Loo.

This low-budget exploitation drama depicts the treatment of women prisoners by the Axis powers near the end of World War II. The film purportedly is based on case histories found in the files of the United Nations Information Office. The weak plot includes scenes of women forced to provide sexual favors for Nazi officers at their club in Shanghai. The Japanese also get into the act of degrading their female captives. The film includes a subplot involving secret agents and a mysterious secret weapon known as the "Cosmic Death Ray." ∎

Women in War (1940), Rep. Dir. John H.
Auer; *Sc.* F. Hugh Herbert, Doris Anderson; *Cast includes:* Elsie Janis, Wendy Barrie, Patric Knowles, Mae Clarke, Dennie Moore, Dorothy Peterson, Billy Gilbert.

The former musical comedy entertainer Elsie Janis stars in this World War II dramatic tribute to the legion of nurses who perform so selflessly in time of war, often under intolerable conditions. Janis is in charge of a group of English nurses working in France. Among them is her own daughter (Wendy Barrie), a former socialite who volunteers for this assignment in lieu of a prison sentence. She falls in love with a British officer (Patric Knowles). The film, one of the earliest to dramatize German air raids and London blackouts, provides enough war scenes of the front lines, villages being bombed and ships being attacked to underscore the director's theme about the horrors of armed conflict. ∎

Woodrow Wilson Film Memorial, The
(1924), Woodrow Wilson Memorial Society. *Dir.* H. F. Dugan.

A documentary covering the political life of President Woodrow Wilson, the film is chiefly concerned with the period from his election to the Presidency until his collapse, the inaugurations of Presidents Harding and Coolidge and Wilson's funeral. Sequences cover incidents leading up to World War I, the draft, the war in Europe and the commemoration of the armistice. Other highlights include the signing of the peace treaty, the return of American troops and the tomb of the Unknown Soldier. ∎

World and the Flesh, The (1932), Par. Dir.
John Cromwell; *Sc.* Oliver H. P. Garrett; *Cast includes:* George Bancroft, Miriam Hopkins, Alan Mowbray, George E. Stone.

The Russian Revolution serves as background for this inept romantic drama involving a rough seaman promoted to commissar and a beautiful aristocrat. A group of aristocrats are frustrated in their plan to flee revolutionary Russia when a sea captain (George Bancroft) and his crew take over the town where the fugitives are hiding. Among them are Miriam Hopkins and her lover, a grand duke (Alan Mowbray). In an attempt to save the lives of her friends, Hopkins distracts the captain by spending the night with him. However, she ends up falling in love. Despite its promising turbulent background, the film quickly succumbs to the familiar romance between a member of royalty and a peasant. Critics attacked the work for its miscasting of the leads and its overacting. Little insight is provided about the causes of the Revolution. ∎

World at War, The (1942), Film Industry.
Sc. Sam Spewack.

A World War II documentary produced by the U.S. government, the film describes the events that led up to the bombing of Pearl Harbor on December 7, 1941. Using familiar newsreel footage and captured German films, the documentary shows the invasions of European countries and the subjugation of the various populations. Scenes of Manchuria and Ethiopia also are included to show the widespread evils of totalitarianism. Actor Paul Stewart handles the narration of this government propaganda film. ■

World in Flames, The (1940), Par. *Dir.* William C. Park; *Sc.* William C. Park.

A documentary showing the turmoil in the world during the 1930s, the film begins with the stock market crash of 1929 and then shifts to conflicts in Germany, Spain and the Far East. There are scenes of the rise of Nazism in Germany as the country moves into other territories and sequences of Japan's drive into China. Newsreel footage derives from several sources, including German propaganda films designed to instill fear in citizens of other countries, as the narrator points out. The work concludes with a statement that the U.S. is better prepared to defend itself than the victims who were forced to succumb to the Nazi onslaught. ■

World in Revolt (1934), Mentone. *Dir.* E. M. Glucksman, Dr. Joseph E. Lee.

A documentary composed of newsreel footage and other shots from various sources, the film outlines the turmoil in the world of the early 1930s. It covers rebellions and insurrections in France, Cuba, China, Italy, India, Ireland, Germany, Austria and Russia, the last of which is given extended treatment concerning the inception and results of that country's revolution. The presentation endeavors to remain neutral in its depiction of each nation's present struggle. The offscreen narrative is handled in an ardent manner by Graham MacNamee, a popular radio and newsreel reporter of the period. ■

World Moves On, The (1934), Fox. *Dir.* John Ford; *Sc.* Reginald Berkeley; *Cast includes:* Madeleine Carroll, Franchot Tone, Reginald Denny, Raul Roulien, Dudley Digges, Stepin Fetchit.

The drama spans many decades as it explores the various interrelationships of two families, the Warburtons and the Girards. They were brought together for business reasons in the early 1800s. The Warburtons are English while the Girards have branches of the firm in both France and Germany. During World War I the two patriarchs of the families are killed when their vessel is torpedoed by their German cousin. Mary Warburton (Madeleine Carroll) is charged with running the textile mill in England. The young capitalist–heroine refuses to turn the factory into a munitions plant. Members of both families are killed in battle as the war machine grinds on. The story then moves to the postwar period. Mary, now a mother, turns to pacifism when she hears rumors of yet another conflict. "Has it ever occurred to you that there are women in the world who are going to become mothers?" she asks. "And you tell me the world is just getting ready to go to war again." The dual-family empire collapses in financial ruin. As Mary and her husband (Franchot Tone) prepare to begin again, rumblings of world rearmament are heard. Hitler and Mussolini flex their military muscles while Russia and Japan listen to the sounds of their own armies on the march. The battle scenes of World War I earlier in the film are exceptionally realistic and grim, depicting men dying from bursts of shrapnel or walls falling in on them. Fox, the film studio, borrowed several excerpts from one of their French war productions and integrated them efficaciously. ■

World, the Flesh and the Devil, The (1959). See Future Wars. ■

World War I (1914–1918). Europe's major powers, after a decade of tilting at each other and having several near brushes with war, were ready for combat by 1914. Cheers greeted the announcement of war in Berlin, Paris and the House of Commons in London. Many believed it would be a short fight of anywhere from six weeks' to several months' duration. But an armistice would not come for four years. An estimated ten million would be killed and another twenty million wounded. Europe would be ravaged by devastation, famine and pestilence. Age-old empires would be destroyed, to be replaced by newly created nations and oppressive dictatorships.

The mood for war resulted from a combination of factors, including, among others, the aggressive policies of Germany, a general armaments race and secret treaties. The assassination by a Serbian patriot of Archduke Franz Ferdinand, heir to the Austro-Hungarian throne, on June 28, 1914, furnished the spark that ignited the explosion. *Storm at Daybreak* (1933), though basically a love story, attempted to illustrate the traditional hatred between Serbia and Austria–Hungary, and recreated the assassination of the Archduke and his wife at Sarajevo.

Using the assassination as an excuse to expand its holdings in the Slavic region of the Balkans, Austria invaded Serbia on July 28. A stunned continent quickly split into two major factions—the Allies (England, France, Russia, Belgium, Serbia and Montenegro) and the Central Powers (Germany, Austria-Hungary and the Ottoman Empire). In a few months 12 nations had entered the conflict. Over the next three years, the number of countries drawn into war grew so that by 1917, only the U.S., among the major nations, was still neutral.

The U.S. gradually moved closer to the Allies as a number of events helped propel U.S. sentiment towards war against Germany. Germany's invasion of tiny, neutral Belgium revolted many Americans. The German policy of unrestricted submarine warfare resulted in the loss of American ships and lives, particularly in the sinking of the British liner *Lusitania* in 1915. Several films referred to the sea tragedy including *Lest We Forget* (1918), which presented the most detailed and graphic depiction of the sinking. The American public became even more incensed following the discovery of a note from Germany's foreign minister to Mexico in which Germany pledged to support Mexico if that country would attack the U.S. British propaganda, meanwhile, had a field day disseminating reports, some exaggerated, of German atrocities.

The U.S. declared war on Germany on April 6, 1917, "to make the world safe for democracy," according to President Wilson. America's entry into the conflict came at an opportune time for the Allies. Russia, soon to be torn by revolution, teetered on the brink of collapse and had to withdraw from the alliance later that year.

The European war spilled over to other parts of the globe, including Africa and Asia. Film studios used these remote, exotic areas as backgrounds. *The Last Outpost* (1935) concerned British troops in the Middle East. *The Lost Patrol* (1934) centered on a handful of British soldiers who stray into the Mesopotamian desert and are attacked by Arabs. East Africa provided the background for several

films. *The African Queen* (1951), with Humphrey Bogart and Katharine Hepburn, depicted German soldiers burning villages. *The Royal African Rifles* (1953), also set in East Africa, concerned a German plot to instigate a native uprising and thereby tie up British troops.

Germany's initial successful opening drive through Belgium and France was stopped at the First Battle of the Marne. But the conflict on the western front bogged down by 1915 in trench warfare which claimed tens of thousands daily in such battles as those at Ypres, Verdun and the Somme that produced no important territorial gains. Several documentaries, including *Somewhere in France* (1915), *Forgotten Men* (1933) and *The Big Drive* (1933), covered the fighting at Verdun and other battles of World War I.

The American Expeditionary Force, commanded by General John J. Pershing, infused new strength on the side of the Allies and helped to stop the German drive on Paris in the second battle of the Marne (1918). Furthermore, Allied offenses at St. Mihiel and the Meuse-Argonne areas (September 12–November 11, 1918) dramatically crushed any remaining hopes of a German victory. Exhausted from years of fighting and burdened with war-weariness and a revolt at home, Germany signed an armistice on November 11, 1918. Around the same time, successful Allied counteroffensives in 1918 on the Italian and Balkan fronts led to the surrender of Austria–Hungary, Bulgaria and Turkey.

Several weapons made their wide-scale debut during the war, including the submarine, machine gun, tank, aircraft and poison gas. The millions of casualties they caused generated a temporary revulsion to war that resulted in the creation of the League of Nations. The German, Austrian, Russian and Turkish empires were dismembered by treaties. A number of former subject nationalities received their independence. Germany, declared the instigator, was saddled with heavy reparations payments. As a result, the country suffered internal postwar economic problems that laid the groundwork for the rise of Hitler and the Nazis in the following decade.

The immensity of the conflict is reflected in more than 400 related American films produced from 1914 through the 1980s. They range from short silent comedies to epic sound dramas, from patriotic documentaries to antiwar works. The films of each decade evoke a different attitude towards the war and the enemy, at times exploiting the conflict in an effort to reflect contemporary social and political values.

Before the U.S. entered the war, American films debated the issues of pacifism and preparedness. In many cases, however, American studios reflected the views of most of the populace by favoring one side. Many dramas appeared in which foreign agents—chiefly German—were portrayed as villains. As early as 1915 German spies in *Over Secret Wires* were shown contacting their submarines about American shipping off the coast of Oregon. Other dramas such as *The Ordeal* (1914) portrayed Germans as brutal killers of civilians. Once the U.S. joined the fighting, American audiences were exposed to more blatant anti-German films. D.W. Griffith's *Hearts of the World* (1918), fairly representative, described the inhabitants of a French village undergoing German atrocities.

Combat dramas of the war were generally vague about specific battles. The romantic plot often took precedence. *Gold Chevrons* (1927), which refers to the Argonne and Chateau-Thierry battles, and *Roaring Rails* (1924), whose opening scenes take place during the battle at Chateau-Thierry, were some exceptions. This is in sharp contrast to early films about the Civil War which specified a particular engagement (*The Battle of Gettysburg, The Battle of Shiloh, With Longstreet at Seven Pines*). Documentaries, however, dealt with specifics; e.g., *Crashing Through to Berlin* (1918) covered several major battles and *Following the Flag to France* (1918) showed Pershing and U.S. troops landing in France. Postwar films recreated several battles. Both the 1932 and 1957 versions of *A Farewell to Arms* included the collapse of the Italian army during its retreat from Caporetto. William Wellmam's *Wings* (1927) presented a re-enactment of the St. Mihiel offensive. The battle sequences in *Sergeant York* (1940) allegedly take place in the Argonne sector.

World War I films made during the 1920s dropped most of the propaganda and patriotism. More importantly, they slowly stripped away the enemy's bestial image. *The Four Horsemen of the Apocalypse* (1921) was the first major postwar film to treat the topic of war generally and World War I specifically—without the usual patriotism and propaganda. *Isn't Life Wonderful?* (1924) director D.W. Griffith, who had previously turned out

a handful of anti-German films, showed deep sympathy for the German people who are suffering a series of hardships in the wake of World War I.

Following a temporary lull in war films in the early 1920s—probably because audiences had had their fill of death and destruction—the genre staged a comeback. The success of *The Big Parade* (1925) and *What Price Glory?* (1926) led to a host of other similar films. *Wings* (1927) added a new element by romanticizing the role of the airplane and its pilot, a knight of the sky. Aside from altering the face of the enemy, the war films of this decade added other themes. Some stressed honor, glory and duty. Others began to reflect antiwar sentiments. "There's something rotten about a world that's got to be wet down every thirty years with the blood of boys ..." exclaims Captain Flagg (Victor McLaglen) in *What Price Glory?*

By the 1930s the antiwar theme became the norm. The trend was precipitated by a trio of 1930 productions, *All Quiet on the Western Front, Journey's End* and, to a lesser extent, *The Dawn Patrol*. Gone were the trappings of honor, glory and duty. What remained were scared, tired soldiers who were just trying to survive in a war they viewed as senseless. Documentaries also shifted their viewpoint. While some, like *The Big Drive* (1933), attempted to put the war in historical perspective, most condemned the conflict. *Forgotten Men* (1933), *Dealers in Death* (1934), *The Unknown Soldier Speaks* (1934) and *Horrors of War* (1940) either attacked the arms merchants, stressed the waste of human lives or generally made a plea to put an end to all wars.

Perhaps Donald Crisp in the World War I air drama *The Dawn Patrol* (1938) best expressed the views of this type of film when he ponders over an English officer's death. "A gallant gentleman died this afternoon. And for what? What have all these deaths accomplished? So many fine chaps who have died and are going to die in this war and in future wars." Dramas continued this trend until 1939 with *Nurse Edith Cavell*. As new storm clouds then gathered over Europe, nations began to rearm and American films ended their flirtation with pacifism.

World War I movies made in America almost invariably dealt with only the three major allies—England, France and the U.S.—particularly in their choice of principal characters. Belgium was used chiefly as an innocent and helpless symbol of Germany's depravity and aggression. Italy's role, inconsequential in Hollywood's view, provided very few heroic characters. In terms of social background, spy dramas and sophisticated characters, the studios preferred England over France. American movie audiences were already familiar with English types and probably felt more comfortable with these settings.

Several World War I films were made after World War II. They included documentaries (*The Guns of August* in 1964), airplane dramas (*The Blue Max* in 1966) and romantic spy tales (*Darling Lili* in 1970). Two exceptional entries, Stanley Kubrick's searingly cynical *Paths of Glory* (1957) and Dalton Trumbo's disturbing *Johnny Got His Gun* (1971), although set during World War I, were powerful antiwar statements about all armed conflicts. See also Antiwar Films, Preparedness, Propaganda. ■

World War II (1939–1945). Tension crackled through Europe's capitals during the summer of 1939 as the war that hardly anybody wanted seemed to be moving closer to reality. Adolf Hitler, the emotionally driven leader of Nazi Germany, shrilly pressed his demands during August upon neighboring Poland for the return of the Baltic port of Danzig and a section of Poland that had been part of eastern Germany (Prussia) but was given to Poland as an outlet to the sea after World War I. Though faced by a build-up of the Nazi war machine on its borders, Poland, reassured of British and French support, firmly refused to accede to the Nazi dictator's demands. At 5:45 A.M. on September 1, 1939, the war of nerves ended and a real war began as German units crossed the border. Two days later France and England honored their alliance with Poland and declared war on Germany. Hitler soon stunned the world as he unveiled a new form of warfare, the "Blitzkrieg"—a high-intensity, coordinated air and ground attack using motorized units—that vanquished Poland in a matter of weeks.

The outbreak of a major war should have come as no surprise. The Axis powers of Germany, Italy and Japan had already compiled a record of aggression in the years immediately preceding the Polish invasion. In Asia, Japan had first seized China's northern province of Manchuria in 1931–1932 and followed with an invasion of the rest of China in 1937. Fascist Italy under Mussolini, beginning in 1935, embarked on the dictator's fantasy of creating a modern Roman empire and, over the next few years, conquered the East African nation of Ethiopia and Albania in Europe. The Nazis, after reinstating the military draft and beginning to rearm Germany in 1935, sent troops into the demilitarized Rhineland on the border of France, then annexed Austria and Czechoslovakia. The fact that no major war had broken out as a result of all these incidents prior to September 1939 probably gave Hitler and many Germans a feeling of confidence that war would somehow always be averted.

Several months after Poland's defeat Hitler turned his attention to western Europe, where, in the spring of 1940, his Nazi juggernaut conquered Denmark, Norway, the Netherlands, Belgium and Luxembourg. The Nazi military machine forced the British army off the continent and subdued France. But anti-Nazi resistance movements soon emerged on the continent, followed quickly by a series of Hollywood dramas echoing this defiance. In *Edge of Darkness* (1943), for instance, an elderly teacher (Morris Carnovsky) enlightens a German officer on why the Nazi New Order is doomed to failure: "What you don't understand is that the individual man must stand against you like a rock."

Hitler in the fall of 1940 determined to destroy the last impediment to his control of western Europe—England. Only the spectacular success of the gallant British fliers who held off the more numerous German air force and destroyed many of the invasion barges on the French coast during the Battle of Britain (1940–1941) prevented Hitler from mounting a cross-channel invasion of England. Winston Churchill's famous tribute to the courageous pilots of the R.A.F. ("Never in the field of human conflict was so much owed by so many to so few") was echoed in several documentaries, including *Battle of Britain* (1943).

Though badly weakened, Britain survived through a combination of personal courage by its people and a growing stream of supplies coming across the North Atlantic from a neutral but increasingly friendly U.S. *Mrs. Miniver* (1942), starring Greer Garson in the title role, epitomizes the courage and strength of the English people who are determined not to surrender. But the "bridge of ships" between the U.S. and Britain suffered a high rate of loss in vessels and seamen from Nazi submarine wolf packs in the Battle of the North Atlantic. The terrors of submarine warfare were graphically recounted in *Action in the North Atlantic* (1943), a tense drama about the U.S. Merchant Marine. The finale in that film includes a voice-over by President Roosevelt: "The goods will be delivered where they are needed and when they are needed. Nothing on land, in the air, on the sea or under the sea shall prevent our final victory."

Germany, stymied by British resistance and with nothing to fear from Russia with whom she had signed a non-aggression pact in August 1939, next moved into the Balkans. By mid-1941 the Nazis had conquered Greece, Crete, and Yugoslavia and forced the remaining Balkan nations to accept a puppet alliance relationship. Documentaries such as those from the "March of Time" series ("Inside Nazi Germany" (1938) and "Peace—by Adolf Hitler," released in 1941) and director Frank Capra's highly acclaimed "Why We Fight" series described Hitler's rise to power and his aggressive military policies.

An overconfident Hitler, in June 1941, invaded Russia, an event that many historians believe was Hitler's biggest mistake. Russia's vastness, the numbing cold of its winters and a willingness by its people to trade lives and territory for time to recoup would eventually sap Hitler's military strength as no other enemy had been able to do. Following deep advances in the first year of fighting that carried German troops to within 25 miles of Moscow, the Nazi military machine was stopped by the Russian winter of 1941–1942 and the first successful Soviet counteroffensive.

Japan's sneak air attack (December 7, 1941) on Pearl Harbor in Hawaii crippled a large part of the U.S. Pacific fleet and brought the U.S. fully into the war. The bombing was recreated in several dramas, most notably in *Tora! Tora! Tora!* (1970). Japan quickly extended its power through the western Pacific, easily taking islands such as Wake, Guam and the Philippines, and swept into southeast Asia. Hollywood immediately turned these losses into films known as "heroic defeats," depicting the bravery of American defenders in such dramas as *Wake Island* (1942), *Corregidor* (1943) and *Bataan* (1943).

The second half of 1942 marked the turning point of the war. An American naval victory over the Japanese at the Battle of Midway stemmed the Japanese advance. The film *Midway* (1976) caught the intensity and importance of the battle. General MacArthur, commander of the American Pacific campaign, initiated an island-hopping campaign, beginning with the invasion of Guadalcanal, to carry the war closer to the Japanese home islands. *Guadalcanal Diary* (1943), made while the event was still fresh in the public's mind, recreated the invasion in one of the better World War II action films. Succeeding American invasions saw the erosion of Japan's dreams of empire and resulted in a stream of films showing American troops defeating the Japanese in the Pacific, including *Wing and a Prayer* (1944) and *Back to Bataan* (1945).

Meanwhile, in the west, Germany's Field Marshal Rommel, who had initially made spectacular gains in North Africa, tasted defeat for the first time in 1942 from Britain's General Montgomery at El Alamein. Combined Allied forces of British, Americans and Free French, under the command of General Eisenhower, retook North Africa by mid-1943. These battles were re-enacted in several desert war films such as *The Desert Fox* (1951) and *Patton* (1970), which partly concerned General Patton's role in North Africa. Germany began its long, final retreat on the Russian front after being stopped at the Battle of Stalingrad in the winter of 1942–1943. Other Russian successes followed in the spring of 1943. Such documentaries as *The Battle of Russia* (1943) and dramas as *The North Star* (1943) and *Days of Glory* (1944) eulogized the Soviet stand against the Nazi invaders.

By 1943 the Allies in Europe were nibbling at the home territory of the Axis as first Sicily fell and then Italy surrendered in September after it had been invaded. *The Story of G.I. Joe* (1945), *A Walk in the Sun* (1945) and *Anzio* (1968) took place during these battles. On June 6, 1944, Allied forces, under Eisenhower, invaded the French coast at Normandy. *The Longest Day* (1962) recreated the massive D-Day invasion in great detail. The Allies recaptured France and pushed on into Germany. *Battleground* (1949) and *Battle of the Bulge* (1965) depicted Germany's desperate counterattack to stop the Allied advance. *The Big Red One* (1980) gave a stirring summary of the war in the west by tracing one

American division's experiences on several major fronts. The Russians captured Berlin on May 2, 1945. Hitler committed suicide, and Germany surrendered unconditionally on May 9, 1945.

In Asia Japanese ground forces had bogged down against the Chinese who, though unable to drive out the invaders, did manage to tie down large elements of enemy troops. China's war effort was sustained by American supplies that originally came by air over the Himalayan "hump" and increased with the reopening of the Burma Road (January 1945). *Burma Convoy* (1941) captured some of the problems and actions of the war in southeast Asia. Japan's cities came under steady attack from airfields in China and on captured islands. After President Truman authorized two atom bombs to be dropped on the cites of Hiroshima and Nagasaki, Japan surrendered on September 2, 1945. *Above and Beyond* (1952) dealt with the pilot who flew over Hiroshima with the first atomic bomb.

World War II was by far the most global of conflicts, dwarfing even World War I in the number of people involved and in the geographical spread of fighting. The human and financial costs stagger belief. An estimated 35 million combatants and civilians were killed. Another estimated 10 million died in Nazi concentration camps. The Soviet Union alone suffered 7,500,000 casualties. China recorded the second highest number of battle casualties with 2,200,000, not counting those who had died before 1937 during a period of undeclared war with Japan. The economic costs were staggering, totaling in the trillions of dollars between war expenditures and destroyed property. The conflict left a power vacuum in eastern Europe that the U.S.S.R. exploited, foisting Communist regimes in those areas that its armies liberated. The war weakened or destroyed the old colonial empires of Italy, France and Britain and accelerated the rise of nationalism as new nations arose in Asia and Africa. The wholesale destruction and suffering resulted in the formation of a new world body, the United Nations, entrusted with the hopeful task of preventing other future catastrophes.

Hollywood turned out more than 600 dramas, comedies and musicals related to World War II. The films embraced other genres as well, such as spy films, serials, cartoons, short subjects and documentaries. Those re-leased during the conflict were generally propaganda-oriented. Studios made the bulk of their war films prior to 1943. Fearing that audiences were beginning to tire of them, Hollywood then began to drift back into traditional escapism.

The government produced hundreds of training films and sponsored scores of documentaries concerning different branches of service and various aspects of the war. They were directed by such major figures as Frank Capra, John Ford and William Wyler. Postwar films, exemplified by *The Best Years of Our Lives* (1946), examined the physical and emotional problems of veterans. "Last year it was 'Kill Japs.' This year it's 'Make money,' " reflects a former sergeant who is having difficulties adjusting to a bank job.

The following decades saw the face of the enemy change, especially in action-oriented World War II films. With Japan and West Germany transformed into America's allies in the Cold War, the enemy now shifted to weak or corrupt officers, as in *Attack!* (1956); politicians, as in *Command Decision* (1948); or the nature of war itself, as in *The Americanization of Emily* (1964). Perhaps one of the last lines in the film *The Longest Day* best sums up the common soldier's view of war. "Here we are," a seriously wounded British soldier (Richard Burton) says to a G.I. separated from his outfit while a dead German soldier lies motionless nearby. "I'm crippled, you're lost and he's dead." See also Documentary, Home Front, Propaganda Films: World War II, Sino–Japanese War, Veterans, and specific battles and individuals. ∎

Wounded Knee, Battle of (December 29, 1890). Neither the Indians nor the Seventh Cavalry were expecting or seeking a fight when the two confronted each other at Wounded Knee Creek in southwest South Dakota. As daylight broke on the gray storm-threatening morning of December 29, 1890, Col. James Forsyth's 500 horse soldiers, supported by four cannon, completely surrounded the small tepee village of about 350 Sioux under Chief Big Foot, bedridden with pneumonia. The Indians, poorly armed, did not seem to pose a threat to Forsyth's orders to disarm them and thus prevent any chance of further conflict.

Forsyth's instructions stemmed from a series of clashes that had erupted in recent weeks between troopers and Indians because of the "Ghost Dance" that led those who participated to believe they were impervious to the bullets of the white man. The dance influenced Indians to be more defiant of white rule. When soldiers tried to break up the ritual, or seize the arms of those tribesmen who took part, fighting developed that resulted in deaths on both sides, including the accidental killing of famed Sioux leader, Chief Sitting Bull.

As Forsyth's men began to disarm the Sioux warriors, a few resisted and tension grew. A medicine man stamped about, telling his tribesmen not to give up their weapons, and not to fear the soldiers, for their Ghost Shirts would protect the Indians from harm. One soldier grabbed an Indian's weapon; it went off and immediately both sides started firing. A murderous close-range rampage broke out with combatants using guns, knives and clubs. After the two sides were separated, the artillery opened up on the village. An hour later the carnage ended with 150 Indians killed and another 50 wounded. The army reportedly lost 25 dead and 39 wounded.

It wasn't a large battle insofar as numbers were concerned, but its importance far outweighed the size of the conflict. It underscored the bad feeling that existed between the Sioux and white society for three decades. It was, furthermore, the last major engagement between Indians and whites in the United States. The Sioux, as well as all the other tribes, realized their way of life had been crushed forever. This was the last major Indian battle in United States History. Surprisingly, the conflict was rarely depicted in films. The Battle of Wounded Knee became the climactic highlight of *The Adventures of Buffalo Bill* (1914), with William Cody playing himself. It also played a part in *Soldier Blue* (1970), which gave a more accurate account of the massacre. Indian spokesmen attacked the 1914 controversial film as an inaccurate account of the battle while several historical societies criticized the work for other historical inaccuracies. See also Crazy Horse, George Custer, Sioux Wars, Sitting Bull. ■

Wrath of God, The (1972), MGM. *Dir.* Ralph Nelson; *Sc.* Ralph Nelson; *Cast includes:* Robert Mitchum, Frank Langella, Rita Hayworth, John Colicos, Victor Buono.

A renegade priest (Robert Mitchum) helps liberate a terrorized Latin-American town in this action drama set in 1920 during a rebellion. Rita Hayworth, as the mother of a demented son (Frank Langella), decides to battle against the insurgents. She provides the romantic interest as well. John Colicos portrays an army colonel. Victor Buono and Ken Hutchinson play soldiers of fortune who join Mitchum in his struggle against Langella. There is sufficient action in this tale, supposedly a satire, including a climactic shootout. ■

Wyandot Indians. See Huron Indians. ■

Wyoming (1928), MGM. *Dir.* W. S. Van Dyke; *Sc.* Madeleine Ruthven, Ross B. Wills; *Cast includes:* Tim McCoy, Dorothy Sebastian, Charles Bell, William Fairbanks.

Two children, bound together by a pledge of friendship, become mortal enemies as adults in this routine action drama involving clashes between the U.S. Cavalry the Indians. Tim McCoy portrays a lieutenant in the cavalry while his boyhood friend (Charles Bell), now the grown son of an Indian chief, takes to the warpath. The young warrior breaks a treaty when he attacks a wagon train that he thinks is intruding upon Indian land. The cavalry, led by McCoy, comes to the rescue of the pioneers, but the hot-headed brave is stopped only when his own father kills him. ■

Wyoming Valley Massacre. See *The Spirit of '76* (1917). ■

X-Y-Z

X Marks the Spot (1942). See Home Front. ∎

Yank in Indo-China, A (1952), Col. *Dir.* Wallace A. Grissell; *Sc.* Samuel Newman; *Cast includes:* John Archer, Douglas Dick, Jean Willes, Maura Murphy.

Two American fliers who run their own freight service in Indo-China resist Communist Chinese guerrillas in this low-budget action drama. John Archer and Douglas Dick portray the fliers who challenge the Red Chinese by blowing up their supplies. They then escape through the jungle with two young women, played by Jean Willes and Maura Murphy. The film provides the conventional elements of this type of chase plot, including the group's capture and final escape. They are saved when the United Nations forces arrive in time to destroy the guerrilla base. ∎

Yank in Korea, A (1951), Col. *Dir.* Lew Landers; *Sc.* William Sackheim; *Cast includes:* Lon McCallister, William Phillips, Bret King, Larry Stewart.

This Korean War drama follows the enlistment, training and combat activities of one soldier, played by Lon McCallister. During a battle in Korea, he invokes the anger of his fellow soldiers when he acts recklessly, thereby exposing them to unnecessary hazards. But his participation in the destruction of an ammunition dump and other heroic deeds wins back their trust and friendship. William Phillips portrays McCallister's sergeant and pal. The film utilizes newsreel footage for some of the battle sequences. ∎

Yank in Libya, A (1942), PRC. *Dir.* Albert Herman; *Sc.* Arthur St. Claire; *Cast includes:* H. B. Warner, Walter Woolf King, Joan Woodbury, Parkyakarkus.

A routine World War II drama about an American war correspondent who uncovers a Nazi gun-smuggling ring in Libya, the film is short on action or war sequences. Walter Woolf King plays the curious reporter while veteran actor H.B. Warner portrays a local British consul. Radio comedian Parkyakarkus supplies the much-needed comic relief in this low-budget tale. ∎

Yank in the R.A.F., A (1941), TCF. *Dir.* Henry King; *Sc.* Daniel Ware, Karl Tunberg; *Cast includes:* Tyrone Power, Betty Grable, John Sutton, Reginald Gardiner, Ralph Byrd.

A blend of World War II romance and propaganda, the film concerns a carefree American pilot (Tyrone Power) who enlists in the Royal Air Force to be near his former sweetheart (Betty Grable). On his first trip to England, Power meets Grable, who is working as an entertainer and volunteer with the Ambulance reserve. The film, which emphasizes the romance and several of Gable's musical numbers, leaves little room for the war sequences. The cocky Power reforms once he witnesses the courage of the British people. The evacuation of Dunkirk, the highlight of the film, is dramatically depicted, as the planes of the R.A.F. provide air cover for the troops and ships below. Other scenes related to the war include bombing raids and a forced landing behind German lines. ∎

Yank in Viet-Nam, A (1964), AA. *Dir.* Marshall Thompson; *Sc.* Jane Wardell, Jack Lewis; *Cast includes:* Marshall Thompson, Enrique Magalona, Mario Barri.

Some of the first American troops embark for Saigon during the early years of the Vietnam War. *A Yank in Viet-Nam* (1964).

A U.S. Marine major, whose helicopter is downed by the Viet Cong, becomes involved with Vietnamese guerrillas in this action drama of the early days of the Vietnam War. Marshall Thompson portrays the leatherneck officer who joins a small guerrilla band in their efforts to free a captured native doctor. He manages to find time to romance the captive's daughter (Kieu Chinh). Enrique Magalona plays the guerrilla chief. The film includes several effective action sequences but rarely explores the background of the war or America's involvement in the conflict. ∎

Yank on the Burma Road, A (1942), MGM. *Dir*. George B. Seitz; *Sc*. Gordon Kahn, Hugo Butler, David Lang; *Cast includes*: Laraine Day, Barry Nelson, Stuart Crawford, Keye Luke.

The Sino-Japanese War is the background for this low-budget drama in which an American hero (Barry Nelson) is hired by the Chinese to lead a convoy of trucks carrying medical supplies to Chungking. Laraine Day portrays a young American wife searching for her husband who supposedly has defected to the Japanese. The film provides some action sequences near the end when Chinese forces battle and defeat Japanese troops encamped in the nearby hills. ∎

Yankee Buccaneer (1952), U. *Dir*. Frederick de Cordova; *Sc*. Charles K. Peck, Jr.; *Cast includes*: Jeff Chandler, Scott Brady, Suzan Ball, Joseph Calleia.

Jeff Chandler is at the helm of this sea adventure set chiefly in the Caribbean during the early 1800s. He is the captain of a U.S. frigate assigned to pose as a pirate ship so that he may learn the location of other pirate vessels that have been preying upon commercial shipping. Scott Brady, who portrays his newly appointed first officer, clashes with the stern captain who resents the lieutenant's unorthodox methods which include the infraction of regulations and his chumminess with the crew. Suzan Ball plays a beautiful Portuguese refugee bent on overthrowing the king of her native land, but the transportation of the gold from South America to accomplish this task is being threatened by the pirate fleet under the control of Del Prado, a corrupt Spanish governor of the West Indies. The men of the American ship, led by Chandler and Brady, attack the governor's stronghold, capture Del Prado and discover the whereabouts of the pirate fleet in this well-mounted but conventional melodrama. ■

Yankee Doodle Dandy (1942), WB. *Dir.* Michael Curtiz; *Sc.* Robert Buckner, Edmund Joseph; *Cast includes:* James Cagney, Joan Leslie, Walter Huston, Richard Whorf, Irene Manning, George Tobias, Rosemary DeCamp, Jeanne Cagney.

Warner Bros.' musical biography of George M. Cohan, released during World War II, is a tribute both to the grand American showman of Broadway and the American way of life. Filled with patriotic songs and family cohesiveness, the film romanticizes the life of the Four Cohans, starring James Cagney as George M., his real-life sister Jeanne Cohan as his sister Josie and Walter Huston and Rosemary DeCamp as the parents. Young George would announce at the end of each performance: "My mother thanks you, my father thanks you, my sister thanks you and I thank you." The story is told in flashback by Cagney to President Franklin D. Roosevelt when the entertainer is called to the White House to receive the Congressional Medal of Honor for his immortal World War I song, "Over There." "A man may give his life to his country in many different ways," the President says. " 'Over There' is as powerful as a cannon. We need more songs to express America." "Where else could a simple guy like me," Cagney muses, "come in and talk things over with the top man?" To which Roosevelt replies: "Well, that's about as good a definition of America as I ever heard."

George M. Cohan was born on the Fourth of July, and he informed the world of the fact through his songs and shows. Attacked by some critics for excessive flag-waving, Cohan continued to write his patriotic songs. His exuberant and aggressive personality, captured in this film, exemplified the America of his period.

The film also illustrates how a commercial Hollywood product could be used politically. President Roosevelt, who gave permission to have himself impersonated, certainly was aware of the impact the film would have. The nation was engaged in a struggle against to-talitarianism. What better way to reach a national audience for propaganda purposes as well as for political ends? The film had no difficulty in succeeding in both areas. ■

"Yankee Doodle in Berlin" (1919), Lesser. *Dir.* F. Richard Jones; *Cast includes:* Bothwell Browne, Ford Sterling, Mal St. Clair, Marie Provost, Bert Roach.

A Mack Sennett World War I comedy short, the film centers on an American flier, portrayed by Bothwell Browne, who is sent to Berlin to get strategic war maps from the Kaiser. Browne, dressed as a woman, has the German leaders competing for his attentions in this zany comedy. ■

Yankee Doodle, Jr. (1922), Cineart. *Dir.* Jack Pratt; *Sc.* Ralph Spence; *Cast includes:* J. Frank Glendon, Zelma Morgan, Victor Sarno.

This film farce takes place in a fictitious South American country beset by revolution. The spoiled son of a fireworks millionaire (J. Frank Glendon) reluctantly agrees to learn the family business by becoming a salesman. He randomly selects San Mariano as the place to begin his new career. Once he reaches the South American country, he becomes embroiled in a revolution led by a local malcontent. A comical battle ensues in which Glendon uses his supply of fireworks to rout the rebels who have besieged the president's palace. His quick and heroic actions win him a large fireworks order from the grateful ruler and the love of the man's daughter (Zelma Morgan).

Hollywood studios turned out hundreds of films during the silent and sound periods using revolutions and rebellions as backgrounds, while often managing to display a penchant for evenhandedness. They sided with the peasantry in dramas and with the aristocracy in farces. This was especially true if the hero came from the upper class, as he did in this romantic comedy. These farces, sometimes set in fictitious lands that were thinly disguised banana republics or petty principalities, evinced little concern for the people or their problems. ■

Yankee Pasha (1954), U. *Dir.* Joseph Pevney; *Sc.* Joseph Hoffman; *Cast includes:* Jeff Chandler, Rhonda Fleming, Mamie Van Doren, Lee J. Cobb, Bart Roberts.

The days of the Barbary pirates, prior to the Tripolitan War (1800–1805), dominate this adventure drama about an American frontiersman who journeys to Morocco to rescue a New England woman whom he has fallen in love with. Rhonda Fleming plays the beautiful captive who is sold into the harem of a Moroccan womanizer (Bart Roberts). Jeff Chandler, as the transplanted backwoodsman, works as a rifle instructor for a local chieftain's guards while he searches for Fleming. When he locates her, U.S. sailors from a recently docked ship help him storm Roberts' fortress for the climactic battle and rescue. A sea battle occurs earlier in the film when a pirate ship attacks the American vessel with Fleming and her father aboard. Lee J. Cobb plays a sultan in this routine tale.

The film is set in 1800, on the eve of the Tripolitan War. Until that conflict, the U.S. and other nations were forced to pay tribute to Moroccan pirates for the privilege of sailing the Mediterranean. The power of these pirates is reflected in the arrogance of one of the local Moroccan sultans who boasts: "Every American is our slave, or why else do they pay us tribute?" Later in the film an American captain voices his disgust in this system of tribute and anticipates the ensuing war. "Someday we'll be able to sail through the Mediterranean without our government having to buy our safety." ■

Yanks (1979), U. *Dir.* John Schlesinger; *Sc.* Colin Welland, Walter Bernstein; *Cast includes:* Richard Gere, Lisa Eichorn, Vanessa Redgrave, William Devane.

This wartime drama, set in England prior to D-Day, 1944, explores the romantic relationships between American soldiers and young Englishwomen. With more than one million Yanks stationed in England by 1944 and most of the local young men away fighting the war, these liaisons were inevitable. They ranged from the earthy to the elevated. Chick Vennera portrays a G.I. who beds and weds his girlfriend (Wendy Morgan) rather quickly. Richard Gere plays a sensitive Yank whose strong love for Lisa Eichorn prevents him from consummating the sexual act. William Devane, as a lonely American officer whose wife back home is ready to divorce him, carries on a platonic affair with a British officer's wife (Vanessa Redgrave) whose husband is away at the front.

The film, which depicts the period with care and great detail, touches upon other issues aside from the possible seduction of the entire English female population (which led to the popular phrase that the Yanks were "overpaid, oversexed and over here"). Eichorn's parents, who are concerned about her relationship with a local boy she is expected to marry when he returns from the war, frown upon her association with Gere. America's racism spills over into an English dancehall. When a black G.I. dances with an English girl, a brawl erupts between white soldiers and black.

America's armed forces during World War II were generally segregated. When the U.S. sent large numbers of troops to England in preparation for the invasion of mainland Europe, black service units were included. Many Britons, unaware of America's racial policies, extended their hospitality to the blacks as well as other G.I.s. The U.S. military frowned upon this relaxed socialization between the black soldiers and the English people, especially the latter's women, fearing that this new-found freedom may lead to postwar problems in the States. The British Government went along with the official American policy although many of its citizens ignored it. Committed to maintain the status quo, the American military came down hard on any blacks who broke these rules. Discontented black troops protested, and sporadic racial incidents erupted, including a race riot in Bamber Bridge, Lancashire, in 1943. President Truman finally ended segregation in the armed forces in 1948. ■

Yanks Ahoy (1943), UA. *Dir.* Kurt Neumann; *Sc.* Eugene Conrad, Edward Seabrook; *Cast includes:* William Tracy, Joe Sawyer, Marjorie Woodworth, Minor Watson, Walter Woolf King.

Another in the series of service comedies featuring William Tracy and Joe Sawyer as two brawling sergeants, the film provides only minimal humor in its slapstick routines. This entry continues Tracy's uncanny knack for memorizing anything, a talent that gets him sent overseas together with Sawyer. Eventually, he and his antagonist are responsible for the capture of a Japanese submarine, albeit a small, two-man vessel. ■

Yanks Are Coming, The (1942). See Musicals. ■

Yellow Tomahawk, The (1954), UA. *Dir.* Lesley Selander; *Sc.* Richard Alan Simmons; *Cast includes:* Rory Calhoun, Peggie Castle, Noah Beery, Warner Anderson.

A callous, intractable U.S. Cavalry major sparks an Indian uprising in this familiar action drama. Warner Anderson, as the cold-blooded officer, needlessly slaughters a band of Cheyenne women and children. He further provokes the Indians when he begins to construct a military outpost on their land, a violation of a long-standing treaty. A young warrior (Lee Van Cleef) vows revenge on the major and his troop. Rory Calhoun, as a Wyoming scout and friend of the warrior, has all he can do to prevent the inevitable battle. When the Indians attack and decimate Anderson's troops, Calhoun is forced to kill Van Cleef with the same bow that represented their friendship. Peggie Castle provides the romantic interest for Calhoun. ■

Yellowneck (1955), Rep. *Dir.* R. John Hugh; *Sc.* Nat S. Linden; *Cast includes:* Lin McCarthy, Steven Courtleigh, Berry Kroeger, Harold Gordon.

Five Confederate deserters, or "yellownecks," as they were called, escape into the dangerous Florida Everglades. Intending to journey to Cuba, the men encounter a variety of obstructions, including the heat, reptiles and warring Seminoles, as they desperately fight their way to the sea. Allegedly, a boat is waiting to take them to Cuba. Stephen Courtleigh portrays an alcoholic colonel who is ashamed of his actions. Lin McCarthy plays a sergeant who is fed up with the stupidity of the endless war. Each of the party dies a horrible death except for a young soldier (Bill Mason) who reaches the sea to find no boat waiting. ■

Yorktown campaign (1781). British General Cornwallis' mistaken belief that Britain continued to control the sea was the first stage in a campaign that would eventually bring victory to the rebels of the American Revolution. The general decided to fortify Yorktown to protect the entry to the York River and await supplies and reinforcements. General George Washington, with the aid of French troops, was quick to march on the Virginia town and lay down a siege. France's Admiral de Grasse, meanwhile, blockaded the 7,000 British forces by sea. On October 17, 1781, Cornwallis, completely sur-

rounded, surrendered in less than two weeks to Washington and his French allies. This was the last military campaign of the war although sporadic fighting, chiefly in the south, continued for another year.

Two historical dramas about the American Revolution recount Cornwallis' capitulation in fairly accurate terms—the silent film *Janice Meredith* (1924) and *The Howards of Virginia* (1940), with Cary Grant and Martha Scott. ■

You Came Along (1945), Par. *Dir.* John Farrow; *Sc.* Robert Smith, Ayn Rand; *Cast includes:* Robert Cummings, Lizabeth Scott, Don DeFore, Charles Drake, Julie Bishop.

A sentimental drama of three World War II pilots on a tour to sell war bonds, the film tells of their romances and their comradeship. Robert Cummings plays one of the American pilots who does not have long to live. Lizabeth Scott portrays a Treasury Department worker in charge of the tour. She falls in love and marries Cummings, accepting the circumstances of his condition. Don DeFore and Charles Drake play the doomed flier's friends. ■

You Can't Ration Love (1944). See Home Front. ■

"You Nazty Spy" (1940). See War Humor. ■

Young Americans. See *Down in San Diego* (1941). ■

Young and the Brave, The (1963), MGM. *Dir.* Francis D. Lyon; *Sc.* Beirne Lay, Jr.; *Cast includes:* Rory Calhoun, William Bendix, Richard Jaeckel, Richard Arlen.

A small band of American soldiers fight their way back to their lines through enemy territory in this low-budget action drama set during the Korean War. Helped by a small Korean orphan and his dog, the G.I.s, who have escaped their captors, manage to elude the North Koreans. Both Rory Calhoun and William Bendix portray sergeants in this routine story. The cards are stacked against the stereotyped enemy who have murdered the boy's parents for aiding the Americans. ■

Young Daniel Boone (1950), Mon. *Dir.* Reginald LeBorg; *Sc.* Clint Johnston, Reginald LeBorg; *Cast includes:* David Bruce,

Kristine Miller, Damian O'Flynn, Don Beddoe.

The usual conflicts between frontiersmen and Indians provide the background for this 18th-century outdoor drama. Folk hero Daniel Boone (David Bruce) sets out to rescue two white girls captured by the hostiles. He also finds time to uncover a French spy (Damian O'Flynn) in this low-budget film. Kristine Miller portrays one of the damsels in distress and the bride of the famous frontiersman who accompanies him to Kentucky as the tale concludes. ■

Young Eagles (1930), Par. *Dir.* William A. Wellman; *Sc.* William S. McNutt, Grover Jones; *Cast includes:* Charles "Buddy" Rogers, Jean Arthur, Paul Lukas, Stuart Erwin, Frank Ross.

A World War I aviation drama, the film co-stars Jean Arthur as an American spy posing as a German. An American flier (Charles Rogers) who has fallen for her becomes disillusioned when he learns that she has run off with a German aviator. Once she gains the necessary information, she transmits it to American authorities. Rogers, of course, forgives her when he discovers the truth. The film provides several air battles, none of which compared to those in *Wings*, which also starred Rogers and turned out by the same director. Some of the footage was borrowed from *Wings*. The German, played by Paul Lukas, was treated with more sympathy than he would have been had this film been made during the war. The film has been singled out as the first 1930s spy drama with a World War I background. ■

Young Lions, The (1958), TCF. *Dir.* Edward Dmytryk; *Sc.* Edward Anhalt; *Cast includes:* Marlon Brando, Montgomery Clift, Dean Martin, Hope Lange, Barbara Rush, May Britt, Maximilian Schell.

Based on Irwin Shaw's best seller, the film covers the experiences of a German officer and two American privates during World War II while focusing as well on the values of both the German and American home fronts. Marlon Brando plays the German officer who before the war believes Hitler will improve the lives of the German people. "I'm not political," he says in 1938, attempting to justify the Nazis to a pretty American tourist, "but I think they stand for something hopeful in

Germany." As the war continues and Brando witnesses the horrors of the conflict, he grows disillusioned with Nazism. In one scene a young soldier says: "I promised my father I'd kill a Frenchman for him." A few scenes later his wish is fulfilled, but he also is killed in the battle. "I'm sure his father is very happy now," Brando says cynically. Later in the film he hears cries of torture inflicted by the Gestapo in a closed room. "I do not think it's possible to remake the world from the basement of this dirty little police station," he says to his superior (Maximilian Schell), a staunch Nazi.

Paralleling his story is that of two American G.I.s. Montgomery Clift portrays a serious-minded soldier who is confronted with anti-Semitism in his barracks. Although shorter and weaker than the four bullies, he challenges them one at a time to a fight. He is badly beaten each time, although he wins the last battle. Dean Martin plays a Broadway singer who is trying to dodge the draft until he faces the realities about his own character and the war. Martin and Clift become good friends. They are separated for a time when Martin's transfer comes through. While he is safe in London, Clift and the others in his company are fighting in Europe. Martin, conscience-stricken, asks for another transfer to his old outfit. The stories of the three principals—Brando, Clift and Martin—converge outside a concentration camp. Seeing the wretched victims of the camp and hearing the commandant complain to him that he is too shorthanded to kill the remaining prisoners are the final assaults upon Brando's conscience. He smashes his machine gun in a rage and staggers down a hill. While comforting his friend Clift, who has just witnessed the human remnants of the camp, Martin sees Brando in the distance and shoots him. The last scene of the film shows Clift returning to his wife and child. In the original novel the ending is quite different. Brando remains unrepentant. He shoots the character played by Clift and is himself killed by the Martin character.

The film is reminiscent of *All Quiet on the Western Front* (1930) and other similar dramas in at least one respect. Hollywood repeated its practice of using a prominent American actor in the role of a sympathetic German soldier. In the case of *The Young Lions*, Brando was at the peak of his popularity. ■

Young Warriors, The (1967), U. Dir. John Peyser; *Sc.* Richard Matheson; *Cast includes:* James Drury, Steve Carlson, Jonathan Daly, Robert Pine.

A World War II drama intended to show the effects of war on the young men who are asked to fight it, this low-budget film features James Drury as the sergeant in charge of a handful of green G.I.s. The story centers on Steve Carlson, who plays a young soldier who matures after his experience in battle. The other infantrymen have stereotyped roles. The film includes several large action sequences, some of which have been borrowed from other works. ■

You're in the Army Now (1941). See Service Comedy. ■

You're in the Navy Now (1951). See Service Comedy. ■

Zapata, Emiliano. See *Viva Zapata!* (1952). ■

Zeppelin. See Aircraft in War. ■

Zeppelin's Last Raid, The (1917), Par. Dir. Thomas H. Ince; *Sc.* C. Gardner Sullivan; *Cast includes:* Howard Hickman, Enid Markey.

One of the few pacifist films of the period, this silent drama suggests that the struggle within the German people for democratic ideals was crushed by their oppressive and war-crazed Kaiser. The commander of a Zeppelin (Howard Hickman) who is in love with a pacifist (Enid Markey) is persuaded by her to join the Legion of Liberty. The secret movement is dedicated to bringing peace and democracy to the warlike nations of Central Europe. When the commander is ordered to bomb a city, he refuses. His crew mutinies and he is forced to shoot some of them. Mortally wounded in the gun battle, he decides to blow up the airship rather than rain destruction on the city below. The silent antiwar film was produced by the same crew that turned out *Civilization* one year earlier.

The film was unique for its time in not condemning the entire German people or depicting them all as a brutal, bestial race intent on raping and pillaging their neighbors. Instead, it showed them simply as a misdirected people who were duped by the Kaiser and his military advisers. ■

Appendix A
Film Biographies Arranged by Subject

SUBJECT	TITLE	YEAR
Alexander	Alexander the Great	(1956)
Boom, Carrie ten	Hiding Place, The	(1975)
Brown, John	Seven Angry Men	(1955)
Cavanaugh, Frank	Iron Major, The	(1943)
Cavell, Edith	Nurse Edith Cavell	(1939)
	Woman the Germans Shot, The	(1918)
Clive, Robert	Clive of India	(1935)
Clum, John Philip	Walk the Proud Land	(1956)
Conwell, Russell	Johnny Ring & the Captain's Sword	(1921)
Custer, George A.	Custer of the West	(1967)
	They Died With Their Boots On	(1941)
Eichmann, Adolf	Operation Eichmann	(1961)
Frank, Anne	Diary of Anne Frank, The	(1959)
Gabaldon, Guy	Hell to Eternity	(1960)
Geronimo	Geronimo	(1939)
	Geronimo	(1962)
Goebbels, Joseph	Enemy of Women	(1944)
Guevara, Che	Che!	(1969)
Hall, Bert	Romance of the Air, A	(1918)
Halsey, William F.	Gallant Hours, The	(1960)
Hamilton, Lady Emma	That Hamilton Woman	(1941)
Hayes, Ira	Outsider, The	(1961)
Hess, Dean	Battle Hymn	(1956)
Hitler, Adolf	Hitler	(1962)
	Hitler Gang, The	(1944)
Hoskins, John M.	Eternal Sea, The	(1955)
Houston, Sam	First Texan, The	(1956)
	Conqueror, The	(1917)
James, Jesse	Jesse James	(1927)
Joan of Arc	Joan of Arc	(1948)
Jones, John Paul	John Paul Jones	(1959)
Khan, Genghis	Genghis Khan	(1965)
Lincoln, Abraham	Abraham Lincoln	(1924)
	Abraham Lincoln	(1930)
	Lincoln Cycle, The	(1917)

London, Jack	Jack London	(1943)
MacArthur, Douglas	MacArthur	(1977)
Madison, Dolly	Magnificent Doll	(1946)
Marcus, David	Cast a Giant Shadow	(1966)
McConnell, Joseph	McConnell Story, The	(1955)
Morgan, John F.	Morgan's Raiders	(1918)
Murphy, Audie	To Hell and Back	(1955)
Nightingale, Florence	White Angel, The	(1936)
Patton, George	Patton	(1970)
Peat, Harold	Private Peat	(1918)
Quantrill, William	Quantrill's Raiders	(1958)
Reed, Tom	Reds	(1981)
Rickenbacker, Edward	Captain Eddie	(1945)
Rommel, Irwin	Desert Fox, The	(1951)
Roosevelt, Theodore	Fighting Roosevelts, The	(1919)
Schmid, Al	Pride of the Marines	(1945)
Terasaki, Gwendolyn	Bridge to the Sun	(1961)
Villa, Pancho	Villa Rides	(1968)
	Viva Villa	(1934)
	Life of General Villa, The	(1914)
Wassell, Corydon	Story of Dr. Wassell, The	(1944)
Wead, Frank	Wings of Eagles, The	(1957)
York, Alvin	Sergeant York	(1941)
Zapata, Emiliano	Viva Zapata!	(1952)

Appendix B
Academy Award-Winning War-Related Films

YEAR	TITLE
1927–28:	Wings (Best Picture)
1929–30:	All Quiet on the Western Front (Best Picture, Best Director)
1932–33:	Cavalcade (Best Picture, Best Director)
1935:	Informer, The (Best Director, Best Actor)
1939:	Gone With the Wind (Best Picture, Best Director, Best Actress)
1941:	Sergeant York (Best Actor)
1942:	Mrs. Miniver (Best Picture, Best Director, Best Actress)
1942:	Yankee Doodle Dandy (Best Actor)
1943:	Casablanca (Best Picture, Best Director)
1943:	Watch on the Rhine (Best Actor)
1946:	Best Years of Our Lives, The (Best Picture, Best Director, Best Actor)
1946:	To Each His Own (Best Actress)
1951:	African Queen, The (Best Actor)
1953:	From Here to Eternity (Best Picture, Best Director)
1953:	Stalag 17 (Best Actor)
1961:	Judgment at Nuremberg (Best Actor)
1970:	Patton (Best Picture, Best Director, Best Actor)
1978:	Deer Hunter, The (Best Picture, Best Director)
1978:	Coming Home (Best Actor, Best Actress)
1981:	Reds (Best Director)
1982:	Sophie's Choice (Best Actress)
1986:	Platoon (Best Picture, Best Director)

APPENDIX C
A List of Wars and Related Films

ABENAKI WARS (1675–1725)

Northwest Passage   (1940)

AFGHANISTAN WAR (1979–)

Rambo III   (1988)

ALGERIAN-FRENCH WARS (1830–1847)

Bugler of Algiers, The	(1914)
Dishonored Medal, The	(1914)
Love and Glory	(1924)
Song of Love, The	(1924)

ALGERIAN WAR OF 1954–1962

Lost Command   (1966)

AMERICAN CIVIL WAR (1861–1865)

Abraham Lincoln	(1924)
Abraham Lincoln	(1930)
According to the Code	(1916)
Advance to the Rear	(1964)
Alvarez Kelly	(1966)
Arizona Bushwhackers	(1968)
Barbara Frietchie	(1908)
Barbara Frietchie	(1915)
Barbara Frietchie	(1924)
Battle of Gettysburg, The	(1914)
Battle, The	(1911)
Beguiled, The	(1971)
Birth of a Nation, The	(1915)
Black Dakotas, The	(1954)
Blue and the Grey or Days of '61	(1908)
Border River	(1954)
Charley One-Eye	(1973)
Copperhead, The	(1920)
Coquette, The	(1910)
Court Martial	(1928)
Coward, The	(1915)

Crisis, The	(1916)
Dan	(1914)
Dark Command, The	(1940)
Despatch Bearer, The	(1907)
Desperados, The	(1969)
Drums in the Deep South	(1951)
Escape From Fort Bravo	(1953)
Fastest Guitar Alive, The	(1967)
Field of Honor, The	(1917)
Friendly Persuasion	(1956)
Frontier Scout	(1938)
Fugitive, The	(1910)
General Spanky	(1937)
General, The	(1927)
Girl Spy Before Vicksburg, The	(1911)
Gone With the Wind	(1939)
Gray Sentinel, The	(1913)
Great Day in the Morning	(1956)
Guerrilla, The	(1908)
Guns of Fort Petticoat, The	(1957)
Hands Up	(1926)
Heart of Lincoln, The	(1915)
Heart of Maryland, The	(1915)
Heart of Maryland, The	(1927)
Hearts in Bondage	(1936)
Held by the Enemy	(1920)
Her Father's Son	(1916)
Highest Law, The	(1921)
His Trust	(1911)
His Trust Fulfilled	(1911)
Honor of His Family, The	(1910)
Horse Soldiers, The	(1959)
House With Closed Shutters, The	(1910)
In Old Kentucky	(1909)
Incident at Phantom Hill	(1966)
Jesse James	(1927)
Jim Bludso	(1917)
Johnny Ring & the Captain's Sword	(1921)

Journey to Shiloh	(1968)
Kansas Raiders	(1950)
Last Outpost, The	(1951)
Last Rebel, The	(1918)
Lincoln Cycle, The	(1917)
Lincoln in the White House	(1939)
Little Yank, The	(1917)
Madam Who?	(1918)
Man From Dakota, The	(1940)
May Blossom	(1915)
Morgan's Last Raid	(1929)
Morgan's Raiders	(1918)
No Drums, No Bugles	(1971)
Only the Brave	(1930)
Operator 13	(1934)
Pride of the South, The	(1913)
Quantrill's Raiders	(1958)
Raid, The	(1954)
Ransomed or a Prisoner of War	(1910)
Rebel City	(1953)
Red Badge of Courage, The	(1951)
Red Mountain	(1951)
Revolt at Fort Laramie	(1957)
Road to Richmond, The	(1910)
Rocky Mountain	(1950)
Romance of Rosy Ridge, The	(1947)
Rose of the South	(1916)
Secret Service	(1931)
Seven Angry Men	(1955)
Shenandoah	(1965)
Siege at Red River	(1954)
Sinews of War, The	(1913)
So Red the Rose	(1935)
Southern Yankee, The	(1948)
Southerners, The	(1914)
Springfield Rifle	(1952)
Stirring Days in Old Virginia	(1909)
Tap Roots	(1948)
Thirteen Fighting Men	(1960)
Those Without Sin	(1917)
Time for Killing, A	(1968)
Two Flags West	(1950)
Vanquished, The	(1953)
Virginia City	(1940)
War Time Sweetheart, A	(1909)
Warrens of Virginia, The	(1915)
Warrens of Virginia, The	(1924)
When Lovers Part	(1910)
With Lee in Virginia	(1913)
Yellowneck	(1955)

AMERICAN REVOLUTION (1775–1783)

America	(1924)
Betsy Ross	(1917)
Brave Women of '76	(1909)
Cardigan	(1922)
Drums Along the Mohawk	(1939)
Governor's Daughter, The	(1909)
Heart of a Hero, The	(1916)
Howards of Virginia, The	(1940)
Janice Meredith	(1924)

John Paul Jones	(1959)
Johnny Tremain	(1957)
Man Without a Country, The	(1917)
Scarlet Coat, The	(1955)
1776	(1972)
1776, or Hessian Renegades	(1909)
Spirit of '76, The	(1917)
Spy, The	(1914)
Swamp Fox, The	(1914)
Washington at Valley Forge	(1914)

ANGLO-SAXON REBELLIONS (1066–1174)

Adventures of Robin Hood, The	(1938)
Black Rose, The	(1950)
Ivanhoe	(1952)

ANGLO-SPANISH WARS (1587–1729)

Sea Hawk, The	(1940)
Seven Seas to Calais	(1963)

APACHE WARS (1871–1876)

Ambush	(1949)
Apache	(1954)
Apache Drums	(1951)
Apache Rifles	(1964)
Apache Uprising	(1966)
Apache Warrior	(1957)
Arrowhead	(1953)
Battle at Apache Pass, The	(1952)
Broken Arrow	(1950)
Conquest of Cochise	(1953)
Deserter, The	(1971)
Duel at Diablo	(1966)
Escape From Fort Bravo	(1953)
Fighting Blood	(1911)
Fort Apache	(1948)
Fort Bowie	(1958)
Fort Massacre	(1958)
Fort Yuma	(1955)
Geronimo	(1939)
Geronimo	(1962)
Geronimo's Last Raid	(1912)
I Killed Geronimo	(1950)
Indian Uprising	(1952)
Last Outpost, The	(1951)
Major Dundee	(1965)
Only the Valiant	(1951)
Rio Grande	(1950)
She Wore a Yellow Ribbon	(1949)
Taza, Son of Cochise	(1954)
Thunder of Drums, A	(1961)
Tomahawk Trail	(1957)
Ulzana's Raid	(1972)
Walk the Proud Land	(1956)
War Drums	(1957)

AUSTRALIAN CONVICT REVOLTS (1800s)

Captain Fury	(1939)

AUSTRO-ITALIAN WARS (1859, 1866)

Lady in Ermine, The	(1927)

BALKAN WARS (1912–1913)

Captive, The	(1915)

BEAR FLAG REPUBLIC REVOLT (1846)

Bold Caballero, The	(1933)
Californian, The	(1937)
Kit Carson	(1940)
Lash, The	(1931)

BLACK HAWK WAR OF 1832

Fall of Black Hawk, The	(1912)

BOER WAR (SEE SOUTH AFRICAN WAR)

BOXER REBELLION (1900)

Fifty-Five Days at Peking	(1963)
Foreign Devils	(1928)
Marked Woman, The	(1914)

CHACO WAR (1932–1935)

Dead March	(1937)
Storm Over the Andes	(1935)

CHEYENNE WARS (1864–1878)

Cheyenne Autumn	(1964)
Guns of Fort Petticoat, The	(1957)
Plainsman, The	(1936)
Soldier Blue	(1970)
White Feather	(1955)
Yellow Tomahawk, The	(1954)

COMANCHE WARS (1858–1875)

Comanche	(1956)
Comanche Territory	(1950)
Conquest of Cochise	(1953)
Last of the Comanches	(1952)
War Party	(1965)

CRIMEAN WAR (1854–1856)

Charge of the Lancers	(1954)
Charge of the Light Brigade, The	(1936)
White Angel, The	(1936)

CRUSADES (1095–1291)

Crusades, The	(1935)
King Richard and the Crusaders	(1954)
Richard, the Lion-Hearted	(1923)
Saracen Blade, The	(1954)

CUBAN REVOLTS OF 1930–1933

Gun Runners, The	(1958)
We Were Strangers	(1949)
World in Revolt	(1934)

CUBAN REVOLUTION (1956–1959)

Che!	(1969)
Rebellion in Cuba	(1961)

CUBAN WAR OF INDEPENDENCE (1895–1898)

Dawn of Freedom, The	(1910)
Santiago	(1956)

FRANCO-PRUSSIAN WAR (1870–1871)

Mademoiselle Fifi	(1944)
Standard Bearer, The	(1908)

FRENCH AND INDIAN WAR (1754–1763)

Battles of Chief Pontiac	(1952)
Fort Ti	(1953)
Iroquois Trail, The	(1950)
Last of the Mohicans, The	(1920)
Last of the Mohicans, The	(1936)
Last of the Red Men	(1947)
Pathfinder, The	(1952)
Seats of the Mighty	(1914)
When the Redskins Rode	(1951)
Winners of the Wilderness	(1927)

FRENCH INDO-CHINA WAR (1946–1954)

China Gate	(1957)
Jump Into Hell	(1955)
Quiet American, The	(1958)

FRENCH REVOLUTION (1789–1799)

Charlotte Corday	(1914)
Fighting Guardsman, The	(1945)
Gambling With Death	(1909)
Madame Sans-Gene	(1925)
Marie Antoinette	(1938)
Nursing a Viper	(1909)
Oath and the Man, The	(1910)
Orphans of the Storm	(1921)
Reign of Terror	(1949)
Scaramouche	(1923)
Start the Revolution Without Me	(1970)
Tale of Two Cities, A	(1917)
Tale of Two Cities, A	(1936)

GLORIOUS REVOLUTION (1688–1689)

Captain Blood	(1924)
Captain Blood	(1935)
Dangerous Maid	(1923)

GRECO-PERSIAN WARS (500–449 B.C.)

300 Spartans, The	(1962)

GREEK CIVIL WAR (1944–1949)

Eleni	(1985)
Guerrilla Girl	(1953)

HOLY ROMAN EMPIRE-PAPACY WARS
(1228–1250)

Flame and the Arrow, The   (1950)

HUNDRED YEARS' WAR (1337–1457)

Joan of Arc   (1948)
Joan the Woman   (1917)
Quentin Durward   (1955)
St. Joan   (1957)

HUNGARIAN REVOLT (1956)

Beast of Budapest   (1958)
Journey, The   (1959)

HURON WARS (1760s)

Deerslayer, The   (1957)
Last of the Mohicans   (1920)
Last of the Mohicans   (1935)

INDIAN (SEPOY) MUTINY (1857–1858)

Beggar of Cawnpore, The   (1916)
Bengal Brigade   (1954)
Campbells Are Coming, The   (1915)
Khyber Patrol   (1954)
King of the Khyber Rifles   (1953)
Rogue's March   (1952)
Rose of the World   (1918)
Sepoy's Wife, The   (1910)
Soldiers Three   (1951)
Storm Over Bengal   (1938)
Stronger Than Death   (1920)
Wee Willie Winkie   (1937)

IRAQI REBELLION OF 1935

I Cover the War   (1937)

IRISH REBELLIONS (1798, 1916–1921,
1969–   )

Beloved Enemy   (1936)
Informer, The   (1935)
Ireland in Revolt (doc.)   (1921)
Key, The   (1934)
Outsider, The   (1979)
Plough and the Stars, The   (1937)
Shake Hands With the Devil   (1959)
Whom the Gods Destroy   (1916)

ISRAEL'S WAR OF INDEPENDENCE
(1948–1949)

Cast a Giant Shadow   (1966)
Exodus   (1960)
Judith   (1966)
Sword in the Desert   (1949)

KIOWA WAR OF 1874

Two Flags West   (1950)
War Arrow   (1954)

KOREAN WAR (1950–53)

All the Young Men   (1960)
Annapolis Story, An   (1955)
Bamboo Prison, The   (1954)
Battle Circus   (1953)
Battle Flame   (1959)
Battle Hymn   (1956)
Battle Taxi   (1955)
Battle Zone   (1952)
Bridges at Toko-Ri, The   (1954)
Cassino to Korea (doc.)   (1950)
Cease Fire (doc.)   (1953)
Combat Squad   (1953)
Death of a Dream (doc.)   (1950)
Dragonfly Squadron   (1954)
Eternal Sea, The   (1955)
First Forty Days, The (doc.)   (1950)
Fixed Bayonets   (1951)
Flight Nurse   (1953)
Glory Brigade, The   (1953)
Hell's Horizon   (1955)
Hold Back the Night   (1956)
Hook, The   (1963)
Hunters, The   (1958)
I Want You   (1951)
Inchon   (1981)
Japanese War Bride   (1952)
Jet Attack   (1958)
Korea Patrol   (1951)
M*A*S*H   (1970)
Manchurian Candidate, The   (1962)
Marines, Let's Go   (1961)
Men in War   (1957)
Men of the Fighting Lady   (1954)
Mr. Walkie Talkie   (1952)
Nun and the Sergeant, The   (1962)
One Minute to Zero   (1952)
Operation Dames   (1959)
Pork Chop Hill   (1959)
Prisoner of War   (1954)
Rack, The   (1956)
Retreat, Hell!   (1952)
Return From the Sea   (1954)
Sabre Jet   (1953)
Sayonara   (1957)
Sniper's Ridge   (1961)
Steel Helmet, The   (1951)
Submarine Command   (1951)
Tank Battalion   (1958)
Target Zero   (1955)
This Is Korea! (doc.)   (1951)
Time Limit   (1957)
Tokyo File 212   (1951)
Torpedo Alley   (1953)
War Hunt   (1962)
Why Korea? (doc.)   (1951)
Yank in Indo-China, A   (1952)
Yank in Korea, A   (1951)
Young and the Brave, The   (1963)

MAU MAU UPRISING (1952–1956)

Something of Value	(1957)

MEXICAN REVOLUTION (1910–1921)

Bandido	(1956)
Barbarous Mexico (doc.)	(1913)
Eagle's Wings, The	(1916)
Fighter, The	(1952)
Five Man Army	(1970)
Life of General Villa, The	(1914)
Stronghold	(1952)
Treasure of Pancho Villa, The	(1955)
Villa Rides	(1968)
Viva Villa	(1934)
Viva Zapata!	(1952)
Wings of the Hawk	(1953)

MEXICAN WAR OF 1846–1848

California	(1927)
California Romance, A	(1923)
For the Honor of Old Glory	(1914)
Frontier Uprising	(1961)
Kit Carson	(1940)
Pirates of Monterey	(1947)

MODOC WAR OF 1872–1873

Drum Beat	(1954)

MOHAWK WARS (1700s)

America	(1924)
Drums Along the Mohawk	(1939)
Mohawk	(1956)
Mohawk's Way, A	(1910)

MORO WAR (1901–1913)

Last Man, The	(1916)
Real Glory, The	(1939)
Tides of Hate	(1917)

NAPOLEONIC WARS (1803–1815)

Captain Horatio Hornblower	(1951)
Conquest	(1937)
Desiree	(1954)
Divine Lady	(1929)
Fighting O'Flynn, The	(1949)
Love and Death	(1975)
Love and War	(1909)
Price of Victory, The	(1911)
Pride and the Passion, The	(1957)
Purple Mask, The	(1955)
Sea Devils	(1953)
Secret of St. Ives, The	(1949)
That Hamilton Woman	(1941)
Tyrant of the Sea	(1950)
War and Peace	(1956)

NICARAGUAN CIVIL WARS (1925–1933, 1978–1979, 1982–)

Flight	(1929)
Last Plane Out	(1983)

Marines Are Coming, The	(1935)
Marines Fly High, The	(1940)
Under Fire	(1983)
Women in Arms (doc.)	(1981)

PENINSULAR WAR (1808–1814)

Pride and the Passion, The	(1957)

PHILIPPINE INSURRECTION (1899–1902)

Across the Pacific	(1926)
Cavalry Command	(1963)

ROMAN CIVIL WARS
(49–44 B.C., 43–31 B.C.)

Cleopatra	(1963)
Julius Caesar	(1953)
Serpent of the Nile	(1953)

RUSSIAN REVOLUTION (1917)

Bavu	(1923)
British Agent	(1934)
Captain of the Guard	(1930)
Doctor Zhivago	(1965)
Fall of the Romanoffs, The	(1917)
Last Command, The	(1928)
Meet the Prince	(1926)
Mockery	(1927)
Red Dance, The	(1928)
Reds	(1981)
Scarlet Dawn	(1932)
Scarlet Lady, The	(1928)
Song of the Flame	(1930)
Surrender	(1927)
Tempest	(1928)
Three Legionnaires	(1937)
Volga Boatman, The	(1926)
World and the Flesh, The	(1932)

RUSSO-FINNISH WAR (1939–1940)

Ski Patrol	(1940)

RUSSO-JAPANESE WAR (1904–1905)

Affair of Three Nations, An	(1915)
Breath of the Gods, The	(1920)
Jack London	(1943)

RUSSO-TURKISH WAR (1877–1878)

Michael Strogoff	(1910)
Michael Strogoff	(1914)
Soldier and the Lady, The	(1937)

SANUSI ANTI-BRITISH REVOLT
(1915–1917)

Burning Sands	(1922)
Flame of the Desert	(1919)

SEMINOLE WARS (1817–1818, 1835–1842)

Seminole	(1953)
Seminole Uprising	(1955)

SEVEN WEEKS WAR (1866)

Lady in Ermine, The	(1927)

SHAWNEE WARS (1774–1814)

Brave Warrior	(1952)
Daniel Boone, Trail Blazer	(1957)

SINO-JAPANESE WAR (1937–1945)

Burma Convoy	(1941)
China	(1943)
China Doll	(1958)
China Girl	(1942)
China Sky	(1945)
Dragon Seed	(1944)
Flying Tigers	(1942)
Four Hundred Million, The	(1939)
International Settlement	(1938)
Kukan (doc.)	(1941)
Lady From Chungking	(1943)
Night Plane From Chungking	(1943)
North of Shanghai	(1939)
Shadows Over Shanghai	(1938)
Yank on the Burma Road, A	(1942)

SIOUX WARS (1862–1891)

Adventures of Buffalo Bill, The	(1914)
Black Dakotas, The	(1954)
Britton of the Seventh	(1916)
Bugles in the Afternoon	(1952)
Chief Crazy Horse	(1955)
Custer's Last Fight	(1912)
Custer's Last Stand	(1936)
Great Sioux Massacre, The	(1965)
Great Sioux Uprising, The	(1953)
Gun That Won the West, The	(1955)
Indian Fighter, the	(1955)
Little Big Horn	(1927)
Little Big Horn	(1951)
Red Tomahawk	(1967)
Run of the Arrow	(1957)
Saskatchewan	(1954)
Savage, The	(1952)
Sitting Bull	(1954)
Sitting Bull at Spirit Lake Massacre	(1927)
They Died With Their Boots On	(1941)
Tomahawk	(1951)

SOUTH AFRICAN WAR (1899–1902)

Boer War, The	(1914)
Cavalcade	(1933)
Girl Scout, The	(1909)
Highlander's Defiance, The	(1910)
Judgment House, The	(1915)
Light That Failed, The	(1939)
Second in Command, The	(1915)
Torn Allegiance	(1984)
Untamed	(1955)

SPANISH-AMERICAN WAR (1898)

Across the Pacific	(1926)
Dawn of Freedom, The	(1910)
Denial, The	(1925)
Fighting Roosevelts, The	(1919)
Masters of Men	(1923)
Rough Riders, The	(1927)
Tangle, The	(1914)
Tearing Down the Spanish Flag	(1898)

SPANISH CIVIL WAR (1936–1939)

Behold a Pale Horse	(1964)
Blockade	(1938)
Confidential Agent	(1945)
Fallen Sparrow, The	(1943)
For Whom the Bell Tolls	(1943)
Good Fight, The (doc.)	(1984)
Last Train From Madrid, The	(1937)

SUDANESE WAR (1896–1899)

Four Feathers	(1915)
Four Feathers	(1929)

TEN YEARS' WAR (1868–1878)

Bright Shawl, The	(1923)

TEXAS WAR OF INDEPENDENCE (1836)

Alamo, The	(1960)
Conqueror, The	(1917)
First Texan, The	(1956)
Heroes of the Alamo	(1938)
Last Command, The	(1955)
Man From the Alamo, The	(1953)
Man of Conquest	(1939)
Martyrs of the Alamo, The	(1915)

TRIPOLITAN WAR (1800–1805)

Barbary Pirate	(1949)
Old Ironsides	(1926)
Tripoli	(1950)

TROJAN WAR (1200 B.C.)

Helen of Troy	(1953)

VIETNAM WAR (1956–1975)

Annihilators, The	(1985)
Apocalypse Now	(1979)
AWOL	(1972)
Boys in Company C, The	(1978)
Combat Shock	(1986)
Coming Home	(1978)
Crazy World of Julius Vrooder, The	(1974)
Dear America: Letters . . . (doc.)	(1988)
Deer Hunter, The	(1978)
Don't Cry, It's Only Thunder	(1982)
84 Charlie Mopic	(1989)
Face of War, A (doc.)	(1968)
Full Metal Jacket	(1987)

Gardens of Stone	(1987)	America Under Fire (doc.)	(1937)
Go Tell the Spartans	(1978)	America's Answer (doc.)	(1918)
Good Morning, Vietnam	(1987)	Anybody's War	(1930)
Green Berets, The	(1968)	Arms and the Girl	(1917)
Hail, Hero!	(1969)	Army Surgeon	(1942)
Hamburger Hill	(1987)	As in a Looking Glass	(1916)
Hanoi Hilton, The	(1987)	Barbed Wire	(1927)
Hearts and Minds (doc.)	(1974)	Battle and Fall of Przemysl (doc.)	(1915)
In the Year of the Pig (doc.)	(1969)	Battle of Paris, The	(1929)
Inside North Vietnam (doc.)	(1967)	Battles of a Nation, The (doc.)	(1915)
Introduction to the Enemy (doc.)	(1975)	Behind the Door	(1920)
Iron Triangle, The	(1989)	Behind the Front	(1926)
Jacknife	(1989)	Belgian, The	(1917)
Limbo	(1972)	Berlin via America	(1918)
Losers, The	(1970)	Better 'Ole, The	(1926)
Missing in Action	(1984)	Beware!	(1919)
Missing in Action 2: The		Beyond Victory	(1931)
Beginning	(1985)	Big Drive, The (doc.)	(1933)
Off Limits	(1988)	Big Parade, The	(1925)
Operation CIA	(1965)	Birth of a Race, The	(1919)
Outside In	(1972)	Black Watch, The	(1929)
P.O.W. The Escape	(1986)	Blaze o' Glory	(1930)
Parades	(1972)	Block-Heads	(1942)
Platoon	(1986)	Blue Eagle, The	(1926)
Purple Hearts	(1984)	Blue Max, The	(1966)
Rambo: First Blood Part II	(1985)	Body and Soul	(1931)
Rolling Thunder	(1977)	Bond, The	(1918)
Search and Destroy	(1981)	Bonnie Annie Laurie	(1918)
Some Won't Go (doc.)	(1969)	Border Wireless, The	(1918)
There Is No 13	(1974)	Boss of Camp 4	(1922)
To the Shores of Hell	(1966)	British Intelligence	(1940)
Tracks	(1976)	Bud's Recruit	(1918)
Uncommon Valor	(1983)	Captain Eddie	(1945)
War at Home, The (doc.)	(1979)	Captain Swagger	(1928)
War Is Hell	(1964)	Captured!	(1933)
Welcome Home, Soldier Boys	(1972)	Case of Sergeant Grischa, The	(1930)
Yank in Vietnam, A	(1964)	Chances	(1931)
		Charmer, The	(1917)
		Child Thou Gavest Me, The	(1922)
WAR OF 1812 (1812–1814)		Civilian Clothes	(1920)
		Claws of the Hun	(1918)
Brave Warrior	(1952)	Closed Gates	(1927)
Buccaneer, The	(1938)	Cock of the Air	(1932)
Buccaneer, The	(1958)	Come On In	(1918)
Captain Caution	(1940)	Comrades	(1928)
Magnificent Doll	(1946)	Convoy	(1927)
Mutiny	(1952)	Corporal Kate	(1926)
		Cradle of Courage	(1920)
WAR OF THE AUSTRIAN SUCCESSION		Crashing Through to Berlin (doc.)	(1918)
(1740–1748)		Crimson Romance	(1934)
Celebrated Case, A	(1914)	Cross Bearer, The	(1918)
		Crowded Hour, The	(1925)
WORLD WAR I (1914–1918)		Dangerous Business	(1920)
		Dangerous Days	(1920)
Ace of Aces	(1933)	Dark Angel, The	(1925)
Adele	(1919)	Dark Angel, The	(1935)
Afraid to Fight	(1922)	Dark Road, The	(1917)
African Queen, The	(1951)	Dark Star, The	(1919)
After the War	(1918)	Darling Lili	(1970)
After Tonight	(1933)	Daughter Angele	(1918)
Alias Mike Moran	(1919)	Daughter of Destiny	(1918)
Alien Enemy, An	(1918)		
All Quiet on the Western Front	(1930)		

Daughter of France, A	(1918)	Ham and Eggs at the Front	(1927)
Dawn Patrol, The	(1930)	Hard Boiled Haggerty	(1927)
Dawn Patrol, The	(1938)	Havoc	(1925)
Dealers in Death (doc.)	(1934)	Heart of Humanity, The	(1918)
Devil Dogs	(1928)	Heart Trouble	(1928)
Dishonored	(1931)	Heartbreak	(1931)
Dog of the Regiment	(1927)	Hearts of the World	(1918)
Doing Their Bit	(1918)	Hell Below	(1933)
Don't Write Letters	(1922)	Hell in the Heavens	(1934)
Doomed Battalion, The	(1932)	Hell's Angels	(1930)
Dough Boys	(1930)	Hell's Holiday (doc.)	(1933)
Draft 258	(1918)	Her Country First	(1918)
Duggan of the Dugouts	(1928)	Her Country's Call	(1917)
Eagle and the Hawk, The	(1933)	Her Debt of Honor	(1918)
Enemy, The	(1928)	Her Man o' War	(1926)
Ever in My Heart	(1933)	Heroes All (doc.)	(1931)
False Faces, The	(1919)	Highest Trump, The	(1919)
Farewell to Arms, A	(1932)	His Buddy's Wife	(1925)
Farewell to Arms, A	(1957)	His Foreign Wife	(1927)
Fields of Honor	(1918)	His Master's Voice	(1925)
Fighting Sixty-Ninth, The	(1940)	Honest Man, An	(1918)
Firefly of France, The	(1918)	Honor First	(1922)
Fires of Faith	(1919)	Horrors of War (doc.)	(1940)
First World War, The (doc.)	(1934)	Hotel Imperial	(1927)
Flames of Chance	(1918)	Hotel Imperial	(1939)
Flying With the Marines (doc.)	(1918)	How Uncle Sam Prepares (doc.)	(1917)
Follow the Girl	(1917)	Humming Bird, The	(1924)
Following the Flag to France		Hun Within, The	(1918)
(doc.)	(1918)	I Want My Man	(1925)
For Better, for Worse	(1919)	I'll Say So	(1918)
For France	(1917)	In Again—Out Again	(1917)
For Liberty	(1917)	In Pursuit of Polly	(1918)
For the Freedom of the East	(1919)	Inside the Lines	(1918)
For the Freedom of the World	(1917)	Inside the Lines	(1930)
For Valour	(1917)	Into No Man's Land	(1928)
Forever After	(1926)	Iowa Under Fire (doc.)	(1924)
Forgotten Men (doc.)	(1933)	Iron Major, The	(1943)
Fountain, The	(1934)	Joan of Plattsburg	(1918)
Four Horsemen of the		Johanna Enlists	(1918)
Apocalypse, The	(1921)	Johnny Got His Gun	(1971)
Four Sons	(1928)	Journey's End	(1930)
Friendly Enemies	(1925)	Kaiser's Finish, The	(1918)
Fugitive Road	(1934)	Kaiser's Shadow, The	(1918)
Gay Diplomat, The	(1931)	Kaiser, or the Beast of Berlin, The	(1918)
Gay Retreat, The	(1927)	Keep 'em Rolling	(1934)
Gentleman From America	(1923)	Kiss Barrier, The	(1925)
Gigolo	(1926)	Kultur	(1918)
Girl Who Stayed at Home, The	(1919)	Lafayette Escadrille	(1958)
Gold Chevrons (doc.)	(1927)	Lafayette, We Come!	(1918)
Golden Dawn	(1930)	Lancer Spy	(1937)
Goodbye Kiss, The	(1928)	Last Outpost, The	(1935)
Gown of Destiny, The	(1917)	Last Parade, The	(1931)
Great Deception, The	(1926)	Leech, The	(1922)
Great Impersonation, The	(1921)	Legion of the Condemned	(1928)
Great Love, The	(1918)	Legionnaires in Paris	(1927)
Greater Glory, The	(1926)	Lest We Forget	(1918)
Greatest Power, The	(1917)	Light of Victory, The	(1919)
Greatest Thing in Life, The	(1918)	Light, The	(1919)
Green Temptation, The	(1922)	Lilac Time	(1928)
Guns of August, The (doc.)	(1964)	Little American, The	(1917)
Half Shot at Sunrise	(1930)	Little Miss Hoover	(1918)

Sons o' Guns	(1936)
Soul of Bronze, The	(1921)
Spirit of '17	(1918)
Spirit of the Red Cross, The	(1918)
Spirit of the U.S.A., The	(1924)
Sporting Venus, The	(1925)
Spuds	(1927)
Spy, The	(1917)
Stamboul Quest	(1934)
Stolen Orders	(1918)
Storm at Daybreak	(1933)
Strong Man, The	(1926)
Submarine Patrol	(1938)
Suicide Fleet	(1931)
Sun-Up	(1925)
Surrender	(1931)
Suspicion	(1918)
Suzy	(1936)
Swat the Spy	(1918)
Tell That to the Marines	(1918)
This Hero Stuff	(1919)
This Mad World	(1930)
Three Faces East	(1926)
Three Faces East	(1930)
Three of Many	(1916)
Three Sisters	(1930)
Thunder Afloat	(1939)
Till I Come Back to You	(1918)
Till We Meet Again	(1936)
Tin Hats	(1926)
To Hell With the Kaiser	(1918)
Today We Live	(1933)
Tomorrow Is Forever	(1946)
Too Fat to Fight	(1918)
Top Sergeant Mulligan	(1928)
Treason	(1917)
True Heaven	(1929)
23 1/2 Hours' Leave	(1919)
Two Arabian Knights	(1927)
Unbeliever, The	(1918)
Uncle Sam of Freedom Ridge	(1920)
Under False Colors	(1917)
Under Four Flags (doc.)	(1918)
Under the Black Eagle	(1928)
Unknown Love, The	(1919)
Unknown Soldier Speaks, The (doc.)	(1934)
Unknown Soldier, The	(1926)
Unpardonable Sin, The	(1919)
Victory of Conscience, The	(1916)
Vive La France	(1918)
Volunteer, The	(1917)
Von Richtofen and Brown	(1971)
Wandering Fires	(1925)
Wanted for Murder	(1918)
War and the Woman	(1917)
War Bride's Secret, The	(1916)
War Horse, The	(1927)
War Nurse	(1930)
War's End (doc.)	(1934)
Wasted Lives	(1923)

Waterloo Bridge	(1940)
We Americans	(1928)
We're in the Navy Now	(1926)
What Price Glory	(1952)
What Price Glory?	(1926)
When Men Desire	(1919)
White Cliffs of Dover, The	(1944)
White Sister, The	(1915)
White Sister, The	(1923)
White Sister, The	(1933)
Who Goes There?	(1917)
Who Was the Other Man?	(1917)
Why America Will Win	(1918)
Why This War? (doc.)	(1939)
Wife or Country	(1918)
Wife Savers	(1928)
Winding Stair, The	(1926)
Wings	(1927)
Wisconsin Under Fire (doc.)	(1924)
Wolves of Kultur	(1918)
Woman Disputed, The	(1928)
Woman From Monte Carlo, The	(1932)
Woman I Love, The	(1937)
Woman of Experience, A	(1931)
Woman the Germans Shot, The	(1918)
Womanhood, the Glory of the Nation	(1917)
Woodrow Wilson Film Memorial (doc.)	(1924)
World Moves On, The	(1934)
Yankee Doodle in Berlin	(1919)
Young Eagles	(1930)

WORLD WAR II (1939–1945)

About Face	(1942)
Above and Beyond	(1952)
Above Suspicion	(1943)
Abroad With Two Yanks	(1944)
Across the Pacific	(1942)
Action in Arabia	(1944)
Action in the North Atlantic	(1943)
Address Unknown	(1944)
Adventures of a Rookie, The	(1943)
Aerial Gunner	(1943)
After Mein Kampf (doc.)	(1961)
Air Force	(1943)
Air Raid Wardens	(1943)
All My Sons	(1948)
All This and World War II (doc.)	(1976)
All Through the Night	(1941)
Allotment Wives	(1945)
Ambush Bay	(1966)
American Guerrilla in Philippines	(1950)
Americanization of Emily, The	(1964)
Angry Hills, The	(1959)
Anzio	(1968)
Appointment in Berlin	(1943)
Appointment in Tokyo (doc.)	(1945)
Arise, My Love	(1940)
Armored Command	(1961)
Army Wives	(1944)

Assignment in Brittany	(1943)	Casablanca	(1942)
At the Front in North Africa		Castle Keep	(1969)
(doc.)	(1943)	Catch-22	(1970)
Atlantic Convoy	(1942)	Charlie Chan in Panama	(1940)
Attack on the Iron Coast	(1968)	Chetniks	(1943)
Attack! (doc.)	(1944)	China Doll	(1958)
Attack!	(1956)	China Venture	(1953)
Away All Boats	(1956)	China's Little Devils	(1945)
Back to Bataan	(1945)	Cipher Bureau	(1938)
Background to Danger	(1943)	Clay Pigeon, The	(1949)
Bamboo Blonde, The	(1946)	Cloak and Dagger	(1946)
Bataan	(1943)	Clock, The	(1945)
Battle at Bloody Beach	(1961)	Command Decision	(1948)
Battle Cry	(1955)	Commandos Strike at Dawn, The	(1942)
Battle for Russia (doc.)	(1943)	Confessions of a Nazi Spy	(1939)
Battle for the Marianas, The (doc.)	(1944)	Confirm or Deny	(1941)
Battle of Blood Island	(1960)	Conspirators, The	(1944)
Battle of Britain (doc.)	(1943)	Corregidor	(1943)
Battle of Midway, The (doc.)	(1942)	Corvette K-225	(1943)
Battle of the Bulge	(1965)	Counter-Attack	(1945)
Battle of the Bulge—Brave Rifles	(1966)	Counter-Espionage	(1942)
Battle of the Coral Sea, The	(1959)	Counterfeit Traitor, The	(1962)
Battle Stations	(1956)	Counterpoint	(1967)
Battleground	(1949)	Crash Dive	(1943)
Beach Red	(1967)	Crisis (doc.)	(1939)
Beachhead	(1954)	Cross of Lorraine, The	(1943)
Beachhead to Berlin (doc.)	(1944)	Cry Havoc	(1943)
Beasts of Berlin	(1939)	Cry of Battle	(1963)
Behind the Enemy Lines (doc.)	(1945)	D-Day, the Sixth of June	(1956)
Behind the Rising Sun	(1943)	Danger in the Pacific	(1942)
Bell for Adano, A	(1945)	Dangerous Partners	(1945)
Berlin Correspondent	(1942)	Dangerously They Live	(1942)
Best Years of Our Lives, The	(1946)	Darby's Rangers	(1958)
Betrayal From the East	(1945)	Dawn Express, The	(1942)
Betrayed	(1954)	Day of Battle (doc.)	(1943)
Between Heaven and Hell	(1956)	Days of Glory	(1944)
Big Noise, The	(1944)	Deadly Game, The	(1941)
Big Red One, The	(1980)	December 7, 1941 (doc.)	(1942)
Biloxi Blues	(1988)	Decision Before Dawn	(1951)
Black Dragons	(1942)	Deep Six, The	(1958)
Black Fox, The (doc.)	(1963)	Desert Fox, The	(1951)
Black Parachute, The	(1944)	Desert Rats, The	(1953)
Blood and Steel	(1959)	Desert Song, The	(1943)
Bold and the Brave, The	(1956)	Desperate Journey	(1942)
Bombardier	(1943)	Destination Gobi	(1953)
Bomber's Moon	(1943)	Destination Tokyo	(1943)
Bombs Over Burma	(1942)	Destroyer	(1943)
Born to Love	(1931)	Devil Pays Off, The	(1941)
Bowery Blitzkrieg	(1941)	Devil With Hitler, The	(1942)
Brady's Escape	(1984)	Devil's Brigade, The	(1968)
Breakthrough	(1950)	Diary of Anne Frank, The	(1959)
Bridge at Remagen, The	(1969)	Dirty Dozen, The	(1967)
Bridge to the Sun	(1961)	Dive Bomber	(1941)
Brought to Action (doc.)	(1945)	Don't Go Near the Water	(1957)
Buck Privates Come Home	(1947)	Doughboys in Ireland	(1943)
Busses Roar	(1942)	Doughgirls, The	(1944)
Caine Mutiny, The	(1954)	Down in San Diego	(1941)
Cairo	(1942)	Eagle Squadron	(1942)
Captain Newman, M.D.	(1963)	Edge of Darkness	(1943)
Captains of the Clouds	(1942)	Eight Iron Men	(1952)
Careful, Soft Shoulders	(1942)	El Alamein	(1953)

Empire of the Sun	(1987)	God Is My Co-Pilot	(1945)
Enchanted Cottage, The	(1945)	Golden Earrings	(1947)
Enemy Agents Meet Ellery Queen	(1942)	Government Girl	(1943)
Enemy Below, The	(1957)	Great Dictator, The	(1940)
Enemy General, The	(1960)	Great Escape, The	(1963)
Enemy of Women	(1944)	Great Impersonation, The	(1942)
Ensign Pulver	(1964)	Guadalcanal Diary	(1943)
Escape	(1940)	Gung Ho!	(1943)
Escape From Hong Kong	(1942)	Guy Named Joe, A	(1943)
Escape in the Desert	(1945)	Hail the Conquering Hero	(1944)
Escape to Glory	(1940)	Half Way to Shanghai	(1942)
Espionage Agent	(1939)	Halls of Montezuma	(1950)
Eve of St. Mark, The	(1944)	Hangmen Also Die	(1943)
Executioners, The (doc.)	(1961)	Happy Land	(1943)
Exile Express	(1939)	Heaven Knows, Mr. Allison	(1957)
Extraordinary Seaman, The	(1969)	Hell in the Pacific	(1968)
Face in the Rain	(1963)	Hell Is for Heroes	(1962)
Fall in	(1943)	Hell Squad	(1958)
Farewell to the King	(1989)	Hell to Eternity	(1960)
Father Goose	(1964)	Hellcats of the Navy	(1957)
Federal Fugitives	(1941)	Her Sister's Secret	(1946)
Fighter Attack	(1953)	Here Come the Waves	(1944)
Fighter Squadron	(1948)	Hey, Rookie	(1944)
Fighting Coast Guard	(1951)	Hidden Enemy, The	(1940)
Fighting Lady, The (doc.)	(1944)	Hiding Place, The	(1975)
Fighting Seabees, The	(1944)	High Barbaree	(1947)
First Comes Courage	(1943)	Hillbilly Blitzkrieg	(1942)
First to Fight	(1967)	Hitler	(1962)
First Yank Into Tokyo	(1945)	Hitler Gang, The	(1944)
Five Branded Women	(1960)	Hitler's Children	(1942)
Five Fingers	(1952)	Hitler's Hangman	(1943)
Five Graves to Cairo	(1943)	Hitler—Dead or Alive	(1942)
Flat Top	(1952)	Hold Back the Dawn	(1941)
Fleet That Came to Stay, The		Hollywood Canteen	(1944)
(doc.)	(1945)	Home of the Brave	(1949)
Flight for Freedom	(1943)	Homecoming	(1948)
Fly by Night	(1942)	Horizontal Lieutenant, The	(1962)
Flying Blind	(1941)	Hornet's Nest	(1970)
Flying Leathernecks	(1951)	Hostages	(1943)
Flying Wild	(1941)	Hotel Berlin	(1943)
Follow the Boys	(1944)	Hour Before the Dawn, The	(1944)
Force of Arms	(1951)	House on 92nd Street, The	(1945)
Foreign Agent	(1942)	Human Comedy, The	(1943)
Foreign Correspondent	(1940)	I Escaped From the Gestapo	(1943)
Forever and a Day	(1943)	I Love a Soldier	(1944)
Four Horsemen of the		I Was an American Spy	(1951)
Apocalypse, The	(1961)	I'll Be Seeing You	(1944)
Four Jills in a Jeep	(1944)	Identity Unknown	(1945)
Four Sons	(1940)	Imitation General	(1958)
Francis	(1950)	Immortal Sergeant, The	(1943)
Friendly Enemies	(1942)	Impostor, The	(1944)
Frogmen, The	(1951)	In Enemy Country	(1968)
From Here to Eternity	(1953)	In Harm's Way	(1965)
Fury in the Pacific (doc.)	(1945)	In Love and War	(1958)
G. I. Honeymoon	(1945)	In Our Time	(1944)
Gallant Hours, The	(1960)	International Lady	(1941)
Gangway for Tomorrow	(1943)	International Squadron	(1941)
Genocide	(1982)	Invisible Agent	(1942)
Get Going	(1943)	Is Paris Burning?	(1966)
Girls of Pleasure Island, The	(1953)	Joan of Paris	(1942)
Go for Broke	(1951)	Joe Smith, American	(1942)

Prison Ship	(1945)	Situation Hopeless, But Not	
Prisoner of Japan	(1942)	Serious	(1965)
Private Navy of Sgt. O'Farrell,		Ski Troop Attack	(1960)
The	(1968)	Sky Commando	(1953)
Proud and the Profane, The	(1956)	Sky Murder	(1940)
PT 109	(1963)	Slaughterhouse Five	(1972)
Purple Heart Diary	(1951)	Smashing of the Reich (doc.)	(1962)
Purple Heart, The	(1944)	Snafu	(1945)
Purple V, The	(1943)	So Ends Our Night	(1941)
Pursuit to Algiers	(1945)	So Proudly We Hail	(1943)
Quick and the Dead, The	(1963)	Soldier's Story, A	(1984)
Quiet Please, Murder	(1942)	Something for the Boys	(1944)
Raid on Rommel	(1971)	Somewhere I'll Find You	(1942)
Raiders of Leyte Gulf	(1963)	Son of Lassie	(1945)
Raiders of the Lost Ark	(1981)	Song of Russia	(1943)
Rainbow Island	(1944)	South Sea Woman	(1953)
Ramparts We Watch, The	(1940)	Spy Ship	(1942)
Rationing	(1944)	Spy Train	(1943)
Ravagers, The	(1965)	Square of Violence, The	(1963)
Red Ball Express	(1952)	Stage Door Canteen	(1943)
Remember Pearl Harbor	(1942)	Stalag 17	(1953)
Report From the Aleutians (doc.)	(1943)	Stand By for Action	(1942)
Reunion	(1942)	Standing Room Only	(1944)
Reunion in France	(1942)	Star Spangled Rhythm	(1942)
Rookies in Burma	(1943)	Steel Claw, The	(1961)
Rosie the Riveter	(1944)	Storm Over Lisbon	(1944)
Rough, Tough and Ready	(1945)	Story of Dr. Wassell, The	(1944)
Run Silent, Run Deep	(1958)	Story of G.I. Joe, The	(1945)
Sabotage Squad	(1942)	Strange Death of Adolph Hitler,	
Saboteur	(1942)	The	(1943)
Safecracker, The	(1958)	Strange Holiday	(1946)
Sahara	(1943)	Submarine Alert	(1943)
Salute for Three	(1943)	Submarine Base	(1943)
Salute to the Marines	(1943)	Submarine Raider	(1942)
Samurai	(1945)	Submarine Seahawk	(1959)
San Pietro (doc.)	(1945)	Suicide Attack (doc.)	(1951)
Sands of Iwo Jima	(1949)	Suicide Battalion	(1958)
Screaming Eagles	(1956)	Sullivans, The	(1944)
Sea Chase, The	(1955)	Sultan's Daughter, The	(1944)
Sealed Cargo	(1951)	Sunday Dinner for a Soldier	(1944)
Searching Wind, The	(1946)	Sundown	(1941)
Secret Agent of Japan	(1942)	Surrender—Hell!	(1959)
Secret Command	(1944)	Swing Shift	(1984)
Secret Enemies	(1942)	Swing Shift Maisie	(1943)
Secret Invasion, The	(1964)	Tampico	(1944)
Secret of Santa Vittorio, The	(1969)	Tank Commandos	(1959)
Secret War of Harry Frigg, The	(1968)	Tanks Are Coming, The	(1951)
Secrets of Scotland Yard	(1944)	Tarawa Beachhead	(1958)
Secrets of the Underground	(1943)	Target Unknown	(1951)
See Here, Private Hargrove	(1944)	Tarzan Triumphs	(1943)
Sergeant Mike	(1945)	Tarzan's Desert Mystery	(1943)
Seven Women From Hell	(1961)	Task Force	(1949)
Seventh Cross, The	(1944)	Taste of Hell, A	(1973)
Shadow of Terror	(1945)	Television Spy	(1939)
She's in the Army	(1942)	Tender Comrade	(1943)
Sherlock Holmes & the Secret		That Nazty Nuisance	(1943)
Weapon	(1942)	Then There Were Three	(1961)
Sherlock Holmes in Washington	(1943)	There's Something About a	
Ship Ahoy	(1942)	Soldier	(1944)
Since You Went Away	(1944)	They Came to Blow Up America	(1943)
		They Dare Not Love	(1941)

They Got Me Covered	(1943)	Up in Arms	(1944)
They Live in Fear	(1944)	Up Periscope	(1959)
They Met in Bombay	(1941)	Victors, The	(1963)
They Raid by Night	(1942)	Victory	(1981)
They Were Expendable	(1945)	Victory at Sea (doc.)	(1954)
Thin Red Line, The	(1964)	Victory Through Air Power (doc.)	(1943)
Thirteen Rue Madeleine	(1946)	Voice in the Wind	(1944)
Thirty Seconds Over Tokyo	(1944)	Voice of Terror, The	(1942)
Thirty-Six Hours	(1964)	Von Ryan's Express	(1965)
This Above All	(1942)	Wackiest Ship in the Army, The	(1960)
This Is the Army	(1943)	Wake Island	(1942)
This Land Is Mine	(1943)	Walk in the Sun, A	(1945)
This Man's Navy	(1945)	War Against Mrs. Hadley, The	(1942)
Thousand Plane Raid, The	(1969)	War Department Report (doc.)	(1943)
Thousands Cheer	(1943)	War Lover, The	(1962)
Three Came Home	(1950)	War Town (doc.)	(1943)
Three Russian Girls	(1944)	Warkill	(1967)
Thunderbirds	(1952)	Watch on the Rhine	(1943)
Thunderbolt (doc.)	(1945)	Waterfront	(1944)
Tiger Fangs	(1943)	We Accuse (doc.)	(1945)
Till We Meet Again	(1944)	We Are the Marines (doc.)	(1942)
Time to Love and a Time to Die,		We've Never Been Licked	(1943)
A	(1958)	What Are We Fighting For? (doc.)	(1943)
To Be or Not to Be	(1942)	What Did You Do in the War,	
To Be or Not to Be	(1983)	Daddy?	(1966)
To Have and Have Not	(1944)	What Next, Corporal Hargrove?	(1945)
To Hell and Back	(1955)	When Hell Broke Loose	(1958)
To the Shores of Iwo Jima (doc.)	(1945)	When Johnny Comes Marching	
To the Shores of Tripoli	(1942)	Home	(1943)
Tobruk	(1966)	When the Lights Go On Again	(1944)
Tokyo Rose	(1945)	When Willie Comes Marching	
Tomorrow the World	(1944)	Home	(1950)
Tonight We Raid Calais	(1943)	Which Way to the Front?	(1970)
Too Late the Hero	(1970)	Who Shall Live–Who Shall Die?	
Top Man	(1943)	(doc.)	(1981)
Tora! Tora! Tora!	(1970)	Wife Takes a Flyer, The	(1942)
Torpedo Boat	(1942)	Wild Blue Yonder, The	(1951)
Torpedo Run	(1958)	Will It Happen Again? (doc.)	(1948)
Train, The	(1964)	Wing and a Prayer	(1944)
Tramp, Tramp, Tramp	(1942)	Winged Victory	(1944)
True Glory, The (doc.)	(1945)	Wings for the Eagle	(1942)
Twelve O'Clock High	(1949)	Wings of Eagles, The	(1957)
Two Down and One to Go (doc.)	(1945)	Wings Over the Pacific	(1943)
Two Tickets to London	(1943)	With the Marines at Tarawa (doc.)	(1944)
Two Weeks to Live	(1943)	Women in Bondage	(1943)
Two Yanks in Trinidad	(1942)	Women in the Night	(1948)
Two-Man Submarine	(1944)	Women in War	(1940)
U-Boat Prisoner	(1944)	World at War, The (doc.)	(1942)
U.S.S. Teakettle	(1951)	World in Flames, The (doc.)	(1940)
Uncertain Glory	(1944)	Yank in Libya, A	(1942)
Under Fire	(1957)	Yank in the R.A.F., A	(1941)
Underground	(1941)	Yanks	(1979)
Underground Agent	(1942)	Yanks Ahoy	(1943)
United We Stand (doc.)	(1942)	Yanks Are Coming, The	(1942)
Unseen Enemy	(1942)	You Came Along	(1945)
Until They Sail	(1957)	You Can't Ration Love	(1944)
Unwritten Code, The	(1944)	You're in the Army Now	(1941)
Up From the Beach	(1965)	Young Lions, The	(1958)
Up Front	(1951)	Young Warriors, The	(1967)